E10
W35

Vosida
got fwat
back

Routledge Handbook of the Law of Armed Conflict

The law of armed conflict is a key element of the global legal order yet it finds itself in a state of flux created by the changing nature of warfare and the influences of other branches of international law. The *Routledge Handbook of the Law of Armed Conflict* provides a unique perspective on the field covering all the key aspects of the law as well as identifying developing and often contentious areas of interest.

The handbook will feature original pieces by international experts in the field, including academics, staff of relevant NGOs and (former) members of the armed forces. Made up of six parts in order to offer a comprehensive overview of the field, the structure of the handbook is as follows:

Part I: Fundamentals
Part II: Principle of distinction
Part III: Means and methods of warfare
Part IV: Special protection regimes
Part V: Compliance and enforcement
Part VI: Some contemporary issues

Throughout the book, attention is paid to non-international conflicts as well as international conflicts with acknowledgement of the differences. The contributors also consider the relationship between the law of armed conflict and human rights law, looking at how the various rules and principles of human rights law interact with specific rules and principles of international humanitarian law in particular circumstances.

The *Routledge Handbook of the Law of Armed Conflict* provides a fresh take on the contemporary laws of war and is written for advanced level students, academics, researchers, NGOs and policymakers with an interest in the field.

Rain Liivoja is a Senior Lecturer and Society in Science – Branco Weiss Fellow at Melbourne Law School, University of Melbourne, Australia, and Affiliated Research Fellow of the Erik Castrén Institute of International Law and Human Rights, University of Helsinki, Finland.

Tim McCormack is a Professor of Law at Melbourne Law School, University of Melbourne, Australia, and the Special Adviser on International Humanitarian Law to the Prosecutor of the International Criminal Court, The Hague, the Netherlands.

Routledge Handbook of the Law of Armed Conflict

Edited by Rain Liivoja and Tim McCormack

Routledge
Taylor & Francis Group

LONDON AND NEW YORK

First published 2016
by Routledge
2 Park Square, Milton Park, Abingdon, Oxon OX14 4RN

and by Routledge
711 Third Avenue, New York, NY 10017

Routledge is an imprint of the Taylor & Francis Group, an informa business

British Library Cataloguing in Publication Data
A catalogue record for this book is available from the British Library

Library of Congress Cataloging in Publication Data
Names: Liivoja, Rain, editor. | McCormack, Timothy L. H., editor.
Title: Routledge handbook of the law of armed conflict / edited by Rain Liivoja and Tim McCormack.
Other titles: Handbook of the law of armed conflict
Description: Milton Park, Abingdon, Oxon : Routledge, 2016. | Includes bibliographical references and index.
Identifiers: LCCN 2015037705| ISBN 9780415640374 (hbk) | ISBN 9780203798362 (ebk)
Subjects: LCSH: War (International law)
Classification: LCC KZ6385 .R685 2016 | DDC 341.6–dc23
LC record available at http://lccn.loc.gov/2015037705

ISBN: 978-0-415-64037-4 (hbk)
ISBN: 978-0-203-79836-2 (ebk)

Typeset in Bembo
by Wearset Ltd, Boldon, Tyne and Wear

MIX
Paper from
responsible sources
FSC® C013056

Printed and bound in Great Britain by
TJ International Ltd, Padstow, Cornwall

Contents

Contents

Contents

Contributors

The chapters to this book have been written by the contributors in their individual capacities. Their contributions do not represent the views of any government, international organisation, tribunal or any other institutions with which they may currently have, or previously had, an affiliation.

Nelleke van Amstel is a Project Coordinator for the Geneva Centre for the Democratic Control of Armed Forces (DCAF) on the topic of private security governance and regulation. She is mainly responsible for support to the implementation of the International Code of Conduct for Private Security Service Providers (the ICoC), along with the promotion of other international and national standards to increase oversight and accountability of the private security sector. Prior to joining DCAF, she worked for the Netherlands Red Cross as a legal adviser on International Humanitarian Law, as a trainee at the ICRC Unit for Relations with Arms Carriers and as a research assistant for Geneva Call on the topic of legal obligations for armed non-state actors. She holds an LLM from the Geneva Academy of International Humanitarian Law and Human Rights and an LLM in International and European law from Groningen University.

Louise Arimatsu has been an Associate Fellow with the International Law programme at Chatham House since 2009. Between 2006 and 2011, she taught international law at University College London and the London School of Economics. She is a graduate of the University of Nottingham (LLM) and the London School of Economics (PhD) and her areas of expertise include international criminal law, international humanitarian law, refugee law and international human rights law. She was the Managing Editor of the *Yearbook on International Humanitarian Law* from 2009 until 2012. She is currently involved in a number of research projects including an investigation with the UN Special Rapporteur on Human Rights and Counter-Terrorism into the Snowden disclosures.

Roberta Arnold is a Public Prosecutor in the Canton Ticino, Switzerland, and a Military Investigating Magistrate, Swiss Military Justice, holding the rank of specialist officer. She has previously worked at the Office of the Attorney General of Switzerland, the Military Academy at ETH Zurich and the Swiss Federal Department of Defence. Roberta earned a PhD from the University of Bern with the publication *The ICC as a New Instrument for Repressing Terrorism*, which was recognised with the Walther Hug Prize and the Francis Lieber Honorable Mention Award. She has published widely on military law, international criminal law and international humanitarian law. A member of the IIHL and the International Society for Military Law and the Law of War, she is the Editor-in-Chief of the *Military Law and the Law of War Review*.

Luis Benavides LLB (National University of Mexico), LLM and PhD (Graduate Institute of International Studies, Geneva) has worked for the UN High Commissioner for Human Rights, the Administrative Tribunal of the World Bank, the Ministry of Foreign Affairs of Mexico and Mexico's Ombudsman's Office. He is a member of the Editorial Board of the *Mexican Yearbook of International Law* and a former member of the Editorial Board of *International Legal Materials*. In 2013 he was appointed the international humanitarian law expert for the UN Panel of Experts concerning the Sudan. He is currently an International Law Professor at the Instituto Tecnológico Autónomo de México.

James P Benoit currently serves as the Assistant to the Deputy General Counsel (Management) for the US Department of the Navy's Office of the General Counsel (OGC). Prior to joining OGC, he served for 20 years in the US Navy Judge Advocate General's (JAG) Corps, attaining the rank of Commander. His final assignment on active duty was as the International Law Advisor in the Office of the Chief Prosecutor, Military Commissions. Immediately before that, he served as the Legal Advisor to the US Military Representative to NATO in Brussels. He has earned an LLM from George Washington, a JD from the University of the Pacific, and both a BS and an MBA from Cornell University. He teaches Law of the Sea at George Washington as an adjunct professor.

Eyal Benvenisti is the Whewell Professor of International Law at the University of Cambridge, the Director of the Lauterpacht Centre for International Law and the co-Editor of the *British Yearbook of International Law*. His second edition of *The International Law of Occupation* was published by Oxford University Press in 2012.

Elizabeth Chadwick has been a Reader by research at Nottingham Trent University since 2007. She has a longstanding research interest in the area of laws of armed neutrality, and has contributed the chapter on 'Neutrality' for *Oxford Bibliographies in International Law* (edited by Anthony Carty) (2014). Her main research and teaching interests lie in the fields of international humanitarian law, the self-determination of 'peoples', international terrorism and international crimes. She is the author of *Self-Determination in the Post-9/11 Era* (Routledge 2011), as well as of a number of book chapters and journal articles on a variety of related topics. Other teaching interests include intellectual property law.

Emily Crawford is co-director of the Sydney Centre for International Law, and lectures in public international law and international humanitarian law at the University of Sydney. She has a PhD in law from the University of New South Wales, and her current research focuses on irregular participation in armed conflict, including cyber warfare, targeted killings, private military and security companies, and drone warfare. She is a member of the New South Wales Red Cross IHL Committee and the International Law Association Committee on Non-State Actors. She is also co-rapporteur on the ILA Study Group on Cybersecurity, Terrorism and International Law.

Robert Cryer is Professor of International and Criminal Law at the University of Birmingham. His teaching and research interests are in international law, criminal law, humanitarian law and legal theory. He is the author of, *inter alia*, *Prosecuting International Crimes: Selectivity and the International Criminal Law Regime* (CUP 2005, with Neil Boister), *The Tokyo International Military Tribunal: A Reappraisal* (OUP 2008), and *An Introduction to International Criminal Law and Procedure* (3rd edn, CUP 2014, with Håkan Friman, Darryl Robinson and Elizabeth Wilmshurst). He is co-editor of the *Journal of Conflict and Security Law* (OUP).

Shane Darcy is a lecturer at the Irish Centre for Human Rights, National University of Ireland Galway. He teaches and researches in the areas of international humanitarian law, international criminal law, business and human rights and transitional justice. He has published articles in journals such as *Journal of Conflict and Security Law*, *Journal of International Criminal Justice*, *Leiden Journal of International Law*, *Yearbook of International Humanitarian Law* and *Military Law Review*. He is the author of *Collective Responsibility and Accountability under International Law* (Transnational 2007) and co-editor of *Judicial Creativity at the International Criminal Tribunals* (OUP 2010, with Joseph Powderly). In 2010, he was awarded the Journal of International Criminal Justice Prize. He is an Associate Editor of *Criminal Law Forum*.

Helen Durham is Director of International Law and Policy at the ICRC and was previously Director of International Law and Strategy at the Australian Red Cross. She is admitted as a Barrister and Solicitor of the Supreme Court of Victoria and is a Senior Fellow at Melbourne Law School. She has a Doctorate of Juridicial Science from Melbourne Law School with a focus on international humanitarian law and international criminal law. She has been involved in a range of field operations with the ICRC (in the Pacific and South Asia) as well as being part of the delegation to the negotiations for the ICC in Rome and New York. She spent time as Director of Research for the Asia Pacific Centre for Military Law and is widely published on IHL related matters.

Alison Duxbury is a Professor of Law at the Melbourne Law School. She is also an Associate Director of the Asia Pacific Centre for Military Law and a member of the Board of Directors of the International Society for Military Law and the Law of War. Her major research interests are in the fields of international law, international institutional law and human rights law. Her publications include 'The Curious Case of the Australian Military Court' (2010) 10 *Oxford University Commonwealth Law Journal* 155 and *The Participation of States in International Organisations: The Role of Human Rights and Democracy* (CUP 2011).

Caitlin Dwyer is an Associate at Markotich Lawyers in Melbourne. In 2013, she was the Associate to the Honourable Justice Lasry of the Supreme Court of Victoria and, prior to that, she served as the Tim Hawkins Memorial Scholar assisting the Special Adviser on International Humanitarian Law to the Prosecutor of the International Criminal Court in The Hague.

William J Fenrick taught international humanitarian law/law of armed conflict and international criminal law at Dalhousie Law School in Halifax, Canada from 2005 to 2010. He was a Senior Legal Adviser in the Office of the Prosecutor (OTP) of the International Criminal Tribunal for the Former Yugoslavia from 1994 until the end of 2004. At the ICTY, he was the head of the Legal Advisory Section which provided international and comparative law advice to the OTP, and also the Senior Adviser on Law of Armed Conflict. From 1992 to 1994 he was a member of the Commission of Experts established under Security Council Resolution 780 investigating war crimes allegations in the former Yugoslavia and, as such, he was responsible for legal matters and for on-site investigations. From 1974 to 1994 he was a military lawyer in the Canadian Forces specialising in the law of armed conflict and operational law.

Dieter Fleck is Former Director, International Agreements and Policy, Federal Ministry of Defence, Germany. He is Honorary President of the International Society for Military Law and the Law of War, Member of the Advisory Board of the Amsterdam Center for International Law, Member of the Editorial Board of the *Journal of International Peacekeeping* and Rapporteur of the International Law Association's Committee on Nuclear Weapons, Non-Proliferation and Contemporary International Law.

Charles Garraway CBE is a Fellow at the Human Rights Centre, University of Essex and Vice President of the International Humanitarian Fact-Finding Commission. He served for 30 years as a legal officer in the United Kingdom Army Legal Services, as a criminal prosecutor and as an adviser in the law of armed conflict and operational law. On retirement in 2003, he worked for the Foreign Office on transitional justice issues in Iraq before taking up the Stockton Chair in International Law at the United States Naval War College, Newport, Rhode Island for the year 2004/2005. He was a Visiting Professor at King's College London from 2002 to 2008, teaching the Law of Armed Conflict, and an Associate Fellow at Chatham House from 2005 to 2012. He worked for the British Red Cross from 2007 to 2011 and now works as an independent consultant. He was appointed CBE in 2002 and awarded an Honorary Doctorate by the University of Essex in 2012. From 2008 to 2013, he was the General Editor of the *United Kingdom Manual on the Law of Armed Conflict*.

Emanuela-Chiara Gillard is a Senior Research Fellow at the Oxford Institute for Ethics, Law and Armed Conflict, and a Research Fellow at the European University Institute Individualisation of War Project. From 2007 to 2012 she was Chief of the Protection of Civilians Section in the Policy Development and Studies Branch of the United Nations Office for Coordination of Humanitarian Affairs. For eight years prior to joining OCHA in 2007, she was a legal adviser at the International Committee of the Red Cross. Before joining the ICRC, she was a legal adviser at the United Nations Compensation Commission. From 1995 to 1997 she was a research fellow at the Lauterpacht Research Centre for International Law at the University of Cambridge. She holds a BA in law and an LLM from the University of Cambridge. She is a Solicitor of the Supreme Court of England and Wales.

Nobuo Hayashi is a Senior Legal Adviser at the International Law and Policy Institute, based in Oslo, Norway. He specialises in international humanitarian law, international criminal law and public international law. He has over 15 years' experience in these areas, performing advanced research, publishing and editing scholarly works, authoring court submissions, advising international prosecutors, and speaking at academic and diplomatic conferences. His most significant works cover military necessity, threat of force, and the law and ethics of nuclear weapons.

Ian Henderson AM, BSc, LLB, LLM, PhD, is a legal officer with the Royal Australian Air Force. He has taught operations law to military audiences in Australia and internationally, and he participated in the 2007 Asia-Pacific regional workshop leading towards the development of the Harvard *Manual on International Law Applicable to Air and Missile Warfare* (2009). Along with a number of articles and book chapters, he is the author of *The Contemporary Law of Targeting: Military Objectives, Proportionality and Precautions in Attack under Additional Protocol I* (Martinus Nijhoff 2009).

Chris Jenks is an Assistant Professor of Law and Director of the criminal justice clinic at the SMU Dedman School of Law in Dallas, Texas, where he teaches and writes on international humanitarian law. He is the co-author of a law of armed conflict textbook, co-editor of a forthcoming war crimes textbook and served as a peer reviewer of both the *Tallinn Manual on the International Law Applicable to Cyber Warfare* and the US Army's field manual on the law of land warfare. He has published articles and book chapters on child soldiers, detention, drones, lethal autonomous weapon systems, extraordinary rendition and peacekeeping. Prior to joining the SMU faculty in 2012, he served for more than 20 years in the US military, first as an infantry officer and then as a judge advocate.

Frits Kalshoven is Professor *emeritus* of International Law and International Humanitarian Law at the University of Leiden. Having served as an officer in the Dutch Navy (1945–1967), he was lecturer and subsequently Professor at the University of Leiden (1967–1989). He has been a participant in numerous international conferences and expert meetings on the development of IHL. He was the first chairman of the UN Commission of Experts to investigate war crimes in the former Yugoslavia (1992–1993), as well as a member (1991–2001) and president (1997–2001) of the International Humanitarian Fact-Finding Commission ex API art 90. In 2003, he was awarded the Henry Dunant Medal of the International Red Cross and Red Crescent Movement for his work on international humanitarian law. He is the author of *Belligerent Reprisals* (Martinus Nijhoff 1971, republished 2005), *Reflections on the Law of War* (collected papers, Martinus Nijhoff 2007) and *Constraints on the Waging of War* (4th edn, CUP 2011, with Liesbeth Zegveld).

Patrick Keane AM, LLB (Hons), LLM, is a legal officer with the Royal Australian Air Force. He has taught operations law to military audiences in Australia and internationally. He has extensive experience in the application of operations law at the tactical, operational and strategic levels.

Jann Kleffner is Professor of International Law and Head of the International Law Centre at the Swedish Defence University. His research is on public international law, with a special focus on the law of armed conflict and peace operations, *jus ad bellum*, international criminal law and human rights law (particularly in armed conflicts). He holds LLM and PhD degrees from the University of Amsterdam Law School and has been a fellow of the Institute for International and Comparative Law in Africa at the University of Pretoria, the Geneva Academy of International Humanitarian Law and Human Rights, and of DePaul University Law School, Chicago, USA. He has served as expert and consultant for a number of states, inter-governmental and non-governmental organisations, including the United Nations, the International Committee of the Red Cross, the International Criminal Court and the International Criminal Tribunal for the Former Yugoslavia. He has also advised law firms in the areas of the law of armed conflict and international criminal law, in addition to fulfilling a number of editorial functions.

Dino Kritsiotis is Chair of Public International Law at the University of Nottingham, where he heads the International Humanitarian Law Unit of the Human Rights Law Centre. Since 2011, he has been a regular member of Oxford University's Summer Masters Programme in International Human Rights Law and he co-convenes, with Anne Orford (Melbourne) and JHH Weiler (Florence), the Annual Junior Faculty Forum for International Law. He completed his law studies at the University of Wales College of Cardiff, and at the University of Cambridge, where he obtained his LLM in international law with distinction in 1992. He also holds a Diploma of International Humanitarian Law, also awarded with distinction, by the International Committee of the Red Cross in 1993. His teaching and research interests concern international law and the use of force, international humanitarian law, general international law, as well as the history and theory of international law. He is widely published in these fields.

Kobi Leins has managed programmes and teams in the areas of administrative law and justice, humanitarian law, human rights law, and disarmament with the United Nations, the International Committee of the Red Cross and the International Service for Human Rights. With a commercial litigation background, in 2006, she worked with an international NGO to advocate for the adoption of the Declaration of Indigenous Peoples' Rights. In 2005, she liaised with states, scientists and stakeholders to raise awareness of, and compliance with, the Biological Weapons and Chemical Weapons Conventions. In 2004, she worked as a Legal Officer at the United Nations Compensation Commission under the auspices of a Security Council Resolution analysing and presenting claims for environmental damage following Iraq's invasion of Kuwait in 1991. More recently, she prepared a matrix for review of domestic compliance with the Chemical Weapons Convention. She is currently a PhD candidate at the University of Melbourne.

Michelle Lesh holds a BA/LLB (Hons) from Monash University and a PhD from the University of Melbourne. She was a Post-Doctoral Fellow at the Hebrew University of Jerusalem. She has served as a foreign law clerk for Chief Justice Barak (Ret.) at Israel's Supreme Court, as the principal researcher for the Turkel Commission Report on Investigating Alleged Violations of the Law of Armed Conflict, and as a human rights officer at UN Office of the High Commissioner for Human Rights. Most recently she worked as an assistant to Israel's Deputy Attorney-General for International Law. Her publications include 'A Critical Discussion of the Second Turkel Report and How it Engages with the Duty to Investigate under International Law', *YBIHL* (2013) and 'Interplay as regards Conduct of Hostilities' in Jann Kleffner & Erika de Wet (eds), *Convergence and Conflicts of Human Rights (IHRL) and International Humanitarian Law (IHL) in Military Operations* (Pretoria University Law Press 2014). She is working on a monograph entitled *Israel's Policy of Targeted Killing and International Humanitarian Law*.

David Letts is an Associate Professor at the Australian National University College of Law and Commodore (retired) following a navy career of nearly 32 years. His naval service included roles at sea as a Logistics Officer and service as a Legal Officer including Fleet Legal Officer, Deputy Director Operations and International Law, Chief Legal Adviser to the UNTAET/UNMISET Force Commander in East Timor and Chief of International Law in the Multi-National Force, Baghdad, Iraq. His final military legal role was Deputy Inspector General of the Australian Defence Force. He has an LLM (International Law) from ANU, is a graduate of Harvard Business School's Advanced Management Program and has been a visiting fellow at Cambridge University's Lauterpacht Centre for International Law. He is a member of the teaching faculty at the International Institute of Humanitarian Law, Sanremo, Italy and is currently Co-Director of the Centre for Military and Security Law at ANU.

Rain Liivoja is a Senior Lecturer and Society in Science – Branco Weiss Fellow at Melbourne Law School. He is also an Affiliated Research Fellow of the Erik Castrén Institute of International Law and Human Rights, University of Helsinki. His research interests include the law of armed conflict, the law of treaties, state jurisdiction and comparative military justice. He is a member of the Board of Directors of the International Society for Military Law and the Law of War, a member of the Australian Red Cross International Humanitarian Law Advisory Committee (Victorian Division), chair of the International Peace and Security Interest Group of the Australian and New Zealand Society of International Law, and book review editor of the *Finnish Yearbook of International Law*. He holds a doctorate in international law from the University of Helsinki.

Noam Lubell is Professor of Law of Armed Conflict, and Head of the School of Law at the University of Essex, UK. In previous years he has taught in a number of academic institutions in Ireland, Israel, the UK and the US. In addition to his academic work, during the last 15 years he has worked for NGOs as International Law Adviser, and Director of a Prisoners and Detainees

Project. He has also provided consultancies and training in human rights law and the laws of armed conflict, for international bodies such as Amnesty International, government bodies and the BBC. He is the Rapporteur of the International Law Association's Committee on the Use of Force, and holds the Swiss Chair of International Humanitarian Law at the Geneva Academy. He has published on a variety of topics in the field of international law, including on self-defence, new technologies and the scope of the battlefield, and is the author of the book *Extra-territorial Use of Force against Non-state Actors* (OUP 2010).

Elliot Luke holds an LLM from the University of Cambridge, an MSc in Development Studies from the London School of Economics and Political Science, a JD from the University of Melbourne and a BA from University College London. From 2012 to 2014, he was a Research Fellow at Melbourne Law School, where he worked with Professors John Tobin and Philip Alston to produce a comprehensive commentary on the United Nations Convention on the Rights of the Child. During this time, he was twice a Scholar in Residence at the Center for Human Rights and Global Justice at NYU School of Law. Prior to his legal career, he worked for a number of NGOs in Australia and Latin America as a researcher and campaigner in the field of human rights.

Tim McCormack is a Professor of Law at Melbourne Law School, an Adjunct Professor of Law at the University of Tasmania Law School and the Special Adviser on International Human-itarian Law to the Prosecutor of the International Criminal Court. He is currently a Fulbright Senior Scholar, Charles H Stockton Distinguished Scholar-in-Residence in the Stockton Center for the Study of International Law at the US Naval War College in Newport, Rhode Island and James Barr Ames Visiting Professor at Harvard Law School. He was the Foundation Australian Red Cross Professor of International Humanitarian Law (1996–2010) and Foundation Director of the Asia Pacific Centre for Military Law (2001–2010) at Melbourne Law School. He is co-editor-in-chief (with Sir Christopher Greenwood) of the *International Humanitarian Law Series* (Martinus Nijhoff) and Correspondents' Reports Editor for the *Yearbook of International Human-itarian Law* (Springer).

Rob McLaughlin is an Associate Professor of Law at the Australian National University. He recently retired from full-time naval service as a Seaman and then Legal Officer in the Royal Australian Navy (Captain), having served in East Timor and Iraq, and on maritime constabulary operations. His postings included Fleet Legal Officer, Strategic Legal Adviser, Director of Operations and International Law, and Director Naval Legal Service. He is a member of the faculty of the International Institute for Humanitarian Law, a member of the Australian Red Cross IHL Committee and is currently co-director of the Centre for Military and Security Law at ANU. He holds a PhD from the University of Cambridge.

Jackson Nyamuya Maogoto is currently a Senior Lecturer at the University of Manchester. He holds a Bachelor of Laws with First Class Honours from Moi University (Kenya); three postgraduate degrees from the University of Cambridge (Masters in Law), University of Tech-nology Sydney (Masters in Law) and University of Melbourne (Doctorate in Law). His teaching and research interests are in public international law (encompassing international criminal law, international human rights and humanitarian law), outer space law and cyber warfare. He has published extensively in his fields of teaching and research interest.

Eve Massingham is an International Humanitarian Law (IHL) Officer with the Australian Red Cross and a PhD candidate with the School of Law at the University of Queensland. As a British

Council Chevening Scholar at Kings College London, she completed a Master of Laws focusing on IHL and international law on the use of force. She also holds a Master of International Development, Bachelor of Laws (Hons) and Graduate Diploma of Legal Practice. She is admitted as a solicitor of the Supreme Courts of Queensland and New South Wales and the High Court of Australia. She has worked in private legal practice and as an Associate to a Federal Court Judge. She has also spent time as an Army Reserve Officer and as an intern with the Office of the Prosecutor of the International Criminal Court. She has published articles and book chapters on IHL and on international law on the use of force.

Robert J Mathews is Head of the Nuclear, Biological and Chemical Arms Control Unit in the Defence Science and Technology Group of Australia's Department of Defence. In this capacity, he has served as scientific adviser to various Australian delegations associated with the Chemical Weapons Convention since 1984. He has also provided support for the Australia Group export licensing measures since its inception in 1985, and in the efforts to strengthen the Biological Weapons Convention, including in the Asia-Pacific region. He is also a Principal Fellow within the Asia Pacific Centre for Military Law at Melbourne Law School. In this capacity, since 1991 he has been involved in various projects including consideration of the challenges to International Humanitarian Law (IHL) and arms control law posed by advances in science and technology and the resulting emerging military technologies. He has been a member of various committees, including Australian Red Cross IHL committees and the Organisation for the Prohibition of Chemical Weapons (OPCW) working groups, and was recently named as the first Recipient of the 'OPCW-The Hague' award, based on his contribution to achieving a world free of chemical weapons.

Bruce Oswald is an Associate Professor in the Melbourne Law School at the University of Melbourne. He is also the Director of the Asia Pacific Centre for Military Law (APCML). He was a Jennings Randolph Senior Fellow (October 2012 to June 2013) at the United States Institute of Peace in Washington, DC, USA. He has served in the Australian Regular Army as a legal officer, and has seen operational service in Rwanda, the Former Yugoslavia, East Timor, Iraq and Afghanistan. He continues to serve in the Army Reserves as a Colonel.

Jadranka Petrovic currently teaches and researches at Monash University. She has completed extensive studies in law, including her doctoral studies, at the Melbourne Law School. Her research interests and publications are in the international legal protection of cultural property in armed conflict and in a number of other areas of international law.

Nancie Prud'homme holds a PhD from the National University of Ireland, Galway which examined the intersection between international human rights and humanitarian law. She has worked at the School of Law, University of Essex as Projects Director for the International Centre on Human Rights and Drug Policy. Prior to that she was based at the Irish Centre for Human Rights, National University of Ireland, Galway, where she directed the EU–China Human Rights Network Project and led a project on the human rights situation of the Rohingyas in Western Burma. She also holds an MSc in Psychology from the University of Essex, and her current work combines psychology with the protection of victims of human rights and humanitarian law violations.

Sasha Radin is Editor-in-Chief of *International Law Studies* and Associate Director of Research at the Stockton Center at the United States Naval War College. She is also a PhD candidate at Melbourne Law School.

Michael N Schmitt is Charles H Stockton Professor and Director of the Stockton Center at the United States Naval War College. He is also Professor of Public International Law at the University of Exeter Law School in the United Kingdom, Fellow at Harvard Law School's Program on International Law and Armed Conflict, Senior Fellow at the NATO Cooperative Cyber Defence Centre of Excellence in Estonia, and General Editor of *International Law Studies*. He served as a legal adviser to the Turkel Commission on the Gaza blockade, Director of the *Tallinn Manual on the International Law Applicable to Cyber Warfare* project, and as a member of the drafting team for the *Harvard Manual on International Law Applicable to Air and Missile Warfare*.

Daphna Shraga holds an LLB and an LLM from Tel-Aviv University, and a PhD from the Graduate Institute of International and Development Studies, Geneva. Between 1979 and 1985, she served in the International Law Branch of the Israeli Judge Advocate General's Unit, joined the UN Office of Legal Affairs in 1989 and served as a Principal Legal Officer in the Office of the Legal Counsel until 2012. She is the author of various articles on the UN-based international and mixed tribunals, politics and justice in the establishment of international tribunals and the role of the Security Council, the applicability of international humanitarian law to peacekeeping operations, the applicability of the laws of occupation to UN transitional administrations, the Security Council as a promoter and enforcer of human rights, and responsibility of international organisations. She has lectured at the Florence Academy of European Law and Melbourne Law University School, and, as of 2012, at Tel-Aviv and the Hebrew Universities.

Mirko Sossai is Assistant Professor of international law at the Department of Law, University 'Roma Tre', Italy. Previously, he was research fellow at the LUISS Guido Carli University in Rome. He holds a PhD in international law from the University of Sienna (2005) and a degree *cum laude* from the University of Padua (2001). He published a monograph in Italian on the prevention of terrorism in international law and edited with Christine Bakker the book *Multilevel Regulation of Military and Security Contractors: The Interplay between International, European, and Domestic Norms* (Hart 2012).

Kelisiana Thynne is a Regional Legal Adviser for the International Committee of the Red Cross (ICRC) based in Kuala Lumpur, Malaysia and covering South-East Asia. She was previously the Director of Capability and Research Manager at the Australian Civil–Military Centre, Legal Adviser to the Afghanistan Delegation of the ICRC and Regional Legal Adviser to the ICRC Pacific Regional delegation. She has also worked for the Office of International Law in the Australian Attorney-General's Department, the Women's Initiatives for Gender Justice (an NGO dealing with gender issues at the International Criminal Court) and was Associate to an Australian Federal Judge. She has a Master of Laws from the University of Sydney, and a Bachelor of Laws (Honours) and a Bachelor of Arts (Honours) from the Australian National University.

John Tobin is a Professor in the Melbourne Law School at the University of Melbourne. He has a combined commerce/law degree with honours and a PhD from the University of Melbourne. He also has an LLM with distinction from the University of London. In 2006, he was a Visiting Professor at both the American Academy of Human Rights and Humanitarian Law, Washington College of Law, American University and in the Law School at New York University. In 2011 he was the Senior Scholar in Residence at the Center for Human Rights and Global Justice at NYU Law School. He has also published numerous reports and articles on human rights, especially children's rights. His book, *The Right to Health in International Law*, was published by OUP in 2012. He is an Advisory Board member to the *Melbourne Journal of International Law* and *International Journal of Children's Rights*. He is also a member of several Advisory Committees and working groups for government bodies and NGOs. Prior to becoming an academic he worked as a commercial lawyer, legal aid lawyer with Victoria Legal Aid and was a legal officer with the Department of Justice.

David Turns is a Senior Lecturer in International Law at the Defence Academy of the United Kingdom (Cranfield University), after being a Lecturer in Law at the University of Liverpool (1994–2007) and a Part-Time Lecturer in the Law Department of the London School of Economics and Political Science (1990–1994). In 2002, he was a Visiting Professor at the Institute for International Law and International Relations, University of Vienna, Austria. He specialises in public international law, with particular focus on military operations and international humanitarian law, the legality of the use of force and international criminal law. He graduated from the London School of Economics and Political Science with undergraduate (LLB) and postgraduate (LLM in International Law) degrees in 1990 and 1992 respectively. He was called to the Bar of England and Wales by the Honourable Society of the Inner Temple in 1992.

Bethany Wellington developed an interest in IHL and the rights of civilian victims of conflict as a student and research assistant at the Melbourne Law School, University of Melbourne. She graduated with first class honours in 2013 and currently works as a lawyer at the multinational law firm K&L Gates.

Abbreviations

ACHR	American Convention on Human Rights (22 November 1969) 1144 UNTS 143
Additional Protocol I/API	Protocol Additional (I) to the Geneva Conventions of 12 August 1949, and Relating to the Protection of Victims of International Armed Conflicts (8 June 1977) 1125 UNTS 3
Additional Protocol II/APII	Protocol Additional (II) to the Geneva Conventions of 12 August 1949, and Relating to the Protection of Victims of Non-International Armed Conflicts (8 June 1977) 1125 UNTS 609
Adelaide LR	*Adelaide Law Review*
ADIL	*Annual Digest of Public International Law Cases* (Longmans, Green & Co 1932–1938) and *Annual Digest and Reports of Public International Law Cases* (Butterworth & Co 1940–1955)
ADIZ	air defence identification zone
AG	Australia Group
AHG	Ad hoc Group
AJCL	*American Journal of Comparative Law*
AJIL Supp	*American Journal of International Law Supplement*
AJIL	*American Journal of International Law*
Albany LR	*Albany Law Review*
American University ILR	*American University International Law Review*
American University JILP	*American University Journal of International Law and Policy*
American University LR	*American University Law Review*
AMIS	African Union Mission in Sudan
AMISOM	African Union Mission in Somalia
AP Commentary	Yves Sandoz, Christophe Swinarski and Bruno Zimmermann (eds), *Commentary on the Additional Protocols of 8 June 1977 to the Geneva Conventions of 12 August 1949* (ICRC/Martinus Nijhoff 1987)
APC	*Armée Populaire Congolaise* (Congolese Popular Army)
ARIO	Articles on the Responsibility of International Organizations
ARSIWA	Articles on Responsibility of States for Internationally Wrongful Acts
ATS	Alien Tort Statute
AU	African Union

Australian ILJ	*Australian International Law Journal*
BFSP	*British and Foreign State Papers*
Boston University ILJ	*Boston University International Law Journal*
Buffalo LR	*Buffalo Law Review*
BW	biological weapons
BWC	Convention on the Prohibition of the Development, Production and Stockpiling of Bacteriological (Biological) Weapons and on their Destruction (10 April 1972) 1015 UNTS 163
BYBIL	*British Year Book of International Law*
C-RAM	counter rocket, artillery and mortar
California Western ILJ	*California Western International Law Journal*
Canadian YBIL	*Canadian Yearbook of International Law*
Case Western Reserve JIL	*Case Western Reserve Journal of International Law*
CAT	Convention against Torture and Other Cruel, Inhuman or Degrading Treatment or Punishment, UNGA Res 39/46 (10 December 1984) 1465 UNTS 85
CCF	continuous combat function
CCM	Convention on Cluster Munitions (30 May 2008) 2688 UNTS 39
CCW	Convention on Prohibitions or Restrictions of Use of Certain Conventional Weapons which may be Deemed to be Excessively Injurious or to have Indiscriminate Effects (10 October 1980) 1342 UNTS 137
CDDH	*Conférence diplomatique sur la réaffirmation et le développement du droit international humanitaire applicable dans les conflits armés –* Diplomatic Conference on the Reaffirmation and Development of International Humanitarian Law applicable in Armed Conflicts (1974–1977)
CED	International Convention for the Protection of All Persons from Enforced Disappearances, UNGA Res 61/177 (20 December 2006)
CEDAW	Convention on the Elimination of All Forms of Discrimination against Women, UNGA Res 34/180 (18 December 1979) 1249 UNTS 13
CESCR	*Committee on Economic, Social and Cultural Rights*
Chinese JIL	*Chinese Journal of International Law*
CIHL	ICRC, *Customary IHL* (online database), www.icrc.org/customary-ihl
CIL	customary international law
CIWS	close-in weapon system(s)
CNS	central nervous system
Columbia HRLR	*Columbia Human Rights Law Review*
Columbia JTL	*Columbia Journal of Transnational Law*
Cornell ILJ	*Cornell International Law Journal*
CRC	Convention on the Rights of the Child, UNGA Res 44/25 (20 November 1989) 1577 UNTS 3
CSR	corporate social responsibility

CTBT	Comprehensive Nuclear-Test Ban Treaty (24 September 1996) 35 ILM 1439
CTBTO	Comprehensive Nuclear-Test Ban Treaty Organization
CUP	Cambridge University Press
CW	chemical weapons
CWC	Convention on the Prohibition of the Development, Production, Stockpiling and Use of Chemical Weapons and on their Destruction (13 January 1993) 1974 UNTS 45
DCS	distributed control system
Denver JILP	*Denver Journal of International Law and Policy*
Dickinson JIL	*Dickinson Journal of International Law*
DPH	direct participation in hostilities
DRC	Democratic Republic of the Congo
ECCC	Extraordinary Chambers in the Courts of Cambodia
ECHO	European Commission's Humanitarian and Civil Protection Department
ECHR	[European] Convention for the Protection of Human Rights and Fundamental Freedoms (4 November 1950) CETS no 5
ECmHR	European Commission of Human Rights
ECOSOC	Economic and Social Council
ECtHR	European Court of Human Rights
ECtHR GC	Grand Chamber of the European Court of Human Rights
EECC	Eritrea–Ethiopia Claims Commission
EEZ	exclusive economic zone
EJIL	*European Journal of International Law*
Emory ILR	*Emory International Law Review*
ENDC	Eighteen Nation Disarmament Committee
ENMOD	Convention on the Prohibition of Military or Any Other Hostile Use of Environmental Modification Techniques (18 May 1977) 1108 UNTS 151
ERQ	explosive remnants of war
EU	European Union
FBW	fly-by-wire
Fordham ILJ	*Fordham International Law Journal*
FPLC	*Forces Patriotiques pour la libération du Congo* (Patriotic Forces for the Liberation of Congo)
FRY	Federal Republic of Yugoslavia
GCI Commentary	Jean Pictet (ed), *Commentary: I Geneva Convention for the Amelioration of the Condition of the Wounded and Sick in Armed Forces in the Field* (ICRC 1952)
GCII Commentary	Jean Pictet (ed), *Commentary: II Geneva Convention for the Amelioration of the Condition of Wounded, Sick and Shipwrecked Members of Armed Forces at Sea* (ICRC 1960)
GCIII Commentary	Jean Pictet (ed), *Commentary: III Geneva Convention Relative to the Treatment of Prisoners of War* (ICRC 1960)
GCIV Commentary	Jean Pictet (ed), *Commentary: IV Geneva Convention Relative to the Protection of Civilian Persons in Time of War* (ICRC 1958)

Geneva Convention I/GCI	Geneva Convention (I) for the Amelioration of the Condition of the Wounded and Sick in Armed Forces in the Field (12 August 1949) 75 UNTS 31
Geneva Convention II/GCII	Geneva Convention (II) for the Amelioration of the Condition of Wounded, Sick and Shipwrecked Members of Armed Forces at Sea (12 August 1949) 75 UNTS 85
Geneva Convention III/GCIII	Geneva Convention (III) relative to the Treatment of Prisoners of War (12 August 1949) 75 UNTS 135
Geneva Convention IV/GCIV	Geneva Convention (IV) relative to the Protection of Civilian Persons in Time of War (12 August 1949) 75 UNTS 287
George Washington ILR	*George Washington International Law Review*
Georgetown JIL	*Georgetown Journal of International Law*
GICCW	Government Industry Conference against Chemical Weapons
GICNT	Global Initiative to Combat Nuclear Terrorism
Hague Regulations/HR	Hague Regulations regarding the Laws and Customs of Land Warfare, annexed to Hague Convention (IV) regarding the Laws and Customs of Land Warfare (18 October 1907) 205 CTS 277
Harvard ILJ	*Harvard International Law Journal*
Harvard LR	*Harvard Law Review*
Harvard NSJ	*Harvard National Security Journal*
Hasting LJ	*Hastings Law Journal*
Hertfordshire LJ	*Hertfordshire Law Journal*
HMSO	Her Majesty's Stationary Office
HPCR	Program on Humanitarian Policy and Conflict Research
HRAW	Hague Rules of Air Warfare
HRC	Human Rights Committee
HRQ	*Human Rights Quarterly*
HRDDP	Human Rights Due Diligence Policy on United Nations Support to non-United Nations Security Forces
IAC	international armed conflict
IACmHR	Inter-American Commission on Human Rights
IACtHR	Inter-American Court of Human Rights
IAEA	International Atomic Energy Agency
IAM	International Assistance Mission
IAU	investigation of alleged use
ICA	incapacitating agent
ICC	International Criminal Court
ICCPR	International Covenant on Civil and Political Rights, UNGA Res 2200A (XXI) (16 December 1966) 999 UNTS 171
ICESCR	International Covenant on Economic, Social, and Cultural Rights, UNGA Res 2200A (XXI) (16 December 1966) 993 UNTS 3
ICJ	International Court of Justice
ICL	international criminal law

ICLQ	*International and Comparative Law Quarterly*
ICoC	International Code of Conduct for Private Security Services Providers
ICoCA	ICoC Association
ICRC	International Committee of the Red Cross
ICS	industrial control systems
ICTR Statute	Statute of the International Criminal Tribunal for Rwanda (8 November 1994, with later amendments)
ICTR	International Criminal Tribunal for Rwanda
ICTY Statute	Statute of the International Tribunal for the Prosecution of Persons Responsible for Serious Violations of International Humanitarian Law Committed in the Territory of the Former Yugoslavia since 1991 (25 May 1993, with later amendments)
ICTY	International Criminal Tribunal for the Former Yugoslavia
IDF	Israel Defence Forces
IED	improvised explosive device
IEL	international environmental law
IGO	international (intergovernmental) organisation
IHL	international humanitarian law
IHRL	international human rights law
IIHL	International Institute of Humanitarian Law
IJCR	*International Journal of Children's Rights*
IJTJ	*International Journal of Transitional Justice*
ILA	International Law Association
ILC	International Law Commission
ILS	International Law Studies
IMT	International Military Tribunal
IMTFE	International Military Tribunal for the Far East
INTERFET	International Force for East Timor
International Organizations LR	*International Organizations Law Review*
Irish YBIL	*Irish Yearbook of International Law*
IRRC	*International Review of the Red Cross*
ISAF	International Security Assistance Force
Israel LR	*Israel Law Review*
Israel YBHR	*Israel Yearbook on Human Rights*
Italian YBIL	*Italian Yearbook of International Law*
JCSL	*Journal of Conflict and Security Law*
JEM	Justice and Equality Movement
JICJ	*Journal of International Criminal Justice*
JILT	*Journal of International Law and Trade*
JLIS	*Journal of Law, Information and Science*
KLA	Kosovo Liberation Army
LAWS	lethal autonomous weapon system(s)
Leiden JIL	*Leiden Journal of International Law*
LNTS	*League of Nations Treaty Series*
LOAC	law of armed conflict
LONW	law of naval warfare

LQR	*Law Quarterly Review*
Max Planck YBUNL	*Max Planck Yearbook of United Nations Law*
Melbourne JIL	*Melbourne Journal of International Law*
MGS	Military Group Site
Michigan JIL	*Michigan Journal of International Law*
Military LR	*Military Law Review*
MINUSCA	United Nations Multidimensional Integrated Stabilization Mission in the Central African Republic
MINUSMA	United Nations Multidimensional Integrated Stabilization Mission in Mali
MINUSTAH	United Nations Stabilization Mission in Haiti
MONUC	United Nations Organization Mission in the Democratic Republic of the Congo
MONUSCO	United Nations Organization Stabilization Mission in Democratic Republic of the Congo
MPEPIL	Rüdiger Wolfrum (ed), *The Max Planck Encyclopedia of Public International Law* (OUP 2008–), www.mpepil.com
NATO	North Atlantic Treaty Organisation
Netherlands ILR	*Netherlands International Law Review*
NGO	non-governmental organisation
NIAC	non-international armed conflict
North Dakota LR	*North Dakota Law Review*
Notre Dame LR	*Notre Dame Law Review*
NPT	Treaty on the Non-Proliferation of Nuclear Weapons (1 July 1968) 729 UNTS 161
NVA	North Vietnamese Army
NWCR	*Naval War College Review*
NYBIL	*Netherlands Yearbook of International Law*
NYU JILP	*New York University Journal of International Law and Policy*
NYU Law Review	*New York University Law Review*
OAG	organised armed groups
OEWG	open-ended intergovernmental working group
ONUC	*Opération des Nations Unies au Congo* (United Nations Operation in the Congo)
OPCW	Organisation for the Prohibition of Chemical Weapons
OSCE	Organization for Security and Co-operation in Europe
OTP	Office of the Prosecutor
OUP	Oxford University Press
PCA	Permanent Court of Arbitration
PCIJ	Permanent Court of International Justice
Pennsylvania State ILR	*Pennsylvania State International Law Review*
PLC	programmable logic controller
PMSC	private military and security company
POW	prisoner of war
PSI	Proliferation Security Initiative
R2P	responsibility to protect
RCA	riot control agent
RCADI	*Recueil des Cours de l'Académie de Droit International de la Haye*

RCWS	remotely controlled weapon station
RDMDG	*Revue de Droit Militaire et de Droit de la Guerre/Military Law and Law of War Review*
RMP	Royal Military Police
ROE	rules of engagement
Rome Statute	Rome Statute of the International Criminal Court (17 July 1998, with later amendments) 2187 UNTS 90
RPA	remotely piloted aircraft
RPV	remotely piloted vehicle
RTP	Responsibility to protect
RUF	Revolutionary United Front
Saskatchewan LR	*Saskatchewan Law Review*
SCADA	supervisory control and data acquisition
SCSL	Special Court for Sierra Leone
SPA	Service Prosecuting Authority
Stanford LPR	*Stanford Law and Policy Review*
Temple LR	*Temple Law Review*
Texas ILJ	*Texas International Law Journal*
TMWC	*Trial of the Major War Criminals before the International Military Tribunal, Nuremberg* (International Military Tribunal, 1947–1949)
Tulane JICL	Tulane Journal of International and Comparative Law
TWC	*Trials of War Criminals before the Nuernberg Military Tribunals under Control Council Law No. 10* (US Government Printing Office 1949–1953)
UAV	unmanned (or uninhabited) aerial vehicle
UCAV	unmanned combat aerial vehicle
UDHR	Universal Declaration of Human Rights, UNGA Res 217A (III) (10 December 1948)
UK	United Kingdom
UN Charter	Charter of the United Nations (26 June 1945, with later amendments)
UN	United Nations
UNAMID	United Nations–African Union Mission in Darfur
UNAMIR	United Nations Assistance Mission for Rwanda
UNAMSIL	United Nations Mission in Sierra Leone
UNCC	United Nations Compensation Commission
UNCLOS	United Nations Convention on the Law of the Sea (10 December 1982) 1833 UNTS 397
UNEP	United Nations Environment Programme
UNHCR	United Nations High Commissioner for Refugees
UNITAF	Unified Task Force (Somalia)
University of Pennsylvania JIL	*University of Pennsylvania Journal of International Law*
UNMIK	United Nations Interim Administration Mission in Kosovo
UNMISET	United Nations Mission of Support in East Timor
UNMISS	United Nations Mission in South Sudan
UNOSOM II	United Nations Operation in Somalia
UNSC	United Nations Security Council

UNSCOM	United Nations Special Commission
UNTAC	United Nations Transitional Authority in Cambodia
UNTAES	United Nations Transitional Administration for Eastern Slavonia
UNTAET	United Nations Transitional Administration in East Timor
UNTEA	United Nations Temporary Executive Authority
UNTS	*United Nations Treaty Series*
UNWCC	United Nations War Crimes Commission
UPC	*Union des Patriotes Congolais* (Union of Congolese Patriots)
US	United States
Utrecht LR	*Utrecht Law Review*
Vanderbilt JTL	*Vanderbilt Journal of Transnational Law*
Virginia JIL	*Virginia Journal of International Law*
Virginia LR	*Virginia Law Review*
VRS	*Vojska Republike Srpske* – Serb forces within Bosnia and Herzegovina
Washington & Lee LR	*Washington and Lee Law Review*
WEL	warfare environmental law
WMD	weapons of mass destruction
YBIHL	*Yearbook of International Humanitarian Law*
YJIL	Yale Journal of International Law

Table of treaties

Table of cases

Arbitration Panels

International Criminal Tribunals

Human Rights Treaty Bodies

Foreword

by Fatou Bensouda

War, with all its devastation – to lives, to property, to culture, to communities and to the environment – has been a tragically ubiquitous feature throughout every stage of human history. My own continent of Africa is not immune from this blight. Instead, it, as well as many other parts of the world, has been wracked by human misery resulting from armed conflict. Spectacular advances in science, medicine, industry, technology, communications, travel, exploration, architecture, agriculture and the exploitation of natural resources have sadly not been matched by comparable advances in the peaceful settlement of disputes, disarmament or in the prevention of armed conflict.

The Law of Armed Conflict, or International Humanitarian Law, would not be necessary in an utopian world. If armed conflict never broke out, the legal regulation of the conduct of hostilities and minimum standards of protection for victims would be pleasantly superfluous. If no atrocities were perpetrated, no international criminal trials would be necessary and victims, their families, their communities, their world, would be free of this scourge. This ideal world is certainly worth working for and important for all generations to aspire to. But, alas, it is not the reality we are confronted with and it is certainly not the reality the International Criminal Court (ICC) deals with on a daily basis.

The publication of this volume of essays follows the recent 150th anniversary of the 1864 Geneva Convention for the Amelioration of the Condition of the Wounded in Armies in the Field – the world's first multilateral treaty regulating the conduct of military hostilities. A century-and-a-half of developments in the law – of treaty-making and of customary international law – make this particular body of rules one of the older fields of International Law. But despite this rich heritage, the popular view of the Law of Armed Conflict has often been that it is observed more in the breach than in the compliance. For many years, this body of law was considered the exclusive preserve of military lawyers, of the International Committee of the Red Cross faithfully toiling for development in the law as well as increased respect for it, and of those relatively few academics interested in the study of it. In the 1980s, for example, only a small number of Law Schools around the world taught a designated course in the Law of Armed Conflict. In the absence of international criminal courts and tribunals to enforce the law, to render accountable those accused of serious violations of the Law of Armed Conflict, this body of law was perhaps not taken as seriously as it could or should have been.

The past 20 years – since the UN Security Council established the International Criminal Tribunal for the Former Yugoslavia, in 1993, and the following year, in 1994, the International Criminal Tribunal for Rwanda – has witnessed an impressive proliferation of international criminal courts and tribunals and, arguably more importantly, increased expectations around the world that impunity for atrocity is unacceptable and must be checked by the force of law. It is difficult to imagine the Rome Diplomatic Conference even occurring, much less successfully resulting in the establishment of the ICC, without the earlier facilitation of a receptive international environment.

The contemporary existence of international courts and tribunals empowered to try individuals accused of egregious international crimes has transformed the Law of Armed Conflict into an integral part of mainstream International Law. Today, the Law of Armed Conflict is taught in many law schools around the world and the demand for knowledge in the field has palpably increased. I am convinced that the ICC, which I have the privilege to serve as Prosecutor, has contributed to that shift. As the world's first permanent international criminal court, with the *potential* to have jurisdiction anywhere in the world, our very existence has encouraged States to take more seriously their own national responsibilities for investigating alleged war crimes as well as other offences falling within the ambit of the Court's subject matter jurisdiction, and for bringing to trial those allegedly responsible for such offences. Whilst this is not, by any means, all that the Court has achieved to date, I do consider it a significant development and one for which the institution of the Court can take some credit.

I am delighted that my Special Adviser on International Humanitarian Law, Professor Tim McCormack, has joined his colleague Dr Rain Liivoja, to co-edit this impressive volume of essays on the Law of Armed Conflict. By virtue of his involvement with my Office, Professor McCormack knows only too well how integral the Law of Armed Conflict is to our work. Article 21 of the Rome Statute enumerates the law applicable to the work of the Court. Apart from the Statute, the Elements of the Crimes and the Rules of Procedure and Evidence themselves, the Court is also directed explicitly to 'applicable treaties and the principles and rules of international law, including the established principles of the international law of armed conflict'. In addition, the Introduction to the section of the Elements of the Crimes dealing with Article 8 War Crimes explicitly states that

> the elements for war crimes under article 8, paragraph 2, of the Statute shall be interpreted within the established framework of the international law of armed conflict including, as appropriate, the international law of armed conflict applicable to armed conflict at sea.

Understanding and applying this body of law is mandatory for our institution.

The editors have assembled a stellar cast of contributors from many countries and regions of the world. The authors have taken innovative approaches to their topics and explained not only the existing legal rules but also current challenges and trends for further development of the law. This new volume of essays is a welcome addition to the literature in the field and most useful to practitioners, researchers and academics alike. I am sure that staff within my Office will certainly benefit from this impressive publication.

Prosecutor of the International Criminal Court
The Hague
June 2015

Introduction

Rain Liivoja and Tim McCormack

A quarter of a century ago, the law of armed conflict, also known as international humanitarian law, was considered an esoteric area of international law – the domain of military lawyers, the International Committee of the Red Cross (and the global Red Cross and Red Crescent Movement) and those few academics interested in the subject matter. Very few universities in the world offered courses in the field and there was relatively little popular awareness of the legal regulation of armed conflict. The transformation has been spectacular and several factors have contributed to the 'mainstreaming' of this area of international law.

One key factor has been transformative media reporting. CNN's real-time coverage of the Gulf War in 1991 was a major breakthrough – bringing the conduct of the armed conflict on to television screens in lounge rooms around the world. Twenty-four years later, that sort of media reporting looks positively antiquated. Since then we have witnessed 'embedded' journalists reporting in real-time literally from inside the theatre of battle. More recently still, the global advent of smart phones and social media has resulted in real-time eye-witness reporting of the conduct of hostilities and its deleterious impact on victims.

Technological change has not occurred in a vacuum. The proliferation of international criminal courts and tribunals – commencing with the establishment by the UN Security Council of the International Criminal Tribunal for the former Yugoslavia in 1993 and the International Criminal Tribunal for Rwanda in 1994, and culminating in the world's first permanent international criminal court in 2002 – has raised global expectations that those responsible for atrocities should be held accountable. Too often accountability seems chimerical but the existence of global justice mechanisms and the reality of ongoing war crimes trials only fuel expectations. Those same tribunals apply the law of armed conflict on a daily basis, constantly contributing jurisprudence and developing our understanding of the law. Career paths for prosecutors, defence counsel, judges and legal advisers guarantee a thirst for knowledge and understanding of the law.

The law itself is constantly challenged and experiences a dynamic process of adaptation. Precision-guided munitions, asymmetric conflict, urban warfare, the use of human shields, counter-insurgency operations, remotely piloted vehicles and increasingly autonomous weapon systems all raise questions about the adequacy of the existing legal framework and whether or not new law is required for specific novelties in the way conflict is waged.

It was an honour for us to be invited to edit the *Routledge Handbook on the Law of Armed Conflict*. The invitation afforded us an opportunity to gather a group of established and emerging scholars from around the world and to invite them to write on their designated topic not only

1

from the perspective of the established *lex lata* but also to consider emerging issues, the increasing influence of related fields of study and critical challenges to the interpretation and/or application of the particular subject matter. We are delighted with the results: with the team of authors we have assembled, with the range of perspectives presented and with the quality of the analysis produced.

We thank each of our authors for their contributions and for taking so seriously our request to engage in analysis of the emerging challenges in their respective subject areas. We are most grateful to Katie Carpenter, Mark Sapwell, Stephen Gutierrez and Olivia Manley from Routledge for their support, encouragement and their long-suffering. We also thank Melissa Peach for her editorial assistance, and Hannah Riley for seeing the manuscript through to publication. It has been a pleasure for us to work with each and every one of them.

Part I
Fundamentals

The law of armed conflict (LOAC) is the branch of international law that seeks to place limitations on the use of violence in an armed conflict with a view to sparing those who do not directly participate in hostilities and restricting violence to the amount necessary to achieve the aim of the conflict, which is to weaken the military potential of the adversary. LOAC is thus distinct from the international law that establishes the prohibition of the use of force in international relations and the exceptions to that prohibition (Chapter 1).

The idea that restraint should be exercised in armed conflict is not of recent vintage. Quite the opposite: rudimentary rules governing warfare can be found in antiquity and, during the Middle Ages, a highly elaborate, if grossly imperfect, code of chivalry developed in medieval Europe. The 'modern' LOAC, however, has developed from the middle of the nineteenth century with the adoption of a series of treaties dealing with particular aspects of warfare (Chapter 2).

LOAC does not deal with each and every instance of violence; it only applies in armed conflict. International law distinguishes between two types of armed conflict – international and non-international – and regulates these somewhat differently. Thus, any application of the substantive rules of LOAC must be preceded by an assessment as to the existence and the legal character of the armed conflict (Chapter 3).

LOAC has the same range of sources as international law generally. In view of the historical development and humanitarian nature of LOAC, however, some of these sources have particular significance, or idiosyncrasies, with implications on the application of the law in practice (Chapter 4).

In regulating or moderating the use of violence in armed conflict, LOAC must strike a precarious balance between multiple interests that are sometimes in competition (Chapter 5). Particularly significant in this regard are considerations of military necessity and humanity, as well as the concepts of chivalry and sovereignty, in the development of LOAC rules.

It has become increasingly accepted that LOAC does not govern the conduct of belligerents in an armed conflict to the exclusion of other branches of international law. In particular, international human rights law continues to apply in armed conflict and its rules interact in different ways with those of LOAC (Chapter 6).

1

War and armed conflict

The parameters of enquiry

Dino Kritsiotis

Perhaps the very first truism to confront any scholar or student of the international laws of war or armed conflict is that these laws operate on the essential premise that a war or armed conflict has come into existence in a legal sense – that is, as a matter of international law. After all, it is that condition of 'war' or 'armed conflict' that presents the organising logic and design of these laws. It is *that* condition which supplies the *raison d'être* for the intervention of international law and, for better or for worse, it articulates what these laws are actually *for*. Recognising the possibilities of this condition in its various historical iterations,[1] international law thus counterpoised the laws of war against the so-called laws of peace,[2] proceeding from 'some kind of more or less definite boundary between times of war and times of peace'.[3]

Evidence of this *summa divisio* of the discipline of international law – of this fragmentation between war and peace occurring at its very core – can be gleaned from the 1868 St Petersburg Declaration, where the Contracting Parties assumed an undertaking 'in case of war among themselves',[4] and the 1904 Hague Convention relative to Hospital Ships, which addressed its Contracting Powers 'in case of war between two or more of them'.[5] Furthermore, as part of this thematic organization of international relations, the whole purpose of treaties of peace was to draw to a formal close the state of war and confirm the return to a state or condition of peace as far as the law was concerned: as Emer de Vattel informed us in his *The Law of Nations* (1758), the treaty of peace occurs '[w]hen the belligerent powers have agreed to lay down their arms, the agreement or contract in which they stipulate the condition of peace and regulate the manner in which it is to be

---

1 Christopher Greenwood, 'The Concept of War in Modern International Law' (1987) 36 *ICLQ* 283.
2 Hence, Stephen C Neff has written of a 'distinct "institution" or "state" of war' – and of a 'set of rules peculiar to war' – in his *War and the Law of Nations: A General History* (CUP 2005) 15. Carsten Stahn has written more recently how these 'types of rules' – ie the laws of peace and the laws of war – 'were treated as alternative frameworks': see Carsten Stahn, '*Jus Post Bellum*: Mapping the Discipline(s)' (2008) 23 *American University ILR* 311, 316.
3 Neff, *War* (n 2) 15.
4 Declaration Renouncing the Use, in Time of War, of Explosive Projectiles under 400 Grammes Weight ('St Petersburg Declaration') (11 December 1868) 138 CTS 297.
5 (21 December 1904) 197 CTS 331, art 3(1).

restored and supported',[6] an incredibly important mechanism if it is to be believed that upon their activation the laws of war came to replace the laws of peace in their solemn entirety.[7]

The laws of war, then, announced the arrangements – most specifically, the rights and obligations – that would obtain *during* warfare,[8] and it is for this reason that they attracted the Latin rubric of the *jus in bello*.[9] As such, they should be properly distinguished from the laws of the *jus ad bellum* which itemise the rights (and, presumably, also the obligations) of states to pursue or to inaugurate warfare in their international relations. For international law, there was thus an understandable sequence of the affliction of public violence as between sovereigns, with the *jus ad bellum* appearing earlier in chronological order than the *jus in bello* – although, to be sure, the laws of the *jus in bello* possess a much older pedigree than those of the *jus ad bellum*.[10] Even so, with their shared concentration on matters of war or *bellum*, we can appreciate why both of these corpuses – that of the *jus ad bellum* and the *jus in bello* – might attract the same designation of the laws *of* war,[11] for each in their own way involve laws *of* – that is, pertaining to or *concerning* – war. That said, at a separate level of analysis, it must be recalled that the laws of the *jus ad bellum* are predicated upon the existence of a state of peace *inter partes*, whose operation precedes any outbreak of public violence or any set of hostilities. As such, the preferred anchoring of the *jus ad bellum* would appear to be within the realm of the laws of *peace*,[12] a position that is sure to be reinforced by the fact that international law no longer provides for 'war' as the common denominator between the *jus ad bellum* and the *jus in bello*: whereas the former are defined by the occurrence of 'force', the latter are now activated by an 'armed conflict' and it cannot be assumed that these fields share an exact coincidence.[13]

As for the laws of war *stricto sensu* (or *jus in bello*), these pronounced upon the detail of the legal relationship as applicable between belligerent states,[14] whereas the legal relationship

---

6 Emer de Vattel, *The Law of Nations, or, Principles of the Law of Nations Applied to the Conduct and Affairs of Nations and Sovereigns* (1758) (Béla Kapossy and Richard Whatmore eds, Liberty Fund 2008) bk IV, ch II, s 9. See further Randall Lesaffer (ed), *Peace Treaties and International Law in European History: From the Late Middle Ages to World War One* (CUP 2008).

7 Note Arnold D McNair advising against such 'generalizations' – and 'hasty generalizations' at that: 'The Functions and Differing Legal Character of Treaties' (1930) 11 *BYBIL* 100, 102.

8 It was Hugo Grotius who alerted us to how 'practice' had asserted more of an expansive conception of war than that provided by Cicero, where war was 'a contention by force': in his seminal *De Jure belli ac pacis* (1625), Grotius wrote that 'the practice has prevailed to indicate by that name [ie war], not an immediate action, but a state of affairs; so that war is the state of contending parties, considered as such': bk I, ch I, s 2.

9 Consider Robert Kolb, 'Origin of the Twin Terms *jus ad bellum/jus in bello*' (1997) 37 *IRRC* 553.

10 And, of more recent vintage altogether, to complete this order is the *jus post bellum* – a product of post-Cold War concerns such as transformative occupation, peace-building and international territorial administration – although this, too, comes with its own antecedents: see Jens Iverson, 'Transitional Justice: *Jus Post Bellum* and International Criminal Law: Differentiating the Usages, History and Dynamics' (2013) 7 *IJTJ* 413.

11 As is common in the literature, and maintained by Yoram Dinstein amongst others, that '[t]he law of war in its totality is subdivided into the *jus in bello* ... and the *jus ad bellum*' in *The Conduct of Hostilities under the Law of International Armed Conflict* (2nd edn, CUP 2010) 3.

12 As appears to be the approach, for example, of Adam Roberts and Richard Guelff (eds), *Documents on the Laws of War* (3rd edn, OUP 2000) 1. Note, also, that certain violations of the laws of peace were characterised as 'crimes against peace' in the Nuremberg Charter (8 August 1945) 82 UNTS 279, art 6(a).

13 The position of the ICJ in *Military and Paramilitary Activities in and Against Nicaragua (Nicaragua v US)* [1986] ICJ Rep 14, ¶ 216 ('[c]learly, [the] use of force *may* in some circumstances raise questions of such law') needs to be contrasted with that of the Appeals Chamber of the ICTY in *Prosecutor v Tadić (Decision on the Defence Motion for Interlocutory Appeal on Jurisdiction)* (Case no IT-94-1, ICTY Appeals Chamber, 2 October 1995) ¶ 70 (an international armed conflict exists '*whenever* there is a resort to armed force') (emphases supplied). See further Dino Kritsiotis, 'The Tremors of *Tadić*' (2010) 43 *Israel LR* 262, 278–279.

14 As per J M Spaight, *War Rights on Land* (Macmillan 1911) 5 – or, better, as between *belligerents*, for the laws of war made accommodation for the so-called 'recognition of belligerency' in the context of civil wars. See Lassa Oppenheim, *International Law: A Treatise* (Longmans 1906) vol II, 86.

between belligerent and non-belligerent states stood to be governed by the laws of neutrality,[15] and the relations as between non-belligerent states continued to be located within the laws of peace.[16] So, within this overall framework developed by international law, the occurrence of a state or condition of war actually yielded consequences on multiple fronts aside from the activation and application of the laws of war, making clear that the determination as any change of the status quo of a given relationship could not and should not be lightly made.[17] Importantly, the whole point of the laws of war was to admit a separate framework for action as between states so that, amongst other things, '[t]he soldier has the right to kill another soldier',[18] and where 'military operations could be mounted against ... enemies *en masse*, without any need for the scrupulous provision of proof of guilt in each individual case, as ordinary law enforcement required.'[19] Behaviour that international law would ordinarily condemn and regard as impermissible, the laws of war would thus anticipate and make *permissible* within the context of the privilege bestowed on combatants to participate in and also to undertake such hostilities.[20]

15 As the preamble of the Hague Convention (V) Respecting the Rights and Duties of Neutral Powers and Persons in Case of War on Land (18 October 1907) 205 CTS 299 provided, its High Contracting Parties acted '[w]ith a view to laying down more clearly the rights and duties of neutral Powers *in case of war on land* and regulating the position of the belligerents who have taken refuge in neutral territory' (emphasis supplied). See also Hague Convention (XIII) concerning the Rights and Duties of Neutral Powers in Naval War (18 October 1907) 205 CTS 395 ('in the event of naval war') and, further, Erik Castrén, *The Present Law of War and Neutrality* (Academia Scientiarum Fennica 1954) 423 ('neutrality presupposes war between some Powers'). On the significance of these laws under the regime of the Charter of the United Nations, consider Patrick M Norton, 'Between the Ideology and the Reality: The Shadow of the Law of Neutrality' (1976) 17 *Harvard ILJ* 249.
16 See further Greenwood (n 1).
17 Declarations of war were but one method to the initiation of warfare according to Oppenheim – alongside 'committing certain hostile acts of force against another State'; Oppenheim (n 14) 102; see also ibid 105. This position is in contradistinction to human rights treaties which 'themselves make no mention of the types of situation in which the provisions are to apply': Louise Doswald-Beck, *Human Rights in Times of Conflict and Terrorism* (OUP 2011) 5. Such treaties, however, demarcate that certain measures of derogation are possible 'in time of war' as well as other public emergencies: ECHR art 15 and ACHR art 27 ('Suspension of Guarantees'). Cf ICCPR art 4 ('[i]n time of public emergency which threatens the life of the nation') and the Arab Charter on Human Rights (22 May 2004) art 4(1) ('[i]n exceptional situations of emergency which threaten the life of the nation'). See further Rosalyn Higgins, 'Derogations under Human Rights Treaties' (1976) 48 *BYBIL* 281.
18 Françoise Hampson, 'Human Rights Law and International Humanitarian Law: Two Coins or Two Sides of the Same Coin?' (1991) 1 *Bulletin of Human Rights* 46, 48.
19 Neff, *War* (n 2) 19.
20 Otherwise known by the name of combatant immunity. Instructions for the Government of Armies of the United States in the Field, General Order No 100 ('Lieber Code') (24 April 1863) art 57 makes provision for the fact that

    [s]o soon as a man is armed by a sovereign government and takes the soldier's oath of fidelity, he is a belligerent; his killing, wounding, or other warlike acts are not individual crimes or offenses. No belligerent has a right to declare that enemies of a certain class, colour, or condition, when properly organized as soldiers, will not be treated by him as public enemies.

    Or, as is explained in the *Commentary* to API,

    the combatants' privilege ... provides immunity from the application of municipal law prohibitions against homicides, wounding and maiming, or capturing persons and destruction of property, so long as these acts are done as acts of war and do not transgress the restraints of the rules of international law applicable in armed conflict. Those who enjoy the combatant's privilege are also legitimate targets for the adversary's attacks until they become *hors de combat* of prisoners of war.

    See Michael Bothe, Karl Josef Partsch and Waldemar A Solf, *New Rules for Victims of Armed Conflicts* (Martinus Nijhoff 1982) 243.

This set of enabling arrangements set forth by international law was not of course to be taken to mean that any and all violence would constitute 'war' for the purposes of the laws of war: the Instructions for the Government of Armies of the United States in the Field (or Lieber Code) of April 1863 went out of its way to explain how '[p]ublic war is a state of armed hostility between sovereign nations or governments' and that '[i]t is a law and requisite of civilized existence that men live in political, continuous societies, forming organized units, called states or nations, whose constituents bear, enjoy, suffer, advance and retrograde together, in peace and in war'.[21] Nor did the condition of war become the occasion for gratuitous or uncontrolled violence during warfare, since the Lieber Code made plain that permissible violence could not occur at the hands of '[m]en, or squads of men, who commit hostilities, whether by fighting, or inroads for destruction or plunder, or by raids of any kind, without commission, *without being part and portion of the organized hostile army*',[22] or, indeed, of those whom it labelled armed prowlers.[23] The laws of war thus contained a series of prohibitions or 'prohibitive' laws,[24] compliance with which was to become essential in making the distinction between lawful and unlawful combatants,[25] and, thus, to the award, conferral or revocation of prisoner-of-war status.[26]

As the introduction to this important and impressive volume, this chapter engages several preliminary, overarching or recurring themes that arise throughout the work. It will commence by investigating the relationship – spelt out in terms of the principle of equal application – between the *jus ad bellum* and the *jus in bello*, providing a brief synopsis of the content of the *jus ad bellum* and what this means (or might mean) for the application of the *jus in bello*. We shall then turn to consider the genealogy and structure of this law – of why, where and how it evolved in the first place – before outlining the developments that occurred after the Second World War which set down the foundations for the subject that remain with us through to this day. The next section engages the *provenance* (or, better, *provenances*) of the laws of war or, as they are now known in view of these developments, the laws of armed conflict,[27] and presents a particular appreciation of the projected relevance of the Geneva Conventions (and their Additional Protocols) from a reading of the treaties themselves: the dual infrastructure of international and non-international armed conflicts is explained, as is the possibility of belligerent occupation occurring within the context of *international* armed conflicts.[28] In the penultimate section of the chapter, some consideration is given to the diverse character of this law – that is, the nature of the propositions that are set forth and, in turn, the question of to *whom* such propositions are addressed. It will be seen that the expansive embrace of the Lieber Code – where 'all men who belong[ed] to the rising *en masse* of the hostile country'[29]

---

21 Art 20. This explains why any crossfire with pirates would not amount to 'war' in the legal sense of that term: Douglas Guilfoyle, 'The Laws of War and the Fight Against Somali Piracy: Combatants or Criminals?' (2010) 11 *Melbourne JIL* 1, and, also, Michael H Passman, 'Protections Afforded to Captured Pirates under the Law of War and International Law' (2008) 33 *Tulane Maritime Law Journal* 1.

22 Lieber Code (n 20) art 82 (emphasis added).

23 Ibid art 84.

24 As it was put in *US v List et al* 11 TWC 1247, 1 (1950).

25 As per Brussels Declaration Concerning the Laws and Customs of War (27 August 1874) 1 *AJIL Supp* 96, art 9. Cf Lieber Code (n 20) art 49.

26 Hence HR arts 1–3 and GCIII art 4.

27 A hint of this change is evident from the GCs and APs themselves: whereas GCIII art 4(A)(2)(d) makes mention of 'the laws and customs of war', API art 43(1) refers to 'the rules of international law applicable in armed conflict'. See also API arts 2(b), 31(3), 31(4), 37, 44(2), 49(3), 57(4), 59(4) and 59(7)).

28 And, throughout, there shall be recourse to the position of custom – as famously emphasised by Theodor Meron, *Human Rights and Humanitarian Norms as Customary Law* (Clarendon 1989).

29 Art 49(2). See also Gerry Simpson, 'Paris 1793 and 1871: *Levée en masse* as Event' in Fleur Johns, Richard Joyce and Sundhya Pahuja (eds), *Events: The Force of International Law* (Routledge 2011) 81.

and those 'citizens who accompany an army for whatever purpose, such as sutlers, editors, or reports of journals, or contractors'[30] took their place alongside the 'public enemy armed or attached to the hostile army for active aid'[31] – is a theme very much continued through to the present time, though it now contends with the narrative of human rights that has been popularised since the adoption of the Universal Declaration of Human Rights in December 1948.[32] The final section of the chapter contains some concluding reflections of the themes and analyses that have brought us to that point, and which might be useful to bear in mind as one makes one's way through the chapters of this volume.

1 The principle of equal application

In order to configure the precise relationship between the *jus ad bellum* and *jus in bello*, it should be recalled at the outset that, as originally conceived, the laws of war were never intended to prohibit or to abolish 'recourse to war for the solution of international controversies'.[33] Rather, the laws of war accepted war as a going concern, which called out for moderation and even regulation – an idea that possesses ancient cultural and religious roots.[34] The notion of restricting recourse to war defines the interest of the *jus ad bellum* – and came as a much later development in international law as the 1907 Hague Convention (II) and the 1928 Kellogg–Briand Pact demonstrate.[35] Its most recent iteration exists in the form of Article 2(4) of the UN Charter, which prohibits all members of the UN 'from the threat or use of force against the territorial integrity or political independence of any state, or in any other manner inconsistent with the Purposes of the United Nations',[36] as well as the Charter framework that makes provision for individual and collective self-defence under Article 51 as it does for actions authorised by the Security Council in accordance with Chapter VII of the Charter.[37] This framework is enjoined by the prohibition of intervention that is not, as such, articulated in the Charter,[38] but which is well-established as a matter of custom and which has been argued to admit its own exceptions for state action (for example, the right of humanitarian intervention or the right of pro-democratic intervention).[39]

---

30 Art 50(1).

31 Art 49(1). See further Sibylle Scheipers, *Unlawful Combatants: A Genealogy of the Irregular Fighter* (OUP 2015).

32 See however Samuel Moyn, *The Last Utopia: Human Rights in History* (Harvard University Press 2010).

33 The formulation of the General Treaty for the Renunciation of War as an Instrument of National Policy ('Kellogg–Briand Pact') (27 August 1928) 94 LNTS 57, art I. See also Roberts and Guelff (n 12) 28.

34 See *Legality of the Threat or Use of Nuclear Weapons (Advisory Opinion)* [1996] ICJ Rep 226, Dissenting Opinion of Judge Weeramantry, 478–482.

35 Hague Convention (II) on the Limitation of Employment of Force for Recovery of Debts (18 October 1907) 205 CTS 250; Kellogg–Briand Pact (n 33).

36 A principle applicable, too, to non-members of the UN on account of its customary status: *Nicaragua* (n 13) ¶ 188.

37 And which, as per art 53 of the Charter, includes 'regional arrangements or agencies for enforcement action' acting under the authority of the Council.

38 UN Charter art 2(7) notwithstanding.

39 See Christopher Greenwood, 'Self-Defence and the Conduct of International Armed Conflict' in Yoram Dinstein and Mala Tabory (eds), *International Law at a Time of Perplexity: Essays in Honour of Shabtai Rosenne* (Kluwer 1989) 273, 274; Dino Kritsiotis, 'Topographies of Force' in Michael N Schmitt and Jelena Pejic (eds), *International Law and Armed Conflict: Exploring the Faultlines – Essays in Honour of Yoram Dinstein* (Martinus Nijhoff 2007) 29.

These developments concerning the *jus ad bellum* – or, perhaps more accurately, the *jus contra bellum*[40] – contrast with the much earlier development of the *jus in bello*: international law caught as it was in the grip of the increasing violence of the nineteenth century with no permanent apparatus for international dispute resolution had

> consequently no alternative but to accept war, independently of the justice of its origin, as a relation which the parties to it may set up if they choose, and to busy itself only in regulating the effects of the relation.[41]

And this it did to vivid and enduring effect with the first multilateral endeavour of its kind: the 1864 Geneva Convention with its key provision that '[w]ounded or sick combatants, to whatever nation they may belong, shall be collected and cared for'.[42]

This Convention and the ones that followed are sure to explain, at least in part, why the laws of war have also attracted the designation of 'international humanitarian law', for their focus has been on 'the central issue of the treatment of the individual, whether civilian or military',[43] but, as the Tokyo District Court was to remind us in *Ryuichi Shimoda v The State* in 1963, and as the contributions to this collection will make repeatedly clear, 'international law respecting war is not formed only by humane feelings, but it has as its basis both military necessity and efficiency and humane feelings, and is formed by weighing these two factors'.[44] That term has thus come with its detractors,[45] with some even concluding that '[e]xamination of the historical development of these laws reveals that despite noble rhetoric to the contrary, the laws of war have been formulated deliberately to privilege military necessity at the cost of humanitarian values'.[46] One can thus appreciate why the

40 Consider Olivier Corten, *The Law Against War: The Prohibition on the Use of Force in Contemporary International Law* (Hart 2010) 51.

41 William Edward Hall, *International Law* (Clarendon 1880) 52. Or, perhaps better put, 'international law has dealt with war as a state of fact which it has hitherto been powerless to prevent': Richard R Baxter, 'So-Called "Unprivileged Belligerency": Spies, Guerrillas, and Saboteurs' (1951) 28 BYBIL 323, 323–324. See also the preamble of the 1899 Hague Convention (II) with Respect to the Laws and Customs of War on Land (29 July 1899) 189 CTS 429 (where the High Contracting Parties considered that 'while seeking means to preserve and prevent armed conflicts among nations, it is likewise necessary to have regard to cases where an appeal to arms may be caused by events which their solicitude could not avert').

42 Geneva Convention for the Amelioration of the Condition of the Wounded in Armies in the Field (22 August 1864) 129 CTS 361, art 6. See further Frits Kalshoven, 'The history of international humanitarian law treaty-making' ch 2 in this volume. This is not to deny the presence of bilateral or customary iterations of the laws of war before this period: indeed, the Lieber Code (n 20) was an exercise in 'restatement, or summary of the *existing* laws of war, rather than actual new legislation.' See Stephen C Neff, *Justice in Blue and Gray: A Legal History of the Civil War* (Harvard University Press 2010) 57.

43 Roberts and Guelff (n 12) 2. Or, as it has been put by Lauterpacht, 'their object is to safeguard, within the limits of the stern exigencies of war, human life and some other fundamental human rights'. See Hersh Lauterpacht, 'The Limits of the Operation of the Laws of War' (1953) 30 BYBIL 206, 214. See also A W B Simpson, 'The Agincourt Campaign and the Law of War' (1995) 16 *Michigan JIL* 653, 653 (concentrating on the 'function' of this corpus, ie 'humanizing war, so far as this is possible, by making it less nasty than it otherwise might be').

44 (1963) 32 ILR 626.

45 Among whom we would include Geoffrey Best, *Humanity in Warfare* (Columbia University Press 1980) 16–17, where he said the term

> could be seen as implying that the laws of war have an exclusively humanitarian purpose, when their evolution has in fact reflected various practical concerns of states and their armed forces on the ground other than those which may be considered humanitarian.

46 Chris af Jochnick and Roger Normand, 'The Legitimation of Violence: A Critical History of the Laws of War' (1994) 35 *Harvard ILJ* 49, 50. See also Theodor Meron, 'Francis Lieber's Code and the Principle of Humanity' (1998) 36 *Columbia JTL* 269.

'laws of war' or its more modern appellation of the 'laws of armed conflict',[47] resting on the twin normative currents of the 'Geneva law' (concerning the protection of victims of warfare) and 'Hague law' (concerning the means and methods of warfare), has proved far less controversial.[48]

Be this as it may, the inspiration and logic for the innovation of the 1864 Geneva Convention stemmed from the carnage present on the battlefield at Solferino in June 1859, as witnessed and then monumentalised in Henri Dunant's *A Memory of Solferino*, where some form of legal intervention was urged.[49] The idea of the resulting Convention was to extend the humanitarian hand of assistance to all wounded combatants *irrespective of their identity or the side on which they fought*, so that the principle of equal application is in fact embedded in the earliest manifestations of the modern canon,[50] in other words well before the arrival of any formalised system of rules known as the *jus ad bellum*.

The most recent invocation of this principle occurs in the 1977 Additional Protocol I, whose preamble reaffirms that the provisions of the four Geneva Conventions as well as of the Protocol

> must be fully applied in all circumstances to all persons who are protected by those instruments, without any adverse distinction based on the nature or origin of the armed conflict or on the causes espoused by or attributed to the Parties to the conflict.[51]

At the same time, we need to be aware of the fact that High Contracting Parties to all four Geneva Conventions have undertaken to respect and to ensure respect for the Conventions – *and to do so in all circumstances*.[52] The significance and appeal of the principle of equal application thus very much continues to resonate through to the modern period,[53] for its foundations are as much philosophical as they are pragmatic. As Michael Walzer has maintained, it is not necessarily the decision of those who are engaged in the thick of hostilities to have entered those hostilities in the first place:

47 See n 28.
48 Frits Kalshoven and Liesbeth Zegveld, *Constrains on the Waging of War: An Introduction to International Humanitarian Law* (4th edn, CUP 2011) 8–24. See however Theodor Meron, 'The Humanization of Humanitarian Law' (2000) 94 *AJIL* 239.
49 See Henry Dunant, *A Memory of Solferino* (ICRC 1959 [1862]) 126.
50 See Caroline Moorehead, *Dunant's Dream: War, Switzerland and the History of the Red Cross* (Carroll & Graf 1998) 29. See further David Rodin and Henry Shue (eds), *Just and Unjust Warriors: The Moral and Legal Status of Soldiers* (OUP 2008).
51 Notwithstanding the fact that the 'nature or origin' of armed conflicts 'in which peoples are fighting against colonial domination and alien occupation and against racist regimes in the exercise of their right of self-determination' affected their classification status as far as API is concerned: see nn 63 and 103.
52 GCI–IV common art 1. In line with this reasoning, *GCI Commentary* 27 advises that

> the words 'in all circumstances' mean that, as soon as one of the conditions of application for which Article 2 provides is present, no Power bound by the Convention can offer any valid pretext, legal or other, for not respecting the Convention in all its parts. The words 'in all circumstances' mean in short that the application of the Convention does not depend on the character of the conflict. Whether a war is 'just' or 'unjust', whether it is a war of aggression or of resistance to aggression, the protection and care due to the wounded and sick are in no way affected.

53 See eg Observance by United Nations forces of International Humanitarian Law, Secretary-General's Bulletin, UN Doc ST/SGB/1999/13 (6 August 1999) s 1(1). See also Adam Roberts, 'The Principle of Equal Application of the Laws of War' in Rodin and Shue (eds) (n 50) 226, 227; Christopher Greenwood, 'The Relationship between *jus ad bellum* and *jus in bello*' (1983) 9 *Review of International Studies* 221; Keiichiro Okimoto, *The Distinction and Relationship between* jus ad bellum *and* jus in bello (Hart 2011).

[B]y and large we don't blame a soldier, even a general, who fights for his own government. He is not the member of a robber band, acting sometimes at great personal risk in a way he thinks is right. We allow him to say what an English soldier says in Shakespeare's *Henry V*: 'We know enough if we know we are the king's men. Our obedience to the king wipes the crime of it out of us.' Not that his obedience can never be criminal; for when he violates the rules of war, superior orders are no defence. The atrocities that he commits are his own; the war is not. It is conceived, both in international law and in ordinary moral judgment, as the king's business – a matter of state policy, not of individual volition, except when the individual is king.[54]

According to this 'moral reality of war',[55] no adverse consequences should attach to any combatant even if it were possible to determine with luminous clarity whether they were acting on behalf of a state engaged in an unjust or illegal war.[56] That said, while the principle of equal application draws upon a cogent and even compelling combination of logic and historical practice,[57] there are occasional traces of reasoning from the *jus ad bellum* to be found within the detail of the *jus in bello*: the international law of belligerent occupation, for instance, is activated under the 1907 Hague Regulations when '[t]he authority of the legitimate power [has] in fact passed into the hands of the occupant';[58] Geneva Convention III sets forth separate standards for the classification of combatants depending on whether they are '[m]embers of the armed forces of a Party to the conflict, as well as members of militia or volunteers corps forming part of such armed forces'[59] as opposed to '[m]embers of other militia and members of other volunteers corps, including those of organized resistance movements, belonging to a Party to the conflict and operating in order outside their own territory, even if this territory is occupied';[60] Additional Protocol I allows derogation from its prohibition to attack, destroy, remove or render useless objects indispensable to the survival of the civilian population[61] where 'the vital requirements of any Party to the conflict in defence of its national territory against invasion',[62] and, furthermore, Additional Protocol I exempts those armed conflicts 'in which peoples are fighting against colonial domination and alien occupation and against racist régimes in the exercise of their right of self-determination' from consideration as non-international armed conflicts and places them within the scope of international armed

---

54 Michael Walzer, *Just and Unjust Wars: A Moral Argument with Historical Illustrations* (4th edn, Basic Books 2006) 39. The reference to *Henry V* is from Act 4, Scene 1.

55 Ibid 37.

56 And it should be borne in mind that even a self-defending state can act in contravention of the *jus ad bellum*: 'the fact that one or more of the parties to a conflict chooses to regard itself as being in a state of war does not relieve it of the necessity to confine its action what it is permissible in self-defence'. See Greenwood, 'Self-Defence' (n 39) 286. This calls into the question the operation of the principle of proportionality as a matter of the *jus ad bellum* – which understands the quantum of force measured as a whole – as opposed to the *jus in bello* which engages a much more specific metric within the law governing targeting: see David Kretzmer, 'The Inherent Right to Self-Defence and Proportionality in *jus ad bellum*' (2013) 24 *EJIL* 235, 236–237. See also Roberts and Guelff (n 12) 2 and 9.

57 See Roberts (n 53) 230–237.

58 HR art 43 (emphasis supplied).

59 GCIII art 4(A)(1).

60 Ibid art 4(A)(2).

61 API art 54(2).

62 Ibid art 54(5).

conflicts.[63] For the most part, however, the applicable law professes its relevance to all sides in a given armed conflict,[64] and this is really as it should be – for 'it is impossible to visualize the conduct of hostilities in which one side would be bound by the rules of warfare without benefiting from them and the other side would benefit from them without being bound by them'.[65]

2 Genealogy and structure

No one considering the development of the laws of war since the 1864 Geneva Convention can escape the importance of its principles, which also came to be applied to naval warfare with the 1899 Hague Convention (III).[66] Furthermore, the provisions of the 1864 Geneva Convention were consolidated and supplemented by the 1906 Geneva Convention,[67] which, in turn, was applied to naval warfare by virtue of the 1907 Hague Convention (X).[68] The emphasis of these documents – as well as those of the 1856 Declaration Respecting Maritime Law[69] and the 1868 St Petersburg Declaration – was very much to put the regulation of warfare on a 'contractual footing'.[70]

This emphasis was emphatically reinforced by the general participation clause (*clausula si omnes*) of Hague Convention (IV), which provided that the Convention and the annexed Regulations 'do not apply except between Contracting Powers, and then only if all the belligerents are parties to the Convention'.[71] Potentially, this clause could have thwarted any successful war crimes prosecutions brought at the end of the Second World War on account

---

63   Ibid art 1(4). However, the qualification of these armed conflicts as international armed conflict is not automatic and is subject to the procedural stipulation set out in art 96(3). See further David E Graham, 'The 1974 Diplomatic Conference on the Law of War: A Victory for Political Causes and a Return to the "Just War" Concept of the Eleventh Century' (1975) 32 *Washington and Lee LR* 25.

64   See n 53.

65   Lauterpacht (n 43) 212.

66   Hague Convention (III) on the Adaptation to Maritime Warfare of Principles of Geneva Convention of 1864 (29 July 1899) 187 CTS 443.

67   Geneva Convention for the Amelioration of the Condition of the Wounded and Sick in Armies in the Field (6 July 1906) 202 CTS 144.

68   Hague Convention (X) for the Adaptation to Maritime War of the Principles of the Geneva Convention (18 October 1907) 15 LNTS 340, 205 CTS 359.

69   (30 March 1856) 115 CTS 1.

70   As is maintained by John Westlake, *International Law* (2nd edn, CUP 1913) pt II, 62. See in particular St Petersburg Declaration (n 4) (which 'is not applicable to non-Contracting Parties, or Parties who shall have not acceded to it' and 'will also cease to be compulsory from the moment when, in a war between Contracting or Acceding Parties, a non-Contracting Party or a non-Acceding Party shall join one of the belligerents'); to similar effect, Hague Declaration (IV, 2) concerning Asphyxiating Gases (29 July 1899) 187 CTS 453; Hague Declaration (IV, 3) concerning Expanding Bullets (29 July 1899) 187 CTS 459; Hague Declaration (XIV) Prohibiting the Discharge of Projectiles and Explosives from Balloons (18 October 1907) 205 CTS 403. For an ascription of these declarations as '[t]he first treaties governing the conduct of warfare [which] were framed as prohibitions imposed upon states parties to a conflict which operated to benefit individuals, rather than as obligations imposed or rights conferred on individuals', see Kate Parlett, *The Individual in the International Legal System: Continuity and Change in International Law* (CUP 2011) 178. Later on the same page, the description is of 'protective obligations on parties to the conflict, rather than rights conferred on individuals'.

71   Art 2. See the discussion of Nagendra Singh and Edward MacWhinney, *Nuclear Weapons and Contemporary International Law* (Martinus Nijhoff 1989) 42–45, and Meron, 'Humanization' (n 48) 247–248. Singh and MacWhinney actually consider (at 42) that 'when dealing with conventions relating to war such a clause when absent should be implied in the treaty'.

of the fact a number of belligerent states were not parties to this Convention,[72] but the Nuremberg Tribunal found that:

> [t]he rules of land warfare expressed in the Convention undoubtedly represented an advance over existing international law at the time of their adoption [b]ut the Convention expressly stated that it was an attempt 'to revise the general laws and customs of war', which it thus recognized to be then existing, but by 1939 these rules laid down in the Convention were recognized by all civilized nations, and were regarded as being declaratory of the laws and customs of war which are referred to in Art. 6 (*b*) of the Charter [of the International Military Tribunal at Nuremberg].[73]

The 1949 Geneva Conventions adopted an altogether different approach from their outset, with the High Contracting Parties giving 'prominent position'[74] to the undertaking made in the very first (and common) article to the Conventions – that is to respect and to ensure respect for these Conventions in all circumstances.[75] This formulation has been regarded as a worthy advance on the stipulations set forth in the 1929 Geneva Conventions,[76] and it produces an arrangement that departs in significant measure from what had gone before:

> By undertaking at the very outset to respect the clauses of the Convention, the Contracting Parties draw attention to the special character of that instrument. It is not an engagement concluded on the basis of reciprocity, binding each party to the contract only in so far as the other party observes its obligations. It is rather a series of unilateral engagements solemnly contracted before the world as represented by the other Contracting Parties. Each State contracts obligations *vis-à-vis* itself and at the same time

---

72 Ditto for the First World War, eg Germany: Coleman Phillipson, *International Law and the Great War* (Fisher Unwin 1915) 158. See further Lauri Hannikainen, 'The Finnish Civil War 1918 and its Aftermath' in Laura Hannikainen, Raija Hanski and Allan Rosas (eds), *Implementing Humanitarian Law Applicable in Armed Conflicts: The Case of Finland* (Martinus Nijhoff 1992) 8, 38.

73 *US et al v Göring et al*, 1 TMWC 171, 253–254 (1946); similarly *US et al v Araki et al*, 22 Tokyo War Crimes Trial 48413, 48491 (International Military Tribunal for the Far East 1948).

74 *GCI Commentary* 25. The obligation appears at the tail-end of the 1929 Geneva Conventions, in the section dealing with application and execution of the Convention: see Convention for the Amelioration of the Condition of the Wounded and Sick in Armies in the Field (27 July 1929) 118 LNTS 303, art 25(1) and Convention Relative to the Treatment of Prisoners of War (27 July 1929) 118 LNTS 343, art 82(1).

75 GCI–IV art 1; similarly API art 1(1), though there is no equivalent provision in APII. See further Frits Kalshoven, 'The Undertaking to Respect and to Ensure Respect in All Circumstances: From Tiny Seed to Ripening Fruit' (1999) 2 *YBIHL* 3 and Carlo Focarelli, 'Common Article 1 of the 1949 Geneva Conventions: A Soap Bubble?' (2010) 21 *EJIL* 125. Meron, 'Humanization' (n 48) 248 regards this stipulation of the Conventions as 'epitomizing the rejection of reciprocity and the insistence on the automatic application of the Conventions'.

76 Note, though, 1929 Geneva Wounded and Sick Convention (n 74) art 25:

> [t]he provisions of the present Convention shall be respected by the High Contracting Parties in all circumstances. If, in time of war, a belligerent is not a party to the Convention, its provisions shall, nevertheless, be binding as between all the belligerents who are parties thereto

and 1929 Geneva Prisoners of War Convention (n 74) art 82: '[i]n time of war if one of the belligerents is not a party to the Convention, its provisions shall, nevertheless, remain binding as between the belligerents who are parties thereto'.

vis-à-vis the others. The motive of the Convention is such a lofty one, so universally recognized as an imperative call of civilization, that one feels the need for its assertion, as much because of the respect one has for it oneself as because of the respect for it which one expects from one's opponent, and perhaps even more for the former reason than for the latter.[77]

That the undertaking is cast in such categorical language and extends to 'all circumstances' is, perhaps, a curious formulation for the Conventions to make in view of the fact that they go on to establish a dichotomised structure that distinguishes *between* what these circumstances might involve in practice. The Conventions then proceed to develop differing arrangements and expectations depending on which of these *circumstances* actually prevails at any given point in time, requiring a distinction to be made between 'all cases of declared war or of any other armed conflict which may arise between two or more of the High Contracting Parties, even if the state of war is not recognized by one of them' (otherwise known as *international armed conflicts*) in Common Article 2 to the Geneva Conventions[78] and those 'armed conflict[s] not of an international character occurring in the territory of one of the High Contracting Parties' (or *non-international armed conflict*) in Common Article 3 of those same Conventions. It is perhaps worth recalling in this respect that the earlier iteration of 'all circumstances' from the 1929 Geneva Conventions was taken to mean the circumstances of peace as well as war.[79]

---

77 *GCI Commentary* 25. Consider, further, the thesis of Lea Brilmayer, 'From "Contract" to "Pledge": The Structure of International Human Rights Agreements' (2006) 77 *BYBIL* 163. GCI–IV common art 2(3) does, however, appear to envisage a role for reciprocity with its stipulation that

> [a]lthough one of the Powers in conflict may not be a party to the present Convention, the Powers who are parties thereto shall remain bound by it in their mutual relations. They shall furthermore be bound by the Convention in relation to the said Power, if the latter accepts and applies the provisions thereof.

78 Though the language of 'armed conflict' had been known before: see Hague Convention (II) with Respect to the Laws and Customs of War on Land (29 July 1899) 189 CTS 429, preamble ('while seeking means to preserve peace and prevent armed conflicts among nations'); see also Hague Convention (III) for the Adaptation to Maritime Warfare of the Principles of the Geneva Convention of 22 August 1864 (29 July 1899) 187 CTS 443, art 1(1) of 1899 ('at the beginning or during the course of hostilities'). Critically for our purposes, the concept of war had become discredited and even subject to ridicule: Edwin M Borchard, '"War" and "Peace"' (1933) 27 *AJIL* 114, 115 ('[i]s it not a strange doctrine that would make the *existence* of war depend upon recognition by anybody?').

79 See n 76. And, even here, note the qualification recalled by Pictet:

> The commentator on the 1929 Convention held that the intention behind these words was to emphasize the general obligation imposed by the Convention, and to make it plain that the Convention must be respected in peace as well as in war *in the case of those of its provisions which are applicable both in peace and war.* He added: 'Can it be that the words "in all circumstances" were meant to imply civil war? We do not think so ... The obligation between the States is international. But it is eminently desirable that the opposing parties in a civil war should be in mind the humane provisions of the Convention for the observance as between themselves'.
>
> *GCI Commentary* 26 (emphasis supplied)

On the issue of the regulation of civil war prior to the institutionalisation of armed conflicts, see Antonio Cassese, 'The Spanish Civil War and the Development of Customary Law Concerning Internal Armed Conflict' in Antonio Cassese (ed), *Current Problems of International Law: Essays on UN Law and on the Laws of Armed Conflict* (Giuffrè 1975) 287.

This division of realms between international and non-international armed conflicts was very much intended and deliberate,[80] and has come to inform the direction of a good deal of subsequent conventional law – such as the 1954 Hague Convention for the Protection of Cultural Property in the Event of Armed Conflict,[81] the 1977 Additional Protocol (I) Relating to the Protection of Victims of *International Armed Conflicts*,[82] the 1977 Additional Protocol (II) Relating to the Protection of *Non-International Armed Conflicts*[83] – and, it would appear, the *lex lata* of international custom.[84] And the occurrence of one *form* of armed conflict as opposed to another has significant legal ramifications on the ground: as the Geneva Conventions indicate, the occurrence of an international armed conflict triggers the plenary application of the Conventions – that is, the Conventions as a whole in their forbidding entirety[85]

80 See Sandesh Sivakumaran, *The Law of Non-International Armed Conflict* (OUP 2012) 41.
81 (14 May 1954) 249 UNTS 240, art 19(1) of which provides that:

> [i]n the event of an armed conflict not of an international character occurring within the territory of one of the High Contracting Parties, each party to the conflict shall be bound to apply, as a minimum, the provisions of the present Convention which relate to respect for cultural property.

See also Second Protocol to the Hague Convention for the Protection of Cultural Property in the Event of Armed Conflict (26 March 1999) 2253 UNTS 212, art 3.
82 Although API art 1(3) suggests an exact coincidence with the scope of the application of the Geneva Conventions for international armed conflicts – '[t]his Protocol, which supplements the Geneva Conventions of 12 August 1949 for the protection of war victims, shall apply in the situations referred to in Article 2 common to those Conventions' – it is clear that art 1(4) of the Protocol intends an expanded version of this concept: see n 63. Again, references to 'war' in the Protocol are confined to the figurative sense of that term: 'the laws of war' (arts 23(1) and 67(4)); 'methods or means of warfare' (arts 35, 36 and 55(1)); 'weapons, projectiles and material and methods of warfare' (art 35(2)); 'ruses of war' (art 37(2)); 'prisoners of war' (arts 41(3), 44–47, 67(2), 77(3) and 85(4)); 'any land, air or sea warfare' (art 49(3)); 'method of warfare' (art 54(1)); 'warfare' (art 55(1)); 'war crimes' (arts 75(7) and 85(5)); and 'right of war correspondents' (art 79(2)). In APII, 'war' is in fact not even mentioned.
83 Defined in much more restrictive terms that GCI–IV common art 3 (which provides simply for 'each Party to the [non-international armed] conflict'), APII provides for its material field of application in art 1(1):

> all armed conflicts which are not covered by Art. 1 of the Protocol Additional to the Geneva Conventions of 12 August 1949, and relating to the Protection of Victims of International Armed Conflicts *and which take place in the territory of a High Contracting Party between its armed forces and dissident armed forces or other organized armed groups which, under responsible command, exercise such control over a part of its territory to enable them to carry out sustained and concerned military operation and to implement this Protocol* [emphasis supplied].

See further Geoffrey Best, *War & Law Since 1945* (Clarendon 1994) 74.
84 In March 2005, ICRC published its study on *Customary International Humanitarian Law* with 161 rules in total, of which 143 are applicable in international *and* non-international armed conflicts (including eight rules which are 'arguably' customary international law) – and where there would appear to be no distinction in the *forms* of *non-international armed conflict* as per the conventional structure: see Jean-Marie Henckaerts, 'Study on Customary International Humanitarian Law: A Contribution to the Understanding and Respect for the Rule of Law in Armed Conflict' (2005) 87 *IRRC* 175, 178.
85 This is a rather broad-brush claim, one that is often made, that is in fact in need of qualification as some of the provisions of the Conventions *do* anticipate their relevance 'in time of peace as in time of' – unspecified – 'war' or 'during hostilities' (again, unspecified), eg on dissemination (GCI–IV common art 47/48/127/145). See also the third para of GCI–IV common art 49/50/129/146 – that '[e]ach High Contracting Party shall take measures necessary for the suppression of *all acts contrary to the provisions of the present Convention other than the grave breaches* [contained herein]' (emphasis supplied).

– with the exception of Common Article 3 of the Geneva Conventions. This is because Common Article 3 was designed with the specific purpose of *non-international armed conflicts* in mind: it contains the baseline protections tailored for that very context.[86]

It is for this reason that Common Article 3 has been referred to as a 'convention in miniature',[87] for it presents a discrete 'framework'[88] convention that sets out the bare minimum of obligations for all parties to non-international armed conflicts.[89] In other words, as a matter of the overall operation of the Conventions, the existence of a non-international armed conflict means that the remaining protections of the Geneva Conventions are not automatically applicable,[90] as Common Article 3 does go on to provide that '[t]he Parties to the conflict should further endeavour to bring into force, by means of special agreements, *all or part of the other provisions of the present Convention*',[91] a stipulation that very much reinforces the dichotomised structure of the Geneva Conventions outlined earlier. Factoring the developments of the 1977 Additional Protocols I and II, as well as those of customary international humanitarian law, we can tabulate this structure and general significance of the Conventions and Protocols as Figure 1.1.

This structure – based as it is on the Geneva Conventions and the Additional Protocols – has, for the most part, served its original purposes, but it has also been tested at recurring intervals within practice,[92] whether in the form of the hostile relations between Israel and the Gaza Strip or with Hezbollah in Lebanon,[93] the 'war on terror' between the United States and al-Qaeda,[94] the recent relations between Kenya and al-Shabab[95] or between the self-proclaimed Islamic State and those states which are involved in military action against it.[96] Specifically, the question has been whether – and, if so, what aspect of – the international law

---

86 See Tom Grant, 'Who Can Make Treaties? Other Subjects of International Law' in Duncan B Hollis (ed), *The Oxford Guide to Treaties* (OUP 2012) 125, 141.

87 *GCI Commentary* 48.

88 The term (which covers 'the general norms and institutions of the regime – for example, its objective, principles, basic obligations, and institutions … [t]hen, the protocols build on the parent agreement through the elaboration of additional (and more specific) commitments and institutional arrangements') seems apposite here: Daniel Bodansky, 'The Framework Convention/Protocol Approach', WHO/ NCD/TFI/99.1, 15.

89 See Sivakumaran (n 80) 54.

90 This qualification – of the remaining *protections* of the Geneva Conventions – is advised because there are other aspects of the Conventions dealing with procedural matters (eg repression of abuses and infractions) that relate to (or do not exclude) common art 3: hence common art 49(3)/50(3)/129(3)/146(3) ('[e]ach High Contracting Party shall take measures necessary for the suppression of all acts contrary to the provisions of the present Convention *other than the grave breaches* defined in [common art 50/51/130/147]' (emphasis supplied)).

91 See further Frédéric Siordet, *Les Conventions de Genève et la guerre civile* (ICRC 1950) and Colin Smith, 'Special Agreements to Apply the Geneva Conventions in Internal Armed Conflicts: The Lessons of Darfur' (2007) 2 *Irish YBIL* 91.

92 Especially after the Cold War, though consider W Michael Reisman and James Silk, 'Which Law Applies to the Afghan Conflict?' (1984) 82 *AJIL* 459.

93 Françoise J Hampson, 'The Relationship between International Humanitarian Law and Human Rights Law from the Perspective of a Human Rights Treaty Body' (2008) 90 *IRRC* 549, 556.

94 Kenneth Roth, 'The Law of War in the War on Terror: Washington's Abuse of "Enemy Combatants"' (2004) 83 *Foreign Affairs* 2; Ruth Wedgwood, 'Fighting a War under its Rules' (2004) 83 *Foreign Affairs* 126.

95 In particular view of the events in Nairobi in September 2013: Nicholas Kulish, Mark Mazzetti and Eric Schmitt, 'Carnage in Mall shows Resilience of Terror Group' *New York Times* (23 September 2013) A1.

96 See eg Robin Wright, 'The Illusion of a Hostage Policy' *New Yorker* (3 February 2015).

of belligerent relations regulates hostilities between state and non-state actors who are acting out with the standard appreciation of non-international armed conflicts as contained in Common Article 3 of the Geneva Conventions.[97] Is the framework devised by the Conventions, and then developed by Additional Protocol II, sufficient so as to account for, or be adapted to, such hostilities?[98] Or has the time come for a new *form* of armed conflict to be incorporated within this framework?[99]

There is also the matter – touched upon in the Protocols by way of the development of the Conventions and illustrated in the last rung of our graphic overleaf – of the precise nature of the relationship between international and non-international armed conflicts, and of the possibilities for the *internationalisation* of non-international armed conflicts with the invariable consequence of the *extent* of the applicable law that that change will bring in its wake. This is separate to the mechanism of the 'special agreement' anticipated by Common Article 3 of the Conventions,[100] which might only result in the gradual conscription of the full corpus of norms applicable in an *international* armed conflict for *non-international* armed conflicts. Rather, our concern relates to the opportunities for the *internationalisation* of a non-international armed conflict whereby its *form* is revised in its entirety and where this occurs at a particular moment or point in time: we have already adverted to the recognition of belligerency,[101] which has fallen out of use but which could conceivably make a return in practice,[102] and the arrangement made in Additional Protocol I for peoples fighting against colonial domination and alien occupation and against racist regimes in the exercise of their right of self-determination.[103] However, the internationalisation of non-international armed conflicts

---

97 As compared with that contained in APII.

98 So, in *Hamdan v Rumsfeld*, 548 US 557, 631–632 (2006) the US Supreme Court said:

> Although the official commentaries accompanying common Art. 3 indicate that an important purpose of the provision was to furnish minimal protection to rebels involved in one kind of 'conflict not of an international character' … the commentaries make clear 'that the scope of the Article must be as wide as possible'.… In fact, limiting language that would have rendered common Art. 3 applicable 'especially [to] cases of civil war, colonial conflicts, or wars of religion,' was omitted from the final version of the Article, which coupled broader scope of application with a narrower range of rights than did earlier proposed iterations.… Common Art. 3, then, is applicable here and … requires that Hamdan be tried by a 'regularly constituted court affording all the judicial guarantees which are recognized as indispensable by civilized peoples'.

> See also Elizabeth Wilmshurst, 'Introduction' in Elizabeth Wilmshurst (ed), *International Law and the Classification of Conflicts* (OUP 2012) 1; Philippe Sands, *Torture Team: Deception, Cruelty and the Compromise of Law* (Allen Lane 2008) 41.

99 As is argued by Roy S Schondorf, 'Extra-State Armed Conflicts: Is there a Need for a New Legal Regime?' (2004) 37 *NYU JILP* 1. See further Geoffrey S Corn, '*Hamdan*, Lebanon, and the Regulation of Hostilities: The Need to Recognize a Hybrid Category of Armed Conflict' (2007) 40 *Vanderbilt JTL* 295.

100 Special agreements are also envisaged for *international* armed conflicts: see eg GCI arts 10, 15, 23, 28, 31, 36, 37 and 52 – as well as art 6 (where 'High Contracting Parties may conclude other special agreements for all matters concerning which they may deem it suitable to make separate provision').

101 See n 14.

102 As was attempted by President Hugo Chavez of Venezuela in respect of the FARC in Colombia in January 2008: Chris Kraul, 'Chavez keeps up Campaign to get Rebels off Terrorist List' *Los Angeles Times* (20 January 2008). See further Felicity Szesnat and Annie R Bird, 'Colombia' in Wilmshurst (ed) (n 98) 203, 222.

103 See n 63.

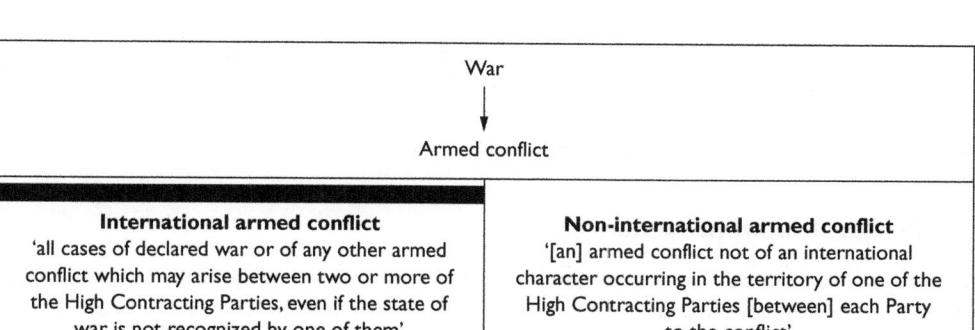

War

↓

Armed conflict

International armed conflict	**Non-international armed conflict**
'all cases of declared war or of any other armed conflict which may arise between two or more of the High Contracting Parties, even if the state of war is not recognized by one of them' (Common Article 2 of Geneva Conventions)	'[an] armed conflict not of an international character occurring in the territory of one of the High Contracting Parties [between] each Party to the conflict' (Common Article 3 of Geneva Conventions)

Applicable law

↓   ↓   ↓

1949 Geneva Conventions (except Common Article 3)	Common Article 3 of 1949 Geneva Conventions
	+
	1977 Second Additional Protocol (where applicable, ie, 'all armed conflicts which are not covered by Art. 1 of the Protocol Additional to the Geneva Conventions of 12 August 1949, and relating to the Protection of Victims of International Armed Conflicts and which take place in the territory of a High Contracting Party between its armed forces and dissident armed forces or other organized armed groups which, under responsible command, exercise such control over a part of its territory to enable them to carry out sustained and concerned military operation and to implement this Protocol')
+	
1977 First Additional Protocol	↓
	Second Additional Protocol
	+
+	
Customary international humanitarian law	Customary international humanitarian law

Internationalisation of non-international armed conflicts

1. Recognition of Belligerency

2. National Liberation Movements: Article 1 (4) + Article 96 (3) of 1977 Second Additional Protocol

3. Agency

Figure 1.1

can also occur in the event that there is intervention from another state,[104] or if it is the case that a relationship of agency has been established between that other state and one of the parties to the non-international armed conflict, that is, 'some of the participants in the internal armed conflict act on behalf of that other State'.[105]

3 The question of provenance

Although it is clear that Common Article 2 and Common Article 3 of the Geneva Conventions intend separate demarcations for the *provenances* of their respective laws,[106] nowhere are their core concepts – of international and non-international armed conflicts – subjected to sustained definition,[107] a matter that relates to both the commencement as well as the conclusion of a given armed conflict.[108] Yet, it is the case that *both* of these provisions enjoin a specific set of histories, ideas, traditions and practices and it is this context that should inform our initial understanding of the purported scope material fields of application: Common Article 2, for example, does not invest exclusive significance in the concept of 'war' for the activation of its laws for, we are advised, it is the existence of an 'armed conflict which may arise between two or more of the High Contracting Parties, even if the state of war is not recognized by one of them' that now matters – so that 'war' is now but *one* instance of an international armed conflict.[109] In contrast, Common Article 3 does not discriminate between the different *forms* of non-international armed conflict with which it is concerned, but this position has now changed since Additional Protocol II only addresses those non-international armed conflicts

> which take place in the territory of a High Contracting Party between its armed forces and dissident armed forces or other organized armed groups which, under responsible command, exercise such control over a part of its territory as to enable them to carry out sustained and concerted military operations and to implement this Protocol.[110]

Importantly, within customary international law, it has been said that non-international armed conflicts occur when there is 'protracted armed violence between governmental

---

104 See Hans-Peter Gasser, 'Internationalized Non-International Armed Conflicts: Case Studies of Afghanistan, Kampuchea, and Lebanon' (1983) 33 *American University LR* 145, 147.

105 *Prosecutor v Tadić* (Case no IT-94-1-A, ICTY Appeals Chamber, 15 July 1999) ¶ 84.

106 As is confirmed by Additional Protocols I and II – but, also, by art 1(4): *supra* n 56.

107 Yet I have argued elsewhere that there are elements of definition presented in the Conventions themselves when one compares what is said for Common Art 2 to what is said for Common Art 3 – and, then, taking account of what is provided for in both Additional Protocols: Kritsiotis, 'The Tremors of *Tadić*' (n 13).

108 See eg Derek Jinks, 'The Temporal Scope of Application of International Humanitarian Law in Contemporary Conflicts' Background Paper prepared for the Informal High-Level Expert Meeting on the Reaffirmation and Development of International Humanitarian Law, Cambridge, MA, 27–29 January 2003, www.hpcrresearch.org/sites/default/files/publications/Session3.pdf.

109 Although consider the proposition that this position represented the status quo as it stood when the Geneva Conventions were adopted: Baxter (n 41) 323.

110 Art 1(1). No such specification exists for the material field of application of common art 3. The relation of APII to common art 3 is thus of an entirely different order to the relation of API to the Geneva Conventions – for API art 1(3) provides that the Protocol 'which supplements the Geneva Conventions ... shall apply in the situations referred to in Art. 2 common to those Conventions'.

authorities and organized armed groups or between such groups within a State',[111] a definition that – at least on its face – does not discriminate between different forms of non-international armed conflict.[112]

The fact that an international armed conflict can occur by virtue of a 'declared war' alone means that, in theory, the Geneva Conventions can become applicable without a single gunshot being fired between High Contracting Parties – a prospect that is sure to seem counter-intuitive to the reader of the Conventions as it might not at all be clear how or why their laws would be relevant in the *absence* of a single act of violence.[113] Be this as it may, this formulation within Common Article 2 recalls the period prior to the Conventions when war could commence 'through committing certain hostile acts of force against another State',[114] or via a declaration of war ('a communication of one State to another that it considers a condition of war existing between them').[115] This traditional focus on the subjective position of states as reflected in the practice of declarations of war proved far too erratic in the end as a device for triggering the laws of war,[116] and explains why the Geneva Conventions settled upon the much more encompassing concept of an (international) armed conflict where '[t]he occurrence of de facto hostilities is sufficient'.[117]

---

111 *Tadić (Jurisdiction)* (n 13) 70. This formulation does appear to side more with the thrust of common art 3 rather than the framework of APII – but the language of 'protracted' armed violence captures the theme from the Protocol that it 'shall not apply to situations of internal disturbances and tensions, such as riots, isolated and sporadic acts of violence and other acts of a similar nature'. Furthermore, CIHL and Rome Statute arts 8(2)(c) and 8(2)(e) do not distinguish between different forms of non-international armed conflicts – in the same way it makes explicit the rules applicable in international *and* non-international armed conflicts.

112 See further the ICRC, 'How is the Term "Armed Conflict" Defined in International Law?' Opinion Paper (March 2008), www.icrc.org/eng/assets/files/other/opinion-paper-armed-conflict.pdf.

113 In fact, the laws of war have traditionally included arrangements for the treatment of resident enemy nationals: see Oppenheim (n 14) 106 and 109–110, and Spaight (n 14) 28–33. See further Lord McNair and A D Watts, *The Legal Effects of War* (4th edn, CUP 1966) 76 and Bernadette Walsh, 'Detention and Deportation of Foreign Nationals in the United Kingdom during the Gulf Conflict' in Peter Rowe (ed), *The Gulf War 1990–91 in International and English Law* (Routledge 1993) 304. See also GCIV arts 35–46 and the suggestion that the Geneva Conventions would be applicable if 'following frontier incidents, the Government concerned adopted security measures, such as internment, against the nationals of the other State who are in its territory'. See *GCIV Commentary* 59.

114 Oppenheim (n 14) 102. The examples given at ibid 104: occupation of a part of foreign territory, an inroad into a foreign country, the blockade of a harbour, an attack at the frontier, an attack on a man-of-war and the capture of a merchantman.

115 Oppenheim (n 14) 103. Oppenheim reporting, too, of the possibility of 'a proclamation and manifesto of a State that it considers itself at war with another State': ibid 102. Where a declaration of war was issued, its significance would surpass any subsequent occurrence of hostilities: 'the war is considered to have been commenced with the date of its declaration although hostilities may not have been commenced till a much later date': ibid 103 (¶ 94).

116 Notwithstanding 1907 Hague Convention (III): 'The Contracting Powers recognize that hostilities between themselves must not commence without previous and explicit warning, in the form either of a declaration of war, giving reasons, or of an ultimatum with conditional declaration of war.' These requirements were not to be regarded as customary at that time (see Spaight (n 14) 21) and, according to *GCIV Commentary* 17–18: 'Since 1907 experience has shown that many armed conflicts, displaying all the characteristics of a war, may arise without being preceded by any of the formalities laid down in the 1907 Hague Convention.'

117 See *GCIV Commentary* 20.

And we find that this metric – that is, of observable de facto hostilities – is one that repeats itself with commendable regularity throughout the Conventions: Geneva Convention I, for example, makes reference to 'the commencement of hostilities'[118] as it does 'the end of hostilities'.[119] Furthermore, a 'time of peace' is defined by reference to 'the outbreak of hostilities',[120] where some of the provisions are actually made contingent '[u]pon the outbreak and during the course of hostilities'.[121] The Geneva Conventions thus convey a rather particular appreciation of their own sense of their relevance – and, by framing certain obligations with reference to *from* or *upon* or even *at* the outbreak of hostilities,[122] the impression is cast that this determination will be obvious and free from difficulty when practice has tended to counsel otherwise.[123] And Additional Protocol I follows suit: it also invokes the language of 'the outbreak of hostilities'[124] as well as 'the beginning of hostilities',[125] making reference, too, to 'the end of active hostilities'.[126] For the most part, then, it would appear that the virtue of an international armed conflict is that it possesses a determinable start, followed by its course or duration[127] and, of course, an identifiable conclusion.[128]

Yet, connecting with a theme from the 1864 Geneva Convention,[129] the Geneva Conventions shall also be applicable in 'cases of partial or total occupation of the territory of a High Contracting Party' – and 'even if the said occupation meets with no armed resistance'.[130] This latter specification was designed to account for experiences of the Second World War 'which saw territories occupied without hostilities' and where 'the Government of the occupied [territory] consider[ed] that armed resistance was useless'.[131] This approach does add an important perspective to the expectation of de facto hostilities, but, *in ultimo*, the question of

---

118 GCI art 17(3).

119 Ibid art 17(4); also, GCIII arts 67 ('at the close of hostilities'), 111 ('until the close of hostilities'), 118(1) ('after the cessation of active hostilities') and 118(2) ('the cessation of hostilities'); GCIV arts 45(2) ('after the cessation of hostilities'), 46, 130(3), 133(1), 133(3) and 134 ('the close of hostilities').

120 GCI art 23(1), 28(2), 31(2) and 40(3). See further GCII art 42(3); GCIII arts 21(3), 43(1), 58(1) and 112(1) ('[u]pon the outbreak of hostilities'). Cf GCIII art 33(2)(b) ('at the outbreak of hostilities').

121 As indeed is the case with GCI art 23(2); see also arts 28(2), 28(3) and 48; GCII arts 33 and 49; GCIII arts 33(3), 109(2), 109(3) and 128; GCIV arts 14(1), 45(5), 70(2), 14(2), 132(2) and 145.

122 See nn 118–121.

123 For unsettled it be: Howard S Levie, 'The Status of Belligerent Personnel "Splashed" and Rescued by a Neutral in the Persian Gulf Area' (1990-91) 31 *Virginia JIL* 611.

124 API art 60(2).

125 Ibid art 73.

126 Ibid art 33(1).

127 Ibid art 79(1) ('areas of armed conflict'). Also actions, offences or reasons 'related to the armed conflict' (arts 75(3), 75(4), 75(5), 75(6), 76(2), 76(3), 77(4) and 77(5)) and 'in time of armed conflict' (arts 82, 83(1) and (2)).

128 Hence, art 75(6): 'Persons who are arrested, detained or interned for reasons related to the armed conflict shall enjoy the protection provided by this Article until their final release, repatriation or re-establishment, even after the end of the armed conflict.' Also art 99(1).

129 Which provided that hospital and ambulance personnel 'may, even after enemy occupation, continue to discharge their functions in the hospital or ambulance which they serve, or may withdraw to rejoin the units to which they belong': 1864 Geneva Convention art 3(1) alongside the 'defeat of the enemy armed forces on land', Oppenheim (n 14) 113 regarded the 'occupation and administration of the enemy territory' as the means by which the purpose of war – 'the overpowering of the enemy' – was to be achieved.

130 Common art 2(2).

131 See *GCIV Commentary* 21.

belligerent occupation remains one of fact that should be decided in accordance with the 1907 Hague Regulations which require that territory is 'actually placed under the authority of the hostile army'.[132]

By an extension of this logic, belligerent occupations can thus come to a 'close'[133] in the same manner in which they came to pass – involving a determination of fact based on realities on the ground. In truth, the same could be maintained for international armed conflicts given the objective dispensation set forth in the Geneva Conventions,[134] but the view has been held that – as a matter of custom – the law of armed conflict applies from the 'initiation' of such conflicts 'and extends beyond the cessation of hostilities until a general conclusion of peace is reached'.[135] This calls to mind the old instrument of the treaty of peace, once the most common mechanism for ending a state of war though it was of course open to belligerents to 'abstain from further acts of war and glide into peaceful relations without expressly making peace through a special treaty'.[136]

As part of their fundamental mission, treaties of peace do need to be distinguished from armistices for this latter cohort of agreements do not bring to a formal close the state of war: in fact, Oppenheim remarked that 'they ought not to be called a temporary peace, because the condition of war remains between the belligerents themselves, and between the belligerents and neutrals on all points beyond the mere cessation of hostilities'.[137] That said, in more recent times, it has been contended that the armistice has experienced a diversification of meaning from its original designation of the suspension of hostilities[138] to the modern position where:

> the locution employed in the general practice of States for a suspension of hostilities is cease-fire (or truce).... As for armistice, in the current practice of States, it denotes a termination of hostilities; even though it does not introduce peace in the full sense of that term. The decisive point is that a modern armistice completely divests the Parties of the right to renew military operations at any time and under any circumstances whatever.

---

132 HR art 42. See further Oppenheim (n 14) 173, and Adam Roberts, 'What is a Military Occupation?' (1984) 55 *BYBIL* 249.

133 As anticipated by GCIV art 77. However, consider GCIV art 6(2):

> In the case of occupied territory, the application of the present Convention shall cease one year after the general close of military operations; however, the Occupying Power shall be bound, for the duration of the occupation, to the extent that such power exercises the functions of government in such territory, by the provisions of the following Articles of the present Convention: 1 to 12, 27, 29 to 34, 47, 49, 51, 52, 53, 59, 61 to 77, 143.

The transient nature of belligerent occupations is also implicit in HR art 43.

134 And considered earlier at n 117. See further Marko Milanovic, 'The End of Application of International Humanitarian Law' (2014) 96 *IRRC* 163.

135 *Tadić (Jurisdiction)* (n 13) ¶ 70.

136 And subjugation of the adversary: Oppenheim (n 14) 275. Yoram Dinstein identifies implied mutual consent, *debellatio* and unilateral declarations as other means by which the formal termination of war can be secured: see *War, Aggression and Self-Defence* (5th edn, CUP 2012) 48. See also W Michael Reisman, 'Stopping Wars and Making Peace: Reflections on the Ideology and Practice of Conflict Termination in Contemporary World Politics' (1998) 6 *Tulane JICL* 5, 6.

137 Oppenheim (n 14) 243.

138 And where it was 'interchangeable in substance with a truce or a modern cease-fire': Dinstein, *War* (n 136) 41–42. See also Reisman (n 136) 16.

By putting an end to war, an armistice today does not brook resumption of hostilities as an option.[139]

Violations of the traditional armistice therefore stood to be governed by (or, better, within) the framework of the laws of war – rather than the *jus ad bellum* of the laws of peace – as is evident from Articles 36–41 of the 1907 Hague Regulations.[140]

No such detailed arrangements append to the conclusion of 'situations' of non-international armed conflict from either Common Article 3 of the Geneva Conventions or from Additional Protocol II.[141] However, the commentary to Additional Protocol II maintains that its application could cease '*after* the end of hostilities',[142] for some of its specifications actually attach to 'the end of the armed conflict'.[143] So, while the occurrence of hostilities defines some of the elements of Common Article 3 – '[p]ersons taking no active part in the hostilities[144] – and Additional Protocol II –

[a]t the end of hostilities, the authorities in power shall endeavor to grant the broadest possible amnesty to persons who have participated in the armed conflict, or those deprived of their liberty for reasons related to the armed conflict, whether they are interned or detained,[145]

– it is also clear that the protections might not be confined to this temporal framework: Common Article 3 issues its prohibitions for 'any time and in any place whatsoever',[146] a formulation that is repeated for the fundamental guarantees announced in Additional Protocol II.[147] A distinction

---

139 Dinstein, *War* (n 136) 42. As evidence of this current practice, Dinstein adduces the 1949 General Armistice Agreements between Israel and Egypt, Lebanon, Jordan and Syria as well as the 1953 Panmunjom Agreement Concerning Military Armistice in Korea where '[t]he metamorphosis in the perception of armistice reached its zenith': ibid 43. If this is so, it is not fully clear why South Korea has endeavoured – especially under President Roh Moo-hyun – to conclude a peace treaty, and why such a move has been persistently resisted by the US: see Choe Sang-Hun, 'South Korea's Leader Calls for Haste on Treaty to End Korean War' *New York Times* (14 November 2007). That this new version of armistice 'does not introduce peace in the full sense of that term' – or, ibid 43, does 'not produce peace in the full meaning of the term' – is explained on the grounds that '[w]hereas a treaty of peace is multi-dimensional (both negating war and providing for amicable relations . . .), an armistice agreement is restricted to the negative aspect of the demise of war': ibid 47.

140 See further Sydney D Bailey, 'Cease-Fires, Truces, and Armistices in the Practice of the UN Security Council' (1977) 71 *AJIL* 461.

141 As per GCI–IV common art 62/61/141/157. Consider, further, the obligation of the parties to the conflict to 'further endeavour to bring into force, by means of special agreements, all or part of the other provisions of the present Convention': see text at n 91.

142 Emphasis supplied. Or, as it is put, 'the end of its applicability' of APII: *AP Commentary* 1360. The silence of the text is used as an opportunity to defer to logic – as this 'means that the rules relating to armed confrontations are no longer applicable after the end of hostilities'; the measures taken restricting people's liberty 'taken for reasons related to the conflict' should however 'cease at the end of active hostilities': ibid. See in particular arts 2(2) and 4(1).

143 Art 2(2).

144 Common art 3(1).

145 Art 6(5).

146 Common art 3(1). Furthermore, the protections for the wounded and sick – who 'shall be collected and cared for' – are not qualified by any reference to hostilities: common art 3(2).

147 Art 4(2). Also, see art 2(1) regarding the personal field of application ('all persons affected by an armed conflict as defined [in this Protocol]') and art 5(1) regarding persons whose liberty has been restricted ('for reasons related to the armed conflict'). Note, too, the distinction drawn in art 13 between 'military operations' and rules that 'shall be observed in all circumstances', art 13(1).

does therefore need to be drawn between the end of active hostilities and the general close of hostilities, with practice tending to side with the latter consideration,[148] but it is surely open to parties to non-international armed conflicts to seek and to achieve a 'peaceful settlement' of some sort.[149]

In theory, the end of an international or non-international armed conflict marks the close of the laws related to both sets of circumstances established by international law – but some have argued that, together with the concept of belligerent occupation, the neat categories put forward by the Geneva Conventions and retained by the Additional Protocols are not sufficient to meet the challenges of the modern world:[150] Adam Roberts, for example, has concentrated on the phenomenon of transformative (belligerent) occupations of the order of the Israeli-occupied territories in the Middle East (1967), Northern Cyprus (1974) and Iraq (2003) which involve 'fundamental changes in the constitutional, social, economic, and legal order within an occupied territory'[151] and which 'typically arises *after* a war – whether civil or international – and/or after a foreign military intervention; and it is likely to end in a different way, as a stable government emerges in the territory itself. In such circumstances', he reasons, 'the *jus in bello* is unlikely to be a perfect fit [and] [i]t might even be tempting to invoke an emerging or future *jus post bellum* as a better basis for handling these situations.'[152]

At base, the problem of the normative infrastructure is that it posits that the belligerent occupant 'shall take all the measures in his power to restore, and ensure, as far as possible, public order and safety, while respecting, unless absolutely prevented, the laws in force in the country'.[153] The organisational premise of this law means that '[t]here is not an atom of sovereignty in the authority of the occupant',[154] but some of the experiences after the Second World War have emphasised that this is a 'cautious, even restrictive assumption in the laws of war' where 'occupying powers should respect the existing laws and economic arrangements within the occupied territory, and should therefore, by implication, make as few changes as possible'.[155] Hence the inclination towards developing a further – and, very importantly, separate – aspect of the corpus for regulating *bellum*, 'a new umbrella labeled *jus post*

---

148 Sivakumaran (n 80) 253; indeed, the law does make provision for this distinction: text at nn 142–143.

149 As was identified in *Tadić (Jurisdiction)* (n 13) ¶ 70.

150 As per the earlier discussion at nn 93–99.

151 Adam Roberts, 'Transformative Military Occupation: Applying the Laws of War and Human Rights' (2006) 100 *AJIL* 580, 580.

152 Ibid 619. On the speculative or tentative nature of this field, see Inger Österdahl and Esther van Zadel, 'What will *Jus Post Bellum* mean? Of New Wine and Old Bottles' (2009) 14 *JCSL* 175 (where the *jus post bellum* is defined (at 178) as 'a broad regulatory framework which contains substantive legal rules governing transitions from conflict to peace, as well as rules on the interplay of these substantive rules in case of conflict'). With its emphasis on transition, this characterisation suggests that we remain within the state of war or armed conflict – and, thus, presumably the *jus in bello* – and raises the fundamental question as to why we do not argue for a more comprehensive regulatory framework within that context or rubric. At another point of their defence, Österdahl and van Zadel, refer to 'a new category of law applicable in the post-conflict phase' as 'both needed and useful': ibid 185. See more generally Eric Patterson (ed), *Ethics Beyond War's End* (Georgetown University Press 2012).

153 HR art 43.

154 Lassa Oppenheim, 'The Legal Relations between an Occupying Power and the Inhabitants' (1917) 33 *LQR* 363, 364.

155 Roberts (n 151) 580.

bellum',[156] notwithstanding the fact that the law confers a rather broad compass of power on the belligerent occupant 'to restore, and ensure, as far as possible, public order and safety' in the territory it has occupied,[157] as it does an escape clause from the requirement it makes to respect the laws in force therein.[158] Furthermore, the law of belligerent occupation is not to be treated alone: it assumes the existence of the laws of the displaced sovereign, and, in its advisory opinion in *Legal Consequences of the Construction of A Wall in the Occupied Palestinian Territory* in July 2004, the ICJ concluded that

> while the jurisdiction of States is primarily territorial, it may sometimes be exercised outside the national territory. Considering the object and purpose of the International Covenant on Civil and Political Rights, it would seem natural that, even when such is the case, States parties to the Covenant should be bound to comply with its provisions.[159]

Further afield, in the context of non-international armed conflicts, Christine Bell has argued that the contents of peace agreements have begun to 'show some steps' in a similar direction,[160] and that, taken as a whole, their contents are deserving of their own treatment and even designation. She has further suggested that the *lex pacificatoria*:

> can be understood as a transnational area of law that like all forms of transnational law 'is built on a process of convergence of ideas, across national boundaries'. The *lex* hovers between three possible conceptions of its nature: first a set of persistent practice of peacemakers that take on a normative quality through their persistent use across conflicts; second, an autonomous legal regime responding to transitions from conflict – what some now describe as a *ius post bellum*; and third, an emerging body of rules capable of standing as an alternative to a tainted and partisan domestic law.[161]

As articulated, the *lex pacificatoria* posits itself as broader in its scope and ambition than the proposed *jus post bellum* and comprises three principal components: the normative force of

---

156 Ibid 582. Stephen Neff recalls 'certain general conceptual features' of the *jus victoriae* which, he reminds us, 'was never, so to speak, a "thing in itself" in the sense of being a free-standing body of law about peace-making as such': Stephen C Neff, 'Conflict Termination and Peace-Making in the Law of Nations: A Historical Perspective' in Carsten Stahn and Jann K Kleffner (eds), Jus Post Bellum: *Towards a Law of Transition from Conflict to Peace* (Asser 2008) 77, 79.

157 HR art 43. See further Yoram Dinstein, *The International Law of Belligerent Occupation* (CUP 2009) 91.

158 HR art 43 ('while preventing, unless absolutely prevented, the laws in force in the country'). As recognised by Roberts (n 151) 582 ('this suggestion has been tempered by awareness of the importance of effective implementation of the present body of occupation law, which is seen as remaining relevant to many problems raised in modern occupations').

159 *Legal Consequences of the Construction of a Wall in the Occupied Palestinian Territory (Advisory Opinion)* [2004] ICJ Rep 136 ¶ 109. As far as the ICCPR is concerned, the Court concluded that '[i]n the exercise of the powers available to it on [the] basis [of an occupying power], Israel is bound by the provisions of the International Covenant on Economic, Social and Cultural Rights': ibid ¶ 112. This set of considerations is sure to affect whether the applicable international law is 'insufficient' to the demands or expectations placed upon it, as per Carsten Stahn, '*Jus Post Bellum*: Mapping the Disciplines' in Stahn and Kleffner (eds) (n 156) 93, 98.

160 Christine Bell, *On the Law of Peace: Peace Agreements and the* Lex Pacificatoria (OUP 2008) 273.

161 Ibid 288, citing H Patrick Glenn, 'A Transnational Concept of Law' in Peter Cane and Mark Tushnet (eds), *The Oxford Handbook of Legal Studies* (OUP 2003) 839, 859.

peace agreements (or, as it is termed, the 'literal laws of the peacemaker');[162] the idea of hybrid self-determination (as experienced through state redefinition, disaggregation of power and dislocation of power)[163] and, finally, the dynamics of 'a "new law" of third party enforcement'.[164] And it is in this context that we are invited to view one of the possible effects of the *lex pacificatoria* 'as a set of normative expectations that shape how peacemakers attempt to reconcile the use of amnesties with the international law that claims regulatory force'.[165] That said, if it is true that '[t]his law of the peacemaker potentially forms part of a broader "law of peace"',[166] it is not clear why this shift of provenance to an emerging *lex pacificatoria* is made necessary if the law on amnesties for Additional Protocol II is conceived in terms of 'the end of hostilities'[167] as well as the broader pragmatism of these conventional arrangements.[168]

4 Structure of commitments

We have already adverted to the 'prohibitive' nature of much of what passes for the law of armed conflict,[169] but, in terms of the range of propositions at stake in this field, this does not convey the fact that the law furnishes certain *entitlements* for taking action as well: Additional Protocol I, for example, confirms that attacks can be undertaken against military objectives in the event of hostilities – but confines this possibility to military objectives,[170] and while Additional Protocol I outlaws belligerent reprisals against protected persons and objects,[171] civilians and the civilian population,[172] civilians objects,[173] cultural objects and places of worship,[174] objects indispensable to the survival of the civilian population,[175] natural environment,[176] and works or installations containing dangerous forces (such as dams, dykes and nuclear electrical generating stations),[177] custom provides for greater latitude in terms of the 'right' of taking belligerent reprisals.[178]

---

162 Ibid 286.
163 Ibid 108.
164 Ibid 22.
165 Ibid 240. Amnesties, too, are the concern of Neff, 'Conflict' (n 156) 90 in the context of the *jus post bellum* for non-international armed conflicts.
166 Bell (n 160) 5.
167 As per APII art 6(5).
168 See the discussion at nn 142–143 and 148–149.
169 See test at n 24.
170 API art 52(2) (defined as 'those objects which by their nature, location, purpose or use make an effective contribution to military action and whose total or partial destruction, capture or neutralization, in the circumstances ruling at the time, offers a definite military advantage').
171 Ibid art 20.
172 Ibid art 51(6).
173 Ibid art 52(1).
174 Ibid art 53(c).
175 Ibid art 54(4) (as defined in art 54(2)).
176 Ibid art 55(2).
177 Ibid art 56(4) (as defined in art 56(1)).
178 Hence, CIHL r 145 ('[w]here not prohibited by international law, belligerent reprisals are subject to stringent conditions'). Cf CIHL r 148 on non-international armed conflicts ('[p]arties to non-international armed conflicts do not have the right to resort to belligerent reprisals. Other countermeasures against persons who do not or who have ceased to take a direct part in hostilities are prohibited'). See further Christopher Greenwood, 'The Twilight of the Law of Belligerent Reprisals' (1989) 20 *Netherlands YBIL* 35, and Meron, 'Humanization' (n 48) 249 (that 'the domain of legitimate reprisals [has] shr[u]nk dramatically').

All of this said, it is appropriate for us to bear in mind that, as far as their application is concerned, the Geneva Conventions and Additional Protocols do not confine themselves to High Contracting Parties as sole addressees for action; High Contracting Parties, it is true, assume the greater burden of the commitments of the Conventions and Protocols, so that it stands to reason that it is the High Contracting Parties that are engaged 'to respect and to ensure respect for the present Convention in all circumstances'[179] as well as 'to enact any legislation necessary to provide effective penal sanctions for persons committing, or ordering to be committed, any of the grave breaches of' the Conventions,[180] which is further to any of the common rules to be applied to all parties to an armed conflict in consequence of the principle of equal application.[181] The Geneva Conventions and Additional Protocols are, thus, home to differential arrangements that are contingent on the *identification* of the actor or actors in question,[182] and, from this framework and the chapters that follow in this edited volume, there can be no doubt about the *plurality* of actors that are assumed to be involved in armed conflicts: at one point, for example, the 1907 Hague Regulations turn their attention to the *levée en masse* (in other words, '[t]he inhabitants of a territory which has not been occupied, who, on the approach of the enemy, spontaneously take up arms to resist the invading troops'),[183] to the besieged,[184] and to the work of governments,[185] relief societies[186] and officers in command;[187] as far as Common Article 3 of the Geneva Conventions is concerned, 'each Party' to a non-international armed conflict must by definition mean that it is *not* a High Contracting Party,[188] and '[a]n impartial humanitarian body, such as the International Committee of the Red Cross, may offer its services to the Parties to the conflict'.[189] Furthermore, it is stated that the provisions of the Conventions shall

> constitute no obstacle to the humanitarian activities of the International Committee of the Red Cross or any other impartial humanitarian organization [which] may, subject to the consent of the Parties to the conflict concerned, undertake for the protection of wounded and sick, medical personnel and chaplains, and for their relief.[190]

Yet, if these components represent the overall thematic organisation of the laws of the Geneva Conventions and Additional Protocols, there is also the perception that the system

---

179 GCI–IV common art 1.
180 GCI–IV common art 49(1)/50(1)/129(1)/146(1) – and where, in common art 49(2)/50(2)/129(2)/146(2) each High Contracting Party 'shall be under the obligation to search for persons alleged to have committed, or to have ordered to be committed, such grave breaches, and shall bring such persons, regardless of their nationality, before its own courts'.
181 See text at n 53.
182 An excellent example is the 'system' of the Protecting Power, on which, see API art 5.
183 HR art 2; see further, GCIII art 4(A)(2) and (6).
184 HR art 27.
185 Ibid art 7.
186 Ibid art 15.
187 Ibid art 26. See also art 33.
188 Otherwise there would be no point in making a separate set of arrangements for non-international armed conflicts.
189 GCI–IV common art 3.
190 GCI art 9.

affords 'individual rights',[191] and how these might relate to the *human* rights elsewhere assured by international law.[192] To be sure, the 1929 Geneva Convention Relative to the Treatment of Prisoners of War did invoke the language of 'rights' to frame some of its commitments – '[p]risoners of war have the right to have their person and their honour respected';[193] they shall also 'have the right to inform the military authorities in whose power they are of their requests with regard to the conditions of captivity to which they are subjected'[194] – and, in an apparent continuation of this theme, the Geneva Conventions announce by way of a common and oft-neglected provision that the wounded, sick, shipwrecked, prisoners-of-war and protected persons 'may in no circumstances renounce in part or entirely the rights secured to them by the present Convention'.[195]

Part of the concern inspiring this formulation was the 'profound modifications' in the legal or political structure encountered by nationals of states as a result of hostilities,[196] but it is also important to observe that the terms of the Geneva Conventions have been conceived according to the *status* of their respective addressees,[197] and that, separate to any notion of 'rights', the language often used to describe the work that these Conventions do is in terms of the 'protections' and 'benefits' they

191 See eg Meron, 'The Geneva Conventions and Public International Law' (2009) 91 *IRRC* 619, 624. The term 'individual rights' is also used in *GCIV Commentary* 79. So, for purposes of illustration, the position on *levées en masse* (n 183) is not framed in terms of the 'rights' of the inhabitants who come together to resist invading troops – but, rather, is addressed to the armed forces of High Contracting Parties as it is provided that these inhabitants 'shall be regarded as belligerents if they carry arms openly and if they respect the laws and customs of war'. Cf the formulation in GCIII art 4(A)(2) and (6).

192 See further Dietrich Schindler, 'Human Rights and Humanitarian Law: Interrelationship of the Laws' (1982) 31 *American University LR* 935. On the individual and human rights, consider, also, Yoram Dinstein, 'Human Rights: Implementation through the UN System' (1995) 89 *ASIL Proceedings* 242, 243. Both of these scholars emphasise the complaint and scrutiny infrastructure of human rights treaties, separate to the consequences anticipated for violations of the Geneva Conventions and Additional Protocols – which, in increasing measure, embrace a system of penal repression: Antonio Cassese, 'On the Current Trends Towards Criminal Prosecution and Punishment of Breaches of International Humanitarian Law' (1998) 9 *EJIL* 2.

193 Art 3(1).

194 Art 42(1); also, art 42(2): 'They shall also have the right to address themselves to representatives of the protecting Powers to indicate to them the points on which they have complaints to formulate with regard to the conditions of captivity.' Furthermore, according to art 62(1), the prisoner-of-war 'shall be advised of his right [to assistance by a qualified counsel of his choice, and, if necessary, to have recourse to the services of a competence interpreter] by the detaining Power, in due time before the trial' and '[e]very prisoner of war shall have the right of appeal against any sentence rendered with regard to him, in the same way as individuals belonging to the armed force of the detaining Power' under art 64. These 'rights' are separate to those of the High Contracting Powers, eg 'to conclude special conventions on all questions relative to prisoners of war, on which it seems to them expedient to have particular regulations' (art 83(1)) and to denounce the Convention (art 96(1)).

195 Common art 7/7/7/8 (and, indeed, by special agreements referred to earlier in the same Conventions). However, the 1929 Geneva Wounded and Sick Convention (n 74) makes less reliance on the language of 'rights': '[t]he right of requisition recognized for belligerents by the laws and customs of war, shall only be exercised in case of urgent necessity and only after the welfare of the wounded and sick has been secured' (art 16(2)); '[i]n cases of loss [of their armlets or the certificates of identity belonging to medical personnel] they have the right to obtain duplicates' (art 21(5)); medical units 'shall also have the right, so long as they shall lend their services to a belligerent, to fly their national flag' (art 23(2)). Reference is also made to 'the privileges of the Convention' (art 16(1); see also art 18(4)).

196 *GCIV Commentary* 73 (eg occupation, *debellatio*, change of government or civil war).

197 Or, that the Conventions 'provide certain categories of people with a status which does not depend on any political events which may occur': ibid.

provide.[198] Indeed, notwithstanding the wording of this common provision of the Conventions,[199] it has been translated as 'intimating to States party to the Convention[s] that they could not release themselves from their obligations towards protected persons, even if the latter showed expressly and of their own free will that that was what they desired'.[200]

'Rights' within the Conventions have nevertheless been 'affirmed' in certain quarters,[201] 'doubtless under the influence of the theoretical trends which also resulted in the Universal Declaration of Human Rights' of the same period – and which has 'led to define in concrete terms a concept which was implicit in the earlier Conventions'.[202] Yet, as one moves from theory to practice and towards the practical application of these rights, 'to assert that a person has a right is to say that he possesses ways and means of having that right respected, and that any violation thereof entails a penalty', but all of this was absent from the original (that is, 1864) Geneva Convention.[203] Nevertheless, the narrative of criminal repression – or the invocation of international criminal law – becomes a much more tangible force with the advent of the 1949 Geneva Conventions,[204] but it is also the case that Protecting Powers were designed to serve as a 'means open to [protected] persons for the defence of their rights'.[205]

198 Ibid ('protection of the Convention', 'the persons who benefit by [the Convention]'); ibid 74 ('partial or total renunciation of the protection accorded to [protected persons] by the Convention', 'renounce the benefits of the Convention', 'Conventions designed to protect the individual'); ibid 75 ('standards of treatment which depend as little as possible, for their application, on the wishes of those concerned'); ibid 76 ('[r]ules of this kind were *in the common interest* and could be renounced by the beneficiaries only under the pressure of external circumstances, against which it was the very purpose of the Convention to protect them', '[r]eference might also be made in municipal law to the rules for the protection of the person', 'keen desire to provide war victims with complete protection',) and ibid 77 (*re* provisions of the Congress of Vienna relating to the slave trade: 'the protection of the individual'). See also GCI–IV common art 6(2)/6(2)/6(2)/7(2) – that wounded, sick, shipwrecked, prisoners-of-war and protected persons

> shall continue to have the benefit of such agreements as long as the [respective] Convention is applicable to them, except where express provisions to the contrary are contained in the aforesaid or in subsequent agreements, or where more favourable measures have been taken with regard to them by one or other Parties to the conflict.

Finally, see the criticism developed by Hampson, 'Human Rights Law' (n 18) 49.

199 See n 192.
200 *GCIV Commentary* 74.
201 Ibid 77. See also Meron, 'Humanization' (n 48) 251.
202 *GCIV Commentary* 77.
203 Which contains 'nothing on the subject': ibid 78. The subsequent 1907 Hague Convention (IV) (n 71) provided in art 3, simply, that '[a] belligerent party which violates the provisions of the said Regulations shall, if the case demands, be liable to pay compensation. It shall be responsible for all acts committed by persons forming part of its armed forces'.
204 Specifically, the arrangement made for grave breaches. As Schindler (n 192) 941 observes, however, '[a] peculiarity of the law of war is that its rules are directly binding on individuals'; see further, Theodor Meron, 'International Criminalization of Internal Atrocities' (1995) 89 *AJIL* 554 and Denise Plattner, 'The Penal Repression of Violations of International Humanitarian Law Applicable in Non-International Armed Conflicts' (1990) 30 *IRRC* 409.
205 GCI–IV common art 8/8/8/9. So, according to *GCIV Commentary* 78: '[i]t through the Protecting Power that protected persons will be able most readily to obtain the intervention in their behalf of their state of origin'. This mechanism has not been put to great use, however: Cassese (n 192) 4. Consider, too, the role of the ICRC in GCI–IV common arts 9/9/9/10 and 10/10/10/11, which 'enjoys prerogatives under the Convention which will enable it to act in the interests of the protected persons': *GCIV Commentary* 78. According to *GCIV Commentary* 84:

> the problem also arises with regard to violation of the rights of protected persons by their own Governments. Although the Convention contains no formal indication in this respect, it is justifiable to consider that the terms of art 7 may entail an important consequence. It should be possible in States which are parties to the Convention and which recognize that any violation of individual rights is justiciable, for the rules of the Convention, which are assimilable with those rights, to be evoked before an appropriate national court by the protected person who has suffered the violation.

That said, it is also clear that any 'system' of individual rights coming forward from the Geneva Conventions and Additional Protocols is *itself* the subject of evolution and change, and this cannot but take account of the overall environment in which such rights are used and presumed to operate:

> Undoubtedly, owing to the still undeveloped character of international law, the safeguards protecting the rights conferred on persons to whom the Convention relates are by no means complete, effective, or automatic as those of national legislations. Nevertheless, [the 'rights' provision of the Conventions] is of the greatest assistance to all protected persons. It allows them to claim the protection of the Convention, not as a favour, but as a right, and in case of violation, it enables them to employ any procedure available, however rudimentary, to demand respect for the Convention[s'] terms. Hence the importance of the dissemination of the Convention[s] ... with special reference to the individual character of the rights which the Convention[s] confer.[206]

Finally, assuming that any system of '[r]ights entails obligations',[207] the question arises as to who is to assume these obligations as a matter of fact and of law: that the rights of the Conventions shall not be renounced does appear to suggest that an *obligation* of some sort might be placed on the self-same holders of these rights to that end,[208] but the ICRC has explained that 'the general effect of the Conventions was to impose obligations on the *States* which were parties to the Convention rather than on individuals' – and it is this context that framed the provision made for individual rights.[209]

---

206 *GCIV Commentary* 79. Indeed, it is maintained (ibid 76) that:

> [h]ad [the authors of those solemn instruments] wanted to lay down the wishes of those victims as a condition of application, they would not have failed to provide safeguards and forms of procedure permitting those wishes to be expressed freely, knowing as they did not great the possibilities of misinterpretation were in wartime.

> For example, in *Avena and Other Mexican Nationals (Mexico v United States of America)* [2004] ICJ Rep 12, ¶ 40, the ICJ observed that 'the individual rights of Mexican nationals under [art 36(1)(b)] of the [1961] Vienna Convention [on Consular Relations]' – which provides in part that:

> > [w]ith a view to facilitating the exercise of consular functions relating to nationals of the sending State[,] ... if he so requests, the competent authorities of the receiving State shall, without delay, inform the consular post of the sending State if, within its consular district, a national of that State is arrested or committed to prison or to custody pending trial or is detained in any other manner

> but makes no mention of 'rights' as such – 'are rights which are to be asserted, at any rate in the first place, within the domestic legal system of the United States'. Furthermore, ibid ¶ 40, the Court spoke of the 'special circumstances of interdependence of the rights of the State and of individual rights', in that 'violations of the rights of the individual under art 36 may entail a violation of the rights of the sending State, and ... violations of the rights of the latter may entail a violation of the rights of the individual'. See further Bruno Simma and Carsten Hoppe, 'From *LaGrand* and *Avena* to *Medellin*: A Rocky Road to Implementation' (2005) 14 *Tulane JICL* 7.

207 *GCIV Commentary* 79.

208 That is, 'can also be considered as obligations directly incumbent on the persons protected': ibid.

209 Ibid 79–80 (emphasis supplied). Note how the invocation of 'rights' informs some of the obligations presented in, eg GCI art 40(4) ('[i]n no circumstances may the said personnel be deprived of their insignia or identity cards nor of the right to wear the armlet') and API art 32 ('the activities of the High Contracting Parties, of the Parties to the conflict and of the international humanitarian organizations mentioned in the Conventions and in this Protocol shall be prompted mainly by the right of families to know the fate of their relatives').

It is worth bearing in mind, too, that the Conventions – and their Protocols[210] – do not actually confine themselves to *binding* states to particular courses of action; other belligerent actors can also be so bound,[211] and, alongside the mechanism for individual accountability instituted by the Conventions and the Protocols,[212] we are presented with an ever-effective infrastructure for upholding these laws that is sure to be encountered many times in the pages that follow.[213]

---

210 For APII, see n 83 – and, with its provision concerning those 'fighting against colonial domination and alien occupation and against racist regimes in the exercise of their right of self-determination', API: n 63.
211 See Sandesh Sivakumran, 'Binding Armed Opposition Groups' (2006) 55 *ICLQ* 369.
212 See Meron, 'International Criminalization' (n 204).
213 One that forms the foundations of the approach of Rome Statute art 8.

2
The history of international humanitarian law treaty-making

Frits Kalshoven

The law of armed conflict has a long history behind it. Examples of conduct foreshadowing today's principles and rules have been found in the records of ancient armed conflicts.[1] Over time, incidental practice developed into a body of customary law. Then, in the mid-nineteenth century, states began to conclude treaties to govern the conduct of war. This is where we find our starting point.

1 First Steps (1850–1880)

The first three treaties on international humanitarian law (IHL) were concluded in the period 1850–1880, each one on a specific aspect of warfare. Two other documents that covered the generality of warfare are mentioned as well because of their great influence on subsequent treaty-making.

1.1 Declaration of Paris (1856)

In the Crimean War (1853–1856) between Russia and a coalition including Turkey, France and Great Britain, warships of the latter two states were engaged in cutting off Russia's imports and exports, whether carried on enemy or neutral vessels. Disputes arising out of such acts of naval warfare were a matter for national prize courts, and these frequently held different views. In order to avoid the occurrence of such differences of opinion among their courts, France and Great Britain in 1854 agreed not to issue letters of marque,[2] or to permit their warships to seize enemy goods on neutral vessels or neutral goods on enemy vessels.

On 30 March 1856, at the Congress of Paris,[3] the belligerent parties signed the Treaty of Paris that brought the war to an end. The Congress thereupon signed the Declaration of Paris[4]

---

1 See eg Leslie C Green, *The Contemporary Law of Armed Conflict* (3rd edn, Manchester University Press 2008) 26–29.
2 Letters mandating private vessels (so-called 'privateers') to capture enemy vessels and bring these before prize courts to be sold.
3 At the time, a meeting of Austria, France, Prussia, Russia, Sardinia-Piedmont, Turkey and Great Britain.
4 115 CTS 1.

which reaffirmed the above rules, on the understanding that goods qualifying as contraband remained open to seizure. The Declaration also prohibited privateering and provided that a blockade, to be binding, must be effective.

That same year, another 45 of the then-existing states acceded to the Declaration.

1.2 Geneva Convention (1864)

On 8 November 1862, a pamphlet appeared in Geneva that described in detail a battle that had been fought on 24 June 1859 near Solferino (northern Italy) between armies of Austria and of France and Piedmont-Sardinia, leaving some 40,000 dead and wounded of all parties. It also described the attempts at evacuating the wounded, irrespective of allegiance, to Castiglione and other nearby localities, and the efforts made to have them taken up and cared for by the inhabitants. Its author, Henry Dunant, a Swiss banker who by happenstance had come to play a central role in the process of collecting and caring for the wounded of Solferino, concluded his *A Memory of Solferino*[5] with two suggestions: (1) in time of peace, permanent aid societies should be created in all countries, so as to have, at the outbreak of war, qualified volunteers available to bring aid to the wounded of all parties; and (2) the principle underlying the functioning of such societies should be embodied in an internationally agreed and properly ratified document.

A Memory of Solferino fell on fertile soil; public opinion at the time was susceptible to notions of social cooperation and improvement of the public weal, and the example of Florence Nightingale and her colleagues treating British wounded soldiers in a hospital on Turkish soil had made people's minds ripe for Dunant's suggestions. Matters moved rapidly: in 1863, a Committee of Five set up in Geneva (with Dunant one of them) convened a conference of state representatives that concluded, *inter alia*, that committees should be created in every country with the task to prepare in peacetime, in contact with their government, for the volunteers' wartime activities; and volunteers in action would wear, 'as a uniform distinctive sign, a white armlet with a red cross'.[6]

Implementing Dunant's second suggestion, a diplomatic conference convened by the Swiss Federal Council on 22 August 1864 adopted the Geneva Convention for the Amelioration of the Condition of the Wounded in Armies in the Field, laying down the principles that 'wounded and sick combatants', no matter their nationality, 'shall be collected and cared for'; that 'ambulances and military hospitals' accommodating such persons 'shall be recognised as neutral and, as such, protected and respected'; that members of the local population who take up wounded shall be equally protected and 'shall remain free' – indeed, generals of the warring parties 'shall make it their duty to notify the inhabitants of the appeal made to their humanity'.[7] And, last but not least, the Convention introduced a 'distinctive and uniform flag' bearing 'a red cross on a white ground'.[8]

With that, the foundations for a system for the 'amelioration of the condition of the wounded and sick of armies in the field' had been laid. The Committees would become the National Red Cross (later also Red Crescent) Societies, and the Geneva Committee, the ICRC. And a treaty had been adopted that could be hoped to support the infant organisational structure.

---

5 *Un Souvenir de Solferino* was privately printed and distributed by Dunant. Much later it was republished more than once, eg by the Institut Henry-Dunant (1969).
6 Resolutions of the Geneva International Conference (26–29 October 1863), reprinted in Dietrich Schindler and Jiří Toman (eds), *The Laws of Armed Conflict* (4th edn, Martinus Nijhoff 2004) 361, art 8.
7 129 CTS 361, arts 6, 1, 5.
8 Ibid art 7.

1.3 St Petersburg Declaration (1868)

While a 'soldier in the field' could be wounded by any of the weapons in use, the rifle bullet was the most common among them. Bullets were solid objects. So had been the cannon ball, but this had largely been replaced with the artillery shell. In the same trend, explosive bullets were being designed in several countries. Russia in 1863 had used such a munition to blow up enemy ammunition carts, and a new type produced in 1867 would explode upon contact with a 'soft target' (say, a human body).[9] And 'rifle-shells' tested by British forces in India, while apparently useful for range-finding in the mountains, might have a 'profound effect on enemy morale' as well.[10]

Should the explosive bullet be welcomed, or banned? Like the ordinary bullet, the explosive bullet could eliminate just one person, at the cost of inflicting very grave wounds, similar to those caused by the burst of an artillery shell. Was this extra damage justifiable? There was the potential effect on soldiers' morale. For some, like the British, this could be an argument in favour of the rifle shells when used against enemy forces. Others might fear for the morale of their own troops and, thus, come to the opposite conclusion.

Fear for the morale of own armed forces probably was at the root of the initiative, taken in 1868 by the Russian Czar, Alexander III, to convene a meeting at St Petersburg to discuss a ban on use of the new projectiles. The 16-state International Military Commission decided accordingly and, on 11 December 1868, signed a Declaration renouncing the use of 'any projectile of a weight below 400 grammes, which is either explosive or charged with fulminating or inflammable substances'.[11] With that, the introduction of the rifle shells was effectively forestalled. Artillery shells, being above that weight, remained unaffected, in spite of their well-known wounding capacity.

The Declaration proclaims that 'the necessities of war ought to yield to the requirements of humanity': a principle that may be said to lay at the root of the law of armed conflict.[12] As well, the war effort should be directed against 'the military forces of the enemy', not against entire populations; and it should be limited to 'weaken[ing]' the enemy forces, by 'disabl[ing] the greatest possible number of men'. Weapons therefore should not 'uselessly aggravate the sufferings of disabled men, [n]or render their death inevitable'. The logical further conclusion follows: weapons which might cause such effects 'would, therefore, be contrary to the laws of humanity' – and the lightweight explosive projectiles would be a case in point.

In a final paragraph, the contracting states reserved to themselves to deal with future weapons developments, in order to 'conciliate the necessities of war with the laws of humanity'.

1.4 Lieber Code (1863)

In 1863, a field manual for an armed conflict saw the light of day in Washington. The conflict was the American Civil War (1861–1865) between the United States and the Confederation, and the document, the 'Instructions for the Government of Armies of the United States in the

---

9 See www.icrc.org/ihl.nsf/INTRO/130?OpenDocument.

10 Frits Kalshoven, 'Conventional Weaponry: The Law from St. Petersburg to Lucerne and Beyond' in Michael A Meyer (ed), *Armed Conflict and the New Laws* (BIICL 1989) 251, reprinted in Frits Kalshoven, *Reflections on the Law of War* (Martinus Nijhoff 2007) 377, 378.

11 Declaration Renouncing the Use, in Time of War, of Explosive Projectiles under 400 Grammes Weight ('St Petersburg Declaration') (11 December 1868) 138 CTS 297.

12 'Limitation and restraint of course are, of all principles pervading the law of war, the most central and crucial': Geoffrey Best, *Humanity in Warfare* (Columbia University Press 1980) 157.

Field', promulgated as General Orders No 100 by President Abraham Lincoln. While written for an internal war, the document largely reflected the existing laws and customs of war: after all, their main author, Francis Lieber, had earlier been a German professor of law. The 157 articles of the Lieber Instructions (or Lieber Code, as they are usually named) have strongly influenced the subsequent efforts at codifying the law of war.

One issue, singled out here because of its lasting importance, concerns the fate of irregular fighters. Two articles are relevant. Article 82 provides that men who in unoccupied territory commit hostilities without being part of the hostile army 'shall be treated summarily as highway robbers or pirates'. And Article 85 deals summarily with similar activities in occupied territory: those who 'rise in arms' against the occupant are 'war rebels' and 'may suffer death, whether they rise singly, in small or large bands, and whether called upon to do so by their own, but expelled, government or not'. I return to these issues later in the chapter.

1.5 Brussels Declaration (1874)

In Europe, the Franco-German War (1870–1871) had once again brought to light the lack of 'precision and authority' of the existing customary law, leading to much discussion and an appeal to the authorities to 'dissipate the existing fog'.[13] Particularly urgent issues included bombardment, occupation and, of course, the definition of combatants. The time had clearly come for an international conference on these matters.

Accordingly, on 27 July 1874, on the initiative of the Czar, 15 European states convened in Brussels to discuss a Russian draft text.[14] On 27 August, the conference concluded its work with the presentation of two documents: a Final Protocol, duly signed by the participating states and explaining what had been done and in what spirit; and a 'Project of an International Declaration Concerning the Laws and Customs of War',[15] characterised in the Protocol as

> a conscientious inquiry of a nature to serve as a basis for an ulterior exchange of ideas, and for the development of the provisions of the Convention of Geneva of 1864 and of the Declaration of St. Petersburg of 1868.

The Russian project had actually included several of the rules of the Geneva Convention of 1864, exposing them to amendment at the conference. That the Convention needed redrafting was well known. However, the ICRC felt that the Brussels Conference, with many officers on the delegations, would not be the proper forum for this undertaking, and on its request the Geneva rules were removed from the project.[16] A simple referral remained, to the effect that the fate of the sick and wounded remained governed by the Convention of 1864, 'save such modifications as the latter may undergo'.[17] With that, the law of war had split into two branches,[18] each following its own path of development: one, known as the law of Geneva; the other, after the venue where the 'ulterior exchange of ideas' would result in regulations of land warfare being adopted, as the law of The Hague.

13 Gustave Moynier, *La Révision de la Convention de Genève: Etude Historique et Critique, suivie d'un Projet de Convention Revisée* (ICRC 1898) 7–8.
14 Jean de Breucker, 'La Déclaration de Bruxelles de 1874 concernant les Lois et Coutumes de la Guerre' (1974) 27 *Chronique de Politique Etrangère* 22, 88–95.
15 1 *AJIL Supp* 96.
16 Moynier (n 13) 8.
17 Brussels Declaration (n 15) art 35.
18 De Breucker (n 14) 72.

Before moving on, we note how Brussels dealt with Lieber's 'highway robbers and pirates' and 'war rebels'. After much debate, with Belgium and the Netherlands opposing Germany, the first rule was replaced with the provision that the population of non-occupied territory rising in defence against an invading army must be regarded as combatants 'if they respect the laws and customs of war'.[19] And the harsh 'war rebel' rule was simply left out, thus leaving the matter of armed resistance in occupied territory to the unwritten – and uncertain – law of nations.[20]

2 The turn of the century

The main events in this next period were the two 'International Peace Conferences' held at The Hague, one from 18 May to 29 July 1899 (Hague I), and the next from 15 June to 18 October 1907 (Hague II). While results on the theme of 'peace and disarmament' remained modest, the negotiations on 'mitigating the horrors of war' have yielded a rich harvest of conventions and declarations on the laws of war on land (at Hague I) and at sea (at Hague II).

2.1 Warfare on land

Hague I adopted the Hague Convention (II) on Land Warfare with annexed Regulations on Land Warfare.[21] The Regulations had been drafted on the basis of the Brussels Declaration of 1874. Hague II confined itself to minor alterations. References in this section are to the 1907 version.[22]

Warfare on land was the business of states' armies. They qualified as 'belligerents', the 'laws, rights, and duties of war' applied to them, and combatants who fell into enemy hands had 'a right to be treated as prisoners of war':[23] a situation for which Chapter II of the Regulations provided a complete regime. The 'militia and volunteer corps' of the time qualified as well, provided they were commanded by 'a person responsible for his subordinates', had a 'fixed distinctive emblem recognizable at a distance', 'carried arms openly' and 'conducted their operations in accordance with the laws and customs of war'.[24] These four conditions actually reflected the normal condition of states' armies.

Not everything was permitted, as expressed in the general principle that '[t]he right of belligerents to adopt means of injuring the enemy is not unlimited'.[25] There followed a list of prohibitions, out of which we mention the bans on use of 'poison or poisoned weapons' and of 'arms, projectiles, or material calculated to cause unnecessary suffering'.[26] Connected to these prohibitions were two declarations adopted at Hague I, one prohibiting the use of projectiles diffusing 'asphyxiating or deleterious gases', and the other (building on St Petersburg) that of so-called dum-dum bullets.

Bombardment of undefended localities was prohibited, 'by whatever means':[27] a phrase showing that the notion of bombs dropped out of the air was no longer a mere fancy. In bombarding defended towns and similar places, where civilians would be living as well, a warning

19 Brussels Declaration (n 15) art 10.
20 De Breucker (n 14) 50–54.
21 189 CTS 429.
22 205 CTS 277.
23 Ibid art 3.
24 Ibid art 1.
25 Ibid art 22.
26 Ibid art 23(a), (e).
27 Ibid art 25.

was required, 'except in cases of assault'.[28] Attempts should also be made to spare buildings devoted to 'religion, art, science, or charitable purposes, historic monuments, hospitals, and places where the sick and wounded are collected', unless they were being used for military purposes: the first rules on protection of objects singled out for their cultural or medical importance.[29]

An invasion of foreign territory could expect resistance by the local army, but by members of the population as well: Lieber's 'highway robbers or pirates'. Brussels had classified them as combatants, provided they respected the laws of war. The Hague now was less lenient: they would not 'qualify' as belligerents and might at best be 'regarded' as such (and not sanctioned for their actions), but this only if they had started their actions 'on the approach of the enemy', 'spontaneously' and 'without having had time to organise themselves' into true armies, and they also must 'respect the laws and customs of war' and 'carry arms openly'.[30] Surely a list of requirements that betrays the limited sympathy the major powers could muster for such a so-called *levée en masse* opposing their invading armies.

Occupation of enemy territory entailed an obligation for the occupant to rule it, as far as the territory was 'actually placed under the authority of the hostile army'.[31] The occupant must do whatever he can 'to restore, and ensure, as far as possible, public order and safety'. On the other hand, the temporary 'authority of the legitimate power' in his hands did not turn him into the sovereign legislator: he must, 'unless absolutely prevented, [respect] the laws in force in the country'.[32]

What about Lieber's 'war rebels'? The Regulations are once again silent on armed resistance in occupied territory. Yet, this time the 'silence' was not absolute. After difficult negotiations, with Russia and Germany on one side and Belgium on the other, the chairman of the commission discussing the Regulations, Fedor de Martens (an Estonian serving the Czar) read out the text of a preambular paragraph based on a Belgian draft.[33] It stated that although not everything could have been regulated, unforeseen cases would not be 'left to the arbitrary judgment of military commanders': in such cases 'the inhabitants and the belligerents' would 'remain under the protection and the rule of the principles of the law of nations, as they result from the usages established among civilised peoples, from the laws of humanity, and the dictates of the public conscience'. The clause, in effect, would become famous as the Martens Clause.

The Regulations did not by themselves constitute a treaty: they were 'annexed' to the Convention, and ratifying states undertook to issue instructions to their armed forces 'in conformity' with the Regulations.[34] While this left the Regulations in the realm of customary law, they had been thoroughly examined and negotiated, and Hague II wrote into the Convention that a belligerent state which violated their provisions would, 'if the case demands, be liable to pay compensation'.[35] The conclusion may be that by 1907, the Regulations had turned into a sort of written or 'hard' customary law.

---

28 Ibid art 26.
29 Ibid art 27.
30 Ibid art 2.
31 Ibid art 42.
32 Ibid art 43.
33 Rik Coolsaet, 'La Belgique et la Première Conférence de la Paix de La Haye (1899)', file 1899b.pdf on CD annexed to Frits Kalshoven (ed), *The Centennial of the First International Peace Conference: Reports & Conclusions* (Kluwer 2000).
34 1907 Hague Convention (IV) (n 22) art 1.
35 Ibid art 3.

2.2 Naval warfare

Warfare at sea always was fundamentally different from land warfare in that the high seas were no man's land, open to the shipping of all nations. Territorial seas, at the time usually three nautical miles wide, were under the jurisdiction of the coastal state, whether belligerent or neutral. Hague II codified the law for many situations flowing from this scheme. This included striking a balance between the belligerents' interests and those of neutral shipping and neutral coastal states. A few lines must suffice to introduce this part of the law of war.

Sea warfare was conducted by warships: vessels built, registered, equipped and manned as such. However, merchant vessels could be converted to warships; they then must meet a list of conditions guaranteeing their recognisability. As for weaponry, limits were set to the use of automatic contact mines, first of all to limit the risks for commercial shipping: in principle, they had to become harmless once they were no longer under control. Limits of a different order governed the bombardment by warships of cities and other inhabited places on the shore: bombardment of undefended localities was strictly prohibited, and fire directed at other localities could solely be aimed at military works and other enumerated objects that qualified as military objectives.

Rules governing the impact of the war on shipping included such disparate matters as the departure of neutral vessels from belligerent harbours at the outbreak of war, the inviolability of postal correspondence on board neutral and enemy vessels, and the immunity from capture of fishing vessels and small local traders.

Hague II had not by far codified the law for every conceivable situation; as noted in the preamble of Convention (XI) on certain cases of capture, the codified law did not affect 'the common law now in force with regard to the matters which that law has left unsettled'.[36] Mention is made, in this respect, of the Convention (XII) on the international prize court.[37] The convention remaining unratified, the court was never created.

2.3 Geneva law

The first Geneva Convention, written in 1864 without a basis in practice, was marked for revision from its early days.[38] As noted, Russia had included some of its provisions in the project for the Brussels Declaration of 1874; with this attempt warded off, the Declaration referred to the Convention of 1864, with such 'modifications as the latter may undergo'. The same clause subsequently came to figure in the Hague Regulations of 1899.[39] In 1906, a new Geneva Convention finally replaced the old one (and the Regulations of 1907 no longer referred to 'modifications').

The Geneva Convention of 1906 was as long and practical as the Convention of 1864 had been short and experimental. It dealt extensively with the condition of the wounded and sick (including the dead), the personnel – both military and that of volunteer aid societies – of

---

36 Convention (XI) relative to certain Restrictions with regard to the Exercise of the Right of Capture in Naval War (18 October 1907) 205 CTS 367.
37 Convention (XII) Relative to the Creation of an International Prize Court (18 October 1907) 205 CTS 381.
38 Moynier (n 13) 5–13.
39 1899 Hague Regulations (n 21) art 21.

'sanitary' formations and their 'materièl', and the distinctive emblem.[40] Some broad strokes may suffice.

The wounded and sick must be 'respected' (ie not harmed) and, positively, 'cared for', 'without distinction of nationality' and 'by the belligerent in whose power they are'.[41] If this was the enemy, they also became prisoners of war. Then, the local population could play a role as well; to that end, 'military authority' could 'make an appeal to the charitable zeal of the inhabitants'.[42]

Elaborating the principles, the Convention dealt with such matters as the possession and use of weapons by the personnel of a sanitary establishment and the guards; the work in their proper functions by sanitary personnel who have fallen in the power of the enemy; and the power of a belligerent intercepting an evacuation convoy, 'if required by military necessity', to break it up, therewith 'charging himself with the care of the sick and wounded whom it contains'.[43]

A final point: since the emblem had been open to abuse, the parties undertook to take the necessary legislative and practical measures to prevent and repress such abuses.[44]

The Hague Convention (X) of 1907 adapted the principles of 1906 to maritime warfare. It introduced the 'hospital ship': a vessel built or equipped 'solely with a view to assisting the wounded, sick and shipwrecked'.[45] Hospital ships could be operated by a belligerent state or by a voluntary aid society in that state or in a neutral state. They had to be painted white, with a broad horizontal band around the ship: green for the state-operated or 'military' hospital ship, red for the other ones; and, apart from national flags, they flew 'the white flag with a red cross'.[46] Their task was to 'afford relief and assistance to the wounded, sick, and shipwrecked of the belligerents without distinction of nationality'.[47] However, belligerents to that end could also 'appeal to the charity of the commanders of neutral merchant ships, yachts, or boats to take on board and tend the sick and wounded':[48] a nice parallel to land warfare's appeal by 'military authority' to the 'charitable zeal of the inhabitants'.

A final note on the treaties mentioned in this section: they all were written for, and applied in 'war', a situation that was either declared or could be recognised from the facts. Rather than describing this, the treaties set forth in detail the relations among the belligerents that were, or were not, or were no longer, parties to a given treaty. Most ruinous was the 'si omnes' clause: when a non-party state joined a war between parties, the treaty was no longer applicable between the original parties as well.

3 The interbellum

As noted, the outbreak of the World War had prevented the planned third Hague peace conference. Striking features of that war had been the endless trench warfare on the French–German border, with the thousands upon thousands of victims; the introduction of British tanks, stopped

---

40 Convention for the Amelioration of the Condition of the Wounded and Sick in Armies in the Field (6 July 1906) 202 CTS 144.
41 Ibid art 1.
42 Ibid art 5.
43 Ibid arts 8, 12, 17.
44 Ibid art 27.
45 Convention (X) for the Adaptation to Maritime Warfare of the Principles of the Geneva Convention (18 October 1907) 205 CTS 359.
46 Ibid art 5.
47 Ibid art 4.
48 Ibid art 9.

by the ever heavier German machine guns; the use by Germany and Great Britain of lethal gas; the rapid development of air warfare, including the bombing of industrial and other non-military targets; and submarine warfare, both against enemy warships and commercial shipping.

The League of Nations, established in 1920,[49] had peace, not war, on its agenda. Yet, law of war issues came up in meetings under its auspices. Thus, a five-power conference (US, Great Britain, France, Italy and Japan) held in Washington in 1922 on the limitation of armaments took positions on submarine warfare and the use of chemical weapons. However, most interesting was its decision to have an international Commission of Jurists elaborate rules of aerial warfare and wartime control of wireless telegraphy.

3.1 Hague Rules of Air Warfare (1923)

The Commission of Jurists met at The Hague. It was composed of six teams, one from each of the parties to the conference and one from the Netherlands. In 1923 it presented its results, usually indicated as Hague Rules. The Rules on wireless telegraphy mainly had to do with neutrality.[50] In contrast, the 62 articles of the Rules of Air Warfare provided a complete set of rules on this novel, three-dimensional form of warfare, with chapters on the participants (the 'belligerents'), hostilities, relations to enemy and neutral aircraft, etc.[51]

The chapter on hostilities opened with the statement that '[t]he use of tracer, incendiary or explosive projectiles by or against aircraft' was permitted.[52] This confirmed practice; as noted in the rule, it also overruled the 1868 St Petersburg Declaration: a clear case of customary law setting aside a rule of treaty law.

The first rule on air bombardment was a radical ban on the practice of terror bombing.[53] Then, for a bombardment to be legitimate, it had to be 'directed at a military objective', that is, an object figuring on an exclusive list and the destruction or injury of which 'would constitute a distinct military advantage to the belligerent'. Moreover, any objective located in a city or other civilian habitation could only be bombed if this locality was situated in the 'immediate vicinity of the operations of the land forces'.[54] So, in today's terms: no strategic bombing. And where bombardment was permissible, special care should be taken of objects selected for their cultural or medical importance.[55]

The 1923 Hague Rules were never signed. Yet, they have not been without influence; as one author had it: 'Although the rules were not ratified, both sides [to the Second World War] publicly acclaimed their adherence and accused their opponents of violations.'[56] And on 30 September 1938, a short while before the outbreak of the war, the League Assembly adopted a resolution which, without referring to the Hague Rules, reaffirmed the ban on intentional bombing of civilian populations. It stated that only identifiable military objectives could be

---

49 Covenant of the League of Nations, being Articles 1–26 of the Treaty of Versailles (28 June 1919) 225 CTS 188.

50 17 *AJIL Supp* 242.

51 17 *AJIL Supp* 245.

52 Ibid pt II, ch IV, art 18.

53 Ibid art 22.

54 Ibid art 24.

55 Ibid art 25, reaffirming HR art 27.

56 Richard H Wyman, 'The First Rules of Air Warfare' (1984) 82 *Air University Review*, www.airpower. au.af.mil/airchronicles/aureview/1984/mar-apr/wyman.html.

attacked, and attacks must take care that civilian populations in the vicinity were not bombed through negligence.[57]

3.2 Geneva Gas Protocol (1925)

The use of poison and poisonous weapons, since long prohibited under customary law and in writing since the Hague Regulations of 1899/1907, came up in the post-First World War debate, if only as a consequence of the use of various types of gas by both sides in trench warfare. A clause in the treaty concluded at the Washington conference of 1922 on the use of submarines and noxious gases in warfare placed on record the parties' assent to the existing prohibition, their agreement 'to be bound thereby as between themselves' and their invitation to 'all other civilized nations to adhere thereto'.[58] However, the treaty never entered into force.

The legal regulation of the use of noxious gas resurfaced again in 1925, at an international conference in Geneva on the international arms trade. Prompted by a French proposal, the conference also adopted the so-called Geneva Gas Protocol.[59] Like the Washington treaty, the Protocol reaffirmed the existing prohibition on wartime use of poison gases, liquids etc, to which it added the use of 'bacteriological methods of warfare'. In the course of time, it would be ratified or acceded to by 137 states; the United States ratified after 50 years, in 1975.

While the Protocol was silent on whether a belligerent attacked with gas would be entitled to respond in kind, many states expressly reserved their right to such a response. A number of them have since withdrawn this reservation. Apart from that, none of the 188 states which since have become party to the Chemical Weapons Convention can be deemed to have retained such a right, given the text of Article 1 by which each state party accepts 'never under any circumstances ... [t]o use chemical weapons'.

3.3 Naval warfare

Submarine warfare during the First World War, with its innumerable victims on the high seas, had led to the insight that the applicable law needed to be reaffirmed. With the Washington treaty of 1922 unratified, a next attempt was made at the 1930 London conference on naval armaments. The conference adopted a treaty, Part IV of which codified two principles 'accepted as established rules of international law': 'In their actions with regard to merchant ships, submarines must conform to the rules of international law to which surface vessels are subject.' And, cases of resistance apart, no warship, 'whether surface vessel or submarine', may sink a merchant vessel 'without having first placed passengers, crew and ship's papers in a place of safety'. Although this treaty also failed to attract sufficient ratifications, Part IV was saved: on 6 November 1936, again in London, a Procès-verbal containing the verbatim text of Part IV was signed and entered into force that same day.[60] It was ultimately accepted by 39 states.[61]

---

57 Protection of Civilian Populations against Bombing from the Air in Case of War, League of Nation Assembly Res (30 September 1938), reprinted in Schindler and Toman (n 6) 329.
58 Treaty Relating to the Use of Submarines and Noxious Gases in Warfare (6 February 1922) 25 LNTS 202, art 5.
59 Protocol for the Prohibition of the Use of Asphyxiating, Poisonous or Other Gases, and of Bacteriological Methods of Warfare (17 June 1925) 94 LNTS 65.
60 173 LNTS 353.
61 Adam Roberts and Richard Guelff, *Documents on the Laws of War* (3rd edn, OUP 2000) 1145.

3.4 Geneva Conventions (1929)

In 1929, a diplomatic conference held in Geneva adopted two Conventions: one, on the wounded and sick of armies in the field; and the other, on the treatment of prisoners of war.

The new Convention for the wounded and sick replaced the Convention of 1906, bringing it up-to-date in the light of the First World War practice. We single out one interesting clause on application. It provided that 'the provisions of the present Convention shall be respected [by the parties] in all circumstances'.[62] As explained by the former secretary-general of the conference, the phrase served to remind the parties of their obligation to apply in peace time the rules in the Convention written for that period. He added that he did not believe it implied application in civil war as well, no matter how desirable this might be.[63]

The Convention on the treatment of prisoners of war completed the provisions in Chapter II of the Hague Regulations of 1899/1907. Here too, experiences of the First World War were worked into the text. We just mention the labour of prisoners of war, their relations with the authorities (through a representative of their choice) and with the outside world, and their punishment, whether disciplinary or judicial, for acts committed before or during imprisonment.[64] One major achievement was the prohibition of reprisals:[65] the infliction of forms of maltreatment in response to similar behaviour by the enemy. Another point of interest was the description of a protecting-power system, by which a state charged with the protection of a belligerent's interests could send representatives to control the situation of prisoners of war in the hands of the other belligerent.[66]

We note that the prisoners-of-war Convention contains the same 'all circumstances' provision,[67] making it all the more improbable that the drafters would have had civil war in mind. And, a last point, the same articles in both Conventions do away with the 'si omnes' clause, specifying that they remain binding if non-parties are among the belligerents.

Herewith, Geneva law had come to cover the wounded and sick (and shipwrecked) and the prisoners of war. Still absent was the civilian population, a category that during the First World War had suffered badly in many countries.[68] The 1929 diplomatic conference did not have the matter on its agenda. Yet, it adopted a resolution recommending that steps be taken towards the conclusion of a convention on the protection of civilians in enemy or occupied territory.[69] A text drafted by the ICRC to that end found approval in the Red Cross world, but by the time the Swiss authorities could have convened the next diplomatic conference, the next war had started.[70]

---

62 Convention for the Amelioration of the Condition of the Wounded and Sick in Armies in the Field (27 July 1929) 118 LNTS 303, art 25.
63 Paul des Gouttes, *La Convention de Genève du 27 juillet 1929: Commentaire* (ICRC 1930) 186–187.
64 Convention relative to the Treatment of Prisoners of War (27 July 1929) 118 LNTS 343.
65 Ibid art 2.
66 Ibid art 86.
67 Ibid art 82.
68 Matthew Stibbe, 'The Internment of Civilians by Belligerent States during the First World War and the Response of the International Committee of the Red Cross' (2006) 41 *Journal of Contemporary History* 5.
69 Final Act of the Diplomatic Conference of 1929 (27 July 1929), reprinted in Schindler and Toman (n 6) 406, ¶ vi.
70 Draft International Convention on the Condition and protection of Civilians of Enemy Nationality who are on Territory Belonging to or Occupied by a Belligerent (recommended by the XV International Red Cross Conference, Tokyo, 1934), reprinted in Schindler and Toman (n 6) 445.

In sum, the interbellum brought a very modest harvest of IHL treaty law: on Hague law, the 1925 Gas Protocol and the 1936 Procès-verbal on submarine warfare; and on Geneva law, the two Conventions of 1929. Efforts such as the 1923 Hague Rules on air warfare and the 1938 League Assembly resolution on bombardment were useful but insufficient. And work on the protection of civilian populations had just begun.

4 The aftermath of the Second World War up to the present

The Second World War once again brought untold misery, with the holocaust and the 'atomic bomb' as horrendous culminating points. Once this war terminated, the creation of the UN was a sign of hope, and so was the establishment of the Nuremberg and Tokyo Tribunals which dealt with the major war criminals of the Axis Powers.[71] At the same time, warfare continued, this time of another type: the decolonisation wars or wars of national liberation.

IHL treaty law had been developing over this entire period, at the outset still according to the Geneva and Hague split. In the 1970s, the two fields could be seen to merge. The present section reflects this development.[72]

4.1 Geneva Conventions (1949)

In 1949, a diplomatic conference in Geneva produced four Conventions, three to replace the Conventions of 1906 and 1929, and the fourth for the protection of civilians – at last!

The Conventions are characterised by a number of common provisions. Common Article 1 reaffirms the phrase, introduced in 1929, that states parties 'undertake to respect and to ensure respect [for each Convention] in all circumstances'. The phrase is widely interpreted as allowing states not party to an armed conflict to urge the parties thereto to respect the law.[73]

Like their predecessors, the Conventions apply in 'war', completed now in Common Article 2 with 'any other armed conflict' between two or more states. The new, more objective clause offers outsiders (other states, the UN, the ICRC) a tool to urge application of the Conventions.

A major step forward has been the adoption of Common Article 3. This by now famous provision lays down minimum rules that must be applied by all the parties to an internal armed conflict that occurs within the territory of a state. The rules protect persons who do not, or no longer, take part in the hostilities: they must always be 'treated humanely, without any adverse distinction founded on race, colour, religion or faith, sex, birth or wealth, or any other similar criteria'. Prohibited in particular are all kind of 'violence to life and person', 'outrages upon personal dignity', hostage taking, summary executions, etc.

A last element common to the four Conventions mentioned here is the introduction of 'grave breaches': select acts, committed wilfully against protected persons or property.[74] The Conventions do not themselves provide sanctions for these acts, nor do they open a road to international adjudication. Rather, it is for the states parties to make the acts publishable in their domestic legislation.

---

71 Agreement for the Prosecution and Punishment of the Major War Criminals of the European Axis ('London Agreement') (8 August 1945) 82 UNTS 280.
72 Convention on the Prevention and Punishment of the Crime of Genocide, UNGA Res 260 (III) (9 December 1948) 78 UNTS 277 is not treated here, since it does not regulate the conduct of war.
73 See also Frits Kalshoven, 'The Undertaking to Respect and Ensure Respect in all Circumstances: From Tiny Seed to Ripening Fruit' (1999) *YBIHL* 3, reprinted in Kalshoven, *Reflections* (n 10) 665.
74 GCI art 49; GCII art 50; GCIII art 129; GCIV art 146.

In Geneva Convention III, the list of protected persons has been completed with the members of 'organised resistance movements, belonging to a Party to the conflict and operating in or outside their own territory, even if this territory is occupied'[75] – Lieber's 'war rebels' at long last brought under protection, always on the understanding that they respect the four conditions set forth in the Hague Regulations of 1899/1907.

As for the newcomer: Geneva Convention IV does not protect against bombardment or any other effects of hostilities. It does aim to protect against other, often equally serious effects of war on freedom, security and health. Thus, a Part on 'general protection of populations against certain consequences of war' deals with agreed 'safety zones' for qualifying groups of persons, protection of civilian hospitals and of land, sea and air transport of wounded and sick civilians, child welfare and family news, etc.[76] One singularly important provision obliges all states, whether belligerent or not, to allow the free passage of medical, hospital and religious consignments, as well as of essential foodstuffs etc for 'children under fifteen, expectant mothers and maternity cases'.[77]

Specific protection is accorded 'protected persons', categories of persons defined as 'those who, at a given moment and in any manner whatsoever, find themselves, in case of a conflict or occupation, in the hands of a Party to the conflict or Occupying Power of which they are not nationals'.[78] Geneva Convention IV provides in detail for the 'status and treatment' of these persons. Selected here are the rules aiming to prevent a repetition of the events that occurred in the Second World War when, the moment the United States joined the war, it interned the Japanese persons living in the country. Internment remains permitted, but only when this is absolutely necessary for reasons of state security, and under periodical review by a competent court or administrative board.[79] In occupied territory as well, internment remains possible.[80] For either case of internment, Geneva Convention IV provides a detailed set of regulations, much like the rules for prisoners of war in Geneva Convention III.[81]

4.2 Hague Convention (1954)

Monuments and other types and sizes of cultural objects had been exposed during the Second World War to all kinds of maltreatment, from wanton destruction to forced exportation. The Hague Regulations were of course totally inadequate, and new treaty law on the subject was urgently needed. To that end, an intergovernmental conference convened by UNESCO met in 1954 in The Hague, and on 14 May 1954 it adopted the Convention for the Protection of Cultural Property in the Event of Armed Conflict.[82]

The Convention distinguishes general and special protection. General protection covers all objects that fall under the description of 'movable or immovable property of great importance to the cultural heritage of every people', from 'monuments of architecture' to 'important collections of books'.[83] Under the heading 'respect', both parties to the conflict are urged to refrain

---

75 GCIII art 4(A)(2).
76 GCIV pt II.
77 Ibid art 23.
78 Ibid art 4.
79 Ibid arts 41–43.
80 Ibid art 78.
81 Ibid arts 79–141; cf GCIII arts 21–48.
82 249 UNTS 240.
83 Ibid art 1.

from any act that might put such a protected object at risk.[84] Objects may be marked with an emblem that consists of a blue-and-white shield.[85]

In contrast, special protection can only be granted to a limited number of refuges sheltering movable objects or centres containing immovable items, that are situated far from any object that might be regarded as a military objective, and are not themselves used for a military purpose.[86] For a refuge or centre to be granted the special protection requires a long process that ends with its inscription in a register held at UNESCO.[87] Few objects have actually been so registered.

The provisions on application of the Convention are copies of the relevant rules in the Geneva Conventions.[88] As another sign of the closing gap between the two branches of IHL, the provisions of the Convention that 'relate to respect for cultural property' are declared applicable in non-international armed conflicts as well.[89]

The conference also adopted a Protocol, aimed against the practice of exportation of cultural property.[90] In a detailed set of rules, the parties undertake to prevent the practice or, where it has occurred, to help mending the consequences.

4.3 Protocols I and II Additional to the 1949 Geneva Conventions (1977)

On 8 June 1977, after four years of negotiations, the Diplomatic Conference on the Reaffirmation and Development of International Humanitarian Law Applicable in Armed Conflicts in Geneva adopted two Protocols additional to the 1949 Conventions, one for international armed conflicts and the other for non-international armed conflicts. (The conference, after its French acronym, is referred to as the CDDH.)

Preparations for the event went back to 1956, when the ICRC published Draft Rules for the Limitation of the Dangers Incurred by the Civilian Population in Time of War.[91] Welcomed in 1957 by the XIXth International Conference of the Red Cross, the text drew few reactions from governments. Then, in December 1968, the UN General Assembly adopted Resolution 2444 (XXIII) which in few words affirmed three principles formulated in 1965 at the XXth International Conference of the Red Cross: no unlimited right for belligerent parties to adopt means of injuring the enemy, prohibition of attacks directed against the civilian population, and distinction at all times between combatants and civilians 'to the effect that the latter be spared as much as possible'. Soon thereafter, government and Red Cross expert meetings had begun preparing for the diplomatic conference.[92]

---

84 Ibid art 4.
85 Ibid arts 6, 16.
86 Ibid art 8.
87 Ibid art 8(6).
88 Ibid art 18; cf GCI–IV art 2.
89 Ibid art 19.
90 249 UNTS 358.
91 Schindler and Toman (n 6) 339.
92 Frits Kalshoven, 'The Conference of Government Experts on the Reaffirmation and Development of International Humanitarian Law Applicable in Armed Conflicts, 24 May–12 June, 1971' (1971) 2 *Netherlands YBIL* 68, and 'The Conference of Government Experts on the Reaffirmation and Development of International Humanitarian Law Applicable in Armed Conflicts (Second Session), 3 May–2 June, 1972' (1972) 3 *Netherlands YBIL* 18, reprinted in Kalshoven, *Reflections* (n 10) 33 and 57, respectively.

Opened in 1974, with the Vietnam war coming to an end, the CDDH spent most of its first session on the qualification of decolonisation wars: international or internal? It decided by over-whelming majority, and in conformity with the position long taken by the majority at the UN General Assembly, that wars of national liberation had to be recognised as international armed conflicts.[93]

With liberation wars thus brought within the ambit of Additional Protocol I, its provision on application is completed with a paragraph stating that liberation wars are included among the situations where the 1949 Geneva Conventions are applicable.[94] Another provision opens the possibility for 'the authority representing' a people fighting a liberation war to unilaterally 'undertake to apply the Conventions and this Protocol': from the moment the depositary (Switzerland) receives this undertaking, and assuming the colonial power is party to the Protocol, the Conventions and the Protocol are in force and binding on all the parties to the conflict.[95] However, this is a rather theoretical construct that has not been applied in practice.

The decision of 1974 also necessitated another look at the term 'combatant'. As with the classical irregular fighter in occupied territory, the officially recognised liberation fighter could not very well be expected to wage war according to the rules written for traditional armies. The solution, finally found in direct contact between the US and Vietnamese heads of delegation, is in two parts: (1) a redefinition of the term 'armed forces' brings the state armies and other armed groups under the same rules, and (2) the irregulars are granted some flexibility in meeting the obligation of all combatants to distinguish themselves from civilians whenever they are 'engaged in an attack or in a military operation preparatory to an attack'.[96] Several states in ratifying Additional Protocol I have added their understanding that apart from wars of liberation, the latter rule will apply solely in occupied territory. The US, for its part, completely rejects the new rule as favouring terrorism. With that, it may be said to revert to, nay surpass, Lieber's classification of irregular fighters in occupied territory as 'war rebels'.

The use by the US of defoliants in Vietnam led to yet another renovation in Additional Protocol I: the set of 'basic rules' (no unlimited right to choose methods or means of warfare, no weapons 'of a nature to cause superfluous injury') was completed with the prohibition 'to employ methods or means of warfare which are intended, or may be expected, to cause wide-spread, long-term and severe damage to the natural environment'.[97]

With Geneva and Hague law flowing into a single stream, Additional Protocol I has sections on the 'wounded, sick and shipwrecked', 'methods and means of warfare' and 'combatant and prisoner-of-war status', as well as a long section headed 'civilian population' that shows when, how and to what extent civilians can be protected against the vicissitudes of warfare. To many, this complete set of rules for the protection of civilians against 'dangers arising from military operations' is the greatest achievement of the CDDH. Without going any further into the details of Additional Protocol I, it may be noted that as of December 2015, 174 states are party to it and the most important non-party, the US, accepts many of its provisions as customary law.

93 Frits Kalshoven, 'The First Session of the Diplomatic Conference on Reaffirmation and Development of International Humanitarian Law Applicable in Armed Conflicts, Geneva, 20 February–29 March, 1974' (1974) 5 *Netherlands YBIL* 3, reprinted in Kalshoven, *Reflections* (n 10) 101.
94 API art 1(4).
95 Ibid art 96(3).
96 Ibid arts 43, 44; see also Frits Kalshoven, 'The Diplomatic Conference on Reaffirmation and Development of International Humanitarian Law Applicable in Armed Conflicts, Geneva, 1974–1977' in Kalshoven, *Reflections* (n 10) 181, 197
97 API art 35.

Fewer words are spent here on Additional Protocol II. It is applicable in select non-international armed conflicts. The conflict must be between the armed forces of a state party and 'armed groups which, under responsible command, exercise such control over a part of its territory as to enable them to carry out sustained and concerted military operations and to implement this Protocol'.[98] A last-minute compromise between the many states who wanted no Protocol at all and those who aimed at a text as close to Additional Protocol I as possible, Additional Protocol II has no rules on 'methods and means of warfare' or 'combatant and prisoner-of-war status', and but a few on protection of the civilian population. It does make provision for the 'humane treatment' of all persons who take no direct part in hostilities: a set of provisions that borrows from Common Article 3 of the 1949 Conventions, completed with human rights. As well, a section on 'wounded, sick and shipwrecked' provides the basics of this oldest part of Geneva law. Additional Protocol II has been accepted by 168 states.

4.4 Convention on Conventional Weapons (1980)

Even before the CDDH, the feeling had become widespread that not only the 'methods of warfare' but certain 'means of warfare' should be tackled too. Attention went in particular to weapons such as small-calibre rifle munitions, landmines and incendiary weapons, and the action sought was not prohibition of possession (a disarmament measure) but prohibition or limitation of use. The CDDH not being empowered to negotiate a treaty on these matters, pressure from the 'activists' resulted in the establishment of an ad hoc committee that examined these matters throughout the four sessions of the conference, thus preparing the ground for further action. Its final report induced the CDDH to recommend that a government conference be speedily convened to carry the matter further. Taking up the suggestion, the UN General Assembly resolved in December 1977 that such a conference be held in 1979.[99]

After due preparation, the UN Conference on Prohibitions or Restrictions of Use of Certain Conventional Weapons Which May be Deemed to be Excessively Injurious or to Have Indiscriminate Effects met in Geneva in two sessions: one in September 1979 and the second in September/October 1980. On 10 October 1980, it adopted a Convention with the same long name but usually referred to as the Convention on Certain Conventional Weapons (CCW).[100]

The CCW is an umbrella to which Protocols can be annexed that contain the substantive rules on use of given weapons. The list of Protocols includes mines and booby traps (II), incendiary weapons (III), blinding laser weapons (IV) and 'explosive remnants of war' (V) including unexploded bomblets of cluster munitions. Both on anti-personnel mines and cluster munitions separate conventions have been adopted, in 1997 and 2008 respectively, which complete the prohibition on their use with a ban on possession, production, etc.

The scope of application of the CCW was originally identical to that of Additional Protocol I: international armed conflicts, including wars of liberation. The fact that non-international armed conflicts were not included soon proved unfortunate, given the increase of such situations. Fortunately, the CCW provides for review conferences.[101] The second review conference decided in December 2001 to expand the application of the CCW and the annexed protocols to all non-international armed conflicts. This revision of Article 1 has been in force since 18 November 2003.

---

98 APII art 1(1).
99 UNGA Res 32/152 (19 December 1977).
100 1342 UNTS 137.
101 Ibid art 8.

4.5 Second Protocol to the 1954 Hague Convention (1999)

An international conference at The Hague, organised jointly by the Netherlands government and UNESCO, in March 1999 adopted a Second Protocol to the Convention of 1954.[102] It largely rewrites the part of the Convention on general protection in terms of Additional Protocol I. It also replaces the part on special protection with a system of 'enhanced protection' of objects that qualify as 'cultural heritage of the greatest importance to humanity' and meet further stringent conditions. The system rests on registration on a list maintained by the Committee for the Protection of Cultural Property in the Event of Armed Conflict, being the executive organ of the Protocol that consists of the representatives of 12 states parties. Like other recent products, the Second Protocol is applicable in all armed conflicts, whether international or non-international.[103]

4.6 Protocol III Additional to the 1949 Geneva Conventions (2006)

In 2006, two narrowly connected issues were resolved that had emerged in 1949 when Israel signed the Geneva Conventions under the reservation that although it respected the use by others of the red cross or crescent, it would itself 'use the Red Shield of David as the emblem and distinctive sign of the medical services of its armed forces'. Israel clearly would never change its position, and the international community proved equally unwilling to accept an additional emblem for a single state. In consequence, the Magen David Adom Society could not be admitted to the Red Cross and Red Crescent Movement. The same applied to the Palestine Red Crescent Society, since Palestine was not a recognised state.

Both problems were finally resolved in a series of manoeuvres that on 21 June 2006 enabled the Movement to accept both candidates. The central piece was the adoption, on 8 December 2005, by an ad hoc diplomatic conference, of Protocol III Additional to the 1949 Geneva Conventions.[104] This introduces a new emblem, defined as 'a red frame in the shape of a square on edge on a white ground' and referred to as the 'red crystal'. It can be used as a protective emblem (emphasising the protected status of the person or object carrying it) and, in limited circumstances, as an indicative emblem with another, unrecognised, emblem (say, the Red Shield of David) at its centre. Additional Protocol III, in force since 14 January 2007, on 22 November 2007 was ratified by Israel.

With this purely Geneva bit of news, we conclude our history of the law of armed conflict. More could have been written about recent developments, in particular in the sphere of international criminal law, but this would have made the present chapter much too long. For these further developments, the reader may be referred to the relevant other chapters of this volume.

102 2253 UNTS 212.
103 Ibid arts 3, 22.
104 2404 UNTS 261.

3

Conflict characterisation

Caitlin Dwyer and Tim McCormack

After the Prosecution's closing submissions had concluded in Lubanga, *the first trial completed at the International Criminal Court, Professor Ben Ferencz, prosecutor from Nuremberg, who had delivered the final section of the final address, was approached by a young lawyer who said: 'Professor Ferencz, I just wanted to say how inspiring it was to hear your words today. This is an exciting time for international criminal justice, and to hear you pass on the baton from Nuremberg to the ICC was just magnificent.'*

Professor Ferencz responded:
'Well, did you hear the guy before me? It's not hard to be inspiring after that – the characterisation of the conflict? Who cares about that stuff?'

It may seem anachronistic that different rules apply to international armed conflicts (IAC) and non-international armed conflicts (NIAC), and that the legal character of an armed conflict can have significant consequences for combatants, civilians and victims of alleged war crimes. The ICRC, in the lead up to the 1949 Diplomatic Conference, had proposed that the Conventions should apply to any situation of armed conflict regardless of its legal character but that proposal was rejected by states.[1] Irrespective of the desirability of a simplification in approach, the current state of the law of armed conflict (LOAC) maintains the distinction between the two categories of armed conflict.

Section 1 of this chapter briefly outlines the significance of the distinction between IAC and NIAC. Section 2 outlines the treaty provisions relevant to the characterisation of conflicts and identifies the lack of a treaty definition of an armed conflict. Instead, the threshold criteria for an IAC and a NIAC have been developed in the international criminal jurisprudence and that has created its own issues. Section 3 examines the question of how to characterise armed conflicts, and proposes two key principles: (1) that the legal character of an armed conflict is

---

1 *GCI Commentary* 29 reproduces the text of the ICRC's proposal: 'The present Convention is applicable between the High Contracting Parties from the moment hostilities have actually broken out, even if no declaration of war has been made and *whatever the form that such armed intervention may take*' (emphasis added).

determined by the nature of the parties to it; and (2) that the only armed conflict which is international is one between two or more opposing states.

1 Significance of the distinction

The body of rules applicable to an IAC is more comprehensive than that applicable to a NIAC. As a consequence, acts that constitute war crimes in the context of an IAC are not necessarily war crimes in a NIAC.[2] To apply different rules in this way may seem arbitrary: why should one civilian be entitled to less protection from the laws of war than another, simply because the conflict he or she is unwittingly caught up in is non-international?[3] This arbitrariness takes on even greater significance given that the majority of conflicts since the Second World War have been non-international and that these conflicts have also created the largest number of victims.[4]

The distinction has its origins in the genesis of LOAC. When negotiating the Geneva Conventions of 1864, 1906, 1929 and finally 1949, states were concerned with securing rights for their own military personnel and civilian population and did so by granting reciprocal rights to other states. States were not concerned with creating rights or protections for non-state armed groups who may one day be fighting against them. Indeed, it was not until 1949, after the Spanish Civil War, that the first multilateral treaty provision even addressed armed conflict not involving two opposing states: Article 3 common to the four Geneva Conventions. Even then, states were careful not to permit that provision to be misinterpreted to give non-state armed groups authority or legitimacy – Common Article 3 declares that its application 'shall not affect the legal status of the Parties to the conflict'. This is a key concern of states and the main reason why the distinction between IAC and NIAC is unlikely to be dissolved: states will not extend legitimacy to non-state armed groups and, more specifically, they will not commit themselves to granting members of such groups combatant privilege or prisoner of war (POW) status.[5]

---

2 For a detailed discussion of the disparity of war crimes in IACs compared to NIACs in the Rome Statute, see eg Tim McCormack, 'The Challenges of Applying Article 8 of the Rome Statute' in Suzannah Linton, Gerry Simpson and William A. Schabas (eds), *For the Sake of Present and Future Generations: Essays in Honour of Roger Clark* (Martinus Nijhoff 2015) ch 21.

3 See eg discussion in *Prosecutor v Tadić (Appeal Judgment)* (Case no IT-94-1-A, ICTY Appeals Chamber, 15 July 1999) ¶ 97.

4 See: ICRC, Introduction to APII, www.icrc.org/applic/ihl/ihl.nsf/INTRO/475?OpenDocument; M Cherif Bassiouni, 'The New Wars and the Crisis of Compliance with the Law of Armed Conflict by Non-State Actors' (2008) 98 *Journal of Criminal Law & Criminology* 711, 712: 'Since the end of World War II, an estimated 250 conflicts have taken place on almost every continent in the world, resulting in estimated casualties ranging from seventy million to 170 million, most of whom were non-combatants'; see also ibid 745–748 for examples.

5 At the Diplomatic Conference of 1949 a proposal to prohibit prosecution for taking part in a NIAC failed and at the Diplomatic Conference of 1974–1977, a proposal to grant POW status to those involved in NIAC failed: see Sandesh Sivakumaran, 'Re-envisaging the International Law of Internal Armed Conflict' (2011) 22(1) *EJIL* 219, 244 and the sources cited therein. See also Bassiouni (n 4) 731. For an exposition of the differences in the detention regimes, see Chris Jenks, 'Detention under the law of armed conflict' ch 17 in this volume.

Thus, although the gap between the two bodies of law has narrowed significantly[6] and there are many arguments for completely abandoning the distinction,[7] the distinction remains.

The absence of combatant privilege and POW status are the most significant and likely the most enduring differences between IAC and NIAC. They also carry significant consequences for individuals which are examined elsewhere.[8] Other distinctions between the two sets of laws include that no rules regulate the occupation of territory by a non-state armed group[9] and that the level of specificity of obligations is far greater in IAC than NIAC. A further consequence of the continued distinction between the two sets of law is the difference in the types of conduct which are criminalised. There are 14 crimes in the Rome Statute which apply only in IAC, including disproportionate attacks and attacks on civilian objects.[10] Even where seemingly the same conduct has been criminalised, there may be significant distinctions in the provisions.

2 The definition of an 'armed conflict'

2.1 Scope of application and lack of definition

The relevant treaty provisions on scope of application of the Geneva Conventions provide no definition of an 'armed conflict'. Common Article 2, for example, states that each respective Convention applies to:

> all cases of declared war or of any other armed conflict which may arise between two or more of the High Contracting Parties, even if the state of war is not recognized by one of them. The Convention shall also apply to all cases of partial or total occupation of the territory of a High Contracting Party, even if the said occupation meets with no armed resistance.

Common Article 3 provides no definitional clarification and simply applies to 'armed conflicts not of an international character occurring in the territory of one of the High Contracting Parties'.

Additional Protocol II applies by virtue of its Article 1(1) to:

> all armed conflicts ... which take place in the territory of a High Contracting Party between its armed forces and dissident armed forces or other organized armed groups which, under

6 See eg the discussion in Sivakumaran (n 5) in particular 222–236.

7 See *Prosecutor v Tadić (Appeals Chamber Decision on the Defence Motion for Interlocutory Appeal on Jurisdiction)* (Case no IT-94-1, ICTY Appeals Chamber, 2 October 1995) ¶¶ 96–98 and 119; *Prosecutor v Lubanga* (Case no ICC-01/04-01/06, ICC Trial Chamber I, 14 March 2012) ¶ 539 and the sources cited therein; James Stewart, 'Towards a Single Definition of Armed Conflict in International Humanitarian Law: A Critique of Internationalized Armed Conflict' (2003) 85 *IRRC* 313; Deidre Willmott, 'Removing the Distinction Between International and Non-International Armed Conflict in the Rome Statute of the International Criminal Court' (2004) 5 *Melbourne JIL* 196.

8 For example, see Emily Crawford, 'Combatants' ch 7 in this volume, for a discussion on the status of the members of organised armed groups captured by the US in Afghanistan.

9 Sivakumaran (n 5) 243–244.

10 See Rome Statute, Elements of Crimes, arts 8(2)(b)(iv) and 8(2)(b)(ii) respectively. See also attacking or bombarding undefended locations (art 8(2)(b)(v)); killing or wounding a combatant who has surrendered (art 8(2)(b)(vi)); improper use of emblems/uniforms (art 8(2)(b)(vii)); abolishing rights of nationals of hostile party (art 8(2)(b)(xiv)); compelling nationals to fight against own side (art 8(2)(b)(xv)); poison (art 8(2)(b)(xvii)); gases etc (art 8(2)(b)(xviii)); exploding bullets (art 8(2)(b)(xix)); indiscriminate or disproportionate weaponry (art 8(2)(b)(xx)); use of human shields (art 8(2)(b)(xxiii)); directing attacks against Red Cross (art 8(2)(b)(xxiv)); and starvation (art 8(2)(b)(xxv)).

responsible command, exercise such control over a part of its territory as to enable them to carry out sustained military operations.

The closest the treaty provisions get to a definition occurs in Article 1(2) of Additional Protocol II where we learn what an armed conflict is not: '[t]his Protocol shall not apply to situations of internal disturbances and tensions, such as riots, isolated and sporadic acts of violence and other acts of a similar nature, as not being armed conflicts'.

Unsurprisingly, the Rome Statute follows the terminology of the various treaty provisions, including the qualifications in Article 1(2) of Additional Protocol II, and provides no general definition of 'armed conflict'. The Elements of the Crimes for each of the war crimes offences in Article 8 of the Rome Statute require the Prosecution to prove that the relevant conduct took place in the context of an armed conflict – either an IAC or a NIAC depending upon the particular offence charged. Again, however, the Elements only impose the requirement and do not offer any definitional clarification.

The ICRC Commentaries on Common Article 2 deal more explicitly with the definition of armed conflict:

It remains to ascertain what is meant by 'armed conflict'. . . . Any difference arising between two States and leading to the intervention of armed forces is an armed conflict within the meaning of Article 2, even if one of the Parties denies the existence of a state of war. It makes no difference how long the conflict lasts, or how much slaughter takes place. The respect due to human personality is not measured by the number of victims. Nor, incidentally, does the application of the Convention necessarily involve the intervention of cumbrous machinery. It all depends on circumstances. If there is only a single wounded person as a result of the conflict, the Convention will have been applied as soon as he has been collected and tended, the provisions of Article 12 observed in his case, and his identity notified to the Power on which he depends. All that can be done by anyone: it is merely a case of taking the trouble to save a human life![11]

This section of the ICRC's Commentary constitutes the foundation upon which the requirements for the existence of an armed conflict have been articulated in the jurisprudence of the international criminal courts and tribunals. The seminal declaration comes from the ICTY Appeals Chamber decision in *Tadić* and draws heavily on the wording in the ICRC *Commentary*:

An armed conflict exists whenever there is a resort to armed force between States or protracted violence between governmental authorities and organized armed groups or between such groups within a State. International humanitarian law applies from the initiation of such armed conflicts and extends beyond the cessation of hostilities until a general conclusion of peace is reached; or, in the case of internal conflict, a peaceful settlement is achieved. Until that moment, international humanitarian law continues to apply in the whole territory of the warring States, or, in the case of internal conflict, the whole territory under the control of a party, whether or not actual combat takes place there.[12]

---

11 *GCI Commentary* 32.
12 *Tadić (Jurisdictional Appeal)* (n 7) ¶ 70.

This particular formulation is repeated *verbatim* in all subsequent ICTY and ICTR jurisprudence as well as in all relevant ICC case law.[13]

2.2 International armed conflict

It is now well established in international criminal jurisprudence that an IAC exists 'whenever there is resort to armed force between States'. This is a low threshold. As the ICC Pre-Trial Chamber described in *Bemba*, using the language of the ICRC *Commentary*, the threshold is met when any difference between two states leads to the intervention of armed forces and it 'makes no difference how long the conflict lasts, or how much slaughter takes place'.[14] The law applicable to IACs will then apply until a general conclusion of peace is reached. It should be noted that this must be a practical peace. The signing of peace agreements, even if they eventually result in the end of hostilities, will not prevent the laws of war applying if peace has not yet been reached on the ground.[15]

To demonstrate just how low the threshold for an IAC is, Christopher Greenwood cites the example of a US Air Force pilot shot down over Lebanon's Bekaa Valley in the early 1980s by a Syrian surface-to-air missile. The pilot safely ejected from the aircraft and parachuted to ground. Washington promptly announced that Geneva Convention III applied to the IAC between the US and Syria and that the pilot was, therefore, entitled to POW status and the legal protections attached to it.[16]

There is an alternative view that suggests a higher threshold is a more appropriate reflection of what states consider to be the law. For example, the ICJ in its judgment in the *Nicaragua* case alluded to the possibility that not all resort to armed force between states triggers the application of LOAC. The *Nicaragua* case dealt principally with the *jus ad bellum* although there are also important statements by the Court on the *jus in bello*. In examining the 'international

---

13 See *Prosecutor v Tadić* (Case no IT-94-1-T, ICTY Trial Chamber, 7 May 1997) ¶¶ 561–562; *Prosecutor v Kunarac, Kovac and Vucovic* (Case nos IT-96-23 and IT-96-23/1-A, ICTY Appeals Chamber, 12 June 2002) ¶ 56; *Prosecutor v Kordić and Čerkez* (Case no IT-95-14/2-A, ICTY Appeals Chamber, 17 December 2004) ¶ 336; *Prosecutor v Delalić, Mucić, Delić and Landžo (Čelebići Camp)* (Case no IT-96-21-T, ICTY Trial Chamber, 16 November 1998) ¶ 183; *Prosecutor v Krnojelac* (Case no IT-97-25-T, ICTY Trial Chamber II, 15 March 2002) ¶ 51; *Prosecutor v Naletilić and Martinović* (Case no IT-98-34, ICTY Trial Chamber, 31 March 2003) ¶ 225; *Prosecutor v Limaj, Bala and Musliu* (Case no IT-03-66-T, ICTY Trial Chamber, 30 November 2005) ¶ 84; *Prosecutor v Haradinaj, Balaj and Brahimaj (Trial Judgment)* (Case no IT-04-84-T, ICTY Trial Chamber, 3 April 2008) ¶ 37; *Prosecutor v Delić* (Case no IT-04-83-T, ICTY Trial Chamber I, 15 September 2008) ¶ 40; *Prosecutor v Milutinović, Šainović, Ojdanić, Pavković, Lazarević and Lukić* (Case no IT-05-87-T, ICTY Trial Chamber, 26 February 2009) vol I, ¶ 125; *Prosecutor v Boškoski and Tarčulovski* (Case no IT-04-82-T, ICTY Trial Chamber II, 10 July 2008) ¶ 175; *Prosecutor v Đorđević* (Case no IT-05-87/1, ICTY Trial Chamber II, 23 February 2011) ¶ 1522; *Prosecutor v Haradinaj, Balaj and Brahimaj (Retrial Judgment)* (Case no IT-04-84bis-T, ICTY Trial Chamber, 29 November 2012) ¶ 392; *Prosecutor v Aleksovski* (Case no IT-95-14/1-T, ICTY Trial Chamber, 25 June 1999) ¶¶ 43–44; *Prosecutor v Furundžija* (Case no IT-95-17/1-T, ICTY Trial Chamber, 10 December 1998) ¶ 59; *Prosecutor v Blaškić* (Case no IT-95-14-T, ICTY Trial Chamber, 3 March 2000) ¶¶ 63–64; *Prosecutor v Krstić* (Case no IT-98-33-T, ICTY Trial Chamber, 2 August 2001) ¶ 481; *Prosecutor v Stakić* (Case no IT-97-24-T, ICTY Trial Chamber, 31 July 2003) ¶ 568. This definition has also been applied outside criminal jurisprudence, see Sivakumaran (n 5) 233 and the sources cited therein.

14 *Prosecutor v Bemba (Decision on the Confirmation of Charges)* (Case no ICC-01/05-01/08, ICC Pre-Trial Chamber III, 15 June 2009) ¶ 222, citing *GCI Commentary* 32.

15 See *Tadić (Trial Judgment)* (n 13) ¶ 566.

16 Christopher Greenwood, 'International Humanitarian Law and United Nations Military Operations' (1998) 1 *YBIHL* 3, 7.

humanitarian law applicable to the dispute' the Court stated that '[c]learly, use of force in some circumstances *may* raise questions of such law'.[17] The implication here is that not all 'resort to force between States' will raise questions of LOAC. Katharina Ziolkowski argues that a 'use of force' by one state against another triggering the application of the *jus ad bellum* will usually cross the threshold of an IAC and so also trigger the application of the *jus in bello* 'with the possible exception of quick, discrete and "surgical" use of force in the meaning of Article 2(4) [of the] UN Charter without further retort by the victim'.[18]

The precise delimitation of the threshold for an IAC is complicated. Nils Melzer argues, for example, that 'while the domestic concentration of troops in a border area is not sufficient to trigger an international armed conflict, mutual hostilities nonetheless are not required'.[19] Instead, Melzer asserts that an IAC requires a 'minimal transgression which expresses the belligerent intent' of the acting state against another and any armed interference by one state with another's 'sphere of sovereignty' is sufficient.[20] While for Ziolkowski the quintessential 'quick, discrete and surgical' strike not triggering an IAC was the Israeli bombing of Osirak in 1981, presumably Melzer would characterise Israel's action as triggering an IAC since Israel clearly deployed arms against Iraq's 'sphere of sovereignty'.[21]

Perhaps the real answer as to how states view the threshold of an IAC has to do with the consequences that flow from another state's resort to lethal military force. Perhaps, when an airforce pilot parachutes from a stricken aircraft over enemy territory, when civilians are incidentally killed in large numbers as a result of a strike on a military objective or when civilians are wilfully targeted, states are much more likely to invoke LOAC and to demand its observance or to demand accountability for those who have allegedly violated it. In other situations of resort to lethal military force perhaps states are more willing not to assert the existence of an IAC. It may be a relatively easy thing for an international criminal court or tribunal to speak in absolute terms because, inevitably, by the time a case comes to trial before such a body, the alleged conduct has resulted in extensive injury, damage and loss of life.

If uncertainties persist in relation to the precise threshold for an IAC arising from kinetic force, those uncertainties are exacerbated in resort to virtual force. The Group of Experts responsible for drafting the *Tallinn Manual on the International Law Applicable to Cyber Warfare* were divided on the requisite threshold of violence to constitute an IAC from cyber attacks. For example, some of the experts would consider a cyber operation that resulted in a small fire in a military installation sufficient to constitute an IAC. Other experts disagreed and argued for a higher threshold of extent, duration or intensity of violence.[22]

---

17 *Military and Paramilitary Activities in and against Nicaragua (Nicaragua v US) (Merits)* [1986] ICJ Rep 14, ¶ 216.

18 Katharina Ziolkowski, 'Computer Network Operations and the Law of Armed Conflict' (2010) 49 *RDMDG* 47, 68.

19 Nils Melzer, *Targeted Killing in International Law* (OUP 2008) 250.

20 Ibid.

21 This hypothetical disagreement ignores the observation of Yoram Dinstein that Israel and Iraq were in 1981 (and still technically are today) in a state of war because Iraq did not sign an armistice agreement with Israel in 1949 – let alone negotiate a final peace treaty. In fact, Iraqi forces have re-engaged in armed hostilities against the state of Israel multiple times since 1949. So, for Dinstein, Osirak was a legitimate military objective and could be targeted in the ongoing IAC between Israel and Iraq. See Yoram Dinstein, *War, Aggression and Self-Defence* (4th edn, CUP 2005) 47–48 and 186.

22 See Commentary to Rule 22, ¶ 12. See further Rain Liivoja, Kobi Leins and Tim McCormack, 'Emerging technologies of warfare' ch 35 in this volume, s 2.2.3.

2.3 Non-international armed conflict

The threshold for a NIAC is more complex again. The jurisprudence, relying on the seminal statement in *Tadić*, identifies two requisite elements: (1) the involvement of 'organised armed groups' (OAG) and, (2) that the violence reach a certain threshold level of intensity.[23] The ICTY Trial Chamber held that both of these criteria should be used 'solely for the purpose, as a minimum, of distinguishing an armed conflict from banditry, unorganized and short-lived insurrections, or terrorist activities, which are not subject to international humanitarian law'.[24] The ICC Trial Chamber has applied this 'sole purpose' concept to the requirement of intensity.[25]

As outlined in the passage from *Tadić* extracted above, once a NIAC has commenced, LOAC continues to apply until a 'peaceful settlement' is reached.[26] In this regard, the distinction between hostilities and armed conflict is crucial;[27] a reduction in the intensity or scope of the violence will not necessarily amount to peaceful settlement. Indeed, in *Lubanga*, the ICC Trial Chamber found that the armed conflict continued in Ituri from the end of May 2003 until at least 13 August 2003 without referring to any incidents of hostilities between armed groups during that final stage of the conflict. Instead, to demonstrate that peaceful settlement had not been reached, the Chamber referred to attacks upon civilians, the UN Security Council's authorisation for a Multinational Force to deploy to the area to restore security and the subsequent provision of a Chapter VII mandate to the UN peacekeepers already on the ground.[28]

2.3.1 Organised armed groups

In *Lubanga*, the ICC Trial Chamber held that to be 'organised', armed groups must have 'a sufficient degree of organization, in order to enable them to carry out protracted armed violence'.[29] The Chamber noted that the requirement of organisation is a limited one which should be applied flexibly, and outlined a non-exhaustive list of potentially relevant factors including:[30]

- the group's internal hierarchy;
- the command structure and rules;
- the extent to which military equipment, including firearms, are available;

---

23 See eg *Lubanga* (n 7) ¶¶ 534–538; *Prosecutor v Lubanga (Decision on the Confirmation of Charges)* (Case no ICC-01/04-01/06, ICC Pre-Trial Chamber I, 29 January 2007) ¶¶ 232–234; *Tadić (Trial Judgment)* (n 13) ¶ 562; *Đorđević* (n 13) ¶¶ 1522 and 1526; *Limaj* (n 13) ¶¶ 84, 94–134; *Haradinaj (Trial Judgment)* (n 13) ¶¶ 60, 63–88; *Prosecutor v Mrkšić, Radić and Šljivančanin* (Case no IT-95-13/1-T, ICTY Trial Chamber, 27 September 2007) ¶ 407.

24 *Tadić (Trial Judgment)* (n 13) ¶ 562, citing GCII Commentary 33; GCIII Commentary 37. See also *Limaj* (n 13) ¶¶ 84 and 89; *Haradinaj (Trial Judgment)* (n 13) ¶ 38; *Đorđević* (n 13) ¶ 1522; *Boškoski* (n 13) ¶ 175.

25 *Lubanga* (n 7) ¶ 538; citing *Đorđević* (n 13) ¶ 1522.

26 See also *Tadić (Jurisdictional Appeal)* (n 7) ¶¶ 67 and 69; *Lubanga* (n 7) ¶ 548; *Prosecutor v Gotovina, Čermak and Markač* (Case no IT-06-90-T, ICTY Trial Chamber, 15 April 2011) ¶ 1694.

27 See also *Prosecutor v Halilovic* (Case no IT-01-48-T, ICTY Trial Chamber, 6 November 2005) fn 72.

28 *Lubanga* (n 7) ¶ 548.

29 *Lubanga* (n 7) ¶ 536; see also *Lubanga (Confirmation Decision)* (n 23) ¶ 233–234; *Prosecutor v Mbarushimana (Decision on the Confirmation of Charges)* (Case no ICC-01/04-01/10, ICC Pre-Trial Chamber I, 16 December 2011) 103; *Haradinaj (Trial Judgment)* (n 13) ¶ 60; *Haradinaj (Retrial Judgment)* (n 13) ¶ 197.

30 *Lubanga* (n 7) ¶ 537. See also *Limaj* (n 13) ¶ 89–90 and the sources cited therein; *Boškoski* (n 13) ¶¶ 199–203; *Haradinaj (Trial Judgment)* (n 13) ¶ 60; *Haradinaj (Retrial Judgment)* (n 13) ¶ 395; *Đorđević* (n 13) ¶ 1526 and the cases cited therein.

- the force or group's ability to plan military operations and put them into effect; and
- the extent, seriousness and intensity of any military involvement.

Consistently with ICTY and ICC jurisprudence,[31] as well as academic commentary,[32] the Chamber discarded any additional requirements that may have been imported from Article 1(1) of Additional Protocol II.[33] The article provides, in part, that the Protocol shall apply to all armed conflicts which:

> take place in the territory of a High Contracting Party between its armed forces and dissident armed forces or other organized armed groups which, under responsible command, exercise such control over a part of its territory as to enable them to carry out sustained and concerted military operations and to implement this Protocol.

The rejection by international criminal courts and tribunals of possible additional threshold requirements such as control over physical territory or responsible command is appropriate. Additional Protocol II is not generally regarded as declaratory of customary international law.[34] More specifically, the Protocol was not intended to provide further definition to the notion of an 'armed conflict not of an international character' as covered by Common Article 3 but was intended to provide stricter rules to be applied in more limited circumstances. The goal of reducing the likelihood of states ignoring or disputing the Protocol's application by providing specific, objective criteria was prioritised over the consequence that the rules of Additional Protocol II would only be applied in a more limited range of conflicts.[35] As such, there is no basis on which to import its requirements to the broader notion of NIAC. If any ambiguity about the impact of Additional Protocol II on the scope of customary international legal thresholds for the existence of a NIAC emerged post-1977, it has since evaporated. The drafting history of Article

31 *Lubanga (Confirmation Decision)* (n 23) ¶ 233; *Mbarushimana (Confirmation Decision)* (n 29) ¶ 103; *Tadić (Jurisdictional Appeal)* (n 7) ¶ 70; *Đorđević* (n 13) ¶¶ 1522 and 1526; *Limaj* (n 13) ¶¶ 85–87; *Haradinaj (Retrial Judgment)* (n 13) ¶¶ 393 and 395; *Haradinaj (Trial Judgment)* (n 13) ¶ 60; *Boškoski* (n 13) ¶ 197. Cf *Prosecutor v Katanga and Ngudjolo (Decision on the Confirmation of Charges)* (Case no ICC-01/04-01/07, ICC Pre-Trial Chamber II, 30 September 2008) ¶ 234, noting that a factual finding does not amount to a decision that it is a legal prerequisite.

32 Knut Dörmann, *Elements of War Crimes under the Rome Statute of the International Criminal Court: Sources and Commentary* (CUP 2002) 386–387 referring to Georges Abi-Saab, 'Non-international Armed Conflicts' in UNESCO/Henry Dunant Institute (eds), *International Dimensions of Humanitarian Law* (Martinus Nijhoff 1988) 237; Christopher Greenwood, 'Scope of Application of Humanitarian Law' in Dieter Fleck (ed), *The Handbook of Humanitarian Law in Armed Conflict* (OUP 1995) 48.

33 *Lubanga* (n 7) ¶ 536.

34 Antonio Cassese, 'The Geneva Protocols of 1977 and Customary International Law' (1984) 3 *UCLA Pacific Basic Law Journal* 55, 109–113; Christopher Greenwood, 'Customary Law Status of the 1977 Additional Protocols' in Astrid Delissen and Gerard Tanja (eds), *Humanitarian Law of Armed Conflict Challenges Ahead* (Martinus Nijhoff 1991) 93, 112–113; Eve la Haye, *War Crimes in Internal Armed Conflicts* (CUP 2008) 104–128; Theodor Meron, *Human Rights and Humanitarian Norms as Customary International Law* (OUP 1989) 72, n 199.

35 See APII art 1(1) which declares that the Protocol 'develops and supplements Article 3 common to the Geneva Conventions of 12 August 1949 without modifying its existing conditions of application'. See also *AP Commentary* ¶¶ 4446–4479 (particularly 4453); *Boškoski* (n 13) ¶ 197; Message from the President of the United States Transmitting the Protocol II Additional to the Geneva Conventions of August 12, 1949, and Relating to the Protection of Victims of Noninternational Armed Conflicts, Concluded at Geneva on June 10, 1977 (US Government Printing Office 1987) 7–8; Report of the Secretary General Pursuant to Paragraph 5 of Security Council Resolution 955 (1994), UN Doc S/1995/134 (13 February 1995) ¶ 12.

8(2)(f) of the Rome Statute demonstrates that states rejected the inclusion of the requirements of Additional Protocol II.[36]

Nevertheless, in *Bemba*, Pre-Trial Chamber II determined that 'responsible command' was a necessary component of organisation. However, the Chamber then defined this as entailing 'some degree of organization ... including the possibility to impose discipline and the ability to plan and carry out military operations'.[37] This accords with statements by the ICTY Trial Chambers, both that the 'leadership of the group must, as a minimum, have the ability to exercise some control over its members so that the basic obligations of Common Article 3 of the Geneva Conventions may be implemented'[38] and that the degree of organisation 'need not be the same as that required for establishing the responsibility of superiors for the acts of their subordinates within the organisation, as no determination of individual criminal responsibility is intended under this provision of the Statute'.[39] So expressed, such criteria are already implied by the requirement of organisation: when the adjective 'organised' is used to describe an 'armed group', the word itself denotes a notion of hierarchy. Therefore, while these criteria may be seen as a useful way to further define or describe the requirement of organisation, there is no utility, and indeed a danger, in labelling such a requirement 'responsible command' as if it were an additional threshold criterion.

In the *Lubanga* judgment, the five paragraphs devoted to determining that there were at least three OAG operating in Ituri during the relevant period[40] stand in stark contrast with the extensive analysis undertaken by the ICTY in relation to the identification of parties to various Balkan armed conflicts.[41] It is acknowledged that the level of analysis in the ICTY decisions went beyond what was *necessary* to establish organisation. It is also acknowledged that the threshold of organisation is a low one and the fact that an armed group is able to engage in hostilities over a prolonged period of time is of itself significant evidence of organisation. Nevertheless, it may have been appropriate for Trial Chamber I in *Lubanga* to engage in more than a cursory examination of the question: the Chamber in effect stated its conclusions rather than elucidated its reasoning. This approach is especially surprising as the relevant groups were deemed not to have participated in many of the hostilities referred to as relevant to the intensity analysis.[42]

2.3.2 Intensity

The intensity of the conflict relates to the requirement that the violence be more than sporadic or isolated. ICC Pre-Trial Chamber II has stated:

---

36 The precursor to art 8(2)(f) which appeared in a Bureau Proposal on 10 July 1998 included the requirements of APII in the second sentence and these requirements were rejected: see William Schabas, *The International Criminal Court: A Commentary on the Rome Statute* (OUP 2010) 205 and the sources cited therein.

37 *Bemba (Confirmation Decision)* (n 14) ¶ 234. See also *Katanga and Ngudjolo* (n 31) ¶ 234, noting that a factual finding does not amount to a decision that it is a legal prerequisite.

38 *Haradinaj (Retrial Judgment)* (n 13) ¶ 393; *Đorđević* (n 13) ¶ 1525; *Boškoski* (n 13) ¶ 196 citing *GCII Commentary* 34. However, *Haradinaj (Trial Judgment)* (n 13) ¶ 60 where no such requirement is outlined.

39 *Limaj* (n 13) ¶ 89; *Mrkšić* (n 23) ¶ 408.

40 See *Lubanga* (n 7) ¶¶ 543–547. See also *Mbarushimana (Confirmation Decision)* (n 29) ¶¶ 104–106, noting the lower standard of proof at confirmation stage (Rome Statute art 61(7)).

41 See eg *Limaj* (n 13) ¶¶ 94–134; *Haradinaj (Trial Judgment)* (n 13) ¶¶ 64–89; *Haradinaj (Retrial Judgment)* (n 13) ¶¶ 18–170 and 406–411; *Đorđević* (n 13) ¶¶ 1537–1578; *Boškoski* (n 13) ¶¶ 250–291.

42 *Lubanga* (n 7) ¶¶ 547–548.

The Statute requires any armed conflict not of an international character to reach a certain level of intensity which exceeds that of internal disturbances and tensions, such as riots, isolated and sporadic acts of violence or other acts of a similar nature.[43]

The ICC Trial Chamber found the following factors are relevant to making such an assessment:[44]

- the seriousness of attacks and potential increase in armed clashes;
- the spread of attacks over territory and over a period of time;
- the increase in the number of government forces;
- the mobilisation and the distribution of weapons among both parties to the conflict; and
- whether the conflict has attracted the attention of the UN Security Council, and, if so, whether any resolutions on the matter have been passed.

However, in the confirmation decision in *Mbarushimana*,[45] Pre-Trial Chamber I did not examine intensity in this way. It concluded that there were 'substantial grounds to believe that, from at least 20 January 2009 until at least 31 December 2009, an armed conflict not of an international character took place in the North and South Kivus'.[46] However, the only assessment of intensity was as follows:

> an armed conflict of a certain intensity took place in the Kivu provinces of the DRC between the FDLR and the FARDC-RDF (from 20 January 2009 to 25 February 2009) and between the FDLR and the FARDC, at times in conjunction with the United Nations Organization Mission in the Democratic Republic of the Congo ('MONUC') (from 2 March 2009 to 31 December 2009). In particular, the Chamber finds substantial grounds to believe that the relevant armed conflict in the eastern DRC began on 20 January 2009, when the Rwanda Defence Forces (RDF) entered the territory of the DRC for the purpose of participating in a joint operation with the FARDC, known as Umoja Wetu, aimed at forcefully dislodging the FDLR from its bases in the North Kivu and enabling willing FDLR troops to demobilise and reintegrate into civilian life in Rwanda. On 25 February 2009, RDF troops began departing from North Kivu and a follow up military operation, Kimia II, was launched by the FARDC, supported by the MONUC forces, across the North and South Kivus with the purpose of neutralising the FDLR by preventing it from reoccupying former positions, as well as by cutting its lines of economic sustenance. This operation started on 2 March 2009 and lasted until 31 December 2009.[47]

This analysis does not establish 'intensity' as required by LOAC. The Chamber focused on the existence and purpose of a mission, which contemplated the use of force. Although this may be relevant, it is not of itself sufficient to satisfy the requirement of intensity. Indeed, in *Limaj*, in response to an argument that the purpose of the Serbian army's presence in Kosovo was to ethnically cleanse and not to engage in hostilities, the ICTY Trial Chamber found that 'the purpose of the armed forces to engage in acts of violence or also achieve some further objective is …

---

43 *Bemba (Confirmation Decision)* (n 14) ¶ 225. See also arts 8(2)(d) and (f).
44 *Lubanga* (n 7) ¶ 538 citing *Mrkšić* (n 23) ¶ 407. See also *Limaj* (n 13) ¶ 90; *Haradinaj (Retrial Judgment)* (n 13) ¶ 394, citing *Đorđević* (n 13) ¶ 1523 and the cases cited therein.
45 *Mbarushimana (Confirmation Decision)* (n 29) ¶¶ 95–107.
46 Ibid ¶ 107.
47 Ibid ¶ 95 (citations omitted).

irrelevant' because the 'determination of the existence of an armed conflict is based solely on two criteria: the intensity of the conflict and organisation of the parties'.[48]

The proper approach to determine the existence of a NIAC is to assess the intensity *of the violence or hostilities* between the parties.[49] In *Bemba*, for example, it was not when the rebel leader Bozize planned the coup against the incumbent President Patasse but when Bozize launched an attack on the city of Bangui, which was followed by further hostilities, that the NIAC began.[50] Certainly, when there is a stated mission which contemplates the use of force against a particular group, the degree of violence or scale of the hostilities needed to meet the intensity requirement may be less than in other situations. However, the criterion remains the same – there must be an outbreak of hostilities of a certain intensity before a NIAC can be said to exist.

Unfortunately, the Rome Statute is not clearly drafted in this regard. Article 8(2)(f) refers to 'protracted armed conflict between governmental authorities and organized armed groups or between such groups'. Although this is useful insofar as it identifies the requirement of 'organised armed groups', the use of the adjective 'protracted' does nothing to clarify the definition of 'armed conflict'. In this sense, it can be contrasted with the phrase 'protracted violence' used in *Tadić*.[51] Nevertheless, the Court is to apply, subject to the words of the Statute, the 'established principles of the international law of armed conflict'[52] which include the jurisprudential definition of NIAC.[53]

2.3.3 Is there a distinction between Articles 8(2)(c) and 8(2)(e) of the Rome Statute?

A question remains as to whether Article 8(2)(c) and (e) of the Rome Statute have a different scope of application. The second sentence in Article 8(2)(f), stating that the offences in Article 8(2)(e) apply 'to armed conflicts that take place in the territory of a State when there is protracted armed conflict between governmental authorities and organized armed groups or between such groups', does not appear in Article 8(2)(d). The only phrase in the sentence which may modify or add some further requirement to the criteria for a NIAC is 'protracted armed conflict' which implies a minimum temporal period. In *Lubanga*, the ICC Trial Chamber did not discuss this phrase, only assessing the requirements of OAG and intensity.[54] In *Bemba*, the ICC Pre-Trial Chamber refrained from determining whether 'protracted' required any further threshold to be met, finding only that, if so, five months was sufficient.[55] The Pre-Trial Chambers have stated that protracted 'focuses on the need for the armed groups in question to have the ability to plan and carry out military operations for a prolonged period of time'.[56] This in itself, introduces no new element to the Chambers' treatment of the requirement that the armed groups be organised. The best interpretation of 'protracted armed conflict' is that it is a reference

---

48 *Limaj* (n 13) ¶ 170.
49 *Tadić (Jurisdictional Appeal)* (n 7) ¶ 70; *Limaj* (n 13) ¶ 93. See eg the assessments in *Lubanga* (n 7) ¶¶ 547–548; *Đorđević* (n 13) ¶¶ 1532–1536 and *Haradinaj (Retrial Judgment)* (n 13) ¶¶ 402–405 and 410 and in particular *Haradinaj (Trial Judgment)* (n 13) ¶¶ 40–49 where the Trial Chamber conducts a review of the application of the intensity requirement in previous decisions.
50 *Bemba (Confirmation Decision)* (n 14) ¶ 243.
51 *Tadić (Jurisdictional Appeal)* (n 7) ¶ 70; *Tadić (Trial Judgment)* (n 12) ¶¶ 561–562.
52 Rome Statute art 21(1)(b).
53 *Bemba (Confirmation Decision)* (n 14) ¶ 234.
54 See *Lubanga* (n 7) ¶ 538.
55 *Bemba (Confirmation Decision)* (n 14) ¶¶ 235 and 255.
56 *Lubanga (Confirmation Decision)* (n 23) ¶ 234. See also *Mbarushimana (Confirmation Decision)* (n 29) ¶ 103.

to the *Tadić* phrase 'protracted violence', and adds nothing beyond the requirement of intensity imported by that phrase.[57]

The structure of Article 8 does not suggest that there should be a distinction between the meaning of 'conflict not of an international character' in Article 8(2)(c) and (e). Article 8(2)(c) criminalises 'serious violations of article 3 common to the four Geneva Conventions' and applies only to those taking no active part in hostilities.[58] Article 8(2)(e) criminalises 'other serious violations of the laws and customs applicable in armed conflicts not of an international character'. These 'other serious violations' derive largely from the 1899 and 1907 Hague Regulations and from Additional Protocol II and victims include both fighters as well as civilians.[59] The ICTY referred to the same definition of NIAC whether it was considering violations of Common Article 3 or of the laws and customs of war outside the scope of that provision.[60] Although some of the acts prohibited by Article 8(2)(e) derive from Additional Protocol II,[61] many do not, and, as mentioned above, the drafting history of that article makes clear that the provision was not intended to reflect the Protocol's narrow scope of application.[62]

Given that the content of any additional requirement imposed by Article 8(2)(f) is difficult to discern and that there is no theoretical or historical basis for a distinction between Articles 8(2)(c) and (e), the same definition of NIAC should be applied to both provisions, despite the principle that the words of a treaty should be given meaning.[63] The approach of the ICC Chambers has been to apply the same requirements for NIACs in respect of both Articles 8(2)(c) and (e) and this approach is supported by a majority of academic commentators.[64]

3 Characterising conflicts

The key determining principle for the legal character of an armed conflict is the nature of the parties to that conflict: conflicts between two or more states are international and all other conflicts are properly characterised as non-international. This is the approach of the Geneva

---

57 This was the approach adopted in *Boškoski* (n 13) ¶ 197; *Prosecutor v Milosević (Decision on Motion for Judgment of Acquittal)* (Case no IT-02-54-T, ICTY Trial Chamber, 16 June 2004) ¶ 20. See also Michael Cottier, William J Fenrick, Patricia Viseur Sellers and Andreas Zimmerman, 'Article 8 War Crimes' in Otto Triffterer (ed), *Commentary on the Rome Statute of the International Criminal Court* (Beck 1999) 285.

58 *Bemba (Confirmation Decision)* (n 14) ¶ 237.

59 Schabas (n 36) 197, 205.

60 See eg *Prosecutor v Orić* (Case no IT-03-68-T, ICTY Trial Chamber II, 30 June 2006) ¶¶ 254, 259, 262; *Prosecutor v Strugar (Trial Judgment)* (Case no IT-01-42-T, ICTY Trial Chamber II, 31 January 2005) ¶¶ 215, 216, 220, 224, 228–229; *Krnojelac* (n 13) ¶¶ 51, 61, 353; *Prosecutor v Galić (Trial Judgment)* (Case no IT-98-29-T, ICTY Trial Chamber I, 5 December 2003) ¶¶ 9, 138.

61 See eg the discussion in *Lubanga* (n 7) ¶ 542.

62 Above (n 36).

63 *Corfu Channel (UK v Albania)* [1949] ICJ Rep 4, 24; *Anglo-Iranian Oil Co (Jurisdiction) (UK v Iran)* [1952] ICJ Rep 93, 105.

64 Schabas (n 36) 205 citing: Theodor Meron, 'The Humanization of Humanitarian Law' (2009) 94 *AJIL* 239, 260; Anthony Cullen, 'The Definition of Non-International Armed Conflict in the Rome Statute of the International Criminal Court: An Analysis of the Threshold of Application Contained in Article 8(2)(f) (2007) 12(3) *JCSL* 419; Michael Bothe 'War Crimes' in Antonio Cassese, Paolo Gaeta and John R W D Jones (eds), *The Rome Statute of the International Criminal Court: A Commentary* (OUP 2002) 379, 423; Claus Kress, 'War Crimes Committed in Non-International Armed Conflict and the Emerging System of International Criminal Justice' (2001) 30 *Israel YBHR* 103, 118; Sandesh Sivakumaran, 'Identifying an Armed Conflict not of an International Character' in Carsten Stahn and Goran Sluiter (eds), *Emerging Practice* (Brill 2009) 363, 373 and 377.

Conventions: Common Article 2 provides that the Conventions apply to any 'conflict which may arise between two or more of the High Contracting Parties', that is, states. Common Article 3 applies to 'armed conflict not of an international character', meaning that it applies to all armed conflicts not covered by Article 2, that is all conflicts which do not involve two (or more) states opposed to each other.[65] This key principle was correctly identified in the *Bemba (Confirmation Decision)* where Pre-Trial Chamber II held that the only conflicts which are international are those in which states oppose each other 'through their respective armed forces or other actors acting on behalf of the State'.[66]

When assessing the character of a conflict, there is a tendency to rely upon the concept of the 'internationalisation' of a pre-existing NIAC. This concept rose to prominence in the jurisprudence of the ICTY[67] and was described in the *Lubanga (Confirmation Decision)* as follows:

> The Chamber considers an armed conflict to be international in character if it takes place between two or more States.... In addition, an internal armed conflict that breaks out on the territory of a State may become international – or, depending on the circumstances, be international in character alongside an internal armed conflict – if (i) another State intervenes in

---

65 The only exception to this is API art 1(4) which is not a customary rule. It treats as international, conflicts which involve non-state forces fighting against 'colonial domination and alien occupation and against racist regimes in the exercise of their right of self determination'.

66 *Bemba (Confirmation Decision)* (n 14) ¶ 223. See also *Lubanga* (n 7) ¶¶ 540–541 and 563–565 (save for on the issue of occupation); *Mbarushimana (Confirmation Decision)* (n 29) ¶¶ 100–102; *Prosecutor v Aleksovski (Joint Opinion of the Majority)* (Case no IT-95-14/1-T, ICTY Trial Chamber, 25 June 1999) ¶ 8; *Tadić (Jurisdictional Appeal)* (n 7) ¶¶ 72–77; *Hamdan v Rumsfeld et al*, 548 US 557, 630 (US Supreme Court 2006); Philip Alston, Report of the Special Rapporteur on Extrajudicial, Summary or Arbitrary Executions, Mission to Afghanistan, UN Doc A/HRC/11/2/Add.4 (6 May 2009) ¶ 1; Jelena Pejic, 'Status of Armed Conflicts' in Elizabeth Wilmshurst (ed), *Perspectives on the ICRC Study on Customary International Humanitarian Law* (CUP 2007) 92–93; Lindsay Moir, *The Law of Internal Armed Conflict* (CUP 2002) 50–51; Liesbeth Zegveld, *Accountability of Armed Opposition Groups in International Law* (CUP 2002) 24, 136; Roy Schondorf, 'The Targeted Killings Judgement: A Preliminary Assessment' (2007) 5 *JICJ* 301, 304; David Kretzmer, 'Targeted Killing of Suspected Terrorists: Extra-Judicial Executions or Legitimate Means of Defence?' (2005) 16(2) *EJIL* 171, 195; Andrew Carswell, 'Classifying the Conflict: A Soldier's Dilemma' (2009) 91 *IRRC* 143, 154; Geneva Academy of International Humanitarian Law and Human Rights, Rule of Law in Armed Conflicts Project, 'Qualification of Armed Conflicts', www.geneva-academy.ch/RULAC/qualification_of_armed_conflict.php; Gabor Rona, 'Interesting Times for International Humanitarian Law: Challenges from the "War on Terror"' (2003) 27(2) *Fletcher Forum on World Affairs* 44, 58; ICRC, 'International Humanitarian Law and the Challenges of Contemporary Armed Conflicts' Report of the 31st International Conference of the Red Cross and Red Crescent (2011), www.icrc.org/eng/assets/files/red-cross-crescent-movement/31st-international-conference/31-int-conference-ihl-challenges-report-11-5-1-2-en.pdf, 8–10; Helen Duffy, *The 'War on Terror' and the Framework of International Law* (CUP 2005) 253; ICRC, 'How is the Term "Armed Conflict" Defined in International Humanitarian Law?' Opinion Paper (2008), www.icrc.org/eng/assets/files/other/opinion-paper-armed-conflict.pdf, 3; Dietrich Schindler, 'The Different Types of Armed Conflicts According to the Geneva Conventions and Protocols' (1979) 163 *RCADI* 147; Marco Sassòli, 'Transnational Armed Groups and International Humanitarian Law' HPCR Occasional Paper No 6 (Program on Humanitarian Policy and Conflict Research, Harvard University, Winter 2006) 8–9.

67 Although this concept was already identified in the scholarship, see Hans-Peter Gasser, 'Internationalized Non-International Armed Conflicts: Case Studies of Afghanistan, Kampuchea and Lebanon' (1983) 33 *American University LR* 145.

that conflict through its troops (direct intervention), or if (ii) some of the participants in the internal armed conflict act on behalf of that other State (indirect intervention).[68]

So expressed, it suggests a temporal element or a change to the status quo which is not necessarily accurate. For example, the conflict between the state of Bosnia and Herzegovina and the non-state armed group of the VRS (*Vojska Republike Srpske* – Serb forces within Bosnia and Herzegovina) was always international because the VRS was either under the control of the rump-state of Yugoslavia or under Serbian control.[69]

3.1 Direct intervention by a foreign state's forces

The concept of internationalisation of an armed conflict has been misinterpreted and misapplied. For example, in *Katanga and Ngudjolo*, Pre-Trial Chamber I found that the intervention of Ugandan Government forces in the conflict between OAG in the territory of the DRC rendered that conflict international.[70] The Trial Chamber seemed to rely upon the passage just extracted. However, the *Tadić* judges stated that an internal armed conflict *may* become international when either direct or indirect intervention by states' armed forces occurs. The proper approach is to apply the key principle to this concept – direct and indirect intervention *will* internationalise a conflict where it results in two states opposing each other. As Uganda did not oppose any other state, its trans-border involvement in the conflicts in Ituri did not create an IAC, as found in *Lubanga*.[71]

The ICTY never faced this precise scenario as all instances of direct trans-border intervention by state armed forces involved two (or more) states opposed to each other.[72] However, in the context of discussing the test for indirect intervention, the ICTY Appeals Chamber made the following relevant statement:

> This question is not a generalised one as to whether an armed conflict has become 'internationalised' in any broad sense of the term; nor is it to be determined by reference to criteria of unmanageable plasticity. The question is a precise one as to whether there is an 'armed conflict ... between two or more of the High Contracting Parties ...' to the Fourth Geneva Convention. Barring a 'declared war' between them, it is only if there is such a conflict that the Convention applies. But whether or not there is such a conflict turns *ex hypothesi*, on whether one state is using force against the other.[73]

---

68 *Lubanga (Confirmation Decision)* (n 23) ¶ 209, referring to *Armed Activities on the Territory of the Congo (Democratic Republic of the Congo v Uganda)* [2005] ICJ Rep 168. However, the passage derives from the *Tadić (Appeal Judgment)* (n 3) ¶ 84 and was widely applied by that tribunal. See also *Katanga and Ngudjolo* (n 31) ¶ 238; *Bemba (Confirmation Decision)* (n 14) ¶ 220.

69 *Prosecutor v Brđanin* (Case no IT-99-36-T, ICTY Trial Chamber II, 1 September 2004) 154.

70 *Katanga and Ngudjolo* (n 31) ¶ 240.

71 *Lubanga* (n 7) ¶ 567. Cf *Katanga and Ngudjolo* (n 31) ¶ 240.

72 See eg *Prosecutor v Kordić and Čerkez* (Case no IT-95-14/2-T, ICTY Trial Chamber, 26 February 2001) ¶¶ 109, 145, where Croatian Government forces both directly and indirectly intervened in a conflict between the Bosnian Croats (HVO) and the forces of the state of Bosnia and Herzegovina; *Brđanin* (n 69) ¶ 154 where the Former Republic of Yugoslavia had effective control of the VRS who was fighting against the forces of the state of Bosnia and Herzegovina.

73 *Tadić (Jurisdictional Appeal)* (n 7) ¶ 26.

That extra-territorial military activity will only create an IAC if it pits two states against each other is supported in the literature[74] and evidenced by state practice.[75] As outlined in the Prosecution Closing Brief in *Lubanga*:[76] in 1971, states rejected a proposal by the ICRC to apply the whole of LOAC to a NIAC where one or both of the parties is assisted by the armed forces of a third state;[77] the drafters of the ICTR Statute determined in Articles 1 and 7 that the law of NIAC was to apply to the acts of Rwandan nationals even outside the physical territory of Rwanda; and states whose troops are currently, or were recently, deployed in Afghanistan to assist the Afghan Government in its armed conflict against the Taliban, such as the US, UK, Australia and Germany consider themselves to be (or to have been) engaged in a NIAC.[78]

3.2 Indirect intervention by a foreign state

As foreshadowed, a state does not have to be directly engaged in the conflict through its official armed forces in order to be a party to an armed conflict. OAG that are acting under the 'overall control' of a state will be treated as an organ of the state for the purposes of the legal characterisation of an armed conflict. The test has been expressed as follows: 'it must be proved that the State wields overall control over the group, not only by equipping and financing the group, but also by coordinating or helping in the general planning of its military activity'.[79]

The threshold of 'overall control' is high. In *Lubanga*, the Trial Chamber found that the evidence of influence by states over armed groups did not establish 'overall control'. In that particular case, evidence of Kinshasa sending trainers and weapons to the APC,[80] and of Rwanda

---

74 See Nico Schrijver and Larissa van den Herik (eds), *Leiden Policy Recommendations on Counter-terrorism and International Law* (1 April 2010) ¶ 63; Yuval Shany, 'Extra-Territorial Self-Help: Between Pragmatism and Legal Doctrine' in Guido Ravasi and Gian Luca Beruto (eds), *International Humanitarian Law and Other Legal Regimes: Interplay in Situations of Violence* (Nagard 2005) 83; Marco Sassòli, 'The Status of Persons Held in Guantanamo Bay under International Humanitarian Law' (2004) 2 *JICJ* 96, 99.

75 Cf *Public Committee against Torture in Israel et al v the Government of Israel et al* (Case no HCJ 769/02, Supreme Court of Israel, 13 December 2006) ¶ 18, stating that the conflict between Israel and terrorist organisations in places which are not subject to Israeli belligerent occupation is an international armed conflict because *inter alia* an armed conflict of an international character is 'one that crosses the borders of the state'.

76 ICC Office of the Prosecutor, Prosecution's Closing Brief in *Prosecutor v Lubanga* (Doc no ICC-01/04-01/06, ICC Trial Chamber I, 1 June 2011) ¶ 34.

77 Stewart (n 7) 313 citing ICRC, *Report on the Work of the Conference of Government Experts* (Geneva 1971) ¶ 284.

78 The US Supreme Court arguably made this assessment in *Hamdan v Rumsfeld* (n 66) 629. See also David Turns, '*Jus ad Pacem in Bello*? Afghanistan, Stability Operations and the International Laws Relating to Armed Conflict' in Michael Schmitt (ed), *The War in Afghanistan: A Legal Analysis* (US Naval War College 2009) 388, 404: 'from the official point of view of the United Kingdom, the ongoing hostilities in Afghanistan and Iraq are in effect treated as internal conflicts in which UK forces are participating on the side of the governments of those States'; Christian Schaller, 'Military Operations in Afghanistan and International Humanitarian Law' SWP Comments No 7 (German Institute for International and Security Affairs 2010), www.swp-berlin.org/fileadmin/contents/products/comments/2010C07_slr_ks.pdf. Additionally, in Somalia, the US and UN forces did not regard themselves as parties to an IAC rather, they applied the law of NIAC: Greenwood, 'United Nations Military Operations' (n 16) 26.

79 *Tadić (Appeal Judgment)* (n 3) ¶ 131. See also ibid 137; *Lubanga* (n 7) ¶ 541; *Lubanga (Confirmation Decision)* (n 23) ¶ 211; *Bemba (Confirmation Decision)* (n 14) ¶ 223; *Prosecutor v Aleksovski* (Case no IT-95-14/1-A, ICTY Appeals Chamber, 24 March 2000) ¶¶ 131–134; *Prosecutor v Delalić, Mucić, Delić and Landžo* (Case no IT-96-21-A, ICTY Appeals Chamber, 20 February 2001) ¶ 26; *Kordić (Appeal Judgment)* (n 13) ¶¶ 306–307.

80 *Lubanga* (n 7) ¶ 553.

supporting the UPC/FPLC by supplying uniforms and weapons, providing training and, on the word of one witness, 'issuing orders and making Rwanda's support conditional with compliance' still did not reach the requisite threshold of 'overall control'.[81] In *Brđanin*, where the ICTY Trial Chamber found that the VJ (*Vojska Jugoslavije* – the army of the Federal Republic of Yugoslavia) had overall control of the VRS, the evidence was overwhelming:

- the VRS was made up of ex-VJ soldiers who remained when the VJ withdrew from the territory;
- their salaries were still paid by Belgrade;
- the aim and objectives of the groups were identical;
- the VJ provided equipment, fuel, ammunition and reserves if they were requested; and
- the UN Security Council acknowledged the 'continued involvement and control of Belgrade over the Bosnian Serb Army and demanded the cessation of all forms of outside interference'.[82]

In creating the test of 'overall control' in the *Tadić* jurisdictional appeal, the ICTY Appeals Chamber sought to 'overrule' the test of 'effective control' formulated by the ICJ in *Nicaragua*.[83] Although there has been debate about the proper interpretation of the 'effective control' test, the Court seemed to require that for the acts of paramilitary groups to be attributable to a state, the paramilitaries must 'act in "complete dependence" on the State, of which they are ultimately merely an instrument' and must be 'so closely attached [to the state] as to appear to be nothing more than its agent'.[84] In the *Bosnian Genocide Case*,[85] the ICJ found that the test of 'effective control' was not met in respect of FRY control of the VJ, despite the *Tadić* findings of FRY 'overall control' of the VJ described above.[86] In *Nicaragua* the Court held that US:

> participation, even if preponderant or decisive, in the financing, organizing, training, supplying and equipping of the contras, the selection of its military or paramilitary targets, and the planning of the whole of its operation, is still insufficient in itself, on the basis of the evidence in the possession of the Court, for the purpose of attributing to the United States the acts committed by the contras in the course of their military or paramilitary operations in Nicaragua.[87]

This 'effective control' test clearly sets a higher threshold than the 'overall control' test articulated by the ICTY Appeals Chamber in *Tadić* and consistently applied by both the ICTY and the ICC since. An obvious question arises as to how to reconcile the disparate tests for the requisite level of control (and which of them takes precedence?) It is clear that the ICJ and the ICTY/ICTR/ICC are considering different issues: the ICJ is deciding on issues of state respons-

81 *Lubanga* (n 7) ¶¶ 554–555.
82 *Brđanin* (n 69) ¶¶ 145–153.
83 *Tadić (Appeal Judgment)* (n 3) ¶¶ 115–145.
84 *Nicaragua* (n 17) ¶¶ 106 and 109; *Application of the Convention on the Prevention and Punishment of the Crime of Genocide (Bosnia and Herzegovina v Serbia and Montenegro)* [2007] ICJ Rep 14 ¶ 392; *Prosecutor v Tadić (Separate and Dissenting Opinion of Judge McDonald)* (Case no IT-94-1-T, ICTY Trial Chamber, 7 May 1997) 295. Cf *Tadić (Appeal Judgment)* (n 3) ¶¶ 111–114.
85 *Bosnian Genocide* (n 84) ¶ 394.
86 Ibid 402.
87 *Nicaragua* (n 17) ¶ 115.

ibility – whether or not the respondent state in contentious legal proceedings can be held to be in violation of certain international legal obligations; and the international criminal courts and tribunals are deciding individual criminal responsibility. In 2007, in *Bosnian Genocide*, the ICJ explained that different tests are applied as a result of different judicial purposes, stating:

> the degree and nature of a State's involvement in an armed conflict on another State's territory which is required for the conflict to be characterized as international, can very well, and without logical inconsistency, differ from the degree and nature of involvement required to give rise to that State's responsibility for a specific act committed in the course of the conflict.[88]

The ICJ's 'effective control' test requires proof of an extraordinary level of control, to the point that some commentators query whether it is ever likely to be met.[89] To require such a level of control to determine that an armed conflict is international may unduly restrict the application of the law of IAC.[90] However, the ICTY Appeals Chamber has disagreed with the ICJ's 'different tests for different purposes' approach and found that there is no distinction between the questions of attribution for state responsibility and internationalisation for conflict characterisation.[91] Whichever rationale is applied for its continued use, the 'overall control' test is now the preferred basis for characterisation of an armed conflict in which one state is involved indirectly through the proxy of a non-state organised armed group. There was an opportunity for states to reject the 'overall control' test and adopt a different formulation in the drafting of the Rome Statute, but that opportunity was not seized.[92]

3.3 Concurrent conflicts

If the only conflicts which are international are those in which two states oppose each other through their official or de facto armed forces, the question arises as to how to characterise a conflict which involves multiple state and non-state parties? One possibility involves multiple separate armed conflicts occurring in the same region at the same time, each being characterised by reference to the parties to it. That one state may be subject to different regimes depending

---

88 *Bosnian Genocide* (n 84) ¶ 404. See also *Aleksovski (Appeal Judgment)* (n 79) ¶ 146; Theodor Meron, 'Classification of Armed Conflict in the Former Yugoslavia: Nicaragua's Fallout' (1998) 92 *AJIL* 236, 237; David B Tyner, 'Internationalization of War Crimes Prosecutions: Correcting the International Criminal Tribunal for the Former Yugoslavia's Folly in Tadic' (2006) 18 *Florida Journal of International Law* 843, 872–876

89 See Tyner (n 88) 845 and the sources cited therein.

90 See *Aleksovksi (Appeal Judgment)* (n 79) ¶ 146; *Delalić (Appeal Judgment)* (n 79) ¶ 23–24; Meron (n 88) 241–242; Stefan Talmon, 'The Responsibility of Outside Powers for Acts of Secessionist Entities' (2009) 58(3) *ICLQ* 493, 513–517 (advocating for the use of the overall control test); Tyner (n 88) 880–885 advocating for a lower standard than effective control. However, he does not link this to any threshold for IAC, seemingly arguing that as long as not all international involvement is sufficient to internationalise a conflict then the test will be appropriate.

91 *Tadić (Appeal Judgment)* (n 3) ¶¶ 103–105. See also Eve La Haye, *War Crimes in Internal Armed Conflict* (CUP 2008) 17; Gerhard Werle, *Principles of International Criminal Law* (TMC Asser Press 2009) 371.

92 See Vienna Convention on the Law of Treaties (23 May 1969) 1155 UNTS 331, arts 33(3)(c) and 33(4).

on the party it is fighting is contemplated in Common Article 2 to the Geneva Conventions.[93] The concept of concurrent conflicts was first judicially recognised in *Nicaragua* where the ICJ held that:

> The conflict between the *contras'* forces and those of the Government of Nicaragua is an armed conflict which is 'not of an international character.' The acts of the *contras* towards the Nicaraguan Government are therefore governed by the law applicable to conflicts of that character; whereas the actions of the United States in and against Nicaragua fall under the legal rules relating to international conflicts.[94]

In *Lubanga*, the Trial Chamber found that Ugandan direct intervention and military occupation of part of the physical territory of the Ituri District of the DRC did not alter the fact that the UPC was a party to a concurrent NIAC.[95] The Chamber stated that:

> The Appeals Chamber of the ICTY has recognized that, depending on the particular actors involved, conflicts taking place on a single territory at the same time may be of a different nature. The Chamber endorses this view and accepts that international and non-international conflicts may coexist.[96]

In *Đorđević*, the ICTY trial Chamber found that a NIAC existed in Kosovo between Serbian forces and the KLA, at the same time that an IAC existed between NATO and the FRY.[97] Similarly, it is assumed that when NATO forces commenced their aerial bombing campaign in Libya, there was an IAC between the various NATO member states involved in the bombing and Libya, concurrent with the separate NIAC occurring between Libyan Government forces and Libyan rebel groups.

Any armed conflict fought by an organised armed group will be non-international unless the group is under the 'overall control' of a state and fighting against the forces of another state. When those conditions are met, Article 4A(2) of Geneva Convention III provides that members of groups 'belonging to a Party to the conflict' will be entitled to POW status if they fulfil certain criteria such as wearing a distinctive sign and carrying arms openly.

The very fact that the ICTY Appeals Chamber treated the legal character of the conflict as a matter for the Trial Chambers, constitutes an acceptance of the importance of the factual realities in any given situation, in favour of a generic approach which may not adequately

---

93 Which reads in part:

> Although one of the Powers in conflict may not be a party to the present Convention, the Powers who are parties thereto shall remain bound by it in their mutual relations. They shall furthermore be bound by the Convention in relation to the said Power, if the latter accepts and applies the provisions thereof.

94 *Nicaragua* (n 17) ¶ 219.
95 *Lubanga* (n 7) ¶¶ 563–656.
96 *Lubanga* (n 7) ¶ 540 (citations omitted), referring to *Tadić (Jurisdictional Appeal)* (n 7) 72–77 and Otto Kimminich, *Shutz der Menschen in bewaffneten Konflikten: Zur Fortwentwicklung des humanitären Völkerrechts* (Kaiser 1979) 126 et seq; Gerhard Werle, *Principles of International Criminal Law* (2nd edn, Asser 2009) 372 and marginal note 997. See also *Prosecutor v Fofana (Decision on Preliminary Motion on Lack of Jurisdiction Materiae: Nature of the Armed Conflict)* (Case no SCSL-2004-14-AR72(e), SCSL Appeals Chamber, 25 May 2004) ¶ 27; Yoram Dinstein, *War, Aggression and Self-Defence* (5th edn, CUP 2012) 6; Schindler (n 66) 150.
97 *Đorđević* (n 13) ¶¶ 1579, 1580.

reflect nuances at any given moment.[98] While some have argued, for example, that the whole of the armed conflict in the Balkans should have been characterised as international because the war was a result of the breakdown of one state and the emergence of several others,[99] such an approach fails to take into account two important considerations. First, in many conflicts, an overarching characterisation will simply not be possible. In Ituri, for example, multiple non-state armed groups were fighting for control of the region, with DRC, Uganda and Rwanda all having various interests and influences in the conflict. Such a complex factual situation is not susceptible to characterisation by any intuitive process. Second, OAGs often lack the capacity, training and history of state armed forces and are perhaps less likely to be able to understand and implement the laws of IAC. Requiring compliance with only the simpler laws of NIAC may increase the likelihood of compliance.[100] Even if this is inaccurate,[101] compliance with the law must be achievable for it to be relevant.

The question then arises as to how a state fighting both an IAC and NIAC simultaneously is to apply the law. Once an armed conflict breaks out: 'international humanitarian law continues to apply in the whole territory of the warring States or, in the case of internal conflicts, the whole territory under the control of a party, whether or not actual combat takes place there'.[102] However, the rejection of the idea that a war between two states will automatically internationalise all armed conflicts occurring within the physical territory in which the hostilities occur, means that the law of NIAC must govern relations between the state and the non-state armed group.[103] This does not mean that the state will be absolved of all obligations which arise purely from the law of IAC when it engages with the OAG. For example, it will still be bound by Additional Protocol I during these engagements and therefore activity which would be in breach of this Protocol – such as disproportionate attack and attacks on civilian objects – will remain unlawful and punishable, even if not prohibited in NIAC. However, it would be hoped that the state would apply the higher standards of the law of IAC as a matter of policy. The absurdity of civilians gaining greater protection from a state's military activities against an OAG simply because there is a simultaneous IAC occurring reinforces the need to homogenise certain areas of LOAC.

---

98 *Prosecutor v Tadić (Separate Opinion of Judge Li)* (Case no IT-94-1, ICTY Appeals Chamber, 2 October 1995) ¶¶ 17–19; *Final Report of the Commission of Experts* (Established by Security Council Resolution 780 (1992)) UN Doc S/1994/674 (24 May 1994) ¶ 44; Government of the United States of America, *Amicus Curiae* Brief presented in *Prosecutor v Tadić* (Case no IT-94-1-T, 25 July 1995) 25–35; James C O'Brien, 'The International Tribunal for Violations of International Humanitarian Law in the Former Yugoslavia' (1993) 87 *AJIL* 639, 647–648; Theodor Meron, 'War Crimes in Yugoslavia and the Development of International Law' (1994) 88 *AJIL* 78, 81–82; George H Aldrich, 'Jurisdiction of the International Criminal Tribunal for the Former Yugoslavia' (1996) 90 *AJIL* 64, 66–67.

99 See eg *Prosecutor v Aleksovski (Dissenting Opinion of Judge Rodrigues)* (Case no IT-95-14/1-T, ICTY Trial Chamber, 25 June 1999) ¶ 22.

100 See Sivakumaran (n 5) 255–258.

101 See eg Bassiouni (n 4) in particular 765–769, 785–789, where he discusses various factors influencing compliance with LOAC.

102 *Tadić (Jurisdictional Appeal)* (n 7) ¶ 70. See also *Delalić (Trial Judgment)* (n 13) ¶¶ 185, 209; *Kordić (Trial Judgment)* (n 72) ¶ 27; *Kunarac (Appeal Judgment)* (n 13) ¶ 57; *Naletilić* (n 13) ¶ 194; *Limaj* (n 13) ¶ 84. Cf *Stakić* (n 13) ¶¶ 571–572 which focus on whether there was a conflict in the region in question.

103 See eg *Lubanga* (n 7) ¶ 551: 'In situations where conflicts of a different nature take place on a single territory, it is necessary to consider whether the criminal acts under consideration were committed as part of an international or a non-international conflict.'

3.4 Military occupation

The second paragraph of Common Article 2 to the Geneva Conventions clarifies that, in addition to armed conflicts between sovereign nation states, the Conventions also apply 'to all cases of partial or total occupation of the territory of a High Contracting Party, even if the said occupation meets with no armed resistance'. The inclusion of this paragraph in Common Article 2 has resulted in the entrenching of the proposition that the law (both conventional and customary) applicable to IACs also applies to situations of military occupation. Even if there is no exchange of military hostilities and so no armed conflict involving the forces of the occupying power, the law applicable to IACs nevertheless applies. In such situations, for example, the occupying power will still owe Geneva Convention IV obligations to the occupied civilian population.

One prominent, albeit contested, example of the application of Geneva Convention IV in the context of a military occupation is Israel's administration of East Jerusalem and the West Bank.[104] The official Israeli Government position is that the Convention does not apply *de jure*. Israel's argument – centring on the second paragraph of Common Article 2, which requires that the occupation pertain to the 'territory of a High Contracting Party' – is that in the 1967 war in which Israel conquered and subsequently occupied East Jerusalem and the West Bank, Jordan was not sovereign over that territory.[105] In the *Wall* advisory opinion, the ICJ dismissed the Israeli interpretation of paragraph 2 by applying a purposive test to its reading of paragraphs 1 and 2 of Common Article 2.[106] The Court also explained that the majority of states, the UN Security Council, the UN General Assembly and the ICRC all agree that Geneva Convention IV does apply *de jure* to the Israeli occupation.[107]

The effect of military occupation on the legal characterisation of an armed conflict has been judicially considered by the ICC. The ICJ in the *DRC v Uganda* case found that Uganda had occupied a substantial part of the physical territory of the Ituri District in the DRC until the withdrawal of Ugandan forces in June 2003.[108] The ICC Pre-Trial Chamber in the Confirmation of Charges Decision against Thomas Lubanga followed the lead of the ICJ and decided that, because the Ugandan Armed Forces were in occupation of part of the District of Ituri at the relevant time, the armed conflict in which the UPC participated was an IAC *ab initio*.[109]

The Prosecution challenged the blanket conflict characterisation of the Pre-Trial Chamber in the closing submissions of the Lubanga Trial. In its judgment, the ICC Trial Chamber considered the facts of the relevant armed conflict and, particularly, that Lubanga's UPC (an OAG) was involved in an armed conflict with other OAGs. The Chamber found that 'the Ugandan military occupation of Bunia airport did not change the legal nature of the conflict' between the UPC and other OAG which occurred some physical distance from the area occupied by Ugandan forces and did not involve sovereign nation states opposed to each other.[110] Consequently, the

---

104 The legal situation with Gaza is more complicated. Israel withdrew its armed forces from Gaza in 2005 but continues to enforce strict controls over sea, air and land access into and out of all of Gaza except for the southern border (which Gaza shares with Egypt) and the Rafah land-crossing into and out of Egypt.
105 See *Legal Consequences of the Construction of a Wall in the Occupied Palestinian Territory (Advisory Opinion)* [2004] ICJ Rep 136, ¶¶ 90 and 93.
106 Ibid ¶ 95.
107 Ibid ¶¶ 96–99.
108 *DRC v Uganda* (n 68) ¶ 177.
109 See *Lubanga (Confirmation Decision)* (n 23) ¶ 220.
110 *Lubanga* (n 7) ¶ 565.

Trial Chamber altered the Pre-Trial Chamber's characterisation of the armed conflict and found that the UPC was engaged at all relevant times in a NIAC.[111]

4 Concluding remarks

The key findings from our framework of analysis are that: an armed conflict is characterised by reference to the parties to it; there may be armed conflicts of different legal characters occurring on the same territory contemporaneously; and a state may be engaged in both an IAC and a NIAC concurrently. The lack of a treaty definition of 'armed conflict' has resulted in the formulation of a definition and the identification of relevant threshold criteria through international criminal jurisprudence. Sometimes the tests for the relevant thresholds for IACs and NIACs have been misconstrued. There are also some 'grey areas', such as whether there is a requirement of 'responsible command' for a group to be party to a NIAC and there are some 'black spots', that is, questions which have not been addressed in the jurisprudence, such as whether the Rome Statute creates two different thresholds for NIACs. Despite these ongoing uncertainties, the international jurisprudence has provided greater clarity around issues of characterisation than has hitherto been the case.

There are some pragmatic and compelling arguments in favour of a unitary set of rules applicable in both IACs and NIACs but the ICC can hardly facilitate such a development. The Rome Statute reflects the prevailing multilateral view that the distinction still has its place and the organs of the Court are not in a position to challenge the treaty parameters that have been set. Any removal of the distinction will only occur through multilateral negotiation.

---

111 Ibid ¶¶ 566 and 567.

4
Sources of the law of armed conflict

Jann Kleffner

The law of armed conflict (LOAC) emanates from the same legal sources as general public international law. Accordingly, LOAC is found primarily in treaties and customary international law, in addition to general principles of law,[1] legally binding unilateral acts and legally binding resolutions of intergovernmental organisations. Furthermore, judicial decisions and international legal scholarship constitute subsidiary sources.[2] These sources and their idiosyncratic features in the context of LOAC will be addressed in turn (Sections 1–6). The subsequent section addresses LOAC rules as norms of *jus cogens* and as *erga omnes* obligations (Section 7). We will then turn to an examination of the Martens Clause and its legal significance (Section 8), followed by a section that examines the situation in which several states with different legal obligations interact and operate jointly (Section 9), before some concluding remarks will be offered (Section 10).

1 Conventional law of armed conflict

In accordance with contemporary public international law, conventional law of armed conflict is set forth in international agreements governed by international law between subjects of international law, whether embodied in a single instrument or in two or more related instruments and whatever its particular designation (agreement, convention, protocol, charter, statute etc).[3] The primary subjects with the required treaty-making capacity are states, but other actors such as intergovernmental organisations or organised armed groups are also endowed with that capacity.[4]

To date, states have adopted more than 50 conventions that set forth rules that specifically regulate various aspects of armed conflicts, starting with the 1856 Paris Declaration Respecting

---

1 Cf ICJ Statute art 38(1)(a)–(c)
2 Cf ibid art 38.
3 Vienna Convention on the Law of Treaties (23 May 1969) 1155 UNTS 331 ('VCLT'), art 2(1)(a).
4 As to organised armed groups, see eg GCI–IV common art 3(c).

Maritime Law[5] and culminating most recently with the 2008 Convention on Cluster Munitions.[6] Not all of the LOAC treaties that have been adopted in the past are today applicable. Some of these treaties have never entered into force,[7] while others have become obsolete, for instance because they have been overtaken by subsequent treaties addressing the same subject matter[8] or because the technology they regulate has ceased to be utilised in armed conflict.[9]

1.1 Categorisation

The following broad categories of LOAC treaties can be distinguished. First, one can distinguish between various LOAC treaties on the basis of the subject matter that they cover. Some are concerned with the protection of victims of armed conflicts, most importantly the 1949 Geneva Conventions addressing the issues of the protection of the wounded, sick and shipwrecked, of prisoners of war and civilians. Second, other treaties address methods and means of warfare, such as certain tactics and strategies and specific weapons. The 1907 Hague Convention (IV) on War on Land and its annexed Regulations and the 1980 Certain Conventional Weapons Convention and its Protocols are examples.[10] A third category is treaties that regulate naval and air warfare, such as the 1907 Hague Convention (X) on Maritime Warfare.[11] Fourth, a number of LOAC conventions specifically address the protection of cultural property in armed conflicts, most notably the 1954 Hague Convention for the Protection of Cultural Property and its Protocols.[12] Last, but not least, conventions that regulate the criminal repression of war crimes (and other international crimes such as genocide and crimes against humanity) constitute a fifth category, such as the 1998 Rome Statute of the International Criminal Court. However, a number of LOAC treaties do not fit neatly into this categorisation on the basis of the subject matter that is addressed. Most notable in that respect is the 1977 Additional Protocol I, which sets forth rules pertaining to the protection of war victims,[13] to methods and means of warfare,[14] to the

---

5 Declaration of Paris (30 March 1856) 115 CTS 1. Although called a 'Declaration' its nature as a treaty in the sense of public international law is confirmed by the final clause, which reads that '(t)he present Declaration is not and shall not be binding, except between those Powers who have acceded, or shall accede, to it'.

6 (30 May 2008) 48 ILM 357. See also Frits Kalshoven, 'The history of international humanitarian law treaty-making' ch 2 in this volume. For a complete list, see the treaty database of the International Committee of the Red Cross, www.icrc.org/ihl.

7 See eg Treaty Relating to the Use of Submarines and Noxious Gases in Warfare (6 February 1922) 16 *AJIL Supp* 57.

8 Examples are the Geneva Convention for the Amelioration of the Condition of the Wounded in Armies in the Field (22 August 1864) 129 CTS 361, Geneva Convention for the Amelioration of the Condition of the Wounded and Sick in Armies in the Field (6 July 1906) 202 CTS 144 and Convention for the Amelioration of the Condition of the Wounded and Sick in Armies in the Field (27 July 1929) 118 LNTS 303, which were superseded by GCI.

9 See eg Hague Declaration (IV, 1) concerning the Prohibition of the Discharge of Projectiles and Explosives from Balloons or by Other New Analogous Methods (29 July 1899) 187 CTS 456.

10 (18 October 1907) 205 CTS 277.

11 Hague Convention (X) for the Adaptation to Maritime Warfare of the Principles of the Geneva Convention (18 October 1907) 205 CTS 359.

12 Convention for the Protection of Cultural Property in the Event of Armed Conflict (14 May 1954) 249 UNTS 240; Protocol for the Protection of Cultural Property in the Event of Armed Conflict (14 May 1954) 249 UNTS 358; Second Protocol to the Hague Convention for the Protection of Cultural Property in the Event of Armed Conflict (26 March 1999) 2253 UNTS 212.

13 Se API pts II, III (s 2) and IV.

14 See pt III (s 1), also certain provisions in pt IV pertain to the conduct of hostilities.

protection of cultural property[15] and to the criminal repression of grave breaches of that Protocol (that is, war crimes).[16]

A further categorisation can be made based on whether the treaty in question is designed to apply to (a certain type of) armed conflict(s) generally, or whether it constitutes a conflict-specific ad hoc regulation, referred to as 'special agreements'.[17] The focus in the present chapter is on the former category, and a few examples of treaties belonging to it have already been given. 'Special agreements', on the other hand, can address all matters concerning which it is deemed suitable to make separate provision. Indeed, the Geneva Conventions contain several provisions which expressly foresee such special agreements to be concluded.[18] An example are special agreements pertaining to the release and repatriation of prisoners of war[19] and civilian internees,[20] such as the 1974 Agreement on the Repatriation of Prisoners of War and Civilian Internees between Bangladesh, India and Pakistan. Furthermore, all agreements foreseen in Article 3 common to the 1949 Geneva Conventions – which invites the parties to a non-international armed conflict 'to bring into force ... all or part of the other provisions' of the Conventions – fall into this latter category of conflict-specific ad hoc regulation. However, such 'special agreements' are subject to the general caveat that they may not undercut the protection flowing from general LOAC treaties.[21]

1.2 Conventional LOAC in international armed conflicts vs non-international armed conflicts

The density of conventional rules pertaining to international armed conflicts differs markedly from those that apply in non-international armed conflicts. Although one can discern a certain increase in treaties that (also) apply in non-international armed conflicts, the latter remain an exception to the former: the bulk of LOAC treaty provisions apply to armed conflicts between two or more states, whereas only Article 3 common to the 1949 Geneva Conventions, the 1977 Additional Protocol II, and a limited number of other treaties or individual treaty provisions[22] apply to non-international armed conflicts. Consequently, the regulation of international armed

---

15 See art 53.
16 See pt V (s 2).
17 Cf eg GCI–IV common art 3; GCI–III art 6; GCIV art 7; Cultural Property Convention (n 12) arts 19(2) and 24.
18 Cf GCI arts 10, 15, 23, 28, 31, 36, 37 and 52; GCII arts 10, 18, 31, 38, 39, 40, 43 and 53; GCIII arts 10, 23, 28, 33, 60, 65–67, 72, 73, 75, 109, 110, 118, 119, 122 and 132; GCIV arts 11, 14, 15, 17, 36, 108, 109, 132, 133 and 149.
19 Cf GCIII arts 118–119.
20 Cf GCIV arts 132–133.
21 Cf GCI–III art 6(1) 2nd sentence; GCIV art 7(1) 2nd sentence; Cultural Property Convention (n 12) art 24(2).
22 These include the Cultural Property Convention (n 12) and its Second Protocol (n 12), the Convention on the Prohibition of the Development, Production, Stockpiling and Use of Chemical Weapons and on their Destruction (13 January 1993) 1974 UNTS 45 ('CWC'), the Convention on the Prohibition of the Development, Production and Stockpiling of Bacteriological (Biological) Weapons and on their Destruction (10 April 1972) 1015 UNTS 163 ('BWC'), the CCW (as amended in 2001), the Convention on the Prohibition of the Use, Stockpiling, Production and Transfer of Anti-Personnel Mines and on the Destruction ('Ottawa Convention') (18 September 1997) 2056 UNTS 211, the Rome Statute, the Convention on the Rights of the Child, UNGA Res 44/25 (20 November 1989) 1577 UNTS 3 and the Optional Protocol thereto on the Involvement of Children in Armed Conflict, UNGA Res 54/263 (25 May 2000) 2173 UNTS 222, and the Convention on Cluster Munitions (30 May 2008) 48 ILM 357.

conflicts in general conventional LOAC is more detailed and specific. This is without prejudice to the specific regulation of non-international armed conflicts through special agreements, such as those foreseen in Common Article 3, as referred to above.[23]

1.3 Applicability of law of treaties

In principle, LOAC treaties are subject to the general law of treaties. In other words, the conclusion and entry into force, observance, application and interpretation, amendment and modification, the invalidity, termination and suspension of the operation of LOAC treaties are subject to the rules that international law sets forth for treaties in general, unless a divergent or supplementary regulation of these matters can be deduced from the LOAC treaty in question.[24] As far as LOAC treaties between states are concerned, the general regulation is set forth in the 1969 Vienna Convention on the Law of Treaties (the 'Vienna Convention').

Against the background of the residual regulation through the general law of treaties, a number of specific aspects deserve mentioning in the context of LOAC treaties.

First, the texts of LOAC treaties are usually adopted as the result of multilateral conferences, at times preceded by (lengthy) negotiating processes.[25] While these processes remain an essentially state-centric exercise, non-governmental organisations have become crucial actors. The ICRC assumes an exceptional role in that regard in as much as it is endowed by states with the mandate 'to prepare any development [of international humanitarian law]'.[26] Multilateral conferences operate according to their own Rules of Procedure that govern matters such as the composition of delegations, the election of officers, the establishment of different committees, the conduct of business and voting during the conference, languages in which the conference is to be conducted, etc.[27]

Second, the majority of LOAC treaties allow states parties to formulate reservations.[28] States frequently make use of that possibility[29] whose formulation, acceptance or objection and legal effects, as well as other relevant aspects are governed by the general law of treaties.[30]

---

23 On the latter, see Sandesh Sivakumaran, *The Law of Non-International Armed Conflict* (OUP 2012) 124–133.

24 LOAC treaties regularly contain provisions on matters such as authentic languages, signature, ratification, accession, deposition, entry into force, relation to earlier treaties and denunciation, see eg GCI 55–64; GCII 54–63; GCIII 133–143; GCIV 150–159.

25 See eg for API and APII, the Diplomatic Conference on the Reaffirmation and Development of International Humanitarian Law Applicable in Armed Conflicts, 1974–1977, which was preceded by a Conference of Government Experts in 1971–1972 and other preparatory work. For the more recent Convention on Cluser Munition, see Virgil Wiebe, John Borrie and Declan Smyth, 'Introduction' in Gro Nystuen and Stuart Casey-Maslen (eds), *The Convention on Cluster Munitions: A Commentary* (OUP 2010) 1, esp 11–36.

26 Statutes of the International Red Cross and Red Crescent Movement, adopted by the 25th International Conference of the Red Cross at Geneva in October 1986 and amended by the 26th International Conference of the Red Cross and Red Crescent at Geneva in December 1995 and by the 29th International Conference of the Red Cross and Red Crescent at Geneva in June 2006, art 5(2)(g) (emphasis added).

27 For these Rules of Procedure for the Diplomatic Conference on the Reaffirmation and Development of International Humanitarian Law Applicable in Armed Conflicts, see *Official Records of the Diplomatic Conference on the Reaffirmation and Development of International Humanitarian Law Applicable in Armed Conflicts* (Swiss Federal Political Department 1978) vol II.

28 For exceptions, see CWC art 22; Ottawa Convention (n 22) art 19; Cluster Munitions Convention (n 22) art 19.

29 As an example, more than 20 out of the 196 states parties to GCI–IV and 39 out of the 174 states parties to API have made reservations, see ICRC treaty database (n 6).

30 Cf VCLT (n 3) arts 19–23.

Third, in the course of the historical evolution of conventional LOAC, states have not infrequently adopted successive treaties relating to the same subject matter. The 1864, 1906, 1929 and 1949 Geneva Conventions for the Amelioration of the Condition of the Wounded in Armies in the Field are examples. In general treaty law, the application of such successive treaties is governed by Article 30 of the Vienna Convention. However, many LOAC treaties contain specific provisions that clarify the relation to earlier treaties relating to the same subject matter. For example, the Preamble of the 1949 Geneva Convention I provides that the Convention's purpose was the revision of the 1929 Geneva Convention. It can be deduced from that formulation that parties to both conventions consider the 1949 Geneva Convention I to govern their mutual relations. Another example is Article 1(1) of Additional Protocol II, which clarifies that 'it develops and supplements Article 3 common to the Geneva Conventions of 12 August 1949 without modifying its existing conditions of application'. Such specific regulations of the relations between earlier and successive LOAC treaties relating to the same subject matter take precedence over the residual regulation set forth in Article 30 of the Vienna Convention.

Fourth, as far as the interpretation of LOAC treaties is concerned, the general rule applies that these treaties 'shall be interpreted in good faith in accordance with the ordinary meaning to be given to the terms of the treaty in their context and in the light of its object and purpose'.[31] While that context consists, amongst other matters, of treaties and instruments adopted in connection to LOAC treaties,[32] an interpretation also needs to be informed by subsequent agreements between the parties regarding the interpretation of the treaty or the application of its provisions, any subsequent practice in the application of the treaty which establishes the agreement of the parties regarding its interpretation and any relevant rules of international law applicable in the relations between the parties.[33] In other words, much as other treaties, LOAC treaties need to be interpreted not in isolation but in the broader context of the actual application and interpretation of the respective treaty and the legal relations between the parties to it. The reference to the interpretation of a treaty 'in the light of its object and purpose' also invites us to consider that object and purpose of LOAC treaties. While the specifics may be confined to the individual treaty (for example, the object and purpose of regulating a specific weapon through a Protocol to the 1980 Convention on Certain Conventional Weapons (CCW)),[34] LOAC treaties have in common the broader object and purpose of striking a reasonable balance between humanitarian considerations, on the one hand, and considerations of military necessity, on the other hand. Accordingly, the interpretation of LOAC treaties needs to be guided by a balanced and nuanced approach, rather than by the dominance of one of the two considerations.

Fifth, several LOAC conventions contain provisions that address the legal relations between states parties and third states as well as the legal consequences for the mutual relations between states parties to the respective LOAC treaty of the fact that a state that is not party to that treaty is a party to the armed conflict. Thus, the 1949 Geneva Conventions provide that

[a]lthough one of the Powers in conflict may not be a party to the present Convention, the Powers who are parties thereto shall remain bound by it in their mutual relations. They

---

31 Cf ibid art 31(1).
32 Cf ibid art 31(2).
33 Cf ibid art 31(3).
34 Convention on Prohibitions or Restrictions on the Use of Certain Conventional Weapons Which May be Deemed to be Excessively Injurious or to Have Indiscriminate Effects (10 October 1980) 1342 UNTS 137.

shall furthermore be bound by the Convention in relation to the said Power, if the latter accepts and applies the provisions thereof.[35]

Such provisions supplement the relevant general regulation in the Vienna Convention on the Law of Treaties.[36]

Sixth, Article 60(5) of the Vienna Convention expressly stipulates that the general rules on the termination or suspension of the operation of a treaty as a consequence of its breach[37] is inapplicable 'to provisions relating to the protection of the human person contained in treaties of a humanitarian character, in particular to provisions prohibiting any form of reprisals against persons protected by such treaties'. This express regulation thus confirms the outlawing of belligerent reprisals against protected persons set forth in the 1949 Geneva Conventions and the 1977 Additional Protocol I.[38]

2 Customary LOAC

A second source of LOAC is customary international law, consisting of 'a general practice accepted as law'[39] that is in principle binding upon all states (except in the case of a state persistently objecting to being bound by the customary rule in question). The two constitutive elements of customary international law are, first, practice that is extensive and virtually uniform occurring in such a way as to show a general recognition that a legal rule has evolved,[40] and, second, the belief that such practice is legally required, prohibited or allowed (also referred to as *opinio juris sive necessitates*). No rule of customary international law can evolve if one of the two elements is missing. Practice alone does not constitute law, nor does practice that is sparse or inconsistent. Likewise, the belief alone that a certain practice is legally required, prohibited or allowed is insufficient for a rule of customary international law to evolve.

While broad agreement exists as to the general requirement of the two aforementioned constitutive elements for a rule of customary international law to come into existence, considerable scholarly debate surrounds the precise contours of practice and *opinio juris*, as well as other aspects of customary international law.[41] These debates persist both in the general realm of customary international law and in the specific context of the law of armed conflict. In addition, norms of customary international law often-times evolve gradually.[42] Consequently, the determination whether and at what point in time an (alleged) rule of customary international law has come into existence is not an easy task. Furthermore, a generally applicable and universally accepted methodology for making such a determination and a central institution tasked with making that determination are absent. Indeed, systematic and comprehensive studies of customary international law akin to those conducted by the ICRC in the field of the law of armed conflict (see below 3.1) are very exceptional.

---

35 Cf GCI–IV common art 2(3). The identical rule applies in relation to the API: see art 3. See also CCW art 1 and the similar provision in Cultural Property Convention (n 12) art 18(3).
36 Cf VCLT (n 3) arts 34–38.
37 Cf ibid art 60(1)–(3).
38 See Shane Darcy, 'Reciprocity and reprisals' ch 28 in this volume.
39 Cf ICJ Statute art 38(1)(b).
40 Cf *North Sea Continental Shelf (Germany v Denmark; Germany v The Netherlands)* [1969] ICJ Rep 3, ¶ 74.
41 For a general description of the main controversies, see Tullio Treves, 'Customary International Law' *MPEPIL* (2006).
42 On the temporal aspect of state practice and the possibility of so-called 'instant custom', see ibid ¶¶ 24–25.

The following sections have to be considered against the foregoing background and with the awareness that certain aspects of the formation of customary international law remain controversial and unclear.

2.1 Background and methodology of the ICRC Customary International Humanitarian Law Study

In 1995, the twenty-sixth International Conference of the Red Cross and Red Crescent mandated the ICRC to engage in a study on the customary rules of the LOAC applicable in international and non-international armed conflicts.[43] The result was published in 2005.[44]

In their assessment of customary international law, the authors of the Study selected official state practice that included both physical acts, such as battlefield practice, the use of certain weapons and the treatment provided to different categories of persons, and verbal acts, including military manuals, national legislation and case law and instructions to the armed forces.[45] They included practice of the various branches of government (executive, legislative, adjudicative), but not decisions of international courts and tribunals, although the latter feature in the Study as 'persuasive evidence' that a rule of customary international law exists.[46] In addition, the practice of international organisations is being included as it 'can contribute to the formation of customary international law', although the weight accorded to any particular resolution negotiated and adopted by international organisations or conferences depends, in the view of the authors, 'on its content, its degree of acceptance and the consistency of state practice outside it'.[47] In light of the ICRC's mandate from states 'to work for the faithful application of international humanitarian law applicable in armed conflicts and ... to prepare any development thereof', official ICRC statements have also been included as relevant practice.[48] The practice of organised armed groups, on the other hand, is not considered to constitute state practice, but has been included as 'other practice', notwithstanding the lack of clarity surrounding the legal significance of such non-state practice.[49]

As far as *opinio juris* is concerned, the authors of the Study acknowledged that 'it proved very difficult and largely theoretical to strictly separate elements of practice and legal conviction'.[50] They distinguished between three types of rules: prohibitions, obligations and permissions. They noted with regard to the former that constitutive practice:

> includes not only statements that such behaviour is prohibited and condemnations of instances where the prohibited behaviour did take place, possibly combined with justifications or excuses from the criticised State, but also physical practice abstaining from the prohibited behaviour. If the practice largely consists of abstention combined with silence, there will need to be some indication that the abstention is based on a legitimate expectation to that effect from the international community.

---

43 Twenty-sixth International Conference of the Red Cross and Red Crescent, Geneva, 3–7 December 1995, Res 1, International Humanitarian Law: From Law to Action; Report on the Follow-up to the International Conference for the Protection of War Victims (1996) 310 *IRRC* 58.

44 Jean-Marie Henckaerts and Louise Doswald-Beck (eds), *Customary International Humanitarian Law* (CUP 2005).

45 Ibid xxxii.

46 Ibid xxxiv.

47 Ibid xxxv–xxxvi.

48 Ibid xxxv.

49 Ibid xxxvi.

50 Ibid xl.

Practice establishing the existence of an obligation ... can be found primarily in behaviour in conformity with such a requirement. The fact that it is a legal requirement, rather
than one reflecting courtesy or mere comity, can be found by either an expression of the
need for such behaviour, or by criticism by other States in the absence of such behaviour.
It may also be that, following criticism by other States, the criticised State will explain its
abstinence by seeking justification within the rule.

Practice establishing the existence of a rule that allows a certain conduct ... can be found
in acts that recognise the right to behave in such a way without actually requiring such
behaviour. This will typically take the form of States undertaking such action, together
with the absence of protests by other States.[51]

The authors further posit that:

[w]hen there is sufficiently dense practice, an *opinio juris* is generally contained within that
practice and, as a result, it is not usually necessary to demonstrate separately the existence
of an *opinio juris*. *Opinio juris* plays an important role, however, in certain situations where
the practice is ambiguous, in order to decide whether or not that practice counts towards
the formation of custom. This is often the case with omissions, when States omit to act or
react but it is not clear why.[52]

The authors also note an idiosyncrasy of LOAC in as much as many of its rules require
abstention from certain conduct and that:

omissions pose a particular problem in the assessment of *opinio juris* because it has to be
proved that the abstention is not a coincidence but based on a legitimate expectation.
When such a requirement of abstention is indicated in statements and documents, the existence of a legal requirement to abstain from the conduct in question can usually be proved.
In addition, such abstentions may also occur after the behaviour in question created a
certain controversy, which also helps to prove that the abstention was not coincidental,
although it is not always easy to conclude that the abstention occurred because of a sense
of legal obligation.[53]

In a separate section on the impact of treaty law on the formation of customary international
(humanitarian) law, the authors explain the inclusion of the ratification, interpretation and
implementation of LOAC treaties, including reservations and interpretative declarations, because
these aspects 'help assess how States view certain rules of international law'.[54] The authors recall
four different ways in which treaties may interact with custom, identified by the International
Law Association:

[A treaty] can provide evidence of existing custom; it can provide the inspiration or model
for the adoption of new custom through State practice; it can assist in the so-called 'crystallisation' of emerging custom; and it can even give rise to new custom of 'its own impact' if
the rule concerned is of a fundamentally norm-creating character and is widely adopted by

51 Ibid xxxix–xl.
52 Ibid xl.
53 Ibid xli.
54 Ibid xlii–xliii.

States with a view to creating a new general legal obligation. There can be no presumption that any of these interactions has taken place and in each case it is a matter of examining the evidence.[55]

However, the authors also explain their caution in considering widespread ratification of a treaty, in as much as they do not consider such ratification to be in and of itself sufficient for the existence of a customary rule of LOAC. Instead, they consider widespread ratification to be 'only an indication and [which] has to be assessed in relation to other elements of practice, in particular the practice of States not party to the treaty in question'.[56] Based on the aforementioned methodological considerations, the wealth of material collected in the course of the Study was examined and the authors formulated a set of 161 rules of customary LOAC.

One of the most significant outcomes of the Study is that it suggests a very close approximation between the law of international armed conflict and the law of non-international armed conflicts. Out of the total of 161 Rules, no less than 149 are concluded to apply in non-international armed conflict, as opposed to 159 which are applicable in international armed conflicts.

2.2 Criticisms of the ICRC Customary International Humanitarian Law Study

While the ICRC Customary International Humanitarian Law Study has met with widespread acknowledgement because of its depth and the wealth of material that it assembles, because it is being cited by international courts and tribunals and because it has been received positively by a number of states, it has also been subjected to criticisms.[57]

Some of these criticisms concern the overall methodology underpinning the findings in the Study.

The US Government, for instance, posited that the Study frequently fails to apply in a rigorous way the otherwise generally appropriate approach to assessing state practice that the Study's introduction describes.[58] In its view, the status of certain purported rules as customary law is questionable because the state practice cited is insufficiently dense.[59] The US Government also objected to the type of material that was included as state practice, criticising for instance that too much emphasis is laid on written materials, such as military manuals and other guidelines by states, as opposed to actual operational practice by states during armed conflict.[60] Other criticisms of the US Government concerned the inclusion of, and weight given to, the statements of non-governmental organisations, the lack of weight given to negative practice especially of non-states parties to relevant treaties and to the practice of specially affected states.[61] Furthermore, the US Government took issue with the Study's approach to *opinio juris*, objecting to the conflation of practice and *opinio juris* and to the significance of military manuals as evidence of *opinio juris*, coming to the conclusion that:

---

55 Ibid xliii–xliv.
56 Ibid xliv.
57 For a collection of essays that discuss the study, its methodology and its rules and a critical analysis of them, see eg Elizabeth Wilmshurst and Susan Breau (eds), *Perspectives on the ICRC Study on Customary International Humanitarian Law* (CUP 2011).
58 John B Bellinger and William J Haynes, 'A US Government Response to the International Committee of the Red Cross's Customary International Humanitarian Law Study' (2007) 89(866) *IRRC* 443, 444.
59 Ibid 444–445.
60 Ibid 445.
61 Ibid.

the practice volumes generally fall far short of identifying the level of positive evidence of opinio juris that would be necessary to justify concluding that the rules advanced by the Study are part of customary international law and would apply to States even in the absence of a treaty obligation.[62]

Yoram Dinstein opined that the breadth of statements that have been included as state practice 'is going too far'.[63] He also objects to the inclusion of the practice of non-governmental organisations, including the ICRC, and the weight given to that practice.[64] He further questions the inclusion of certain documents as 'military manuals', whereas, in his opinion, they do not possess that status in their respective states and he points to an inaccuracy concerning Israeli practice.[65] Yoram Dinstein also questions the way in which the authors of the Study made use of practice emanating from the ICRC's archive.[66]

The general criticisms of the overall methodology underlying the ICRC Customary IHL Study have also been applied to specific Rules in the Study. A number of legal scholars and some states have expressed reservations about the customary status of individual Rules and/or their extension to non-international armed conflicts as a matter of customary international law.[67]

3 General principles of law

Article 38(1)(c) of the ICJ Statute identifies 'general principles of law recognized by civilized nations' as a third, distinct source of international law. While the process of norm generation in the context of these general principles remains to some extent controversial, the majority view today holds that general principles of law can originate from any of the following five bases.[68] First, general principles may be derived from municipal law, either through a comparative exercise or, as the use of general principles of law by the ICJ seems to suggest, through an intuitive exercise.[69] Second, general principles may emanate from international relations, distilled through 'a comparative method ..., coupled with a generalizing assessment of the international legal rules in question'.[70] Third, principles recognised in legal relations in general, such as the principle of good faith, can produce general principles of law in the sense of Article 38(1)(c) of the ICJ Statute.[71] Fourth, principles of legal logic may constitute such general principles of law.[72] Fifth, general principles can be developed from a particular treaty regime or other international

---

62 Ibid 446–447. For a response to the US criticisms, see Jean-Marie Henckaerts, 'Customary International Humanitarian Law: A Response to US comments' (2007) 89(866) *IRRC* 473.

63 Yoram Dinstein, 'The ICRC Customary International Humanitarian Law Study' in Anthony M Helm (ed), *The Law of War in the 21st Century: Weaponry and the Use of Force* (US Naval War College 2006) 99, 102.

64 Ibid 102–103.

65 Ibid 103.

66 Ibid 104.

67 See, among others, the various contributions in Wilmshurst and Breau (n 57) pt III; Bellinger and Haynes (n 58) 448–471; Dinstein (n 63) 105–109; David Turns, 'Weapons in the ICRC Study on Customary International Humanitarian Law' (2006) 11 *JCSL* 201, 211–235; James Benoit, 'Mistreatment of the Wounded, Sick and Shipwrecked by the ICRC Study on Customary International Humanitarian Law' (2008) 11 *YBIHL* 175.

68 Rüdiger Wolfrum, 'General International Law (Principles, Rules, and Standards)' *MPEPIL* (December 2010) ¶¶ 28–53.

69 Ibid ¶¶ 30–32.

70 Ibid ¶ 33.

71 Ibid ¶¶ 37–38.

72 Ibid ¶¶ 39–40.

instruments through a comparative approach that considers whether and to what extent a particular principle has developed from a fundamental rule in one particular international treaty into a principle of a more general scope through express invocation in national or international case law and in doctrine and through its reaffirmation in resolutions of international organisations or statements of international conferences.[73]

Article 38(1)(c) of the ICJ Statute lists general principles of law as a source of international law without further qualification and thus suggests that such principles constitute a source of international law with equal rank to international conventional and customary law. However, the drafting history of Article 38(1)(c) (and its predecessor provision in the Statute of the Permanent Court of International Justice (PCIJ)), as well as the resort to general principles as a source of international law in the jurisprudence of international courts and tribunals suggests that general principles of law have a primarily supplementary function.[74] While this does not diminish the standing of general principles of law as an independent source of international legal obligation in their own right, resort to general principles of law as a source of international law generally does not occur if and when the legal question at hand can be answered by resort to pertinent rules of international conventional and customary law.

In the context of LOAC, the regulatory density through treaties and customary law is such that (express) and exclusive resort to general principles of law does not occur frequently. In this respect, it is revealing that the ICJ in its jurisprudence does not rely on general principles of law in the sense of Article 38(1)(c) when deciding questions of LOAC. If it refers to 'principles' in that context, it instead refers to '[general] principles [and rules] *of humanitarian law*', at times in conjunction with a reference to pertinent treaty provisions or customary international law.[75] This in turn raises the question of the potential relationship between 'general principles of law' as a source of international law, on the one hand, and (general) principles of LOAC, on the other hand. Suffice it to observe in the present context that many, if not all, of the basic principles of LOAC identified would lend themselves to a classification as 'general principles of law' of the fifth type described above. The principles of distinction, proportionality and protection as well as the prohibition of using means and methods of warfare which are of a nature to cause superfluous injury and unnecessary suffering are a red thread throughout various LOAC treaties and other international instruments. They are frequently invoked in national or international case law and in doctrine as well as reaffirmed frequently in resolutions of international organisations or statements of international conferences. As such, these fundamental rules have developed into principles of a more general scope that apply outside particular treaties. Indeed, some of the LOAC principles, such as distinction and the prohibition of superfluous injury and unnecessary

---

73 Ibid ¶¶ 41–53.
74 On the supplementary role of general principles, see ibid ¶¶ 58–59. See also Rome Statute art 21(1)(c), expressly granting such supplementary status to general principles of law.
75 See eg *Military and Paramilitary Activities in and against Nicaragua (Nicaragua v United States of America) (Merits)* [1986] ICJ Rep 14, ¶ 215 ('principles of humanitarian law underlying the specific provisions of Convention No. VIII of 1907'), 218 ('fundamental general principles of humanitarian law'), 219 ('principles are to be looked for in the provisions of Article 3 of each of the four Conventions of 12 August 194'), 220 ('general principles of humanitarian law to which the Conventions merely give specific expression'), 225 ('general principles of humanitarian law'), 256; *Armed Activities on the Territory of the Congo (Democratic Republic of the Congo v Uganda)* [2005] ICJ Rep 168, ¶ 215 ('rules and principles of international human rights law and international humanitarian law'); *Legal Consequences of the Construction of a Wall in the Occupied Palestinian Territory (Advisory Opinion)* [2004] ICJ Rep 136, ¶ 37; *Legality of the Threat or Use of Nuclear Weapons (Advisory Opinion)* [1996] ICJ Rep 226, ¶¶ 42, 51, 78 ('cardinal principles contained in the texts constituting the fabric of humanitarian law'), 79 ('intransgressible principles of international customary law') 83, 85, 86.

suffering, are referred to as 'basic rules' in treaty provisions[76] and as 'principle' or 'general principles' in the ICRC Customary Law Study,[77] thus confirming that they constitute generic legal norms that underlie the more specific rules of LOAC, which is characteristic of legal principles.[78] As a result, LOAC principles find a triple basis in the sources of international law: they emanate from international conventional and customary law while at the same time constituting general principles of law in the sense of Article 38(1)(c) of the ICJ Statute.

The existence of basic LOAC principles that (also) qualify as general principles of law raises another issue pertinent to the relevance of 'principles' in LOAC. That issue pertains to the passage in the Martens Clause that stipulates that in cases not covered by international agreements civilians and combatants 'remain under the protection and authority of the *principles of international law derived from established custom, from the principles of humanity and from the dictates of public conscience*'.[79] It is clear from the wording that the 'principles of international law' referred to are distinct from 'general principles of law' in the sense of Article 38(1)(c) of the ICJ Statute. This is evident from the proclaimed bases for the 'principles of international law' that the Martens Clause refers to: such principles are 'derived from established custom, from the principles of humanity and from the dictates of public conscience'. Such a process of norm-generation differs markedly from the process of norm-generation of 'general principles of law' in the sense of Article 38(1)(c) of the ICJ Statute described in the foregoing. We will return to the value and significance of the Martens Clause as a source of LOAC below (Section 8).

4 Unilateral acts

It has long been recognised that unilateral acts of states can produce legal obligations under international law. This is notably the case if and when it can be deduced from the circumstances surrounding the unilateral act that the latter is accompanied by an intent to be bound as a matter of international law.[80] The pertinent case law and doctrine regarding unilateral acts as a source of international law are primarily concerned with the unilateral acts of states.[81] Within the

---

76 See eg API arts 35(2) and 48.
77 See eg CIHL rr 1–6 ('The Principle of Distinction') and 70–71 ('General Principles on the Use of Weapons').
78 For the distinction between the two concepts of legal principles and legal rules, see Ronald Dworkin, *Taking Rights Seriously* (Harvard University Press 1977) 25, explaining that legal principles, as opposed to legal rules, 'do not set out legal consequences that follow automatically when the conditions provided are met'. Rather, they incorporate into the law general goals and values, regularly specifying neither their subjects and their content in detail nor their conditions of application: ibid 22–23.
79 Cf the wording of API art 1(2) and the CCW preamble, which differ to some extent from earlier versions of the Martens Clause, especially as far as the reference to 'principles of humanity' are concerned, with earlier versions referring instead to 'the laws of humanity', see eg Preamble to Hague Convention No IV (1907), and arts 63/62/142/158 Geneva Conventions.
80 Cf *Nuclear Tests (Australia v France)* [1974] ICJ Rep 253, ¶ 43.
81 See in particular *Legal Status of Eastern Greenland (Denmark v Norway)* [1933] PCIJ Series A/B No 53, ¶ 71; *Nicaragua* (n 75); *Frontier Dispute (Burkina Faso/Republic of Mali)* [1986] ICJ Rep 554; *Armed Activities on the Territory of the Congo (New Application: 2002) (Democratic Republic of the Congo v Rwanda) (Jurisdiction and Admissibility)* [2006] ICJ Rep 6; Guiding Principles Applicable to Unilateral Declarations of States Capable of Creating Legal Obligations, in Report of the International Law Commission – Fifty-Eighth Session, UN Doc A/61/10 (2006) ch IX; Unilateral Acts of States: Report of the Working Group – Conclusions of the International Law Commission Relating to Unilateral Acts of States, UN Doc A/CN.4/L.703 (20 July 2006).

specific context of LOAC, states do at times make unilateral declarations and they can produce legal effects provided that the respective state intended them to do so.[82]

However, one of the idiosyncratic features of LOAC is that non-state actors who are parties to a non-international armed conflict, that is, organised armed groups, can produce LOAC obligations by way of unilateral acts. Indeed, besides customary LOAC and special agreements, such as those foreseen in Common Article 3, unilateral acts have become an important source of LOAC in non-international armed conflicts as far as organised armed groups are concerned. These acts frequently consist of declarations through which the organised armed group in question expresses its intent to be bound by (certain) LOAC treaties, commitments made to the ICRC, to UN bodies or to Switzerland as the Depository of the Geneva Conventions and Additional Protocols thereto.[83] As far as the substance of these declarations is concerned, they can either be of a general nature and include entire LOAC treaties, or they can concern particular rules or issues for instance in the form of 'Deeds of Commitment' made under the auspices of *Geneva Call* to ban anti-personnel mines and to further the protection of children from the effects of armed conflict.[84] Frequently, such declarations (and LOAC obligations that emanate from other sources) are internalised into the regulatory framework governing the conduct of organised armed groups through instructions, codes of conduct, internal regulations and 'legislation'.[85]

5 Binding resolutions of international organisations

Applicable binding resolutions of inter-governmental organisations may be the source for obligations under LOAC. The most pertinent (potential) example in that respect would be a binding resolution adopted by the Security Council in accordance with Chapter VII of the UN Charter through which the Council imposes upon parties to an armed conflict LOAC obligations, or creates LOAC rights, independently of any applicable treaties or customary law. Such a possibility remains hypothetical however. The Security Council has not acted in this way as legislator in the field of LOAC thus far. Yet, that possibility cannot be excluded.[86]

Furthermore, the Security Council has at times adopted Chapter VII resolutions that abrogate from certain LOAC rules. More specifically, Security Council Resolution 1483 on the situation in Iraq, adopted under Chapter VII of the UN Charter, provided for several abrogations from the law of belligerent occupation by granting the occupying powers (US and UK) several specific rights and imposing on them certain responsibilities which conflicted with the rights and obligations of an occupying power under the law of belligerent occupation as enshrined in the 1907 Hague Regulations, the 1949 Geneva Convention IV and customary international humanitarian law.[87] In such a case, the addressee(s) of the relevant binding Security Council Resolution must give precedent to the obligations under the Resolution by virtue of Article 103 of the UN

---

82 For some examples, see Sivakumaran (n 23) 113–114.
83 Ibid 118–122.
84 See generally, www.genevacall.org and the list of signatories of Deeds of Commitment www.geneva-call.org/resources/list-of-signatories/list-of-signatories.htm.
85 Sivakumaran (n 23) 133–141.
86 See Georg Nolte, 'The Different Functions of the Security Council with Respect to Humanitarian Law' in Vaughan Lowe, Adam Roberts, Jennifer Welsh and Dominik Zaum (eds), *The United Nations Security Council and War: The Evolution of Thought and Practice since 1945* (OUP 2008) 532.
87 For discussion, see David Scheffer, 'The Security Council and International Law on Military Occupations' in Lowe *et al* (eds) (n 86) 596–605.

Charter, provided that the Security Council acts in accordance with the UN Charter and the imposed obligations are compatible with *jus cogens* norms.[88]

6 Subsidiary sources

Article 38(1)(d) lists judicial decisions and the teachings of the most highly qualified publicists of the various nations, as subsidiary means for the determination of rules of law. In other words, irrespective of the potential value of judicial decisions for the process of customary law formation (to the extent that they amount to state practice and/or *opinio juris*), they do not constitute more than subsidiary sources in their own right, together with legal doctrine. That holds true in the context of LOAC as much as in all other areas of international law.

Judicial decisions in LOAC matters can be rendered by domestic, internationalised and international courts and tribunals. Indeed, there has been a significant increase in LOAC litigation in these fora over the years, not the least before international(ised) criminal tribunals tasked with the prosecution of war crimes and before domestic courts.[89]

One of the characteristic features of LOAC concerning 'the teachings of the most highly qualified publicists of the various nations' – or 'legal doctrine' in its alternative designation – is that it does not only include academic publications, such as books and articles in academic journals. Rather, the ICRC has engaged in various exercises through which it has developed its own position as regards the interpretation of existing law. Such exercises include the ICRC Commentaries to the 1949 Geneva Conventions and its 1977 Additional Protocols[90] – a very widely referenced work – but also various expert consultations,[91] some of which have led to the adoption of an official ICRC position vis-à-vis a given issue.[92] The ICRC's contribution to legal doctrine is of particular weight in light of its express mandate 'to work for the understanding and dissemination of knowledge of international humanitarian law applicable in armed conflicts and to prepare any development thereof'.[93]

7 *Jus cogens* and *erga omnes* obligations

International law recognises a hierarchically superior category of norms, *jus cogens* or peremptory norms of general international law, defined as norms 'accepted by the international community of States as a whole as a norm from which no derogation is permitted and which can be modified only by a subsequent norm of general international law having the same character'.[94] As the

---

88 See generally on constraints of the Chapter VII powers of the Security Council, Rudolf Bernhardt, 'Article 103' in Bruno Simma (ed), *The Charter of the United Nations: A Commentary* (2nd edn, OUP 2002) 1295–1302.

89 For a useful online database, see Oxford Reports on International Law, opil.ouplaw.com/home/ ORIL.

90 *GCI Commentary, GCII Commentary, GCIII Commentary, GCIV Commentary, AP Commentary*. The Commentaries are currently being updated.

91 See eg ICRC, 'Clarification Process on the Notion of Direct Participation in Hostilities under International Humanitarian Law (Proceedings)' (30 June 2009), www.icrc.org/eng/resources/documents/ article/other/direct-participation-article-020709.htm; Tristan Ferraro, 'Occupation and Other Forms of Administration of Foreign Territory: Expert Meeting – Report' (ICRC, March 2012), www.icrc. org/eng/assets/files/publications/icrc-002-4094.pdf.

92 See ICRC, *Interpretive Guidance on the Notion of Direct Participation in Hostilities under International Humanitarian Law* (ICRC 2009).

93 Cf Statutes of the Movement (n 26) art 5(2)(g).

94 Cf VCLT (n 3) art 53.

definition makes clear, *jus cogens* does not constitute a source of international law in its own right. Peremptory norms are part of *general* international law and hence flow from customary international law, although they regularly find simultaneous expression in conventional international law and general principles. The essence of the status of a norm as *jus cogens* is that it possesses a specific hierarchical pedigree, endowed with specific legal consequences, such as that conflicting treaties are void[95] and that grounds precluding the wrongfulness of conduct are unavailable.[96] While there is some uncertainty as to exactly which norms of international law have the character of *jus cogens*, the basic rules of LOAC are widely held to fall into that category.[97] Consequently, if states (and *mutatis mutandis* other subjects of international law) were to conclude a treaty that conflicts with one or more LOAC norms that possess *jus cogens* status, such a treaty would be void. They would also be barred from invoking any of the grounds precluding the wrongfulness under the international law of state responsibility.

All *jus cogens* norms, including those in the realm of LOAC, also possess the status of obligations *erga omnes*, defined by the ICJ as those 'obligations of a State towards the international community as a whole' which are 'the concern of all States' and involving rights in whose protection 'all States can be held to have a legal interest'.[98] The reverse is not true: not every obligation *erga omnes* necessarily constitutes a peremptory norm of general international law. As far as LOAC is concerned, many (if not all) of its rules do not normatively exhaust themselves in the regulation of the mutual relationship between one party to an armed conflict and another such party. Rather, they are (also) owed to the international community as a whole, or, as far as obligations under a LOAC treaty that is not universally ratified is concerned, to all other states parties to that treaty (obligations *erga omnes partes*).[99]

8 The Martens Clause

Several LOAC treaties contain the so-called Martens Clause according to which, in cases not covered by international agreements, civilians and combatants 'remain under the protection and authority of the *principles of international law derived from established custom, from the principles of humanity and from the dictates of public conscience*'.[100] The normative content and legal force of the Martens Clause has sparked considerable debate.[101] This is especially the case with regard to the latter part of the Clause's reference to 'the principles/laws of humanity' and the 'dictates of public conscience'. While the references to 'the principles of international law derived from established custom' can be conceptualised in conformity with the traditional sources of international law,

---

95 Ibid.
96 Cf Draft Articles on Responsibility of States for Internationally Wrongful Acts, in 'Report of the International Law Commission on the Work of its Fifty-Third Session' UN Doc A/56/10 (November 2001) ('ARSIWA') art 26; Draft Articles on the Responsibility of International Organizations, in the 'Report of the International Law Commission on the Work of its Sixty-Third Session' UN Doc A/66/10 (2011) ('ARIO') art 26.
97 Fragmentation of International Law: Difficulties arising from the Divergence and Expansion of International Law – Report of the Study Group of the International Law Commission: Finalized by Martti Koskenniemi, UN Doc A/CN.4/L.682 (13 April 2006) ¶ 33, with further references.
98 *Barcelona Traction, Light and Power Co Ltd (Belgium v Spain) (Second Phase)* [1970] ICJ Rep 3, ¶ 33.
99 *Wall* (n 75) ¶¶ 155–159.
100 See n 79.
101 For that discussion in general, see amongst others: Theodor Meron, 'The Martens Clause, Principles of Humanity, and Dictates of Public Conscience' (2000) 94 *AJIL* 78; Antonio Cassese, 'The Martens Clause: Half a Loaf or Simply Pie in the Sky?' (2000) 11 *EJIL* 187; Rupert Ticehurst, 'The Martens Clause and the Laws of Armed Conflict' (1997) 37 *IRRC* 125.

'principles/laws of humanity' and the 'dictates of public conscience' cannot. However, an expansive interpretation to the effect that the Martens Clause's reference to principles of humanity and dictates of public conscience provides a positive source of LOAC in its own right akin to conventional, customary or general principles of LOAC is neither borne out by state practice that could establish an agreement between states on such an interpretation[102] nor can one deduce such an understanding from the case law of international courts and tribunals.[103]

It is therefore submitted that, as long as, and to the extent that, the principles of humanity and dictates of public conscience mentioned in the Martens Clause have not found their expression in a treaty provision, a rule of customary international law, or another source of positive international law, they do not constitute a source of LOAC. Principles of humanity and dictates of public conscience may be driving forces for the development of the law, but they do not constitute the law.

9 Legal interoperability

In contemporary armed conflicts, states frequently operate jointly, either in the form of ad hoc 'coalitions of the willing' or as member states of international organisations. States with differing legal obligations conduct military operations in these multinational contexts, raising the question whether and to what extent international law in general, and LOAC in particular, provides any guidance on the legal interoperability between troop contributing states.

The fundamental starting point in that regard is the quintessential precondition for a state to be bound by a rule of international law, namely its consent to the rule in question. The consent to be bound by a treaty rule can be expressed in various ways,[104] whereas the consent to be bound by a rule of customary international law is encapsulated in the expression of the constitutive, subjective element of *opinio juris* (including the non-objection to the (emerging) rule). In other words, no state can be subjected to a rule of international law without its consent.[105] In armed conflicts in which states operate jointly, the requirement of consent entails that in principle all individual states remain subject to only those rules that they have accepted individually. Conversely, no state can evade its LOAC obligations by referring to the fact that another troop contributing state has not accepted a given LOAC obligation. This underlying principle is epitomised by the common rule in the 1949 Geneva Conventions that

> [a]lthough one of the Powers in conflict may not be a party to the present Convention, the Powers who are parties thereto shall remain bound by it in their mutual relations. They

---

102 Cf VCLT (n 3) art 31(3)(b). For the disparate submissions of a number of states on the meaning of the Martens Clause in the course of the proceedings before the ICJ that preceded its Advisory Opinion on *Nuclear Weapons* (n 75), see the summary in Ticehurst (n 101).

103 As to the ICJ, nothing in *Nuclear Weapons* (n 7575) suggests such an interpretation, which led some judges to dissent from it and express a different opinion, see eg ibid Dissenting Opinion of Judge Shahabuddeen, 375–428, 406–411. The ICTY has applied the Martens Clause as an aid to *interpret* a given rule of positive international law – see eg *Prosecutor v Kupreškić* (Case no IT-95-16-T, ICTY Trial Chamber, 14 January 2000) ¶ 525 – and as a justification to emphasise *opinio juris* over state practice when establishing a rule of customary international law – ibid ¶ 527. Neither of these constructions suggests that the principles of humanity and dictates of public conscience, to which the Martens Clause refers, constitute independent sources of international law.

104 Cf VCLT (n 3) arts 11–17.

105 This holds equally true to rules of a *jus cogens* nature, as per the definition of what constitutes a rule of *jus cogens*, namely a rule that is 'accepted by the international community of States *as a whole*' (emphasis added) and hence includes the acceptance by all states.

shall furthermore be bound by the Convention in relation to the said Power, if the latter accepts and applies the provisions thereof.[106]

However, neither general international law nor any specific rule of LOAC prohibit states that are subject to a given obligation under LOAC to engage in military cooperation and operations with states that are not subject to that same obligation.[107]

Whether and to what extent it is the LOAC obligations of the troop contributing state that are applicable to the conduct of its troops that are placed at the disposal of another state or international organisation, is a complex matter. However, it would stand to reason that the applicability of LOAC rules (and other primary rules of international law) mirrors the attribution of conduct on the level of the secondary rules of state responsibility and the responsibility of international organisations for internationally wrongful acts. Underlying the rules on attributing conduct is the notion that the conduct of state organs placed at the disposal and under the effective control of another state or international organisation thus become, as matter of law, the conduct of that other state or international organisation.[108] It would be only logical to construe the primary rules that govern such conduct in the same way, namely to subject the troops that are placed at the disposal of another state or international organisation to the rules that are binding on that other state or international organisation – rather than to the primary rules of the troop contributing state – if and when that other state or international organisation exercises effective control over the conduct of the troops. A different construction would lead to an incoherent result that conduct is being attributed to one subject of international law (the other state or international organisation) that constitutes a breach of an international legal obligation of another subject (the troop contributing state).

A related, but distinct, legal problem concerns the question whether and to what extent states are legally barred from putting their troops at the disposal of another state or international organisation whose LOAC obligations undercut those of the troop contributing state. The rule that states are under an obligation to respect and ensure respect of LOAC[109] and certain rules in the law of international responsibility[110] would seem to militate at least against a deliberate circumvention of the obligations of a troop contributing state by putting its troops at the disposal of another state or international organisations.

On the operational level, questions that differences in LOAC obligations – or, for that matter, in the interpretation of pertinent LOAC rules – raise, are addressed to some extent on the level of Rules of Engagement and through caveats. The latter enable a given troop contributing state not to partake in a given operation or to abstain from engaging in certain conduct that it considers gives rise to concerns in relation to its LOAC obligations.

10 Concluding remarks

The sources of LOAC are embedded into the general framework and doctrine of sources of public international law. However, the aforementioned sections have brought to the fore a number of idiosyncratic features. These features do not only concern the two main sources of

---

106 Cf GCI–IV common art 2(3).
107 Cf the express recognition to that effect in Cluster Munitions Convention (n 22) art 21(3). The same principle applies outside the specific context of that Convention as a matter of general international law.
108 Cf ARSIWA (n 96) art 6; ARIO (n 96) art 7.
109 Cf GCI–IV common art 1; API art 1(1); CIHL r 139.
110 Cf in particular ARIO (n 96) art 61(1).

conventional and customary law. One example in that respect is the importance that unilateral acts assume in LOAC, in particular in the context of non-international armed conflicts and adopted by organised armed groups. Another is the role of the ICRC in the promotion and development of LOAC, and its adoption of interpretive positions, which renders it a highly authoritative actor in the realm of sources that is unique to LOAC. Furthermore, the basic rules of the LOAC are widely accepted to possess *jus cogens* status. Together with the nature of LOAC obligations as obligations *erga omnes*, this hierarchical superiority confirms that LOAC is part and parcel of the basic tenets of the international legal order.

5
Basic principles

Nobuo Hayashi

This chapter illustrates the normative process through which the law of armed conflict (LOAC) creates its rules. It does so by identifying major 'ingredients' of the process, elucidating their interplay and reflecting on the consequences that the interplay entails vis-à-vis positive LOAC rules. In addition to military necessity and humanity, chivalry and sovereignty will also be considered where appropriate.

Key to this inquiry is the idea that LOAC has been developed with a view to striking a realistic balance between military necessity and humanity and that, accordingly, the law 'accounts for' them.[1] What is meant by this has remained obscure, however, and this obscurity has given rise to different opinions.

---

1 Declaration Renouncing the Use, in Time of War, of Explosive Projectiles Under 400 Grammes Weight (29 November to 11 December 1868) 138 CTS 297 ('St Petersburg Declaration'); Convention (IV) Respecting the Laws and Customs of War on Land (18 October 1907) 205 CTS 277; *In re von Lewinski* (1944) 16 ADIL 509, 512 ('*von Manstein*'); US Department of the Army, *The Law of Land Warfare* (1956) 4; *AP Commentary* ¶ 1389; Frédéric de Mulinen, *Handbook on the Law of War for Armed Forces* (ICRC 1987) 83; UK Ministry of Defence, *The Manual of the Law of Armed Conflict* (OUP 2004) 23, 442 ('UK Manual'); Thomas Erskine Holland, *The Laws of War on Land (Written and Unwritten)* (OUP 1908) 13; N C H Dunbar, 'The Significance of Military Necessity in the Law of War' (1955) 67 *Juridical Review* 201, 212; G I A D Draper, 'Military Necessity and Humanitarian Imperatives' (1973) 12 *RDMDG* 129, 142; Geoffrey Best, 'The Restraint of War in Historical and Philosophical Perspective' in Astrid J M Delissen and Gerard J Tanja (eds), *Humanitarian Law of Armed Conflict Challenges Ahead: Essays in Honour of Frits Kalshoven* (Nijhoff 1991) 3, 5; Chris af Jochnick and Roger Normand, 'The Legitimation of Violence: A Critical History of the Laws of War' (1994) 35 *Harvard ILJ* 49, 53; A P V Rogers, *Law on the Battlefield* (2nd edn, Manchester University Press 2004) 4; Eyal Benvenisti, 'Human Dignity in Combat: The Duty to Spare Enemy Civilians' (2006) 39 *Israel LR* 81, 81; Christopher Greenwood, 'Historical Development and Legal Basis' in Dieter Fleck (ed), *The Handbook of International Humanitarian Law* (2nd edn, OUP 2008) 1, 37–38; Nils Melzer, *Targeted Killing in International Law* (OUP 2008) 290; Gary D Solis, *The Law of Armed Conflict: International Humanitarian Law in War* (CUP 2010) 269; Michael N Schmitt, 'Military Necessity and Humanity in International Humanitarian Law: Preserving the Delicate Balance' (2010) 50 *Virginia JIL* 795, 798.

1 Reason-giving considerations in LOAC norm-creation

1.1 Military necessity[2]

In its material context, military necessity embodies a twofold truism. It is in the belligerent's self-interest to do what is militarily necessary and to avoid what is unnecessary. Conversely, it is against its self-interest to let go of necessities of war or encumber itself with non-necessities. Material military necessity is a matter of calculating the degree of cogency between the means taken or considered, on the one hand, and the ends sought, on the other, under the circumstances prevailing or anticipated at the relevant time. To say that 'Doing this is militarily necessary' is simply to signify that the act conduces towards the materialisation of a given military end to some degree.

A given act's military necessity vis-à-vis its goal depends on the availability of other reasonably attainable goals and other reasonably conducive acts, as well as the prevailing circumstances. For the Allies during the Second World War, the destruction of the Monte Cassino Abbey was, all else being equal, arguably more militarily necessary in order to conquer the monastery hill than if the goal had been to compel the German forces to divert their resources from the Anzio beachhead.[3] An act is also capable of military necessity assessments given enough pertinent facts. Allied commanders drew reasonable though dissimilar conclusions about the military necessity of the Abbey's destruction based on the facts then available to them.[4] An act's military necessity or non-necessity is susceptible neither to being taken out of its particular circumstances nor to being generalised. Whatever one's assessment of the destruction of the Monte Cassino Abbey may be, one cannot determine in general and a priori whether destroying a building sitting atop a topographically dominant elevation is militarily necessary or unnecessary.

In the context of LOAC norm-creation, military necessity embodies indifference.[5] Conduct is normatively indifferent where the two propositions 'It is permitted to perform it' and 'It is permitted to refrain from it' are both true simultaneously.[6] Military necessity permits the performance of what is militarily necessary and the forbearance of what is militarily unnecessary. It also tolerates the former's forbearance and the latter's performance, however, because neither victory nor defeat is per se of concern to LOAC. The law does not make it its business to ensure that each belligerent maximises its prospect of success or minimises its prospect of failure. LOAC's framers have no reason to obligate militarily necessary behaviour or prohibit militarily unnecessary behaviour.

As reason-giving considerations, military necessity is generalised and stipulatory. The material question was whether a given act was or would be militarily necessary, in view of its particular purpose and circumstances. The question here is what LOAC should do about this kind of act, *once* it is agreed that it would generally be militarily necessary or unnecessary vis-à-vis an otherwise legitimate kind of military purpose. There may well be no military necessity to intern prisoners of war (POWs) in certain specific cases. Nevertheless, interning POWs is generally

---

2 Nobuo Hayashi, 'Contextualising Military Necessity' (2013) 27 *Emory ILR* 189.

3 Nigel de Lee, 'Moral Ambiguities in the Bombing of Monte Cassino' (2005) 4 *Journal of Military Ethics* 129, 133; Reuben E Brigety II, 'Commentary: Moral Ambiguities in the Bombing of Monte Cassino' (2005) 4 *Journal of Military Ethics* 139, 140.

4 Marten Blumenson, *The Mediterranean Theater of Operations: Salerno to Cassino* (US Army Center of Military History 1993) 403 (Gen Tuker in favour), 404 (Gen Freyberg in favour), 405–406 (Gen Clark against), 413 (Gen Walker against), 415 (President Roosevelt in favour).

5 Nobuo Hayashi, 'Military Necessity as Normative Indifference' (2013) 44 *Georgetown JIL* 675.

6 G H von Wright, 'Deontic Logic' (1951) 60 *Mind* 1, 3–4.

deemed militarily necessary.[7] Normative military necessity prompts LOAC's framers to leave the belligerent at liberty to intern or decline to intern its POWs.[8]

In the juridical context of positive LOAC, military necessity operates exclusively as an exception. Military necessity clauses attached to certain LOAC rules, such as that which prohibits property destruction in occupied territory,[9] exceptionally authorise behaviour deviating from the rules' principal prescriptions as long as such behaviour fulfils four cumulative requirements. First, the measure must be taken primarily for some specific military purpose. Second, the measure must be required for the purpose's attainment. Third, the purpose must be in conformity with LOAC. Fourth, the measure itself must otherwise be in conformity with LOAC.[10] If not, or no longer, in fulfilment of these requirements, the deviant conduct reverts to being governed by the principal prescriptions, and it becomes unlawful. The conduct's unlawfulness emanates from its breach of the principal rule, *not* its lack of military necessity or the now inoperative exceptional clause.

Assessing juridical military necessity involves interpreting the relevant rules and clauses vis-à-vis the particular set of facts at issue. In the *Hostages* case, the US Military Tribunal at Nuremberg applied Article 23(g) of the Hague Regulations to the 'scorched earth' policy to which the German forces resorted in Finmark, northern Norway, in 1944.[11] It was found that '[t]here is evidence in the record that there was no military necessity for this destruction and devastation'.[12]

Various perspectives on military necessity have been proposed. It was once argued that military necessity pleas are, or should be, admissible *de novo* in support of conduct at odds with unqualified LOAC rules. Thus, the material military necessity of given belligerent conduct overrides any LOAC provisions that prescribe contrary action. The *Kriegsräson* doctrine, so named after the German maxim 'Kriegsräson geht vor Kriegsmanier' ('Necessities of war override rules of war'), remained influential among German military and international lawyers until the end of the Second World War.[13] Since its rejection at post-war trials,[14] *Kriegsräson* has been

---

7 Sibylle Scheipers, 'Introduction: Prisoners of War' in Sibylle Scheipers (ed), *Prisoners in War* (OUP 2010) 1, 7–8.

8 HR art 5; GCIII art 21. But, see API art 41(3).

9 GCIV art 53.

10 Nobuo Hayashi, 'Requirements of Military Necessity in International Humanitarian Law and International Criminal Law' (2010) 28 *Boston University ILJ* 39, 62–94.

11 *US v List (Hostages)* 11 TWC 757, 1296–1297 (1950).

12 Ibid 1296. Nevertheless, the tribunal declined to find the accused guilty of the crime charged. It did so on the ground that he honestly, albeit erroneously in retrospect, believed Finmark's devastation to be militarily necessary. See ibid 1296–1297. For what has come to be known as the 'Rendulic rule' of no second guessing, see Brian J Bill, 'The Rendulic "Rule": Military Necessity, Commander's Knowledge, and Methods of Warfare' (2009) 12 *YBIHL* 119.

13 Isabel V Hull, '"Military Necessity" and the Laws of War in Imperial Germany' in Stathis N Kalyvas, Ian Shapiro and Tarek Masoud (eds), *Order, Conflict, and Violence* (CUP 2008) 352, 359–374; Coleman Phillipson, *International Law and the Great War* (Fisher Unwin 1915) 133–138; James Wilford Garner, *International Law and the World War* (Longman 1920) vol i, 278–282; vol ii, 195–198; Dunbar, 'Significance' (n 1) 203–204, 207–208; William V O'Brien, 'The Meaning of "Military Necessity" in International Law' (1957) 1 *World Polity* 109, 119–137; Geoffrey Best, *Humanity in Warfare: The Modern History of the International Law of Armed Conflicts* (Methuen 1983) 172–179; Mika Nishimura Hayashi, 'The Martens Clause and Military Necessity' in Howard M Hensel (ed), *The Legitimate Use of Military Force: The Just War Tradition and the Customary Law of Armed Conflict* (Ashgate 2008) 135, 137–138; Solis (n 1) 265–268.

14 *In re Rauter* (1949) 16 ADIL 526, 543; *In re Burghoff* (1949) 15 ADIL 551, 554–557; *Hostages* (n 11) 1255–1256, 1272–1273, 1296; *von Manstein* (n 1) 512–513; *US v Krupp von Bohlen und Halbach (Krupp)*, 9 TWC 1340 (1950); *US v von Leeb (High Command)* 11 TWC 1, 541 (1951).

thoroughly discredited.[15] It is widely accepted today that military necessity has no place outside specific exceptional clauses.[16]

Some authorities go further. In their view, military necessity functions as a layer of normative restraint additional to positive LOAC.[17] This position – let us call it 'counter-*Kriegsräson*' – entails two major assertions. First, as reason-giving considerations, military necessity condemns militarily unnecessary conduct. Second, these considerations survive the process of LOAC norm-creation. Consequently, an act otherwise lawful according to positive LOAC nevertheless becomes unlawful on account of its lack of material military necessity. As seen below, neither assertion is correct.

Military necessity has occasionally been equated with military objective, particularly in international criminal law.[18] This equation is unhelpful, since the former pertains to *conduct* whereas the latter pertains to *objects*.[19] Where given conduct is militarily necessary or unnecessary, LOAC's framers have reason to permit it or tolerate it. Where an object constitutes a military objective or a civilian object, it becomes principally liable to or immune from attacks.[20]

---

15 Office of the Judge Advocate General, Canadian Forces, *Law of Armed Conflict at the Operational and Tactical Levels* (2001) ¶ 202.5 ('Canadian Manual'); UK *Manual* (n 1) 23; Georg Schwarzenberger, *International Law as Applied by International Courts and Tribunals: The Law of Armed Conflict* (Stevens & Sons 1968) 136; Greenwood, 'Historical Development' (n 1) 38; Solis (n 1) 269.

16 US Department of the Army (n 1) 4; US Navy, US Marine Corps and US Coast Guard, *The Commander's Handbook on the Law of Naval Operations*, NWP 1-14M/MCWP 5-12.1/COMDTPUB P5800.7A (July 2007) ¶ 5.3.1 ('*Commander's Handbook*'); Canadian Manual (n 15) ¶ 202.5; UK *Manual* (n 1) 22–23, 442; Percy Bordwell, *The Law of War Between Belligerents: A History and Commentary* (Callaghan 1908) 5; Elihu Root, 'Opening Address' (1921) 15 *ASIL Proceedings* 1, 3; Dunbar, 'Significance' (n 1) 202; Robert W Tucker, *The Law of War and Neutrality at Sea* (US Naval War College 1957) 33–37; Draper (n 1) 138, 142; Frits Kalshoven, *Belligerent Reprisals* (Sijthoff 1971) 366; International Law Commission, *Report on the International Law Commission on the Work of its Thirty-Second Session*, UN Doc A/35/10 (1980) 45–46; *AP Commentary* ¶¶ 1386, 1405; de Mulinen (n 1) 82–83; Henri Meyrowitz, 'The Principle of Superfluous Injury or Unnecessary Suffering: From the Declaration of St. Petersburg of 1868 to Additional Protocol I of 1977' (1994) 299 *IRRC* 98, 108; Donald A Wells, 'The Limits of War and Military Necessity' (1988) 19 *Journal of Social Philosophy* (1988) 3; Jean Pictet, *Development and Principles of International Humanitarian Law* (Nijhoff 1985) 88; Georges Abi-Saab and Luigi Condorelli, 'Réponses à la Question 1, b)' (2000) 33 *Revue Belge de Droit International* 406, 407–408; Robert Kolb, *Ius in Bello: Le Droit International des Conflits Armés* (Helbing & Lichtenhahn 2003) 57; Leslie C Green, *The Contemporary Law of Armed Conflict* (3rd edn, Manchester University Press 2008) 147–148; Yoram Dinstein, *The Conduct of Hostilities under the Law of International Armed Conflict* (2nd edn, CUP 2010) 6.

17 Schwarzenberger (n 15) 135; Telford Taylor, *Nuremberg and Vietnam: An American Tragedy* (Corgi Childrens 1970) 34; Meyrowitz (n 16) 107; Federic L Borch, 'Targeting After Kosovo: Has the Law Changed for Strike Planners?' (2003) 56 *NWCR* 64, 66; Greenwood, 'Historical Development' (n 1) 36–37, 38; Gabriella Venturini, 'Necessity in the Law of Armed Conflict and International Criminal Law' (2010) 41 *Netherlands YBIL* 45, 48–50; Henry Shue, 'Civilian Protection and Force Protection' in David Whetham (ed), *Ethics, Law and Military Operations* (Palgrave Macmillan 2011) 135, 136–137; Melzer, *Targeted Killing* (n 1) 286; *Commander's Handbook* (n 16) ¶ 5.3.1; UK *Manual* (n 1) 22; Nils Melzer, 'Keeping the Balance between Military Necessity and Humanity: A Response to Four Critiques of the ICRC's Interpretive Guidance on the Notion of Direct Participation in Hostilities' (2010) 42 *NYU JILP* 831, 910.

18 *Prosecutor v Strugar* (Case no IT-01-42-T, Trial Chamber II, 31 January 2005) ¶ 295; *Prosecutor v Brđanin* (Case no IT-99-36-A, Appeals Chamber, 3 April 2007) ¶ 337; *Prosecutor v Strugar* (Case no IT-01-42-A, Appeals Chamber, 17 July 2008) ¶ 330; Kriangsak Kittichaisaree, *International Criminal Law* (OUP 2001) 274 n 68.

19 API art 52(2).

20 Ibid art 52(1).

Military necessity has also been treated synonymously with proportionality.[21] When calculating material military necessity, something approximating proportionality may characterise the measures taken vis-à-vis the goal sought. It is unclear, however, whether proportionality constitutes distinct reason-giving considerations in LOAC norm-creation. Nor would it operate as a clause exceptionally modifying the normative content of a principal LOAC rule. It is rather an element in the LOAC rule that establishes the lawfulness or unlawfulness of an attack directed at a military objective.[22]

Any difference between military necessity and military advantage or convenience might be seen as one of degrees. The former might involve the act's indispensability, whereas the latter might encompass indispensability as well as mere gain, superiority or expediency. It is doubtful whether the indispensability of belligerent conduct is a viable distinguishing feature here.[23] Could it be, alternatively, that military advantage compares the belligerent's position vis-à-vis its adversary's but military necessity does not? Here, too, although military advantage may certainly be construed in this manner, it does not follow that the notion cannot be understood without reference to such comparisons. Normatively, military advantage could easily function as reason-giving considerations in LOAC norm-creation. The law's framers would have very good reasons to leave militarily advantageous conduct permitted[24] and militarily disadvantageous conduct tolerated.

The clearest difference between the two notions lies in their juridical significance. No positive LOAC rules expressly admit military advantage or convenience as an exception to their principal prescriptions. Acts not in fulfilment of the four aforementioned requirements may be regarded as military advantage or convenience ineligible for deviation from LOAC rules that envisage military necessity pleas.[25]

1.2 Humanity

It has been observed that humanity is difficult to define.[26] Humanity has been described as: a notion that 'forbids the infliction of suffering, injury, or destruction not actually necessary for the accomplishment of legitimate military purposes';[27] a synonym with the prohibition of superfluous injury and unnecessary suffering;[28] an equivalent to the Martens Clause;[29] a vehicle through which international human rights law has made its way into the regulation of armed

---

21 David Luban, 'Military Necessity and the Cultures of Military Law' (2013) 26 *Leiden JIL* 315, 343–345.
22 API art 51(5)(b).
23 Arguably, no *conditio sine qua non* characterises military necessity. See Hayashi, 'Contextualising Military Necessity' (n 2).
24 W Hays Parks, 'Means and Methods of Warfare' (2006) 38 *George Washington ILR* 511 n 25 (citing Edward R Cummings).
25 Roger O'Keefe, *The Protection of Cultural Property in Armed Conflict* (CUP 2006) 122–123 (referring to Eisenhower's General Order No 68, 29 December 1943); *von Manstein* (n 1) 522; Draper (n 1) 134; Melzer, *Targeted Killing* (n 1) 291–292; Solis (n 1) 264.
26 Robin Coupland, 'Humanity: What is It and How Does It Influence International Law?' (2001) 83 *IRRC* 969; Kjetil Mujezinovic Larsen and Camilla Guldahl Cooper, 'Conclusions' in Kjetil Mujezinović Larsen, Camilla Guldahl Cooper and Gro Nystuen (eds), *Searching for a 'Principle of Humanity' in International Humanitarian Law* (CUP 2012) 355–357.
27 UK *Manual* (n 1) 23.
28 Meyrowitz (n 16) 98; Geoffrey S Corn, 'Principle of Humanity' *MPEPIL* (2012) ¶¶ 1, 4.
29 UK *Manual* (n 1) 23; Nishimura Hayashi (n 13) 136–137; Jochen von Bernstorff, 'Martens Clause' *MPEPIL* (2012) ¶ 14.

conflicts;[30] and an equivalent to what the ICJ in its *Corfu Channel* judgment referred to as 'elementary considerations of humanity'.[31]

Perhaps it is easier to consider what humanity *does* in relation to LOAC. It would appear that specific belligerent acts can be described as humane or inhumane (just as they can be described as militarily necessary or unnecessary). Frank Richards, a First World War veteran, recalled his November 1914 action at a village called Englefontaine:

> When bombing dug-outs or cellars it was always wise to throw bombs into them first and have a look around them after. But we had to be very careful in this village as there were civilians in some of the cellars. We shouted down them to make sure. Another man and I shouted down one cellar twice and receiving no reply were just about to pull the pins out of our bombs when we heard a woman's voice cry out and a young lady came up the cellar steps. As soon as she saw us she started to speak rapidly in French and gave both of us a hearty kiss. She and the members of her family had their beds, stove and everything else of use in the cellar which they had not left for some days. They guessed an attack was being made and when we first shouted down had been too frightened to answer. If the young lady had not cried out when she did we would have innocently murdered them all.[32]

It seems clear that Richards acted humanely in this episode. Had he chosen to throw the bombs into the cellar, he would have acted inhumanely albeit perhaps 'wisely'.

In LOAC norm-creation, acts such as assuming some risks of self-endangerment in favour of civilians, and caring for the wounded and sick, would be deemed consistent with humanity and affirmatively demanded by it. Humanity would unhesitatingly condemn – that is, demand that one refrain from – plunder, torture and the like as inhumane. Elsewhere, however, humanity may exhibit indifference. Examples include the conclusion of agreements recognising hospital zones and localities,[33] and the censoring of communications between POWs and the exterior.[34] Philosophers acknowledge that morality in society encompasses not only duties and obligations but also those qualities that go beyond them.[35] The same may be said *mutatis mutandis* of humanity in LOAC norm-creation.

The 'pointer' at which the 'humanity of duty' ends and the 'humanity of aspiration' begins is a highly contentious matter.[36] In the Englefontaine episode, Richards considered it 'wise' to 'throw bombs into cellars first and have a look around them after'. He also clearly found it morally troubling to do so, however. In fact, he found it so morally troubling that he decided *not* to do the wise thing. Instead, Richards, together with his colleague, chose to risk self-endangerment by shouting into the cellar. Michael Walzer observes:

---

30 Theodor Meron, 'The Humanization of Humanitarian Law' (2000) 94 *AJIL* 239.

31 Yoram Dinstein, 'The Principle of Proportionality' in Larsen, Cooper and Nystuen (eds) (n 26) 73; *Legality of the Threat or Use of Nuclear Weapons (Advisory Opinion)* [1996] ICJ Rep 226 ¶ 79.

32 Frank Richards, *Old Soldiers Never Die* (Amazon 2001) 310; Michael Walzer, *Just and Unjust Wars: A Moral Argument with Historical Illustrations* (4th edn, Basic Books 2006) 152, 154.

33 This humane conduct nevertheless remains a matter of humanitarian permission. See Raymund T Yingling and Robert W Ginnane, 'The Geneva Conventions of 1949' (1952) 46 *AJIL* 393, 400.

34 Similarly, this inhumane conduct nevertheless remains a matter of humanitarian toleration.

35 H L A Hart, *The Concept of Law* (OUP 1961) 177–178; Lon L Fuller, *The Morality of Law* (rev edn, Yale University Press 1969) 4, 15–27, 30–32.

36 Fuller has conceded as much, at least in relation to the 'pointer' at which the 'morality of duty' yields to the 'morality of aspiration'. See ibid 9–13, 27–30.

Innocently murder, because they had shouted first; but if they had not shouted, and then killed the French family, it would have been, Richards believed, murder simply. And yet he was accepting a certain risk in shouting, for had there been German soldiers in the cellar, they might have scrambled out, firing as they came. It would have been more prudent to throw the bombs without warning, which means that military necessity would have justified him in doing so.... And yet Richards was surely doing the right thing when he shouted his warning. He was acting as a moral man ought to act; he is not an example of fighting heroically, above and beyond the call of duty, but simply of fighting well. It is what we expect of soldiers.[37]

Contemporary thinkers debate whether the risk of self-endangerment of the kind assumed by Richards is what humanity only permits, or what it demands.[38]

Juridically, humanity functions as an exception. There are positive LOAC rules, for example Article 49 of Geneva Convention IV,[39] which expressly admit exceptions on humanitarian grounds or, at any rate, on grounds that are arguably analogous. Deviating from the principal prescriptions of these rules is lawful insofar as it is in fact humane to do so in the manner specified by the exceptional clauses. The question is whether humanity may also function as a justification or excuse vis-à-vis positive LOAC. Can humanity be invoked *de novo* in support of belligerent behaviour deviating from an unqualified LOAC rule, *à la* '*Humanitätsräson*'?[40] Or, for that matter, can there be a 'counter-*Humanitätsräson*' whereby humanity operates as an additional layer of normative restraint over positive LOAC? We will address these questions below.

1.3 Chivalry and other considerations

Chivalry is a third and sometimes overlooked 'ingredient' in the process of LOAC norm-creation. As with humanity, it appears more fruitful to focus on chivalry's normative and juridical functions in relation to LOAC than to decipher its content.[41]

Chivalry appears indifferent regarding certain kinds of belligerent conduct but not so regarding others. Thus, it prompts LOAC's framers to tolerate certain techniques of deception as ruses of war and yet condemn certain others as perfidy or treachery. One may ask whether chivalry is admissible *de novo* as a justification or excuse for deviation from positive LOAC (a '*Ritterlichkeitsräson*'?)[42] or an additional layer of normative restraint thereon (a 'counter-*Ritterlichkeitsräson*'?).

---

37 Walzer, *Just and Unjust Wars* (n 32) 152, 154 (emphasis in original).

38 Ibid 152, 154, 305–306; Avishai Margalit and Michael Walzer, 'Israel: Civilians & Combatants' *New York Review of Books* (14 May 2009); David Luban, 'Risk Taking and Force Protection' in Yitzhak Benbaji and Naomi Sussmann (eds), *Reading Walzer* (Routledge 2014) 277; Henry Shue, 'Civilian Protection and Force Protection' in Whetham (ed) (n 17) 135, 138; David Whetham, 'The Just War Tradition: A Pragmatic Compromise' in ibid 65, 83.

39 GCIV art 49 (principally prohibiting forcible transfers of residents in occupied territory yet exceptionally authorising their temporary evacuations 'if the security of the population ... so demand[s]').

40 '*Humanitätsräson geht vor Kriegsmanier*' ('Necessities of humanity override rules of war'), so to speak. This author is indebted to Mareile Kaufmann for her assistance in German.

41 Rain Liivoja, 'Chivalry without a Horse: Military Honour and the Modern Law of Armed Conflict' in Rain Liivoja and Andres Saumets (eds), *The Law of Armed Conflict: Historical and Contemporary Perspectives* (Tartu University Press 2012) 75.

42 Similarly, '*Ritterlichkeitsräson geht vor Kriegsmanier*' ('Necessities of chivalry override rules of war').

Sovereignty also functions as reason-giving considerations in LOAC norm-creation. They may exhibit indifference in some matters, for example the regulation of non-international armed conflicts, whereas they demand specific behaviour and condemn others on matters of neutrality.

2 Dynamics of considerations interplay

Reason-giving considerations interact with one another in three distinct ways. They are: (a) where all the relevant considerations permit or demand the same behaviour ('norm alignment'); (b) where one set of considerations permits particular behaviour, whereas another set demands contrary behaviour ('norm contradiction'); and (c) where two or more sets of considerations demand mutually incompatible behaviour ('norm conflict'). This chapter primarily examines the binary interplay between military necessity and humanity.

2.1 Norm alignment and joint satisfaction

It has been suggested that military necessity and humanity find themselves in 'diametrical opposition'[43] and that its resolution involves 'dialectical compromise'.[44] In fact, they can and do align themselves; moreover, their alignment is far more pervasive than 'rare'.[45]

That performing certain conduct is deemed both inhumane and militarily unnecessary is a widely accepted notion indeed. For Carl von Clausewitz, committing needless brutalities – for example putting prisoners to death and devastating cities and countries – was, first and foremost, a sign of ineffective and unintelligent fighting.[46] Similar observations have been made regarding pillaging indiscriminately,[47] murdering POWs,[48] plundering private or public property,[49] raping women and ill-treating populations of occupied territories,[50] attacking civilians,[51] abusing detained persons during counter-insurgency operations,[52] sadistic acts of cruelty[53] and bombarding undefended localities.[54]

Where military necessity permits and humanity demands the conduct's forbearance, the belligerent satisfies both considerations by refraining from it. LOAC may 'account for' this possibility by validly positing a rule unqualifiedly prohibiting the said behaviour.[55] This rule extinguishes all liberties to perform the conduct that military necessity may otherwise tolerate. Examples include LOAC rules unqualifiedly prohibiting killing POWs,[56] bombarding

43 Yoram Dinstein, *The Conduct of Hostilities under the Law of International Armed Conflict* (1st edn, CUP 2004) 16.
44 Schmitt, 'Military Necessity' (n 1) 801.
45 Yoram Dinstein, 'Military Necessity' *MPEPIL* (2010) ¶¶ 3–4.
46 Carl von Clausewitz, *On War* (Michael Howard and Peter Paret eds tr, Knopf 1993) 85. See also R B Brandt, 'Utilitarianism and the Rules of War' (1972) 1 *Philosophical and Public Affairs* 145, 155.
47 Henry Sidgwick, *The Elements of Politics* (Macmillan 1891) 256.
48 Brandt (n 46) 154–155.
49 Ibid 155; Louise Doswald-Beck and Sylvain Vité, 'International Humanitarian Law and Human Rights Law' (1993) 293 *IRRC* 94, 99.
50 Brandt (n 46) 155.
51 Kenneth James Keith, 'The Present State of International Humanitarian Law' (1980) 9 *Australian YBIL* 13, 34.
52 US Army and Marine Corps, *Counterinsurgency Field Manual* (University of Chicago Press 2007) 251.
53 Doswald-Beck and Vité (n 49) 99.
54 Dinstein, 'Military Necessity' (2010) (n 45) ¶ 3; UK *Manual* (n 1) 90.
55 Brandt (n 46) 154–155.
56 GCIII art 13.

undefended localities,[57] shooting persons descending from aircraft in distress[58] and generally maltreating persons *hors de combat*.[59]

Joint satisfaction can also be performance based. The idea that it is strategically expedient to fight ethically in counterinsurgency with a view to earning the support of local residents is hardly new.[60] The same has been said of certain measures taken during belligerent occupation[61] and a doctrine of aerial warfare known as effects-based operations.[62] Here, too, LOAC 'accounts for' this possibility when it validly posits rules unqualifiedly obligating the conduct's perform-ance.[63] The law thereby extinguishes any contrary liberties on the belligerent's part to behave otherwise as may be tolerated by military necessity.

The fact that some belligerent acts are amenable to joint satisfaction of this character does not mean that LOAC's framers always validly posit rules unqualifiedly obligating its pursuit. It is, as noted earlier, not per se of concern to LOAC whether the belligerent fights competently or incompetently. Where this type of joint satisfaction is available, military necessity permits its pursuit and only tolerates its non-pursuit. The relative scarcity of these rules can also be explained by the fact that the framers may let *third* considerations permitting its non-pursuit, such as sovereignty, prevail.[64]

2.2 Norm contradiction and joint satisfaction

Where given conduct is a matter of indifference, there is neither any duty to perform it nor any duty to refrain from it. If, then, one norm stipulating such indifference regarding particular behaviour is juxtaposed vis-à-vis another norm stipulating a duty to perform it – or to refrain from it, as the case may be – the two norms contradict each other. They do so because both cannot be true simultaneously. Joint satisfaction nevertheless results where the addressee acts according to the duty. Norm contradiction becomes problematic if, but only if, the addressee avails him or herself of the liberty and thereby leaves the contrary duty unsatisfied.

---

57 HR art 25.
58 API art 42(1).
59 Ibid art 41(1).
60 John A Nagl, *Learning to Eat Soup with a Knife: Counterinsurgency Lessons from Malaya and Vietnam* (Praeger 2002) 87–107; David Galula, *Counterinsurgency Warfare: Theory and Practice* (Praeger 1964) 52; US Army and Marine Corps (n 52) 245–246.
61 Geoffrey Best, 'Restraints on War by Land Before 1945' in Michael Howard (ed), *Restraints in War: Studies in the Limitation of Armed Conflict* (OUP 1979) 17, 28–29; Brandt (n 46) 155.
62 David A Deptula, *Effects-Based Operations: Change in the Nature of Warfare* (Aerospace Education Founda-tion 2001); Michael N Schmitt, 'Effects-Based Operations and the Law of Aerial Warfare' in Wolff Heintschel von Heinegg and Volker Epping (eds), *International Humanitarian Law Facing New Challenges: Symposium in Honour of Knut Ipsen* (Springer 2007) 21, 37.
63 API art 57(3) (obligating the attacking party to choose the least injurious amongst those military objectives offering similar military advantage); Brandt (n 46) 155.
64 The *si omnes* clauses exemplify strictly historical instances where considerations of sovereignty amongst adversarial powers resulted in the non-application in certain circumstances of LOAC rules which would otherwise have created unqualified obligations. Similarly, in 1949, the ICRC failed to rally states in its effort to expand the scope of application of the four Geneva Conventions in their entirety to all types of armed conflict. See David A Elder, 'The Historical Background of Common Article 3 of the Geneva Convention of 1949' (1979) 11 *Case Western Reserve JIL* 37, 41–54; Georges Abi-Saab, 'Non-International Armed Conflicts' in UNESCO (ed), *International Dimensions of Humanitarian Law* (UNESCO 1988) 217, 220; Lindsay Moir, *The Law of Internal Armed Conflict* (CUP 2002) 24–29. The same is true of the defeat of numerous would-be APII provisions. See Abi-Saab, 'Non-International Armed Conflicts' (n 64) 230–233; Moir (n 64) 91–96.

At issue here is a situation where humanity demands what military necessity only tolerates or the former condemns what the latter permits. The belligerent jointly satisfies both sets of considerations by acting in accordance with humanity. LOAC norm-creation deals with joint satisfaction of this kind in five ways. In one, LOAC validly posits a rule *unqualifiedly* obligating its pursuit. Thus, the law categorically bans the denial of quarter,[65] attacks on the civilian population or on individual civilians not directly participating in hostilities,[66] deliberate infliction of terror amongst civilians,[67] their starvation as a method of combat,[68] recruitment of children into the armed forces and their use in hostilities,[69] use of POWs[70] or protected persons[71] as human shields, hostage-taking[72] and permanent forcible transfers and deportations.[73] Those framing these rules have elected to let humanity's condemnation trump military necessity's contrary permission.[74] Similarly, LOAC unqualifiedly obligates the release of POWs with provisions in unusual conditions of combat.[75] By validly positing this rule, the law extinguishes any liberty on the belligerent's part to act otherwise as may be permitted by military necessity.

Second, a LOAC rule may *principally* obligate the pursuit of joint satisfaction but exceptionally authorise its non-pursuit. Consider, for example, those rules principally prohibiting yet exceptionally authorising the destruction of property,[76] the destruction of captured enemy and neutral merchant vessels,[77] and temporary evacuations of residents in occupied territories.[78] Conversely, the following acts are principally obligatory yet exceptionally optional: the Detaining Power allowing internees to receive shipments which may meet their needs;[79] combatants distinguishing themselves from the civilian population;[80] attacking parties giving effective

---

65 HR art 23(d); API art 40. See also Morris Greenspan, *The Modern Law of Land Warfare* (University of California Press 1959) 103; Dinstein, *Conduct of Hostilities* (n 16) 7.
66 API art 51(1), 51(3).
67 Ibid art 51(2).
68 Ibid art 54(1).
69 Ibid art 77(2). See also Peter Rowe, 'The Obligation of a State under International Law to Protect Members of its Own Armed Forces during Armed Conflict or Occupation' (2006) 9 *YBIHL* 3, 17–18.
70 GCIII art 23.
71 GCIV art 28.
72 Ibid art 34.
73 Ibid art 49.
74 Marshall Cohen, 'Morality and the Laws of War' in Virginia Held, Sidney Morgenbesser and Thomas Nagel (eds), *Philosophy, Morality, and International Affairs* (OUP 1974) 71, 74.
75 API art 41(3). See also Dinstein, *Conduct of Hostilities* (n 16) 7.
76 HR art 23(g); GCIV art 49. See also Brandt (n 46) 155–160; Doswald-Beck and Vité (n 49) 100. This includes the destruction of cultural property and objects indispensable to the survival of the civilian population. For cultural property, see Convention for the Protection of Cultural Property in the Event of Armed Conflict (14 May 1954) 249 UNTS 240, art 4(2); Second Protocol to the Hague Convention of 1954 for the Protection of Cultural Property in the Event of Armed Conflict (26 March 1999) 38 ILM 769, art 6 ('Hague Cultural Property Protocol II'); Doswald-Beck and Vité (n 49) 100.
77 *San Remo Manual on International Law Applicable to Armed Conflicts at Sea* (IIHL 1995) ¶ 102 ('*San Remo Manual*').
78 GCIV art 49.
79 Ibid art 108. This provision envisages situations where 'military necessity require[s] the quantity of such shipments to be limited', implying that otherwise impermissible limitations are exceptionally permissible insofar as they actually happen to be militarily necessary.
80 API art 44(3). This duty is partially waived when, 'owing to the nature of the hostilities an armed combatant cannot … distinguish himself' in accordance with it.

advance warning;[81] and belligerents allowing civil defence organisations to work.[82] Here, LOAC's framers have elected, in principle, to let humanitarian condemnations and demands take precedence over contrary liberties permitted by military necessity. Where these rules apply, the belligerent is obligated to pursue the joint satisfaction demanded by humanity and tolerated by military necessity – unless, and to the extent that, non-pursuit proves militarily necessary in a particular situation.

Third, certain LOAC rules *indeterminately* obligate the pursuit of joint satisfaction. Examples arguably include those rules concerning proportionality in attacks[83] and the use of weapons of a nature to cause superfluous injury and unnecessary suffering,[84] as well as those obligating humane but militarily unnecessary action 'as far as military considerations permit',[85] 'whenever circumstances permit'[86] and 'to the maximum extent feasible'.[87] The process of their norm-creation has left the priority between military necessity and humanity unsettled. The non-pursuit of joint satisfaction is authorised to the extent permitted by military necessity, while its pursuit is obligated to the extent demanded by humanity. The rules themselves do not specify the point at which the former gives way to the latter. Their framers effectively transfer the burden of discovering this point to the rules' addressees and adjudicators.

Fourth, there are some types of belligerent conduct over which LOAC rules only *exceptionally* obligate the pursuit of joint satisfaction. Take, for example, the declaration and establishment of a blockade[88] and the denial by the blocking party of free passage of essential goods to blockaded ports.[89] The framers of these rules have principally elected to let military necessity's permission trump humanity's contrary demands. The belligerent is at liberty to act as permitted by military necessity not only where it is in fact militarily necessary to do so; the same liberty remains in place even if it is not. This liberty not to pursue joint satisfaction exceptionally ceases where its pursuit does in fact prove humane.

Fifth, LOAC may *decline* or *fail* to obligate the pursuit of joint satisfaction altogether. It may *decline* to do so by validly positing rules unqualifiedly authorising non-pursuit. Such is the case

---

81 HR art 26; API art 57(2); Julius Stone, *Legal Controls of International Conflict: A Treatise on the Dynamics of Disputes- and War-Law* (Rinehart & Co 1954) 622–623; Rogers (n 1) 88. Belligerents need not give such warning if 'circumstances do not permit' (such as assault requiring an element of surprise).

82 API art 62(1). That is, 'except in cases of imperative military necessity'.

83 Doswald-Beck and Vité (n 49) 100; Schmitt, 'Military Necessity' (n 1) 804–805; Luban, 'Risk Taking' (n 38) 294–296.

84 St Petersburg Declaration (n 1); HR art 23(e). See also *Nuclear Weapons* (n 31) 586–587 (Judge Higgins, dissenting); Yves Sandoz, 'International Humanitarian Law in the Twenty-First Century' (2003) 6 *YBIHL* 3, 8; Parks (n 24) n 25; *Commentary on the HPCR Manual on International Law Applicable to Air and Missile Warfare* (Harvard University 2010) 66.

85 That is, eg leaving a part of a party's medical personnel and materiel with the wounded and sick to assist in the latter's care should the party in question be compelled to abandon them to the enemy. See GCI art 12. See also, Convention for the Amelioration of the Condition of the Wounded and Sick in Armies in the Field (6 July 1906) 202 CTS 144, art 1 ('so far as military conditions permit'); Convention for the Amelioration of the Condition of the Wounded and Sick in Armies in the Field (27 July 1929) 118 LNTS 303, art 1 ('as far as military exigencies permit'); *GCI Commentary* 141–142.

86 That is, eg searching, collecting and evacuating the wounded, sick, shipwrecked and dead. See Jean-Marie Henckaerts and Louise Doswald-Beck, *Customary International Humanitarian Law* (CUP 2005) 396, 406; GCI art 15; GCII art 18; Doswald-Beck and Vité (n 49) 100.

87 That is, eg removing movable cultural property from the vicinity of military objectives and avoiding locating military objectives near cultural property. See Hague Cultural Property Protocol II (n 76) art 8.

88 That is, unless the blockade has the sole purpose of starving the civilian population or is disproportionately injurious to the civilian population. See *San Remo Manual* (n 77) ¶¶ 93, 102.

89 That is, unless the denial leaves the civilian population inadequately supplied. See *San Remo Manual* (n 77) ¶ 103.

regarding the Detaining Power interning POWs,[90] the belligerent searching and controlling medical vessels[91] and the Occupying Power confiscating state property in occupied territory which may be used for military operations.[92] The belligerent also remains at liberty to disable eligible enemy combatants, deliberately inflict terror amongst them or starve them as a method of combat. As regards these acts, LOAC's framers have elected to grant permissions of military necessity unfettered precedence over contrary demands of humanity. It in no way matters whether, at a given moment, availing oneself of the former permission is militarily necessary or unnecessary; nor does it matter whether contrary action happens to be humane or inhumane. Acting as demanded by humanity, and thereby acting in joint satisfaction, is now entirely optional.

As for the law's *failure*, one may look to the ICJ's agnosticism regarding the lawfulness or otherwise of nuclear weapons in certain circumstances;[93] and the ICRC's concession that it is unclear whether customary LOAC prohibits belligerent reprisals against civilians during hostilities.[94] Similarly, no LOAC rule appears to obligate civilians taking a direct part in hostilities, continuously or otherwise, to distinguish themselves from those taking no such part.[95]

Is there a generally liberal or prohibitive presumption for conduct not specifically regulated by positive LOAC? A conservative reading of the Martens Clause would hold that it merely safeguards the continued application of customary LOAC rules.[96] Read more progressively, the Clause would represent a framework through which LOAC rules are to be interpreted.[97] As seen below, while indifferent considerations such as military necessity do not create additional layers of normative significance, affirmative considerations may.

Norm contradiction also occurs between permissions of military necessity and demands of chivalry. It has led to the adoption, *inter alia*, of LOAC rules prohibiting improper use of enemy uniforms,[98] direct participation in hostilities by paroled or repatriated POWs and by those sick, wounded or shipwrecked who have been returned[99] and treachery.[100] The military necessity–chivalry interplay also underlies LOAC rules authorising the detention and search of *parlementaires*,[101] and the absence of prohibition against espionage per se.[102]

---

90 HR art 5; GCIII art 21.

91 GCII art 31.

92 HR art 53.

93 *Nuclear Weapons* (n 31) ¶ 97.

94 Henckaerts and Doswald-Beck (n 86) 520–523. See also UK *Manual* (n 1) 420–421; Jean-François Quéguiner, 'The Principle of Distinction: Beyond an Obligation of Customary International Humanitarian Law' in Hensel (ed) (n 13) 161, 174–175; Schmitt, 'Military Necessity' (n 1) 820–822.

95 Nobuo Hayashi, 'Continuous Attack Liability without Right or Fact of Direct Participation in Hostilities: *The ICRC Interpretive Guidance* and Perils of a Pseudo-Status' in Joanna Nowakowska-Małusecka (ed), *International Humanitarian Law: Antecedents and Challenges of the Present Time* (Branta 2010) 56, 75–76.

96 Theodor Meron, 'The Martens Clause, Principles of Humanity, and Dictates of Public Conscience (2000) 94 *AJIL* 78, 87–88; Dinstein, 'Proportionality' (n 31) 72–73.

97 *Prosecutor v Kupreškić* (Case no IT-95-16-T, Trial Chamber, 14 January 2000) ¶¶ 525–527; Antonio Cassese, 'The Martens Clause: Half a Loaf or simply Pie in the Sky?' (2000) 11 *EJIL* 187.

98 HR art 23(f); API art 39(2). See also Bordwell (n 16) 283.

99 HR arts 10, 12; Lassa Oppenheim, *International Law: A Treatise* (Ronald F Roxburgh ed, 3rd edn, Longmans 1921) 192; GCII art 16.

100 HR art 23(b); Rome Statute arts 8(2)(b)(xi), 8(2)(e)(ix).

101 HR arts 33, 34.

102 Ibid art 24; Oppenheim (n 99) 222–223; Dinstein, *Conduct of Hostilities* (n 16) 241; HPCR, *Manual on International Law Applicable to Air and Missile Warfare* (Harvard University 2009) ¶ 119.

2.3 Norm conflict

Two norms conflict with each other where one obligates its addressee to perform a given act and the other prohibits the same act. The logical impossibility of joint obedience to which two conflicting norms give rise does not preclude the logical possibility of their valid co-existence. Conflicting norms may validly co-exist, even within one legal system.[103] It would nevertheless be a functional shortcoming of a legal system if it contained valid yet conflicting norms.[104]

Similarly, it would be seriously detrimental to LOAC's functionality if two conflicting sets of reason-giving considerations involved in its norm-creation led to the adoption of conflicting rules. The law endeavours to avoid them by letting one set trump the other or by devising a compromise between them. Indifferent considerations, such as military necessity, do not obligate conduct and therefore do not become involved in norm conflicts. At stake here are those considerations that are *not* indifferent. For instance, one set of humanitarian considerations demands that the Detaining Power not medically intervene with a POW, whereas another set of humanitarian considerations arguably demands such intervention in certain circumstances. Article 13 of Geneva Convention III embodies a compromise struck between them. The same may be said *mutatis mutandis* of Article 78(1) of Additional Protocol I. This article principally prohibits evacuations of children to a foreign country yet arguably obligates their temporary evacuations where 'compelling reasons of the health or medical treatment of the children or, except in occupied territory, their safety, so require'.

3 Consequences of considerations interplay

To what consequences does the interplay between reason-giving considerations in the process of LOAC norm-creation give rise? In particular, do these considerations operate as lawfulness criteria in addition to positive LOAC?

As noted earlier, unqualified LOAC rules extinguish all contrary liberties permitted or tolerated by indifferent considerations. The latter considerations have thus been 'accounted for' and, consequently, do not modify an act's lawfulness or otherwise established by the former rules. It is arguable, however, that the same may not be said so readily of conflicting demands and condemnations.

3.1 Military necessity – Kriegsräson and counter-Kriegsräson

Kriegsräson asserts that, although LOAC does account for military necessity, it cannot be construed so that the belligerent is denied the option to do what it needs to succeed. Where rules are formulated without an express military necessity exception, it merely means that military necessity and the law are considered *generally* in agreement over the normative content of these rules. Whenever there *is* a collision, the former prevails over the latter.

Kriegsräson is unacceptable because it purports to justify all militarily necessary conduct even where it is already unqualifiedly outlawed in positive LOAC. Rejecting *Kriegsräson* amounts to rejecting the idea that military necessity somehow 'rights' or 'repairs' the unlawfulness of such

---

103 Georg Henrik von Wright, 'Value, Norm, and Action in My Philosophical Writings' in Georg Meggle (ed), *Actions, Norms and Values: Discussions with Georg Henrik von Wright* (de Gruyter 1999) 11, 21; Ota Weinberger, 'Logical Analysis in the Realm of Law' in ibid 300; H L A Hart, 'Kelsen's Doctrine of the Unity of Law' in H L A Hart, *Essays in Jurisprudence and Philosophy* (OUP 1983) 309, 325.

104 Hart, 'Kelsen's Doctrine' (n 103) 325–326.

conduct. Variations of the same theme, for example self-preservation,[105] self-defence[106] and impracticality,[107] are to be rejected for the same reason.

Counter-*Kriegsräson* is perhaps most forcefully stated in the following passage:

> [A] direct attack against an otherwise legitimate military target constitutes a [LOAC] violation … if that attack is not required for the submission of the enemy with a minimum expenditure of time, life and physical resources … [T]he fact that [LOAC] does not prohibit direct attacks against combatants does not give rise to a legal entitlement to kill combatants at any time and any place so long as they are not *hors de combat* within the meaning of Article 41(2) AP I. Strictly speaking, although the absence of such a prohibition is undisputedly intentional, it constitutes no more than a strong presumption that, in a situation of armed conflict, it will generally be militarily necessary to kill, injure, or capture combatants of the opposing armed forces in order to bring about the submission of the adversary with a minimum expenditure of time, life and physical resources. It does not permit the senseless slaughter of combatants where there manifestly is no military necessity to do so, for example where a group of defenceless soldiers has not had the time to surrender, but could clearly be captured *without additional risk to the operating forces*.[108]

On this view, the mere fact that LOAC accounts for military necessity does not leave the belligerent at liberty to do what is, in fact, militarily unnecessary. Where LOAC rules are unqualifiedly formulated, it simply means that whatever these rules authorise is deemed generally militarily necessary – 'no more than a strong presumption', in other words. Where there is a collision between conduct being militarily unnecessary, on the one hand, and it being otherwise lawful according to positive LOAC, on the other, the former 'wrongs' or 'vitiates' the latter. Where the military necessity for particular belligerent conduct does not exist or ceases to exist, the law, all things considered, prohibits it.

Counter-*Kriegsräson* is predicated on two perceptions of military necessity *qua* reason-giving considerations in LOAC norm-creation. First, some aspects of military necessity survive the process and act as a residual lawfulness modifier. Put differently, LOAC does *not* fully account for military

---

105 Stone (n 81) 352–353. But see N C H Dunbar, 'Military Necessity in War Crimes Trials' (1952) 29 *BYBIL* 442, 443; Schwarzenberger (n 15) 136; Walzer, *Just and Unjust Wars* (n 32) 305; Marshall Cohen, 'Morality and the Laws of War' in Held *et al* (eds) (n 74) 71, 76–78; Dinstein, 'Military Necessity' (2010) (n 45) ¶¶ 10–11.

106 *Nuclear Weapons* (n 31) 262–263. But see ibid 590 (Judge Higgins, dissenting), 513–520 (Judge Weeramantry, dissenting); Luigi Condorelli, 'Le Droit International Humanitaire, ou l'Exploration par la Cour d'une Terra à Peu Près Incognita pour Elle' in Laurence Boisson de Chazournes and Philippe Sands (eds), *International Law, the International Court of Justice and Nuclear Weapons* (CUP 1999) 229, 244–245; Christopher Greenwood, 'Jus in bellum and Jus in bello in the Nuclear Weapons Advisory Opinion' in ibid 247, 264; Judith Gardam, 'Necessity and Proportionality in Jus ad Bellum and Jus in Bello' in ibid 275, 292; Marcelo G Kohen, 'The Notion of "State Survival" in International Law' in ibid 293, 310; Nishimura Hayashi (n 13) 143–144; Dinstein, *Conduct of Hostilities* (n 16) 85–86; Solis (n 1) 269; Greenwood, 'Historical Development' (n 1) 36–37.

107 Hilaire McCoubrey, 'The Nature of the Modern Doctrine of Military Necessity' (1991) 30 *RDMDG* 215, 237.

108 Melzer, *Targeted Killing* (n 1) 287–288 (emphasis in original; footnotes omitted).

necessity. Second, those aspects that remain unaccounted for are *not* indifferent. As seen above, these perceptions are both erroneous. Counter-*Kriegsräson* remains unconvincing.[109]

3.2 Humanity – Humanitätsräson *and counter-*Humanitätsräson?

It stands to reason that pleas arising *de novo* from indifferent considerations of humanity are inadmissible. Holding otherwise would amount to accepting the idea that, like *Kriegsräson*, acting as permitted yet not demanded by humanity somehow 'repairs' or 'rights' the act's unlawfulness. In other words, a strictly indifferent *Humanitätsräson* is untenable. Nor, for that matter, is a strictly indifferent counter-*Humanitätsräson*: the belligerent's failure to do what is permitted by humanity would not render that failure unlawful if it otherwise remains lawful in positive LOAC.

Humanity's demands and condemnations are perhaps more complex. These aspects may in fact survive the process through which LOAC validly posits its rules. It is possible that a LOAC rule unqualifiedly obligating or prohibiting given conduct does not resolve such genuine norm conflicts as may exist with contrary humanitarian demands.[110] Article 118 of Geneva Convention III stipulates that '[p]risoners of war shall be released and repatriated without delay after the cessation of active hostilities'.[111] That this provision creates an unqualified obligation finds support in its drafting history[112] as well as some scholarly writings.[113] A situation may arise where a Detaining Power finds itself torn between Article 118 and a humanitarian demand of non-repatriation. This dilemma arose in the aftermath of the Korean War,[114] the Iran–Iraq War[115] and the Gulf War.[116]

Has Article 118's adoption compulsorily resolved the norm conflict by letting the duty of repatriation trump the conflicting humanitarian demand that may arise in specific cases? Neither *lex specialis*[117] nor *jus cogens*[118] offers a satisfactory alternative here, as it is unqualified LOAC rules

---

109 Dapo Akande, 'Clearing the Fog of War? The ICRC's Interpretive Guidance on Direct Participation in Hostilities' (2010) 59 *ICLQ* 180, 192; Schmitt, 'Military Necessity' (n 1) 835; Michael N Schmitt, 'The Interpretive Guidance on the Notion of Direct Participation in Hostilities: A Critical Analysis' (2010) 1 *Harvard NSJ* 5, 41, 43.

110 In truth, genuine norm conflicts are by no means unique LOAC. On the contrary, they are a fact of life generally. The specific manner in which solutions are found for the norms' addressees varies from one body of positive law to another.

111 GCIII art 118.

112 Final Record of the Diplomatic Conference of Geneva of 1949, vol 2-A, 324, 462; *GCIII Commentary* 542–543.

113 Horst Fischer, 'Protection of Prisoners of War' in Fleck (ed) (n 1) 367, 416.

114 *GCIII Commentary* 543–546.

115 John Quigley, 'Iran and Iraq and the Obligations to Release and Repatriate Prisoners of War after the Close of Hostilities' (1989–1990) 5 *American University JILP* 73, 81–83.

116 Peter Rowe, 'Prisoners of War in the Gulf Area' in Peter Rowe (ed), *The Gulf War 1990-91 in International and English Law* (Routledge 1993) 203, citing *The Times* (5 March 1991) and ICRC *Bulletin*, no 184 (May 1991); ICRC, *Annual Report 1991* (ICRC 1991) 101, 102. It is now UK policy that 'prisoners of war should not be repatriated against their will'. See UK *Manual* (n 1) 205.

117 Repatriating or not repatriating POWs after the cessation of hostilities is possibly one area where international human rights law and international refugee law prohibiting repatriation in certain situations would function as the *lex specialis* relative to LOAC obligating repatriation in all situations.

118 For a discussion as to whether *non-refoulement* has attained *jus cogens* status, see Walter Kälin, Martina Caroni and Lukas Heim, 'Article 33, para. 1, 1951 Convention' in Andreas Zimmermann (ed), *The 1951 Convention Relating to the Status of Refugees and its 1967 Protocol: A Commentary* (OUP 2011) 1327, 1347–1348.

themselves that supposedly account for military necessity and humanity, and it is this fact that supposedly renders military necessity and humanity pleas inadmissible *de novo*.[119] Nor does the argument that the subsequent custom has modified Article 118, with the result that the provision now has an implicit exceptional humanity clause, remedy the difficulty. This remedy would not have been available to those during the Korean War grappling with the norm conflict created when Article 118 was validly posited in 1949.

An affirmative *Humanitätsräson* offers an arguably more cogent explanation. The mere fact that Article 118 unqualifiedly obligates post-hostilities POW repatriation has not resolved the norm conflict. It is not clear whether, all things considered, the *unqualifiedness* of the prescriptions contained in Article 118 vis-à-vis conflicting humanitarian demands was, in 1949, or has since been, conclusive for LOAC. The idea that the latter demands may have survived the process of LOAC norm-creation accommodates the possibility that humanitarian pleas *de novo* in support of non-repatriation are not inadmissible vis-à-vis Article 118.

Nor, for that matter, is an affirmative counter-*Humanitätsräson* inconceivable. A LOAC rule may decline or fail to obligate what humanity demands or, in any event, unqualifiedly obligate less than what humanity demands.[120] Where this occurs, acting in accordance with humanitarian demands entails pursuing, and exceeding, the joint satisfaction envisaged in the rule. If it were agreed that humanity demands 'capture rather than kill,' and if it were true that the process of LOAC norm-creation through which the lawfulness of 'killing rather than capturing' has come to be validly secured does not fully account for such demands, *then* it might be argued that killing rather than capturing is, all things considered, unlawful under LOAC.[121]

3.3 Chivalry – Ritterlichkeitsräson *and* counter-Ritterlichkeitsräson?

For the same reasons, both an indifferent *Ritterlichkeitsräson* and an indifferent counter-*Ritterlichkeitsräson* are safely rejected. What may not are their affirmative variations, and especially an affirmative counter-*Ritterlichkeitsräson*.[122]

4 Conclusion

The precise content of military necessity, humanity, chivalry and the like will continue to stir debate. This chapter nevertheless shows that their functions relative to LOAC can be illuminated. The normative characteristics of these notions shape the dynamics of their interplay in the context of LOAC norm-creation, as well as the consequences of such interplay vis-à-vis positive

119 Yoram Dinstein, 'Military Necessity' (1982) 3 *MPEPIL* 274, 274; Dinstein, *Conduct of Hostilities* (2004) (n 43) 18–19; Dinstein, *Conduct of Hostilities* (2010) (n 16) 6–7; Dinstein, 'Military Necessity' (2010) (n 45) ¶ 7; Schmitt, 'Military Necessity' (n 1) 805.
120 There is a standing 'invitation to exceed that minimum' established in common art 3. See *GCI Commentary* 52.
121 Jeff McMahan, 'The Morality of War and the Law of War' in David Rodin and Henry Shue (eds), *Just and Unjust Warriors: The Moral and Legal Studies of Soldiers* (OUP 2008) 19, 37; ICRC, *Interpretive Guidance on the Notion of Direct Participation in Hostilities under International Humanitarian Law* (ICRC 2009) 82; Nils Melzer, 'The ICRC's Clarification Process on the Notion of Direct Participation in Hostilities under International Humanitarian Law' in Christian Tomuschat, Evelyne Lagrange and Stefan Oeter (eds), *The Right to Life* (Nijhoff 2010) 151, 162.
122 Rain Liivoja, 'Law and Honour: Normative Pluralism in the Regulation of Military Conduct' in Jan Klabbers and Touko Piiparinen (eds), *Normative Pluralism and International Law: Exploring Global Governance* (CUP 2013) 143.

LOAC. The fact that military necessity is always indifferent not only confirms the fallacy of *Kriegsräson* but also invalidates the idea that belligerent conduct consistent with positive LOAC becomes unlawful by virtue of its lack of military necessity alone. In contrast, affirmative aspects of humanity and chivalry may survive the process of LOAC norm-creation and operate as additional layers of lawfulness determination over positive LOAC. In view of its potentially far-reaching ramifications, the latter idea requires further careful scrutiny.

6

Impact of human rights law

Noam Lubell and Nancie Prud'homme

The question of whether human rights law impacts upon the regulation of armed conflict became a vital issue to address following the adoption of the Charter of the United Nations in 1945. The Charter identified human rights as one of the four founding purposes of the United Nations[1] and included provisions upon which a universal system for the protection of human rights could be built.[2] The Charter thereby affirmed that human rights were no longer part of the exclusive jurisdiction of each member of the United Nations but a subject of international concern and a branch of public international law.

The establishment of human rights law as an international legal framework raised the question of its application during armed conflict and its relation to the law of armed conflict. At first, strict separation and compartmentalisation of the law of armed conflict (LOAC) and international human rights law (IHRL) was advocated. For instance, the late Professor Colonel Draper, leading scholar and LOAC expert writing on the relationship between human rights and LOAC noted that '[t]he attempt to confuse the two regimes of law is unsupportable in theory and inadequate in practice. The two regimes are not only distinct but are diametrically opposed.'[3] The reasons for advocating such separation were rooted at many different levels. Notably, the two fields became part of public international law at different times, initially developed independently of one another and were seemingly divergent in their objectives, scope of application, norms, implementing mechanisms and the environments in which they apply.[4] These arguments were used to sustain that human

---

1 UN Charter art 1(3).
2 Ibid art 55(c). For more details on this provision see Rüdiger Wolfrum and Eibe Riedel, 'Article 55 (c)' in Bruno Simma *et al.* (eds), *The Charter of the United Nations: A Commentary* (3rd edn, OUP 2012) vol II, 1565.
3 G I A D Draper, 'Humanitarian Law and Human Rights' (1979) *Acta Juridica* 199, reprinted in M A Meyer and H McCoubrey (eds), *Reflections on Law and Armed Conflicts: The Selected Works on the Laws of War by the Late Professor Colonel G I A D Draper, OBE* (Kluwer, The Hague 1998) 149.
4 See generally on the early development of international humanitarian law and international human rights law Jean Pictet, *Development and Principles of International Humanitarian Law* (Martinus Nijhoff 1985) 5–25; David Levinson (ed), *The Wilson Chronology of Human Rights* (Wilson 2003) 1–19; Paul Gordon Lauren, *The Evolution of International Human Rights* (2nd edn, University of Pennsylvania Press 2003) 1–36; Rene van der Wolf and Willem-Jan van der Wolf (eds), *Laws of War and International Law* (Wolf 2002) vol 1, 9–18.

rights and LOAC are two distinct branches of international law that should be kept apart in two tight compartments and not interact.[5]

Over time, and especially from the 1960s and holding of the Tehran Conference,[6] the separatist approach to international human rights law and LOAC was rejected; it appeared no longer desirable or feasible to consider the legal frameworks as completely foreign to one another. The Tehran Conference discussed at length the application of human rights in times of armed conflict and became a decisive event for the relationship between international human rights law and LOAC. In its proclamation it linked the existence of armed conflicts with human rights violations, highlighted the impact of conflicts on human rights and called upon the international community to react to those situations. At the institutional level during these times, the United Nations and the International Committee of the Red Cross started to show interest in exploring and developing the interplay between the two legal frameworks.

While marked differences exist in the scope of application of international human rights law and LOAC, it remains that the disciplines are both applicable in situations of armed conflict. As international humanitarian and human rights norms and bodies developed, and the occurrence of non-international armed conflict increased, the impact of each field on the other became clearer. Their relationship and need for linking them has been acknowledged for decades now. Most experts agree that the disciplines cannot be totally dissociated from one another and there is a desire to see productive interaction between the two fields of international law.

The interaction between international human rights law and LOAC has great practical importance both at the protection and the implementation levels. For example, the applicability of human rights law might affect how and when armed forces resort to lethal force in specific circumstances. Likewise, how the interplay between the disciplines is construed can affect the legal protection and guarantees given to individuals detained during a conflict. The interpretation of the interplay between the disciplines can further determine whether a given state will or will not be found responsible for human rights violations occurring in the context of fighting and on the means of redress that will be available to alleged victims.

The existence of these two potentially applicable legal frameworks in a situation of armed conflict creates concurrent and sometimes competing protections and obligations. Legal uncertainties in such contexts rarely ensure protection of individuals and can lead to interpretation of the law that risks being impractical on the ground. The discussion has now moved beyond whether human rights law impacts upon the law of armed conflict, or if the two disciplines interact. The existence of a relationship between international human rights law and LOAC is now widely accepted. Their concurrent application is at present more or less a fait accompli but there remain debates on the nature of their interaction.

This chapter examines four central issues that need to be addressed to assess the impact of human rights law on the law of armed conflict and vice versa. It discusses the applicability and extraterritorial applicability of human rights law during armed conflict. It highlights certain areas where human rights law and the law of armed conflict can influence each other. It examines how the interplay between the disciplines has been articulated, and provides suggestions on how

---

5 See Michel-Cyr Djiena Wembou and Daouda Fall, *Le Droit International Humanitaire: Théories et Réalités Africaines* (L'Harmattan 2000) 66–67; Hector Gros Espiell, 'Human Rights: Concept and Standards' in Janusz Symonides (ed), *Humanitarian Law and Human Rights* (Ashgate 2000) 345, 352; Raúl Emilio Vinuesa, 'Interface, Correspondence and Convergence of Human Rights and International Humanitarian Law' (1998) 1 *YBIHL* 70; Dietrich Schindler, 'The International Committee of the Red Cross and Human Rights' (1979) 208 *IRRC* 3; Draper (n 3) 145.
6 'Proclamation of Tehran' Final Act, International Conference on Human Rights, Tehran, 22 April to 13 May 1968, UN Doc A/CONF 32/41 (1968), preamble.

to move forward to clarify the interplay and develop tools to better articulate the interaction between the disciplines.

1 Continued applicability during armed conflict and extraterritorial applicability of human rights law

The debate over the applicability of international human rights law during armed conflict often conflates two issues that require separate attention: that of continued applicability of human rights law once the applicability of LOAC has been triggered by an armed conflict; and the separate matter of whether human rights obligations can apply to extraterritorial conduct. The distinction between these issues is apparent when considering the fact that the continued applicability concern will arise in non-international armed conflicts of a type that occur within the territory of the state, thus requiring an answer only to the first question. Likewise, concerns over the applicability of human rights obligations extraterritorially is a matter that is not confined to wartime, and can arise outside situations of armed conflict.

The fact that international human rights law remains applicable even after an armed conflict has triggered the applicability of LOAC, is now firmly established and cannot be reasonably contested. It has been affirmed repeatedly and in no uncertain terms by the ICJ in a combination of case law and advisory opinions.[7] The treaty sources themselves also demonstrate that human rights do not dissipate into thin air once a conflict breaks out. Recalling that at the heart of the concept of human rights is the preservation of human dignity and protection from abuse of power, it is no surprise that human rights remain of utmost concern during times of war. Notably, when human rights treaties mention states of emergency, including war, they allow for certain limitations on rights through the derogation mechanism, but keep a significant portion of human rights obligations as binding even in such times, and thus designed to apply in periods of armed conflict.[8] Indeed, international human rights monitoring bodies have continued to hold states to their human rights obligations in cases covering circumstances in which LOAC was also applicable.[9] The continued applicability of human rights law is therefore grounded in its legal origin, and confirmed by international bodies. But one should not confuse *whether it applies*, with the question of *how it is implemented*. In other words, criticism of applying human rights obligations to circumstances of armed conflict are misplaced if they challenge the very applicability of international human rights law, but this does not relieve the need to further examine the precise modalities of application. Derogation from certain aspects of specific obligations, as mentioned above, is perhaps the most obvious manner in which the actual application of human rights might differ during a conflict. The question of how human rights obligations – while remaining applicable – might be interpreted and applied in a contextual approach that takes the armed conflict into account, will be returned to in greater detail in a later section.

---

7 *Legality of the Threat or Use of Nuclear Weapons (Advisory Opinion)* [1996] ICJ Rep 226, ¶ 25; *Legal Consequences of the Construction of a Wall in the Occupied Palestinian Territory (Advisory Opinion)* [2004] ICJ Rep 136, ¶ 106; *Armed Activities on the Territory of the Congo (Democratic Republic of the Congo v Uganda)* [2005] ICJ Rep 168, ¶ 216.

8 ICCPR art 4, ECHR art 15, ACHR art 27.

9 *Abella v Argentina* (Case no 11.137, Report no 55/97, IACmHR, 18 November 1997); HRC, 'General Comment 29: States of Emergency (Article 4)' UN Doc CCPR/C/21/Rev.1/Add.11 (31 August 2001) ¶ 3; Committee on Economic, Social and Cultural Rights, 'Concluding Observation: Israel' UN Doc E/C.12/1/Add.69 (31 August 2001); *Al-Skeini and Others v UK* (App no 55721/07, ECtHR GC, 7 July 2011).

With the general question of continued applicability answered, the separate matter of extra-territorial applicability must now be examined. When faced with an internal armed conflict, as are a weighty proportion of all armed conflicts in recent decades, the applicability of inter-national human rights law cannot be questioned on these grounds. The picture, however, changes once we examine the conduct of states occurring beyond their borders. As a side note, it should be mentioned that in most cases this will arise in the context of international armed conflicts, but the question is equally relevant to non-international armed conflicts which include extraterritorial elements (for example, cross-border operations against members of armed groups).[10] In addition, it must be stressed that this is a question that requires settling within the realm of analysis of human rights law itself, and is separate from the question of interplay with LOAC. This is because extraterritorial applicability of human rights obligations is an issue that covers a wider scope than conflict operations.[11] It must therefore be addressed independently; if it transpires that human rights obligations do apply to extraterritorial conduct, we then must return to the separate existing question of the interplay between the two bodies of law and how the obligations must be interpreted in practice.

Two primary challenges present themselves as potential obstacles to extraterritorial human rights obligations: a legal and textual argument attempting to demonstrate that the international human rights treaties were designed to only apply within a state's borders; and a claim that any expectation of extraterritorial obligations fails the test of practicability and cannot be realistically managed when it comes to implementation.[12] The treaty-based arguments rest on the fact that human rights treaties tend to speak of obligations owed to individuals subject to the jurisdiction of the state, thus seemingly excluding individuals outside its territory.[13] Moreover, the Inter-national Covenant on Civil and Political Rights (ICCPR) goes further than just mentioning jurisdiction, and speaks specifically of individuals 'within its territory and subject to its jurisdiction'.[14] Nevertheless, as strong as these arguments might seem at first glance, a detailed examination demonstrates that they do not prevent the applicability of extraterritorial human rights obligations.

First, as to the ICCPR, an examination of the drafting process reveals that the inclusion of the reference to territory was designed to prevent the possibility that an individual living abroad would be able to bring a human rights claim against their state of nationality in a matter over which it had no control.[15] This has a clear logic when applied to such circumstances. The same logic is, however, completely misplaced when applied to circumstances in which it is the state itself which crosses borders and takes direct action which impinges upon an individual's rights. The drafting process therefore reveals that the reference to territory was not intended to exclude the latter circumstances. As for the reference to jurisdiction, the analysis is more complex, but

10 There are many examples in which states take cross-border military action against armed groups, including: Israel vs Hezbollah in Lebanon, Turkey vs PKK in Iraq, US vs Al-Qaida in Afghanistan, Colombia vs FARC in Ecuador, and a host of cross-border operations by DRC's neighbours into its territory. For an analysis of how to classify such situations, see Elizabeth Wilmshurst (ed), *International Law and the Classification of Conflicts* (OUP 2012).

11 For an analysis of extraterritorial human rights obligations, see Noam Lubell, *Extraterritorial Use of Force against Non-State Actors* (OUP 2010) ch 8; see also Marko Milanovic, *Extraterritorial Application of Human Rights Treaties: Law, Principles, and Policy* (OUP 2011).

12 Michael J Dennis, 'Non-Application of Civil and Political Rights Extraterritorially during Times of International Armed Conflict' (2007) 40 *Israel LR* 453.

13 ACHR art 1; AmCHR art 1; ICCPR art 2.

14 Ibid.

15 Commission on Human Rights, 'Summary Record of the Hundred and Ninety-Fourth Meeting' UN Doc E/CN.4/SR.194 (1950) ¶¶ 15–16.

ultimately arrives at a similar conclusion.[16] Interpretations of jurisdiction generally tend to point to the authority of a state to take a certain action such as legislating or enforcing legislation.[17] Perceived in this manner, being within the jurisdiction of a state would mean being in a situation in which the state has the authority to pass laws or enforce the law in a way that impacts upon the individual. But this notion of jurisdiction fails to meet the objective of protection that human rights law is destined to provide. Consider its application in circumstances in which State A sends its agents on a covert mission into the territory of State B, to illegally abduct an individual, and that following the abduction, these state agents torture and summarily execute the individual, all while remaining in State B. State A did not have the required jurisdictional authority to engage in such acts. If the human rights obligations were dependent on an interpretation of jurisdictional authority, it would mean that by virtue of acting without authority a state would be exempt from accountability for its action. Illegality of the act would provide the perpetrator with impunity for its consequences. This clearly goes against the very object and purpose of the human rights treaties, and cannot be the correct interpretation. Instead, the notion of jurisdiction in human rights treaties must be understood in the context of their obligations, and indeed has been done so by a number of human rights bodies. The approach of these bodies has been to find that by virtue of the circumstances of the case or the act in question, a state might bring the individual within its jurisdiction for the purposes of human rights obligations.[18]

There are a number of circumstances which can be used to demonstrate this approach, many of them particularly pertinent to situations of armed conflict. The first of these is situations of military occupation. In these circumstances, despite acting extraterritorially and not being the sovereign power, the occupying state is considered to be bound by international human rights law in its dealing with the population of the occupied territory.[19] In many ways, this is the easiest of the examples, since the very fact of being an occupying power means that the state has been found through LOAC to have an element of control and authority, and having displaced the regular authorities it is natural that the rights of the population are found to rest in its hands. This has been affirmed in numerous cases, and is considered to fulfil what is sometimes referred to as the test of control over territory. In such situations the state is considered to be responsible for the whole spectrum of potentially applicable (depending, for example, on the treaties in force) human rights obligations.[20]

---

16 See analysis in Lubell, *Extraterritorial Use of Force* (n 11) 207–213.

17 Martin Dixon and Robert McCorquodale, *Cases and Materials on International Law* (OUP 2003) 268; 'In its broadest sense, the jurisdiction of a State may refer to its lawful power to act and hence to its power to decide whether and, if so, how to act': Bernard Oxman, 'Jurisdiction of States' in *Encyclopedia of Public International Law* (Elsevier 1997) vol III, 55, 55.

18 For examples, see *Cyprus v Turkey* (App no 6780/74 and No 6950/75, ECtHR, 26 May 1975) ¶ 8; *X v UK* (App no 7547/76, ECtHR, 15 December 1977); *Alejandre et al v Cuba* ('*Brothers to the Rescue*') (Case no 11.589, Report no 86/99, IACmHR, 29 September 1999) ¶ 23; *Coard et al v US* (Case no 10.951, Report no 109/99, IACmHR, 29 September 1999) ¶ 37; *Issa and Others v Turkey* (App no 31821/96, ECtHR, 16 November 2004) ¶ 72.

19 *Wall* (n 7) ¶¶ 107–112; *DRC v Uganda* (n 7) ¶¶ 216–220; HRC, 'Concluding Observations: Israel' UN Doc CCPR/C/79/Add.93 (18 August 1998); CESCR, 'Concluding Observations: Israel' UN Doc E/C.12/1/Add.69 (31 August 2001); Walter Kälin, 'Report on the Situation of Human Rights in Kuwait under Iraqi Occupation' UN Doc E/CN.4/1992/26 (15 January 1992) ¶¶ 55–59; *Loizidou v Turkey (Preliminary Objections)* (App no 15318/89, ECtHR, 23 March 1995) ¶¶ 62–64; *Cyprus v Turkey* (App no 25781/94, ECtHR, 10 May 2001) ¶ 77.

20 *Al-Skeini and Others v UK* (n 9) ¶ 138.

Matters get more complicated absent control over a large territorial area, but human rights obligations can still remain applicable. For example, if a state has control over a detention facility, it will be bound by human rights law in relation to the detainees therein. This too is emerging as relatively hard to argue against.[21] As a brief reminder, it must be stressed at this stage that one cannot adequately respond to these arguments by asserting that LOAC will have the answer even if human rights law does not apply, since a number of extraterritorial scenarios can and have occurred also in situations outside armed conflict and in which LOAC is not there to provide an alternative.[22] We therefore need an independent answer as to the applicability of human rights law. The interplay with LOAC, if it applies, is a question to be answered at the next stage.

Clarity and agreement begin to fade when we turn to circumstances where there is no control over territory or even a single facility, and in which we speak of control over an individual or aspects of the individual's life. It is however submitted here that both logic and case law support a limited extension of human rights obligations to such situations. The applicability of human rights obligations in the above mentioned occupation and detention scenarios did not depend on consent of the territorial state, but on the control exerted over the population under the acting state's thumb. What if the detention facility was not a formal prison, but a makeshift detention camp, or simply state agents who are holding abducted individuals in a secret location? As far as the power relationship between the state and the individuals is concerned, the scenario is the same, and human rights obligations must apply.[23] Likewise the same logic is clear even if there is no lengthy detention, but a short operation in which state agents grab hold of an individual and kill him/her.[24] Until this point, it is probably not hard to convince that some elements of human rights obligations (for example, the right to life) should apply. But what if the state agents do not physically grab hold of the individual, and instead shoot him/her from ten feet away? Excluding this from the purview of human rights obligations, would simply create an incentive to shoot and kill, rather than detain.[25] This, however, raises the question of how far it can be stretched – should it apply not just to shooting an individual from a few feet away, but also to bombing from a distance, or a targeted missile strike launched from an

---

21 *Hess v UK (Admissibility)* (App no 6231/73, ECmHR Plenary, 28 May 1975) (1975) 2 D&R 72; *Coard v US* (n 18) ¶ 37; *Request for Precautionary Measures Concerning the Detainees at Guantanamo Bay, Cuba* (IACHR, 12 March 2002) 41 ILM (2002) 532; *Al-Skeini et al v Secretary of State for Defence* [2004] EWHC 2911, ¶¶ 286–288; *Al-Skeini and others v Secretary of State for Defence* [2007] UKHL 26, ¶ 106; *Al-Saadoon and Mufdhi v UK* (App no 61498/08, ECtHR, 30 June 2009) ¶¶ 86–89.

22 *Hess v UK* (n 21).

23 *Lopez Bourgos v Uruguay* (Comm no 52/1979, HRC, 29 July 1981), UN Doc CCPR/C/OP/1 (1984) 88; *Celiberti de Casariego v Uruguay* (Comm no 56/1979, HRC, 29 July 1981), UN Doc CCPR/C/OP/1 (1984) 92.

24 *Issa and Others v Turkey* (App no 31821/96, ECtHR, 16 November 2004) ¶¶ 71–72.

25 See Lubell, *Extraterritorial Use of Force* (n 11) 220–227; and especially the discussion of killing from a distance in Martin Scheinin, 'Extraterritorial Effect of the International Covenant on Civil and Political Rights' in Fons Coomans and Menno T Kamminga (eds), *Extraterritorial Application of Human Rights Treaties* (Intersentia 2004) 73, 77–78;

   Attempts by the respondent governments in *Bankovic* to distinguish *Issa* rested on the at best tenuous argument that the victims were technically in the custody of Turkish forces and therefore within Turkish 'jurisdiction' – simply shooting suspects is apparently immune from scrutiny, so long as you are careful not to arrest them first!
   Hurst Hannum, 'Remarks, Bombing for Peace: Collateral Damage and Human Rights' (2002) 96 *ASIL Proceedings* 95, 98.

unmanned aerial vehicle? These are questions that are still the matter of debate.[26] The position taken here is that the object and purpose of international human rights law, the majority of case law by human rights bodies and the logical conclusion of the above arguments, is that human rights law obligations can apply in such circumstances. However, two important caveats must be introduced: first, that unless we are in circumstances in which the state has control and authority over the territory – in which case it is bound by all applicable human rights treaties – then the applicable obligations will only be those which the state has the power to control directly. In other words, when state agents point a sniper rifle at the head of an individual, they certainly have control over the person's right to life, but one would not expect a claim over the right to trade union membership to be particularly pertinent to the case.[27] Second – and vital in the context of the current examination – while the above establishes the applicability of a human rights obligation, it still remains to be determined how this obligation must be interpreted in practice if the situation is one in which LOAC also applies.

To conclude this section, in both the matter of continued applicability of human rights law during conflict, and in the question of extraterritorial applicability of such obligations, it is therefore imperative to understand the difference between the question of whether human rights obligations *can* apply, as opposed to the modality of *how* they might apply. In most cases some form of human rights obligations will be applicable, but the circumstances and context can have profound implications on how these obligations must be implemented in practice. The following sections will demonstrate how the joint applicability of human rights and LOAC impact upon the interpretations of both bodies of law, and suggest possibilities for a practical approach to their implementation.

2 Areas of direct influence

The cross-over areas between LOAC and international human rights law are endless, and the manifestation of the human rights impact on LOAC takes many forms. This section will illustrate a number of select issues in which the interaction demonstrates the potential for positive engagement between the bodies of law, even if at times challenging. One of the most obvious areas to begin with is the regulation of detention and trial. Both bodies of law have numerous rules in this sphere and the applicability of human rights obligations in relation to detention is amongst the least controversial, as far as the earlier discussion on challenges to applicability. Moreover, human rights law might allow for forms of administrative/security detention as envisaged in LOAC, although derogation may be required.[28] A simple reverting to one body of law while disregarding the other does not provide a solution, since neither body has all the answers to all detention issues. For example, LOAC does not contain clear enough guidance for

---

26 *Bankovic et al v Belgium et al (Decision on Admissibility)* (App no 52207/99, ECtHR, 12 December 2001) appeared to negate applicability in circumstances of aerial bombardment, ¶¶ 59–60; human rights obligations were found however in Cuba's shooting down of a civilian plane outside national airspace, in *Alejandre v Cuba* (n 18) ¶¶ 25, 53; Moreover, there have been numerous ECHR cases before and after Bankovic, that take a wider approach to extraterritorial applicability, including *Issa v Turkey* (n 18); *Isaak and Others v Turkey (Admissibility)* (App no 44587/98, ECtHR, 28 September 2006); *Ocalan v Turkey* (App no 46221/99, ECtHR, 12 May 2005) ¶ 91; *Al-Skeini and Others v UK* (n 9).

27 Orna Ben-Naftali and Yuval Shany, 'Living in Denial: The Application of Human Rights in the Occupied Territories' (2003–2004) 37 *Israel LR* 17, 64; Lubell, *Extraterritorial Use of Force* (n 11) 227–231.

28 Françoise Hampson, 'Detention, the "War on Terror" and International Law' in Howard M Hensel (ed), *The Law of Armed Conflict: Constraints on the Contemporary Use of Military Force* (Ashgate 2005) 131, 142–145.

detention during non-international armed conflicts,[29] while human rights law does not contain the detailed rules for prisoners of war. The bodies of law must therefore work together, filling in the gaps in each other's arsenal. When LOAC requires a fair trial, for example, it is human rights law which can provide us with an understanding of the elements required to determine whether a specific procedure meets the necessary standard. There are many other such instances, and the ICRC study on customary international law provides an excellent example of the interlacing of human rights and LOAC in regulation of detention and trial.[30]

Another area where the interaction is clearly necessary, is in situations of military occupation. On the one hand, an occupying power will, by nature, be the governing authority of a territory, controlling the lives of the population. As such, their human rights are under its control, and it has clear legal obligations in this regard.[31] On the other hand, LOAC has a clear set of detailed rules for regulating situations of military occupation.[32] Again, in most cases this does not cause a direct contradiction, and the two bodies of law can work comfortably together. However, challenges do arise in a number of areas, the first of these being the extent to which the occupying power must go beyond non-interference with rights and provision of basic supplies, and whether it has the same scope of positive duties arising from human rights obligations as it would in its own territory. It would be unreasonable and impractical to pretend that an occupied territory – especially if it is on another continent – can immediately upon commencement of occupation come under the maximalist level of human rights obligations. While human rights obligations will apply, there must be a contextual approach to determining the level at which the rights must be fulfilled. This does not absolve the occupying power from its obligations to respect, protect and fulfil the rights of the inhabitants. These obligations do, in principle, apply; but it does mean that each case must be examined in the context of the circumstances and that the level of obligations be interpreted in a manner that can be practically implemented.[33]

The question of use of force during occupation is another area which raises challenges with regard to the interplay, as it also does in certain other types of military action such as peace support operations.[34] In both these situations, a military force is likely to be patrolling the streets in civilian areas. Indeed, it is recognised by military forces that operations of this type can require rules of engagement that resemble law enforcement rather than the direct resort to lethal force allowed by LOAC. However, LOAC does not provide the detailed rules on use of force for policing type activities, as these are found in the law enforcement and human rights framework.[35] The regulation of policing type activities carried out by the military amongst the civilian

---

29   While there are cases in which lack of adequate infrastructure and resources constitutes an impediment to the establishment of a proper detention regime, the dearth of legal norms – especially in non-international armed conflicts – also constitutes an important obstacle to safeguarding the life, health and dignity of those who have been detained.
ICRC, 'Strengthening Legal Protection for Victims of Armed Conflicts: Draft Resolution and Report' (October 2011) 9

30   CIHL rr 87–105 with commentaries.
31   See cases cited in n 19.
32   See GCIV.
33   For detailed analysis leading to this approach, see Noam Lubell, 'Human Rights during Military Occupation' (2012) 885 *IRRC* 317.
34   See the debates as reflected in the ICRC, 'Occupation and other Forms of Administration of Foreign Territory: Expert Meeting' (2012) 109–130.
35   UN Basic Principles on the Use of Force and Firearms by Law Enforcement Officials, UN Doc A/CONF.144/28/Rev.1 (1990) 112; UN Code of Conduct for Law Enforcement Officials, UNGA Res 34/169 (17 December 1979).

population would therefore have to draw, at least in part, from the relevant international human rights law guidelines on use of force.

One of the areas with significant repercussions but not always given adequate attention, is the potential impact of human rights law in relation to investigations of acts occurring in armed conflict. Although LOAC can require investigations in certain circumstances, there may be perceived differences between LOAC and human rights law in this regard. For example, while under LOAC there is a need for investigation if there appears to have been a violation which amounts to a war crime,[36] civilian deaths which appear to be lawful under LOAC (for example, circumstances whereby it was indisputably within the proportionality formula) might fall outside this obligation;[37] there is also a question as to the type of investigation (if any) required for violations of LOAC that do not amount to war crimes.[38] Human rights law, however, could arguably require an investigation for most civilian deaths,[39] and thus of incidents which might fall outside those requiring an investigation under LOAC. This potential disparity in the trigger for investigation is one of the areas in which the interplay between the bodies of law reveals a tension which is still in the process of being resolved.[40] Notwithstanding, human rights bodies have shown a willingness to accept that the precise shape of investigations conducted in the context of armed conflict cannot always reasonably be expected to meet the same standards as peace time domestic police investigations.[41] Many aspects of an investigation, from collection of forensic

---

36 This is most clearly the case with regard to the grave breaches regime, but also goes beyond this and stems, for example, from the duties to ensure respect and suppress violations, and from customary international law; see analysis of customary international law in CIHL commentary to r 158; for examinations of the duty to investigate and a number of possible approaches to its implementation, see Amichai Cohen and Yuval Shany, 'Beyond the Grave Breaches Regime: The Duty to Investigate Alleged Violations of International Law Governing Armed Conflicts' (2011) 14 *YBIHL* 37; Michael N Schmitt, 'Investigating Violations of International Law in Armed Conflict' (2011) 2 *Harvard NSJ* 31; Sasha Radin and Michael N Schmitt, 'Investigations under international humanitarian law' ch 32 in this volume; Turkel Commission, 'Second Report: Israel's Mechanisms for Examining and Investigating Complaints and Claims of Violations of the Laws of Armed Conflict According to International Law' (February 2013).

37 The incidental death or injury of a civilian during an armed conflict, conversely, does not necessarily give rise to an automatic suspicion of criminality; it will be the context in which the incidental death or injury occurred that will determine whether there is a reasonable suspicion of the perpetration of a war crime. Any such reasonable suspicion will immediately trigger an investigation.
Turkel Commission (n 3637) 102

38 The Turkel Commission was of the opinion that war crimes require an *investigation*, while other violations require 'some form of *examination*'. Ibid 99.

39 *Isayeva, Yusupova and Bazayeva v Russia* (App nos 57947/00, 57948/00 and 57949/00, ECtHR, 24 February 2005) ¶ 208; 'The Court has held that the procedural obligation under Article 2 continues to apply in difficult security conditions, including in a context of armed conflict'. *Al-Skeini and Others v UK* (n 9) ¶ 163–164.

40 For suggestions for reconciling some of the tensions in the regulation of investigations, see Cohen and Shany (n 36).

41 The Court takes as its starting point the practical problems caused to the investigatory authorities by the fact that the United Kingdom was an Occupying Power in a foreign and hostile region in the immediate aftermath of invasion and war. These practical problems included the breakdown in the civil infrastructure, leading inter alia to shortages of local pathologists and facilities for autopsies; the scope for linguistic and cultural misunderstandings between the occupiers and the local population; and the danger inherent in any activity in Iraq at that time. As stated above, the Court considers that in circumstances such as these the procedural duty under Article 2 must be applied realistically, to take account of specific problems faced by investigators.
Al-Skeini and Others v UK (n 9) ¶ 168

evidence to using experts at the alleged scene of crime might be difficult – if not impossible – to fulfil on the battlefield.[42] Once again, therefore, the obligation under human rights law does exist and can have an impact with regard to the obligations of the military, but the specificities of the obligation must be interpreted in context. A final point on this matter, is that the perceived 'intrusion' of human rights law investigations into armed conflict would most likely be avoided if the military ensured that breaches of LOAC were investigated and dealt with adequately and promptly as already required.[43] In practice, cases that come before human rights bodies tend to be of the type that would have required investigation also under LOAC, due to circumstances which raised allegations of breaching LOAC and not only human rights law.

3 Concurrent application of human rights law and the law of armed conflict

As discussed, the potential impact of human rights law in areas regulated by LOAC is clear. What remains is the need to clarify their interplay and identify the manner in which the concurrent application can work in practice. The ICJ played a key role in addressing the relationship between international human rights law and the law of armed conflict. It sought to clarify their concurrent application in the Advisory Opinions on the *Legality of the Threat or Use of Nuclear Weapons*[44] and the *Legal Consequences of the Construction of a Wall in the Occupied Palestinian Territory*,[45] and in the *DRC v Uganda* case.[46]

In response to the discussion on the applicability of the right to life during armed conflict,[47] the Court stated in the Advisory Opinion on the Legality of the *Threat or Use of Nuclear Weapons* that:

> the protection of the International Covenant of Civil and Political Rights does not cease in times of war, except by operation of Article 4 of the Covenant whereby certain provisions may be derogated from in a time of national emergency. Respect for the right to life is not, however, such a provision. In principle, the right not arbitrarily to be deprived of one's life applies also in hostilities. The test of what is an arbitrary deprivation of life, however, then falls to be determined by the applicable lex specialis, namely, the law applicable in armed conflict which is designed to regulate the conduct of hostilities. Thus whether a particular loss of life, through the use of a certain weapon in warfare, is to be considered an arbitrary deprivation of life contrary to Article 6 of the Covenant, can only be decided by reference to the law applicable in armed conflict and not deduced from the terms of the Covenant itself.[48]

The ICJ thereby acknowledged that while certain derogations are allowed, international human rights law continues to apply during armed conflicts. The judges affirmed the interconnectedness of international human rights law and the law of armed conflict. They offered the use of the *lex specialis* principle as a tool to articulate the concurrent application of the two fields of law, supporting the continued application of human rights law during conflict while granting

---

42 Ibid.
43 See n 36.
44 *Nuclear Weapons* (n 7).
45 *Wall* (n 7).
46 *DRC v Uganda* (n 7).
47 *Nuclear Weapons* (n 7) ¶ 24.
48 Ibid ¶ 25.

some degree of primacy to LOAC over international human rights law at least in relation to the right to life.

The ICJ addressed the concurrent application of international human rights law and the law of armed conflict for a second time in the *Wall* opinion. The Court rejected the position held by Israel[49] that human rights treaties do not apply in the Occupied Territories due to the ongoing armed conflict to which LOAC applies exclusively.[50] The judges used both LOAC and human rights law to support their conclusion in the Advisory Opinion, stating that:

> the protection offered by human rights conventions does not cease in case of armed conflict, save through the effect of provisions for derogation of the kind to be found in Article 4 of the International Covenant on Civil and Political Rights.[51]

The ICJ further suggested there are in fact three possibilities when considering how to articulate the concurrent application of international human rights law and LOAC:

> As regards the relationship between international humanitarian law and human rights law, there are thus three possible situations: some rights may be exclusively matters of international humanitarian law; others may be exclusively matters of human rights law; yet others may be matters of both these branches of international law. In order to answer the question put to it, the Court will have to take into consideration both these branches of international law, namely human rights law and, as lex specialis, international humanitarian law.[52]

While ultimately using the *lex specialis* principle to support its reasoning, the ICJ appeared to propose a somewhat novel approach to clarify the interplay between the disciplines, suggesting that both branches will govern concomitantly.

The ICJ again addressed the interplay between LOAC and international human rights law in the *DRC v Uganda* case in 2005.[53] Therein the judges reiterated their position held in the *Wall* and accordingly 'concluded that both branches of international law, namely international human rights law and international humanitarian law, would have to be taken into consideration'.[54]

---

49 Israel, 'Implementation of the International Covenant on Economic, Social and Cultural Rights: Second Periodic Report' UN Doc E/1990/6/Add.32 (3 August 2001) ¶¶ 5–8.

50 Ibid ¶ 102, citing the Report of the Secretary-General prepared pursuant to General Assembly resolution ES-10/13, 'Illegal Israeli actions in Occupied East Jerusalem and the Rest of the Occupied Palestinian Territory' UN Doc A/ES-10/248 (24 November 2003), Annex I, ¶ 4:

> Israel denies that the International Covenant on Civil and Political Rights and the International Covenant on Economic, Social and Cultural Rights, both of which it has signed, are applicable to the occupied Palestinian territory. It asserts that humanitarian law is the protection granted in a conflict situation such as the one in the West Bank and Gaza Strip, whereas human rights treaties were intended for the protection of citizens from their own Government in times of peace.

> See Israel, 'Implementation of the International Covenant on Civil and Political Rights: Second Periodic Report' UN Doc CCPR/C/ISR/2001/2 (20 November 2001) ¶ 8. See also Committee on the Rights of the Child, 'Summary Record of the 829th meeting' UN Doc CRC/C/SR.829 (2002) ¶¶ 39–42. Therein Israel also rejects the applicability of the Convention on the Rights of the Child to the West Bank and the Gaza Strip.

51 *Wall* (n 7) ¶ 106.

52 Ibid.

53 *DRC v Uganda* (n 7) ¶ 216.

54 Ibid.

Significantly, the ICJ did not this time mention that LOAC should be considered as *lex specialis*. In this case the Court appeared to advocate the use of a complementary approach to the concurrent application of international human rights law and LOAC, whereby each field should inform, rather than displace, the other.

Although the ICJ appeared to provide direction for addressing the interplay, its pronouncements lacked detail on how the interplay ought to be applied. The Court first proposed the *lex specialis* principle as a tool to articulate the concurrent application and subsequently suggested a complementary approach to the topic, but without developing the foundations of such a model. There is, therefore, a need for coherent legal reasoning supporting the articulation of the interplay between international human rights law and LOAC. The examination and critical appraisal of the theory of *lex specialis* is a vital step in this direction.

The *lex specialis* principle is remarkably vague and can be used to support several, and often diametrically opposed, arguments. The logic of this principle has been used by the USA, Israel and Russia to argue that in situations of armed conflict LOAC applies exclusively, displacing or excluding the whole international human rights framework.[55] In contrast, the *lex specialis* principle has been interpreted to mean that, depending on the situation at hand, either one of the legal frameworks could be the more specific one.[56] Finally, it has been used to support a combined application of the two fields.[57] Simply, the vagueness of the *lex specialis* maxim, and its consequential broad scope, allows this theory to be interpreted in all directions. This is the opposite of clarification, and is far from being a solution. In many cases, it also fails to offer a practical result. While it is correct to assert that the use of the LOAC framework is crucial to the assessment of the taking of life between combatants during international armed conflict, the *lex specialis* principle seems of less assistance for many other problems of co-application. For instance, the application of the *lex specialis* principle in cases of potential violations of the right to life is not readily transposable to situations of non-international armed conflict, where there is less agreement on the definition of individual status and associated rules of targeting, and LOAC

---

55 These arguments were rejected by the HRC. See eg HRC, 'Concluding Observations: United States of America' UN Doc CCPR/C/USA/CO/3/Rev.1 (18 December 2006); HRC, 'Concluding Observations: Israel' UN Doc CCPR/C/ISR/CO/3 (3 September 2010). The ICJ also reiterated the concurrent application of international humanitarian and human rights treaties, in response to Russia's argument rejecting the application of the International Convention on the Elimination of All Forms of Racial Discrimination, UNGA Res 2106 (XX) (21 December 1965) 660 UNTS 195 on the basis that the dispute rather concerned international humanitarian law. *Application of the International Convention on the Elimination of All Forms of Racial Discrimination (Georgia v Russia) (Provisional Measures) (Order)* [2008] ICJ Rep 353, ¶¶ 79, 83, 95–97, 110–112.

56 See for instance Report of the Office of the High Commissioner on the Outcome of the Expert Consultation on the Issue of Protecting the Human Rights of Civilians in Armed Conflict, UN Doc A/HRC/14/40 (2 June 2010) ¶ 14.

57 For instance, in the context of targeted killing of suspected terrorists, Kretzmer proposed that 'the applicable system must be a mixed model, which incorporates features of international human rights law'. David Kretzmer, 'Targeted Killing of Suspected Terrorists: Extra-Judicial Executions or Legitimate Means of Defence?' (2005) 16 *EJIL* 171, 171. See also Orna Ben-Naftali and Keren R Michaeli, 'We Must not Make a Scarecrow of the Law: A Legal Analysis of the Israeli Policy of Targeted Killings' (2003) 36 *Cornell ILJ* 233; Ben-Naftali and Shany (n 27); Marco Sassòli and Laura M Olson, 'The Relationship between International Humanitarian and Human Rights Law where it Matters: Admissible Killing and Internment of Fighters in Non-International Armed Conflicts' (2008) 871 *IRRC* 599, 626. For challenges with the mixed model approach see Yuval Shany, 'Human Rights and Humanitarian Law as Competing Legal Paradigms for Fighting Terror' in Orna Ben-Naftali (ed), *International Humanitarian Law and International Human Rights Law* (OUP 2011) 13; Kenneth Watkin, 'Controlling the Use of Force: A Role for Human Rights Norms in Contemporary Armed Conflict' (2004) 98 *AJIL* 1, 34.

norms therefore become less clear.[58] The relationship between LOAC and human rights law requires a complex cross-fertilisation that might need to combine a number of elements and rules from both fields at the same time. Similarly, in the case of detention during armed conflict, there is no simple solution of juxtaposing a single LOAC rule against a single human rights rule, and choosing between them. In such cases a complex myriad of rules must be taken into account simultaneously on matters such as the status and circumstances of the given detainee (prisoner of war, member of armed group, civilian in occupied territory, civilian in internal conflict and so on), the type of detention (administrative, preventative, on a criminal charge) and more. Likewise, it is unclear how the *lex specialis* principle could assist in articulating the interplay between LOAC and economic, social and cultural rights, for example, in relation to obligations concerning the right to health during occupation. Although LOAC contains health-related obligations, it is in international human rights law that the detailed understanding of the right to health is to be found.[59] The *lex specialis* principle is not a practical or workable model to articulate the complexity of the relationship between LOAC and human rights law.

Accordingly, closer inspection reveals that although *lex specialis* is an established and long-used principle that developed in other areas of law, it is neither an appropriate nor useful tool in the current context.[60] It has unfortunately become entrenched in the discourse and is mistakenly assumed to answer the complex question of concurrent application. Moreover, its uncritical acceptance has often become a method to avoid the 'tedious' elaboration of a detailed approach to clarify the interplay between the disciplines. There would be far greater chance of progress if the *lex specialis* principle were dethroned from its position as the primary tool for articulating the interplay between human rights and LOAC. Indeed, the Human Rights Committee has wisely left aside the *lex specialis*-based articulation of the relationship between international human rights law and LOAC, affirming that:

> the Covenant [on Civil and Political Rights] applies also in situations of armed conflict to which the rules of international humanitarian law are applicable. While, in respect of certain Covenant rights, more specific rules of international humanitarian law may be specially relevant for the purposes of the interpretation of Covenant rights, both spheres of law are complementary, not mutually exclusive.[61]

Arguably, by discarding the reference to *lex specialis* in the *DRC v Uganda* case, the ICJ has also retreated from the simplistic application of this principle, proposing an alternative approach more likely to respect the nature of each field of law. It has become clear that we must identify other avenues to develop and crystallise a complementary use of international human rights law and LOAC in order to operationalise their interplay in a practical manner.

---

58 For a complete explanation of the categorisation of members of non-state groups, see Lubell, *Extraterritorial Use of Force* (n 11) ch 6, s 1.5.

59 For example, see CESCR, 'General Comment no 14: The Right to the Highest Attainable Standard of Health (Art. 12)' UN Doc E/C.12/2000/4 (11 August 2000).

60 Nancie Prud'homme, 'Lex Specialis: Oversimplifying a More Complex and Multifaceted Relationship?' (2007) 40 *Israel LR* 356.

61 HRC, 'General Comment no 31: Nature of the General Legal Obligation Imposed on States Parties to the Covenant' UN Doc CCPR/C/21/Rev.1/Add.13 (29 March 2004) ¶ 11. See also HRC, 'General Comment 29' (n 9) ¶¶ 3, 9, 11, 16.

4 Conclusion: operationalising the interplay between LOAC and human rights law

An increasing number of bodies have adopted a complementary approach. For instance, in 1997, the Inter-American Commission on Human Rights in the *Abella* case,[62] examined a petition regarding violations of the American Convention on Human Rights, during a situation alleging the summary execution, disappearance and torture of individuals following combat at the La Tablada army barracks between the Argentinian military and over 40 armed persons. The Commission explained therein the applicable legal framework[63] and in light of the facts qualified the events at La Tablada as a non-international armed conflict which 'triggered application of the provisions of Common Article 3, as well as other rules relevant to the conduct of internal hostilities'.[64] It used LOAC to decide whether the alleged violations were legitimate under human rights law, and on the basis of that answer ruled on violations of the American Convention. In its conclusions, the Commission accordingly only stated violations of the American Convention, which were informed by the LOAC framework.

Institutions have also adopted a complementary approach in relation to the issue of detention. For example, the ICRC Customary International Humanitarian Law Study provides in Rule 99 that '[a]rbitrary deprivation of liberty is prohibited'[65] in international as well as non-international armed conflict. The wording of Rule 99 uses terms that are found in the human rights framework rather than in humanitarian treaty law. A detailed framework for deprivation of liberty does not explicitly exist in humanitarian treaty law applicable in non-international armed conflict.[66] The Study appears to state the need to rely upon human rights law to interpret the meaning of arbitrary deprivation of liberty in the context of non-international armed conflict.[67] Human rights law is used in the ICRC study to assess both the acceptable grounds for deprivation of liberty, as well as the necessary procedural requirements.[68] It uses human rights law to interpret LOAC in such a way as to include the principle of legality, as well as the stated procedural requirements otherwise absent from humanitarian treaty law. The ICRC study provides a strong example of a complementary application of human rights and LOAC.

The members of the UN fact-finding mission on Gaza established by the Human Rights Council in 2009[69] also adopted a complementary approach, for instance when examining allegations of killing of civilians involving a deliberate attack on police facilities which led to the death of 99 police officers.[70] It examined more specifically whether the police in Gaza needed to be

---

62 *Abella v Argentina* (n 9)

63 Ibid ¶¶ 149–153.

64 Ibid ¶ 156.

65 CIHL r 99.

66 CIHL commentary to r 99. As it is noted in the ICRC study, GCI–IV common art 3 and APII rather provide for the humane treatment of civilians and persons *hors de combat*.

67 CIHL commentary to r 99.

68 Ibid.

69 HRC, 'The Grave Violations of Human Rights in the Occupied Palestinian Territory, Particularly Due to the Recent Israeli Military Attacks against the Occupied Gaza Strip' UN Doc A/HRC/S-9/2 (2009). The President of the Human Rights Council announced in April 2009 the appointment of Justice Richard Goldstone as head of the fact-finding mission, as well as three additional experts – Professor Christine Chinkin, Ms Hina Jilani and Colonel Desmond Travers. See UN, 'Richard J. Goldstone Appointed to Lead Human Rights Council Fact-Finding Mission on Gaza Conflict' Press Release (3 April 2009), www.ohchr.org/EN/NewsEvents/Pages/DisplayNews.aspx?NewsID=8469&LangID=E.

70 'Human Rights in Palestine and Other Occupied Arab Territories' Report of the United Nations Fact-Finding Mission on the Gaza Conflict, UN Doc A/HRC/12/48 (25 September 2009) ¶¶ 33, 424–429.

regarded as part of the civilian population under LOAC, and whether Israel had respected the principle of distinction between civilians/civilian objects and combatants/military objectives as provided for under the LOAC framework. The report also discussed the violation of the right to life and prohibition of arbitrary killings under international human rights law. The report concluded that international human rights law and LOAC were jointly applicable to the situation in general, and also applied the appropriate rules of each field together, taking each other into account. Following this, the report declared violations of the right to life under international human rights law only in relation to the individuals killed who were not legitimate targets under LOAC, and whose deaths came about in the context of a disproportionate attack under the latter body of law.[71] The joint complementary application therefore produced a result in which there is no conflict of rules, but rather a mutually reinforcing conclusion.

The starting point of the complementary approach is that the operationalisation of the interplay cannot be made solely by comparing two opposing rules and choosing between them, but must be through an approach that respects the specificities of each field, where LOAC and human rights law apply in such a way as to feed into each other, and take each other into account when addressing a situation. The complementary approach is nuanced, requiring a case by case concurrent application of LOAC and human rights law where each field is interpreted in light of the other. Although there are virtually endless potential scenarios, it is still possible – and vital – to identify in advance certain types of circumstances, such as detention or force during military occupation, and to reach a practicable agreed approach. It is suggested that, through practice and further clarification processes involving all stakeholders, agreement in principle can be reached over the best approaches to be tailored for specific types of situations. Ultimately, it is inescapable that the two legal frameworks apply concurrently, and the impact of human rights law on the regulation of armed conflict is palpable. While this does on occasion create tension between these bodies of law, in more situations than is usually assumed there are in fact available interpretations to apply them together without contradiction. For the difficult cases, the intricacy of the relationship is such that the *lex specialis* principle cannot provide a simple one-size-fits-all solution. There is a growing recognition of the need to continue and develop approaches for complementary application of LOAC and human rights law that is both practicable and recognises their respective objectives.

71 Ibid ¶ 1923:

> that Israel, by deliberately attacking police stations and killing large numbers of policemen ... during the first minutes of the military operations, failed to respect the principle of proportionality between the military advantage anticipated by killing some policemen who might have been members of Palestinian armed groups and the loss of civilian life (the majority of policemen and members of the public present in the police stations or nearby during the attack). Therefore, these were disproportionate attacks in violation of customary international law. The Mission finds a violation of the right to life (ICCPR, article 6) of the policemen killed in these attacks who were not members of Palestinian armed groups.

Part II
Principle of distinction

At the core of LOAC stands the principle of distinction. In its contemporary form, the principle is expressed under the heading of 'Basic rule' in Article 48 of Additional Protocol I:

> In order to ensure respect for and protection of the civilian population and civilian objects, the Parties to the conflict shall at all times distinguish between the civilian population and combatants and between civilian objects and military objectives and accordingly shall direct their operations only against military objectives.

Civilians are defined negatively as those persons who are not combatants (Article 50(1) of the Protocol). Likewise, civilian objects as those objects that are not military objectives (Article 52(1) of Protocol). The definition of combatants (Chapter 7) and objects that are military objectives (Chapter 8) is thus crucial for the application of the principle of distinction.

Giving more substance and precision to the principle of distinction, contemporary LOAC contains detailed rules on the 'respect' and the 'protection' that is due to civilians and civilian objects (Chapter 9). However, such protection is forfeited when civilians directly participate in hostilities (Chapter 10).

7
Combatants

Emily Crawford

It is one of the 'fundamental and intransgressible principle[s]'[1] of international humanitarian law (IHL) that participants in an armed conflict observe the principle of distinction. Parties to the conflict must 'at all times distinguish between civilians and combatants. Attacks may only be directed against combatants.'[2] Inherent in this principle is the need to define who is considered a combatant – one who is lawfully permitted to take active and direct part in the hostilities.[3] This chapter examines the origins and evolution of combatant status, discusses the current rules regarding who may be considered a combatant under international law and what consequences follow when combatant status is denied. This chapter will also explore whether international law is evolving to include new categories of persons entitled to combatant status.

1 The historical development of combatant status

Since the beginnings of recorded history, there are examples of nations and empires setting down criteria for the selection of soldiers for combat.[4] These criteria usually revolved around physical attributes – a certain minimum height or age usually being the determining factor. For example, the armies of Ramses II required that soldiers measure at least one metre in height;[5] Philip V of Macedon conscripted all boys over the age of 16 in his war against the Romans.[6] There are even examples of categories of persons who would be exempted from military service – early Hebrew laws excluded those who have 'built a new home and not dedicated it [or] planted a vineyard and not eaten of it'.[7]

---

1 *Legality of the Threat or Use of Nuclear Weapons (Advisory Opinion)* [1996] ICJ Rep 226, 257.
2 CIHL r 1.
3 Knut Ipsen, 'Combatants and Non-Combatants' in Dieter Fleck (ed), *The Handbook of Humanitarian Law in Armed Conflicts* (2nd edn, OUP 2009) 66.
4 See generally Alexander Gillespie, *A History of the Laws of War, Vol I: The Customs and Laws of War with Regards to Combatants and Captives* (Hart 2011) 12–26
5 Gillespie (n 4) 13; Doyne Dawson, *The First Armies* (Cassell 2001) 150.
6 Gillespie (n 4) 15.
7 The Book of Deuteronomy 20:8, 20:4–7.

What distinguished these laws from modern international rules regarding participants in armed conflicts is their plurality, not their universality; the rules that applied in Egypt were not applicable in Assyria. Each nation was free to set their own rules regarding who may be permitted to join the armed forces or fight for their country in battle. The idea that there should be a universal set of criteria determining who may or may not participate in armed conflict is a comparatively recent occurrence, only developing as a result of certain geo-political developments, such as the emergence of the nation state, the centralisation of governmental authority typified by the Westphalian system and the advent of internationally agreed upon rules between those nations and governmental authorities.[8] Warfare was now considered the sole domain of the state and its standing armies;[9] armed conflict was an instrument of national policy, and not the private enterprise of feudal lords or city-states.[10] As such, it was considered necessary to set down criteria for who may be lawfully permitted to engage in armed conflict.[11]

The first legal instrument to define what constituted a 'lawful combatant' was the Lieber Code. The Code was named for its author, Francis Lieber, a law professor who, during the US Civil War and at the behest of President Lincoln, spearheaded the drafting of a 'Code of Regulations for the government of armies in their field, as authorised by the laws and usages of war'.[12] The result was the Instructions for the Government of Armies of the United States in the Field, promulgated as General Order No 100 and containing 157 articles.[13] Article 57 made reference to a 'belligerent' in the following way: 'so soon as a man is armed by a sovereign government and takes the soldier's oath of fidelity, he is a belligerent; his killing, wounding, or other warlike acts are not individual crimes or offenses'.

Also included in the Lieber Code definition of combatant was the participant in a *levée en masse*. *Levée en masse*, the spontaneous uprising of the civilian population against an invading force, was a concept that had its origins in the French Revolution[14] and was outlined in Articles 52 and 53 of the Lieber Code, which provided that

> if the people of that portion of an invaded country which is not yet occupied by the enemy, or of the whole country, at the approach of a hostile army, rise, under a duly authorized levy 'en masse' to resist the invader, they are now treated as public enemies, and, if captured, are prisoners of war.

---

8 See generally Hugo Grotius, *De jure Belli ac Pacis* (1625) bk I, ch V. See also G I A D Draper, 'Combatant Status: An Historical Perspective'(1972) 11 *RDMDG* 135, 136–140; Kenneth Watkin, 'Warriors Without Rights? Combatants, Unprivileged Belligerents, and the Struggle over Legitimacy' HPCR Occasional Paper Series, Program on Humanitarian Policy and Conflict Research (Harvard University 2005) 12, www.hpcrresearch.org/sites/default/files/publications/OccasionalPaper2.pdf.

9 Draper (n 8) 139.

10 See Karl von Clausewitz, *On War* (Penguin 1968) 119; the idea that 'war is a mere continuation of policy by other means'; and Stephen Neff, *War and the Law of Nations: A General History* (CUP 2005) 161–166.

11 Draper (n 8) 139–140.

12 Jordan Paust, 'Dr Francis Lieber and the Lieber Code' (2001) 95 *ASIL Proceedings* 112, 114.

13 General Orders No 100: Instructions for the Government of Armies of the US in the Field (24 April 1863) ('Lieber Code').

14 See Alan Forrest, '*La Patrie en Danger*: The French Revolution and the First *Levée en Masse*' in Daniel Moran and Arthur Waldron (eds), *The People in Arms: Military Myth and National Mobilisation since the French Revolution* (CUP 2003) 9.

Though only a 'domestic' legal instrument, the Lieber Code would go on to have a profound influence in future international law-making endeavours in Europe.[15] The Code was generally regarded as reflecting the law of that day regarding conduct in all armed conflicts, not just in civil wars.[16] In the years following the American Civil War, the Lieber Code was adapted by England, France and Germany for their own military manuals.[17] Similar codes were also adopted by Prussia, the Netherlands, Russia, Argentina and Spain.[18]

At the same time, endeavours were underway in Europe to introduce international laws governing state conduct in armed conflict. To that end, the first Geneva Convention of 1864 introduced international laws to protect the wounded and sick in armies in the field.[19] The Convention necessarily took lawful combatants into account in its ambit, but without defining the elements that comprised lawful combatancy. It was not until 1874 when the first attempt to produce an internationally accepted definition of combatant status came about, during the Brussels Conference of 1874 in its Project of an International Declaration concerning the Laws and Customs of War.[20] Article 9 of the Declaration states:

the laws, rights and duties of war apply not only to armies but also to militia and volunteer corps fulfilling the following conditions:

1   that they be commanded by a person responsible for his subordinates;
2   that they have a fixed distinctive emblem recognisable at a distance;
3   that they carry arms openly;
4   that they conduct their operations in accordance with the laws and customs of war.

The Brussels Declaration also added, in Article 10, the category of *levée en masse* to the list of lawful combatants. Six years later, in 1880, the *Oxford Manual on the Laws of War*[21] elaborated on the Brussels Declaration, to include naval crews within the definition of lawful combatants. However, neither the Brussels Declaration nor the *Oxford Manual* were adopted as binding international agreements.[22] Despite this lack of binding force, both the Declaration and the Manual were influential instruments, in that they informed the debate and eventual definition of combatants that was accepted in the internationally binding Hague Regulations of 1899 and 1907, both of which outline rules for who may be considered a combatant.[23] Under Article 1 of the 1907 Hague Regulations, 'belligerents' must fulfil the four criteria as outlined in the Brussels Declaration.

---

15 Christopher Greenwood, 'International Humanitarian Law (Laws of War): Revised Report for the Centennial Commemoration of the First Hague Peace Conference 1899' in Frits Kalshoven (ed), *The Centennial of the First International Peace Conference* (Kluwer 2000) 167.
16 R R Baxter, 'The First Modern Codification of the Law of Armed Conflict: Francis Lieber and General Order No. 100' (1963) 25 *IRRC* 171.
17 Paust (n 12) 114.
18 Theodor Meron, 'Francis Lieber's Code and Principles of Humanity' (1998) 36 *Columbia JTL* 269, 278–280.
19 Convention for the Amelioration of the Condition of the Wounded in Armies in the Field (22 August 1864) 129 CTS 361.
20 Project of an International Declaration Concerning the Laws and Customs of War (27 August 1874) 1 *AJIL Supp* 96.
21 *Oxford Manual of the Laws of War on Land* (Institute of International Law, 9 September 1880) reprinted in J B Scott (ed), *Resolutions of the Institute of International Law, Dealing with the Law of Nations* (OUP 1916).
22 See Christopher Greenwood, 'Historical Development and Legal Basis' in Fleck (ed) (n 3) 24.
23 HR arts 1–2.

This definition of combatant stood until the end of the Second World War. When the time came to debate the Geneva Conventions in 1949, the drafters clarified and expanded on the Hague criteria. The experiences during the Second World War regarding the involvement of partisan and resistance fighters in Europe prompted a re-evaluation of the criteria for lawful combatancy.[24] In response to advocacy undertaken by the ICRC during the war,[25] the Conference of Government Experts[26] and the 1949 Diplomatic Conference[27] that drafted and debated the Geneva Conventions came to the agreement that partisans and other resistance fighters should, under specific conditions, be awarded combatant status, and all attendant rights and responsibilities connected to such status. Thus, the 1949 Diplomatic Conference adopted significantly expanded rules regarding combatants. Additional categories of combatant were added when the Geneva Conventions were reaffirmed and developed in the 1970s, taking into account changes in the conduct of armed conflict during the post-Second World War environment.[28]

2 The rules regarding combatants in international armed conflicts

The relevant treaty provisions regarding combatant status are now contained in Article 13(1)–(2) of Geneva Conventions I and II, Article 4A(1)–(3) and (6) of Geneva Convention III and Articles 43–44 of Additional Protocol I. As outlined in Article 4A of Geneva Convention III, combatants are those who fall into the following categories:

1 Members of the armed forces of a Party to the conflict as well as members of militias or volunteer corps forming part of such armed forces.

2 Members of other militias and members of other volunteer corps, including those of organised resistance movements, belonging to a Party to the conflict and operating in or outside their own territory, even if this territory is occupied, provided that such militias or volunteer corps, including such organised resistance movements, fulfil the following conditions:

(a) that of being commanded by a person responsible for his subordinates;
(b) that of having a fixed distinctive sign recognisable at a distance;
(c) that of carrying arms openly;
(d) that of conducting their operations in accordance with the laws and customs of war.

3 Members of regular armed forces who profess allegiance to a government or an authority not recognised by the Detaining Power.

...

6 Inhabitants of a non-occupied territory, who on the approach of the enemy spontaneously take up arms to resist the invading forces, without having had the time to form themselves into regular armed units, provided they carry arms openly and respect the laws and customs of war.

---

24 *GCI Commentary* 52–64.
25 See *Report of the International Committee of the Red Cross on its activities during the Second World War* (ICRC 1948) i, 517–535.
26 See *Report on the Work of the Conference of Government Experts* (ICRC 1947) 103–110.
27 See *Final Record of the Diplomatic Conference of Geneva of 1949* (Swiss Federal Political Department 1949) vol IIA, 237–244; vol IIB, 269–272; vol III, 58–62.
28 See Caitlin Dwyer and Tim McCormack, 'Conflict characterisation' ch 3 in this volume.

Under the Geneva rules, regular armed forces as well as partisan and resistance fighters, and participants in a *levée en masse*, are to be considered combatants. For partisan and resistance fighters, the crucial elements for recognition are adherence to the laws of armed conflict, being commanded by a person who is responsible for his or her subordinates and observing the principle of distinction – by distinguishing themselves from the civilian population through the wearing of fixed distinctive emblems and the open carrying of weaponry. For those involved in a *levée en masse*, the open carrying of arms is also required as is adherence to the laws of armed conflict, though the element of group organisation is not necessary.

In terms of the substantive understanding of these four provisions, the first of the provisions – that of being commanded by a person responsible for his subordinates – is essentially straightforward. In an international armed conflict, any irregular armed group must be commanded by a person who is ultimately responsible for their conduct. This provision serves multiple functions – it enables parties to the conflict to conduct their operations according to an internal disciplinary system in compliance with the laws of armed conflict,[29] it provides for a chain of command and accountability which has important implications regarding command responsibility[30] and it excludes from the protection regime private individuals who take up arms in 'private wars'.[31]

The second requirement is that of having a fixed distinctive sign. The distinctive sign can take any number of forms – from a full uniform to a sash, coat, emblem or armband. Even the wearing of camouflage is not precluded by this provision. As noted by Dinstein, 'the issue is not whether combatants can be seen, but the lack of desire on their part to create the false impression that they are civilians'.[32] The critical element is that the distinctive sign be the same for all members of the group, and used only by them. The philosophy behind this provision is ensuring that all persons who are directly participating in the hostilities are identifiable as such from a distance.

The requirement of carrying arms openly is similar to that of the fixed distinction sign – both stem from the need for all persons in a conflict zone to be able to identify members of the armed forces or armed groups. 'Carrying arms openly' does not literally mean the constant visible carriage of firearms or weapons – which has led Solis to speculate 'how can a weapon be carried openly, yet not visibly?'[33] However, the *Commentaries* to the Conventions make it clear that:

> although the difference may seem slight, there must be no confusion between carrying arms 'openly' and carrying them 'visibly' or 'ostensibly' ... [this provision] is not an attempt to prescribe that a hand-grenade or a revolver must be carried at belt or shoulder rather than in a pocket or under a coat. The enemy must be able to recognised partisans as combatants in the same way as members of regular armed forces, whatever their weapons. Thus, a civilian could not enter a military post on a false pretext and then open fire, having taken unfair advantage of his adversaries.[34]

The relevant element of the provision, like that of the distinctive sign, is that ability to identify someone as a direct participant in the hostilities; thus, such participants must 'abstain

29 Geoff Corn, Victor Hansen, Richard Jackson, Chris Jenks, Eric Talbot Jensen and James Schoettler Jr, *The Law of Armed Conflict: An Operational Approach* (Wolters Kluwer 2012) 137.
30 Ibid; see also Robert Cryer, 'Individual liability in international law' ch 31 in this volume.
31 Gary Solis, *The Law of Armed Conflict: International Humanitarian Law in War* (CUP 2010) 196.
32 Yoram Dinstein, *The Conduct of Hostilities under the Law of International Armed Conflict* (CUP 2004) 38.
33 Solis (n 31) 196.
34 *GCIII Commentary* 61.

from creating the false impression that he is an innocent civilian … he must carry his arms openly in a reasonable way, depending on the nature of the weapon and the prevailing circumstances'.[35]

The remaining criterion is the requirement that all participants conduct their operations in accordance with the laws and customs of war. This restates the requirement placed on all members of the armed forces – both regular and irregular – that all are 'bound to conform in the conduct of their operations to the recognized standards of the international humanitarian law'.[36]

The four criteria in Article 4A(2) apply to irregulars – partisans and resistance fighters – only; however, as noted by Corn et al, the very notion of 'regular' armed forces implies that the four criteria exist as a normative foundation to which irregulars must also adhere: 'it would be counterintuitive to require members of militia groups to meet these requirements while releasing members of regular armed forces from an analogous obligation'.[37] However, there are differing consequences between regulars and irregulars regarding non-compliance with the rules. In order to be afforded lawful combatant status (and POW treatment) irregulars, both as a group and individually, must comply with the four criteria. Occasional failure by individuals in the group to comply with the criteria will not result in the group as a whole being denied protected status, though individual responsibility may well attach to any acts amounting to war crimes. However, if the group, as whole, fails to observe some or all of the criteria in 4A(2), then individuals within that group are denied protected combatant status – regardless of whether they have complied fully with the 4A(2) criteria. Some scholars have criticised this as a form of collective punishment.[38]

To the 1949 Geneva Conventions classifications of combatant, Additional Protocol I adds a new type of armed conflict to the category of international armed conflict – 'wars of national liberation', defined as

> armed conflicts in which peoples are fighting against colonial domination and alien occupation and against racist régimes in the exercise of their right of self-determination, as enshrined in the Charter of the United Nations and the Declaration on Principles of International Law concerning Friendly Relations and Co-operation among States in accordance with the Charter of the United Nations.[39]

Additional Protocol I also adds new persons to the category of combatant, defined in Article 43(1) as follows:

> The armed forces of a Party to a conflict consist of all organized armed forces, groups and units which are under a command responsible to that Party for the conduct of its subordinates, even if that Party is represented by a government or an authority not recognized by an adverse Party. Such armed forces shall be subject to an internal disciplinary system which, 'inter alia', shall enforce compliance with the rules of international law applicable in armed conflict.

---

35 Dinstein, *The Conduct of Hostilities* (n 32) 39.
36 W Thomas Mallison and Sally Mallison, 'The Juridical Status of Irregular Combatants under the International Humanitarian Law of Armed Conflict' (1977) 9 *Case Western Reserve JIL* 39, 59.
37 Corn *et al* (n 29) 138.
38 Mallison and Mallison (n 36) 63.
39 API art 1(4).

Protocol I attenuates the strict criteria for irregulars that is outlined in the 1949 Geneva Conventions. Under Article 4A(2) of Geneva Convention III, irregular fighters must, in order to be granted combatant status, carry their arms openly and wear a fixed, distinctive insignia, recognisable at a distance. Such provisions are at odds with the very nature of resistance warfare. The requirement of wearing a fixed visible insignia seemed an unfeasible provision to include in a treaty concerning guerrilla warfare.[40] As noted in the *Commentary* to Additional Protocol I:

> As a practical matter, it was recognised early ... that the prerequisites that members of such movements bear fixed distinctive signs visible at a distance, and that they carry arms openly, virtually precludes the use of the provision. Only rarely have members of organised resistance movements ... been able to comply with all of the conditions of art 4A(2). In order to accomplish their mission, they must work secretly, wear no uniform or distinguishing sign, and withhold their identity prior to their attack. Realisation of the inadequacy of this provision to provide privileged combatant status for those who fight regular military forces in colonial wars and struggles for self-determination gave rise to strong initiatives to relax or abolish the 1949 Geneva Conventions standards for 'freedom fighters'.[41]

Thus, Article 44(3) recognises that 'there are situations in armed conflicts where, owing to the nature of the hostilities an armed combatant cannot so distinguish himself' and provides that such a combatant will not lose his combatant status so long as he

> carries his arms openly (a) during each military engagement, and (b) during such time as he is visible to the adversary while he is engaged in a military deployment preceding the launching of an attack in which he is to participate.

However, this article does not extend to regular armies the right to engage in guerrilla tactics. Article 44(7) specifies that the article is 'not intended to change the generally accepted practice of States with respect to the wearing of the uniform by combatants assigned to the regular, uniformed armed units of a Party to the conflict'.[42]

The intent of Articles 43–44 and Additional Protocol I as a whole was to acknowledge and regulate wars of national liberation and those who fought in them; as noted in the *Commentary* to Protocol I:

> guerrilla fighters will not simply disappear by putting them outside the law applicable in armed conflict, on the basis that they are incapable of complying with the traditional rules of such law. Neither would this encourage them to at least comply with those rules which they are in a position to comply with, as this would not benefit them in any way.

---

40 For the debate at the Diplomatic Conference regarding the exact meaning of insignia that is 'visible at a distance', see CDDH/III/SR.55-56, from 22 April 1977; also, the comments from the French delegation in Committee III at the second Session of the Diplomatic Conference, regarding the unrealistic nature of distinction requirements for resistance fighters as outlined in GC III art 4A(2), 14 CDDH 537, 538 (CDDH/III/SR.33-SR.36). Similar comments were made by Norway (CDDH/III/SR.33-36; CDDH at 400, 537). See further Michael Bothe, Karl Partsch and Waldemar Solf (eds), *New Rules for Victims of Armed Conflicts: Commentary on the Two 1977 Protocols Additional to the Geneva Conventions of 1949* (Martinus Nijhoff 1982) 245.

41 Bothe *et al* (eds) (n 40) 245.

42 See further *AP Commentary* ¶ 1723.

The Diplomatic Conference has therefore made an effort to identify this phenomenon and cannot be criticised for so doing.[43]

However, the Diplomatic Conference was indeed criticised for its endeavours to expand the category of combatant. Both during and following the Diplomatic Conference, a number of states including the US, Israel, India and Pakistan voiced their concerns regarding the Protocol.[44] Commentators denounced the Protocol as 'law in the service of terror',[45] arguing that the Diplomatic Conference had gone out of its way to accommodate radicals and terrorists, rather than acting to compel radical groups to curtail their own behaviour to comply with the existing laws of armed conflict.[46]

The predominant concern regarding the expansion of combatant status was that Additional Protocol I, and Article 44 specifically, had undermined one of the fundamental

> *quid pro quos* of humanitarian law: in exchange for making yourself more easily distinguishable from the civilian population (and as a result facilitating the ability of the enemy to lawfully attack you), the law granted you the benefit of POW status with its accordant combatant immunity.[47]

The objection to Article 44 was thus that such a provision

> would reduce the protection of civilians to vanishing point. Members of the opposing armed forces would come to regard every civilian as likely to be a combatant in disguise and, for their own protection, would see them as proper targets for attack.[48]

Indeed, it was this very concern that stopped US President Ronald Reagan from submitting Additional Protocol I to the Senate for ratification, stating concerns regarding an instrument which would

> grant combatant status to irregular forces even if they do not satisfy the traditional requirements to distinguish themselves from the civilian population and otherwise comply with the laws of war. This would endanger civilians among whom terrorists and other irregulars attempt to conceal themselves. These problems are so fundamental in character that they cannot be remedied through reservations ... we must not, and need not, give recognition and protection to terrorist groups as a price for progress in humanitarian law.[49]

---

43 Ibid ¶ 1684.
44 See comments in *Official Records VI*, CDDH/SR.40 and 41, 121–155, 178–181, 183–186, 189–192 and *Official Records XV*, CDDH/III/SR.55 and 56, 155–187.
45 Douglas Feith, 'Law in the Service of Terror: The Strange Case of the Additional Protocol' (1985) 1 *National Interest* 36, 36.
46 Abraham Sofaer, 'Terrorism and the Law' (1985–1986) 64 *Foreign Affairs* 901, 912–915.
47 Geoffrey Corn, 'Thinking the Unthinkable: Has the Time Come to Offer Combatant Immunity to Non-State Actors?' (2011) 22 *Stanford LPR* 253, 274.
48 UK Ministry of Defence, *Manual of the Law of Armed Conflict* (OUP 2004) ¶ 4.5.1.
49 Message from the President of the United States transmitting the Protocol II Additional to the Geneva Conventions of August 12, 1949, and Relating to the Protection of Victims of Noninternational Armed Conflicts, Concluded at Geneva on June 10, 1977 (29 January 1987).

As of December 2015, 174 states are parties to Additional Protocol I, with 13 states having lodged reservations relating to Article 44;[50] and 23 states are not party to Protocol I.[51] Rules 4 and 106 of the ICRC CIHL study affirm the customary status of Articles 43 and 44,[52] despite continuing opposition to the Protocol from states such as the US.[53]

3 The rules regarding participants in non-international armed conflicts

There is no combatant status for non-state participants in non-international armed conflicts. Common Article 3, and the only other dedicated international instrument regulating conduct in non-international armed conflicts, Additional Protocol II, both recognise that non-state parties will, obviously, take direct part in non-international armed conflicts[54] – such participation is not an internationally wrongful act.[55] However, neither instrument legitimises or immunises such participation. Furthermore, neither instrument provides the extensive protections for such 'domestic' fighters that are offered for combatants in an international armed conflict.[56]

4 The importance of combatant status: combatant immunity

Designation as a lawful combatant brings with it certain privileges, such as entitlement to prisoner of war (POW) status upon capture.[57] The other major right that attaches to combatant status is known as 'combatant immunity'. Lawful combatants, so designated under IHL, will not face prosecution for their war-like acts at the cessation of hostilities, provided they conducted themselves in accordance with the laws of armed conflict.[58] Though the phrase 'combatant

---

50 These include Argentina, Australia, Canada, France, Germany, Ireland, Italy, Japan, South Korea, Netherlands, New Zealand, Spain and United Kingdom.

51 These are Andorra, Azerbaijan, Bhutan, Eritrea, India, Indonesia, Iran, Israel, Kiribati, Malaysia, Marshall Islands, Myanmar, Nepal, Niue, Pakistan, Papua New Guinea, Singapore, Somalia, Sri Lanka, Thailand, Turkey, Tuvalu and United States of America.

52 CIHL rr 4 and 106.

53 See Letter from John Bellinger III, Legal Adviser to the US Department of State and William Haynes II, General Counsel, U.S. Department of Defense, Initial response of U.S. to ICRC study on Customary International Humanitarian Law with Illustrative Comments (3 November 2006), www.state. gov/s/l/2006/98860.htm.

54 Common art 3 refers to 'Persons taking no active part in the hostilities, including members of armed forces who have laid down their arms and those placed "hors de combat"'; APII art 4 refers to 'all persons who do not take a direct part or who have ceased to take part in hostilities'.

55 R R Baxter, 'So-Called "Unprivileged Belligerency": Spies, Guerrillas, and Saboteurs' (1951) 28 *BYBIL* 323, 344. Nathaniel Berman concurs, stating

> engagement in combat by those not covered by the combatants' privilege, assuming no war crimes have been committed, is not illegal *per se* under *international* law. Rather, since such acts are not immunised by international law, the contending parties are free to punish individuals engaged in such activities under their own law.
>
> 'Privileging Combat? Contemporary Conflict and the Legal Construction of War'
> (2004) 43 *Columbia JTL* 1, 14.

56 See Emily Crawford, *The Treatment of Combatants and Insurgents under the Law of Armed Conflict* (OUP 2010), specifically ch 3.

57 See Chris Jenks, 'Detention under the law of armed conflict' ch 17 in this volume.

58 Yoram Dinstein, 'The Distinction between Unlawful Combatants and War Criminals' in Yoram Dinstein and Mala Tabory (eds), *International Law at a Time of Perplexity: Essays in Honour of Shabtai Rosenne* (Martinus Nijhoff 1989) 104–105; Waldemar Solf, 'The Status of Combatants in Non-International Armed Conflicts under Domestic Law and Transnational Practice' (1983–1984) 33 *American University LR* 53, 57–58.

immunity' is not explicitly used in the Geneva Conventions or the Additional Protocols, its substance is found in Article 43(2) of Additional Protocol I, which states that 'combatants ... have the right to participate directly in hostilities'.[59] As outlined in a *Commentary* to Additional Protocol I,

> the combatants' privilege ... provides immunity from the application of municipal law prohibitions against homicides, wounding and maiming, or capturing persons and destruction of property, so long as these acts are done as acts of war and do not transgress the restraints of the rules of international law applicable in armed conflict. Those who enjoy the combatant's privilege are also legitimate targets for the adversary's attacks until they become *hors de combat* or prisoners of war. The essence of prisoner of war status under the Third Convention is the obligation imposed on a Detaining Power to respect the privilege of combatants who have fallen into its power.[60]

5 The consequences of denial of combatant status: unlawful combatants

A person who takes direct part in hostilities[61] without falling under any of the categories enumerated in Article 4A of Geneva Convention III or Articles 43–44 of Protocol I will not be considered a lawful combatant – that is to say, someone entitled to the combatant's privilege, and to POW status. This goes to the heart of the principle of distinction – a civilian may not take direct part in hostilities and simultaneously enjoy the immunity from attack that comes with civilian status: 'a person is not allowed to wear simultaneously two caps: the hat of a civilian and the helmet of a soldier'.[62]

Under the Geneva Conventions and Additional Protocol I, only two categories of person are pre-emptively designated as 'unlawful combatants' – spies[63] and mercenaries.[64] However, neither the Geneva Conventions nor the Additional Protocols explicitly use the term 'unlawful combatant'. Rather, it is left to states to determine how they wish to deal with 'persons taking a direct part in hostilities without being entitled to do so and who therefore cannot be classified as prisoners of war on falling into the power of the enemy'.[65]

As such, one can look to domestic case law and legislation to examine the origins and development of the concept of 'unlawful combatant'. One of the earliest usages of the term can be traced to the US Supreme Court case *ex parte Quirin*.[66] In that case, seven German servicemen had covertly entered the US in 1942, abandoned their uniforms and then proceeded to carry out acts of sabotage. In handing down their decision, the US Supreme Court determined that there was a legal category of unlawful combatant:

---

59 The idea of combatant immunity has been recognised in a number of fora, such as the Nuremberg Trials: *US v List* 11 TWC 757, 788 (1948). Though not specifically mentioned in the Conventions, the notion of combatant immunity can be inferred from provisions in the Conventions themselves, namely GCIII arts 82, 87–89. See Derek Jinks, 'Protective Parity and the Laws of War' (2004) 79 *Notre Dame LR* 1493, 1502.

60 Bothe *et al* (eds) (n 40) 243–244.

61 See Michelle Lesh, 'Direct participation in hostilities' ch 10 in this volume.

62 Dinstein, *The Conduct of Hostilities* (n 32) 29.

63 See also HR arts 29–31 re spies.

64 API arts 46(1), 47(1); see Leslie Green, 'The Status of Mercenaries in International Law' (1978) 8 *Israel YBHR* 9.

65 Knut Dörmann, 'The Legal Situation of "Unlawful/Unprivileged Combatants"' (2003) 85 *IRRC* 45, 45.

66 *Ex parte Quirin et al*, 317 US 1 (1942).

By universal agreement and practice, the law of war draws a distinction between the armed forces and the peaceful populations of belligerent nations and also between those who are lawful and unlawful combatants. Lawful combatants are subject to capture and detention as prisoners of war by opposing military forces. Unlawful combatants are likewise subject to capture and detention, but in addition they are subject to trial and punishment by military tribunals for acts which render their belligerency unlawful.[67]

A more modern enunciation of the concept of unlawful combatancy exists in the US Military Commissions Act of 2009, amending the Military Commissions Act of 2006, which refers to 'unprivileged enemy belligerent' in Section 948a, defining such a person as:

an individual (other than a privileged belligerent) who –

(A) has engaged in hostilities against the United States or its coalition partners;
(B) has purposefully and materially supported hostilities against the United States or its coalition partners;

or

(C) was a part of al Qaeda at the time of the alleged offense under this chapter.[68]

The category of 'unlawful combatant' exists also in Israel, under the Detention of Unlawful Combatants Law in 2002,[69] defining unlawful combatants as 'anyone taking part – directly or indirectly – in hostilities against the State of Israel, who is not entitled to a prisoner of war status under Geneva Convention (III)'.[70] This legislation allows for administrative detention of unlawful combatants,

on grounds of State security, but it is subject to judicial review by a (civilian) District Court (both initially and every six months thereafter) … an unlawful combatant can be held in detention as long as hostilities by the force to which he belongs have not been terminated.[71]

6 Problems with the category of 'unlawful combatant'

There is nothing controversial in the determination that civilians may not participate in armed conflicts unless they do so within the strictures of preordained categories such as *levée en masse*. What is questionable is whether there is a category additional to that of combatant and civilian.

---

67 Ibid 30–31.
68 Military Commission Act of 2009, 10 USC §§ 948a et seq.
69 Detention of Unlawful Combatants Law, 2002, 1834 *Sefer Hahukim* (Laws of the State of Israel, Hebrew) 192.
70 Dinstein, *The Conduct of Hostilities* (n 32) 31.
71 Ibid 32. The intent of Israeli law, in denying combatant status and providing for indefinite detention, is to ensure that suspects are unable to claim that their acts are committed in the context of an armed struggle against the State of Israel. The definition of unlawful combatant under Israeli law is thus quite wide, encompassing both terrorist organisations and those who cause harm to the State of Israel. Indeed, a Israeli case, *Barghouti*, made reference to unlawful combatants as a category which includes terrorist organisation members and enemy forces who take direct part in terrorist and hostile acts against Israelis, but who, if captured, are not entitled to POW status: *State of Israel v Marwan Barghouti* (District Court of Tel Aviv and Jaffa, Criminal Case no 092134/02, 12 December 2002) ¶ 11.2.

Does international law recognise a third category, that of unlawful combatant, one who is neither civilian nor combatant?

This question of a potential 'third status' under IHL has come in for intense scrutiny over the last decade, in large part due to the so-called '9/11' attacks on the United States. Following the 9/11 attacks, the United States declared a 'war on terrorism'.[72] After a joint resolution passed US Congress on 18 September 2001 authorising the president to use lethal military force,[73] the US began air and ground strikes against the Taliban regime in Afghanistan.[74] This was followed by the invasion of Iraq in 2003,[75] and the ongoing strikes against targets in additional states including Yemen, Somalia and Pakistan.[76] Both abroad and in its own territory, the US instituted a policy of detention for persons arrested in connection with the 'war on terror'. Many of the foreign detainees were taken to the US military base in Guantánamo Bay in Cuba.

The initial US position regarding all foreign nationals detained was that neither Taliban nor al-Qaeda fighters were to be considered POWs under Geneva law – they were instead 'unlawful combatants'.[77] Though the US eventually changed its position on captured Taliban fighters, the Bush administration continued to assert that al-Qaeda fighters were 'unlawful combatants' and therefore not entitled to any form of Geneva protection.[78] The US Government also determined that any detainees in Guantánamo would not be able to challenge their detention in a US Federal Court via petition for a writ of *habeas corpus*.[79]

The US approach seemed to take the descriptive nature of the term 'unlawful combatant' and use it as a legal status by which to characterise al-Qaeda operatives. By designating such persons as 'unlawful', it seemed as if the US was attempting to deny any recourse to the law – domestic and international – that such 'unlawful' persons might have otherwise enjoyed. As noted by Fletcher and Ohlin,

---

72 US President George W Bush used the term in an address to a Joint Session of Congress on 20 September 2001. In the televised address, President Bush stated that the US 'war on terror begins with al-Qaeda, but it does not end there. It will not end until every terrorist group of global reach has been found, stopped and defeated.' The full transcript is available at www.whitehouse.gov/news/releases/2001/09/20010920-8.html.

73 The US Congress sanctioned the 'war on terror' in Authorization for Use of Military Force against Terrorists, Pub L 107–140, 115 Stat 224, 18 September 2001.

74 'On This Day: US Launches Air Strikes Against the Taleban' *BBC News* (7 October 2001), news.bbc.co.uk/onthisday/hi/dates/stories/october/7/newsid_2519000/2519353.stm.

75 Patrick Cockburn, 'A Decade has Passed since the Invasion of Iraq, but the Debate Goes On' *Independent* (13 June 2013), www.independent.co.uk/news/world/middle-east/a-decade-has-passed-since-the-invasion-of-iraq-but-the-debate-goes-on-8658241.html.

76 See generally the ongoing project by the Bureau of Investigative Journalism on US drone strikes at www.thebureauinvestigates.com/category/projects/drones.

77 See the Memorandum of 9 January 2002 from John Yoo, Deputy Assistant Attorney General, and Robert Delahunty, Special Counsel, US Department of Justice, to William Haynes, General Counsel, US Department of Defense (DoD); in which they express their legal opinion that both Taliban and al-Qaeda detainees do not merit any form of protections under any of the Geneva Conventions: excerpted in Karen Greenberg and Anthony Dratel (eds), *The Torture Papers: The Road to Abu Ghraib* (CUP 2005) 38–117.

78 See the White House Fact Sheet, 'Status of Detainees at Guantánamo' (7 February 2002), www.whitehouse.gov/news/releases/2002/02/20020207-13.html. The US Government agreed to apply GCIII to captured Taliban, but not to al-Qaeda detainees. This is despite US Department of Justice advice to Alberto Gonzalez, Counsel to the President, that neither Taliban nor al-Qaeda detainees warranted Geneva protections. See the Memo to Alberto Gonzalez from the Office of the Assistant Attorney General, excerpted in Greenberg and Dratel (eds) (n 77) 136–143.

79 See Memorandum for William Haynes II, General Counsel, US Department of Defense from Deputy Assistant Attorneys-General Patrick Philbin and John Yoo, excerpted in Greenberg and Dratel (eds) (n 77) 29–37.

when combatants are unlawful, the argument goes, they are subject to the burdens of combatancy (they can be killed), but they have no reciprocal rights … the phrase unlawful combatant as used today combines the aspect of unlawful from the law of crime and the concept of combatant from the law of war. For those thus labelled, it is the worst of all possible worlds.[80]

Indeed, there was almost uniform resistance to US attempts to proclaim a 'Geneva' status of 'unlawful enemy combatant'.[81] The overwhelming response was that the US had attempted to stretch the law too far, by trying to restrict the applicability of international law in their conflict with al-Qaeda,[82] and that they had tried to create a category of persons without rights under the law.[83]

The attempts by the US Government to limit the protections and remedies offered to persons deprived of their liberty, both under international and US domestic law, were challenged several times in the US Supreme Court. These challenges came in the cases *Hamdi v Rumsfeld*,[84] *Rasul v Bush*[85] and *Rumsfeld v Padilla*,[86] and culminated in two cases – *Hamdan v Rumsfeld*[87] and *Boumediene v Bush*[88] – where the Supreme Court rejected the US Government's attempt to deny access to petitions for a writ of *habeas corpus*, affirmed the universality of Common Article 3 for all armed conflicts other than international conflicts between opposing sovereign nation states, and held that the provisions of Common Article 3 are applicable as a basic set of fundamental rules to be observed in all armed conflicts.[89] Partly in response to these court decisions, the US

80 George Fletcher and Jens David Ohlin, *Defending Humanity* (OUP 2008) 183.
81 See eg Human Rights Watch, 'Background Paper on Geneva Conventions and Persons Held by U.S. Forces' (29 January 2002), www.hrw.org/legacy/backgrounder/usa/pow-bck.pdf; Leila Zerrougui (Chairperson-Rapporteur of the Working Group on Arbitrary Detention), Leandro Despouy (Special Rapporteur on the independence of judges and lawyers), Manfred Nowak (Special Rapporteur on torture and other cruel, inhuman or degrading treatment or punishment), Asma Jahangir (Special Rapporteur on freedom of religion or belief) and Paul Hunt (Special Rapporteur on the right of everyone to the enjoyment of the highest attainable standard of physical and mental health), 'Situation of Detainees at Guantánamo Bay' UN Commission on Human Rights, UN Doc E/CN.4/2006/120 (27 February 2006); Martin Scheinin (Special Rapporteur on the promotion and protection of human rights and fundamental freedoms while countering terrorism), 'Mission to the United States of America' UN Human Rights Council, UN Doc A/HRC/6/17/Add.3 (22 November 2007); European Parliament Resolution on the Detainees in Guantanamo Bay, Doc P5_TAPROV(2002)0066 (7 February 2002); 'Merkel criticises Guantanamo Bay' *BBC News* (7 January 2006), news.bbc.co.uk/1/hi/world/europe/4590912.stm (quoting German Chancellor Angela Merkel); see also Amnesty International, 'Guantánamo: A Decade of Damage to Human Rights' Doc AMR 51/103/2011 (December 2011).
82 See generally Dörmann (n 65) 48–49; Sylvia Borelli, 'Casting Light on the Legal Black Hole: International Law and Detentions Abroad in the "War on Terror"' (2005) 87 *IRRC* 39; George Fletcher, 'Black Hole in Guantánamo Bay' (2004) 2 *JICJ* 121; Marco Sassòli, 'The Status of Persons Held in Guantánamo under International Humanitarian Law' (2004) 2 *JICJ* 96.
83 See *R (Abbasi and another) v Secretary of State for Foreign and Commonwealth Affairs* [2002] EWCA Civ 159, ¶ 64, where the Court of Appeals states that Guantánamo detainees have been 'arbitrarily detained in a legal black-hole'.
84 *Hamdi v Rumsfeld*, 542 US 507 (2004).
85 *Rasul v Bush*, 542 US 446 (2004).
86 *Rumsfeld v Padilla*, 542 US 426 (2004). For an assessment of the 2004 cases, see Terry Gill and Elies van Sliedregt, 'Guantánamo Bay: A Reflection on the Legal Status and Rights of "Unlawful Enemy Combatants"' (2005) 1 *Utrecht LR* 28.
87 *Hamdan v Rumsfeld*, 548 US 557 (2006).
88 *Boumediene v Bush*, 553 US 723 (2008).
89 See *Hamdan* (n 87) 66–69 (Stevens J).

Obama administration changed the legislative terminology from 'unlawful combatant' to 'unprivileged enemy belligerent'.[90]

It is true that persons who participate in armed conflict without being permitted to do so do not enjoy either combatant privilege or POW rights. However, to reach the conclusion that such persons lose all legal rights is untenable. Even spies and mercenaries must be guaranteed fair trial rights, for example.[91] One cannot extrapolate a new international category under IHL when the origin of such a category is a single case in a domestic judicial system – *ex parte Quirin*. Furthermore, a case decided during time of war, several years before the almost universal adoption of the Geneva Conventions, seems insufficient grounds to formulate an entirely new status, especially in the face of such overwhelming international resistance. Indeed, the Israeli Supreme Court declined to recognise 'unlawful combatants' as a third category of persons under Geneva law, stating that neither treaty nor customary IHL provide any basis for proclaiming such a category.[92]

The adoption of the Geneva Conventions must be seen as superseding any interpretation of the law of armed conflict which sanctions stripping any person detained in relation to an armed conflict of any sort of legal protection or status. Indeed, the *Commentary* to the Conventions makes this point:[93]

> Every person in enemy hands must have some status under international law: he is either a prisoner of war and, as such, covered by the Third Convention, a civilian covered by the Fourth Convention, [or] a member of the medical personnel of the armed forces who is covered by the First Convention. *There is no intermediate status*; nobody in enemy hands can fall outside the law.[94]

Therefore, an 'unlawful combatant' in an international armed conflict will find international legal protection under another instrument, most likely the Fourth Convention. As Dörmann argues,

> a textual interpretation of the Conventions can only lead to the conclusion that all persons who are not protected by GC I-III, thus also persons who do not respect the conditions which would entitle them to POW status/treatment, are covered by GCIV.[95]

7 The future law of combatant status

As this chapter has demonstrated, combatant status is unique to international armed conflicts only. However, there is emergent debate in the literature regarding whether combatant status could ever be extended to include participants in non-international armed conflicts.[96] The development of the customary international law relating to non-international armed conflicts

---

90 See the change in terminology from the Military Commissions Act of 2006 to the Military Commissions Act of 2009.
91 API art 75.
92 HCJ 769/02 *The Public Committee Against Torture in Israel et al v the Government of Israel* [2006] 2 IsrLR 459, ¶ 28 ('*Targeted Killings*'). See also William Fenrick, 'The *Targeted Killings* Judgment and the Scope of Direct Participation in Hostilities' (2007) 5 JICJ 332, 334.
93 Antonio Cassese, *International Law* (2nd edn, OUP 2005) 410.
94 *GCIV Commentary* 51 (original emphasis).
95 Dörmann (n 65) 48–49.
96 Corn (n 47).

over the last 40 years has filled in many of the lacunae in the law of non-international armed conflict.[97] The growing influence of international human rights law has also increased the quantum of available protections for persons caught up in non-international armed conflicts.[98] The legal gap between regulating international and non-international armed conflicts has narrowed to the point where a number of voices have called for the possibility of a uniform application of the laws of armed conflict to all kinds of armed conflict.[99]

Whether such a development will ever eventuate seems unlikely – at least for the foreseeable future. At every stage in the development of the treaty law of armed conflict, the inclusion of new categories of combatant was highly contested.[100] The contentious debates regarding the concept of direct participation in hostilities and the legal rights afforded to such persons suggests that combatant status will remain a highly contested category. It seems unlikely that states will willingly allow rebels and insurgents to have international immunity from the operation of domestic treason and criminal laws.

However, there is some basis for the argument that combatant immunity in non-international armed conflicts is possible – in the amnesty provision in Article 6(5) of Protocol II, which provides:

> At the end of hostilities, the authorities in power shall endeavour to grant the broadest possible amnesty to persons who have participated in the armed conflict, or those deprived of their liberty for reasons related to the armed conflict, whether they are interned or detained.[101]

Effectively a type of retroactive combatant immunity, the amnesty provision in Article 6(5) of Protocol II at least suggests the possibility of combatant immunity in non-international armed conflicts. Indeed, it is noteworthy that Article 6(5) was adopted by consensus during the Diplomatic Conferences that adopted the Additional Protocols.[102]

Granting amnesty at the cessation of hostilities for participation in the conflict is not obligatory; states are encouraged to grant amnesty, but need not do so. However, despite the lack of

---

97 See the Report of the UN Commission of Enquiry on Darfur Pursuant to Security Council Resolution 1564 of 18 September 2004 (25 January 2005) ¶ 159, www.un.org/news/dh/sudan/com_inq_darfur. pdf; the ICTY in the *Prosecutor v Tadić (Decision on the Defence Motion for Interlocutory Appeal on Jurisdiction)* (Case no IT-94-1-AR72, ICTY Appeals Chamber, 2 October 1995) 96–127; see also Emily Crawford, 'Blurring the Lines between International and Non-International Armed Conflicts: The Evolution of Customary International Law Applicable in Internal Armed Conflicts' (2008) 15 *Australian ILJ* 29.

98 See generally Christopher Greenwood, 'Human Rights and Humanitarian Law: Conflict or Convergence?' (2010) 43 *Case Western Reserve JIL* 491; Theodor Meron, 'Convergence of International Humanitarian Law and Human Rights Law' in Daniel Warner (ed), *Human Rights and Humanitarian Law: The Quest for Universality* (Martinus Nijhoff 1997).

99 See eg the ICTY in *Tadić (Interlocutory Appeal)* (n 97) 96–97; Lindsay Moir, 'Towards the Unification of International Humanitarian Law?' in Richard Burchill, Nigel White and Justin Morris (eds), *International Conflict and Security Law: Essays in Memory of Hilaire McCoubrey* (CUP 2005); Emily Crawford, 'Unequal Before the Law: The Case for the Elimination of the Distinction Between International and Non-International Armed Conflict' (2007) 20 *Leiden JIL* 441.

100 See the debate over participants in *levée en masse* at the Hague Conferences in *Report to the Hague Conferences of 1899 and 1907* (James Scott ed, Clarendon 1917) 139–142; debate over partisans at the Geneva Conference, *Final Record of the Diplomatic Conference of Geneva of 1949*, vol IIA, 469; and debate over guerrilla and national liberation fighters at the 1977 Conferences in *Official Records XIV*, CDDH/III/SR.33-36, 317–385, 447–556.

101 This is confirmed and elaborated on in CIHL r 159.

102 See *Official Records VII*, CDDH/Sr.50, 97.

a legal imperative, state practice has demonstrated a number of instances where states have granted amnesties for participants in non-international armed conflicts. These amnesties have taken a number of forms, including special agreements, legislation and, in some instances, general declarations by the authorities in power.[103]

The granting of amnesty does not, arguably, have the same legal weight as combatant immunity. Participants in a non-international armed conflict cannot assume that they will be granted amnesty at the end of the armed conflict in the same way a combatant in an international armed conflict can rely on his combatant immunity. However, the prevalence of amnesty agreements does demonstrate that states have been generally inclined towards the granting of amnesties in non-international armed conflicts.

Until states are willing to accept universal combatant status in all types of armed conflict, it seems likely that the current categories of combatant will remain fixed, applying only in international armed conflicts.

---

103 For a general outline of the extant amnesty agreements, see Jean-Marie Henckaerts and Louise Doswald-Beck, *Customary International Humanitarian Law* (CUP 2005) vol ii, pt 2, 4017–4044.

8

Military objectives

David Turns

The operational effectiveness of the contemporary international law of armed conflict is predicated on one of the most fundamental principles of the modern law: namely, the principle of distinction, which the ICJ has labelled the first of the 'cardinal principles' of international humanitarian law, because it is 'aimed at the protection of the civilian population and civilian objects and establishes the distinction between combatants and non-combatants; States must never make civilians the object of attack'.[1] The principle of distinction has been implicit in the enunciation of earlier, more generalised, rules of LOAC: 'The right of belligerents to adopt means of injuring the enemy is not unlimited';[2] 'The attack or bombardment, by whatever means, of towns, villages, dwellings or buildings which are undefended is prohibited'.[3] As such, the principle of distinction operates both as an essential component of the legal protection afforded to the civilian population and to individual civilians, and as a crucial element in the legal regulation of the conduct of hostilities; it is enshrined both in treaty provision[4] and as a norm of customary international law.[5] The universally accepted contemporary formulation appears in Article 48 of Additional Protocol I, which reads as follows:

> In order to ensure respect for and protection of the civilian population and civilian objects, the Parties to the conflict shall at all times distinguish between the civilian population and combatants and between civilian objects and military objectives and accordingly shall direct their operations only against military objectives.

The wording makes it evident that, insofar as inanimate objects are concerned,[6] it is necessary to give effect to the rule by distinguishing military objectives from civilian objects; since the law

---

1 *Legality of the Threat or Use of Nuclear Weapons (Advisory Opinion)* [1996] ICJ Rep 226, ¶ 78.
2 HR art 22.
3 HR art 25.
4 API art 48.
5 The essence of the principle is restated in CIHL r 1 (in relation to persons); CIHL r 7 (in relation to objects).
6 This chapter does not deal with the principle of distinction as between persons, ie combatants and civilians; as to the generalities of which, see Emily Crawford, 'Combatants' ch 7 in this volume.

does not define civilian objects other than in negative terms, the definition of military objectives per se assumes a critical importance. What precisely, therefore, is a military objective?[7] With the demise of the doctrines of 'total war' since the end of the Second World War, it is no longer permissible to be as blithely cynical in answering this question as in an earlier era, as evinced by the following exchange in the British House of Commons, during a debate on aerial bombardments in the Spanish Civil War:

> THE PRIME MINISTER: The difficulty [with military objectives] arises when one of the forces engaged in aerial warfare, being accused of deliberate bombing of civilians, deny that they were bombing civilians or that it was deliberate, and allege that they were in pursuit of military objectives. Again, what is a military objective? Surely these are not matters which can be passed over as if they were of no importance. Suppose a church is used as the headquarters of a division. Is that a military objective or is it not?
> MR S O DAVIES: It depends upon what side it is on.[8]

The advent of the modern rules on targeting operations with the adoption of Additional Protocol I in 1977, as interpreted in practice in contemporary armed conflicts since the First Gulf War in 1991, has resulted in the development of a modern legal concept of the military objective – a concept that in its general parameters is reasonably clear and very widely agreed. This is mostly true even of states, like the US and Israel, which have refused to become parties to the Protocol as a whole. The concept has acquired general applicability across the spectrum of armed conflict and in all the known domains of warfare. This chapter will outline the development of the concept and the formulation of the definition in law, along with its interpretation and selected problems that have arisen in practice in recent military operations and are likely to be relevant to future operations. The discussion will be necessarily limited by the requirements of time and space but the scope will seek to provide a reasonably comprehensive overview of this crucial area of modern operational law and practice.

1 Background and historical development

Notwithstanding the fact that the laws and customs of war had maintained some elementary notions of the difference between combatants and non-combatants (and the general permissibility of attacking only the former) since ancient times,[9] a concept of objects as military objectives only began to emerge with the evolution of modern methods and means of warfare from the late nineteenth century onwards. The earliest codificatory instruments and manuals of modern LOAC contained no reference at all to military objectives as a legal concept, other than obliquely and in the most general of terms, by reference to the Clausewitzian concept of military necessity; this was notably the case in relation to warfare on land.[10] Throughout much of the history

---

7 The term 'military objective' is used in this chapter in its legal sense under IHL, that is, in reference to inanimate objects (buildings, installations etc) as lawful objects of attack in specific military operations; not in its politico-military doctrinal sense, in reference to the broader aims and objectives of a war or campaign.

8 Hansard, *HC Debs* (21 June 1938) vol 337 col 938.

9 Leslie Green, *The Contemporary Law of Armed Conflict* (3rd edn, Manchester University Press 2008) 26–32.

10 See General Orders No 100: Instructions for the Government of United States Armies in the Field (24 April 1863) arts 15–17; Brussels Declaration concerning the Laws and Customs of War (27 August 1874) art 13(g); *Oxford Manual of the Laws of War on Land* (9 September 1880) art 32(b).

of warfare, however, developments in LOAC have often been prompted by technological advances. The age-old practice of naval bombardment, combined with the development of modern naval artillery during the late nineteenth century[11] and of the 'all-big-gun' battleship in the early years of the twentieth century,[12] led to the inclusion of clauses defining – by explicit exclusion from the prohibition on bombardment of 'undefended ports, towns, villages, dwellings or buildings' – permissible targets in the 1907 Hague Convention (IX) concerning Bombardment by Naval Forces in Time of War[13] and the 1913 *Oxford Manual of the Laws of Naval War*.[14] Both of these instruments excluded, '[m]ilitary works, military or naval establishments, depots of arms or war "matériel," workshops or plants which could be utilized for the needs of the hostile fleet or army, and the war-ships [*sic*] in the harbour' from the scope of the prohibition on bombardment of undefended places.

The elaboration of details as to objects that might lawfully be targeted, however, was inextricably bound up with the development of aerial warfare from the second decade of the twentieth century. Balloons had made their earliest significant appearance in warfare during the American Civil War (1861–1865), when limited use of tethered balloons for observation was made by the Union Army Balloon Corps; the first transmission of battlefield intelligence to enable accurate indirect artillery fire was sent by telegraph from Dr Thaddeus Lowe's balloon observing Confederate positions at Falls Church, Virginia.[15] Although a first abortive attempt at dropping ordnance from the air against an enemy target was made as early as the mid-nineteenth century,[16] it was the advent of powered flight that enabled the first offensive air operations in the second decade of the twentieth century. The very first country to deploy powered aircraft in battle was Italy, during the Italo-Turkish War (1911–1912), when aircraft were used both in the anticipated reconnaissance role (including as spotters to correct inaccurate artillery fire) and to bomb Turkish infantry positions in the Libyan desert[17] – although the Italians also had the more dubious distinction in that conflict of becoming the first nation to lose aircraft to hostile fire from the ground.[18] Already in these operations there was a foretaste of the bitterness pro-

11 See Marshall J Bastable, 'From Breechloaders to Monster Guns: Sir William Armstrong and the Invention of Modern Artillery, 1854–1880' (1992) 33(2) *Technology and Culture* 213. Explosive shells were first used in the Crimean War (1853–1856), by the Russians in the attack on the Turkish fleet at Sinope and by the French in the bombardment of the Russian forts at Kinburn.

12 Although generally attributed to the British First Sea Lord Admiral Sir John Fisher, who designed and built the first 'dreadnought' battleship for the Royal Navy in 1906, the idea appears to have been first articulated in print by the Italian naval engineer Vittorio Cuniberti in 1903: see Nicola Zotti, 'Cuniberti: the creator of the monocaliber battleship' *L'Indipendente* (11 August 2013), www.lindipendente.eu/wp/en/2013/08/11/cuniberti/.

13 (18 October 1907) 205 CTS 345, arts 1–2.

14 Arts 25–26.

15 US Centennial of Flight Commission, 'Balloons in the American Civil War', http://centennialofflight.net/essay/Lighter_than_air/Civil_War_balloons/LTA5.htm. It appears, however, that the French Revolutionary armies were the first to make use of a balloon for military reconnaissance, at the Battle of Fleurus during the War of the First Coalition (1792–1797): US Centennial of Flight Commission, 'Military Use of Balloons During the Napoleonic Era', http://centennialofflight.net/essay/Lighter_than_air/Napoleon's_wars/LTA3.htm.

16 The Austrians launched 200 pilotless balloons carrying bombs against the city of Venice, which had proclaimed its independence as the Republic of San Marco during the First Italian War of Independence (1848–1849), but the wind sent them back over the Austrian positions: US Centennial of Flight Commission, 'Military Use of Balloons in the Mid- and Late Nineteenth Century', http://centennialofflight.net/essay/Lighter_than_air/military_balloons_in_Europe/LTA4.htm.

17 Cdre William H Beehler, *The History of the Italian–Turkish War, September 29, 1911, to October 18, 1912* (Advertiser-Republican 1913) 31, 34, 98.

18 James D Crabtree, *On Air Defense* (Praeger 1994) 9.

voked by every aerial bombing campaign since: on several occasions during the conflict, the Ottoman Red Crescent formally protested that its clearly marked field hospitals, as well as a cemetery, had been illegally attacked by both aeroplanes and airships of the Italian forces. Each such allegation was summarily denied by the Italian authorities, who accused the Turks of deliberately propagating malicious falsehoods.[19] The first known attempt to bomb a city from the air occurred during the First Balkan War (1912–1913), when Bulgarian aircraft dropped primitive 22-pound bombs on the fortified Turkish city of Adrianople, after leafleting the city from the air with threats that it would be destroyed if it did not surrender.[20] Strategic bombing doctrines were first coherently formulated by the German, British and Italian air forces during the First World War, leading directly to modern notions of airpower: already by the time of the Second World War it had become apparent that no belligerent could hope to win a war without control of the air over the battlespace, and the concept of industrialised total war during that conflict sealed the delivery of destruction to specific targets from the air as the method of choice for prosecuting a successful war.

Although it was the technological developments just outlined that led to the adoption of LOAC rules concerning military objectives, even the *lex lata* struggled to keep up with them, at least initially. In this context it is interesting that one of the earliest adopted international instruments relating to methods and means of warfare imposed a blanket prohibition, with no attempt to consider the different targets at which such launchings might or might not be directed.[21] Even when such considerations were explicitly introduced a few years later,[22] they were arguably more in the nature of an exclusionary extension to the pre-existing customary rule prohibiting attacks on an 'open city'[23] than a formulation of a new rule per se. Nevertheless, state practice in strategic bombing operations during the First World War largely confirmed that the Hague Convention (IX) list of objects not exempt from attack, even in undefended localities, effectively constituted the first set of specified military objectives in the modern codified LOAC.[24] That experience during the Great War informed the work of the Commission of Jurists, which met in The Hague in 1922–1923 and produced the first – and, to date, the only – international legal instrument of its kind: the Hague Rules of Aerial Warfare,[25] the most significant development of which was their explicit adoption of the notion of 'military objective' as a legal concept. Interestingly in light of their states' subsequent practice during the Second World War, it has been noted that the British and American delegations to the Commission took diametrically opposed approaches to this concept: the British attached great importance to the term 'military objective' without ever actually attempting to define it, whereas the Americans preferred to list specific designated military objects which could legitimately be bombed, while studiously avoiding any use of that term.[26]

---

19 For the exchange of correspondence, see 'La Guerre en Tripolitaine' (1912) *Bulletin International des Sociétés de la Croix-Rouge* 43(169) 75–83; ibid 43(170) 174–180; ibid 43(171) 268–272; ibid 43(172) 330–333.

20 Michael Paris, *Winged Warfare: The Literature and Theory of Aerial Warfare in Britain, 1859–1917* (Manchester University Press 1992) 110–111.

21 Hague Declaration (IV, 1) to Prohibit, for the Term of Five Years, the Launching of Projectiles and Explosives from Balloons, and Other Methods of Similar Nature (29 July 1899) 187 CTS 456.

22 See above, text to nn 13–14.

23 See HR art 25; *US v Ohlendorf et al (Einsatzgruppen)* 4 TWC 411 (US Military Tribunal at Nuremberg, 1948) 467; CIHL r 37.

24 J M Spaight, 'Air Bombardment' (1923–1924) 4 *BYBIL* 21, 23–25.

25 (1923) 17 *AJIL Supp* 245.

26 W Hays Parks, 'Air War and the Law of War' (1990) 32 *Air Force LR* 1, 28.

Article 24(1) of the Hague Rules provided that in order for aerial bombardment to be legitimate, it had to be directed at a military objective; paragraph (2) then provided a list of such objectives. These were as follows: 'military forces; military works; military establishments or depots; factories constituting important and well-known centres engaged in the manufacture of arms, ammunition or distinctively military supplies; lines of communication or transportation used for military purposes'; the wording of the paragraph implies that this list was intended to be exhaustive. The article also introduced the earliest explicit formulation of the rule of proportionality: bombardment of civilian objects (where located in the immediate vicinity of land operations) was legitimate, 'provided that there exists a reasonable presumption that the military concentration [targeted] is sufficiently important to justify such bombardment, having regard to the danger thus caused to the civilian population'.[27] The Hague Rules' listing of military objectives (albeit in a short and patently non-exhaustive list) and their formulation of proportionality were very significant pointers to the future: state practice evidenced their partial acceptance, even if not as strictly binding legal obligations,[28] and many of the provisions pioneered in the Rules have since been revisited in later instruments.[29]

The last pre-war attempt at legal development in this field was the Draft Convention for the Protection of Civilian Populations Against New Engines of War, which was produced by the International Law Association in 1938.[30] This sought *inter alia* to prohibit the bombardment of defended towns when military objectives could not be 'clearly recognized',[31] and aerial bombardment not directed at 'combatant forces or belligerent establishments [these were defined in Article 2] or lines of communication or transportation used for military purposes'.[32] It also proscribed attacks on undefended localities, but it defined these in such restricted terms that in practice hardly any city in Europe would have benefitted from its protection:

A town, port, village or isolated building shall be considered undefended provided that not only (a) no combatant troops, but also (b) no military, naval or air establishment, or barracks, arsenal, munition stores or factories, aerodromes or aeroplane workshops or ships of war, naval dockyards, forts, or fortifications for defensive or offensive purposes, or entrenchments ... exist within its boundaries or within a radius of 'x' kilometres from such boundaries.[33]

Such was the lack of consensus that, despite widespread international agreement on the need for some sort of international legal framework to regulate aerial bombardment,[34] neither the Hague Draft Rules nor the Draft Amsterdam Convention was ever even opened for signature. Thus, at the start of the Second World War, there was no binding treaty in force specifically governing aerial warfare and only the most general principles concerning military objectives could be said to have passed into customary international law, namely, that they needed to be

---

27 Hague Rules (n 25) art 24(4).
28 Both sides during the Second World War cited the Rules when accusing each other of violating the laws of war in respect of aerial warfare: Adam Roberts and Richard Guelff, *Documents on the Laws of War* (3rd edn, OUP 2000) 140.
29 Ibid 141.
30 Amsterdam Convention (2 September 1938) reprinted in Dietrich Schindler and Jiří Toman, *The Laws of Armed Conflicts* (Martinus Nijhoff 1988) 223.
31 Ibid art 3.
32 Ibid art 5(1).
33 Ibid art 2.
34 For example, see *League of Nations Official Journal, Special Supplement No 177 – Sino-Japanese Conflict – Appeal by the Chinese Government* (1937).

'legitimate, identifiable military objectives'.[35] By this time, the world had already had a taste of the horrors to come: the Japanese bombing of Shanghai in the so-called 'January 28 Incident' (1932) and the bombing of Guernica by the Luftwaffe's Condor Legion and the *Aviazione Legionaria*, at the behest of the Nationalists, in 1937 during the Spanish Civil War heralded the use of aerial bombardment as a method of 'total war', that was to culminate in the dropping of the atomic bombs by the Americans on Hiroshima and Nagasaki in 1945. As part of the doctrine of 'total war', in such operations entire cities or districts were treated as legitimate targets for bombardment,[36] with little or no attempt to distinguish between individual objects within them – a practice known euphemistically as 'area bombardment' (alternative terms included 'carpet bombing', 'saturation bombing', 'obliteration bombing' or, from the German and Japanese perspective, 'terror bombing').[37] As its chief British proponent put it, in unrepentant retrospective: 'International law can always be argued pro and con, but in this matter of the use of aircraft in war there is, it so happens, no international law at all.'[38]

2 The modern law

2.1 The basic definition

The experience of the 1930s and 1940s and the fact that at that time, 'each belligerent determined what should be understood by [military] objectives as it pleased [and] their ideas often differed considerably, depending on whether the territory concerned was their own, enemy territory, or territory of an ally occupied by enemy forces', led to a general recognition that, 'a restrictive definition [of military objectives] was necessary if the essential distinction between combatants and civilians and between civilian objects and military objectives was to be maintained'.[39] After the Second World War, however, the 1949 Geneva Conventions focused exclusively on the humanitarian protection of victims of armed conflicts and – despite such protection being legally predicated upon the fundamental principle of distinction – did not venture to define military objectives as such. Perhaps the reason for such reticence at the time, as was apparently the case when Additional Protocol I was being negotiated three decades later, was what the ICRC in particular saw as, 'a problem of a moral nature . . .: should a humanitarian treaty describe objects which may be attacked?'[40] Actually, when seen in the light of centuries of a permissive tradition built into the laws and customs of war, whereby the law specified what was permitted as well as what was prohibited, the problem does not seem so acute. In any event, whatever the precise scruples were, they were overcome at the Geneva Diplomatic Conference which resulted in the adoption of the 1977 Additional Protocols. After restating the negative

---

35 As stated by British Prime Minister Neville Chamberlain in the House of Commons (see Hansard, *HC Debs* (21 June 1938) vol 337 cols 937–938), and subsequently adopted by unanimous resolution of the Assembly of the League of Nations: 'Protection of Civilian Populations Against Bombing From the Air in Case of War' (30 September 1938) *League of Nations Official Journal, Special Supplement No 182*, 15–16.

36 In the case of the atomic bombs dropped on Japan, the weapons themselves were only suitable for use against a target the size of a city as they were incapable of distinguishing between different objects.

37 See generally Igor Primoratz (ed), *Terror from the Sky: The Bombing of German Cities in World War II* (Bergbahn 2010).

38 Marshal of the Royal Air Force Sir Arthur Harris, *Bomber Offensive* (first published 1947, Pen & Sword Military Classics 2005) 177.

39 *AP Commentary* ¶ 2000.

40 Ibid ¶ 2015.

definition of civilian objects *a contrario* military objectives, the following is then stated in Article 52(2) of Additional Protocol I:

> Attacks shall be limited strictly to military objectives. In so far as objects are concerned, military objectives are limited to those objects which by their nature, location, purpose or use make an effective contribution to military action and whose total or partial destruction, capture or neutralization, in the circumstances ruling at the time, offers a definite military advantage.

Despite being contained in a treaty to which by no means all the major military powers in the world are parties, the rules for targeting operations in the Protocol – including the above-cited definition of military objectives – were quickly recognised as significant enough that they were accepted as reflecting customary international law. The Protocol is currently binding on 174 states[41] – that is to say, a very large majority of states in the world. Already by the time of the First Gulf War in 1991 (fewer than 15 years after the adoption of the Protocol and at a time when neither the US nor the UK was legally bound by its provisions as a matter of treaty obligation),[42] its provisions on the selection of targets, precautions in attack and protection of the civilian population were accepted and applied in effect by the Coalition forces;[43] official accounts of military operations by both states repeatedly emphasised that only 'military targets' were attacked.[44] Current US doctrine, while not restating Additional Protocol I per se since the US continues to object to other aspects of that instrument and is not formally bound by it, nevertheless reflects its provisions substantively in its currently authoritative illustrative list of '[p]roper objects of attack':

> enemy warships and military aircraft, naval and military auxiliaries, naval and military bases ashore, warship construction and repair facilities, military depots and warehouses, petroleum/oils/lubricants storage areas, docks, port facilities, harbors, bridges, airfields, military vehicles, armor, artillery, ammunition stores, troops concentrations and embarkation points, lines of communication and other objects used to conduct or support military operations ... also ... geographic features, such as a mountain pass, and buildings and facilities that provide administrative and personnel support for military and naval operations such as barracks, communications and command and control facilities, headquarters buildings, mess halls and training areas.

---

41 ICRC, 'Treaties and States Parties to Such Treaties', www.icrc.org/applic/ihl/ihl.nsf/Treaty.xsp?doc umentId=D9E6B6264D7723C3C12563CD002D6CE4&action=OpenDocument.

42 The UK finally ratified API (along with APII) in 1998, but the US has not ratified to the present day, and seems unlikely to do so in the foreseeable future; for a useful distillation of the US attitude to these instruments, see Michael J Matheson, 'The United States Position on the Relation of Customary International Law to the 1977 Protocols Additional to the 1949 Geneva Conventions' (1987) 2 *American University JILP* 419.

43 See Michael N Schmitt, 'The Law of Targeting' in Elizabeth Wilmshurst and Susan Breau (eds), *Perspectives on the ICRC Study on Customary International Humanitarian Law* (CUP 2007) 131–134.

44 For example, US Department of Defense, 'Final Report to Congress on the Conduct of the Persian Gulf War – Appendix O: The Role of the Law of War' (1992) 31 *ILM* 615; Letter dated 30 January 1991 from the Permanent Representative of the United States of America to the United Nations addressed to the President of the Security Council, UN Doc S/22173; Letter dated 13 February 1991 from the Permanent Representative of the United Kingdom of Great Britain and Northern Ireland to the United Nations addressed to the President of the Security Council, UN Doc S/22218.

Proper objects of attack also [may] include enemy lines of communication, rail yards, bridges, rolling stock, barges, lighters, industrial installations producing war-fighting products, and power generation plants.[45]

Other non-party states to Additional Protocol I, like Israel, have expressly recognised the Article 52(2) definition of military objectives as reflecting customary international law,[46] and that status has also been recognised by international tribunals.[47]

2.2 Scope of application

2.2.1 Classification of armed conflict

Additional Protocol I is expressly stated to apply only in situations of international armed conflict: that is, 'declared war or ... any other armed conflict which may arise between two or more of the High Contracting Parties',[48] as well as, 'armed conflicts in which peoples are fighting against colonial domination and alien occupation and against racist régimes in the exercise of their right of self-determination'.[49] The definition of military objectives in the *lex scripta* is theoretically unique to situations of international armed conflict, since Additional Protocol II (on the protection of victims in non-international armed conflicts) does not contain any provisions as to either the methods and means of warfare or the selection of targets. The basic rule of distinction reiterated in Article 48 of Additional Protocol I derives from the legal separation of combatants from civilians, categories of personal status which as such do not exist in non-international armed conflicts, where the law speaks of 'persons who do not take a direct part or who have ceased to take part in hostilities'[50] apart from those who attract special protection by reason of having been deprived of their liberty or of being wounded, sick or shipwrecked. Civilians are certainly mentioned in the context of non-international armed conflicts,[51] but are not defined in either a positive or a negative sense; and since there is no category of combatant status per se in such conflicts, it is not surprising that there is equally no provision as to military objectives.

---

45 US Navy, US Marine Corps and US Coast Guard, *The Commander's Handbook on the Law of Naval Operations*, NWP 1-14M/MCWP 5-12.1/COMDTPUB P5800.7A (July 2007) ¶ 8.2.5, www.usnwc. edu/getattachment/a9b8e92d-2c8d-4779-9925-0defea93325c/1-14M_(Jul_2007)_(NWP). It is interesting to note that the historical American predilection for listing specific types of legitimate targets without relying on the term 'military objectives' (cf Parks (n 26) 33) continues to this day. On the other hand, certain other American official publications quote from and comment on the Article 52(2) definition of military objectives without identifying the specific treaty source: see US Joint Chiefs of Staff, *Joint Publication 3-60: Joint Targeting* (31 January 2013) Appendix A ¶ 4(b), http://cfr.org/content/publications/attachments/Joint_Chiefs_of_Staff-Joint_Targeting_31_January_2013.pdf.
46 For example, Israel Ministry of Foreign Affairs, 'Responding to Hezbollah Attacks from Lebanon: Issues of Proportionality' (25 July 2006) 2, www.mfa.gov.il/mfa/aboutisrael/state/law/pages/responding%20to%20hizbullah%20attacks%20from%20lebanon-%20issues%20of%20proportionality%20july%202006.aspx; Israel Ministry of Foreign Affairs, 'The Operation in Gaza: Factual and Legal Aspects' (29 July 2009) ¶ 101, www.mfa.gov.il/mfa/foreignpolicy/terrorism/palestinian/pages/operation_in_gaza-factual_and_legal_aspects.aspx.
47 *Eritrea v Ethiopia (Partial Award, Western Front, Aerial Bombardment and Related Claims: Eritrea's Claims 1, 3, 5, 9–13, 14, 21, 25 and 26 (Partial Award)* (2005) 26 RIAA 291 (Eritrea–Ethiopia Claims Commission) ¶ 14.
48 GCI–IV common art 2, referenced in API art 1(3).
49 API art 1(4).
50 APII art 4(1).
51 Ibid arts 13–18.

On the other hand, since at least the mid-1990s there has been a clear tendency to assimilate certain rules of the law in international armed conflicts to non-international armed conflicts also. This trend was first publicised in a very general sense in case law by the ICTY,[52] while treaty instruments adopted in the succeeding years confirmed it. This was notably the case in respect of the definition of military objectives from Additional Protocol I, which was incorporated *verbatim* in Article 2(6) of the Amended Protocol II to the 1980 Convention on Certain Conventional Weapons[53] and in Article 1(f) of the Second Protocol to the 1954 Hague Convention for the Protection of Cultural Property in the Event of Armed Conflict;[54] both of these instruments are expressly applicable in situations of non-international armed conflict. Restatements of the law in international documents produced since have reiterated that at customary international law the definition of military objectives from Additional Protocol I applies to non-international as well as international armed conflicts.[55] Certain states in any event apply the definition and its associated targeting rules as a matter of doctrine in all armed conflicts, irrespective of their formal characterisation;[56] although this may be seen as a policy choice rather than an actual legal obligation, as has been the case in Coalition operations in Afghanistan.[57] Nevertheless, in light of developments over the last 20 years, it is now uncontroversial to assert conclusively that the definition of military objectives from Additional Protocol I is applicable in non-international armed conflicts also.

2.2.2 Domains of warfare

As has already been discussed, until the adoption of Additional Protocol I there was no international law instrument in force which provided a definition of military objectives for aerial warfare, although there was such a pre-existing definition in force for naval warfare (specifically, for naval bombardment of targets on land).[58] With the adoption and consolidation of the newly articulated definition and targeting rules in the Protocol, however, it was sensibly decided to extend their reach to all the then-known domains of warfare:

> The provisions of [Articles 48–67 of Additional Protocol I] apply to any land, air or sea warfare which may affect the civilian population, individual civilians or civilian objects on land. They further apply to all attacks from the sea or from the air against objectives on land but do not otherwise affect the rules of international law applicable in armed conflict at sea or in the air.[59]

---

52 See *Prosecutor v Tadić (Decision on the Defence Motion for Interlocutory Appeal on Jurisdiction)* (Case no IT-94-1, ICTY Appeals Chamber, 2 October 1995) ¶¶ 100–127.

53 Protocol on Prohibitions or Restrictions on the Use of Mines, Booby-Traps and Other Devices (10 October 1980) 1342 UNTS 168 (as amended 3 May 1996), UN Doc CCW/CONF.I/16.

54 249 UNTS 240.

55 CIHL r 8; *The Manual on the Law of Non-International Armed Conflict With Commentary* (IIHL 2006) ¶ 1.1.4.1.

56 For example, UK Ministry of Defence, *Joint Doctrine Publication 3-46: Legal Support to Joint Operations* (2nd edn, 2010) ¶ 130, www.mod.uk/DefenceInternet/MicroSite/DCDC/OurPublications/JDWP/Jdp346LegalSupportToJointOperations2ndEdition.htm.

57 Headquarters International Security Assistance Force/United States Forces-Afghanistan, *COMISAF's Tactical Directive* (30 November 2011), www.pksoi.org/document_repository/doc_lib/20111105%20nuc%20tactical%20directive%20revision%204%20%28releaseable%20version%29%20r%5B1%5D.pdf.

58 HCIX art 2.

59 API art 49(3).

Thus, modern restatements of the law of targeting operations in both the maritime[60] and aerial[61] warfare operational environments use the same definition of military objectives. To the extent that these domains of warfare are just over a century old (in the case of aerial warfare) and very much older (in the case of maritime warfare), the *lex lata* is uncontroversial in this respect.

Arguably less certain is the position in respect of the newest domains of warfare, or those that, whilst acknowledged as possible in theory, are yet to emerge in practice. In respect of outer space, international law has since the 1960s been moving consistently in the general direction of ensuring that militarisation of the environment does not take place, and there is no known instance of armed conflict taking place in outer space. On the one hand, Blount has argued cogently that the law of international armed conflict (including the Additional Protocol I definition of military objectives) must necessarily apply by logical extension in the event of any space conflict. On the other hand, the same author has noted that the physical particularities of the space environment may make it very difficult to apply the rule of distinction correctly in practice: for example, it may be all but impossible to verify the identity of targets at first hand and distinguish military satellites from the virtually identical myriad of different civilian satellites already in use in outer space; such targeting operations would then be highly dependent, even more than is the case in conventional operations, on the availability of accurate intelligence.[62] 'Soft law' in the relatively new domain of cyberspace adopts exactly the same approach as the *San Remo* and *Harvard Manuals* in restating the Additional Protocol I definition of military objectives as being applicable in cyber operations.[63] Unlike war in outer space, which as stated above remains a somewhat hypothetical possibility for the time being, war in cyberspace is not only possible but has actually already occurred, albeit on a limited scale and without apparently incurring either direct physical destruction of intangible objects or human casualties or fatalities.[64] Nevertheless, the capability for cyber operations to cause death or injury to persons and physical damage or destruction to objects is undisputed, and it has been correctly argued that such operations would amount to 'attacks' in the sense of IHL,[65] and would therefore be governed by the relevant provisions of Additional Protocol I.[66] Insofar as military objectives are concerned, and as will be discussed further below, special difficulties for targeting in the cyber environment are likely to be posed by the prevalence of 'dual-use objects' and the unforeseeable and unintended effects of attacks, which will have serious consequences for the precautions which Additional Protocol I requires commanders to take in planning and launching attacks. Nevertheless, in sum, the applicability of the Additional Protocol I definition of military objectives across all

---

60 See *San Remo Manual on International Law Applicable to Armed Conflicts at Sea* (IIHL 1994) r 40

61 See *HPCR Manual on International Law Applicable to Air and Missile Warfare* (Harvard University 2009) r 1(y).

62 See P J Blount, 'Targeting in Outer Space: Legal Aspects of Operational Military Actions in Space' (2012) *Harvard NSJ*, http://harvardnsj.org/2012/11/targeting-in-outer-space-legal-aspects-of-operational-military-actions-in-space/.

63 M Schmitt (ed), *Tallinn Manual on the International Law Applicable to Cyber Warfare* (CUP 2013) r 38.

64 Apart from a few instances of 'cyberattacks' that occurred without any context of armed conflict (eg Estonia in 2007, Iran in 2010), peripheral cyber operations have been noted in the context of conventional kinetic armed conflicts in Georgia (2008) and Gaza (2012); their effect was exclusively psychological and restricted to propaganda.

65 '"Attacks" means acts of violence against the adversary, whether in offence or in defence': API art 49(1). See also *Tallinn Manual* (n 63) r 30.

66 Michael N Schmitt, 'Cyber Operations and the *Jus in Bello*: Key Issues' (2011) 87 *International Law Studies* 89.

the currently existing and envisaged domains of warfare appears to be beyond questioning as a matter of principle.

2.3 Elements of the definition

There are two elements to the Article 52(2) definition of military objectives, which must be simultaneously met in order for a given object to be a legitimate target for attack: the object must make an effective contribution to enemy military action by reason of its 'nature, location, purpose or use', and its destruction, capture or neutralisation must have a 'definite military advantage' for the attacker. The application of these criteria is time-sensitive: that is, they must be assessed according to 'the circumstances ruling at the time' of the attack – except in respect of its 'nature', an object that was not a military objective hours or even minutes ago may suddenly become one, and vice versa. Although this temporal aspect may seem arbitrary, it is an inevitable corollary of modern technology and the speed with which circumstances may change in the contemporary battlespace. Attacking commanders must take precautions: in particular, they must do everything feasible to verify that they are attacking military objectives,[67] to choose means and methods of attack that will avoid or minimise collateral damage[68] and to give effective advance warning to the civilian population of attacks which may affect them.[69]

2.3.1 'Nature'

The 'nature' of an object is generally the most straightforward aspect in assessing whether or not it may lawfully be targeted; it refers to the intrinsic character of the object as being of, or belonging to, the armed forces of a party to an armed conflict. Such objects are always going to be legitimate military objectives, irrespective of where they are or what they are doing in relation to frontline hostilities, and during an armed conflict they may in theory[70] be attacked in any place and at any time, without prior warning. They include such obvious military assets as barracks, tanks, transport and equipment, fortifications, military aircraft, warships, staff headquarters, defence ministry buildings and installations, airbases and naval port facilities. Thus, the Argentine Navy cruiser ARA *General Belgrano*, torpedoed and sunk by a British submarine during the Falklands War (1982), was plainly a military objective by nature – legally it was of no significance that at the time of her sinking she was sailing away from the British Task Force and arguably presented no *immediate* threat.[71]

2.3.2 'Location'

Almost any object that is not intrinsically military may nonetheless acquire a military significance in a particular operation by reason of its geographical situation, 'either because it is a site that must be seized or because it is important to prevent the enemy from seizing it, or otherwise because it is a matter of forcing the enemy to retreat from it'.[72] Bridges, roads and railway lines are obvious examples of such objects. Although the NATO attack on the Leskovac railway

---

67 API art 57(2)(a)(i).
68 Ibid art 57(2)(a)(ii).
69 Ibid art 57(2)(c).
70 Subject to API art 57(2)(b), on which see further below.
71 See Hansard, *HC Debs* (4 May 1982) vol 23 cols 29–30.
72 *API Commentary* ¶ 2021.

bridge in eastern Serbia during the Kosovo War (1999) has attracted much notoriety because of the unfortunate and unintended civilian casualties that resulted from the fact that a passenger train was crossing it at the moment of attack, the bridge was correctly targeted as 'part of a re-supply route being used for Serb forces in Kosovo':[73] its location had rendered its destruction of military significance to the NATO campaign. At ratification of Additional Protocol I, a number of states made interpretative statements or declarations regarding this criterion, to the effect that a specific area of land may be a military objective if its location renders it important for military operations[74] – for example, a hill that provides a vantage point, or a mountain pass that provides the best route of advance against an enemy position. Conversely, however, designating an entire area of land and treating, for example, all vehicles travelling within it as military objects – as Israel allegedly did in respect of the area south of the Litani River during the Second Lebanon War (2006)[75] – would not comply with this aspect of the law.

2.3.3 'Purpose or use'

These two criteria are usefully considered together as being interlinked, rather than separately, for their essence is the same and the only difference between them is temporal: as it has concisely been expressed, '"[p]urpose" means the future intended use of an object while "use" means its present function'.[76] Actual use is obviously easier to determine conclusively and accurately than intended future use, knowledge of which will depend on accurate up-to-date intelligence. Although it would be tempting for a commander to infer from a previous pattern of conduct by the enemy that they are likely to make use of certain objects for military purposes, such a con-clusion without evidence of actual use in the instant situation would be difficult to justify in law. For example, whilst it has long been recognised that Israel's irregular enemies in Gaza (Hamas) and Lebanon (Hezbollah) have a 'well-known and cynical practice of establishing positions close to civilian or United Nations installations',[77] that would not justify any systematic targeting of such installations in future operations on the assumption that their purpose will turn them into military objectives. On the other hand, even an object that is normally immune from attack – such as a school or a hotel – will lose its protection and become a military objective if it is actu-ally used for military purposes.[78] In the 2006 conflict in Lebanon, Israel claimed that air strikes on civilian residential buildings, health facilities including ambulances, and civilian convoys, were justifiable on the basis that Hezbollah was actually using them to fire rockets and transport weapons and fighters.[79] The Protocol requires that if there is any doubt as to whether or not a civilian object is actually being used for military purposes, 'it shall be presumed not to be so used'.[80]

---

73 ICTY, 'Final Report to the Prosecutor by the Committee Established to Review the NATO Bombing Campaign Against the Federal Republic of Yugoslavia' (2000) 39 *International Legal Materials* 1257 ¶ 58.

74 Roberts and Guelff (n 28) 500 (Australia), 502 (Canada), 505 (Germany), 507 (Italy), 508 (Netherlands, New Zealand), 509 (Spain), 511 (UK).

75 UN Human Rights Council Mission to Lebanon and Israel, UN Doc A/HRC/2/7 (2 October 2006) ¶ 41.

76 UK Ministry of Defence, *The Manual of the Law of Armed Conflict* (OUP 2004) ¶ 5.4.4(e).

77 UN Security Council Official Records, 3654th Meeting, UN Doc S/PV.3654 (18 April 1996) 14 (statement of Mr Biørn Lian (Norway)).

78 *AP Commentary* ¶ 2022.

79 Mission to Lebanon and Israel (n 75) ¶¶ 46–48.

80 API art 52(3).

2.3.4 'Effective contribution to military action'

This is a somewhat vague phrase, one which the ICRC *Commentary* does not comment on and which it has been noted is open to different possible interpretations;[81] as such, it is unsurprising that considerable latitude is afforded to commanders who are making the assessment. The preferred approach seems to be that 'military action' has 'a wide meaning equating to the general prosecution of the war' and 'effective contribution' does not require the kind of direct causation needed for direct participation in hostilities by individual civilians: accordingly, legitimate military objectives far to the rear of the zone of combat – an armaments factory, for example – may still be targeted on the basis that their contribution to military action is effective, albeit indirect in relation to specific hostilities.[82] Uncertainties over the nature of the 'effective contribution' lie at the heart of the controversy surrounding the US concept of economic targets, as will be discussed below.

2.3.5 'Definite military advantage'

This part of the test is related to the fundamental principle of military necessity as an enabling or permissive factor for military forces in the conduct of operations. In essence it is intended to preclude decisions to proceed with an attack being based on a military advantage that is too remote, indeterminate or only potential[83] – as Rogers suggests: '[it] excludes a fanciful estimate of the military advantage or one that is not based on proper information; or it means a concrete and perceptible military advantage rather than a hypothetical and speculative one'.[84] The military advantage in question must also be that which is 'anticipated from the attack considered as a whole and not only from isolated or particular parts of the attack'.[85] Just because a given object satisfies the other criteria in Article 52(2) to qualify as a military objective does not mean that it will always be *necessary* to attack it: in a war of manoeuvre on the ground, for example, it may be that attacking commanders elect for reasons of military utility and necessity to bypass certain enemy strongpoints, notwithstanding that they would obviously be legitimate military objectives under the law. However, that choice – the option *not* to attack a valid military objective – should be understood as being of a moral nature rather than a matter of legal obligation.

2.4 Areas of controversy

2.4.1 Collateral damage, proportionality and human shields

Even if a given object satisfies the Article 52(2) criteria and qualifies as a military objective, it will not always be lawful to attack it, depending on the application (if relevant) of the principle of proportionality. As long as there are no civilians or civilian objects in the vicinity – as in the cases of a warship on the high seas, a military communications system housed in a remote and otherwise uninhabited mountainous or desert area, or an unmanned aerial vehicle in the air – there is no need to consider the doctrine of proportionality. However, if the proximity of civilians or civilian objects creates a likelihood of collateral damage, Additional Protocol I requires the attacking commander to consider whether, 'the attack may be expected to cause incidental

---

81 Heather Harrison Dinniss, *Cyber Warfare and the Laws of War* (CUP 2012) 188.
82 See A P V Rogers, *Law on the Battlefield* (2nd edn, Manchester University Press 2004) 67.
83 *AP Commentary* ¶ 2024.
84 Rogers (n 82) 65.
85 UK *Manual* (n 76) ¶ 5.4.4(j).

loss of civilian life, injury to civilians, damage to civilian objects, or a combination thereof, which would be excessive in relation to the concrete and direct military advantage anticipated'; if it would, then the attack should be cancelled or suspended.[86] Where a choice of different military objectives is possible, the one estimated to carry the lowest collateral damage should be selected, although this obligation only applies as such if the objectives in question would produce 'a similar military advantage'.[87]

Many contemporary military operations take place in asymmetric conflicts, which are often set in an urban environment where the civilian population is still largely *in situ* and the defending party, being at a military/technological disadvantage vis-à-vis the attacker, deliberately operates within and among that civilian population. The attacking commander's task is thus fraught with difficult conundrums: for example, how to weigh up the military advantage of killing an enemy commander or destroying a mobile rocket launcher against the likelihood of serious damage to an adjacent school or house of worship, or dozens (or more) of likely or potential civilian casualties. If the defenders are using the presence or movement of civilians 'in attempts to shield military objectives from attacks',[88] as was done by the Iraqis during the First Gulf War,[89] how (if at all) is that factored in to the proportionality equation? Equally, to what extent – if at all – should a commander's imperative to complete his mission successfully at a minimum cost to his own troops ('force protection') form part of the proportionality assessment? These are difficult questions, of both morality and law,[90] which cannot be answered here as they are not strictly part of the question of the *definition* of military objectives; but they are a critical consequence of the designation of such objectives and their selection for attack.

2.4.2 'Dual-use objects'

'Dual-use objects' are 'objects which have some civilian uses and some actual or potential military use'.[91] Given their prevalence in modern industrialised states it is unfortunate that they are not defined in Additional Protocol I, but recognised examples in customary international law include communications and transportation systems, petrochemical complexes and 'manufacturing plants of certain types'.[92] Issues of collateral damage and proportionality, as highlighted in the previous sub-section, will invariably be central to the question of when such objects may be attacked. However, since dual-use objects are essentially nothing more than acknowledged military objectives that have a typically high risk of collateral damage because of their normal partially civilian use, it would be doctrinally incorrect to assert that there is any general or specific prohibition on attacking them – rather, special care and precautions in attack will need to be taken when targeting them. A now-classic example is NATO's targeting of the Serbian state-owned national broadcaster, *Radio-televizija Srbije* (RTS), in downtown Belgrade during the Kosovo War. The facility was deliberately selected for attack due to its wartime use as a back-up command, control

---

86 API art 57(2)(b).

87 Ibid art 57(3).

88 Ibid art 51(7).

89 Final Report to Congress (n 44) 624–627 (use of civilians as human shields); Letter dated 22 January 1991 from the Permanent Representative of Kuwait to the United Nations addressed to the President of the Security Council, UN Doc S/22128 (use of prisoners of war as human shields).

90 For extended discussions, see Joseph Holland, 'Military Objective and Collateral Damage: Their Relationship and Dynamics' (2004) 7 *YBIHL* 35; Noam Neuman, 'Applying the Rule of Proportionality: Force Protection and Cumulative Assessment in International Law and Practice' (2004) 7 *YBIHL* 79.

91 ICTY Final Report (n 73) ¶ 37.

92 Ibid.

and communications network for the Serbian military and security forces, but NATO was careful to attack in the middle of the night, when the building would be at its emptiest, and the resulting civilian casualties (some 16 or 17 persons) were deemed, 'unfortunately high but ... not ... clearly disproportionate'.[93] Ethiopia's bombardment of the Hirgigo power station during its war with Eritrea in 1998–2000 was the subject of an arbitration award, wherein the power station was found to have been a lawful military objective because it provided the electric power necessary for the operation of the port and naval base at Massawa, which itself was a valid military objective.[94] Israel's choice of dual-use objects for attack during its operations in Lebanon and Gaza in recent years has also been investigated, with rather more mixed results.[95]

The issue of dual-use objects and the circumstances in which they may be targeted is likely to be of particular significance in the context of the possibility of future cyberwars: since so many computer networks are simultaneously of military and civilian use, special care will need to be given to the likelihood of collateral damage. It is highly likely that such damage could be some way down the chain of causation (the 'law of unintended consequences' – for example, a network that provides support for a hospital, the national electricity grid or civil air traffic control) or that a particular targeted network serves objects that, in addition to military functions in wartime, are indispensable for the survival of the civilian population[96] or contain dangerous forces.[97] The scope for mistakes and/or unforeseeable 'knock-on' damage to assets other than those directly targeted will be especially large in the cyber context.

2.4.3 Economic targets

In its current formulation of a military doctrine and practice dating back as far as the American Civil War, the US holds that, '[e]conomic objects of the enemy that indirectly but effectively support and sustain the enemy's war-fighting capability may also be attacked'.[98] This expansive interpretation of the notion of legitimate military objectives can be traced back to the Civil War practice of deliberately destroying Confederate cotton stocks, on the basis that the entire Southern economy rested on cotton and the proceeds of its sale abroad almost exclusively financed and sustained the Confederacy's continuing war effort, despite the fact that it had far fewer war-sustaining resources than the North. The practice received judicial approval in a series of cases during and after the war[99] and has remained part of US doctrine ever since. It was evident in General William T Sherman's 'March to the Sea' through Georgia in 1864, in which he ordered the systematic destruction of Confederate infrastructure – particularly railways and cotton mills – with a view to destroying the Confederacy's physical capacity to continue the war.[100] Outside

---

93 See ibid ¶¶ 71–79.
94 *Eritrea's Claims* (n 47) ¶¶ 106–121.
95 See 'Responding to Hezbollah Attacks' (n 46) 5–6; Mission to Lebanon and Israel (n 75) ¶¶ 49–51; The Operation in Gaza (n 46) ¶¶ 233–236.
96 API art 54.
97 Ibid art 56.
98 *Commander's Handbook* (n 45) ¶ 8.2.5.
99 *Mrs Alexander's Cotton*, 69 US 404 (1864), 419–420; *Lamar v Browne*, 92 US 187 (1875), 194; *Young v United States*, 97 US 39 (1877), 59–61.
100 See Headquarters Military Division of the Mississippi, Special Field Orders No 120 (9 November 1864) in US War Department, *The War of the Rebellion: A Compilation of the Official Records of the Union and Confederate Armies* (Government Printing Office 1892) Ser 1 – Vol XXXIX (Pt III) 713; for analysis, Thomas G Robisch, 'General William T Sherman: Would the Georgia Campaigns of the First Commander of the Modern Era Comply with Current Law of War Standards?' (1995) 9 *Emory ILR* 459.

America it also accorded with the views of another famously stern practitioner of war, General Helmut von Moltke, the Chief of the Prussian and German General Staff, who signalled his reaction to the adoption of the *Oxford Manual* in 1880, in part, as follows:

> The greatest good deed in war is the speedy ending of the war, and every means to that end, so long as it is not *reprehensible*, must remain open. In no way can I declare myself in agreement with the Declaration of St Petersburg that the sole justifiable measure in war is 'the weakening of the enemy's military power'. No, all the sources of support for the hostile government must be considered, its finances, railroads, foodstuffs, even its prestige.[101]

Despite consistent application by the US, most recently in the targeting of mobile oil refineries in Iraq,[102] the view that 'war-sustaining' or purely economic targets are legitimate military objectives has not found acceptance in the military doctrine and practice of other states – the British position, for example, is that such objects do not of themselves make an *effective* contribution to *military* action, nor would their destruction confer a *definite* military advantage, and they therefore fall outside the parameters of permissible targets under Article 52(2).[103] This is an area of operational law which is likely to be problematic in terms of interoperability within multinational coalitions, since the US interpretation of the law on this point is at odds with that of the UK and virtually all other states; in practice, however, this will likely continue to result in certain targeting operations being tasked exclusively to the US partners within a coalition.

2.4.4 Enemy morale

The targeting of enemy morale as such is not generally considered acceptable as a military objective in the modern law, despite extensive practice to the contrary during both World Wars. As with attacks on economic targets, the notion of destroying an enemy civilian population's morale originated in modern warfare with General Sherman's tactics during the American Civil War. Sherman tellingly summed up his views on how modern 'total war' should be conducted, by reference to his 1864 Savannah Campaign, in the following terms:

> We are not only fighting hostile armies, but a hostile people, and must make old and young, rich and poor, feel the hard hand of war, as well as their organized armies. I know that this recent movement of mine through Georgia has had a wonderful effect in this respect. Thousands [of Southerners] who had been deceived by their lying papers into the belief that we were being whipped all the time, realized the truth, and have no appetite for a repetition of the same experience.[104]

During the First World War, Germany initiated the deliberate bombing of cities with its Zeppelin raids from 1915, in an unsuccessful attempt to force the British civilian population to demand that its government sue for peace; in spite of the failure of this approach, comprehensive doctrines of strategic bombing in order to target the morale of an enemy for psychological effect were expounded in the interwar period by Marshal of the Royal Air Force Sir Hugh

---

101 'On the Nature of War by Helmut Moltke (the Elder)' (11 December 1880), wwi.lib.byu.edu/index. php/On_the_Nature_of_War_by_Helmut_Moltke_the_Elder (emphasis in original).
102 Kenneth Watkin, 'Targeting "Islamic State" Oil Facilities' (2014) 90 *International Law Studies* 499.
103 Rogers (n 82) 70–71.
104 W T Sherman to Maj Gen H W Halleck (24 December 1864) in *The War of the Rebellion* (n 100) ser 1, vol XLIV 798, 799.

Trenchard in the UK,[105] General Billy Mitchell in the US[106] and General Giulio Douhet in Italy.[107] The latter in particular had a seminal influence on strategic bombing during the Second World War, when both sides deliberately aimed to destroy the 'will of the people' to continue the fight, by bombing their cities to saturation in a policy euphemistically known as 'area bombardment': the 'terror raids' on Rotterdam and Coventry, the 'Blitz' on major cities around Britain in 1940 and the firebombing of Hamburg, Dresden and Tokyo, were so many grim markers along the way of 'total war'.

Today, such tactics are expressly ruled out: the modern law clearly forbids deliberate attempts to terrorise the civilian population as such.[108] The slightly more subtle aspect of 'area bombardment' against notionally legitimate but separate targets is equally proscribed by way of the ban on indiscriminate attacks ('bombardment by any methods or means which treats as a single military objective a number of clearly separated and distinct military objectives located in a city, town, village or other area containing a similar concentration of civilians or civilian objects').[109] Although it is occasionally suggested that targeting enemy media on the basis that it purveys hostile propaganda is acceptable,[110] it is unlikely that there is sufficient *opinio juris* to justify asserting this as a proposition of international law.[111] However, if the broadcasting either directly contributes to military action (for example, by broadcasting instructions to military units) or amounts to incitement to war crimes or similar illegal acts, it would probably be acceptable.[112] Hitherto a relatively unusual area of the law with few precedents,[113] this may well assume greater prominence with the seemingly inexorable rise of social media, coupled with the potential for cyber operations: Kenyan operations against Al-Shabaab in Somalia and the 2012 Gaza conflict are likely to be significant pointers to future trends as the opposing sides traded accusations and self-promotion on Twitter and in live blogs.[114] It is not surprising that the weaker, non-state parties to the conflicts should have found such methods attractive and useful; arguably more interesting is the reciprocal interest taken by the opposing state forces, and the possibility of social media becoming a more extensive battlespace in conflicts of the future – complete with the potential for a corresponding expansion of target sets.

105 See Scot Robertson, 'The Development of Royal Air Force Strategic Bombing Doctrine between the Wars: A Revolution in Military Affairs?' (1998) XII(1) *Air and Space Power Journal* 37.
106 See Lt Col Peter R Faber, 'The Development of US Strategic Bombing Doctrine in the Interwar Years: Moral and Legal?' (1996–1997) 7 *United States Air Force Academy Journal of Legal Studies*, www. usafa.edu/df/dfl/documents/JLS Volume 7/morleg.pdf.
107 See Giulio Douhet, *The Command of the Air* (first published 1921, Dino Ferrari tr, Coward-McCann, 1942).
108 API art 51(2).
109 Ibid art 51(5)(a).
110 For example, ICTY Final Report (n 73) 1277–1278 (NATO attack on RTS); Frank J Gaffney Jr, 'Take Out Al Jazeera' *Fox News* (29 September 2003), www.foxnews.com/story/2003/09/29/take-out-al-jazeera/ (American attack on Al Jazeera in Iraq); 'Responding to Hezbollah Attacks' (n 46) 6 (Israeli attack on the Al Manar Television station in Lebanon); 'Israeli Airstrikes target Palestinian TV Station in Gaza' *Ma'an News Agency* (29 July 2014), www.maannews.net/eng/viewdetails. aspx?id=716837.
111 ICTY Final Report (n 73) 1278–1279.
112 Rogers (n 82) 82–83.
113 Rare examples are the prosecution of Julius Streicher (newspaper publishing) and Hans Fritzsche (radio broadcasting) by the International Military Tribunal at Nuremberg after the Second World War: see *Prosecutor v Ruggiu* (Case no ICTR-97-32-1, Trial Chamber I, 1 June 2000).
114 David Smith, 'Al-Shabaab in War of Words with Kenyan Army on Twitter' *Guardian* (13 December 2011), www.theguardian.com/world/2011/dec/13/al-shabaab-war-words-twitter; Uri Friedman, 'Israel Defense Forces live Blogs Gaza Offensive' *Foreign Policy* (14 November 2012), http://foreign policy.com/2012/11/14/israel-defense-forces-live-blogs-gaza-offensive/.

3 Conclusion

Despite the fact that it is one of the most recent areas of development in IHL and that its formulation as binding law derives exclusively from a treaty that was adopted less than 40 years ago to which a substantial number of militarily significant states still refuse to become parties to, the concept of the military objective has assumed paramount importance in the conduct of contemporary military operations. With the advent of aerial warfare and its rise to domination of the modern battlespace, the designation of military objectives – together with the precautions to be taken in attacking them – has become absolutely critical to success; not just in the military sense, but, perhaps even more importantly, in the political, diplomatic and public relations senses too. The 'CNN effect' of rolling news reporting from conflict zones and the ubiquitous nature of modern journalism, coupled with the adage that 'bad news sells' and the rise of social media, has meant that sympathy for a state engaged in an armed conflict will rapidly be forfeited if it is not seen to be observing the rules. That those rules, and notably the definition of military objectives in Additional Protocol I, have become such a universal reference point (even in the lexicon of states that are not legally bound by the Protocol) is testament to their usefulness and durability; moreover, they are so flexible and adaptable that, in the absence of any discernible international appetite for making new law on the subject, they are likely to continue to serve the changing character of warfare for the foreseeable future.

9

Protection of civilians in the conduct of hostilities

Emanuela-Chiara Gillard

International humanitarian law is based on the premise that war must be fought between combatants. Individual civilians and civilian populations enjoy general protection against dangers arising from military operations and in the conduct of military operations constant care must be taken to spare them.[1]

A number of specific rules give more detailed substance to this general principle, starting with the principle of distinction and including the prohibition of attacks against civilians, indiscriminate attacks and rules on precautions. The rules outlined below are complemented, *inter alia*, by those on combatants, military objectives, direct participation in hostilities, humanitarian relief and reprisals or particular categories of persons, such as women, children or displaced persons.

The interplay between human rights and international humanitarian law (IHL) is complex.[2] For present purposes it suffices to note that there is general agreement that conduct of hostilities – the focus of the present chapter – is an area where the rules of IHL are the *lex specialis*.[3] Consequently, reference will only be made to this body of law.

1 Protection of civilians: a progressive codification

The first treaty to lay down specific protections for the civilian population was the 1949 Geneva Convention IV relative to the Protection of Civilian Persons in Time of War.[4] Despite its broad title, the Convention only contains a small number of provisions applicable to *all* civilians in

---

1 API arts 51(1) and 57(1).
2 See Noam Lubell and Nancie Prud'homme, 'Impact of human rights law' ch 6 in this volume.
3 See eg Cordula Droege, 'The Interplay between International Humanitarian Law and International Human Rights Law in Situations of Armed Conflict' (2007) 49 *Israel LR* 310, 347.
4 A small number of provisions of the Regulations to the Hague Convention (IV) of 1907 (arts 23–28) afford indirect protection to civilians during hostilities. Indirect inasmuch as they prohibit attacks against undefended towns, villages, dwellings and buildings, rather than against civilians per se. Section III, dealing with military authority over the territory of the hostile state, provides some additional safeguards.

states involved in armed conflict.[5] The majority of the rules only apply to 'protected persons' within the meaning of the Convention: persons who 'find themselves, in case of a conflict or occupation, in the hands of a Party to the conflict or Occupying Power of which they are not nationals'.[6]

Geneva Convention IV was a significant development as it laid down important safeguards specifically for protected persons, such as the prohibitions on human shields, collective punishment and reprisals, as well as guarantees during occupation, but it did not contain rules regulating conduct of hostilities. Consequently, certain cardinal rules for the protection of the civilian population – some already considered customary at the time, including most notably, the principle of distinction and the prohibition on attacking civilians[7] – were not codified.[8]

It was only in Additional Protocol I that states codified rules on the conduct of hostilities in meaningful detail, including in terms of the protections to be afforded to civilians. Additional Protocol I lays down, *inter alia*, the principle of distinction, the prohibition against indiscriminate attacks and precautions in attack and defence. Importantly also, the protections in this instrument apply to *all* civilians and not just those in the hands of a party of which they are not nationals. As pointed out in the ICRC *Commentary*, '[i]n protecting civilians against the dangers of war, the important aspect is not so much their nationality as the inoffensive character of the persons to be spared'.[9]

Only a small number of treaty rules regulate conduct of hostilities in non-international armed conflicts.[10] Article 4(2) of Additional Protocol II contains a non-exhaustive list of prohibited acts: collective punishment, taking of hostages, acts of terrorism, pillage; and some basic rules setting out fundamental principles in far less detail than Additional Protocol I.[11] Article 13 grants the civilian population and individual civilians general protection from the dangers arising from military operations and prohibits attacks against civilians and acts or threats of violence whose primary aim is to spread terror. The Protocol does not address indiscriminate attacks or precautions.

This being said, many – but not all – of the rules regulating conduct of hostilities found in Additional Protocol I are considered customary and also applicable in non-international conflict.[12]

---

5 GCIV arts 13–26.
6 GCIV art 4.
7 See eg *AP Commentary* ¶¶ 1826 and 1864; W Hays Parks, 'The Protection of Civilians from Air Warfare' (1998) 27 *Israel YBHR* 65, 72.
8 The 1949 Diplomatic Conference was not tasked with revising the HR, but this left a serious gap in codified humanitarian law. *AP Commentary* ¶ 1829–1830.
9 *AP Commentary* ¶ 1909.
10 Although GCI–IV common art 3 requires persons not taking active part in hostilities to be treated humanely and prohibits violence to life and person, this provision does not relate to conduct of hostilities. Rather, it aims to ensure humane treatment for persons in the power of a party to a non-international armed conflict. Michael Bothe, Karl-Josef Partsch and Waldemar Solf, *New Rules for Victims of Armed Conflict: Commentary on the Two 1977 Protocols Additional to the Geneva Conventions of 1949* (2nd edn, Martinus Nijhoff 2013) 769.
11 A more detailed draft instrument had been elaborated during the Diplomatic Conference, but it was reduced considerably before the final plenary sessions once it became apparent that it would not be acceptable to all participants. *AP Commentary* ¶¶ 4405–4418.
12 CIHL pt I (rr 1–24). For divergent views see eg Elizabeth Wilmshurst (ed), *Perspectives on the ICRC Study on Customary International Humanitarian Law* (CUP 2007).

2 The principle of distinction

The principle of distinction requires belligerents to distinguish at all times between combatants and civilians and to direct attacks exclusively against combatants or civilians taking direct part in hostilities, for the duration of such participation.[13]

The principle is the keystone of IHL. Although it was only codified, in relation to international armed conflicts, in Article 48 of Additional Protocol I, it has long been considered customary – in both international and non-international armed conflicts. The ICJ considers it one of the 'cardinal principles' of IHL and of the 'intransgressible principles of international customary law'.[14]

In relation to non-international armed conflicts, during the Diplomatic Conference leading to the adoption of Additional Protocol II, language which may be interpreted as a recognition of insurgent parties or as granting rights to their members was removed, including references to 'parties to the conflict' and 'combatants'.[15] Paradoxically, this means that Additional Protocol II does not actually contain the principle of distinction, as it was impossible to formulate it without resorting to terms that would have been problematic.[16] However, the principle is implicit in the prohibition in Article 13(2) on attacking the civilian population or individual civilians.

2.1 Who is a civilian?

Article 50(1) of Additional Protocol I defines civilians negatively as anyone who is not a member of the armed forces. This approach highlights the fact that civilians and combatants are two mutually exclusive categories and that 'there is no undistributed middle between the categories of combatants ... and civilians'.[17] In case of doubt a person is to be considered a civilian.[18]

The civilian population comprises all persons who are civilians.[19] The presence within the civilian population of persons who are not civilians does not deprive it of its civilian character and protections.[20]

In non-international armed conflicts, for the reasons stated above, Additional Protocol II does not contain any reference to combatants, making it impossible to define civilians in the same negative manner. Although the Protocol refers both to civilians and to the civilian population, these terms are left undefined. Absent any reference to combatants or members of the organised group, the inference is that everyone who is not a member of a state's armed forces is a civilian and thus protected from attack unless she or he takes direct part in hostilities and loses protection for the duration of such participation.

The ICRC Interpretive Guidance on Direct Participation in Hostilities suggests an innovative approach, drawing a distinction between those members of an armed group who assume a continuous combat function and who, it considers, can be targeted at all times and persons who

---

13 The principle is broader in scope and also requires distinguishing between military objectives other than combatants and civilian objects. The focus of the present chapter is the protection of civilian persons and for reasons of space reference will not be made to civilian objects, even though they are also protected and their destruction can have significant adverse effects on civilian populations.

14 *Legality of the Threat or Use of Nuclear Weapons (Advisory Opinion)* [1996] ICJ Rep 226 ¶¶ 78 and 79.

15 CIHL commentary to r 5.

16 *AP Commentary* ¶¶ 4405–4418.

17 Yoram Dinstein, *The Conduct of Hostilities under the Law of International Armed Conflict* (2nd edn, CUP 2010) ¶ 304.

18 API art 50(1).

19 API art 50(2).

20 API art 50(3).

either take direct part in hostilities in a sporadic manner or who carry out functions within the group that do not amount to direct participation in hostilities.[21]

2.2 What constitutes an attack?

For the purpose of IHL the term 'attack' covers acts of violence against the adversary – whether in offence or defence.[22] Although this may appear counter-intuitive, both types of violence can have adverse effects on civilians and, consequently, must be regulated.

Parties must respect the rules protecting from the effects of hostilities vis-à-vis their own nationals too, for example if they find themselves in territory that has fallen under the control of the enemy, against which their state of nationality is carrying out attacks;[23] and also during the 'invasion phase': when a state's armed forces carry out attacks against invading forces, they must comply with the rules protecting the civilian population.[24]

3 Attacks against civilians

For the purpose of conduct of hostilities,[25] the principal consequence of civilian status is the entitlement to general protection from the dangers arising from military operations. Such protection is given effect, first and foremost, by the prohibition of directing attacks against the civilian population or individual civilians.[26]

The prohibition is absolute;[27] considered customary in international and non-international armed conflicts[28] and a war crime under the Rome Statute in both situations.[29]

The targeting must be intentional. Civilian casualties are not unlawful if they arise in the course of discriminate attacks against military objectives, or as a result of human error or mechanical malfunction.[30] The committee reviewing NATO's bombing campaign against Yugoslavia discusses a number of attacks that caused extensive civilian casualties, not one of which was found to be in violation of the law.[31]

---

21 ICRC, *Interpretive Guidance on the Notion of Direct Participation in Hostilities under International Humanitarian Law* (ICRC 2009) 31–36. For divergent views on this and other elements of the Guidance see eg 'Forum: The ICRC Interpretive Guidance on the Notion of Direct Participation in Hostilities under International Humanitarian Law' (2010) 42 *NYU JILP* 637.
22 API art 49.
23 *AP Commentary* ¶¶ 1877 and 1891.
24 Frits Kalshoven and Liesbeth Zegveld, *Constraints on the Waging of War* (4th edn, CUP 2011) 98.
25 Civilian status also has consequences for the framework for deprivation of liberty.
26 API art 51(2) and APII art 13(2).
27 This point was highlighted by the ICTY Appeals Chamber, which rectified a Trial Chamber's assertion that '[t]argeting civilians or civilian property is an offence *when not justified by military necessity*' (emphasis added) by underscoring that 'there is an absolute prohibition on the targeting of civilians'. *Prosecutor v Blaškić* (Case no IT-95-14-T, ICTY Trial Chamber, 3 March 2000) ¶ 180 and (Case no IT-95-14-T, ICTY Appeals Chamber, 29 July 2004) ¶ 109 respectively.
28 CIHL r 1.
29 Rome Statute arts 8(2)(b)(i) and 8(2)(e)(i) respectively.
30 Dinstein (n 17) ¶ 309.
31 See eg the discussion of the attacks on the Djakovica Convoy; the RTS: and Korisa Village in Part B of the Final Report to the Prosecutor by the Committee Established to Review the NATO Bombing Campaign Against the Federal Republic of Yugoslavia, 8 June 2000 ('NATO Report'), ¶¶ 58–79 and 86–89.

Civilians lose their immunity from attack if they carry out acts that amount to direct participation in hostilities, for the duration of such participation.[32] Despite its centrality to the rules on conduct of hostilities, treaty law provides no guidance as to what constitutes direct participation in hostilities.[33]

4 Spreading terror

A related prohibition is that of acts or threats of violence whose primary purpose is to spread terror among the civilian population. The prohibition is applicable in international and non-international armed conflicts[34] and is considered customary in both.[35]

This rule bans the practices resorted to, principally since the advent of air warfare, of launching attacks whose primary, if not sole, objective is the morale of the civilian population so as to undermine its support for the leadership and its determination to continue the war.[36]

Although violations of this prohibition are not grave breaches of Additional Protocol I, nor are among the Rome Statute war crimes, the ICTY found that they gave rise to individual criminal responsibility under its Statute as violations of the laws or customs of war, provided they entailed death or injury.[37] A number of defendants were charged and some found guilty of this offence.

In *Galic*, the defendant was found guilty of overseeing a protracted campaign of shelling and sniping upon civilian areas of Sarajevo and the civilian population with the primary purpose of spreading terror.[38] In *Milošević*, the defendant was found guilty of ordering a campaign of sniping and shelling, including with modified airbombs – indiscriminate weapons which serve no military purpose – whose primary purpose was spreading terror among the civilian population.[39]

The prohibition covers acts whose *intentional* and *primary* purpose is to spread terror, but not attacks against military objectives which, because of their intensity, cause incidental terror in the civilian population.[40]

All the ICTY cases relate to attacks against unlawful targets: the civilian population and civilian objects. There are no instances in which the attacks were against military objectives and, therefore, permissible, but had the primary purpose of terrorising the civilian population. This has led to suggestions that attacks against an unlawful target are a condition precedent for violations of this rule.[41] While apparently supported by ICTY practice, such an approach is

---

32 API art 51(3) and APII art 13(3). Civilians do not just lose their entitlement to immunity from attack but also to all the protections of the section/part of the relevant Protocol on 'General Protection from the Effects of Hostilities'/'Civilian Population' for the duration of their direct participation in hostilities.

33 But, see ICRC, *Interpretive Guidance* (n 21); for a discussion, see Michelle Lesh, 'Direct participation in hostilities' ch 10 in this volume.

34 API art 51(2) and APII art 13(2). See also the related prohibitions of 'all measures of intimidation or of terrorism' of protected persons in GCIV art 33 and of 'acts of terrorism' against persons who do not take a direct part in hostilities or who have ceased to do so in APII art 4(2)d.

35 CIHL r 2.

36 For a historical review see Parks (n 7) 77.

37 *Prosecutor v Galić* (Case no IT-98-29-T, ICTY Trial Chamber I, 5 December 2003) ¶ 130.

38 Ibid ¶ 597. The indictments against Karadžić and Mladić include similar charges. *Prosecutor v Karadžić (Third Amended Indictment)* (Case no IT-95-5/18-PT, ICTY, 27 February 2009) ¶¶ 76–82 and *Prosecutor v Mladić (Fourth Amended Indictment)* (Case no IT-09-92-PT, ICTY, 16 December 2011) ¶¶ 14–18.

39 *Prosecutor v Milošević* (Case no IT-98-29/1-T, ICTY Trial Chamber III, 12 December 2007) ¶ 978.

40 See eg the British Military Manual according to which the prohibition 'does not apply to terror caused as a by-product of attacks on military objectives or as a result of genuine warnings of impending attacks on such objects'. UK Ministry of Defence, *The Manual of the Law of Armed Conflict* (OUP 2004) ¶ 5.21.1.

41 Michael N Schmitt, 'The Law of Targeting' in Wilmshurst (n 12) 131, 140.

duplicative. As attacks against civilians are already unlawful, the prohibition of attacks whose primary purpose is spreading terror would be redundant, not adding anything to existing rules – unless perhaps as an aggravating factor in an already unlawful attack.[42]

The absence of practice relating to attacks against legitimate objectives could be attributed to the limited jurisprudence on this issue and the difficulties in determining whether the primary purpose of an attack against a military objective is indeed terrorising the civilian population.

On this last point, according to the ICTY, such a purpose could be inferred from the circumstances of the acts or threats of violence – that is, their nature, timing and duration. Attacks during ceasefires or long-term and persistent attacks against civilians, as well as indiscriminate attacks, could be taken as indications of the intent to spread terror. The location of the attacks is also significant. For example, the fact that, during the siege of Sarajevo, civilians were targeted in places they visited during daily activities, such as marketplaces, water distribution points and public transportation also provided strong indicia of such intent.[43]

5 Indiscriminate attacks

In addition to direct attacks against civilians, IHL also prohibits indiscriminate attacks. These target military – and therefore legitimate – objectives but are unlawful nonetheless because of the civilian casualties or risk thereof they entail. The prohibition flows from the principle of distinction and aims to limit the adverse impact on civilians of attacks against military objectives.

The prohibition is considered customary in both international and non-international armed conflicts.[44] In relation to the former it is codified in considerable detail in Article 51 Additional Protocol I. A similar provision was included in a draft of Additional Protocol II but was removed when the text was simplified.[45]

Indiscriminate attacks that are disproportionate committed in international armed conflicts are war crimes under the Rome Statute.[46]

5.1 What is an indiscriminate attack?

The general prohibition of indiscriminate attacks in Article 51(4) of Additional Protocol I is followed by an explanation of what constitutes such attacks:

a   attacks which are not directed at a specific military objective;
b   attacks which employ a method or means of combat which cannot be directed at a specific military objective; or
c   attacks which employ a method or means of combat the effects of which cannot be limited as required by the Protocol;

---

42 The Trial Chamber in *Milošević* appears to have taken this approach, explaining that

> [t]he first sentence [of art 51 API] incorporates a general prohibition of attacks on civilians, while the second sentence prohibits a specific form of attacks on civilians.... [T]he crime of terror, therefore, constitutes an 'aggravated', more serious form of, unlawful attack on civilians.
>
> *Milošević* (n 39) ¶¶ 873 and 882

43 Ibid ¶ 881.
44 CIHL r 11.
45 *AP Commentary* ¶ 4416.
46 Rome Statute art 8(2)(b)(iv).

and consequently, in each such case, are of a nature to strike military objectives and civilians or civilian objects without distinction.

Attacks not directed at a specific military objective cover two types of attacks: first, attacks whose intended targets are military objectives but in which no attempt is made to direct the munition towards a specific objective, as in the case of unaimed fire into enemy-controlled territory; and, second, attacks which combine distinct and separate military objectives in a single target area. This aspect of the prohibition thus relates to *how* weapons are used rather than to weapons that are inherently impossible to use discriminately.

The prohibition of attacks that employ a means or method of combat that cannot be directed at a specific military objective focuses on the weapons and whether they are capable of being directed at a specific military target.

This type of attack was considered by the ICTY in *Martić*. A Trial Chamber found that firing non-guided projectiles with cluster-warheads at densely populated civilian areas from the extreme of their range was an indiscriminate attack because of the high dispersion error of the projectiles when launched at maximum range, which made it impossible for them to strike specific targets.[47] More recently, the Independent Commission of Inquiry on Syria found that attacks by barrel bombs dropped into urban areas from helicopters flying at high altitudes were indiscriminate.[48]

What constitutes an acceptable margin of error in the accuracy with which weapons can be fired, and thus precludes their use from being indiscriminate, evolves in keeping with technological advances.[49] The law does not set precise parameters – a wise approach as shown by the difficulties encountered by the ICTY in the case of *Gotovina* discussed below.

Finally, the prohibition of attacks whose effects cannot be limited as required by Additional Protocol I broadens the notion of indiscriminate attacks significantly. First, it focuses on the *effects* of attacks rather than merely on their intended target. Second, it requires such effects to be limited in accordance with Additional Protocol I more broadly and not just the principle of distinction. This includes, most notably, the rules on the protection of the environment.[50]

To avoid falling foul of this aspect of the prohibition, the effects of an attack must be controllable both in space – that is, in terms of the areas affected – and over time. An initially lawful attack against a military objective may nonetheless be unlawful if it has the potential of harming civilians in the long run, like unexploded cluster submunitions fired in civilian areas.

Unless the use of a particular weapon is specifically prohibited, as is the case for anti-personnel mines and cluster-munitions[51] for example, its compliance with this aspect of the prohibition of indiscriminate attacks must be assessed on a case-by-case basis, considering factors such as the nature of the weapon used, the location of the attack and the duration of its harmful effects.[52]

---

47 *Prosecutor v Martić* (Case no IT-95-11-T, ICTY Trial Chamber, 12 June 2007) ¶¶ 462–463.
48 Report of the Independent International Commission of Inquiry on the Syrian Arab Republic, UN Doc A/HRC/25/65 (12 February 2014), ¶ 86.
49 Schmitt, 'Law of Targeting' (n 41) 152.
50 API arts 35(3) and 55.
51 Convention on the Prohibition of the Use, Stockpiling, Production and Transfer of Anti-Personnel Mines and on their Destruction (18 September 1997) 2056 UNTS 211; Convention on Cluster Munitions (30 May 2008) 2688 UNTS 39. The use of these weapons by states not parties to the treaties remains subject to the general rules of IHL. Both weapons can cause civilian casualties when used in an attack and also pose a long-term threat.
52 For instance, Schmitt proffers the example of the use of perishable toxins in areas in which only combatants are present as an attack with a biological weapon which would prima facie not violate the rule. Schmitt, 'Law of Targeting' (n 41) 154.

Resort to explosive weapons during fighting in densely populated areas in recent conflicts is having a devastating effect on civilians. The common feature of explosive weapons is that they are indiscriminate within their zones of blast and fragmentation effect, which makes their use in populated areas highly problematic. Concerns have been raised by the ICRC, which, in view of the significant likelihood of indiscriminate effects, recommended that resort to explosive weapons with a wide impact area be avoided in densely populated areas.[53] At the request of the UN Secretary-General, the United Nations Office for the Coordination of Humanitarian Affairs is compiling military practice and policy in the use of explosive weapons in populated areas in order to promote a change in practice. Separately, several States have begun a process to develop a political declaration through which States would recognise the problem and commit to take steps to address it.[54]

5.2 Two examples of indiscriminate attacks

Having laid down this three-pronged definition, Additional Protocol I then gives two examples of indiscriminate attacks: those which treat as a single military objective a number of clearly separated and distinct military objectives and disproportionate attacks.[55]

The first example refers to attacks like the area bombardments of the Second World War, which targeted as a single objective a number of clearly separate and distinct military objectives in a built-up area. Arguably, the example is redundant as already covered by Article 51(4)(a) of Additional Protocol I, but was inserted to put to rest any argument that such attacks may be lawful.[56] Only attacks against 'true' target areas are permissible: areas whose entirety constitutes a military objective or where several such objectives are so intermingled that they are practically inseparable and can thus only be attacked together.[57]

The ICTY considered this form of indiscriminate attack in an appeal relating to the 1995 Croatian offensive to re-take Krajina. The Trial Chamber in *Gotovina* had found the defendant, a commander of the operation, guilty of a joint criminal enterprise to commit war crimes and crimes against humanity. The decision hinged on a determination that Gotovina had ordered indiscriminate artillery attacks against civilians and civilian objects in four towns that had led to the displacement of some 20,000 civilians.[58]

The Trial Chamber found that legitimate military objectives existed in the towns and based its assessment of the lawfulness of any attack on a presumption that any artillery projectile impacting *within* 200 metres of a legitimate target was deliberately fired at that target, while all impact sites located *more* than 200 metres from a legitimate target were evidence of an unlawful attack. The Trial Chamber gave no explanation of the basis for adopting this margin of error.

---

53 ICRC, 'International Humanitarian Law and the Challenges of Contemporary Armed Conflicts', Doc 32IC/15/11 (October 2015) 47–53, www.icrc.org/en/document/international-humanitarian-law-and-challenges-contemporary-armed-conflicts. More generally see John Borrie and Maya Brehm, 'Enhancing Civilian Protection from Use of Explosive Weapons in Populated Areas: Building a Policy and Research Agenda' (2011) 93(883) *IRRC* 809.

54 Report of the Secretary-General on the Protection of Civilians in Armed Conflict, UN Doc S/2015/453 (18 June 2015) ¶¶ 30 and 63. See also, Summary report of OCHA-Chatham House Expert Meeting on Reducing the Humanitarian Impact of the Use of Explosive Weapons in Populated Areas, London, 23–24 September 2013, https://docs.unocha.org/sites/dms/Documents/Expert%20Meeting%20on%20EWIPA%20-%20Summary%20Report.pdf.

55 API art 51(5).

56 Stefan Oeter, 'Methods and Means of Combat' in Dieter Fleck, *The Handbook of International Humanitarian Law* (2nd edn, OUP 2008) 204.

57 Ibid.

58 *Prosecutor* v *Gotovina* (Case no IT-06-90-T, ICTY Trial Chamber I, 15 April 2011).

Although only some 5 per cent of the sample artillery impact sites considered by the Trial Chamber were beyond the 200 metre range, it nonetheless inferred that the defendant had ordered the targeting of the entire towns and civilian populations rather than military targets located therein.[59]

In 2012 the Appeals Chamber overturned the decision. It found that the Trial Chamber had erred in not providing an evidentiary basis for its adoption of the 200 metre rule, particularly because it related to a highly technical subject: the margin of error of artillery weapons in particular conditions.[60] In the absence of support for the 200 metre rule, and in view of its centrality to the finding of unlawful shelling, the Appeals Chamber acquitted the defendant.

6 Disproportionate attacks

The second example of indiscriminate attacks referred to in Additional Protocol I are disproportionate attacks, that is, those 'which may be expected to cause incidental loss of civilian life, injury to civilians, damage to civilian objects, or a combination thereof, which would be excessive in relation to the concrete and direct military advantage anticipated'.[61]

This prohibition is perhaps the most evident manifestation of the balance between military necessity and considerations of humanity running through IHL.[62]

A norm that only existed in general terms at the time of its codification in Additional Protocol I,[63] and absent from Common Article 3 Geneva Conventions and Additional Protocol II, the prohibition of disproportionate attacks is now considered customary in both international and non-international armed conflicts.[64] Its violation in international armed conflicts is a grave breach of Additional Protocol I and a war crime under the Rome Statute.[65]

Although Additional Protocol I refers to disproportionate attacks as an example of indiscriminate attacks, distinction and proportionality are in fact two related but distinct principles, which share the objective of protecting civilians during attacks against military objectives.

---

59 Ibid ¶¶ 1911, 1923, 1935 and 1943. The Trial Chamber's judgment was the subject of considerable criticism. See eg W Huffmann, 'Margin of Error: Potential Pitfalls of the Ruling in *The Prosecutor v Ante Gotovina*' (2012) 211 *Military LR* 1.

60 *Prosecutor v Gotovina* (Case no IT-06-90-A, ICTY Appeals Chamber, 16 November 2012) ¶ 61. The Appeals Chamber also criticised the adoption of a single standard of margin of error to the artillery shelling of all four towns, despite witness evidence that factors such as wind speed and the differences in firing-range could affect the margin of error. Ibid ¶ 60.

61 API art 51(5)(b).

62 See eg Michael N Schmitt, 'Military Necessity and Humanity in International Humanitarian Law: Preserving the Delicate Balance' (2010) 50 *Virginia JIL* 797; Eyal Benvenisti, 'Human Dignity in Combat: the Duty to Spare Enemy Civilians' (2006) 39 *Israel LR* 81.

63 For a historical review see Judith Gardam, *Necessity, Proportionality and the Use of Force* (CUP 2004) 85.

64 CIHL r 14.

65 API art 85(3)(b) and Rome Statute art 8(2)(b)(iv). Both provisions adopt a more stringent standard than the prohibitions in API arts 51(5)(b) and 57(2)(a)(ii). For individual criminal responsibility to arise under API art 85(3)(b), the attack must have been launched *in the knowledge* that it will cause excessive loss of life, injury to civilians or damage to civilian objects, and death or serious injury to body or health must actual arise. This is a higher standard than the expectation that such casualties or damage would arise referred to in API arts 51(5)(b) and 57(2)(a)(ii). See *AP Commentary* ¶¶ 3477–3481. Similarly, the war crime under Rome Statute art 8(2)(b)(iv) requires the *knowledge* that the attack will cause incidental loss of life or injury to civilians or damage to civilian objects which would be *clearly* excessive in relation to the concrete and direct *overall* military advantage anticipated. For a view of whether the addition of the words 'clearly' and 'overall' actually alter the prohibition see eg Knut Dörmann, *Elements of Crime under the Rome Statute of the International Criminal Court* (CUP 2003) 169–170.

For an attack to be lawful it must comply with both principles. Proportionality is an additional requirement that attacking forces must comply with over and above the rules relating to discrimination. Conversely, an indiscriminate attack cannot be justified on grounds of proportionality.[66]

Although a clear and fundamental rule of IHL, proportionality is notoriously difficult to apply in practice, as it requires evaluating and balancing against each other two dissimilar and non-quantifiable values: military advantage and civilian casualties and damage.

The difficulties inherent in applying the test were outlined in detail by the committee reviewing NATO's bombing campaign against Yugoslavia:

49   The questions which remain unresolved once one decides to apply the principle of proportionality include ...:

(a)   What are the relative values to be assigned to the military advantage gained and the injury to non-combatants and or the damage to civilian objects?
(b)   What do you include or exclude in totaling your sums?
(c)   What is the standard of measurement in time or space? and
(d)   To what extent is a military commander obligated to expose his own forces to danger in order to limit civilian casualties or damage to civilian objects?

50   The answers to these questions are not simple. It may be necessary to resolve them on a case by case basis, and the answers may differ depending on the background and values of the decision maker.[67]

6.1 Concrete and direct military advantage

Upon ratification of Additional Protocol I a number of states expressed their understanding that the military advantage to be considered is that expected from the attack as a whole rather than from isolated or particular parts thereof.[68]

This approach was adopted in the Rome Statute war crime, which speaks of 'the concrete and direct *overall* military advantage anticipated'.[69] This is but one of the ways in which the war crime is narrower than the prohibition in Additional Protocol I, the others are discussed below. Of course, nothing precludes the imposition of more onerous requirements for the establishment of individual criminal responsibility than for state responsibility for violation of the same rule.

At one end of the spectrum, it is clear that military advantage is not to be assessed bullet-by-bullet or, probably, even in relation to attacks against individual military targets.[70] At the other end, it is equally evident that it is not long-term political advantages that must be considered, nor winning the war.[71] According to some military manuals it is the advantage anticipated from

---

66   *AP Commentary* ¶¶ 1972, 1979 and 2207. This point was emphasised in an explanatory note to the elements of crime of Rome Statute art 8(2)(b)(iv). See Dörmann (n 65) 163. See also Gardam (n 63) 94.
67   NATO Report (n 31) ¶¶ 48–49.
68   See the statements of Belgium and the virtually identical ones of Australia, Canada, Germany, Italy, the Netherlands, New Zealand, Spain and the UK, referred to in Dörmann (n 65) 170.
69   Rome Statute art 8(2)(b)(iv), emphasis added.
70   William J Fenwick, 'Targeting and Proportionality during the NATO Bombing Campaign against Yugoslavia' (2001) 12 *EJIL* 489, 499.
71   Dörmann (n 65) 164.

'the military campaign or operation of which the specific attack forms part', rather than that arising from isolated or particular parts thereof.[72]

By way of example, in the 1991 Gulf war, US forces calculated the expected military advantage of particular 'target sets'. For instance, with regard to the railways and bridges set, with some exceptions, the value of any particular Iraqi bridge, in isolation, was not great. But the specific proportionality analysis adopted by the US measured the overall value of the set against the total casualties that strikes against it were likely to cause.[73]

What is clear is that the same yardstick must be adopted in calculating expected military advantage and the corresponding expected civilian casualties and damage. The latter too must be assessed on the basis of the same operation as a whole rather than of individual strikes.[74]

An unsettled question is whether avoiding casualties among the attacking forces and preserving military equipment – so-called 'force protection' – constitutes a military advantage to be factored into proportionality assessments. Some states declared upon ratification of Additional Protocol I that force protection constituted such a military advantage.[75]

There is a marked divergence of views among commentators. Some argue that preserving personnel and equipment to fight future battles is self-evidently a military advantage. Their opponents consider that factoring force protection into a proportionality calculation risks decisively blurring that analysis.[76]

A possible compromise position is to treat force protection as a relevant tactical gain that can be factored into proportionality assessments, provided the expected military advantage meets the 'concrete and direct' standard and is not too indirect or abstract – a determination to be made on a case-by-case basis.[77]

6.2 Civilian casualties

Not every civilian death or injury is a violation of IHL. The law is premised on the reality that civilian casualties are a tragic but usually unavoidable consequence of armed conflict. What is prohibited are casualties either resulting from direct or indiscriminate attacks or expected to be excessive compared to the anticipated military advantage of the attack causing them.

It is not just the civilian casualties[78] expected immediately and directly by an attack that must be factored into a proportionality assessment. Expected indirect or secondary casualties caused by the 'reverberating' effects of the attack must also be considered.

Such secondary effects are particularly problematic when dual use facilities are attacked. The issue came to prominence following the Coalition's targeting of the Iraqi electricity generation and distribution grid in 1991 and the knock-on effect on other facilities dependent on electricity, including water-distribution, purification and sewage-treatment facilities and medical

---

72 See eg Australian and Canadian military manuals referred to in Dörmann (n 65) 172.

73 Michael W Lewis, 'The Law of Aerial Bombardment in the 1991 Gulf War' (2003) 97 *AJIL* 481, 494.

74 Dörmann (n 65) 173.

75 Australia and New Zealand. The Australian and Canadian military manuals also include force protection among the elements that make up military advantage. CIHL, vol II, r 14, ¶¶ 161, 167 and 169.

76 See the review of arguments in Robin Geiss, 'The Principle of Proportionality: "Force Protection" as a Military Advantage' (2012) 45 *Israel LR* 71.

77 Ibid.

78 API art 51(5)(b) requires consideration of 'loss of civilian life, injury to civilians, damage to civilian objects, or a combination thereof'. As explained, the present chapter does not address civilian objects.

establishments, leading to the deaths of tens of thousands of civilians. It also significantly affected agricultural production by reducing irrigation capacity.[79]

In subsequent conflicts, efforts were made to avoid similar reverberating effects. For example, NATO in Yugoslavia attacked power distribution rather than generation facilities. This had the military aim of disrupting power supply without the long-term incapacitation of electrical generation capability. With similar concerns in mind, Coalition forces in Iraq in 2003 used weapons that short-circuited rather than destroyed electrical targets.[80]

A further possible broadening of the range of civilian casualties to be considered was suggested by the ICTY Trial Chamber in *Kupreškić*, which found that 'in case of repeated attacks, all or most of them falling within the grey area between indisputable legality and unlawfulness, it might be warranted to conclude that the cumulative effect of such acts' may be such to render them unlawful.[81]

At present there is little if any support for this approach – starting from within the ICTY itself[82] – which could lead to the counter-intuitive result that a series of attacks, not unlawful if assessed individually, could, when considered as a whole, be disproportionate.

6.3 A speculative assessment

A further challenge in applying the proportionality test is the fact that it is not based on certainties but, instead, requires the balancing of two speculative outcomes: *expected* civilian casualties and *anticipated* military advantage.[83]

States have emphasised that the proportionality assessment must be made on the basis of the information available at the time of planning and executing the attack, and not retrospectively with the benefit of hindsight.[84]

Information on the actual effects of attacks is, of course, relevant in ensuring future operations comply with the law. In this respect it has been suggested that in addition to the *ex ante* review of the likely effects of an attack required by the rules on precautions, an *ex post facto* review should also be effected. Some states already carry out this review internally; what is proposed is rendering the results of such analyses public and ultimately subjecting them to some form of judicial supervision.[85]

---

79 See eg J W Crawford, 'The Law of Noncombatant Immunity and the Targeting of National Electrical Power Systems' (1997) 21 *Fletcher Forum of World Affairs* 101, 102; and Lewis (n 73) 504–507.

80 Human Rights Watch, 'Civilian Deaths in the NATO Air Campaign' (February 2000) and Michael N Schmitt, 'The Conduct of Hostilities during Operation Iraqi Freedom: An International Humanitarian Law Assessment' (2003) 6 *YBIHL* 73, 93.

81 *Prosecutor v Kupreškić* (Case no IT-95-16-T, ICTY Trial Chamber, 14 January 2000) ¶ 526.

82 NATO Report (n 31) ¶ 52.

83 The crime in Article 8(2)(b)(iv) Rome Statute adopts a more onerous standard for this aspect of the rule too, requiring *knowledge* that a particular attack *will* cause clearly excessive damage.

84 CIHL vol II, pt 1, ¶¶ 331–335.

85 Amichai Cohen and Yuval Shany, 'A Development of Modest Proportions: the Application of the Principle of Proportionality in the Israeli Supreme Court Judgment on the Lawfulness of Targeted Killings' ILFHUJ Research Paper No 5-07, April 2007. See also Marco Sassoli and Lindsey Cameron, 'The Protection of Civilian Objects: Current State of the Law and Issues de Lege Ferenda' in Natalino Ronzitti and Gabriella Venturini (eds), *The Law of Air Warfare: Contemporary Issues* (Eleven International 2006), 35, 64.

6.4 Excessiveness – a subjective standard

The essence of proportionality is the prohibition of excessive expected civilian casualties compared to the expected military advantage.[86] Determining what is excessive entails a subjective evaluation and, as pointed out in the NATO Report,

> answers may differ depending on the background and values of the decision maker. It is unlikely that a human rights lawyer and an experienced combat commander would assign the same relative values to military advantage and to injury to noncombatants.[87]

The report recommends that the determination of relative values be that of the 'reasonable military commander'.[88]

It is unlikely that such a commander exists, as the determination is inextricably connected with the subjective perspective of the party carrying out the assessment and the shifting tides of battle. The difference in value attributed to the military advantage from an attack is likely to be particularly marked in asymmetrical conflicts.[89]

To some degree the ICTY took this subjective element into account in the test it suggested in *Galić*, namely, whether 'a reasonably well-informed person in the circumstances of the actual perpetrator, making reasonable use of the information available to him or her, could have expected excessive civilian casualties to result from the attack'.[90]

Ultimately, the subjective evaluation must be above all a question of common sense, reached reasonably and in good faith.[91]

7 Human shields

Additional Protocol I reiterates the well-established prohibition on resort to human shields – that is, using persons protected by IHL to deter attacks against military objectives.

Despite a longstanding prohibition, resort to such practices – and condemnation thereof – is not a recent phenomenon. Examples date from the American Civil War to numerous modern conflicts including the placing by Saddam Hussein of foreign nationals in the proximity of military objectives in Iraq in 1991;[92] and that by Bosnian Serb forces of UN peacekeepers and military observers at potential targets of the 1995 NATO air campaign.[93]

Recent increased resort to human shields has been attributed to the asymmetry characterising many modern conflicts, where, confronted with overwhelming technological superiority, weaker parties have used human shields to prevent attacks they cannot thwart by conventional means.[94]

---

86 In this respect too the crime in Rome Statute art 8(2)(b)(iv) adopts a more onerous standard, requiring civilian casualties to be *clearly* excessive.
87 NATO Report (n 31) ¶ 49.
88 Ibid.
89 See Michael N Schmitt, 'Asymmetrical Warfare and International Humanitarian Law' (2007) 62 *Air Force Law Review* 1, 28.
90 *Galić* (n 37) ¶ 58.
91 *AP Commentary* ¶ 2208; Dörmann (n 65) 165.
92 See eg Parks (n 7) 98.
93 *Prosecutor v Karadžić (Prosecution's Marked-Up Indictment)* (Case no IT-95-5/18-I, ICTY, 19 October 2009) ¶¶ 83 et seq.
94 See eg Schmitt, 'Asymmetrical Warfare' (n 89) 18.

s can deter attacks in two ways. They can affect proportionality assessments,
'se lawful attacks on military objectives disproportionate. Possibly even more
ne of close public scrutiny of certain conflicts, regardless of its actual legiti-
gainst a military objective protected by human shields causes civilian casu-
ndermine support for the attacker and be perceived as immoral.[95]

7.1 Scope of the prohibition

In international armed conflicts, Geneva Convention III and Geneva Convention IV expressly prohibit the use of certain categories of protected persons as human shields.[96] Article 51(7) of Additional Protocol I, the most comprehensive expression of the rule, expands the prohibition to all civilians.

In non-international armed conflicts, Additional Protocol II does not mention human shields but such practices would deprive civilians of the general protection against the dangers arising from military operations granted by Article 13. The prohibition on human shields is considered customary in both international and non-international armed conflicts.[97] 'Utilising the presence of civilians or other protected persons to render certain points, areas or military forces immune from military operations' in international conflicts is a war crime in the Rome Statute in international armed conflicts.[98]

7.2 Elements of the prohibition

The prohibition is absolute. This is in contrast with the related rule on precautions in defence which requires parties 'to the maximum extent feasible' to endeavour to remove civilians from the vicinity of military objectives and to avoid locating military objectives within or near densely populated areas.[99]

A broad range of possible practices are prohibited: placing civilians in the proximity of military objectives; placing military objectives in the proximity of civilians; and using the movement of civilians to shield military objectives. Such movements could be spontaneous, as in the case of civilians fleeing fighting, or compelled, as in the case of civilians being forced to act as screens for moving troops. Although there is a tendency to focus on the defensive use of human shields to protect military objectives, the prohibition is equally applicable when civilians are used to provide cover for offensive military operations, like when combatants attack the enemy while sheltering behind civilians.[100]

For the prohibition to apply, civilians must be intentionally stationed near military objectives – or, conversely, military objectives among civilians – in order to deter attacks. Their mere presence in proximity to combatants and other military objectives, often inevitable during fighting in populated areas, is not a violation.

---

95 Michael N Schmitt, 'Human Shields in International Law' (2009) 38 *Israel YBHR* 7, 22.
96 GCIII art 23 and GCIV art 28 prohibit using prisoners of war or persons protected by GCIV respectively as human shields.
97 CIHL r 97.
98 Rome Statute art 8(2)(b)(xxiii).
99 API art 58.
100 For example, in 2003 irregular Iraqi forces engaged Coalition forces from behind women and children. Schmitt, 'Human Shields' (n 95) 35.

Finally, recourse by one side to human shields does not affect its opponent's obligations.[101] This means that the presence of human shields does not preclude an attack on a 'protected' military objective. But any attack must nonetheless comply with the rules on targeting including the prohibition on indiscriminate attacks.

7.3 Voluntary human shields

The prohibition on human shields is clear and well-established. The more recent phenomenon of 'voluntary' human shields – civilians who willingly locate to military objectives to deter attacks – raises more complex legal questions.

Recent examples of such practices include Serbian civilians who gathered on bridges in Belgrade to prevent their bombing during the 1999 NATO campaign and foreign nationals who travelled to Iraq in 2002–2003 to shield strategic locations such as oil refineries and power stations ahead of expected Coalition military strikes.

While inferring the intent to shield is usually straightforward, determining whether there is genuine consent to do so is more difficult. This issue was central in Israel's Supreme Court decision on the Israel Defence Force's 'early warning' procedure. The tactic, used in operations to arrest suspects, relied upon consenting neighbours to relay warnings of impending operations to residents to allow them to leave the premises and suspects to surrender. The Court found the procedure unlawful *inter alia* because

> in light of the inequality between the occupying force and the local resident, it is not to be expected that the local resident will reject the request.... A procedure is not to be based upon consent, when in many cases the consent will not be real.[102]

Although consent is evident in certain situations, most notably when activists are involved, in others ascertaining whether it is freely given is difficult. This is problematic in view of the position adopted by some commentators that the voluntary nature of the shielding affects the protections to which the persons in question are entitled.

Treaty law does not expressly mention voluntary human shields and there are divergent views as to whether the rules discussed above apply to them or whether the fact they are not acting under compulsion means they lose their immunity from attack. This also affects the obligations of the party benefitting from their presence and of the attacker.

There is a marked divergence of views as to whether voluntary shielding amounts to direct participation in hostilities. The experts participating in the elaboration of the ICRC's Interpretive Guidance were unable to reach agreement.[103]

According to the Guidance, deliberate abuse by civilians of their entitlement to protection in order to shield a military objective does not automatically amount to direct participation in

---

101 API art 51(8).
102 *Adalah (Legal Center for Arab Minority Rights in Israel) et al v Commander of the Central Region (Early Warning)* (Case no HCJ 3799/02, Supreme Court of Israel, 23 June 2005) ¶ 24.
103 ICRC, *Interpretive Guidance* (n 21) 57; Lesh (n 33) s 2.2. See also the reports of the meetings when human shields were discussed: Second Expert Meeting on the Notion of Direct Participation in Hostilities, 25–26 October 2004, Summary Report, 6–7; Fourth Expert Meeting on the Notion of Direct Participation in Hostilities, 27–28 November 2006, Summary Report, 44–46; Fifth Expert Meeting on the Notion of Direct Participation in Hostilities, 5–6 February 2008, Summary Report, 70–72. There was agreement that *involuntary* human shields could not be considered as taking direct part in hostilities. Ibid.

hostilities. Whether it does must be determined on a case-by-case basis. For it to do so, their behaviour must be capable of directly causing the requisite threshold of harm, namely 'likely to adversely affect the military operations or military capacity of a party to an armed conflict or inflicting death, injury or destruction on persons or objects protected against direct attack'.[104]

In ground operations, civilians who provide physical cover to fighters or inhibit the movements of enemy forces can be considered as taking direct part in hostilities, as their acts pose a physical obstacle between the attacking forces and the intended target, directly adversely affecting military operations. In contrast, in air warfare, where the presence of civilians around a military objective does not impair the attacker's capacity to identify and destroy the target, their involvement does not amount to direct participation. While the presence of voluntary human shields in such circumstances could shift the parameters of the proportionality assessment to the detriment of the attacker, increasing the probability that the expected incidental harm would be excessive, the obstacle they pose is a legal rather than a physical one: they do not actually and physically prevent the attack, but merely render it unlawful. Consequently, the resulting harm is indirect and they cannot be considered as taking direct part in hostilities.[105]

The alternative view is that voluntary human shields take actual steps to prevent harm to military objectives and in so doing they contribute to military action in a direct casual way. Consequently, their actions amount to direct participation.[106]

If voluntary human shields are considered as taking direct part in hostilities, they are not entitled to the protections in Part IV, Section I of Additional Protocol I – including the prohibition on resort to human shields. The rule simply does not come into operation and there can be no question of it being violated. Although this may appear counterintuitive, it in fact allows the attacking party to target the shielded objective without having to take proportionality concerns into account – at least not in relation to the voluntary human shields. Obviously, other civilian casualties and damage to civilian property must be considered in the proportionality calculation.

If, on the other hand, voluntary human shields are not considered as taking direct part in hostilities, they retain their entitlement to the protections in the abovementioned Part of Additional Protocol I, including the prohibition on human shields. The party benefitting from their actions is in violation of this rule and is required, to the maximum extent feasible, to remove them from the vicinity of the military objective.[107]

The obligations of the attacking party also depend on whether the voluntary human shields are considered as taking direct part in hostilities. If they are, they are not entitled to immunity from attack for the duration of such participation and the risk of their death or injury need not be taken into account in assessing the proportionality of an attack.

If, on the other hand they are not taking direct part in hostilities, they retain their immunity from attack and their presence does not affect the obligations of the attacking party which, consequently, must refrain from attacking them per se and must also take their expected death or injury into account when assessing the proportionality of the attack. As pointed out by critics, this approach effectively allows a defender to 'immunise' a target if it allows a sufficient number of voluntary human shields to protect it and thus benefit from its violation of the law.[108]

---

104 ICRC, *Interpretive Guidance* (n 21) 47.
105 Ibid 56–57.
106 Schmitt, 'Human Shields' (n 95) 41.
107 For an analysis of when failure to remove civilians from the vicinity of military objectives becomes acquiescence and resort to human shields, see Jean-Francois Queguiner, 'Precautions under the Law Governing the Conduct of Hostilities' (2006) 88(864) *IRRC* 793, 815.
108 Ibid 42.

A third approach has been proposed, applicable to both voluntary and compelled human shields. It treats them as not directly participating in hostilities and, consequently, entitled to immunity from attack but then affords 'reduced weight' to the risk of their death or injury in proportionality assessments so as not to provide undue advantage to the party benefitting from their presence in violation of its obligations.[109]

8 Precautions

In the conduct of military operations constant care must be taken to spare the civilian population. Additional Protocol I lays down a series of precautionary measures to give practical effect to this premise. Precautions are of particular importance when hostilities take place in urban areas, where civilians are at greatest risk of being caught up in the fighting.

Articles 57 and 58 of Additional Protocol I set out precautions to be taken in attack and against the effects of attack respectively. These rules are complementary. Failure by one side to take precautions does not absolve the other of its obligations, and effective protection of the civilian population requires a combination of precautions taken by both sides.

The duty to take precautions is not absolute. It is a duty to act in good faith to take practicable measures.[110] Parties must do 'everything feasible' to verify objectives are indeed military;[111] take 'all feasible precautions' to avoid or minimise incidental civilian casualties[112] and give advance warning 'if circumstances permit'.[113] Similarly, precautions against the effects of attacks must be implemented 'to the maximum extent feasible'.[114]

At the time of the negotiations of Additional Protocol I a number of delegations stated that by 'feasible precautions' they understood everything that was 'practicable' or practically possible taking into account all the circumstances at the time of the attack, including those relevant to the success of military operations.[115]

Whether adequate precautionary measures have been adopted cannot be determined on the basis of a single attack – a bigger sample is necessary.[116] But where civilian casualties continue to occur, precautions should be adjusted. The successive measures adopted by ISAF in Afghanistan to reduce civilian casualties from air strikes discussed below are a case in point.

Full implementation of precautionary measures can probably only be expected from higher levels of command, who have all the necessary information for target identification and proportionality assessments as well as the authority to select means and methods of attack. However, forces at a more operational level actually executing attacks also have a degree of responsibility. They must be aware of the general principles and, in certain circumstances, may be in the best position to determine whether an attack must be cancelled.[117]

---

109 See eg UK *Manual* (n 40) ¶ 5.22.1.
110 Fenwick, 'Targeting and Proportionality' (n 70) 501.
111 API art 57(2)(a)(i).
112 API art 57(2)(a)(ii).
113 API art 57(3).
114 API art 58.
115 *AP Commentary* ¶ 2198. This approach was enshrined in art 3(4) Protocol II to the CCW, which specifies that '[f]easible precautions are those precautions which are practicable or practically possible taking into account all circumstances ruling at the time, *including humanitarian and military considerations*' (emphasis added). Military considerations include those pertaining to force protection. See eg Benvenisti (n 62) 93, who, like others, considers that the duty to minimise harm to civilians does not entail an obligation for the attacker to assume personal life-threatening risks.
116 NATO Report (n 31) ¶ 29.
117 *AP Commentary* ¶ 2197.

The obligation to take all feasible precautions is considered customary in both international and non-international armed conflicts.[118] Its violation does not entail individual criminal responsibility. This being said, a failure to take all feasible precautions may amount to a disproportionate attack, which is a grave breach of Additional Protocol I and a war crime in international armed conflicts under the Rome Statute.[119]

8.1 Precautions in attack

Having laid down the general obligation to spare civilians, Article 57 of Additional Protocol I then sets out a series of measures to be taken by those planning or deciding upon an attack to give effect to it: rules relating to identification of targets; choice of means and methods of attack; warnings; and the duty to consider alternative military targets.

In recognition of the numerous and often complex legal issues raised by the conduct of hostilities, military legal advisers have played an increasingly prominent role in the planning and implementation of military operations to provide general guidance and, in some cases, strike-specific advice to promote compliance with IHL.[120]

8.1.1 Identification

Those planning or deciding attacks must do everything feasible to verify that the intended targets really are military objectives.[121] Accurate identification of objectives is obviously an essential step for the application in practice of the principle of distinction.

To give effect to this obligation effective intelligence-gathering systems to collect and evaluate information concerning potential targets must be established, and forces must be instructed to use available technical means to properly identify targets during operations.[122]

Despite these measures, errors in identification occur. For example, in 1999 NATO aircraft mistakenly targeted the Chinese Embassy in Belgrade, killing three civilians and injuring 15 others. The attack was made in the mistaken belief that the Embassy premises were the Directorate for Supply and Procurement – considered a military target because of its role in military procurement.[123]

Always during the campaign against Yugoslavia, NATO aircraft initially attacked targets while flying at an altitude that put them beyond the reach of Serbian defences, a tactic, critics argued, that led to civilian casualties, as it reduced the precision of its strikes.[124] The NATO Report found that there was nothing inherently unlawful about the practice. Commanders had to take practicable measures to distinguish military objectives from civilians. The minimum altitude adopted may have meant targets could not be verified with the naked eye but other technologies allowed them to effectively comply with this obligation in the vast majority of cases.[125]

---

118 CIHL r 15.
119 API art 85(3)(b) and Rome Statute art 8(2)(b)(iv).
120 For an in-depth analysis of *inter alia* the role of JAGs in US military operations see Janina Dill, *Legitimate Targets? Social Construction, International Law, and US Bombing* (OUP 2014).
121 API art 57(2)(a)(i).
122 NATO Report (n 31) ¶ 29.
123 Ibid ¶¶ 80–85.
124 See eg Human Rights Watch, 'Civilian Deaths' (n 80) 21.
125 NATO Report (n 31) ¶ 56.

8.1.2 Precautions in choice of means and methods of attack

Once a military target has been accurately identified, appropriate means and methods of attack must be selected to avoid civilian casualties. Only if this is not possible may they be 'minimised'.[126]

A variety of measures can be taken to minimise civilian casualties, starting with the choice of weapons. Technological advances enable belligerents who can afford them to use increasingly accurate weapons, like precision-guided munitions, which can reduce civilian casualties. With the same objective, following the extensive casualties caused by the reverberating effects of the destruction of the Iraqi power grid in 1991, during the campaign against Serbia the US used 'soft bombs': bomblets that dispersed large numbers of chemically treated carbon-graphite filaments that short-circuited electrical power distribution equipment without causing long-term or irreparable damage.[127]

The choice of timing and location of attacks is also important. During the Second World War, Allied bombardments against factories considered military objectives were carried out when they were empty so as to destroy the factories without killing the workers.[128] Similarly, in 2003 Coalition bombing of Iraqi urban areas was carried out at night when civilians were less likely to be on the streets.[129]

The choice of location of attacks is equally significant. For example, rather than attacking railway stations, usually located within cities, a similar military advantage can be obtained by destroying railway lines in less populated areas.

These and other measures to reduce civilian casualties are ordinarily set out in rules of engagement and other instruments, which may be modified to avoid the repetition of errors and further minimise civilian casualties.[130]

For example, since 2008, ISAF has adopted a number of tactical directives and other measures in order to reduce civilian casualties from air strikes and other operations and to increase support among the Afghan population. Faulty identification of intended targets has been a recurring problem and, in an attempt to remedy this, key elements of the successive instructions included:

- limitation of the use of force, in particular, close air support, against residential compounds and other locations likely to produce civilian casualties;[131]
- authorisation to use air-to-ground munitions and indirect fire against residential areas only to be granted in very limited situations;[132]

---

126 API art 57(2)(a)(ii).
127 W J Fenwick, 'The Law Applicable to Targeting and Proportionality after Operation Allied Force: A View from the Outside' (2000) 3 *YBIHL* 53, 74.
128 AP Commentary, ¶ 2200.
129 Human Rights Watch, 'Off-Target: The Conduct of the War and Civilian Casualties in Iraq' (2003) 17.
130 For example, during the campaign against Serbia, NATO modified its rules of engagement to reduce risks to civilians. After a refugee convoy was mistakenly attacked, the altitude restriction of 15,000 feet to fly above Serbian defences was relaxed and before launching attacks visual confirmation was required that civilians were not present. Fenwick, 'Targeting and Proportionality' (n 70) 501.
131 Revised Tactical Directive of 2 July 2009, www.nato.int/isaf/docu/official_texts/Tactical_Directive_090706.pdf.
132 Ibid.

- instructions to presume, until otherwise apparent, that every Afghan is a civilian, all compounds are civilian structures and that civilians are present in every location where there is evidence of human habitation;[133]
- permission to use aerial-delivered munitions on civilian dwellings only as a last resort in situations of self-defence.[134]

8.1.3 Prohibition of disproportionate attacks

The next precautionary measure requires parties to refrain from launching indiscriminate attacks[135] – a reiteration of the prohibition of such attacks in Article 51 of Additional Protocol I discussed above.

8.1.4 Duty to cancel or postpone attacks

Article 57(2)(b) of Additional Protocol I addresses the next stage in the attack process: a target has been identified and appropriate means and methods for attacking it have been selected, but in the interval between the decision and the execution of the attack it becomes apparent either that the chosen target is not in fact a military objective or that the attack would be disproportionate. In such circumstances the attack must be cancelled or suspended.

As already stated, all those involved in the attack planning and execution process must take precautionary measures. Persons actually executing an attack have a particular role to play, as they are the most 'proximate' to the target and in a position to determine whether it has in fact been properly identified and to note any unexpected civilian presence. Although unlikely to have the authority to call off a strike, they should be required to transmit this information to those directing the operation.

The NATO Report gives an example of the application of this measure. A convoy of refugees was mistakenly identified as Serbian military vehicles and put under sustained aircraft attack, causing over 70 civilian deaths. The attack was suspended once doubts assailed the military planners, as Serbian forces did not normally travel in such large convoys, and slower aircraft confirmed the true identity of the vehicles.[136]

8.1.5 Warnings

Effective advance warning must be given of attacks that may affect the civilian population, unless circumstances do not permit.[137]

---

133 COMISAF Tactical Directive, 30 November 2011, www.isaf.nato.int/images/docs/20111105%20 nuc%20tactical%20directive%20revision%204%20(releaseable%20version)%20r.pdf.

134 Fragmentary order of June 2012 referred to in UNAMA/OHCHR, Afghanistan Mid-Year Report 2012 on the Protection of Civilians in Armed Conflict (July 2012) 38.

135 API art 57(2)(a)(iii).

136 NATO Report (n 31) ¶¶ 63–70. See also Anthony Rogers, 'Zero-Casualty Warfare' (2000) (837) IRRC 165, 174.

137 API art 57(2)(c). See also arts 4(2) and 5(2) Protocol II to the CCW and arts 3(10), 3(11) and 6(4) of Protocol II as amended in 1996 for warning requirements for these weapons.

Some recent conflicts have witnessed a dramatic increase in the number, scope and specificity of warnings issued – probably as a result of strategic self-imposed restrictions to avoid the adverse publicity associated with civilian casualties, rather than for legal reasons.[138]

The purpose of warnings is to allow civilians to take shelter or leave the area and to allow the party defending against the effect of attacks to take appropriate measures to protect the population. To be effective warnings must thus be timely, sufficiently specific and comprehensible to allow this to happen. What constitutes an effective warning to a large extent depends on the specific circumstances of the attack: the nature and location of the target and the means and methods of attack used.

Civilians who do not take heed of a warning and remain in a dangerous location, do not lose their entitlement to protection.

Warnings are only required for attacks that may affect civilians. This is understood as those that may cause civilian casualties.[139] There is no duty to give warnings of attacks in areas where there are no civilians left.[140] However, it should not be assumed that no civilians remain in an area merely because a warning has been issued.

The timing of warnings must be such as to give civilians sufficient time to move away from the intended target. General warnings in relation to areas where attacks will be carried out must allow the population to evacuate, and their timing should take into account factors such as the number of people who must leave, the area likely to be affected, the availability of means of transport, the state of roads and the location of possible destinations.[141]

The time lapse between warning and attack on a specific target is likely to be much shorter, but must nonetheless be sufficient to enable civilians to seek temporary shelter elsewhere.

Striking the correct balance between humanitarian and military considerations can be difficult. The time lapse between warning and attack must not allow the enemy sufficient time to remove weapons that might have been the object of attack in the intended target. Conversely, warnings given too much in advance may give the impression that the intended attack has been cancelled. For example, the NATO strike on the television tower in Belgrade was criticised *inter alia* because a warning had been issued 11 days before the attack and this lapse of time, some argue, could have led civilians to believe the attack had been cancelled.[142]

Warnings may be general in nature, instructing the population to leave areas with military targets or extremely precise, like Israel's – criticised – practice of 'roof knocking': firing warning shots with small munitions at the roofs of intended targets.

General warnings may be followed by more specific ones indicating which targets are going to be attacked imminently. What matters is whether the warnings are sufficiently precise to allow the affected population to move to areas of safety.

Israel was criticised for not having issued instructions to the civilian population as to the measures to take to avoid harm in the conflicts in Lebanon in 2006 and Gaza in 2008.[143]

---

138 Pnina Sharvit Baruch and Noam Neuman, 'Warning Civilians Prior to Attack under International Law' in Raul A 'Pete' Pedrozo and Daria P Wollschlaeger (eds), *International Law and the Changing Character of War* (US Naval War College 2011) 360–361.

139 Ibid 375.

140 UK *Manual* (n 40) ¶ 5.32.8.

141 Sharvit Baruch and Neuman (n 138) 379.

142 See eg Queguiner (n 107) 808.

143 Report of the Commission of Inquiry on Lebanon pursuant to Human Rights Council Res S-2/1*, A/HRC/3/2 (23 November 2006) ¶ 157; Report of the United Nations Fact Finding Mission on the Gaza Conflict, A/HRC/12/48 (25 September 2009) ('Goldstone Report') ¶¶ 500–542. For a critique of this aspect of the Goldstone Report, see Schmitt, 'Military Necessity and Humanity' (n 62) 827.

From a legal point of view, responsibility for this type of measure lies with the side defending from the effects of attack. From a practical point of view, the attacker is unlikely to have the necessary information to enable it to give reliable instructions.

Warnings have been issued in a variety of ways, depending on the situation, most frequently by dropping leaflets and radio broadcasts, but many other possibilities exist.

During the 2006 Lebanon war, in addition to leaflets and broadcasts, Israel also made pre-recorded telephone calls in Arabic to residents in the vicinity of intended targets and had phone conversations with local authorities. Similar methods were employed during the various rounds of hostilities in Gaza, as well as the more controversial practice of 'roof-knocking'.[144]

Earlier instruments required warnings to be given to the authorities.[145] Additional Protocol I is silent on the matter. In recent practice, warnings tended to be given directly to the population – as this was possible and is probably the most effective method.

Ultimately what matters is that the warnings reach those likely to be affected in a language or other form they understand.

There is no obligation to issue a warning if circumstances do not permit, for example if there is insufficient time to do so like when troops have to respond to an attack or come across a target unexpectedly or where the element of surprise is essential to the success of an operation or the security of the attacking forces.[146]

8.1.6 Target selection

The final precautionary measures requires parties, when several objectives exist whose destruction would provide a similar military advantage, to select the one, the attack on which may be expected to cause the least danger to civilians.[147]

Examples of the implementation of this precautionary measure include the attacks by Coalition forces in Iraq in 2003 of electrical power distribution rather than generation facilities, as the latter are harder to repair so their incapacitation causes longer hardship to the civilian population; as well as attacks against telecommunications cables rather than facilities.[148]

Effectively, this rule provides some guidance for the practical application of the prohibition on disproportionate attacks and, to a degree is already covered by the requirement to take measures to avoid or minimise civilian casualties.

8.2 Passive precautions

While the majority of rules regulating the conduct of hostilities require parties to take measures to spare civilians in the territory under the enemy's control, those on precautions against the effects of attacks or 'passive precautions' shift the focus and lay down measures a party must take to protect the civilian population within *its* control.

The duty to adopt passive precautions is not absolute: measures must be adopted 'to the maximum extent feasible'. Some consider that this expression sets a less exacting standard than the 'feasibile precautions' to be taken in attack, as reflected in the terms employed in the specific

---

144 Sharvit Baruch and Neuman (n 138) 368–371, 387.
145 See eg HR art 26.
146 UK *Manual* (n 40) ¶ 5.32.8.
147 API art 57(3).
148 See eg Schmitt 'The Conduct of Hostilities' (n 80) 93–94.

precautionary measures: 'endeavour' to remove the civilian population and 'avoid' locating military objectives in densely populated areas.[149]

Failure by the defending party to take precautions does not preclude its opponent from carrying out an attack. In so doing it must take the precautionary measures incumbent upon it.

Article 58 of Additional Protocol I lays down two specific precautionary measures aimed at separating civilians from military objectives, an essential first step in ensuring their protection, and concludes with a general requirement to adopt other precautionary measures.

8.2.1 Removal of the civilian population

Article 58(a) of Additional Protocol I requires parties to endeavour to remove the civilian population under their control from the vicinity of military objectives. This duty is expressly without prejudice to the prohibition on displacing the civilian population in situations of occupation, unless required by imperative military reasons or the security of the population.

During the Second World War, a number of states evacuated children from major cities. In recent conflicts, the tendency has been for civilians to leave areas of fighting of their initiative and by their own means.

8.2.2 Avoid locating military objectives within densely populated areas

Article 58(b) of Additional Protocol I requires parties to avoid locating military objectives within or near densely populated areas. This covers both fixed objectives, like military bases, and mobile ones like troops and weapons.

Again, the requirement is to do what is feasible. For example, the expansion of cities may cause military bases originally constructed in less densely populated areas to end up within or in close proximity to cities. Their relocation is not required.

In some recent conflicts the militarily weaker party has been accused of intentionally locating military objectives within and carrying out attacks from densely populated areas. For example, during the 2006 Lebanon war, Israel claimed that its attacks on civilian areas were justified and the civilian toll exacerbated by Hezbollah's practice of storing weapons in civilian homes and firing rockets from within populated areas.[150] Similar assertions were made by Israel in relation to Palestinian fighters in Gaza in 2008.[151]

The prohibition on resort to human shields does not extend to the intentional use of civilian objects to deter attacks on military objectives. Such practices therefore only violate the duty to take passive precautions.

149 See eg Sassoli and Cameron (n 85) 71. This lower standard reflects the position of smaller states that expressed concerns during the negotiations of the APs about the practical possibility of separating military objectives from the civilian population. CIHL commentary to r 11.
150 The extent of these practices is disputed. See eg Human Rights Watch, 'Why they Died: Civilian Casualties in Lebanon during the 2006 War' (September 2007) 53–56.
151 Palestinian fighters were accused of launching attacks from within civilian areas and from protected sites such as schools and mosques and using civilian and protected sites as bases for military activity. See eg Goldstone Report (n 143) ¶¶ 439–498.

8.2.3 Other measures

Finally, Article 58(c) of Additional Protocol I requires parties to take the other necessary precautions to protect civilians under their control from the dangers resulting from military operations.

Obvious examples include the construction of shelters and the installation of systems for issuing alerts. More complex possibilities also exist, for example air-defence systems like the 'Iron Dome' missile system employed by Israel to intercept short-range and artillery shells that would otherwise strike populated areas.

10
Direct participation in hostilities

Michelle Lesh

The principle of distinction, a 'cardinal'[1] rule of LOAC, requires criteria by which to identify who is a combatant and who is a civilian. Asymmetrical warfare has revealed in new ways that this golden rule is susceptible to abuse because the categories of combatant and civilian are 'bleeding together'.[2] The reason that there is difficulty in determining who is a civilian and who is a combatant is twofold. The first issue relates to the prevalence of non-state actors in contemporary armed conflict. It is often difficult to determine who the fighters are, whether they act in a manner typical of combatants and the parameters of the battlefield in which they operate. The second issue relates to the preferred methods of warfare of states. Because fighting so often occurs in urban areas and because most states rely heavily on air power, there are inevitably many civilian casualties.

Under LOAC, the premise on which civilian status rests is protection from attack. The principle of distinction articulates this foundational rule.[3] This principle is 'inseparable'[4] from the principle of the protection of the civilian population.[5] This is based on the presumption that civilians are not engaged in the hostilities around them.

Article 51(3) of Additional Protocol I (for international armed conflicts (IACs)) and Article 13(3) of Additional Protocol II (for non-international armed conflicts (NIACs)) articulate the limits to the scope of protected civilian status: 'Civilians shall enjoy the protection afforded by this Section, unless and for such time as they take a direct part in hostilities.'[6] Civilians who participate in hostilities are often referred to by the acronym DPH. The legal consequence of DPH is the loss of protected civilian status without becoming entitled to the rights given to

---

1 *Legality of the Threat or Use of Nuclear Weapons (Advisory Opinion)* [1996] ICJ Rep 226, 256 ¶ 78.
2 Gerry Simpson, 'Paris 1793 and 1871: *Levée en Masse* as Event' in Fleur Johns, Richard Joyce and Sundhya Pahuja (eds), *Events: The Force of International Law* (Routlege 2011) 80.
3 API art 48.
4 *AP Commentary* ¶ 1911.
5 API art 51(2).
6 API art 51(3). This notion is replicated in other embodiments of LOAC. See GCI–IV art 3; Rome Statute art 8.2(b)(i), 8.2(e)(i). See also UK Ministry of Defence, *The Manual of the Law of Armed Conflict* (OUP 2004) ¶ 5.3.2; *The Manual on the Law of Non-International Armed Conflict: With Commentary* (IIHL 2006) r 2.1.1.2.

combatants.[7] Defining DPH has proven to be problematic.[8] The meaning of these words set out in Article 51(3) has ignited intense debate.

A major development in this area of the law occurred with the publication of the ICRC Interpretive Guidance on Direct Participation in Hostilities ('Guidance') in 2009. Also relevant is the judgment of the Israeli Supreme Court in the *Targeted Killing* case. Although this is a domestic court decision, applicable to the practice of one particular state, at the time it was handed down (2006) it signified a contribution to international debate surrounding this vague provision of the law. Scholarly debates have also assisted in deciphering how to apply this provision. These debates have occurred largely amongst governmental, non-governmental, military and academic experts who were invited by the ICRC to participate in the meetings over a period of five years that culminated in the Guidance.[9] The meetings did not always result in unanimous conclusions when applying the rules to particular scenarios. The wide spectrum of legal controversies that emerged can generally be divided into the 'broad' and 'narrow' definitional approaches. The broad approach favours a wide interpretation for the circumstances in which civilian protection is forfeited and the narrow approach prefers a restricted interpretation for loss of civilian protection. At this stage it is sufficient to note that the Guidance has opened up dialogue and influenced the debate in this area.[10] The arguments of this chapter will engage with those of the Guidance, the most comprehensive legal document on the meaning of 'civilians directly participating in hostilities'.

1 'Take a direct part'

Analysis of the meaning of DPH will be divided into the participation of individuals and groups. Individuals who participate in hostilities reflect the language of Article 51(3), which delineates the forfeiture of protected status in its individual form. The first part of the discussion will focus on what acts constitute 'direct participation'. The second part of the analysis will focus on the period for which civilian protection is lost.

The meaning of 'direct' in the context of DPH is concerned with the type of acts which establish the loss of civilian protection. The Guidance creates three cumulative criteria for determining whether a specific act qualifies as DPH: threshold of harm, causal link and belligerent nexus.[11] The requirements collectively depict the relevant conduct undertaken by individual civilians during hostilities.

1.1 Threshold of harm

This requirement is concerned with the meanings of 'hostilities' and 'attack'. The specific act in question must be likely to harm (as opposed to actually harming) a party to the conflict. To reach the threshold of harm, the act must be likely to cause military harm or death, injury and

---

7 *AP Commentary* ¶ 1942.

8 CIHL practice to r 6.

9 See ICRC, 'Overview of the ICRC's Expert Process (2003–2008)' (2009), www.icrc.org/eng/assets/ files/other/overview-of-the-icrcs-expert-process-icrc.pdf.

10 Dieter Fleck, 'Direct Participation in Hostilities by Non-State Actors and the Challenge of Compliance with International Humanitarian Law' (2010) 4 *Public Diplomacy Magazine* 40.

11 ICRC, *Interpretive Guidance on the Notion of Direct Participation in Hostilities under International Humanitarian Law* (ICRC 2009) 46. See also Nils Melzer, *Targeted Killing in International Law* (OUP 2008) 276, 341–346. This chapter was written before the publication of the United States Department of Defense Law of War Manual June 2015. The Manual's approach to DPH represents a significant contribution to the debate and it can be said, broadly, to position itself somewhere between the ICRC Guidance and the *Targeted Killing Case*.

destruction.[12] This definition is supported by the Additional Protocol I Commentary's discussion of Article 51(3): 'Hostile acts should be understood to be acts which by their nature and purpose are intended to cause actual harm to the personnel and equipment of the armed forces.'[13] The *Targeted Killing* case adopts a similar understanding of hostile acts, which include hostile acts against civilians.[14]

The Guidance uses various illustrative examples to explain what it means by adversely affecting the military operations and capacity of a party to the conflict,[15] and what would qualify as direct attacks against civilians and civilian objects.[16] Examples of acts by non-state actors that would meet the threshold of harm include launching rockets (irrespective of their range or impact), the indefinite incarceration of a prisoner of war (POW)[17] and an individual who provides a member of an organised armed group (OAG)[18] with crucial tactical targeting information about the location of enemy soldiers taking cover in a nearby house.[19]

The requirement does not cover actions that enhance the party's military capabilities. This is legitimate in the sense that, for example, donations for military equipment should rightly not be covered. The exclusive focus on harm has, however, been criticised.[20] The Guidance would not cover actions undertaken by non-state actors that do not negatively affect the enemy but enhance the OAG who is a party to the conflict, for example. Forms of capacity-building such as the build-up of weapons or the recruitment of fighters to organisations like al-Qaeda or Islamic State (IS, also known as ISIS, ISIL or Daesh) would not fall within the meaning of 'adverse harm'.[21]

1.2 Causal link

Direct causation requires a direct causal link between the specific act and the likely harm that would result from it. This harm, according to the Guidance, should be brought in one causal step.[22] Only acts that are themselves one step causally distant from the harm they are likely to cause, or acts that are 'an integral part'[23] of them, deprive civilians of their protection.[24] The one causal step approach has received support from some commentators.[25] Others have criticised it,

---

12 ICRC, *Interpretive Guidance* (n 11) 47.
13 *AP Commentary* ¶ 1942. The Guidance nonetheless diverges from the accepted definition in its position that not all actions that take place during the armed conflict amount to 'hostilities' in the context of DPH. See ibid 41; Melzer, *Targeted Killing* (n 11) 243, 276.
14 *Public Committee against Torture in Israel v Government of Israel* ('*Targeted Killing*') [2006] HCJ 769/02 ¶ 33.
15 ICRC, *Interpretive Guidance* (n 11) 48.
16 Ibid 49.
17 See ICRC, 'Third Expert Meeting on the Notion of Direct Participation in Hostilities' (2005) 15–16, www.icrc.org/eng/assets/files/other/2005-09-report-dph-2005-icrc.pdf.
18 The concept of 'organised armed group' is not clearly defined in the law.
19 See ICRC, 'Second Expert Meeting on the Notion of Direct Participation in Hostilities' (2004) 5–6, www.icrc.org/eng/assets/files/other/2004-07-report-dph-2004-icrc.pdf.
20 Michael N Schmitt, 'Deconstructing Direct Participation in Hostilities: The Constitutive Elements' (2010) 42 *NYU JILP* 697, 713–725.
21 For criticism see Michael N Schmitt, 'The Interpretive Guidance on the Notion of Direct Participation in Hostilities: A Critical Analysis' (2010) 1 *Harvard NSJ* 1, 27.
22 ICRC, *Interpretive Guidance* (n 11) 53.
23 For a discussion of the causal proximity test and constituting an 'integral part' of military operations see ICRC, 'Fourth Expert Meeting on the Notion of Direct Participation in Hostilities' (2006) 46–48, www.icrc.org/eng/assets/files/other/2006-03-report-dph-2006-icrc.pdf.
24 ICRC, *Interpretive Guidance* (n 11) 54–55.
25 Dapo Akande, 'Current Developments: Clearing the Fog of War? The ICRC's Interpretive Guidance on Direct Participation in Hostilities' (2010) 59 *ICLQ* 188.

particularly on the grounds that it does not take into account the gathering of intelligence.[26] To see what is at issue, it is necessary to consider an example.

Suppose that Taliban fighters[27] emplace an improvised explosive device (IED) at an International Security Assistance Force (ISAF) camp in Afghanistan at 5 pm on a Saturday afternoon killing five Coalition service members. The planting of the IED is the act that is one step causally distant from the deaths it causes. Assume that the Taliban fighters assembled the IED two days earlier in a nearby village in the Helmand Province in preparation for detonating it in the camp on that Saturday afternoon. Based on his elaboration of the Guidance's causal requirement,[28] it would seem that Melzer would distinguish their activity of assembling the IED from the activity of the person who assembles IEDs in a factory for the purpose of the conflict more generally. On Melzer's account, the activities of the Taliban fighters in assembling the IED should be considered an 'integral part' of the act that is one step causally distant from deaths in the ISAF camp (though those activities occurred two days earlier 40 kilometres away) whereas the activity of the person in the factory should not. The activity of the person assembling IEDs in the factory would not be one step causally distant from the deaths in the ISAF camp, even if the Taliban fighters had used an IED the factory worker had assembled (assuming that the fighters merely took it from a stockpile of IEDs in a warehouse). Melzer would also regard the fighter's actions of loading the IED on to a truck, driving the truck to the site of the attack and laying the IED as integral to the act of detonating it.

The approach taken by the Guidance to direct participation is often considered narrow (though there are accounts that are even more so).[29] Certainly it is narrower than the approach taken in the *Targeted Killing* case, according to which people who plan and direct operations are usually held to be causally responsible for the effects of those operations even though the effects are mediated by the agency of others.[30] Most significantly, the Court did not limit its interpretation of 'direct' to the person(s) 'committing the physical act of attack'.[31] Chief Justice (Ret.) Barak looked at the whole chain of command involved in an attack. He concluded: 'those who have sent him [the perpetrator of an attack] as well, take "a direct part". The same goes for the person who decided upon the act, and the person who planned it.'[32]

Evidently the accounts the Guidance and *Targeted Killing* case offer of 'direct participation' is mirrored in their accounts of 'indirect participation'.[33] This has been a popular approach in

---

26 Schmitt, 'The Constitutive Elements' (n 20) 727–729. For a response to this criticism see: Nils Melzer, 'Keeping the Balance between Military Necessity and Humanity: A Response to Four Critiques on the ICRC's Interpretive Guidance on the Notion of Direct Participation in Hostilities' (2010) 42 *NYU JILP* 831, 867. See also William H Boothby, *The Law of Targeting* (OUP 2012) 154–156.

27 The Guidance includes collective actions as part of its understanding of direction causation. See ICRC, *Interpretive Guidance* (n 11) 54–55.

28 Melzer, 'Keeping the Balance' (n 26) 865–869.

29 Vincent-Joël Proulx, 'If the Hat Fits, Wear It, if the Turban Fits, Run for Your Life: Reflections on the Indefinite Detention and Targeted Killing of Suspected Terrorists' (2005) 56 *Hastings LJ* 801, 886.

30 *Targeted Killing* (n 14) ¶¶ 34, 35.

31 Ibid ¶ 37.

32 Ibid. For a similar view on what counts as 'direct' see eg Yoram Dinstein, *The Conduct of Hostilities under the Law of International Armed Conflict* (2nd edn, CUP 2010) 146–152; Gary Solis, *The Law of Armed Conflict: International Humanitarian Law in War* (CUP 2010) 542–545; Boothby, *The Law of Targeting* (n 26) 156–157; Turkel Commission, 'The Public Commission to Examine the Maritime Incident of 31 May 2010: Report: Part One' (January 2011), www.turkel-committee.gov.il/files/wordocs/8808report-eng.pdf, ¶ 201. It should be noted that the Office of the Prosecutor of the ICC took a different position from the Turkel Commission in its assessment of the legal status of the individuals on board the *Mavi Marmara*. See n 38.

33 ICRC, *Interpretive Guidance* (n 11) 43.

determining the meaning of Article 51(3).[34] The examples that are regularly appealed to are the ammunition truck driver, human shields and the bomb-maker. It is commonly agreed that the driver delivering ammunition to an active firing position at the front line engages in DPH.[35] There is, however, disagreement as to whether IED-making counts as 'direct' or 'indirect'[36] participation in hostilities and there is controversy due to various interpretations of the legal status of human shields, in particular whether voluntary human shields count as DPH.[37]

1.3 B elligerent nexus

The final criterion set out in the Guidance is 'belligerent nexus'. In order to count as DPH, acts by members of an OAG must be clearly detrimental to a party to the conflict. It is not enough that the actions, for example, strengthen the OAG. There are two limbs to this requirement, which are a culmination of the previous two steps. The act must 'be specifically designed to directly cause the required threshold of harm in support of a party to the conflict *and* to the detriment of another'.[38] Criticism levelled at this criterion states that it should not require both limbs but rather one or the other.[39]

---

34 See *AP Commentary* ¶ 1944; IACmHR, 'Third Report on the Human Rights Situation in Colombia' (26 February 1999) ¶ 53–57, www.cidh.org/countryrep/Colom99en/chapter.4a.htm; *Prosecutor v Akayesu (Judgment)* (Case no ICTR-96-4-T, 2 ICTR Trial Chamber, September 1998) ¶ 629.

35 *Targeted Killing* (n 14) ¶ 35; Yoram Dinstein, 'Distinction and Loss of Civilian Protection in International Armed Conflicts' in Michael D Carsten (ed), *International Law and Military Operations* (US Naval War College 2008) 183, 191–192; W Hays Parks, 'Air War and the Laws of War' (1990) 32 *Air Force LR* 134; Cf A P V Rogers, 'Direct Participation in Hostilities: Some Personal Reflections' (2009) 48 *RDMDG* 143, 152 who suggests the act does not amount to direct participation; ICRC, *Interpretive Guidance* (n 11) 56. The Guidance distinguishes this form of 'direct' participation from other scenarios involving a driver transporting ammunition.

36 See ICRC, *Interpretive Guidance* (n 11) 53 n 123; Kenneth Watkin, 'Opportunity Lost: Organized Armed Groups and the ICRC "Direct Participation in Hostilities" Interpretive Guidance' (2010) 42 *NYU JILP* 641, 681; William J Fenrick, 'ICRC Guidance on Direct Participation in Hostilities' (2009) 12 *YIHL* 287, 293.

37 See *Targeted Killing* (n 14) ¶ 36; ICRC, *Interpretive Guidance* (n 11) 56; Melzer, *Targeted Killing* (n 11) 35, 345–346; ICRC, Second Expert Meeting (n 19) 6–7; ICRC, Fourth Expert Meeting (n 23) 44–46; ICRC, Sixth Meeting of Experts on the Notion of Direct Participation in Hostilities (2008) 70–72, www.icrc.org/eng/assets/files/other/2008-05-report-dph-2008-icrc.pdf. See also Michael N Schmitt, 'Human Shields in International Humanitarian Law' (2009) 47 *Columbia JIL* 292; Rewi Lyall, 'Voluntary Human Shields, Direct Participation in Hostilities and the International Humanitarian Law Obligations of States' (2008) 9 *Melbourne JIL* 313.

38 ICRC, *Interpretive Guidance* (n 11) 58 (emphasis added). The Office of the Prosecutor (OTP) of the International Criminal Court, in its preliminary investigation into the situation on board the *Mavi Marmara*, found that the passengers' resistance to the Israel Defense Forces' interception and boarding of the vessel did not amount to DPH and therefore the passengers were not deprived of their protected civilian status. Based on its application of the three criteria of the Guidance, the OTP concluded that '[t]he information available does not indicate that the crew and passengers' actions were specifically designed to support Hamas by harming Israel'. In relation to the passengers who used violence against the IDF soldiers, the Report specified that 'their acts were intended to oppose Israel's enforcement of the blockade in furtherance of the flotilla's humanitarian and political focused objectives, … rather than specifically designed to support a party to the conflict'. See the OTP of the ICC, 'Situation on Registered Vessels, of Comoros, Greece and Cambodia Article 53(1) Report' (6 November 2014) ¶¶ 48–53. The subsequent Pre-Trial Chamber and Appeal Chamber decisions on this situation did not address the substantive issue of DPH.

39 Schmitt, 'The Interpretive Guidance' (n 21) 34; Boothby, *The Law of Targeting* (n 26) 155–156.

Four situations (individual self-defence, exercise of power or authority over persons or territory, civil unrest and inter-civilian violence) are discussed in the Guidance in order to highlight what does *not* count as a belligerent nexus.[40] The Guidance does acknowledge that there are practical difficulties in determining the belligerent nexus. One such example would be Sunni residents fleeing from Ramadi, the capital of Anbar province when fighting is taking place between the Iraqi armed forces and fighters belonging to ISIS. The residents are adversely affecting the military operations of the Iraqi armed forces because they are blocking a strategically important area that allows the soldiers access to the city. However, the conduct of the residents does not specifically support ISIS by causing harm to the Iraqi armed forces operation and therefore a belligerent nexus would not be evidenced.

The Guidance is trying to emphasise that in relation to belligerent nexus the specific act must be an integral part of the hostilities between parties that form the basis of the armed conflict between those parties. This highlights the way in which this requirement is very much linked to causation. The belligerent act, according to the Guidance, must be of a specifically military nature and 'so closely linked to the subsequent execution of a specific hostile act that they already constitute an integral part of that act'.[41] The Guidance would require the individual's specific act to be an integral part of, for example, the launching of rocket-propelled grenades. Would the people who work smuggling goods in the underground tunnels connecting Gaza with Egypt have a belligerent nexus to the armed conflict between Israel and Hamas? The answer is that they almost certainly would not, though there may be circumstances in which the smuggling of goods through the tunnels would count as integral to an act that is one step causally distant from the harm it is likely to cause. If, however, unlike the Guidance, one accepts the position that the threshold of harm requirement should also include enhancement of the military capacity of one side rather than just adversely affecting the enemy, then arguably the belligerent nexus requirement should extend to include the enhancement notion. In that case one would have a more extended idea of which goods smuggled through the underground tunnels would count as having a belligerent nexus to the conflict.

1.4 Grey areas

The three requirements of the Guidance cover many of the ambiguities concerning DPH. The requirements do not, however, cover all grey areas and in acknowledging this, the Guidance suggests that in cases of doubt, civilian protection should apply.[42] On the face of it, this approach to doubtful cases is consistent with Article 50(1) Additional Protocol I.[43] Some commentators, however, argue that it is a misapplication of Article 50(1), which is concerned with whether an individual is a civilian or a combatant, not whether he or she is a civilian or a civilian in DPH. Therefore, these commentators argue, affording protection in 'doubtful cases' does not apply to grey areas of DPH.[44] The approach of the Guidance contrasts with the *Targeted Killing* case's

40 ICRC, *Interpretive Guidance* (n 11) 61–63.

41 Ibid 65–66.

42 Ibid 74. See also, Christof Heyns, Report of the Special Rapporteur on Extrajudicial, Summary or Arbitrary Executions, UN Doc A/68/382 (13 September 2013) ¶ 67; Office of the Prosecutor, 'Situation on Comoros' (n 38) ¶ 54; Tom Ruys, 'Licence to Kill? State Sponsored Assassination under International Law' (2009) KU Leuven Faculty of Law, Working Paper 28, www.law.kuleuven.be/iir/nl/onderzoek/wp/WP76e.pdf.

43 API art 50; *AP Commentary* ¶ 1920.

44 Schmitt, 'The Constitutive Elements' (n 20) 736–737; Watkin, 'Opportunity Lost' (n 36) 665–666; Boothby, *The Law of Targeting* (n 26) 149, 158.

support for Schmitt's position that grey areas should be interpreted liberally (that is, 'in favour of finding direct participation').[45] As stated at the outset of this chapter, the *Targeted Killing* case's general interpretation of DPH falls into the 'broad approach'. It is important to note, however, that adopting a 'broad approach' generally to DPH does not necessarily require adopting a 'liberal approach' to grey areas. That is because the broad approach could interpret forfeiture of protected civilian status to cover a wide range of activities, yet when uncertainty exists about whether an individual has engaged in those activities, it could consider that individual to be a civilian.[46] Adopting a cautious rather than a liberal approach to grey areas is not in the least in tension with reasons for adopting the broad approach more generally. When there is uncertainty, the benefit of the doubt should be given to the individual and protection should be granted.

2 'For such time'

Following the evaluation of which acts constitute 'direct', the factor that must be considered is the time for which protection is lost. There are two aspects that need to be determined separately in order to establish the meaning of 'for such time'. The first establishes the beginning and end of hostilities. This sets the parameters of the relevant period to assess when DPH begins and when it finishes. The second establishes the legal consequences of the 'revolving door theory'.[47] How do the pauses between acts of violence affect a person's legal protection from direct attack?

The narrow approach to 'for such time' interprets the loss of civilian protection as lasting for the duration of the specific act.[48] This is based on a strict textual reading of the phrase 'unless and for such time' in Article 51(3).[49] Upon completion of the specific act, protection is returned. This rules out, to a certain extent, figures higher up in the command structure of the OAG from ever losing their protection. Because they do not carry out belligerent acts but rather recruit or plan them, it is difficult to pinpoint a specific time frame when they would be considered to partake in hostilities in a way that deprives them of their protection. This relates to what counts as preparatory acts. As noted earlier, the Guidance specifies that preparatory measures and deployment must be 'of a specifically military nature and so closely linked to the subsequent execution of a specific hostile act that they already constitute an integral part of that act'.[50] The

---

45 *Targeted Killing* (n 14) ¶ 34; Michael N Schmitt, 'Direct Participation in Hostilities and 21st Century Armed Conflict' in Horst Fischer (ed), *Crisis Management and Humanitarian Protection* (Berliner WissenschaftsVerlag 2004) 509. For a development in Schmitt's position on degree of doubt as to status see Michael N Schmitt and John J Merriam, 'The Tyranny of Context: Israeli Targeting Practices in Legal Perspective' (2015) 37 *University of Pennsylvania JIL* 53, 125, http://papers.ssrn.com/sol3/papers.cfm?abstract_id=2593629.

46 Melzer, *Targeted Killing* (n 11) 339.

47 See Parks, 'Air War' (n 35) 118.

48 ICRC, *Interpretive Guidance* (n 11) 43.

49 This interpretation has received wide support: *AP Commentary* ¶ 1492 ; IACHR, 'Third Report on the Human Rights Situation in Colombia' (n 34) ¶ 55; *Abella v Argentina* (Case no 11.137, IACHR, 18 November 1997) ¶ 189; *Prosecutor v Blagojević (Judgment)* (Case no IT-02-60-T, ICTY Trial Chamber, 17 January 2005) ¶ 544; Amnesty International, 'Israel and the Occupied Territories: State Assassinations and Other Unlawful Killings' (2001) 29, www.amnesty.org/en/library/info/MDE15/005/2001/en; Cassese, 'Expert Opinion' (n 29) 7–8, 18, 20; Yael Stein, 'By Any Name Illegal and Immoral' (2003) 17 *Ethics and International Affairs* 127, 129.

50 ICRC, *Interpretive Guidance* (n 11) 65–66.

Guidance provides examples to further clarify this approach.[51] Concern has been raised that this amounts to a restrictive definition.[52]

In terms of when a specific act ends, the Guidance stipulates that this occurs after the individual is physically separated from the operation, for example with the removal of weapons and the resumption of activities distinct from the operation.[53] Importantly, the Guidance notes that there does not have to be a temporal or geographic proximity to the execution of the specific act in order for it to count as 'for such time'. Therefore if weapons are collected with the intention of laying mines or mounting a suicide attack of any kind one month later it could still count as satisfying 'for such time'.

The 'specific act' approach to 'for such time' perceives the 'revolving door' as a welcome restriction[54] because civilians who participate sporadically *should* regain their protection in the intervals between attacks.[55] This approach has been criticised for failing to take into account 'the persistent civilian participator'.[56] Moreover, by limiting the interpretation of 'for such time' to the specific act and by focusing on the tactical aspect of DPH, with little reference to the planning and execution of future attacks,[57] critics claim that the Guidance does not adequately remove the 'revolving door' threat.[58] A restrictive approach for the duration of the loss of protection is based on a fear that without such an approach the civilian population will be at risk.[59] It is an attempt to impose further restraints on state armed forces.[60]

By way of contrast, the interpretation adopted by the *Targeted Killing* case of 'for such time' is an attempt to respond adequately to the 'revolving door' concern.[61] In the Court's view, an individual civilian who directly participates in hostilities loses his or her protection and can be targeted at all times 'until he or she unambiguously opts out of hostilities through extended non-participation or an affirmative act of withdrawal'.[62] This means the individual can be attacked 'between episodes of participation'.[63] The stated overriding aim of this approach is to create a situation that ensures the greatest level of protection for the civilian population.[64] Critics of this approach, however, claim that continuous DPH has precisely the opposite effect: harming the civilian population.[65]

---

51 Ibid.
52 Bill Boothby, '"And for Such Time As": The Time Dimension to Direct Participation in Hostilities' (2010) 42 *NYU JILP* 741.
53 ICRC, *Interpretive Guidance* (n 11) 67. Cf *Targeted Killing* (n 14) ¶ 33 which ruled that taking part in hostilities does not require the use of a weapon. See also Turkel Commission (n 32) ¶¶ 197–198, 217.
54 Melzer, *Targeted Killing* (n 11) 347.
55 Ibid 347, 352–353.
56 Ibid 357.
57 Watkin, 'Opportunity Lost' (n 36) 660.
58 Schmitt, 'The Interpretive Guidance' (n 21) 38.
59 A P V Rogers, *Law on the Battlefield* (3rd edn, Manchester University Press 2012) 15; Cassese, 'Expert Opinion' (n 29) 20. See also Marco Sassòli, 'Targeting: The Scope and Utility of the Concept of "Military Objectives" for the Protection of Civilians in Contemporary Armed Conflicts' in David Wippman and Matthew Evangelista (eds), *New Wars, New Laws? Applying the Laws of War in 21st Century Conflicts* (Martinus Nijhoff 2005) 201.
60 Jann Kleffner, 'From "Belligerents" to "Fighters" and Civilians Directly Participating in Hostilities: On the Principle of Distinction in Non-International Armed Conflicts One Hundred Years after the Second Hague Peace Conference' (2007) *Netherlands ILR* 315, 332.
61 *Targeted Killing* (n 14) ¶ 40.
62 Schmitt, 'The Interpretive Guidance' (n 21) 38.
63 Boothby, 'And for Such Time As' (n 52) 767–768. See also *Targeted Killing* (n 14) ¶ 39; Watkin, 'Opportunity Lost' (n 36) 686.
64 Boothby, 'And for Such Time As' (n 52) 760.
65 Melzer, *Targeted Killing* (n 11) 341.

3 Groups who directly participate in hostilities

Following the analysis of individual civilians who lose their protection, this section will consider whether members of OAGs lose their protection from attack by virtue of their function in that group. With the growth of non-state actors participating in armed conflict, applying the notion of OAG for the purposes of targeting has had growing appeal.[66] Indeed, this approach originated from the Guidance, and the notion of 'organised armed groups' is increasingly reflected in state practice.[67]

According to the Guidance, there are three elements that make up an OAG: sufficient degree of military organisation, 'belonging to a party to the conflict' and 'continuous combat function' (CCF). All three elements must be fulfilled in order for its members to forfeit protection from attack.

3.1 Organisation

A sufficient degree of military organisation is an expected and uncontroversial element of an OAG.[68] Some commentators focus on the need for a group to conduct itself under a command structure. They propose that basic military staff structure (personnel, intelligence, operations, logistics, civil–military relations and signals) can be applied in assessing DPH.[69] The comparison to command structure has been criticised for failing to address sufficiently the practical difficulties of civilians participating on an unorganised, sporadic basis.[70]

3.2 Belonging to a party

The requirement of 'belonging to a party to the conflict' is an import of a requirement that generally relates to entitlement to POW status.[71] Admittedly, some confusion does exist as to the meaning of belonging to a party given the different contexts in which it exists in the treaty law.[72] Some critics have claimed that the Guidance utilises the notion of 'belonging to a party' to determine conflict characterisation. The Guidance states that OAGs engaged in violence against a party to an IAC without *belonging to another party to the same conflict* are civilians in that IAC. OAGs operating within the broader context of an IAC *without belonging to a party to that conflict* could be regarded as a separate party to a NIAC. This has led some commentators to raise

---

66 Examples of non-state actors involved in conflicts include ISIS, Boko Haram, Al-Shabaab, Houthis, Izz al-Din al-Qassam Brigades, the United Armed Forces of Novorossiya, the Colombian National Liberation Army and the Lord's Resistance Army

67 See eg Government of Israel, 'The 2014 Gaza Conflict 7 July – 26 August 2014: Factual and Legal Aspects' (May 2015) 156, http://mfa.gov.il/ProtectiveEdge/Documents/IDFConduct.pdf; Schmitt and Merriam (n 45) 112–113.

68 Watkin, 'Opportunity Lost' (n 36) 674.

69 Ibid. See also Geoffrey Corn and Chris Jenks, 'Two Sides of the Combatant Coin: Untangling Direct Participation in Hostilities from Belligerent Status in Non-International Armed Conflict' *University of Pennsylvania JIL* 33 (2011) 313, 333–334; Hilly Moodrick-Even Khen, 'Can We Now Tell What "Direct Participation in Hostilities" Is? HCJ 769/02 *The Public Committee against Torture in Israel v the Government of Israel*' (2007) 40 *Israel LR* 213, 239–240.

70 Melzer, *Targeted Killing* (n 11) 340.

71 For criticism that this is misplaced see Schmitt, 'The Interpretive Guidance' (n 21) 17–18.

72 See eg Katherine Del Mar, 'The Requirement of "Belonging" under International Humanitarian Law' (2010) 21 *EJIL* 105, 108, 115–117.

the question of whether the Guidance is stating there are two conflicts occurring simultaneously whereby two distinct bodies of law would apply to a situation not factually distinct.[73] This would mean that at one stage of the Libya conflict the Benghazi rebels were civilians directly participating in the IAC between the Gaddafi regime and coalition states and they were also possibly armed forces in a separate NIAC between the Gaddafi regime and the Benghazi rebels.

3.3 Continuous combat function

The third requirement of the Guidance for collective forfeiture of protected civilian status is CCF.[74] This determines whether a person is targetable at all times and this is established through assessing their function in an OAG. Their function must be *continuously* to take part in hostilities. Uniform and behaviour are indications used to identify CCF[75] and the three cumulative criteria (threshold of harm, causal link and belligerent nexus) are applied to the *function* (as opposed to the specific act) to determine whether the CCF criterion is satisfied. The CCF criterion, which in effect treats OAGs as the equivalent to regular armed forces, was a way to respond to concerns that a narrow interpretation of individual civilians directly participating in hostilities (that is, loss of protection for a specific act) was unrealistic on the battlefield. Nonetheless, there have been criticisms that CCF function remains too restrictive[76] and that CCF is too permissive.[77]

It appears that the Guidance is replacing the 'membership approach' that had previously developed in the discourse on DPH with its CCF approach. The membership approach argues that OAGs that fulfil the same function as combatants are subject to the same targeting rules as armed forces.[78] Members of such groups, however, cannot be combatants because they fail to fulfil the criteria of Article 4 Geneva Convention III. One of the motivating factors behind support for the membership approach is that it would be counterintuitive for members of such groups to be characterised as civilians in the context of detention (that is, they do not receive combatant privilege) and members of the armed forces in the context of targeting.[79]

A significant difference between the membership and CCF approaches is that rather than focusing on membership of a group in order to establish civilian loss of protection, the Guidance looks at the specific function in the group to establish the legal status equivalent to members of the armed forces.[80] It has been contended that in doing so the Guidance is applying different

---

73 Watkin, 'Opportunity Lost' (n 36) 651. For a rejection of Watkin's critique see Melzer, 'Keeping the Balance' (n 26) 841–842.

74 ICRC, *Interpretive Guidance* (n 11) 33.

75 Ibid 35.

76 See Boothby, *The Law of Targeting* (n 26) 150–152.

77 Philip Alston, Report of the Special Rapporteur on Extrajudicial, Summary or Arbitrary Executions, UN Doc A/HRC/14/24/Add.6 (28 May 2010) ¶ 65–67.

78 Kenneth Watkin, 'Controlling the Use of Force: A Role for Human Rights Norms in Contemporary Armed Conflict' (2004) 98 *AJIL* 1, 17; Kleffner (n 60) 330.

79 Schmitt, 'The Interpretive Guidance' (n 21) 17. There are, however, commentators who do not support the membership approach. See Sassòli, 'Targeting' (n 59) 200–201. See also Colonel Mark 'Max' Maxwell, 'Rebutting the Civilian Presumption: Playing Whack-A-Mole Without a Mallet?' in Claire Finkelstein, Jens David Ohlin and Andrew Altman (eds), *Targeted Killings: Law and Morality in an Asymmetrical World* (OUP 2012) 54, 56.

80 ICRC, *Interpretive Guidance* (n 11) 32–33.

criteria for targeting regular state armed forces and 'others'.[81] Melzer defends the focus on function by arguing that it is a way to complement the formal notion of membership, which is recognised for state armed forces.[82] In addition to criticism of the distinction the Guidance makes between regular and irregular armed forces, criticism has also been levelled over the limited range of functions regarded as entailing membership. The broad approach to membership 'involves a much broader range of activity'[83] in what constitutes 'functional'.[84] In groups with mixed functions it will be more difficult to ascertain which members have combat function.[85] There appears to be agreement that political and religious leaders, members in the 'political wing' of the group, financial contributors and informants will be civilians who may directly participate in hostilities sporadically.[86]

4 Restraints on the use of force

The Guidance includes Section IX, which declares that LOAC requires restraints on the use of force. It states that 'the kind and degree of force which is permissible against persons not entitled to protection against direct attack must not exceed what is actually necessary to accomplish a legitimate military purpose in the prevailing circumstances'.[87] The Guidance supports its position with reference to the principles of humanity and necessity.[88] This interpretation by the Guidance has received both support[89] and criticism.[90]

---

81 Watkin, 'Opportunity Lost' (n 36) 671–672, 690.
82 Melzer, 'Keeping the Balance' (n 26) 845. The status determination for targeting used by the Guidance in its concept of CCF has been criticised on various grounds. See Corn and Jenks, 'Two Sides of the Combatant Coin' (n 69); Françoise J Hampson, 'Direct Participation in Hostilities and the Interoperability of the Law of Armed Conflict and Human Rights Law' in Raul A Pedrozo and Daria P Wollschlaeger (eds), *International Law and the Changing Character of War* (US Naval War College 2011) 187.
83 Watkin, 'Opportunity Lost' (n 36) 683.
84 *Targeted Killing* (n 14) ¶ 35.
85 Hamas, for example. See Gershon Baskin, 'Assassinating the Chance for Calm' *Daily Beast* (15 November 2012), www.thedailybeast.com/articles/2012/11/15/assassinating-the-chance-for-calm.html.
86 Melzer, *Targeted Killing* (n 11) 320. See also Ruys, 'Licence to Kill?' (n 42) 28; David Kretzmer, 'Targeted Killing of Suspected Terrorists: Extra-Judicial Executions of Legitimate Means of Defence?' (2005) 16 *EJIL* 171, 200; Asa Kasher and Amos Yadlin, 'Assassination and Preventive Killing' (2005) 25 *SAIS Review of International Affairs* 41, 54.
87 ICRC, *Interpretive Guidance* (n 11) 77.
88 See eg ibid 82. See also Jann K Kleffner, 'Section IX of the ICRC Interpretive Guidance on Direct Participation in Hostilities: The End of *Jus in Bello* Proportionality as We Know it?' (2012) 45 *Israel LR* 35, 37–42.
89 Alston, Report of the Special Rapporteur (n 77) 23 ¶ 76; Ryan Goodman, 'The Power to Kill or Capture Enemy Combatants' (2013) 24 *EJIL* 850. Goodman is a supporter of Section IX but he attempts to strengthen its basis by securing it more firmly in the law through analysing treaty law, state practice, drafting history, Pictet's work and UN positions. This should be read in conjunction with the other aspect of his argument, which focuses on the definition of *hors de combat*. For a critique of Goodman's thesis see: Geoffrey S Corn, Laurie R Blank, Chris Jenks and Eric Talbot Jensen, 'Belligerent Targeting and the Invalidity of a Least Harmful Means Rule' (2013) 89 *International Law Studies* 536.
90 See W Hays Parks, 'Part IX of the ICRC "Direct Participation in Hostilities" Study: No Mandate, No Expertise and Legally Incorrect' (2010) 42 *International Law and Politics* 769; Charles Garraway, '"To Kill or Not to Kill?" Dilemmas on the Use of Force' (2010) 15 *JCSL* 499, 506–507; Rogers, 'Direct Participation in Hostilities' (n 35) 158;

The Guidance has been criticised for stating that such restraints are required by LOAC, regardless of the conflict characterisation.[91] The Guidance did nonetheless state that in practice, such considerations are likely to become more relevant where a party to the conflict exercises effective territorial control during an occupation or a NIAC.[92] Indeed, Article 5 of Geneva Convention IV, which covers situations of occupation, deals directly with arrest.[93] The principle of superfluous injury and unnecessary harm is another area of LOAC that indirectly concerns arrest because it has been interpreted to mean that if a soldier can be put out of action by capturing him or her then the soldier should not be wounded.[94]

Notably, the Guidance refers to the *Targeted Killing* case to support its position on restraints on the use of force.[95] Certain commentators have questioned this reliance on the judgment.[96] The *Targeted Killing* case, in its less drastic measures requirement, establishes an obligation to arrest. Chief Justice (Ret.) Barak explicitly states the way in which this requirement has been influenced by international human rights law: 'among the military means, one must choose the means whose harm to the human rights of the harmed person is smallest'.[97] Moreover, human rights sources are referenced in order to support this precondition.[98] Significantly, the judgment places limits on the arrest requirement: it cannot be applied if it exposes soldiers' lives to a great risk.[99] The judgment's caveat demonstrates the way its interpretation of the human rights obligation has been tempered by LOAC concerns.

Section IX of the Guidance has undoubtedly caused controversy over whether LOAC requires restraints on the use of force. The question of capture over kill – especially in the context of targeting operations against civilians directly participating in hostilities – is a pertinent one.[100] In this debate, the human rights law arrest requirement is often evoked.[101] Many human rights law sources (both soft and hard law) insist that the right to life cannot be deprived arbitrarily.[102] The meaning of 'arbitrary' has been interpreted broadly and the use of lethal force

---

91 Parks, 'No Mandate' (n 90) 788 (fn 64).

92 ICRC, *Interpretive Guidance* (n 11) 80–81.

93 GCIV art 5.

94 API art 35(2). See ICRC, Fourth Expert Meeting on the Notion of 'Direct Participation in Hostilities under IHL' (2006) Background Document, 47, www.icrc.org/eng/assets/files/other/2006-02-background-doc-icrc.pdf; Fifth Expert Meeting on the Notion of 'Direct Participation in Hostilities under IHL' (2008) 19, www.icrc.org/eng/resources/documents/article/other/direct-participation-article-020709.htm; Goodman 'The Power to Kill' (n 87) 839–852; Kleffner 'Section IX' (n 88) 44–45. Another provision of LOAC that accounts for the question of capture over kill is denial of quarter. See API art 41(b).

95 ICRC, *Interpretive Guidance* (n 11) 81.

96 Parks, 'No Mandate' (n 90) 793.

97 *Targeted Killing* (n 14) ¶ 40.

98 Ibid ¶ 40; See *McCann v UK* (App no 18984/91, ECtHR GC, 27 September 1995) ¶ 236; Aharon Barak, 'Proportional Effect: The Israeli Experience' (2007) 14 (on file with the author).

99 For discussion of this requirement see Kenneth Watkin, 'Maintaining Law and Order During Occupation: Breaking the Normative Chains' (2008) 41 *Israel LR* 175, 196–197.

100 See eg Parks, 'No Mandate' (n 90) 783–785: for rebuttal see Melzer, 'Keeping the Balance' (n 26) 894–913.

101 The author has addressed the debate more exhaustively elsewhere: Michelle Lesh, 'Interplay as Regards Conduct of Hostilities' in Jann Kleffner and Erika de Wet (eds), *Convergence and Conflicts of Human Rights (IHRL) and International Humanitarian Law (IHL) in Military Operations* (Pretoria University Law Press 2014).

102 See ICCPR art 6: 'every human being has the inherent right to life. This right shall be protected by law. No one shall be arbitrarily deprived of his life.' Similar provisions have been incorporated in UDHR art 3; ECHR art 2; African Charter on Human and Peoples' Rights (27 June 1981) 1520 UNTS 217, art 4; ACHR art 4(1). See also ICCPR art 9.

must be limited to circumstances strictly proportionate to the nature of the threat.[103] Arrest is the common law enforcement measure employed in human rights law.

The complexity of the LOAC and human rights law interface will not be comprehensively addressed here.[104] It is sufficient to note that it is no longer considered a cut-and-dry matter that LOAC governs wartime and that human rights governs peacetime. A more sophisticated understanding of the legal regimes has emerged. There is increasing support that non-derogable human rights, such as the right to life, continue to apply beyond peacetime,[105] including during IACs,[106] NIACs[107] and occupation.[108] This is based on the notion that LOAC and human rights law share 'a common core of fundamental standards which are applicable in all times'.[109]

5 Conclusions

The legal meaning of loss of civilian protection during armed conflict is best understood in the context of DPH. Interpretations of DPH has been developed in relation to individuals and groups in an attempt to cover the complex range of situations in which non-state actors and OAGs are parties to, or involved in, armed conflicts. Interpretation of the legal rules and best practice will undoubtedly shape our understanding of how loss of civilian protection is understood in the twenty-first century. The contribution of the Guidance has influenced the development of these legal rules and it is an appropriate starting point from which states, international organisations and other important actors in the international community can further clarify the current state of the law.

There is a paradox that lies at the heart of the debate surrounding the meaning of DPH. Both sides of the debate (those who take the narrow approach and those who take the broad approach) feel compelled to adopt the positions they do because of a deeply felt obligation to protect the civilian population during times of armed conflict and to minimise human suffering and death. How can commitment to this uncontroversial tenet of LOAC lead to such radically different approaches? Part of the answer, lies in differing perceptions of states and their armed forces. On the one hand Melzer is concerned that in the absence of clear restrictions on the scope of DPH:

> armed forces operating in a hostile environment might be inclined to consider any civilian showing the slightest enmity as directly participating in hostilities, which would amount to a de facto presumption of loss of protection irreconcilable with the fundamental principle of distinction.[110]

---

103 *Guerrero v Columbia* (Comm no R.11/45, HRC, 5 February 1979) UN Doc A/37/40 (1982) (30 April 1982) ¶ 13.2; *McCann* (n 98) ¶ 236; Basic Principles on the Use of Force and Firearms by Law Enforcement Officials art 1, www2.ohchr.org/english/law/firearms.htm; Principles on the Effective Prevention and Investigation of Extra-Legal, Arbitrary and Summary Executions, UN Doc E/RES/1989/65 (24 May 1989) art 1. For a detailed discussion of what constitutes 'arbitrary' deprivation under international human rights law, see Phillip Alston, Report of the Special Rapporteur on Extrajudicial, Summary or Arbitrary Executions, UN Doc A/61/311 (5 September 2006) ¶¶ 33–45.
104 See Noam Lubell and Nancie Prud'homme, 'Impact of human rights law' ch 6 in this volume.
105 *Legal Consequences of the Construction of a Wall in the Occupied Palestinian Territory (Advisory Opinion)* [2004] ICJ Rep 136 ¶ 106.
106 *Nuclear Weapons* (n 1) ¶ 240.
107 *Abella* (n 49) ¶¶ 151–171.
108 *Bankovic v Belgium and others* (App no 52207/99, ECtHR GC, 12 December 2001).
109 *Prosecutor v Delalić* (Case no IT-96-21-A, ICTY Appeals Chamber, 20 February 2001) ¶ 149.
110 Melzer, *Targeted Killing* (n 11) 333.

On the other hand, Schmitt warns that: '[as] only states make international law, through either treaty or practice (customary law), IHL necessarily takes account of state's military requirements on the battlefield. Indeed, norms that unduly hamper military operations have little hope of emerging'.[111]

The different approaches are also due, in part, to the fact that there is no morally neutral account of what counts as state interests or what counts as 'unduly hampering'. Surely what Schmitt and Melzer believe constitute 'unduly' are very different. It is true that states make law but the hope is that in time, they will make law in the interests of a community of nations, constituted as a community, because each nation is for the most part impartially answerable to international law, rather than only pressing their own interests narrowly conceived. It is important to remember that the interests of states are not separable from the interests of the citizens of those states. The citizens of a state might believe that it is inherent in their very conception of their national interests, that their state be answerable to international law for reasons that are partly moral. This is not a constraint on an otherwise morally neutral conception of the pursuit of 'state interest': it is part of their very conception of 'state interest'.

In conclusion, it seems fitting to turn to Lauterpacht and to reflect on his famous depiction of the tenuous nature of LOAC: 'if international law is, in some ways, at the vanishing point of law, the law of war is, perhaps even more conspicuously, at the vanishing point of international law'.[112] Lauterpacht's dictum has been extended and appropriated elsewhere.[113] Nonetheless, it is hard to resist applying it to this analysis. If the laws of war are, in some ways, at the vanishing point of law, the legality of targeting is, perhaps even more conspicuously, at the vanishing point of the laws of war. This is illuminated most clearly in the discussion of the forfeiture of civilian protection and what it means to be a civilian directly participating in hostilities.

---

111 Schmitt, 'The Interpretive Guidance' (n 21) 11.
112 Hersch Lauterpacht, 'The Problem of the Revision of the Law of War' (1952) 29 *BYBIL* 382.
113 See eg Rogers, *Law on the Battlefield* (n 59) 2.

Part III
Means and methods of warfare

According to a foundational principle of LOAC, codified in Article 35(1) of Additional Protocol I, '[i]n any armed conflict, the right of the Parties to the conflict to choose methods or means of warfare is not unlimited'. In this context, means of warfare refer to weapons and projectiles, whereas methods of warfare mean tactics – the ways in which weapons are used.

LOAC limits the choice of means and methods of warfare in a number of ways. On the one hand, there are a handful of general rules, in particular the prohibitions to use means and methods that are inherently indiscriminate, or of a nature to cause superfluous injury or unnecessary suffering (codified in Articles 51(4)(b) and 35(2) of Additional Protocol I, respectively).

These general rules are complemented by weapon-specific restrictions relating to certain conventional weapons (Chapter 11), as well as to chemical and biological weapons (Chapter 12). International law does not expressly prohibit nuclear weapons, but there are treaties relating to nuclear non-proliferation and the efforts that are being, or should be, made to achieve nuclear disarmament (Chapter 13).

The regulation of specific methods of warfare tends to be more domain-specific. Thus, restrictions placed on particular methods of land warfare constitute a fairly discrete subset of LOAC rules (Chapter 14). In the naval and air warfare contexts, however, the regulation of methods is closely intertwined with the regulation of means, as well as with questions of the law of the sea and of airspace (Chapters 15 and 16).

11
Conventional weapons

Mirko Sossai

1 An historical overview of the prohibitions and restrictions on the use of conventional weapons

Conventional weapons are not formally recognised as a distinct category under the law of armed conflict. Within the framework of UN initiatives on conventional disarmament, their definition is negatively expressed: it is understood to mean all weapons other than weapons of mass destruction.[1] The latter 'include atomic explosive weapons, radio-active material weapons, lethal chemical and biological weapons'.[2]

Under international humanitarian law, the use of certain conventional weapons could be either limited or prohibited. In circumstances of prohibition, the ban could be either absolute or relative: whereas some weapons could be used by way of reprisal, in recent conventions states undertake 'never in any circumstances' to use them.

The more recent multilateral treaties are characterised by a close relationship between disarmament law and the law of armed conflict. They are aimed at eliminating an entire category of weapons by prohibiting not only the use but also the development, production, acquisition, stockpiling, retention or use of them, and by requiring their destruction. Along with the model of the 1993 Convention on Chemical Weapons,[3] both the 1997 Anti-Personnel Landmines Convention[4] (Ottawa Convention) and the 2008 Convention on Cluster Munitions[5] (CCM) belong to this category. Though these disarmament treaties do take into account humanitarian concerns, it should be borne in mind that disarmament law and international humanitarian law on weaponry seek to achieve different objectives: both branches of law are aimed at reducing the destructive potential of war, but while the former serves the purpose of lessening the

1 Study on Conventional Disarmament, UN Doc A/39/348 (1985) 6.
2 UN Department of Political and Security Council Affairs, *The United Nations and Disarmament 1945–1970* (UN 1970) 28.
3 Convention on the Prohibition of the Development, Production, Stockpiling and Use of Chemical Weapons and on their Destruction (13 January 1993) 1974 UNTS 45.
4 Convention on the Prohibition of the Use, Stockpiling, Production and Transfer of Anti-Personnel Mines and on their Destruction (18 September 1997) 2056 UNTS 211.
5 Convention on Cluster Munitions (30 May 2008) 2688 UNTS 39.

probability of the outbreak of war, the primary aim of the law of armed conflict is to preserve certain core humanitarian values during hostilities.[6]

Limitations on the use of weapons in war were introduced already within the framework of the early codifications of the law of armed conflict. The 1868 St Petersburg Declaration out-lawed projectiles of a weight below 400 grammes, which are either explosive or charged with fulminating or inflammable substances.[7] The weight limit was arbitrarily set with the purpose of distinguishing between explosive artillery and rifle munitions,[8] and nowadays that element has been regarded as obsolete.[9] However, the importance of that legal instrument is related to the rationale behind the specific ban: the Preamble significantly refers to 'arms which uselessly aggravate the sufferings of disabled men, or render their death inevitable'. The principles embod-ied in the Declaration were turned into an autonomous rule by Article 23(e) of both the 1899 and 1907 Hague Regulations, which state in the authentic French version: 'il est notamment interdit ... d'employer des armes, des projectiles ou des matières propres à causer des maux superflus'. While the 1899 English translation referred to weapons 'of a nature to cause superflu-ous injury', the 1907 text was changed in weapons 'calculated to cause unnecessary sufferings'. The linguistic issue was subsequently eliminated by Article 35 Additional Protocol I, which reaffirms that basic principle by referring to both expressions.[10] At the Hague Peace Conferences of 1899 and 1907, states also introduced specific prohibitions on the use of poison and poisoned weapons, as well as of bullets that expand or flatten easily in the human body (dum-dum bullets).[11]

It took another three-quarters of a century to adopt a new legal instrument regulating certain conventional weapons. At the beginning of the 1970s, the employment of new means of combat during the Vietnam War, such as fragmentation weapons, napalm and small-calibre high-velocity bullets, prompted a renewed interest on the matter. Modern efforts to impose addi-tional restrictions and prohibitions began with various expert meetings convened by the ICRC before and during the 1974–1977 Diplomatic Conference on the Reaffirmation and Develop-ment of International Humanitarian Law.[12] Notwithstanding lengthy discussions on the topic, also in the context of an ad hoc committee, no agreement regarding the use of specified weapons was reached at the Diplomatic Conference. Rather, Additional Protocol I reaffirms and develops a set of general principles governing the employment of methods and means of warfare. Not only does it restate the cornerstone principle of 'no unlimited right' and the ban on weapons 'of

6 See Christopher Greenwood, 'The Law of Weaponry at the Start of the New Millennium' in Michael N Schmitt and Leslie C Green (eds), *The Law of Armed Conflict: Into the New Millennium* (US Naval War College 1998) 185.

7 Declaration Renouncing the Use, in Time of War, of Explosive Projectiles under 400 Grammes Weight ('St Petersburg Declaration') (11 December 1868) reprinted in (1907) 1 *AJIL Supp* 95.

8 Frits Kalshoven, 'Arms, Armaments and International Law' (1985-II) 191 *RCADI* 182.

9 Subsequent practice has modified the prohibition under the 1868 St Petersburg Declaration: since the First World War, exploding anti-aircraft bullets have been constantly used and art 18 of the 1923 Hague Rules of Air Warfare had already provided that the 'use of tracer, incendiary or explosive pro-jectiles by or against aircraft is not prohibited'. Customary international law nowadays prohibits only the anti-personnel use of such projectiles in both international and internal armed conflicts. Cf CIHL r 78.

10 See *AP Commentary* ¶ 1426.

11 HR art 23(a); Declaration (IV, 3) concerning Expanding Bullets (29 July 1899) 187 CTS 459. The 1907 Hague Convention (VIII) disciplines both the laying of automatic submarine contact mines and the use of torpedoes. See Rob McLaughlin and David Letts, 'Law of naval warfare' ch 15 in this volume.

12 Michael Bothe, Karl Josef Partsch and Waldemar A Solf, *New Rules for Victims of Armed Conflict: Com-mentary on the Two 1977 Protocols Additional to the Geneva Conventions of 1949* (Nijhoff 1982) 197.

a nature to cause superfluous injury or unnecessary suffering', but it also addresses new categories of prohibited weapons: those intended 'to cause widespread, long-term and severe damage to the natural environment' and those that are by nature indiscriminate. Nevertheless, at its final session the Diplomatic Conference adopted a resolution which recommended the convening of a conference exclusively devoted to restrictions on conventional weapons. That is precisely what happened two years later under the auspices of the UN: the two sessions of the conference held in 1979 and 1980 led to the adoption of the Convention on Certain Conventional Weapons (CCW).[13]

The brief historical overview shows that states have so far adopted two different approaches to the banning of weapons: they have either identified general criteria forbidding unspecified categories of weapons which cause consequences contrary to international humanitarian law (IHL) or agreed on explicit treaty prohibitions barring the use of certain weapons. While the former has the advantage of having both vast coverage and a continuing force of expansion, that keep the prohibitions up to date with technological developments,[14] it suffers from vagueness: general standards inevitably leave room for divergent interpretations. The latter is aimed at overcoming uncertainty through a precise definition of the forbidden weapons. But its main flaw is the risk of obsolescence, as states might be tempted to circumvent the ban by developing new weapons.

However the two regulatory approaches should be considered as mutually supportive rather than opposing each other. The existence of explicit prohibitions 'does not exhaust the meaning of the general principles'.[15] In this regard, states are obliged to assess the legality of new weapons they study, develop or acquire, in order to establish whether their employment would be prohibited under some or all circumstances. Article 36 Additional Protocol I requires contracting parties to adopt a domestic mechanism of evaluation, but inadequate national implementation, as well as the lack of both recognised standards of review and an independent compliance-monitoring authority, have so far limited the efficacy of such a provision in preventing the introduction of cruel and excessively injurious weapons.[16] In any case, a differentiation should be made between the employment of weapons that are by their very nature and design prohibited per se and the unlawful use of otherwise lawful weapons.[17]

---

13 Convention on Prohibitions or Restrictions on the Use of Certain Conventional Weapons which may be Deemed to be Excessively Injurious or to have Indiscriminate Effects (10 October 1980) 1342 UNTS 137. See J Ashley Roach, 'Certain Conventional Weapons Convention: Arms Control or Humanitarian Law?' (1984) 105 *Military LR* 3; William Hays Parks, 'Conventional Weapons and Weapon Reviews' (2007) 8 *YBIHL* 55, 74.

14 Antonio Cassese, 'Means of Warfare: The Traditional and the New Law' in Antonio Cassese (ed), *The New Humanitarian Law of Armed Conflict* (Editoriale Scientifica 1979) 161.

15 Roger S Clark, 'Methods of Warfare that Cause Unnecessary Suffering or are Inherently Indiscriminate: A Memorial Tribute to Howard Berman' (1997–1998) 28 *California Western ILJ* 379, 385.

16 Cf Isabelle Daoust, Robin Coupland and Rikke Ishoey, 'New Wars, New Weapons? The Obligation of States to assess the Legality of Means and Methods of Warfare' (2002) 84 *IRRC* 345.

17 See *AP Commentary* ¶ 1469: art 36:

> is intended to require States to analyze whether the employment of a weapon for its normal or expected use would be prohibited under some or all circumstances. A State is not required to foresee or analyze all possible misuses of a weapon, for almost any weapon can be misused in ways that would be prohibited.

See Yoram Dinstein, *The Conduct of Hostilities under the Law of International Armed Conflict* (2nd edn, CUP 2010) ¶ 214.

2 Role and potential of the Convention on Conventional Weapons

Although the 1980 CCW was negotiated under the auspices of the UN, it falls within the category of the treaties on the law of armed conflict, since it mainly refers to the use of certain weapons which may be deemed excessively injurious or to have indiscriminate effects. In any case it contains some arms control aspects. The first element to be emphasised is that the CCW is an 'umbrella treaty', as it only addresses its scope of application, accession and the withdrawal, and the amendment procedure. It does not include substantive provisions, which are left to its now five protocols. This represented a compromise solution within the UN Conference, aimed at promoting the widest possible participation by way of a flexible approach. Each protocol addresses a category of weapons and a certain margin of discretion is indeed left to the ratifying states, as they must become party to at least two of the protocols in existence at the relevant time.[18]

The CCW seeks to address the flaws of the above-mentioned regulatory approaches, on the one hand by establishing links between the specific bans and the general principles, and, on the other, by envisaging the possibility of negotiating new protocols, in order to take into account technological developments in the field of weapon systems. The CCW has been therefore described as a living process,[19] particularly thanks to its review conferences that are convened every five years.

Reference to general principles of IHL, including an explicit formulation of the Martens Clause, is made in the preamble of the CCW: they therefore represent the context in light of which the specific provisions of the Protocols need to be read, under the general rule of interpretation in the Vienna Convention of the Law of Treaties.[20] It is noteworthy that the preamble not only recalls the fundamental principles of *jus in bello*, but it also recognises a *jus ad bellum* dimension, that is, the efforts towards general and complete disarmament as a means to avoid recourse to the use of force in international relations, in accordance with Article 2(4) of the UN Charter.

Commentators regarded the CCW as a modest achievement, because of its scope of application limited to the law of international armed conflicts, the exclusion of certain weapons of concern, such as flechettes and small-calibre bullets, the lack of a monitoring mechanism and the possibility for 'unwilling states' to influence both the adoption and the content of new Protocols. It has been observed that military considerations have taken prevalence over humanitarian concerns.[21]

Various attempts have been made in recent years to overcome the inadequacies of the CCW and to expand its reach. In 2001, the second Review Conference extended the scope of application of its Protocols to cover also 'situations referred to in Article 3 common to the Geneva Conventions of 12 August 1949', in other words non-international armed conflicts. A compliance mechanism was established in 2006, based on voluntary declarations by states parties, that submit their annual national reports to the CCW Implementation Support Unit. Like any

---

18 William J Fenrick, 'New Developments in the Law concerning the Use of Conventional Weapons in Armed Conflict' (1981) 9 *Canadian YBIL* 229.

19 William H Boothby, *Weapons and the Law of Armed Conflict* (OUP 2009) 107.

20 Vienna Convention on the Law of Treaties (23 May 1969) 1155 UNTS 331, art 31(1): 'A treaty shall be interpreted in good faith in accordance with the ordinary meaning to be given to the terms of the treaty in their context and in the light of its object and purpose.'

21 Knut Dörmann, 'Conventional Disarmament: Nothing New on the Geneva Front' in Thomas Giegerich (ed), *A Wiser Century? Judicial Dispute Settlement, Disarmament and the Laws of War 100 Years after the Second Hague Peace Conference* (Duncker & Humblot 2009) 143.

other system based on the exchange of information, the quality of the data risks being undermined by irregular participation and incomplete reporting.

Furthermore, other Protocols have been adopted: in addition to the original three Protocols on non-detectable fragments (I), mines, booby traps and other devices (II) and incendiary weapons (III), respectively, the first Review Conference approved Protocol IV prohibiting the use of blinding laser weapons and an amended Protocol II, while Protocol V on explosive remnants of war was adopted in 2003.

A fundamental aspect of Protocol I is the rationale behind its prohibition 'to use any weapons the primary effect of which is to injure by fragments which in the human body escape detection by X-rays', that is the protection of combatants. Non-detectable fragments are indeed a clear example of a means of warfare 'of a nature to cause superfluous injury or unnecessary sufferings'.[22] The same general principle underlies Protocol IV, which bans a particular type of weapon before it was used on the battlefield: laser weapons 'specifically designed, as their sole combat function or as one of their combat functions, to cause permanent blindness to unenhanced vision'. Therefore, normal use of lasers on the battlefield, for range-finding and target designation, fall outside this definition.[23] Laser weapons are not indiscriminate in that they can always be directed against a specific target but permanent blinding, being irreversible, is not militarily necessary and is recognised as superfluous injury or unnecessary sufferings.[24] Protocol IV also contains a disarmament element as it prohibits the transfer of blinding laser weapons to any state or non-state entity.

The main rationale behind the other three Protocols is increasing the protection of the civilian population. The regulation of incendiary weapons was regarded as the real *raison d'être* for the CCW, in consideration of the extensive use of napalm in Vietnam. The comprehensive ban proposed by various delegations did not find support at the UN Conference: Protocol III imposes restrictions on the use of incendiary weapons, in particular by stating that 'it is prohibited in all circumstances to make any military objective located within a concentration of civilians the object of attack'. What is significant is the definition. In recent times it has been debated whether Protocol III includes white phosphorus as a prohibited incendiary weapon. An answer in the affirmative depends on whether white phosphorus is a component of a munition which 'is primarily designed to set fire to objects or to cause burn injury to persons through the action of flame, heat, or combination thereof', or whether, on the contrary, the munition is designed to provide illumination of the battlefield, therefore having only incidental incendiary effects.[25] Much criticism was directed at the use of munitions containing white phosphorus particularly by the Israel Defence Forces (IDF) during the Operation Cast Lead in the Gaza Strip. According to various reports, the firing of white phosphorus shells caused injury to civilians and damage to civilian objects.[26] Though not a party to Protocol III, Israel claimed that its policy did not violate

---

22 See A P V Rogers and Paul Malherbe, *Model Manual on the Law of Armed Conflict* (ICRC 1999) 45.

23 Cf Louise Doswald-Beck, 'New Protocol on Blinding Laser Weapons' (1996) 36(312) *IRRC* 272.

24 UK Ministry of Defence, *The Manual of the Law of Armed Conflict* (OUP 2004) 116.

25 Iain J MacLeod and A P V Rogers, 'The Use of White Phosphorus and the Law of War' (2007) 10 *YBIHL* 75. The issue of the misuse of white phosphorus munitions against civilians arose at the Fourth Review Conference of the CCW in November 2011: the final Document reflects the disagreement among the delegations regarding the adequacy of the protections under Protocol III. See CCW CCW/CONF.IV/4/Add.1 (14-25 November 2011). On the different positions taken by the contracting parties on the topic, cf Human Rights Watch and the Harvard Law School International Human Rights Clinic, 'Incendiary Weapons: Government Positions and Practices' (April 2012), www.hrw.org/sites/default/files/related_material/arms_incendiary_0412.pdf.

26 See Report of the United Nations Fact-Finding Mission on the Gaza Conflict, UN Doc A/HRC/12/48 (25 September 2009) ¶ 1919.

its provisions and the IDF eventually decided 'to significantly reduce its use of smoke shells containing white phosphorus during the conduct of hostilities in urban areas'.[27] Therefore, in July 2013, the Israeli Supreme Court, sitting as the High Court of Justice, decided that there was no need to adjudicate a petition on that matter: nevertheless, the Court recommended to conduct a thorough examination of the issue.[28] It is to be noted that Protocol III is not intended to protect combatants: however, state practice is consistent with the view that incendiary weapons may not be used against them if such use would cause unnecessary suffering.[29]

Protocol II with its amendments and Protocol V are aimed at addressing the problem of the humanitarian impact of two types of weapons, which have been perceived by public opinion as particularly cruel because of their horrific consequences on the civilian population during and after hostilities: mines and cluster munitions.

The purpose of Protocol II was to prohibit the employment of mines, booby traps and other devices in certain circumstances, particularly all forms of indiscriminate use. Article 4 is aimed at restricting their use 'in any city, town, village or other area containing a similar concentration of civilians' in which there is no actual or imminent combat between ground forces. The Protocol includes both limitations on the use of remotely delivered mines and a ban on certain types of booby traps, such as those in the form of an apparently harmless portable object, by reference to 'the rules of international law applicable in armed conflict relating to treachery and perfidy'. One of the merits of Protocol II is its broad scope of application which covers a wide category of weapons. However, it does not adequately address the question of the use of anti-personnel landmines. Though they were not a major issue at the 1980 Conference, the public support for a complete ban increased after the end of the Cold War thanks to the commitment of NGOs, through the International Campaign to Ban Landmines. But the amended Protocol of 1996 contains a general prohibition only against anti-personnel mines which are not detectable. It is nonetheless a highly complicated instrument which introduces a series of clearer restrictions.[30] It also deals with the post-conflict legacy of landmines, by specifying that information relating to all minefields and mined areas must be recorded. The same purpose of minimising the risks to the civilian population characterises the 2003 Protocol V on explosive remnants of war (ERW), defined as unexploded or abandoned explosive ordnance: the recording requirements are aimed at facilitating the clearance, removal or destruction of ERW by the party in control of the territory. But the obligations under Protocol V, which entered into force in November 2006, are not retroactive.[31] As for the existing ERW, Article 7 only contains a weak obligation for states parties 'in a position to do so' to provide assistance 'as far as necessary and feasible'.

Though Amended Protocol II includes restrictions on anti-vehicles mines, since 2001 there has been discussion among states parties on how to reduce the humanitarian impact of mines

---

27 See 'IDF Clarifies Policy regarding White Phosphorus', www.idf.il/1283-18901-en/Dover.aspx.

28 HCJ 4146/11 *Yoav Hess et al v Chief of Staff* (Supreme Court of Israel, 9 July 2013). See Ido Rosenzweig, Amichai Cohen and Yuval Shany, 'High Court of Justice Rejects Petition against IDF Use of White Phosphorus' (August 2013) 56 *Terrorism and Democracy*, http://en.idi.org.il/analysis/terrorism-and-democracy/issue-no-56/high-court-of-justice-rejects-petition-against-idf-use-of-white-phosphorus.

29 CIHL commentary to r 85.

30 See Alan Bryden, *International Law, Politics, and Inhumane Weapons: The Effectiveness of Global Landmine Regimes* (Routledge 2013).

31 Louis Maresca, 'A New Protocol on Explosive Remnants of War: The History and Negotiation of Protocol V to the 1980 Convention on Certain Conventional Weapons' (2004) 86 *IRRC* 815, 830.

other than anti-personnel mines. The Fourth Review Conference tried to revive the work on that topic by convening an open-ended meeting of experts in 2012.[32]

Another element of interest is related to the permissibility of the use in reprisal of the conventional weapons covered by the CCW. First of all, there is no doubt that the use of incendiary weapons against the civilian population *by way of reprisal* is prohibited, even though there is no explicit prohibition in Protocol III comparable to the one contained in Protocol II with regard to mines, booby traps and other devices.[33] It remains instead debatable whether Protocol IV, since it does not contain the phrase 'in all circumstances', permits the use of blinding laser weapons against the armed forces of the adverse party by way of reprisal.[34]

3 The recourse to alternative fora: the Anti-Personnel Landmines Convention and the Convention on Cluster Munitions

Article 8 of the CCW has represented at the same time the legal basis and the justification for the requirement of consensus in the adoption of additional protocols at review conferences.[35] Indeed, reaching consensus during negotiations has been regarded as enhancing the subsequent ratification of an international agreement by the widest possible number of parties: it goes without saying that universal acceptance is essential in the context of bans on the use of weapons. But decision-making by consensus has often meant the production of texts which represented the minimum common denominator among competing national interests.

The unsatisfactory results achieved within the framework of the CCW for the content of Amended Protocol II led a group of like-minded states, with the active support of the ICRC and civil society actors, to seek an alternative forum in order to negotiate, under different voting procedures, a complete ban on the use of landmines. The Ottawa Convention, adopted in September 1997, is the successful outcome of that initiative: the formulation of Article 1 makes clear the comprehensive character of the Convention, as states undertake 'never under any circumstances to use anti-personnel mines'. It follows that reprisals are forbidden under the Ottawa Convention. The definition of landmines, as those mines 'designed to be exploded by the presence, proximity or contact of a person and that will incapacitate, injure or kill one or more persons', does not contain the term 'primarily' before 'designed' and therefore differs from the one included in Amended Protocol II:[36] the total ban also covers all dual-purpose mines, as long as one of its functions is to be detonated by a person.[37] Article 5 specifies that the obligation to destroy involves 'the destruction of all anti-personnel mines in mined areas under its jurisdiction or control'. Although the Convention has been widely ratified, it remains far from universally adopted: the list of the current 160 states parties does not include Russia, China or the United

---

32 Final Document of the Fourth Review Conference CCW/CONF.IV/4/Add.1 (Geneva, 14–25 November 2011) 15 December 2011.

33 Frits Kalshoven and Liesbeth Zegveld, *Constraints on the Waging of War: An Introduction to International Humanitarian Law* (4th edn, CUP 2011) 187.

34 Boothby (n 19) 53.

35 In 1980 the UN Conference adopted the CCW and the first three protocols by consensus. Cf CCW art 8: 'Such a conference may agree, with the full participation of all States represented at the conference, upon additional protocols which shall be adopted in the same manner as this Convention.'

36 Dinstein, *The Conduct of Hostilities* (n 17) 74.

37 Stefan Oeter, 'Methods and Means of Combat' in Dieter Fleck (ed), *The Handbook of International Humanitarian Law* (2nd edn, OUP 2008) 119, 141.

States, all of which decided not to join the treaty, in particular for its lack of a geographical exception for the minefields in the demilitarised zone between North and South Korea.[38]

Within the framework of CCW, the requirement of consensus has more recently conditioned the discussion on a draft protocol on cluster munitions. Given the impasse in the negotiations at the Third Review Conference in 2006,[39] at the final day of that meeting Norway announced that it would convene an international conference in Oslo to start a process towards the ban of cluster munitions.[40] The 2008 CCM builds on the comprehensive model of the recent international agreements covering both disarmament and IHL aspects: the usual formula 'never under any circumstances' reflects the general prohibition of all use, stockpiling, production and transfer of cluster munitions. Its scope of application therefore covers non-international armed conflicts: what represents a novelty is the explicit reference in the preamble to 'armed groups distinct from the armed forces of a State', which 'shall not, under any circumstances, be permitted to engage in any activity prohibited to a State Party to this Convention'.[41] Like the 1997 Ottawa Convention, the CCM does not admit reservations.

The ban, though comprehensive, is not absolute: the definition of cluster munitions, one of the most challenging issues during the negotiations, is broadly framed – a conventional munition that is designed to disperse or release explosive submunitions each weighing less than 20 kilograms, and includes those explosive submunitions – but it provides for several exceptions, including munitions designed only to emit smoke or produce electrical effects, and munitions having specific characteristics which avoid indiscriminate area effects.

Not only does the CCM contain requirements for stockpile destruction, clearance and risk education, it clearly addresses assistance to victims. Whereas both the Ottawa Convention and Protocol V refer to 'assistance for the care and rehabilitation and social and economic reintegration' for those parties 'in a position to do so',[42] Article 5 of the CCM specifies a series of measures for the fulfilment of this new positive obligation[43] to 'adequately provide age- and gender-sensitive assistance, including medical care, rehabilitation and psychological support, as well as provide for their social and economic inclusion'.

However, a high price has been paid to attain the goal of universality, even during the negotiation process towards the adoption of the CCM. At the very last moment of the Dublin Conference, a compromise formula was reached as regards to the relations with states not party to the Convention, in order to limit the scope of the prohibition of assisting anyone to engage in forbidden activity.[44] Concerns were expressed by NATO countries about the effects of the Convention on their military relationships with the United States, which was considered unlikely to join the Convention. Article 21(3) allows states parties to 'engage in military cooperation and operations with states not party to this Convention that might engage in activities

---

38 Stuart Maslen, *Anti-Personnel Mines Under Humanitarian Law: A View from the Vanishing Point* (Intersentia/Transnational 2001) 85.

39 The negotiations over a protocol on cluster munitions continued in parallel within the context of the CCW: but the Review Conference in November 2011 finally failed to adopt the text.

40 See Karen Hulme, 'The 2008 Cluster Munitions Convention: Stepping Outside the CCW Framework (Again)' (2009) 58 *ICLQ* 219.

41 Bonnie Docherty, 'Breaking New Ground: The Convention on Cluster Munitions and the Evolution of International Humanitarian Law' (2009) 31 *HRQ* 934; Sandesh Sivakumaran, *The Law of Non-International Armed Conflict* (OUP 2012) 409.

42 Ottawa Convention art 6(3); Protocol V art 8(2).

43 Cf Eric David, 'La Convention de 2008 sur les Armes à Sous-Munitions' (2009) 113 *Revue Générale de Droit International Public* 785, 800.

44 CCM art 1(1)(c).

prohibited to a State Party'.[45] The provision simply appears to address an issue of legal interoperability in the context of a coalition force,[46] but it also introduces some elements of ambiguity that could undermine the comprehensive character of the CCM. To give just one example, it is unclear whether an aircraft equipped with cluster munitions may be based within the jurisdiction of a state party.[47]

4 Conventional weapons in non-international armed conflicts

The question of bans and restrictions on the use of weapons in non-international armed conflicts was addressed by the ICTY in the *Tadić* case as follows:

> Elementary considerations of humanity and common sense make it preposterous that the use by states of weapons prohibited in armed conflict between themselves be allowed when States try to put down rebellion by their own nationals on their own territory. What is inhumane, and consequently proscribed in international wars, cannot but be inhumane and inadmissible in civil strife.[48]

In recent years treaty law on weaponry has been extended to non-international armed conflict. The 'never under any circumstances' formula confirms the applicability of both the Ottawa Convention and the CCM to that scenario. By the amendment adopted in 2001, the CCW and its Protocols now cover 'situations referred to in Article 3 common to the Geneva Conventions of 12 August 1949' for those states having ratified it.[49]

It is noteworthy that the ICRC Customary International Humanitarian Law study considered the extension of the CCW's scope of application as an indication that the notion of the equality of application of IHL rules in international and non-international armed conflicts 'was gaining currency within the international community'.[50] Indeed, the ICRC study is based on the assumption that state practice in many respects does not distinguish between the two types of armed conflicts:[51] as for the means of warfare, 'states generally do not have a different set of military weapons for international and non-international armed conflicts'.[52] Therefore, customary international law becomes one of the driving forces towards the convergence of the two largely treaty-based legal regimes.

Ten Rules of the ICRC study deal with different categories of conventional weapons: respectively, poison, expanding bullets, exploding bullets, weapons causing injury by non-detectable

---

45 Torfinn Arntsen, 'Article 21' in Gro Nystuen (ed), *The Convention on Cluster Munitions: A Commentary* (OUP 2010) 541, 571 et seq; Tommaso Di Ruzza, 'The Convention on Cluster Munitions: Towards a Balance between Humanitarian and Military Considerations?' (2008) 47 *RDMDG* 405.
46 Cf *HPCR Manual on International Law Applicable to Air and Missile Warfare* (2009) r 164.
47 Natalino Ronzitti, 'Modern Means of Warfare: The Need to Rely upon International Humanitarian Law, Disarmament, and Non-proliferation Law to achieve a Decent Regulation of Weapons' in Antonio Cassese (ed), *Realizing Utopia: The Future of International Law* (OUP 2012) 553, 558.
48 *Prosecutor v Tadić (Decision on the Defence Motion for Interlocutory Appeal on Jurisdiction)* (Case no IT-94-1, ICTY Appeals Chamber, 2 October 1995) ¶ 119.
49 For those states that have not accepted the amendment, some commentators have argued that Protocol III and IV are in any case applicable to internal armed conflict.
50 Jean-Marie Henckaerts and Louise Doswald-Beck, *Customary International Humanitarian Law* (CUP 2005) vol I, xxxv.
51 Walter Kälin, 'The ICRC's Compilation of the Customary Rules of Humanitarian Law' in Giegerich (ed) (n 21) 417 at 424.
52 CIHL commentary to rr 70, 71, 72, 73.

fragments, booby traps, landmines, incendiary weapons and blinding laser weapons.[53] The recognition of the customary nature of restrictions and prohibitions contained in CCW Protocols I to IV and, above all, their extension to cover non-international armed conflicts have been strongly criticised because of the absence of meaningful state practice.[54] However, the point has been made that the use of those conventional weapons is forbidden because of the application of the general principles rather than because the specific ban has acquired customary status.[55] Another author suggests that more time and practice is needed for the emergence of a custom applicable to internal armed conflicts, even if he acknowledges that half the states in the world are party to the CCW protocols and practice appears to be increasingly consistent with their substantive provisions.[56] In 2004 the Eritrea–Ethiopia Claims Commission acknowledged that certain norms in Protocol II 'such as those concerning recording of mine fields and prohibition of indiscriminate use',[57] belong to customary law.

In ascertaining treaty-generated custom,[58] the main question is which international practice is relevant. The position taken by the ICRC study in relation to conventional weapons is strictly linked to its methodology: specifically, as for the impact of treaty law on the formation of new custom, the weight given to the practice of non-contracting states[59] and specially affected states.[60]

5 Is it permissible to use expanding bullets for extraterritorial law enforcement?

The ban on a specific weapon during wartime should not be necessarily construed in absolute terms, in the sense that it does not exclude that its use could be permissible in other circumstances. While the ICRC study affirms that state practice establishes that the prohibition of expanding bullets is a norm of customary international law applicable in both international and non-international armed conflicts, it also acknowledges that states consider such bullets necessary for certain law enforcement purposes:

> in particular where it is necessary to confront an armed person in an urban environment or crowd of people, expanding bullets may be used by police to ensure that the bullets used do not pass through the body of a suspect into another person and to increase the chance that once hit, the suspect is instantly prevented from firing back.[61]

In consideration of the analogous interface between the law of armed conflict and law enforcement, the use of bullets which expand or flatten easily in the human body has been

---

53 CIHL r 72, 77–86; cf *Manual on the Law of Non-International Armed Conflict* (IIHL 2006) 31, ¶ 2.2.2.

54 David Turns, 'Weapons in the ICRC Study on Customary International Humanitarian Law' (2006) 11 *JCSL* 201.

55 Steven Haines, 'Weapons, Means and Methods of Warfare' in Elizabeth Wilmshurst and Susan Breau (eds), *Perspectives on the ICRC Study on Customary International Humanitarian Law* (CUP 2007) 273

56 William Boothby, 'Weapons, Prohibited' in *MPEPIL*, ¶ 32.

57 *Eritrea v Ethiopia (Partial Award: Central Front – Eritrea's Claims 2, 4, 6, 7, 8 and 22)* (2004) 26 *RIAA* 115, 129.

58 *North Sea Continental Shelf (Germany/Denmark; Germany/Netherlands)* [1969] ICJ Rep 3, 43. See Maurice H Mendelson, 'The Formation of Customary International Law' (1998) 272 *RCADI* 155, 294; Yoram Dinstein, 'The Interaction between Customary International Law and Treaties' (2006) 322 *RCADI* 243, 303, 376.

59 See CIHL practice to r 79 on weapons primarily injuring by non-detectable fragments.

60 See CIHL practice to r 86 on blinding laser weapons.

61 CIHL commentary to r 77.

associated with the employment of riot control agents (RCA).[62] Under Article 1(5) of the CWC, state parties undertake 'not to use riot control agents as a method of warfare', whereas Article II(9)(d) permits the use of chemicals for 'law enforcement including domestic riot control purposes'.[63]

For both types of weapons the question is whether they are simply prohibited during an armed conflict or whether their use is allowed for law enforcement purposes in that scenario.[64] The starting point of this analysis is that in the conduct of hostilities, the use of both RCA and expanding bullets against combatants or civilians directly participating in hostilities[65] is forbidden. One should not necessarily stretch this parallel analysis too far: whereas expanding bullets severely incapacitate and kill with immediate effect, RCA are non-lethal and the ban on their use as a method of warfare is aimed at impeding their use in combination with lethal weapons, for instance as a method of cave combat, as well as avoiding an escalation to an exchange of lethal chemical agents.

The core aspect is that military forces do exercise law enforcement tasks in the context of an ongoing armed conflict, especially in situations of *occupatio bellica* and non-international armed conflicts. As for the former, the law of armed conflict defines the limits of the permitted law enforcement activities when a territory is effectively placed under foreign military authority: expanding bullets could be used by the occupying force in its capacity as the power responsible for public law and order, for controlling political demonstrations and other forms of civil unrest. Such bullets are useful in situations of law enforcement, because they do not pass through the body of the targeted person and, therefore, minimise the risk of injury for bystanders.[66] This purpose also specifies the type of munitions and means of delivery that could be employed: as noted in CIHL,

> the bullets used by police forces ... are fired from a pistol and accordingly deposit less energy than a rifle bullet; the conclusion is therefore reached that the type of expanding bullet that is used by the police is different to that prohibited to the military.[67]

---

62 Kenneth Watkin, 'Chemical Agents and Expanding Bullets: Limited Law Enforcement Exceptions or Unwarranted Handcuffs?' (2006) 36 *Israel YBHR* 43.

63 See Robert J Mathews, 'Chemical and biological weapons' ch 12 in this volume.

64 See Nils Melzer, 'Conceptual Distinction and Overlaps between Law Enforcement and the Conduct of Hostilities' in Terry D Gill and Dieter Fleck (eds), *The Handbook of the International Law Military Operations* (OUP 2010) 33:

> the generic concept of law enforcement comprises all territorial and extraterritorial measures taken by a State or other collective entity to maintain or restore public security, law and order or to otherwise exercise its authority or power over individuals, objects or territory.

65 See Michelle Lesh, 'Direct participation in hostilities' ch 10 in this volume; ICRC, *Interpretive Guidance on the Notion of Direct Participation in Hostilities under International Humanitarian Law* (ICRC 2009).

66 Nils Melzer, *Targeted Killing in International Law* (OUP 2008) 416: 'Although not perfectly balanced, this accurately reflects the fact that the tolerance for collateral damage is significantly greater in the conduct of hostilities than it is under the law enforcement paradigm.'

67 CIHL commentary to r 77. The rifles used at the time of the Hague Conference fired a bullet which delivers approximately 3,000J of energy, while the average ammunition for police handguns and machine pistols carries approximately 500J of energy. It follows the expanding handgun ammunition typically does not cause a wound as large as that caused by an expanding rifle bullet. Cf Robin Coupland and Dominique Loye, 'The 1899 Hague Declaration concerning Expanding Bullets, a Treaty Effective for more than 100 Years faces Complex Contemporary Issues' (2003) 85 *IRRC* 136.

Human rights law is also of relevance in the determination of the standards that a specific bullet should satisfy, as the employment of specific weapons should not result in an arbitrary deprivation of life or in an infliction of torture and other cruel, inhuman or degrading treatment.[68] It is to be stressed that: 'rules and regulations on the use of firearms by law enforcement officials should include guidelines that ... prohibit the use of those firearms and ammunition that cause unwarranted injury or present an unwarranted risk'.[69]

The same line of reasoning should be applied in situations of internal armed conflicts, where the distinction between law enforcement and other military operations is even more relevant. Indeed, recognising permitted uses of expanding bullets outside the conduct of hostilities does not challenge the existence of a customary rule prohibiting their use as a means of combat.[70]

The discussion has again arisen on the occasion of the adoption of an amendment to Article 8 of the Rome Statute, which extends the ICC's jurisdiction over the war crime of employing bullets which expand or flatten easily in the human body, to cover those acts committed during an armed conflict not of an international character.[71] In order to broaden the use of expanding bullets during civil wars, there were attempts at the Review Conference in Kampala to draft the Elements of Crimes differently from those adopted for international armed conflicts. In the end, the elements of crimes were not changed, but the resolution containing the amendments to Article 8 of the Rome Statute, adopted by the Review Conference introduces some ambiguity. After noting that the elements of crime 'specify that the conduct took place in the context of and was associated with an armed conflict, which consequently confirm the exclusion from the Court's jurisdiction of law enforcement situations', the preamble of the resolution affirms that 'the crime is committed *only* if the perpetrator employs the bullets to uselessly aggravate suffering or the wounding effect upon the target of such bullets, as reflected in customary international law'.[72] But the *mens rea* element does not require a specific intent, which would narrow the scope of this war crime, but merely that the perpetrator 'was aware that the nature of the bullets was such that their employment would uselessly aggravate suffering or the wounding effect'.

Consequently, states parties might be tempted not only to qualify as 'law-enforcement' military operations having a clear belligerent nexus,[73] but also to assume that the employment of expanding bullets is permitted in specific situations other than pure law enforcement, including for the conduct of hostilities.[74]

---

68 See *McCann et al v UK* (App no 18984/91, ECtHR Grand Chamber, 27 September 1995). Cf HRC, 'General Comment no. 6: The Right to Life (art. 6)' (30 April 1982):

> States parties should take measures not only to prevent and punish deprivation of life by criminal acts, but also to prevent arbitrary killing by their own security forces. The deprivation of life by the authorities of the State is a matter of the utmost gravity. Therefore, the law must strictly control and limit the circumstances in which a person may be deprived of his life by such authorities.

69 Basic Principles on the Use of Force and Firearms by Law Enforcement Officials (7 September 1990).

70 *Contra: The Manual on the Law of Non-International Armed Conflict with Commentary* (IIHL 2006) 35: 'it is doubtful whether this age-old prohibition can be regarded as applicable in non-international armed conflicts'.

71 Amendments to art 8 of the Rome Statute, RC/Res 5 (2010).

72 Ibid (emphasis added).

73 Robin Geiss, 'Poison, Gas and Expanding Bullets: The Extension of the List of Prohibited Weapons at the Review Conference of the International Criminal Court in Kampala' (2011) *YBIHL* 335, 346.

74 Alfons Vanheusden, William Hays Parks and William H Boothby, 'The Use of Expanding Bullets in Military Operations: Examining the Kampala Consensus' (2011) 50 *RDMDG* 535.

6 The misuse of conventional weapons as a criminal offence

The use of prohibited weapons not only constitutes an international wrongful act, but might also involve the criminal liability of the perpetrator:[75] both the Ottawa Convention and the CCM require states to consider the employment of the respective weapon as a criminal offence under their domestic law.[76]

As for the CCW and associated protocols, they merely contain a list of prohibitions and restrictions, with the notable exception of Amended Protocol II: the implementation of the *due diligence* obligation to prevent and suppress violations of its provisions by persons or on territory under its jurisdiction or control, comprises 'appropriate measures to ensure the imposition of penal sanctions against persons who, in relation to an armed conflict ... wilfully kill or cause serious injury to civilians and to bring such persons to justice'.[77]

In addition, the use of certain 'classical' conventional weapons constitutes an international crime: under Article 8 of the 1998 Rome Statute, employing poison or poisoned weapons, of employing asphyxiating, poisonous or other gases and all analogous liquids, materials or devices and of employing bullets which expand or flatten easily in the human body, are crimes within the jurisdiction of the ICC, as serious violations of the laws and customs applicable in international armed conflict and, after the Kampala Review Conference, also in armed conflicts not of an international character. The amendment adopted in 2010 undoubtedly reconciles Article 8 of the Statute with existing customary international law: at the Rome Diplomatic Conference the omission was more the result of a political compromise, as part of the final package deal which had brought the deletion of all references to weapons of mass destruction, rather than the expression of the belief that the use of poison, gas or expanding bullets would be lawful in internal armed conflicts.[78]

However, the original proposal for amendments submitted by Belgium[79] was much more extensive with regard to both international and non-international armed conflicts, as it added to the list of war crimes the use of anti-personnel landmines as well as 'weapons as defined by and in violation of' CCW Protocol I and IV on non-detectable fragments and blinding laser weapons respectively. But the proposal failed to receive broad consensus at the Assembly of States Parties in November 2009, and it was therefore dropped.[80]

7 Conclusion: is international humanitarian law on weaponry still adequate for present-day warfare?

The outcome of the Kampala Review Conference has again prompted the question whether the existing law on weaponry, and specifically the list of forbidden weapons, adequately addresses the realities of present-day armed conflicts.[81]

One might wonder indeed how the restrictions and prohibitions on certain bullets, which were drafted at the end of the nineteenth century, can respond to the challenges posed both by

---

75 Ronzitti (n 47) 558.
76 Ottawa Convention art 9; CCM art 9.
77 APII art 14.
78 Herman von Hebel and Darryl Robinson, 'Crimes Within the Jurisdiction of the Court' in Roy S Lee (ed), *The International Criminal Court: The Making of the Rome Statute* (Kluwer 1999) 79, 113.
79 Belgium: Proposal of Amendments, UN Doc C.N.733.2009.TREATIES-8, (29 September 2009). See Roger S Clark, 'The "Weapons Provision" and its Annex: The Belgian Proposals' in Roberto Bellelli (ed), *International Criminal Justice* (Ashgate 2010) 489.
80 Resolution ICC-ASP/8/Res.6 (26 November 2009).
81 See Geiss (n 73) 349.

modern warfare scenarios and by the advances in military technology. In recent years, the efforts by Switzerland to negotiate a CCW Protocol on small-calibre weapon systems proved to be unsuccessful: suffice it here to observe that the crucial element of the Swiss proposal was that the legality of a bullet should be determined by its amount of energy deposit and not necessarily by its construction.[82] Much controversy still surrounds the use of depleted uranium projectiles, particularly for the effects on health. But such munitions are not yet regulated by specific treaty provisions, since they do not fall within any category of existing conventional weapons. They nonetheless remain subject to the general principles of IHL as do all categories of weapons – conventional weapons and weapons of mass destruction.[83] As for the impact of technological advances, criticism has been levelled against the future introduction of fully autonomous weapon systems,[84] after the widespread deployment of unmanned vehicles. Legal debate has blossomed over whether the use of robotics as a means of warfare would, in some or all circumstances, be prohibited by the existing rules of IHL.[85] Pursuant to the decision taken by the 2013 Meeting of High Contracting Parties to the CCW, a meeting of experts was convened to discuss the questions, from a technical, ethical, legal and military viewpoint, posed by emerging technologies in the area of lethal autonomous weapons systems (LAWS).[86] Interestingly, the debate on the legal aspects covered not only the issue of the compatibility of LAWS with key principles of IHL (for example, distinction, proportionality and precautions in attack) but also the possible existence of accountability gaps. In other words, the very notion of autonomy might raise questions of command and control, particularly as regards whether or to what extent decisions can be lawfully delegated to LAWS.[87]

Despite technological advances, the most commonly available weapons in situations of internal armed conflicts are light and rarely complex: for instance, handguns, assault rifles like the Kalashnikov, mortars and portable rocket launchers of the RPG-7 type. Over the last decade, there has been increasing awareness of the direct and indirect effects on the civilian population created by the poorly regulated arms trade and the illicit trafficking of arms: hundreds of thousands of people have been killed or injured by conventional weapons.[88] Great expectations have been raised by the elaboration and the adoption of the Arms Trade Treaty, to control international transfers of conventional arms.[89] Its scope of application includes the military

---

82 Cf Coupland and Loye (n 67) at 139.
83 Avril McDonald, Jann K Kleffner and Brigit Toebes (eds), *Depleted Uranium Weapons and International Law* (Asser 2008). On the application of general IHL principles to all categories of weapons see *Legality of the Threat or Use of Nuclear Weapons (Advisory Opinion)* [1996] ICJ Rep 226, ¶ 79.
84 Human Rights Watch, 'Losing Humanity: The Case against Killer Robots' (November 2012), www.hrw.org/sites/default/files/reports/arms1112ForUpload_0_0.pdf.
85 See Rain Liivoja, Kobi Leins and Tim McCormack, 'Emerging technologies of warfare' ch 35 in this volume; Michael N Schmitt and Jeffrey S Thurnher, '"Out of the Loop": Autonomous Weapon Systems and the Law of Armed Conflict' (2013) 4 *Harvard NSJ* 231.
86 Report of the 2014 informal Meeting of Experts on Lethal Autonomous Weapons Systems (LAWS), CCW/MSP/2014/3 (11 June 2014).
87 See Thilo Marauhn, 'An Analysis of the Potential Impact of Lethal Autonomous Weapons Systems on Responsibility and Accountability for Violations of International Law' Presentation on the occasion of the CCW expert meeting on lethal autonomous systems, Geneva, 13–16 May 2014, www.unog.ch.
88 William Hague, Laurent Fabius, Guido Westerwelle and Ewa Björling, 'Why this Arms Trade Treaty is Essential' *Guardian* (2 July 2012).
89 See the text in UN Doc A/CONF.217/2013/L.3 (27 March 2013). The Arms Trade Treaty was adopted by the UN General Assembly on 2 April 2013 with Resolution 67/234 B and opened for signature on 3 June 2013. The treaty entered into force on 24 December 2014.

equipment categories already covered by the UN Register on Conventional Arms:[90] battle tanks, armoured combat vehicles, large-calibre artillery systems, combat aircraft, attack helicopters, warships, missiles or missile systems, small arms and light weapons.

The cornerstone of any regime of arms transfers is the obligation to 'respect and ensure respect' for international humanitarian law under Common Article 1 of the four Geneva Conventions of 1949. As noted by the ICRC '[t]o ensure that violations of humanitarian law are not facilitated by unregulated access to arms and ammunition, arms transfer decisions should include a consideration of whether the recipient is likely to respect this law'.[91] Apart from the cases of prohibited transfers already contemplated in the relevant agreements, states that produce and export arms should therefore assess whether the transfer of conventional arms could be used to commit or facilitate a serious violation of IHL.[92]

---

90 The UN Register was created by the UN General Assembly Resolution 46/36L, in order to

> prevent excessive and destabilizing accumulation of arms, ... to promote stability and strengthen regional or international peace and security [and to] enhance confidence, promote stability, help states to exercise restraint, ease tensions and strengthen regional and international peace and security.

91 ICRC, 'Arms Transfer Decisions, Applying International Humanitarian Law Criteria' (May 2007) 3.
92 Cf Arms Trade Treaty art 7.

12

Chemical and biological weapons

*Robert J Mathews**

The use of poisons and poisoned weapons as a method of warfare has been practised since ancient times, ranging from poisoned arrows and spears, to poisoning wells and food supplies, to the dispersion of toxic gases and the release of disease-causing agents. The first recorded use of poisonous gases as a method of warfare dates back at least as far as 431–402 BCE when the Spartans burnt mixtures of sulphur and pitch when besieging Athenian cities.[1] A similar mixture of toxic chemicals (subsequently called 'Greek Fire') was used by the Byzantine navy in the seventh century.[2] Other early examples of chemical warfare include the dispersion smoke containing toxic compounds of arsenic.[3] Likewise, biological warfare since the Middle Ages has included the poisoning of food and wells, and the deliberate spread of diseases, including by catapulting diseased bodies and excrement over city walls, the use of plague against Swedish troops in 1710 and the use of smallpox against American Indians in 1763.[4]

Historically, efforts aimed at the prohibition of use in warfare of poisons and poisoned weapons, which are now generally referred to as chemical and biological weapons (CBW), have

* The research for this chapter was undertaken as part of the Program on the Regulation of Emerging Military Technologies (PREMT), which is supported by the Australian Research Council's *Discovery Projects* funding scheme (project number DP130100432).

1 See eg Harry Salem, Michael Fessel and Bryan Ballantyne, 'Inhalation Toxicology of Riot Control Agents' in Harry Salem and Sidney A Katz, *Inhalation Toxicology* (3rd edn, CRC 2014) 213.

2 'Greek fire' caused both the release of toxic vapours, and incendiary effects against the wooden-hulled battleships. See eg Alex Roland, 'Secrecy, Technology, and War: Greek Fire and the Defence of Byzantium, Technology and Culture' (1992) 33 *Technology and Culture* 655.

3 Adrienne Mayor, *Greek Fire, Poison Arrows and Scorpion Bombs: Biological and Chemical Warfare in the Ancient World* (Overlook 2003) 23–39.

4 Mark Wheelis, 'Biological Warfare before 1914' in Erhard Geissler and John Ellis van Courtland Moon, *Biological and Toxin Weapons: Research, Development and Use from the Middle Ages to 1945* (OUP 1999) 8.

been essentially through the law of armed conflict (LOAC).[5] These early LOAC agreements include the 1899 and 1907 Hague Conventions[6] and the 1925 Geneva Protocol.[7]

Commencing in the late 1960s, there have been serious efforts by the international community to strengthen the prohibitions of CBW enshrined in the 1899 and 1907 Hague Conventions and the 1925 Geneva Protocol, primarily through disarmament treaties, in particular the 1972 Biological Weapons Convention (BWC)[8] and the 1993 Chemical Weapons Convention (CWC).[9] These treaties have aimed at prohibiting not just the use of CBW, but also the prohibition of the development, production, acquisition, stockpiling and transfer of these weapons.

This chapter commences with an overview of the efforts to prohibit the use of CBW by means of the 1899 and 1907 Hague Conventions and 1925 Geneva Protocol. This is followed by a brief discussion of the negotiation of the BWC and CWC, including efforts to strengthen the BWC. The chapter then outlines the role of other international agreements in helping to achieve these humanitarian objectives in our changing world. The chapter concludes with reflections on some of the current and future challenges to the prohibition of CBW.

1 Efforts to prohibit chemical and biological weapons through LOAC provisions

The prohibition of use in warfare of poisons, including toxic chemicals and pathogens, seems almost as ancient as the weapons themselves. Prohibition of the use of poisons and poisoned weapons include the Manu laws of India (dating from prior to 500 BCE), as well as ancient Chinese, Greek and Roman law and law derived from the Koran.[10] By the latter part of the nineteenth century, it was generally accepted that the use of poisons and poisoned weapons in armed conflict was contrary to the law of nations. But the various early norms were not always fully respected.

The 'Lieber Code', an instruction signed by President Abraham Lincoln in 1863, represented a significant early attempt to codify the laws of war. Article 16 of the Lieber Code states that 'It does not admit to the use of poison in any way', and Article 70 states 'The use of poison in any

---

5 The 'law of armed conflict' (LOAC) refers to that part of international law which is concerned with the limits to acceptable war-time conduct (*jus in bello*). LOAC is sometimes referred to as 'international humanitarian law' (IHL). Where considered more appropriate, in particular, when quoting references, the term IHL will be used in this chapter.

6 See in particular Hague Convention (II) with Respect to the Laws and Customs of War on Land (29 July 1899) 189 CTS 429; Hague Declaration (IV, 2) on the Use of Projectiles the Object of Which is the Diffusion of Asphyxiating or Deleterious Gases (29 July 1899) 187 CTS 453; Hague Convention (IV) regarding the Laws and Customs of War on Land (18 October 1907) 205 CTS 277.

7 Protocol for the Prohibition of the Use of Asphyxiating, Poisonous or Other Gases, and of Bacteriological Methods of Warfare (17 June 1925) 94 LNTS 65.

8 Convention on the Prohibition of the Development, Production and Stockpiling of Bacteriological (Biological) Weapons and on their Destruction (10 April 1972) 1015 UNTS 163 ('BWC').

9 Convention on the Prohibition of the Development, Production, Stockpiling and Use of Chemical Weapons and on their Destruction (13 January 1993) 1974 UNTS 45 ('CWC').

10 See eg Julian Perry Robinson, 'The Negotiation of the Chemical Weapons Convention: A Historic Overview' in Michael Bothe, Natalino Ronzitti and Allan Rosas (eds), *The New Chemical Weapons Convention: Implementation and Prospects* (Kluwer 1998) 17.

manner, be it to poison wells, or food, or arms, is wholly excluded from modern warfare. He that uses it puts himself beyond the pale of the law and the usages of war.'[11]

In 1874 the representatives of 15 European states met in Brussels, to examine a draft agreement concerning the laws and customs of war, which had been prepared by the Russian Government based in part on the provisions of the Lieber Code. The subsequent Declaration of the Brussels Conference prohibited *inter alia*, 'the employment of poison or poisoned weapons'.[12] This Declaration was never ratified because not all governments were willing to accept it as a binding treaty. However, the provisions included in this Declaration formed the basis of the discussion on arms control and disarmament in the 1899 and 1907 Hague Conferences.[13]

The 1899 Hague Conference was the first international conference[14] that successfully addressed the regulation of the conduct of warfare. One of the objectives of the Conference was to reinforce the earlier prohibitions on the use in warfare of poisons and poisoned weapons[15] through a multilaterally negotiated agreement. At that time, these prohibitions were generally understood to include the large-scale release of toxic chemicals and biological agents (disease).[16] In addition to the prohibition of the 'use of poisons or poisoned weapons',[17] the Conference also prohibited the 'use of projectiles for the diffusion of asphyxiating or deleterious gases'.[18] Thus, the 1899 Hague Conference was significant in that, for the first time, the historical norms against the use of CBW were enshrined in multilaterally agreed treaties.

However, the limited effectiveness of these prohibitions developed through the Hague Conference soon became apparent with the extensive use of chemical warfare during the First

11 This Code, prepared during the American Civil War by Francis Lieber and endorsed by President Lincoln, dictated how soldiers should conduct themselves in wartime. Although the provisions were binding only on the armed forces of the United States, they were considered to correspond to a great extent to the other laws and customs of war existing at that time. See eg Dietrich Schindler and Jiří Toman, *The Laws of Armed Conflicts* (Martinus Nijhoff 1988) 3.

12 Project of an International Declaration Concerning the Laws and Customs of War (Brussels Declaration) (27 August 1874) 1 *AJIL Supp* 96, art XIII(a).

13 James Brown Scott (ed), *The Reports of The Hague Conferences of 1899 and 1907* (Clarendon 1917) 137.

14 The conference was 'international' in the sense that participation was not limited to European states, but included states from the Americas and Asia.

15 The *Oxford English Dictionary* defines a poison as

[a]ny substance which, when introduced into or absorbed by a living organism, destroys or injures health, irrespective of mechanical means or thermal changes. Popularly applied to a substance capable of destroying life by rapid action, and when taken in small quantity.

Thus, the term 'poison' includes synthetic chemicals, toxins and pathogenic materials. It is interesting to note that this meaning of 'a poison' has remained essentially unchanged at least as far back as the thirteenth century, although the alternative spelling 'poyson' was sometimes used as late as the eighteenth century. See *The Oxford English Dictionary* (2nd edn, OUP 1989) vol xii, 2.

16 See eg Anders Boserup, *The Problem of Chemical and Biological Warfare, Volume III: CBW and the Law of War* (SIPRI 1973) 93–96. In this document, Boserup refers to the fact that as early as March 1918, representatives of the military authorities of US, France, UK, Belgium, Italy and Portugal had informed the ICRC that they considered the use of toxic and asphyxiating gases as being included in the prohibition of poison. With respect to biological weapons, Boserup referred to negotiation records of the 1899 Hague Conventions (including reference to the Brussels Conference of 1874), which indicate that the term 'poison or poisoned weapons' was also intended to include the spreading of disease on enemy territory.

17 1899 Hague Regulations art 23(a).

18 Hague Declaration (IV, 2). This Declaration was based on a proposal by Russia. See Scott (n 13) 12, 131; Arthur Eyffinger, *The 1899 Hague Peace Conference: The Parliament of Man, the Federation of the World* (Kluwer 1999) 238.

World War, with more than 1.25 million casualties from chemical weapons (CW), including more than 100,000 fatalities.[19] It has been estimated that more than 120,000 tonnes of toxic chemicals were used during the First World War.[20] However, there was limited use of biological weapons (BW) during the First World War, which were targeted primarily at the horses required for transportation of military equipment as part of the various war efforts.[21]

The large-scale of use of CW during the First World War was widely condemned by the international community. For example, in an appeal to the belligerents on 6 February 1918, the International Committee of the Red Cross stated that:

> We wish to-day to take a stand against a barbaric innovation.... This innovation is the use of asphyxiating and poisonous gas, which will it seems increase to an extent so far undreamed of.... We protest with all the force at our command against such warfare which can only be called criminal.[22]

In 1920, there were preliminary discussions within the newly established League of Nations on the feasibility of developing a comprehensive verifiable chemical disarmament treaty. However, on the issue of the verification of 'non-production' of chemical weapons within the chemical industry, it was concluded that 'it would be useless to seek to restrict the use of gases in wartime by prohibiting or limiting their manufacture in peacetime'.[23] After failure of an alternative proposal by several major military powers that would have allowed states with advanced chemical industry to develop and stockpile CW but not transfer them to states with less developed chemical industry,[24] diplomats eventually settled for an agreement on the prohibition of the use of CBW, based on the principles of LOAC.

To this end, the International Conference on the Control of the International Trade in Arms, Munitions, and Implements of War, convened in Geneva in 1925 under the auspices of the Council of the League of Nations, negotiated the text of the Geneva Protocol. While the major motivation for the Protocol was the extensive use of CW in the First World War, there was also agreement to include the prohibition of use of BW. The early draft Protocol text proposed the prohibition of the use in war of 'asphyxiating, poisonous or other gases, all analogous liquids, materials or devices'.[25] At that time, many of the negotiators considered that this

19 See eg ICRC, 'ICRC in WWI: Overview of Activities' (11 January 2005), www.icrc.org/eng/resources/documents/misc/57jqgq.htm.

20 Report of the UN Secretary-General, Chemical and Bacteriological (Biological) Weapons and the effects of their possible use: Report of the Secretary-General (UN 1969) 1.

21 This included attempts to infect horses and cattle with glanders and anthrax. See eg Julian Perry Robinson, *The Problem of Chemical and Biological Warfare, Volume I: The Rise of CB Weapons* (SIPRI 1971) 216.

22 ICRC (n 19). The statement made by the ICRC on 6 February 1918 was included in an appeal against the use of poisonous gases, intended to convince the belligerents to renounce these weapons. In an effort to curb this alarming escalation in means of warfare, the ICRC invoked the 1899 and 1907 Hague Regulations, which prohibit the use of poisoned weapons, and the 1899 Hague Declaration (IV, 2) prohibiting the use of projectiles which diffuse asphyxiating gases.

23 Victor Lefebure, *The Riddle of the Rhine: Chemical Strategy in Peace and War* (The Chemical Foundation 1923) 249–252.

24 Jozef Goldblat, *The Problem of Chemical and Biological Warfare, Volume IV: CB Disarmament Negotiations, 1920–1970* (SIPRI 1974) 58–66. This proposal was not popular with many of the countries which did not have the industrial capability to produce their own CW.

25 This terminology had been developed in the Treaty of Peace between the Allied and Associated Powers and Germany (Treaty of Versailles) (28 June 1919) 225 CTS 188, art 171, intended to prohibit the use of these weapons by Germany. See Goldblat (n 24) 42.

terminology captured both CW and BW.[26] However, in the concluding phase of the negotiations, the delegation of Poland expressed its preference for a specific reference to BW, and proposed the inclusion of the words 'agree to extend this prohibition to the use of bacteriological methods of warfare'. This proposal was not opposed by other delegations.[27]

The 1925 Geneva Protocol represented a mixed achievement. The instrument did represent a collective response to the horrors of the use of CW in the First World War; however, it suffered from some major limitations. First, it represented a compromise – as already mentioned above, several states had been keen to achieve an agreement on the comprehensive prohibition of chemical and biological weapons, including the prohibition of developing and stockpiling CBW, while other states wanted to retain the option of maintaining a stockpile of CBW. The resultant prohibition only on *use* was the best that could be achieved at that time.[28] Second, many states parties entered reservations on reciprocal use of CW and BW so that the Protocol ended up constituting a de facto prohibition on first use in warfare rather than a comprehensive prohibition on any use in warfare[29]. Third, the Protocol only prohibited the use of CBW in warfare and not in those conflict situations where war had not formally been declared.[30]

There were also other limitations, perhaps less apparent to the drafters of the Protocol. One was that, based on the reference to 'bacteriological methods of warfare', one could argue that pathogens other than bacteria would not be covered by the Protocol (an obvious example being the smallpox virus, which was used for biological warfare in the eighteenth century and apparently stockpiled in large quantities in the twentieth century).[31] This apparent deficiency in the 1925 Geneva Protocol had been remedied by the 1960s, with the UN referring to the prohibition of 'bacteriological (biological) weapons', the term which was subsequently chosen for Article I of the BWC.[32] In addition, until the early 1980s, there were no internationally recognised procedures in place to investigate allegations of use of CBW.[33]

Unfortunately the 1925 Geneva Protocol, at least in part as a result of some of these limitations, did not prevent the use of CBW by its states parties – even in wars against other states parties. In particular, CW have been used at various times since the First World War despite the existence of the Protocol. Authenticated use of CW since 1925 include Spanish forces in Morocco (1925), Italian forces in Libya (1930), Soviet forces intervening against Muslim

26 Based on the *Oxford English Dictionary* definition of 'poisonous', it would be difficult to argue that the terminology 'all analogous poisonous liquids, materials or devices liquids' would not include contagious disease-causing agents, as well as toxic synthetic chemicals and toxins. See *The Oxford English Dictionary* (n 15) 2–3.

27 For example, during this negotiation, the French representative stated that he thought the original formula developed by the Drafting Committee was wide enough to cover bacteriological warfare, but that France had no objection to making an explicit reference to BW, as proposed by Poland. See Goldblat (n 24) 68.

28 In other words, states parties to the 1925 Geneva Protocol were still able to develop, produce and stockpile CBW.

29 In this respect, for those holding the view that the 'prohibition of poison and poison weapons' included the prohibition of the large-scale release of toxic chemicals and biological agents, the 1925 Geneva Protocol was, in fact, a weaker prohibition on the use of CBW than the prohibitions enshrined in the 1899 and 1907 Hague Conventions.

30 For a more detailed discussion about some of the limitations of the 1925 Geneva Protocol, see Timothy L H McCormack, 'International Law and the Use of Chemical Weapons in the Gulf War' (1990) 21 *California Western ILJ* 1, 5–10.

31 Although, as discussed above, the words 'all analogous poisonous liquids, materials or devices' would include all disease-causing agents, not just bacteria.

32 UN Secretary-General (n 20) 2.

33 A situation which was not adequately remedied until the 1980s (as discussed in s 3.1).

insurgents in Sinkiang (1934), Italian forces in Ethiopia (1935–1940), Japanese forces in China (which included use of BW as well as CW) (1937–1945), Egyptian forces intervening in the Yemeni civil war (1963–1967), Iraqi forces against Iran in the Gulf War (1983–1988) and Iraqi forces in Iraqi Kurdistan (1987–1988).[34] It is interesting to note that there was no CBW used in the European theatres during the Second World War.[35]

The widespread use of CW from the early twentieth century until the late 1980s demonstrated the limited effectiveness of the relevant provisions of the 1899 Hague Convention and the 1925 Geneva Protocol. Unfortunately, the early UN Resolutions supporting the 1925 Geneva Protocol had limited effect on strengthening the Protocol. For example, the General Assembly called for strict observance of the 1925 Geneva Protocol and invited all states to accede to this Protocol,[36] and requested the UN Secretary-General to prepare a report on CBW for consideration by the Eighteen Nation Disarmament Committee (ENDC).[37]

Subsequently the ICRC, in its Customary International Humanitarian Law study concluded that the prohibition on the use of CW and BW had become customary international humanitarian law, in both international and non-international armed conflicts.[38]

While the provisions of the 1925 Geneva Protocol and the CWC were not able to prevent the use of CW in Syria in 2013, the recognition that the earlier prohibitions on the use of CBW were now customary international law, even in non-international armed conflicts, together with the CWC and the other recent international agreements including the UN Secretary-General's investigation of alleged use (IAU) mechanism (discussed in Sections 2 and 3) did enable the UN to play a key role in confirming the use of CW in Syria. Following international pressure, Syria acceded to the CWC and its CW stockpile was promptly destroyed under strict verification, thus preventing what could have been considerably greater loss of life and suffering due to CW (discussed further in Section 2.2.2).

2 Supporting LOAC provisions through disarmament treaties

2.1 Efforts to negotiate a comprehensive 'CBW Treaty'

Following the conclusion of the negotiation of the Nuclear Non-Proliferation Treaty (NPT)[39] by the ENDC in 1968, the decision was taken for the ENDC and subsequent Geneva disarmament committees[40] to attempt to develop a treaty that would address the deficiencies in the

---

34 Information compiled by Harvard Sussex CBW Program. See www.sussex.ac.uk/Units/spru/hsp.

35 It has been argued that CBW were not used in the European theatre in the Second World War primarily because of concerns about 'retaliation in kind', rather than out of respect for the provisions of the 1925 Geneva Protocol. See eg Robinson (n 21) 294–335.

36 UNGA Res 2162 B (XXI) (5 December 1966).

37 UNGA Res 2452 A (XXIII) (20 December 1968). The Geneva-based ENDC was established in 1962 with five members from the Western Bloc (Canada, France, Italy, UK, US), five members from the Eastern Bloc (Bulgaria, Czechoslovakia, Poland, Romania, Soviet Union), and eight members from the Non-Aligned Movement (NAM) (Brazil, Burma, Ethiopia, India, Mexico, Nigeria, Sweden, United Arab Republic).

38 See Jean-Marie Henckaerts, 'Study on Customary International Humanitarian Law: A Contribution to the Understanding and Respect for the Rule of Law in Armed Conflict' (2005) 87(857) *IRRC* 175–212. See in particular CIHL rr 73, 74, 75 and 76.

39 Treaty on the Non-Proliferation of Nuclear Weapons (1 July 1968) 729 UNTS 161.

40 In 1969, there was an expansion in membership of the ENDC to 26 members, and its name was changed to the Conference of the Committee on Disarmament (CCD). The ENDC and CCD were forerunners to the Conference on Disarmament (CD), which currently has 65 members.

earlier LOAC provisions by comprehensively banning both CW and BW, including their development, production and stockpiling. One of the major motivations for the negotiation of such a treaty was the large-scale use of herbicides and irritants in the Vietnam conflict, which many states had regarded as chemical warfare.[41] The decision by the USA to destroy its BW stockpile and ratify the 1925 Geneva Protocol was also a major factor in the agreement to negotiate a comprehensive CBW Treaty. In addition, the release in 1969 of the report commissioned by the UN Secretary-General included a strong call for the conclusion of an agreement to eliminate CBW.[42]

With respect to a comprehensive prohibition of CW, there was a major difference of view among the participants in the Geneva disarmament committee. In particular, the Western countries argued that because CW were regarded as being of military significance, had been used on a large scale in armed conflict and were still being stockpiled in large quantities, compliance with a comprehensive prohibition on CW would need to be monitored through detailed declarations and intrusive international inspections, to ensure the security of all parties. In contrast, the Eastern European countries were opposed to intrusive verification measures. However, with respect to a comprehensive prohibition of BW, there appeared to be general assessments by both the Western countries and the Eastern European countries that a comprehensive prohibition of BW would not require intrusive verification of compliance. The rationale for this position was that 'BW were of little military utility' and had not been used in war on any significant scale. Therefore, it was argued that cheating under a BW ban would not yield important advantages to the cheating party.[43]

Based on the arguments presented above, the Western countries argued that a treaty to ban BW could be achieved relatively quickly without serious security risks if it was treated separately from a ban on CW (see Section 2.3.1).[44] Thus, the decision was taken to divide the earlier LOAC prohibitions of use of poisons/CBW into two separate treaties.

2.2 The Chemical Weapons Convention

2.2.1 Negotiation of the CWC

The negotiation of the CWC commenced in 1972 in Geneva. Between 1972 and 1984, various efforts to progress negotiations were made. These included 'exploratory discussions' within the Geneva disarmament committee, bilateral negotiations between the USA and USSR, and the

---

41 In 1969, UNGA Res 2603 A (XXIV) (16 December 1969) put forward a formal definition of chemical weapons, which included irritant agents and herbicides. It was adopted with 80 votes in favour, three against (Australia, Portugal and USA) and 36 abstentions (including most Western states).

42 UN Secretary-General (n 20). The report urged 'all States to accede to the Geneva Protocol of 1925', and 'all countries to reach agreement to halt the development, production and stockpiling of all chemical and bacteriological (biological) agents for purposes of war and to achieve their effective elimination from the arsenal of weapons'.

43 See eg Thomas Dashiell, 'A Review of US Biological Warfare Policies' in Brad Roberts (ed), *Biological Weapons: Weapons of the Future* (Center for Strategic and International Studies 1993) 4.

44 However, more recently, commentators have suggested that the major powers did assess that biological weapons were of significant military value, but considered that it would be too difficult to negotiate verification provisions that would be able to verify adequately the BWC. See eg Julian Perry Robinson, Thomas Stock and Ronald Sutherland, 'The Chemical Weapons Convention: The Success of Chemical Disarmament Negotiations' *SIPRI Yearbook 1993* (1993) 712–713.

establishment of an Ad hoc Working Group on Chemical Weapons. Some progress was made through these various initiatives, but it was slow and limited.

Several developments in the 1980s provided a catalyst for more substantive progress: confirmed large-scale use of CW by Iraq in 1984, and concerns that other countries might consider CW proliferation as a security option; admission by the USSR in 1987 that it possessed CW and its hosting of an international meeting of disarmament negotiators at one of its CW facilities (following on from the advent of glasnost and perestroika), and its acceptance of the concept of challenge inspection for verification of compliance with a CW convention; and the solid support of the international chemical industry associations for a future Convention, obtained in September 1989 at the Government Industry Conference Against Chemical Weapons (GICCW) in Canberra.[45]

Following an 'end-game' process initiated by Australia, the negotiation of the CWC was finally concluded in the Conference on Disarmament in Geneva in 1992. This agreement was recognised as being a revolution in arms control and disarmament. It was the first comprehensively verifiable multilateral treaty to completely ban an entire class of weapons, and firmly limit and monitor activities that may contribute to the production of those weapons through the establishment of a new international organisation, the Organisation for the Prohibition of Chemical Weapons (OPCW).[46]

2.2.2 Current status of the CWC

Since its entry into force, the CWC has been increasingly seen as one of the most (if not the most) successful arms control and disarmament treaties. The OPCW has been recognised as playing a critical role in the success of the CWC, including the verification of destruction of all declared CW stockpiles and related equipment, to the extent that the OPCW was awarded the Nobel Peace Prize in 2013. By the end of 2015, 63,445 tonnes (90 per cent) of the 70,493 tonnes declared stockpile of chemical agent had been destroyed.[47]

The verification of declared chemical industry facilities, designed to provide assurance that there will be no new CW produced, is also regarded as proceeding very effectively. By the end of 2014, there had been more than 2,000 routine inspections of declared industry sites. In September 2013, several OPCW inspectors were members of the inspection team requested by the UN Secretary-General to investigate the alleged use of CW, which confirmed the large-scale use of sarin (nerve agent) in Syria. In May 2014, the OPCW conducted the first of several investigations in Syria, which confirmed that chlorine (choking agent) had been used 'systematically and repeatedly' as a weapon in villages in Northern Syria.[48] The OPCW has provided chemical security guidelines to states parties to reduce the possibility that dual-purpose chemicals

---

45 The Government Industry Conference against Chemical Weapons (GICCW or the 'Canberra Conference'), hosted by Australia, brought together 375 delegates from 66 countries and four organisations, with approximately half of the delegates from the chemical industry.

46 For information on the CWC 'end-game' and a summary of the provisions of the CWC, see Martine Letts, R J Mathews, T L H McCormack and Chris Moraitis, 'The Conclusion of the Chemical Weapons Convention: An Australian Perspective' (1993) 14 *Arms Control* 311.

47 Eight states parties have declared CW stockpiles to the OPCW: Albania, India, Iraq, Libya, South Korea, Syria, Russia and the USA. By the end of 2014 Iraq, Libya, Russia and USA have yet to complete destruction of their CW agent stockpiles.

48 See 'OPCW Fact-Finding Mission: "Compelling Confirmation" that Chlorine Gas used as a Weapon in Syria' (10 September 2014), www.opcw.org/news/article/opcw-fact-finding-mission-compelling-confirmation-that-chlorine-gas-used-as-weapon-in-syria.

such as chlorine (used extensively in the production of many commercial chemicals and for water purification) cannot be obtained and used for hostile purposes.[49]

In the early 2000s, there was considerable progress with universality through various OPCW Action Plans and outreach activities.[50] By the end of 2015, there were 192 states parties to the CWC.[51] Based on information that has been provided to the OPCW by states parties, 186 of the states parties have established a national authority, 141 states parties have informed the OPCW of the legislative and administrative measures that they have taken to implement the CWC and 89 states parties have legislation covering all key areas.[52]

2.3 The Biological Weapons Convention

2.3.1 Negotiation of the BWC

As discussed above, in 1969, the Western countries argued that a treaty to ban BW could be achieved relatively quickly without serious security risks if it was treated separately from a ban on CW. Accordingly, a draft BWC treaty text was prepared by the UK in 1969, which proposed prohibiting the development, production, stockpiling and use of biological weapons. Two years of negotiation followed with some inevitable adjustments to the proposed text. The UN General Assembly commended the draft treaty on biological weapons on 16 December 1971. The BWC was opened for signature on 10 April 1972 and entered into force on 5 March 1975. The BWC was the first true multilateral disarmament treaty, being the first Convention to comprehensively ban an entire class of weapons.[53]

2.3.2 Identifying and addressing weaknesses in the BWC

Though the BWC marked an important landmark in arms control, allegations of clandestine production or use of BW subsequent to its entry into force resulted in assessments by many states parties that the BWC was seriously weak and lacked credibility because it contained no effective verification provisions.[54] In particular, an outbreak of anthrax at Sverdlovsk in the USSR in 1979 raised concerns about compliance with BWC obligations;[55] and the UN Special

---

49 See eg 'International Meeting on Chemical Safety and Security' (8 November 2012), www.opcw.org/international-meeting-on-chemical-safety-and-security/.

50 These activities were motivated, at least in part, by recognition that universality and full and effective implementation of the Convention by all states parties would raise the barriers to CW terrorism (discussed further in s 4.2).

51 There are only four UN member states not party to the CWC: Egypt, the Democratic Republic of Korea and South Sudan are non-signatories; and Israel is a signatory state yet to ratify the treaty.

52 For more detailed information on the current status of the CWC, see www.opcw.org.

53 For more information on the negotiations, and a summary of the agreed provisions, see Goldblat (n 24) 322–325.

54 For example, intelligence assessments provided in the early 1990s by the USA and Russian Federation concluded that about eight countries either had, or were seeking, an offensive BW capability. See US Congress, Office of Technology Assessment (OTA), 'Proliferation of Weapons of Mass Destruction: Assessing the Risks' OTA-ISC-559 (August 1993) 65; Yevgeny Primakov, 'New Challenge after the Cold War: The Proliferation of Weapons of Mass Destruction' Report by the Foreign Intelligence Service of the Russian Federation (1993).

55 In 1992, President Yeltsin admitted that there had been an offensive BW programme during the previous 20 years, and acknowledged that the Sverdlovsk anthrax outbreak was the result of military research to make biological weapons. See *SIPRI Yearbook 1993* (1993) 287–288.

Commission (UNSCOM) in the early 1990s revealed an offensive BW programme in Iraq.[56] To compound the problem, the advances in biotechnology since the mid-1970s which had increased the capability to manufacture a number of highly useful biological products (including agricultural and pharmaceutical products) on an industrial scale, could also be used to produce biological agents for weapons purposes.

Various initiatives to strengthen the BWC have subsequently been undertaken, including confidence-building measures (CBMs) introduced by the Second Review Conference in 1986,[57] the development of an Article V Multilateral Consultative Mechanism,[58] efforts to conclude a Protocol to strengthen the BWC and, since 2002, an intersessional process (ISP) focused on enhanced national implementation.

2.3.3 Efforts to negotiate a protocol to strengthen the BWC

By the early 1990s, most BWC states parties had accepted that the BWC was in need of additional strengthening through the development of compliance monitoring procedures. There was also a sense of optimism, in the euphoria following the end of the Cold War and following conclusion of the negotiation of the CWC in 1992, that the time was then right to commence negotiation of a legally binding instrument to strengthen the BWC.

In September 1994, a Special Conference of States Parties of the BWC agreed to establish an Ad hoc Group (AHG) with a mandate to 'consider appropriate measures, including possible verification measures, and draft proposals to strengthen the Convention to be included in a legally binding instrument'.[59]

The first session of the AHG took place in January 1995. Despite early progress based on the verification, assistance and international cooperation provisions contained in the CWC Text,[60] by early 2001, the AHG had been unable to produce a consensus text. A 'Compromise Text' developed by the Chair of the AHG was presented to the twenty-third session of the AHG in May 2001. Several BWC states parties expressed concerns about various aspects of the text, in

---

56 Iraq's BW programme embraced a comprehensive range of agents and munitions. Agents included anthrax, botulinum toxin, ricin and the BW delivery systems ranged from tactical weapons (eg artillery shells) through to strategic weapons (eg aerial bombs and missile warheads filled with anthrax). See Report of the Secretary-General on the Status of the Implementation of the Special Commission's Plan for the Ongoing Monitoring and Verification of Iraq's Compliance with Relevant Parts of Section of Security Council Resolution 687 (1991), UN Doc S/1995/864 (11 October 1995).

57 Requested information covers high containment facilities (including Bio-Safety Level 4 facilities), unusual outbreaks of disease, publications, conferences and exchanges of personnel in areas relevant to the BWC. Additional CBMs were introduced by the Third Review Conference in 1991, including declarations of vaccine production facilities, legislation (including export controls) and defensive and past offensive research and development of BW.

58 The Article V Consultation Process was used for the first (and, so far, only) time in 1997, in relation to an allegation of use of BW, at the request of Cuba. The particular allegation by Cuba was that a US government aircraft had deliberately released a crop-destroying insect pest (*Thrips Palmi*) over Cuba in an attempt to damage its agricultural sector. For more information, see 'News Chronology: 5 May 1997' (September 1997) 37 *Harvard Sussex CBW Bulletin* 15; 'News Chronology, 15 December 1997' (March 1998) 39 *Harvard Sussex CBW Bulletin* 31.

59 See Special Conference of the States Parties to the Convention on the Prohibition of the Development, Production and Stockpiling of Bacteriological (Biological) and Toxin Weapons and on their Destruction (Geneva, 19–30 September 1994): Final Report, Doc BWC/SPCONF/1 (1994) ¶ 36.

60 Annabelle Duncan and R J Mathews, 'Development of a Verification Protocol for the Biological Weapons Convention' in John B Poole and Richard Guthrie (eds), *Verification 1996: Arms Control, Peacekeeping and the Environment* (Westview/VERTIC 1996) 151–170.

particular the USA which publicly rejected the text.[61] As a result, the Fifth Review Conference convened in November/December 2001 finished on an unhappy note, and was suspended until November 2002.

2.3.4 The intersessional process to strengthen the BWC

The events of 9/11 and the posting of letters containing anthrax to US Senators in late 2001 led to a decision at the reconvened Fifth BWC Review Conference in November 2002 to conduct an intersessional programme of work to consider topics designed to strengthen the BWC through improved national implementation measures.[62] This programme comprised annual meetings of states parties preceded by meetings of experts focusing on improved national legislation and better national oversight over dangerous pathogens, enhancing international capabilities to deal with alleged cases of biological weapons use and strengthening and broadening national and international efforts for disease surveillance, and codes of conduct for scientists.[63]

The Sixth BWC Review Conference convened in November 2006 agreed to extend this ISP with a continuing focus on national implementation and, in addition, agreed to the establishment of a three-person Implementation Support Unit to promote universality and more effective implementation of the Convention.[64] To complement the ISP in Geneva, there have been several regional workshops conducted to assist states in different regions to encourage universality of the BWC and to fulfil their national obligations.[65]

2.3.5 Current status of BWC

As of December 2015, there were 173 states parties to the BWC. Based on discussions at various BWC meetings and informal discussions, it appears that approximately 60 states parties had enacted the necessary national implementation measures, and that approximately another 60 states parties had made substantial progress in the development of their national legislation.[66] Two of the major causes of the delays, especially in many of the smaller states parties, has been the lack of legal resources and delays in getting parliamentary approval of the legislative measures. The more limited progress with increasing the BWC membership and enactment of the

---

61 R J Mathews, 'Efforts to Strengthen the Biological Weapons Convention stalled as Review Conference Suspended' (June 2002) *Journal of the ANZ Association of Advancement of Science* 3.

62 Fifth Review Conference of the States Parties to the Convention on the Prohibition of the Development, Production and Stockpiling of Bacteriological (Biological) and Toxin Weapons and on their Destruction (Geneva, 19 November–7 December 2001 and 11–22 November 2002): Final Document, Doc BWC/CONF.V/17 (2002) 17.

63 For a useful summary of the BWC ISP, see Piers D Millet, 'The Biological Weapons Convention: Content, Review Process and Efforts to Strengthen' in Kathryn McLaughlin and Kathryn Nixdorff (eds), *The BWPP Biological Weapons Reader* (BWPP 2009) 19.

64 Sixth Review Conference of the States Parties to the Convention on the Prohibition of the Development, Production and Stockpiling of Bacteriological (Biological) and Toxin Weapons and on their Destruction (20 November–8 December 2006): Final Document, Doc BWC/CONF.VI/6 (2006) 19–21.

65 These have included workshops hosted by a number of states parties to the Convention, including Australia, Indonesia and the US. In addition, there have been several regional workshops hosted by a number of international organisations including the European Union, Interpol, the International Committee of the Red Cross (ICRC) and the World Health Organization (WHO).

66 As discussed in s 4.2, one of the motivations for obtaining greater universality and more effective national implementation has been the recognition that universality and full and effective implementation by all states parties would raise the barriers to bio-terrorism.

necessary national implementation measures, when compared to the CWC, is at least in part because of the 'institutional deficit' of the BWC.[67]

While many states parties argue that the BWC ISP is no substitute for a Protocol, it is generally accepted that the ISP is playing a valuable role in supporting the objectives of the Convention, including through enhanced national implementation measures and greater cooperation among relevant agencies and the non-government sectors.[68]

2.4 The relationship between the BWC and CWC and LOAC CBW prohibitions

It is clear from the third preambular paragraph of the BWC that the BWC was not intended to replace the 1925 Geneva Protocol but to strengthen it. Similarly, the fourth and sixth preambular paragraphs of the CWC make clear that the CWC was intended to reaffirm and complement the obligations assumed under the 1925 Geneva Protocol. Similarly, it is clear from the provisions of the 1925 Geneva Protocol that the Protocol was not intended to replace earlier treaties prohibiting this form of warfare (for example, the 1899 Hague Convention).[69]

3 Other agreements that support the LOAC-based prohibitions of use of CBW

3.1 UN Secretary-General's mechanism

Concerns about the possible use of CBW in the late 1970s led to the adoption in December 1980 of UN General Assembly Resolution 35/144C. Under this Resolution, the UN General Assembly requested that the UN Secretary-General investigate the alleged use of CW/toxins in South-East Asia and Afghanistan.[70] Investigations were conducted, but the teams were unable to reach a definitive conclusion as to whether CW had been used.

The subsequent UN General Assembly Resolution (37/98D), adopted in December 1982 broadened the mandate of the UN Secretary-General's mechanism to include alleged use of BW as well as CW. Resolution 37/98D required the UN Secretary-General to compile and maintain lists of qualified experts to conduct field investigations as well as lists of reference laboratories capable of analysing relevant samples (which could include biomedical samples and/or

---

67 The draft Protocol to strengthen the BWC, rejected in August 2001, included provisions for the establishment of a new organisation, the Organisation for the Prohibition of Biological Weapons (OPBW), to oversee the operation of the BWC and its proposed Protocol. The absence of such an international organisation has been referred to as the 'Institutional Deficit'. See Nicholas Sims, 'Strengthening Structures for the Biological and Toxin Weapons Convention: Options for Remedying the Institutional Deficit' (2006) 3 *Disarmament Forum* 17.

68 For more detailed information on the current status of the BWC see, www.unog.ch/bwc.

69 The provisions of the 1925 Geneva Protocol, include 'Whereas the prohibition of such use has been declared in Treaties to which the majority of Powers of the world are Parties' and

That the High Contracting Parties, so far as they not already Parties to Treaties prohibiting such use, accept this prohibition to the use of bacteriological methods of warfare and agree to be bound as between themselves according to the terms of this declaration.

70 The basis of this approach is the UN Secretary-General's authority, under UN Charter art 99, to bring matters that may constitute a threat to international peace and security to the attention of the Security Council and allows the Secretary-General to engage in fact-finding with respect to such issues.

environmental samples). An 80-page report on guidelines for the conduct of such investigations was also prepared.[71]

During 1983 and early 1984, there were several allegations by Iran to the UN Security Council that Iraq was using CW in the Iraq–Iran war. In response, under UN General Assembly Resolution 37/98D, the UN Secretary-General initiated an investigation of use of CW in the Iraq-Iran war. The initial UN Investigation, which took place in March 1984, confirmed that sulphur mustard blister agent and tabun nerve agent were being used, and that there were many CW casualties.[72] Subsequent UN investigations confirmed the continued use of CW by Iraq against Iran until 1987. However, other investigations, including the alleged use of CW in Mozambique in 1992, were not able to produce a definitive result.[73]

The UN Secretary-General's Mechanism was used in 2013 to investigate reports of large-scale use of CW in Syria.[74] The UN investigation mechanism was used rather than OPCW investigation because Syria was not a state party at the time that the attacks took place. After completing the investigation three weeks later, the UN reported that it had confirmed the use of the nerve agent sarin in the Ghouta attack, and had collected clear and convincing evidence that surface-to-surface rockets containing sarin had been used in the Ghouta area of Damascus. The UN report was careful not to blame either side for the CW attack.[75]

3.2 CBW export controls

As already discussed, by mid-1984 it had become clear that Iraq had used large quantities of sulphur mustard blister agent and smaller quantities of tabun nerve agent, and was increasing the use of CW against Iran. Furthermore, Iraq was seeking to acquire CW precursors for more toxic nerve agents (including sarin and VX), and was obtaining at least some of these CW precursor chemicals from 'Western' companies. At the same time, Iraq was developing a broadly based chemical industry sector using 'Western' engineering companies, which it was judged could eventually result in an indigenous CW production capability.

In response, 15 countries, namely Australia, Canada, Japan, New Zealand, USA and the (then ten) countries in the European Union[76] placed export licensing control measures on various CW precursor chemicals which Iraq was known to be seeking for CW purposes. However, by mid-November 1984, it was recognised that despite these export controls, Iraq was still obtaining the precursors and producing CW. It was realised that Iraq was probably

---

71 Gabriele Kraatz-Wadsack, 'Preparing for and Implementing the UN Secretary-General's Mechanism for the Investigation of the Alleged Use of Chemical and Biological Weapons' *ASA Newsletter* (March 2009) 1, www.asanltr/newsletter.

72 'Report of the Specialists Appointed by the Secretary-General to Investigate Allegations by the Islamic Republic of Iran Concerning the Use of Chemical Weapons: Note by the Secretary-General' UN Doc S/16433 (1984).

73 See Jonathon B Tucker and Raymond A Zilinskas, 'UN Field Investigations: The Historical Record' (April 2002) 32 *Arms Control Today* 12–13.

74 The largest-scale chemical weapons attack during the Syrian Civil War occurred on 21 August 2013 when several opposition-controlled or disputed areas of Ghouta, a suburb of Damascus, were struck by rockets containing the chemical warfare agent sarin. It has been estimated that more than 1,400 people were killed in the sarin attacks. The Syrian Government and opposition each blamed the other for the attack. For more information see, www.opcw.org.

75 Åke Sellstrom, Scott Cairns and Maurizio Barbeschi, 'United Nations Mission to Investigate Allegations of the Use of Chemical Weapons in the Syrian Arab Republic: Report of the Alleged Use of Chemical Weapons in the Ghouta Area of Damascus on 21 August 2013' (13 September 2013).

76 At that time, there were ten member countries of the European Union: Belgium, Denmark, France, Federal Republic of Germany, Greece, Ireland, Italy, Luxembourg, the Netherlands and the UK.

'shopping around' based on the variations in the different countries' control lists. In response, Australian officials suggested it would be useful to convene an informal meeting of the 15 countries in an effort to harmonise the various national export control lists.

The first meeting took place on 28 June 1985 at the Australian Embassy in Brussels and subsequently became known as the Australia Group (AG).[77] Between 1985 and 1987, the AG developed a list of CW-precursor chemicals for export control.[78] By the end of 1987, it had become clear that the AG export controls on CW precursor chemicals had slowed Iraqi CW precursor procurement, forced Iraq to seek alternative suppliers of preferred chemicals from either 'front companies' or non-AG supplier countries and had forced Iraq either to go back to earlier stages in CW production processes or choose less efficient production routes.[79]

From early 1988, there were increasing concerns about the proliferation and use of CBW, following the large-scale use of nerve agent against civilians at Halabja (in March 1988), and evidence that 'countries of concern' were developing an interest in offensive BW programmes. These concerns led to the UN Security Council Resolution 620,[80] and led the AG participants to increase the size of the CW precursor export control list, and the development of export control lists containing dual-use chemical and biological production equipment, as well as pathogens and toxins.[81]

Since its inception, the AG has remained an informal 'like-minded' group with the flexibility to adapt to changing international relations, science and technology, and security environment. Membership has increased from 15 to 41 countries, and the various control lists have been further developed and revised based on various changing circumstances.[82]

In the aftermath of the events of 9/11 and anthrax letters, the Proliferation Security Initiative (PSI) was launched, based on the recognition that diplomacy, treaty law, export control licensing measures and other non-proliferation arrangements may not always prevent a state or non-state actor from acquiring materials and equipment for weapons of mass destruction (WMD) and their delivery systems. The PSI has become a global effort that aims to stop trafficking of WMD and related materials to and from states and non-state actors of proliferation concern.[83]

---

77 The countries invited to the first meeting were those 15 countries which had already put in place export controls on CW precursor chemicals. The European Commission was also invited to send observers, which it did (two observers). There were 33 people at the first meeting.

78 For a more detailed discussion, see R J Mathews, 'Comparison of the Chemicals on the Australia Group Control List with those in the CWC Schedules' (1993) 21 *CBW Conventions Bulletin* 1.

79 Indeed by 1988, Iraq had formed an 'Anti-Australia Group Committee' in Baghdad, tasked with keeping track of current AG export control lists and trying to find alternative suppliers. (Information provided by a former UNSCOM official, based on interviews conducted in Iraq in 1991.)

80 UNSC Res 620 (26 August 1988), *inter alia*: 'Condemns resolutely the use of chemical weapons'; 'Encourages the Secretary-General to carry out promptly investigations', 'Calls upon all States to continue to apply, or establish or to strengthen strict controls on the export of chemical products serving for the production of chemical weapons' and 'Decides to consider immediately, taking into account the investigations of the Secretary-General, appropriate and effective measures'.

81 For a more detailed discussion, see R J Mathews, 'The Development of the Australia Group Export Control Lists of Biological Pathogens, Toxins and Dual-use Equipment' (2004) 66 *CBW Conventions Bulletin* 1.

82 R J Mathews, 'CBW Export Controls and the 'Web of Prevention': A Practitioners Perspective' in Brian Rappert and Caitríona McLeish (eds), *A Web of Prevention: The Life Sciences, Biological Weapons and the Governance of Research* (Earthscan 2007).

83 Susan Koch, 'Proliferation Security Initiative: Origins and Evolution' Centre for the Study of Weapons of Mass Proliferation Occasional Paper 9 (National Defense University Press 2012).

3.3 UN Security Council Resolution 1540

The importance of membership of, and adherence to, the BWC and CWC has taken on even greater significance since the events of 9/11 and the anthrax mail letters. It is recognised that small countries which have not been able to ratify treaties, have no implementing legislation in place to criminalise the activities prohibited by the BWC and CWC, and do not have effective security measures in place related to dual-use biological and chemical equipment and materials may become 'safe havens' for terrorist groups which may decide to use such countries as a location to develop CBW device for terrorist purposes.

On 28 April 2004, the UN Security Council unanimously adopted Resolution 1540 under Chapter VII of the UN Charter which affirms that the proliferation of nuclear, chemical and biological weapons and their means of delivery constitutes a threat to international peace and security. The Resolution obliges all UN Member States, *inter alia*, to refrain from supporting by any means non-state actors from developing, acquiring, manufacturing, possessing, transporting, transferring or using nuclear, chemical or biological weapons and their delivery systems.

Under Resolution 1540, in an effort to ensure that all UN Member States are implementing these domestic measures effectively, there were reporting requirements to a UN Security Council Committee (the '1540 Committee'), which was to convene for two years. The first country reports were required within six months of adoption of Resolution 1540. However, it soon became clear that many UN Member States would require substantially longer than the two years anticipated by the UN Security Council.

As a result of the limited number of country responses, the Security Council recognised that full implementation of Resolution 1540 by all states will be a long-term task that will require ongoing efforts at national, regional and international levels. As a consequence, the Security Council has extended the mandate of the 1540 Committee several times.[84]

At the time of writing, 176 UN Member States had provided one or more reports to the Resolution 1540 Committee, and 17 UN Member States are still to provide a report.[85]

3.4 The Rome Statute – use of CBW as a war crime

There have been attempts to raise barriers to the use of CBW through efforts to incorporate the employment of CBW as a war crime under the provisions of the Rome Statute and ICC.

The Rome Statute established four core international crimes: genocide, crimes against humanity, war crimes and the crime of aggression. In the negotiation of the war crimes provisions, there was no apparent disagreement among negotiators that the use of CBW should be included as a war crime. However, there was disagreement as to whether the use of nuclear weapons should be included in the war crime provisions. In the subsequent stand-off, a number of delegations would only accept reference to CBW as defined in the CWC and BWC if the use of nuclear weapons was also included as a war crime.[86]

---

84 UNSC Res 1673 (27 April 2006), Res 1810 (25 April 2008) and Res 1977 (20 April 2011). The latter resolution extends the mandate of the 1540 Committee until 2021.
85 For more information on the implementation of UNSC Res 1540 see, www.un.org/en/sc/1540.
86 Kara Allen, Scott Spence and Rocío Escaurianza Leal, 'Chemical and Biological Weapons Use in the Rome Statute: A Case for Change' VERTIC Brief Number 14 (February 2011), www.vertic.org/media/assets/Publications/VB%2014.pdf.

The resulting 'back-room deal' saw no reference to nuclear weapons, and CBW were described using the terminology of the earlier LOAC agreements.[87] Thus, under the provisions of Article 8(2)(b)(xvii) of the Rome Statute, war crimes include 'employing poison or poisoned weapons'; and under the provisions of Article 8(2)(b)(xviii), 'employing asphyxiating, poisonous or other gases, and all analogous liquids, materials or devices'.

It would be difficult to argue, based on the terminology used in Article 8(2)(b)(xviii), that the use of CW (including riot control agents as a method of warfare) would not be captured by the Rome Statute war crime provisions. However, despite the clear scientific meaning of the term 'poison', in particular its meaning when used in the historic CBW prohibitions (as discussed in Section 1), in recent years a number of legal advisers have taken a more narrow interpretation of the terminology 'poisons or poisoned weapons' that would exclude the large-scale use of CBW.[88] Likewise, a number of legal advisers have interpreted 'employing asphyxiating, poisonous or other gases, and all analogous liquids, materials or devices' as not including the use of BW. This is clearly an issue that needs to be clarified before the ICC is requested to consider dealing with alleged users of BW under the ICC.[89] A possible alternative to a formal amendment, which does not appear to have been considered yet, would be the development of an agreed 'understanding' by the states parties that for the purposes of the Rome Statute, the employment of 'poisons or poisoned weapons' in Article 8(2)(b)(xvii) and the 'poisonous' substances listed in Article 8(2)(b)(xviii) would include the large scale use of BW.[90]

4 Future challenges to the prohibition of use of CBW

4.1 Changing security environment and nature of warfare

The security environment has changed considerably in recent decades, not least as a result of the end of the Cold War and the events of 9/11. In particular, the borderlines between war, civil war, large-scale violations of human rights, revolutions and uprisings, insurgencies and terrorism as well as organised crime are becoming increasingly blurred.[91]

This has resulted in the changing nature of military operations, including greater involvement in law enforcement (including counter-terrorism) and peacekeeping roles. The CWC allows the use of certain toxic chemicals, including riot control agents (RCAs) as defined in

---

87 Philippe Kirsch QC and Daryl Robinson, 'Reaching Agreement at the Rome Conference' in Antonio Cassese, Paola Gaeta and John R W D Jones (eds), *The Rome Statute of the International Criminal Court: A Commentary* (OUP 2002) 79–80.

88 There are a range of views on this issue. See eg Wil D Verwey, *Riot Control Agents and Herbicides in War* (Sijthoff 1977) 205–225; Anne Van Wynen Thomas and A J Thomas Jr, *Legal Limits on the Use of Chemical and Biological Weapons* (Southern Methodist University Press 1970) 45–57; Jean Pascal Zanders, 'International Norms against Chemical and Biological Warfare: An Ambiguous Legacy' (2003) 8 *JCSL* 391.

89 Clarifying that all use of CBW would be covered by the Rome Statute was the objective of an unsuccessful proposed amendment to the Rome Statute by Belgium at the First Review Conference of the Rome Statute in 2009.

90 In this regard, it should be noted that where there has been a lack of clarity in technical terms within a treaty, eg the CWC, states parties have developed 'understandings' of the meanings of those terms rather than attempt to amend the Convention. See eg Lisa Woolomes Tabassi, *OPCW: The Legal Texts* (Asser 2009) 157–201.

91 See eg Note by the OPCW Director-General, 'Report of the Advisory Panel on Future Priorities of the Organisation for the Prohibition of Chemical Weapons' OPCW Report Number S/951/2011 (25 July 2011) 4–5.

CWC Article II(7), to be used for law enforcement purposes[92] but not as a method of warfare.[93] Concerns have been expressed that this provision has created a loophole which may result in use of CBW in armed conflict situations. A key issue is at what point does an operation of this type transition from being a 'law enforcement' operation to 'armed conflict'? And, in particular, in what ways will the changing nature of the operation require adapting the rules of engagement, including the possibility of the military peacekeeping force being able to use RCAs for defensive purposes to save lives, even after the operation is assessed as to have become a 'non-international armed conflict'.

4.2 CBW terrorism

While the likelihood of the large-scale use of CBW in major inter-state conflicts may have declined in recent decades, there has been no corresponding decline in civil wars, revolutions, insurgencies and terrorism events.

Indeed, there have been attempts by terrorist groups to acquire and use improvised CBW devices since the 1970s, including the Aum Shinrikyo's attempts to acquire and use anthrax and sarin in Tokyo in the early to mid-1990s. However, since 9/11 and the anthrax letter incidents of late 2001, the attempts of terrorist groups to acquire non-conventional weapons have become a focus of particular attention. In particular, reports that al-Qaeda has been seeking to acquire or develop improvised CBW have exacerbated these concerns.[94]

The potential roles of the BWC and CWC in raising barriers to CB terrorism have been recognised since the mid-1990s[95] and these arms control agreements are becoming an increasingly valuable part of the 'counter-terrorism toolbox'.[96] Since early 2002, in response to the post-9/11 security environment, there have been increasing efforts to strengthen the treaties (and, since 2004, UN Security Council Resolution 1540) through more effective national implementation measures, including domestic legislation, security of dual-use materials, equipment and technology, and outreach and codes of conduct for the relevant scientific communities. The international community has recognised that for the various arms control measures and UN Resolutions to be an effective part of the 'counter-terrorism toolbox', there also needs to be considerable cooperation between the arms control community[97] and other international agencies,[98] as well as government officials, scientific researchers and industry representatives who have not traditionally been involved with WMD arms control activities.

---

92 CWC art II(9)(d).

93 CWC art I(5).

94 See eg Evidence to US Senate Armed Services Committee Hearing, *Worldwide Threat: Converging Dangers in a Post 9/11 World*, 107th Congress, Washington DC, 19 March 2002.

95 See eg BWC Conference of the States Parties, Fourth Review Conference, *Final Declaration*, Doc BWC/CONF.IV/9 (25 November to 6 December 1996) 17; *Report of the First Special Session of the Conference of the States Parties to Review the Operation of the Chemical Weapons Convention (First Review Conference): 28 April – 9 May 2003*, OPCW Conference of the State Parties, OPCW Doc RC-1/5 (9 May 2003) 5.

96 Robert J Mathews, 'WMD Arms Control Agreements in the Post-September 11 Security Environment: Part of the Counter-Terrorism Toolbox' (2007) 8 *Melbourne JIL* 292, and references therein.

97 For example, the IAEA, the OPCW, the UN Institute for Disarmament Research, the ICRC and government officials with arms control responsibilities.

98 This includes Interpol, the EU, the WHO, the Food and Agriculture Organization, the World Organisation for Animal Health, the International Union of Pure and Applied Chemistry, the European Chemical Industry Council, the UN Institute for Training and Research and the World Customs Organization.

4.3 Rapid advances in the life sciences

In recent years, there have been rapid advances in the life sciences, including the 'convergence' of biology and chemistry, and nanotechnology.[99] It is recognised that these advances promise many benefits to humankind, including more efficient food production, improvements to medicines and to health care, the generation of renewable energy sources and the enhancement of pollution management. There are also many potential benefits of the convergence of chemistry and biology (and related aspects of nanotechnology) for the protection against CBW, including development of enhanced equipment for the detection of CBW agents, medical countermeasures, decontamination, and laboratory analysis and identification techniques, including bioforensics.

However, there are also potential negative implications for the CBW prohibition as a result of these advances; including the possibility that the advances could be mis-used for the production of toxic chemicals, including toxins and bio-regulators (sometimes called 'mid-spectrum agents),[100] in quantities that may be suitable for large-scale use for CW purposes, and large-scale novel production of pathogens for use as BW. This includes concerns that the advances in the life sciences may enable the construction of complex biologically active molecules that could interfere with life processes including development, inheritance, reproduction, sensation and cognition.[101]

With the increasing convergence of chemistry and biology, it is increasingly the same science base underpinning both treaties. One particularly concerning aspect of convergence is the development of classes of chemicals which act on the central nervous system (CNS) in a manner which is commonly (but inaccurately) referred to as 'incapacitating' (for example, fentanyl analogs and other opioids).[102] These chemicals are highly toxic (some with lethality comparable to VX nerve agent). The development of these chemicals and the improved understanding of their mechanisms of action are being driven by medical research, including the development of new anaesthetics. It has been suggested that these chemicals may have a potential role in law enforcement as so-called 'incapacitating agents' (ICAs), however recent studies have concluded that it is currently not possible to deliver such 'ICAs' for law enforcement purposes in a 'safe' manner.[103] Several CWC states parties have recently stated that they have not (and are not)

---

99 See eg Robert J Mathews, 'The Convergence of Chemistry and Biology: Implications for the CWC' *OPCW Today* (August 2012) 20–21.

100 See eg National Research Council, *Life Sciences and Related Fields: Trends Relevant to the Biological Weapons Convention* (National Academies Press 2011) 88–90.

101 See eg Matthew Meselson, 'Averting the Hostile Exploitation of Biotechnology' (June 2000) 48 *Harvard-Sussex CBW Bulletin* 16–19.

102 The prominence of this issue was raised following the Moscow Theatre siege in October 2002, during which Russian special forces used a 'disabling chemical' (fentanyl analogs) when storming the Dubrovka theatre. The Russian Health Ministry later announced that 129 of the 763 hostages had died, of whom all but five had been killed by the toxic chemical. See 'News Chronology: 26 October 2002' (December 2002) 58 *Harvard-Sussex CBW Bulletin* 45–46.

103 Concerns have also been expressed that the convergence of chemistry and biology may blur the current distinctions between RCAs and 'ICAs', and that 'ICAs' being developed for Law Enforcement purposes may subsequently be used as a method of warfare. Toxins or bioregulators (covered by the provisions of both the BWC and CWC) may be developed as either RCAs or ICAs. See Katie Smallwood, Ralf Trapp, Robert Mathews, Beat Schmidt and Leiv K Sydnes, 'Impact of Scientific Developments on the Chemical Weapons Convention (IUPAC Technical Report)' (2013) 85 *Pure and Applied Chemistry* 857.

producing CNS-acting chemicals for law enforcement purposes, and have sought similar assurances from other states parties.[104]

Another concern which has been raised is whether the advances in S&T, including nano-technology, may result in the development of novel materials that could be used as CBW which may not fall within the scope of either the BWC or CWC. Two examples which have been hypothesised are nano-materials that may asphyxiate without 'chemical action', and assemblies of atoms (sometimes called 'nano-robots') that may simulate the action of a pathogen.[105] It has been suggested that possible ways to address such a development could be through negotiation of brief supplementary provisions or ad hoc treaty law.[106] However, another option, which does not appear to have been considered yet and which may be more readily achievable, would be for the states parties of the BWC and CWC to prepare statements for endorsement at their respective Review Conferences which confirm that all such novel materials are captured by the prohibition of CBW, even if there are arguments that a particular material may not be covered by the definitions of BW and CW contained in BWC or CWC.[107] In any case, as discussed in Section 1, such materials would be captured by the language of the 1899 and 1907 Hague Conventions prohibiting 'poison and poisoned weapons' and by the 1925 Geneva Protocol.

5 Reflections and concluding comments

As outlined in this chapter, the ancient taboos and norms against the use of CW and BW have proved far from adequate in preventing the use of these weapons, even after these norms had been enshrined in multilaterally negotiated LOAC agreements, including the 1899 and 1907 Hague Conventions and the 1925 Geneva Protocol. The efforts of the international community since the late 1960s to strengthen the prohibitions of CBW have resulted in the BWC and CWC, supported by various complementary international agreements, which in combination, have been largely recognised as a success story and are generally regarded to have greatly reduced the possibility of large-scale use of CBW as a method of warfare.

So while there remain concerns that a few states may have retained CW stockpiles[108] and that CW may still be used in armed conflict, the overall view, based on recent developments is that the threat of the large-scale use of 'traditional' CW in armed conflict with large number of

---

104 See eg Australian Working Paper, 'Weaponisation of Central Nervous System Acting Chemicals for Law Enforcement Purposes' C-19/NAT.1 (14 November 2014).

105 See eg Robert D Pinson, 'Is Nanotechnology Prohibited by the Biological and Chemical Weapons Conventions?' (2004) 22 *Berkley Journal of International Law* 279. In this article, Pinson refers to the possibility of nano-materials that may condense in the lungs causing asphyxiation.

106 William H Boothby, *Conflict Law: The Influence of New Weapons Technology, Human Rights and Emerging Actors* (Asser 2014) 184–185.

107 If considered useful, the states parties of the BWC and CWC could agree to convene a combined meeting of experts which could develop guidelines or recommendation on the monitoring and/or national regulation of relevant nanotechnology to ensure that any such technology will not be used for purposes prohibited by the BWC or CWC.

108 For example, the Washington-based 'Arms Control Association' has listed a number of states which have been alleged to either possess, or are developing, stockpiles of CW or BW. States on this list include Egypt, Israel and North Korea, which are not states parties to either the BWC or CWC. For more information see, www.armscontrol.org/factsheets/cbwprolif.

casualties has declined significantly in recent years, especially following the elimination of Syria's CW.[109] Similarly, the threat of large-scale use of 'traditional' BW in armed conflict with large number of casualties also appears to have declined significantly since the end of the Cold War and the destruction of Iraq's BW stockpile in the early 1990s.

The strengthening of these LOAC provisions through disarmament law exemplifies the close relationship between LOAC and disarmament law. This has been expressed by noted arms-control expert, Jozef Goldblat, as follows:

> All laws of war suffer from one common weakness: the rules of conduct established for belligerents in time of peace may not resist the pressure of military expedience generated in the course of hostilities, and the attempts to 'humanise' war may sometimes prove futile. The danger that the weapons prohibited may, under certain circumstances, be resorted to – as has occurred on several occasions – will not disappear as long as these weapons remain in the arsenals of States.[110]

Hence the intrinsic link between the development of the humanitarian laws of war and progress in the field of disarmament.

However, despite the successes of these international agreements, events such as recent use of CW in Syria provide a stark reminder that the international community cannot afford to become complacent, particularly while there are still states which may possess stockpiles of CBW and which have chosen to remain outside the disarmament treaty regimes, and while many states parties have not yet fully implemented national implementation and other treaty obligations. And it also reminds us of the continuing importance of the LOAC agreements, including the associated UN Secretary-General's mechanism and the customary international law status of the LOAC agreements, including when CBW is being used in the territory of a non-state party.[111]

As discussed above, we live in a changing world, and there is still much to be done to ensure that these agreements remain effective. The legal regimes supporting the prohibition of CBW will be increasingly challenged, and the various challenges will be addressed more effectively with greater levels of cooperation between the BWC and CWC communities. This includes making every effort to ensure respect for the scope of the prohibitions contained in the 1899 and 1907 Hague Conventions and the 1925 Geneva Protocol, as well as universality and full and effective national implementation of all treaties and other agreements. In this respect, the importance of cooperative efforts between international players, relevant domestic government

---

109 For example, in an interview on 17 November 2014 on the role of the UN and OPCW in the elimination of Syria's CW stockpile, the Director-General of the OPCW, Ambassador Ahmet Üzümcü, stated

> This determination and this united position as well as our success in Syria have pushed the threshold for use of CW quite high. No country now, I think, could defend in a legitimate way, leaving aside legally, the use of these substances. In fact, I do not see any country able to use CW anymore. The reaction will be very firm.

See, www.the-trench.org/uzumcu-interview.

110 Jozef Goldblat, *Agreements for Arms Control: A Critical Survey* (SIPRI 1982) 89.

111 For a discussion of this issue, see William Boothby, *Weapons and the Law of Armed Conflict* (OUP 2009) 129–139.

agencies, and between governments and civil society, including the relevant scientific and industrial communities, cannot be over-emphasised.[112]

There is certainly no room for complacency. It is useful and salutary in this context to recall the words of Charles Flowerree, former US Ambassador for Disarmament who, when discussing arms control agreements, suggested:

> The means by which these agreements survive and adapt to changing conditions after they enter into force deserve as much attention as the negotiations that produced them in the first place. They cannot simply be left to fend for themselves.[113]

---

112 See eg Julian Perry Robinson, 'The Impact of Pugwash on the Debates over Chemical and Biological Weapons' in Allison L C de Cerreno and Alexander Keynan (eds), *Scientific Cooperation, State Conflict: The Roles of Scientists in Mitigating International Discord* (New York Academy of Sciences 1998) 224–252.

113 Charles C Flowerree, 'On Tending Arms Control Agreements' *Washington Quarterly* (Winter 1990) 199–214.

13
Nuclear weapons in international law

*Dieter Fleck**

The legality of the threat or use of nuclear weapons was not being assessed when the atomic bomb was developed during the Second World War. Instead, all relevant deliberations had concentrated on how to end that war quickly without considering questions related to the future role of nuclear weaponry. Important rules of international law which inform a professional legal assessment today, including the UN Charter, have entered into force only after the first and so far only case when nuclear weapons were used. Furthermore, the role of nuclear weapons has undergone important changes since the end of superpower confrontation during the Cold War, and so have the challenges posed by their existence. Hence any legal assessment must consider the different historic phases for the role of nuclear weapons in military planning and decision-making. Different branches of international law are relevant in this respect. It is in this broader context that the role of states and non-state actors in the development of pertinent principles and rules are to be considered.

The present chapter will discuss the role of nuclear weapons in the different phases since their existence and undertake a legal assessment of their use (Section 1). Various achievements towards the legal regulation of nuclear armament will be evaluated (Section 2); and emerging open issues for research and government action in the coming years will be addressed (Section 3). The chapter is not limited to considerations under the law of armed conflict; it shows that conclusions to be drawn on the current role of nuclear weapons and their legal regulation in the contemporary world requires an assessment of a larger spectrum of issues (Section 4).

1 The threat or use of nuclear weapons: a phased legal assessment

Nuclear weapons are capable of inflicting mass destruction and causing long-term devastation of targeted areas. In addition, radioactive fallout can create severe health problems in wide geographical areas for many decades. These effects cannot be effectively limited to military objectives or to the territories of the parties to an armed conflict.

* The author may express his gratitude to Professor Masahiko Asada, Graduate School of Law, Kyoto University, and Professor Timothy McCormack, Melbourne Law School, for critical comments on an earlier draft of this chapter. The text incorporates developments up to September 2014.

233

1.1 Hiroshima and Nagasaki: the difference between decisions taken at the time and assessments made in retrospect

The bombing of Hiroshima and Nagasaki on 6 and 9 August 1945, which led to Japan's surrender in the Second World War, was without precedence in history. About 140,000 of the 350,000 inhabitants of Hiroshima and 70,000 of the 270,000 living in Nagasaki died by the end of that year; larger numbers of men, women and children were severely injured and incapacitated for their lifetime. As early as January 1946 the UN General Assembly established an Atomic Energy Commission with the mandate to 'make proposals for the elimination from national armaments of atomic weapons and all other major weapons adaptable for mass destruction'.[1] That task is still unaccomplished and it has become increasingly difficult over time. In fact the development of nuclear weaponry has continued on a larger scale. Between 1945 and 1996, when the Comprehensive Nuclear-Test-Ban Treaty[2] was opened for signature, more than 2,000 nuclear tests were carried out all over the world. A number of nuclear weapons tests had been performed in the Marshall Islands (during the UN Pacific Islands territories trusteeship) and in the Sahara Desert, ignoring severe health damage of local populations.[3] Even years after nuclear weapons tests had been outlawed in the atmosphere, in outer space and under water by the 1963 Partial Nuclear Test Ban Treaty,[4] such tests were performed in the Pacific region (near Mururoa Atoll and Fangastaufa Island), yet the ICJ declared that inasmuch as France had undertaken the obligation to hold no further nuclear tests in the atmosphere in the South Pacific, the dispute had thus disappeared, the claim no longer had any object and there was nothing on which to give judgment.[5]

1.2 East–West confrontation: mutual deterrence and arms control

In the decades following the Second World War nuclear deterrence between the two superpowers became an essential element of security policy, successfully averting the use of nuclear weapons by preventing all-out war between the East and West.[6] It was the success of that policy that has often marginalised debates, however relevant,[7] on the legality of the use of nuclear weapons. In fact, in a 'practice significantly supported for almost 50 years by their allies and other States sheltering under their nuclear umbrella', nuclear powers still maintain 'a posture of readiness to launch nuclear weapons 365 days a year, 24 hours of every day', and in very few

---

1 UNGA Res 1(I) (24 January 1946).
2 Comprehensive Nuclear-Test-Ban Treaty (CTBT), UN Doc A/50/1027 (24 September 1996) Annex.
3 See testimony by the delegation of the Marshall Islands, referred to in *Legality of the Threat or Use of Nuclear Weapons (Advisory Opinion)* [1996] ICJ Rep 226, Dissenting Opinion of Judge Koroma, 569–570.
4 Treaty Banning Nuclear Weapon Tests in the Atmosphere, in Outer Space, and under Water (5 August 1963) 480 UNTS 43.
5 *Nuclear Tests (Australia v France and New Zealand v France)* [1974] ICJ Rep 253 and 457. See also *Request for an Examination of the Situation in Accordance with Paragraph 63 of the Court's Judgment of 20 December 1974 in the Nuclear Tests (New Zealand v France) Case (Order)* [1995] ICJ Rep 288.
6 For a comprehensive assessment, see Michael Quinlan, *Thinking about Nuclear Weapons: Principles, Problems, Prospects* (OUP 2009) 21–45.
7 See eg Georg Schwarzenberger, *The Legality of Nuclear Weapons* (Stevens 1958); Nagendra Singh, *Nuclear Weapons and International Law* (Stevens 1959); Ian Brownlie, 'Some Legal Aspects of the Use of Nuclear Weapons' (1965) 14 *ICLQ* 437.

international crises the use of nuclear weapons was threatened.[8] Diplomatic activities, far from seeking the abolition of nuclear weapons altogether, have concentrated on the improvement of communications to reduce the risk of outbreak of nuclear war,[9] to prohibit the emplacement of nuclear weapons on the seabed,[10] prohibit any military use of Antarctica,[11] the Moon and other celestial bodies[12] and the obligation not to place in orbit around the Earth any objects carrying nuclear weapons or station such weapons in outer space.[13] A first regional treaty prohibited nuclear weapons in Latin America and the Caribbean,[14] an example later to be followed in other populated regions of the world.[15]

The 1968 Nuclear Non-Proliferation Treaty (NPT)[16] provides a comprehensive legal structure of rights and obligations to protect mankind from nuclear aggression and accidental extinction by promoting three main goals, convincingly described as the three pillars of the Treaty, that is, peaceful use of nuclear energy, non-proliferation of nuclear weapons and nuclear disarmament. The NPT offers incentives for the research, production and use of nuclear energy for peaceful purposes; it provides that each state party undertakes not to provide any source, equipment or fissionable material to any non-nuclear-weapon state for peaceful purposes, unless it shall be subject to safeguards and inspections by the International Atomic Energy Agency (IAEA); and it includes an obligation of each of the parties to the Treaty to pursue negotiations on complete nuclear disarmament under strict and effective international control. Although

---

8 Statement by Vice-President Schwebel referring to state practice in his Dissenting Opinion in *Nuclear Weapons* (n 3).

9 See Memorandum of Understanding regarding the Establishment of a Direct Communications Link, US–USSR (20 June 1963) 472 UNTS 163; Agreement on Measures to Improve the USA–USSR Direct Communications Link, US–USSR (30 September 1971) 806 UNTS 402; Agreement on Measures to Reduce the Risk of Outbreak of Nuclear War, US–USSR (30 September 1971) 807 UNTS 57; Agreement on the Prevention of Nuclear War, US–USSR (22 June 1973) 917 UNTS 85; Agreement to Expand the US–USSR Direct Communications Link, US–USSR (17 July 1984) TIAS 11428; Agreement on the Establishment of Nuclear Risk Reduction Centres, US–USSR (15 September 1987) 1530 UNTS 379; Agreement on Notifications of Launches of Intercontinental Ballistic Missiles and Submarine-Launched Ballistic Missiles, US–USSR (31 May 1988) 27 ILM 1200; Memorandum of Agreement on the Establishment of a Joint Center for the Exchange of Data from Early Warning Systems and Notifications of Missile Launches, US–Russia (4 June 2000) State Dept No 00-73, 2000 WL 1121378; Memorandum of Understanding on Notifications of Missile Launches (16 December 2000) State Dept No 01-15, 2000 WL 33125447; Agreement Concerning the Future Consultation Procedure for Implementation of the Agreement of September 30, 1971 on Measures to Reduce the Risk of Outbreak of Nuclear War between the US and USSR, US–Russia (25 June 2004) State Dept No 04-193, 2004 WL 2387596. See also multilateral Convention on Early Notification of a Nuclear Accident (26 September 1986) IAEA Doc INFCIRC/335, 1439 UNTS 275 and Convention on Assistance in the Case of a Nuclear Accident or Radiological Emergency (26 September 1986) IAEA Doc INFCIRC/336, 1457 UNTS 133.

10 Treaty on the Prohibition of the Emplacement of Nuclear Weapons and Other Weapons of Mass Destruction at the Seabed and the Ocean Floor and in the Subsoil Thereof (11 February 1971) 955 UNTS 115.

11 Antarctic Treaty (1 December 1959) 402 UNTS 71.

12 Treaty on Principles governing the Activities of States in the Exploration and Use of Outer Space, Including the Moon and Other Celestial Bodies ('Outer Space Treaty') (27 January 1967) 610 UNTS 205; Agreement Governing the Activities of States on the Moon and Other Celestial Bodies (Moon Agreement) (18 December 1979) 1363 UNTS 3.

13 Outer Space Treaty (n 12).

14 Treaty for the Prohibition of Nuclear Weapons in Latin America ('Treaty of Tlatelolco') (14 February 1967) 634 UNTS 326.

15 See s 2.3.

16 Treaty on the Non-Proliferation of Nuclear Weapons (1 July 1968) 729 UNTS 161.

extended indefinitely in 1995, the NPT has not succeeded in limiting nuclear weapons to the five defined nuclear-weapon states (China, France, Russia, the UK and the US). Instead, the number of nuclear powers already includes or is widely believed to include four non-parties to the NPT: Israel,[17] India and Pakistan,[18] and North Korea.[19] Iranian attitudes to their national nuclear programmes in defiance of the IAEA inspections regime have raised severe international criticism.[20] This development shows that the nuclear threat is an element far beyond bipolar East–West confrontation today. Any successful solution will require multilateral efforts for which, as historic examples have shown,[21] there is no unified procedure.[22]

When the law of armed conflict was reaffirmed and further developed by the 1977 Additional Protocols to the Geneva Conventions of 1949, a number of states formally expressed their view, uncontested by any other party, that the 'new rules introduced by Additional Protocol I' were intended to apply to conventional weapons, irrespective of other rules of international law applicable to other types of weapons, with the result that these rules do not 'influence, regulate, or prohibit the use of nuclear weapons'.[23] There is consensus that those 'new rules' include (1) the rules protecting the environment,[24] (2) the rules elaborating the principle of proportionality in the protection of the civilian population,[25] (3) the prohibition of reprisals against the civilian population and civilian objects.[26] In the text of all declarations made it has been left open whether more rules of Additional Protocol I could be considered as being 'new'. Widespread, long-term and severe damage to the natural environment was specifically prohibited in 1977,[27]

---

17 Israel is believed to possess the largest and most sophisticated nuclear arsenal outside the five declared nuclear-weapon states.

18 See UNSC Res 1172 (6 June 1998); Agreement on Reducing the risk from Accidents Relating to Nuclear Weapons, Pakistan–India (21 February 2007), www.stimson.org/research-pages/agreement-on-reducing-the-risk-from-accidents-relating-to-nuclear-weapons; Agreement for Cooperation Concerning Peaceful Uses of Nuclear Energy, US–India (US–India 123 Agreement) (10 October 2008), www.state.gov/documents/organization/122068.pdf.

19 The Democratic People's Republic of Korea, a former party to the NPT, had declared its withdrawal from the Treaty on 12 March 1993, but suspended that declaration on 11 June 1993. On 10 January 2003 it declared an 'immediate effectuation of its withdrawal from the NPT' see, www.atomicarchive.com/Docs/Deterrence/DPRKNPTstatement.shtml. The Security Council has requested North Korea to retract its withdrawal and abandon all nuclear weapons and existing nuclear programmes in a complete, verifiable and irreversible manner, see UNSC Res 1718 (14 October 2006), UNSC Res 1874 (12 June 2009) and UNSC Res 2087 (22 January 2013). See Jonathan D Pollack, *No Exit: North Korea, Nuclear Weapons and International Security* (Routledge/IISS 2011).

20 See s 2.2.

21 Belarus, Kazakhstan and Ukraine (after the fall of the USSR), and South Africa after the end of the apartheid regime), had given up their nuclear weapons. Earlier, Argentina, Australia, Brazil, Iran, Iraq, South Korea and Taiwan, acting in different context in the early 1990s, have abandoned alleged nuclear weapons programmes and acceded to the NPT as non-nuclear-weapon states.

22 For a short legal assessment of different nuclear arms control activities, see Dieter Fleck, 'Nuclear Arms Control' in Roland Robertson and Jan Aart Scholte (eds), *Encyclopedia of Globalization* (Routledge 2006) vol 3, 896.

23 Statements made on ratification of API by Belgium, Canada, France, Germany, Italy, the Netherlands, Spain, UK and – on signature – by the US, see Adam Roberts and Richard Guelff, *Documents on the Laws of War* (3rd edn, OUP 2000) 499–512.

24 API arts 35(3), 55.

25 API arts 57, 58.

26 API arts 51(6), 52(1), 53(c), 54(4), 55(2) and 56(4). Frits Kalshoven, 'Arms, Armaments and International Law' (1985-II) 191 *RCADI* 183, 287; Frits Kalshoven and Lisbeth Zegveld, *Constraints on the Waging of War: An Introduction to International Humanitarian Law* (4th edn, CUP 2011) 118.

27 Convention on the Prohibition of Military or Any Other Hostile Use of Environmental Modification Techniques (ENMOD) (18 May 1977) 1108 UNTS 151.

without expressly mentioning nuclear weapons. The Rome Statute[28] established the jurisdiction of the ICC with respect to the crime of genocide, crimes against humanity, war crimes and the crime of aggression, but again no specific reference to the use of nuclear weapons was made.

1.3 Nuclear weapons in a multipolar world: incentives and problems for ensuring non-proliferation and nuclear disarmament

The UN General Assembly frequently declared with large majorities that the use of nuclear weapons would be violating the UN Charter. Yet in contrast to other weapons of mass destruction,[29] there is as yet no international convention expressly prohibiting the use of nuclear weapons. General prohibitions of indiscriminate warfare, of unnecessary suffering and of poison are part of the rules and principles of the law of armed conflict, but their application to nuclear weapons in the particular circumstances of their potential use remains controversial.

In its Advisory Opinion on *The Legality of the Threat or Use of Nuclear Weapons* of 8 July 1996[30] the ICJ, following a request by the General Assembly,[31] offered legal advice on a question that was put in general and abstract form.[32] This Opinion, and the parallel Opinion which was handed down per request of the World Health Organization,[33] raised a wide spectrum of international legal issues.[34] Only those related to the threat or use of nuclear weapons shall be discussed here. The Court stated by 11 votes to three with Judges Koroma, Shahabuddeen and Weeramantry dissenting, that there is in neither customary nor conventional international law any comprehensive and universal prohibition of the threat or use of nuclear weapons as such.[35] All judges unanimously underlined that a threat or use of force by nuclear weapons that is contrary to Article 2(4) of the UN Charter and that fails to meet all the requirements of Article 51 is unlawful,[36] and that a threat or use of nuclear weapons

> should also be compatible with the requirements of international law applicable in armed conflict, particularly those of the principles and rules of international humanitarian law, as well as with the specific obligations under treaties and other undertakings which expressly deal with nuclear weapons.[37]

28 Rome Statute; Amendment to Article 8 (10 June 2010) Annex I to Resolution RC/Res 5; Amendment to the ICC Statute on the Crime of Aggression (11 June 2010) Annex I to Resolution RC/Res 6.
29 Convention on the Prohibition of the Development, Production and Stockpiling of Bacteriological (Biological) and Toxin Weapons and on their Destruction (10 April 1972) 1015 UNTS 163; Convention on the Prohibition of the Development, Production, Stockpiling and Use of Chemical Weapons and on their Destruction (13 January 1993) 1974 UNTS 45.
30 *Nuclear Weapons* (n 3).
31 UNGA Res 49/75/K (15 December 1994).
32 Ibid ¶ 11: 'Is the threat or use of nuclear weapons in any circumstance permitted under international law?'/'Est-il permis en droit international de recourir à la menace ou à l'emploi d'armes nucléaires en toute circonstance?'
33 *Legality of the Use by a State of Nuclear Weapons in Armed Conflict (Advisory Opinion)* [1996] ICJ Rep 66.
34 See Laurence Boisson de Chazournes and Phillipe Sands (eds), *International Law, the International Court of Justice and Nuclear Weapons* (CUP 1999).
35 *Nuclear Weapons* (n 3) ¶¶ 23–36, 105(2)(B).
36 Ibid ¶¶ 37–50, 105(2)(C).
37 Ibid ¶¶ 51–89, 105(2)(D).

However, evenly split and only by the President's casting vote, with Vice-President Schwebel and Judges Guillaume, Higgins, Koroma, Oda, Shahabuddeen and Weeramantry dissenting, the Court declared that while:

> the threat or use of nuclear weapons would generally be contrary to the rules of international law applicable in armed conflict, and in particular the principles and rules of humanitarian law … in view of the current state of international law, and of the elements of fact at its disposal, the Court cannot conclude definitively whether the threat or use of nuclear weapons would be lawful or unlawful in an extreme circumstance of self-defence in which the very survival of a State would be at stake.[38]

Finally the Court unanimously confirmed that '[t]here exists an obligation to pursue in good faith and bring to a conclusion negotiations leading to nuclear disarmament in all its aspects under strict and effective international control'.[39]

The controversial statement that there is no comprehensive and universal prohibition of the threat or use of nuclear weapons as such was contested by Judges Koroma, Shahabuddeen and Weeramantry with references to the principles that in any armed conflict the right of the parties to choose methods and means of combat is not unlimited, and that it is prohibited to employ weapons of a nature to cause superfluous injury or unnecessary suffering, as well as the Martens Clause. Together, these rules of customary international law could operate to prohibit the use of nuclear weapons in situations in which proportionality, distinction between military objectives and civilian objects, and the environment are at risk.[40] Reference was also made to specific rules, including Article 23(a) of the 1907 Hague Regulations,[41] the 1925 Geneva Gas Protocol,[42] the 1948 Genocide Convention,[43] human rights conventions and environmental treaties.[44] While these arguments do not direct to an express conventional or customary prohibition of the use of nuclear weapons as such, the approach taken by the three dissenting judges was certainly more problem-oriented and hence more appropriate than assumptions made by others[45] who, following the lines of argument in the *Lotus* case,[46] conclude that if international law does not prohibit particular conduct, that conduct is permitted.

The more controversial question whether the threat or use of nuclear weapons would be lawful or unlawful in an extreme circumstance of self-defence was dividing the Court to an

---

38 Ibid ¶¶ 90–97, 105(2)(E).

39 Ibid ¶¶ 98–103, 105(2)(F).

40 See in particular *Nuclear Weapons* (n 3) Dissenting Opinion of Judge Shahabuddeen.

41 Hague Convention (IV) Respecting the Laws and Customs of War on Land and its Annex: Regulations Respecting the Laws and Customs of War on Land (18 October 1907) 205 CTS 277.

42 Protocol for the Prohibition of the Use of Asphyxiating, Poisonous or Other Gases, and of Bacteriological Methods of Warfare (17 June 1925) 187 CTS 453.

43 Convention on the Prevention and Punishment of the Crime of Genocide (9 December 1948) 78 UNTS 277.

44 See *Nuclear Weapons* (n 3) Dissenting Opinions of Judges Koroma and Weeramantry.

45 See eg Yoram Dinstein, *The Conduct of Hostilities under the Law of International Armed Conflict* (2nd edn, CUP 2010) 85 ('It is ordinarily understood that, if international law does not prohibit a certain conduct, that conduct is lawful.').

46 *SS 'Lotus' (France v Turkey)* [1927] PCIJ Series A No 10. Also *Nuclear Weapons* (n 3) Dissenting Opinion of Judge Shahabuddeen, pt II, refers to the '*Lotus* principle that a State has a right to do whatever is not prohibited under international law', but clearly does so with interpretive constraints from today's perspective under the UN Charter, constraints that may be also supported by an interpretation of the *Lotus* judgment in its historical context.

extent that has increased legal controversies rather than solving them. While many have taken the position that it would have been unwarranted and a departure from the judicial function should the Court have declared the use of nuclear weapons unlawful in all circumstances,[47] others have criticised the judgment for failing to specify those 'extreme circumstance[s] of self-defence in which the very survival of a State would be at stake' and that it could imply that general principles of customary international humanitarian law do not automatically apply to specific weapons.[48] Judge Higgins convincingly shows that the position taken by the majority was unclear and it represented a *non liquet* that should have no place in the Court's jurisprudence:

> I do not consider it juridically meaningful to say that the use of nuclear weapons is 'generally contrary to the rules of international law applicable in armed conflict, and in particular the principles and rules of humanitarian law'. What does the term 'generally' mean? Is it a numerical allusion, or is it a reference to different types of nuclear weapons, or is it a suggestion that the rules of humanitarian law cannot be met save for exceptions?[49]

Judge Higgins acknowledged the need to resolve tensions between competing norms here;[50] but at the same time she expressed doubts whether 'a pronouncement of illegality in all circumstances of the use of nuclear weapons or the answers formulated by the Court … best serve to protect mankind against that unimaginable suffering that we all fear'.[51]

Extreme circumstances of self-defence in which the very survival of a state would be at stake would not exempt any party to an armed conflict from compliance with relevant rules of international humanitarian law, as such exemptions are not provided for therein. But the right of self-defence cannot be denied, not even if recourse to nuclear weapons is 'the last available means by way of which the victimized State could exercise its right under Article 51 of the Charter'.[52]

Whether such a situation could occur in reality has not been unanimously perceived in the Cold War and it has become open to even more doubts in recent years. While in abstract terms there may be agreement that 'military advantage' must be one related to 'the very survival of a State or avoidance of infliction (whether by nuclear or other weapons of mass destruction) of vast and severe suffering on its own population',[53] states would hesitate to make this part of their operational planning and the ICJ 'rightly regards that evidence as

---

47 Christopher J Greenwood, 'The Advisory Opinion on Nuclear Weapons and the Contribution of the International Court to International Humanitarian Law' (1997) 37(316) *IRRC* 65, 73. See also Richard A Falk, 'Nuclear Weapons, International Law and the World Court: A Historic Encounter' (1997) 91 *AJIL* 64, 73.

48 Timothy L H McCormack, 'A Non Liquet on Nuclear Weapons: The ICJ Avoids the Application of General Principles of International Humanitarian Law' (1997) 37(316) *IRRC* 76, 89.

49 *Nuclear Weapons* (n 3) Dissenting Opinion of Judge Higgins, ¶¶ 25–36.

50 Ibid ¶ 41:

> We live in a decentralized world order, in which some States are known to possess nuclear weapons but choose to remain outside of the non-proliferation treaty system; while other such non-parties have declared their intention to obtain nuclear weapons; and yet other States are believed clandestinely to possess, or to be working shortly to possess nuclear weapons.

51 Ibid.

52 *Nuclear Weapons* (n 3) Separate Opinion by Judge Fleischhauer, ¶ 3.

53 *Nuclear Weapons* (n 3) Dissenting Opinion of Judge Higgins, ¶ 21.

uncertain'.[54] Scholarly examples of compatibility of use of nuclear weapons with international humanitarian law – low yield tactical nuclear weapons used to destroy an underground bunker (far removed from a civilian population) or the destruction of a military objective on the high seas (miles away from a densely populated civilian area) – have not been referred to by nuclear powers in their submissions to the ICJ in relation to the Advisory Opinion,[55] nor indeed 'may it be assumed that such types of weapons (perhaps to be used against submarines, or in deserts) can suffice to represent for a nuclear weapon State all that is required for an effective policy of deterrence'.[56] As stressed by the Red Cross and Red Crescent movement at its thirty-first International Conference (2011), it is 'difficult to envisage how any use of nuclear weapons could be compatible with the rules of international humanitarian law, in particular the rules of distinction, precaution and proportionality'.[57] Far from denying the right of self-defence in extreme situations in which the very survival of a state would be at stake, existing doubts may be related to the probability of such factual situations rather than to the contents of a legal rule. Yet it is to be admitted that in the absence of an express legal prohibition questions as to the legality of the threat or use of nuclear weapons in extreme situations will prevail.

The unanimous reminder by the Court of the obligation of states 'to pursue in good faith and bring to a conclusion negotiations leading to nuclear disarmament in all its aspects under strict and effective international control'[58] deliberately confirms the existence of a legal obligation of what had been referred to a few months before by the Security Council as no more than a political goal:[59] the Court underlined that Article VI of the NPT recognised 'an obligation to negotiate in good faith a nuclear disarmament' that goes beyond 'a mere obligation of conduct' (*pactum de negotiando*), and includes 'an obligation to achieve a precise result' (*pactum de contrahendo*).[60] The Court did not see this obligation as being created by the NPT, it rather used the phrase 'recognition by Article VI'. Some authors, and, indeed, the President of the ICJ have stated that this part of the Advisory Opinion is an expression of customary international law today,[61] an aspect that points pressure on non-parties to the NPT (for example, Israel, India, Pakistan and North Korea) to participate in negotiations on nuclear disarmament. Yet no further consequences have been drawn by the Court itself. Vice-President Schwebel in his Dissenting Opinion treated paragraph 105(2)F of the judgment as a mere *dictum*, as this issue had not been submitted to the Court and argued out

---

54 Ibid ¶ 18.
55 See eg Letter dated 16 June 1995 from the Legal Adviser to the Foreign and Commonwealth Office of the United Kingdom of Great Britain and Northern Ireland, together with Written Comments of the United Kingdom, www.icj-cij.org/docket/files/95/8802.pdf.
56 *Nuclear Weapons* (n 3) Dissenting Opinion of Judge Higgins, ¶ 30.
57 ICRC, 'Working Towards the Elimination of Nuclear Weapons' Background Document CD/11/4.1 (26 November 2011), www.icrc.org/eng/resources/documents/report/nuclear-background-document-2011-11-26.htm.
58 *Nuclear Weapons* (n 3) ¶ 105(2)F.
59 UNSC Res 984 (11 April 1995):

> 8. *Urges* all States, as provided for in Article VI of the Treaty on the Non-Proliferation of Nuclear Weapons, to pursue in good faith on effective measures relating to nuclear disarmament and on a treaty on general and complete disarmament under strict and effective international control which remains a universal goal.

60 *Nuclear Weapons* (n 3) ¶ 99.
61 *Nuclear Weapons* (n 3) Declaration by President Bedjaoui, ¶ 23; Michael Bothe, 'Weapons of Mass Destruction, Counter-Proliferation' *MPEPIL* (September 2012) ¶ 12.

before it. He called it 'another anodyne asseveration of the obvious', if applied to the parties to the NPT, but 'a dubious holding' if applied to non-parties. Representatives of nuclear-weapon states still tend to suggest that Article VI is of rather limited scope.[62]

The scope of Article VI is broader than the portion of the text that was summarised by the Court. Instead of establishing 'an obligation to pursue in good faith and bring to a conclusion negotiations leading to nuclear disarmament in all its aspects under strict and effective international control', as the Court had underlined, the article provides that

[e]ach of the Parties to the Treaty undertakes to pursue negotiations in good faith on effective measures relating to cessation of the nuclear arms race at an early date and to nuclear disarmament, and on a treaty on general and complete disarmament under strict and effective international control.

Hence three different objectives – cessation of the nuclear arms race, nuclear disarmament and general disarmament – are put in context in the NPT and they are connected with different conditions, as confirmed by the treaty text, its negotiating history and the practice of states parties.[63] While the character of Article VI as a legal obligation is not to be disputed, a convincing implementation in all its aspects is yet to be found. The initiative for a world free of nuclear weapons launched by President Obama in April 2009, even after the encouraging first step achieved with the 2010 New START Treaty,[64] still requires a long way to go, before successful cooperation in a multipolar world may lead to further results. The readiness for nuclear disarmament is still limited by security concerns, a lack of confidence-building and control. Missile

---

62 Christopher A Ford, 'Debating Disarmament: Interpreting Article VI of the Treaty on the Non-Proliferation of Nuclear Weapons' (2007) 14(3) *Nonproliferation Review* 401; Quinlan (n 6) 153–156, 171–177; but see the critical review by Daniel H Joyner, *Interpreting the Nuclear Non-Proliferation Treaty* (OUP 2011) 95–108.

63 See George Bunn and Roland M Timerbaev, 'Nuclear Disarmament: How Much have the Five Nuclear Powers Promised in the Non-Proliferation Treaty?' in John Rhinelander and Adam Scheinman (eds), *At the Nuclear Crossroads* (University Press of America 1995) 11–29 and notes. See also Shannon N Kile, 'Russian-US Nuclear Arms Control' (2012) *SIPRI Yearbook* 355.

64 Treaty on Measures for the Further Reduction and Limitation of Strategic Offensive Arms, US–Russia (8 April 2010) 50 ILM 342. For ratification proceedings in Russia and the United States, see Shannon N Kile, 'Nuclear Arms Control and Non-Proliferation'(2011) *SIPRI Yearbook* 363, 370–371. On 25 January 2011, the Russian State Duma adopted a draft law on the New START Treaty ratification with two formal statements, one addressed to the Russian President:

As the US has withdrawn from the Soviet-US Treaty on the limitation of anti-ballistic missile systems, special significance has to be attached to maintaining missile defense systems and all their components at a designated level of preparedness for improvement in case of a military threat against Russia.

The other was addressed to the international community: 'The State Duma considers the deployment of the US non-strategic nuclear weapons outside the US unjustified and not complying with today's Euro-Atlantic relations.' The US ratification text specifies that the correlation between strategic offensive weapons and missile defence addressed in the preamble 'does not impose a legal obligation on the parties', with the effect that the US cannot be constrained in its missile defence activities. The Russian document asserts otherwise. Russian Foreign Minister Sergei Lavrov, referring in that context to the withdrawal clause in the event of an emergency, stated: 'We are convinced that the implementation of the full-scale global missile defense by the U.S. will be precisely such an emergency.' See gsn.nti.org/gsn/nw_20110201_4215.php.

defence against possible nuclear attacks is still seen as a potential threat rather than a stabilising factor for (common) peace efforts.[65]

A critical comparison of different national approaches in contemporary nuclear strategies might offer useful parameters for legal evaluation. Yet there are limits for gaining access to relevant information, as important aspects of nuclear strategies remain classified.[66] A comparison between more recent policy developments in nuclear strategies remains desirable in this context. Various, albeit different, signals have been sent by Russia's new military doctrine and policy for nuclear deterrence until 2020, and recent developments in the US, while other nuclear powers have proven much less communicative on this issue.

A clarification of a state's right to use nuclear weapons, against the backdrop of fundamental threats to its survival, remains an essential element of any meaningful discussion of nuclear disarmament. In this context both the scope of the threat and the means available to respond are to be evaluated. It remains difficult to arrive at common conclusions here; nevertheless further analysis in this area is necessary. A particular challenge is the right of pre-emptive/anticipatory self-defence in response to threats of development, acquisition and possession of nuclear weapons. The different roles of intermediate range and strategic nuclear weapons as opposed to tactical nuclear weapons and the different requirements for their verification should be considered in this context. Specific legal aspects arise from nuclear sharing as a concept in NATO's policy of nuclear deterrence, which involves member states without nuclear weapons of their own in political and military planning processes.

65 Tom Sauer, *Eliminating Nuclear Weapons: The Role of Missile Defense* (Hurst 2011). There are, however, also encouraging other developments. The Carnegie Endowment, addressing the risks of reliance on nuclear deterrence has advocated NATO–Russian cooperation on missile defence, which should be started at shorter range and later extended to strategic systems. A joint proposal was developed by Wolfgang Ischinger, Igor Ivanov and Sam Nunn, 'Toward a Stronger European Security' *Moscow Times* (8 December 2009); Wolfgang Ischinger, 'Ein Dach für das Haus Europa' *Frankfurter Allgemeine Zeitung* (20 June 2011). At the NATO–Russia Council (Sochi, 4 July 2011), NATO Secretary-General Anders Fogh Rasmussen and Russian Foreign Minister Sergei Lavrov could not confirm progress on NATO–Russian cooperation on missile defence, but Rasmussen:

> invited Russia to consider ways of linking our two separate systems together. We want to see two systems that would exchange information to make the defence of NATO territory and of Russia territory more effective. Because this would make us both safer. And it would prove that the best way to more security is through more cooperation.
>
> www.nato.int/cps/en/natolive/opinions_76041.htm.

66 For general information, see *Deterrence and Defence Posture Review*, adopted by heads of state and government participating in the meeting of the North Atlantic Council in Chicago on 20 May 2012, www.nato.int/cps/en/SID-BC1BD788-68E2C019/natolive/official_texts_87597.htm; Nuclear Posture Review Debate, www.defencetalk.com/tag/nuclear-posture-review; Военная доктрина Российской Федерации (Military Doctrine of the Russian Federation), approved by Decree of the President of the Russian Federation (5 February 2010), news.kremlin.ru/ref_notes/461; United Press International, 'Russia plans New Defense Strategy' (24 April 2012), www.upi.com/Top_News/World-News/2012/04/24/Russia-plans-new-defense-strategy/UPI-81581335293440; Andrei Zagorski, 'Russia's Tactical Nuclear Weapons: Posture, Politics and Arms Control' *Hamburger Beiträge zur Friedensforschung und Sicherheitspolitik* no 156 (Institut für Friedensforschung und Sicherheitspolitik an der Universität Hamburg 2011); Chinese State Council, *China's National Defense in 2010* (Information Office of the Chinese State Council, March 2011).

1.4 The challenge of terrorist access: limits of control and the need to address root causes

Any legal assessment of the threat or use of nuclear weapons would be incomplete if possibilities of access to such weapons by non-state actors remained unconsidered. Even if it may be more realistic to imagine other weapons of mass destruction, that is, chemical or biological weapons in the hands of non-state actors, nuclear scenarios in non-international armed conflicts and terrorist activities of larger scale cannot be excluded. This underlines the importance of vertical non-proliferation, that is, the denial of access to non-state actors, in addition to horizontal restrictions in the cooperation between states.

Following alarming reports that enriched fissionable material, mainly from the former USSR, is being freely smuggled across international borders in Central Asia, and considering that the scope of the only existing international convention on this subject matter[67] at this time, was limited to nuclear material used for peaceful purposes and did not cover nuclear material of a military nature, new conventions have been adopted for the suppression of terrorist bombings,[68] and the suppression of other acts of nuclear terrorism.[69] Under the former treaty states parties are obliged to penalise any unlawful delivery and detonation of explosive devices; the latter extends that obligation to any unlawful possession or use of radioactive material.

In 2006, the UN General Assembly adopted a comprehensive counter-terrorism strategy which aims to develop legal and operational frameworks for cooperation in suppressing terrorist networks, capacity-building to suppress them and control of relevant materials.[70] The Security Council has taken relevant measures, in a number of cases acting under its Chapter VII powers.[71] The US has formed a 'coalition of the willing' to foster multilateral responses including the Proliferation Security Initiative (PSI)[72] and the Global Initiative to Combat Nuclear Terrorism (GICNT).[73] The EU has taken several initiatives including the EU Strategy Against Proliferation of Weapons of Mass Destruction in 2003.[74]

Should vertical non-proliferation prove unsuccessful, alarming scenarios would become reality. Deterrence of non-state actors would work differently from existing experience in international relations between states. The same would apply to any confidence-building measures.

---

67 Convention on the Physical Protection of Nuclear Material (CPPNM), IAEA Doc INFCIRC/274/ Rev 1 (26 October 1979) 1456 UNTS 101; Amendments to the Convention on the Physical Protection of Nuclear Material, IAEA Doc GOV/INF/2005/10-GC(49)/INF/6 (8 July 2005).
68 International Convention for the Suppression of Terrorist Bombings, UNGA Res 52/164 (15 December 1997) 2149 UNTS 256.
69 International Convention for the Suppression of Acts of Nuclear Terrorism, UNGA Res 59/290 (13 April 2005) 2445 UNTS 89.
70 UNGA Res 60/288 (20 September 2006).
71 See in particular UNSC Res 1540 (28 April 2004). For ongoing activities of the Council see, www. un.org/terrorism/securitycouncil.shtml.
72 See US Department of State, 'Proliferation Security Initiative', www.state.gov/t/isn/c10390.htm; Michael Byers, 'Proliferation Security Initiative (PSI)' *MPEPIL* (June 2007).
73 See US Department of State, 'The Global Initiative to Combat Nuclear Terrorism', www.state.gov/t/ isn/c18406.htm.
74 See Jana Hertwig, *Die Europäische Union und die Bekämpfung der Verbreitung von Massenvernichtungswaffen: Theorie und Praxis der europäischen Nichtverbreitungsstrategie* (Peter Lang 2010). For an assessment of present activities, see Natalino Ronzitti (ed), *Coordinating Global and Regional Efforts to Combat WMD Terrorism* (Istituto Affari Internazionali 2009).

2 Public responsibility: challenges for international organisations and civil society

Approximately 20,500 tactical and strategic nuclear warheads may still exist today, of which more than 5,000 are deployed and nearly 2,000 are kept in a state of high operational alert.[75] An estimated 95 per cent is in US or Russian custody; yet the number of states with access to nuclear weapons tends to increase. Furthermore, unlawful access by non-state actors cannot be excluded. As this is an alarming notion for regional and global security, the need for effective efforts towards nuclear disarmament and confidence-building requires resolute action by states.

2.1 Negative and positive security assurances

In 1968, when the NPT was adopted, the Security Council welcomed

> the intention expressed by certain states that they will provide support and immediate assistance, in accordance with the UN Charter, to any non-nuclear-weapon state Party to the Treaty on the Non-Proliferation of Nuclear Weapons that is a victim of an act or an object of a threat of aggression in which nuclear weapons are used.[76]

The value of any such 'positive assurance' remains questionable. It may be unacceptable for states to receive military assistance without specific request. Inasmuch as the commitment is to take action within the Security Council to ensure that the Council takes appropriate measures to provide, in accordance with the Charter, necessary assistance, it is reflecting no more than existing obligations under the Charter with respect to threats to the peace, breaches of the peace and acts of aggression. Members of the Security Council could hardly limit such assistance to states parties to the NPT. Yet the idea was further pursued in context with the NPT's indefinite extension in 1995, when the Council used the same words with respect to positive security assurances by certain nuclear-weapon states.[77]

At the same time the Council took note

> with appreciation of the statements made by each of the nuclear-weapon States ..., in which they give security assurances against the use of nuclear weapons to non-nuclear-weapon States that are Parties to the Treaty on the Non-Proliferation of Nuclear Weapons.[78]

Such 'negative security assurances', too, have a long history which is not free from controversy.[79] An important exception declared by France, UK, US and Russia relates to

---

75 See Shannon N Kile, Vitaly Fedchenko, Phillip Schell and Hans M Kristensen, 'World Nuclear Forces' (2012) *SIPRI Yearbook* 307–350.

76 UNSC Res 255 (19 June 1968) ¶ 2.

77 UNSC Res 984 (11 April 1995) ¶ 7.

78 Ibid ¶ 1.

79 A first proposal made to this effect by Soviet Premier Alexei Kosygin in a message to the Eighteen-Nation Committee on Disarmament on 1 February 1966, suggested 'a clause on the prohibition of the use of nuclear weapons against non-nuclear states parties to the treaty, which have no nuclear weapons on their territory': Disarmament Commission, Official Records: Supplement for 1966 (UN 1967) 8–10, cf Mohamed I Shaker, *The Nuclear Non-Proliferation Treaty: Origin and Implementation 1959-1979* (Oceana 1980), vol II, 473 et seq. One of the states in which US nuclear weapons were deployed was the Federal Republic of Germany, a possible target of hundreds of Soviet missiles and thousands of Soviet tanks at that time.

the case of an invasion or other attack on [the declaring State], its armed forces, its allies, or on a State towards which it has a security commitment, carried out or sustained by such non-nuclear-weapon State in association or alliance with a nuclear-weapon State.[80]

Thus a first use of nuclear weapons is not excluded by these four states. Only China has undertaken 'not to be the first to use nuclear weapons at any time or under any circumstances'.[81]

The security assurances of 6 April 1995 were made in the form of unilateral declarations, after consultation with the other nuclear-weapon states. On the same date, the NPT Review Conference adopted a declaration, stating that 'further steps should be considered to assure non-nuclear-weapon states party to the Treaty against the use or threat of use of nuclear weapons. These steps could take the form of an internationally legally binding instrument.'[82] This proposal which was reiterated at the 2010 Review Conference,[83] has not been implemented so far, except in nuclear-weapon-free zones (see below, Section 2.3). It still requires further initiatives. Also the debate on no-first-use commitments which was of some significance during the Cold War,[84] might be revived in new contexts. In any event, more transparency is required at the international level, to make security assurances more meaningful.

2.2 The IAEA safeguards system and other control mechanisms

The IAEA safeguards provide a most professional tool for comprehensive verification of compliance with relevant obligations.[85] Yet in international security affairs control mechanisms cannot effectively work without cooperation. This is currently to be seen in the case of Iran's alleged non-compliance with IAEA safeguards. Following unsuccessful measures taken by the Security Council,[86] talks between China, France, Germany, Russia, the UK, the US ('E3 + 3') and Iran are being conducted, but so far these talks have not led to final results in terms of confidence-building and full compliance. The IAEA has indicated that Iran has carried out activities relevant to the development of a nuclear explosive device (that is: efforts, some successful, to procure nuclear related and dual use equipment and materials by military-related individuals and entities; efforts to develop undeclared pathways for the production of nuclear material; acquisition of nuclear weapons development information and documentation from a

---

80 See UN Docs S/1995/261 (Russia), S/1995/262 (UK), S/1995/263 (US), S/1995/264 (France) and S/1995/265 (China) (6 April 1995).

81 UN Doc S/1995/265 (6 April 1995) ¶ 1. See John W Lewis and Xue Litai, 'Making China's Nuclear War Plan' (2012) 68(5) *Bulletin of the Atomic Scientists* 45.

82 Principles and Objectives for Nuclear Non-Proliferation and Disarmament, UN Doc NPT/CONF.1995/32/DEC.2 (9 December 1996).

83 Final Document of the 2010 NPT Review Conference, UN Doc NPT/CONF.2010/50 (Vol I) (May 2010) 21, ¶ I.C.

84 See Josef Goldblat, *Arms Control: A Guide to Negotiations and Agreements* (Sage 1994) 197–199.

85 See Paul C Szasz, *The Law and Practices of the International Atomic Energy Agency* (IAEA 1970); Reinhard H Rainer and Paul C Szasz, *The Law and Practices of the International Atomic Energy Agency 1970–1980* (IAEA 1993); Laura Rockwood, 'The IAEA Safeguards System' *International Nuclear Law: History, Evolution and Outlook* (OECD Nuclear Energy Agency 2010) 243–269.

86 UNSC Res 1696 (31 July 2006) demanded that Iran shall suspend all enrichment-related and reprocessing activities, including research and development, to be verified by the IAEA. This demand, extended by UNSC Res 1737 (23 December 2006) to work on all heavy-water-related projects, including the construction of a research reactor moderated by heavy water, and sanctioned by a Council Committee to decide *inter alia* on individual travel restrictions and the freezing of funds, was reaffirmed by UNSC Res 1747 (24 March 2007), 1803 (3 March 2008) and 1835 (27 September 2008) without, however, being complied with by Iran.

clandestine nuclear supply network; and work on the development of an indigenous design of a nuclear weapon including the testing of components); consequently the IAEA has expressed serious concerns regarding possible military dimensions to Iran's nuclear programme.[87] Efforts towards a diplomatic settlement are to be continued. They may be considered as being most relevant for Iran itself, a country which is almost surrounded by nuclear-weapon states, many of them not even defined as such in Article IX(3) of the NPT, and which has been encircled by foreign troops following 11 September 2001.[88]

2.3 Nuclear-weapon-free zones

Apart from the Antarctica, outer space and the seabed,[89] nuclear-weapon-free zones have also been established in populated areas. South America,[90] the South Pacific (Australia, Cook Islands, Fiji, Kiribati, Nauru, New Zealand, Niue, Papua New Guinea, Solomon Islands, Tonga, Tuvalu, Vanuatu and Western Samoa),[91] South-East Asia (Brunei Darussalam, Cambodia, Indonesia, Laos, Malaysia, Myanmar, Philippines, Singapore, Thailand and Vietnam),[92] Africa[93] and Central Asia (Kazakhstan, Kyrgyzstan, Tajikistan, Turkmenistan and Uzbekistan)[94] have accepted the obligation to ban production, purchasing and deployment of nuclear weapons, their components and other nuclear explosive devices on their territories including their respective continental shelves and Exclusive Economic Zones. A zone free from weapons of mass destruction in the Middle East is presently under discussion.[95]

In response to international challenges[96] nuclear-weapon states party to the NPT have regularly committed themselves to negative security assurances with respect to nuclear-weapon-free zones. These commitments are declared in a protocol attached to the respective treaty. Like commitments by states not party to the NPT who are known or believed to also

---

87 Report by the Director General of the IAEA, 'Implementation of the NPT Safeguards Agreement and Relevant Provisions of Security Council Resolutions in the Islamic Republic of Iran' IAEA Doc GOV/2011/65 (8 November 2011); see Joint Statement on a Framework for Cooperation, signed by the Director General of the International Atomic Energy Agency (IAEA) and the Vice-President of the Islamic Republic of Iran (11 November 2013), www.iaea.org/newscenter/pressreleases/2013/prn201321.html; Joint Statement by EU High Representative Catherine Ashton and Iran Foreign Minister Zarif (24 November 2013), www.eeas.europa.eu/statements/docs/2013/131124_02_en.pdf; Joint Plan of Action (24 November 2013) adopted by the 'EU3 + 3' and Iran, www.reuters.com/article/2013/11/24/us-iran-nuclear-agreement-text-idUSBRE9AN0BQ20131124.

88 Jalil Roshandel, 'The Nuclear Controversy in the Context of Iran's Evolving Defence Strategy' in Shannon N Kile (ed), *Europe and Iran: Perspectives on Non-Proliferation* (OUP/SIPRI 2005) 46, 51; Hossein Mousavian 'The Iranian Nuclear Dispute: Origins and Current Options' *Arms Control Today* (July/August 2012) www.armscontrol.org/2012_07-08/The_Iranian_Nuclear_Dispute_Origins_and_Current_Options; Tariq Rauf and Robert Kelley, 'Nuclear Verification in Iran, in *Arms Control Today* (September 2014), http://legacy.armscontrol.org/act/2014_09/Features/Nuclear-Verification-in-Iran.

89 Notes 10–13 and accompanying text, above.

90 Treaty of Tlatelolco (n 14).

91 South Pacific Nuclear Free Zone Treaty (Rarotonga Treaty) (6 August 1985) 1445 UNTS 177.

92 Treaty on the South-East Asia Nuclear Weapon Free Zone (Bangkok Treaty) (15 December 1995) 1981 UNTS 129.

93 African Nuclear-Weapon-Free Zone Treaty (Pelindaba Treaty) (11 April 1996) 35 ILM 698.

94 Treaty on a Nuclear-Weapon-Free Zone in Central Asia (Semipalatinsk Treaty) (8 September 2006), www.opanal.org/NWFZ/CentralAsia/canwfz_en.htm; Marco Roscini, 'Something Old, Something New: The 2006 Semipalatinsk Treaty on a Nuclear Weapons-Free Zone in Central Asia' (2008) *Chinese JIL* 593.

95 See NPT Review Conference 2010 (n 83) 29–31.

96 See UNGA Res 3472 (XXX) B (11 December 1975) ¶ 2.

possess nuclear weapons are more problematic. It would be difficult to arrange for binding declarations in such cases that would exclude any recognition of possession of nuclear armaments at the same time.

2.4 The role of states and civil society

Public pressure towards establishing a more effective multilateral regime to achieve and maintain a world without nuclear weapons was visible throughout the Cold War and has increased ever since. Yet multilateral negotiations on nuclear disarmament and a prohibition of the threat and use of nuclear weapons remain at a standstill, although the 2010 NPT Review Conference again referred to the proposal to conduct 'negotiations on a nuclear weapons convention or agreement on a framework of separate mutually reinforcing instruments, backed by a strong system of verification'.[97] A prominent plea for a world free from nuclear weapons has been made by Henry Kissinger, George Schultz, William Perry and Sam Nunn.[98] Similar pleas were made by former Foreign Secretary Douglas Hurd,[99] former Prime Minister Malcolm Fraser[100] and former German statesmen including Helmut Schmidt, Richard von Weizsäcker and Hans-Dietrich Genscher, who also developed practical steps to be taken for implementation.[101]

The International Movement of the Red Cross and Red Crescent has repeatedly pointed to the catastrophic humanitarian consequences of any use of nuclear weapons and the need for a legally binding international instrument that will prohibit the use of such weapons and lead to their elimination.[102]

While these initiatives have received a wide international echo, they have not led to immediate political action by governments so far (see Section 3.6).

3 Gaps in legal regulation: general principles and their role in practice

In view of the voluntary character of treaty law, the reference to existing gaps is disputable in general.[103] This is all the more relevant for treaties on arms control and non-proliferation.[104] Hence no gaps in law will be discussed here, but gaps in prescription deriving from factual behaviour of states and non-state actors as compared with the declared policy goals which are expressed in the three pillars of the NPT.

---

97 NPT Review Conference 2010 (n 83) 20; Tim Wright, 'Negotiations for a Nuclear Weapons Convention: Distant Dream or Present Possibility?' (2009) 10 *Melbourne JIL* 217.

98 See Henry A Kissinger, George P Schultz, William J Perry and Sam Nunn, 'Toward a Nuclear-Free World' *Wall Street Journal* (15 January 2008).

99 Douglas Hurd, Malcolm Rifkind, David Owen and George Robertson, 'Start Worrying and Learn to Ditch the Bomb' *The Times* (London, 30 June 2008).

100 Malcolm Fraser, Gustav Nossal, Barry Jones, Peter Gration, John Sanderson and Tilman Ruff, 'Imagine There's No Bomb' *Age* (Melbourne, 8 April 2009).

101 Helmut Schmidt, Richard von Weizsäcker, Egon Bahr and Hans-Dietrich Genscher, 'Für eine atomwaffenfreie Welt' *Frankfurter Allgemeine Zeitung* (9 January 2009).

102 See n 57.

103 Jörg Kammerhofer, 'Gaps, the Nuclear Weapons Advisory Opinion and the Structure of International Legal Argument between Theory and Practice' (2009) 80 *BYBIL* 333, 354–360.

104 Dieter Fleck, 'Consequences of Withdrawal from Non-Proliferation Obligations and the Need for Dispute Settlement' in Daniel H Joyner and Marco Roscini (eds), *Non-Proliferation Law as a Special Regime* (CUP 2012) 250.

3.1 Implementation of the Comprehensive Test-Ban Treaty

A first such gap is to be seen in the failure of states so far to achieve a worldwide comprehensive nuclear test ban and make it legally binding. Annex 2 of the 1996 Comprehensive Nuclear-Test-Ban Treaty (CTBT)[105] lists 44 states which participated in the negotiations of the Treaty and possessed nuclear power or research reactors at the time. In accordance with Article XIV CTBT these 44 states must become parties for the Treaty to enter into force. Three of them (India, North Korea and Pakistan) have not yet signed the Treaty and an additional five states (China, Egypt, Iran, Israel and the US) have signed but not yet ratified. Even after the CTBT was opened for signature, nuclear tests were conducted by India (1998), Pakistan (1998), and North Korea (2006 and 2009).

The Preparatory Commission for the Comprehensive Nuclear-Test-Ban Treaty Organization (CTBTO), founded in 1996, is tasked with building up the verification regime of the CTBT in preparation for the Treaty's entry into force as well as promoting the Treaty's universality. It is an interim organisation based in Vienna with over 260 staff from over 70 countries.[106]

3.2 The fissile material cut-off treaty

While the US, UK, Russia, and France have officially declared an end to their production for weapons and China has unofficially halted its production, India and Pakistan (and possibly Israel and North Korea) continue to produce fissile material for nuclear weapons. A fissile material cut-off treaty which would ban the production of fissile material for nuclear weapons purposes, that is, principally highly enriched uranium and plutonium, has not been achieved so far.[107]

3.3 Prevention of an arms race in outer space

A convention on the prevention of an arms race in outer space could consolidate and expand existing obligations,[108] hitherto confined to the placement of weapons of mass destruction in orbit around the Earth and the stationing of such weapons in outer space, is yet to be negotiated.[109]

3.4 Nuclear and radiation safety and protection

Accidents in nuclear power plants, such as those in Chernobyl 1986 and Fukushima 2011, have increased global awareness of the risks of nuclear radiation. Yet IAEA activities to control nuclear and radiation safety[110] are limited to peaceful uses of nuclear energy.

National nuclear safety agencies are assumingly excluded from military arsenals and little is known about safety standards and control within the latter. International cooperation on this

---

105 See n 2.
106 See www.ctbto.org.
107 Federation of American Scientists, 'Factsheet on the Fissile Material Cutoff Treaty (FMCT)', www.fas.org/nuke/control/fmct/.
108 See n 10 and accompanying text.
109 Federation of American Scientists, 'Factsheet on the Prevention of an Arms Race in Outer Space (PAROS)', www.fas.org/nuke/control/paros/index.html.
110 See eg IAEA, 'International Nuclear and Radiation Safety Experts Conclude IAEA Peer Review of Slovenia's Regulatory System' Press Release 2011/18 (4 October 2011), www.iaea.org/newscenter/pressreleases/2011/prn201118.html.

matter is limited and complicated.[111] Relevant information is strictly classified and nuclear-weapon states under the NPT would deny any acknowledgement of 'nuclear status' to any other state that may have gained nuclear weapons.

3.5 Dispute settlement

The lack of an obligatory dispute settlement may be one of the most notable gaps in this context. As any dispute on issues of nuclear non-proliferation may affect peace and security on a global scale, further action by the Security Council will be called for. Yet recent experience, in particular on North Korea and Iran, shows that the means at hand for the Council, may not be the most effective. Measures under Chapter VII may be necessary as a means of last resort, but they hardly provide effective remedies for the root causes of disputes. They sometimes undermine other important goals of the UN, may have negative social impacts and deny cooperation with the target state rather than encouraging it. As meaningful steps of escalation are often not available, premature sanctions may even weaken the authority of the Council to take action as a last resort.

Such considerations should lead to strengthen forms of peaceful settlement of disputes, as called for under Article 2(3) of the UN Charter, and to develop appropriate forums and procedures for such activity. The UN Secretary-General and competent international organisations such as the IAEA are challenged here to take appropriate initiatives in an effective and timely manner.

3.6 General and complete nuclear disarmament under strict and effective international control

While large numbers of nuclear warheads still exist,[112] reliance on nuclear weapons for deterrence is widely considered as increasingly hazardous and decreasingly effective. It appears realistic to conclude:

> So long as any State has such weapons – especially nuclear arms – others will want them. So long as any such weapons remain in any State's arsenal, there is a high risk that they will one day be used, by design or accident. Any such use would be catastrophic.[113]

In contrast to these considerations, several states pursue activities to further develop and/or modernise nuclear weapons, missile systems and platforms. It is true that the nature of the problem requires a consideration of future threats, the most relevant aspects of which will be hardly foreseeable. This should caution expectations for effective measures of nuclear disarmament within foreseeable timeframes. Yet it may also be considered that there can be security benefits of early advances on further cuts to nuclear weapon stockpiles.[114]

---

111 For an exchange between UK and India, and UK and Pakistan, see Quinlan (n 6) 133–149.
112 See n 75.
113 See Weapons of Mass Destruction Commission, 'Weapons of Terror: Freeing the World of Nuclear, Biological and Chemical Arms' (2006), www.blixassociates.com/final-report; Michael Spies and John Burroughs (eds), *Nuclear Disorder or Cooperative Security? U.S. Weapons of Terror, the Global Proliferation Crisis, and Paths to Peace* (May 2007), wmdreport.org/ndcs/online.
114 See International Commission on Nuclear Non-Proliferation and Disarmament, 'Eliminating Nuclear Threats: A Practical Agenda for Global Policymakers' (November 2009), icnnd.org/reference/reports/ent. See also Malcolm Chalmers, *Less is Better: Nuclear Restraint at Low Numbers* (Routledge 2012).

4 Conclusions and outlook

While the complexity of the topic and its importance for global security requires further study and combined activities,[115] some general conclusions may be drawn here to support and inform continued efforts in this field:

1   A comprehensive legal assessment of issues related to nuclear weapons cannot be confined to international humanitarian law; it has to consider the impact of other branches of international law, in particular human rights, environmental law, arms control and disarmament law.
2   The question whether nuclear weapons development, acquisition and possession can be justified remains linked to scenarios that should be perceived even if an actual use of such weapons would be unlawful in hindsight.
3   The legality of the threat or use of nuclear weapons is influenced by existing security threats triggering the development, production, testing, stockpiling and transfer of those weapons and their carrier systems. The right of pre-emptive/anticipatory self-defence has to be considered in this context.
4   The question whether the threat or use of nuclear weapons could be justified in an armed conflict, depends on circumstances that are extremely remote and less likely today than under the conditions of the Cold War.
5   Efforts to close open gaps in the present treaty system, most particularly the implementation of the 1996 Comprehensive Test Ban Treaty, the conclusion of a Fissile Material Cut-off Treaty, the prevention of an arms race in outer space, an enhancement of nuclear and radiation safety and protection, and an improvement of peaceful settlement of any dispute on these matters, may also facilitate steps for reaching the ultimate goal of nuclear disarmament and remain relevant even after that goal has been reached.
6   The need for general and complete nuclear disarmament under strict and effective international control requires strict compliance with the 1968 Treaty on the Non-Proliferation of Nuclear Weapons and reliable cooperation by non-parties to that Treaty.
7   Even a verifiable prohibition of the development, production and stockpiling of nuclear weapons and on their complete destruction would not eliminate the knowledge of relevant activities; neither would it effectively ensure that terrorist actors could not get hold of such weapons. Nevertheless concrete steps towards outlawing nuclear weapons remains as essential for peace and security as the prohibitions of chemical and biological weapons that are already part of international law today.

---

115 See International Law Association, 'Work Plan for the Committee on Nuclear Weapons, Non-Proliferation & Contemporary International Law' (29 August 2011), www.ila-hq.org/en/committees/index.cfm/cid/1025.

14
Methods of land warfare

William J Fenrick*

One might well regard the traditional methods of waging land warfare as battle, devastation and siege. This chapter will begin by addressing quarter, the extent of the obligation to accept surrender. Devastation, starvation and siege will then be addressed. The chapter will conclude by addressing permissible and impermissible deception; and espionage and sabotage. Targeting issues and the weapons used in battle are addressed in other chapters.[1] The discussion will be closely linked to the ICRC Customary International Humanitarian Law Study (CIHL) as Rules 46 to 69 of the Study constitute the most recent attempt at a relatively comprehensive overview of the topics addressed in the chapter. It must be observed, however, that the CIHL focused more on prohibitions than permissions, with the result that methods of warfare such as siege warfare and espionage are not fully addressed.

Treaty-based roots for the laws concerning means and methods of land warfare are, for the most part, found in Hague Law provisions. The Lieber Code of 1863, which was adopted by Federal forces in the American Civil War of 1861–1865 (a non-international armed conflict but one on a massive scale), prohibits the denial of quarter,[2] limits the right of one side to exercise control over the property of the other or of its nationals,[3] prohibits acting in bad faith,[4] explicitly permits starvation as a method of war,[5] addresses espionage and sabotage,[6] and permits ruses and prohibits perfidy.[7]

---

* An earlier version of this chapter appeared as 'Specific Methods of Warfare' in Elizabeth Wilmshurst and Susan Breau (eds), *Perspectives on the ICRC Study on Customary International Humanitarian Law* (CUP 2007) ch 9. Parts of that chapter are reproduced here with the kind permission of Cambridge University Press.

1 See Part II of this volume regarding the principle of distinction and chs 11–13 on particular weapons.
2 Instruction for the Government of Armies of the United States in the Field, General Orders no 100 ('Lieber Code') (24 April 1863), reprinted in Dietrich Schindler and Jiří Toman (eds), *The Laws of Armed Conflict* (4th edn, Martinus Nijhoff 2004) 3, arts 60–62, 66.
3 Ibid arts 31, 34–38, 44–45, 72–73.
4 Ibid art 11.
5 Ibid arts 17–18.
6 Ibid arts 83–84, 88, 98–100, 102, 104.
7 Ibid art 101.

The 1907 Hague Regulations also address methods of land warfare: denial of quarter, treacherous killing or wounding, improper use of flags of truce and enemy uniforms, and destruction or seizure of enemy property,[8] ruses of war,[9] pillage,[10] spies[11] and treatment of property in occupied territory.[12]

The 1949 Geneva Conventions, insofar as they regulate international conflict, do not address denial of quarter, deception, communication with the enemy or starvation as a method of warfare. Geneva Convention IV supplements the Hague Regulations and repeats the prohibition of pillage,[13] addresses treatment of property in occupied territory[14] and addresses provision of relief supplies in occupied territory.[15] Geneva Convention I contains specific rules applicable to military medical units.[16] Geneva Convention III indicates what items found with prisoners of war are not to be considered booty.[17] Further, the Geneva Conventions list 'extensive destruction and appropriation of (protected) property, not justified by military necessity and carried out unlawfully and wantonly' as grave breaches.[18] Common Article 3 of the Conventions implicitly prohibits denial of quarter in non-international armed conflicts.

Additional Protocol I addresses what have traditionally been regarded as both Hague law and Geneva law issues, in fact effecting a merger of the two branches of the law of armed conflict. The Protocol deals with denial of quarter,[19] military property assigned to civil defence purposes,[20] (for the first time in a treaty) prohibits starvation of civilians as a method of warfare,[21] addresses relief in favour of the civilian population in areas under enemy control,[22] defines and prohibits perfidy while clearly indicating that ruses of war are permissible[23] and prohibits improper use of certain distinctive emblems, including, in certain circumstances, enemy uniforms.[24]

Additional Protocol II, which applies to non-international armed conflicts, prohibits denial of quarter,[25] prohibits starvation of civilians as a method of warfare[26] and prohibits misuse of the distinctive emblem of the red cross.[27]

Most recently, the Rome Statute, which is, of course, prospective, indicates grave breaches of the Geneva Conventions are war crimes,[28] and goes on to prohibit for international armed conflicts: making improper use of flags of truce, distinctive emblems and enemy uniforms,[29]

8 HR art 23.
9 Ibid art 24.
10 Ibid arts 28, 47.
11 Ibid arts 29–31.
12 Ibid arts 46, 49–54.
13 GCIV art 33.
14 Ibid art 53.
15 Ibid art 59–63.
16 GCI arts 33, 35.
17 GCIII art 18.
18 GCI art 50; GCII art 51; GCIV art 147.
19 API art 40–42 and 85.
20 Ibid arts 22, 23, 30, 67.
21 Ibid art 54.
22 Ibid arts 68–71.
23 Ibid arts 37.
24 Ibid arts 38, 39.
25 APII art 4.
26 Ibid art 14.
27 Ibid art 12.
28 Rome Statute art 8(2)(a).
29 Ibid ¶ (b)(vii).

treacherous killing or wounding,[30] denial of quarter,[31] destroying or seizing enemy property without military necessity,[32] pillage[33] and starvation of civilians as a method of warfare.[34] For non-international armed conflicts, prohibited acts include: pillage,[35] treacherous killing or wounding,[36] denial of quarter[37] and destroying or seizing the adversary's property without military necessity.[38]

1 Denial of quarter

Quarter is mercy (essentially the right to life) granted to an opponent on the condition that the opponent surrenders. Ordering that no quarter will be given, threatening an opponent with no quarter or conducting hostilities on the basis of no quarter is prohibited by a basic and long-standing rule of customary international humanitarian law reflected in CIHL Rule 46. It is most unlikely anyone would challenge its existence or content. The rule is also contained in Article 40 of Additional Protocol I (adopted by consensus) and in Article 4 of Additional Protocol II (adopted by consensus). It is of particular importance to military commanders. This rule is amplified by CIHL Rule 47 which states:

> Attacking persons who are recognized as *hors de combat* is prohibited. A person *hors de combat* is:
>
> (a) Anyone who is in the power of an Adverse Party;
> (b) Anyone who is defenceless because of unconsciousness, shipwreck, wounds or sickness; or
> (c) Anyone who clearly expresses an intention to surrender;
>
> Provided he or she abstains from any hostile act and does not attempt to escape.

This, too, is a longstanding rule of customary international humanitarian law applicable to both international and non-international conflict. It is also contained in Articles 41(1) and 85(3)(e) of Additional Protocol I (both adopted by consensus) and, implicitly, in Common Article 3 of the Geneva Conventions and in Article 4 of Additional Protocol II (adopted by consensus).

Persons who are *hors de combat* under Rule 47(a) and (b) do not pose a threat to an attacker and compliance with these parts of the Rule should not be difficult under normal circumstances. It must, however, be emphasised that once a person is in the power of an adverse party, as the result of a surrender or otherwise, that person may not be attacked even if it is extremely difficult to keep or evacuate prisoners. For example, if a reconnaissance patrol captures a combatant then it may not kill the prisoner even if his or her presence makes mission accomplishment difficult or impossible.

The only real issue is how does one interpret and apply Rule 47(c). In particular, does the person purportedly attempting to surrender actually have the intent and capacity to do so and

30 Ibid ¶ (b)(xi).
31 Ibid ¶ (b)(xii).
32 Ibid ¶ (b)(xiii).
33 Ibid ¶ (b)(xvi).
34 Ibid ¶ (b)(xxv).
35 Ibid ¶ (e)(v).
36 Ibid ¶ (e)(ix).
37 Ibid ¶ (e)(x).
38 Ibid ¶ (e)(xii).

has he or she demonstrated that intent in a timely fashion? It is clear that the simple fact that troops are retreating does not demonstrate an intent to surrender. The Report on United Kingdom Practice in the CIHL cited a former British Director of Army Legal Services who, adverting to an incident in the 1982 Falklands Conflict, stated that UK soldiers were not required to risk their own lives in granting quarter. He added that capture was to take place when circumstances permitted and that, as an example, it might not be practicable to accept surrender of one group of enemy soldiers while under fire from another group.[39] Somewhat similarly, the Report on US Practice referred to an incident in the 1990–1991 Gulf War in which tanks equipped with earthmoving plough blades breached trench lines then turned and filled in the trenches entombing Iraqi defenders.[40] The US defended this practice and asserted

> a soldier who fights to the very last possible minute assumes certain risks. His opponent either may not see his surrender, may not recognize his actions as an attempt to surrender in the heat and confusion of battle, or may find it difficult (if not impossible) to halt an onrushing assault to accept a soldier's last minute effort at surrender.[41]

As a hypothetical, one might also envisage a situation in which troops behind their own lines are overflown by aircraft of an attacking force. Such troops may purport to indicate an intent to surrender by downing arms or putting their hands up, for example. If, however, these troops are not in a position where, because of their location and the resources available to the attacking side, they have the physical capacity to surrender, one might query whether they remain potentially subject to legitimate attack. Persons purporting to surrender must possess both the intent and the capacity to surrender. If an offer to surrender is impossible of acceptance, attack is permissible.

The rule prohibiting denial of quarter is further amplified by CIHL Rule 48 which applies to both international and non-international conflicts and prohibits attacks directed against persons parachuting from an aircraft in distress during their descent. This rule was first codified in Article 42 of Additional Protocol I and, at that time it was not adopted by consensus because some states were of the view that persons landing in their own territory could not be regarded as *hors de combat*. At the present time, there appears to be a general consensus that all persons parachuting from aircraft in distress should be regarded as *hors de combat* and therefore immune from attack. Once parachutists have landed they would normally be regarded as ceasing to be *hors de combat* and therefore subject to the normal attack rules. The commentary to the Rule suggests that such parachutists landing in territory under the control of the adverse party should be given an opportunity to surrender unless it is apparent they are engaging in a hostile act.[42] Rule 48 does not apply to troops who are airborne as part of a military operation and are not bailing out in distress.

2 Devastation, starvation and siege

Attempting to coerce an opponent by devastating his territory, laying siege to his towns and fortresses, and starving his civilians and military personnel has, unfortunately, been a common

---

39 CIHL practice pt VI to r 47(c).
40 CIHL practice pt VI to r 47(b).
41 Ibid.
42 CIHL commentary to r 48.

military practice from time immemorial.[43] Indeed, in the American Civil War, Union generals such as Sherman and Sheridan switched to tactics emphasising devastation precisely because attempts to immunise civilian property from seizure or destruction appeared to be prolonging the war. As recently as the Second World War, legal rulings by the victors on the vanquished imposed relatively limited restrictions on devastation and siege as methods of war. In the *Hostages Trial*, a US Tribunal in Germany acquitted General Rendulic on a charge related to devastation of the Norwegian province of Finnmark which Rendulic carried out to hinder what he anticipated would be a Russian attack in the area. In fact, Soviet forces were not planning such an attack but Rendulic was acquitted because he honestly and reasonably perceived such an attack as imminent and he regarded the destruction of property as justified by military necessity.[44] In the *High Command Case*, another US Tribunal held that under existing customary law a besieging commander was permitted to fire on civilians attempting to escape from Leningrad in order to drive them back into the city and increase the pressure on the defending commander to surrender.[45] Another factor related to the issue of siege warfare is that commanders are extremely reluctant to commit their forces to fighting in built up areas containing large numbers of civilians such as cities or towns because such fighting is extremely likely to result in high casualties among the attacking forces and among the civilians in the area.[46] As an example, in the American attack on Manila in 1945, when American forces were attempting to drive Japanese forces out of a city inhabited by Filipinos allied to the Americans, 16,000 Japanese soldiers died, American forces lost 1,000 killed and 5,000 wounded, Manila was devastated and the bodies of 100,000 Filipino civilians were found in the rubble, most of them killed in the exchange of fire between American and Japanese forces.[47]

According to CIHL Rule 50 '[t]he destruction or seizure of the property of an adversary is prohibited unless required by imperative military necessity' both in international and non-international conflicts. For international armed conflicts this is a longstanding part of customary law codified in Article 23(g) of the Hague Regulations among other places. More recently, for non-international conflicts, it is prohibited by Article 8(2)(e)(xii) of the Rome Statute. Leaving aside the Rome Statute provision which is prospective, one might query whether the evidentiary basis for the application of this rule to non-international conflicts is substantially stronger than the evidentiary basis for Rule 49 (considered below) and the CIHL could not conclude whether or not Rule 49 applied to non-international conflicts. Perhaps it is considered more appropriate to apply Rule 50 to such conflicts because of its more general nature.

---

43 See as examples: for the ancient period, Paul Bentley Kern, *Ancient Siege Warfare* (Indiana University Press 1999); for the medieval period, Sean McGlynn, *By Sword and Fire: Cruelty: Cruelty and Atrocity in Medieval Warfare* (Phoenix 2009), Maurice H Keen, *The Laws of War in the Late Middle Ages* (Routledge/Keegan Paul 1965); Richard L C Jones, 'Fortifications and Sieges in Western Europe, *c.*800–1450' in Maurice Keen, *Medieval Warfare: A History* (OUP 1999) 163; for the practice of chevauchee or devastation in the medieval period see in particular, Clifford J Roger, *War Cruel and Sharp: English Strategy Under Edward III, 1327–1360* (Boydell 2000); for the siege of Quebec in 1759 and devastation of the surrounding countryside, see Dan Snow, *Death or Victory: The Battle of Quebec and the Birth of Empire* (Allen Lane 2009); for the American Civil War, see Mark E Neely Jr, *The Civil War and the Limits of Destruction* (Harvard University Press 2007) and Noah Andre Trudeau, *Southern Storm: Sherman's March to the Sea* (Harper 2008).
44 *US v List et al (Hostages Trial)* 11 TWC 1230, 1296 (US Military Tribunal at Nuremberg, 1947).
45 *US v von Leeb et al (High Command Trial)* 11 TWC 462, 563 (US Military Tribunal at Nuremberg, 1947).
46 Alice Hills, *Future Wars in Cities: Rethinking a Liberal Dilemma* (Frank Cass 2004).
47 R Smith, *Trimph in the Philippines* (USGPO 1963) 237–308 (account of the battle), 306–307 (casualty figures).

As worded, Rule 50 might be regarded as applicable to both the destruction of property in territory under the control of an adversary by means of an attack and to destruction of property belonging to an adversary in territory under the control of the party by other means. If it does, then 'imperative military necessity' must be equated with the 'definite military advantage' derived from an attack on a military objective (Rule 8). One might query whether this is practicable or desirable. For all practical purposes, Rule 50 has been applied in such a way by a Trial Chamber of the ICTY.[48] In that case, in substance, the court held that an attack which resulted in damage to a civilian object and which was directed at the civilian object was not required by imperative military necessity. Presumably the court would also have decided that an attack which was directed at a military objective but which resulted in excessive/disproportionate damage to civilian objects could not be justified by imperative military necessity. Whether the approach adopted by the ICTY will be followed in future remains to be seen.[49]

CIHL Rule 49 states: 'The parties to the conflict may seize military equipment belonging to an adverse party as war booty.' Although one may query the precise parameters of war booty, there is no question that this rule is well embedded in customary law related to international armed conflict. The compilers/authors of the CIHL were, however, unable to identify a rule of customary law which would either permit or prohibit such seizures in non-international armed conflicts. One might debate this conclusion as, presumably, whether formally labelled war booty or not, the parties to non-international armed conflicts seize and use military equipment belonging to the adverse party whenever possible. It is suggested that a more rigorous approach, perhaps an unnecessarily rigorous approach, has been adopted concerning the identification of rules related to permissible activities concerning property than concerning the identification of other rules related to non-international armed conflict. That being said, it must be noted that, if one assumes seizure or destruction of military equipment belonging to an adverse party is always required by imperative military necessity, Rule 49 is subsumed under Rule 50 and Rule 50 does apply to all conflicts.

Rule 49 indicates seizure must be by an adverse party and for an adverse party. It does not legitimize seizure for private purposes, such as war trophies. It also limits the scope of such seizures. There are special rules applicable to military medical units set forth in Geneva Convention I, and to medical ships and aircraft and to material and buildings of military units permanently assigned to civil defence organisations set forth in Additional Protocol I.[50] War booty includes all enemy military equipment or property captured or found on the battlefield except for the personal belongings and protective gear of prisoners of war. If private property found on the battlefield includes arms, ammunition, military equipment or military papers it may also be seized as booty. Booty may be used without restriction and need not be returned to an adversary on the cessation of hostilities.

---

48 *Prosecutor v Strugar* (Case no IT-01-42-T, ICTY, 31 January 2005). Strugar was convicted for the shelling of the Old Town of Dubrovnik for a violation of art 3(d) of the ICTY Statute which, among other things, penalised destruction or wilful damage done to institutions dedicated to religion and to historic monuments but the analysis of culpability involved essentially similar legal issues. The Old Town of Dubrovnik is generally regarded as constituting, in entirety, a cultural or historic monument. The Trial Chamber was satisfied that the elements of related charges for attacking civilian objects and for causing devastation not justified by military necessity were established but held that the art 3(d) charge most effectively encapsulated the prohibited conduct.

49 As a former staff member of the ICTY Office of the Prosecutor, the author must observe that prosecutors will tend to adopt a defensible practice of multiple charging unless there is substantial jurisprudence indicating only one charge is appropriate, in order to ensure that the prohibited conduct is accurately identified to the satisfaction of the Trial Chamber.

50 GCI arts 33, 35; API arts 22, 23, 30, 67 respectively.

Pillage involves the forcible taking of property for private purposes from the Adverse Party or from persons linked to the Adverse Party. Pillage and plunder are synonyms. Pillage is prohibited in both international and non-international conflicts (CIHL Rule 52). This rule is a longstanding part of customary law and is, in substance, a specific application of the general principle of law prohibiting theft. The rule is also codified in Article 33 of Geneva Convention IV and in Article 4 of Additional Protocol II.

CIHL Rule 53 prohibits the use of starvation of the civilian population as a method of warfare in both international and non-international conflict. Starvation of civilians as a method of warfare was first prohibited by treaty in Article 54 of Additional Protocol I and Article 14 of Additional Protocol II. Prior to the adoption of the Additional Protocols in 1977, starvation of civilians was regarded as an acceptable method of warfare. Since then it would appear from the CIHL to have developed into a rule of customary law applicable to all conflicts. One might query the extent to which this development applies to long established methods of warfare such as siege. If the authorities in an encircled area make a conscious decision to choose guns over butter with the result that civilians in the encircled area are deprived of essential foodstuffs, presumably it would be inappropriate to accuse the commander of the encircling forces of using starvation as a method of warfare. The CIHL itself states: 'The prohibition of starvation as a method of warfare does not prohibit siege warfare as long as the purpose is to achieve a military objective and not to starve a civilian population.'[51] One might query whether this rather modest qualifier is sufficient.

One highly respected but relatively conservative legal writer, Yoram Dinstein, has subjected Article 54 of Additional Protocol I (and, by implication, Article 14 of Additional Protocol II) to ferocious criticism where siege warfare is concerned as, in his view, there is no alternative means, other than assault, which is almost always extremely costly to all, for bringing about the capture of defended towns.[52] Dinstein concluded his observations on the starvation prohibition as follows:

> It stands to reason that the practice of States will not confirm the sweeping abolition of siege warfare affecting civilians. Possibly, a construction of the language of Article 54 will be arrived at, whereby siege warfare will continue to be acquiesced with – notwithstanding civilian deprivations – at least in those circumstances when the besieging force is willing to assure civilians a safe passage out.[53]

A P V Rogers, another highly respected writer but one who normally tends to adopt a more liberal/progressive position than that of Professor Dinstein, has also expressed concerns about the viability of a strict application of Article 54 to a siege situation.[54] Considering the importance of the issue, it might well have been appropriate for the authors of the CIHL to have included more extensive rules similar to those in the recent UK *Manual* related to siege, which is a specific method of warfare highly relevant to the starvation issue.[55] In particular, one should note the UK *Manual* which states:

---

51 Jean-Marie Henckaerts and Louise Doswald-Beck (eds), *Customary International Humanitarian Law* (CUP 2005) vol 1, 188.
52 Yoram Dinstein, *The Conduct of Hostilities Under the Law of International Armed Conflict* (CUP 2004) 133–137.
53 Ibid 137.
54 A P V Rogers, *Law on the Battlefield* (3rd edn, Manchester University Press 2012) 140–142.
55 UK Ministry of Defence, *The Manual of the Law of Armed Conflict* (OUP 2004) ¶ 5.34 for sieges.

The military authorities of the besieged area might decide not to permit the evacuation of civilians or the civilians themselves might decide to stay where they are. In those circumstances, so long as the besieging commander left open his offer to allow civilians and the wounded and sick to leave the besieged area, he would be justified in preventing any supplies from reaching that area.[56]

CIHL Rule 54 is a corollary to Rule 53 and it prohibits attacking, destroying, removing or rendering useless objects indispensable to the survival of the civilian population in both international and non-international conflicts. As with Rule 53, the first treaty law prohibitions of such attacks are contained in Article 54 of Additional Protocol I and Article 14 of Additional Protocol II. Both articles list examples of such objects including foodstuffs, agricultural areas for the production of foodstuffs, crops, livestock, drinking water installations and supplies and irrigation works. The lists are not intended to be exhaustive and the commentary to Rule 54 suggests other items might well be included such as medical supplies and means of shelter.[57] The commentary also adverts to two exceptions to the rule referred to in Additional Protocol I: (i) the objects may be attacked if they are used as sustenance solely for combatants or otherwise in direct support of military action provided, in the latter case, that such action does not starve the civilian population or force its movement (Article 54(3)), and (ii) a state may, on the basis of imperative military necessity, use a 'scorched earth policy' on and in defence of national territory against invasion. The commentary suggests, however, that neither exception applies to non-international armed conflict because they are not referred to in Additional Protocol II.[58]

The Rule has been criticised as overly broad in a recent decision of the Eritrea-Ethiopia Claims Commission.[59] In that decision, the Commission, which is evaluating claims in an international armed conflict, was required to determine customary law relating to attacks on a water reservoir. It held that:

> the provisions of Article 54 [of Additional Protocol I] that prohibit attacks against drinking water installations and supplies that are indispensable to the survival of the civilian population for the specific purpose of denying them for their sustenance value to the adverse Party had become part of customary international humanitarian law by 1999.[60]

The same decision concluded that the ICRC Study 'concludes that a broader prohibition than the one stated in Article 54(2) has become customary law. The Commission need not, and does not, endorse the study's broader conclusion.'[61] It would appear, however, that the scope of Rule 54 standing alone is narrowed by the study commentary.

CIHL Rules 55 and 56 are designed to facilitate the provision of assistance to the civilian population while allowing parties to the conflict to maintain control over the process. Both apply to international and non-international conflict. Rule 55 states: 'The parties to the conflict must allow and facilitate rapid and unimpeded passage of humanitarian relief for civilians in need, which is impartial in character and conducted without any adverse distinction, subject to their right of control.' This Rule is an abbreviated version of Article 23 of Geneva Convention

---

56 Ibid ¶ 5.34.3.
57 CIHL commentary to r 54.
58 Ibid.
59 *Eritrea v Ethiopia (Partial Award: Western Front, Aerial Bombardment and Related Claims, Eritrea's Claims 1, 3 ,5, 9–13, 14, 21, 25 and 26)* (2005) 26 RIAA 291.
60 Ibid 28–30.
61 Ibid fn 23.

IV and of Article 70 of Additional Protocol I. There is no analogous provision in Additional Protocol II. It would appear to balance the requirements of the parties to the conflict to exercise control over activities in areas within their power with the need for passage of humanitarian relief to civilians. Optics notwithstanding, the parties do retain a substantial degree of control over the process. Because of this factor, it should be acceptable as a customary law rule for all conflicts. Rule 56 states: 'The parties to the conflict must ensure the freedom of movement of authorized humanitarian relief personnel essential to the exercise of their functions. Only in case of imperative military necessity may their movements be temporarily restricted.' This Rule is a slightly modified version of Article 71(3) of Additional Protocol I. There is no analogous provision in Additional Protocol II. As with Rule 55 above, the parties do retain a degree of control over the process and, because of this, it should be an acceptable customary rule for all conflicts. Although Article 71(4) of Additional Protocol I is not referred to in the Rule or the related commentary, perhaps it is included by implication. It states:

> Under no circumstances may relief personnel exceed the terms of their mission under this Protocol. In particular, they shall take account of the security concerns of the Party in whose territory they are carrying out their duties. The mission of any of the personnel who do not respect these conditions may be terminated.

3 Permissible and impermissible deception

CIHL Rule 57 states that the following rule applies to both international and non-international conflicts: 'Ruses of war are not prohibited as long as they do not infringe a rule of International Humanitarian Law.' This rule is an extremely useful statement of the obvious. No military commander views combat as a fair fight. If the odds are even, something is wrong. Most recently, Article 37(2) of Additional Protocol I has codified this area of the law as follows:

> Ruses of war are not prohibited. Such ruses are acts which are intended to mislead an adversary or to induce him to act recklessly but which infringe no rule of international law applicable in armed conflict and which are not perfidious because they do not invite the confidence of an adversary with respect to protection under the law.

There is no similar provision in the final version of Additional Protocol II but the applicability of the Rule to non-international armed conflict is unlikely to be questioned. Belligerent forces are expected to be on guard against legitimate ruses but they are entitled to expect their opponents to comply with applicable international humanitarian law. The list of permissible ruses is never closed. The current UK *Manual* gives several examples, including surprises and ambushes.[62]

Additional rules of CIHL prohibit the improper use of the white flag of truce, of the distinctive emblems of the Geneva Conventions, of the United Nations emblem and uniform, of other internationally recognised emblems, of the flags, military emblems, insignia or uniforms of the adverse party and of the flags, military emblems, insignia or uniforms of states not party to the conflict.[63] All of the rules apply to international armed conflict and, with the arguable exceptions of the enemy and non-party uniform rules, to non-international conflicts.

---

62 UK *Manual* (n 17) ¶ 5.17.2.
63 CIHL rr 58–63.

The one contentious rule in this list is Rule 62 which states: 'Improper Use of the Flags or Military Emblems, Insignia or Uniforms of the Adversary Is Prohibited.' The commentary concludes this rule is customary for international armed conflicts and should also apply on non-international armed conflicts when the parties to the conflict do in fact wear uniforms. This conclusion is quite reasonable. The question, however, is: what is improper use? There has been a longstanding debate on this issue in which, generally speaking, representatives of major military powers argue that enemy military uniforms could be worn except in combat while representatives of smaller military powers argue that use of enemy uniforms is prohibited in a much wider range of circumstances. Prior to the development of Additional Protocol I, the applicable rule would appear to have been the so-called Skorzeny Rule. In the Trial of Otto Skorzeny following the Second World War, all of the accused were acquitted by an American court because the prosecution did not establish the accused, German soldiers, had actually worn American uniforms in combat during the Ardennes Offensive in December 1944 although it had established they wore such uniforms in the operational area.[64] Although an American court acquitted Skorzeny and his co-accused in their trial in 1947, 18 members of Skorzeny's unit who were captured in US uniforms during the Ardennes Offensive were executed as spies shortly thereafter.[65]

Article 39(2) of Additional Protocol I states: 'It is prohibited to make use of the flags or military emblems, insignia or uniforms of adverse Parties while engaging in attacks or in order to shield, favour, protect or impede military operations.' Quite obviously, this rule imposes much greater restrictions on the use of enemy uniforms than the Skorzeny Rule. The only Party to Additional Protocol I which has reserved on Article 39(2) is Canada, for reasons probably impossible to decipher at the present time. Before and since the adoption of Additional Protocol I, many states have continued to have some of their forces make use of enemy uniforms in a variety of circumstances. The respected American author, W Hays Parks, has compiled a substantial but not exhaustive list of examples of use of enemy uniforms in a variety of circumstances by several countries.[66] Although this list is extremely impressive, it is by no means clear what legal weight should be assigned to it as one cannot determine whether states authorised these acts on the assumption they were legally permissible or as a calculated risk taken in defiance of the applicable legal norms.

The commentary tends to beg the question of the parameters of permissible use of enemy uniforms by stating 'It cannot be concluded that the wearing of enemy uniforms outside of combat would be improper.'[67] It is submitted that, bearing in mind present state practice, the following less anaemic formulation must be preferred: 'the wearing of enemy uniforms outside of combat is permitted'. This approach is not applicable to military aircraft. As the insignia on military aircraft cannot be changed in mid-flight, any use of enemy insignia on military aircraft in areas where they might be engaged in operations is prohibited.

Although ruses of war are permissible, the CIHL indicates that killing, injuring or capturing an adversary by resort to perfidy is prohibited in both international and non-international conflicts.[68] This is a longstanding rule of customary international law. The final version of

---

64 *US v Skorzeny* 9 LRTWC 90, 90–93 (General Military Government Court of the US Zone of Germany, 1947).

65 James J Weingartner, 'Otto Skorzeny and the Laws of War' (1991) 55 *Journal of Military History* 207, 217–218, referred to in W Hays Parks, 'Special Forces Wear of Non-Standard Uniforms' (2003) 4 *Chicago JIL* 493, 545.

66 Parks (n 65) Annex, 545–560.

67 Henckaerts and Doswald-Beck (n 51) vol I, 216.

68 CIHL r 65.

Additional Protocol II does not contain a perfidy provision. It is codified and defined in Article 37(1) of Additional Protocol I which states in part:

> It is prohibited to kill, injure or capture an adversary by resort to perfidy. Acts inviting the confidence of an adversary to lead him to believe that he is entitled to, or is obliged to accord, protection under the rules of international law applicable in armed conflict, with intent to betray that confidence, shall constitute perfidy.

The same provision goes on to give the following examples of perfidy:

(a) the feigning of an intent to negotiate under a flag of truce or of a surrender;
(b) the feigning of an incapacitation by wounds or sickness;
(c) the feigning of civilian, non-combatant status; and
(d) the feigning of protected status by the use of signs, emblems or uniforms of the United Nations or of neutral or other States not Parties to the conflict.

These examples are just that, examples. They are prohibited in all conflicts, not merely international conflicts. It should be noted that improper wearing of enemy uniforms as referred to in Rule 62 above is not perfidious because international humanitarian law (IHL) does not require a party to a conflict to accord protection to soldiers wearing its own uniforms.

The commentary notes that the Hague Regulations prohibit 'to kill or wound treacherously' while Additional Protocol I prohibits 'to kill, injure or capture an adversary by resort to perfidy' and asserts, quite reasonably, that killing, injuring or capturing by resort to perfidy are all prohibited under customary law.[69] Although Articles 8(2)(b)(xi) and (e)(ix) of the Rome Statute use the Hague Regulations formulation in listing war crimes, the risk of killing or injuring is so high in attempting to capture by means of perfidy that excluding capture from Rule 65 is nonsensical.

The Commentary to this Rule discusses what it refers to as 'treacherous attempt upon the life of an enemy' and what might also be referred to as 'assassination'.[70] It appears to regard assassination as being embraced in entirety by either or both of treacherous killing or attacking civilian(s). One might question whether a separate rule is needed for this particular topic. Bearing in mind the range of state practice as referred to in the customary law study, the potential significance of the topic, even in wartime, and the desirability of addressing closely related issues such as outlawry and offering rewards, it is submitted that the general adoption of rules essentially similar to the rules in the current UK *Manual* addressing both assassination and outlawry would be desirable and justifiable. These state:

> 5.13 Whether or not the killing of a selected individual is lawful depends on the circumstances of the case. There is no rule dealing specifically with assassination, but the following rules would be applicable in such a case:
>
> a. attacks may not be directed against civilians, . . .
> b. attacks must be limited to military objectives, including enemy combatants, . . .
> c. only combatants have the right to participate directly in hostilities,
> d. enemy combatants may not be killed by resort to perfidy, . . .

69 CIHL commentary to r 65.
70 Ibid.

5.14 The proscription or outlawing or of the putting of a price on the head of an enemy individual or any offer for an enemy 'dead or alive' is prohibited.

5.14.1 The prohibition extends to offers of rewards for the killing or wounding of all enemies, or of a class of enemy persons, such as officers. On the other hand, offers of rewards for the capture unharmed of enemy personnel generally or of particular enemy personnel would be lawful.[71]

4 Espionage and sabotage

The parties to an armed conflict routinely gather information or intelligence about their adverse parties by all available means in order to conduct their operations effectively. Indeed, they must do so in order to comply with their various legal obligations such as the obligation to observe the principle of distinction when making targeting decisions. On the other hand, the adverse party can be expected to use all available countermeasures to prevent the gathering of accurate information. One of the methods used to gather information, even in these technologically sophisticated times, is spying or espionage.

The basic legal rules concerning espionage remain those in Articles 29–31 of the Hague Regulations and these provisions can be regarded as part of customary law. In brief, under these articles: (a) a spy is a person who, acting clandestinely or under false pretences, (b) obtains or endeavours to obtain information behind enemy lines, (c) with the intention of communicating it to the hostile party. A person who gathers information openly, for example, as a member of a uniformed military party on a reconnaissance mission behind enemy lines, is not a spy. Espionage is not a war crime and neither the spies themselves nor those who send them on missions are war criminals.[72] On the other hand, because effective espionage can confer a substantial advantage on the party making use of the tool, the other party is entitled to punish captured spies, often severely, under their national law or the law in effect in occupied territory following a fair trial. One might observe that, if spying was a war crime, the party using spies would be prohibited from so doing and would also be obligated to punish spies after they return from their mission. Instead, spies are often rewarded or decorated for successful missions and, indeed, Article 31 of the Hague Regulations provides that a spy who is captured by the adverse party after returning to his own armed forces must be treated as a prisoner of war and may not be punished for his or her acts of spying.

Sabotage is normally regarded as action taken by individuals or small units operating in enemy controlled territory to damage or destroy material, works or installations in that territory.[73] Sabotage can, in some circumstances, be an extremely discriminate method of warfare which minimises the risk to civilians and civilian objects. Whether or not acts of sabotage are lawful under IHL depends on a variety of factors: (a) is the object attacked a military objective? (b) is the damage anticipated from the attack in compliance with the principle of proportionality? and (c) how is the attack carried out? and (d) what is the status under IHL of the individuals carrying out the attack? If the object attacked is a military objective and the damage anticipated from the attack is not expected to infringe the proportionality principle, there is no violation of

71 UK *Manual* (n 17) ¶¶ 5.13–5.14.1.
72 R R Baxter, 'So-Called "Unprivileged Belligerency": Spies, Guerrillas, and Saboteurs' (1951) 28 *BYBIL* 323, 330–331.
73 Pietro Verry, *Dictionary of the International Law of Armed Conflict* (ICRC 1992) 101.

IHL as such, for the same reasons as the commission of acts of espionage do not violate IHL.[74] On the other hand, as sabotage can confer a substantial advantage on the party making use of this method of war, captured saboteurs may be tried and severely punished by the adverse party under its national law or the law in effect in the occupied territory unless the saboteurs can establish they had combatant status when the acts of sabotage were committed.

5 Conclusions

Leaving aside weapons and targeting, which are addressed elsewhere, the legal issues related to methods of land warfare discussed in this chapter would not appear to be ripe for revisiting. Although one might argue about particular applications of the law, the IHL concerning denial of quarter, permissible and impermissible deception, espionage and sabotage appears to be relatively straightforward. The only area where it is considered some additional discussion and analysis might be helpful is that of devastation, starvation and siege, particularly siege warfare. Although one might like to think that siege is an obsolete method of warfare, it is not. It is a fact that, in contemporary society, the civilian population and civilian objects are often intermixed with military forces and military objectives. A legal fiat that 'this must not be done' is simply unworkable as urban spaces are not, or at least are rarely, designed with future armed conflict in mind. Further, fighting in urban areas or Fighting In Built Up Areas (FIBUA is the military acronym) is dreaded by all military commanders who wish to limit death or injury to their own forces or to the civilian population. A generally agreed approach to the application of the principle prohibiting starvation as a method of warfare to siege situations would be helpful. Such an approach must take account of both military and humanitarian requirements. A simple statement that starvation is always prohibited even in siege situations will not contribute to the primary purpose of IHL, the reduction of civilian suffering in armed conflict.

74 Baxter (n 72).

15
Law of naval warfare
David Letts and Rob McLaughlin

The law of naval warfare (LONW) is a specialised component of international humanitarian law (IHL), focused upon the application of fundamental IHL principles to maritime operational conduct. Contextually, this encompasses both the unique nature of the maritime environment and a long history of mediated resolutions to tensions between trade, maritime communications and maritime security, common heritage and sovereignty, and armed conflict and neutrality. Perhaps because of this mediating function, LONW has rarely kept pace with either tactical or technological developments in maritime operations,[1] although it has (at least since the 1990s) responded efficiently to norm crystallisation in terms of the general management and regulation of the maritime domain. This tendency to lag tactics and technology defines what is perhaps the core thematic challenge faced by the LONW: the scant likelihood of naval armed conflict occurring in the 'classic' way envisaged when much of the black letter law was crafted. This is not to say that situations do not arise where traditional LONW clearly applies – the maritime aspects of the 2003 Iraq War (such as visit and search, albeit with the complicating overlay of a UN Security Council (UNSC) sanctions regime in parallel operation), and the 2006 blockade with respect to the Israel–Lebanon conflict, provide two recent examples of relatively traditional applications of LONW. The form and nature of challenges to the utility and interpretation of traditional LONW vary widely, but are illustrated in four discrete, but indicative, issues: (1) non-international armed conflict (NIAC) at sea (and in particular some of the as-yet unresolved issues that surround the application of LONW to Sri Lankan maritime operations against the LTTE (the Tamil Tigers),[2]

---

1 D P O'Connell, *The Influence of Law on Seapower* (Naval Institute Press 1975) xiii.
2 For background on the maritime dimensions of the final years of the NIAC in Sri Lanka, see Justin O Smith, *Maritime Interdiction in Counterinsurgency: The Role of the Sri Lankan Navy in the Defeat of the Tamil Tigers* (thesis, US Naval Postgraduate School 2010) 46–58, www.dtic.mil/dtic/tr/fulltext/u2/a524725. pdf; see also Martin N Murphy, 'Maritime Threat: Tactics and Technology of the Sea Tigers' *Jane's Intelligence Review* (1 June 2006).

and the Gaza Flotilla incident);[3] (2) the seduction of paradigm blurring – from constabulary operations into armed conflict operations – that is a defining operational factor of the incidence of maritime terrorism[4] (although this is also of course a broader IHL challenge); (3) issues of status raised by increased mixing of military and civilian crews and personnel at sea,[5] along with the increased potential for civilians to be characterised as taking a direct part in hostilities at sea;[6] and (4) the unavoidable interpretive challenges that weaponised technologies such as cyber, and unmanned and even autonomous surface and subsurface combat vehicles[7] portend for traditional black letter LONW, as equally as for broader IHL. This chapter, however, will focus upon the historical development of the LONW, rather than its likely responses to these many current and future challenges.

This chapter will address the LONW narrowly defined – that is, IHL which applies to armed conflict at sea. To this end, the overlapping issues of maritime law enforcement, and UNSC resolution and sanctions enforcement, are not dealt with except insofar as is necessary to highlight a relevant distinction or point. The chapter begins with a brief assessment of the way in which uniquely maritime thematic concerns have influenced the development of LONW, focusing upon two of these as indicative examples: the oceans as the venue of armed conflict at sea, and the overt 'stakeholder' status of maritime trade and commerce as an influence upon the development of LONW (Section 1). The chapter then progresses to an account of the major instruments, cases and soft law sources of LONW (Section 2). This is followed by an analysis of those 'means and methods' issues which are generally unique to LONW, but remain of enduring utility – issues such as blockade, visit and search, and naval mine warfare (Section 3).

1 Thematic issues which overlay the application of IHL at sea

In considering the nature and substance of LONW, it is important briefly to note the thematic issues which attend the application of IHL at sea, and which – consequently – are vital to understanding how LONW has developed and is applied. These contextual influences are many, but it will suffice to describe briefly two closely entwined – indeed iterative – thematic factors, which will indicate the form and colour of these influences.

---

3 General Assembly, Human Rights Council, 'Report of the International Fact-Finding Mission to Investigate Violations of International Law, including International Humanitarian and Human Rights Law, Resulting from the Israeli Attacks on the Flotilla of Ships carrying Humanitarian Assistance' UN Doc A/HRC/15/21 (27 September 2011); The Turkel Commission, 'Report (Part 1) of the Public Commission to Examine the Maritime Incident of 31 May 2010' (January 2011); 'Report of the Secretary-General's Panel of Inquiry on the 31 May 2010 Flotilla Incident' (September 2011); Turkish National Commission of Inquiry, 'Report on the Israeli Attack on the Humanitarian Aid Convoy to Gaza on 31 May 2010' (February 2011).
4 Gal Luft and Anne Korin, 'Terrorism goes to Sea' *Foreign Affairs* (November/December 2004); Michael D Greenberg, Peter Chalk, Henry H Willis, Ivan Khilko and David S Ortiz, *Maritime Terrorism: Risk and Liability* (RAND 2006); Stuart Kaye, 'Threats from the Global Commons: Problems of Jurisdiction and Enforcement' (2007) 8 *Melbourne JIL* 185; Douglas Guilfoyle, *Shipping Interdiction and the Law of the Sea* (CUP 2009); Natalie Klein, *Maritime Security and the Law of the Sea* (OUP 2011); Rob McLaughlin, '"Terrorism" as a Central Theme in the Evolution of Maritime Operations Law since 11 September 2001' (2011) *YBIHL* 391.
5 Elan R Ghazal and Manik V Suri, 'Blurring the Civilian–Combatant Line: Legal Implications of Deploying US Civilian Mariners in the Libyan Theatre' *Harvard NSJ* (online) (16 August 2012), http://harvardnsj.org/2012/08/blurring-the-civilian-combatant-line-legal-implications-of-deploying-u-s-civilian-mariners-in-the-libyan-theater/.
6 For example, the contentious findings in the Turkel Commission *Report* (n 3) ¶¶ 192–201 characterising some of those aboard the vessels as 'civilians taking a direct part in hostilities'.
7 Hitoshi Nasu and Rob McLaughlin (eds), *New Technologies and the Law of Armed Conflict* (Asser 2014).

1.1 The venue for armed conflict at sea

The foremost contextual influence on the nature and substance of LONW is the fact that one venue for armed conflict at sea is the maritime global commons – waters seaward of states' territorial seas. Clearly, armed conflict in sovereign waters – internal waters, territorial waters and archipelagic waters – is anticipated and governed by LONW, but the domain concerns in these areas are in many ways analogous to fighting on a belligerent's land territory, and do in fact concern fighting in the national airspace of the adversary. Similarly, the sovereign waters of neutral states are treated in LONW in essentially the same manner as their land territory and national airspace, with the non-IHL-based caveat that the right of innocent passage through neutral territorial seas and archipelagic waters (and the right of transit passage through certain straits and sea lanes) is available equally to all belligerents, unless limited or suspended, with cause, by the neutral coastal state as part of its careful maintenance of that neutrality.[8]

Beyond the domain of sovereign waters, however, is a vast battlespace over which no belligerent can generally claim sovereignty. This battlespace comprises the contiguous zone,[9] exclusive economic zone (EEZ)[10] and high seas,[11] and airspace above each,[12] which for ease of reference may be collectively termed 'international waters' (and international airspace).[13] These waters are distinct from internal waters, territorial sea and archipelagic waters in that they are not subject to territorial sovereignty. Certainly, there are sovereign rights in various components of international waters – the 'FISC' rights (fiscal, immigration, sanitary and customs) in the contiguous zone,[14] resource, environmental and structure rights in the EEZ,[15] shared rights in uses of the high seas[16] – but for the purposes of armed conflict at sea, international waters are common space over which no belligerent is capable of asserting a superior sovereign claim.

This defining contextual factor is fundamental to understanding the development and application of LONW. Whereas land-based international armed conflict (including within national airspace) by definition involves a transgressed territorial sovereignty – and in practice tends to limit the actions of, and thus attention necessary to, neutrals in the area of operations – armed conflict in international waters takes place in a venue that maintains its underlying essence and legal character as a commons. Neutrals continue to utilise international waters without significant legal restriction (although common sense will often ensure that traffic diverts around sites of confrontation).[17] One consequence – as shall become evident below – is that LONW spells out in great detail how and why belligerents may interact with neutral vessels.

---

8 *San Remo Manual on International Law Applicable to Armed Conflicts at Sea* (IIHL 1994) ('*San Remo Manual*') rr 10–12, pt II.

9 United Nations Convention on the Law of the Sea (10 December 1982) 1833 UNTS 397 ('UNCLOS'), art 33.

10 Ibid pt V.

11 Ibid pt VII.

12 Ibid art 2(2) ('This sovereignty [over the territorial sea] extends to the air space over the territorial sea').

13 For example, US Navy, US Marine Corps and US Coast Guard, *The Commander's Handbook on the Law of Naval Operations*, NWP 1-14M/MCWP 5-12.1/COMDTPUB P5800.7A (July 2007) ¶ 1.6.

14 UNCLOS (n 9) art 33(1).

15 Ibid arts 56(1)(a), 60.

16 Ibid arts 87, 90.

17 For example, the 'customary belligerent right to control neutral vessels and aircraft in the immediate vicinity of naval operations'– *San Remo Manual* (n 8) r 108; German Navy, *Commander's Handbook: Legal Bases for the Operations of Naval Forces* (2002) ¶ 303, http://lgdata.s3-website-us-east-1.amazonaws.com/docs/905/454602/German_Naval_Handbook.pdf; Richard Jaques (ed), *Maritime Operational Zones Manual* (US Naval War College 2006) 4-2–4-6.

Similarly, whilst triggers for IHL on land or in national airspace are often contingent upon or associated with a breach of territorial sovereignty, posture and interactions between potential belligerents in international waters do not necessarily carry with them a precursor breach of territorial sovereignty.[18]

This general proposition is frayed by unilateral expedients which purport to turn an interaction in international waters into a sovereign territorial incident via mechanisms such as dubious maritime claims, questionable domestic legislation purporting to require permission for warship passage (primarily in territorial seas and archipelagic waters, but in some cases extending into international waters through excessive claims of security authority)[19] and protest at military activity on the high seas.[20] However, as a general rule, interactions between vessels in international waters – even in times of tension – do not carry with them quite the same level of sovereign offence as a transgression by troops or aircraft into land territory or national airspace. Although it related to a different maritime zone – one which is understood in modern law of the sea terms as a strait used for international navigation, in which there is no right for the coastal state to hinder or suspend transit passage – this issue remains the political and legal essence of the *Corfu Channel case*:[21] ships, especially warships, can give offence at sea, but this is a lesser form of sovereignty irritant than crossing a land or air border. At the same time, however, if it is possible that an attack upon a single warship may constitute a use of force that gives rise to the right of national self-defence under Article 51 of the UN Charter and customary international law – as confirmed in the *Oil Platforms* case[22] – then it is also clearly arguable that the same act would simultaneously constitute a de facto limited situation of international armed conflict.

1.2 Trade and commerce as a direct 'stakeholder' in LONW

A second, related factor – whilst it may initially appear anomalous – is that LONW is explicitly and comprehensively designed to ensure the continuity of economic activity. This is entirely consistent with the underlying purpose of most legal regimes relating to the sea – to facilitate international trade and commerce. Given that more than 90 per cent of world trade is conducted

---

18 For example, Rob McLaughlin, 'Dangerous Waters and International Law: The *Corfu Channel Case*, Warships, and Sovereignty Irritants' in Karine Bannelier, Theodore Christakis and Sarah Heathcote (eds), *The ICJ and the Evolution of International Law: The Enduring Impact of the Corfu Channel Case* (Routledge 2012) 164.

19 For example, Syria's claim to regulate, via prior permission, the innocent passage of warships, 'ships of a dangerous nature', submarines and other diving vessels through the Syrian Territorial Sea: Definition Act of Internal Waters and Territorial Sea Limits of the Syrian Arab Republic, Law no 28 (19 November 2003) art 9(1), www.un.org/Depts/los/LEGISLATIONANDTREATIES/PDFFILES/syr_2003e. pdf; and Vietnam's claim to security jurisdiction in the Contiguous Zone. See the analysis in US Department of Defense, *Maritime Claims Reference Manual*, DoD 2005.1-M (2005, updated May 2014), www.jag.navy.mil/organization/documents/mcrm/Vietnam2014.pdf.

20 For example, India's Declaration on 29 June 1995, upon ratification of UNCLOS:

> The Government of the Republic of India understands that the provisions of the Convention do not authorize other States to carry out in the exclusive economic zone and on the continental shelf military exercises or manoeuvres, in particular those involving the use of weapons or explosives without the consent of the coastal State.
>
> www.un.org/depts/los/convention_agreements/convention_declarations.htm

21 *Corfu Channel (UK v Albania)* [1949] ICJ Rep 4, ¶ 30.

22 *Oil Platforms (Iran v US)* [2003] ICJ Rep 161, ¶¶ 65–72.

by sea,[23] and the fact that the sea remains the lifeline of the world economy, LONW has explicitly crystallised as a fundamental purpose within its regulatory scope the requirement to facilitate – or at least ensure minimal hindrance of – ongoing maritime communications. This purpose – reflected in the detailed rules for dealing with neutral (merchant) shipping, and the minimal interference permitted of belligerents in relation to neutrals in international waters – is almost unique in the broader IHL lexicon which (perhaps apart from IHL relating to occupation) generally does not directly address the economic aspects or consequences of armed conflict.

The importance of this additional influence on LONW is best illustrated via a comparison. For maritime operations just before and during the 2003 conflict in Iraq, the extant Security Council resolutions authorised a sanctions regime dating from Resolution 661 (6 August 1990). Resolution 1447 (4 December 2002) had, at that time, reconfirmed the sanctions regime (as amended from time to time, including via Resolution 986 (14 April 1995) which permitted limited oil/petroleum trade to recommence) as extant for a further 180 days – that is, until June 2003.[24] The UNSC Sanctions Committee[25] was generally the source of import and export approvals to and from Iraq – including under the 'Oil-for-Food' programme and the technicalities of the dual-use technology import restrictions. These matters were managed on a procedural level through UN letters of approval to import or export, which were issued on the authorisation of the Committee.

LONW, however, recognises a markedly *different* procedure for characterising the acceptability of goods for passing through the visit and search cordon at sea (for this is what was in place during the Iraq War in 2003).[26] This process centres on the concept of 'contraband'. The *San Remo Manual* defines contraband as 'goods which are ultimately destined for territory under the control of the enemy and which may be susceptible for use in armed conflict'.[27]

It should be noted that the term 'contraband' is regularly misused in the media (and military operations). For many, 'contraband' encompasses all those articles subject to a sanctions regime, however the two classes of items are quite distinct. First, as identified above, contraband concerns items susceptible for use in armed conflict by the enemy. Contraband does not generally include food, educational materials or medical supplies. The Iraq sanctions regime, on the other hand, was much wider and regulated many of these items. Second, contraband relates to goods going into the enemy's territory, not goods coming out. In fact, although there is some debate about the issue, the general position is that where the right of visit and search is being exercised (as opposed to blockade), belligerents are limited to dealing with *inbound* maritime traffic. Trade goods – including oil – coming out of the enemy's territory, even if the financial return from those exports might be used to support military operations, are not contraband under LONW.[28] The sanctions process, on the other hand, is markedly different from contraband and covers *all in- and outbound goods*. Thus oil could only be exported under a Sanctions Committee letter of

23 For 2012, world trade carried by sea was 8.7 billion tons: UNCTAD, *Review of Maritime Transport 2012* (2012) Table 1.3, http://unctad.org/en/PublicationsLibrary/rmt2012_en.pdf.

24 UNSC Res 1447 (4 December 2002) operative ¶ 1.

25 UNSC Res 1284 (17 December 1999) operative ¶¶ 17–18.

26 For example, *Operational Zones Manual* (n 17) C-63: MARLO Advisory Bulletin 03-08 (21 March 2003).

27 *San Remo Manual* (n 8) r 148.

28 Belligerents have at times, however, claimed the right to interdict as contraband both goods going into the territory of the adversary, and goods coming out of the territory of the adversary regardless of the neutral flag of the vessel – eg the account of the US–UK correspondence on this matter during the First World War, summarised in George Grafton Wilson, *International Law Situations, with Solutions and Notes 1933* (US Naval War College 1933) esp 18.

approval, which was in turn tied to the Oil for Food programme. The distinguishing factor is clearly the LONW's additional purpose of facilitating (or at the very least, leaving space for) continued non-interference with trade and maritime communications during armed conflict.

2 Key sources of international humanitarian law: maritime context

The traditional starting point for consideration of the modern sources of law applicable to armed conflict at sea is the 1856 Paris Declaration Respecting Maritime Law.[29] This does not imply prior absence of agreements between states, or practice among states, during periods of war. Nor does it indicate that non-European states had not entered into arrangements that dealt with warfare in the maritime domain.[30] However, such arrangements, regardless of their geographic location, did not amount to a widely accepted and universally applied legal framework that could be considered representative of an international legal norm.[31]

2.1 Paris Declaration 1856

The fulcrum for the Paris Declaration was the Crimean War (1853–1856 involving Russian Imperial forces and British, French and Turkish (Ottoman) forces), particularly in relation to how rules for the capture of property at sea might be aligned between France and Britain. Both states made declarations on this issue in 1854 and although originally intended to apply only during the Crimean War, at the subsequent peace negotiations in Paris in 1856 the *Declaration of Paris* was adopted as the final act of the parties assembled. The Declaration focused upon four issues: privateering, goods being transported by a neutral flag vessel, neutral goods being transported under enemy flag and blockade. The Declaration abolished the practice of privateering (authorisation given by a state to a private vessel to attack and seize foreign shipping and cargo during times of war), regulated enemy and neutral property onboard enemy and neutral ships, and required that blockades must be effective in order to be binding. The Declaration was signed by the seven states participating in the Paris peace negotiations, but was subsequently acceded to, or its principles adopted by, other states. It has undoubtedly attained the status of customary international law (CIL).[32]

2.2 Hague 1907

Although naval warfare issues were discussed at the 1899 Hague Peace Conference, the proposed declarations relating to asphyxiating or deleterious gases in the naval context were ultimately vetoed and did not proceed. At the 1907 Hague Peace Conference, however, regulation of naval warfare was extensively considered and most of the current legal framework governing

---

29 (30 March 1856) 61 British State Papers 155, reprinted in Adam Roberts and Richard Guelff, *Documents on the Laws of War* (3rd edn, OUP 2001) 48.

30 Literature regarding the codification of the law of the sea and the law of naval warfare is almost entirely focused on what may be termed a 'Euro-centric' view. This situation is not unique to LONW: see R R Baxter, 'The Law of War' in Maarten Bos (ed), *The Present State of International Law and Other Essays written in Honour of the Centenary Celebration of the International Law Association 1873–1973* (Kluwer 1973) 118.

31 Roberts and Guelff (n 29) 47.

32 Ibid.

naval warfare is set out in eight of the conventions that were concluded there.[33] There is little contemporary relevance for at least three of these conventions. Hague Convention (VI) relating to the Status of Enemy Merchant Ships at the Outbreak of Hostilities[34] did not receive wide acceptance among states and during the First World War it became apparent that adherence to the Convention's provisions was highly disparate, even amongst signatory states. In the Second World War there was further lack of adherence to the Convention's requirements, and it is no longer generally regarded as part of the law of naval warfare.[35] Hague Convention (X) for the Adaptation to Maritime Warfare of the Principles of the Geneva Convention (of 6 July 1906)[36] is no longer relevant because its provisions have been incorporated into Geneva Convention II. Hague Convention (XII) relative to the Establishment of an International Prize Court[37] never entered into force as it was only signed by one state (Nicaragua) in 1909. A naval conference held in London in 1908 and 1909 attempted to reinvigorate this issue, but the subsequent 1909 Declaration of London[38] was never ratified by any state.

The remaining five 1907 Hague Conventions remain relevant, to varying degrees, within LONW. Hague Convention (VII) relating to the Conversion of Merchant Ships into Warships[39] reflected an issue that emerged during the 1870 Franco-Prussian war when the King of Prussia sought to create a German navy from volunteer vessels, raising concerns regarding the prohibition on privateers in the Paris Declaration.[40] Over the next few decades there was some evidence of state practice in converting merchant ships into warships at the outbreak of hostilities and the practice certainly occurred during the Russo-Japanese war of 1904–1905. Accordingly, the issue was addressed at the 1907 Hague Peace Conference with signatories agreeing on a system to facilitate legitimate conversions. Significantly, the Convention established the fundamental aspects of the definition of a warship.[41] However, the Convention did not resolve whether conversion may occur on the high seas; nor did it deal with the question of how reconversion to merchant vessel status would occur. State practice since 1907, particularly during the two World Wars, saw many instances of merchant vessels being converted into warships. The use of merchant raiders by the German Navy during the Second World War was perhaps the most widespread among belligerents, and British Admiralty intelligence reports in 1940 indicated that more than 800 German vessels could potentially be used for this purpose.[42] In one battle, between the cruiser HMAS *Sydney* and the German raider HSK *Kormoran* off the coast of Western Australia on 19 November 1941, *Sydney* was sunk with the loss of all hands. This remains the worst disaster in Australian naval history.[43] In terms of underlying rationale – that is,

---

33 On the 1899 Hague Peace Conference and the US veto of this provision in Committee, then joined with a British veto in the Conference, see A T Mahan, *Report to the Commission of the United States of America to the International Conference at the Hague* (31 July 1899), http://avalon.law.yale.edu/19th_century/hag99-06.asp.

34 1 *AJIL Supp* 127.

35 Roberts and Guelff (n 29) 67.

36 2 *AJIL Supp* 153.

37 Ibid 174.

38 Declaration concerning the Laws of Naval War (26 February 1909) 3 *AJIL Supp* 186 ('London Declaration').

39 2 *AJIL Supp* 133.

40 See n 29.

41 Hague Convention (VII) arts 2–5 (n 39); *San Remo Manual* (n 8) r 13(g). Roberts and Guelff (n 29) 96.

42 Confidential Admiralty Fleet Order 422 (21 March 1940) quoted in Terence R H Cole (Commissioner), *The Loss of HMAS Sydney II* (Department of Defence of Australia 2009) i, 173.

43 *Sydney*'s entire crew of 645 died in the battle with *Kormoran*; the latter recorded 82 deaths from the battle.

of providing a means of distinguishing between warships and merchant vessels in times of war – the reality of state practice during the two World Wars, and the Iran–Iraq war in the 1980s,[44] indicates variable adherence to the strict requirements of the Convention.

Hague Convention (VIII) relative to the Laying of Automatic Submarine Contact Mines[45] sought to address an issue that had steadily increased in importance during the nineteenth century as the use of sea mines as a method of warfare became more prevalent.[46] In order to possess a credible mine threat, a state need only have the capability and means of deploying mines. Their potency and low detectability automatically required an opposing belligerent to consider the possibility that mines had actually been deployed. During the 1904–1905 Russo-Japanese War, Russia sought access to a port that would not be subject to seasonal closures due to adverse weather conditions, such as those that affected Vladivostok. Port Arthur, a Chinese port, had been leased to Russia and was being used by the Russian fleet as its base. With some success, Russia and Japan both used contact mines to try and counter each other's presence in the vicinity of Port Arthur. However, damage caused to neutral shipping by mines led to concern regarding their use – not only during war but also once hostilities had ceased. Hague Convention (VIII) attempted to deal with this by placing restrictions upon how automatic contact mines could be used by belligerents and neutral powers, specifying post-hostilities obligations.[47] State practice during the two World Wars, and since, saw departures from the requirements of the Convention, particularly in relation to the requirement for notification.[48] One aspect of the Convention that has drawn criticism is that its provisions only apply to one particular type of mine. The *San Remo Manual* has addressed this lacuna through a more expansive definition in an attempt to create an encompassing description that would apply to a mine regardless of the detonation technology employed.[49]

The contemporary relevance of Hague Convention (IX) concerning Bombardment by Naval Forces in Time of War[50] has been clearly demonstrated on a number of occasions during the past 30 years.[51] At first glance it may appear that aspects of the Convention relate to naval warfare concepts that are largely confined to history. For example, Article 1 of the Convention provides: 'The bombardment by naval forces of undefended ports, towns, villages, dwellings or buildings is forbidden. A place cannot be bombarded solely because automatic submarine contact mines are anchored off the harbour.'

It is difficult to envisage an undefended port, town or village existing in the twenty-first century in the same way as contemplated in 1907. Further, the requirement to distinguish between military objectives and civilian objects is now clearly specified in Additional Protocol I

---

44 There were numerous attacks against shipping during the September 1980 to August 1988 Iran–Iraq war. A summary of hostile maritime activity occurring in the Persian Gulf during this period can be found in *Oil Platforms* (n 22) ¶¶ 23–25.

45 2 *AJIL Supp* 138.

46 Sea mines were used during the Crimean War, the American Civil War, the Boxer rebellion in China and the Russo-Japanese war.

47 In particular, see Hague Convention (VIII) arts 1–5 (n 45).

48 The ICJ has considered aspects of the law relating to the use of mines in *Corfu Channel* (n 21); *Military and Paramilitary Activities in and against Nicaragua (Nicaragua v US)* [1986] ICJ Rep 14; *Oil Platforms* (n 22).

49 *San Remo Manual* (n 8) rr 80–92; see also the accompanying Explanation, ibid 168–176. For a recent legal evaluation see the Naval Mine Warfare Forum in (2014) 90 *International Law Studies*.

50 2 *AJIL Supp* 146. The term 'Bombardment' has been replaced in modern usage with 'Naval Gunfire Support' or 'Naval Fires' and includes the use of missiles and other projectiles that are fired/launched from a naval platform against a land target.

51 For example, naval gunfire was used in the Falklands War 1982, Lebanese Civil War 1984, Iran–Iraq War 1980–1988, Gulf War 1991, Gulf War 2003.

and in customary international law.[52] Accordingly, this part of the Convention is somewhat unremarkable in the modern context. Article 2 of the Convention established the circumstances in which naval forces can use 'artillery' to attack military objectives and these, too, are now largely reflected in Additional Protocol I.[53] Adherence to the provisions of the Convention during the two World Wars was undermined by several instances of indiscriminate bombardment, or targeting that did not have a military purpose. However, naval gunfire was used to support operations during the Korean and Vietnam wars and remains an important part of the suite of options available to naval forces. In terms of relatively recent naval operations, the United States Navy deployed two battleships, USS *Missouri* and USS *Wisconsin*, to the Persian Gulf in 1991 where they provided support using both land attack missiles and their 16-inch guns. In 2003, the assault on the Al Faw Peninsula by British Royal Marines was accompanied by the use of naval gunfire in support of the ground forces[54] and reports of the accuracy and effect of the naval gunfire employed during that campaign have reinforced its continued value.[55]

Hague Convention (XI) relative to Certain Restrictions with regard to the Exercise of the Right of Capture in Naval War[56] deals with three specific issues. Articles 1 and 2 stipulate rules for respecting the inviolable nature of 'the postal correspondence of neutrals or belligerents, whatever its official character may be, found on board a neutral or enemy ship'. The continuing relevance of this part of the Convention may be questioned on the basis of state practice during the two World Wars,[57] the advent of air transport for postal items and electronic transmission of information. The second matter dealt with by the Convention was a codification of some customary exemptions from capture that existed for certain vessels: coastal fishing vessels, local traders and vessels on religious, scientific or philanthropic missions. This exemption applied if the vessel remained employed in the exempt role and ceased if the vessel took 'any part whatever in hostilities'. Perhaps the most famous example of a belligerent deviating from this requirement occurred during the evacuation of Allied forces from Dunkirk in May/June 1940 when hundreds of small craft assisted the evacuation of forces from France to England. The third matter dealt with by the Convention concerned how the crews of captured enemy merchant vessels would be treated and it provides, in general terms, that they would not be treated as prisoners of war. State practice during the two World Wars resulted in enemy merchant mariners being interned or made prisoner of war although crews from neutral states were not treated in this way provided they had not engaged in hostilities.[58]

The final maritime-specific Convention from the 1907 Hague Conference is Hague Convention (XIII) concerning the Rights and Duties of Neutral Powers in Naval War.[59] This Convention sets out the key requirements to be observed by both neutral powers and warships of belligerents in the ports and waters of neutral states. One of the significant requirements of

---

52 See generally *Prosecutor v Tadić (Decision on the Defence Motion for Interlocutory Appeal on Jurisdiction)* (Case no IT-94-1, ICTY Appeals Chamber, 2 October 1995) ¶¶ 96–127.

53 API arts 35–59

54 The operation, involving Royal Navy and Royal Australian Navy ships, became known as 'Five Inch Friday'. See www.awm.gov.au/collection/REL31406/.

55 For a contemporary account of the action involving HMAS *Anzac* see, www.defence.gov.au/news/navynews/editions/4605/topstories/story06.htm.

56 2 *AJIL Supp* 167.

57 Roberts and Guelff (n 29) 127 note that state practice during the two World Wars resulted in merchant ships being sunk in many cases without warning. In those cases where vessels were captured mail was invariably seized, examined and either censored or confiscated.

58 Ibid 128.

59 2 *AJIL Supp* 202.

the Convention is the '24-hour rule' which applies to both the time permitted for a belligerent warship to remain in a neutral port[60] and the time period between departure from port of belligerent warships and merchant vessels.[61] Application of the Convention's principles occurred in 1939 when the German pocket-battleship *Admiral Graf Spee* was damaged during an encounter with three ships (HMS *Ajax*, HMS *Exeter* and HMS *Achilles*) from the British Royal Navy[62] off the coast of South America. The *Graf Spee* sought refuge in the Uruguayan port of Montevideo where the ship remained for three days. Initially, attempts were made by British authorities to force the Uruguayan authorities to expel the *Graf Spee* from the port as soon as possible. However the British subsequently sought to delay the departure of the *Graf Spee* by arranging for British and French merchant vessels to sail from the port at intervals close to 24 hours so that time could be 'bought' for additional British warships to steam to the area. The outcome of these actions was that the captain of the *Graf Spee*, in the belief that a superior allied force was waiting for him just outside neutral Uruguayan waters, took his ship to sea on 17 December 1939 and scuttled it in the River Plate estuary.

2.3 London Declaration 1909

The next step in the codification of the law of naval warfare occurred with the 1909 London Declaration,[63] which attempted to deal with some of the issues left unresolved following the 1907 Hague Conference – in particular, questions relating to the establishment of an international prize court, clarification of aspects of the law relating to blockades and contraband, convoys involving neutral vessels and the problem of 'un-neutral service'. However, despite the London Declaration being signed by all ten participating states on 26 February 1909, it was never ratified by any state and therefore never entered into force. A number of states did attempt to abide by the London Declaration during the First World War but it proved problematic to implement and was thus abandoned.[64] In terms of contemporary application, at least one of the subjects dealt with by the London Declaration – an international prize court – has little or no relevance in modern naval warfare. Conversely, the continued use of blockade as a method of warfare in a variety of guises and conflicts warrants further attention (below).[65]

2.4 Oxford Manual 1913

The absence of a manual that specifically, and comprehensively, dealt with LONW was the impetus behind the Institute of International Law establishing a special commission in 1910 to develop a code that crystallised the laws and customs of naval warfare. The special commission's work resulted in 'the Institute at its Oxford session, on 9 August 1913, adopting the following Manual, based on the right of capture'.[66] Detailed assessment of the issues covered in the Manual

---

60 Ibid arts 12, 13
61 Ibid art 16 – the rationale being that a neutral state should take action to prevent hostilities taking place in its territory and immediate environs.
62 HMS *Achilles* was assigned to the New Zealand Division of the British Royal Navy at the time of the battle with *Graf Spee*, www.navymuseum.co.nz/second-world-war-1939-1945/atlantic/battle-of-the-river-plate-1.
63 London Declaration (n 38).
64 Roberts and Guelff (n 29) 127.
65 For consideration of blockade as a method of warfare, see s 3.1.
66 Oxford Manual of Naval War (9 August 1913) preamble, reproduced in Natalino Ronzitti (ed), *The Law of Naval Warfare* (Martinus Nijhoff 1988) 278.

is beyond the scope of this chapter, but it should be noted that the Manual's status as a restatement of the law applicable at the time is not universally accepted.[67] Regardless, however, it is noteworthy that the Manual represents another step along the journey of codification of LONW.

2.5 Developments 1918–1939

Further instruments that emerged between the two World Wars, which have affected LONW in a variety of ways, include the 1922 Washington Treaties,[68] the 1930 London Treaty[69] and the 1936 London Proces-Verbal.[70] The importance of the Washington Naval Armament Treaty lies in its regulation of an anticipated build-up of naval forces among the major naval powers of the time, which in turn led to a focus on improvements in weapon systems and technology as a means of countering the Treaty's impact. The Washington Submarine Treaty, the 1930 London Treaty and the 1936 London Proces-Verbal, helped to shape the law relating to submarine warfare – despite lack of entry into force of the Washington Submarine Treaty, expiration of most of the 1930 London Treaty, and significant deviation from the requirements of each instrument during the Second World War.[71]

The comments of Professor R R Baxter in describing the status of LONW as it evolved during both the World Wars are illuminating:

> The law, whether conventional or customary, which was in force at the outbreak of the First World War was already highly politically charged, representing as it did a preliminary squaring off for war and an attempt to reconcile the interests of the major maritime powers with those of other States. Where this classic body of law now stands it is difficult to say, for a number of forces have been at work to obscure its contours and bleach its colours almost to vanishing point.[72]

There is little doubt that the practice of belligerents on both sides of the conflict during the Second World War did not conform, in all respects, to either customary or codified LONW.[73] Nevertheless, following the completion of hostilities in 1945, attempts to promote codification of laws that specifically relate to naval warfare have been generally unsuccessful. The obvious exception is Geneva Convention II but its focus is not on 'how' naval warfare should be conducted at sea, but rather to provide a regime for the protection of those wounded, sick and shipwrecked in warfare at sea.[74] Another significant development in broader IHL which fundamentally affects naval warfare is those provisions of Additional Protocol I that regulate the means

---

67 Compare comments by Pietro Verri in Ronzitti (n 66) 339–340; Roberts and Guelff (n 29) 574; *San Remo Manual* (n 8) 61.

68 Treaty for the Limitation of Naval Armament (6 February 1922) 25 LNTS 202; Treaty Relating to the Use of Submarines and Noxious Gases in Warfare (6 February 1922) 16 *AJIL Supp* 57 which has not entered into force as France has not ratified it.

69 Treaty for the Limitation and Reduction of Naval Armaments (Part IV) (22 April 1930) 112 LNTS 88.

70 Process-Verbal Relating to the Rules of Submarine Warfare set Forth in Part IV of the Treaty of London of 22 April 1930 (6 November 1936) 173 LNTS 353.

71 See n 84 below.

72 Baxter (n 30) 119.

73 Ibid 119–120; *San Remo Manual* (n 8) 122, 175; Roberts and Guelff (n 29) 96, 103, 111, 120.

74 For a more detailed discussion of GCII's protection regime, see James Benoit, 'Wounded and sick, and medical services' ch 18 in this volume.

and methods of warfare. Certainly, not all states are party to Additional Protocol I,[75] and there is some difference of opinion among academic writers regarding 'whether and to what extent the provisions of Additional Protocol I apply to naval warfare at all'.[76] However, a significant number of states do consider that Additional Protocol I applies in the maritime context, and that many of its provisions reflect customary international law.[77]

It is also relevant to note the impact of codification of the law of the sea on naval warfare.[78] One area where there has been significant change wrought by the UN Convention on the Law of the Sea (UNCLOS) 1982, is the creation of maritime zones which affect the areas in which naval warfare may legitimately be waged (see below). The UNCLOS has also formalised a number of passage regimes[79] although differing views exist among states regarding the applicability of elements of these regimes to warships, including submarines and air capable ships, which reflect the national interests of the states involved. As noted in Section 1.1, some states seek to enforce a requirement for warships to give prior notification of, or seek prior permission for, the exercise of innocent passage through their territorial sea.[80] These attempts to regulate passage by warships are arguably contrary to UNCLOS Article 17 and are actively resisted by most navies. In relation to military activities in a state's EEZ[81] some states have made declarations under UNCLOS Article 310 which purport to prohibit other states from undertaking military activities in their EEZ.[82] Again, most of the world's navies resist such claims either in doctrine or in practice.[83]

There are two other areas that are relevant as sources of LONW. First, there have been a number of judicial decisions that affect discrete areas of naval warfare. For example, the operational practice of German U-boats in the Second World War was one of the key issues in the trial of Admiral Dönitz at the Nuremberg International Military Tribunal. Arguments were raised in Dönitz's defence regarding allied naval practice during the war, and although he was convicted of some of the charges against him, there were a number of instances excluded from consideration by the tribunal:

> Dönitz is charged with waging unrestricted submarine warfare contrary to the Naval Protocol of 1936, to which Germany acceded, and which reaffirmed the rules of submarine warfare laid down in the London Naval Agreement of 1930.

---

75 As of December 2015, there are 174 states parties to API.

76 Wolff Heintschel von Heinegg, 'The Current State of the Law of Naval Warfare: A Fresh Look at the San Remo Manual' in Anthony M Helm (ed), *The Law of War in the 21st Century: Weaponry and the Use of Force* (US Naval War College 2006) 260, 278, where the author briefly discusses this topic in the context of 'the famous dispute between Meyrowitz and Rauch'.

77 Detailed discussion of API is provided in chs 8, 9, 10 and 14, in this volume; specific aspects of API that relate to methods and means of naval warfare are discussed in s 4 below.

78 Although it is recognised that codification of the law of the sea pre-dates UNCLOS 1982 (n 9), discussion in this chapter will be limited to UNCLOS 1982 due to the wide acceptance of UNCLOS among states as being reflective of both codified and customary law.

79 For example, ibid arts 17–32 (innocent passage in the territorial sea), 37–44 (transit passage in straits used for international navigation), 53–54 (archipelagic sea lanes passage).

80 E D Brown, *The International Law of the Sea* (Dartmouth 1994) i, 65.

81 UNCLOS (n 9) arts 55–75 describe the regime of EEZ, which is defined under art 57 as a zone that 'shall not extend beyond 200 nautical miles from the baselines from which the breadth of the territorial sea is measured'. High seas freedoms of navigation and overflight exist in the EEZ per arts 58, 87.

82 See eg India's Declaration (n 20); see also *San Remo Manual* (n 8) 81–82; Brown, *International Law of the Sea* (n 80) 241–243; Natalie Klein, *Maritime Security and the Law of the Sea* (OUP 2011) 46–54.

83 This issue was discussed extensively in George V Galdorisi and Alan G Kaufman, 'Military Activities in the Exclusive Economic Zone: Preventing Uncertainty and Defusing Conflict' (2002) 32 *California Western ILJ* 253.

The Prosecution has submitted that on 3 September 1939 the German U-Boat arm began to wage unrestricted submarine warfare upon all merchant ships, whether enemy or neutral, cynically disregarding the Protocol; and that a calculated effort was made throughout the war to disguise this practice by making hypocritical references to international law and supposed violations by the Allies....

Shortly after the outbreak of war the British Admiralty, in accordance with its *Handbook of Instructions* of 1938 to the Merchant Navy, armed its merchant vessels, in many cases convoyed them with armed escort, gave orders to send position reports upon sighting submarines, thus integrating merchant vessels into the warning network of naval intelligence. On 1 October 1939 the British Admiralty announced British merchant ships had been ordered to ram U-Boats if possible.

In the actual circumstances of this case, the tribunal is not prepared to hold Dönitz guilty for his conduct of submarine warfare against British armed merchant ships.

In view of all of the facts proved, and in particular of an order of the British Admiralty announced on 8 May 1940, according to which all vessels should be sunk at night in the Skagerrak, and the answer to interrogatories by Admiral Nimitz stating that unrestricted submarine warfare was carried on in the Pacific Ocean by the United States from the first day that Nation entered the war, the sentence of Dönitz is not assessed on the ground of his breaches of the international law of submarine warfare.[84]

This judgment provides some evidence of state practice regarding submarine warfare during the Second World War, noting that belligerents on both sides of the conflict did not always act in accordance with the law regulating naval warfare in general, and submarine warfare in particular.

Judicial and arbitral decisions are also useful in determining the level of force, and the context in which force can be escalated, when undertaking a naval blockade or a visit and search operation. For example, *The I'm Alone*[85] and *The Red Crusader*[86] cases make it clear that the use of potentially lethal force in an operation where such force cannot objectively be justified is not permitted. Although both of these cases refer to incidents that occurred when LONW did not apply, they are nevertheless instructive as there are a number of situations within an armed conflict, especially where neutral vessels or protected persons are involved, when caution must be exercised in dealing with persons that are encountered.[87]

Finally, LONW has benefitted significantly from a number of 'soft law' publications, such as the 1913 *Oxford Manual* and the 1994 *San Remo Manual*, in its development. In relation to the *San Remo Manual*, its stated purpose is to provide 'a contemporary restatement – together with some progressive development – of the law applicable to armed conflicts at sea'.[88] Despite not having treaty status, the comprehensive process undertaken in drafting the *San Remo Manual*, and the widespread reference to the rules therein by academic publicists and states in national military/naval manuals, has led to the Manual obtaining, arguably, status as a subsidiary means of determining international law.[89] In addition, a number of states have made their international

---

84 *US et al v Göring et al*, 1 TMWC 171, 311–313 (International Military Tribunal at Nuremberg, 1946).
85 *The I'm Alone* (1935) 3 UNRIAA 1609 (Canada–US Special Joint Commission).
86 *The Red Crusader* (1962) 35 ILR 485.
87 This issue was considered in *The M/V 'Saiga' (No 2) (Saint Vincent and the Grenadines v Guinea)* (Case no 2, International Tribunal for the Law of the Sea, 1 July 1999).
88 *San Remo Manual* (n 8) opening page.
89 ICJ Statute art 38(1)(d).

law or LONW manuals available publicly[90] and these 'operational' publications have also served both to describe each state's understanding of the applicable law and to outline the practice expected of commanders in myriad operational situations. The most recent publication in this lineage of soft law development in the LONW is the 2009 San Remo *Rules of Engagement Handbook*.[91]

3 Means and methods of warfare in the maritime context

Many aspects of IHL means and methods – such as the Additional Protocol I targeting rules noted above – apply equally to LONW as they do to other conflict domains. However, there are some means and methods, of contemporary relevance,[92] that were specifically designed for the unique maritime context.

3.1 Blockade[93]

There is a link between the use of blockade in naval warfare and the declaration of special maritime zones by belligerents, as both purport to restrict ordinary passage rights to some extent. The distinction between the two is that blockade seeks to completely prevent vessels of all nations (that is, enemy and neutral) from entering or leaving a port or coastal area, whereas the declaration of a zone may not involve attempts at such exclusion. Blockade has long been recognised as a method of naval warfare,[94] although during the latter part of the twentieth century there were assertions that the law relating to blockade was 'now mainly of historical significance'.[95] However, blockade ('by ... sea ... forces') is specifically mentioned in Article 42 of the UN Charter as a measure that the Security Council has occasionally authorised,[96] although this reference to blockade is not generally considered to be a direct reference to LONW blockade. State practice during the twentieth century and the early part of the twenty-first century has reinforced the relevance of LONW on blockade but has been inconsistent in terms of application of the key formal requirements of a blockade – that it be effective, that it be publicly declared and that it not interfere with the rights of neutral vessels and states.[97] During the Second World War 'the formal blockade of ports or coasts belonging to or occupied by the enemy ... had for all practical purposes been replaced by the effective closure of entire sea areas to all non-friendly commercial shipping'.[98] Nevertheless, there have been a number of occasions in which

90 For example, *Royal Australian Navy Manual of International Law,* Australian Book of Reference 5179 (Australian Department of Defence 1998); *Commander's Handbook* (n 13). UK, German and Canadian publications are also readily available.
91 Alan Cole, Phillip Drew, Rob McLaughlin and Dennis Mandsager, *Rules of Engagement Handbook* (IIHL 2009).
92 It is not possible to deal adequately with all of the methods and means of naval warfare in this chapter so only selected topics that are unique and particular to LONW are discussed. The *San Remo Manual* is a convenient starting point for more detailed discussion of other methods and means of naval warfare. See also Ronzitti (n 66).
93 Although blockade can apply to vessels/aircraft and ports/airfields, discussion in this chapter will be limited to the maritime environment.
94 Paris Declaration (n 29) principle 4; London Declaration (n 38) arts 1–21; see also *Operational Zones Manual* (n 17) 4-20–4-29.
95 Frits Kalshoven in Ronzitti (n 66) 274; see also *San Remo Manual* (n 8) 176. These views are in contrast with those expressed in the *Operational Zones Manual* (n 17) 4-28–4-29.
96 For example UNSC Res 665 (25 August 1990) following the Iraq invasion of Kuwait in 1990.
97 *San Remo Manual* (n 8) 176–179.
98 Kalshoven (n 95) 274.

blockades have been used during armed conflicts since the Second World War – including the Korean War, Vietnam War, 1971 India/Pakistan War, 1967/1973 Israeli/Arab Wars[99] and by Israel against Hezbollah in South Lebanon in 2006 and against Hamas in Gaza in 2009. The Gaza blockade also highlighted differences of opinion regarding the application of blockade in international armed conflicts and non-international armed conflicts.[100]

3.2 Maritime zones

One area of naval warfare employed by states in a variety of ways is the promulgation and use of maritime zones[101] during periods of conflict. The use of 'operational zones' had occurred during the First World War and this practice was widely employed during the Second World War and subsequent conflicts.[102] However, there is divergence of opinion in relation to the legality of declaring maritime zones at all, the type of zones that might legitimately be established and the effect upon vessels of all states following the declaration of a maritime zone.[103] The *San Remo Manual* notes that a 'variety of names have been given to these zones, such as exclusion zones, military areas, barred areas, war zones or operational zones'.[104] There have also been a variety of ways in which maritime zones have been employed during conflict, including the somewhat controversial declaration of a zone or 'defensive bubble' around warships as they undertake passage or conduct operations,[105] as well as states declaring large portions of ocean space to be subject to some form of maritime zone regime – as occurred, for example, during the Second World War, the Falklands War and the Iran–Iraq War in the 1980s.

The key issue in attempting to determine the effect of a maritime zone is to understand its impact upon ships in the region. Declaration of a maritime zone does not remove the obligation placed upon a belligerent only to attack those targets that may lawfully be attacked in accordance with LONW. This issue achieved particular prominence during the Falklands War when the Argentine cruiser *Belgrano* was sunk, allegedly outside the exclusion zone that had been established by Britain around the Falkland Islands.[106] Similarly, the mere declaration of a maritime

---

99 *Operational Zones Manual* (n 17) 4–28.

100 Wolff Heintschel von Heinegg, 'Methods and Means of Naval Warfare in Non-International Armed Conflicts' in Kenneth Watkin and Andrew J Norris (eds), *Non-International Armed Conflict in the Twenty-first Century* (US Naval War College 2012) 211–212; James Farrant, 'The Gaza Flotilla Incident and the Modern Law of Blockade' (2013) 66(3) *NWCR* 81–83.

101 The term 'maritime zone' is used to describe zones, however identified, that are established by a belligerent under the laws of naval warfare and is distinct from the zones that are established under UNCLOS.

102 Baxter (n 30) 119; *San Remo Manual* (n 8) 181; Ronzitti (n 66) 39–41; *Operational Zones Manual* (n 17) 4-1–4-4.

103 *San Remo Manual* (n 8) 181.

104 Ibid.

105 *Operational Zones Manual* (n 17) 4-10–4-16 notes two approaches by states: a 'defensive bubble' in relation to Argentine vessels and aircraft that moved its geographic location in concert with British naval forces as they approached the South Atlantic was declared by the British Government on 23 April 1982 during the Falklands War; in 2003 as preparations for offensive operations against Iraq were being undertaken by United States Navy forces in the Eastern Mediterranean Sea a series of Notices to Mariners (NOTMARs) and Notices to Airmen (NOTAMs) were issued declaring that US forces were operating at a heightened state of readiness and that all vessels and aircraft should navigate with extreme caution in the vicinity of the US ships.

106 Although this assertion was made at the time of the sinking, some recent reporting has suggested otherwise: David Wilkes, 'Belgrano was "Fair Target" as it was headed into Falklands Exclusion Zone and NOT Back to Port, according to Top Secret Dossier' *Daily Mail* (26 December 2011).

zone does not legally affect the passage rights of vessels that exist under UNCLOS[107] but it may serve to highlight that caution should be exercised – by, for example, neutral vessels if they transit through such a zone. Importantly, there is a difference between declaring that a maritime zone exists in a remote and infrequently accessed area of ocean (such as the South Atlantic) and making such a declaration in the busy waterways of (for example) the South China Sea. A further possibility is that belligerents may wish to attempt to limit the geographical location of the conflict to certain defined areas – a maritime zone declaration may assist in this regard.

3.3 Visit and search

The right for a belligerent to conduct visit and search over enemy or neutral merchant vessels is distinct from the right of visit which may be exercised under the UNCLOS,[108] with the latter being a peacetime right applicable in limited circumstances. The belligerent right of visit and search has a number of discrete variables depending upon the circumstances encountered on each occasion. For example, it may be necessary to divert a vessel to a port or anchorage so that inspection of the vessel and/or its cargo can occur safely in the prevailing sea conditions – it would be almost impossible to conduct safely a comprehensive search of a large, modern container vessel in anything but the most benign sea state – but such diversion must be based on a reasonable suspicion that the vessel is carrying contraband, is of an enemy character or on some other criteria that would enliven the belligerent right to visit and search the vessel. Another live question is whether the right exists in relation to NIACs – an issue hotly debated in terms of the Spanish Civil War,[109] and of enduring resonance given the recent Sri Lankan conflict and – depending upon legal characterisation – the Israel–Palestinian conflict.

There is no right for a belligerent to visit and search a vessel if it is being escorted under neutral state convoy as the responsibility for checking the material being transported in those vessels lies with the state exercising operational control over the convoy.[110] This obligation extends to ensuring that the convoy of neutral vessels is not heading for an enemy port. However, if enemy or neutral merchant vessels are being escorted under enemy convoy, then this fact alone would be enough to expose those vessels to the risk of attack. Resistance to visit and search can result in forfeiture of the normal protection from attack that merchant vessels otherwise enjoy.

3.4 Mine warfare

The use of mines, both at sea and in the land environment, is an aspect of warfare that has constantly attracted attention given the potential for indiscriminate outcomes affecting parts of the population entitled to protection from such effects. As noted earlier, 1907 Hague Convention (VIII)[111] attempted to deal with naval mine warfare – but as it existed over a century ago. However, the use of mines is not only an issue of historical interest. Mines are a relatively inexpensive weapon and have been deployed in almost every maritime conflict over the past

---

107 UNCLOS (n 9) arts 17–19, 38–39, 52–54.

108 Ibid art 110.

109 For example, Robert R Wilson, 'Recognition of Insurgency and Belligerency' (1937) 31 *ASIL Proceedings* 136; Fred K Nielsen, 'Insurgency and Maritime Law' (1937) 31 *ASIL Proceedings* 144; 'Discussion' (1937) 31 *ASIL Proceedings* 153.

110 Ronzitti (n 66) 268; *San Remo Manual* (n 8) 197–199.

111 1907 Hague Convention (VIII) (n 45).

century.[112] Technological advances have resulted in new types of mines being developed[113] and the provisions of Hague Convention (VIII), strictly interpreted, are not applicable to mines other than automatic contact mines. The *San Remo Manual* notes there are some basic principles that derive from Hague Convention (VIII) and customary international law that inform the law regarding naval mine warfare.[114] These key principles are: mines may only be used to achieve a legitimate military outcome, belligerents must retain some control over mines they have deployed and/or have the ability to render a mine safe if such control is lost, notification of mine fields must occur and the location of a mine field must be recorded so that the area can be cleared once hostilities have ceased. These principles have been reinforced by the ICJ on a number of occasions, including in the *Corfu Channel* case,[115] *Nicaragua* case[116] and the *Oil Platforms* case.[117]

3.5 Bombardment

The final means of maritime warfare that will be considered in this chapter is bombardment, the contemporary relevance of which was discussed above in the context of the 2003 Gulf War. One of the key issues that emerged was a requirement that those authorising the engagement 'fully understood their legal obligations in relation to precautions in attack'.[118] These obligations are not unique and reflect the provisions of Hague Convention (IX), relevant portions of Additional Protocol I and customary international law.[119]

The principle of distinction is of fundamental importance in bombardment as a means of warfare. There is no doubt that when deploying kinetic force belligerents must distinguish between combatants and civilians, as well as refrain from attacks against civilian/protected objects.[120] This requirement translates into a positive obligation, at multiple levels in the command chain, to ensure that only legitimate military targets are attacked. In a deliberate targeting scenario, where time is available to assess properly the likely consequences of bombardment, this obligation is not very difficult to meet. However, naval bombardment can often occur in a time-sensitive manner, especially when providing close support to an ongoing land operation. It does not matter what means of effecting bombardment are employed as the principles involved apply regardless of the method of delivery. Accordingly, the deployment of a land attack missile from a naval platform and the use of a warship's main gun system will require the same targeting considerations in order to ensure the outcome complies with the law. Indiscriminate attacks, of any type, are not permitted.

---

112 For example, mines were used in both World Wars, the Korean War, the Vietnam War, the 1980–1988 Iran–Iraq War, the 2003 Gulf War and during the 2011 Libyan conflict: see Heintschel von Heinegg (n 100) 221.

113 Types of mines include limpet mines (attached to a vessel's hull), moored/drifting/floating/bottom contact mines, remote controlled mines, magnetic/acoustic/pressure mines. There are also mines with special characteristics such as aerial delivery, torpedo propulsion, hydrostatic depth control and 'daisy-chain' mines.

114 *San Remo Manual* (n 8) 169–176.

115 *Corfu Channel* (n 21).

116 *Nicaragua* (n 48).

117 *Oil Platforms* (n 22).

118 Neil Brown, 'Legal Considerations in Relation to Maritime Operations against Iraq' in Raul A Pedrozo (ed), *The War in Iraq: A Legal Analysis* (US Naval War College 2010) 133.

119 For extensive discussion of these requirements, see *San Remo Manual* (n 8) 113–124.

120 See *Prosecutor v Strugar* (Case no IT-01-42-T, ICTY Trial Judgment, 31 January 2005).

4 Conclusion

LONW clearly seeks to explain and apply the fundamental principles of IHL within a maritime context. Although there are different factors and contextual variables at play, the irreducible and fundamental IHL principles applicable in LONW are the same as for any other environment – 'attack', 'military necessity' and 'proportionality' are defined in the same way at sea as they are ashore. But LONW is more than a merely mechanical application of general IHL principles within the maritime context; it is also a dialogue between IHL and the need to facilitate neutral trade in the margins of armed conflicts, the need to navigate the implications of common heritage and sovereignty in the conduct of armed conflict at sea and the need to accommodate the often unique applications of technology within the maritime operational domain. LONW is also an area of IHL in which the status of, and almost customary respect accorded to, a number of soft law instruments (such as the *San Remo Manual*) is well established – perhaps to an unparalleled degree. As responsive as this approach of applying IHL principles to the maritime domain via soft law instruments has proven to be, however, even some of these almost customary crystallisations have themselves begun to date. Indeed, there has been no substantial, encompassing, progressive soft law instrument – or even revision of an existing instrument – since the *San Remo Manual*. LONW has often been accused of lagging both technological advance and operational practice at sea, and whilst undoubtedly to some extent true, this criticism can unfairly tarnish in its generality – LONW is not a moribund discipline; indeed it is arguably one of the more dynamic components of IHL in general. However, there are new and renewed challenges to IHL interpretation and application – such as NIAC, civilians taking a direct part in hostilities, organised armed group, cyber[121] and autonomous weapons capabilities – which have not yet been adequately examined, debated and assessed in terms of their maritime applications and consequences. If LONW is to remain relevant and authoritative, it must – over the course of the next decade – engage with and respond to such emerging and re-emerging IHL challenges as they manifest in the maritime domain. In doing so, however, LONW must not ignore or seek to nullify the enduring contextual influences – and the unique accommodations of those interests – that have long underpinned its relevance and utility.

---

121 The forthcoming *Tallinn 2.0 Manual* will include a chapter dealing with the challenges that arise from cyber operations at sea.

16

Air and missile warfare

Ian Henderson and Patrick Keane

Compared with land and naval warfare, air and missile warfare is a relatively recent phenomenon. Unsurprisingly, therefore, the law that applies to air missile warfare draws on both of the other domains, either directly or indirectly, for relevant legal rules and principles. This chapter covers legal rules and principles which clearly apply to air and missile warfare and where the manner of application is reasonably uncontroversial, a further group of rules and principles where there is significant agreement on broad application but not necessarily the specifics and also those issues which remain areas of active controversy.

1 Rules on air warfare

There is limited treaty law dealing specifically with air and missile warfare, and what treaty law does exist mainly deals with medical aircraft.[1] However, there are two works of significant interest.

1.1 Status of 1923 Hague Rules of Air Warfare

As early as 1920, the ICRC recognised the need for clarity in the rules that applied to air warfare. Accordingly, a Commission of Jurists, made up of experts from France, Italy, Japan, the Netherlands, the UK and the US met at The Hague and a set of 'Rules of Air Warfare' ('HRAW') was adopted by them in 1923. Unfortunately for scholars of the law of air warfare, the HRAW were never set out in a treaty or in any other way officially endorsed as international law. Nevertheless, it is certainly suggested by some that the HRAW are generally recognised as constituting customary international law.[2]

---

1 See GCI ch VI; API arts 24–31.
2 *AP Commentary* ¶ 1637, fn 13. The HRAW are referred to by the ICTY as being 'considered to be an authoritative interpretation of the law'. *Prosecutor v Galić* (Case no IT-98-29-T, ICTY Trial Chamber, 5 December 2003) fn 103; *Prosecutor v Galić* (Case no IT-98-29-A, ICTY Appeals Chamber, 30 November 2006) fn 275.

1.2 Status of the 2009 Harvard Manual on the Law Applicable to Air and Missile Warfare

In 2009, the Program on Humanitarian Policy and Conflict Research (HPCR) at Harvard University published the *Manual on International Law Applicable to Air and Missile Warfare*, which summarises in 175 rules the various extant treaties and the eminent authors' assessment of customary international law as it applies specifically to the air environment.[3] There is also a *Commentary* on the *Manual* which 'clarifies the prominent legal interpretations and indicates differing perspectives'.[4] The purpose of the *AMW Manual* is to restate international law governing air and missile warfare.

When one looks at the manner in which it was produced, it is an inescapable conclusion that the *AMW Manual* contains the collated writings of many of 'the most highly qualified publicists of various nations'[5] on the topic of international law applicable to air and missile warfare. Like the *San Remo Manual on International Law Applicable to Armed Conflicts at Sea* (1994),[6] so the *AMW Commentary* may come to be regarded as a subsidiary means to determine international law applicable to air and missile warfare. As such, the *AMW Manual* is a highly persuasive, but not authoritative, exposition of the relevant law.

2 Definitions

2.1 State aircraft

The 1944 Chicago Convention defines 'aircraft' as any machine that can derive support in the atmosphere from the reactions of the air other than the reactions of the air against the Earth's surface.[7]

There is no exclusive definition for the term 'state aircraft' but aircraft used in military, customs and police services are deemed to be state aircraft.[8] It is open for states to assert that aircraft falling outside these three categories should still be regarded as state aircraft but there is potential for disagreement between states. States may assert that an aircraft on a civil aircraft register, owned by private entities and crewed by employees or contractors, is a state aircraft when it is in use for a government purpose. For example, under domestic law the US may designate chartered aircraft as state aircraft.[9] Conversely, there is no obligation upon other states to treat such aircraft as state aircraft.

Most states have existing administrative communication mechanisms for seeking 'diplomatic clearance' for state aircraft to overfly or land in the territory of other states. It is likely that states would utilise these mechanisms to achieve consensus on the status of particular aircraft.

3　*HPCR Manual on International Law applicable to Air and Missile Warfare* (2009), www.ihlresearch.org/amw/ ('*AMW Manual*').

4　*Commentary on the HPCR Manual on International Law applicable to Air and Missile Warfare* (2010), www. ihlresearch.org/amw/manual ('*AMW Commentary*') iii.

5　Per ICJ Statute art 38(1)(d).

6　*San Remo Manual on International Law Applicable to Armed Conflicts at Sea* (IIHL 1994) ('*San Remo Manual*').

7　Convention on International Civil Aviation (7 December 1944) 15 UNTS 295, annex 1 ('Chicago Convention'); *AMW Manual* (n 3) S A.

8　Ibid art 3.

9　See 49 USC § 40125(c)(1)(C).

2.2 Military aircraft and their crews

Under HRAW, to be regarded as a military aircraft, an aircraft must:

    (i) be operated by the armed forces of a State;
    (ii) bear the military markings of that State;
    (iii) be commanded by a member of the armed forces; and
    (iv) be controlled, manned or preprogrammed by a crew subject to regular armed forces discipline.[10]

Only military aircraft may carry out attacks on military objectives.[11] This proscription is likely to extend to any activity that may only be carried out lawfully in accordance with a belligerent right. There are of course numerous military activities that can be carried out lawfully without a belligerent right under the law of armed conflict.

Civil aircraft and non-military state aircraft being used by states for military purposes may constitute military objectives. Learned publications have provided indicative lists of activities which may render an aircraft liable to attack as a military objective.[12] Participation in one of the listed activities does not automatically render an aircraft a military objective: the general principles of international law regarding military objectives must always be satisfied. Indeed, even military aircraft must meet the tests under general principles of international law to be a legitimate military objective and this must be judged in the circumstances of the particular conflict.

To be afforded combatant status under the law of armed conflict, the crew of a military aircraft need to distinguish themselves from the civilian population. In a properly marked military aircraft, this can be achieved merely by being on board the aircraft and there is no positive requirement to wear distinguishing military uniforms. Of course, wearing such uniforms is useful in case the crew are separated from the aircraft in hostile territory (either by forced landing or through bailing out).[13] There is no requirement for such uniforms to bear badges of rank.[14] No such requirement exists with respect to land or naval warfare, and there is no reason under either treaty or customary international law to import such a restriction into aerial warfare.

2.3 Medical aircraft

For the purposes of the law of international armed conflict, medical aircraft are those exclusively employed for the removal of wounded and sick and for the transport of medical personnel and equipment.[15] Medical aircraft may be military aircraft, albeit lacking the combatant status of the latter, but may also be civilian aircraft. A substantial body of treaty law has been developed governing the protection of, and operating procedures for, medical aircraft.[16] Apart from the rules related to the marking of aircraft with distinctive emblems, there is limited evidence of state practice relying upon the treaty regime for the protection of medical aircraft, particularly the

---

10 HRAW arts 3 and 14; *San Remo Manual* (n 6) ¶ 13(j); *AMW Manual* (n 3) S A, ¶ 1(x).
11 HRAW art 15; *AMW Manual* (n 3) S D, r 17
12 *San Remo Manual* (n 6) ¶ 63; *AMW Manual* (n 3) r 27.
13 See HRAW art 15.
14 But see UK Ministry of Defence, *The Manual of the Law of Armed Conflict* (OUP 2004) ¶ 12.10.4 (as amended) ('UK *Manual*').
15 GCI art 36.
16 Ibid arts 36 and 37; API arts 24–31.

rules relating to the procedures to be adopted in various zones of the battlefield. It appears that states prefer to rely upon operational security and force protection measures for the protection of medical aircraft, rather than the forbearance of the adversary in accordance with the law of international armed conflict.

2.4 Unmanned aerial vehicles

Unmanned (or uninhabited) aerial vehicles (UAV) are aircraft that are either remotely piloted or operate autonomously. Other common terms include 'remotely piloted aircraft' ('RPA', the current term being preferred in some military circles), 'drone' (a term frequently used in the media), 'armed drone' and, when some form of armament is also involved, sometimes 'unmanned combat aerial vehicle' ('UCAV').[17] A UAV is the aircraft element of a system, comprising one or more aircraft (which can be expendable or recoverable and can carry lethal or non-lethal payloads), a flight control station, and information and retrieval or processing stations.[18] There are over 1,000 different makes and models of UAV on the market or in development in more than 50 countries; coming in fixed wing, rotorcraft and lighter-than-air flying machines; sized from micro UAVs that fit in the palm of a hand to 25,000-pound turbojets with wingspans wider than a Boeing 737.[19]

The legal issues discussed have generally concerned the use of force, the status of the operators of the aircraft (for example, military or civilian intelligence agent), the status of the intended target or the injury and damage caused to other than the intended target. None of these issues are unique to UAV. Comparatively little attention has been paid to legal issues concerning the aircraft themselves; however, the rise in the use and variety of UAV highlight some interesting legal issues. The main question is whether a UAV can be a 'military aircraft' for the purposes of the law of armed conflict.

In view of the definition of 'military aircraft' given above, the first point to note is that a UAV operated by a civilian intelligence agency may well be a state aircraft, but will *ipso facto* not be a military aircraft.

Second, the issue of markings on a military aircraft are highlighted by UAV. As UAV become smaller and smaller in size, the bearing of the military markings of a state appear to become less practically relevant. This is also true for stealth aircraft. While it is not yet possible to be definitive on this point, it may be that this aspect of the customary international law applicable to military aircraft is losing its legal significance.[20]

Third, being commanded by a member of the armed forces is not the same as being operated. Whether the aircraft is controlled, manned or pre-programmed by a crew subject to regular armed forces discipline is a separate question. The person who exercises command is the person who 'exercises authority over that aircraft'.[21] While authority can be exercised via manipulation of the flight controls, that is not a prerequisite. And with respect to a UAV, as the aircraft itself

---

17 See generally *AMW Commentary* (n 4) rr 1(dd) and (ee) and commentary.
18 Michael Sullivan, 'DOD could Achieve Greater Commonality and Efficiencies among its Unmanned Aircraft Systems', submission to the hearing by the Subcommittee on National Security and Foreign Affairs, Committee on Oversight and Government Reform, US House of Representatives, on 'Rise of the Drones: Unmanned Systems and the Future of War', 4, http://oversight.house.gov.
19 Douglas Marshall, 'Unmanned Aerial Systems and International Civil Aviation Organization Regulations' (2009) 85 *North Dakota LR* 693, 694–695 (internal footnotes omitted).
20 See generally Ian Henderson, 'International Law Concerning the Status and Marking of Remotely Piloted Aircraft' (2011) 39 *Denver JILP* 615.
21 *AMW Commentary* (n 4) r 1(x), ¶ 4.

is already being operated remotely, there seems to be no reason why a commander could not then also be remote from the operator.

Finally, UAV highlight the issue of the status of the crew. While customary international law indicates that the crew should be subject to regular armed forces discipline, it is clear from article 4(A)(4) of Geneva Convention III that at least some members of the crew may comprise civilian members. In the context of the UAV, 'crew' refers to those who are remotely operating or flight programming autonomous UAV.[22] It is unclear whether these accompanying civilians need to be subject to armed forces discipline for an aircraft to be a military aircraft.

3 Rules governing state aircraft

3.1 Navigation rights for state aircraft

State aircraft are not required to comply with the legal and navigation regimes for international civil aviation that are mandatory for civil aircraft. State aircraft may navigate freely in international airspace, paying due regard to the safety of navigation of civil aircraft.[23]

State aircraft require the permission of other states for entry to territorial airspace and entry of a state aircraft to territorial airspace without permission may be an internationally wrongful act. The exceptions to this requirement are where state aircraft are exercising transit passage or archipelagic sea lane passage (see below) and arguably *force majeure* (also discussed below).

3.2 Sovereign immunity of aircraft

Under customary international law, state aircraft attract the same character of sovereign immunity enjoyed by warships and other public vessels. There is no treaty law directly on point but there are a number of references in treaties which support this conclusion.[24] Therefore, state aircraft are exempt from laws regarding boarding, search, inspection and taxation in the absence of special stipulation. Permission for state aircraft to enter the territory of a foreign state is customarily in the form of diplomatic clearance. States may attempt to impose limitations on sovereign immunity as conditions for the grant of such clearance. These are matters to be negotiated between states but customarily the principle of foreign sovereign state immunity is observed.

Less settled is the status of the crew and passengers of a state aircraft when present in a foreign state. The extent of the immunity of the crew of public vessels and state aircraft while disembarked is not dealt with in treaty law and may be subject to interpretation by states and/or to bilateral agreement between states. If the correlation between state aircraft and public vessels extends to the crew, then members of the crew of a state aircraft who have disembarked the aircraft continue to enjoy certain immunity from local jurisdiction when on official business.

A further area of controversy is the extent of sovereign immunity of state aircraft that enter the territory of a foreign state without permission due to an emergency (for example, due to adverse weather, mechanical or medical emergency).

---

22 Ibid ¶ 6.
23 Chicago Convention (n 7) art 3 requires states to have due regard, when issuing regulations for their state aircraft, for the safety of navigation of civil aircraft.
24 United Nations Convention on the Law of the Sea (10 December 1982) 1833 UNTS 3 ('UNCLOS') arts 42(5) and 236. In relation to military aircraft, see also the Convention Relating to the Regulation of Aerial Navigation (13 October 1919) 11 LNTS 173 ('Paris Convention') art 32.

There is a specific duty on states to assist civil aircraft in distress under treaty law[25] but this does not extend to state aircraft.[26] Public vessels have a right under treaty law to stop and anchor in the territorial sea of a foreign state if rendered necessary by distress[27] and a right under customary law of entry to the ports or internal waters to shelter in order to preserve human life. Arguably, state aircraft should have an analogous right to land on foreign territory in emergency in order to preserve human life. The extent to which the state aircraft would enjoy sovereign immunity in these circumstances is the subject of doubt, though if the entry to foreign territory were lawful it should continue to have the same status as a public vessel in similar circumstances.[28]

3.3 State consortium aircraft

Aircraft are expensive to own and to operate. Defence budgets may not be able to afford large numbers of aircraft or the necessary maintenance and training infrastructure. While smaller states may only require a level of military capability that could be delivered by a small number of aircraft, there is a certain base level of infrastructure cost regardless of fleet size. For these reasons, states may seek to cooperate in the development of air capability by operating a fleet of aircraft collectively. This is a different concept from aircraft operated by an international organisation with legal personality. The aircraft would not be owned or operated exclusively by any state or international organisation but would be consortium aircraft used interchangeably by the various cooperating states. The concept of consortium aircraft poses a number of legal challenges for cooperating states.

Consortium aircraft would present conceptual challenges for non-participating states when the consortium aircraft sought access to state territory. Most aircraft, state and civil, are listed on a national register, usually distinguished by a tail number. The unique individual tail number indicates in which country the aircraft is registered and whether the aircraft is on a civil or state aircraft register. The register is more than just for identification purposes. It is part of the system of technical and operational airworthiness for aircraft in that state and indicates to other states the standards that have been applied in allowing the aircraft to be registered and operated. This allows other states to exercise discretion in authorising that aircraft to enter territorial airspace and operate out of airfields. States operating consortium aircraft would be required to deal with the issue of registration in a way that was acceptable to other states.

There is a question as to whether customary international law still requires a state aircraft to be on a single state register. In the early days of aviation there were specific requirements for aircraft to be on state register and not on the register of more than one state.[29] These requirements were not replicated in the international civil aviation regime but this did not seek to replace customary law for state aircraft.

Ultimately, the requirement for single state registration emanates from theories of state responsibility. Other states may be hesitant to give access to consortium aircraft unless an understanding can be reached about which country is responsible for the aircraft and its actions. This is particularly relevant in the area of liability for damage caused by the aircraft. The actions of state aircraft are imputed to the responsible state and it is likely that states would demand clarity

---

25 Chicago Convention (n 7) art 25.
26 Ibid art 3(a).
27 UNCLOS (n 24) art 18(2).
28 Ibid art 32.
29 Paris Convention (n 24) arts 5–8.

on state responsibility for the aircraft on any given flight. Practically speaking, it should be possible for an airframe either to move between registers, or otherwise to be attributable to specific states in a manner that satisfies both customary law and the need for state responsibility.

Thorny issues would arise for consortium aircraft in the event of an international armed conflict involving one or more of the participating states. Would the consortium aircraft be a valid military objective within the armed conflict only when operated by the state that is participating in the conflict? Would other participants in the consortium, who are neutral in the conflict, be acting inconsistent with neutrality if they conform to the terms of the consortium arrangement and share the aircraft with a belligerent party?

This is an area of considerable legal complexity and worthy of further exploration if consortium arrangements become more common.

4 Zones

4.1 National and international airspace

The principal divisions for airspace are national airspace and international airspace. States exercise full sovereignty over the national airspace above their land and territorial sea.[30] State aircraft may not enter national airspace of another state without authorisation by special agreement or otherwise.[31] States have granted civil aircraft of other states certain freedoms to enter national airspace for the purposes of international transportation and commerce.[32]

There is no settled limit to the maximum altitude of national airspace and the beginning of outer space. Various methodologies have been suggested for the upward delimitation of national airspace (and the earthward delimitation of outer space) principally using spatial, functional and scientific characteristics. The matter is not settled and there is little merit in restating the various proposals, as they have been set out in detail in other learned publications.[33] The formulation proposed by the *AMW Manual* that ' "air" or "airspace" means the air up to the highest altitude at which an aircraft can fly and below the lowest possible perigee of an earth satellite in orbit'[34] is from the functional school; and while persuasive,[35] it cannot be regarded as a final statement on the law.

4.2 Transit passage and archipelagic sea lane passage

State aircraft enjoy similar transit rights to public vessels through territorial and archipelagic waters of foreign states for both international straits and archipelagic sea lanes. All aircraft, including state aircraft, may exercise transit passage above straits which are used for international navigation between one part of the high seas or an exclusive economic zone and another part of the high seas or an exclusive economic zone[36] and through the territorial seas and archipelagic

---

30 Ibid art 1; Chicago Convention (n 7) art 1; *Military and Paramilitary Activities in and against Nicaragua (Nicaragua v US)* [1986] ICJ Rep 14, ¶ 251.
31 Chicago Convention (n 7) art 3.
32 Ibid ch II, arts 5–16.
33 Gbenga Oduntan, 'The Never Ending Dispute: Legal Theories on the Spatial Demarcation Boundary Plane between Airspace and Outer Space' (2003) 1(2) *Hertfordshire LJ* 64; Dean Reinhardt, 'The Vertical Limit of State Sovereignty' (2007) 72 *Journal of Air Law and Commerce* 65.
34 *AMW Manual* (n 3) r 1(a).
35 See s 1.2, above.
36 UNCLOS (n 24) art 38.

waters of archipelagic states above archipelagic sea lanes.[37] Aircraft do not enjoy rights of innocent passage in the territorial airspace of other states.[38]

Aircraft exercising transit or archipelagic sea lane passage are required to refrain from any activities other than those incident to their normal modes of continuous and expeditious transit, unless rendered necessary by *force majeure* or distress,[39] and particularly any threat or use of force against bordering states. This limitation does not preclude state aircraft from engaging in activities that are consistent with their security, the security of accompanying surface and subsurface forces, nor does the limitation prevent ships from launching and recovering aircraft.[40]

More delicate questions arise with respect to the use of sensors for purposes unrelated to the safety of navigation or the security of the aircraft or accompanying vessels. The use of sensors for general intelligence collection against targets in bordering states would not constitute a threat or use of force, nor a violation of the principles of international law embodied in the UN Charter. However, the use of sensors for purposes unrelated to continuous and expeditious transit would appear to be proscribed by treaty law. There would appear to be no prohibition against incidental collection of information through use of sensors for purposes associated with transit in the normal mode. It would generally be regarded as the normal mode for aircraft in transit to have all passive sensors (that is, sensors that receive some bandwidth of the electromagnetic spectrum) activated and to use active sensors (sensors that involve the transmission of some bandwidth of the electromagnetic spectrum and receiving a return from that transmission) for the purpose of air navigation and security.

There would not appear to be any prohibition under international law on the collection of intelligence by aircraft during a flight that has received diplomatic clearance for entry to national airspace. States may seek to impose conditions regarding the use of aircraft systems as conditions of diplomatic clearance. Given the lack of jurisdiction over activities on the aircraft, if an aircraft was suspected of acting in breach of conditions of a diplomatic clearance, the territorial state would be entitled to revoke diplomatic clearance and demand that the aircraft depart its territory.

4.3 Exclusion zones

Exclusion zones are a mechanism utilised by states in armed conflict to restrict navigation in specified areas. Exclusion zones do not have a basis in treaty law and states may seek to justify the declaration of exclusion zones in theories of national self-defence and military necessity. Exclusion zones may also be regarded as a measure taken by states in armed conflict to reduce the risk of civilian casualties. It provides notice to aircraft operators, and their insurers, that a certain area is regarded as a zone of active hostilities.

The declaration of an exclusion zone by a state does not alter any right of navigation that exists under international law. Interference with freedom of navigation, without lawful justification, may be regarded as an internationally wrongful act. Entry into an exclusion zone without authority does not justify attack and any attack must also conform to the general principles of the law of armed conflict. Entry by an aircraft to an exclusion zone may provide the belligerent

---

37 Ibid art 53.
38 Aircraft are deliberately excluded from the innocent passage regime set out in UNCLOS (n 24) pt II, s 3.
39 Ibid arts 39 and 54
40 *AMW Commentary* (n 4) r 170 and commentary.

enforcing the zone with some of the indicia that go to identifying an aircraft as a military objective.

Exclusion zones imposed through a resolution of the UN Security Council may have the effect of altering rights of navigation and other aspects of international law within the zone in a manner that is binding upon states.

4.4 Air defence identification zones

Air defence identification zones (ADIZs) are often misunderstood in terms of the applicable law. An ADIZ is an area of airspace that projects outwards from national airspace into international airspace. The authority for an ADIZ does not come from the Chicago Convention, but rather is an aspect of state sovereignty combined, potentially, with national self-defence. The principle purpose of an ADIZ is to help manage the common air picture by way of facilitating early identification of aircraft near a nation's sovereign airspace. As ADIZ operate in international airspace, no extra legal rights accrue to the state that proclaims the ADIZ. Rather, what the zones do is provide a means for facilitating the identification of aircraft that are on course to enter national airspace by making it a condition of entry to national airspace that an aircraft on entering the ADIZ is to identify itself to the relevant state.

Confusion sometimes arises when the states choose to use the presence of a non-identified aircraft in an ADIZ as one of the escalation triggers under its rules of engagement. Entry to an ADIZ without compliance with identification procedures does not, of itself, constitute a belligerent act and does not necessarily justify the use of force in self-defence. State aircraft are entitled under international law to navigate in international airspace and the ADIZ does not create any legal reporting obligation. The threat or use of force against a foreign aircraft navigating within an ADIZ may constitute an internationally wrongful act if not justified under principles of international law.

4.5 No-fly zones

No-fly zones are unique amongst the air zones in that a no-fly zone is imposed over another state's sovereign airspace. The best legal authority for imposing a no-fly zone is a UN Security Council resolution that specifically authorises such a zone. For example, UN Security Council Resolution 1973 (2011), relying on the authority granted under Chapter VII of the UN Charter, imposed a blanket ban (that is, both military and civil) on aircraft operating in Libyan airspace. It is also possible, albeit less persuasive, to derive implied authority for a no-fly zone from a Chapter VII UN Security Council resolution. An example of this approach is UN Security Council Resolution 688 in relation to Iraq. That particular resolution was relied upon by Coalition forces to impose and enforce a no-fly zone despite no specific mention of such a zone appearing in the resolution.

In a scholarly article dealing with no-fly zones, Professor Schmitt states that:

> If a state establishes a no-fly zone in the absence of a Security Council resolution, rules of attack apply within the zone in precisely the same manner as they would outside it. For instance, civilian aircraft violating the zone could not be engaged, as they would constitute civilian objects immune from attack.... However, enforcement of a Security Council-authorized no-fly zone applying to all aircraft ... necessarily alters the equation. A civilian aircraft violating a no-fly zone forfeits its civilian status and becomes a 'military objective,' because it is making an 'effective contribution to military action' and its 'destruction,

capture or neutralization, in the circumstances ruling at the time, offers a definite military advantage' to the states enforcing the no-fly zone. Were this not the case, the establishment of a no-fly zone prohibiting all flights would be meaningless.[41]

With respect, this argument is not without controversy. Rule 105 of the *AMW Manual* states that: '(a) A Belligerent Party is not absolved of its obligations under the law of international armed conflict by establishing "exclusion zones" or no-fly zones. (b) Zones designated for unrestricted air or missile attacks are prohibited.' And Rule 110 of the *AMW Manual* states: 'Subject to the Rules set out in Sections D and G of this Manual, aircraft entering a no-fly zone without specific permission are liable to be attacked.'

There is no reason to conclude that the UN Security Council can alter such significant facets of the law of armed conflict as the distinction between civilian objects and military objectives, or at least not without extremely specific language. It is hard to agree with the conclusion that the mere entry of a civilian aircraft into a no-fly zone automatically means that that aircraft is making an effective contribution to military action and that its capture, destruction or neutralisation will offer a military advantage. Professor Schmitt's argument seems premised on the basis that the imposition of a blanket no-fly zone would be meaningless if civilian aircraft were not liable to attack upon entry into such a zone. That is not necessarily the case. Such aircraft could be liable to forced landing, diversion and even seizure upon landing. While not a perfect analogy, consider UN Security Council resolutions under Chapter VII that impose bans on travel by certain state officials. Such resolutions allow legal mechanisms to be put in place to prohibit travel, and perhaps even a certain level of force to be used if a person attempts to travel, but would be unlikely to be interpreted to permit the use of lethal force to prevent travel contrary to the resolution.

An issue that does not appear to have received any discussion to date is whether the imposition of a no-fly zone is a belligerent act in much the same way as the declaring of a blockade under the law of naval warfare.

5 Means and methods of warfare

5.1 Precautions in attack – human shields

While not unique to aerial warfare, the issue of how to treat human shields in precautions in attack is a significant factor given the role of air power in conducting attacks on significant military objectives. Rule 45 of the *AMW Manual* states that a belligerent party may not use the civilian population to shield lawful targets from attack.[42] Civilians who are present at a military objective in this context are often referred to as 'human shields'. Notwithstanding the prohibition on using human shields, what are the legal consequences vis-à-vis an attack; and, in particular, how does the presence of such human shields affect the proportionality assessment?

The discussion of human shields invariably draws at least a conceptual distinction between involuntary and voluntary human shields;[43] and for some commentators, also a legal distinction. The commentary to Rule 45 of the *AMW Manual* sets out the issues clearly.

41 Michael Schmitt, 'Wings over Libya: The No-Fly Zone in Legal Perspective' (2011) 36 *Yale JIL Online* 45, www.yjil.org/online/volume-36-spring-2011/wings-over-libya-the-no-fly-zone-in-legal-perspective (internal footnotes omitted).
42 See API art 51(7).
43 See eg *AMW Commentary* (n 4) r 45, ¶ 5; and ICRC, *Interpretive Guidance on the Notion of Direct Participation in Hostilities under International Humanitarian Law* (ICRC 2009) 56–58 and 60.

For involuntary human shields, there are essentially two possible positions. There is no significant dispute that involuntary human shields count as civilians in a proportionality analysis, with the only disagreement being whether such human shields count in the usual way or whether a reduced weighting is given to involuntary human shields in the proportionality analysis when compared to other civilians.[44] While sympathetic to the position, it cannot be the law that different types of humans are weighted differently. A human life is a human life and the law does not make distinctions about relative worth.[45]

With respect to voluntary human shields there are three main views. The first view is that voluntary human shields are not counted in the proportionality equation at all because they are civilians taking a direct part in hostilities. The second view is that not only do voluntary human shields count in the proportionality equation but they are given the usual weighting that would apply to any other civilian. A third view is that voluntary human shields do count but are given less weighting in the proportionality analysis when compared to other civilians.[46] Starting with the third position first, this cannot be the law for the same reasons discussed above with respect to involuntary human shields – the law does not make distinctions about the relative worth of different human beings. Which of the first or second positions is the correct one is a more difficult legal conundrum: however, a few points can be made.

First, arguments with respect to the 'intention' of voluntary human shields rendering them civilians taking a direct part in hostilities are misleading. The key issue under the law of armed conflict is effect or potential threat, with the subjective mental state of intention usually being reserved for consideration of offences under international criminal law. Two examples might suffice to explain this point. Conscripts are considered combatants, and therefore lawful targets, just as much as volunteers. Equally a civilian worker inside a military objective (for example, a munitions factory or a military headquarters) does not lose protection from attack merely by voluntarily being present in a clear military objective. Some respected commentators do, however, associate mental state with targetability under the law of armed conflict. For example, Melzer talks about the non-targetability of 'civilians [who] are totally unaware of the role they are playing in the conduct of hostilities'.[47]

Second, it may be that the commentators are looking at the wrong area of law to deal with the issue of voluntary human shields. Tortured mental gymnastics are required to squeeze the concept of a voluntary human shield into the legal notion of direct participation into hostilities, particularly where the human shield is not creating an actual physical obstacle to military operations (for example, physically attempting to block the movement of a military vehicle across a narrow causeway) but are merely attempting to provide by their presence a legal obstacle in the form of affecting the proportionality assessment.

Rather than trying to conclude that this somehow amounts to the legal notion of direct participation in hostilities, it may be the case that a legal argument could be made that such civilians have forfeited a certain element of protection under the law of armed conflict (that is, to be counted in the proportionality assessment) without having lost civilian status. While not a perfect analogy, this would be comparable to the common law legal notion in the law of negligence of *volenti non fit injuria* ('to one who volunteers, no harm is done'). Importantly, the loss of protection would be limited to assessment under the concept of proportionality. It would still be unlawful to

44 *AMW Commentary* (n 4) r 45, ¶ 7.
45 See Ian Henderson, *The Contemporary Law of Targeting: Military Objectives, Proportionality and Precautions in Attack under Additional Protocol I* (Martinus Nijhoff 2009) 215 and 246.
46 *AMW Commentary* (n 4) r 45, ¶ 6.
47 ICRC, *Interpretive Guidance* (n 43) 60.

use prohibited weapons against voluntary human shields, for example, and, if captured, they would be entitled to appropriate protection under the law of armed conflict etc. A further advantage of this form of analysis is that it avoids having to consider whether a voluntary human shield is targetable, for example, while on a bus travelling towards but still some distance away from the military objective, on the basis that they have commenced taking a direct part in hostilities upon movement towards the location at which the direct participation will occur.[48]

A final point worth noting with respect to voluntary human shields is that there is an obligation on the defending belligerent party to at least discourage and in all likelihood take positive steps to remove them from the presence of military objectives.[49]

5.2 Surrender by/to aircraft

While it may initially seem a straightforward issue, the legal concept of surrender both by and to aircraft remains a debated point in the law of armed conflict. Starting with the general proposition it is legally uncontroversial to state that:

> Persons who are *hors de combat* – either because they have clearly expressed an intention to surrender or as a result of sickness, wounds or shipwreck – must not be attacked, provided that they abstain from any hostile act and no attempt is made to evade capture.[50]

Nonetheless, there are two issues that require discussion with respect to air operations. The first issue is even whether an aircraft in the air can validly surrender. Even the terminology is of interest. It is common in the law of naval warfare to talk about a ship surrendering, but of course a ship is itself an inanimate object. The same applies to aircraft. What is really under discussion is surrender by the captain or crew of the aircraft. This point is well illustrated in rule 125 of the *AMW Manual*, which states that: 'Enemy personnel may offer to surrender themselves (and the military equipment under their control) to a Belligerent Party.' Therefore, it is always important to identify whether the crew of the aircraft can validly offer to surrender in various circumstances. In this regard note that Rule 126 of the *AMW Manual* states that: 'It is prohibited to deny quarter to those manifesting the intent to surrender.' In other words, the mere fact that the person offering to surrender is the pilot of an aircraft is not a ground for refusing to accept the offer of surrender.

The UK *Manual* states that 'in air-to-air combat, surrender is usually impracticable and occurs very infrequently'.[51] The concern in the case of aerial warfare is that a 'pilot who remains in his [sic] aircraft cannot be said to have "laid down his arms" or to have "no longer a means of defence"'.[52] While an understandable concern, this does not change the fundamental legal principles. Rule 127 of the *AMW Manual* states:

> Surrender is contingent on three cumulative conditions:
>
> (a) The intention to surrender is communicated in a clear manner to the enemy.
> (b) Those offering to surrender must not engage in any further hostile acts.
> (c) No attempt is made to evade capture.

---

48 On the issue of the temporal connection for direct participation in hostilities including preparations for and return from combat, see ICRC, *Interpretive Guidance* (n 43) 67.
49 *AMW Commentary* (n 4) r 43, ¶ 4.
50 See *AMW Manual* (n 3) r 15(b); API art 41; HR art 23(c).
51 UK *Manual* (n 14) ¶ 12.64.
52 Ibid ¶ 12.6 4.1.

Laying down arms or no longer having a means of defence are not strict requirements of the law. If they were, it would be close to impossible for the captain of a warship ever to surrender short of abandoning ship. Notably, up to this point the rules quoted from the *AMW Manual* have been dealing with general propositions of law applicable to armed conflict. The *AMW Manual* also sets out rules specific to surrender in aerial warfare, namely:

> 128. Aircrews of a military aircraft wishing to surrender ought to do everything feasible to express clearly their intention to do so. In particular, they ought to communicate their intention on a common radio channel such as a distress frequency.
>
> 129. A Belligerent Party may insist on the surrender by an enemy military aircraft being effected in a prescribed mode, reasonable in the circumstances. Failure to follow any such instructions may render the aircraft and the aircrew liable to attack.
>
> 130. Aircrews of military aircraft wishing to surrender may, in certain circumstances, have to parachute from the aircraft in order to communicate their intentions.

As can be seen from the rules themselves, there are no limitations or exceptions for offers to surrender merely because an aircraft is airborne, is in contested or enemy airspace[53] or, for that matter, is offering to surrender to ground forces. This may be contrasted to the UK *Manual* which states, incorrectly in our view, that offers to surrender need only be accepted where the circumstances do not prevent enforcement (using the example of where an engagement has not taken place over enemy territory).

The second issue involves offers of surrender by ground forces to an aircraft, the concern being: how can an aircraft accept such surrender?[54] Notwithstanding views to the contrary,[55] the better view is that where ground or naval forces offer to surrender to an aircraft, that offer must be respected and the feasibility of immediately taking the surrendering combatant into custody is not relevant.[56] In the authors' experiences over many years of being instructed upon and conducting instruction on the law of armed conflict, the very common example when dealing with the topic of surrender is the dilemma for a special forces patrol that is behind enemy lines and comes across enemy forces who promptly surrender. There has never been any debate that the legal point is that they must respect the offer to surrender and not shoot the surrendering combatants, notwithstanding that the special forces mission will be significantly if not completely compromised regardless of whether they take the surrendering combatants into custody or release them on the spot.

Consistent with the concept of surrender, the surrendering combatant must obey any reasonable instructions that are given until such time as they can be taken into custody or it becomes apparent that they will not be taken into custody. In some circumstances, the aircraft may be able to land (particularly if it is a rotary wing), or remain on station pending the arrival of another force element to take the surrendering combatant into custody, or provide directions that are reasonable in the circumstances for the surrendering combatant to move in the direction

---

53 Ibid.
54 See Angus Stickler, 'US Apache Guns down Surrendering Insurgents' *Bureau of Investigative Journalism* (23 May 2010), www.thebureauinvestigates.com/2011/05/23/us-apache-guns-down-surrendering-insurgents; David Leigh, 'Iraq War Logs: Apache Crew Killed Insurgents Who tried to Surrender' *Guardian* (22 October 2010), www.guardian.co.uk/world/2010/oct/22/iraq-war-logs-apache-insurgents-surrender.
55 *AMW Commentary* (n 4) r 15(b), ¶ 8.
56 Ibid r 15(b), ¶ 8, and r 127(c), ¶ 2.

of another force element that can take the surrendering combatant into custody.[57] The point is well made in the *AMW Manual* that offers to surrender must be in good faith, and if forces regularly offer to surrender and then recommence fighting upon an aircraft's departure, future offers of surrender may be treated with suspicion.[58]

6 Interference with aircraft in international airspace

6.1 Interception of neutral aircraft

A number of learned works specify rules of international law concerning the interception of neutral civil aircraft.[59] The interception of neutral civilian aircraft is portrayed as a belligerent right, enjoyed exclusively by belligerent military aircraft. The context for this statement depends upon what is meant by the word 'intercept' in aircraft operations.

State aircraft, which include aircraft in customs and police service as well as military aircraft, are free to navigate in international airspace, with the limitation that they must have due regard for the safety of navigation of civil aircraft.[60] There is no doubt that non–military state aircraft are lawfully entitled to navigate in international airspace and to approach, identify and communicate with civilian aircraft. There is little basis to suggest that these rights would be suspended during international armed conflict or limited to military aircraft.

For the same reason, military aircraft enjoy the right to navigate freely in international airspace and to approach, identify and communicate with aircraft, without relying upon a belligerent right under the law of armed conflict. Hence the word 'intercept' in the context of a belligerent right must have some different meaning to merely approaching, identifying and communicating with an aircraft and must relate to some interference with the navigation or operation of the aircraft that would otherwise be prohibited by international law in the absence of a belligerent right.

6.2 Intelligence collection in international airspace[61]

There is no prohibition in international law on the collection of intelligence by aircraft in international airspace against targets within state territory of a foreign state. It is no different in this regard from the collection of intelligence from space or indeed from terrestrial assets within the territory of the collecting state. States may view the collection of intelligence as a potential threat to national security but this does not necessarily justify the use of lethal force in national self-defence.

In an international armed conflict, the law of armed conflict would allow attack upon military objectives and a state aircraft of the adversary collecting intelligence would likely fall within this category. Outside an existing international armed conflict, states may seek to justify the use of lethal force against a state aircraft collecting intelligence in international airspace on some theory of the right of national self-defence. The collection of intelligence would not, of itself, amount to an armed attack giving rise to a right of self-defence under the UN Charter (query the

---

57 *AMW Commentary* (n 4), r 127(c), ¶ 2.
58 Ibid r 15(b), ¶ 8, and r 127(c), ¶ 3.
59 *San Remo Manual* (n 6) 125; *AMW Manual* (n 3) s U.
60 Chicago Convention (n 7) art 3(c).
61 See also s 4.2, above.

situation where the intelligence collection is preparatory to, or an element of, an imminent armed attack).

In the absence of an armed conflict or imminent armed attack it is likely that the use of lethal force against a state aircraft suspected of collecting intelligence in international airspace would not be justified as an act of national self-defence and would be regarded as an internationally wrongful act and, potentially, an armed attack justifying a lawful response in self-defence.

Different considerations may apply if the aircraft is in fact causing more tangible damage to persons or property (including computer systems or data) within the territorial state through a cyber attack. In that respect the aircraft is no different from any other medium of delivery and the law that applies is the emerging law related to cyber operations.

As an alternative to lethal response, the territorial state may seek to prevent the collection of intelligence through non-lethal means. This could include harassing or buzzing the collecting aircraft or using electronic counter measures to defeat the collecting aircraft's sensors. There is no prohibition on taking such measures, noting however that state aircraft are free to navigate in international airspace and any action that caused a hazard to the safety of air navigation may constitute an internationally wrongful act.

7 Coalition warfare

Legal issues associated with coalition warfare are not unique to aerial warfare but do play a prominent part due to the nature of air operations. It is not unusual for a strike package to comprise attack aircraft from one nation, support aircraft from another and for the planning and authorising of the attack to have involved officers from both the aircraft contributing nations and other nations in a multinational headquarters.'[F]or the military lawyer, issues of State responsibility for the actions of others are some of the most complex that they encounter in coalition operations.'[62] While the law itself and the legal answers are not yet clear, to some extent the questions are clear.

> (Under what conditions) does ... responsibility lie solely with one actor (and, if so, with whom – the lead-nation, the State whose personnel are committing the internationally wrongful act or the inter-governmental organization under whose authority a State's contingent operates)? Can States and inter-governmental organizations bear concurrent responsibility, and, if so, what should be the principles governing the apportioning of the applicable consequences, including reparation for injury?[63]

Imagine the scenario of a UN Security Council sanctioned peace enforcement operation. States A and B wish to support but to avoid 'boots on the ground', State A contributes intelligence, surveillance and reconnaissance UAV and State B augments State A's UAV crew with both operators and analysts. State C uses both the intelligence provided to conduct military operations.

---

62 Alan Cole, 'Legal Issues in Forming the Coalition' in Michael Schmitt (ed), *The War in Afghanistan: A Legal Analysis* (US Naval War College 2009) 141, 148.

63 Swedish National Defence College and Amsterdam Centre for International Law, 'Research Project: Responsibility in Multinational Military Organisations' (2009), http://users.ox.ac.uk/~sann2029/abstract-responsibility-in-multinational-mil-op.pdf. For an interesting research project on state responsibility, see *SHARES: Research Project on Shared Responsibility in International Law*, www.sharesproject.nl/.

To determine potential legal liability, the main legal decision points in a military operation must be identified;[64] and then liability for those decisions is based on the law that deals with the responsibility of states and international organisations. The starting point, therefore, is the work of the International Law Commission on the articles on Responsibility of States for Internationally Wrongful Acts prepared by the International Law Commission,[65] along with the draft articles on the Responsibility of International Organizations.[66] While neither set of articles are treaties and have no direct force of law by themselves, both are potentially a useful black-letter expression of what may constitute customary international law,[67] particularly when being cited with some authority.[68] Based on those articles and the case law to date,[69] some broad propositions can be put forward.

While it has been suggested that all members of a coalition should bear joint responsibility for the internationally wrongful acts of any other member, that is not the law.[70] Rather, the critical legal question is whether a state exercised effective control over the actions of a component of a coalition military force. The mere ability to exercise control is not sufficient. The question is who did exercise specific control in the particular circumstances?[71] Also, a state is only responsible to the extent that its own conduct has contributed to the internationally wrongful act[72] and even then only where the act of State C would have been unlawful if committed by State A.[73] Where State A and State C's international legal responsibilities vary such that what would be an unlawful act for State C is not an unlawful act for State A,[74] then State A does not attract liability under this article.

---

64 See eg the six-step LOAC targeting process that was developed and adopted by Australia in the lead up to the 2003 Gulf War. Air Marshal Angus Houston, 'The Law of Armed Conflict and Contemporary Air Operations: The ADF Approach' Speech delivered at the Solferino Seminar, Weston Creek, 11 May 2004, www.defence.gov.au/raaf/corporate/leaders/Solferino%20Seminar.pdf. For more detailed explanation of the process, see Henderson (n 45) 237–238.

65 'Responsibility of States for Internationally Wrongful Acts' Report of the International Law Commission on the Work of its Fifty-Third session, UN Doc A/56/10 (2001).

66 'Responsibility of International Organizations: Texts and Titles of Draft Articles 1 to 67' International Law Commission on the Work of its Sixty-Third Session, UN Doc A/CN.4/L.778 (2011).

67 See Caitlin Bell, 'Reassessing Multiple Attribution: The International Law Commission and the *Behrami and Saramati* decision' (2010) 42 *NYU JILP* 501, 520–521.

68 See eg *Al-Jedda v UK* (App no 27021/08, ECtHR GC, 7 July 2011) ¶¶ 56 and 84.

69 The key cases of interest currently are: *Nicaragua* (n 30); *Armed Activities on the Territory of the Congo (Democratic Republic of the Congo v Uganda)* [2005] ICJ Rep 168; *Application of the Convention on the Prevention and Punishment of the Crime of Genocide (Bosnia and Herzegovina v Serbia and Montenegro)* [2007] ICJ Rep 91; *Behrami v France; Saramati v France (Admissibility)* (App nos 71412/01 and 78166/01, ECtHR GC, 2 May 2007); *Al-Jedda* (n 68). See also *Mustafić-Mujić et al v The Netherlands* (Case no 200.020.173/01, Court of Appeal in The Hague, 5 July 2011), http://zoeken.rechtspraak.nl/detailpage.aspx?ljn=BR5386; *Nuhanović v The Netherlands* (Case no 200.020.174/01, Court of Appeal in The Hague, 5 July 2011), http://zoeken. rechtspraak.nl/detailpage.aspx?ljn=BR5388. See generally Richard C Gross and Ian Henderson, 'Multinational Operations' in Geoffrey S Corn, Rachel E VanLandingham and Shane R Reeves (eds), *U.S. Military Operations: Law, Policy, and Practice* (OUP 2015) 341–370.

70 Torsten Stein, 'Coalition Warfare and Differing Legal Obligations of Coalition Members under International Humanitarian Law' in Andru E Wall (ed), *Legal and Ethical Lessons of NATO's Kosovo Campaign* (US Naval War College 2002) 317, 334.

71 'State Responsibility' Report of the International Law Commission on the Work of its Fifty-Third Session, UN Doc A/56/10 (23 April to 1 June and 2 July to 10 August 2001), 68–69, http://untreaty. un.org/ilc/reports/2001/2001report.htm.

72 Ibid, 66–67.

73 Ibid.

74 For example, State B is a party to a treaty obligation that is not binding (either as matter of treaty or customary international law) on State A.

Finally, it is worth noting that it may also be possible for more than one entity to share legal responsibility. For example, Article 47 of the articles on Responsibility of States for Internationally Wrongful Acts provides that '[w]here several States are responsible for the same internationally wrongful act, the responsibility of each State may be invoked in relation to that act'. This article does not deal with determining whether State A is internationally responsible for the acts of State C, but rather states that both States A and C can be concurrently liable.[75]

---

75 See Bell (n 67).

Part IV
Special protection regimes

In addition to the general protection of civilians and civilian objects (discussed in Part II) and the regulation of means and methods of warfare (Part III), LOAC makes special provision for particular categories of persons and objects:

- persons detained as a result of the conflict, including prisoners of war and civilian internees (Chapter 17);
- the wounded and the sick, as well as those tasked with their care (Chapter 18);
- women (Chapter 19);
- children (Chapter 20);
- cultural property (Chapter 21);
- the natural environment (Chapter 22);
- those involved in the delivery of humanitarian relief (Chapter 23);
- those involved in peacekeeping operations (Chapter 24).

Additionally, discrete subsets of LOAC rules apply in circumstances where one state party to an armed conflict exercises authority over the territory of another (occupation) (Chapter 25) and in relation to states that have chosen to remain outside the conflict (neutrality) (Chapter 26).

Part IV

Special protection regimes

17
Detention under the law of armed conflict

Chris Jenks

Despite recent hard earned experience during international and non-international armed con-flicts in places like Afghanistan and Iraq, and in peacekeeping missions around the world,[1] the international community continues to struggle practically and conceptually with detention of belligerents. The struggle includes questions ranging from when individuals may be detained and for how long, to determining the applicable legal regime. While this myriad of issues is vexing, they are neither as new,[2] nor the applicable law as lacking,[3] as has been argued.

This chapter addresses what to some has become a legal Gordian Knot[4] – detention during armed conflict. Similarly to Alexander's approach of cutting the knot, this chapter takes a prag-matic approach to detention.

This chapter will begin by providing an overview of the traditional law of armed conflict (LOAC) applicable to detention during international armed conflict (IAC). The 1949 Geneva Conventions, supplemented by Additional Protocol I, create a binary detention system in IAC – status-based detention of prisoners of war (POWs) and conduct-based detention or internment of civilians. Next the chapter will provide an overview of the LOAC applicable to

---

1 Notably MONUSCO, the UN Mission in the Democratic Republic of the Congo. In 2013 the UN Security Council issued a resolution creating an intervention brigade with the mission to take offensive action to 'neutralize' the armed groups threatening stability in eastern DRC. See UNSC Res 1925 (28 May 2010). This has led to the UN conducting offensive operations, which at some point will entail capturing members of the armed groups. Where such detainees would be housed, under whose control, under what conditions and when/how/and to whom they would be released are all unclear.

2 For one of many examples of previous conflicts involving non-state actors, see Thomas Pakenham, *The Boer War* (Abacus 1991) (describing the Second Boer War in South Africa, which featured belligerents who did not wear military uniforms, violations of the laws and customs of war by both sides and, in terms of detention, one of the first concentration camps. British military interned the families of Boer Commandos).

3 See Alberto Gonzales, 'Decision RE Application of the Geneva Convention on Prisoners of War to the Conflict with al Qaeda and the Taliban' Memorandum for the President (25 January 2002) (referring to the Geneva Convention's limitations on questioning prisoners of war as 'obsolete' and other provisions as 'quaint').

4 See generally Geoffrey Corn and Eric Talbot Jensen, 'Untying the Gordian Knot: A Proposal for Deter-mining the Applicability of the Laws of War to the War on Terror' (2008) 81 *Temple LR* 787. As the title suggests, Corn and Jensen's analysis is at the broader normative level of what law could or should apply.

non-international armed conflicts (NIAC). From there the chapter will explain several of the contemporary challenges to that traditional IAC model. The first of these challenges is the inverse relationship between the prevalence of the types of armed conflict and the amount of law strictly applicable to those conflicts. While almost all of the wartime detention law applies to IAC, the vast majority of contemporary armed conflicts are NIAC for which little law exists. Thus even to the extent that the 1949 Geneva Conventions framework could be useful in guiding contemporary detention operations, the Conventions do not formally apply. The chapter then discusses how, even if the Conventions were to apply, there would still be difficulties: should non-state actors, like members of al-Qaeda, be detained as prisoners of war or civilian internees? What does the answer to that question mean in terms of their treatment and subsequent release?

The chapter concludes by proposing that the 1949 Geneva Conventions and the 1977 Additional Protocols, outmoded and seemingly inapplicable though they may be in some respects, offer the most thorough, humane, realistic and readily available option for determining how to treat and when to release non-state actors detained during a NIAC. This chapter proposes to cut the legal Gordian Knot with a policy sword, intermingling types and applications of the law of armed conflict and conflating treatment standards from Geneva Convention III with the civilian internment and release provisions of Geneva Convention IV.

1 Authority to detain in international armed conflict

The LOAC does not provide positive authority to detain. Indeed the LOAC does not, in and of itself, provide authority for conduct of any kind. Rather the LOAC consists of international rules designed to humanise armed conflict to the extent possible by limiting its effects. That said, detention is considered within the nature of,[5] or inherent to,[6] armed conflict, at least during IAC.

The vast majority of the LOAC on detention, notably all four of the 1949 Geneva Conventions and Additional Protocol I, is only triggered by IAC. Given that, reviewing the traditional model of detention in IAC before addressing detention in NIAC is appropriate.

2 IAC model: POWs and civilian internment

The traditional model of detention in armed conflict is based on IAC − state on state warfare with a clear end. This is not surprising given the development of the 1949 Geneva Conventions in the aftermath of the Second World War, which involved global-scale armed conflict between

---

5 The US Supreme Court confronted the issue of authority to detain in *Hamdi v Rumsfeld*, a case brought by a US citizen detained during hostilities in Afghanistan. While acknowledging that the domestic law authorising 'all necessary and appropriate force' did not refer to detention, the Court stated that 'detention to prevent a combatant's return to the battlefield is a fundamental incident of waging war' a proposition on which the Court claimed 'universal agreement and practice': *Hamdi v Rumsfeld*, 542 US 507, 519 (2004). See *Ex parte Quirin*, 317 US 1, 31 (1942), stating that

> [l]awful combatants are subject to capture and detention as prisoners of war by opposing military forces. Unlawful combatants are likewise subject to capture and detention, but in addition they are subject to trial and punishment by military tribunals for acts which render their belligerency unlawful.

6 Jelena Pejic, 'The Protective Scope of Common Article 3: More than Meets the Eye' (2011) 93 *IRRC* 189, 207 (stating that '[i]n the ICRC's view, both treaty and customary IHL contain an inherent power to intern').

the multi-state Axis forces and the multi-state Allies. The ends of the various conflicts were unequivocal, with Italy, Germany and finally Japan signing formal instruments of surrender.

The trigger for the application of this law is found in what is known as Common Article 2, so named because it is the same in each of the four 1949 Geneva Conventions. Common Article 2 states that the Geneva Conventions 'shall apply to all cases of declared war or of any other armed conflict which may arise between two or more of the High Contracting Parties, even if the state of war is not recognized by one of them'.[7]

When there is an IAC, in terms of detention the relevant conventions are Geneva Convention III, devoted to POWs, and Geneva Convention IV, which details regulations for the treatment of internees, civilians detained/interned as security threats.

2.1 Geneva Convention III: status-based detention of POWs

At a strategic level, capturing members of the opposing force in armed conflict is one of numerous measures employed as part of an overall effort to bring the enemy in the collective sense to submission. At a narrower, tactical or operational level, by capturing and incapacitating members of the opposing force the capturing force ensures it does not face those same members in future engagements.

Capturing a member of the enemy force is based on their status as such, not on an individualised assessment of their threat.[8] The LOAC presumes that belligerent operatives 'are part of the military potential of the enemy and it is therefore always lawful to attack [and thus to capture] them for the purpose of weakening that potential'.[9] As the ICRC acknowledges, '[p]risoners of war may be interned ... for no individual reason. The purpose of this internment is not to punish them, but only to hinder their direct participation in hostilities and/or to protect them'.[10]

To qualify for POW status under Geneva Convention III, an individual must fall in one of the following categories listed in Article 4(A) of the Convention:

(1) Members of the armed forces of a party to the conflict as well as members of militia or volunteer corps forming part of such armed forces.

(2) Members of other militias and members of other volunteer corps, including those of organized resistance movements, belonging to a Party to the conflict and operating in or outside their own territory, even if this territory is occupied, provided that such militias or volunteer corps, including such organized resistance movements, fulfill the following conditions:

---

7 See GCIII–IV common art 2. Note the prescient nature of the trigger not to require a declaration of war but link the application of the Geneva Conventions to the existence of armed conflict between states. Indeed since the Second World War while there have been numerous armed conflicts, there have been few declarations of war. Some of the few post-1949 conventions declarations of war include the 1978 war between Somalia and Ethiopia, the 1980 Iran–Iraq War, the 1982 war between the UK and Argentina and the 2005 conflict between Chad and Sudan. In terms of the Geneva Conventions only applying to High Contracting Parties, every state in the world has signed or acceded to the Conventions.

8 See Geoffrey S Corn, Laurie R Blank, Chris Jenks and Eric Talbot Jensen, 'Belligerent Targeting and the Invalidity of a Least Harmful Means Rule' (2013) 89 *International Law Studies* 536.

9 Marco Sassòli and Laura M Olson, 'The Relationship between International Humanitarian and Human Rights Law where it Matters: Admissible Killing and Internment of Fighters in Non-International Armed Conflicts' (2008) 90 *IRRC* 599, 606.

10 Marco Sassòli, Antoine A Bouvier and Anne Quintin, *How Does Law Protect in War?* (3rd edn, ICRC 2011) 10.

(a) that of being commanded by a person responsible for his subordinates;

(b) that of having a fixed distinctive sign recognizable at a distance;

(c) that of carrying arms openly;

(d) that of conducting their operations in accordance with the laws and customs of war.

(3) Members of regular armed forces who profess allegiance to a government or an authority not recognized by the Detaining Power.

(4) Persons who accompany the armed forces without actually being members thereof, such as civilian members of military aircraft crews, war correspondents, supply contractors, members of labour units or of services responsible for the welfare of the armed forces, provided that they have received authorization from the armed forces which they accompany, who shall provide them for that purpose with an identity card similar to the annexed model.

(5) Members of crews, including masters, pilots and apprentices, of the merchant marine and the crews of civil aircraft of the Parties to the conflict, who do not benefit by more favourable treatment under any other provisions of international law.

(6) Inhabitants of a non-occupied territory, who on the approach of the enemy spontaneously take up arms to resist the invading forces, without having had time to form themselves into regular armed units, provided they carry arms openly and respect the laws and customs of war.

Notably, only categories (1), (2), (3) and (6) involve combatants, meaning those imbued with the right to directly participate in hostilities.[11] As will be discussed later, categories (4) and (5) are civilians who are nonetheless entitled to POW status and treatment, but who lack the right to participate directly in hostilities.

Where there is doubt concerning whether or not a belligerent who has fallen into the hands of the enemy belongs to one of the POW categories, Article 5 of Geneva Convention III provides that 'such persons shall enjoy the protection of the present Convention until such time as their status has been determined by a competent tribunal'. Until such an 'Article 5 tribunal' determines otherwise, the default setting or rebuttable presumption is that a captured belligerent is entitled to POW status.

POW status means an individual is entitled to be treated under the terms of Geneva Convention III.[12] The Convention provides robust and detailed protections at all stages. Part III of the Convention is titled 'Captivity' and is broken into sections and corresponding protections. Section I deals with the beginning of captivity and Section II about internment of POWs. Section II is subdivided into chapters which cover issues including quarters, food and clothing

---

11 Military medical and religious personnel exclusively engaged in the care of the sick and wounded, while members of the armed forces are considered non-combatants as they do not have the right to directly participate in hostilities. When captured, they are not POWs but rather are 'retained personnel'. Essentially a capturing force may retain them to provide spiritual and medical assistance to POWs but must release them as soon as they are not required to provide such assistance. See GCIII art 33. See further James P Benoit, 'Wounded and sick, and medical services' ch 18 in this volume.

12 Returning to those categories of POWs who are combatants and have the right to direct participation, with that right comes the combatant's privilege, meaning that combatants 'cannot be held criminal responsible for lawful belligerent acts [like shooting and killing an enemy soldier] during wartime': Laurie R Blank and Gregory P Noone, *International Law and Armed Conflict: Fundamental Principles and Contemporary Challenges in the Law of War* (Aspen 2013) 243.

of POWs, hygiene and medical attention, religious, intellectual and physical activities, discipline, rank of POWs and transfer of POWs after their arrival in a POW camp. Section III covers POW labour, Section IV deals with POW financial resources, Sections V and VI address POW relations with the exterior and the authorities respectively. The result is a full panoply of protections, including the right to humane treatment, protection from insults and public curiosity, equal treatment, free maintenance and medical care and freedom from reprisals.

Under Geneva Convention III, '[p]risoners of war shall be released and repatriated without delay after the cessation of active hostilities'.[13] Even before the cessation of hostilities, indeed throughout the conflict, state parties 'are bound to send back to their own country, regardless of number or rank, seriously wounded and seriously sick prisoners of war'.[14]

This is yet another demonstration of the alternating over and under breadth of the LOAC. States may detain members of the enemy force based on their status as a member of the force. And the belligerent need not pose a threat at the time of capture. But because the purpose of the POW detention regime is to incapacitate and prevent belligerents from returning to the fight, POW detention lasts only as long as the underlying conflict. The status-based POW detention regime is fundamentally different from when detaining civilians, who may be detained or interned based on their conduct and only for so long as they pose a security threat.

2.2 Geneva Convention IV: conduct-based internment of civilians

Geneva Convention IV addresses the protection of civilians in time of armed conflict.[15] The level and type of protections depends on the location of the civilian and the manner in which the civilian is experiencing the impact of hostilities. All persons who are not taking an active part in the hostilities receive the protections Common Article 3 affords.[16] The elderly, women and children, those in occupied territories, all receive additional protections. But Geneva Convention IV also recognises that under certain circumstances civilians may be detained, not because of *who* they are but for what they are *doing*. So in contrast to the status-based POW detention regime, the detention of civilians is conduct based. Nonetheless, before evaluating what conduct makes a civilian liable for internment, inquiry into who exactly qualifies as a civilian is required.

13 GCIII art 118.
14 GCIII art 109.
15 The need for this protection stems, at least in part, from the fact that civilians are killed or wounded in almost every armed conflict in far greater numbers than combatants. In a story on the sixtieth anniversary of the 1949 Geneva Conventions the BBC claimed that 'in World War I, the ratio of soldiers to civilians killed was 10 to one. In The Second World War it became 50-50, and today the figures are almost reversed – up to 10 civilians for every one soldier'. Imogen Foulkes, 'Geneva Conventions' Struggle for Respect' *BBC News* (8 August 2009), news.bbc.co.uk/2/hi/europe/8196166.stm. For a more contemporary representation, the number of Afghan civilians killed in 2013 (2,959) considerably exceeds the sum total of all US fatalities in Afghanistan from 2001 through 2013 (2,313). See UNAMA, 'Civilian Casualties in Afghan Conflict Rise by 14 per cent in 2013' Press Release (8 February 2014), unama.unmissions.org/Portals/UNAMA/human%20rights/Feb_8_2014_PoC-report_2013-PR-ENG-final.pdf; iCasualties, 'Operation Enduring Freedom', icasualties.org/oef.
16 Similar to common art 2 discussed above, common art 3 is so named because it is the same in each of the 1949 Geneva Conventions. Common art 3 requires that those not actively participating in the armed conflict be treated humanely and protected from violence, being made a hostage, outrages upon personal dignity and the passing of sentences and the carrying out of executions without a pronouncement by a regularly constituted court. See GCIII–IV art 3.

The definition of civilian is not as straightforward as might be expected. Despite Geneva Convention IV being devoted to civilians, the Convention does not formally define the term.[17] It was not until 1977 and Additional Protocol I that the first treaty definition of civilian emerged. Recognising the difficulty in drafting a comprehensive list of everyone considered a civilian, the drafters of Additional Protocol I chose to adopt a definition of exclusion, or a negative definition. Under Article 50 of Additional Protocol I, a civilian is *anyone* who does not fall under one of the combatant categories of POW from Geneva Convention III.[18]

Article 78 of Geneva Convention IV recognises that '[i]f an occupying power considers it necessary, for imperative reasons of security' then it may intern civilians.[19] The civilians in an Article 78 context are citizens and residents of an occupied territory. For example, Iraqis living in Baghdad following the US invasion of Iraq in 2003. Article 78

> relates to people who have not been guilty of any infringement of the penal provisions enacted by the Occupying Power, but that Power may, for reasons of its own, consider them dangerous to its security and is consequently entitled to restrict their freedom of action.[20]

Thus Article 78 envisions the need for preventative or security-based detention of civilians during armed conflict. As will be discussed later in the chapter, it is this kind of risk-based detention, albeit in NIAC, not IAC, that generates both discussion and controversy.

Important as detaining a civilian who poses a security risk is, Article 78 doesn't define or quantify the risk. Instead, commentary to a different but related section of Geneva Convention IV sheds some, but not much, light on the predicate requirements of 'imperative reasons of security'. Article 42 of Geneva Convention IV deals with interning civilians of enemy nationality living in the territory of a belligerent. So while Article 78 dealt with an Iraqi living in Baghdad under US occupation of Iraq, Article 42 involves an Iraqi who was living in the US during the armed conflict. If US did not repatriate the Iraqi civilian to Iraq, Article 42 provides a limited basis for the US to detain that Iraqi civilian if the security concerns of the US render such detention absolutely necessary.

---

17 Instead, GCIV art 4 defines the individuals whom the Convention protects as 'those who at a given moment and in any manner whatsoever, find themselves, in case of a conflict of occupation in the hands or persons a Party to the conflict or Occupying Power of which they are not nationals'.

18 More specifically, API states that

> a civilian is any person who does not belong to one of the categories of persons referred to in [GCIII] Article 4(a)(1) [members of the force], (2) [members of militias who meet the required conditions], (3) [members of regular armed forces who profess allegiance to a government of authority not recognised by the detaining power] and (6) [*levée en masse*].

As previously discussed, that leaves two categories of POWs – persons accompanying the force without actually being members thereof (GCIII art 4(a)(4)) and members of merchant marine and civil aircraft crews (GCIII art 4(a)(5)). These individuals are thus civilians but civilians entitled to POW status and treatment.

19 Elsewhere in GCIV the predicate for internment is if it is 'absolutely necessary'. See GCIV art 42. The difference between the two articles is that unlike art 42, art 78

> relates to people who have not been guilty of any infringement of the penal provisions enacted by the Occupying Power, but that Power may, for reasons of its own, consider them dangerous to its security and is consequently entitled to restrict their freedom of action.

> *GCIV Commentary* 368

Nonetheless, the commentary states that internment must 'observe the stipulations of article 43'. Ibid.

20 *GCIV Commentary* 368.

In addressing what is meant by terms like 'security of the State', the Commentary to Article 42 states that the drafters did not believe it was possible to define the term and that it's left 'very largely to Governments to decide the measure of activity prejudicial to the internal or external security of the State which justifies internment or assigned residence'.[21] The Commentary does provide that

> the mere fact that a person is a subject of an enemy Power cannot be considered as threatening the security of the country where he is living; it is not therefore a valid reason for interning him or placing him in assigned residence. To justify recourse to such measures the State must have good reason to think that the person concerned, by his activities, knowledge or qualifications, represents a real threat to its present or future security.[22]

Significantly, the Commentary 'stresses the exceptional character of measures of internment' and that only 'absolutely necessity ... and only then if security cannot be safeguarded by other, less severe means'.[23]

Status as an internee[24] means an individual is entitled to the protections of Section IV of Part II of Geneva Convention IV. This section explains where internment camps may (and may not) be located, how they are to be marked and the protective measures they must provide internees to shield them from the hazards of war. There are separate sections for food and clothing to be provided to internees, religious and physical activities, personal property and financial resources, administration and discipline, relations with the exterior and penal and disciplinary sanctions. These provisions are similar to the POW treatment provisions from Geneva Convention III but somewhat less detailed.

Because such internment is conduct based, there is a greater temporal limitation on its duration than the 'end of hostilities' of status-based POW detention. The decision to intern a civilian is subject to an initial review 'as soon as possible by an appropriate court or administrative board' designated by the detaining power and at least semi-annual review thereafter.[25]

Notably judicial review, while permissible, is not required. Recognising that a dangerous and austere battlefield environment may not allow judicial review, the LOAC allows an administrative board to review civilian internment. The key to such a board is that 'where the decision is an administrative one, it must be made not by one official but by an administrative board offering the necessary guarantees of independence and impartiality'.[26] Periodic reviews of internment under the LOAC are automatic and are conducted 'with a view to favourably amending the initial decision if circumstances permit'.[27]

---

21 *GCIV Commentary* 257–258. Detention of a civilian who is alleged to have violated a penal provision of the detaining power is governed by art 42. The procedures for art 42 detention are laid out in art 43. While internment under art 78 is different from that under art 42, the Commentary to art 78 states that internment must 'observe the stipulations of article 43'. *GCIV Commentary* 368.

22 *GCIV Commentary* 257–258. The Commentary states that where a state has 'serious and legitimate reason to think that [individuals] are members of organizations whose object is to cause disturbances, or that they may seriously prejudice its security by other means, such as sabotage or espionage' and where 'Subversive activity carried on inside the territory of a Party to the conflict or actions which are of direct assistance to an enemy Power both threaten the security of the country' internment may be appropriate. But this only restarts the definition inquiry: what constitutes serious and legitimate reason or subversive activity?

23 *GCIV Commentary* 257–258.

24 This chapter does not address another administrative measure an occupying power may impose under GCIV, that of assigning residences to certain civilians.

25 GCIV art 43.

26 *GCIV Commentary* 260.

27 Ibid 261.

In explaining the periodic review requirement, the Commentary states that 'no protected person should be kept in assigned residence or in an internment camp for a longer time than the security of the Detaining State demands'.[28]

Thus the LOAC provides significant information for when and how civilians and, as previously discussed, combatants may be detained. There is varying amount of guidance on treatment conditions, more for POWs than for civilians. And for release, there is more information, as there should be, for review and release of conduct-based civilian detention than status-based POW captivity. All in all, the civilian and POW detention regimes extant in IAC have retained their utility. Indeed these systems form the basis for military training, manuals and regulations on detention.[29] The challenges arise not so much from detention in IACs but in NIACs. And this threshold question of the quantum of law available is made more difficult by non-state actors and armed conflicts without clear ends.

3 Non-international armed conflict

3.1 Authority to detain

Unlike in an IAC, during NIAC, there is an ongoing debate about whether LOAC provides authority to detain.

One view is that '[i]t is logical that … since [in a NIAC] there is no conflict between two or more sovereigns, the [law] of non-international armed conflict should be silent, in deference to national law, on questions of detention'.[30] That national law tends to be domestic criminal law and procedure, allowing law enforcement to detain individuals only based on their conduct, not based on their status or concerns they pose a security threat.

On the other side of the debate is the claim that even the limited amount of LOAC applicable to NIAC implicitly recognises authority to deprive people of their liberty. Under this argument, LOAC's

> reference to 'persons, hors de combat by … detention' and 'regularly constituted courts' in Common Article 3, and to persons 'interned' in the Second Additional Protocol, Articles 5 and 6, are superfluous if not understood to be accompanied by an authority to detain or intern respectively.[31]

---

28 Ibid. The Commentary also provides that the review procedures from GCIV are the minimum standard and that in conducting reviews at least twice a year that

> the responsible authorities will be bound to take into account the progress of events – which is often rapid – and changes as a result of which it may be found that the continuing internment or assigned residence of the person concerned are no longer justified.

29 See, among others, US Army Regulation 190–198, Enemy Prisoners of War, Retained Personnel, Civilian Internees and Other Detainees (1 October 1997).

30 Gabor Rona, 'An Appraisal of US Practice Relating to Enemy Combatants' (2007) 10 *YBIHl* 232, 241; see also Lawrence Hill-Cawthorne and Dapo Akande, 'Locating the Legal Basis for Detention in Non-International Armed Conflicts: A Rejoinder to Aurel Sari' *EJIL:Talk!* (2 June 2014), www.ejiltalk.org/locating-the-legal-basis-for-detention-in-non-international-armed-conflicts-a-rejoinder-to-aurel-sari.

31 David Tuck, 'Detention by Armed Groups: Overcoming Challenges to Humanitarian Action' (2011) 93 (883) *IRRC* 765; see also Ezequiel Heffes, 'Detention in NIACs: A Pledge in Favor of the Application of IHL' *Opinio Juris* (16 May 2014), http://opiniojuris.org/2014/05/16/guest-post-detention-niacs-pledge-favour-application-ihl/.

This argument reflects the tension, almost a clash, between the law enforcement/human rights paradigm for detention and that of LOAC. Indeed the disagreement on the issue of LOAC authority to detain in NIAC only increased in May 2014, following the High Court of England and Wales' decision in *Mohammed v Ministry of Defence*.[32] There, the High Court ruled that at least as applied to the United Kingdom, LOAC does not provide detention authority in NIAC. The Court considered the LOAC applicable to NIAC and stated that

> [n]either [the relevant portions of the Geneva Conventions nor Additional Protocol II] contains any express statement that it is lawful to deprive persons of their liberty in an armed conflict to which these provisions apply. All that they do is to set out certain minimum standards of treatment which must be afforded to persons who are detained during such an armed conflict.[33]

Underpinning the Court's decision that LOAC does not provide authority to detain in NIAC is that there is such little law from which to draw.

3.2 NIAC model of detention

There is some, albeit not much, in the way of 'black-letter' LOAC concerning detention in NIAC. Common Article 3 of the four 1949 Geneva Conventions, but applying to NIACs, refers to members of the armed forces placed in detention in its categorisation of 'persons taking no active part in hostilities'.[34] Common Article 3 provides an important minimum standard of treatment in detention, that those not actively participating in the armed conflict be treated humanely and protected from violence, from being made a hostage, from outrages upon personal dignity and from the passing of sentences and the carrying out of executions without a pronouncement by a regularly constituted court.[35]

---

32 *Serdar Mohammed v Ministry of Defence* [2014] EWHC 1369 (QB).

33 Ibid ¶ 239 (QB). The Court then took note of the argument of the UK Ministry of Defence that a power to detain is implicit in GCI–IV common art 3 and APII. Ibid. The Court went so far as to acknowledge that '[t]his argument has the support of some academic writers and of the International Committee of the Red Cross', mentioning in particular Jelena Pejic, a legal adviser to the ICRC, who has written that '[i]nternment is … clearly a measure that can be taken in non-international armed conflict, as evidenced by the language of [APII], which mentions internment in Articles 5 and 6 respectively'. Ibid ¶ 240, quoting Jelena Pejic, 'Procedural Principles and Safeguards for Internment/Administrative Detention in Armed Conflict and other Situations of Violence' (2005) 87(858) *IRRC* 375, 377. The Court then rejected this approach: ibid ¶¶ 241–246.

34 On its face, common art 3 would seem to only apply to a NIAC, but courts in the US and Europe have ruled that its baseline level of protections apply in all armed conflicts, however characterised. See *Hamdan v Rumsfeld*, 548 US 557 (2006). See also *Military and Paramilitary Activities in and against Nicaragua (Nicaragua v US)* [1986] ICJ Rep 14, ¶ 218, stating that

> Common Article 3 which is common to all four Geneva Conventions of 12 August 1949 defines certain rules to be applied in the armed conflicts of a non-international character. There is no doubt that, in the event of international armed conflicts, these rules also constitute a minimum yardstick, in addition to the more elaborate rules which are also to apply to international conflicts; and they are rules which, in the Court's opinion, reflect what the Court in 1949 called 'elementary considerations of humanity'.

> *Prosecutor v Tadić (Decision on the Defence Motion for Interlocutory Appeal on Jurisdiction)* (Case no IT-94-1-A, ICTY Appeals Chamber, 2 October 1995) ¶ 98 (holding that common art 3 is customary international law and applicable in both NIAC and IAC).

35 See GCIII–IV art 3.

The only other LOAC potentially applicable to NIAC is Additional Protocol II to the 1949 Geneva Conventions.[36] Article 5 of Additional Protocol II provides guidance on 'persons whose liberty has been restricted'[37] while Article 6 discusses 'penal prosecutions'.[38] Yet despite the informative sounding titles of those articles, neither they nor any other part of Additional Protocol II provides details of how detention in NIAC is to be conducted.[39]

Supplementing this limited body of law however is considerable custom and practice. For example, the ICRC, in its Customary International Law Study, identified a number of detention issues in NIAC for which custom has developed in the form of practice, military manuals and United Nations Documents.[40] The ICRC is also 'leading a major consultation process on how to strengthen legal protection for persons deprived of their liberty in relation to NIAC'.[41] The United Nations has issued operating procedures for detention in peace operations, many of which occur during NIAC.[42] Additionally, Denmark led the recent Copenhagen Process, a multi-year effort involving representatives from other countries, regional and international organisations, and civil society which developed principles designed to guide the conduct of detention in international military operations.[43] These approaches are important reminders that in the absence of detailed law, LOAC-based custom, practice and policy offer alternatives to fill the lacuna.

4 Challenges and a proposal

4.1 Quantum of law vs prevalence of conflict

As outlined above, while there are references to detention in the bodies of law governing both IACs and NIACs, there is an unhelpful inverse relationship between the amount of law available and the applicability of that law. In the aftermath of the Second World War, NIACs are far

---

36 Potentially applicable as not all NIACs trigger APII. For APII to apply, there must be an armed conflict which is not an IAC and

> which take place in the territory of a High Contracting Party between its armed forces and dissident armed forces or other organized armed groups which, under responsible command, exercise such control over a part of its territory as to enable them to carry out sustained and concerted military operations and to implement this Protocol.
>
> APII art 1(1)

37 APII art 5.
38 APII art 6.
39 Pejic (n 33) 377.
40 See CIHL rr 118–128. These rules cover the provision of necessities to persons deprived of their liberty, accommodation for women and children, location of internment and detention centres, pillage of personal belongings, recording and notification of personal details, ICRC access, correspondence, visits, respect for convictions and religious practices, release and return.
41 See ICRC, 'The ICRC's Work on Strengthening Legal Protection' (31 January 2014), www.icrc.org/eng/what-we-do/other-activities/development-ihl/strengthening-legal-protection-ihl-detention.htm.
42 United Nations' Interim Standard Operating Procedures for Detention in United Nations Peace Operations (25 January 2010).
43 See the Copenhagen Process on the Handling of Detainees in International Military Operations, 'Principles and Guidelines' (19 October 2012), um.dk/en/~/media/UM/English-site/Documents/Politics-and-diplomacy/Copenhangen%20Process%20Principles%20and%20Guidelines.pdf.

more prevalent[44] but for which there is far less law, both in general and as applied to detention.[45]

An armed conflict involving non-state actors, even disparately located in several countries, cannot constitute an IAC. Thus the more extensive law that governs detention in IACs is inapplicable. The lack of law applicable to NIACs poses one, but certainly not the only, challenge.

To apply IAC detention provisions in NIAC could be part of the solution, necessarily grounded in policy not law. Professor Ryan Goodman has articulated a three-part rationale for a policy of applying the law governing IAC to NIACs against non-state actors like al-Qaeda:

> The first is a reactive reason; simply put, many commentators and practitioners have applied the law of international armed conflict to the conflict with al-Qaeda by analogy. It's a prevalent practice that's used, for example, in debates about whether or not we can hold fighters until the cessation of hostilities and with or without access to an attorney. The analog or the referent in those discussions is often international armed conflict. And if that's a prevalent mode of discourse or argument, then we at least need to conflict, to evaluate those kinds of claims.
>
> A second reason is an affirmative one. On my view, it's valid to use the law of international armed conflict as an analogy. In fact, if we have to think of an analogy, it's the closest fit or closest approximation – especially the Fourth Geneva Convention – for questions of who may be detained and what types of activities on the part of civilians are subject to detention. That is, the rules contained in the Civilians Convention, are the closest analog that we have and therefore the best reference point for trying to approximate what the law of armed conflict should look like or will look like when it applies in a non international scenario like the conflict with al-Qaeda.
>
> The third reason is the strongest, and it's an affirmative argument not just by way of analogy. The argument here is that the law in international armed conflict establishes an outer boundary of permissive action. The idea is fairly simple, which is that the law of armed conflict uniformly involves more exacting, more restrictive obligations on parties in international armed conflict than in non international armed conflict. We could even state this point as a maxim: if states have authority to engage in particular practices in an international armed conflict, they a fortiori possess the authority to undertake the same practices in non international armed conflict, or simply put, whatever is permitted in international armed conflict is permitted in non international armed conflict. Therefore, if the law of armed conflict permits a state to detain civilians in international armed conflict, the law of armed conflict surely permits states to detain civilians in a non international armed conflict. The same logic does not apply to prohibitions or proscriptive rules: it does not follow that

---

44 For example, according to NATO, in 2000 there were 25 armed conflicts around the world. NATO, 'Statistics on Armed Conflicts around the World', nato.gov.si/eng/topic/threats-to-security/statistics. Of those, only one, the conflict between India and Pakistan, was of an international nature. See also Armed Conflict Database, acd.iiss.org.

45 The ICRC asserts that there are four key areas in which LOAC governing detention in NIAC 'falls short': (i) conditions of detention, (ii) protection for especially vulnerable groups of detainees, (iii) grounds and procedures for internment and (iv) transfers of detainees from one authority to another. ICRC, 'Detention in Non-international Armed Conflict: The ICRC's Work on Strengthening Legal Protection' (31 January 2014), www.icrc.org/eng/what-we-do/other-activities/development-ihl/strengthening-legal-protection-ihl-detention.htm.

if the law of armed conflict forbids states from engaging in a practice in international armed conflict that the law would also forbid states from engaging in that practice in non international armed conflict.[46]

Professor Goodman's approach ameliorates, but does not fully solve, the problem. Applying the robust IAC law to NIAC still results in difficulties. The first of these is the inability for status-based detention based on Geneva Convention III because non-state actors do not qualify as POWs.

4.2 Challenge posed by non-state actors

The problem is not that the Geneva Conventions make no provision for non-state actors, they do. In IAC, members of militias or volunteer corps who make up the armed forces of a party to the conflict qualify for POW status and treatment.[47] Even militias or volunteer corps which do not directly comprise the armed forces of a party may qualify for POW status and treatment.[48] And, interestingly, there is not a geographic limitation; the provisions of Geneva Convention III apply to militias operating 'in or outside their territory'.[49]

Nonetheless, even if Geneva Convention III applied to NIAC, its provisions would not apply to most non-state actors involved in current or recent armed conflicts. That's because the non-state actors do not make up the military of a party to the conflict or comply with the conditions for free-standing militias or volunteer corps.[50]

Consider the armed conflict in Afghanistan following the September 11 attacks. At the outset the conflict was an IAC, a war between two high contracting parties to the Geneva Conventions, the US and Afghanistan. Status as an IAC triggered at least the potential for the application of Geneva Convention III governing POWs.

Members of al-Qaeda could potentially qualify for POW status and treatment as members of a militia. But there does not seem to be a credible argument that al-Qaeda complies with the predicate requirements of a command structure, fixed distinctive sign, carrying their arms openly and following the LOAC.

The assessment of the Taliban, then representing the government of Afghanistan, is more difficult. In denying the Taliban POW status, the US claimed that even if the Taliban constituted the armed forces of Afghanistan they would still need to meet with the four-part test. This argument was criticised as not being supported by a plain reading of the text of Geneva

---

46 Ryan Goodman, 'The Second Annual Solf-Warren Lecture in International and Operational Law' (2009) 201 *Military LR* 237. For persuasive arguments for applying the law of international armed conflict to non-international armed conflict, particularly in the area of detention, see Sassóli and Olson (n 9).

47 GCIII art 4.

48 See s 2.1 above.

49 GCIII art 4.

50 Following the 9/11 attacks, the US considered the status under international humanitarian law both of the Taliban, which constituted the government of Afghanistan at the time, and of al Qaeda, which based its terrorist organisation in Afghanistan with Taliban consent. George W Bush, 'Humane Treatment of Taliban and al Qaeda Detainees' Memorandum (7 February 2002), www.pegc.us/archive/ White_House/bush_memo_20020207_ed.pdf; Jay S Bybee, 'Status of Taliban Forces under Article 4 of the Third Geneva Convention of 1949' Memorandum Opinion for the Counsel to the President (7 February 2002), www.fas.org/irp/agency/doj/olc/taliban.pdf (Status of Taliban Forces Memorandum Opinion).

Convention III;[51] yet the argument finds support from the ICRC and is persuasive at a normative level. In terms of the ICRC support, the commentary to Geneva Convention III, in explaining another category of persons who qualify for POW status, refers to the attributes of armed forces as 'they wear uniform, they have an organized hierarchy and they know and respect the laws and customs of war'.[52]

More broadly, if the armed forces of a party to the conflict do not have to meet the four conditions a perverse result follows whereby members of regular armed forces would be governed by lower standards than those applicable to militia and volunteer forces.[53]

The answer, and its not a new one, is again rooted in policy — treat unprivileged belligerents as POWs. It is somewhat surprising that the US wrestled with the question of whether to classify the Taliban and al-Qaeda as POWs. In previous conflicts the US detained individuals and treated them under the terms of a status to which they did not qualify as a matter of law. During the Korean conflict, the US did not recognise the legitimacy of Chinese intervention. Regardless of the accuracy of that view, the significance is that the US did not believe that members of the Chinese Army qualified as POWs as a matter of law, but treated them as such as a matter of policy.

Similarly, during the Vietnam War, the US, along with its allies,[54] joined South Vietnam in fighting an array of enemies associated with North Vietnam. Some, like the North Vietnamese Army (NVA), were clearly entitled to POW status and treatment. With respect to other forces, notably the Viet Cong, the US nonetheless held Article 5 tribunals[55] and determined they were not POWs. Nonetheless, the US then treated the Viet Cong as POWs as a matter of policy, and housed them in camps adjacent to the POW camps for captured NVA.[56] Key to the US approach

---

51 See Silvia Borelli, 'Casting Light on the Legal Black Hole: International Law and Detentions Abroad in the "War on Terror"' (2005) 87 *IRRC* 39.
52 *GCIII Commentary* 63.
53 See Status of Taliban Forces Memorandum Opinion (n 50) 5. As the US Department of Justice indicated (emphasis in original),

> [t]here is no evidence that any of the GPW's drafters or ratifiers believed that members of the regular armed forces ought to be governed by *lower standards* in their conduct of warfare than those applicable to militia and volunteer forces.

54 Notably Australia, New Zealand, the Republic of Korea and Thailand.
55 In Vietnam, the US conduct of art 5 tribunals was little more than bringing the captured individual before an US Army officer who inquired about the circumstances of capture and afforded the individual the opportunity to provide input. See also Geoffrey Corn, Eric Talbot Jensen and Sean Watts, 'Understanding the Distinct Function of the Combatant Status Review Tribunals: A Response to Blocher' (2007) 116 *Yale Law Journal Pocket Part* 327 (describing how the US identified, as a matter of policy, groups qualifying for POW status, including Viet Cong Main Forces, Viet Cong Local Forces, North Vietnamese Army Units and Organised Forces of Irregular Guerillas and Self-Defence Forces who had not engaged in terrorism, sabotage or spying. US Military Assistance Command, Vietnam, Directive No 381–346, Military Intelligence: Combined Screening of Detainees (27 December 1967), reprinted in Howard Levie, *Documents on Prisoners of War* (US Naval War College 1979) 748).
56 Blank and Noone (n 12) 2330–2334 (quoting the former Military Assistance Command Vietnam (MACV) Staff Judge Advocate George Prugh on detention operations during the Vietam War):

> [v]irtually none of [the] classic [IAC] conditions existed.... It was certainly arguable that many Viet Cong did not meet the criteria of guerillas entitled to prisoner of war status under Article 4, [GCIII]. However, civil incarceration and criminal trial of the great number of Viet Cong was too much for the civil resources at hand.

Blank and Noone then provide a copy of the MACV policy directive which required that members of the Viet Cong would be classified and treated as POWs.

was that the policy application of Geneva Convention III to the Viet Cong was nearly identical to the legal application of the Convention to the NVA. The ICRC, in reviewing the treatment conditions of both the NVA and Viet Cong, labelled the US instruction to apply Geneva Convention III as a matter of policy:

> a brilliant expression of a liberal and realistic attitude.... This text could very well be a most important one in the history of the humanitarian law, for it is the first time ... that a government goes far beyond the requirements of the Geneva Convention in an official instruction to its armed forces.[57]

Treating unprivileged belligerents in NIAC as POWs means the detainees receive the benefits of the treatment provision of Geneva Convention III but they are still not entitled to the combatant's privilege.[58] Thus the capturing force may still prosecute them for their violations of the LOAC.[59]

But even this second policy act does not fully address the problem because status-based POW detention does not require review of detention and assumes a clear end point, which in many NIACs does not exist.

4.3 Reviewing and ending status-based detention

Regardless of whether one reaches the conclusion that the Taliban and al-Qaeda were entitled to POW treatment as matter of law or of policy, a practical concern with the application of Geneva Convention III remains. The concern flows not from what Geneva Convention III provides, but in what it does not. The application of Geneva Convention III yields a robust guide on POW treatment conditions, from quarters, food, clothing, hygiene, medical attention, to religious, intellectual and physical activities. What it doesn't do is provide much in the way of guidance on release. That is not a criticism of the Convention but a statement of its inherent limitations given that the detention regime is status based.

---

57 United States Army Center of Military History, 'The US Army in Vietnam, Prisoners of War and War Crimes', www.history.army.mil/books/Vietnam/Law-War/law-04.htm. During Vietnam, the US provided an example of how applying LOAC as a matter of policy can yield tangible, meaningful results. More recently the US provided an example of how unexplained, unverifiable policy actions yield little. In 2006 the US Department of Defense issued a directive claiming as a matter of policy, the US military would comply with the more robust IAC law 'during all armed conflicts, however characterized': Department of Defense Directive 2311.01E, Law of War Program (9 May 2006) ¶ 4.1, www.dtic.mil/whs/directives/corres/pdf/231101e.pdf. Yet as of this writing, some eight years later, what exactly that policy decision means remains unclear. With which conventions or parts of conventions governing the conduct of hostilities is the US complying? Without knowing that, how would the ICRC or international community know if and how well the US is doing as it says it is?

58 But, see Geoff Corn, 'Thinking the Unthinkable: Has the Time Come to Offer Combatant Immunity to Non-State Actors?' (2011) 22 *Stanford LPR* 253 (discussing affording non-state actors POW status and combatant immunity).

59 Even here there is potential for helpful conflation between IAC and NIAC law and GCIII and GCIV. API contains a list of fundamental guarantees on the treatment of persons in the power of a party to a conflict recognised as customary international law. In particular, API art 75 provides process rights akin to those from the ICCPR. The vast majority of the world, some 174 states, are party to API. But for those states that are not, portions of API, including art 75, are binding as customary international law, a point even the US acknowledges. White House, 'New Actions on Guantanamo and Detainee Policy' Fact Sheet (7 March 2011), www.whitehouse.gov/the-press-office/2011/03/07/fact-sheet-new-actions-guant-namo-and-detainee-policy.

Geneva Convention III applies 'from the time [a qualifying person] fall[s] into the power of the enemy and until their final release and repatriation'.[60] As previously discussed, in terms of timing of release, the Convention states only that 'prisoners of war shall be released and repatriated without delay after the cessation of hostilities'.[61]

Geneva Convention III presupposes status as an immutable quality, once a belligerent qualifies for POW treatment their status remains as a POW for the duration of the conflict.[62] If during the war in the Falklands, the British detained a uniformed member of the Argentine Army, that individual's status remains constant, a member of the armed forces of a party to the conflict.

But the conclusion of NIACs involving non-state actors who increasingly operate from more than one state and are aligned to varying degrees with other organised armed groups is not so straightforward.[63] Returning to the Falklands example, there are not gradients of being a member of the armed forces of Argentina, either one is or is not. But there are degrees of membership in groups like al-Qaeda as well as questions about the effect is one were to renounce their membership.

Geneva Convention IV security detention review mechanisms could bridge the gaps created by status in NIAC not lending itself to the binary IAC detention regime and by the uncertainty of when NIACs end.

This would mean semi-annual reviews of whether the detainee still poses an imperative security threat. Consistent with Geneva Convention IV these reviews would be held automatically and occur with a rebuttable presumption that the detainee no longer poses a security threat. An administrative board could conduct the reviews so long as there are sufficient indicia of independence and impartiality. The board could still comprise members of the capturing party's armed forces. But the board members would need to be under a separate chain of command.[64] Whatever decisions the board recommends could be subject to review but the only permissible modification would be those in the detainee's favour. This means that where the board recommends continued detention, a higher level of the capturing party's government could reverse that detention and direct release. But where the board recommends release, the review could not reverse that decision.[65]

---

60 GCIII art 5.
61 GCIII art 118.
62 And under GCIII art 7, 'prisoner of war may in no circumstances renounce in part or in entirety the rights secured to them' under the Convention.
63 Consider the dynamic relationship between al-Qaeda groups, in Pakistan and Afghanistan but previously in Iraq and in the Arabian peninsula and al-Qaeda in the Maghreb. See 'Letter to al-Zarqai from al-Zawahri' *MSNBC* (11 October 2005), www.nbcnews.com/id/9666242/ns/world_news-terrorism/t/letter-al-zarqawi-al-zawahri (describing communication between the head of al-Qaeda in Pakistan and the head of al-Qaeda in Iraq); Helen Collis and Hayley Peterson, 'Head of al Qaeda in Pakistan Ayman al-Zawahri communicated with Nasser al-Wuhayshi, the Head of al Qaeda in the Arabian Peninsula' *Daily Mail* (4 August 2013) (describing communication between the head of al-Qaeda in Pakistan and his counterpart in Yemen).
64 While this seems counter-intuitive, it can and is done. For example, in the US, military defence counsel, military judges and those serving as inspector generals are placed in a separate chain of command and are only subject to that command's orders and evaluation.
65 This is similar to how the US conducts administrative boards to determine whether or not to discharge service members. Whatever decision the board makes is reviewed and can be modified, but only to the service member's benefit. See US Army Regulation 635–200, Active Duty Enlisted Administrative (6 June 2005).

5 Conclusion

Geneva Conventions III and IV provide a solid detention framework for IAC. Geneva Convention III recognises broad, status-based detention. It provides considerable guidance on treatment, but is of limited use in terms of release. Geneva Convention IV applies a higher, conduct-based threshold for detention. The treatment provisions of Geneva Convention IV are less robust than for Geneva Convention III, but unlike status-based POW detention, civilian conduct-based detention provides for a review process.

A hybrid application of Geneva Conventions III and IV could thus form the basis of a NIAC detention regime – apply the Geneva Conventions as a matter of policy to NIACs, to allow for status-based detention of non-state actors but treatment as a POW. Such detention would then be subject to the review process from Geneva Convention IV.

Allowing status-based detention of non-state actors would result in over breadth, more individuals being detained than would the case if the detaining entity were forced to identify specific threat-based actions warranting detention. But there are some implicit checks on how such detention would occur. Were a military to believe an individual a member of al-Qaeda and ordered his detention, and it turned out the individual while sympathetic to al-Qaeda was not a member as such or conducting any activities at al-Qaeda's behest, the individual would be released no later than following the first six month review. And while six months of unnecessary detention is problematic, it's a finite problem. And in a counter-insurgency environment, status-based detention of non-state actors would in some ways be self-regulating. A military commander who detains too many people on the basis of status who do not in fact pose a security threat will undermine their relationship with the local populace and their perceptions of legitimacy.

There will inevitably be over- or under-breadth in any detention system and indeed any law or legal system. The question is who should incur the risks or pay the costs. Between members of an armed force who comply with the LOAC, the civilian population and non-state actors, non-state actors should bear the risk of inevitable over-breadth from a status-based detention regime.

This approach is vulnerable to criticism. But much of the criticism, while legally correct, is practically unhelpful.[66] This chapter operates on the assumption that following a 'successful' deconstruction of this proposal, critics must shift to positivism and a proposed solution. And any solution would seem, by definition, to look a lot like some combination of Geneva Conventions III and IV. Moreover, there are considerable advantages, practically and in establishing legitimacy, of tethering a detention regime to the world's most ratified treaty and which has formed the basis for how militaries around the world train to conduct detention operations.

---

66 In a similar vein, this chapter ignores the discussion of whether there are only two categories of individuals, prisoners of war or civilian, or if there is some alternate category involving unprivileged belligerents. The majority view is that under API's negative definition of civilian – a civilian is any person who does not belong to a POW qualifying category – the universe is binary: if someone is not a POW then they are a civilian. See API art 50(1). The ICRC *Commentary* however notes that 'things are not always so straightforward' and that an individual who did not qualify as a matter of law as a POW would still be treated as such. *AP Commentary* ¶¶ 1761, 1736. But the debate of whether there are two or more categories of actors on the battlefield does not meaningfully advance the debate of detention treatment and release of non-state actors.

18
Wounded and sick, and medical services

James P Benoit

The origins of the law of armed conflict (LOAC) are perhaps not surprisingly found in the area of caring for the wounded and sick, as the most obvious persons who require protection from war.[1] 'The treatment of the wounded and sick has been at the heart of international humanitarian law since its modern inception.'[2]

Although historical examples of caring for the wounded and sick certainly exist (for example, Florence Nightingale in the Crimean War from 1854–1856), the pivotal moment under LOAC in this respect was the Battle of Solferino in 1859. Jean Henri Dunant, a Swiss businessman, personally witnessed the end and horrific aftermath of one of the bloodiest battles in the nineteenth century, prompting him to write a short book *Un Souvenir de Solférino*.[3] This vivid description of approximately 40,000 soldiers lying dead or dying on the battlefield with inadequate medical attention served as the catalyst both for the creation in 1863 of the precursor to today's ICRC, and for an international conference that adopted the first Geneva Convention for the Amelioration of the Condition of the Wounded and Sick in Armed Forces in the Field in 1864. Subsequent international conferences led to expanded LOAC protections, and thus Dunant should be considered the founder of modern LOAC. The Second World War confirmed the need to clarify, revise and extend LOAC, which led to the adoption of the four Geneva Conventions of 1949.

Based upon this lengthy pedigree, the LOAC norms protecting those who are *hors de combat* by virtue of their wounds or illness would appear to be largely resolved, with clear rules of either customary international law (CIL) or treaty law addressing all conceivable issues. For example, the ICRC Customary International Humanitarian Law (CIHL) Study included three seemingly innocuous 'Rules' for handling the wounded, sick and shipwrecked.[4] Cambridge University Press subsequently published a companion book (both complementary and complimentary) that omitted any discussion of these CIL norms because they 'were regarded as uncontroversial and

---

1 See generally Frits Kalshoven, 'The history of international humanitarian law treaty-making' ch 2 in this volume.
2 Sandesh Sivakumaran, *The Law of Non-International Armed Conflict* (OUP 2012) 273.
3 Henry Dunant, *A Memory of Solferino* (ICRC 1986 [1862]).
4 CIHL rr 109–111.

an example of Rules where the authors of the Study have comprehensively encapsulated the law'.[5] Sadly, caring for the wounded and sick remains fraught with avoidance, ambiguity and misapplication.

This chapter endeavours to describe the framework in this fundamental area, as well as to highlight contentious and emerging areas of thought. It will analyse each of the various protected groups (that is, wounded and sick, medical and religious personnel, medical units and establishments, and medical transports) individually, providing the definition, legal status and the specific obligations to 'respect and protect' each group (which generally means not only not to attack them, but also to affirmatively come to their aid). Just a reminder at the outset that Common Article 2 limits the application of the specific protections contained in the four Geneva Conventions to international armed conflict (IAC). However, Common Article 3 provides a 'mini-convention' that extends basic guarantees to non-international armed conflict (NIAC), including treating 'those placed *hors de combat* by sickness, wounds … humanely'.[6] The only other Common Article 3 requirement regarding the wounded and sick is that they 'shall be collected and cared for'.[7] Additional Protocol II further elaborates on the specific protections extended to wounded and sick in a subset of NIAC.[8]

In addition, many provisions of human rights treaties remain applicable during armed conflict.[9] Moreover, armed conflict may not be used as a justification to violate *jus cogens* norms (that is, peremptory principles from which no derogation is permitted).[10] General human rights protections for wounded and sick best fit under the ICCPR's rubrics of the right to life, and the right not to be 'subjected to torture or to cruel, inhuman or degrading treatment or punishment.

---

5 Elizabeth Wilmshurst and Susan Breau (eds), *Perspectives on the ICRC Study on Customary International Humanitarian Law* (CUP 2007) ix. See also Susan Breau, 'Protected Persons and Objects' in ibid 169; George Aldrich, 'Customary International Humanitarian Law: An Interpretation on Behalf of the International Committee of the Red Cross' (2006) 76 *BYBIL* 503, 522; Michael Bothe, 'Customary International Humanitarian Law: Some Reflections on the ICRC Study' (2005) 8 *YBIHL* 143, 171 (stating rather conclusorily that these three ICRC Study rules 'show[ed] that the new rules contained in AP I have become customary law').

6 GCI arts 3(1), 12; APII arts 2(1) (adding the grounds of language, political or other opinion, and national or social origin), 4(1), 7(2), 9(2); CIHL rr 88, 109–110. Cf ICCPR arts 2(1), 26.

7 GCI art 3(2).

8 See Caitlin Dwyer and Tim McCormack, 'Conflict characterisation' ch 3 in this volume. By its terms, APII only applies where the non-governmental forces 'exercise such control over a part of [the government's] territory as to enable them to carry out sustained and concerted military operations': APII art 1(1). For those states that have ratified API, which includes wars of national liberation within its definition of IAC, APII would also not cover these conflicts. Other types of NIAC (eg where non-governmental forces do not control any territory) continue to be controlled by common art 3, so long as the hostilities have risen to the level of an armed conflict. See generally *GCI Commentary* 49–52; *Prosecutor v Tadić (Decision on the Defence Motion for Interlocutory Appeal on Jurisdiction)* (Case no IT-94-1, ICTY Appeals Chamber, 2 October 1995) ¶¶ 67–70. If the US ever ratifies APII, it would most likely do so with the understanding that it applies to all types of NIAC covered by common art 3. Department of State Letter of Submittal to The President VIII (13 December 1986) and Attachment 1, Detailed Analysis of Provisions at 2, 7, attached to President Reagan's Letter of Transmittal to the Senate of Protocol II Additional to the 1949 Geneva Conventions, and Relating to the Protection of Victims of Non[-]international Armed Conflicts (29 January 1987), www.loc.gov/rr/frd/Military_Law/pdf/protocol-II-100-2.pdf.

9 See Noam Lubell and Nancie Prud'homme, 'Impact of human rights law' ch 6 in this volume.

10 See eg Convention Against Torture and Other Cruel, Inhuman or Degrading Treatment or Punishment, UNGA Res 39/46 (10 December 1984) 1465 UNTS 85, art 2(2); ICCPR arts 4(2), 6(3); Convention on the Prevention and Punishment of the Crime of Genocide, UNGA Res 260 (III) (9 December 1948) 78 UNTS 277, art 1. Cf ICCPR arts 4(1), 4(3).

In particular, no one shall be subjected without his free consent to medical or scientific experimentation.'[11] To do so, also constitutes a war crime in both IAC and NIAC.[12]

Perhaps because of the perception of this area of LOAC as being 'settled', there is a relative paucity of modern scholarship on the topic.[13] Nevertheless, caring for the wounded and sick remains important in modern warfare. For example, in the ongoing NIAC in Afghanistan, the Afghan Army is concerned about having to use its own ambulances, which are much slower and more dangerous than NATO's medical evacuation (medevac) helicopters. Pending the withdrawal of NATO forces, the Afghan Army anticipated that it would often lose the 'golden hour' (that is, the window of opportunity to save a victim of severe trauma).[14] There are also current concerns about medical facilities still not being respected and protected: 'violence – in all its forms – against health facilities and personnel represents one of the most serious yet neglected humanitarian issues of today'.[15] Even medical evacuation convoys and offices of the widely respected ICRC are not immune from attack.[16]

1 Wounded and sick

Even the initial definition of who qualifies as 'wounded and sick' is not without controversy. As a matter of historical record, the scope of Geneva Convention I and its precursors has been limited to '[w]ounded or sick combatants'. Moreover, to be precise, 'wounded and sick' is shorthand for combatants who are actually *hors de combat* because of wounds and sickness – if a combatant continues to fight despite a broken leg, she is not entitled to protection because she is still participating in hostilities.[17]

The categories of persons to whom Geneva Convention I and Geneva Convention II apply are coterminous with those categories of persons whom are entitled to prisoner of war (POW) status upon capture.[18] Thus, 'civilian personnel who are searching for shipwrecked civilians' are not protected by Geneva Convention II,[19] but would need to look to Geneva Convention IV for protection.[20] This does not detract from the general principle that '[c]ivilian medical care remains the primary responsibility of the civilian authorities'.[21] In fact, Geneva Convention IV

---

11 ICCPR arts 6(1), 7.

12 Rome Statute art 8(2)(b)(x) and (e)(xi).

13 But, see Peter Maurer, 'Op-ed: Medical Care in the Line of Fire' *InterCrossBlog* (21 May 2013); James Benoit, 'Mistreatment of the Wounded, Sick and Shipwrecked by the ICRC Study on Customary International Humanitarian Law' (2008) 11 *YBIHL* 175.

14 See generally Kevin Sieff, 'Without US Helicopters, Afghans Struggle to Save Wounded' *Washington Post* (19 May 2013).

15 Maurer (n 13).

16 AP, 'Syrian Troops attack Convoy evacuating Wounded from Key Rebel Town, Killing 7, Activists Say' *Washington Post* (31 May 2013); Azam Ahmed, 'Suicide Bombers Attack a Red Cross Compound in Eastern Afghanistan' *New York Times* (30 May 2013).

17 API art 8(a); *AP Commentary* ¶ 306. Moreover, 'the feigning of an incapacitation by wounds or sickness' is one of the classic forms of perfidy. API art 37(1)(b); CIHL r 65; *AP Commentary* ¶¶ 1502, 1505.

18 See generally GCI arts 13–14; GCII arts 13 (extending many protections to shipwrecked as well), 16; *GCI Commentary* 143–144, *GCII Commentary* 94–95.

19 *GCII Commentary* 205.

20 GCIV arts 16, 63; *GCI Commentary* 145, *GCII Commentary* 96, *GCIV Commentary* 45.

21 The Judge Advocate General's Legal Center and School ('TJAGLCS'), *US Army Operational Law Handbook* (2012) ('*OPLAW Handbook*') 18; TJAGLCS, *Law of Armed Conflict Deskbook* (2012) ('*LOAC Deskbook*') 46. Note that these two TJAGLCS publications are for instructional purposes, and are not official publications of the US Army, let alone the US Government. *OPLAW Handbook* ii; *LOAC Deskbook* ii.

specifically excludes wounded and sick combatants from its definition of 'protected persons' (who are civilian persons in time of war, generally enemy nationals and inhabitants of occupied territories).[22] As will be seen, while the protections under Geneva Convention IV for wounded, sick and shipwrecked civilians are somewhat comparable to their military counterparts under Geneva Convention I and Geneva Convention II, they are certainly not identical.

Representing the zenith of humanitarian treaties, Additional Protocol I sought to blur this distinction by expanding the definition of wounded, sick and shipwrecked not only to include civilians, but also 'maternity cases, newborn babies and other persons who may be in need of immediate medical assistance or care, such as the infirm or expectant mothers'.[23] As Professor Dinstein so aptly notes, '[i]t is obvious from this text that some of those enjoying the status of "wounded" and "sick" are neither wounded nor sick (eg newborn babies)'.[24] The ICRC *Commentary* to Additional Protocol I recognises that this article deviates from the earlier Geneva Conventions.[25] The ICRC CIHL Study endorses this 'important innovation in relation to the Conventions' by claiming that the expanded protections are now a matter of CIL.[26] However, this conclusion rests on surprisingly thin state practice.[27] Additional Protocol II supplements Common Article 3 by providing specific protections for wounded, sick and shipwrecked in a NIAC, but without ever defining its terms.[28]

One of the problems with Additional Protocol I muddying the distinction between wounded, sick and shipwrecked combatants, and their civilian counterparts, is that combatants and civilians have very different statuses during armed conflict. Wounded, sick and shipwrecked combatants are entitled to POW status upon capture, and after being medically treated, are automatically placed into captivity.[29] On the other hand, wounded, sick and shipwrecked civilians are entitled to the protected status of civilians.[30] Civilians may only be interned under certain conditions (for example, 'security of the Detaining Power').[31]

Other than the general admonition to 'respect and protect' them, the first enumerated protection is to treat the wounded and sick humanely, without any adverse distinction other than medical triage.[32] '[A]ny wounded or sick person ... is entitled to respect and humane treatment and the care which his condition requires.'[33] The principle of humane treatment, besides incorporating the ICCPR's prohibitions on violence to life and person, the taking of hostages, outrages upon personal dignity, etc, which are enumerated as prohibited acts in Common Article 3, also incorporates other aspects, such as the prohibitions against enforced disappearances and

---

22 GCIV art 4; *GCIV Commentary* 50–51.

23 API art 8.

24 Yoram Dinstein, *The Conduct of Hostilities under the Law of International Conflict* (CUP 2004) 143.

25 *AP Commentary* ¶¶ 304, 312.

26 CIHL commentary to rr 109, 138.

27 Benoit (n 13) 196–199. But, see Sivakumaran (n 2) 273 (positing that the obligations of common art 3 already extend to 'persons who do not take an active part in hostilities, [and therefore] it includes the civilian wounded and sick as well as wounded and sick fighters').

28 APII pt III.

29 See generally GCI arts 13–14; GCII arts 13, 14–16; GCIII arts 15, 17, 21; *GCI Commentary* 143–144, *GCII Commentary* 94–95; CIHL r 3, 106; Emily Crawford, 'Combatants' and Chris Jenks, 'Detention under the law of armed conflict' chs 7 and 17 in this volume.

30 See generally GCIV arts 4, 27; Emanuela-Chiara Gillard, 'Protection of civilians in the conduct of hostilities' ch 9 in this volume; CIHL r 5.

31 GCIV arts 41–43, 68, 78–79.

32 GCI art 12; GCII art 12; API art 10; APII arts 4(1), 7(2); CIHL r 110; *LOAC Deskbook* (n 21) 48–49.

33 *GCI Commentary* 145; *GCII Commentary* 96.

forced labour.[34] The obligation to treat persons humanely also appears in ad hoc agreements in NIACs, although these agreements often are not followed in practice.[35]

The next enumerated protection is to 'take all possible measures' to search for, collect and protect the wounded and sick, a requirement that applies to both IAC and NIAC.[36] 'But there are times when military operations will make the obligation to search for the fallen impracticable.'[37] For example, in the 1991 Gulf War, 'US policy ... was not to search for casualties in Iraqi tanks or armored personnel carriers because of concerns about unexploded ordnance.'[38] Since these duties commence at the battlefront, the duty to 'protect' includes the duty to evacuate to a safer location, especially 'from a besieged or encircled area'.[39] If the wounded and sick cannot be evacuated, '[t]he Party to the conflict which is compelled to abandon wounded or sick to the enemy shall, as far as military considerations permit, leave with them a part of its medical personnel and material to assist in their care'.[40] However, there is a temporal distinction between when the obligation arises on land ('[a]t all times, and particularly after an engagement') vice at sea ('[a]fter each engagement').[41] The difference in wording between Geneva Convention I and Geneva Convention II 'tacitly accept[s] the view of the Government experts ... that the words "after each engagement" were better suited to the special conditions prevailing at sea'.[42] Thus the treaty law obligation for soldiers to search for and collect the wounded and sick begins earlier in an engagement (that is, during the heat of the land battle, if possible, perhaps during a lull in fighting), whereas sailors are permitted to wait for a naval battle to have ended before searching for and collecting the wounded, sick and shipwrecked.[43]

Having briefly explored the fundamental protections of searching for, collecting, protecting and treating the wounded and sick humanely, it is time to revisit the definition of who qualifies as 'wounded and sick' deserving of these protections. As already mentioned, Geneva Convention I and Geneva Convention II were historically limited to protecting combatants who are placed *hors de combat* because of wounds or sickness, and then are cared for, and subsequently detained as POWs.[44] Wounded and sick civilians historically were treated as civilians by civilian medical personnel at civilian hospitals.[45] While the protections under Geneva Convention IV for wounded, sick and shipwrecked civilians are somewhat comparable to their military counterparts under Geneva Convention I and Geneva Convention II, they are certainly not identical.

Specifically, the duties to search for, collect and evacuate civilian wounded, sick and shipwrecked under Geneva Convention IV are limited to searching for the wounded and assisting

---

34 Sivakumaran (n 2) 257–258.
35 Ibid 256–257 (listing examples of such agreements and the violations thereof).
36 GCI arts 3(2), 15; GCII arts 3(2), 18; APII art 8.
37 *GCI Commentary* 151.
38 *LOAC Deskbook* (n 21) 50.
39 GCI art 15; GCII art 18; *GCI Commentary* 150, 152, 155–157, *GCII Commentary* 83, 121–122, 134–136, 154–155.
40 GCI art 12.
41 Compare GCI art 15; APII art 8 *with* GCII art 18.
42 *GCII Commentary* 132. See also *AP Commentary* ¶¶ 4650–4651, 4653; Dinstein (n 24) 143–144 (exploring the differences between the duty to search for and collected the wounded and sick under GCI and GCII).
43 But, see CIHL r 109 (glossing over this temporal distinction by adopting a more generic 'whenever circumstances permit' standard, with neither explanation nor citations to supporting state practice); Benoit (n 13) 204–205 (criticising this aspect of the CIHL Study).
44 See generally GCI arts 13–14; GCII arts 13, 16; *GCI Commentary* 143–144, *GCII Commentary* 94–95.
45 GCIV arts 4, 35–43, 79–135; *GCI Commentary* 145; *GCII Commentary* 96, 205; *GCIV Commentary* 45, 50–51; *OPLAW Handbook* (n 21) 18.

the shipwrecked '[a]s far as military considerations allow', and removing the wounded and sick from besieged or encircled areas, but only if 'local agreements' have been reached by the parties to the conflict.[46] Table 18.1 illustrates the limited protections for civilian wounded, sick and shipwrecked provided in Geneva Convention IV.[47]

Contrast these fairly limited protections owed to civilians with the more robust duties owed to combatants:

1 '[a]t all times, and particularly after an engagement, ... without delay, take all possible measures to search for and collect the [shipwrecked,] wounded and sick';
2 '[w]henever circumstances permit, [arrange] an armistice or a suspension of fire ... to permit the removal, exchange and transport of the wounded left on the battlefield; and
3 conclude 'local arrangements ... for the removal or exchange of wounded and sick from a besieged or encircled area'.[48]

There are thus lacunae (shaded in grey Table 18.1) in the duties to search for, collect and evacuate civilian wounded, sick and shipwrecked under Geneva Convention IV. For example, there is no explicit mention of an obligation to search for or to collect sick civilians in either Geneva Convention IV or in its ICRC *Commentary*.

As discussed earlier, Additional Protocol I sought to fill these lacunae by expanding the definition of wounded, sick and shipwrecked to include not only civilians, but also expectant mothers, newborn babies and the infirm.[49] This significant expansion of the definition of wounded and sick has serious potential ramifications for military operations. Twenty-five years earlier, the ICRC *Commentary* had noted:

> Article 13 [of Geneva Convention I and Geneva Convention II] cannot ... in any way entitle a belligerent to refrain from respecting a wounded person, or to deny him the requisite treatment, even where he does not belong to one of the categories specified in the Article. Any wounded person, whoever he may be, must be treated by the enemy in accordance with the Geneva Convention. When a wounded person falls into the enemy's

Table 18.1 Duties towards civilian wounded, sick and shipwrecked under Geneva Convention IV

	Wounded	*Sick*	*Shipwrecked*
Search for	'search for the ... wounded' (Article 16)		
Collect			'assist the shipwrecked' (Article 16)
Evacuate	'remov[e] from besieged or encircled areas, of wounded' (Article 17)	'remov[e] from besieged or encircled areas, of ... sick' (Article 17)	

46 GCIV arts 16–17.
47 Benoit (n 13) 195.
48 GCI art 15; GCII art 18; GCIV art 17.
49 API art 8(a); *AP Commentary* ¶¶ 304, 312; CIHL commentary to r 109.

hands, the latter will have ample time to consider, at the proper time and place, what his status is, and whether he is or is not a prisoner of war. At most, Article 13 will serve to determine under what Convention the wounded man is to be respected and cared for.[50]

However, while it would be difficult to argue against the logic of treating civilian wounded who 'fall[] into the enemy's hands' presumably at or near the field of battle and injured as a result of military operations, it is more difficult to justify Additional Protocol I's requirement not only to search for sick civilians, but also 'to come to [the] defence, to lend help and support [to]' expectant mothers, newborn babies and the medically infirm.[51] This goes well beyond Geneva Convention IV's admonition to respect and protect the infirm and expectant mothers '[a]s far as military considerations allow',[52] which recognises the fact that saving civilians is the responsibility of the civilian authorities – 'the military is not required to provide injured civilians with medical care in a combat zone.'[53]

For example, if a military convoy suffers an improvised explosive device (IED) attack, certainly one would expect the responding medical personnel to search for, collect, protect and treat the wounded convoy personnel (be they military or civilian), as well as any local civilians wounded either in the attack or subsequent military operations, especially if no civilian medical treatment facility is readily available. For example, '[i]t is US policy that "[c]ivilians who are injured, wounded, or become sick as a result of military operations may be collected and provided initial medical treatment in accordance with theater policies"'.[54]

However, is it reasonable for Additional Protocol I to require the military medical personnel responding to an IED attack also to search the surrounding neighbourhood(s) for expectant mothers, newborn babies and the medically infirm, and to evacuate them to a safer location? What if the expectant mother does not want to leave her family's home, despite its proximity to a recent IED attack? How long should the military medical treatment facility continue treating the expectant mother – only until her baby is born, or through the first critical year of life? It is a far cry from treating civilians wounded during military operations, to usurping the local civilian medical professionals' responsibility to treat those requiring medical care in their communities.

In any event, treating wounded and sick civilians (for example, providing emergency care in cases where life, limb or eyesight would be jeopardised without immediate intervention) does not deprive a medical unit of its protection.[55] Moreover, 'inspired by the events at Solferino', military commanders may appeal to the civilian population and local aid societies to assist in the treatment of the wounded and sick.[56]

Two miscellaneous matters regarding the wounded, sick and shipwrecked remain. The first is to:

> record as soon as possible, in respect of each wounded, sick or dead person of the adverse Party falling into their hands, any particulars which may assist in his identification.

---

50 *GCI Commentary* 145; *GCII Commentary* 96.
51 API art 10; *AP Commentary* ¶ 446; CIHL commentary to r 109.
52 GCIV art 16.
53 *LOAC Deskbook* (n 21) 46.
54 Ibid citing the US Department of the Army, *The Medical Company Tactics, Techniques, and Procedures*, Field Manual 4-02.6 (2002) ¶ A-4.
55 GCI art 22; *GCI Commentary* 202–205.
56 GCI art 18; GCII art 21; API art 17; *GCI Commentary* 184–193; *GCII Commentary* 151–153; *AP Commentary* ¶¶ 718–731. See also GCIV art 19 (authorising civilian hospitals to treat military wounded and sick).

> These records should if possible include: ... serial number; [full name] ... date of birth; ... date and place of capture or death; ... particulars concerning wounds or illness, or cause of death.[57]

Recording details regarding the wounded, sick, shipwrecked and dead, and forwarding them through the ICRC to the adverse belligerent facilitates accounting and searching for the missing.[58] This protection is similar to that extended to detained POWs and interned civilians.[59]

The final protection is to dispose of the dead properly.[60] Due to inherent personal, moral and religious sensitivities in this area, the relevant treaty rules are fairly detailed. Medical examinations of the deceased are encouraged, 'with a view to confirming death, establishing identity and enabling a report to be made'.[61] Presumably this recommendation to conduct a medical examination 'if possible' should be deferential to religious sensitivities about desecrating the human body, although there is no mention of this in the ICRC *Commentary*.[62] The dead should be buried in individual (as opposed to mass) graves 'as far as circumstances permit', and 'if possible according to the rites of the religion to which they belonged'.[63] Bodies may only be cremated for hygienic or religious reasons (for example, Hindus and Buddhists),[64] 'or in accordance with [a POW's or civilian internee's] express wish to this effect'.[65] Graves are preferably to be grouped by nationality, and are to be maintained, respected 'and [their exact locations] marked so that they may always be found', with a view that after hostilities have ended the bodies may be subsequently exhumed and transported 'to the home country' if requested.[66] 'Grouping in this manner will make it possible for countries to pay collective tribute to their dead at a later date.'[67] Towards this end, the relevant articles refer to the use of a 'double identity disc' (colloquially known as dogtags), with one disc remaining on the body, and one being forwarded along with the dead person's personal effects.[68] Due to practical considerations, there are no requirements either to conduct cremations at sea, or to mark the exact location of burials at sea.[69] The only treaty requirements regarding the dead in a NIAC are 'to search for the dead, prevent their being despoiled, and decently dispose of them'.[70] Although the ICRC CIHL Study recognised that '[t]here is no treaty provision explicitly requiring measures to identify the dead prior to their disposal in the context of a [NIAC]', it found that a CIL norm exists to that effect,[71] and also recognised 'a growing trend' in CIL towards returning the remains of the dead in a NIAC to their families upon request.[72]

---

57 GCI arts 16–17; GCII arts 19–20; API art 33(2); CIHL commentary to rr 116, 117, 123.
58 CIHL commentary to rr 98, 117.
59 GCIII art 122; GCIV art 138.
60 CIHL r 115.
61 GCI art 17; GCII art 20; GCIII art 120.
62 *LOAC Deskbook* (n 21) 51.
63 GCI art 17; GCII art 20; GCIII art 120; GCIV art 130; CIHL commentary to r 115.
64 GCI art 17.
65 GCIII art 120; GCIV art 130; *GCI Commentary* 179; CIHL commentary to r 115.
66 GCI art 17; GCIII art 120; GCIV art 130; API art 34(1); *GCI Commentary* 181; CIHL commentary to rr 114, 116.
67 *GCI Commentary* 180.
68 GCI arts 16–17; GCII arts 19–20. Surprisingly, there is no similar requirement for handling a deceased POW's dogtags, although '[t]his was probably an oversight on the part of the drafters of the Third Convention and by analogy, one may assume that the Detaining Power should follow the same procedure in the case of deceased prisoners of war'. *GCIII Commentary* 565.
69 GCII art 20.
70 APII art 8; CIHL r 115.
71 CIHL r 116.
72 CIHL commentary to r 114.

2 Medical and religious personnel

The definition of medical and religious personnel is slightly less controversial, and certainly includes '[m]edical personnel proper', that is those 'exclusively engaged in' assisting wounded, sick, dying and dead combatants, such as 'doctors, surgeons, dentists, chemists, orderlies, nurses, stretcher-bearers, etc'.[73] The definition also includes the administrative staff that manage the medical units and establishments. To be 'exclusively engaged' in providing medical services, the assignment must be permanent. In 1949, Geneva Convention I was expanded to include medical personnel charged with 'the prevention of disease' (for example, providing inoculations, or disinfecting the water supply). In 1977, Additional Protocol I extended protection to civilian medical personnel as well.[74]

Medical and religious personnel also includes chaplains (that is, military clerics, of whatever faith) who are 'attached to the armed forces', even though they 'need not be exclusively or even partially assigned to the wounded and sick'.[75] Additional Protocol I extends protection to civilian clerics as well.[76] However, religious staff (for example, chaplain assistants) are not expressly included within the definition of protected persons (unlike their medical counterparts). The US does not recognise chaplain assistants as protected persons, but rather as combatants charged with protecting chaplains in combat situations.[77] Thus, while the US issues special identification cards (DD Form 1934) to the full spectrum of medical personnel and to chaplains (as noncombatants), it only issues regular armed forces identification cards to chaplain assistants.[78]

Medical and religious personnel also may include personnel of national Red Cross societies and other relief organisations, but only if the state provides notification of 'the names of the societies which it has authorized, under its responsibility, to render assistance to the regular medical service of its armed forces'.[79]

Personnel only temporarily assigned to certain medical duties are treated as 'auxiliary medical personnel'.[80] However, Article 25 of Geneva Convention I provides a very short list of temporary medical duties that qualify for protection: 'hospital orderlies, nurses or auxiliary stretcher-bearers'. Rather than being illustrative, this list is exclusive.[81] Thus, an administrative assistant permanently assigned to a hospital would be a protected person (because s/he is 'exclusively engaged in' operating a medical establishment), while one only temporarily so assigned would not (because administrative personnel are not one of the three categories of enumerated 'auxiliary medical personnel'). However, auxiliary medical personnel may not be that common in practice.[82] Somewhat confusing through a modern lens, the list of auxiliary medical personnel includes nurses, who are more likely today to be permanently assigned to medical duties, and thus would constitute protected persons. Only military personnel temporarily assigned as nurses would constitute 'auxiliary medical personnel' (for example, a cook who has also been trained to function as a back-up nurse when needed). However, although auxiliary medical personnel are entitled to protection on the battlefield, once captured, they become ordinary POWs, while

---

73 *GCI Commentary* 218.
74 See generally GCI art 24; *GCI Commentary* 218–219; API art 8(c); CIHL r 25.
75 GCI art 24; GCII arts 36–37; *GCI Commentary* 220; API art 8(d); CIHL r 27.
76 API art 15(5).
77 Jonathan Odom, 'Beyond Arm Bands and Arms Banned: Chaplains, Armed Conflict, and the Law' (2002) 49 *Naval LR* 22–23.
78 GCI art 40; GCII art 42; API art 43(2).
79 GCI art 26.
80 GCI art 25; *GCI Commentary* 221.
81 *GCI Commentary* 222.
82 *LOAC Deskbook* (n 21) 55.

their permanently assigned medical counterparts become 'retained personnel' entitled to repatriation.[83]

Another distinction between temporary and permanently assigned medical personnel and chaplains involves identification. Permanently assigned medical personnel and chaplains are issued a special identification card, and encouraged to wear an armlet (also known as a brassard) with the distinctive emblem on their left arm, presumably at all times, in order to be recognised as such from afar.[84] However, medical personnel in recent conflicts have removed their distinguishing brassard because they felt it led to them being specifically targeted. Auxiliary medical personnel may wear a special brassard, but only 'while carrying out medical duties', and only displaying 'the distinctive sign in miniature' (for example, a mini red cross, or mini red crescent) to distinguish the armlet from those worn by permanently assigned medical personnel.[85] Note that states expanded the distinctive emblems used by medical personnel and relief societies to include a red crystal (that is, diamond) in 2005, in order to avoid any political or religious connotation associated with using either a red cross or red crescent.[86] The red crystal is also intended to avoid any future proliferation of other distinctive emblems that might undermine the protections afforded by displaying one of the three distinctive emblems.[87]

Geneva Convention II expands the definition of medical and religious personnel to include 'personnel of hospital ships' (that is, ship crewmembers).[88] Thus, all personnel assigned to a hospital ship (however temporarily) are protected so long as they are actually assigned to the ship. For example, an engineman temporarily assigned to work in the engine room of a hospital ship would be included in the definition of medical personnel, although he would only be treated as 'auxiliary personnel' if he were temporarily assigned to serve as a stretcher-bearer on land.

The LOAC has always treated medical personnel and chaplains differently from their brothers- and sisters-in-arms, with a 'status *sui generis*'.[89] However, this has not always been the case in practice. Belligerent parties in the First World War found 'that it was necessary to retain enemy medical personnel to assist in the care of prisoners of war, and held up repatriation for lengthy periods'.[90]

Article 12 of the 1929 First Geneva Convention sought to remedy this practice by expressly providing that exclusively engaged medical personnel and chaplains:

> may not be retained after they have fallen into the hands of the enemy. In the absence of an agreement to the contrary, they shall be sent back to the belligerent to which they belong as soon as a route for their return shall be open and military considerations permit. Pending their return they shall continue to carry out their duties under the direction of the enemy; they shall preferably be engaged in the care of the wounded and sick of the belligerent to which they belong.

83 GCI arts 29–30.
84 GCI art 40. Although this article provides that permanently assigned medical personnel and chaplains '*shall* wear' the armlet, the ICRC *Commentary* provides that 'all permanent medical personnel and chaplains *are entitled* to wear the armlet' (emphasis added). *GCI Commentary* 309. The logical reconciliation of these two seemingly disparate statements is that permanently assigned medical personnel and chaplains *should* wear the distinctive brassard if they wish to be recognised as such from afar. Wearing the brassard merely facilitates identification of protected persons – it does not confer protected status on them. CIHL commentary to r 30, 156; *AP Commentary* ¶ 4717.
85 GCI art 41.
86 APIII art 2(2).
87 *LOAC Deskbook* (n 21) 63.
88 GCII art 36; *GCII Commentary* 203–205.
89 *GCI Commentary* 239.
90 Ibid 235.

Although this provision appears to require repatriation at the earliest opportunity, given the caveat regarding an agreement, it was not surprising in the Second World War that

> the belligerent Powers agreed among themselves to retain in the camps a considerable number of the medical personnel in their hands, to assist in the care of the prisoners of war … repatriation was, in consequence, infrequent, incomplete and extremely dilatory.[91]

'Great Britain and Italy, for example, retained 2 doctors, 2 dentists, 2 chaplains, and 12 medical orderlies for every 1,000 POWs.'[92] Germany even retained 'reserves' of medical personnel in case they were needed, but used them in the interim for non-medical work.[93]

After the Second World War experience, the updated Geneva Convention I recognised the military requirement to retain medical personnel and chaplains, but 'only in so far as the state of health, the spiritual needs and the number of prisoners of war require'.[94] They are entitled to continue to carry out their medical and spiritual duties, in addition to receiving all of the benefits of POWs, but 'shall not … be required to perform any work outside their medical or religious duties'.[95] '[I]t was thought desirable that prisoners should be cared for by their own countrymen, speaking the same language and using methods of treatment to which the prisoners were accustomed.'[96] Repatriation remains the rule, with retention of medical personnel and chaplains permitted only when 'indispensable'.[97] However, '[s]ince World War II, this is one of the least honored provisions of the convention. US medical personnel in Korea and Vietnam were neither repatriated nor given retained person status.'[98] 'The US practice is that retained persons will be assigned to POW camps in the ratio of 2 doctors, 2 nurses, 1 chaplain, and 7 enlisted medical personnel per 1,000 POWs.'[99]

In terms of safeguards, permanent medical personnel and chaplains merely have an overarching protection 'to be respected and protected in all circumstances'.[100] This classic and all-encompassing formulation

> make[s] it quite clear that medical personnel are to be respected and protected at all times and in all places, both on the battlefield and behind the lines, and whether retained only temporarily by the enemy or for a lengthy period.[101]

No other guidance was felt necessary, either in Geneva Convention I or its ICRC *Commentary*. Although the protection of permanent medical personnel and chaplains is not made expressly conditional on them abstaining from committing acts harmful to the enemy (unlike medical units), this condition is implied.[102] Like medical units, medical personnel should not lose their protections if they possess small arms to defend themselves and their patients against marauders.[103]

---

91 Ibid 237.
92 *LOAC Deskbook* (n 21) 53.
93 *GCI Commentary* 237.
94 GCI art 28.
95 Ibid; *GCI Commentary* 246–248, 251–253, 256; GCIII arts 33, 35.
96 *GCI Commentary* 241, 247.
97 GCI art 30; GCII art 37; *GCI Commentary* 240–241, 244–245.
98 *LOAC Deskbook* (n 21) 53 n 9.
99 Ibid 54.
100 GCI art 24.
101 *GCI Commentary* 220.
102 Ibid 221.
103 CIHL commentary to r 25.

As alluded to earlier, permanent medical personnel and chaplains may be captured by the enemy, but the ICRC *Commentary* to Article 28 of Geneva Convention I clarifies that:

> when speaking of the passing of medical personnel and chaplains into enemy hands, [Article 28] uses the words 'who fall into the hands of the adverse Party'. The wording implies that the capture of medical personnel must be a matter of chance and depend upon fluctuations at the battle front; for it is hardly conceivable that a belligerent should deliberately try to capture such personnel. An organized 'medical hunt' would certainly be a sorry sight and completely contrary to the spirit of the Geneva Convention. On the other hand one can well imagine a fighting unit coming upon a group of medical personnel and leaving them to carry on their duties, and the medical staff, for their part, not taking in flight when enemy forces draw near.[104]

Thus, there is conflicting advice in the guidance to medical personnel regarding evading capture. Medical units are told that '[t]hey must refrain from all aggressive action and may not use force to prevent the capture of their unit by the enemy' (else risk losing their protection) yet '[i]t is, on the other hand, perfectly legitimate for a medical unit to withdraw in the face of the enemy'.[105] But medical personnel are also told that it is perfectly reasonable 'not [to take] flight when enemy forces draw near'.[106] Seeking to harmonise this seemingly disparate guidance yields the conclusion that permanent medical personnel and chaplains may seek to evade capture, but that they are not required to do so. This is consistent with the fact that once captured, permanent medical personnel and chaplains are treated as retained personnel. Since they are not POWs, they have no duty to subsequently escape (which their state otherwise might require).[107] Moreover, retained medical personnel and chaplains obtain all of the benefits afforded to regular POWs, but are entitled to repatriation earlier than their POW comrades.[108] Since auxiliary medical personnel are only entitled to protection on the battlefield,[109] they may have more of an incentive to evade capture!

3 Medical units and establishments

Although not expressly defined in the Geneva Conventions, the definition of medical units and establishments is fairly self-evident:

> Medical units may be either mobile, or in fixed establishments. Fixed establishments are, as their name indicates, permanent buildings used as hospitals or stores. Mobile units are defined as establishments which can move from place to place as circumstances require following the movement of the troops. It is field hospitals and ambulances which are in particular referred to, but it is not necessary for them to be accommodated in shelters or tents; an establishment in the open, however small, is a medical unit if its object is to collect the wounded.[110]

---

104 *GCI Commentary* 242.
105 Ibid 203 and n 1, 204; CIHL commentary to r 25.
106 *GCI Commentary* 242.
107 Ibid 255–256; Code of Conduct for Members of the Armed Forces of the United States, Executive Order 10631 (17 August 1955) art III.
108 GCI arts 28, 30; GCIII arts 33, 35; *GCI Commentary* 244–245.
109 GCI art 29.
110 *GCI Commentary* 194–195; CIHL r 28.

Moreover, '[a] group of medical orderlies, however small – one, even – must be regarded as a medical unit'.[111]

The protected status of military medical units and establishments is expressly provided in Geneva Convention I: 'Fixed establishments and mobile medical units of the Medical Service may in no circumstances be attacked, but shall at all times be respected and protected by the Parties to the conflict.'[112] 'However, incidental damage to medical facilities situated near military objectives is not a violation of the LOAC.'[113] Moreover, this protection from attack does not prevent medical units and establishments from being captured by the enemy, who may continue to operate them as medical units and establishments.[114] Although not expressly mentioned, '[Geneva Convention I] does not confer immunity from search by the enemy on medical units, establishments, or transports'.[115]

The only requirements for protection are that medical units and establishments must be 'of the Medical Service', and may not perform any non-medical military function, else they risk losing their protection. Such non-medical military functions include sheltering soldiers, storing arms or ammunition, etc.[116] This is the medical unit equivalent of 'refraining from hostilities' by a wounded or sick combatant in order to retain protected status. However, before losing their protected status, medical units must be warned of their transgression(s), and have a reasonable time either to cease the harmful acts or to evacuate the wounded and sick.[117] Moreover, performing certain *de minimis* acts related to their medical function, and done in good faith will not deprive medical units and establishments of their protection. These acts expressly include possessing small arms and/or sentries for protection against attack (but not against capture), possessing small arms and ammunition taken from the wounded and sick, treating civilians and the presence of veterinarians (who treat military working animals).[118] 'In contrast, placing machine guns, grenade launchers, mines, light antitank weapons, etc., around a medical unit *would* cause a loss of protection.'[119] Thus, while Article 24 of Geneva Convention I explicitly requires that '[m]edical personnel [must be] exclusively engaged in medical duties in order to be protected', Geneva Convention I implicitly imposes the same requirement on medical units and establishments. The Rome Statute classifies intentionally attacking protected medical units as a war crime in both IAC and NIAC.[120]

Unlike shore-based medical units, hospital ships have absolute protection, not only from attack, but also from capture, regardless of whether there are any wounded, sick or shipwrecked aboard.[121]

---

111 *GCI Commentary* 312.
112 GCI art 19; see also GCII art 23 (protecting medical units from naval bombardment or attack from the sea); GCIV art 18 (protecting civilian hospitals from attack); API art 12; CIHL r 28; Rome Statute arts 8(2)(b)(xxiv), (e)(ii) and (e)(iv) (classifying intentional attacking medical facilities as a war crime in both IAC and NIAC).
113 *OPLAW Handbook* (n 21) 18.
114 GCI art 19; *GCI Commentary* 197–198.
115 US Department of the Army, *Army Law of Land Warfare*, Field Manual 27-10 (1956) ¶ 221; *LOAC Deskbook* (n 21) 56.
116 GCI arts 19, 21, 22; API art 13; *GCI Commentary* 196, 200–201; CIHL r 28.
117 GCI art 21; API art 13; *GCI Commentary* 201–202.
118 GCI art 22; APII art 11; *GCI Commentary* 202–205.
119 *LOAC Deskbook* (n 21) 57 (emphasis in original).
120 Rome Statute arts 8(2)(b)(ix) and (e)(ii).
121 GCII arts 22, 24–26; *GCII Commentary* 158–162, 204. See also GCI art 20 (protecting hospital ships from attack from land); GCIV art 21 (protecting vessels carrying wounded and sick civilians).

> The difference is fully justified: a hospital ship could no longer carry out its duties if it were deprived of its personnel and crew, for those [persons] constitute, so to speak, an integral part of the ship. As has been said, the ship would be merely a derelict.[122]

However, there are two conditions to receiving such absolute protection: (1) they must be exclusively assigned to assist, treat and transport wounded, sick and shipwrecked; and (2) their names and characteristics must have been properly notified to the parties to the conflict at least ten days before being so employed 'in order to guarantee the security of hospital ships'.[123] Even if a hospital ship is in port when the port 'falls into the hands of the enemy', the hospital ship must be permitted to leave port instead of being captured.[124] However, like their shore-based counterparts, hospital ships may lose their protected status if 'they are used to commit, outside their humanitarian duties, acts harmful to the enemy'.[125]

Traditionally, hospital ships were limited to 'purely deflective means of defence, such as chaff and flares'.[126]

> However, due to the changing threat environment in which the red cross symbol is not recognised by various hostile groups and actors as indicating protected status, the United States views the manning of hospital ships with defensive weapons systems, such as anti-missile defence systems or crew-served weapons to defend against small boat threats as prudent (Anti-Terrorism/Force Protection) measures, analogous to arming crew members with small arms, and consistent with the humanitarian purpose of hospital ships and duty to safeguard the wounded and sick.[127]

If such weapons are purely used defensively, that should not deprive them of protection.[128]

Another limitation on hospital ships that has evolved with technology is the prohibition against using 'a secret code for their wireless or other means of communication'.[129] The requirement for hospital ships to transmit 'in the open' was established 'so that belligerents could verify that hospital ships' communications systems were being used only in support of their humanitarian function and not as a means of communicating information that would be harmful to the enemy'.[130] With modern navies relying on encrypted communications systems, the more modern rule is that hospital ships may use cryptographic equipment for communications, so

---

122 *GCII Commentary* 204.

123 GCII art 22; *GCII Commentary* 158–162.

124 GCII art 29.

125 GCII arts 34–35; *GCII Commentary* 158–159. See also GCII art 30 (promise by state parties not to use hospital ships for any military purpose), art 33 (promise by state parties not to use '[m]erchant vessels which have been transformed into hospital ships ... [for] any other use throughout the duration of hostilities').

126 *San Remo Manual on International Law Applicable to Armed Conflicts at Sea* (IIHL 1994) ¶ 170 ('*San Remo Manual*').

127 US Navy, US Marine Corps and US Coast Guard, *The Commander's Handbook on the Law of Naval Operations*, NWP 1-14M/MCWP 5-12.1/COMDTPUB P5800.7A (July 2007) ¶ 8.6.3 ('*Commander's Handbook*'); Michael Sirak, 'US Navy Seeks to Revise Laws of War on Hospital Ships' *Jane's Defence Weekly* (19 August 2003).

128 Richard J Grunawalt, 'Hospital Ships in the War on Terror: Sanctuaries or Targets?' (2005) 58 *NWCR* 89, 109–112.

129 GCII art 34.

130 *Commander's Handbook* (n 126) ¶ 8.6.3.

long as they do not transmit intelligence data.[131] Finally, parties to the conflict may search, temporarily detain (up to seven days), and embark a commissioner or neutral observer aboard hospital ships to ensure strict compliance with the rules.[132]

States may seek to enlarge geographically the protection of wounded and sick, medical personnel, and medical units and establishments by designating hospital zones – however, they must be mutually recognised by belligerent parties in order to be effective.[133] Annex I to Geneva Convention I provides a draft agreement between belligerent parties recognising hospital zones, and setting certain conditions upon them, such as no military operations or work conducted therein, being far removed from military objectives, etc.[134] There apparently has been some use of hospital zones in both IAC and NIAC, based upon written agreements.[135]

4 Medical transports

The definition of medical transports is also fairly obvious, if not expressly defined, and historically included one or more military vehicles operating on land (road or rail), or inland waterways, and engaged in a humanitarian function.[136] Additional Protocol I expanded the definition to include civilian ambulances.[137] Medical aircraft are covered by separate provisions,[138] as are hospital ships.[139]

The protected status of medical transports operating on land (or inland waterways) is expressly provided in Geneva Convention I: 'Transports of wounded and sick or of medical equipment shall be respected and protected in the same way as mobile medical units.' A properly marked ambulance is the archetypal example of a mobile medical unit, and thus must be exclusively engaged in the search for, collection, transport or treatment of the wounded or sick, and may not be used to perform any non-medical function, else it risks losing its protection.[140] The 'exclusively engaged' requirement is made explicit for medical aircraft,[141] and for hospital ships.[142]

Like other medical units, military (but not Red Cross) ambulances may be captured by the enemy, who may then use them as they wish, so long as they 'ensure the care of the wounded and sick they contain'.[143] However, if the enemy uses a former medical transport for another purpose (for example, transporting war materiel), then they must remove the protected emblem to avoid repeating 'the serious abuses which occurred during the Second World War', as well

---

131 *San Remo Manual* (n 125) ¶ 171; Dinstein (n 24) 171; *Commander's Handbook* (n 126) ¶ 8.6.3.
132 GCII art 31.
133 GCI art 23.
134 GCI, annex I, arts 1–13; *GCI Commentary* 415–429.
135 CIHL commentary to r 35.
136 *GCI Commentary* 280; see generally GCI art 35; API art 21 (which uses the terminology 'medical vehicles' to refer to medical transports on land – API art 8(h)); CIHL r 29.
137 API art 8(g).
138 GCI arts 36–37; API arts 24–31.
139 GCII art 22; API art 22.
140 GCI arts 21, 35, 39; API art 21; *GCI Commentary* 194–195, 280; Rome Statute arts 8(2)(b)(xxiv), (e)(ii) (classifying intentionally attacking medical transports as a war crime in both IAC and NIAC).
141 GCI art 36.
142 GCII arts 22, 34–35.
143 GCI arts 34–35; *GCI Commentary* 282–283.

as committing a grave breach of Geneva Convention I.[144] Captured ambulance drivers are treated as retained medical personnel, assuming they are exclusively assigned as such.[145] Although not expressly mentioned, as the quintessential type of mobile medical unit, a military ambulance may not use force to prevent its capture, although it presumably may try to evade capture without using force.[146] Unfortunately, ambulances continue to be used perfidiously in modern armed conflicts.

The status of medical aircraft is far more complex. Properly marked medical aircraft exclusively engaged in humanitarian functions are only protected from attack 'while flying at heights, times and on routes specifically agreed upon between the belligerents concerned'.[147] This is because 'the speed of modern aircraft makes identification by color or markings useless. Only previous agreement could afford any real safeguard.'[148] Thus, while the default rule is that ambulances are protected from attack (unless or until they are used to commit 'acts harmful to the enemy'), medical aircraft are only protected if the opposing belligerents have provided their consent by entering into a specific agreement detailing their flight plans.[149] Moreover, medical aircraft are prohibited from flying over enemy territory and 'shall obey every summons to land' for inspection to confirm their exclusively humanitarian function.[150] Unlike medical units, there is no express requirement to warn medical aircraft straying either into enemy territory or off their previously agreed flight paths.[151] However, the ICRC *Commentary* posits the expectation that: 'every belligerent conscious of his duty would warn the offending plane by radio or order it to land ... before resorting to extreme measures'.[152]

A question often arises whether a medevac aircrew may report what they have observed while on a humanitarian mission, without risking the loss of their protected status. At least one unofficial US military publication claims that:

> [r]eporting information acquired incidentally to the aircraft's medical mission does not cause the aircraft to lose its protection. Medical personnel are responsible for reporting information gained through casual observation of activities in plain view in the discharge of their duties. This does not violate the law of armed conflict or constitute grounds for loss of protected status. For example, a Medevac aircraft crew could report the presence of an

---

144 GCI arts 44, 53; GCII arts 44, 45; API art 38; APII art 12; *GCI Commentary* 281–282; Rome Statute art 8(2)(b)(vii). The commentary to GCI provides:

> [a]fter the wounded have been taken to the rear under the protection of the red cross sign, there will be a great temptation to load the empty vehicles returning to the front with war material. If the emblem then remains on the loaded vehicles, there is a grave breach of the Convention, even if the sign has simply been left on through negligence or because there has been no time to remove it.
>
> *GCI Commentary* 281–282

Although misusing the distinctive emblem is not one of the enumerated 'grave breaches', that list 'is not to be taken as exhaustive'. *GCI Commentary* 371. API includes misusing the distinctive emblem as a grave breach if it is used perfidiously, and 'caus[es] death or serious injury'. API art 85(3)(f). Such use may also constitute perfidy. API arts 37(1)(d), 38(1), 85(3)(f); CIHL r 65.

145 *GCI Commentary* 218–219, *GCII Commentary* 205; *AP Commentary* ¶ 3987.

146 Cf *GCI Commentary* 203–204.

147 GCI art 36; GCII art 39; GCIV art 22. See also *San Remo Manual* (n 125) ¶¶ 54, 177.

148 *LOAC Deskbook* (n 21) 59; *GCI Commentary* 288.

149 *GCI Commentary* 288.

150 GCI art 36; GCII art 39; GCIV art 22; API art 30.

151 Compare GCI art 21 *with* GCI art 36.

152 *GCI Commentary* 291–292.

enemy patrol if the patrol was observed in the course of its regular mission and not as part of an information gathering mission outside its medical duties.[153]

Additional Protocol I slightly modified the regime protecting medical aircraft, depending on their specific geographical area of operations. Additional Protocol I retained the default rule that medical aircraft are not protected in hostile skies (enemy territory or 'the contact zone') unless the opposing belligerents have entered into a specific agreement detailing their flight plans.[154] Additional Protocol I codifies the expectation that if the enemy recognises a medical aircraft flying above its area without (or in deviation from) an agreement, 'that Party shall make all reasonable efforts to give the order to land ... and ... to allow the aircraft time for compliance, before resorting to an attack against the aircraft'.[155] However, medical aircraft flying above areas controlled by friendly forces (that is, friendly skies) are 'not dependent on any agreement with an adverse Party' in order to be respected and protected against attack.[156] Nevertheless, notifying the adverse belligerent may be necessary '[f]or greater safety ... in particular when such aircraft are making flights bringing them within range of surface-to-air weapons systems of the adverse Party'.[157] Additional Protocol I also introduced additional optional distinctive signals to identify medical aircraft.[158] Although Additional Protocol I is not binding on the US as a matter of treaty law, the US 'support[s] the principle that known medical aircraft be respected and protected when performing their humanitarian functions'.[159] Nevertheless, despite these modifications, there does not appear to be any state practice implementing Additional Protocol I's new medical aircraft protection regime.

Although Additional Protocol I includes 'the conveyance by land, water or air' under the rubric of 'medical transports', it maintains the traditional distinction between the protections afforded to medical vehicles on land, medical aircraft and hospital ships.[160] In contrast, Additional Protocol II uses the same expansive definition of medical transports, but conflates the traditional distinction between the protections afforded ambulances versus medical aircraft in a NIAC.[161] This may be due to the fact that in a NIAC, most (if not all) medical transports presumably will belong to the state. Nevertheless, treaty rules cannot ignore the realities of modern warfare: '[b]attlefield realities determine whether treaty texts agreed to in the comfortable diplomatic atmosphere of Geneva are, at the end of the day, practicable'.[162] Thus, the ICRC *Commentary* to Additional Protocol II recognised that medical aircraft in a NIAC were at risk of being attacked, unless they followed the traditional notification procedures.[163]

---

153 *LOAC Deskbook* (n 21) 60.
154 API arts 26–27.
155 API art 27(2).
156 API art 25.
157 Ibid.
158 API art 18(5), annex I, arts 6–8 (subsequently amended in 1993).
159 Michael Matheson, 'The Sixth Annual American Red Cross-Washington College of Law Conference on International Humanitarian Law: A Workshop on Customary International Law and the 1977 Protocols Additional to the 1949 Geneva Conventions' (1987) 2 *American University JILP* 423–424.
160 API arts 8(f)–(j), 21–31.
161 APII art 11; *AP Commentary* ¶¶ 4712–4714; CIHL r 29.
162 William Hays Parks, 'Comments on the ICRC Customary Law Study' (Unpublished Manuscript, 28 September 2005) 1.
163 *AP Commentary* ¶ 4718; *LOAC Deskbook* (n 21) 60, n 17 (providing operational examples).

5 Conclusions

Despite the lengthy history of protecting those who are placed *hors de combat* by virtue of their wounds or illness, issues remain with each of the protected groups, either in their definition, legal status or specific protections against harm. For example, does the category of 'wounded and sick' include civilians as well as combatants, even if their injuries or illnesses are unrelated to military operations? Has Additional Protocol I gone too far by including expectant mothers, newborn babies and the infirm within this rubric? What are the repercussions of operational commanders and medical personnel extending their missions to include searching for, collecting, treating and evacuating these groups? What are the temporal and geographical boundaries to these obligations?

Although LOAC has always treated medical personnel and chaplains with a unique status different from their brothers- and sisters-in-arms, this has not always been respected in practice. Repatriation of retained medical personnel in the Second World War was infrequent, incomplete and untimely, and medical personnel were made to perform non-medical work, which the updated Geneva Convention I sought to remedy. Moreover, although medical personnel are protected from attack unless or until they commit acts harmful to the enemy, medical personnel in recent conflicts have removed their distinguishing brassard because they felt it led to them being specifically targeted.

Similarly, hospital ships have had to rethink relying on their inherent vulnerability to remain protected, particularly in light of modern terrorist threats. Thus, the decision to arm US hospital ships with .50-calibre machine guns, to defend against small boat and other terrorist attacks, was probably sound. Yet despite modern threats, hospital zones continue to be used in both IAC and NIAC.

Medical transports are not without their issues. Ambulances continue to be used perfidiously in modern armed conflicts. Additional Protocol II uses an expansive definition of medical transports, to include any type of conveyance by land, water or air. Yet treaty rules developed in the clear air of Geneva cannot ignore battlefield realities, such as the need for prior agreements to ensure medical aircraft are protected from attack.

As we have seen, the proper treatment of the wounded and sick, and medical services resides at the core of international humanitarian law. Yet their proper respect and protection remains fraught not only with avoidance, ambiguity, and misapplication, but also with intentional violence against them, which is even more troubling. This remains 'one of the most serious yet neglected humanitarian issues of today'.[164]

---

164 Maurer (n13).

19

Women and war

Helen Durham and Eve Massingham

When Francoise Krill wrote her seminal piece on the protection of women under international humanitarian law (IHL) in 1985,[1] it was clear that the Geneva Conventions of 1949 and their Additional Protocols of 1977 were the main sources of the international legal framework aimed at reducing the suffering of women during times of armed conflict. During the 1970s and 1980s, the operational work of the ICRC, and a few other developing norms also assisted in this task,[2] however there was not the depth or breadth of focus upon this issue relative to contemporary reality. Nearing 30 years after Krill's piece, whilst the Geneva Conventions and their Protocols continue to provide the core protections, many other sources of law, albeit some of it soft law, must now supplement a chapter on the protection of women in times of armed conflict.

Today, one can cite a range of UN documents – including Security Council resolutions, Secretary-Generals' Bulletins and other international law instruments – including more human rights treaties and a variety of contributions from civil society, that seek to establish mechanisms of protection for women in times of armed conflict. There is also a body of international criminal law jurisprudence – in particular from the ICTY and ICTR, and also soon to be emerging from the ICC[3] – that adds to our understanding of how these rules are to be interpreted and enforced. The last few decades have also seen an increased number of studies and reflections upon the diverse way armed conflict impacts upon women.[4] Gaining a better understanding of

---

1 Françoise Krill, 'The Protection of Women in International Humanitarian Law' (1985) 25(249) *IRRC* 337.
2 Ibid 362–363; Declaration on the Protection of Women and Children in Emergency and Armed Conflict, UNGA Res 3318 (XXIX) (14 December 1974).
3 For example Jean-Pierre Bemba Gombo is currently before the ICC on charges, as military commander, relating to hundreds of rapes committed by his troops in the Central African Republic campaign during 2002–2003.
4 Charlotte Lindsay, *Women Facing War: ICRC Study on the Impact of Armed Conflict on Women* (ICRC 2001); UN Population Fund, 'Impact of Conflict on Women and Girls Meeting and Report on Mainstreaming Gender in Areas of Conflict and Reconstruction' (2002), www.unfpa.org/upload/lib_pub_file/46_filename_armedconflict_women.pdf; UNICEF, 'The Impact of Conflict on Women and Girls in West and Central Africa and the UNICEF Response' (2005), www.unicef.org/publications/files/Impact_final.pdf; Helen Durham and Tracey Gurd (eds), *Listening to the Silences: Women and War* (Martinus Nijhoff 2005).

the needs of women during war will continue to assist in any attempts to match the legal doctrine with the genuine experiences of those requiring respect, humane treatment, protection and assistance.

That is not to say that specific protections for women in times of war had not already been recognised prior to the Geneva Conventions and their Protocols, but rather that such recognition had been anything but comprehensive and enforced. Furthermore, most of the issues relating to protection had tended to focus exclusively on the prohibitions of sexual violence during times of armed conflict rather than identifying wider ways war impacts upon women. In relation to rape, despite a poor record of prosecution, historically a range of prohibitions of such behaviour in wartime can be found. Eriksson notes that 'several early texts, such as the Belli Treatise of 1563, ... held that the crime of rape during wartime was punishable by death'.[5] Parker cites the Treaty on Amity and Commerce of 1785 (between the US and Prussia) as providing 'if war should arise ... all women and children ... shall not be molested in their persons'.[6] The Lieber Code of 1863 provided that all wanton violence committed against persons in the invaded country, including rape, was prohibited under penalty of death – indicating it was considered a very serious offence.[7] Rape was also listed as a crime in the Report Presented to the Preliminary Peace Conference in March 1919 and, as such, intended by the Commission on the Responsibility of the Authors of the War and on Enforcement of Penalties to be among the First World War crimes prosecuted.[8]

This chapter commences with an analysis of the ways women experience armed conflict. It then moves to examine the legal framework of IHL as it pertains to women, in particular the articles that provide specific protections. The range of other provisions, found in human rights law as well as resolutions from the Security Council and jurisprudence from international criminal enforcement mechanisms is then explored. Finally, the broader issue of gender and the laws of war is raised, leading to a conclusion that more work needs to be done to ensure protection of women continues to be a priority during times of armed conflict.

1 Effects of war on women

There is a considerable body of literature which looks at the ways in which women are affected by conflict and their specific needs and requirements during war.[9] This literature, whilst contributing to an important discourse, is not the focus of this chapter, which rather aims to outline the key provisions that provide protection in times of armed conflict. However, two points are worth making about the effects of war on women in order to explain the inclusion of a section in this text. First, as Gardam eloquently puts it '[w]ar exacerbates the inequalities that exist in different forms and to varying degrees in all societies'.[10] This means that the treatment of women during times of armed conflict cannot be examined in isolation from 'peace-time' social views

---

5 Maria Eriksson, *Defining Rape: Emerging Obligations for States under International Law?* (Martinus Nijhoff 2011) 344.

6 Karen Parker, 'Human Rights of Women during Armed Conflict' in Kelly Askin and Dorean Koenig (eds), *Women and International Human Rights Law* (Transnational 2001) 291.

7 Instruction for the Government of Armies of the United States in the Field, General Orders No 100 ('Lieber Code') (24 April 1863) in Dietrich Schindler and Jiří Toman (eds), *The Laws of Armed Conflict* (4th edn, Martinus Nijhoff 2004) 3, art 44.

8 American Society of International Law, 'Commission on the Responsibility of the Authors of the War and on Enforcement of Penalties' (1920) 14 *AJIL* 95, 114.

9 See in particular Lindsay, *Women Facing War* (n 4); Durham and Gurd (eds) (n 4); ICRC, 'Addressing the Needs of Women Affected by Armed Conflict: An ICRC Guidance Document' (2004).

10 Judith Gardam, 'Women, Human Rights and International Law' (1998) 38(324) *IRRC* 422.

on the security and agency of women as part of the general community. If women do not have equality or safety before a conflict commences they have very little chance of strong protections during war. Second, it is now widely recognised that women participate in, and are affected by, war in a variety of ways – to assume automatically that women are only victims during conflict is to miss a substantial part of the story. Across the world women in war are also key figures in political, military and daily life. They demonstrate resilience and resourcefulness, often taking on new challenges as heads-of-households or as community leaders in the absence of men. Whilst often placed in situations of particular risk, women experience conflict, engage in conflict, try to limit conflict and develop systems for their own protection during times of conflict in a multitude of ways.[11]

A study undertaken by the ICRC entitled 'Women Facing War' identified a range of ways armed conflict affects women including their personal safety, sexual violence, displacement, freedom of movement, access to food, shelter, healthcare and sources of livelihoods, hygiene and sanitation, maintenance of the family unit, education and training, as well as religious and cultural practices. Key themes that emerged in relation to legal difficulties experienced by women during and post conflict included access to effective remedies and difficulties in dealing with legal systems when there was a loss of personal documentation.[12] Clearly there are many issues that require further consideration in this area that are beyond the scope of this chapter. It is important to acknowledge this context in relation to the normative legal framework developed to protect women over many years.

It is also widely acknowledged that violence against women, be they civilians or combatants, during war can be used to serve different purposes. In relation to sexual violence much has been written about the use of rape during war. Arguments have been made that sexual violence is used to motivate and reward combatants, that it is a demonstration of superior power over the enemy population or that it is a tool to bring about ethnic cleansing, to humiliate and demoralise and to inflict harm on the most basic unit within society, the family. Women are often victims of sexual violence for gendered reasons as 'symbolic' bearers of their culture or specifically targeted due to their reproductive capacities.[13] As Henry notes, such violence has a long history and rape has 'existed as a lasting legacy of violent conflict throughout the centuries'.[14] Henry notes that:

[d]uring the First and Second World wars, countless numbers of women were raped in concentration camps, military brothels and in occupied areas. In the latter part of the twentieth century, rape was no less ubiquitous: the rape of Bengali women during the nine-month conflict in Bangladesh in 1971 created a national crisis when thousands of women became pregnant and husbands rejected their wives. Sexual violence also forms a

---

11 Anke Biehler, 'Protection of Women in International Humanitarian Law and Human Rights Law' in Roberta Arnold and Noëlle Quénivet (eds), *International Humanitarian Law and Human Rights Law: Towards a new Merger in International Law* (Brill 2008) 355, 356; Charlotte Lindsay, 'The Impact of Armed Conflict on Women' in Durham and Gurd (eds) (n 4) 21. See also, Medina Haeri and Nadine Puechguirbal, 'From Helplessness to Agency: Examining the Plurality of Women's Experiences in Armed Conflict' (2010) 92(877) *IRRC* 103.

12 Lindsay, *Women Facing War* (n 4).

13 For a further discussion, see Radhika Coomaraswamy 'Sexual Violence during Wartime' in Durham and Gurd (eds) (n 4) 53; Susan Brownmiller, *Against our Will: Men, Women and Rape* (Simon & Schuster 1975); Alexandra Stiglmayer (ed), *Mass Rape: The War Against Women in Bosnia-Herzegovina* (University of Nebraksa Press 1994); Kelly Dawn Askin, *War Crimes Against Women: Prosecution in International War Crimes Tribunal* (Kluwer 1997).

14 Nicola Henry, *War and Rape: Law, Memory and Justice* (Routledge 2011) 2.

well-remembered part of the Vietnam war due to the rapes committed by American soldiers against civilian Vietnamese women, and the fact that few perpetrators have ever been brought to justice. Likewise during the 1980s conflict in Uganda, women once again suffered the effects of impunity and silence due to widespread forms of rape and sexual violence.[15]

Sadly this narrative continues into the twenty-first century's conflicts, with Physicians for Human Rights reporting in 2002 that an average of 40 women and girls were being raped every day in South Kivu, Democratic Republic of Congo.[16] A total of 53 per cent of respondents who had 'face-to-face' contact with Revolutionary United Front forces during the conflict in Sierra Leone reported experiencing sexual violence[17] and 39.5 per cent of women interviewed in three villages in Darfur, Sudan reported in a 2006 study that they had either been a victim of or witness to sexual assault during the attacks on their villages.[18] Reports from Syria suggest that sexual assaults on women and girls are also sadly a feature of that conflict.[19] These statistics are more than sobering considering current efforts to ensure that sexual violence is not accepted as a customary feature of armed conflict.

Whilst women have traditionally been looked at exclusively as victims during time of armed conflict, their role in peace-making as well as directly participating in hostilities needs to be understood and incorporated into the legal discourse. The raft of provisions dealing with women as prisoners of war indicates that the drafters of the major IHL instruments understood that women are likely to be part of the fighting forces and this factor is even more prevalent now. Women can also be perpetrators of crimes under IHL, including the most serious of crimes, as was confirmed by the ICTR convicting Pauline Nyiramasuhuko, Rwanda's former minister of Family Affairs and Women's Development, of genocide.[20] Pauline Nyiramasuhuko was convicted by the ICTR of conspiracy to commit genocide, genocide (she is the first women in history to be convicted of genocide), extermination rape and persecution as crimes against humanity and violence to life and outrages on personal dignity as war crimes. More recently, the ICC issued an arrest warrant for Simone Gbagbo as a co-perpetrator of crimes against humanity in Côte D'Ivoire during 2010. The warrant is the first issued for a woman by the ICC and includes charges relating to rape and other sexual violence.[21]

The need to continue a dialogue on the way armed conflict affects women and the way women affect armed conflict is necessary to ensure that the legal framework adequately reflects the reality experienced during war.

---

15 Ibid 2–3 (citations omitted).
16 Physicians for Human Rights, 'War-Related Sexual Violence in Sierra Leone: A Population-Based Assessment' (2002) 3.
17 Physicians for Human Rights, 'Statement for the Record' US Senate Committee on the Judiciary, Human Rights and the Law Subcommittee – Rape as a Weapon of War: Accountability for Sexual Violence in Conflict (1 April 2008) 5, s3.amazonaws.com/PHR_other/rape-as-a-weapon-of-war.pdf.
18 Physicians for Human Rights 'Darfur: Assault on Survival' (2006) 31, s3.amazonaws.com/PHR_Reports/darfur-assault-on-survival.pdf.
19 Human Rights Watch, 'Syria: Sexual Assault in Detention' (15 June 2012), www.hrw.org/fr/node/108048.
20 *Prosecutor v Nyiramasuhuko et al* (Case no ICTR-98-42-T, Trial Chamber II, 24 June 2011) ¶¶ 38–40.
21 *Prosecutor v Gbagbo (Warrant of Arrest)* (Case no ICC-02/11-01/12, Pre-Trial Chamber III, 29 February 2012, unsealed 22 November 2012).

2 Equality of protection under international humanitarian law

IHL is premised on equality of protection. Numerous provisions refer to the notion of respect and protection being afforded without adverse distinction founded on sex as well as on other grounds.[22] This goes to the heart of IHL as a regime aimed at the reduction of suffering and the mitigation of the effects of war – regardless of 'race, colour, religion or faith, sex, birth or wealth'.[23] Therefore the starting point of any analysis of IHL as it relates to women is that they are afforded the same protections as that granted to men, either as civilians, combatants or those *hors de combat*. As well as a prohibition on discrimination, IHL also acknowledges women will have specific requirements and needs and addresses this accordingly. Thus there are a range of specific provisions to be found within the Geneva Conventions and their Protocols that grant protection for women. These additional protections often reflect the biological and physiological requirements that women may have (such as pre- and post-natal care, monthly hygiene or requirements of nursing mothers). However, they also deal with social views that may judge women more harshly as combatants or position women as more vulnerable to sexual violence. To deal with these issues there are requirements within IHL for women prisoners of war not to be more severely punished than a male member and the need for separation in detention, as will be discussed below. In this respect, distinctions on the basis of sex are only prohibited to the extent they are unfavourable or adverse. This is confirmed in a number of specific articles – for example Article 14 of Geneva Convention III states that '[w]omen shall be treated with all the regards due to their sex and shall in all cases benefit by treatment as favourable as that granted to men'.

3 Specific protection under international humanitarian law for women in times of conflict

3.1 Protection against abuse

Rape and other forms of sexual violence are clearly prohibited by IHL. Whilst sexual violence is not an atrocity that is suffered exclusively by women (men are also victims of sexual violence in war) as noted, sadly rape is a horrific reality for many women and girls during turbulent times. The prohibition against sexual violence is an established rule of customary international law applicable in both international and non-international armed conflicts.[24] This prohibition is derived from a number of sources dating back to the Lieber Code,[25] including the Geneva

---

22 GCI art 12; GCIV art 13; API arts 9, 75; APII art 2.
23 See GCI–IV common art 3.
24 CIHL r 93.
25 Lieber Code (n 7) art 44 provided that:

> All wanton violence committed against persons in the invaded country, all destruction of property not commanded by the authorized officer, all robbery, all pillage or sacking, even after taking a place by main force, all rape, wounding, maiming, or killing of such inhabitants, are prohibited under the penalty of death, or such other severe punishment as may seem adequate for the gravity of the offense. A soldier, officer or private, in the act of committing such violence, and disobeying a superior ordering him to abstain from it, may be lawfully killed on the spot by such superior.

Ibid art 47 provided that:

> Crimes punishable by all penal codes, such as arson, murder, maiming, assaults, highway robbery, theft, burglary, fraud, forgery, and rape, if committed by an American soldier in a hostile country against its inhabitants, are not only punishable as at home, but in all cases in which death is not inflicted, the severer punishment shall be preferred.

Conventions, and seen in more recent sources such as the 1998 Rome Statue of the International Criminal Court.[26] Within the Geneva Conventions the first reference to rape is found in Article 27 of Geneva Convention IV which states that '[w]omen shall be specifically protected against any attack on their honour, in particular against rape, enforced prostitution, or any form of indecent assault'.

Over many years concerns have been raised that this provision focuses upon the concept of 'honour' of a woman rather than her dignity or well-being.[27] International law, like all documents, is a product of the time of its drafting and since 1949 the Additional Protocols have updated the manner in which sexual violence is described within IHL treaties and also broadened the prohibition beyond women. For example Article 75(2)(b) of Additional Protocol I expressly prohibits against either sex 'outrages upon personal dignity, in particular humiliating and degrading treatment, enforced prostitution and any form of indecent assault'. Article 76 of Additional Protocol I confirms this prohibition, specifically against women by stating '[w]omen shall be the object of special respect and shall be protected in particular against rape, forced prostitution and any other form of indecent assault'. As noted previously the prohibitions on sexual violence are relevant in all classifications of conflict, international and non-international, and to confirm this Additional Protocol II prohibits 'outrages upon personal dignity, in particular humiliating and degrading treatment, rape, enforced prostitution and any form of indecent assault'.[28]

In the late 1990s discussions focused on the fact that rape is not specifically listed as a 'grave breach' of the Geneva Conventions and Additional Protocol I.[29] The 'grave breach' provisions place upon the High Contracting Parties 'the obligation to search for persons alleged to have committed, or to have ordered to be committed, such grave breaches, and shall bring such persons, regardless of their nationality, before its own courts'.[30] The lack of specific listing of rape as one of these crimes was of concern. Whilst it was always understood that sexual violence falls within the scope of 'wilfully causing great suffering or serious injury to body or health' there were calls for further clarity around the status of the crime of rape and other acts of sexual violence.

With the creation of the ad hoc ICTY and ICTR an opportunity to re-visit the classification of these crimes under IHL occurred. The ICTY Statute has the capacity to prosecute those accused of grave breaches of the Geneva Conventions (Article 2) as well as specifically listing rape as a crime against humanity (Article 5). The ICTR Statute dealing with violations of Article 3 Common to the Geneva Conventions and Additional Protocol II (Article 4) identified 'outrages upon personal dignity, in particular humiliating and degrading treatment, rape, enforced prostitution and any form of indecent assault' as a war crime as well as rape being a crime against humanity (Article 3).

Adding weight to the development of protections against sexual abuse during armed conflict, the Rome Statute of the ICC has the most comprehensive list of prohibitions during international and non-international armed conflict. Article 8(2)(b)(xxii), dealing with war crimes states that it is a serious violation of the laws and customs applicable in international armed conflict to commit '[r]ape, sexual slavery, enforced prostitution, forced pregnancy ... enforced

26 Rome Statute, arts 7(1)(g), 8(b)(xxii) and 8(e)(vi).
27 Gardam (n 10) 424.
28 APII art 4(2)(e).
29 See Christine Chinkin, 'Women: The Forgotten Victims of Armed Conflict' in Helen Durham and Tim McCormack (eds), *The Changing Face of Conflict and the Efficacy of International Humanitarian Law* (Kluwer 1999) 23.
30 GCI art 50; GCII art 51; GCIII art 130; GCIV art 147.

sterilization, or any other form of sexual violence also constituting a grave breach of the Geneva Conventions'. This is repeated in Article 8(2)(e)(vi) dealing with cases of armed conflict not of an international character. Rape is also specifically listed in the ICC as a crime against humanity in Article 7(g) and gender is recognised as a category of persecution under Article 7(h). As will be discussed later, the jurisprudence, in particular at this stage from the two ad hoc tribunals, has made it now abundantly clear that any form of sexual violence is condemned as a serious war crime as well as having been successfully prosecuted as torture, a crime against humanity and genocide.

3.2 Protection for pregnant women and mothers of young children

Following on from the capacity within IHL to afford protections based on need, the role that women play as mothers is one that is specifically recognised during times of armed conflict. Understanding that children and those who care for them face a range of vulnerabilities, the Geneva Conventions and their Protocols make specific provision for the care both of children (a topic to be addressed in the next chapter of this book) and of mothers of young children. Pregnant women and mothers of children under the age of seven years are entitled to preferential treatment:

- when in the territory of a party to the conflict they shall benefit from any preferential treatment to the same extent as the nationals of the state concerned (Geneva Convention IV Article 38);
- an occupying power may not hinder the application of preferential measures adopted prior to occupation in regards to food, medical care and protection against the effects of war which favour pregnant women and mothers of children under the age of seven (Geneva Convention IV Article 50);
- expectant and nursing mothers shall be given additional food, in proportion to their physiological needs (Geneva Convention IV Article 89);
- pregnant women and new born babies are to have the same protection as that accorded to the sick and wounded (API Article 8(a));
- the conclusion of agreements for their release from places of internment with priority (API Articles 76(2) and 132);
- prohibition of the use of the death penalty against such women (API Article 76(3)).[31]

3.3 Protection for women detainees

In both international and non-international armed conflicts the Protocols provide for the accommodation of women 'whose liberty has been restricted for reasons related to the armed conflict' in quarters separate from men's and under the immediate supervision of women.[32] This is unless men and women of a family are able to be accommodated as a family unit.[33] Geneva Convention IV also provides a couple of additional protections. Article 97 notes that 'a woman internee shall not be searched except by a woman' and Article 119 notes that in

31 See also ICCPR art 6(5) which states that sentence of death shall not be carried out on pregnant women.
32 API art 75(5); APII art 5(2)(a); see also GCIV art 76.
33 API art 75(5); APII art 5(2)(a). API notes that accommodation as a family unit shall be the case 'whenever possible'.

relation to disciplinary punishments, account shall be taken of a number of factors, including the internee's sex.

Geneva Convention IV does also state that if, as an 'exceptional and temporary measure', it is necessary to accommodate women internees in the same place of internment as men, 'the provision of separate sleeping quarters and sanitary conveniences ... shall be obligatory'.[34] The Standard Minimum Rules for the Treatment of Prisoners expressly require, when possible, that women be detained in separate institutions from men and, in situations when both sexes are detained in an institution, that women be allocated separate premises.[35]

3.4 Protection for women prisoners of war

In a similar manner, women prisoners of war are entitled to 'separate dormitories' from men[36] and 'separate conveniences'[37] from men when they are detained. Women are also to be under the supervision of women when undergoing disciplinary punishment.[38] However, unlike female civilian internees,[39] female prisoners of war have no specific rights only to be searched by a woman. Due regard is required to be given to a prisoner's sex, and the Geneva Conventions are clear that women shall in all cases benefit by treatment as favourable as that granted to men.[40] Finally Article 88 of Geneva Convention III makes clear that punishment for offences is to be non-discriminatory: 'In no case may a woman prisoner of war be awarded or sentenced to a punishment more severe ... than a male member of the armed forces of the Detaining Power dealt with for a similar offence.' This highlights the tension sometimes found with social views harshly judging women accused of committing atrocities.[41]

3.5 Protections against the disproportionate impact of the means and methods of warfare on women

As we have noted earlier, whilst much has been made in recent years of the need to acknowledge that women are affected by conflict in a variety of ways and should not be perceived merely as victims, it is clear that the impact of hostilities has a disproportionate effect on women insofar as they comprise a majority of the civilian population. The most fundamental of IHL principles is articulated by Article 48 of Additional Protocol I, which holds that:

> In order to ensure respect for and protection of the civilian population and civilian objects, the Parties to the conflict shall at all times distinguish between the civilian population and the combatants and between civilian objects and military objectives and accordingly shall direct their operations only against military objectives.

---

34 GCIV art 85.
35 Standard Minimum Rules for the Treatment of Prisoners, adopted by the First UN Congress on the Prevention of Crime and the Treatment of Offenders (30 August 1955), approved by ECOSOC Res 663 C (XXIV) (31 July 1957) and 2076 (LXII) (13 May 1977), r 8.
36 GCIII art 25.
37 GCIII art 29.
38 GCIII art 97.
39 See GCIV art 97.
40 GCIII art 14.
41 For further discussion on this point, see Nicole Hogg 'Women's Participation in the Rwandan Genocide: Mothers or Monsters' (2010) 92(877) *IRRC* 69.

This principle is widely agreed to have been incorporated into customary IHL as a norm applicable in both international and non-international armed conflicts.[42] In particular, regarding non-international armed conflict, Article 13 of Additional Protocol II also notes that the civilian population shall not be the object of attack.

Breaches of the principle of distinction, and the other more specific provisions protecting the civilian population from attack (such as the prohibition on indiscriminate attacks pursuant to Article 51 of Additional Protocol I and the required precautions in attack pursuant to Article 57 Additional Protocol I), have a disproportionate effect on women as they often leave women trying to provide for the household and care for the young, elderly and sick in the absence of power, water, health services and other essential civilian infrastructure.

Other general protections which are of particular significance to women include the prohibition on methods of warfare which affect the ability of the civilian population to survive. Article 54 of Additional Protocol I notes that starvation of civilians as a method of warfare is prohibited and Article 55 of Additional Protocol I requires care to be taken to protect the national environment against long-term damage. Article 14 of Additional Protocol II protects objects indispensible to the civilian population in times of non-international armed conflict. Breaches of the prohibitions against pillage, reprisals against protected persons and their property[43] may also disproportionally affect women.

As one of us has previously noted, the use of particular weapons, such as those which continue to maim and kill after the conflict, is also a matter of particular concern to women left undefended in civilian communities.[44] Weapons such as anti-personnel landmines and explosive remnants of war have a devastating effect on the lives of civilians – often long after the conflict has ended – and also hamper reconstruction efforts post-conflict. The Ottawa Convention,[45] the Conventional Weapons Convention[46] and the more recent Convention on Cluster Munitions[47] are positive advances in ensuring that women are afforded greater protection by international law in times of conflict (and post-conflict). However, women continue to suffer, whether injured by these weapons themselves, limited in their ability to undertake tasks such as collecting firewood or water due to the presence of these weapons or having lost family members to these weapons.

The 2005 Human Security Report identifies that, '[w]ith the critically important exception of sexual violence, there is considerable evidence to suggest that men, not women, are more vulnerable to the major impacts of armed conflict'.[48] However, as Haeri and Puechguirbal point out, 'it is women who must pick up the pieces, support their families, raise their children on their own and keep their communities going despite the emotional, physical, and financial losses caused by the absence of their menfolk'.[49] As such, the notion of the right to know the fate of loved ones is another area where the protections afforded by IHL have perhaps a

---

42 CIHL r 1.

43 GCIV art 33.

44 Helen Durham, 'International Humanitarian Law and the Protection of Women' in Durham and Gurd (eds) (n 4) 95, 103–105.

45 Convention on the Prohibition of the Use, Stockpiling, Production and Transfer of Anti-Personnel Landmines and on their Destruction (18 September 1997) 2056 UNTS 211.

46 Convention on Prohibitions or Restrictions on the Use of Certain Conventional Weapons which may be Deemed to be Excessively Injurious or to have Indiscriminate Effects (10 October 1980) 1342 UNTS 137.

47 (3 December 2008) 48 ILM 357.

48 Human Security Centre, *Human Security Report 2005: War and Peace in the 21st Century* (OUP 2005) 102.

49 Haeri and Puechguirbal (n 11) 106.

disproportionate impact on women. The rules, which seek to ensure that capture and detention of persons in association with the armed conflict is carried out in accordance with standards that would allow next of kin to be notified without delay, and that searches are to be conducted for missing persons,[50] acknowledge the humanity of ensuring that people know what has become of their family members, even if that news is not good news.

4 Developments in the twenty-first century

The twenty-first century has seen a particular focus on two aspects of the women and war topic: first, acknowledging and addressing sexual violence; second, acknowledging and addressing the importance of women in the prevention and resolution of conflicts and in peace-building and the importance of their equal participation in the institutions of the world.

It was the atrocities in the former Yugoslavia and Rwanda during the 1990s that led to international attention being directed to the issue of sexual violence against women and girls. This issue has clearly been the focus of much of the recent attention on issues concerning women and war. Unfortunately its prevalence makes this appropriate. Even more unfortunately though, as was mentioned above, it is a problem that the international community had been quite unsuccessful in alleviating. The call of the Security Council pursuant to Resolution 1325 (2000) requiring 'all parties to armed conflict to take special measures to protect women and girls from gender-based violence, particularly rape and other forms of sexual abuse, and all other forms of violence in situations of armed conflict' was an important start. This was followed in 2003 by the Secretary-General's Bulletin on Special Measures for Protection from Sexual Exploitation and Sexual Abuse.[51] This Bulletin, whilst primarily concerned with prohibiting sexual exploitation and sexual abuse by United Nations employees, notes that United Nations forces conducting operations under United Nations command and control are prohibited from committing acts of sexual exploitation and sexual abuse, and have a particular duty of care towards women and children, pursuant to the Secretary-General's Bulletin on Observance by United Nations Forces of International Humanitarian Law.[52]

Security Council Resolution 1820 in 2008 on Women, Peace and Security is seen as the most influential and strong expression of the international community's condemnation of practices that have plagued the history of warfare. The resolution was particularly significant in two respects. It speaks of 'sexual violence, when used or commissioned as a tactic of war' and acknowledges that where a society continues to have sexual violence it is almost impossible to build sustainable peace. The resolution,

> [d]emands that all parties to armed conflict immediately take appropriate measures to protect civilians, including women and girls, from all forms of sexual violence, which could include, inter alia, enforcing appropriate military disciplinary measures and upholding the principle of command responsibility, training troops on the categorical prohibition of all forms of sexual violence against civilians, debunking myths that fuel sexual violence, vetting armed and security forces to take into account past actions of rape and other forms of sexual violence, and evacuation of women and children under imminent threat of sexual violence to safety.

50 See particularly GCI arts 15–17; GCII arts 18–19; GCIII arts 70–71; GCIV arts 25–26; API S III; APII arts 5(2)(b) and 8.
51 UN Doc ST/SGB/2003/13 (9 October 2003).
52 UN Doc ST/SGB/1999/13 (6 August 1999) s 7.

Chairing the debates, the then US Secretary of State Condoleezza Rice stated, '[w]e affirm that sexual violence profoundly affects not only the health and safety of women, but also the economic and social stability of their nations'.[53]

Security Council Resolutions 1888 and 1899 of 2009 report on the implementation of the recommendations set down in resolution 1325 with mixed results – but poor results with respect to the persistence of violence against women. Resolution 1889,

> [s]*trongly condemns* all violations of applicable international law committed against women and girls in situations of armed conflicts and post-conflict situations, *demands* all parties to conflicts to cease such acts with immediate effect, and *emphasizes* the responsibility of all States to put an end to impunity and to prosecute those responsible for all forms of violence committed against women and girls in armed conflicts, including rape and other sexual violence.

It is promising that recent developments have not just focused on women as victims of sexual violence. As part of the positive trend towards providing a wider context for the way armed conflict impacts upon women, and the way women impact upon armed conflict, women must be seen not just as victims of war, but also noted for their contributions to peace.[54] Significantly, Security Council Resolution 1325 reaffirms the importance of women in the prevention and resolution of conflicts and in peace-building and looks to ways to expand the role and contribution of women at all decision-making levels in national, regional and international institutions and in mechanisms for the prevention, management and resolution of conflict.

Further adding, in an increasingly meaningful way, to the discourse is attention focused on the provisions of human rights law which are premised on equality of protection, and which can have application in times of armed conflict. Parker notes, in particular, the Convention of the Elimination of All Forms of Discrimination Against Women (CEDAW)[55] and the Universal Declaration of Human Rights, as examples of human rights law making a significant contribution to the IHL provisions against gender discrimination.[56] These documents, which recognise the importance of equality to peace,[57] recognise the right to gender equality in employment, and the right of women to participate in 'the political and public life of the country ... on equal

---

53 'Secretary of State Rice Speaks on Sexual Violence as an Instrument of Warfare' US Department of State Archive, http://2001-2009.state.gov/g/wi/archives/106103.htm.

54 Report of the Secretary-General on Women, Peace and Security, UN Doc S/2002/1154 (16 October 2002) ¶ 5. Earlier, a watershed moment in the international community's recognition of the link between inequality and discrimination in peacetime and violence against women in armed conflict came in 1995 at the Fourth World Conference on Women was convened by the UN in Beijing which focused on 12 key areas of concern identified as obstacles to the advancement of women in the world including 'the effects of armed or other kinds of conflict on women, including those living under foreign occupation'; an acknowledgement that women experience armed conflict in a different manner from men and thus have specific needs and requirements. The Fourth World Conference on Women culminated in the adoption of the Beijing Declaration and Platform for Action in order to address these concerns. See Beijing Declaration and Platform for Action, Fourth World Conference for Women (15 September 1995) ch 3.

55 UNGA Res 34/180 (18 December 1979) 1249 UNTS 13.

56 Parker (n 6) 308.

57 See the preamble to the CEDAW which notes the cause of peace requires the maximum participation of women on equal terms with men in all fields.

terms with men'.[58] Parker notes they may also be invoked to address gender discrimination in the military.[59]

The Committee on the Elimination of Discrimination against Women (Committee), which makes recommendations on any issue affecting women to which it believes the states parties to the CEDAW should devote more attention to, has been working towards a General Recommendation on Women in Conflict and Post-Conflict Situations. In July 2011, the Committee held a general discussion on women in conflict and post-conflict situations in the context of the particular provisions of the CEDAW including:

- Article 5(a) on the modification of social and cultural patterns of conduct of men and women;
- Article 6 on the suppression of trafficking and exploitation of women;
- Articles 7 and 8 on women's participation in political and public life and their representation in government and at the international level;
- Article 9 on women's rights to a nationality;
- Article 10 on the right to education;
- Article 11 on the right to work;
- Article 12 on the right to health; and
- Article 15(1) on women's equality with men before the law.

This is further evidence of the human rights agenda's recognition of the need for a focus on equality when working towards limiting the effects of armed conflict on women.

Other developments during this period have included the creation in 2010 of the position of Special Representative of the UN Secretary-General on Sexual Violence in Conflict.[60] The international community's most recent attempt to reduce violence and the suffering associated with it, the UN Conference on the Arms Trade Treaty, demonstrated that increasingly during international treaty negotiations attempts are made to include provisions about the way in which such legal frameworks impact on women. The preamble of the Arms Trade Treaty acknowledges that women (and children) 'account for the vast majority of those adversely affected by armed conflict and armed violence'.[61] Further, Article 7(4) requires states parties considering an export of conventional arms to 'take into account the risk of [them] being used to commit or facilitate serious acts of gender-based violence or serious acts of violence against women and children'. Whilst the obligation to take into account the risk of gender-based violence could not be classified as a strong obligation, the reference to gender-based violence demonstrates that this effect of conflict was on the minds of those gathered in New York for the negotiations.

As well as developments in treaty negotiations, there are also good news stories to be heard about the way in which actors are implementing the obligation for humanitarian assistance under IHL.[62] Positive steps in ensuring that, in the delivery of humanitarian assistance, the

---

58 CEDAW arts 7 and 8; see also UDHR arts 21 and 23.
59 Parker (n 6) 308.
60 Margot Wallström, a Swedish politician with a long history of defending women's rights, was appointed to this position in June 2010. Zainab Hawa Bangura, the Minister of Health and Sanitation of Sierra Leone succeeded her in June 2012.
61 Arms Trade Treaty, UNGA Res 67/234B (2 April 2013) 52 ILM 988.
62 See eg GCI–IV common art 3; GCI arts 9, 18; GCII art 9; GCIII art 9; GCIV art 10; API art 17; APII art 18.

effects of conflict on women are understood and addressed and that women's specific needs are taken into account can be highlighted in the example below.

> A lack of agency and control over their own life also creates a number of protection problems for women. For example, if women are not consulted about the location of water points or sanitary facilities, these structures may be constructed in an area that is not safe for women and exposes them to additional risks, such as sexual violence.[63]

5 Accountability

Despite the inclusion of rape in the Commission on the Responsibility of the Authors of the War and Enforcement of Penalties,[64] trials which dealt with First World War crimes did not include a charge for rape. At the Nuremberg and Tokyo war crimes trials neither set of legal proceedings listed rape as a war crime or a crime against humanity.[65] During the Nuremberg trial evidence of rape was actually put before the court, however, rape was not formally prosecuted and the judges did not mention it in their findings.[66] In the Tokyo trials some defendants were prosecuted for rape crimes, but rape was tried only alongside other crimes. The sexual enslavement of comfort women was not a subject of inquiry until much later when a Tribunal was set up to address these crimes in 2000.[67]

Whilst a number of cases of rape were prosecuted at domestic war crimes trials post the Second World War,[68] and indeed Australia carried out the death penalty for this crime on two occasions, the paucity of focus upon these crimes has led many commentators to comment on the 'silent' nature of sexual crimes. However this has changed in the last decade. The jurisprudence of the ICTY has been very influential in shaping the ICC and modern international criminal law more generally. This particularly applies with regards to jurisprudence with respect of crimes of sexual violence. The ICTY notes '[a]lmost half of those convicted by the ICTY have been found guilty of elements of crimes involving sexual violence'.[69] The ICTY's first trial, *Tadić*, which is often cited for many principles of international criminal law, was significant because it included a charge of rape as a crime against humanity.[70]

---

63 Haeri and Puechguirbal (n 11) 106.
64 American Society of International Law (n 8) 114.
65 Henry (n 14) 8; see also Judith Gardam, 'Women and International Humanitarian Law' in William Maley (ed), *Shelters from the Storm: Developments in International Humanitarian Law* (Australian Defence Studies Centre 1995) 210.
66 The word 'rape' does not appear once in the 179-page Nuremberg judgment: Henry (n 14) 35.
67 The Women's International War Crimes Tribunal on Japan's Military Sexual Slavery was held in Tokyo in December 2000. See further Rumi Sakamoto, 'The Women's International War Crimes Tribunal on Japan's Military Sexual Slavery: A Legal and Feminist Approach to the "Comfort Women" Issue' (June 2001) *New Zealand Journal of Asian Studies* 49.
68 Helen Durham and Narrelle Morris, 'Women's Bodies and International Criminal Law: From Tokyo to Rabaul' in Yuki Tanaka, Tim McCormack and Gerry Simpson (eds), *Beyond Victor's Justice? The Tokyo War Crimes Trial Revisited* (Martinus Nijhoff 2010) 283.
69 ICTY, 'Crimes of Sexual Violence', www.icty.org/sid/10312. See also ICTY, 'In Numbers', www.icty.org/sid/10586 which notes that, as of mid-2011, 78 individuals, or 48 per cent of the 161 accused, had charges of sexual violence included in their indictments.
70 *Prosecutor v Tadić (First Amended Indictment)* (Case no IT-94-1, ICTY Appeals Chamber, 1 September 1995).

This was the first time since the Tokyo trial that rape was tried by an international criminal tribunal.[71] As Henry notes,

> Although the rape charges were withdrawn because Witness F was too frightened to testify, the case importantly not only recognized the ramifications of testifying for sexual violence survivors, but also established that rape was part of a widespread campaign of ethnic cleansing against the Muslim population in Bosnia-Herzegovina.[72]

Other cases from the ICTY similarly led to a serious of firsts. Rape was recognised by the ICTY as a crime of 'torture' for the first time in *Čelebiči*.[73] In that case it was the repeated use of rape as a means of torture of two female prisoners in the camp that saw criminal responsibility imposed 'for the first time in the history of international criminal law ... based only on sexual offenses committed against women'.[74] It was in *Kunarac* where rape was first recognised as a crime against humanity[75] and *Furundžija* where rape and sexual assault were sole charges for the first time.[76] *Furundžija* also made it clear that a forced oral act is a degrading act that harms dignity and has reinforced the idea that rape, including oral penetration, can be a form of torture.[77]

The jurisprudence of the ICTR is also significant – in particular, the finding that Jean Paul Akayesu was guilty of genocide. The ICTR found:

> [w]ith regard ... to ... rape and sexual violence, ... they constitute genocide in the same way as any other act as long as they were committed with the specific intent to destroy, in whole or in part, a particular group, targeted as such.[78]

The ICTR noted particularly the effect of the infliction both of serious bodily harm and of mental harm through rape and sexual violence as being 'one of the worst ways to inflict harm'. The ICTR found that the rape and sexual violence committed solely against Tutsi women, 'many of whom were subjected to the worst public humiliation, mutilated, and raped several times, often in public, in the Bureau Communal premises or in other public places, and often by more than one assailant', constituted genocide because it 'resulted in physical and psychological destruction of Tutsi women, their families and their communities'.[79]

The tribunal goes on to note:

> This sexualized representation of ethnic identity graphically illustrates that Tutsi women were subjected to sexual violence because they were Tutsi. Sexual violence was a step in the process of destruction of the Tutsi group – destruction of the spirit, of the will to live, and of life itself.[80]

---

71 Henry (n 14) 72.
72 Henry (n 14) 72 (citations omitted).
73 Henry (n 14) 80; Alona Hagay-Frey, *Sex and Gender Crimes in the New International Law: Past, Present, Future* (Martinus Nijhoff 2011) 90.
74 Hagay-Frey (n 73) 92.
75 Eriksson (n 5) 383.
76 *Prosecutor v Furundžija* (Case no IT-95-17/1, ICTY Trial Chamber, 10 December 1998).
77 Hagay-Frey (n 73) 90.
78 *Prosecutor v Akayesu* (Case no ICTR-96-4-T, Trial Chamber I, 2 September 1998) ¶ 731.
79 Ibid.
80 Ibid ¶ 732.

Whilst the only case concluded before the ICC to date did not deal with sexual violence,[81] other cases currently before the court include charges of mass rapes. Germain Katanga and Mathieu Ngudjolo Chui, commanders of two militia groups, are suspected of orchestrating mass rapes in the Democratic Republic of Congo[82] and Jean-Pierre Bemba Gombo is charged, by virtue of his knowing failure to control the troops he commanded, for hundreds of rapes committed by his troops in the Central African Republic campaign during 2002–2003.[83] Further, in 2012, in a statement to mark International Day of the Girl, ICC Prosecutor Fatou Bensouda asserted that girls 'should not be subjected to rape and sexual violence, nor made to witness brutal sexual attacks' and noted her intention to 'continue to include gender crimes and crimes against children in our charges and to bring the full force of the law to bear on those most responsible for them'.[84]

6 A note about gender and the law of armed conflict

It is being increasingly recognised that having a discourse around 'women and war' is not sufficient to cover all gender-based issues in conflict. 'Gender and war' is increasingly becoming topical, with the international community recognising that vulnerabilities experienced by both men and women on account of their gender are exacerbated by conflict. In particular, the discourse is acknowledging that men are also victims of sexual violence – evidence of which can be seen in cases currently before the courts. In his opening statement in the *Bemba* case, the then ICC Prosecutor Luis Moreno Ocampo put to the court that Bemba was responsible, by virtue of his knowing failure to control the troops he commanded, for hundreds of rapes committed by his troops (mentioned above). Significantly Moreno Ocampo noted:

> [t]he massive rapes were not just sexually motivated; as gender crimes, they were crimes of domination and humiliation directed against women, but also directed against men with authority. These crimes spread terror and devastated communities by means of the cheapest weapon and most available ammunition. Women were raped systematically to assert dominance and to shatter resistance. Men were raped in public to destroy their authority, their capacity to lead.[85]

Further evidence of the need to consider 'gender and war' can be seen when it comes to detainees. That, for example, there is no corollary of the provision in Article 97 of Geneva Convention III, that requires women prisoners of war undergoing disciplinary punishment to be under the immediate supervision of women, has the potential to require review in light of the inclusion of women in the ranks of military police units carrying out roles at detention centres. This was made particularly evident when pictures from Abu Ghraib, demonstrating the involvement of women in sexual violence, grabbed international headlines and challenged

---

81 *Prosecutor v Lubanga* (Case no ICC-01/04-01/06, Trial Chamber I, 14 March 2012).
82 *Prosecutor v Katanga and Ngudjolo Chui (Decision on the Confirmation of the Charges)* (Case no ICC-01/04-01/07, Pre-Trial Chamber, 30 September 2008) ¶ 354.
83 *Prosecutor v Bemba (Confirmation of Charges)* (Case no ICC-01/05-01/08, Pre-Trial Chamber II, 15 June 2009).
84 Statement ICC Prosecutor Fatou Bensouda on International Day of the Girl (11 October 2012), www. icc-cpi.int/NR/exeres/BA002052-64BA-47DD-B712-CBAB371ED331.htm.
85 *Prosecutor v Bemba (Trial Hearing Transcript)* (Case no ICC-01/05-01/08, Trial Chamber III, 22 November 2010) 10.

traditionally held assumptions about the perpetrators and victims of sexual violence.[86] There is no doubt that ensuring that the dignity of all persons is made possible in times of armed conflict must be the subject of further study and discussions.

7 Conclusion

For women across the world, armed conflict means being displaced, being in fear for their safety, not knowing the fate of loved ones, being targeted because they are women, struggling to survive, struggling to access water, food and sanitation facilities and struggling to care for their loved ones. The importance of ensuring there are adequate protections for women through these times of armed conflict is essential. IHL is a legal framework based on equality of protection but also, as discussed in this chapter, acknowledges that women have specific needs. The Security Council, human rights bodies and the humanitarian sector have started paying closer attention to the plight of women during times of war in the last decade. International human rights law is increasingly starting to engage with issues relating to women and their needs in times of armed conflict. As a global community we are also better at recognising that women play a variety of different roles in times of armed conflict – and in peace-building – and are not just victims, but may also have roles including as leaders and as combatants. Despite the progress, it is clear that more needs to be done to ensure that the issue of women and war is kept on the agenda at the highest level of decision-making institutions – including in both national and international frameworks. Continuing to ensure that the realities women experience in times of armed conflict are reflected in the range of legal norms that claim to protect them is an end worth striving towards. Finally, it is important to acknowledge that women also show great resilience in holding communities together during times of war. In the end it is women themselves that often have the best answers to questions about their own protection.

---

86 See further Helen Durham and Katie O'Byrne, 'The Dialogue of Difference: Gender Perspectives on International Humanitarian Law' (2010) 92(877) *IRRC* 39–40.

20

Children and the law of armed conflict

Looking beyond the protection paradigm

John Tobin and Elliot Luke*

The appalling experience of children in armed conflict has motivated the creation of a complex international architecture to ensure their protection. In 2003, the UN Security Council called for 'an era of application' with respect to the various legal norms which the international community has developed in order to protect children associated with armed conflict.[1] This chapter aims to identify the central features and underlying values of these norms. Section 1 provides a brief historical analysis, which reveals a shift in states' attitudes towards children, moving from a historically instrumentalist vision to the contemporary child protectionist paradigm. It also reveals a transformation of the orthodox understanding of the law of armed of conflict. Originally synonymous with international humanitarian law as the *lex specialis* for armed conflict, the contemporary understanding of a state's obligations in times of armed conflict must now encompass international human rights law.

Section 2 examines the content of the legal norms, particularly as they relate to the recruitment of children and their participation in conflict, and seeks to identify the applicable law. This section also outlines a model to navigate the tension and confusion caused by the concurrent application of international humanitarian law standards and international human rights standards concerning children in times of armed conflict.

Finally, Section 3 looks beyond the child protection paradigm that dominates the current understanding and application of the law of armed conflict as it relates to children. It offers some reflections as to the consequences that might flow from the application of a rights-based model to the situation of children associated with armed conflict in which the narrative of victimhood is balanced against a vision of children as agents with evolving capacities.

* This chapter was prepared with the assistance of research funds from ARC Discovery Grant DP 120104 'Children's Rights: From Theory to Practice'. Thanks to Tim McCormack and Rain Liivoja for their comments on earlier drafts of this chapter. All errors remain the authors'.

1 UNSC Res 1460 (30 January 2003) ¶ 1.

1 The evolution of a complex institutional and normative framework

The following historical analysis briefly outlines the development of the law of armed conflict applicable to children and reveals the evolution of a complex system in which various institutional actors have played a significant role in seeking to advance and implement a broad and comprehensive normative framework for the protection of children.

1.1 Late nineteenth to mid-twentieth centuries

At the turn of the twentieth century, there was a growing concern among states for the health and well-being of children, which led to the creation of maternal and infant health clinics across much of the industrialised world.[2] However, instrumentalist considerations provided the motivation for these clinics, which were viewed as 'a scientific and convincing way to produce healthy children who would become productive workers and robust soldiers'.[3] During this period, Westphalian sovereignty was the dominant paradigm of international relations and children were critical to maintaining and expanding states' economic and military strength.[4] Indeed, the involvement in war, which had been a constant throughout history,[5] often took on a romantic allure for many adolescent boys who were impatient for adulthood and for whom war offered an adventure that was impossible to resist.

The atrocities of the First World War, however, destroyed both this illusion and the lives of many children. An active civil society forced states to embrace a more protective agenda with respect to children and, in 1924, the League of Nations adopted the first international human rights instrument, the Geneva Declaration on the Rights of Child.[6] The Declaration reflects a classic child welfare or child protection approach: '[t]he child that is hungry must be fed; the child that is sick must be nursed; and ... [t]he child must be the first to receive relief in times of distress'. Any recognition of a child's agency and evolving autonomy was entirely absent, as was any concern regarding the recruitment and participation of children in armed conflict. This was hardly surprising, however, given that hope of peace stifled any acknowledgement of the possibility of another war.

1.2 Post-Second World War

Such hope, of course, proved to be false. But the carnage of the Second World War acted as a catalyst for the adoption of the Universal Declaration of Human Rights[7] (UDHR) in 1948, an instrument which provides the foundations of the modern system of international human rights. In a reflection of the times, Article 25(2) of the UDHR preserved the child protection model, and provided that motherhood and childhood are each entitled to special care and assistance, and that all children, whether or not born out of wedlock, shall enjoy the same social protection. Significantly, from the perspective of this chapter, the UDHR was perceived to be the antidote to armed conflict and not an instrument for its regulation.

---

2 World Health Organization, *The World Health Report 2005: Make Every Mother and Child Count* (2005) 2–3.

3 Ibid 2.

4 Ibid.

5 David Rosen, 'Child Soldiers, International Humanitarian Law, and the Globalization of Childhood' (2007) 109 *American Anthropologist* 296, 297.

6 Geneva Declaration of the Rights of the Child, League of Nations (26 September 1924).

7 UNGA Res 217A(III) (10 December 1948).

In 1949, the Geneva Conventions[8] effectively bifurcated modern international law into the laws for war and the laws for peacetime. These humanitarian instruments also adopted a child protection paradigm, and this was maintained in Additional Protocols I and II,[9] adopted in 1979 which demanded that 'children shall be the object of special respect'[10] and 'provided with the care and aid they require'.[11] The Additional Protocols also introduced into international law, for the first time, standards regulating the recruitment and participation of children below the age of 15 in armed conflict.

In 1989, the UN General Assembly adopted the Convention on the Rights of the Child (CRC).[12] Notably, it included Article 38, requiring states 'to respect and to ensure respect for rules of international humanitarian law applicable ... in armed conflicts which are relevant to the child'. Hailed by some as an innovation,[13] this provision integrated humanitarian norms into human rights law and initiated the regime interaction that now characterises the contemporary law of armed conflict. However, Article 38 was also decried by many for its apparent failure to provide greater protection against the recruitment and use of children in armed conflict than Additional Protocol I.[14] Many advocates had sought a 'straight 18' prohibition for children's involvement in armed conflict, which would have been consistent with other provisions of the CRC, such as Article 19, which protects children against violence, abuse, injury and neglect. However, several states rejected this approach as being inconsistent with their own practices, which allowed for the recruitment and participation of children aged 15 years and over.[15]

In contrast, the African Charter on the Rights and Welfare of the Child,[16] which came into force in 1990, succeeded where the CRC failed. Article 22 requires states parties to take all necessary measures to ensure that no child (defined as a person under 18 years of age) takes a direct part in hostilities or is recruited by a state's armed forces.

Spurned by the disappointment of the CRC and the standard achieved under the African Charter, in 1992, the newly created Committee on the Rights of the Child began to agitate for an optional protocol to the CRC which would adopt the 'straight 18' approach.[17] In response to its lobbying, the Commission on Human Rights established an open-ended working group

---

8 As of December 2015, GCI–IV have been signed or ratified by 196 states.

9 As of December 2015, there are 174 states party to AP I and 168 to AP II.

10 API art 77(1).

11 APII art 4(3).

12 (2 September 1990) 1577 UNTS 3. The CRC has been ratified by all UN Member States except the USA.

13 See eg Rachel Brett, 'Child Soldiers: Law, Politics, and Practice' (1996) 4 *IJCR* 115, 116; Chen Reis, 'Trying the Future, Avenging the Past: The Implications of Prosecuting Children for Participation in Internal Armed Conflict' (1997) 28 *Columbia HRLR* 629, 642; Geraldine Van Bueren, *The International Law on the Rights of the Child* (Martinus Nijhoff 1995) 349.

14 See eg Carolyn Hamilton and Tabatha Abu El-Haj, 'Armed Conflict: The Protection of Children under International Law' (1996) 5 *IJCR* 1, 36; Van Bueren (n 13) 335; Howard Mann, 'International Law and the Child Soldier' (1987) 36 *ICLQ* 32, 56; Françoise Krill, 'The Protection of Children in Armed Conflicts' in Michael Freeman and Philip Veerman (eds), *The Ideologies of Children's Rights* (Martinus Nijhoff 1992) 347, 354.

15 See Office of the High Commissioner for Human Rights, *Legislative History of the Convention on the Rights of the Child* (United Nations 2007) 775.

16 African Charter on the Rights and Welfare of the Child, Organization of African Unity, OAU Doc CAB/LEG/24.9/49 (29 November 1999) ('African Charter').

17 See Committee on the Rights of the Child, 'Report on the General Day of Discussion on Children in Armed Conflict' UN Doc CRC/C/10 (1992) 23, in particular ¶ 75 ('CRC Report').

to address this proposal in 1994.[18] The UN Secretary-General also appointed Graça Machel as his expert to produce a report on the impact of armed conflict on children. Her 1996 report detailed the atrocious experience of children affected by armed conflict and generated a wave of international initiatives within this area,[19] including the appointment of the UN Secretary-General's Special Representative on Children and Armed Conflict[20] and the adoption of the Cape Town Principles[21] in 1997 by the NGO Working Group on the Convention on the Rights of the Child and UNICEF.

The Rome Statute of the International Criminal Court,[22] adopted in 1998, defined 'war crime' to include conscripting or enlisting children under the age of 15 years or using them to participate actively in hostilities.[23] In 1999 the International Labour Organisation's Convention Concerning the Prohibition and Immediate Action for the Elimination of the Worst Forms of Child Labour[24] prohibited the forced or compulsory recruitment of children for use in armed conflict.[25] Also in the same year, the Security Council adopted Resolution 1261 in which it undertook to give special attention to the protection, welfare and rights of children when taking action aimed at promoting peace and security[26] and requested that the Secretary-General ensure that UN peacekeeping activities include 'appropriate training on the protection, rights and welfare of children'.[27]

1.3 Moving into the twenty-first century

The Optional Protocol to the Convention on the Rights of the Child on the Involvement of Children in Armed Conflict (the 'Optional Protocol') was finally adopted in 2000.[28] Although it does not include a 'straight 18' approach, the standards with respect to the recruitment and participation of children have been raised over and above those of the CRC and the Additional Protocols (discussed below).

In 2001, the Security Council maintained its commitment to addressing the situation of children in armed conflict and adopted a 'name and shame' approach in Resolution 1379, which requested that the Secretary-General include in his annual report a list of states that violate

---

18 Draft Optional Protocol to the Convention on the Rights of the Child: Note by the Secretariat, UN Doc E/CN 4/1994/91 (1994).
19 Graça Machel, 'Impact of Armed Conflict on Children' Report of the Expert of the Secretary-General Submitted Pursuant to UNGA Res 48/157, UN Doc A/51/306 (26 August 1996) ('Machel Report'). A follow-up to the Machel Report was published in 2009: UNICEF, *Machel Study 10-year Strategic Review: Conflict and Children in a Changing World* (Office of the Special Representative of the Secretary-General for Children and Armed Conflict and UNICEF 2009).
20 See generally Office of the Special Representative of the Secretary-General for Children and Armed Conflict, http://childrenandarmedconflict.un.org/.
21 Cape Town Principles and Best Practices on the Recruitment of Children into the Armed Forces and on Demobilization and Social Reintegration of Child Soldiers in Africa (30 April 1997).
22 (17 July 1998) 2187 UNTS 90
23 Rome Statute art 8(2)(c) and (e).
24 ILO Convention Concerning the Prohibition and Immediate Action for the Elimination of the Worst Forms of Child Labour ('Worst Forms of Child Labour Convention') (17 June 1999) General Conference of the International Labour Organization, 87th session Convention no 182.
25 Ibid art 3(a). Note that art 2 states defines a child as a person under 18.
26 UNSC Res 1261 (25 August 1999).
27 Ibid ¶ 19.
28 Optional Protocol to the Convention on the Rights of the Child on the Involvement of Children in Armed Conflict (25 May 2000) 2173 UNTS 222.

international law by recruiting or using children in armed conflict.[29] This was followed in 2003 by Resolution 1460 in which the Security Council supported the Secretary-General's call for 'an era of application' with respect to the relevant international standards.[30] The Security Council's commitment to such an era was further demonstrated in Resolution 1539,[31] which contemplated a dialogue with parties involved in armed conflict and an action plan to end child recruitment.

In the same year, the ICJ handed down its advisory opinion in the *Wall* case,[32] which confirmed that human rights, including those contained in the CRC, apply in times of armed conflict.[33] As a result, the law of armed conflict imported more than just international humanitarian norms. Rather, human rights were now recognised as an integral part of the normative framework regulating the conduct of states during armed conflict.

Frustrated at the lack of impact resulting from its previous resolutions, in 2005 the Security Council adopted Resolution 1612,[34] which has been described as both 'remarkable'[35] and 'groundbreaking'.[36] The resolution establishes a mechanism to monitor and report on six grave violations of international law: killing and maiming of children, recruiting and using child soldiers, attacks against schools or hospitals, rape or other grave sexual violence against children, abduction of children, and denial of humanitarian access for children. This was complemented by the ICC's indictment of Thomas Lubanga Dyilo in 2006 for the use and recruitment of children under the age of 15 in the first proceedings in the ICC.[37]

In 2007, the Paris Principles and Guidelines on Children Associated with Armed Forces or Armed Groups were adopted. These aimed to combat the unlawful recruitment and use of children by armed forces and groups. As of December 2015, 100 member states had endorsed the Principles.

In 2009, Security Council Resolution 1882[38] stressed the importance of effective disarmament, demobilisation and reintegration programmes for children. Further, Resolution 1888[39] contained a commitment to include specific provisions for the protection of children from rape and sexual violence in the mandates of United Nations peacekeeping operations. Moreover, Resolution 1998,[40] passed in 2011, called on member states

---

29 UNSC Res 1379 (20 November 2001) ¶ 16.
30 UNSC Res 1460 (30 January 2003) ¶ 1.
31 UNSC Res 1539 (22 April 2004).
32 *Legal Consequences of the Construction of a Wall in the Occupied Palestinian Territory (Advisory Opinion)* [2004] ICJ Rep136.
33 Ibid ¶ 106. This view was confirmed by the ICJ in *Armed Activities on the Territory of the Congo (DRC v Uganda)* [2005] ICJ Rep 116.
34 UNSC Res 1612 (26 July 2005).
35 Perinaz Kermani Menez, 'Moving from Words to Action in the Modern "Era of Application": A New Approach to Realising Children's Rights in Armed Conflict' (2007) 15 *IJCR* 219, 220.
36 WatchList on Children and Armed Conflict, 'UN Security Council Resolution 1612 and Beyond: Strengthening Protection for Children in Armed Conflict' (May 2009) 4.
37 *Prosecutor v Lubanga (Warrant of Arrest)* (Case no ICC-01/04-01/06, Pre-Trial Chamber I, 10 February 2006).
38 UNSC Res 1882 (4 August 2009).
39 UNSC Res 1888 (30 September 2009).
40 UNSC Res 1998 (12 July 2011). See also UNSC Res 2068 (19 September 2012), in which the Security Council condemned violations of international law involving the recruitment and use of children and expressed concern at continued violations and abuses against children in armed conflict.

to devise ways ... to facilitate the development and implementation of time-bound actions plans, and the review and monitoring by the United Nations country level task force of obligations and commitments relating to the protection of children and armed conflict.

On 14 March 2012, the ICC delivered its first decision, *Prosecutor v Lubanga Dyilo*, in which the defendant was found guilty of conscripting and enlisting children under the age of 15 and using them to participate actively in hostilities.[41] On 26 April of the same year, the Special Court for Sierra Leone found the former President of Liberia, Charles Taylor, guilty of war crimes based partly on his support to RUF rebels in relation to their recruitment and use of children.[42]

1.4 The continual evolution of the paradigm

The successful prosecution of Thomas Lubanga and Charles Taylor provides a strong counterpoint to the early instrumentalist vision of children. Whereas concern for children was once motivated by their potential for soldiery, their recruitment and use is now criminalised. Thus, over the last century, the legal conception of childhood has transformed and an elaborate institutional and normative structure has developed to defend and protect this conception. The remainder of this chapter aims, first, to explore the substance of this normative structure and, second, to assess the possibility of challenging the dominant protectionist conception of childhood with a more progressive approach that recognises the agency and evolving capacities of children.

2 Untangling the normative framework

The international law of armed conflict as it applies to children associated with armed conflict is complex and, with this in mind, this chapter focuses on two illustrative issues:

1   the recruitment and participation of children in armed conflict; and
2   children's legal entitlements under humanitarian law and human rights law outside the sphere of recruitment and participation.

Numerous standards govern the first of these issues and the interaction of regimes, which arises in the second, has destabilised long-held understandings of the law of armed conflict. Thus, the aim of this section is to disentangle the relevant standards and offer a methodology by which to navigate the confusion that arises from the intersection of humanitarian and human rights law.

2.1 The law relating to the recruitment and participation of children

2.1.1 International armed conflict

Article 77(2) of Additional Protocol I to the Geneva Conventions, which applies to international armed conflicts, provides that:

---

41 *Prosecutor v Lubanga Dyilo* (Case no ICC-01/04-01/06, Trial Chamber I, 14 March 2012).
42 *Prosecutor v Taylor* (Case no SCSL-03-01-T, Trial Chamber II, 18 May 2012); also see *Prosecutor v Fofana and Kondewa* (Case no SCSL 004-14-A, Appeals Chamber, 28 May 2008).

> The Parties to the conflict shall take all feasible measures in order that children who have not attained the age of fifteen years do not take a direct part in hostilities.... In recruiting among those persons who have attained the age of fifteen years but who have not attained the age of eighteen years, the Parties to the conflict shall endeavour to give priority to those who are oldest.

The key interpretative questions here relate to the meaning of 'feasible measures' and 'direct' participation. The Commentary to Additional Protocol I explains that 'feasible' should be taken to mean 'capable of being done, accomplished or carried put, possible or practicable'.[43] Significantly, the Commentary on Article 57 of Additional Protocol I rejects the notion that feasibility may be subject to 'the success of the military operation'[44] although this is contested by some member states, including Australia, the UK and the US, which each apply a more restrictive interpretation of what constitutes feasible measures.[45]

As the Committee on the Rights of the Child has observed, the distinction between 'direct' and 'indirect' participation is 'very hard to draw'.[46] Mann suggests that 'direct' requires a 'relationship of adequate causality between the act of participation and its immediate result in military operations', but concedes that it 'cannot clearly be defined and that its use may vary from situation to situation and from conflict to conflict'.[47] The ICRC has stated that 'the notion of direct participation in hostilities refers to specific hostile acts carried out by individuals as part of the conduct of hostilities'.[48] As such, the ICRC has developed its own set of criteria which may be used to determine whether participation amounts to 'direct participation' for the purposes of international humanitarian law:

1   the act must be likely to adversely affect the military operations or military capacity of a party to an armed conflict or, alternatively, to inflict death, injury, or destruction on persons or objects protected against direct attack (threshold of harm), and
2   there must be a direct causal link between the act and the harm likely to result either from that act, or from a coordinated military operation of which that act constitutes an integral part (direct causation), and
3   the act must be specifically designed to directly cause the required threshold of harm in support of a party to the conflict and to the detriment of another (belligerent nexus).[49]

Whilst the ICRC criteria provide useful guidance on this issue, they are not wholly authoritative. For this reason, it is sufficient to note for present purposes the equivocacy of the distinction between direct and indirect participation.[50]

---

43   *AP Commentary* ¶ 3171.
44   Ibid 681–682.
45   Child Soldiers International, 'Louder than Words: An Agenda for Action to End State Use of Child Soldiers' (2012) 47.
46   CRC Report (n 17) ¶ 251.
47   Mann (n 14) 45.
48   ICRC, *Interpretive Guidance on the Notion of Direct Participation in Hostilities under International Humanitarian Law* (ICRC 2009) 45.
49   Ibid 46.
50   This is examined in greater detail in Michelle Lesh, 'Direct participation in hostilities' ch 10 in this volume.

2.1.2 Non-international armed conflicts

Article 4(3)(c) of Additional Protocol II applies to non-international armed conflicts and states that 'children who have not attained the age of fifteen years shall neither be recruited in the armed forces or groups nor allowed to take part in hostilities'. Additional Protocol II therefore offers a higher standard of protection than Additional Protocol I in that it is not qualified by references to 'feasible measures' or 'direct' participation.[51]

2.1.3 The Convention on the Rights of the Child

Articles 38(2) and (3) of the CRC mirror the standards under Additional Protocol I. States parties are required to take feasible measures to ensure that persons under the age of 15 years do not take a direct part in hostilities. As with Additional Protocol I, an absolute prohibition is placed on the recruitment of persons under 15 years, however states are permitted to recruit children over 15. This is often seen to be incongruous with other provisions of the CRC which seek to protect children's best interests,[52] ensure their survival and development[53] and protect them from injury, harm and abuse.[54] This incongruity was recognised during drafting, where many delegates expressed regret that the standards under the CRC failed to afford greater protection than the existing norms under Additional Protocol I and actually offered lesser protection than the standards under Additional Protocol II.[55]

2.1.4 The Optional Protocol to the Convention on the Rights of the Child

The expectation was that the Optional Protocol to the Convention on the Rights of the Child on the Involvement of Children in Armed Conflict would deliver the 'straight 18' approach, and prohibit in absolute terms the recruitment and participation in hostilities of all persons under the age of 18. Although this goal was not met, the Optional Protocol does advance the protection of children in several ways. First, Article 2 prohibits the compulsory recruitment of all persons under the age of 18. Second, Article 1 requires that '[s]tates parties shall take all feasible measures to ensure that members of their armed forces who have not attained the age of eighteen [as opposed to 15] years do not take a direct part in hostilities'. Although this advances on the previous standard, it again remains problematic in that the obligation is qualified by the requirement that states merely take 'feasible' measures to avoid 'direct' participation.[56]

---

51 As to why the standard offered in APII is higher than that of API, Mann (n 14) 50, notes that

> it was widely presumed during the Conference that local 'rebel' groups were better placed to recruit young children to participate in the conflict for extended periods of time. In returning to a stronger prohibition for internal armed conflicts in comparison with that adopted for international conflicts, the participating States were intending to make it more difficult (legally and politically) for the dissident groups within their territory to achieve this perceived military advantage.

52 CRC art 3.
53 CRC art 6.
54 CRC art 19.
55 See generally Office of the High Commissioner for Human Rights (n 15) 775–799; Sharon Detrick, *A Commentary on the United Nations Convention on the Rights of the Child* (Kluwer 1999) 514–516. The USA and USSR refused to provide consensus on the standards under APII: see Office of the High Commissioner for Human Rights (n 15) 796.
56 For a discussion of the Optional Protocol, see Matthew Happold, *Child Soldiers in International Law* (Manchester University Press 2005) 77–81.

The Optional Protocol still allows for the voluntary recruitment of persons under 18, however unlike earlier instruments, it requires states parties to raise the minimum age for voluntary recruitment and ensure that persons under 18 remain entitled to special protection. Thus, states are required to provide a declaration upon ratification containing details of the age at which they permit voluntary recruitment and the procedural safeguards against forced or coerced recruitment. With respect to such safeguards, Article 3(3) provides that as a minimum states must ensure that:

a   recruitment is genuinely voluntary;
b   recruitment is carried out with the informed consent of parents or guardians;
c   recruits are fully informed of the duties involved in military service; and
d   recruits provide reliable proof of age.

Article 4 of the Optional Protocol also provides that armed groups (as distinct from state armed forces) *should not* recruit or use in hostilities persons under 18 years of age. The inclusion of this provision was particularly contentious during drafting as many states viewed it as affirming the legitimacy of non-state armed groups. In response, it was argued that:

> non-governmental armed groups were susceptible to international pressure and reference was made as an example to an armed opposition group which ... declared its willingness to abide by the recruitment standards in the Convention on the Rights of the Child.[57]

The concern remained, however, that 'implied recognition should not be given to non-governmental armed groups and that it would be preferable to see the issue covered in the preamble to the draft optional protocol rather than in its operative part'.[58] It was further noted that it was important to be realistic about the measures available to governments in this context, given that 'non-governmental armed groups were already beyond the pale of the law'.[59] Ultimately the provision was included on the basis that the Optional Protocol ought to address non-state actors directly and provide for criminalisation of actions in violation of the Protocol.'[60]

2.2 Customary international law on the use and recruitment of children

The standards present in the complex normative framework are yet to receive universal ratification. In particular, the higher standards of Additional Protocol II and the Optional Protocol have received only modest ratification (167 and 156 states respectively as at August 2014). As such, there is a question as to whether these standards have achieved the status of customary international law. Matthew Happold has reviewed this issue carefully and concluded that:

> Customary law mandates that states refrain from recruiting children under 15 years of age into their armed forces and take all feasible efforts to ensure children below 15 years do not take a direct (or possibly any) part in hostilities.[61]

57 Committee on the Rights of the Child, Report of the Working Group on a Draft Optional Protocol to the Convention on the Rights of the Child on Involvement of Children in Armed Conflicts on its Third Session, UN Doc E/CN.4/1997/96 (13 March 1997) ¶ 35.
58 Ibid ¶ 37.
59 Ibid.
60 Ibid.
61 Happold (n 56) 99.

Non-state groups are subject to a higher standard, which prohibits both recruitment of children under 15 years of age and their participation in hostilities.[62] There is also evidence of an emerging customary norm prohibiting both states and non-state groups from compulsorily recruiting persons under 18, however this is yet to crystallise, thus limiting its practical application.[63]

2.3 The law relating to the general protection of children associated with armed conflict

The norms regulating the general protection of children associated with armed conflict are numerous. Consequently, the following discussion seeks to identify the core features of the relevant instruments and to offer a means by which to navigate and resolve the tensions created by the interaction of international humanitarian law and international human rights law.[64]

2.4 Geneva Convention IV on the protection of civilians

In the 1940s, it was decided that a draft convention dedicated to the protection of children in armed conflict and civil war 'should be incorporated into the Fourth Geneva Convention'.[65] It is ironic then, that 'children are not specifically included in the only provision [of the Fourth Geneva Convention] stating the principle of special protection'.[66] Despite this omission, several articles of Geneva Convention IV do offer protection to children.[67] Article 27 of Geneva Convention IV expresses the general principle that protected persons (including child civilians) are entitled to humane treatment, respect for their honour, family rights, religious convictions, practices and customs and protection against all acts of violence including rape, forced prostitution and indecent assault. It also prohibits coercion, corporal punishment, torture, collective penalties, reprisals and the taking of hostages. Furthermore, Part II of Geneva Convention IV, which offers general protection against the consequences of war,[68] includes a number of protections relevant to children (generally defined as being under 15) and relating to issues such as hospitals and safety zones, the free passage of food, measures to assist children who are orphaned or separated from their parents and to be educated in accordance with their cultural tradition.[69] Part III of Geneva Convention IV requires the following:

- equal treatment of children under 15 years of age, relative to the nationals of a state;
- occupying powers to take measures to ensure the proper working of all institutions devoted to the care and education of the occupied state;
- a prohibition against compulsion to work for any person under 18;
- a prohibition against the death penalty on any person who was under 18 at the time of the offence and an obligation to pay proper regard to the special treatment due to minors (undefined) who are detained or convicted for offences;[70]

---

62 Ibid.
63 Ibid.
64 For a more fulsome account, see generally Jenny Kuper, *International Law Concerning Child Civilians in Armed Conflict* (OUP 1997) and Hamilton and El-Haj (n 14).
65 Hamilton and El-Haj (n 14) 12.
66 Mann (n 14) 34.
67 For a detailed examination of this protection see: Hamilton and El-Haj (n 14) 9–11, noting that the protections afforded by these articles are 'not particularly powerful'.
68 GCIV Pt II is entitled 'General Protection of Populations against Certain Consequences of War'.
69 GCIV arts 14, 17, 23 and 24.
70 GCIV arts 38(5), 50, 51, 68 and 76.

- the lodgement of child internees with their families;
- additional food for children under 15 in proportion to their needs;
- the education of internee children must be assured; and
- special playgrounds must be reserved for children and young people.[71]

However, these provisions contain several deficiencies. First, they provide no clear definition of a child. Moreover, a number of articles contain protections afforded only to children under 15. This is to be contrasted with the presumption under Article 1 of the Convention that a child is any person under 18. Further age-based entitlements, such as the right of children under seven to be with their mothers if they are in a safety zone,[72] lack a coherent basis for the age distinction and this serves only to impose an unnecessary restriction on the potential protections afforded to children more generally. Article 51, at least, is unambiguous in its prohibition of compulsory work for children, whilst Article 68 prohibits the death penalty for offences committed while the offender was under 18 years of age. In contrast, Article 76, which deals with conditions of detention in occupied territories, contains a provision, which recognises 'the special treatment due to minors', whilst failing to define the term 'minor'.

Even Article 24, which deals with the treatment of children separated from their parents, only applies to children so deprived as a result of war and 'fails to address the needs of children who are still with their parents but have similar problems of maintenance and education'.[73] The discretion inherent in the implementation of this article 'provides a wide field of activity for private institutions and organisations'.[74] This in turn raises the possibility that states will abdicate responsibility for implementation of the article in favour of such organisations.[75] Finally, Article 24 is not a 'child rights' article in the sense of securing the best interests of children but 'rather an expression of parental or family rights and States' concern in retaining their children'.[76] The same complaint applies to Article 82, which allows for interned parents to request the internment of their child without any requirement that the best interests of the child be taken into account.

2.5 Additional Protocol I

Additional Protocol I was designed in part to respond to the failure of Geneva Convention IV to offer special protection to children.[77] It extends the general protection afforded to civilians in international armed conflicts to child civilians.[78] Unlike Geneva Convention IV, this protection aims to protect children from the conduct of hostilities[79] and also grants protection to the civilian population at large. Further, it offers children specific protections under Articles 77 and 78.

Article 77 provides that:

> Children shall be the object of special respect and shall be protected against any form of indecent assault. The Parties to the conflict shall provide them with the care and aid they require, whether because of their age or for any other reason.

71 GCIV arts 82, 89, 94 and 132.
72 GCIV art 14.
73 Hamilton and El-Haj (n 14) 16.
74 Ibid.
75 Ibid 17.
76 Ibid.
77 Kuper (n 64) 78.
78 See API arts 51, 52, 74 and 75.
79 See API art 52; see also Hamilton and El-Haj (n 14) 19–20.

Significantly, it 'is not subject to any restrictions as regards its scope of application; it therefore applies to all children who are in the territory of States at war, whether or not they are affected by armed conflict'.[80] This is significant as certain provisions under Geneva Convention IV apply only to children who fall within a particular category of protected person, such as children in occupied territories.

It also provides that children under 15 years of age, who take a direct part in hostilities and fall into the power of an adverse party, shall benefit from special protection, regardless of whether they are prisoners of war.[81] Children (defined here as persons under 15) who are arrested, detained or interned for reasons related to the armed conflict, shall be held separately from adults, except where families are accommodated together.[82] Moreover, echoing Geneva Convention IV, the death penalty shall not be handed down for persons who were under 18 at the time of their offence.[83]

Article 78 of Additional Protocol I deals with the evacuation of children and adopts a more 'cautious approach'[84] than Article 24 of Geneva Convention IV, in an attempt to address the reality that evacuations had been

> carried out for other reasons, for example, to educate children according to certain political or religious views or to prepare them to serve in the armed forces of a State. Sometimes they had been carried out in conditions such as to result in the children losing their identity or being raised in a manner foreign to that of their family or their country.[85]

Thus, Article 78 provides that evacuation shall not occur unless it is carried out for compelling reasons related to the safety, health or medical treatment of a child. Furthermore, consent from parents or legal guardians must be obtained and the evacuation must be supervised by the Protecting Power.[86]

2.6 Additional Protocol II

Additional Protocol II governs the protection of child civilians in high intensity, non-international armed conflicts.[87] The general protection afforded to children against the effects of armed conflict under Additional Protocol II is similar to that enjoyed under Additional Protocol I. Thus, armed forces are required to distinguish between civilians and those who take part in hostilities, with the former afforded legal protections against being attacked.[88] Furthermore, Additional Protocol II prohibits attacks on objects indispensable to the survival of the civilian population[89] and states that 'all persons who do not take part or who have ceased to take part in hostilities ... are entitled to respect for their person, honour and convictions and religious practices'.[90] Specific

---

80 *AP Commentary* ¶ 3171.
81 API art 77(3).
82 Ibid art 77(4).
83 Ibid art 77(5). For a commentary on the content of API art 77, see *AP Commentary* ¶ 3171.
84 Ibid 909, ¶ 3211.
85 Ibid.
86 For a comprehensive discussion of API art 78, see ibid 907–915.
87 For a comprehensive overview of the protection afforded to children in high intensity non-international armed conflicts, see Kuper (n 64) 66–68 and 95–97.
88 APII art 13(2).
89 Ibid art 14.
90 Ibid art 4(1).

acts of ill treatment such as torture, rape and slavery are prohibited[91] and persons detained or interned are entitled to minimum guarantees[92] and due process rights in any criminal proceedings.[93]

Article 4(3) specifically offers care and aid to children, in particular in relation to their education, religious or otherwise, and their reunification with their families, where they have been temporarily separated. Furthermore, Article 6(4) provides that the 'death penalty shall not be pronounced on persons who were under the age of eighteen years at the time of the offence'.

Article 4(3) represents a watershed in international humanitarian law, since it was the first provision of universal application to children in non-international armed conflicts. However, Additional Protocol II suffers from similar defects to Additional Protocol I. It fails to define 'child' and this potentially limits its application to children over 15. The right to education is drafted from the perspective of a child's parents and contains no requirement to take into account the child's wishes and best interests. The provision for temporary evacuation suffers from the same defect, and the provision dealing with reunification offers nothing that is not already provided under Article 10 of Geneva Convention IV. Finally, the reality is that in any case, Additional Protocol II does 'not apply to the majority of civil wars now current in the international arena'.[94]

2.7 Common Article 3 of the Geneva Conventions

Common Article 3, appearing in each of the Geneva Conventions, provides to child civilians the only source of protection under international humanitarian law in non-international, low intensity armed conflicts, which generally fall outside the scope of the Geneva Conventions and Additional Protocols. With respect to persons taking no active part in hostilities, including children, it prohibits various conduct, including violence to life and person, the taking of hostages, humiliating and degrading treatment and extrajudicial killings.

The general nature of Common Article 3 means that it is too generic to provide any significant protection to children and it specifically fails to address the situation of children affected by armed conflict. Moreover, Maher suggests that Common Article 3 inadequately safeguards against children's participation in new types of warfare, and represents a compromise between states wishing to retain absolute autonomy to deal with internal conflict and states calling for uniform adherence to international standards. The outcome is that Common Article 3 'does little more than protect the most fundamental human values and prescribes no extensive codification of standards applicable to belligerents in internal armed conflicts',[95] and the protections which it affords to children are therefore inadequate.

2.8 The CRC and special protection

Article 38 of the CRC imposes an obligation on states parties 'to respect and to ensure respect for the rules of international humanitarian law applicable ... in armed conflicts, which are relevant to the child'. This deference to international humanitarian law reflects the orthodox

---

91 Ibid art 4(2).
92 Ibid art 5.
93 Ibid art 6.
94 Judith Gardam, *Non-Combatant Immunity as a Norm of International Humanitarian Law* (Martinus Nijhoff 1993) 129.
95 Colleen Maher, 'The Protection of Children in Armed Conflict: A Human Rights Analysis of the Protection Afforded to Children in Warfare' (1989) 9 *Boston College Third World Law Journal* 297, 303. See also Hamilton and El-Haj (n 14) 27.

view at the time the CRC was adopted that international humanitarian law was *lex specialis* in times of armed conflict. Had this orthodoxy been maintained, the special protection afforded to children would have been determined largely by reference to international humanitarian standards. However, in the years since the CRC came into force the contemporary law of armed conflict has changed such that it is now informed both by international humanitarian law *and* by international human rights law. As the ICJ observed in the *Wall* case, human rights law, *including the CRC*, applies during times of armed conflict.[96]

The ICJ anticipated that in order to reconcile the two normative regimes, there would be circumstances in which *either* international humanitarian law *or* international human rights law would be *lex specialis*, and the relationship between the two must be seen as being complementary.[97] Indeed, the broad overlap between the protections offered under each regime reflects their complementarity. For example, with respect to certain issues, such as the evacuation of children, international humanitarian law offers explicit guidance on the substantive measures required in order for the rights of children in this context to be realised. On the other hand, the CRC offers greater guidance with respect to other issues, such as how to deal with juvenile offenders and the health of children.

In reality, however, the CRC offers a far broader and more ambitious range of entitlements to children associated with armed conflict beyond the content of Article 38. This raises the issue of states' capacity to secure these *other* rights during armed conflict. Under the CRC, children have rights to freedom of expression, association, play, leisure, cultural activities, liberty, education, health and an adequate standard of living.[98] They also enjoy an overriding right to have their best interests be a primary consideration in matters which concern them.[99] Moreover, the fact that none of these rights are subject to derogation enables advocates to insist that they be respected during armed conflict. Unsurprisingly, military commanders remain anxious about such claims when they have been operating a paradigm in which the principle of military necessity under international humanitarian law has been used to justify actions which may compromise children's rights.

A fundamental question therefore arises as to whether the regimes that are supposed to cohabitate mutually within the contemporary understanding of the law of armed conflict may suffer from irreconcilable differences.[100] The point to stress here is that, subject to few exceptions, such as torture, the reality is that children's rights remain subject to limitation. The real issue therefore is whether a particular limitation can be justified as being reasonable. As a general rule, the reasonableness of a limitation will depend on:

- whether the limitation of the right was undertaken pursuant to a relevant law;
- whether the limitation pursued a legitimate aim or pressing social need; and
- whether more proportionate measures to achieve the same aim may have been taken.

In turn, proportionality will be contingent on:

- the existence of a rational connection (usually based on evidence) between the measure undertaken and the aim pursued; and

---

96 *Wall* (n 32) ¶ 106.
97 Ibid.
98 See CRC arts 13, 15, 31, 37, 28, 24 and 27, respectively.
99 Ibid art 3.
100 This issue is discussed in more detail in Noam Lubell and Nancie Prud'homme, 'Impact of human rights law' ch 6 in this volume.

- whether a reasonable alternative measure is available which would minimally impair the right in question.[101]

If this process is followed, a child may suffer an interference with his or her right but there will be no violation of that right.

This test with its emphasis on proportionality goes some way to aligning the application of human rights with humanitarian law (which also places significant emphasis on the principle of proportionality, especially in contexts such as targeting). In practical terms, this means that where, for example, a child's best interests must be a primary consideration, this does not mean that the child's interests must automatically trump all other considerations. It does require, however, that decisions made during an armed conflict give genuine consideration to children's interests. Moreover, where these interests are compromised, the state bears the onus of justifying why such an outcome is reasonable.[102]

The conclusion to be drawn from this discussion is that the normative tensions between humanitarian law and human rights law may be less than is commonly assumed. Although this issue requires further consideration, one right that has been largely overlooked in the rush to protect children associated with armed conflict, is their right to participation. It is the potential impact of this right on the law of armed conflict that will now be considered.

3 Looking beyond the protection paradigm: accommodating the agency, voice and evolving capacities of children

The modern sociology of childhood views the child as an active subject with agency and evolving capacity, and not simply a passive object in need of protection.[103] Article 12 of the CRC has played a pivotal role in the expansion of the modern conception of childhood and requires states to 'assure to the child who is capable of forming his or her own views, the right to express those views freely in all matters affecting the child'.

This right, regarded by some commentators as the 'perhaps most radical element' of the CRC,[104] is not unknown in the context of armed conflict. Indeed, in her seminal report, Graça Machel proclaimed that 'young people should be seen ... as survivors and active participants in creating solutions, not just as victims or problems'.[105] But this sentiment is often overlooked in international discussions on armed conflict, which primarily focus on the need to *protect* children.

What then are the consequences of recognising children's evolving capacities and agency for the law of armed conflict? The observations that follow aim to stimulate a discussion with respect to three illustrative issues:

- the voluntariness of child recruitment;
- the criminal responsibility of children for crimes committed during armed conflict; and
- the challenges associated with creating effective mechanisms to facilitate consultation with children.

101 John Tobin, *The Right to Health in International Law* (OUP 2011) 181–184.
102 See Siracusa Principles on the Limitation and Derogation of Provisions in the International Covenant on Civil and Political Rights, UN Doc E/CN.4/1984/4, Annex (1984) art I(A)(12), which states that '[t]he burden of justifying a limitation upon a right ... lies with the state'.
103 See generally Michael Freeman, 'The Sociology of Childhood and Children's Rights' (1998) 6 *IJCR* 433.
104 Lisa Woll, 'Organizational Responses to the Convention on the Rights of the Child: International Lessons for Child Welfare Organizations' (2001) 80 *Child Welfare* 668, 673.
105 Cited in Machel Report (n 19) 11.

3.1 Voluntariness

During the Lubanga trial, evidence was led by psychologist Dr Elizabeth Schauer, who suggested 'that from a psychological point of view children cannot give "informed" consent when joining an armed group'.[106] Her view was based on the assertion that children:

> have limited understanding of the consequences of their choices; they do not control or fully comprehend the structures and forces they are dealing with; and they have inadequate knowledge and understanding of the short- and long-term consequences of their actions.[107]

Dr Schauer concluded 'that children lack the capacity to determine their best interests in this particular context'.[108] This vision of the incompetent child is difficult to reconcile with the concept of a child's evolving capacities, the empirical foundation for which is to be found in current scholarship in developmental psychology.

But Dr Schauer's evidence is consistent with the dominant narrative within the context of armed conflict.[109] It is founded upon the assumption that children who volunteer for military service are invariably motivated by poverty.[110] Thus, it is assumed that a child's choice cannot be genuine, free or fully informed. But Dr Schauer's position is problematic to the extent that it makes no allowance for children's agency and reinforces the rhetoric of victimhood. An approach which views children as rights-bearers would recognise that whilst children who volunteer to join armed services make their own choices, these choices are made 'not in conditions of their own choosing'.[111] This approach allows for the affirmation of the child's capacity and prompts a rhetorical shift from 'paternalism and salvationism'[112] to empowerment and agency. It demands that attention is not simply directed to the prohibition of voluntary recruitment but to the economic and social conditions which underpin a child's decision to join an armed group.

3.2 Criminal responsibility

The idea of children's evolving capacities also has consequences for the question of whether children who commit atrocities during armed conflict can be held criminally responsible for their actions.[113] There are three schools of thought with respect to this issue. The first argues that children remain in a stage of intellectual development and evolving maturity and for this reason should not be held criminally responsible for their actions. The second contends that in the aftermath of a conflict, prosecutors ought to focus on the most responsible, those in leadership positions with command responsibility, and not children.[114] A final view argues that children are

---

106 *Lubanga* (Judgment) (n 41) ¶ 610.
107 Ibid.
108 Ibid.
109 For a précis of the dominant narrative, see Mark A Drumbl, *Reimagining Child Soldiers in International Law and Policy* (OUP 2012) 6.
110 See Machel Report (n 19) 12.
111 Joanna Phoenix, 'In the Name of Protection: Youth Prostitution Reforms in England and Wales' (2002) 22 *Critical Social Policy* 353, 362.
112 Ibid 354.
113 For a more detailed discussion, see generally Drumbl (n 109) and Happold (n 56) 141–160.
114 This was the position adopted by the Prosecutor for the Special Court for Sierra Leone: Happold (n 56) citing SCSL Public Affairs Office, 'Special Court Prosecutor Says He Will Not Prosecute Children' Press Release, 2 November 2002.

capable of forming the requisite *mens rea* for the commission of war crimes and crimes against humanity and in such circumstances they should be liable to prosecution.[115]

The first of these views remains the orthodox position and reflects the dominant narrative of children as victims in need of protection in the context of armed conflict. However, it is difficult to reconcile this vision with the broader and more progressive conception of children under a rights–based approach, as agents with evolving capacities. Thus, it becomes problematic for civil society and bodies such as the Committee on the Rights of the Child to advocate and demand the adoption of this progressive conception of childhood *in all matters concerning children*, but then quarantine children associated with armed conflict from the application of this model. A coherent and consistent application of the progressive vision of children as agents with evolving capacity tends to imply that there will be circumstances where such agency and capacity will mean that children must accept responsibility for their actions, including criminal responsibility in times of armed conflict.

3.3 Consultation and participation

Article 12 of the CRC provides that children have a right to express their views in *all matters affecting* them. There is increasing appreciation for the fact that this right applies to the myriad decisions and practices affecting children both during and after armed conflict. To take just one example, with respect to the determination of reparations, the ICC has explained that '[t]he views of the child victims are to be considered when decisions are made about individual or collective reparations that concern them, bearing in mind their circumstances, age and level of maturity'.[116]

However, this ostensible acknowledgement of the notion of child participation masks the complexities inherent in the creation of systems and processes to allow for the views of children to be considered in a meaningful way. In reality, when the dominant paradigm remains one of salvation, there is a risk that references to an alternative approach encompassing agency and participation may amount to little more than rhetoric. As such, substantial work remains to be done on how to consult with children and facilitate their active participation in matters affecting them in the context of armed conflicts, in a way that is not merely tokenistic.

4 Looking forward: not only to see but to hear children

In its 2012 resolution on Children and Armed Conflict, the Security Council reiterated its 'primary responsibility for the maintenance of international peace and security and in this connection its commitment to address the widespread impact of armed conflict on children'.[117] This passage reflects an instrumentalist concern for the situation of children associated with armed conflict. But, unlike the vision of children as future soldiers to bolster and facilitate the expansion of states early in the twentieth century, the instrumentalist vision of children currently held by the Security Council need not be a cause for concern. This is because the reality is that an aggrieved, abused and neglected cohort of children and young people is hardly a recipe for a stable and functioning state. Moreover, this instrumentalist conception of children is tempered by the Security Council 'stressing the importance of comprehensively *protecting children* in all

---

115 See Drumbl (n 109) 175–180.

116 *Prosecutor v Lubanga (Decision Establishing the Principles and Procedures to be Applied to Reparations)* (Case no ICC-01/04-01/06, Trial Chamber I, 7 August 2010) ¶ 215.

117 UNSC Res 2068 (19 September 2012).

situations of armed conflict' (emphasis added). Thus a humanitarian concern for the welfare of children co-exists as a factor in motivating the Security Council to take action to address the situation of children associated with armed conflict.

Notably absent from the Security Council resolution is the idea of children as agents with evolving capacity and a right to participate in all matters affecting them. This contrasts sharply with the resolutions adopted by the Security Council with respect to women and conflict, where it has emphasised the need to facilitate the 'full, equal and effective' participation of women in the prevention and resolution of conflict.[118] This differential treatment of children should not come as a surprise given that the victimhood narrative remains the dominant conception of children within the law of armed conflict. The challenge, however, is to move beyond this narrative to envision children as agents with evolving capacity and a right to participate in all matters affecting them. This does not require states to abandon protective measures for children associated with armed conflict. But it does mean that the process by which these measures are developed must become a collaborative effort between adults and those children whose experience of living in armed conflict provides them with insights and expertise which adults cannot afford to ignore.

---

118 UNSC Res 1889 (5 October 2009). See also UNSC Res 1325 (31 October 2000); UNSC Res 1820 (19 June 2008); UNSC Res 1888 (30 September 2009); UNSC Res 1960 (16 December 2010).

21
Cultural property

Jadranka Petrovic

Wartime destruction, theft, pillage or misappropriation of cultural property is as old as armed conflict itself. Throughout history countless architectural structures of outstanding historic or artistic value, works of art and other cultural artifacts have been destroyed or plundered during warfare. The Roman destruction of Carthage, the German destruction of the Louvain library, the bombing of Yokohama, Tokyo, Rotterdam, London, Hamburg, Dresden and the irreplaceable monastery of Monte Cassino, the pillage of Jewish art during the Second World War, the use of historical sites in Lebanon, Iraq, Kosovo and Syria for military purposes, the deliberate shelling of the Old City of Dubrovnik (a World Heritage site), the burning of the Sarajevo library, the destruction of the Old Bridge of Mostar and the mausoleums in Mali, the looting of Iraq's national museum and of the magnificent Roman mosaics of Apamea in Syria are only a few examples of the deliberate destruction of humanity's cultural heritage in times of armed conflict. It is impossible to predict how many treasures future generations will be deprived of due to warfare.

International legal protection of cultural property in armed conflict has developed in response to cultural disasters. The body of norms of the LOAC concerning cultural property grew gradually. Today several international legal instruments govern the protection of cultural property in armed conflict. A number of provisions of these instruments have entered the domain of international customary law.

This chapter first briefly surveys the current state of international treaty law governing protection of cultural property in armed conflict and then canvasses the rules of customary international law on the subject. This is followed by consideration of the question of the definition of cultural property and then analysis of modes of cultural property protection. The difference between the rules applicable to international and non-international armed conflicts is also addressed. Finally, the chapter discusses the interaction between the LOAC concerning cultural property and international criminal law and pinpoints some issues emanating from this interaction.

1 Sources

1.1 Treaties

The first international multilateral treaties that provided some protection to cultural property in armed conflict were conventions adopted at the First and Second Peace Conferences at The Hague in 1899 and 1907 respectively. Of particular significance are the 1899 Convention (II) with Respect to the Laws and Customs of War on Land,[1] 1907 Convention (IV) Respecting the Laws and Customs of War on Land[2] and 1907 Convention (IX) Concerning Bombardment by Naval Forces in Time of War.[3] Similarly worded Articles 27 and 56 of the 1899 and 1907 Hague Regulations respectively concern the protection of certain objects in sieges and bombardment and in occupied territories. The 1907 Convention (IX) provides the description of a 'distinctive and visible sign' to be used for objects protected from bombardment by naval forces in time of war.[4]

During both World Wars these three conventions were the only international multilateral treaties that contained legally binding provisions concerning protection of cultural property in armed conflict. However, the extent of the destruction of cultural property during the two World Wars proved that those provisions were ineffective.[5] This revealed the need for a more comprehensive, and a more up-to date treaty that recognised the advances in the techniques of warfare as well as the threats those advances posed to the protection of cultural property. Such a treaty was adopted in 1954.

The Convention for the Protection of Cultural Property in the Event of Armed Conflict (1954 Convention)[6] was adopted in The Hague on 14 May 1954. Together with annexed Regulations for its execution and the Protocol for the Protection of Cultural Property in the Event of Armed Conflict[7] concerning movable cultural property in occupied territories which was adopted on the same day, the 1954 Convention was considered by many as the 'Red Cross Charter for cultural property'.[8] This Convention was the first international multilateral treaty to deal exclusively with the protection of cultural property. Its adoption represented the most significant development in the protection of cultural property in armed conflict. Despite this, the 1954 Convention did not attract widespread ratification. Reinforcement of its rules was attempted through the inclusion of the cultural property-related provisions in the two Additional Protocols to the Geneva Conventions, adopted on 8 June 1977.

Additional Protocol I, applicable to international armed conflict, and Additional Protocol II, applicable to non-international armed conflict, contain several articles relevant to the protection

---

1 Convention (II) with Respect to the Laws and Customs of War on Land, with Annexed Regulations (29 July 1899) 189 CTS 429.
2 Convention (IV) Respecting the Laws and Customs of War on Land with Annexed Regulations (18 October 1907) 205 CTS 277 ('1907 Convention IV').
3 Convention (IX) Concerning Bombardment by Naval Forces in Time of War (18 October 1907) 205 CTS 345.
4 Ibid art 5.
5 See eg Kevin Chamberlain, *War and Cultural Heritage* (Institute of Art and Law 2004); Jadranka Petrovic, *The Old Bridge of Mostar and Increasing Respect for Cultural Property in Armed Conflict* (Martinus Nijhoff 2013) 99.
6 Convention for the Protection of Cultural Property in the Event of Armed Conflict, with Annexed Regulations for the Execution of the Convention (14 May 1945) 249 UNTS 240 ('1954 Convention' and '1954 Hague Regulations').
7 Protocol for the Protection of Cultural Property in the Event of Armed Conflict (14 May 1954) 249 UNTS 358.
8 Jiří Toman, *The Protection of Cultural Property in the Event of Armed Conflict: Commentary on the Convention for the Protection of Cultural Property in the Event of Armed Conflict and its Protocol, signed on 14 May 1954 in The Hague, and on other Instruments of International Law concerning such Protection* (UNESCO 1996), 21.

of cultural property in armed conflict. Two of these articles, namely, Article 53 of Additional Protocol I and Article 16 of Additional Protocol II, in their entirety deal with the 'protection of cultural objects and places of worship'. However, the 1954 Convention remains the paramount instrument for the international protection of cultural property in armed conflict as its application is in no way prejudiced by these two articles.[9]

The cultural disasters emanating from numerous armed conflicts that have occurred since the adoption of the 1954 Convention have exposed its major weaknesses, such as the absence of any definition of specific breaches that give rise to criminal responsibility and the ambiguity surrounding the concept of military necessity. Those specific weaknesses were addressed in the Second Protocol to the 1954 Hague Convention, adopted on 26 March 1999 (1999 Protocol).[10] The Protocol, *inter alia*, specified which breaches of the Convention give rise to criminal responsibility[11] and clarified a waiver of protection on the basis of 'imperative military necessity' pursuant to Article 4(2) of the Convention by linking the notion of military necessity with the concept of 'military objective' as defined in Article 52 of Additional Protocol I.[12]

Although all these legal instruments are interrelated, in each conflict it has to be ascertained precisely which of them is applicable to a party to the conflict to determine the level of protection afforded to certain cultural property. However, some LOAC norms concerning the protection of cultural property have become part of customary law applicable in international and non-international armed conflicts and, as such, are binding on all parties to armed conflicts regardless of the precise legal characterisation of the armed conflict.

1.2 Customary international law

The 1907 Hague Regulations form part of customary international law. Accordingly, Articles 27 and 56 (as well as Article 23(g) concerning military necessity) of these regulations are binding on all states whether or not they are party to the Regulations. This was expressly recognised by the International Military Tribunal (IMT) in Nuremberg which declared that 'by 1939 these rules laid down in the [1907 Hague Convention (IV)] were recognized by all civilized nations, and were regarded as being declaratory of the laws and customs of war'.[13] In 1993, this was affirmed by the UN Secretary-General in his report to the UN Security Council concerning the establishment of the ICTY.[14] I have argued elsewhere that certain parts of the 1954 Convention, especially the provisions governing 'respect for cultural property', are also binding on all states by virtue of customary law.[15] Equally, Article 53 of Additional Protocol I and Article 16 of Additional Protocol II represent statements of general principles which reflect the provisions of the Hague Regulations concerning cultural property and of the entire 1954 Convention and are deemed to be 'the portions of cultural protection law that have most clearly reached customary international law status'.[16]

---

9 Arts 53 and 16 explicitly state that their application is '[w]ithout prejudice to the provisions of the Hague Convention of 14 May 1954'.

10 Second Protocol to the Hague Convention of 1954 for the Protection of Cultural Property in the Event of Armed Conflict (26 March 1999) 2253 UNTS 212 ('1999 Protocol').

11 Ibid art 15. For a discussion on penal sanctions under the 1999 Protocol (n 10), see eg Roger O'Keefe, *The Protection of Cultural Property in Armed Conflict* (CUP 2006) 274–288.

12 1999 Protocol (n 10) art 6.

13 *US et al v Göring et al* 1 TMWC 171, 223 (1946).

14 Report of the Secretary-General Pursuant to Paragraph 2 of the Security Council Resolution 808 (1993), UN Doc S/25704 (3 May 1993) ¶¶ 41–42.

15 See eg Petrovic (n 5) fn 59.

16 Ibid 105 and fn 69, quoting David Meyer, 'The 1954 Hague Cultural Property Convention and its Emergence into Customary International Law' (1993) 11 *Boston University ILJ* 349, 362.

2 Definition of cultural property

The term 'cultural property' was used for the first time in international law in the 1954 Convention. Article 1 of this Convention provides a comprehensive definition of the term, applying it to tangible, human-made (as opposed to nature-made), movable and immovable objects of great importance to the cultural heritage of every people, irrespective of whether they are religious or secular, such as monuments of architecture, art or history, works of art, manuscripts and important collections of books or archives. Article 1 also encompasses buildings whose purpose is to preserve or exhibit movable cultural property, such as museums, and 'centres' containing a large amount of movable and immovable cultural property.

However, it is not always easy to determine what objects exactly enjoy protection within the meaning of Article 1. The reason for this is that the international law which accords protection to cultural property is heavily reliant on domestic law. States determine the scope of application of the 1954 Convention because cultural property 'of great importance to the cultural heritage of every people' is property that is designated as such by national laws on cultural property and is deemed important by the competent national authorities. As national laws differ, there is no uniform definition of cultural property at the national level.[17]

The existence of varied terminology and differences in the scope of application in other international legal instruments that contain provisions concerning cultural property also results in a lack of uniform definition of cultural property at the international level. Articles 27 and 56 of the 1907 Hague Regulations accord protection to a range of objects. However, only some of those objects would qualify as 'cultural' property within the meaning of Article 1 of the 1954 Convention today.

Like Articles 27 and 56 of the Hague Regulations, Article 53 of Additional Protocol I and Article 16 of Additional Protocol II do not use the term 'cultural property'. These two articles merely prohibit acts of hostility directed against three categories of objects, namely, 'the historic monuments, works of art or places of worship' which constitute 'the cultural or spiritual heritage of peoples'. While the Hague Regulations and the 1977 Additional Protocols go a step further in ensuring protection for wider categories of objects than the 1954 Convention, those other objects do not necessarily qualify as 'cultural property' under the 1954 Convention, which, as noted, remains the principal international legal instrument on the protection of cultural property in armed conflict.

The varied terminology among these instruments and their differing scope of application may create confusion when it comes to implementation at the national level. Knowing what objects are protected by the LOAC is of the utmost importance in armed conflict.[18] Decisions at the operational level by military commanders about what constitutes a legitimate military target greatly depend on a clear definition of cultural property. Thus, a more consistent approach to definitions, including terminology, is desirable.

17 For a discussion about the definition of 'cultural property', see generally Roger O'Keefe, 'The Meaning of "Cultural Property" under the 1954 Hague Convention' (1999) 46 *Netherlands ILR* 26. See also, Manlio Frigo, 'Cultural Property v Cultural Heritage: A "Battle of Concepts" in International Law?' (2004) 86 *IRRC* 367

18 Petrovic (n 5) 13.

3 Modes of protection

There are three main systems of protection of cultural property under the 1954 Convention:

- the so-called 'general protection' accorded to all objects that qualify as 'cultural property' within the meaning of Article 1 of the 1954 Convention (that is, property 'of *great* importance to the cultural heritage of every people');
- 'special protection' envisaged for certain cultural property 'of *very great* importance'; and
- 'enhanced protection' for cultural property 'of *the greatest* importance for humanity'.

The 1907 Hague Regulations do not accord to cultural objects any other type of protection except the 'general' or direct protection in Articles 27 and 56.[19] The 1977 Additional Protocols, on the other hand, do provide for dual-level protection for cultural property, namely, indirect protection accorded to all civilian objects[20] (cultural objects are generally 'civilian' in nature) and direct protection accorded to 'historic monuments, works of art, or places of worship which constitute cultural or spiritual heritage of peoples'.[21]

3.1 General protection of cultural property

Under Article 2 of the 1954 Convention, protection of cultural property comprises the safeguarding of, and respect for, cultural property. The Convention (together with its 1999 Protocol) is the only multilateral treaty that includes provisions about the safeguarding of, not just respect for, cultural property. Article 3 of the Convention obligates states to take, at their discretion, peacetime measures in order to protect cultural property situated within their own territory against the foreseeable effects of an armed conflict. Article 5 of the 1999 Protocol refers to some examples of measures that might fall within the rubric of safeguarding, such as preparation of inventories, planning of emergency measures for protection against fire or structural collapse, preparation for the removal of movable cultural property or the provision for *in situ* protection of such property. However, neither the Convention nor the Protocol envisages any repercussions for states in case of their failure to abide by this obligation. In fact, Article 4(5) of the Convention declares unambiguously that the absence of the measures of safeguard does not mean that states may evade the obligations relevant to their 'respect for cultural property'.[22]

'Respect for cultural property' is governed by Article 4 of the 1954 Convention. Pursuant to this article, states must refrain from any use of cultural property and its surroundings, situated within their own territory as well as within the territory of other states, for military purposes and from any act of hostility directed against such property. States also must prohibit, prevent and stop theft, pillage or misappropriation of, and acts of vandalism directed against, cultural property, and must refrain from reprisals against cultural property and from requisitioning movable cultural property situated in another state.

---

19 Ultimately, HR arts 25 and 28 (concerning the protection of objects) provide protection to 'cultural' objects.

20 See API art 52(1). For the applicability of the general prohibition of attacks on civilian objects in both international and non-international armed conflict, see eg *Prosecutor v Strugar* (Case no IT-01-42-T, ICTY Trial Chamber II, 31 January 2005) ¶ 224; *Prosecutor v Tadić* (*Decision on the Defence Motion for Interlocutory Appeal on Jurisdiction*) (Case no IT-94-1, ICTY Appeals Chamber, 2 October 1995) (*Tadić Jurisdiction Decision*) ¶¶ 100, 111 and 127.

21 API art 53; APII art 16.

22 1954 Convention (n 6) art 4(5).

In relation to the first-mentioned obligation in Article 4, the distinction needs to be made between the use of cultural property itself for military purposes and the use of the immediate surroundings of cultural property for such purposes. It should be noted, however, that this article does not specify when cultural property or its surroundings are to be considered to be 'used' for military purposes. As discussed below, Article 8 of the Convention provides some guidance on this subject.

Where the second-mentioned obligation in Article 4 is concerned, the Convention proscribes not only acts of hostility which result in actual damage to, or the destruction of, cultural property but also any act of hostility 'directed' against cultural property. But, as with the use of cultural property for military purposes, the Convention does not provide a definition of acts of hostility.

In accordance with Article 4(2) of the Convention, the only exception to the obligations related to the use of cultural property and its surroundings for military purposes and to the prohibition on attacks against cultural property is imperative military necessity. It follows that not only can the attacking party invoke military necessity when cultural property is being used for military purposes by the opposing party, but also the party that is holding cultural property can do the same where such use is imperatively required by military necessity. Attacks on cultural property in Kosovo in the 1990s by Serb forces where these forces alleged the use of such property for military purposes by the Kosovo Albanians is an example of the former. The use of the Samarra Minaret in Iraq, in 2005, by American forces as a sniper post exemplifies the latter justification.

However, neither Article 4(2), nor the remainder of the Convention, specifically defines the concept of 'imperative military necessity'. This was considered to be one of the major weaknesses of the Convention. As countless attacks on cultural property throughout history of warfare have shown, the concept of military necessity can be very elastic.[23] The often-cited bombing of Monte Cassino in 1943 by the Allied forces[24] and the more recent shelling of the Old City of Dubrovnik in 1991 by the Yugoslav Army[25] are powerful examples of the 'elasticity' of the term 'military necessity'.

The 1977 Additional Protocols provide both indirect and direct protection to cultural property. The former is ensured by Article 52 of Additional Protocol I, protecting objects of cultural property by virtue of their civilian character. This article provides protection for civilian objects by prohibiting attacks on non-military objectives. It defines civilian objects as 'all objects which are not military objectives' and it spells out that civilian objects must not be attacked or be the object of reprisals.[26] Military objectives are limited to objects which 'by their nature, location, purpose or use make an effective contribution to military action *and* whose total or partial destruction, capture or neutralization, in the circumstances ruling at the time, offers a definite military advantage'.[27] If there is doubt whether an object that is normally considered to be civilian, is used to make an effective contribution to military action, the presumption is that an object is not to be so used. In determining whether an object is to be considered a military objective both requirements of the definition must be met and those requirements must be fulfilled *at the time of making a decision and thus not sometime in the past*. As discussed below, the definition of 'military objective' in Article 52(2) of Additional Protocol I remedies the weaknesses

---

23 See eg Patrick Boylan, *Review of the Convention for the Protection of Cultural Property in the Event of Armed Conflict* (UNESCO Publishing 1993) ¶ 4.9.

24 Ibid ¶ 2.44.

25 See eg *Strugar* (n 20) ¶¶ 182, 194, 202–203.

26 API art 52(1).

27 Ibid art 52(2) (emphasis added).

of the 1954 Convention concerning the concept of military necessity. The provisions of Article 52 have become part of customary international law and as such bind all states that are parties to international armed conflict.[28] Additional Protocol II does not contain any corresponding provisions. Nevertheless, the applicability of the general rule that prohibits attacks on civilian objects is also extended to non-international armed conflicts.[29]

Article 53 of Additional Protocol I and Article 16 of Additional Protocol II respectively provide direct protection to cultural property. Pursuant to these articles it is prohibited to direct any acts of hostility against three categories of objects, namely, 'historic monuments, works of art or places of worship'. To be accorded protection, these objects must 'constitute the cultural or spiritual heritage of peoples'. As with the prohibition in Article 4 of the 1954 Convention, this is a strict prohibition; for a violation to have occurred it is not necessary that actual damage to, or destruction of, cultural objects has taken place – it is enough that acts of hostility are being 'directed' against such objects.

Both Articles 53 and 16 also prohibit the use of cultural property 'in support of military effort'. Unlike Article 4 of the 1954 Convention, these articles do not make any reference to the use of immediate surroundings of cultural property for military purposes or of the appliances in use for its protection. However, like the Convention, the 1977 Additional Protocols are silent on the definition of the 'use in support of' military effort. As far as 'military effort' is concerned, a range of both passive and active military activities can fall under the umbrella of this concept.[30]

In contrast to the 1954 Convention, Articles 53 and 16 of the 1977 Additional Protocols I and II respectively do not make any reference to military necessity. Instead, the concept of 'military objective' is to be applied meaning that even if an object of cultural property is being used in support of the military effort that does not automatically turn it into a military target. In accordance with Article 52 of Additional Protocol I, attacks must be limited strictly to military objectives. In other words, the use of the protected object must make an 'effective' contribution to military action. In addition to this, total or partial destruction, capture or neutralisation of such an object must offer a 'definite' military advantage. Such advantage must exist 'at the time' of ruling and not in the past. But even then the right to attack is not unlimited as the principle of proportionality must be respected and other feasible precautionary measures must be taken.[31]

The 1907 Hague Regulations especially protect several categories of objects, only some of which constitute 'cultural property'. In Article 27, the Hague Regulations provide protection in sieges and bombardments to 'buildings dedicated to religion, art, science, or charitable purposes, historic monuments, hospitals, and places where the sick and wounded are collected' provided that these objects are not used 'at the time' for military purposes. On this condition these objects are to be 'spare[d] as far as possible'. While Article 27 does specify that it is not the use of cultural property for military purposes at any point in time but only the use 'at the time' that is relevant here (meaning no past or future (anticipated) use could provide justification for an attack), the Hague Regulations do not define the concept of 'use for military purposes'. For guidance, the ICTY Trial Chamber in *Kordić* resorted to Article 8 of the 1954 Convention, applicable to 'special protection' of cultural property, noting that 'there is little difference between the conditions for according of general and those for the provision of special

28 See eg *Strugar* (n 20) ¶ 223.
29 Ibid ¶ 224.
30 See eg *AP Commentary* ¶ 2078.
31 See API arts 51(5)(b), 57 and 58. See also Petrovic (n 5) 165–166 and fn 244 and 245.

protection'.[32] In this Chamber's view '[t]he fundamental principle is that protection of whatever type will be lost if cultural property ... is used for military purposes, and this principle is consistent with the custom codified in Article 27 of the Hague Regulations'.[33]

Article 56 of the Hague Regulations accords protection to similar categories of objects. Only this article applies to 'military authority over the territory of the hostile state'. Unlike the 1954 Convention and 1977 Additional Protocols, which prohibit attacks 'directed' against cultural property, here the Hague Regulations prohibit all seizure of, destruction or wilful damage 'done' to the protected objects. Thus for a violation of this article to occur it is necessary that these proscribed acts have taken place or that there has been actual destruction or damage to the protected objects.

Pursuant to Article 23(g) of the Hague Regulations, destruction or seizure of enemy's property generally is forbidden. The only exception is imperative military necessity. However, like its successor, the 1954 Convention, the Hague Regulations do not define this concept.

As it has already been noted, the 1999 Protocol addresses the major weaknesses of the 1954 Convention, including the exception of 'imperative military necessity' central to the respect for cultural property. In accordance with Article 6 of this Protocol, imperative military necessity may only be invoked to 'direct' an act of hostility against cultural property

> when and for as long as that property has, by its *function*, been made into a military objective and there is no feasible alternative available to obtain a similar military advantage to that offered by directing an act of hostility against that objective.[34]

This article links the concept of imperative military necessity with the concept of military objective envisaged by Article 52 of Additional Protocol I. However, Article 6 of the 1999 Protocol limits itself only to objects which by their 'function' are made into a military objective. In *Strugar*, the Trial Chamber pointed to the 1999 Protocol in this regard. The Trial Chamber noted that the protection of cultural property is waived 'when and for as long as (i) that cultural property has, by its function [and not by other ways referred to in Article 52(2) of Additional Protocol I], been made into a military objective'.[35]

The same article of the 1999 Protocol also envisages the exception of imperative military necessity

> to use cultural property for purposes which are likely to expose it to destruction or damage when and for as long as no choice is possible between such use of the cultural property and another feasible method for obtaining a similar military advantage.[36]

Additionally, Article 6 of the Protocol specifies the decision-making level[37] and, in case of an attack on a cultural property object which has become a legitimate military objective, it imposes the requirement of an effective advance warning wherever possible.[38]

---

32 *Prosecutor v Kordić* (Case no IT-95-14/2-T, ICTY Trial Chamber III, 26 February 2001) ¶ 362.
33 Ibid.
34 1999 Protocol (n 10) art 6(a) (emphasis added).
35 *Strugar* (n 20) fn 957. See also Jean-Marie Henckaerts, 'New Rules for the Protection of Cultural Property in Armed Conflict' (1999) 835 *IRRC* 593.
36 1999 Protocol (n 10) art 6(b).
37 Ibid art 6(c).
38 Ibid art 6(d).

Respect for cultural property is further reinforced by the obligation of states to take precautions in attack[39] and also precautions against the effects of hostilities.[40] The specific reference is also made to protection of cultural property in occupied territory.[41]

In addition to the safeguarding of and respect for cultural property, the issue of distinctive marking also deserves attention in the context of cultural property protection in armed conflict. The purpose of marking cultural property by a distinctive emblem is to facilitate its recognition in case of an attack. Some have criticised distinctive marking as they believe that such marking provides the enemy with a potential 'target list'.[42] The events in the territory of the former Yugoslavia during the armed conflicts in the 1990s proved that marked cultural property was indeed a particularly favoured target. For instance, the protective flags displaying the distinctive emblem of the 1954 Convention that flew in the Old City of Dubrovnik attracted shelling by the Yugoslav Army forces in 1991.[43]

The 1907 Hague Regulations envisage distinctive marking in Article 27(2). This article imposes a duty on the besieged to mark the presence of the protected buildings or places by 'distinctive and visible signs' and to notify such signs to the enemy beforehand. The Hague Regulations do not, however, describe a distinctive emblem. This question is dealt with in Article 5 of the 1907 Convention IX.

The 1954 Convention also envisages distinctive marking.[44] The distinctive emblem is defined in Article 16 of the Convention and the conditions under which it can be used are specified in the following article. Unlike the Hague Regulations, the 1954 Convention does not impose a duty on the holder of cultural property under the 'general protection' to mark such property. The distinctive marking for such property is entirely at the discretion of the holder of such property. While the absence of a distinctive emblem does not affect the obligation to respect cultural property under general protection, it may, nevertheless, lessen the responsibility of the opposing party in the event of bombardment where the presence of cultural property is not clearly visible.[45]

In contrast to cultural property under 'general protection', cultural property under 'special protection' must be marked with a distinctive emblem.[46] In accordance with Article 20(2) of the 1954 Regulations, the emblem must be clearly visible in daylight from the air as well as from the ground. The duty to mark cultural property under 'special protection' relates to far fewer objects and sites than to cultural property under 'general protection'.

3.2 Special protection of cultural property

Pursuant to Article 8 of the 1954 Convention, only a limited number of refuges intended to shelter movable cultural property in armed conflict, and of centres containing monuments and other immovable cultural property, may be placed under 'special protection'. Such cultural

---

39 Ibid art 7.
40 Ibid art 8.
41 Ibid art 9.
42 See eg Jeffrey Levin, 'Cultural Heritage under Fire' (1992) 7.1 *Conservation Perspectives: The Getty Conservation Institute Newsletter* ¶ 5, www.getty.edu/conservation/publications/newsletters/7_1/cultural.html.
43 See eg Karen Detling, 'Eternal Silence: The Destruction of Cultural Property in Yugoslavia' (1993) 17 *Maryland JILT* 41, 66–68 and nn 155 and 156.
44 1954 Convention (n 6) art 6.
45 See Toman (n 8) 90.
46 1954 Convention (n 6) art 10.

property must be 'of very great importance' and it has to fulfil a number of requirements specified in Article 8, including its entry in the Register of Cultural Property under Special Protection.[47]

The system of special protection accords immunity to cultural property by prohibiting acts of hostility directed against such property and any use of such property or its surroundings for military purposes.[48] The immunity may be withdrawn only in exceptional cases of 'unavoidable military necessity'. In contrast to the vague concept of imperative military necessity in Article 4, Article 11 of the Convention is rather more specific. Article 11(2) provides that immunity shall be withdrawn from cultural property under special protection 'for such time as that necessity continues', that such necessity 'can be established only by the officer commanding force the equivalent of division in size or larger' and that '[w]henever circumstances permit, the opposing Party shall be notified, a reasonable time in advance, of the decision to withdraw immunity'.

For a number of reasons, the system of 'special protection' has been unsuccessful, however. The Register of Cultural Property under Special Protection contains less than a symbolic number of inscriptions (currently, one refuge for sheltering movable cultural property in Austria and three refuges in the Netherlands, and one centre containing monuments – Stato della Citta del Vaticano). This led to the third system of protection of cultural property, the so-called 'enhanced protection' introduced in the 1999 Protocol.

3.3 Enhanced protection of cultural property

The system of enhanced protection is governed by Articles 10–14 of the 1999 Protocol. Under Article 10 of the Protocol three conditions have to be met before cultural property is included in the List of Cultural Property under Enhanced Protection, namely, it must be cultural heritage of the greatest importance for humanity, it must be protected by adequate domestic legal and administrative measures recognising its exceptional cultural and historical value and ensuring the highest level of protection and, finally, it is not used for military purposes or to shield military sites. The system of enhanced protection is aimed at eventually replacing the system of special protection.

In terms of the level of protection for cultural property under general protection and cultural property under enhanced protection ultimately there is not much difference. The only difference between these two systems of protection is that the holder of cultural property under enhanced protection cannot convert such property into a military objective whereas this is possible for the holder of cultural property under general protection. Notwithstanding this, the 1999 Protocol regime is predicted to be more successful than the general protection regime. As discussed, the Protocol addresses the major weaknesses of the 1954 Convention in the meaningful way (that is, clarifies the concept of 'military necessity', specifies offences for breaches of norms of the Convention and introduces the mode of so-called 'enhanced protection' which ultimately 'relaxes' the requirements relevant to the mode of 'special protection').

4 International and non-international armed conflict

Except for Additional Protocol II, all of the discussed legal instruments apply to international armed conflict. However, with the exception of the 1907 Hague Regulations, these instruments also contain provisions extending some protection to cultural property in non-international

---

47 Ibid art 8(6).
48 Ibid art 9.

armed conflict. Article 19 of the 1954 Convention, for example, provides that in the event of such conflict parties to the conflict will be bound, as a minimum, by the most important provision of the Convention – Article 4 regulating respect for cultural property. In addition to this, Article 19 obligates the parties to the conflict to endeavour to bring into force by special agreement all or part of the other provisions of the Convention. Armed conflicts not of an international character are also dealt with in Article 22 of the 1999 Protocol ('This protocol shall apply in the event of an armed conflict not of an international character, occurring within the territory of one of the Parties.').

Additional Protocol II in its entirety governs non-international armed conflicts. This protocol is significantly briefer than Additional Protocol I which governs international armed conflict. However, as discussed, Article 16 of Additional Protocol II and Article 53 of Additional Protocol I which deal with the protection of cultural property are almost identical. The only difference is that Article 16 does not contain references to 'other relevant international instruments' or to the prohibition to make cultural property 'the object of reprisals' whereas both are included in Article 53.

While Additional Protocol II does not contain the general rule prohibiting attacks on civilian objects that is contained in Additional Protocol I, this rule is, nevertheless and as already discussed, considered a norm of customary international law applicable to international and non-international armed conflicts alike.[49] However, some other important provisions relevant to cultural property protection which are included in Additional Protocol I are also absent from Additional Protocol II. For example, only Protocol I contains provisions on grave breaches, where, pursuant to Article 85, attacks directed against cultural property may under certain circumstances qualify as a grave breach and may thus be regarded as a war crime.[50] Additional Protocol II, in contrast, is silent on violations in non-international armed conflicts.

5 The interaction between the LOAC and international criminal law

5.1 Normative level

Article 85 of Additional Protocol I deals with grave breaches of the Protocol. Those breaches are regarded as war crimes, entailing individual criminal responsibility. Subparagraph (4)(d) of this article defines a 'grave breach' in relation to cultural property. However, this is a complex and imprecise provision which goes beyond the Additional Protocol I as it implies special protection of cultural property 'given by special arrangement, for example, within the framework of a competent international organisation'.[51]

Under Article 56 of the 1907 Hague Regulations, all seizure of, destruction of or wilful damage done to protected property 'should' be made the subject of legal proceedings. Similarly soft wording is used in Article 56 of the 1899 Hague Regulations. Article 28 of the 1954 Convention, titled 'sanctions', also using soft wording, spells out that the High Contracting Parties 'undertake to take', within the framework of their ordinary criminal jurisdiction, measures to prosecute and punish those responsible for breaches of the Convention. Notwithstanding the reference to universal jurisdiction in case of such breaches there has been a failure at the implementation level. One of the major reasons for this failure has been the absence of a list of possible violations of the Convention and the concomitant silence of the Convention on the

---

49 See eg *Strugar* (n 20) ¶ 224.
50 See API art 85(4)(d).
51 See eg Toman (n 8) 392. See also, Petrovic (n 5) 202–204.

concrete sanctions that should be imposed. The former was remedied by Article 15 of the 1999 Protocol which obligates states to criminalise five serious violations specified by this article. Under Article 18 of the Protocol, states are under an obligation either to try or to extradite persons responsible for these violations. Concrete sanctions are left to be regulated by domestic law.

5.2 The trials in the aftermath of the World Wars

The first attempt of the international community to react collectively to damage to cultural property occurred in response to the devastation perpetrated during the First World War. After the war, in January 1919, the Allied Commission on Responsibility for War and Guarantees was established with the aim of collecting evidence concerning attacks against cultural property.[52] Based on the subsequently adopted Treaty of Versailles, Germans accused of war crimes would be tried by military tribunals of the victorious Allies.[53] This was rejected by the Germans who even threatened the resumption of the war if the Allies pursued this initiative. Eventually, the Germans agreed to try their nationals for war crimes by their own national court – the *Reichsgericht* in Leipzig – but by applying international law, which would introduce the 'international' component into such trials. However, the Leipzig trials were farcical. Only six out of 896 war crimes suspects were tried and convicted. Those who were imprisoned immediately 'escaped'.

The first truly international enforcement of international law protecting cultural property in armed conflict took place after the Second World War with the establishment of the IMT at Nuremberg. Under Article 6(b) of the IMT Charter, cultural property was covered by 'war crimes' under the rubric of 'plunder of public or private property'. Despite the grave damage that cultural property suffered during the Second World War, such property was not given as prominent place at the IMT as is often assumed. Given the absence of any direct reference to cultural property in the IMT Charter it is not surprising that cultural property did not have a prominent place in the IMT Indictment. The indictment addressed cultural property in an unsystematic manner and squeezed it in between other types of property such as raw materials and agricultural livestock including cows, pigs and poultry. The IMT judgment focused on the 'seizure' of movable cultural property and centred its discussion on the defendant Alfred Rosenberg, the organiser of the 'Einsatzstab Rosenberg', who was infamous for a massive art seizure.[54] Rosenberg was found guilty on all counts of the indictment, including those relating to cultural property,[55] and sentenced to death.[56] In Lippman's words, this sentence constituted 'unprecedented criminal punishment for art theft by international tribunal'.[57]

While the IMT's focus on Rosenberg and on movable cultural property is of special importance, it is regrettable that the IMT judgment did not discuss or explicitly impose punishment for the plunder of cultural property in relation to other defendants who were also involved in the seizure of cultural property. It is also disappointing that the judgment, except for a few tangential references, did not discuss the destruction of immovable cultural property.

---

52 See eg Toman (n 8) 14.
53 Treaty of Peace between the Allied and Associated Powers and Germany (Treaty of Versailles) (28 June 1919) 225 CTS 188.
54 See *US v Göring* (n 13) 411, 495.
55 Ibid 497.
56 Ibid 529.
57 See Matthew Lippman, 'Art and Ideology in the Third Reich: The Protection of Cultural Property and the Humanitarian Law of War' (1998) 17 *Dickinson JIL* 1, 48.

Cultural property was even more 'invisible' in the International Military Tribunal for the Far East (IMTFE) Charter and the IMTFE's indictment and judgment.[58] For example, a great many private and public libraries were destroyed in the Pacific theatre of war, including the National University of Tsing Hua, Peking, where 200,000 out of a collection of 350,000 volumes were destroyed, the University Nan-kài, T'ien-chin, where more than 224,000 volumes were lost as a result of bombing in July 1937 and the University of Nanking, where 10 per cent of collections disappeared after 1939,[59] yet this tribunal did not address specifically these (or any other) losses of cultural property.

The ad hoc nature of these two tribunals reduced their deterrent effect. In the absence of a permanent international enforcement mechanism, cultural property continued to be destroyed from one armed conflict to another with impunity. In the more than 300 armed conflicts that have taken place since the end of the Second World War a countless number of cultural objects has been affected by warfare. However, it was not until the 'cultural genocide' took place in the territory of the former Yugoslavia in the 1990s, following the dissolution of this state, that charges involving cultural property have been dealt with by another ad hoc international criminal tribunal – this time the ICTY.

5.3 Post-IMT and IMTFE tribunals

Unlike the IMT Charter and the IMTFE Charter, the ICTY Statute (although it also does not use the term 'cultural property') explicitly refers to some types of objects that constitute cultural property. Cultural property is directly covered by Article 3(d) of the Statute (which is based on the 1907 Hague Regulations) – seizure of, destruction or wilful damage done to institutions dedicated to religion, charity and education, the arts and science, historic monuments and works of art and science constitutes a violation of the laws or customs of war. Cultural property is also dealt with indirectly by the ICTY Statute, including Article 5(h), as the crime against humanity – persecution.

In contrast to the IMT, the ICTY focuses on immovable cultural property. A number of individuals have been prosecuted, tried and convicted, *inter alia*, for unlawful attacks on cultural property. The so-called 'Dubrovnik' cases relating to the 1991 attack on the Old City of Dubrovnik,[60] Croatia, by the Yugoslav Army, and the *Prlić et al* case,[61] involving the 1993 deliberate destruction of the Old Bridge of Mostar, Bosnia and Herzegovina, by Croat forces, both of which are World Heritage sites, are the most prominent ICTY cases concerning cultural property.

However, due to various factors, including the magnitude of other crimes within the ICTY's jurisdiction and the ICTY's limited resources, cultural property-related offences have been

---

58 *US et al v Araki et al*, 22 Tokyo War Crimes Trial 48413 (International Military Tribunal for the Far East 1948). See Sanja Zgonjanin, 'Destruction of Libraries and Archives as a War Crime' (2005) 40 *Libraries and Culture* 128, 131–134 (discussing the destruction of the Shanghai Library by Japanese forces during the Second World War). See also Hans van der Hoeven and Joan van Albada, *Lost Memory: Libraries and Archives Destroyed in the Twentieth Century* (UNESCO 1996) 4 (referring, *inter alia*, to the 'rape of Nanking', considered as one of the worst atrocities during the Second World War, where as a result of the Sino-Japanese war, which started in 1937, hundreds of thousands of books were lost in China).

59 Van der Hoeven and van Albada (n 58) 8.

60 See eg *Prosecutor v Jokić (Sentencing)* (Case no IT-01-42/1-S, ICTY Trial Chamber I, 18 March 2004); *Strugar* (n 20).

61 See *Prosecutor v Prlić et al (Amended Indictment)* (Case no IT-04-74-AI, ICTY Prosecutor, 16 November 2005); *Prosecutor v Prlić et al* (Case no IT-04-74-T, ICTY Trial Chamber, 29 May 2013).

somewhat marginalised by this tribunal.[62] Despite this, the jurisprudence of the ICTY concerning the unlawful attacks on cultural property, together with lessons learnt from the IMT, has influenced the criminalisation of such attacks by the ICC.

The inclusion of cultural property-related offences among 'the most serious crimes of concern to the international community as a whole'[63] in the Rome Statute demonstrates the determination of the international community to 'put an end to impunity for the perpetrators of these crimes',[64] and, at the same time, emphasises the importance of preserving cultural property. The ICC has jurisdiction over crimes involving cultural property under the rubric of war crimes ('other serious violations of the laws and customs of international law', which is, like Article 3(d) of the ICTY Statute, based on the 1907 Hague Regulations)[65] and crimes against humanity (persecution).[66] Like the ICTY Statute, the Rome Statute takes an anthropocentric approach to cultural property, which creates tension with the universal value of cultural property. With this in mind, and also given the primacy of human life and the magnitude of crimes against human beings (as opposed to crimes against property) usually committed in armed conflicts, as well as the fact that the ICC, like any other international tribunal, deals only with the most serious crimes and only indicts the most serious persons responsible for such crimes, it is unlikely that cultural property-related offences will be much more 'visible' at this court than they have been at the earlier ad hoc tribunals.

Another reason for caution where the prosecution of crimes involving cultural property is concerned relates to the principle of complementarity. Under this principle, the responsibility to prosecute crimes over which the ICC has jurisdiction lies primarily with domestic courts. However, states have been perennially reluctant to prosecute war crimes generally, let alone crimes concerning cultural property. Nevertheless, since the Rome Statute criminalises unlawful attacks on cultural property, the possibility always exists for the prosecution to be carried out at the international level in the event that a national court is unwilling or genuinely unable to act. At the time of writing, one such situation is before the ICC, namely, the Mali situation, involving the destruction of mausoleums and archives in Timbuktu in 2012. *Prosecutor v al-Faqi al-Mahdi* is the first ICC case exclusively concerning wilful attacks on

---

62 For a discussion about the ICTY's approach to cultural property, see eg Theodor Meron, 'The Protection of Cultural Property in the Event of Armed Conflict within the Case-Law of the International Criminal Tribunal for the Former Yugoslavia' (2005) 57 *Museum International* 41; Frits Kalshoven, 'The Protection of Cultural Property in the Event of Armed Conflict within the Framework of International Humanitarian Law' (2005) 57 *Museum International* 61; Micaela Frulli, 'Advancing the Protection of Cultural Property through the Implementation of Individual Criminal Responsibility: The Case-Law of the International Criminal Tribunal for the Former Yugoslavia' (2005) 15 *Italian YBIL* 195; Michael Bothe, 'War Crimes' in Antonio Cassese, Paola Gaeta and John R W D Jones (eds), *The Rome Statute of the International Criminal Court: A Commentary* (2002) 379; Petrovic (n 5).

63 Rome Statute preamble ¶ 4.

64 Ibid ¶ 5. For a discussion on the criminalisation of offences against cultural property taken by the Rome Statute, see eg Michaela Frulli, 'The Criminalization of Offences against Cultural Heritage in Times of Armed Conflict: The Quest for Consistency' (2011) 22 *EJIL* 203; Yaron Gottlieb, 'Criminalizing Destruction of Cultural Property: A Proposal for Defining New Crimes under the Rome Statute of the ICC' (2004–2005) 23 *Pennsylvania State ILR* 857.

65 Ibid arts 8(2)(b)(ix) and 8(2)(e)(iv).

66 Ibid art 7(1)(h).

cultural property.[67] At the same time, another cultural catastrophe, equally warranting the ICC's attention, has been taking place in the ongoing armed conflict in Syria where cultural property has been deliberately targeted for ideological reasons, archaeological sites have been looted on an industrial scale and illicit trafficking in cultural objects has reached an unprecedented level.[68]

6 Conclusion

As with other areas of the LOAC, rules providing protection to cultural property in times of armed conflict have generally developed in response to certain events. This is not necessarily a bad thing. By acknowledging the notion of common heritage and thus recognising that an enemy's cultural property ultimately belongs to all humankind, the international community has been continuously striving to improve protection of precious cultural treasures from the horrors of warfare. Those efforts have resulted in a considerable number of norms which form part of both customary and treaty international law, applicable to international and, to a lesser extent, to non-international armed conflict. Despite some weaknesses, those norms provide for comprehensive protection of cultural property in armed conflict; when combined, they make it almost impossible for belligerents to justify an attack on cultural objects. Although not the only or perfect mechanisms, international tribunals remain important means of enforcing these norms and thereby honouring humanity's duty to protect cultural property.

---

67 *Prosecutor v al-Faqi al-Mahdi* (Case no ICC-01/12-01/15, ICC Pre-Trial Chamber I). Confirmation of charges hearing began on 18 January 2016. Note that the statutes of other international criminal tribunals or 'hybrid' tribunals (mixed international–national tribunals) only sporadically deal with cultural property. ICTR Statute art 4(f) and SCSL Statute art 3(f) directly mention only pillage as a war crime concerned with cultural property. Like the ICTY Statute and the Rome Statute, these two tribunals do not make any reference to the 1954 Convention. Law on the Extraordinary Chambers of Cambodia art 7 is the only provision in the statutes of international criminal tribunals or mixed criminal tribunals which explicitly makes such a reference.

68 See eg UNITAR report by its UNOSAT programme that has revealed large-scale destruction and damage to cultural heritage sites in Syria, including cultural property inscribed on the UNESCO World Heritage List, UNOSAT, 'Satelite-Based Damage Assessment to Cultural Heritage Sites in Syria' (22 December 2014), www.unitar.org/unosat-report-damage-cultural-heritage-sites-syria-calls-scaled-protection-efforts/. See also Jadranka Petrovic and Rebecca Hughes, 'The Syrian Conflict and the Use of Cultural Property for Military Purposes' in Jadranka Petrovic (ed), *Accountability for Violations of International Humanitarian Law: Essays in Honour of Tim McCormack* (Routledge 2015) 136.

22

The protection of the environment

Roberta Arnold

1 Introduction

1.1 A brief history

The birth of modern international environmental law (IEL) can be traced back to the eighteenth and nineteenth centuries,[1] with the adoption of the first public health measures and industrialisation.[2] Timid efforts were also undertaken to limit the negative effects of warfare on the environment, with the adoption of 'anthropocentric'[3] treaties like the 1925 Geneva Gas Protocol.[4] Recognition that the environment itself requires protection from the effects of armed conflicts, however, coincides with the Vietnam War (1955–1970),[5] during which new techniques and methods of warfare were employed – such as the use of 'cloud-seeding', napalm and chemical defoliants – which have resulted in long-term contamination and significant destruction of forests and wildlife.[6] On 16 December 1969, the UN General

---

1 Cf Peter H Sand, *The History and Origin of International Environmental Law* (Edward Elgar 2015)
2 Philippe Sands and Jacqueline Peel, *Principles of International Environmental Law* (3rd edn, CUP 2012) 23–25; Karen Hulme, *War Torn Environment: Interpreting the Legal Threshold* (Martinus Nijhoff Publishers 2004) 6; Jessica C Lawrence and Kevin Jon Heller, 'The Limits of Article 8(2)(b)(iv) of the Rome Statute, the First Ecocentric Environmental War Crime' (2007) 20 *Georgetown International Environmental Law Review* 61, 63 et seq.
3 Julian Wyatt, 'Law-Making at the Intersection of International Environmental, Humanitarian and Criminal Law: The Issue of Damage to the Environment in International Armed Conflict' (2010) 92(879) *IRRC* 593, 606.
4 Protocol for the Prohibition of the Use of Asphyxiating, Poisonous or Other Gases, and of Bacteriological Methods of Warfare (8 February 1928) 2138 UNTS 65.
5 Hulme (n 2) 9 and 72; Stefan Oeter, 'Methods and Means of Warfare' in Dieter Fleck (ed), *The Handbook of Humanitarian Law in Armed Conflicts* (2nd edn, OUP 2008) 116; Wyatt (n 3) 603, 607; Michael N Schmitt, 'Green War: An Assessment of the Environmental Law of International in Armed Conflict' in Michael N Schmitt (ed), *Essays on Law and War at the Fault Lines* (TMC Asser 2012) 361, 372.
6 Sandesh Sivakumaran, *The Law of Non-International Armed Conflict* (OUP 2012) 397; A P V Rogers, *Law on the Battlefield* (2nd edn, Manchester University Press 2004) 163, citing Hilaire McCoubrey; Marco Sassòli, Antoine A Bouvier and Anne Quintin (eds), *How Does Law Protect in War?* (3rd edn, ICRC 2011) ii, case 38, 9.

Assembly endeavoured to extend the scope of the 1925 Geneva Gas Protocol to chemical or biological agents intended to cause disease in or have direct toxic effects on 'man, animals or plants'.[7] The Stockholm Principles, a soft law instrument adopted in 1972, called upon states to cooperate to develop further international law regarding liability for environmental damage and to 'strive to reach prompt agreement, in the relevant international organs, on the elimination and complete destruction of [nuclear] weapons'.[8] To provide more 'teeth', in 1976 states adopted the Convention on the Prohibition of Military or Any Other Hostile Use of Environmental Modification Techniques (ENMOD Convention)[9] and in 1977 Additional Protocols I and II to the Geneva Conventions of 1949. Further endeavours led to the adoption of soft-law tools like the 1982 World Charter for Nature[10] and the 1992 Rio Declaration.[11] In 1992, the UN General Assembly urged member states to take all measures to ensure compliance with existing international law on the protection of the environment during armed conflict and recommended implementation into military manuals and dissemination.[12] In 1994, following the second Gulf War, when extensive pollution was caused by the intentional destruction of over 600 oil wells in Kuwait by the retreating Iraqi army,[13] the ICRC launched its Guidelines on environmental protection during armed conflict.[14] Although the General Assembly did not formally approve them, at its forty-ninth session it invited all states to disseminate and incorporate them into military manuals.[15] A further legal development has been the entry into force of the Rome Statute of the ICC in 2002, codifying certain war crimes against the environment.[16]

Environmental damages have been raised in relation to NATO's Kosovo intervention in 1999, when dozens of industrial sites were bombed, leading to toxic chemical contamination at several hotspots,[17] as well as to the Israel–Lebanese conflict in 2006, when an estimated 12,000 to 15,000 tons of fuel oil were released into the Mediterranean Sea following the bombing of the Jiyeh power station,[18] or Israel's intervention in the Gaza Strip in December 2008–2009, 'severely contaminating soils and potentially contaminating groundwater with rainfall'.[19]

---

7 1925 Gas Protocol (n 4); UNGA Res 2603 (XXIV) (16 December 1969).

8 Declaration of the United Nations Conference on the Human Environment (16 June 1972) 1972 UNYB 319, principles 22 and 26.

9 (10 December 1976) 1108 UNTS 151; see also Hulme (n 2) 11.

10 UNGA Res 37/7 (28 October 1982) ¶¶ 5 and 20.

11 Rio Declaration on Environment and Development, Report of the UN Conference on Environment and Development, Annex I, UN Doc A/Conf. 151/26 (12 August 1992).

12 UNGA Res 47/37 (25 November 1992).

13 United Nations Environment Programme (UNEP), 'Protecting the Environment during Armed Conflict: An Inventory and Analysis of International Law' (November 2009) 6, http://postconflict.unep. ch/publications/int_law.pdf.

14 ICRC, 'Guidelines for Military Manuals and Instructions on the Protection of the Environment in Times of Armed Conflict' Annex, UN Doc A/49/323 (14 August 1994), reprinted in (1996) 36 (311) IRRC 232 ('ICRC Guidelines'); Michael Bothe, Carl Bruch, Jordan Diamond and David Jensen, 'International Law Protecting the Environment during Armed Conflict: Gaps and Opportunities' (2010) 92(879) IRRC 569, 573; Wyatt (n 3) 598.

15 UNGA Res 49/50 (9 December 1994).

16 Rome Statute art 8(2)(b)(iv).

17 UNEP (n 13) 6.

18 Ibid 7.

19 Wyatt (n 3) 598.

In 2009, the United Nations Environment Programme (UNEP) published its report, 'Protecting the Environment during Armed Conflict',[20] which recognises that: 'Modern conflicts also cause extensive destruction and degradation of the environment. In turn environmental damage which often extends beyond the borders of conflict-affected countries, can threaten the lives and livelihoods of people well after peace agreements are signed.'[21]

1.2 The definition of 'environmental law' and 'environment'

IEL, which applies in peacetime, is the legal regime that 'comprises those substantive, procedural and institutional rules of international law which have as their primary objective the protection of the environment'.[22] Warfare environmental law (WEL), a working definition used in this chapter, will instead indicate the legal regime encompassing those provisions of the laws of armed conflict (LOAC) that address the protection of the environment.

With regard to the term 'environment', no universal legal definition exists, yet. Treaty-makers have adopted a piecemeal approach by resorting to scientific definitions that focus on its natural components.[23] In the present chapter, the term will be used in the sense of 'natural environment',[24] which, according to the International Law Commission (ILC),

> should be taken broadly to cover the environment of the human race and where the human race develops, as well as areas the preservation of which is of fundamental importance in protecting the environment. These words therefore cover the seas, the atmosphere, climate, forests and other plant cover, fauna, flora and other biological elements.[25]

1.3 The protection of the environment under the LOAC: a fragmented system

When discussing warfare-related environmental issues, the tendency is to think about the effects of war on the environment, rather than the reverse, such as the fact that the lack of natural resources or guaranteeing control over natural resources may be the cause of armed conflicts.[26] The present chapter will focus on the first scenario.

Direct environmental impacts of hostilities may include the destruction of water supply and irrigation systems, the disruption of health services and health-related problems including death, weapon and chemical contamination, surface water and aquifer contamination, and impacts on fauna and flora. Other impacts may be caused indirectly by the victims of armed conflicts, such as deforestation (firewood collection, charcoal production), spread of diseases, surface and sub-surface pollution, over-exploitation of water, over-fishing, over-grazing, desertification.[27]

---

20 UNEP (n 13).
21 Ibid 6.
22 Sands and Peel (n 2) 17.
23 Sands and Peel (n 2) 18–19; Hulme (n 2) 12.
24 The term environment may be larger and encompass, eg humans and human-made structures. Sands and Peel (n 2) 17; Hulme (n 2) 12; Rogers (n 6) 161.
25 Draft Code of Crimes against the Peace and Security of Mankind, UN Doc A/46/19 (1996) ch IV, commentary to art 46.
26 ICRC, 'Framework for Environmental Management in Assistance Programmes' (2010) 92(879) *IRRC* 747, 749; Mara Tignino, 'Water, International Peace, and Security' (2010) 92(879) *IRRC* 647, 648; see the map of Security Council responses to conflicts linked to natural resources (1948–2011) in UNEP (n 13) 15, 84.
27 ICRC, 'Framework' (n 26) 750.

In protecting the environment, WEL appears extremely fragmented. Provisions can be found in specific and general treaties, at the international and domestic levels, with a humanitarian or criminal law objective. It therefore becomes difficult for the military service member to identify the proper code of conduct to be adopted, unless these principles have been translated into military manuals.

Moreover, these rules may be categorised differently, depending on their objective: (a) as preventive measures, to be adopted already in peacetime; (b) as protective measures, to be adopted during armed conflict, for example when targeting; (c) as enforcement measures, aiming at either damage compensation (via, for instance, the UN Compensation Commission)[28] or criminal prosecution.

The first question, thus, is whether this fragmentation creates gaps in the system and how these may be filled. For instance, some IEL treaties, which may be complementary, provide for their continued application during hostilities; others, however, remain silent or state that they are automatically suspended, terminated or inapplicable in the context of armed conflict. The current view is that IEL treaties do not automatically apply during armed conflict, unless they specifically state so,[29] like, for example, the UN Convention on the Law of the Sea.[30] Once simultaneous applicability of WEL and IEL is determined, the next question is their relationship: the current view is that although complementary, WEL constitutes the *lex specialis* and so takes precedence.[31] It is beyond the scope of this chapter to examine this aspect further, but it should be kept in mind when assessing the impacts of a military operation on the environment.

Another question is the level at which protective measures may be adopted and enforced: for example, the ban of a specific weapon may only be taken at the strategic level, whereas the choice to use a lawful weapon in a context where it may damage the environment may have to be taken at the tactical level, say, by a unit commander. Enforcement may, accordingly, follow different regimes: a state that equips its forces with a weapon, notwithstanding ratification of a treaty banning it, may be accountable under the doctrine of state responsibility; a serviceman who uses a self-made unlawful weapon, instead, may be individually accountable under criminal law, with different consequences.

Enforcement may then be hindered by the armed conflict itself: under such circumstances, the level of overall damages may be so high that priority may be given to the protection of humans, rather than the environment. An example is provided by the lack of importance given to the extinction threat to which the Virunga National Park's mountain gorillas, on the border between Rwanda and the Democratic Republic of Congo, were in 1994, and are still, exposed.[32]

In sum, the major problem seems to be the fact that the environment, in times of war, has generally been protected due to its vital function for the human being, not because of its intrinsic value. The current trend, however, seems to have a somewhat more eco-centric approach, as it will be discussed next.

---

28 The UN Compensation Commission was created by UNSC Res 687 (3 April 1991); Sassòli *et al* (n 6), case 38, 22–23; Bothe *et al* (n 14) 603–604.

29 ICRC Guidelines (n 14) ¶ 5; Bothe *et al* (n 14) 570.

30 Ibid 581.

31 Ibid 580, 591; UNEP (n 13) 5, ¶ 8.

32 'Rwanda's Mountain Gorillas Beating Survival Odds' *Chicago Tribune* (4 September 2000), http://news. nationalgeographic.com/news/2002/09/0904_020904_gorillas.html; 'Congo Conflict puts Endangered Mountain Gorillas in Peril' *Agence France-Presse* (24 September 2012), www.rawstory.com/rs/2012/09/24/congo-conflict-puts-endangered-mountain-gorillas-in-peril/.

1.4 Aims and objectives

The aim of the present chapter is to provide an overview of WEL, highlighting the challenges to be addressed. After the introduction, Sections 2 to 4 will list and examine LOAC instruments addressing the environment, Section 5 will discuss enforcement, whereas Section 6 will draw conclusions.

2 General principles of LOAC applied to the environment

There are four core LOAC principles on the conduct of hostilities: military necessity, distinction, proportionality and limitation in the choice of means and method of warfare. These, as stated in Rule 43 of the ICRC Customary International Humanitarian Law Study, qualify as customary law both in international and non-international armed conflicts and apply in the following manner to the natural environment:

A. No part of the natural environment may be attacked, unless it is a military objective.
B. Destruction of any part of the natural environment is prohibited, unless required by imperative military necessity.
C. Launching an attack against a military objective which may be expected to cause incidental damage to the environment which would be excessive in relation to the concrete and direct military advantage anticipated is prohibited.

2.1 The principle of distinction

Paragraph A of Rule 43 restates the general principle of distinction (Rule 7) in relation to the natural environment. The Study goes on to explain:

> The rule that it is prohibited to attack any part of the natural environment unless it is a military objective is based on the general requirement that a distinction be made between military objectives and civilian objects.... This rule is reflected in Protocol III to the Convention on Certain Conventional Weapons, which provides that 'it is prohibited to make forests or other kinds of plant cover the object of attack by incendiary weapons except when such natural elements are used to cover, conceal or camouflage combatants or other military objectives, or are themselves military objectives'. The military manuals and official statements which consider that an area of land may be a military objective if it meets the required conditions also reflect this.[33]

The rule that the natural environment as a non-military object should be taken into account when planning an attack, in observance of the principle of distinction, has also been restated in the above-mentioned ICRC Guidelines.[34]

2.2 The principle of military necessity

Paragraph B of Rule 43 restates the applicability of the principle of military necessity (Rule 50) to the natural environment.[35] The view that its application to the environment is now a

---

33 CIHL commentary to r 43.
34 ICRC Guidelines (n 14); on their history, see Schmitt (n 5) 392; Rogers (n 6) 161.
35 See also Christopher Greenwood, 'Historical Development and Legal Basis' in Fleck (n 5) 30, ¶ 130.

recognised principle of customary law is supported by the ICRC Guidelines,[36] their restatement in military manuals, national legislation and official statements,[37] the 1996 advisory opinion of the ICJ on *Nuclear Weapons*[38] and the Report of the Committee Established to Review the Bombing Campaign Against the Federal Republic of Yugoslavia (NATO Bombing Report).[39] According to the latter:

> Even when targeting admittedly legitimate military objectives, there is a need to avoid excessive long-term damage to the economic infrastructure and natural environment with a consequential adverse effect on the civilian population. Indeed, military objectives should not be targeted if the attack is likely to cause collateral environmental damage which would be excessive in relation to the direct military advantage which the attack is expected to produce.[40]

2.3 The principle of proportionality

The principle of proportionality with regard to the environment is addressed in Paragraph C of Rule 43 of the ICRC Customary Law Study. The application of the principle to the natural environment as a customary rule is supported by the ICRC Guidelines,[41] official statements[42] and the ICJ advisory opinion on *Nuclear Weapons*.[43] State practice, moreover, shows general acceptance that incidental damage affecting the natural environment must not be excessive in relation to the military advantage anticipated from an attack on a military objective.

This principle applies both in cases of international and non-international armed conflicts, meaning that environmental considerations must be made in all targeting processes.[44]

2.4 The Martens Clause and the principle of humanity

There are other important general principles of the LOAC which apply to the natural environment, in addition to the previous core three. Some argue, for instance, that also the Martens Clause, holding that one must have regard for 'the dictates of the public conscience' as stated in the preamble to the 1907 Hague Convention (IV), and the principle of humanity,[45] applies to environmental concerns.[46] The underlying reasoning is that since the environment is necessary for the survival of the human being, its protection may be enforced by applying to it also those so-called 'anthropocentric general principles' that first have the human being as their focus. This line of reasoning can be read in the conclusion of the NATO Bombing Report:

---

36 ICRC Guidelines (n 14) ¶¶ 8, 9.
37 CIHL practice to r 43; Rogers (n 6) 162.
38 *Legality of the Threat or Use of Nuclear Weapons (Advisory Opinion)* [1996] ICJ Reports 226, ¶ 30.
39 ICTY, Final Report of the Committee Established to Review the NATO Bombing Campaign against the Federal Republic of Yugoslavia (13 June 2000) ('NATO Bombing Report'), www.icty.org/sid/10052.
40 Ibid ¶ 18.
41 ICRC Guidelines (n 14) ¶ 13(c).
42 CIHL practice to r 43.
43 *Nuclear Weapons* (n 38) ¶ 30.
44 Yoram Dinstein, 'Protection of the Environment in International Armed Conflict' (2001) 5 *Max Planck Yearbook of United Nations Law* 523, 525.
45 Adam Roberts, 'Failures in Protecting the Environment' in Peter Rowe (ed), *The Gulf War 1990–91 in International and English Law* (Routledge 1993); Rogers (n 6) 162, n 9.
46 Rogers (n 6) 162 (citing Michael Bothe).

Care shall be taken in warfare to protect the natural environment against widespread, long-term and severe damage. This protection includes a prohibition of the use of methods or means of warfare which are intended or may be expected to cause such damage to the natural environment and thereby to prejudice the health or survival of the population.[47]

2.5 Other general rules of the LOAC

In addition to Rule 43 of the ICRC Customary Law Study, Rules 44 and 45 also address the protection of the environment.[48] Rule 44 provides that:

Methods and means of warfare must be employed with due regard to the protection and preservation of the natural environment. In the conduct of military operations, all feasible precautions must be taken to avoid, and in any event to minimise, incidental damage to the environment. Lack of scientific certainty as to the effects on the environment of certain military operations does not absolve a party to the conflict from taking such precautions.

Pursuant to state practice and military manuals,[49] the obligation to take all feasible precautions to avoid, and in any event to minimise, incidental damage to *civilian objects* equally applies to damage to the natural environment, regardless of the nature of the conflict.[50] This principle is a variation of Article 57 of Additional Protocol I, through which the IEL 'precautionary principle' was extended (in a quite revolutionary fashion)[51] to armed conflicts.[52] The potential effects of an attack should be assessed during the planning phase.[53]

Rule 45, in turn, provides as follows:

The use of methods or means of warfare that are intended, or may be expected, to cause widespread, long-term and severe damage to the natural environment is prohibited. Destruction of the natural environment may not be used as a weapon.

This provision restates Articles 35(3) and 55(1) of Additional Protocol I. Even though the proposal to extend Article 35(3) to non-international armed conflicts (NIAC) was rejected in 1977,[54] it can be found in other instruments applicable to NIAC, such as agreements between parties to conflicts,[55] or several military manuals.[56] As a consequence, Rule 45 can be considered as being applicable to all types of conflicts, international and non-international.

Rule 45 contains an absolute prohibition: if the damage is widespread, long term and severe, or if the destruction of the natural environment is used as a weapon, it is irrelevant whether the

---

47 NATO Bombing Report (n 39) ¶ 14(1).
48 On customary WEL, see also Schmitt (n 5) 415 *et seq.*
49 Namely the *United States Naval Handbook* and the official statements of Argentina and Canada, cited in the CIHL practice to r 44.
50 CIHL commentary to r 44.
51 Bothe *et al* (n 14) 575.
52 See *Nuclear Weapons* (n 38) ¶ 32; CIHL practice to r 44.
53 CIHL commentary to r 44.
54 CIHL commentary to r 45.
55 Memorandum of Understanding on the Application of IHL between Croatia and the Socialist Federal Republic of Yugoslavia, ¶ 6; Agreement on the Application of IHL between the Parties to the Conflict in Bosnia and Herzegovina, ¶ 2.5.
56 CIHL practice to r 45.

conduct may have been justified under the principles of military necessity and proportionality.[57] In this regard, Rule 45 differs from Rule 43, which contains a relative prohibition drawn from the 'Geneva law' according to which the environment is a civilian object that may only be attacked *if* justified under general LOAC principles.[58] The absolute prohibition found in Rule 45 is restated in the ICRC Guidelines[59] and in the UN Secretary-General's Bulletin on Observance by UN forces of IHL.[60]

Some state practice with regard to the (questionable) lawfulness of nuclear weapons may be used to challenge the customary nature of Rule 45. A counterargument in this regard, however, is that the use of nuclear weapons would be unlawful already on the basis of the principle of distinction (that is to say, the prohibition of indiscriminate attacks) and the principle of proportionality,[61] so that no exception to Rule 45's application to the environment would be relevant.

3 LOAC treaties addressing directly the protection of the environment

3.1 The ENMOD Convention

The ENMOD Convention[62] was adopted on 10 December 1976 as a reaction to the US military tactics employed in Vietnam.[63] It applies to all state parties, not just those engaged in conflict.[64] Article I(1) provides that:

> Each State Party to this Convention undertakes not to engage in military or any other hostile use of environmental modification techniques having *widespread, long lasting **or** severe effects* as the means of destruction, damage or injury to any other State Party.

It was the understanding of the drafters that, for the purposes of ENMOD, the terms 'widespread', 'long lasting' and 'severe' shall be interpreted as follows:[65]

a   'widespread' – encompassing an area on the scale of several hundred square kilometres;
b   'long-lasting' – lasting for a period of months, or approximately a season;
c   'severe' – involving serious or significant disruption or harm to human life, natural and economic resources or other assets.

---

57 CIHL commentary to r 45.
58 Karen Hulme, 'Taking Care to Protect the Environment against Damage: A Meaningless Obligation?' (2010) 92(879) *IRRC* 675, 678.
59 ICRC Guidelines (n 14) ¶ 11.
60 UN Secretary-General, Secretary-General's Bulletin: Observance by United Nations Forces of International Humanitarian Law, UN Doc ST/SGB/1999/13 (6 August 1999).
61 CIHL commentary to r 45.
62 See n 9; for an analysis, see Schmitt (n 5) 448.
63 Antoine Bouvier, 'Protection of the Natural Environment in time of Armed Conflict' (1991) 285 (31) *IRRC* 567, 606.
64 Rogers (n 6) 166 (citing Szasz).
65 Understandings, in Report of the Conference of the Committee on Disarmament, UN Doc A/31/27 (1976) vol I, 91–92, www.icrc.org/ihl.nsf/FULL/460?OpenDocument. These Understandings, albeit not incorporated into the Convention, were adopted by the drafters in order to provide additional explanations with regard to some provisions.

This interpretation was intended to apply exclusively to the ENMOD Convention and was not intended to prejudice the interpretation of the same or similar terms used in other international agreements,[66] such as Additional Protocol I or Article 8 of the Rome Statute. Since the aim was to keep a low threshold of application in order to encompass all military manipulations of the environment, the criteria are disjunctive.[67]

Pursuant to Article II: 'the term "environmental modification techniques" refers to any technique for changing – through the deliberate manipulation of natural processes – the dynamics, composition or structure of the Earth, including its biota, lithosphere, hydrosphere and atmosphere, or of outer space'. The actions must have been carried out with military or any other hostile purposes.[68]

In summary, Dinstein lists the following requirements:[69]

- The proscribed action must consist of 'manipulation of natural processes', so that the natural process becomes a weapon. Examples are earthquakes, tsunamis, an upset in the ecological balance of a region; changes in climate and weather patterns (clouds, precipitation, cyclones of various types and tornadic storms); changes in ocean currents, in the ozone layer and the state of the ionosphere.[70] It is unclear whether the use of nuclear weapons may be encompassed.[71]
- The conduct must be deliberate: mere collateral damage is not covered; the interdiction must have a widespread, long-lasting or severe effect on the environment.[72]
- The conduct must cause destruction, damage or injury, albeit the victim of the modification technique does not necessarily have to be the environment itself (a likely target, for instance, may be a major industrial complex); as long as there is a causal nexus between the deliberate act and the result, the damage may go far beyond what was intended or foreseen.
- This damage must be inflicted on another state, whether belligerent or neutral, provided that it is a party to the ENMOD Convention. If the damage affects only the acting state, the conduct is not caught by the treaty.

In Dinstein's view, the ENMOD Convention does not apply *erga omnes* and to areas outside the jurisdiction of all states, like the high seas, unless the activities on the high seas affect the shipping of a state party.[73] However, at the Second ENMOD Review Conference in 1992, the United States stated that the Convention reflected 'the international community's consensus that the environment itself should not be used as an instrument of war',[74] so that the Convention could be argued to be reflective of customary international law.[75]

---

66 Dietrich Schindler and Jiří Toman, *The Laws of Armed Conflicts* (Martinus Nijhoff 1988) 164–169; on the problem of interpretation, see Oeter (n 5) 116, ¶ 403.
67 Hulme (n 2) 91.
68 Understandings (n 65); Rogers (n 6) 164; Dinstein (n 44) 526.
69 Dinstein (n 44) 527 *et seq*.
70 Understandings (n 65); CIHL r 45; Bouvier (n 63) 563; Hulme (n 2) 72.
71 Rogers (n 6) 166.
72 Dinstein (n 44) 528. He argues that since lower-level manipulations of natural processes for hostile purposes are not forbidden, the ENMOD Convention seems to condone military preparations for such activities.
73 Dinstein (n 44) 529.
74 CIHL practice to r 45.
75 CIHL r 45. See however Karen Hulme, 'Climate Change and International Humanitarian Law' in Rosemary Gail Rayfuse and Shirley V Scott (eds), *International Law in Era of Climate Change* (Edward Elgar 2012) 190, 214.

3.2 Additional Protocol I

Under LOAC, the environment is primarily addressed by Additional Protocol I, unless one takes into consideration provisions on the law of occupation, such as Articles 23 and 55 of the Hague Regulations, which are concerned with the non-deprivation of enemy populations of the natural resources they need to survive. Both of these provisions, however, are anthropocentric.

The only provisions of Additional Protocol I specifically protecting the environment, Articles 35(3) and 55, which were influenced by and adopted complementarily to ENMOD,[76] are somewhat more eco-centric. In contrast to Additional Protocol I, however, no analogous norm protecting the environment can be found in the 1977 Additional Protocol II.

The importance of Articles 35(3) and 55 of Additional Protocol I was restated in the *Nuclear Weapons* advisory opinion,[77] but it must be observed that most NATO countries strongly oppose their application to nuclear weapons.[78]

Article 35(3) provides that: 'It is prohibited to employ methods or means of warfare which are intended, or may be expected, to cause widespread, long-term and severe damage to the natural environment.' Article 55 provides that:

1 Care shall be taken in warfare to protect the natural environment against widespread, long-term and severe damage. This protection includes a prohibition of the use of methods or means of warfare which are intended or may be expected to cause such damage to the natural environment and thereby to prejudice the health or survival of the population.

2 Attacks against the natural environment by way of reprisals are prohibited.

At first sight, both norms appear to contain the same obligations, but a thorough examination leads to a different conclusion. Article 35 restates the general principle of limitation in the choice of means and methods of warfare and is partly eco-centric.[79] Article 55, instead, is anthropocentric, a view supported by the fact that it follows Article 54, which deals with the protection of objects indispensable to the survival of the civilian population.[80] Article 35(3) applies everywhere (land, air, sea, high seas),[81] whereas Article 55 is limited to land and territorial waters.[82]

The difference between the two provisions is further reflected by the different threshold of application. In addition to the criteria that the damage must be widespread, long term and severe, Article 55 provides that it must 'thereby prejudice' the health or survival of the population.[83] According to some, however, the second sentence is to be read separately from the first, which is a kind of general 'duty of care' clause,[84] followed by the illustration of how this duty may be met, for example, by avoiding the use of specific weapons. According to some, due to this, it may be argued that the scope of application of Article 55 is broader than that of Article

---

76 Bothe *et al* (n 14) 572; Hulme (n 2) 72. On the history, see Schmitt (n 5) 433 *et seq*.

77 *Nuclear Weapons* (n 38) ¶ 30; Knut Dörmann, *Elements of War Crimes under the Rome Statute of the International Criminal Court: Sources and Commentary* (2003 CUP) 174.

78 See in particular the declarations made by the US and the UK, cited by Bothe *et al* (n 14) 573.

79 *AP Commentary* ¶ 1441.

80 Ibid ¶ 2124.

81 Rogers (n 6) 168 (referring to the views of Michael Bothe, Elmar Rauch and Stephan Witteler).

82 Ibid (referring to the views of Frits Kalshoven and Liesbeth Zegveld).

83 Hulme (n 2) 74 and 78.

84 On the origins, see ibid 80.

35, which lacks an analogous general clause,[85] limiting itself to prohibiting specific means and methods of warfare *tout court*.

Some argue that due to their high threshold of application, in particular the duration criterion, these norms do 'not impose any significant limitation on combatants waging conventional warfare':[86]

> Reference to twenty or thirty years were made by some representatives as being a minimum [duration of damage].... [I]t is impossible to say with certainty what period of time might be involved. It appeared to be a widely shared assumption that battlefield damage incidental to conventional warfare would not normally be proscribed by this provision.[87]

A similar conclusion was reached by the ICTY in its NATO Bombing Report:

> [I]t is thought that the notion of 'long-term' damage in Additional Protocol I would need to be measured in years rather than months, and that as such, ordinary battlefield damage of the kind caused to France in World War I would not be covered. The great difficulty of assessing whether environmental damage exceeded the threshold of Additional Protocol I has also led to criticism by ecologists. This may partly explain the disagreement as to whether any of the damage caused by the oil spills and fires in the 1990/91 Gulf War technically crossed the threshold of Additional Protocol I.[88]

The other requirements were left without explanation, even though the notion 'severe' may be interpreted as meaning the prejudicing of the continued survival of the civilian population or involving the risk of major health problems, whereas 'widespread' may indicate effects which go beyond the standard of several hundred square kilometres set forth by the ENMOD Convention.[89]

UNEP recommends the following interpretation:

> As a starting point ..., the precedents set by the 1976 ENMOD convention should serve as the minimum basis, namely that 'widespread' encompasses an area on the scale of several hundred square kilometres; 'long-term' is for a period of months, or approximately a season; and 'severe' involves serious or significant disruption or harm to human life, natural economic resources or other assets.[90]

A textual reading of the words 'may be expected' suggests that actual damage is not required: a threat is sufficient. The ban is absolute: if the above-mentioned criteria are met, the principles of proportionality and military necessity do not come into play.[91] Collateral damage seems to be caught by Additional Protocol I only if it affects large areas, it lasts for a long period and it causes severe damage to the environment:

---

85 See ibid 74.
86 Bothe *et al* (n 14) 573.
87 Report of the Drafters' Committee, Doc CDDH/215/Rev. 1, ¶ 27; Sassòli *et al* (n 6) 606.
88 Cited by Sassòli *et al* (n 6), case 38, 21.
89 Rogers (n 6) 171.
90 UNEP (n 13) 5, Recommendations ¶ 1.
91 NATO Bombing Report (n 39) ¶ 283; Rogers (n 6) 169; Oeter (n 5) 117, ¶ 403.

the usual collateral damage caused by large military operations in the course of conventional warfare (which can be quite considerable) are thus excluded from the scope of the prohibitions against environmental damage of AP I and accordingly continue to fall under basic requirements of military necessity.[92]

In sum, whereas Article 35(3) contains a general prohibition of means and methods of warfare causing disproportionate damage on the environment, Article 55 additionally contains a 'duty of care' clause, pursuant to which potential damage should be anticipated and prevented. Thus, in assessing the legality of a military operation and the precautionary measures to be taken under Article 57 of Additional Protocol I, environmental considerations are to be included.[93] This process may be facilitated by the inclusion of environmental considerations into military manuals.[94] However, the 'duty of care' clause does not seem to encompass the obligation to take measures (for example, the removal of mines) after the end of the conflict.[95] Such considerations, however, have been made in several arms control treaties, that will be examined later.

Article 56 of Additional Protocol I and Article 15 of Additional Protocol II, which are primarily aimed at protecting works and installations containing dangerous forces and at preventing severe damage to the civilian population that may be caused by the release of such forces, could also apply.[96] Unfortunately they do not explicitly address oil fields and petrochemical plants (which may have been intentionally excluded),[97] so that they do not cover, for instance, the attacks on such installations that occurred during the 1990–1991 Gulf War, the 1999 Kosovo conflict or the 2006 Israel–Lebanon conflict. Nevertheless, such attacks could be in breach of the principle of distinction. Like Article 54(2), Article 56 also applies even when the object (a dam, dyke or nuclear electrical generating station) constitutes a military objective, except in the restricted cases referred to under paragraph 2, that is, when they are used, as a rule, in regular, significant and direct support of military operations and if such attack is the only feasible way to terminate such support.[98]

3.3 The difference between ENMOD and Additional Protocol I

The conditions 'widespread', 'long lasting' and 'severe' under the ENMOD Convention are disjunctive, whereas under Additional Protocol I they are cumulative, so that the threshold of application is lower. Moreover, the prohibition contained in the ENMOD Convention is absolute (no application of the principles of military necessity and proportionality) and refers to the environment in general, not just the 'natural' environment.

The ENMOD Convention defines the criterion 'long lasting' as 'lasting for a period of months, or approximately a season',[99] whereas Additional Protocol I interprets it in terms of decades (20–30 years).[100] This has to do with the fact that the ENMOD Convention addresses

---

92 Oeter (n 5) 117, ¶ 403.
93 Hulme, *War Torn* (n 2) 87.
94 In Switzerland, for instance, there are different manuals and pocket cards containing the rules on the protection of the environment: Manual 51.313 d, www.vtg.admin.ch/internet/vtg/de/home/militaerdienst/allgemeines/uwsa/downloads.html.
95 Hulme (n 2) 83.
96 According to CIHL, this provision constitutes customary law: CIHL r 42.
97 Sassòli *et al* (n 6) 17; Hulme (n 75) 202 *et seq.*
98 Sassòli *et al* (n 6) 17.
99 Understandings (n 65); CIHL r 45; Sassòli *et al* (n 6) 606.
100 Bothe *et al* (n 14) 573; Hulme (n 2) 94.

the deliberate *manipulation* of the environment, as opposed to an intended or expected *result* thereof.[101]

The ENMOD Convention defines 'widespread' as 'an area of several hundred square kilometres'. Since states stipulated that the terms under Additional Protocol I are not to be interpreted in the sense of the ENMOD Convention, to which they are complementary, it may be argued that the term 'widespread' under the Protocol is meant to cover a much larger area.[102]

If environmental consequences occur, the ENMOD Convention applies regardless of whether those were foreseen or intended; Additional Protocol I, by contrast, requires intent on the side of the perpetrator; negligence is not covered. However, if the act was committed with intent, Additional Protocol I applies regardless of whether the conduct led to actual damage.[103]

The ENMOD Convention applies to any hostile use of environmental modification techniques, also in peacetime, whereas Additional Protocol I only applies during armed conflict.[104]

4 Bans on specific types of weapons with effects on the environment

According to the principle of limitation, reflected in Article 22 of the Hague Regulations and Article 35(1) of Additional Protocol I, the right of the parties to the conflict to choose methods or means of warfare is not unlimited. This principle is given further effect in Article 36 of Additional Protocol I, which requires states to ensure that any new weapon, or means or method of warfare, does not contravene existing rules of international law, such as the prohibition of means or methods of warfare that cause widespread, long-term and severe damage to the natural environment. Furthermore, several treaties have been adopted restricting or prohibiting the use of specific weapons that may provide an indirect basis for the protection of the environment.

4.1 Conventional weapons and cluster bombs

The 1980 Convention on Certain Conventional Weapons (CCW)[105] and some of its protocols specifically address the environment. At the outset, paragraph 4 of the Preamble of the CCW echoes Articles 35(3) and 55(1) of Additional Protocol I by stating that 'it is prohibited to employ methods or means of warfare which are intended, or may be expected, to cause widespread, long-term and severe damage to the natural environment'.

More specifically, Article 2(4) of CCW Protocol III, which now also applies to NIAC,[106] provides that:

> It is prohibited to make forests or other kinds of plant cover the object of attack by incendiary weapons except when such natural elements are used to cover, conceal or camouflage combatants or other military objectives, or are themselves military objectives.

---

101 CIHL commentary to r 45.
102 Hulme (n 2) 92.
103 Rogers (n 6) 170.
104 Ibid.
105 Convention on Prohibitions or Restrictions of Use of Certain Conventional Weapons which may be Deemed to be Excessively Injurious or to have Indiscriminate Effects (10 October 1980) 1342 UNTS 137.
106 See ibid amended art 1 (entered into force in 2004).

CCW Protocol II also provides a basis of (indirect) protection of the environment, by trying to limit the effects of mines. The original Protocol II of 1980 merely encouraged cooperation to remove or render minefields ineffective. However, Articles 3(2) and 10 of the 1996 amended version – which qualify as customary law applicable to all armed conflicts[107] – oblige states to remove mines or otherwise render them harmless at the end of hostilities. Similarly, the 1997 Ottawa Convention on Anti-Personnel Mines – also applicable to NIAC[108] – contains the obligation for states to destroy or ensure the destruction of anti-personnel mines in mined areas.[109] Unlike Amended CCW Protocol II, however, the Ottawa Convention lacks reference to parties to the conflict other than states, which appears to exclude non-state groups.[110]

Finally, 2003 CCW Protocol V on explosive remnants of war offers similar guidelines that may protect the environment post-conflict.[111]

Cluster bombs also constitute a threat to the environment, due to the long presence of unexploded subductions after the cessation of hostilities, which makes the affected areas useless. Since bomblets are sometimes undetectable, they can impact, for example, the use of farmland and livestock, not to mention impeding access to shelter and water. The 2008 Convention on Cluster Munitions (CCM)[112] prohibits all use, stockpiling, production and transfer of cluster munitions; its provisions also concern assistance to victims, clearance of contaminated areas and destruction of stockpiles.

4.2 Biological, bacteriological and chemical weapons

The 1925 Gas Protocol prohibits the use of chemical and biological means of warfare, more specifically the employment of 'asphyxiating, poisonous or other gases, and all analogous liquids, materials and devices'. Chemical herbicides could also be encompassed by this prohibition.[113] Research, development, stockpiling and possession of such weapons are, however, not addressed by the Protocol and no control mechanisms or provisions establishing responsibility for violations are foreseen.[114]

The 1972 Biological Weapons Convention (BWC), on the other hand, bans the development, production and stockpiling of biological weapons, not their actual use.[115] This aspect is covered by the 1925 Gas Protocol, which is complementary. Taken together, these two treaties contribute to the protection of the environment, in particular the fauna and the flora.[116]

The 1993 Chemical Weapons Convention (CWC) not only reaffirms the prohibition contained in the 1925 Protocol in relation to chemical weapons and extends it to development,

---

107 CIHL commentary to r 83.
108 Sivakumaran (n 6) 407.
109 Convention on the Prohibition of the Use, Stockpiling, Production and Transfer of Anti-Personnel Mines and on the Destruction (18 September 1997) 2056 UNTS 211, art 5.
110 Ibid.
111 Sassòli et al (n 6) 13; Rogers (n 6) 173;
112 Convention on Cluster Munitions (30 May 2008) 2688 UNTS 39.
113 Peter Rowe, *Defence: The Legal Implications* (Brassey 1987) 117; see UNGA Res 2603 A (XXIV) (16 December 1969).
114 Sassòli et al (n 6) 12. However, a breach of the 1925 Protocol now amounts to a war crime in international armed conflict under art 8(2)(b)(xviii) of the Rome Statute.
115 Convention on the Prohibition of the Development, Production and Stockpiling of Bacteriological (Biological) and Toxin Weapons and on their Destruction (10 April 1972) 1015 UNTS 163.
116 Sassòli et al (n 6) 13.

production, acquisition, stockpiling, retention and transfer,[117] its Verification Annex also prohibits the destruction of chemical weapons by 'dumping in any body of water, land burial and open pit burning'.[118] This convention has the advantage of providing for monitoring and verification mechanisms.

4.3 Nuclear weapons

The three major treaties specifically regulating nuclear weapons are the 1963 Partial Test-Ban Treaty,[119] the 1968 Nuclear Non-Proliferation Treaty (NPT)[120] and the 1996 Comprehensive Nuclear-Test-Ban Treaty (CTBT).[121] There are additionally regional nuclear disarmament treaties.[122] The details of these treaties are examined elsewhere in this book.[123] Out of these specific treaties, however, it should be recalled that the 1963 Partial Test-Ban Treaty, which is concerned with nuclear testing, is particularly relevant for the protection of marine ecosystems.

Since negotiations for Additional Protocol I were based on the general agreement that the use of nuclear weapons would have to be regulated by specific treaties – which have been listed previously – nuclear weapons states in particular have argued that such weapons are not subject to Articles 35(3) and 55 of Additional Protocol I.[124] In the *Nuclear Weapons* advisory opinion, however, the ICJ affirmed the relevance of environmental considerations to assessing the legality of the use of nuclear weapons:

> States must take environmental considerations into account when assessing what is necessary and proportionate in the pursuit of legitimate military objectives. Respect for the environment is one of the elements that go to assessing whether an action is in conformity with the principles of necessity and proportionality.[125]

Moreover, the ICJ referred to UN General Assembly Resolution 47/37, which states that 'destruction of the environment, not justified by military necessity and carried out wantonly, is clearly contrary to existing international law'.[126] The ICJ concluded that:

> while the existing international law relating to the protection and safeguarding of the environment does not specifically prohibit the use of nuclear weapons, it indicates important environmental factors that are properly to be taken into account in the context of the implementation of the principles and rules of the law applicable in armed conflict.[127]

---

117 Convention on the Prohibition of the Development, Production, Stockpiling and Use of Chemical Weapons and on their Destruction (13 January 1993) 1974 UNTS 45, art I.

118 Ibid Annex on Implementation and Verification, pt IV(A), ¶ 13.

119 Treaty Banning Nuclear Weapon Tests in the Atmosphere, in Outer Space, and under Water (5 August 1963) 480 UNTS 43.

120 Treaty on the Non-Proliferation of Nuclear Weapons (1 July 1968) 729 UNTS 161.

121 Comprehensive Nuclear-Test-Ban Treaty, UN Doc A/50/1027 (24 September 1996) Annex, 35 ILM 1439.

122 For a list, see Sassòli *et al* (n 6) 14.

123 See Dieter Fleck, 'Nuclear weapons in international law' ch 13 in this volume.

124 Rogers (n 6) 174.

125 *Nuclear Weapons* (n 38) ¶ 30.

126 Ibid ¶ 32; UNGA Res 47/37 (25 November 1992).

127 *Nuclear Weapons* (n 38) ¶ 33.

4.4 Depleted uranium

There is no specific treaty concerning depleted uranium. The NATO Bombing Report observed that:

> In view of the uncertain state of development of the legal standards governing this area, it should be emphasised that the use of depleted uranium or other potentially hazardous substance by any adversary to conflicts within the former Yugoslavia since 1991 has not formed the basis of any charge laid by the Prosecutor. It is acknowledged that the underlying principles of the law of armed conflict such as proportionality are applicable also in this context.[128]

However, the UN General Assembly has requested the UN Secretary-General to produce reports on their environmental impact.[129] These could lead to the codification in treaty law of norms protecting the environment from depleted uranium armaments.[130]

5 Enforcement

The two alternative enforcement possibilities of WEL are individual criminal responsibility and state responsibility.

5.1 International criminal law

Violations of Articles 35(3) and 55 of Additional Protocol I are not grave breaches pursuant to Article 85 of the Protocol.[131] However, they are punishable under Article 8(2)(b)(iv) of the Rome Statute, which regards it a war crime in an international armed conflict to

> [i]ntentionally launch an attack in the knowledge that such attack will cause incidental loss of life or injury to civilians or damage to civilian objects or widespread, long-term and severe damage to the natural environment which would be clearly excessive in relation to the concrete and direct overall military advantage anticipated.[132]

No analogous provision, however, is to be found in the war crimes list applicable in times of NIAC.[133]

The question is whether, in interpreting the *actus reus* of the war crime stipulated in Article 8(2)(b)(iv), the ICC will rely on Additional Protocol I or on ENMOD. Article 8(2)(b)(iv) is very similar in wording to Article 55 of Additional Protocol I: considering that the criteria under Article 8(2)(b)(iv) are also conjunctive, it can be argued that the tendency will be to rely on Additional Protocol I. Lawrence and Heller argue that in this case the article will become a 'virtual nullity', since the Additional Protocol I standard, as observed by Schmitt, is 'nearly

---

128 ICTY (n 39) ¶ 26.
129 UNGA Res 62/30 (5 December 2007); UNGA Res 63/54 (2 December 2008); see also eg Report of the Secretary General on the Effects of the Use of Armaments and Ammunition containing Depleted Uranium, UN Doc A/65/129 (14 July 2010).
130 Sassòli *et al* (n 6) case 38, 19; Rogers (n 6) 176–177.
131 But, see API art 85(3)(b)–(c).
132 See also Rome Statute art 8(2)(b)(xviii).
133 See Rome Statute art 8(2)(c), (e).

impossible to meet in all but the most egregious circumstances'.[134] By defining as 'severe' only an act that prejudices the health or survival of the population – even admitting that the other criteria are met – damage would not fall under the provision if it has 'only' impacted on the environment. At the same time, it is difficult to predict what kind of damage the ICC would regard as serious enough to rise to the level of an offence, which may be inconsistent with the principle of legality. This aspect, for instance, created a problem in the ICTY's assessment of NATO's bombing campaign against Yugoslavia.[135]

With regard to the *mens rea*, the crime specified in Article 8(2)(b)(iv) of the Rome Statute may be committed with intent (*dolus directus*) or constructive intent (*dolus eventualis*).[136] The question is whether the (constructive) intent must have encompassed also the prejudice to the health or survival of the population as a secondary effect.[137] Unfortunately, the Elements of Crimes do not resolve the matter as they merely state that the accused person must have launched the attack and must have been aware that this would cause widespread, long-term and severe damage to the natural environment.[138] Moreover, by requiring the damage to be of such an extent as to be *clearly* excessive in relation to the concrete and direct overall military advantage anticipated, the Rome Statute provides additionally for a proportionality test,[139] factoring in a military advantage foreseeable by the perpetrator at the relevant time and which may or may not be temporally or geographically related to the object of the attack.[140] The NATO Bombing Report observed that the Rome Statute recognises 'operational reality' and that the use of the word *clearly* ensures that criminal responsibility would be entailed only in cases where the excessiveness of the incidental damage was obvious.[141] It went on to criticise the *mens rea* criteria:

> the requisite *mens rea* on the part of a commander would be actual or constructive knowledge as to the grave environmental effects of a military attack; a standard which would be difficult to establish for the purposes of prosecution and which may provide an insufficient basis to prosecute military commanders inflicting environmental harm in the (mistaken) belief that such conduct was warranted by military necessity.... In addition, the notion of 'excessive' environmental destruction is imprecise and the actual environmental impact, both present and long term, of the NATO bombing campaign is at present unknown and difficult to measure.[142]

In sum, it seems that Article 8(2)(b)(iv) of the Rome Statute does not constitute a panacea for environmental damage caused by armed conflicts. However, as Lawrence and Heller put it, the critique ought not be too severe, because the inclusion of this provision in the Rome Statute still represents 'a significant advance for international law', in that 'for the first time, the world

---

134 Lawrence and Heller (n 2) 68, citing Schmitt (n 5).
135 Lawrence and Heller (n 2) 80.
136 Hulme (n 2) 74.
137 Ibid 76.
138 Elements of Crimes, UN Doc PCNICC/2000/1/Add.2 (2000); Dörmann (n 77) 164–165, 176.
139 Dörmann (n 77) 166; William Fenrick, 'The Rule of Proportionality and Protocol I in Conventional Warfare' (1982) 98 *Military LR* 91; Roberta Arnold, 'Commentary to Article 8(2)(b)(iv)' in Otto Triffterer (ed), *Commentary on the Rome Statute of the International Criminal Court* (2nd edn, Nomos 2008) 338, 341; see also Hulme (n 2) 78.
140 Elements of Crimes (n 138) fn 36, 37; ICTY (n 39) ¶ 50; Dörmann (n 77) 176; Lawrence and Heller (n 2) 86.
141 ICTY (n 39) ¶ 21.
142 ICTY (n 39) ¶ 23; see also Lawrence and Heller (n 2) 75, 82 *et seq.*

community has recognized both that environmental damage caused by unnecessary military attacks should be prohibited even when that damage does not directly harm human interests'.[143]

5.2 State responsibility

Violations of Hague Convention (IV), the ENMOD Convention and Additional Protocol I provisions result in state responsibility, requiring reparations, which have not proven to be very effective with regard to environmental damage.[144]

There are different mechanisms to address disputes related to environmental damage during armed conflict. One of these is the UN Compensation Commission, which was established by the Security Council to process compensation claims relating to the 1990–1991 Gulf War.[145] However, claims for environmental damage have had less success than claims for human damage and there have been very few cases in which countries have been held liable. Nonetheless, according to UNEP, a similar structure could be established as a permanent body, either under the UN General Assembly or under the Security Council, to investigate and decide on alleged violations and handle and process compensation claims.[146]

Another tool is the Permanent Court of Arbitration (PCA), which in 2002 adopted the Optional Rules for Conciliation of Disputes Relating to the Environment and/or Natural Resources. These, according to UNEP, provide the 'most comprehensive set of environmentally tailored dispute resolution procedural rules presently available and could be extended to disputes arising from environmental damage during armed conflict'.[147]

6 Conclusions

The legal protection of the environment may be established in different ways under LOAC. The first possibility is to refer to the general principles of distinction, military necessity and proportionality, in which case also collateral damage to the environment may be encompassed, but which only provide for an indirect basis of protection of the environment.

The second possibility is to refer to specific provisions providing for a direct basis of protection of the environment, such as Articles 35(3) and 55 of Additional Protocol I, or the ENMOD Convention. The disadvantage of this approach, however, is the relatively high threshold of application of these provisions. The triple cumulative standard of Additional Protocol I is nearly impossible to achieve, particularly given imprecise definitions of the relevant terms.[148]

The third possibility is to refer to the legal regime regulating the use of weapons, which may prevent the use of specific tools with negative impacts on the environment. In this case, however, the basis of protection is indirect and new technologies, such as the use of depleted uranium, are not addressed.[149]

Notwithstanding the fragmentation of WEL, it can be concluded that the protection of the environment in times of warfare is comprehensive. At the same time, the recent trend to

---

143 Lawrence and Heller (n 2) 101 *et seq*.
144 Ibid 71; Schmitt (n 5).
145 See UNSC Res 687 (3 April 1991); Hulme (n 2) 12.
146 UNEP (n 13) 6; Lawrence and Heller (n 2) 72.
147 UNEP (n 13) 6.
148 Ibid 4.
149 Ibid.

consider IEL complementary to WEL, which shall nonetheless retain its status as *lex specialis*, may fill the existing gap, as seen with the introduction of the 'duty of care' IEL principle.

Moreover, the appreciation that nowadays armed conflicts are primarily fought between non-state actors has led the international community to recognise, through state practice or by extending the scope of application of specific treaties, like Amended Protocol II to the CCW, the application of WEL to non-international armed conflicts, too.[150]

From the enforcement perspective, although in times of warfare priority is generally given to the protection of human beings and there is still little case law addressing the protection of the environment,[151] it is to be noted that with the adoption of Article 8(2)(b)(iv) of the Rome Statute, breaches of Articles 35(3) and 55 of Additional Protocol I can now be prosecuted as war crimes. This step forward shall be an incentive to states to implement WEL provisions, as already suggested by the ICRC Guidelines, which, at the same time, would provide an alternative to state responsibility for accountability for damage to the environment. Thus, although perfection in this realm is yet to be achieved, positive work is (even though timidly) in progress.

150 Sassòli *et al* (n 6) 23; see however the negative findings of UNEP (n 13) 4.
151 UNEP (n 13) 4; see Lawrence and Heller (n 2).

23

The protection of humanitarian relief

The legal framework

*Alison Duxbury**

On 5 August 2010, ten members of a medical team from the International Assistance Mission (IAM), a Christian aid organisation, were killed in Afghanistan. The group comprised six Americans, a German, a Briton and two Afghanis. Prior to the attack, in 44 years of operations, only four international staff of IAM (and no local staff) had been killed while on duty in Afghanistan.[1] The Taliban claimed responsibility for the attack, accusing the victims of spying and proselytising Christianity – accusations that were denied by IAM, the United States' government and relatives of the victims.[2] Following the attack, the managing director of a British organisation, Afghanaid, described the incident as the 'worst attack on humanitarian workers in 30 years'. She added that '[i]t will have very serious implications and make us revisit our security protocols. It cannot just be business as usual.'[3]

In order to increase 'public awareness about humanitarian assistance activities' and to commemorate those 'who have worked in the promotion of the humanitarian cause and those who have lost their lives in the course of duty' the General Assembly of the United Nations has proclaimed 19 August as World Humanitarian Day.[4] The date was chosen to mark the day that 22 people, including the Special Representative of the Secretary-General, Sérgio Vieira de Mello, died in the Canal Hotel bombing in 2003 in Baghdad. The proclamation of World Humanitarian Day is an acknowledgement of the need both to recognise the work of humanitarian personnel and to protect them from the dangers they face in the field. The legal framework is an important tool in protecting such personnel against violence.

---

* The author would like to thank Christopher Lum, Julia Wang and Kasia Pawlikowski for their research assistance in preparing this chapter.
1 International Assistance Mission, 'On the Death of 10 of the 12 Nuristan Eye Camp Team Members' (Kabul, 9 August 2010), www.iam-afghanistan.org/pressreleases.
2 Ibid; Jon Boone, 'Worst Attack on Humanitarian Workers in 30 Years' *Sydney Morning Herald* (10 August 2010), www.smh.com.au/world/worst-attack-on-humanitarian-workers-in-30-years-20100809-11u7j. html.
3 Farhana Faruqi-Stocker, quoted in Boone (n 2).
4 Strengthening of the Coordination of Emergency Humanitarian Assistance of the United Nations, UNGA Res 63/139 (5 March 2009) ¶ 26.

The attack in August 2010 and the Taliban's accusations are indicative of changes in the global security environment – these changes include the increasing criminality of actions against aid operations and the growing politicisation of violence.[5] Although there are measures that aid agencies can take to reduce such threats, no organisation is immune from attack.[6] The decision of the International Red Cross and Red Crescent Movement in 2011 to initiate the Health Care in Danger project demonstrates the seriousness with which it views attacks against a particular group of humanitarian workers – health care personnel – and the services they deliver.[7] It is against this background that this chapter will address the legal framework for the protection of humanitarian relief operations and their personnel, focusing in particular on the provisions of international humanitarian law. The analysis is designed to answer three interrelated questions. First, who is recognised as a humanitarian worker for the purposes of international law? Second, what are the legal obligations on states to protect humanitarian workers? Finally, are states legally obliged to facilitate humanitarian work and assistance? This third question is different from, but related to, the first two questions. Thus, it is possible to distinguish between the law designed to protect humanitarian workers and the law dealing with the question whether states are obliged to facilitate (and consent to) humanitarian assistance within their borders. However, clearly the questions are related as without protection from attack, the ability of humanitarian workers to undertake humanitarian assistance activities is severely compromised.

1 Context

Before examining these questions, it is necessary to highlight the context in which the law governing the protection of humanitarian personnel is applied. In its 2010 report, Operational Security Management in Violent Environments, the Overseas Development Institute reported the statistics on the incidence of major violence against aid workers in the last decade.[8] The statistics (compiled in the Aid Worker Security Database) demonstrate that in recent years most attacks against aid workers occurred in a small number of highly violent conflicts.[9] There has been an increased rate of attacks in these violent settings, including attacks against national staff. It is also evident that international staff are being targeted and that the motivation of perpetrators is increasingly politically oriented.[10] For example, in 2000 the total number of major incidents of violence against national staff members was 70; by 2009 that number had increased to 205. The number of international staff victims had also increased from 21 in 2000 to 73 in 2009.[11] Although there was a small reduction in the number of attacks in 2009 and 2010 (when compared to the peak number of incidents in 2008), the 2011 Aid Worker Security Report suggests that this is due to 'the shrinking presence of international aid agencies in the most violent

---

5 Overseas Development Institute, 'Operational Security Management in Violent Environments' (December 2010) 8 *Good Practice Review* 1.

6 For example, in 2012 one of the ICRC's staff members in Pakistan was kidnapped and murdered. The ICRC has been active in Pakistan since 1947: see ICRC, 'Pakistan: Kidnapped ICRC Delegate Murdered' ICRC News Release 12/95 (Islamabad/Geneva, 29 April 2012), www.icrc.org/eng/resources/documents/news-release/2012/pakistan-news-2012-04-29.htm.

7 Thirty-Second International Conference of the Red Cross and Red Crescent, 'Health Care in Danger: Respecting and Protecting Health Care' 31IC/11/R5 (2011). For the project's activities and reports, see, www.icrc.org/eng/what-we-do/safeguarding-health-care/solution/2013-04-26-hcid-health-care-in-danger-project.htm.

8 Overseas Development Institute, 'Operational Security Management' (n 5) 275.

9 Ibid 274.

10 Ibid.

11 Ibid 275.

settings … rather than improving security conditions'.[12] Thus, the reduction in the number of projects and personnel in Somalia and Darfur has resulted in a lessening in the number of attacks on aid personnel.[13] However, this reduction in violent incidents appears to be short lived – the 2014 report indicates that 460 aid workers were victims of major attacks in 2013, the highest number recorded in any one year.[14] The report states that '[w]orsening crises in Syria and South Sudan, combined with continued high levels of violence in Afghanistan, Pakistan, and Sudan, made 2013 another record-breaking year for violence against aid workers'.[15] The statistics demonstrate that attacks may be directed against either national or international staff and that there has been an increase in politically motivated attacks as distinct from acts of violence that are economically motivated.[16] Although national staff make up the greatest number of victims (since they comprise the vast majority of staff in the field), on a per capita basis, international staff are more likely to be attacked.[17] This last point may have some relevance when discussing the provisions of international humanitarian law that distinguish between the protections afforded to nationals and non-nationals of a party to a conflict.

The greatest number of violent attacks against humanitarian workers occur in armed conflicts. On that basis, although humanitarian personnel undertake their activities in a variety of situations (including, international or non-international armed conflicts, natural or man-made disasters and situations where a UN peacekeeping operation is deployed), this chapter will focus on the relevant principles of international humanitarian law. This does not mean that outside the sphere of armed conflict humanitarian workers operate in a legal vacuum – numerous provisions of international human rights law require states to respect, promote and protect the rights of individuals within their jurisdiction or under their control. Such provisions can also operate during times of armed conflict. In addition, the International Law Commission has delivered a number of reports under the topic 'protection of persons in the event of disasters', which set out the legal instruments applicable to assistance in the event of natural and man-made disasters.[18] Nevertheless, with the exception of a possible duty to facilitate humanitarian assistance operations (where international human rights law is also relevant), international humanitarian law provides more focused provisions in relation to both defining and protecting humanitarian workers, than any other body of international law.

---

12 Humanitarian Outcomes, 'Aid Worker Security Report 2011: Spotlight on Security for National Aid Workers: Issues and Perspectives' (August 2011) 'Key Findings'.

13 Ibid 5. See also Humanitarian Outcomes, 'Aid Worker Security Report 2014: Unsafe Passage: Road Attacks and their Impact on Humanitarian Operations' (2014) 3, https://aidworkersecurity.org/reports, where attention is drawn to the 'wholesale withdrawal of Médicins Sans Frontières [from Somalia] after 22 years of running medical programmes in the country'.

14 Humanitarian Outcomes, 'Aid Worker Security Report 2014' (n 13) 1.

15 Ibid 2.

16 Overseas Development Institute, 'Providing Aid in Insecure Environments: 2009 Update' (April 2009) 5.

17 Humanitarian Outcomes, 'Aid Worker Security Report 2014' (n 13) 3. See also Caroline Moulins, 'Violent Incidents affecting the Delivery of Health Care: January 2012 to December 2013' (ICRC 2014) 4. This report, which is part of the Health Care in Danger project facilitated by the ICRC, indicates that 'local health-care providers … were the group most affected by violent incidents'.

18 The special rapporteur of the International Law Commission, Eduardo Valencia-Ospina, has submitted seven reports 'Preliminary Report on the Protection of Persons in the Event of Disasters' UN Doc A/CN.4/598 (2008); 'Second Report on the Protection of Persons in the Event of Disasters' UN Doc A/CN.4/615 (2009); 'Third Report on the Protection of Persons in the Event of Disasters' UN Doc A/CN.4/629 (2010); 'Fourth Report on the Protection of Persons in the Event of Disasters' UN Doc A/CN.4/643 (2011); 'Fifth Report on the Protection of Persons in the Event of Disasters' UN Doc A/CN.4/652 (2012); 'Sixth Report on the Protection of Persons in the Event of Disasters' UN Doc A/CN.4/662 (2013); 'Seventh Report on the Protection of Persons in the Event of Disasters' UN Doc A/CN.4/668 (2014).

2 Who is a humanitarian worker? What is humanitarian assistance?

The first question to be considered is: who is a humanitarian worker for the purpose of the legal provisions governing protection? This question is sometimes ignored in the literature – the approach of 'I know one when I see one' appearing to be the dominant attitude to defining a person who works in the humanitarian sector. When listing the type of people who undertake humanitarian work, it is usual to include employees of the ICRC, the national Red Cross and Crescent Societies and non-governmental organisations (NGOs) with a humanitarian purpose. But these are not the only organisations that describe their actions as 'humanitarian'. The work of the United Nations and other international organisations in conflict or disaster settings may encompass a number of activities that can be captured under the heading 'humanitarian'. The term has also been used by some militaries to describe aspects of their work, although members of the armed forces would not be classified as humanitarian workers for the purposes of the law.[19] For example, a 2010 Department of Defence description of Australia's involvement in Uruzgan province in Afghanistan indicated that special forces reservists were involved in building the support of local communities through 'listening to community leaders, conducting medical clinics, providing humanitarian assistance, and conducting community based assessments, in conjunction with Uruzgan's Provincial Police Reserve.... In addition, they were involved in a number of hostile engagements with insurgents.'[20] The use of the term 'humanitarian' by the military is discouraged by the humanitarian sector due to the fear that it may align humanitarian work with the political objectives of a government.[21] In response to opposition by humanitarian agencies towards the militarisation of the word 'humanitarian', the International Commission on Intervention and State Sovereignty preferred the phrase 'responsibility to protect' rather than 'humanitarian intervention' when describing military action undertaken by states for humanitarian purposes.[22] Finally, private security firms may also perceive their work as being broadly humanitarian in nature. In 2006 the Director General of the British Association of Private Security Companies suggested that private security firms are not only providing protective security services, but were increasingly supporting 'post-conflict reconstruction efforts by giving advice and providing services for personal and site protection. They are ... moving into new fields such as state-building, supporting and even providing humanitarian and disaster relief, which includes logistics, communications and energy services.'[23] However, NGOs operating in Afghanistan believe that 'the presence of military actors and contractors executing military-funded stabilisation projects undermines the security of their staff'.[24] These examples demonstrate that the term 'humanitarian' could apply to a number of different types of operations and personnel, and that the term has been appropriated by actors with a diverse range of objectives.

---

19 *GCIV Commentary* 333 states that the protection granted to 'National Red Cross Societies and other relief societies is also extended to special organizations "of a nonmilitary character".'

20 Australian Government Department of Defence, 'One Commando Regiment Army Reservists reach out to Uruzgan' (16 March 2010), www.defence.gov.au/op/afghanistan/gallery/2010/20100316/.

21 For a critical account of the use of humanitarian assistance in counterinsurgency operations, see Jamie Williamson, 'Using Humanitarian Aid to "Win Hearts and Minds": A Costly Failure?' (2011) 93(884) *IRRC* 1035.

22 International Commission on Intervention and State Sovereignty, 'The Responsibility to Protect' (December 2001) ¶¶ 1.40–1.41.

23 Toni Pfanner, 'Interview with Andrew Bearpark' (2006) 88(863) *IRRC* 449, 451.

24 International Crisis Group, 'Aid and Conflict in Afghanistan' (August 2011) 23.

2.1 International humanitarian law

In terms of the relevant legal framework, neither international humanitarian law nor international human rights law provide a definition of 'humanitarian worker' or 'humanitarian personnel'. However, the Geneva Conventions and Additional Protocols protect various people and the tasks they perform on the basis that their work is of a 'humanitarian' character. As a starting point, for the purposes of international humanitarian law, humanitarian personnel would be classified as civilians as they do not fulfil the definition of armed forces and combatants in Additional Protocol I. Article 50 of Additional Protocol I defines a civilian negatively in the sense that a civilian is a person who does not fall within one of the other categories recognised in Geneva Convention III (as prisoners of war) and Article 43 of Additional Protocol I (defining the armed forces of a party to a conflict).

Outside this general classification as civilians, the Geneva Conventions and Additional Protocols recognise the activities of designated people whose work could be described as 'humanitarian' – including the ICRC,[25] national societies of the Red Cross and Crescent movement,[26] 'aid societies',[27] 'relief societies'[28] and 'civil defence organisations'.[29] This last group of organisations perform certain tasks as listed in Additional Protocol I, such as rescue, fire fighting and the provision of emergency accommodation.[30] In addition, the terms 'civilian medical units' and 'civilian medical personnel' are used in Additional Protocol I[31] – the activities of such personnel can also be described as essentially humanitarian. The Geneva Conventions and Additional Protocol I also refer to the work of 'impartial humanitarian organisations'.[32] The Conventions do not define 'impartial', although the commentaries note that an organisation does not have to be neutral to be considered impartial.[33] Additionally, the commentaries state that 'impartiality does not necessarily mean mathematical equality', thus impartiality requires that humanitarian aid is distributed on the basis of need, rather than on the basis of considerations relating to the person who is in need.[34] Consequently, not only must the organisation be impartial, but so must its activities.[35] In this respect, the ICRC's distinction between the principles of impartiality and neutrality is relevant – impartiality requires that an organisation does not discriminate on the basis of race, ethnicity, religion or other grounds and that it gives priority only on the basis of need.[36] Neutrality dictates that an organisation cannot take sides in hostilities or engage in controversies of a political nature.[37] Although neutrality is not required for the work of a humanitarian organisation to be protected by the Conventions and Protocols, the commentaries suggest that 'impartiality benefits greatly from neutrality'.[38] In a similar vein, a 2009 General

25 For example, GCI–III art 9; GCIV arts 10 and 59.
26 For example, GCIV art 63; API art 17; APII art 18.
27 For example, API art 17.
28 For example, GCIII art 125; GCIV art 142; APII art 18.
29 API art 62.
30 API art 61.
31 See API, arts 12(2) and 15.
32 For example, GCI–III art 9; GCIV arts 10 and 59 use the term 'impartial humanitarian organization'. API art 22(2)(b) uses the term 'impartial international humanitarian organization'.
33 *GCI Commentary* 108.
34 Ibid 109
35 *GCIV Commentary* 97.
36 Statutes of the International Red Cross and Red Crescent Movement, adopted by the Twenty-Fifth International Conference of the Red Cross at Geneva in 1986, amended in 1995 and 2006, Preamble.
37 Ibid.
38 *GCII Commentary* 68.

Assembly resolution called upon humanitarian actors to respect the principles of neutrality, humanity, impartiality and independence for the provision of humanitarian assistance.[39] As well as impartiality, the Conventions and Additional Protocol I require that an organisation's work must be 'humanitarian'. The Commentary to Geneva Convention I defines the term 'humanitarian' broadly as 'concerned with the condition of man, considered solely as a human being, without regard to the value which he represents as a military, political, professional or other unit'.[40] The activities carried out by the organisation must be unaffected by 'any political or military consideration' and include subsidiary activities such as sending medical personnel, other staff and equipment, and sending and distributing relief supplies.[41]

2.2 Other international instruments

The Geneva Conventions and Additional Protocols are not the only international instruments which specifically protect the persons or activities of humanitarian workers. The Convention on the Safety of United Nations and Associated Personnel and the Optional Protocol to the Convention provide for the protection of humanitarian NGOs as 'associated personnel' when they are deployed under an agreement with the Secretary-General or a UN specialised agency to carry out activities in support of UN operations.[42] This Convention was designed to combat the increasing violence against UN and associated personnel in various situations outlined in the Convention (and as expanded in its Optional Protocol).[43] However, the Convention does not apply to enforcement actions authorised by the Security Council where the law of armed conflict applies.[44] Furthermore, the need for an agreement with the UN in order for an NGO to fall within the ambit of this Convention means that its application to humanitarian workers is limited.[45] For example, it does not cover the ICRC, as that particular organisation's fundamental commitment to the principle of neutrality may be jeopardised if it were perceived to be acting under the directions of the UN.[46]

Outside these legally binding instruments, a number of other documents are also relevant in defining humanitarian assistance or humanitarian workers. A 2003 resolution of the Institute of International Law, 'Humanitarian Assistance', employs a slightly broader definition of humanitarian assistance than found in the commentaries to the Geneva Conventions. In the view of

---

39 UNGA Res 64/77 (7 December 2009) ¶ 8.

40 *GCI Commentary* 108.

41 Ibid 109.

42 Convention on the Safety of United Nations and Associated Personnel (adopted 9 December 1994, entered into force 15 January 1999) 2051 UNTS 363, art 1 ('UN Safety Convention').

43 Art II(1) of the Optional Protocol extends the situations to which the original Convention applies to include UN operations 'conducted under United Nations authority and control for the purposes of: (a) Delivering humanitarian, political or development assistance in peacebuilding, or (b) Delivering emergency humanitarian assistance'.

44 Art 2(2) of the Convention provides that:

> [t]his Convention shall not apply to a United Nations operation authorized by the Security Council as an enforcement action under Chapter VII of the Charter of the United Nations in which any of the personnel are engaged as combatants against organized armed forces and to which the law of international armed conflict applies.

45 For a discussion of this condition during the drafting of the Convention, see 'Report of the Ad hoc Committee on the Scope of Legal Protection under the Convention on the Safety of United Nations and Associated Personnel' UN Doc A/57/52 (2002) ¶¶ 49–60.

46 Antoine Bouvier ' "Convention on the Safety of United Nations and Associated Personnel": Presentation and Analysis' (2005) 35(309) *IRRC* 638, 655.

the Institute, humanitarian assistance means 'all acts, activities and the human and material resources for the provision of goods and services of an exclusively humanitarian character, indispensable for the survival and the fulfilment of the essential needs of the victims of disasters'.[47] Such disasters include natural and man-made disasters and, importantly for the purposes of this chapter, armed conflicts.[48] Finally, the UN Special Representative on the situation of Human Rights Defenders, a mandate established by the Commission on Human Rights to implement the UN Declaration on Human Rights Defenders,[49] describes human rights defenders as 'people who, individually or with others, act to promote or protect human rights' – this includes 'any human rights concerns'.[50] The clearest examples of human rights defenders are NGOs working with a mandate to protect the standards articulated in human rights treaties. However, the Special Representative on Human Rights Defenders has recognised that the broad definition of a human rights defender could include those who work 'to establish housing, healthcare and sustainable income-generation projects for poor and marginalized communities'.[51] Such personnel may not use the term 'human rights', but would still fall within protections accorded under the Declaration.[52] While the Declaration on Human Rights Defenders does not explicitly provide that human rights defenders must be neutral and impartial, it states that individuals and groups must not undertake activities aimed at the destruction of the rights contained in the Declaration.[53] In addition, human rights defenders must accept the universality of human rights and advocate in a peaceful manner.[54]

Together these treaties and international statements indicate that the term 'humanitarian' may encompass a wide range of activities in a number of different contexts. Although 'impartiality' is not specifically required in all the legal provisions, it would appear to be a necessary aspect of providing true humanitarian assistance.[55] The requirement of independence would also appear to be important, particularly where the legal provisions cite the ICRC as an example of an impartial humanitarian body.[56] Finally, although military organisations may carry out humanitarian activities, this activity would not bring the personnel involved in such operations within the protection accorded to humanitarian personnel in an armed conflict given their association with a party to the conflict. However, separate protection is provided in the Conventions and Protocols for medical personnel.[57]

---

47 Institute of International Law, 'Humanitarian Assistance' (2003) ¶ 1.
48 Ibid ¶ 2.
49 UNCHR Res 2000/61 (26 April 2000).
50 Office of the UN High Commissioner for Human Rights ('UNHCR'), 'Human Rights Defenders: Protecting the Right to Defend Human Rights' Fact Sheet no 29 (2004) 2.
51 Ibid 4–5.
52 Ibid.
53 Declaration on the Right and Responsibility of Individuals, Groups and Organs of Society to Promote and Protect Universally Recognized Human Rights and Fundamental Freedoms, UNGA Res 53/144 (9 December 1998) art 19.
54 UNHCR (n 50) 9–10.
55 For example, see *Military and Paramilitary Activities in and against Nicaragua (Nicaragua v US)* [1986] ICJ Rep 1986, ¶ 243, where the ICJ held that '[a]n essential feature of truly humanitarian aid is that it is given "without discrimination" of any kind'.
56 Kate Mackintosh, 'Beyond the Red Cross: The Protection of Independent Humanitarian Organizations and their Staff in International Humanitarian Law' (2007) 89(865) *IRRC* 113, 116.
57 See James P Benoit, 'Wounded and sick, and medical services' ch 18 in this volume.

3 Legal obligations to protect humanitarian workers

The source of the international legal obligation to protect humanitarian personnel and human-itarian relief operations depends on the type of personnel involved (for example, whether they are employed by the United Nations, the Red Cross or other NGOs) and the type of situation in which the personnel are operating (for example, international or non-international armed conflict). Broadly, the legal provisions are divided into the law which protects humanitarian workers from attack (the law relating to the methods of warfare ('Hague law') and the law which protects the victims of armed conflict ('Geneva law').

3.1 The principle of distinction

As civilians, humanitarian workers are protected from attack by the law prohibiting the targeting of civilians in international and non-international armed conflict. In international armed con-flict, Additional Protocol I provides that the parties to the conflict must 'distinguish between the civilian population and combatants and between civilian objects and military objectives'. Attacks can only be directed against military objectives.[58] In non-international armed conflicts falling within the scope of Additional Protocol II, the civilian population is also specifically protected against attack.[59] The principle of distinction, in both international and non-international armed conflict, is regarded as a principle of customary international law.[60] Civilians only lose their protection if and for such time as they 'take a direct part in hostilities'.[61] The protection from attack for humanitarian personnel and their work, has been significantly progressed by the Rome Statute of the ICC, which provides that it is a war crime in both international and non-international armed conflict to intentionally direct attacks

> against personnel, installations, material, unit or vehicles involved in a humanitarian assist-ance or peacekeeping mission in accordance with the Charter of the United Nations, as long as they are entitled to protection given to civilians or civilian objects under the inter-national law of armed conflict.[62]

A similar provision is found in the Statute of the Special Court for Sierra Leone.[63] These provi-sions leave no doubt that humanitarian personnel and their operations must not be targeted, as both civilians generally, and explicitly, because of the nature of the activities they undertake.

3.2 General protection as civilians

As well as the provisions protecting humanitarian personnel and their operations from attack, humanitarian workers are entitled to protection under 'Geneva law'. At a minimum, as civilians they are entitled to the fundamental guarantees of humane treatment found in Article 75 of

58 API art 48.
59 APII art 13.
60 CIHL r 1, 3.
61 API art 51(3); APII art 13(3).
62 Rome Statute art 8(2)(b)(iii) (international armed conflict); art 8(2)(e)(iii) (non-international armed conflict). However, the threshold requirement contained in art 8(1) (that '[t]he Court shall have juris-diction in respect of war crimes in particular when committed as part of a plan or policy or as part of a large-scale commission of such crimes') would suggest that prosecution for attacks on humanitarian workers will be rare.
63 SCSL Statute art 4(b).

Additional Protocol I (in relation to international armed conflict) and Article 4 of Additional Protocol II and Common Article 3 (in relation to non-international armed conflict). Additionally, a question arises as to whether humanitarian workers are 'protected persons' for the purposes of Geneva Convention IV (the civilian convention). For the most part, Geneva Convention IV is designed to protect persons 'who find themselves ... in the hands of a Party to the conflict or Occupying Power of which they are not nationals'.[64] Nationals of neutral states with normal diplomatic relations with the belligerent state do not fall within this definition, the assumption being that they will be protected through normal diplomatic channels.[65] This definition clearly has implications for humanitarian staff falling within the protective provisions of Geneva Convention IV – a state's own nationals would not be classified as protected persons for the purposes of the Convention,[66] nor would international staff of neutral states where those states have regular diplomatic relations with the belligerent state. Mackintosh suggests that '[i]ronically ... if humanitarian organizations did send staff with the same nationality as the parties to the conflict, they might find that they were better protected'.[67] While this may be the case as a matter of law (or at least, international humanitarian law), as is demonstrated by the statistics compiled in the Aid Worker Security database, although expatriate aid workers are attacked at a higher rate than national staff members, the latter group 'because of their higher numbers and greater exposure in frontline field positions, comprise the vast majority of victims every year'.[68] Leaving aside the definition of protected persons, Part II of Geneva Convention IV provides basic protections to the whole of the populations in the countries in the conflict without distinction on the basis of race or nationality. Of relevance to this discussion is Article 20 which provides that particular types of workers, 'persons regularly and solely engaged in the operation administration of civilian hospitals', must be respected and protected.[69]

3.3 Specific protections for humanitarian personnel

A number of provisions of international humanitarian law specifically protect humanitarian personnel and facilitate their operations. In international armed conflicts, each of the four Geneva Conventions contains a provision enabling the ICRC or 'any other impartial humanitarian organization' to carry out 'humanitarian activities', subject to the consent of the parties to the conflict.[70] During a situation of occupation, the obligation on states is more onerous as the 'Occupying Power shall agree to relief schemes ... and shall facilitate them by all the means at its disposal' if the territory is inadequately supplied.[71] In non-international armed conflict, Additional Protocol II also provides that relief societies (such as the Red Cross) 'may offer their services for the performance of their traditional functions in relation to the victims of the armed

---

64 GCIV art 4.
65 Mackintosh (n 56) 119.
66 The extended definition of protected persons suggested by the ICTY in *Tadić*, whereby weight is given to a person's allegiance to a party to a conflict or ethnicity, as distinct from the 'legal bond of nationality', is unlikely to be of great assistance in protecting humanitarian workers. See *Prosecutor v Tadić* (Case no ICTY-99-IT-94-1-A, ICTY Appeals Chamber, 15 July 1999) ¶¶ 165–166.
67 Mackintosh (n 56) 119.
68 Humanitarian Outcomes, 'Aid Worker Security Report 2011' (n 12) 8. The 2014 report indicates that the organisations that 'suffered the greatest number of attacks were local NGOs and national Red Cross/Crescent Societies. This is not surprising since these actors tend to be the front-line responders in the deep field.' See 'Aid Worker Security Report 2014' (n 13) 3.
69 GCIV art 20.
70 GCI–III art 9; GCIV art 10.
71 GCIV art 59.

conflict' and that medical personnel 'shall be granted all available help in the performance of their duties'.[72] These provisions will be discussed in more detail in Secion 4 of this chapter, suffice to say at this point that although such provisions do not clearly protect humanitarian personnel, the ability of organisations to undertake humanitarian activities depends on a certain level of protection for their personnel.

Explicit protective provisions are included in Additional Protocol I, which provides that relief personnel, civilian medical personnel and civil defence personnel 'shall be respected and protected'.[73] Additional Protocol II provides the same level of protection for medical personnel and medical units.[74] The concept of respect and protection are defined in the commentaries as meaning 'to spare, not to attack' (respect), while protect means 'to come to someone's defence, to lend help and support'.[75] In the commentary to Article 11 of Additional Protocol I (dealing with medical transports), it is stated that respect and protection: 'imply not only the obligation to spare the people and objects concerned, but also to actively take measures to ensure that medical units and transports are able to perform their functions and to give them assistance when necessary'.[76]

Consequently there is both a negative obligation not to attack and a positive obligation to provide assistance where necessary. In the event that humanitarian personnel on a United Nations operation fulfil the definitions in the Convention on the Safety of United Nations and Associated Personnel, then state parties to that Convention are under an obligation to take all appropriate measures to ensure the safety and security of such personnel.[77] The obligation extends to cooperating to prevent crimes against such personnel and to prosecute or extradite offenders.[78] In addition, United Nations personnel benefit from certain privileges and immunities as set out in the Convention on the Privileges and Immunities of the United Nations to enable them to exercise their functions. These privileges and immunities apply to experts 'performing functions for the United Nations' and extend to immunity from arrest and detention and immunity for words spoken or acts done in the course of the performance of the mission.[79] Such provisions protect personnel from actions which may impact on the viability of UN missions.

The plethora of treaty provisions has led the ICRC to conclude in its Study on Customary International Law that it is the principle of customary international law in both international and non-international armed conflicts that 'humanitarian personnel must be respected and protected'.[80] This principle is seen as a corollary of the prohibition on starvation of the civilian population and the rule that the wounded and sick must be collected and cared for.[81] The Study reinforces the customary status of this rule by highlighting that violations have been condemned by states and international organisations alike.[82] Consequently, both the General Assembly and the Security Council have condemned violent acts against humanitarian personnel and United

72 APII arts 18(1), 9(1).
73 See API art 71(2) (relief personnel); art 15 (civilian medical personnel); art 62(1) (civil defence personnel).
74 APII art 9(1) (personnel); art 11(1) (units and transports).
75 *AP Commentary* 146.
76 Ibid 1433.
77 UN Safety Convention (n 42) art 7(2).
78 Ibid arts 13 and 14.
79 Convention on the Privileges and Immunities of the United Nations (13 February 1946) 1 UNTS 15, art VI, s 22(a) and (b).
80 CIHL r 31.
81 Ibid.
82 Ibid.

Nations and associated personnel in complex humanitarian emergencies, and urged states to take the necessary measures to ensure the safety and security of humanitarian personnel either generally, or in relation to specific conflicts.[83]

3.4 The provision of protection

One question that arises in terms of the protection offered to humanitarian personnel is: who should provide such protection? Should the obligation to protect be on the territorial state (the state where the personnel operate), the humanitarian organisations themselves or perhaps UN peacekeeping personnel (in situations where a UN mission has been authorised by the Security Council)? The Additional Protocols indicate that impartial humanitarian personnel (and their consignments) should be respected – this obligation is clearly directed to the parties to a conflict (states). For example, Article 70 of Additional Protocol I provides that the parties 'shall protect relief consignments and facilitate their rapid distribution'.[84] The commentary suggests that this requires a party 'to do its utmost to prevent such relief from being diverted from its legitimate destination'.[85] The commentaries to Article 71(2) (dealing with the duty to respect and protect relief personnel) state that: '[t]he obligation to respect and protect relief personnel applies to all the Parties to the conflict, which should, in particular, inform and instruct the armed forces not to attack such personnel'.[86] The commentary also states that in the event that the protective emblem of the Red Cross is not applicable, then the 'receiving Party' (the territorial state) to the conflict may decide whether they wish to attach an armed escort to the convoy.[87] Consequently, the commentaries envisage the possibility of armed personnel escorting a humanitarian mission. In a situation of occupation, Article 59 of Geneva Convention IV provides that the Occupying Power 'shall facilitate [relief schemes] by all the means at its disposal'. The commentary to this provision does not make reference to armed escorts, but the broad nature of this provision would also suggest that military escorts are a possibility.[88] However, as a practical matter, the use of armed escorts for protection is controversial. A joint working group of the ICRC and the International Federation of Red Cross and Red Crescent Societies came to the conclusion that the use of armed escorts conflicts with a number of Fundamental Principles of the Red Cross movement (not least, impartiality and neutrality) and that they should only be used in situations where 'human lives may be saved only by accepting an armed escort'.[89] Certain (strict) criteria for accepting an escort were suggested by the working group, including the pressing nature of the need and the approval of the party controlling the territory through which a humanitarian convoy may move.[90] Member states may not be equipped to provide security (particularly where territory is outside governmental control) and humanitarian actors may be reluctant to accept government security for reasons of principle where the government is a party to the

---

83 See eg UNSC Res 1502 (2003); UNGA Res 64/77 (7 December 2009); UNSC Res 2003 (2011) ¶ 3 (Darfur); UNSC Res 2036 (2012) ¶ 16 (Somalia).
84 API art 70.
85 *AP Commentary* 828.
86 Ibid 834.
87 Ibid.
88 'The occupation authorities must … co-operate wholeheartedly in the rapid and scrupulous execution of the schemes. For that purpose they have many and varied means at their disposal (transport, stores, facilities for distributing and supervising agencies)': *GCIV Commentary* 320.
89 ICRC and International Federation, Council of Delegates, 'Report on the Use of Armed Protection for Humanitarian Assistance' (1995) 'III Findings and Principles'.
90 Ibid.

conflict.[91] Pursuant to international humanitarian law, the use of military forces to secure a convoy will not change the status of humanitarian personnel as civilians; however, if the armed forces come under attack, then humanitarian workers may be injured or killed as 'incidental loss of civilian life' (collateral damage).[92]

It is possible for humanitarian organisations to provide their own security. Additional Protocol I recognises that civilian medical units retain their protected status even if their personnel are equipped with light individual weapons for their own defence or for that of the wounded and sick in their charge.[93] The commentaries reveal that the prospect of civilian medical personnel carrying arms was controversial, but that it was admitted 'that civilian medical personnel were exposed to the same dangers and had to deal with the same situations as military medical personnel'.[94] Civil defence personnel may also carry light individual weapons for the purpose of maintaining order or for self-defence.[95] Once more, the commentaries describe the discussion surrounding the adoption of this provision as 'heated'[96] with restrictions being put on the type of weapons that may be carried in areas where land fighting is taking, or is likely to take, place.[97]

As an alternative, humanitarian organisations may rely on an armed security escort from a private military security company. Humanitarian organisations are reluctant to discuss these arrangements and the allocation of costs in an organisation's budget is an important consideration.[98] Williamson distinguishes between the provision of armed escorts to enable humanitarian organisations to access locations, and, security systems which may be used to safeguard facilities and households of humanitarian organisations.[99] In situations where humanitarian organisations employ private military and security contractors to obtain access to areas, questions may arise as to the status of such an escort under international humanitarian law. Contractors are classified as civilians rather than combatants as they are not part of the armed forces of a party to a conflict.[100] As civilians, they maintain their protection unless they take a direct part in hostilities. If a humanitarian convoy came under attack and members of a security company responded, then a question arises as to whether the security personnel are directly participating in hostilities (and therefore liable to be targeted). The ICRC's Interpretive Guidance on Direct Participation in Hostilities discounts this possibility by stating that merely by acting in self-defence against attack, a civilian is not taken to have directly participated in hostilities.[101]

---

91 Abby Stoddard and Adele Harmer, 'Supporting Security for Humanitarian Action: A Review of Critical Issues for the Humanitarian Community' (Humanitarian Outcomes 2010) 5. See also comments in the *Good Practice Review*: 'Overly protective state arrangements for aid agencies can increase insecurity due to perception of partiality, and can make it more difficult for agencies to respond impartially to needs by making access dependent on state police or military escorts', in Overseas Development Institute, 'Operational Security Management' (n 5) 23.
92 API art 51(5)(b).
93 API art 13(2)(a).
94 *AP Commentary* 177.
95 API art 65(3).
96 *AP Commentary* 774.
97 API art 65(3).
98 See discussion in Andrew Bearpark, 'The Case for Humanitarian Organizations to Use Private Security Contractors' in Benjamin Perrin (ed), *Modern Warfare: Armed Groups, Private Militaries, Humanitarian Organizations, and the Law* (UBC Press 2012) 157, 164; Stoddard and Harmer (n 91) 6.
99 Jamie Williamson, 'The Use of Armed Security Escorts: A Challenge to Independent and Neutral Humanitarian Action' in Perrin (n 98) 168, 171.
100 For a definition of the 'armed forces of a Party to a conflict', see API art 43.
101 ICRC, *Interpretive Guidance on the Notion of Direct Participation in Hostilities under International Humanitarian Law* (ICRC 2009) 61.

Finally, there may be situations where UN missions authorised by the Security Council have an obligation to protect humanitarian personnel pursuant to a Security Council resolution. The approach of the Security Council in protecting civilians and the difficulties with including a mandate to protect civilians in UN authorised missions are discussed in detail in a report commissioned by the Department of Peacekeeping Operations and the Office for the Coordination of Humanitarian Affairs, *Protecting Civilians in the Context of UN Peacekeeping Operations: Successes, Setbacks and Remaining Challenges*.[102] The report notes that an increasing number of missions are expressly mandated to protect civilians with ten UN peacekeeping operations (by mid-2009) including an authorisation to 'protect civilians under imminent threat of physical violence'.[103] A number of such operations have also been given a mandate to facilitate humanitarian assistance and protect humanitarian personnel. Such missions include MONUC in the Democratic Republic of the Congo where the mission was authorised to 'ensure the protection of civilians, including humanitarian personnel, under imminent threat of physical violence, in particular violence emanating from any of the parties engaged in the conflict',[104] and to 'facilitate humanitarian assistance ... as MONUC deems within its capabilities'.[105] The operation in Darfur (UNAMID) was authorised to facilitate humanitarian assistance, including ('within its capabilities'), 'to ensure the security and freedom of movement of ... humanitarian workers' and to 'facilitate the effective provision of humanitarian assistance and full access to people in need'.[106] More recently, the United Nations Mission in South Sudan (UNMISS) has been authorised to 'provide security for United Nations and humanitarian personnel, installations and equipment necessary for implementation of mandated tasks'.[107] The Force Commander has stated that 'while UNMISS was beholden to ensure that humanitarian organizations could operate safely, some of those organizations were uncomfortable with that arrangement, as it conflicted with humanitarian principles'.[108] This statement accurately captures the obligation, derived from a binding Chapter VII resolution, but also the difficulty, in providing protection to humanitarian personnel.

4 Are states obliged to facilitate humanitarian activities?

The final question to consider is whether states are obliged to facilitate humanitarian activities under international humanitarian law or human rights law. The above Security Council resolutions indicate that there may be situations where a UN mission is mandated to facilitate humanitarian work and protect humanitarian workers within its sphere of operations. The Security Council may also demand that parties to a conflict grant access to humanitarian organisations. For example, in relation to the conflict in Syria the Security Council has demanded 'that all parties, in particular the Syrian authorities, promptly allow rapid, safe and unhindered humanitarian access for United Nations humanitarian agencies and their implementing partners, including

---

102 Victoria Holt and Glyn Taylor (with Max Kelly), *Protecting Civilians in the Context of UN Peacekeeping Operations: Successes, Setbacks and Remaining Challenges* (UN 2009).
103 Ibid 43–44.
104 UNSC Res 1856 (2008) ¶ 3; UNSC Res 1565 (2004) ¶ 4; UNSC Res 1493 (2003) ¶ 25.
105 UNSC Res 1291 (2000) ¶ 7.
106 'The Report of the Secretary-General and the Chairperson of the African Union Commission on the Hybrid Operation in Darfur' UN Doc S/2007/307/REV.1 (2007) ¶ 55(b).
107 UNSC Res 1996 (2011) ¶ 3(b).
108 'In Meeting with Security Council, United Nations Peacekeeping Force Commanders' UN Doc SC/10679 (20 June 2012).

across conflict lines and across borders'.[109] Outside these missions and binding resolutions, a number of provisions of international humanitarian law aim to facilitate humanitarian assistance to civilians, with the treaties and commentaries placing the primary responsibility on the state to provide such assistance. This is clear from legal provisions such as Article 60 of Geneva Convention IV, which states that the presence of relief consignments from impartial humanitarian organisations does not relieve the occupying power of its responsibility to ensure food and medical supplies for a population.[110] In non-international armed conflict, the commentary to Article 18 of Additional Protocol II provides that 'States are primarily responsible for organizing relief' – relief societies 'play an auxiliary role by assisting the authorities in their task'.[111] The resolution of the Institute of International Law on Humanitarian Assistance also emphasises the state's duty with respect to 'the organization, provision and distribution of humanitarian assistance'.[112]

In an international armed conflict the ICRC or any other impartial humanitarian organisation may undertake relief and protection work for wounded, sick and shipwrecked members of the armed forces, prisoners of war and civilians.[113] In non-international armed conflicts, Additional Protocol II provides that relief actions may also be undertaken if the civilian population is 'suffering undue hardship'.[114] The key point is that such work, whether in international or non-international armed conflict, is subject to state consent and control.[115] However, commentators and the commentaries to Additional Protocol I also highlight that the state should not be able to refuse such relief on arbitrary grounds.[116] If starvation would result from a refusal to allow relief activities, then the rule prohibiting the starvation of civilians as a method of warfare would come into play (as would the associated war crime of the intentional starvation of civilians as a method of warfare through the deprivation of objects indispensable for their survival, such as 'wilfully impeding relief supplies' in international armed conflict).[117] Geneva Convention IV

---

109 UNSC Res 2139 (2014) ¶ 6. See also UNSC Res 2165 (2014) ¶ 6.

110 GCIV arts 60, 55 and 56. In API art 69 this is extended to the provision of other supplies 'essential to the survival of the civilian population and objects necessary for religious worship'.

111 *AP Commentary* 1477.

112 Institute of International Law (n 47) III(1).

113 GCI–III art 9; GCIV art 10.

114 APII art 18(2). Common art 3 also provides that an impartial humanitarian body, such as the ICRC, may offer its services to the parties to the conflict.

115 *GCI Commentary* 110. See also API art 70; APII art 18(2). In non-international armed conflicts, consent from any non-state actors controlling or operating in the territory would be necessary from a practical point of view: Felix Schwendimann, 'The Legal Framework of Humanitarian Access in Armed Conflict' (2011) 93(884) *IRRC* 993, 1001.

116 *APII Commentary* 1479:

> The fact that consent is required does not mean that the decision is left to the discretion of the parties. If the survival of the population is threatened and a humanitarian organization fulfilling the required conditions of impartiality and non-discrimination is able to remedy this situation, relief actions must take place.

> See also CIHL r 55; Schwendimann (n 115) 998. However, *GCI Commentary* 110–111 states that belligerent powers 'do not have to give a reason for their refusals. The decision is entirely theirs. But being bound to apply the Convention, they alone must bear the responsibility if they refuse help in carrying out their engagements.'

117 See API art 51(1); APII art 14. CIHL links the rules relating to the provision and facilitation of humanitarian assistance and that dealing with the prohibition of starvation as a method of warfare. Consequently, 'deliberately impeding humanitarian aid ... or restricting the freedom of movement of humanitarian relief personnel ... may constitute violations of the prohibition of starvation'. See CIHL rr 55 and 56. The war crime is found in the Rome Statute art 8(2)(b)(xxv).

also provides that civilians (whether in international armed conflict or in occupied territory) '*shall* have every facility for making applications' to the Protecting Powers, the Red Cross or any other organisation 'that might be able to assist them'.[118] Furthermore, these organisations shall be 'granted all facilities for that purpose by the authority, within the bounds set by military or security considerations'.[119] More broadly, states have a duty to allow the free passage of consignments of medical and hospital stores intended for civilians. Specifically, they should permit 'free passage of all consignments of essential foodstuffs, clothing and tonics intended for children under fifteen, expectant mothers and maternity cases'.[120] This obligation is only subject to defined exceptions, for example, if 'the consignments may be diverted from their destination'.[121] In occupied territories, the obligation on an occupying power is more exacting as National Red Cross and Red Crescent societies, '*shall* be able to pursue their activities in accordance with Red Cross principles' and other relief societies shall also be permitted to continue their activities, subject only 'to temporary and exceptional measures imposed for urgent reasons of security'.[122] Consequently, the threshold to be satisfied in order for relief to be refused is high, suggesting that there is an obligation on states to accept humanitarian relief where such relief is required.[123] This is certainly the view expressed in the ICRC's Study on Customary International Law which provides that it is a rule of customary international law that the parties (in both an international and a non-international armed conflict) 'must allow and facilitate rapid and unimpeded passage of humanitarian relief to civilians in need, which is impartial in character and conducted without any adverse distinction, subject to their right of control'.[124]

International human rights law may also provide some support for an obligation to facilitate humanitarian assistance during armed conflict. It has been recognised that both international humanitarian law and international human rights law may apply during an armed conflict (unless a state has derogated from its obligations under human rights law).[125] Treaties such as the International Covenant on Civil and Political Rights and the International Covenant on Economic, Social and Cultural Rights protect the right to life, the right to an adequate standard of living, including adequate food, clothing and housing, and the right to enjoy the highest attainable standard of physical and mental health.[126] Pursuant to the International Covenant on Economic, Social, and Cultural Rights (ICESCR), state parties have an obligation to 'take steps, individually and through international assistance and cooperation ... to the maximum of its available resources, with a view to achieving progressively the full realisation of the rights recognised in

---

118 GCIV art 30 (emphasis added).
119 Ibid.
120 GCIV art 23.
121 GCIV art 23(a).
122 GCIV art 63 (emphasis added).
123 Rebecca Barber, 'Facilitating Humanitarian Assistance in International Humanitarian Law and Human Rights Law' (2009) 91(874) *IRRC* 371, 391; Swiss Federal Department of Foreign Affairs, *Humanitarian Access in Situations of Armed Conflict: Handbook on the Normative Framework* (2011) 23.
124 CIHL r 55.
125 See discussion in Barber (n 123) 391. See also *Legal Consequences of the Construction of a Wall in the Occupied Palestinian Territory (Advisory Opinion)* [2004] ICJ Rep 136, ¶ 106:

> [T]he Court considers that the protection offered by human rights conventions does not cease in case of armed conflict, save through the effect of provisions for derogation of the kind to be found in Article 4 of the International Covenant on Civil and Political Rights.

126 ICCPR art 1; ICESCR arts 1, 12. See also the Convention on the Rights of the Child (20 November 1989) 1577 UNTS 3; African Charter on Human Rights (20 November 1969) 1520 UNTS 217.

the present Covenant by all appropriate means'.[127] On the basis of such provisions and comments by the Committee on Economic, Social and Cultural Rights regarding the extent of the obligations contained in the ICESCR, Barber concludes that 'international human rights law ... provides a more substantive protection of humanitarian assistance than does international humanitarian law'.[128] In the event that a state is unable to fulfil its obligations to provide such assistance, then there is some support in soft law instruments for a duty on the state to seek assistance from other states or international organisations.[129] Finally, it should be noted that the right of organisations or states to provide humanitarian assistance should be distinguished from the right of civilians to receive such assistance.[130] Yoram Dinstein asserts that '[n]o customary norm has so far crystallized in the international law of armed conflict to establish a general right to humanitarian assistance ... solely because provisions are scarce'.[131] Thus, while international humanitarian law and international human rights law facilitates (and even necessitates) the provision of assistance by humanitarian organisations, such organisations are not under a duty to provide assistance in the event that the state is unable to provide relief.

5 Conclusion

In a 2011 handbook setting out the normative framework for humanitarian access, the Swiss Federal Department of Foreign Affairs highlights that the law is 'an important tool for humanitarian negotiators' where there is a need to negotiate access with parties to a conflict.[132] It provides a 'structured and practical approach to humanitarian access'.[133] Despite this framework, attacks on humanitarian workers have increased, particularly in a small number of violent conflict situations. International humanitarian law provides a number of protections for humanitarian workers against attack and also provisions that facilitate humanitarian access. Although the provisions are not comprehensive (in the sense that the law differs depending on whether the situation is classified as either occupation, international or non-international armed conflict) it is unlikely that amendments to the law would result in a significant reduction in the number of violent attacks against humanitarian personnel. A number of publications set out the key principles for humanitarian actors in gaining access to high risk environments.[134] In addition, the ICRC has recently published a compendium of practical measures for state armed forces 'to mitigate the effect of military operations on the safe access to and delivery of health care'.[135]

127 ICESCR art 2(1).
128 Barber (n 123) 395.
129 Institute of International Law (n 47) III(3). The International Law Commission, in its draft articles on the protection of persons in the event of disasters (which do not apply in situations where IHL is applicable) has included a duty on states to seek assistance where necessary, and not to withhold consent to such assistance on arbitrary grounds (draft arts 10 and 11): see International Law Commission, UN Doc A/66/10 (2011) 255. On the extent of this duty in peacetime, see also J Benton Heath, 'Disasters, Relief, and Neglect: The Duty to Accept Humanitarian Assistance and the Work of the International Law Commission' (2011) 43 *NYU JILP* 419.
130 Yoram Dinstein, 'The Right to Humanitarian Assistance' (2000) 53(4) *NWCR* 77, 78.
131 Ibid 79.
132 Swiss Federal Department of Foreign Affairs (n 123) 9.
133 Ibid.
134 Schwendimann (n 115) 1007. Publications that discuss security and access for humanitarian personnel include David Lloyd Roberts, *Staying Alive: Safety and Security Guidelines for Humanitarian Volunteers in Conflict Areas* (ICRC 2005); Swiss Department of Foreign Affairs, *Humanitarian Access in Situations of Armed Conflict: Field Manual Version 1.0* (2011).
135 ICRC, 'Promoting Military Operational Practice that Ensures Safe Access to and Delivery of Health Care' (2014) 33–42.

It is through such principles and also through a greater dissemination of the law that secure access may be gained. Consequently, commentators have suggested that the focus should not be on the development of new rules, but rather on implementation of the existing rules.[136] However, despite the plethora of legal provisions, there have not been any criminal prosecutions of those associated with attacks against humanitarian workers.[137] The prosecution of those responsible for attacks on humanitarian workers would not only highlight the relevance of the legal provisions but also the seriousness with which such attacks are viewed by the international community.[138]

---

136 For example, Alexander Breitegger, 'The Legal Framework Applicable to Insecurity and Violence Affecting the Delivery of Health Care in Armed Conflicts and Other Emergencies' (2013) 95 *IRRC* 83, 125.
137 Helen Durham and Phoebe Wynn-Pope, 'Protecting the "Helpers": Humanitarian and Health Care Workers during Times of Armed Conflict' (2011) 14 *YBIHL* 327, 344.
138 Ibid 344–345.

24

The applicability of the laws of armed conflict to peacekeeping operations

Daphna Shraga

The debate over the applicability of international humanitarian law (IHL) to UN peacekeeping operations which spanned the 1990s ended with the promulgation of the Secretary-General's Bulletin on the Observance by United Nations Forces of International Humanitarian Law.[1] In the decade that followed, a new and more complex debate emerged over the scope of application of IHL in the specificities of UN operations, the 'duality' of peacekeepers, the application of the laws of occupation to UN transitional administrations, the convergence or divergence of IHL and international human rights law (IHRL), and the responsibility of the UN for violations of IHL or IHRL by members of its peacekeeping operations. It was a debate situated at the intersection of many disciplines: of IHL, IHRL, international criminal law, responsibility of international organisations and privileges and immunities of the organisation and its personnel.

1 The applicability of IHL to peacekeeping operations: a legislative history of the debate

For almost four decades after the Korea operation in the 1950s, the applicability of IHL to peacekeeping operations was conceived as a theoretical assumption, a voluntarily assumed undertaking or a statement of policy, but only rarely as a legally binding obligation. The Congo operation in the 1960s was the sole exception, not only in acknowledging responsibility for violations of the laws of war, but in accepting liability for the largest compensation payment ever made in any single UN operation.[2]

---

1 UN Doc ST/SGB/1999/13 (6 August 1999).
2 Secretary-General's Letter dated 6 August 1965 to the Representative of the Union of Soviet Socialist Republics Concerning Payment of Indemnities to Belgian Citizens Residents of the Democratic Republic of the Congo, UN Doc S/6597. For the settlement agreements on lump-sum payments made by the UN to states whose nationals suffered damages from ONUC military actions see, Exchange of Letters Relating to the Settlement of Claims Filed against the United Nations in the Congo by Belgian Nationals, UN–Belgium (20 February 1965) 535 UNTS 197; see also settlement agreements with Switzerland (3 June 1966) 564 UNTS 193, Greece (20 June 1966) 565 UNTS 3, Luxembourg (28 December 1966) 585 UNTS 147, Italy (18 January 1967) 588 UNTS 197; Jean J A Salmon, 'Les Accords Spaak-U Thant du 26 fèvrier 1965' (1965) 11 *Annuaire Français de Droit International* 468.

By the mid-1990s, a combination of seemingly unrelated developments had converged to bring the question of the applicability of IHL to peacekeeping operations to the fore of the UN agenda. By then, UN operations had grown in number, scope and complexity of mandates. Deployed in conflict situations of extreme brutality where attacks against peacekeepers had dramatically increased, UN forces were compelled to resort to the use of force, both offensive and defensive. As they became willingly or unwillingly involved as a 'party to the conflict', allegations of serious violations of IHL and IHRL in the areas of their deployment began to surface. For the UN, which had ushered in an era of accountability, abuses by peacekeeping personnel engaged in combat could no longer be ignored.

In an incremental process, the UN Secretariat had put in place a normative framework for the conduct of the military activities of peacekeeping operations. In the 1960s, when Regulations for the Force were still promulgated, they provided that the Force shall observe the 'principles and spirit' of the general international conventions applicable to the conduct of military personnel;[3] a formula which in its more elaborated form was included as a standard clause in all Status of Forces Agreements since the early 1990s.[4] It was not, however, until 1999 when the Secretary-General promulgated the Bulletin that the UN explicitly recognised – what by then was widely accepted – that IHL applies to UN peacekeepers when actively engaged in combat.

The application of IHL to UN operations was predicated on the principle that what is customarily applicable to states should also be considered applicable *mutatis mutandis* to the UN as a consequence of its international legal personality, and regardless of its own contribution to the creation of the customary norm. In distilling the core IHL rules for UN forces, the Secretary-General has, thus, circumscribed their material, temporal and territorial scope of application and adapted them to the specificities of UN operations. Accordingly, the Secretary-General's Bulletin (and by implication IHL) applies to members of UN forces when, in situations of armed conflict, they are actively engaged therein as combatants, to the extent and for the duration of their engagement. It applies in enforcement actions when the use of force is authorised in

---

3 Regulations for the United Nations Emergency Force (UNEF), UN Doc ST/SGB/UNEF/1 (20 February 1957) reg 44; Regulations for the United Nations Force in the Congo, UN Doc ST/SGB/ONUC/1 (15 July 1963) reg 43; Regulations for the United Nations Force in Cyprus, UN Doc ST/SGB/UNFICYP/1 (25 April 1964) reg 40.

4 Accordingly, the UN has undertaken to ensure that the Force conducts its operations with full respect for the principles and spirit (later replaced by 'principles and rules') of the general international conventions applicable to the conduct of military personnel, ie the four Geneva Conventions of 1949, their two Additional Protocols of 1977 and the Convention on the Protection of Cultural Property in the Event of Armed Conflict of 1954; the host state has, on its part, undertaken the correlative obligation to treat the UN Force at all times with full respect for the principles and spirit of the general international conventions applicable to the treatment of military personnel.

pursuit of a Chapter VII mandate and in traditional Chapter VI operations when it is permitted in self-defence.[5]

At the time of its adoption, the Secretary-General's Bulletin was critiqued for having included conventional IHL provisions, not yet universally recognised as part of customary international law, and for blurring the distinction between international and non-international armed conflicts. The criticism, on both grounds, was not entirely misplaced.

For the Secretary-General the customary international law nature of the core IHL provisions was both the legal basis for the application of IHL to peacekeeping operations, and a limitation put on the choice of the applicable law. Mindful of the risk that deviating from what is universally considered customary international law would be seen as exceeding his powers and legislating for states, the Secretary-General limited the scope of the Bulletin to the lowest common denominator by which all national contingents would otherwise be bound. The exceptions were the provisions on the prohibitions on using methods of warfare intended to cause widespread, long-term and severe damage to the natural environment, and on rendering useless objects indispensable to the survival of the civilian population causing the release of dangerous forces with consequent severe losses among the civilian population. Given their importance and the devastating effect that violating these prohibitions could wreak on the natural environment and the civilian population at large, their inclusion amounted above all to an undertaking to abide by the highest standard of conduct within the general consensus of states.

The Secretary-General's Bulletin declined to qualify the nature of the conflict in the area of the UN operation, and thus implicitly applied the core IHL norms across the international/non-international divide. While not unaware of the criticism that in so doing the Secretariat might have blurred the distinction between the two regimes, the Secretary-General considered that the applicability of the Bulletin to UN forces regardless of the nature of the operation is consistent with the UN unqualified undertaking in the Status of Forces Agreement to abide by the entirety of the 1949 Geneva Conventions, their 1977 Additional Protocols, as well as the 1954 Cultural Property Convention. It reflected also the realities of peacekeeping operations deployed in situations characterised by aspects of both international and non-international armed conflicts – a

---

5 On the applicability of IHL to peacekeeping operations, in general, and the Secretary-General's Bulletin, in particular, see, D W Bowett, *United Nations Forces: A Legal Study* (Praeger 1964) 484–516; Finn Seyersted, *United Nations Forces in the Law of Peace and War* (Sijthoff 1966) 178–220; Dietrich Schindler, 'United Nations Forces and International Humanitarian Law' in Christophe Swinarski (ed), *Studies and Essays on International Humanitarian Law and Red Cross Principles in Honour of Jean Pictet* (Nijhoff 1984) 521; Richard D Glick, 'Lip Service to the Laws of War: Humanitarian Law and United Nations Armed Forces' (1995) 17 *Michigan JIL* 53; Hilaire McCoubrey and Nigel D White, *The Blue Helmets: Legal Regulation of United Nations Military Operations* (Darmouth 1996); Christopher Greenwood, 'International Humanitarian Law and United Nations Military Operations' (1998) 1 *YBIHL* 3; Brian D Tittemore, 'Belligerents in Blue Helmets: Applying International Humanitarian Law to United Nations Peace Operations' (1997) 33 *Stanford JIL* 61; Jaume Saura, 'Lawful Peacekeeping: Applicability of International Humanitarian Law to United Nations Peacekeeping Operations' (2007) 58 *Hastings LJ* 479; Marten Zwanenburg, 'The Secretary-General's Bulletin on Observance by United Nations Forces of International Humanitarian Law' (2000) 39 *RDMDG* 14; Daphna Shraga, 'The United Nations as an Actor Bound by International Humanitarian Law' in *The United Nations and International Humanitarian Law: Actes du Colloque International de l'Université de Genève* (Pedone 1996) 318, reprinted in (1998) 5(2) *International Peacekeeping* 64; Daphna Shraga, 'UN Peacekeeping Operations: Applicability of International Humanitarian Law and Responsibility for Operation-Related Damage' (2000) 94 *AJIL* 406, 407–408; Luigi Condorelli, 'Les Progrès de Droit International Humanitaire et la Circulaire du Secrétaire Général des Nations Unies du 6 Août 1999' in Laurence Boisson de Chazournes and Verra Gowlland-Debbas (eds), *The International Legal System in Quest of Equity and Universality: Liber Amicorum Georges Abi-Saab* (Springer 2001) 496.

distinctive feature of the conflict in Bosnia and Herzegovina and, at times, the situation in the North-Eastern DRC.

A decade after the promulgation of the Bulletin, general developments in international law and jurisprudence expanded the scope of application of IHL rules on the protection of civilians, repression of war crimes and the prohibition of the use of certain weapons in international armed conflicts to non-international armed conflicts. In dispensing with the distinction between the two, they also validated the Secretariat's initial choice of the core IHL provisions, and their application invariably to international and non-international armed conflicts.[6]

2 The specificities of peacekeeping operations: the 'double-key' test and the duality of peacekeepers

2.1 The 'double-key' test

Under the Secretary-General's Bulletin, for IHL to apply to UN forces two cumulative conditions must be met: the existence of an armed conflict in the area of their deployment, and their actual engagement in the conflict as combatants. While the former triggers the applicability of IHL to the situation in the first place, the latter triggers it in respect of the UN force. Under this 'double-key' or a 'circle-within-a circle' test, it is only if and when they are actively engaged in combat that UN forces are subject to IHL, and this, for the duration of their engagement only. When the UN combat mission ends – and regardless of whether or not the situation as a whole still qualifies as an armed conflict – IHL ceases to apply to the UN operation.[7]

The foremost example of a peacekeeping operation engaged intermittently in combat action was the UN Operation in Somalia (UNOSOM II). Launched in response to the attack on the Pakistani troops on 5 June 1993 by forces of General Mohammed Farah Aideed, UNOSOM II was authorised by Security Council Resolution 837 (1993) 'to take all necessary measures' against all those responsible for the armed attacks. On 12 June 1993, UNOSOM II mounted a military offensive through a series of air and ground operations in South Mogadishu. The UN Commission of Inquiry established by Security Council Resolution 885 (1993) to investigate armed attacks on UNOSOM II personnel described the period following the adoption of Resolution 837 and the continued attacks against UNOSOM II in its efforts to capture Aideed, as a 'virtual war situation between UNOSOM II and the SNA [the Somali National Alliance], as the two sides attacked each other over a period of four weeks'.[8] The 'war' between UNOSOM II and the SNA, however, was part of a larger context of a civil war of total anarchy, widespread

---

6 Daphna Shraga, 'The Secretary-General's Bulletin on the Observance by United Nations Forces of International Humanitarian Law: A Decade Later' (2009) 39 *Israel YBHR* 357; Jean-Marie Henckaerts and Louise Doswald-Beck (eds), *Customary International Humanitarian Law* (CUP 2005) xxix. In its Decision on Jurisdiction in the *Tadić* case, the Appeals Chamber of the ICTY concluded that 'in the area of armed conflict the distinction between interstate wars and civil wars is losing its value as far as human beings are concerned'. *Prosecutor v Tadić (Decision on the Defence Motion for Interlocutory Appeal on Jurisdiction)* (Case no IT-94-1-AR-72, 2 October 1995) ¶ 97.

7 Terry D Gill, 'Legal Characterization and Basis for Enforcement Operations and Peace Enforcement Operations under the Charter' in Terry D Gill and Dieter Fleck (eds), *The Handbook of the International Law of Military Operations* (OUP 2010) 81, 87–88. For a critical view of the intermittent application of IHL to UN forces, see Marten C Zwanenburg, *Accountability under International Humanitarian Law for United Nations and North Atlantic Treaty Organization Peace Support Operations* (E M Meijers Instituut 2004) 199–201.

8 Report of the Commission of Inquiry Established Pursuant to Resolution 885 (1993) to Investigate Armed Attacks on UNOSOM II Personnel, UN Doc S/1994/653 (1 June 1994) ¶ 125.

lawlessness, inter-clan fighting and a total collapse of governmental authority and control. It was a 'war-within-a-war', or – within the meaning of Section 1 of the Secretary-General's Bulletin – a situation of armed conflict in which UN forces were actively engaged as combatants. It was nevertheless implicit in the view of the Commission that at no point in the period leading to and including the attack of 5 June, were UNOSOM II personnel considered combatants and that at the time of the attack they were persons *hors de combat*. For the Security Council, the 'unprovoked attacks' of 5 June against UNOSOM II personnel were considered 'criminal acts' for which those responsible should have been arrested, detained, prosecuted, tried and punished. In the aftermath of the attack on the Pakistani troops, and following the adoption of Resolution 837 on 6 June 1993, more particularly, when UNOSOM II was engaged in combat, IHL would have applied to UN forces as a 'party to the conflict'.

2.2 The duality of peacekeepers as civilians and combatants

The dual nature of peacekeepers as both – though not simultaneously – civilians and combatants is premised on the assumption that in the circumstances of multidimensional peacekeeping operations deployed in conflict situations, the military component of the operation, in the conduct of its *non-military* or routine operational activities, is entitled to protected civilian status. A distinction between peacekeepers as civilians and as combatants, challenging though it may be in the realities of peacekeeping operations, is necessary for the determination of whether and for how long the UN operation becomes a 'party to the conflict', and whether an attack against peacekeepers constitutes an international crime or a lawful act of combat.

The duality of peacekeepers was the underlying premise of the 1994 Convention on the Safety of United Nations and Associated Personnel.[9] The Convention internationalised the crime of attacks against peacekeepers, enjoined the parties to make them punishable by law and 'to prosecute or extradite' the offender. It failed, however, to distinguish between the protective regime of the Convention and IHL, a distinction critical to the qualification of attacks against peacekeepers as international crimes or lawful acts of combat. Furthermore, Article 20 of the Convention ('without-prejudice' clause) which seemingly recognised the mutually inclusive application of IHL and the protective regime of the Convention did little to clarify the ambiguity.[10] It was not until the adoption of the Statute of the ICC in 1998, which expanded the definition of war crimes to include attacks against peacekeepers 'as long as they are entitled to the protection given to civilians or civilian objects under the international law of armed conflict' that the fine line between the protected status of peacekeepers as civilians, and their status as combatants was finally drawn.[11] In the decade that followed, the principle of duality of

9 UNGA Res 49/59 (9 December 1994) 2051 UNTS 363.

10 Art 20(a) provides:

> Nothing in this Convention shall affect … [t]he applicability of international humanitarian law and universally recognized standards of human rights as contained in international instruments in relation to the protection of United Nations operations and United Nations and associated personnel or the responsibility of such personnel to respect such law and standards.

11 Evan T Bloom, 'Protecting Peacekeepers: The Convention on the Safety of United Nations and Associated Personnel' (1995) 89 *AJIL* 621; Christopher Greenwood, 'Protection of Peacekeepers: The Legal Regime' (1996) 7 *Duke JCIL* 185. On the inadequacies of the Convention and recommended measures to strengthen its protective regime, see Report of the Secretary-General, Scope of Legal Protection under the Convention on the Safety of United Nations and Associated Personnel, UN Doc A/55/637 (21 November 2000).

peacekeepers would be the basis for the prosecution of attacks against peacekeepers before virtually all international jurisdictions: the SCSL, the ICTY, the ICTR and the ICC.[12]

In the SCSL, leaders of the Revolutionary United Front were prosecuted, among others, for abducting and detaining hundreds of peacekeepers of the UN Mission in Sierra Leone (UNAMSIL) in various locations in the country in violation of Article 4(b) of the SCSL Statute. In its judgment the Special Court held that throughout the indictment period there was an armed conflict of a non-international character in Sierra Leone, and that UNAMSIL's personnel who took no part in hostilities were at all relevant times deemed civilians and entitled to the same protection. It concluded, therefore, that:

> personnel of peacekeeping missions are entitled to protection as long as they are not taking a direct part in the hostilities – and thus have become combatants – at the time of the alleged offence. Where peacekeepers become combatants, they can be legitimate targets for the extent of their participation in accordance with international humanitarian law.[13]

In the ICTY, Radovan Karadžić was indicted for taking hostage in concert with others, 284 UN peacekeepers and military observers of the UN Protection Force (UNPROFOR) and holding them (as human shields) at various strategic locations in the Republika Srpska. Taking peacekeepers as hostages was not charged as an attack against peacekeepers – a crime not yet in existence at the time of the indictment (or its commission, for that matter) – but as a crime against civilians in violation of Common Article 3(b) of the Geneva Conventions ('taking of hostages').[14] It was nonetheless premised on the principle that, for as long as peacekeepers take no part in hostilities – their presence in the theatre of war notwithstanding – they are entitled to protected civilian status.

Similarly, in the *Bagosora* case, the ICTR found the accused guilty of murder of ten Belgian peacekeepers of the United Nations Assistance Mission for Rwanda (UNAMIR). While elaborating little on the distinction between peacekeepers as civilians and as combatants, the tribunal nonetheless considered the ten Belgian peacekeepers – disarmed at the time of the attack – to be non-combatants. Their murder within the first 24 hours of the Rwandan genocide, therefore, amounted to a crime against humanity and a war crime in violation of Article 3 Common to the Geneva Conventions.[15]

Within the general context of the 'situation' in the Sudan – a 'situation' referred to the Prosecutor of the ICC by Security Council Resolution 1593 (2005) – charges were brought against Idriss Abu Garda, the Chairman of the United Resistance Front (URF), for intentionally directing, with other rebel groups, attacks against personnel, installations, units and vehicles of the African Union Mission in Sudan (AMIS) in the Military Group Site (MGS) in Haskanita, North Darfur; an attack which killed 12 AMIS peacekeeping personnel and wounded eight more.

In its decision on the Confirmation of the Charges, the Pre-Trial Chamber held that at the relevant time, an armed conflict not of an international character existed in Darfur between the government of the Sudan and rebel groups operating in the Darfur region. On the question of

---

12 Mohamed A Bangura, 'Prosecuting the Crime of Attack on Peacekeepers: A Prosecutor's Challenge' (2010) 23 *Leiden JIL* 165.

13 *Prosecutor against Sesay, Kallon and Gbao* (Case no SCSL-04-15-T, Trial Chamber I, 2 March 2009) ¶ 233.

14 *Prosecutor v Karadžić (Prosecution's Marked-Up Indictment)* (Case no IT-95-5/18-PT, ICTY Trial Chamber III, 19 October 2009).

15 *Prosecutor v Bagosora, Kabiligi, Ntabakuze and Nsengiyumva* (Case no ICTR-98-41-T, Trial Chamber I, 18 December 2008) ¶ 2175.

whether the MGS Haskanita retained its protected civilian status at the time of the attack, it held that AMIS was an impartial mission entrusted with an observation mandate, that it was not entitled to use force except in self-defence and to protect African Union (AU) installations and civilians in their immediate vicinity, and that in point of fact it took no direct part in hostilities or used force beyond self-defence. The Pre-Trial Chamber concluded that at the time of the attack on 29 September 2007, the AMIS operation, its personnel and installations at MGS Haskanita were entitled to the protection afforded to civilians and civilian objects,[16] and that the attack against them was a war crime within the meaning of Article 8(2)(e)(iii) of the Rome Statute.

Notwithstanding its consistent application across international jurisdictions, applying the principle of duality in the realities of any given operation remains a challenge; it has been particularly trying in the case of the Intervention Brigade – the military offensive wing of the United Nations Organization Stabilization Mission in the Democratic Republic of the Congo (MONUSCO). Established by Security Council Resolution 2098 (2013) as a dedicated military force under MONUSCO's operational command, the Intervention Brigade was entrusted with the responsibility of 'neutralizing' armed groups with a view to reducing the threat posed by these groups to state authority and civilian security in Eastern DRC.[17] By the same resolution MONUSCO was also authorised to take all necessary measures through its regular forces or the Intervention Brigade to protect civilians under imminent threat of physical violence, protect UN personnel, facilities, installations and equipment and carry out targeted offensive operations, through the Intervention Brigade, to neutralise or disarm armed groups.

The presumption that in multidimensional peacekeeping operations the military component, in the conduct of its routine operational activities is entitled to protected civilian status, is refutable in the case of the Intervention Brigade, whose mandate to carry out targeted offensive operations against armed groups is its sole combat mission. There is little doubt, therefore, that absent a 'civilian mandate' to support the presumption of 'duality of peacekeepers', the Intervention Brigade should be considered 'a party to the conflict', and its members as combatants *at all times* and not only in the conduct of their mandated offensive operations. It would equally be the case for MONUSCO operations while cooperating with the Intervention Brigade in its offensive operations, or when it is otherwise 'actively engaged in combat'. The more difficult and yet unresolved question, however, is whether the engagement of the Intervention Brigade in an offensive operation affects MONUSCO as a whole, and transforms it 'by association' to 'a party to the conflict', and thus a legitimate military target, anywhere, at all times and regardless

---

16 *Prosecutor v Abu Garda (Decision on the Confirmation of Charges: Public Redacted Version)* (Case no ICC-02/05-02/09, Pre-Trial Chamber I, 8 February 2010) ¶¶ 83, 126–132. For lack of sufficient evidence, however, to substantiate Abu Garda's individual criminal responsibility under art 25(3)(a) of the Statute, the Chamber declined to confirm the charges. Relying on its Decision on the Confirmation of Charges against Abu-Garda, the Pre-Trial Chamber confirmed on 7 March 2011 the same charges against two rebel leaders of the Justice and Equality Movement (JEM) Collective Leadership, and the Sudanese Army Unity (SLA-Unity), Bander Abakaer Nourain and Mohammed Jerbo Jamus, respectively, for their responsibility as co-perpetrators of the attack on the AU Mission in Haskanita. *Prosecutor v Abakaer Nourain and Jerbo Jamus (Corrigendum of the 'Decision on the Confirmation of Charges')* (Case no ICC-02/05-03/09, ICC, Pre-Trial Chamber I, 7 March 2011).

17 UNSC Res 2098 (28 March 2013) ¶¶ 9, 12; UNSC Res 2147 (28 March 2014) extended MONUSCO's mandate, including its military offensive arm, the Intervention Brigade, until 31 March 2015.

of whether in any given circumstances members of the UN force are actively engaged in combat.[18]

The creation of the Intervention Brigade which the Security Council underscored was 'on exceptional basis and without creating a precedent',[19] was, in fact, a blue-print for future UN operations. In Mali[20] and the Central African Republic[21] similar auxiliary forces, already deployed in the country (by invitation),[22] were mandated by the Council to intervene in support of elements of the UN operation under imminent and serious threat, or provide them with operational support. Unlike the Intervention Brigade, however, they operated at all times – including when engaged in support of the UN operation – outside the UN command and control structure. Their engagement in combat operations of all kinds, therefore, would not transform the UN operation in question into a 'party to the conflict', or entail for it the application of IHL. It may not, however, shield it from safety and security risks from the other 'party to the conflict', oblivious to the distinction between the military forces.

3 The applicability of the laws of occupation to UN administrations

In the early 2000s a new debate emerged over the applicability of the laws of occupation to UN administrations in control of territories and populations in transition to independence or to a politically agreed status. By then, UN administrations had already been established in West

---

18 Bruce Oswald, 'The Security Council and the Intervention Brigade: Some Legal Issues' (2013) *ASIL Insights* 17; Scott Sheeran and Stephanie Case, 'The Intervention Brigade: Legal Issues for the UN in the Democratic Republic of the Congo' (International Peace Institute, November 2014) 9–11. Acutely aware of the blurred distinction between the Intervention Brigade and MONUSCO's military component, and of the consequential security risks that such may entail for MONUSCO's personnel of all kinds across the DRC, the Security Council requested the Secretary-General regularly to report to it on the 'risks and their implications for the safety and the security for the UN personnel and facilities as a result of the possible operations of the Intervention Brigade' (UNSC Res 2098 (28 March 2013) ¶ 34(b)(vi)). The Council concerns were borne out in the realities of MONUSCO, as evidenced in subsequent Secretary-General Reports on MONUSCO (ie Secretary-General's reports on the United Nations Organization Stabilization Mission in the Democratic Republic of the Congo, UN Doc S/2013/581 (30 September 2013) ¶¶ 66–68, UN Doc S/2013/757 (17 December 2013) ¶¶ 17, 20 and 73, and UN Doc S/2014/157 (5 March 2014) ¶¶ 68–70.

19 UNSC Res 2098 (28 March 2013) ¶ 9.

20 By UNSC Res 2100 (25 April 2013) the Security Council established the United Nations Multidimensional Integrated Stabilization Mission in Mali (MINUSMA). By the same resolution, the Security Council authorised the French troops 'to intervene in support of elements of MINUSMA when under imminent and serious threat upon request of the Secretary-General' (¶ 18), see also UNSC Res 2164 (25 June 2014) ¶ 26.

21 By UNSC Res 2149 (10 April 2014) the Security Council established the United Nations Multidimensional Integrated Stabilization Mission in the Central African Republic (MINUSCA). By the same resolution the Council also authorised the French force, already deployed in the country, from the commencement until the end of MINUSCA's mandate, to 'use all necessary means to provide operational support to elements of MINUSCA, at the request of the Secretary-General' (¶ 47).

22 Karine Bannelier and Theodore Christakis, 'Under the UN Security Council's Watchful Eyes: Military Intervention by Invitation in the Malian Conflict' (2013) 26 *Leiden JIL* 855.

Irian,[23] Cambodia[24] and Eastern Slavonia,[25] with a limited mandate 'to administer' a territory and its population on behalf of the existing or the future sovereign, and a power, however limited, 'to legislate'. But it was only in Kosovo and East Timor that the UN administrations displaced the previous sovereign as the 'source of authority', and assumed all-inclusive administrative and legislative authority in the territory under their administration.[26] It is in these operations also that the analogy, however imperfect, to military occupation and its limitations was most compelling.

For all their similarities, however, in their effective control over the territory and exclusive authority over its inhabitants, UN administrations were fundamentally different from military occupation in their legal basis, founding instruments and the circumstances of their establishment. To begin with, while all UN administrations were established in post-conflict circumstances, none was established in 'Regulation-42 circumstances', nor was the 'administered' territory considered 'occupied' within the meaning of the 1907 Hague Regulations ('a territory actually placed under the authority of the hostile army').[27] Unlike military occupation also, which operates within the limitations of the status quo, UN administrations were established to effectuate political, institutional and legislative changes in the administered territory within the

---

23 The United Nations Temporary Executive Authority (UNTEA) in West New Guinea (West Irian) was established by the 1962 Agreement between Indonesia and the Netherlands endorsed by UNGA Res 1752(XVII), with a mandate to administer the territory in transition from Dutch to Indonesian rule. Rosalyn Higgins, *United Nations Peacekeeping, 1946–1947: Documents and Commentary* (OUP 1970) ii, 91 et seq.

24 The 1991 Agreement on Comprehensive Political Settlement of the Cambodia Conflict called for the establishment of the United Nations Transitional Authority in Cambodia (UNTAC) to be responsible for the organisation and the conduct of the electoral process with all powers of administration and legislation relating to the conduct of the elections. Agreement on a Comprehensive Political Settlement of the Cambodia Conflict, UN Doc S/23177-A/46/608 (30 October 1991); Steven R Ratner, 'The Cambodia Settlement Agreement' (1993) 87 *AJIL* 1.

25 Under the 1995 Basic Agreement on the Region of Eastern Slavonia, Baranja and Western Sirmium between the Government of Croatia and the local Croatian Serb authorities in Eastern Slavonia, the area known as the Republic of Serb-Krajina was to revert to Croatia after four years of war. By Res 1037 (1996) the Security Council decided to establish the United Nations Transitional Administration for Eastern Slavonia, Baranja and Western Sirmium (UNTAES) to oversee the transition to Croatian rule, and in so doing to establish a police force, organise elections for local government bodies, monitor the respect for human rights and establish the normal functioning of all public services in the region.

26 The United Nations Interim Administration Mission in Kosovo (UNMIK) and the United Nations Transitional Administration in East Timor (UNTAET) were established by UNSC Res 1244 (10 June 1999) and 1272 (25 October 1999), respectively.

27 On two occasions, however, in the context of UN-authorised operations, the territory of their deployment could have been considered to have fallen into the hands of the 'hostile' army, and thus 'occupied' within the meaning of art 42 of the 1907 Hague Regulations. In the early stages of the UNITAF and INTERFET operations conducted in Somalia and East Timor under US and Australian-led command, respectively, the territory actually placed under their effective control met the conditions of art 42. In both operations, the Australian contingent applied the laws of occupation to the conduct of its mandated activities in the area of its deployment. See the Statement by the Australian Government in the Meeting of Contracting Parties to the Fourth Geneva Convention, Geneva, 27–29 October 1998 (1999) 2 *YBIHL* 450, 451; Michael J Kelly, 'Responsibility for Public Security in Peace Operations' in Helen Durham and Timothy L H McCormack (eds), *The Changing Face of Conflict and the Efficacy of International Humanitarian Law* (Kluwer 1999) 141; Michael J Kelly, Timothy L H McCormack, Paul Muggleton and Bruce M Oswald, 'Legal Aspects of Australia's Involvement in the International Force for East Timor' (2001) 83(841) *IRRC* 101; Bruce M Oswald, 'The INTERFET Detainee Management Unit in East Timor' (2000) 3 *YBIHL* 347.

limitations of their mandate – the sole and unique source of their authority in the territories under their administration.

But while the laws of occupation did not apply *de jure* (or de facto for that matter) to any of the UN administrations, in the cases of UNMIK and UNTAET, they guided, by analogy, the choice of the applicable law to the UN administration,[28] including the principles of respect for the local law and international human rights standards, the administration of state and socially owned property, the immunity of the UN administration from local jurisdiction and, most importantly perhaps, the limitations imposed on its over-all administrative authority by the principle of non-alienability of sovereignty.

4 The convergence of human rights and IHL in peacekeeping operations

The debate over the convergence of IHL and IHRL in situations of armed conflict, which in the practice of states had already been concluded, has only recently begun in the context of peacekeeping operations, where the very question of the applicability of IHRL to UN operations has yet to be fully acknowledged. In an era when the obligation to respect, protect and fulfil human rights was considered 'territorial' and incumbent upon states alone, it would have been inconceivable to suggest that the UN – having no territory of its own and in no position to affect, in either act or omission, the human rights of individuals – would be subject to human rights obligations enshrined in treaties to which it was not even a party. But with the evolution in the 1990s in the size, nature and mandates of peacekeeping operations, and their growing potential to affect the human rights of individuals in areas of their deployment, the question of the applicability of human rights to UN operations, its legal basis, 'trigger point' and scope, could no longer be avoided.

In establishing the legal basis and 'trigger point' for the applicability of IHRL to peacekeeping operations, an analogy, however imperfect, may be drawn from states' military operations conducted outside their territory. But while for states, human rights obligations apply as a matter of extra-territorial application of their human rights treaties, for the UN, as a non-party to any of these treaties, the customary international law nature of the human rights obligations is the legal basis – the only one, perhaps, with the exception of self-assumed conventional obligations – for the applicability of IHRL to its military operations. Both for states and the UN, however, what triggers the application of IHRL to their military operations is the 'effective control' of either operation over a territory and its population; and its scope of application is determined by the extent of such control and its relevancy to the human right in question. For either entity, it is the capacity to impact the enjoyment of human rights that creates for them both a potential for abuse, and an 'obligation to respect'.[29]

---

28 Tobias H Irmscher, 'The Legal Framework for the Activities of the United Nations Interim Administration Mission in Kosovo: The Charter, Human Rights, and the Law of Occupation' (2001) 44 *German YBIL* 353, 374–395; Erika de Wet, 'The Direct Administration of Territories by the United Nations and its Member States in the Post-Cold War Era: Legal Bases and Implications for National Law' (2004) 8 *Max Planck YBUNL* 291; Steven R Ratner, 'Foreign Occupation and International Territorial Administrations: The Challenges of Convergence' (2005) 16 *EJIL* 695; Daphna Shraga, 'Military Occupation and UN Transitional Administrations: The Analogy and its Limitations' in Marcelo G Kohen (ed), *Promoting Justice, Human Rights and Conflict Resolution through International Law, Liber Amicorum Lucius Caflisch* (Brill 2007) 479; Eyal Benvenisti, *The International Law of Occupation* (2nd edn, OUP 2012) 276–298.

29 Frédéric Mégret and Florian Hoffman, 'The UN as a Human Rights Violator? Some Reflections on the United Nations Changing Human Rights Responsibilities' (2003) 25 *HRQ* 314; Matteo Tondini, 'UN Peace Operations: The Last Frontier of the Extra-territorial Application of Human Rights' (2005) 44 *RDMDG* 175; Jan Wouters, Eva Brems, Stefaan Smis and Pierre Schmitt (eds), *Accountability for Human Rights Violations by International Organizations* (Intersentia 2010).

While the UN has never formally declared the applicability of IHRL to its operations in a manner similar to the promulgation of the Secretary-General's Bulletin on the applicability of IHL to UN forces, in the practice of the organisation, core IHRL and IHL obligations converged to apply to the conduct of UN operations in control of territory and population. The cases of the UN transitional administrations in Kosovo and East Timor, the arrest and detention of persons by members of UN operations and their handover to national authorities, and the conditionality of UN assistance to non-UN forces on their compliance with IHRL and IHL have been the foremost examples.

4.1 The law applicable to the UN administrations in Kosovo and East Timor

The UN transitional administrations in Kosovo and East Timor were entrusted by Security Council Resolutions 1244 (1999) and 1272 (1999), respectively, with overall legislative and executive authority, including in the administration of justice. As the 'virtual governments' in the territories under their administration, they exercised therein exclusive and effective control – a control which triggered for the UN administrations the obligation to respect and promote the quasi-totality of human rights, norms and standards.

In Kosovo and East Timor IHRL and IHL converged to create a normative framework for the UN administration. In both territories, regulations on the applicable law incorporated into the local law core international human rights instruments, binding upon all office-holders in the performance of their public duties.[30] In determining the law governing the administration of the territory, however, where neither local law nor human rights standards alone could provide a normative framework, the principles of the laws of occupation were drawn upon by analogy to fill the gap.

4.2 Arrest and detention by peacekeeping operations

Another form of control, not necessarily over a territory but one which likewise triggers for the UN operation human rights obligations, is control over persons, particularly those finding themselves in the hands of the operation whether as detainees or refuge seekers. In the practice of peacekeeping operations, detention has been the almost inevitable consequence of their engagement in non-international armed conflict or in exercising law and order functions.[31] In regulating internment by UN peacekeeping operations in non-international armed conflict or other situations of violence, IHL rules provided little guidance. The legal regime of detention applicable in international armed conflict or belligerent occupation under Geneva Conventions

---

30 UNMIK Reg No 2000/59 Amending Reg No 1999/24 on the Law Applicable in Kosovo (27 October 2000); UNTAET Reg No 1999/1 on the Authority of the Transitional Administration in East Timor (27 November 1999). UNMIK's undertaking to respect international human rights standards notwithstanding, the administration has been criticised for its human rights record, whether in the protection of minorities, or in its 'executive detention' practices in breach of *habeas corpus* guarantees under ECHR and ICCPR. See Ombudsperson Institution in Kosovo, Special Report No. 3, on the Conformity of Deprivations of Liberty Under "Executive Orders" with Recognized International Standards (29 June 2001); Carsten Stahn, 'Justice Under Transitional Administration: Contours and Critique of a Paradigm' (2005) 27 *Houston JIL* 311, 329–331; Ray Murphy, *UN Peacekeeping in Lebanon, Somalia and Kosovo, Operational and Legal Issues in Practice* (CUP 2007) 279–293.

31 Bruce Oswald, 'The Law on Military Occupation: Answering the Challenges of Detention During Contemporary Peace Operations?' (2007) 8 *Melbourne JIL* 311; Bruce Oswald, 'Detention of Civilians on Military Operations: Reasons for and Challenges to Developing a Special Law of Detention' (2008) 32 *Melbourne University LR* 524.

III and IV, and Additional Protocol I, is, with few exceptions, largely irrelevant to the realities of peacekeeping operations. Deployed in places and situations of non-international armed conflict, or other situations of violence, where IHL is either inapplicable or contains too few and largely inadequate provisions on detention, importing from IHRL norms and standards to supplement or substitute for a virtually non-existent regime has been crucial in developing a coherent legal framework for detention in peacekeeping operations. 'Borrowing' from IHRL has been of particular relevance in establishing the legal basis for detention and its continued lawfulness, conditions of detention and the treatment of detainees, judicial procedural guarantees and accountability for abuse and ill-treatment.[32]

In 2010, the UN Secretariat issued Interim Standard Operating Procedures on Detention in United Nations Peace Operations.[33] Designed to ensure that 'persons detained by United Nations personnel in United Nations peace operations … are handled humanely and in a manner that is consistent with applicable international human rights, humanitarian and refugee law, norms and standards', it combined IHRL and IHL rules to create a single legal regime applicable across operations and situations. The Interim SOP, however, is a framework detention regime adapted to the specificities of peacekeeping operations, which, with the exception of detention in non-international armed conflict, is limited to 48 hours, or until such time as handing over the detainee to the national authorities for prosecution is made possible. The end of the detention period, however brief, does not end the IHRL/IHL obligations of the UN operation, for a new series of obligations relating to the terms and conditions of such transfer will then emerge.

The decision to hand over a detainee, its modalities and its aftermath, including ill-treatment of the detainee by the authorities to which he was transferred, may entail for the UN operation international responsibility within the limitations of the customary international law principle of *non-refoulement*. Borrowed from international refugee law, the principle of *non-refoulement* enjoins the UN operation to condition handover on guarantees of humane treatment, due process and, in case of prosecution and subsequent trial, on the non-imposition of death penalty.[34]

4.3 Conditionality of UN assistance to non-UN forces on compliance with IHL and IHRL

The Security Council has never called upon UN peacekeeping operations to comply with IHL and IHRL in the conduct of their operations in the same way that it has almost routinely called upon all other military forces operating alongside the UN operation to do the same.[35] It was nonetheless keen to ensure that the UN operation is not implicated or is seen to be implicated

---

32 Jelena Pejic, 'Procedural Principles and Safeguards for Internment/Administrative Detention in Armed Conflict and Other Situations of Violence' (2005) 87(858) *IRRC* 375.

33 UN Department of Peacekeeping Operations ref 2010.6 (25 January 2010).

34 Cordula Droege, 'Transfers of Detainees: Legal Framework, *Non-Refoulement* and Contemporary Challenges' (2008) 90(871) *IRRC* 669; Emanuela-Chiara Gillard, 'There's No Place Like Home: State's Obligations in Relation to Transfers of Persons' (2008) 90(871) *IRRC* 703.

35 UNSC Res 2098 (28 March 2013) authorised MONUSCO, through the Intervention Brigade, to carry out targeted offensive operations 'in strict compliance with international law, including international humanitarian law and with the human rights due diligence policy on UN-support to non UN forces (HRDDP)' (¶ 12(b)). UNSC Res 2124 (12 November 2013) underlined 'the importance of AMISOM abiding by all requirements applicable to it under international human rights and humanitarian law', and further underlined 'the need for AMISOM to ensure that any detainees in their custody… are treated in strict compliance with applicable obligations under international humanitarian law and human rights law' (¶ 12).

in facilitating violations of human rights and IHL committed by non-UN military forces supported by the UN operation. For the first time in the DRC, the Security Council adopted a policy conditioning the assistance provided by the United Nations Organization Mission in the Democratic Republic of the Congo (MONUC, later renamed MONUSCO) to non-UN forces on their compliance with IHL and IHRL.[36] The policy later renamed Human Rights Due Diligence Policy on United Nations Support to non-United Nations Security Forces (HRDDP),[37] was made applicable across UN operations in all cases of support and assistance to non-UN forces.[38] Adopted at the time when the International Law Commission (ILC) had just completed its draft Articles on Responsibility of International Organizations, the 'conditionality policy' and its successor the 'Human Rights Due Diligence Policy' reflected a growing awareness that, in the language of Article 14 of the ILC Articles, such assistance might entail for the organisation international responsibility for 'aiding and assisting' in the commission of an internationally wrongful act.[39]

5 Responsibility without accountability: the remaining challenge

The responsibility of the UN for violations of IHL committed by members of its peacekeeping operations, while, in principle, acknowledged,[40] has rarely been attributed to or otherwise assumed by the organisation with any consequence (the Congo operation in the 1960s being the rare exception). The responsibility of the UN for violations of IHRL, whose applicability to

36 Thirtieth Report of the Secretary-General on the United Nations Organization Mission in the Democratic Republic of the Congo, UN Doc S/2009/623 (4 December 2009). In UNSC Res 1906 (23 December 2009) (¶ 22), the Security Council reiterated 'that the support of MONUC to FARDC-led military operations against foreign and Congolese armed groups is strictly conditioned on FARDC's compliance with international humanitarian, human rights and refugee law'. It further called upon MONUC to 'intercede with the FARDC command if elements of a FARDC unit receiving MONUC's support are suspected of having committed grave violations of such laws, and if the situation persists … to withdraw support from these FARDC units'.

37 The HRDDP is contained in the Identical Letters dated 25 February 2013 from the Secretary-General addressed to the President of the General Assembly and to the President of the Security Council, UN Doc A/67/775-S/2013/110 (5 March 2013).

38 The HRDDP was made initially applicable to all UN-assisted military operations conducted in the DRC through the Intervention Brigade, either unilaterally or jointly with government-led forces (UNSC Res 2098 (28 March 2013) ¶ 12(b) and UNSC Res 2147 (28 March 2014) ¶ 33). It was then extended to the UN support provided to the Somali National Army for joint operations conducted with the African Union Mission in Somalia (AMISOM) (UNSC Res 2124 (12 November 2013) ¶¶ 14–16), to military operations conducted jointly with the Malian Defence and Security Forces (UNSC Res 2100 (25 April 2013) ¶ 26, and UNSC Res 2164 (25 June 2014) ¶ 16) and to the UN support to non-UN security forces in the Central African Republic (UNSC Res 2149 (10 April 2014) ¶ 39).

39 Art 14 of the Articles on Responsibility of International Organizations (art 13 in the draft Articles) attributes responsibility to an international organisation for 'aiding and assisting' a state or another international organisation in the commission of an internationally wrongful act, if, in so doing, the 'assisting organization' had knowledge of the circumstances of the internationally wrongful act; UNGA Res 66/100 (9 December 2011) on Responsibility of International Organizations; Report of the International Law Commission on the Work of its Sixty-Third Session, UN Doc A/66/10 (2011) 103–105; Scott P Sheeran, 'A Constitutional Moment? United Nations Peacekeeping in the Democratic Republic of Congo' (2011) 8 *International Organizations LR* 55.

40 For the first time in 1996, the international responsibility of the UN for IHL violations was articulated and circumscribed in the Secretary-General's Report on 'the limitations of UN third-party liability'. Report of the Secretary-General, Administrative and Budgetary Aspects of the Financing of the United Nations Peacekeeping Operations: Financing of the United Nations Peacekeeping Operations, UN Doc A/51/389 (20 September 1996) ¶¶ 6–19.

UN operations has not even been formally acknowledged, has yet to be seriously debated. The cases of sexual exploitation and abuse by members of UN operations, and the outbreak of the cholera epidemic in Haiti allegedly attributed to the UN operation at the time and place of the event, illustrate the acuity of the debate.

While allegations of sexual exploitation and abuse by UN peacekeepers were known to have existed in Bosnia and Herzegovina, Kosovo, Haiti, East Timor and Cambodia throughout the 1990s, and in Burundi, Côte d'Ivoire, Sierra Leone and Liberia since the early 2000s, it was the revelation of the seriousness and scope of the phenomenon in the DRC in 2004 – the worst case ever of sexual exploitation by peacekeepers – that compelled the UN political organs to act. An umbrella term for rape, forced prostitution and sexual violence of all kinds, sexual exploitation constitutes a serious violation of IHL and IHRL. In the realities of peacekeeping operations where sex was 'bartered' for money, work and food and in many cases was nothing short of 'rape in disguise', sexual exploitation was defined in the Secretary-General's Bulletin on Measures to Protect from Sexual Exploitation and Sexual Abuse, as 'any actual or attempted abuse of a position of vulnerability, different power, or trust, for sexual purposes'.[41] From the vantage point of the UN, therefore, sexual exploitation was considered misconduct or a criminal act performed outside the 'official functions' of the organ or the agent and thus not attributable to the organisation.[42] Sexual exploitation of whatever nature, therefore, remained the responsibility of those who had committed it, namely, the peacekeepers, officials or experts on missions, and subject, within the legal limitations imposed (that is, the privileges and immunities of the operation and its personnel), to the jurisdiction of their host state or the state of nationality.[43] The possibility that the UN, as the parent organ of the peacekeeping operation, might be attributed responsibility for lack of due-diligence to prevent this long-standing, widespread practice of sexual exploitation across countries and operations has never been seriously considered.

The cholera epidemic in Haiti, which claimed the lives of more than 8,500 Haitians and sickened over 700,000 more, was due, according to the UN Independent Panel of Experts, to contamination of the Artibonite River with a South-Asian type of the cholera virus as a result

---

41 Secretary-General's Bulletin on Special Measures for Protection from Sexual Exploitation and Sexual Abuse, UN Doc ST/SGB/2003/13 (9 October 2003) s 1.

42 Art 6 of the ILC Articles on Responsibility of International Organizations attributes responsibility to the organisation for conduct of its organ or agent done '*in the performance of functions of that organ or agent*'. In its commentary on this article, the ILC noted:

> The requirement … that the organ or agent acts 'in the performance of functions of that organ or agent' is intended to make it clear that conduct is attributable to the international organization when the organ or agent *exercises functions that have been given to that organ or agent, and at any event is not attributable when the organ or agent acts in a private capacity.*

ILC Articles on Responsibility of International Organizations, International Law Commission, Report on the Work of its Sixty-Third Session, UN Doc A/66/10 (2011) 84.

43 A Comprehensive Strategy to Eliminate Future Sexual Exploitation and Abuse in United Nations Peacekeeping Operations, UN Doc A/59/710 (24 March 2005); Jennifer Murray, 'Who Will Police the Peace-Builders? The Failure to Establish Accountability for Participation of United Nations Civilian Police in the Trafficking of Women in Post-Conflict Bosnia and Herzegovina' (2003) 34 *Columbia HRLR* 475; Muna Ndulo, 'The United Nations Responses to the Sexual Abuse and Exploitation of Women and Girls by Peacekeepers During Peacekeeping Missions' (2009) 27 *Berkley JIL* 127; Róisín Burke, 'Attribution of Responsibility: Sexual Abuse and Exploitation, and Effective Control of Blue Helmets' (2012) 16 *Journal of International Peacekeeping* 1; Tom Dannenbaum, 'Translating the Standard of Effective Control into a System of Effective Accountability: How Liability Should be Apportioned for Violations of Human Rights by Member State Troop Contingents Serving as United Nations Peacekeepers' (2010) 51 *Harvard ILJ* 113.

of human waste.[44] Subsequent independent investigative reports, including clarifications released by members of the UN Panel of Experts, pointed at the Nepalese contingent of the United Nations Stabilization Mission in Haiti (MINUSTAH) stationed close to a tributary of the Artibonite River, as the carrier of the pathogenic strain and the source of the cholera epidemic. Attempts at bringing a claim against the UN for its negligence in not preventing the outbreak of the epidemic and for violating the human rights to life, health, adequate standard of living, clean water and sanitation and an effective remedy, have failed. A petition submitted to the UN Secretariat on behalf of 5,000 victims was rejected as 'non-receivable' under Article 29 of the Convention on the Privileges and Immunities of the United Nations; and the class action submitted against the organisation in the United States District Court of New York was dismissed for lack of subject-matter jurisdiction as all defendants in the class suit enjoyed absolute immunity from jurisdiction. In neither case has the alleged responsibility of the UN for the outbreak of the cholera epidemic been addressed on its merits.[45]

In the absence of a competent jurisdiction to settle the claims between individuals and the organisation and to pronounce on the law of responsibility of international organisations, it falls to the UN voluntarily to assume its responsibility for violations of IHL and IHRL. The UN, however, has little incentive to entertain the claims, and nor do member states which stand to bear the brunt of compensation payment in the event of a (successful) mass claim. And while the state of nationality of the victims can, theoretically at least, exercise its right to 'diplomatic protection' and espouse their claims against the organisation, in practice, few, and fewer still of those heavily dependent on UN assistance, would dare to venture. In reality, none of the countries where massive violations of IHL and IHRL have occurred under 'UN watch' – Bosnia and Herzegovina, Rwanda, Haiti and the DRC – have espoused the claims of their nationals against the UN for its alleged responsibility for the commission of the violations or for failing to prevent them. For as long, therefore, as an institutional accountability framework does not exist and nor does pressure voluntarily to assume its international responsibility, UN accountability for violations of IHL and IHRL by members of its peacekeeping operations will remain its greatest legal, political and moral challenge.

---

44 Final Report of the Independent Panel of Experts on the Cholera Outbreak in Haiti, www.un.org/News/dh/infocus/haiti/UN-cholera-report-final.pdf.

45 José Alvarez, 'The United Nations in the Time of the Cholera' (April 2014) *AJIL Unbound*, www.asil.org/blogs/united-nations-time-cholera.

25
Occupation and territorial administration

Eyal Benvenisti

The principle that European sovereignty was not to be alienated through the use of force, a principle that crystallised in Europe in the Congress of Vienna, found its manifestation in international law of the nineteenth century as part of the laws of war. Sovereignty was to be protected by a regime that prohibited any unilateral change of status during occupation and which delineated the authority of the foreign power between invasion and the re-establishment of peace. Indirectly then, the law of occupation, as part of the laws of war, defined and protected state sovereignty. According to this law, the occupying power is bound to respect and maintain the political and other institutions that exist in that territory, and is responsible for the management of public order and civil life in the territory under its control. The occupation is also limited in time and the occupant has only temporary managerial powers, for the duration of the occupation. The occupant administers the territory on behalf of the sovereign and the occupied population.

The law of occupation operates as a gap filler – in fact the only legal gap filler – that replaces the void that occurs with the temporary ousting of the sovereign government. Because it serves to protect the formal title of the sovereign state, the law of occupation is intimately related to the law of sovereignty. Over the years the changing attitudes about sovereignty and about entitlement to sovereignty also modified the law on occupation, as the principles of self-determination, democracy and human rights pierced the veil of national sovereignty.

Since initially occupation was viewed as a possible by-product of military actions during war, it was colloquially referred to in legal literature as 'belligerent occupation' (while occupation that received the consent of the sovereign was termed 'pacific' occupation). But at least since the adoption of Geneva Convention IV, with its focus on individuals rather than governments, and its scope that encompasses also occupations that 'm[et] no armed resistance',[1] the regime of occupation does not depend on the existence of a formal state of war or on armed resistance to the occupant. Also, as the only gap filler to a situation where the sovereign is precluded by a foreign power from exercising authority in its territory, the scope of the law must extend beyond the confines of war. Therefore the proper definition of occupation is a situation where the forces of one or more states – including peacekeeping forces or forces of international organisations – exercise effective control over a territory of another state without the sovereign's volition.

---

1 GCIV art 2(2).

1 Evolution of the concept of occupation

The law of occupation evolved gradually during the second half of the nineteenth century through deliberations among European governments mainly during the peace conferences in Brussels (1874)[2] and in The Hague (1899, 1907),[3] involving weak and strong governments, as well as scholars. The principle protecting individuals and their property was derived from the earlier distinction between the combatants and non-combatants and the duty to spare the latter from the scourge of war. The obligation to respect the sovereign rights of the ousted government reflects the final stages in the crystallisation of the concept of sovereignty as a national claim for exclusive control over the nation's territory and nationals. This two-pronged concept of occupation became part of general international law by the early twentieth century.[4]

During the twentieth century the law of occupation was often honoured by its breach. Most if not all occupants either failed to recognise the applicability of the law of occupation or implemented it in ways that promoted their own interests at the expense of those of the occupied. Most ousted governments, from exile or upon their return, also accorded little respect to the law, refusing to acknowledge the validity of acts that the occupant had enacted. Another type of challenge emerged during the post-Cold War era by the UN post-conflict administration regimes such as in Kosovo and East Timor (1999), or multilateral regimes endorsed by the UN such as in Somalia (1992), none of which acknowledged the applicability of the law of occupation to their missions (except for the Australian unit in Somalia).[5]

Changing perceptions about the nature of sovereignty have affected both the scope of authority of the occupant and the identity of the stakeholders to whom the occupant was accountable to. The occupant's powers have expanded through time to cover almost all the areas in which modern governments assert legitimacy to police, a far cry from the turn of the century laissez-faire conception of minimal governmental intervention. The emerging principles of self-determination, of human and minority rights, were responsible for the shift in focus regarding the beneficiary of the trust: contemporary attention is paid more to the interests of the indigenous community under occupation rather than to the wishes of the ousted government.

2 Applicable law

Being an integral part of international armed conflicts, the main source of law that regulates occupations is the law of international armed conflict, namely the Hague Regulations, Geneva Convention IV and Additional Protocol I, as well as customary international law. Initially there was a debate about the formal applicability of the general body of human rights law to occupations. Some have claimed that when armed conflict erupts, most 'peacetime' human rights are

---

2 Project of an International Declaration concerning the Laws and Customs of War (Brussels Declaration) (27 August 1874), www.icrc.org/ihl.nsf/FULL/135?OpenDocument.

3 Convention (II) with Respect to the Laws and Customs of War on Land and its Annex: Regulations concerning the Laws and Customs of War on Land, The Hague (29 July 1899) 189 CTS 429; Convention (IV) respecting the Laws and Customs of War on Land and its Annex: Regulations concerning the Laws and Customs of War on Land, The Hague (18 October 1907) 205 CTS 277.

4 On the evolution of the law, see Eyal Benvenisti, *The International Law of Occupation* (2nd edn, OUP 2012) ch 2.

5 See Michael J Kelly, *Restoring and Maintaining Order in Complex Peace Operations* (Martinus Nijhoff 1999).

temporarily superseded by the humanitarian laws of war.[6] But the opposite position ultimately gained the upper hand.[7] The finding that general and regional human rights treaties apply in occupied territories results from two propositions. The first is that the protection offered by human rights conventions does not cease in cases of international armed conflict. The second proposition is that the territorial scope of state parties' obligations under most human rights treaties encompass areas 'under their jurisdiction' which means under their 'effective control', and occupied territories would be included under that definition. Specifically, the ICJ has in 2004 opined that the major human rights treaties, including the 1966 Covenant on Civil and Political Rights (ICCPR), and the 1966 Covenant on Economic, Social and Cultural Rights (ICESCR) apply in situations of military occupation.[8]

The parallel applicability of human rights law along with the Hague and Geneva texts and customary international humanitarian law raises the question of the relationship between the two. Human rights documents may complement the law of occupation in specific issues that are treated in more detail in the former.[9] But the real issue, where human rights law seems to differ most dramatically from the law of occupation, lies in the area of civil and political rights. Civil and political rights are ignored by the Hague and Geneva norms. Realistically, one cannot expect occupants to endanger the security of their forces for the purpose of allowing local residents to enjoy political rights that are usually granted in democracies in peacetime. If the political process is lawfully halted for the duration of the occupation, the suspension of political rights seems to be a sensible consequence. Political rights are often among the first to be suspended by occupants, and this propensity has not been criticised as unlawful in principle. In the interplay between the conflicting interests, the law of occupation concedes that certain civil and political rights will from time to time be subjected to other concerns. Ultimately, as in other cases, the occupant is required to balance its interests against those of the occupied community and the ousted government, while guiding itself

> by the knowledge that the object and purpose of the [human rights] Convention as an instrument for the protection of individual human beings requires that its provisions be interpreted and applied so as to make its safeguards practical and effective.[10]

Thus, as hostilities subside, and security interests permit, the occupant is expected to restore civil and political rights. Under such circumstances, the human rights documents should serve as guidance for re-establishing civil and political rights in the occupied territory. Under certain circumstances, the occupant's human rights obligations towards the local population may require it to modify the local laws in ways that promote their rights. At the same time, its authority to

---

6 See eg Yoram Dinstein, 'Human Rights in Armed Conflict: International Humanitarian Law' in Theodor Meron, *Human Rights in International Law: Legal and Policy Issues* (Clarendon 1985) 345, 350–352 (most human rights exist in peacetime but may disappear completely in wartime); Jean S Pictet, *Humanitarian Law and the Protection of War Victims* (Sijthoff 1975) 15.

7 *Legality of the Threat or Use of Nuclear Weapons, (Advisory Opinion)* [1996] ICJ Rep 226; *Legal Consequences of the Construction of a Wall in the Occupied Palestinian Territory* [2004] *(Advisory Opinion)* ICJ Rep 136; Yoram Dinstein, *The International Law of Belligerent Occupation* (CUP 2009) 69; Benvenisti, *International Law of Occupation* (n 4); Adam Roberts, 'Prolonged Military Occupation: The Israeli-Occupied Territories since 1967' (1990) 84 *AJIL* 44, 72; Yutaka Arai-Takahashi, *The Law of Occupation: Continuity and Changes of International Humanitarian Law, and its Interaction with International Human Rights Law* (Martinus Nijhoff 2009).

8 *Wall* (n 7).

9 Roberts, 'Prolonged Military Occupation' (n 7) 72–73.

10 *Al-Skeini and Others v UK* (App no 55721/07, ECtHR Grand Chamber, 7 July 2011) ¶ 162.

modify the law is now subjected to human rights obligations, including the maintenance of the rule of law.[11]

The strict restrictions against administrative detention are another potential area of serious conflict between human rights law and occupation law.[12] Other rights, such as the rights of minority groups to maintain their culture and their traditional ways of life, also become relevant considerations which must shape the policies that the occupant pursues.

Although certain human rights may be derogated '[i]n time of public emergency which threatens the life of the nation',[13] not all occupations would qualify as such. Indeed, as the House of Lords noted in the context of the occupation of Iraq, '[i]t is hard to think that these conditions could ever be met when a state had chosen to conduct an overseas peacekeeping operation, however dangerous the conditions, from which it could withdraw'.[14]

The application of human rights law might don the occupation administration with a sense of normalcy, and human rights law might be invoked by the occupant to expand its authority and law-making power. This is not necessarily always the case, nor should it be so. The same body of human rights law may impose strict demands on the occupant such as the protection of expectations and the obligation to involve the population in decision-making processes that affect their interests. Generally a healthy suspicion in the occupant's motives should always inform a review of its policies by the various monitoring and adjudicating bodies. Specifically, due to the inherent lack of faith in the impartiality of the occupant, international tribunals should not grant the occupant nearly the same margin of appreciation that sovereigns enjoy. In fact occupants should not enjoy any margin of appreciation.

3 Territorial and temporal scope

3.1 Effective control over foreign territory

Because the occupant's authority does not derive from a right to control but from the fact of control, both questions, of the timing and of territorial scope of the occupation, depend on a factual determination of the occupant's effective control over certain territory. While Article 42 of the Hague Regulations emphasises this territorial test, Geneva Convention IV adds a test of effective control over individuals. While this is a simple proposition, it is all but simple to apply to concrete cases due to the rather vague text from which this the territorial is derived. Although seemingly straightforward, the conditions for occupation it sets forth are subject to diverging interpretations. The authentic text reads: 'Un territoire est considéré comme occupé lorsqu'il se trouve placé de fait sous l'autorité de l'armée ennemie. L'occupation ne s'étend qu'aux territoires où cette autorité est établie et en mesure de s'exercer.' This has been translated as: 'Territory is considered occupied when it is actually placed under the authority of the hostile army. The occupation extends only to the territory where such authority has been established and can be exercised.'

This text leads to a mystery: if the authority 'has been established' ('est établie'), would it not by itself mean that the area is occupied? If so, why add the condition that the authority 'can be exercised' ('en mesure de s'exercer')? And if the latter is redundant, wouldn't the entire second

---

11 On this, see Benvenisti, *International Law of Occupation* (n 4) 103–104.
12 On the tension in the context of the detentions during the occupation of Iraq, see *Al-Jedda v UK* (App no 27021/08, ECtHR Grand Chamber, 7 July 2011); *Hassan v The United Kingdom* (App no 29750/09, ECtHR Grand Chamber, 16 September 2014).
13 ICCPR art 4(1).
14 *R (Al-Jedda) v Secretary of State for Defence* [2007] UKHL 58, ¶ 38 (Lord Bingham).

sentence be redundant too, given the reference in the first sentence to a territory being '*actually placed* under the authority of the hostile army' ('se trouve placé de fait')? This tension between 'actual' or 'potential' control reflects deep disagreement between the drafters on the appropriate test. Initially it was obvious that an army that can control the population will control them, if only to requisition their resources to feed its men and its horses. But with the changing nature of warfare, the diminishing strategic value of local resources, and the heavier obligations towards the occupied population, hostile armies could benefit from the 'actual control' test that would allow them to exercise only military control over the land without burdening themselves with responsibilities flowing from the establishment of governmental institutions to administer civilian life.

The debate boils down to the purpose of the law: to fill the temporary sovereignity void. Therefore, what should count is the absence of indigenous authority when this happens, even the power that refrains from dealing with the local population will nevertheless be considered an occupant and bound by the occupant's obligations. To fill the sovereignty gap and ensure that the occupant is accountable to the occupied population, the test of 'potential' control was preferred.[15] As Adam Roberts observed, occupation law would apply when, *inter alia*, 'the military force has either displaced the territory's ordinary system of public order and govern-ment, replacing it with its own command structure, *or else has shown the clear physical ability to displace it*'.[16] This reflects what Robert Kolb and Sylvain Vité aptly call a functional test: the law of occupation applies whenever the foreign force is capable of exercising some of the authorities that the law expects and indeed requires it to exert as an occupant.[17] Accurately, the EU Com-mission of Inquiry into the conflict between Georgia and Russia did not accept the Russian claim that Russia was not an occupying power over parts of Georgia.[18] It rejected Russia's argu-ment that 'the determining factor in international law necessary to recognise a military presence as an occupation regime is whether the invading state has established effective control over the territory of the country in question *and its population*'.[19] The Commission found that 'to a certain degree, Russian forces were in a position to ensure public order and safety in the territories they were stationed in'.[20] The 'serious lack of action by the Russian troops to prevent violations and protect ethnic Georgians'[21] could not absolve them from their obligations as occupants.

Against the bulk of scholarly opinion and case law, and perhaps reflecting the confusion of the military manuals, the judgment of the ICJ in the *Armed Activities* case[22] seemed to revive the 'actual control' test, and seemed to imply that only direct authority *over a population* amounts to occupation. Appropriately, the EU Commission of Inquiry regarded that statement as address-ing only the evidentiary aspects of the question, as if the ICJ had difficulties ascertaining whether the Ugandan forces were in fact exercising control on DRC territory.[23]

---

15 On this matter, see Benvenisti, *International Law of Occupation* (n 4) 47–49; Eyal Benvenisti, 'Belligerent Occupation' *MPEPIL* (2008).

16 Adam Roberts, 'What is a Military Occupation?' (1984) 55 *BYBIL* 249, 300 (emphasis added).

17 Robert Kolb and Sylvain Vité, *Le Droit de l'Occupation Militaire: Perspectives Historiques et Enjeux Juridiques Actuels* (Bruylant 2009) 143, 149.

18 Independent International Fact-Finding Mission on the Conflict in Georgia ('IIFFMCG'), Report (September 2009) i, 308.

19 Cited ibid (emphasis added).

20 Ibid 373.

21 Ibid.

22 *Armed Activities on the Territory of the Congo (Democratic Republic of the Congo v Uganda)* [2005] ICJ Rep 116, ¶ 173 ('the Court must examine whether ... the said authority was in fact established and exer-cised'). See the critical comments of Judge Koojimans in his separate opinion, ¶¶ 40–41.

23 IIFFMCG (n 18) 305.

The better interpretation of the test for occupation therefore stipulates that occupation begins when the foreign army is in actual control of enemy *territory*, and is *in a position* to establish, if it so wishes, authority over the population. It is irrelevant whether the army actually does so or not.

Because the test is a test of effective territorial control, the territorial and temporal scopes of occupation depend on the facts. It makes no sense to require occupants to be actually able 'to enforce immediately and on the very spot the authority of an occupant',[24] but, instead, the effective control test requires 'the presence of sufficient force following on the cessation of local resistance'.[25] In the *Hostages* case a US Military Tribunal at Nuremberg found that the German army remained an occupant despite the fact that from time to time 'the partisans were able to control sections of these countries at various times', because 'it [was] established that the Germans could at any time they desired assume physical control of any part of the country. The control of the resistance forces was temporary only'.[26] But in the *Einsatzgruppen* trial it was established that 'in many of the areas where the Einsatzgruppen operated, the so-called partisans had wrested considerable territory from the German occupant, and that military combat action of some dimensions was required to reoccupy those areas'.[27] On those occasions the territory was therefore found to be unoccupied (and therefore those partisans were found to have been entitled to be regarded as prisoners of war).

3.2 Additional obligations when exercising control over specific individuals

Geneva Convention IV and Additional Protocol I enumerate several obligations – some negative (such as the prohibition on deportations) some positive (such as the obligation to ensure food and medical supplies to the population) – applicable towards individuals who 'find themselves in the hands of a foreign army'.[28] The invading army must respect the local population wherever it finds them and is precluded, for example, from kidnapping local civilians or transferring them out of the area, even before it establishes effective control there. The picture is more complex with respect to the extent of the positive duties that the invading army has towards the local population (for example, the duty to provide food or medical care, the duty to evacuate from the battle zone) while the war still rages. A careful and constant balancing of security and humanitarian interests will be required.

3.3 Are the airspace and maritime resources occupied as well?

The practice of several occupants has been to treat the territorial waters and the airspace above the occupied territory as subject to the jurisdiction of the occupant.[29] Control over the airspace is clearly a matter that must be regulated by the occupant, if it is expected to function properly. But it is less clear whether the occupant should be regarded as responsible for the use of all the

---

24 Lassa Oppenheim, *International Law: A Treatise* (Longmans, Green & Co 1906) ii, 170.

25 UK War Office, *The Law of War on Land* (HMSO 1958) ¶ 506.

26 *US v List et al (Hostages)* 11 TWC 1230, 1243 (1947).

27 *US v Ohlendorf et al (Einsatzgruppen)* 4 TWC 436, 491–493 (US Military Tribunal at Nuremberg, 1950).

28 GCIV art 4.

29 With respect to airspace, see Theodor Meron, 'Applicability of Multilateral Conventions to Occupied Territories' (1978) 72 *AJIL* 542, 555–556; with respect to maritime resources, see Dinstein, *International Law* (n 7) 47–48 (referring to the Israeli drilling of oil in the continental shelf of the Sinai peninsula belonging to Egypt).

marine resources of the occupied state that are situated off the occupied coast. It would make sense to regard the occupant as the responsible party if, for example, the maritime resources in the Exclusive Economic Zone and the continental shelf serve the economy of the occupied territory, and the ousted government has no access to the coast from the area it controls. If, however, the occupant holds but a sliver of the coast and the population under its control does not depend on the marine resources, its intervention in the management of those resources by the legitimate government is unwarranted. More problematic would be the case when both the occupant and the ousted government have access to parts of the sea from the areas each control, and they need to coordinate the use of the resources. Perhaps the sensible rule in such cases would be to allocate responsibilities and shares as a reflection of the needs of the local populations in the respective areas under the control of the two parties. Such a solution would seem warranted under the rules pertaining to the management of natural resources in occupied territories.

3.4 Occupation through proxies

According to the law on state responsibility, occupation could be recognised when the occupying state prefers to operate through proxies.[30] These proxies could be local insurgents,[31] and they could also be private military companies.[32]

Throughout the history of occupation law, several occupants have sought to evade their obligations by invoking the consent of the sovereign as a pretext to reject the applicability of the law of occupation. They would also purport to recognise new governments (like the Quisling government in Norway or Vichy in France) or states (the Japanese occupation of Manchukuo) whose consent they celebrated. To overcome such claims, it is useful to look into 'the substance of relations [between the ruler and the ruled], not to their legal characterisation as such'.[33] This is why a clear definition of what amounts to consent is crucial. For consent to be valid, it must not be coerced. It must be extended by the recognised government of a recognised state.[34]

---

30 The ICTY encountered internal debate concerning the question what test should apply for the attribution of the proxy to the principal state. In *Prosecutor v Blaškić* (Case no IT-95-14-T, ICTY Trial Chamber, 3 March 2000) ¶¶ 149–150, the Trial Chamber determined that enclaves in Bosnia and Herzegovina controlled by the HVO (Croatian Defence Council) were subject to Croatia's occupation 'through the overall control it exercised over the HVO, the support it lent it and the close ties it maintained with it'. However, in *Prosecutor v Naletilić and Martinović* (Case no IT-98-34-T, ICTY Trial Chamber, 31 March 2003) ¶ 214, the Trial Chamber made the following distinction: there is an essential distinction between the determination of a state of occupation and that of the existence of an international armed conflict. The application of the overall control test is applicable to the latter. A further degree of control is required to establish occupation.
31 Like most recently in the Crimea and the Eastern parts of Ukraine.
32 For the use of private military companies for establishing military presence and arguably occupying some parts of foreign territory, see 'U.S. Relies on Contractors in Somalia Conflict' *New York Times* (11 August 2011).
33 *Prosecutor v Tadić* (Case no IT-94-1, ICTY Appeals Chamber, 15 July 1999) ¶ 168. For a recent judgment along these lines, see *Chiragov v Armenia* (App no 13216/05, ECHR Grand Chamber, 16 June 2015) (examining the nature of the involvement of Armenian troops in Nagorno-Karabakh as key for assigning responsibility to Armenia).
34 Koutroulis notes as a genuine case of invitation the Indian presence in Sri Lanka in 1987 that did not amount to occupation (Vaios Koutroulis, *Le début et la fin du droit de l'occupation* 76–78 (Pedone 2010)).

3.5 How occupation ends?

The conditions that define when occupation begins also identify its termination.[35] The declarations by the occupant on the establishment or dismantling of administration are legally irrelevant. Obviously, occupation can end in a number of ways: with the loss of effective control, namely when the occupant is no longer capable of exercising its authority; through the genuine consent of the sovereign (the ousted government or an indigenous one) by the signing of a peace agreement; or by transferring authority to an indigenous government endorsed by the occupied population through referendum and which has received international recognition.[36] The latter type of ending – recognising indigenous governments – seems to be gaining recognition in recent years. In principle, the acceptance of such an ending runs the risk of providing an incentive for occupants to circumvent the goals of the occupation regime that call for strict adherence to the status quo *ante bellum*. This concern is reflected in Article 47 of Geneva Convention IV which stipulates that the protection of the Convention will remain in force regardless of any changes introduced, as the result of the occupation of a territory, into the institutions or government of the said territory 'by any agreement concluded between the authorities of the occupied territories and the Occupying Power'. But, at the same time, changes endorsed by the entire population of a given country through free and fair referenda or general elections, such as the ones effected in Iraq in 2005, can be expected to be regarded as valid.[37]

Article 6(3) of Geneva Convention IV provides that the application of the Convention in occupied territory 'shall cease one year after the general close of military operations', except that, to the extent that the occupant continues to exercise the functions of government in that territory, it would continue to be bound by several of the provisions of the Convention.[38] With the post-Second World War occupations in mind, the expectation was that, with time, the need to regulate the relationships between the indigenous population and the occupant would diminish. This expectation was far from realistic, and was belied by subsequent events. This provision has not been invoked in the years since, and Additional Protocol I reversed it.[39] However, in a highly controversial statement, the *Wall* Advisory Opinion refers to this time limit, finding that only those articles of the Geneva Convention IV referred to in Article 6(3), remain applicable in the West Bank.[40]

3.6 Is there an obligation to terminate the occupation?

The temporary rule of the occupant also requires it continuously to justify its presence in the foreign country. A legal framework that respects human and peoples' rights can no longer support the thesis that the occupant may hold the territory 'as a pledge of his military success,

---

35 For different types of terminations, see Adam Roberts, 'Occupation, Military, Termination of' *MPEPIL* (2011); see also Roberts, 'What is a Military Occupation?' (n 16) 257–260.

36 See Roberts, 'Occupation' (n 35); Dinstein, *International Law* (n 7) 270–280; Eyal Benvenisti, 'The Law on the Unilateral Termination of Occupation' in Thomas Giegerich (ed), *A Wiser Century? Judicial Dispute Settlement, Disarmament and the Laws of War 100 Years after the Second Hague Peace Conference* (Duncker & Humblot 2009) 371.

37 See the cases of Grenada, Panama, Afghanistan (in 2001); Bangladesh and Cambodia are also examples of acts of national self-determination, but where political reasons delayed wide international recognition. On these cases, see Benvenisti, *International Law of Occupation* (n 4) ch 7.

38 GCIV arts 1–12, 27, 29–34, 47, 49, 51, 52, 53, 59, 61–77, 143.

39 API art 3(b).

40 *Legal Consequences of the Construction of a Wall in the Occupied Palestinian Territory (Advisory Opinion)* [2004] ICJ Rep 136, ¶ 125.

and thereby impress upon the enemy the necessity of submitting to terms of peace'.[41] In the eyes of the drafters of the law of occupation in the nineteenth century, occupations were to be quickly resolved by peace agreements. There was no need to impress upon the occupant the obligation to terminate its rule, indeed it was the occupant's right to hold on to its rightful asset obtained through battle. This vision is long gone. It is incompatible with the obligations towards the population and to the people's right to exercise self-determination. This vision assigns the burden of stalemate on negotiations for the settlement of the conflict between the occupant and the occupied solely with the ousted government. Such an allocation of the burden of stalemate is not conducive to political solutions; rather, it encourages the ousted government to seek military responses. For these reasons the law of occupation ought not to condone an occupant which holds out in bad faith, using its control of the occupied territory as leverage. Indeed, such a position is no different from outright annexation. Instead, a more appropriate system of incentives would denounce such acts as illegal, would view the continued rule of the recalcitrant occupant as an aggression and would treat measures aimed at the occupant's own interests as illegal and void. There is a fine line between reasonable bargaining and obstinate holdout, a line that is very difficult to draw and one upon which there would sometimes be more disagreement than consent. In many instances, however, it would not be too difficult to conclude that there is, beyond reasonable doubt, bad faith on the part of the occupant that could taint its status in the territory under its control.

3.7 Is there an obligation to occupy?

As much as occupants must justify their continued presence, foreign powers may at times carry the burden of establishing an occupation regime. A 'responsibility to occupy' may be part of the more general responsibility to protect. As the UNMIK rule in Kosovo shows, the use of force against foreign armies would be just the first step in a long, arduous and costly period of administration of the territory seized during the military campaign. The resources spent on fighting will pale in comparison with the resources necessary to restore and ensure a stable order, and the commitment to humanitarian intervention requires an even stronger commitment to humanitarian occupation. The Report of the International Commission on Intervention and State Sovereignty on the Responsibility to Protect (2001), rightly pointed out that

> the responsibility [is] not just to prevent and react, but to follow through and rebuild.... [T]here should be a genuine commitment to helping to build a durable peace, and promoting good governance and sustainable development. Conditions of public safety and order have to be reconstituted by international agents acting in partnership with local authorities, with the goal of progressively transferring to them authority and responsibility to rebuild.[42]

This commitment to humanitarian occupation may prove too onerous for governments contemplating possible intervention. This might produce too little intervention, when such is necessary. But states might try to get around this obligation to occupy and administer, and to limit their intervention only to the initial phase of the armed intervention, committing themselves not to occupy the foreign territory. Such a policy could often be not only flawed in terms of the intervener's self-interest but also irresponsible towards the population in the invaded region and a dereliction of a duty.

---

41 Oppenheim (n 24) 167.
42 Report of the International Commission on Intervention and State Sovereignty on the Responsibility to Protect (2001) 39–45.

4 Who can be an occupant?

4.1 General

The texts on the law of occupation address situations where the sovereign in the occupied territory and the occupant are enemies. Article 43 of the Hague Regulations refers to 'the hostile army' and Article 4 of Geneva Convention IV focuses on the need to protect 'Protected Persons', namely 'those who, at a given moment and in any manner whatsoever, find themselves, in case of a conflict or occupation, in the hands of [an] Occupying Power of which they are not nationals', but excluding those who are nationals of the occupant or nationals of a neutral state or of a co-belligerent state, if their state of nationality has normal diplomatic representation in the occupying state.[43] This was probably also the underlying assumption: international law needed to regulate only such situations, as others would be resolved through diplomatic channels. There was also a deeper reason: international law was not regarded as authorised to intervene in inter-state affairs to protect citizens from their respective governments.

Given the emphasis on inter-state enmity, it was not a mistake to infer that the law of occupation did not apply outside that context, as did the 1956 US military manual which stipulated that an 'administration established in friendly territory' such as in 'areas which are freed from enemy occupation' were 'not considered to be occupied'.[44] However, in principle, conflicts of interest between government and governed can arise also in administering 'friendly' territory, or whenever the ruler is not accountable to the ruled. Since contemporary international law has also recognised the obligation to regulate the internal relations between a state and its citizens, there is therefore no reason not to expand the concept of 'hostility' to which Article 42 refers to cover other grounds for 'foreignness' between an administration and the people subjected to its rule.[45] The same goes for the interpretation of the concept of protected persons. The ICTY was correct to expand the scope of the term to encompass other situations of non-allegiance between the army and the inhabitants. Applying Geneva Convention IV to the conflict within Bosnia, the Appeals Chamber of the ICTY, turning to the preparatory work of the Fourth Convention, explained that the Convention

> also intends to protect those civilians in occupied territory who, while having the nationality of the Party to the conflict in whose hands they find themselves, are refugees and thus no longer owe allegiance to this Party and no longer enjoy its diplomatic protection.[46]

At least in certain conflicts, nationality should not be a factor in granting a person a protected status.[47]

---

43 Also not protected are nationals of a state which is not bound by the Convention.

44 US Department of the Army, *Army Law of Land Warfare*, Field Manual 27–10 (1956) ¶ 354 (titled 'Friendly Territory Subject to Civil Affairs Administration Distinguished').

45 The British forces applied the Hague Regulations when they recaptured their 'own' colonies in South-East Asia from the Japanese Army in the Second World War. See Frank S V Donnison, *British Military Administration in the Far East* 1943–6 (HMSO 1956).

46 *Prosecutor v Tadić (Appeal Judgment)* (n 33) ¶ 164.

47 Ibid ¶¶ 166, 168. This interpretation was upheld in subsequent judgments: *Prosecutor v Aleksovski* (Case no IT-95-14/1-A, ICTY Appeals Chamber, 24 March 2000) ¶¶ 151–152; *Prosecutor v Mucić et al* (Case no IT-96-21-A, ICTY Appeals Chamber, 20 February 2001) ¶¶ 81–84; *Naletilić and Martinović* (n 30) ¶¶ 204–208; *Prosecutor v Brđanin* (Case no IT-99-36-T, ICTY Trial Chamber II, 1 September 2004) ¶ 125.

The applicability of the law of occupation to occupation of a 'friendly' territory obviously does not mean that the discretion of the occupant would be as constrained as that of the enemy occupant. But it does mean that the basic idea of an exceptional regime which merits international attention and subject to at least the basic constraints of occupation law also applies to the friendliest of the occupants. Needless to add, international human rights law applies to all these different types of non-allegiance.

4.2 Occupation during non-international armed conflict

For the same reasons, there is no reason to refrain from applying the law of occupation in the internal sphere, namely to non-state actors who control territory. The paradigmatic case of internal occupation is the occupation of parts of Georgia by the secessionist forces of Abkhazia. The EU Commission of Inquiry into the conflict in Georgia in 2008 described a situation in which as a result of the fighting, 'most ethnic Georgians left the upper Kodori Valley. The territory was occupied by Abkhaz forces, supported by Russian paratroopers.'[48] The so-called 'Islamic State' is a non-state actor that controls territory and population. Despite its non-state status and utter disregard of international law, the laws it purports to enact will merit at least some respect due to their shaping of private expectations.[49]

4.3 UN territorial administration

A number of UN interventions to end conflicts in the post-Cold War era assumed authority to provide public order and administer civil life. In some cases this assumption of control was based on an agreement with the local government and hence could be regarded as not subject to the law of occupation. When the assumption of control was based on authority under Chapter VII of the UN Charter, for example in Kosovo (UNMIK 1999) and East Timor (UNTAET 1999), a question was raised whether UN administration should have been regarded as subject to, or at least guided by, the law of occupation, despite the lack of direct military conflict. In principle, the same concerns about potential conflicts of interest between occupant and occupied exists with respect to UN-led occupations. The potential conflict in these settings could be both vis-à-vis the occupied population (or parts thereof), and vis-à-vis the ousted government. The example of the UNMIK administration of Kosovo does not suggest otherwise.[50]

Several arguments have been raised to absolve UN-led occupation from obedience to this law. The UN, some say, is not subject to the laws of war in general and the law of occupation in particular.[51] Furthermore, the ousted sovereign had consented to the exercise of discretion of the Security Council, and the state continues to be bound by its consent. Others have suggested that the law of occupation would apply to the UN, but only when it is directly involved in an

---

48 IIFFMCG (n 18) ii, 290.

49 On the laws promulgated by ISIS see Andrew F March and Mara Revkin, 'Caliphate of Law: ISIS' Ground Rules' *Foreign Affairs* (15 April 2015). On the need to respect private expectations see nn 87–88 and accompanying text.

50 For a critical examination of the UNMIK administration, see Benvenisti, *International Law of Occupation* (n 4) ch 10.

51 Secretary-General's Bulletin: Observance by United Nations Forces of International Humanitarian Law, UN Doc ST/SGB/1999/13 (6 August 1999). On a view supporting the inapplicability of the law (but noting that the law can inspire the administration), see Daphna Shraga, 'Military Occupation and UN Transitional Administrations: The Analogy and its Limitations' in Marcelo G Kohen (ed), *Promoting Justice, Human Rights and Conflict Resolution through International Law: Liber Amicorum Lucius Caflisch* (Martinus Nijhoff 2007) 479.

international armed conflict.[52] Some have suggested that there is simply no need to apply the law of occupation to a trusted institution such as the Security Council. Applying the law of occupation would needlessly restrain it from promoting good governance and human rights in the foreign territory.[53]

Unless the UN administration is based on the free and explicit consent of the sovereign,[54] none of these arguments is ultimately fully convincing.[55] They all share the assumption that the Security Council can be trusted to act as the trustee sovereign, for whom the law of occupation would be a nuisance. But if we consider the fact that the role of the law of occupation is not only to protect the rights of the inhabitants, but also to respect state sovereignty and self-determination, it becomes clear that there are legal limits to UN-led administrations.[56] Occupants may not ignore this obligation even if they are granted the authority to do so by the Security Council acting under Chapter VII because the latter may not disregard norms that have the status of *jus cogens* such as self-determination, and as Oscar Schachter emphasised, when discussing Security Council Resolution 1483 concerning Iraq, the principle of 'sovereign equality' and the right of states to political independence and territorial integrity 'limit the authority of the Council to impose a regime'.[57] The same argument applies with similar force, if not more, for the Security Council's obligation to protect the rights, including the human rights, of the protected persons in occupied territory.[58] If, according to a General Comment of the Human Rights Committee,

> the rights guaranteed under the Covenant belong to the people living in the territory of a State party, and that once the people are accorded the protection of the rights under the Covenant, such protection devolves with territory and continues to belong to them, notwithstanding changes in the administration of that territory,[59]

52 Charles H B Garraway, 'Applicability and Application of International Humanitarian Law to Enforcement and Peace Enforcement Operations' in Terry D Gill and Dieter Fleck (eds), *The Handbook of the International Law of Military Operations* (OUP 2010) 129, 130–131; Christopher Greenwood, 'International Humanitarian Law and United Nations Military Operations' (1998) 1 *YBIHL* 3, 28–30, 33–34; Roberts, 'What is a Military Occupation?' (n 16) 290.

53 David J Scheffer, 'Beyond Occupation Law' (2003) 97 *AJIL* 842, 851 ('liberating armies that operate with international authority, advance democracy, and save civilian populations from atrocities should be regulated by a modern occupation regime that can be created under the UN Charter').

54 For the consent or lack thereof in UN administrations, see Benvenisti, *International Law of Occupation* (n 4) 278.

55 Steven R Ratner, 'Foreign Occupation and International Territorial Administration: The Challenges of Convergence' (2005) 16 *EJIL* 695, 702 ('the legal frameworks governing these two types of operations have witnessed significant convergence. As a result, it becomes more difficult to see them as governed by separate sets of norms').

56 For the view that the UN is or should be subject to the laws of armed conflict and the law of occupation, see Tobias H Irmscher, 'The Legal Framework for the Activities of the United Nations Interim Administration Mission in Kosovo: The Charter, Human Rights, and the Law of Occupation' (2001) 44 *German YBIL* 353, 383–387; Hansjoerg Strohmeyer, 'Collapse and Reconstruction of a Judicial System: The United Nations Mission in Kosovo and East Timor' (2001) 95 *AJIL* 46, 58–59; Umesh Palwankar, 'Applicability of International Humanitarian Law to UN Peacekeeping Forces' (1993) 33 *IRRC* 227.

57 Oscar Schachter, 'United Nations Law in the Gulf Conflict' (1991) 85 *AJIL* 452, 468.

58 Alexandre Faite, 'Applicability of the Law of Occupation to United Nations-Mandated Forces' in Alexandre Faite and Jérémie Grenier (eds), *Report of Expert Meeting on Multinational Peace Operations, Geneva, 11–12 December 2003* (ICRC 2004) 71, 76.

59 General Comment no 26: Continuity of Obligations, UN Doc CCPR/C/21/Add.8/Rev.1 (1997) ¶ 4. On this comment and its applicability to UNMIK in Kosovo, see Benvenisti, *International Law of Occupation* (n 4) 290.

then it is not clear to what extent the Security Council, even acting under Chapter VII, has the right to instruct the occupation regime to ignore these protections. It is also unclear why the law should allow the UN to ignore the accumulated experience with occupations and the discipline that the law of occupation imposes on the administration.[60] The law of occupation provides basic guidelines on the exercise of the otherwise wide-ranging governmental powers by occupants. Recourse to the framework of the law of occupation may enable both the government and the governed to draw upon the rich experience that has accumulated over the years and to inform their policies and expectations. Therefore, there can be no legally valid UN-based regime 'beyond occupation law';[61] the law of occupation also applies to UN-led missions,[62] albeit allowing for a wider interpretation of the scope of the occupant's authority, given the disinterestedness of the occupant or its supervising body.[63]

The law of occupation, as well as human rights law, would certainly apply to states whose forces take part in implementing the UN-led mission. To the extent that the operation is attributed to the member states (rather than to the UN), they would be expected, when complying with the UN mandate, to observe, as much as the text allows them, their general obligations under international law including human rights law.[64] This principle has received sound support from national and international courts in recent years.[65]

5 Authority of occupant

5.1 In general

The occupation administration must attend to three sets of interests: its own security interests, the interests of the ousted government and those of the local population. How to balance these often conflicting interests is one of the major challenges of the law. It is possible to argue that the Hague Regulations betray a preference to the interests of the ousted government when those are in conflict with the interests of the local population. The occupant was expected to fulfil the vacuum created by the ousting of the local government and maintain its bases of power until the conditions for the latter's return were mutually agreed upon. In contrast, the underlying effort of Geneva Convention IV is to focus predominantly on the effort to ensure the interests of the inhabitants. This emphasis is underscored by the complementary application of human rights law that focuses entirely on individuals.

With the advent of the twentieth century and the ever-increasing regulation of markets and other social activities by contemporary governments, and especially as occupations became protracted, the authority of the occupant was increasingly regarded as broader in scope emphasising not only the obligation to 'restore' but also the duty to 'ensure' effective functioning of civil life

---

60 Siobhan Wills, *Protecting Civilians: The Obligations of Peacekeepers* (OUP 2009) 241–244.

61 Cf David J Scheffer, 'Beyond Occupation Law' (2003) 97 *AJIL* 842.

62 See also *Prosecutor v Tadić (Decision on the Defense Motion for Interlocutory Appeal on Jurisdiction)* (Case no IT-94-1-AR72, ICTY Appeals Chamber, 2 October 1995) ¶ 93 (noting that art 1 of the four Geneva Conventions 'lays down an obligation that is incumbent, not only on states, but also on other international entities including the United Nations').

63 Sylvain Vité, 'L'Applicabilité du Droit International de l'Occupation Militaire aux Activités des Organisations Internationales' (2004) 86 *IRRC* 9, 25–26.

64 Jann K Kleffner, 'Human Rights and International Humanitarian Law: General Issues' in Gill and Fleck (eds) (n 52) 51, 76.

65 *R (Al Jedda) v Secretary of State for Defence* [2007] UKHL 58; *Al Jedda v UK* (App no 27021/08, ECtHR, 7 July 2011); see also Joined Cases C-402/05 P and C-415/05 P, *Kadi and Al Barakaat International Foundation v Council and Commission* [2008] ECR I-6351.

in the more general sense. The role of the modern state was so vast that preserving the pre-conflict status quo was often detrimental for the local population. To be able to comply with its human rights obligations, the occupant may at times have the authority and even the obligation to depart from the status quo.

Article 43 of the Hague Regulations provides the gist of the occupant's authority and responsibility: 'The authority of the legitimate power having in fact passed into the hands of the occupant, the latter shall take all the measures in his power to restore, and ensure, as far as possible, public order and safety.' A more accurate rendition of the authoritative French text (which refers to *l'ordre et la vie publics*) posts 'public order *and civil life*' as the spheres of the occupant's authority. During the short-term occupations envisioned by the drafters of the Hague Regulations, these obligations would mean the obligation to restore the order that existed prior to the occupation and to keep it that way, as far as possible, for the brief period anticipated. Upon occupation, the occupant becomes responsible for maintaining public order, and therefore will be held responsible for its omissions in that respect. In its *DRC v Uganda* judgment, the ICJ held that the occupant was responsible for the failure to prevent in the occupied area ethnic conflicts and the recruitment of child soldiers, as well as for not taking appropriate measures to prevent the looting, plundering and exploitation of natural resources.[66]

The duties of the occupant under Geneva Convention IV are far more numerous. It is no longer the disinterested watch guard, but instead a very involved regulator and provider. It is required to ensure the humane treatment of protected persons, without discriminating among them, and to respect, among other things, the protected persons' honour, family rights, religious convictions and practices, and manners and customs,[67] to facilitate the proper working of all institutions devoted to the care and education of children,[68] provide specific labour conditions,[69] ensure food and medical supplies of the population,[70] maintain medical services[71] and agree to relief schemes and to facilitate them by all means at its disposal.[72] Such an expansive view seems to be consonant with the prevalent view, discussed above, that the occupant is bound also by human rights obligations, and that in general it must 'take measures to ensure respect for human rights and international humanitarian law in the occupied territories'.[73]

It should be mentioned that there are also pre- and post-occupation obligations. Either before or after the occupant is able to establish (or continue to maintain) effective control over territory, it is bound by duties under the law on the conduct of hostilities, Geneva Convention IV and human rights law.[74]

5.2 Scope of law-making

Article 43 of the Hague Regulations ends with a restraint on the occupant's authority. In taking measures to restore and ensure public order and civil life, the occupant must proceed 'while respecting, unless absolutely prevented, the laws in force in the country'. The term 'unless absolutely prevented' was inserted to replace the term 'unless necessary' at the insistence of the

---

66 *Armed Activities* (n 22) 244–248.
67 GCIV art 27.
68 GCIV art 51.
69 GCIV art 52.
70 GCIV art 55.
71 GCIV art 56.
72 GCIV art 59.
73 *Armed Activities* (n 22) ¶ 211.
74 For further reading, see Benvenisti, *International Law of Occupation* (n 4) 57–58.

potentially occupied states, to emphasise the occupant's obligation to preserve the status quo also in the legal sphere.[75] This restraint on the occupant's authority creates a tension with its authority and obligation to ensure public order and civil life as elaborated in the previous sections. To reconcile the two requirements of Article 43 it is necessary to suggest that whenever the implementation of the obligation to ensure requires changes of the local laws, these changes will be considered lawful. This conclusion is further bolstered by Article 64 of Geneva Convention IV, which replaced the negative test of 'unless absolutely prevented', with a positive authorisation for the occupant who

> may subject the population of the occupied territory to provisions which are essential to enable the Occupying Power to fulfill its obligations under the present Convention, to maintain the orderly government of the territory, and to ensure the security of the Occupying Power.[76]

Scholars in the post-Second World War period readily conceded legitimate subjects for the occupant's law-making other than military necessity. The welfare of the population was deemed a worthy goal for the occupant to pursue.[77] In addition, especially in light of the oppressive laws that the occupants found in Nazi Germany and other occupied states, some scholars have argued that at times moral arguments, and not only technical difficulties, could be considered as preventing an occupant from respecting local laws and, in fact, requiring change.[78] With the enlargement of the legitimate authority of the occupant came a more lenient view of legislation, leading to suggestions to interpret 'absolutely prevented' as meaning 'necessity', or simply asking for a 'sufficient justification' for changing the law.[79] It would seem that such an expansive scope of authority would be particularly fitting in genuine 'humanitarian' or 'transformative' occupations, provided that the occupant steps back and enables the effective exercise of the collective right to self-determination. This question became the focus of scholarly attention in light of the occupation of Iraq in 2003, and the transformation of the Iraqi state institutions and its economy. The *Law of War Manual* issued in June 2015 by the US Department of Defense offers an extensive list of grounds that may justify changes to the domestic law.[80]

5.3 The occupant's management of international affairs

Nowadays there are few areas of national regulation that are not governed, or at least heavily influenced, by formal or informal international agreements, institutions or other means of interactions. National policy-making routinely involves coordination with foreign governments and

---

75 For further reading, ibid 89–95.
76 Ibid 95–102.
77 Gerhard von Glahn, *The Occupation of Enemy Territory: A Commentary on the Law and Practice of Belligerent Occupation* (University of Minnesota Press 1957) 97; Morris Greenspan, *The Modern Law of Land Warfare* (University of California Press 1959) 224; Odile Debbasch, *L'Occupation Militaire: Pouvoirs Reconnus aux Forces Armees hors de leur Territoire National* (Pichon et Durand–Auzias 1962) 172; Arnold D McNair and Arthur D Watts, *The Legal Effects of War* (4th edn, CUP 1966) 369; Myres S McDougal and Florentino P Feliciano, *Law and Minimum World Public Order: The Legal Regulation of International Coercion* (Yale University Press 1961) 767, 770.
78 See eg McDougal and Feliciano (n 77) 770.
79 Ernst Feilchenfeld, *The International Economic Law of Belligerent Occupation* (Carnegie Endowment for International Peace 1942) 89; Yoram Dinstein, 'The International Law of Belligerent Occupation and Human Rights' (1978) 8 *Israel YBHR* 104, 112.
80 See s 11.9 ('Local Law and Legislation') 763–766.

international bureaucracies. The management of local natural resources might be governed by treaties and subject to regional regimes. The occupant may be faced with several treaties by which the ousted government is bound. Is the occupant bound to comply on behalf of the occupied area with the international obligations assumed by the legitimate government prior to the occupation? Is it authorised to undertake new international obligations for the duration of the occupation? Could such negotiations yield agreements that would be binding after the expiration of the occupation period? And similar questions arise for third countries and treaty bodies: must they accept the occupant as representing the state party? May they negotiate with the occupant?

From the perspective of the law of occupation, it would seem that to the extent that public order and civil life depend on complying with formal international obligations and informal 'soft law' commitments that the ousted government had assumed prior to the occupation, the occupant should regard itself as bound by those obligations.[81] For example, during the occupation of Iraq the occupation authorities justified their redrafting of the Iraqi labour code by recalling that, as a state party to the International Labour Organization (ILO) Conventions 138 and 182, Iraq was obliged to take affirmative steps towards eliminating child labour.[82] Similarly, new undertakings on behalf of the local populations necessary to 'restore and ensure' public order and civil life should also be regarded within the ambit of the occupant's authority to pursue. The law does not restrict the occupant's choice of the legal means it has to realise its duties. Under Article 43 of the Hague Regulations, the occupant may and indeed must, 'take *all the measures in his power* to restore, and ensure, as far as possible, public order and safety'. The law is mainly interested in the occupant's goals, not in the means it uses to further these goals. As put by Schwarzenberger, '[I]n short, the *ratio* of the rule [of Article 43] is to forestall temptations on the part of the Occupying Power to abuse its discretionary and legislative powers.'[83] The same logic would apply with equal force to the authority to coordinate its activities with neighbouring states. This perspective suggests that there should be no a priori restriction on the occupant's authority to negotiate or renegotiate international agreements.

The same conclusion can be gleaned from other areas of international law that seek to ensure that human activity in a certain territory is not harmful to collective interests. To the extent that compliance with existing international undertakings or committing to new obligations promotes global interests such as the reduction of pollution, the optimal utilisation of transboundary water and other resources, the cooperation in the fight against pandemics, those should be encouraged for the benefit of the occupied population, neighbouring states and the entire global community. For example, the Venice Commission opined in 2009 that Russia was expected to comply with the 1951 Geneva Convention on the Status of Refugees,[84] to which Georgia was a party, in the areas of Georgia under Russian occupation.[85]

---

81 Meron (n 29); Eyal Benvenisti, 'Water Conflicts during the Occupation of Iraq, Forthcoming in Agora Future Implications of the Iraq Conflict' (2003) 97 *AJIL* 860; Adam Roberts, 'Transformative Military Occupation: Applying the Laws of War and Human Rights' (2006) 100 *AJIL* 580, 589.

82 Coalition Provisional Authority Order no 89: Amendments to the Labor Code, Law No 71 of 1987, Doc no CPA/ORD/05 (May 2004/89). See also Sylvian Vité, 'The Interrelation of the Law of Occupation and Economic, Social and Cultural Rights: The Examples of Food, Health and Property' (2008) 90 *IRRC* 629, 633.

83 Georg Schwarzenberger, *International Law as applied by International Courts and Tribunals* (Stevens & Sons 1968) ii, 201.

84 (28 July 1951) 189 UNTS 150.

85 Venice Commission, Opinion on the Law on Occupied Territories of Georgia, Opinion no 516/2009, Doc no CDL-AD(2009)015 (78th Plenary Session, 13–14 March 2009) ¶ 17.

In the same vein, the occupant should be encouraged to participate, on behalf of the area it occupies, in regional institutions aimed, for example, at the management of shared natural resources such as water, fisheries and oil. The protection of the interests of all riparian states and peoples dependent on a particular watercourse requires that occupants would be entitled to represent the interests of the occupied territory and its inhabitants in the shared watercourse vis-à-vis neighbouring countries, and at the same time assume responsibility vis-à-vis those states for any harm it causes to them by its own management decisions.

Three caveats are called for. A question of conflict of interests may arise when the occupant is itself a riparian of the same transboundary resource. The Israeli occupation of the West Bank, for example, has put Israeli occupation administration in control of water resources shared by Israel and the West Bank (the Mountain Aquifer) or by Israel, the West Bank and Jordan (the Jordan River).[86] In such cases the concentration of representation of both Israeli and West Bank interests by one authority is an unsatisfactory solution. The second caveat relates to cases of partial occupation of a territory, where the sovereign government controls part of the natural resource, be it a watercourse or an oil field, and conflicts arise between it and the occupant, or between these two and third parties. Awareness to such problematic situations should lead to ad hoc approaches to ensure equitable and sustainable management of the resources in question.

The third and most important caveat relates to occupants who deny the applicability of the occupation regime and instead illegally annex the territory or act through puppet regimes. Because such acts are illegal their consequences are invalid, and the UN Security Council often reminds states of their obligation to regard such acts as legally invalid. States must therefore, for example, refrain from signing new treaties with such regimes. But this caveat contains its own caveat: there are circumstances in which states should disregard the illegality and continue to maintain existing treaty-based relations that benefit the local population. This is emphasised by the ICJ in its *Namibia Advisory Opinion* which admonishes states not to respect 'certain general conventions such as those of a humanitarian character, the non-performance of which may adversely affect the people of Namibia'.[87] The Court also added that '[i]n general, the non-recognition of South Africa's administration of the Territory should not result in depriving the people of Namibia of any advantages derived from international co-operation'.[88] It might be argued that the same concern with the wish not to deprive the inhabitants of the benefit of international cooperation should apply as well to bilateral and regional treaties such as free trade areas which ensure the livelihoods of the occupied inhabitants. For example, one might question the appropriateness of the judgment of the European Court of Justice which decided that farmers in Northern Cyprus, under Turkish rule through a 'Turkish Republic of Northern Cyprus', could not benefit from the Association Agreement which had been signed between the European Community and Cyprus before the occupation, and thereby imposed an effective economic blockade on that part of the island, with consequent severe economic hardships inflicted on the population.[89]

---

86 Sharif S Elmusa, 'Dividing Common Water Resources According to International Water Law: The Case of the Palestinian-Israeli Waters' (1995) 35 *Natural Resources Journal* 223, 225; Eyal Benvenisti and Haim Gvirtzman, 'Harnessing International Law to Determine Israeli–Palestinian Water Rights: The Mountain Aquifer' (1993) 33 *Natural Resources Journal* 543; Jamal L El-Hindi, 'The West Bank Aquifer and Conventions Regarding the Laws of Belligerent Occupation' (1990) 11 *Michigan JIL* 1400.

87 *Legal Consequences for States of the Continued Presence of South Africa in Namibia (South West Africa) notwithstanding Security Council Resolution 276 (1970) (Advisory Opinion)* [1971] ICJ Rep 16 ¶¶ 122, 125.

88 Ibid ¶ 125.

89 C-432/92, *R v Minister of Agriculture, ex parte Anastasiou* [1994] ECR I-3087. For a critical review of this litigation, see Stefan Talmon, 'The Cyprus Question before the European Court of Justice' (2001) 12 *EJIL* 727.

The question remains as to the nature and durability of any agreements concluded between the occupant and other states with respect to the management of the occupied territories in those spheres, such as environment protection, that are regarded under the occupant's jurisdiction. Because the occupant's authority is essentially limited in time − only as long as it exercises effective control − it cannot create rights and obligations among the state parties that will last beyond the period of occupation. To draw from Feilchenfeld, 'though [Article 55] permits the Occupant to let or utilize public land and buildings, sell crops on public land, cut or sell timber, and work mines, *such contract or lease must not extend beyond the termination of the war*'.[90]

The same rationale would apply, I would argue, to agreements between the occupant, as the administrator of the occupied country's natural resources, and neighbouring countries. Such agreements − whether or not formally qualified as treaties under the Vienna Convention on the Law of Treaties[91] − will be valid for the duration of the occupation, but terminate automatically when occupation ends and a new regime comes to power. Such a termination, however, does not suggest that such agreements will not be able to create long-term impact. Any renegotiation of the agreement will have to take into consideration the changed circumstances as a result of the war and occupation, and vested interests that have been crystallised in the meantime. Such uses would, for example, constitute part of the 'factors relevant to equitable and reasonable utilization' specified in Article 6 of the Watercourses Convention.[92]

In general the occupant has no authority to bind the occupied people to international agreements or to other liabilities that would encumber the occupied people beyond the occupation period. Note, however, that while the agreements will not be binding on the returning sovereign, their consequences, and the expectations that people develop in good faith while relying on them, might be given legal recognition.[93]

5.4 Management of property

The provisions in the Hague Regulations provide two types of restrictions on the occupant's use of local resources. One type of restriction relates to the type of the resource, the other relates to the purpose of the contemplated use. The Hague Regulations distinguish primarily between private and public property. Whereas Articles 53 and 55 allow certain uses of public property by occupants, private property is protected by several provisions that prohibit confiscation, pillage and collective punishment.[94] Moreover, Article 33 of Geneva Convention IV protects private property of Protected Persons against reprisals. According to the ICJ in the *DRC v Uganda* judgment, the prohibition on pillage extends also to the exploitation of the foreign country's natural resources.[95] Specific private property that can be used for military purposes (like means of communications and of transportations) may be taken 'but must be restored and compensation fixed

---

90 Feilchenfeld (n 79) 714 (emphasis added).
91 (23 May 1969) 1155 UNTS 331, art 2(1)(a) regards as treaties agreements signed between states, but in this case it will be the occupant, which is distinct from the state, which will be the party to the agreement. On the other hand, art 3 does not rule out other types of agreements subject to this law.
92 Convention on the Law of the Non-Navigational Uses of International Watercourses, UNGA Res 51/229 (21 May 1997).
93 On this, see Benvenisti, *International Law of Occupation* (n 4) ch 12.
94 HR arts 46, 47, 50; GCIV art 33.
95 *Armed Activities* (n 22) ¶ 245.

when peace is made'.[96] Private property may, however, be affected by an occupant under certain circumstances. The occupant is authorised to requisition goods and services in proportion to the resources of the occupied region to accommodate the needs of the army of occupation, but the occupant is obligated to pay for such in cash as far as it is possible.[97] The occupant is also authorised to collect contributions.[98] It is also authorised to collect taxes 'as far as is possible, in accordance with the rules of assessment and incidence in force ... to defray the expenses of the administration of the occupied territory'.[99]

Public property – certain movable public property and most immovable public property – can be used by the occupant. But the utilisation of public property is qualified by two conditions. The first condition relates to the purpose of the use. The occupant may use the different types of property to meet its security needs, to defray the occupation administration's costs and to promote the needs of the local population. It is generally accepted that the occupant may not use them for its own domestic purposes, but rather use them 'to the extent necessary for the current administration of the territory and to meet the essential needs of the population'.[100] This restriction was acknowledged by the occupants of Iraq in 2003, who informed the president of the UN Security Council that they would 'act to ensure that Iraq's oil is protected and used for the benefit of the Iraqi people'. The second condition applies to public immovable property only. Article 55 of the Hague Regulations stipulates that the occupant, being 'only [the] administrator and usufructuary', 'must safeguard the capital of [such] properties, and administer them in accordance with the rules of usufruct'. The usufructuary principle was interpreted as forbidding wasteful or negligent destruction of the capital value, whether by excessive cutting or mining or other abusive exploitation.

The authority and right to use public immovable property for the benefit of the local population extends also to the utilisation of natural resources situated in the occupied territory. Therefore, the utilisation of these resources according to the above-mentioned guidelines would not constitute a violation of the principle of permanent sovereignty over its natural resources, as stated by the ICJ in its *DRC v Uganda* judgment.[101] This judgment also states that the occupant must 'take appropriate measures to prevent the looting, plundering and exploitation of natural resources in the occupied territory'.[102] The same guidelines apply to the management of the environment in the occupied territory and its water resources. The occupant is authorised, and in fact would be obliged, to assume control over natural resources, protect them against overuse and pollution, and allocate them equitably and reasonably among the various domestic users.

6 Concluding remarks

The law of occupation represents an effort to fill the legal and administrative void created when a foreign actor ousts the national authorities and prevents them from exercising their authority

---

96 HR art 53(2).
97 HR art 52.
98 HR art 51.
99 HR art 48. A question has arisen during the Israeli occupation of the West bank and Gaza as to whether an occupant was entitled to introduce new types of taxes (ie a value-added-tax), to which the Israeli court of justice gave a positive answer. HCJ 69/81 *Abu Aita et al v Military Commander of the Judea and Samaria Region et al* (1983) 37 PD(2) 197, 7 Selected Judgments of the Supreme Court of Israel 1.
100 Institute of International Law, Déclaration de Bruges sur le Recours à la Force (2 September 2003).
101 *Armed Activities* (n 22) ¶ 244.
102 Ibid ¶ 248.

in a certain area. The effort, however well intended, is inherently flawed because the void is filled by an authority whose interests often clash with those of the local population and the ousted government. This inherent conflict of interests calls for special attention by third parties that monitor and review the occupant's measures. The detailed law and the rich jurisprudence that has developed over the years is not a reason for complacency. In fact, the practice demonstrates that the legal regime is far from providing a satisfactory answer to the control gap. Therefore, a healthy suspicion in the occupant's motives should always inform the reviewers. The likely partiality of the occupant requires, for example, that international tribunals refrain from granting the occupant the same margin of appreciation that sovereigns enjoy. While not illegal as such, the law of occupation is susceptible to systematic abuse and hence calls for close and constant scrutiny.

26
Neutrality revisited

Elizabeth Chadwick

To understand the operation of laws of armed conflict one should first comprehend the context of, and crucial role played by, rules of armed neutrality.[1] Prior to 1945, when inter-state force was prohibited in UN Charter Article 2(4),[2] policies of armed neutrality permitted a state which had no particular interest in a war occurring elsewhere to abstain from the hostilities and remain 'neutral'.[3] Not only that, but largely for strategic reasons, states were positively encouraged to confine themselves to neutral attitudes and avoid intervention in the conflicts of others. Neutral states remained at peace with each other, while their neutrality as regards the belligerents' conflict could be protected by complying with three essential rules: neutral states did not (1) favour either belligerent,[4] (2) engage in any warlike acts themselves and (3) allow neutral territory to be used by the belligerents.[5] Not surprisingly, as neutral states remained sources of trade and

---

1 A policy of 'armed neutrality' on the outbreak of war between two or more states is distinct from a stance of permanent neutrality (a legal obligation), or the neutrality maintained by humanitarian NGOs and UN peacekeeping units. Michael Bothe, 'The Law of Neutrality' in Dieter Fleck (ed), *The Handbook of International Humanitarian Law* (3rd edn, OUP 2013) 549. See also Hersh Lauterpacht, 'Neutrality and Collective Security' in Elihu Lauterpacht (ed), *Collected Papers: Volume 5 – Settlement of Disputes, War and Neutrality* (CUP 2004) 611; Philip C Jessup and Francis Deak, *Neutrality: Its History, Economics and Law* (4 vols, Columbia University Press 1935–1936).

2 UN Charter art 2(4) states that '[a]ll Members shall refrain in their international relations from the threat or use of force against the territorial integrity or political independence of any State, or in any other manner inconsistent with the Purposes of the UN'.

3 Neutral, 'equal' treatment did not necessarily mean 'identical' treatment, due to extraneous factors such as geographical proximity, pre-existing trade agreements, legal tradition and culture. For a comprehensive overview and list of sources on neutrality, see Elizabeth Chadwick, 'Neutrality' in Anthony Carty (ed), *Oxford Bibliographies in International Law* (OUP 2014), www.oxfordbibliographies.com/view/document/obo-9780199796953/obo-9780199796953-0060.xml.

4 Neutral impartiality was not so much a general duty as a set of specific duties. Neutral non-discrimination, for example, implies the duty to treat belligerents formally, not materially, on the basis of equality. Andrea Gioia, 'Neutrality and Non-Belligerency' in H H G Post (ed), *International Economic Law and Armed Conflict* (Martinus Nijhoff 1994) 51, 80–81.

5 Included within the duty of prevention. Dietrich Schindler, 'Transformations in the Law of Neutrality since 1945' in Astrid J M Delissen and Gerard J Tanja (eds), *Humanitarian Law of Armed Conflict: Challenges Ahead* (Martinus Nijhoff 1991) 367, 379; Gioia (n 4) 81.

supplies despite the outbreak of war, a strategic part of belligerent war planning revolved around assessments as to which states were likely to remain neutral during the next military campaign. Both neutral and belligerent states benefited from this arrangement, while respect for neutral rules benefited the wider peace by helping to confine the spread and devastation of war.

Most crucially, the respective balance between belligerent and neutral state rights and duties rested on one central premise: neutral states could continue to trade peacefully, despite the outbreak of war, but only so long as they permitted the belligerents to monitor neutral trade for purposes of preventing receipt by the enemy of 'prohibited contraband' and other goods useful to that enemy's war effort.[6] Practices based around this fundamental compromise effectively determined the majority of inter-state relations during war, and constituted a 'practical example of that anomaly of a military war and a commercial peace'.[7] Further, as neutrality generally applied only between states, neutral citizens were often left to pursue their own commercial advantages, for example by running maritime blockades in order to sell prohibited contraband to one or other belligerent.[8] This placed the role of 'policing' neutral merchant trade mainly on the belligerents. However, once industrial developments heightened the importance of economic warfare, more powerful state belligerents began to demand increasing levels of 'due diligence' from neutral states. If such demands for neutral due diligence were ignored, a state's neutrality could be made impossible to defend against belligerent encroachment, drawing that neutral into the war, and/or necessitating the payment of compensation to the belligerent for 'un-neutral' service.[9]

For so long as states waged war against each other 'lawfully' for any reason whatsoever, war in practical terms was perceived as a disease having no cure. The fact that 'international law was originally a law of war, and that relations between states in earlier times were essentially of a military nature',[10] led instead to the development of international laws of war designed to achieve greater battlefield conformity and predictability. Starting from about 1648,[11] until the outbreak of the First World War, such laws also included regulations to lessen the effects of war on uninvolved third states – and, in particular, to mitigate the effects of war on belligerent and neutral state legal relations. The First World War in turn marks the point at which the existing laws of war and neutrality appeared to be unequal to the task of restraining new war practices and industrialised armaments. The horrors of this 'total war' mandated afterwards that a cure for war be sought, which effort began with a 'peace programme' instituted by the League of Nations designed to slow the impetus to war. Unfortunately, the League also proved unequal to this task, not least because of the more profound linkage between trade and war, so a renewed attempt to

---

6 F E Smith, *International Law* (Dent 1900) 145; Nicolas Politis, *La Neutralite et la Paix* (Hachette 1935) 39–44. See also the *Caroline* case of 1841: John Bassett Moore, *Digest of International Law* (US Government Printing Office 1906) vol 2, 409, 412; 29 *BFSP* 1137; 30 *BFSP* 195 (involving US inability to defend its neutrality); *Bauer v Marmara et al*, 942 F Supp 2d 31 (DDC 2013), affirmed 774 F 3d 1026 (DC Cir 2014) (US Neutrality Act of 1794 contextualised as a 'bounty' or 'informer' statute, regarding which see *Vermont Agency of Natural Resources v US; ex rel Stevens*, 529 US 765, 774–79 (2000). The 1794 statute financially rewarded citizens for information of wrongdoing.).

7 Charles H Stockton, 'The Declaration of Paris' (1920) 14 *AJIL* 357, referring to the Crimean War (1853–1856).

8 Trade in contraband, or a breach of blockade, was forbidden only by international law. Yoram Dinstein, 'The Laws of Neutrality' (1984) 14 *Israel YBHR* 80, 95–96; Hersh Lauterpacht (ed), *Oppenheim's Treatise on International Law: Volume II – Disputes, War and Neutrality* (7th edn, Longmans 1952) 656.

9 See eg Elizabeth Chadwick, *Traditional Neutrality Revisited* (Kluwer 2002) ch 2.

10 Erik Castrén, *The Present Law of War and Neutrality* (Finnish Academy of Science and Letters 1954) 6.

11 For example, after the Peace of Westphalia made states the supreme administrative entities in international life.

forestall war had to await the aftermath of the Second World War and the 1945 UN Charter, which instrument comprehensively prohibits the unauthorised use of inter-state force in Article 2(4), as reinforced by Security Council collective enforcement powers pursuant to the Charter, Chapter VII.

Where then does the UN Charter leave neutrality? Interestingly, neutrality does indeed continue to operate as a legal institution in the UN era, even though the positive legal obligations of Charter collective security are designed to deter states from attacking each other.[12] Unfortunately, the Security Council is often either unable or unwilling to utilise its enforcement powers to maintain or restore international peace and security, the scope of which includes collective action to resolve any de facto situation which disrupts diplomatic relations and trade.[13] States continue instead to utilise force against each other, and/or to proffer varying degrees of support for unilateral or regional enforcement mechanisms, such as voluntary sanctions regimes, armed interventions, administrative occupations, peace-enforcing and peace-keeping operations, etc. On the other hand, Security Council inaction leaves states free to remain impartial, so neutrality continues to play a vital role in inter-state diplomacy during times of war, not least by offering a tried-and-tested mechanism to deflect forceful entanglements.

In order to discuss these issues, with a view to assessing the current state of armed neutrality, it is intended, first, to provide a brief overview of the 'classical' law of neutrality, after which the impact on neutrality of UN collective security is introduced. The extent to which specific aspects of neutrality have survived in the contemporary era is next examined, after which the potential relevance of neutrality to other uses of state force, including, controversially, during non-international armed conflicts,[14] is then considered. It is concluded that laws of neutrality remain viable in helping to resolve a very wide variety indeed of violent situations.

1 Classical laws of neutrality: a quick overview

So long as war for any reason was deemed the lawful prerogative of sovereign states, states concentrated their efforts on making the 'inexorable necessity'[15] of conflict more predictable, if not always more 'civilised'. Slowly, states conformed their battle rules in accordance with the necessities of a surrounding belligerent environment. For example, land warfare needed to be self-supporting, in the sense that civilians were expected to supply both the defending and attacking/occupying armies. In contrast, maritime warfare was more likely to involve both public and private shipping, and the numbers of persons involved were far fewer. Greater disagreement surrounded specific practices at sea, but the rules developed for land warfare remained rather more basic compared to those for maritime warfare. Over time, inter-state treaties and agreements as to 'civilised' customs and norms for armed conflict (and neutrality) solidified, and contained increasingly onerous standards, particularly to benefit wounded or captured combatants, and civilian populations inhabiting occupied territory. Greater conformity in battlefield behaviour improved military discipline, strengthened the rules of war and neutrality, and instilled a deeper sense of state responsibility concerning the need to temper war's disruption as regards war's growing impact on globalising commercial relations.

12 As imposed by UN Charter arts 24(1) and 25, and as enabled pursuant to art 39. See also art 103.
13 See UN Charter art 27(3).
14 See eg Christopher Greenwood, 'The Applicability of International Humanitarian Law and the Law of Neutrality to the Kosovo Campaign' in Andru E Wall (ed), *Legal and Ethical Lessons of NATO's Kosovo Campaign* (US Naval War College 2002) 35, 44–45.
15 'Preface', The 1880 Oxford Manual of Laws of War on Land, www.icrc.org/ihl.nsf/FULL/140? OpenDocument (quoting Baron Jomini).

'Classical' rules of neutrality also developed in two separate branches: rules for land warfare, and rules for maritime war. The latter included rules concerning naval blockade and the transport of prohibited contraband. As normal commerce between neutral and belligerent states was likely to be interrupted by war, it had long been agreed that neutral vessels and innocent cargoes should be immune from belligerent capture.[16] Nonetheless, belligerent rules governing the transport of 'prohibited contraband' and forbidding its receipt by the enemy were so important they were actually formulated during peacetime, as the very rationale of economic warfare planning required belligerents to be fully prepared to block any and all sources of continuous supply to the enemy. The rules thus permitted belligerents to seize and confiscate ship cargoes (and ships) as 'prize' if they constituted prohibited contraband. Prize captures were often controversial, as each belligerent state established its own 'prize courts' on the outbreak of hostilities,[17] in which the legality of captures under the capturing belligerent's municipal laws could be adjudicated. Prize court practice did in time harmonise certain profiteering opportunities, for example the issue of 'letters of marque' by belligerent governments to authorised privateers was gradually prohibited due to the danger that prize captures could constitute piracy.

Rules of neutrality also evolved in different formats, including 'imperfect', 'benevolent'[18] and 'qualified' neutrality,[19] the most rigorous form being 'absolute' or 'strict'.[20] Two European-wide Armed Neutralities in 1780 and 1800 were especially important,[21] as they were necessitated by the armed struggles which ensued between many European states over their competing colonial interests in the New World. Far-flung colonies made it much more likely that European belligerents could interfere with neutral commerce *anywhere*, such as by stop, search and seizure of contraband, so the European maritime powers were forced to build defensive alliances to protect their rights to continue trading peacefully. The 1780 Armed Neutrality was agreed among Russia, Spain, Denmark, Sweden, Prussia, Austria and joined by the new American states; the second Armed Neutrality, in 1800, was formulated initially by Russia, Denmark, Prussia and Sweden. Following the examples of the 1780 and 1800 Armed Neutralities, interest in more precise rules increased and some further progress was made, but by the outbreak of the Crimean War in 1853, the maritime rules of neutrality again needed harmonisation, particularly as regards maritime captures. The 1856 Declaration of Paris at war's end reiterated and strengthened the

---

16 See eg *Consolato del Mare*, dating from the twelfth century, but first published in 1474 in Barcelona, in Catalan. See Chadwick (n 9) 24.

17 Castrén (n 10) 14 notes that the first prize court was established in France in 1373. See also Hague Convention (XII) Relative to the Creation of an International Prize Court (18 October 1907) 205 CTS 381. See further Eliav Lieblich, 'Guest Post: Update on Israel/Palestine and the Revival of International Prize Law' *Opinio Juris* (14 September 2014), www.opiniojuris.org/2014/09/14/guest-post-update-israelpalestine-revival-international-prize-law (concerning prize proceedings in customary international law, as per *The State of Israel v The Vessel Estelle* (26861-08-13, District Court of Haifa, 31 August 2013)).

18 'Benevolent' neutrality permits one belligerent to be favoured over the other. Lauterpacht (n 8) 662–663. No *legal* distinction exists between benevolent and strict forms of neutrality, but 'benevolent' neutrality was generally more 'unstable and theoretically unjustifiable'. Malbone W Graham Jr, 'Neutrality and the World War' (1923) 17 *AJIL* 704, 720.

19 'Qualified' neutrality signifies a state that is neutral on the whole, but which is obligated by pre-existing treaty obligation to afford some kind of assistance to one of the belligerents. Lauterpacht (n 8) 663.

20 'Strict', 'absolute' or 'perfect' neutrality is a stance of complete impartiality not permitting any assistance whatsoever to a belligerent. Ibid 663.

21 See eg Chadwick (n 9) 182–187. See also the 1818 US Neutrality Law, c 88, s 8, 3 Stat 449, and the 1819 British Foreign Enlistment Act, 59 Geo III c 69.

rules of 1780 and 1800, and, most importantly, prohibited privateering and required blockades to be 'effective'.[22]

The rules for economic warfare at sea became increasingly refined and municipal neutrality laws were also developed (for example, to deter foreign enlistment). The US Civil War (1861–1864) proved that laws of neutrality were equally appropriate to regulate international relations during high-intensity 'civil' wars. In that conflict, specific neutral practices, such as private, neutral shipbuilding for a belligerent, and/or the private loan of money – most usually, to the rebellious Southern Confederate states – were particularly contentious, but far less objectionable was the fact of observing neutrality. The stakes were raised, however, as markets industrialised and widened geographically. The burdens of 'due diligence' then placed on neutral states grew heavier still, demanding

> a diligence proportioned ... to the dignity and strength of the power which is to exercise it ... [and] which prompts the neutral ... to discover ... acts forbidden by its good faith as a neutral and imposes upon it the obligation ... to use all the means in its power to prevent.[23]

Neutral states soon discovered they could protect themselves from belligerent encroachment *only* if possessed of sufficient defensive power, so many were forced to develop increasingly stringent municipal rules of neutrality to control their citizens' activities.

By 1907, Hague Conventions (V) and (XIII) were formulated specifically to regulate neutrality during land and naval warfare, respectively.[24] This process of formalisation however actually weakened the overall influence of neutrality, not least due to the strict, *contractual* approach to treaty compliance common at the time, which caused a loss of legal flexibility.[25] Hague Conventions (V) and (XIII) obligate the belligerents to respect the inviolability of neutral state territory, meaning that belligerents may not lawfully utilise neutral territory for their respective war efforts, such as by attempting to move or store munitions or supplies, or recruiting troops there; similarly, neutral states must prevent the belligerents from using neutral territory. Thereafter, defending state neutrality – even by force – could not be viewed as a hostile

---

22 Declaration Respecting Maritime Law (Declaration of Paris) (30 March 1856) 115 CTS 1. The US however refused to prohibit privateering until its own mid-nineteenth century civil war.

23 See Chadwick (n 9) 19, 48.

24 Hague Convention (V) regarding the Rights and Duties of Neutral Powers and Persons in War on Land (18 October 1907) 205 CTS 299; Hague Convention (XIII) concerning the Rights and Duties of Neutral Powers in Naval War (18 October 1907) 205 CTS 395. Other 1907 conventions pertaining to neutrality are Hague Convention (VII) relating to the Conversion of Merchant Ships into Warships (18 October 1907) 205 CTS 319; Hague Convention (XI) relative to certain Restrictions with regard to the Exercise of the Right of Capture in Naval War (18 October 1907) 205 CTS 367; and Hague Convention (XII) (n 17) (never ratified). See also the unratified Declaration concerning the Laws of Naval War ('London Declaration') (26 February 1909) 208 CTS 338, which in addition to existing rules, also attempted to conform contraband lists, rules for neutral convoy and the obligation to pay compensation in the event of wrongful captures of merchant ships or their cargoes.

25 For example, Hague Convention (V) (n 24) art 20; Hague Convention (VII) (n 24) art 7; Hague Convention (XI) (n 24) art 9; Hague Convention (XII) (n 17) art 51; Hague Convention XIII (n 24) art 28. See also the 1909 London Declaration (n 24) art 66.

act,[26] while neutral states were henceforth obligated to disarm and detain any belligerent military personnel and equipment discovered on neutral territory.[27] These rules endure today. Neutral railway material cannot be requisitioned by a belligerent unless 'absolutely necessary' at which point compensation becomes payable,[28] while belligerents may utilise neutral ports but only to effect emergency ship repairs. Any additional, discretionary, neutral prohibitions must also be applied impartially. All such provisions were and are designed to ensure as broad a peace as is possible, without which the entire economic structure surrounding international trade might collapse.

Overall, neutrality constituted a defensive form of state self-determination, but, ultimately, the many sophisticated laws, municipal codes and diplomatic policies designed to make war more predictable and 'civilised' simply could not compete with the temptations offered by the profits from new industrial weapons utilised during the First World War.[29] Only a paradigm shift as regards force could solve the many post-war challenges, and, encouraged by civil peace societies which had by 1918 existed for more than 50 years,[30] the League of Nations was persuaded to construct an embryonic system of collective security to forestall the future outbreak of war.[31] The League Covenant thus constituted an acknowledgement that a crucial crossroads had been reached as regards the 'disease' of modern war, but here, too, the League would also prove to be ineffective.[32] By the 1930s, states began to revise and strengthen their neutrality barriers and/or to retreat into other isolationist policies and positions.[33] A long and bloody Second World War ended with those drafting the UN Charter in 1945 finally being compelled expressly to prohibit unauthorised inter-state uses of force, thereby effecting the legal paradigm shift required for the maintenance of international peace and security, as is now discussed.

26 Hague Convention (V) (n 24) art 10. Cf Michael N Schmitt, Heather A Harrison Dinniss and Thomas C Wingfield, 'Computers and War: The Legal Battlespace, Background Paper', Informal High-Level Expert Meeting on Current Challenges to International Humanitarian Law (Cambridge, 25–27 June 2004) 15, www.hpcrresearch.org/sites/default/files/publications/schmittetal.pdf (principle of neutrality prohibits cross-border damage inflicted from use of weaponry in belligerent territory).

27 Hague Convention (V) (n 24) ch II.

28 Ibid art 19.

29 See eg Elizabeth Chadwick, 'The "Impossibility" of Maritime Neutrality' (2007) 54 Netherlands ILR 337, 340–352; George Herbert Perris, The War Traders: An Exposure (National Peace Council 1913) 9 ('The great body of the War Trade is now, in fact, a great financial network').

30 Trainin notes that, between 1815 and 1910, 148 international meetings were convened to regulate and control the usages of war, 90 of which were held in the first decade of the twentieth century. I P Trainin, 'Questions of Guerrilla Warfare in the Law of War' (1946) 40 AJIL 534, 536, fn 2.

31 During which a policy of 'differential' neutrality remained available, in support of an 'approved cause'. Graham (n 18) 721; Lauterpacht (n 8) 664, 666. Cf Dietrich Schindler, 'Comments to A. Gioia' in Post (n 4) 121 ('absolute neutrality not admissible under the Covenant'). See also League Covenant art 16; the (unenforceable) General Treaty for the Renunciation of War as an Instrument of National Policy ('Kellog-Briand Pact') (27 August 1928) 94 LNTS 57, which purported to prohibit war as an instrument of national policy. See Edwin Borchard, 'The Multilateral Pact "Renunciation of War"', address delivered at the Williamstown Institute of Politics (22 August 1928), http://avalon.law.yale.edu/20th_century/kbbor.asp.

32 Cf John B Whitton, 'La Neutralité et la Société des Nations' (1927, II) RCADI 453, 479–528, passim, and 530; Edwin Borchard and William Potter Lage, Neutrality for the United States (Yale University Press 1937).

33 See eg Declarations by the European Governments Constituting the Agreement regarding Non-Intervention in Spain, together with a Declaration by the Swiss Government in regard to Its Attitude Toward the Situation in Spain (1936) reprinted in Norman J Padelford, International Law and Diplomacy in the Spanish Civil Strife (Macmillan 1939) appendix 1, 205. No single instrument was signed, as the 'agreement' was a concert of policy.

2 Neutrality and UN collective security

When, in 1945, the new UN organisation chose to surpass League efforts regarding collective security, it reinforced Charter Article 2(4) provisions with Security Council collective enforcement powers,[34] along with Charter Articles 2(5), 25 and 103. Nonetheless, as 'the turn is generally slow' when the direction of international law needs to change,[35] force remains a constant factor in international life, whether in terms of state rights of self-defence against attack pursuant to Charter Article 51,[36] and/or of state domestic control over life within state territorial borders as per Article 2(7). Moreover, the Charter concepts of 'aggression' and 'self-defence' remain somewhat undefined in absolute legal terms,[37] and are notionally directed solely at states in any event. The Security Council often deadlocks when needing to resolve a threat to or breach of international peace and security, due not least to the separate political interests of its Five Permanent Members, and new armaments continue to be developed, sold and utilised.[38] Therefore, the silence of the Charter as to the continued survival of neutrality, per se, has changed little, as broader tendencies of inaction and indecision maintain a clear role for neutrality. In other words, the 'new' Charter paradigm prohibiting inter-state force does not appear in actuality to have greatly altered the fundamental realities, including the framework and balance of neutral rights and duties during armed conflict.[39]

International law continues to be divided between laws of peace and laws of war, the latter taking precedence as the *lex specialis* during international armed conflicts. Therefore, it could still be argued that laws of war continue to ground international law in general, particularly as laws of armed conflict should guide *all* uses of military force, including during peacekeeping operations and unresisted military occupations.[40] While the Security Council can legally authorise collective uses of force (for example, to resolve a threat to international peace and security), states otherwise utilising force (for example, in collective self-defence) must keep the Security Council duly informed. Outside these limited circumstances, states should obtain redress for any legal or political wrongs done to them through peaceful means. Difficulties arise therefore when

---

34 UN Charter ch VII, arts 39–51. See also ch VI, concerning the pacific settlement of disputes, and ch VIII, concerning regional arrangements, such as NATO.

35 As noted in a different context by Niall Ferguson, 'Turning Points' *New York Times* (30 November 2012), www.nytimes.com/2012/11/30/opinion/global/niall-ferguson-turning-points.html.

36 Consider also *Caroline* (n 6), comprising today's customary international law standard for 'necessity': 'instant, overwhelming, and leaving no choice of means, and no moment for deliberation'; Michael Bothe, 'Terrorism and the Legality of Pre-Emptive Force' (2003) 14(2) *EJIL* 227; Niaz A Shah, 'Self-Defence, Anticipatory Self-Defence and Pre-Emption: International Law's Response to Terrorism' (2007) 12 *JCSL* 95; Christian J Tams, 'The Use of Force against Terrorists' (2009) 20 *EJIL* 359; T D Gill, 'The Temporal Dimension of Self-Defence: Anticipation, Pre-Emption, Prevention and Immediacy' (2006) 11 *JCSL* 361; Mary Ellen O'Connell, 'The Myth of Preemptive Self-Defense' (American Society of International Law Task Force on Terrorism, August 2002), www.comw.org/qdr/fulltext/02oconnell.pdf.

37 See Rome Statute art 8 bis and UNGA Res 3314 (XXIX) defining 'aggression' in terms of force only. Consider state rights of self-defence against 'attack', as discussed in *Legal Consequences of the Construction of a Wall in the Occupied Palestinian Territory (Advisory Opinion)* [2004] ICJ Rep 136.

38 See eg European Parliament Resolution on the Use of Armed Drones, Doc 2014/2567(RSP) (27 February 2014); cf the UN Arms Trade Treaty, UNGA Res 64/48 (2 December 2009).

39 See eg *Legal Consequences for States of the Continued Presence of South Africa in Namibia (South West Africa) notwithstanding Security Council Resolution 276 (Advisory Opinion)* [1971] ICJ Rep 16, 93, separate opinion of Judge Ammoun (law of neutrality survives in its entirety).

40 See eg Shane Darcy and John Reynolds, '"Otherwise Occupied": The Status of the Gaza Strip from the Perspective of International Humanitarian Law' (2010) 15 *JCSL* 211; R Russell Buchan, 'The Palmer Report and the Legality of Israel's Naval Blockade of Gaza' (2012) 61(1) *ICLQ* 264.

provocations arise which appear to necessitate the use of force in self-defence,[41] and a state may be unwilling or unable to pursue peaceful means in response – a dynamic which partially helps to account for the vast number of (non-)international armed conflicts since 1945.[42]

Of course, the overt, first deployment of force between states in the contemporary era has been greatly reduced by known Charter provisions, and Security Council enforcement powers include both the power to adopt non-forceful sanctions pursuant to Charter Article 41 and/or forceful measures pursuant to Article 42.[43] Unfortunately, the Council by no means is required to utilise its Chapter VII powers,[44] and mischievous 'opportunities' can arise from Security Council deadlock. Further, Charter Article 2(4) may indeed represent a peremptory international norm having the character of supreme law,[45] but Charter Articles 2(4) and 51 remain clouded by subjective political intent. The variety of coercive means available to states, whether utilised in self-defence, or as measures short of force (for example, economic countermeasures, self-help and/or diplomatic reprisal), mean that allegations of 'aggression' and 'self-defence' (however construed) are likely to be heard as a crisis escalates. More problematic is the fact that no Charter counterpart to Article 2(4) exists to restrain domestic state uses of force, even though domestic force, too, can spiral out of control, cross territorial borders and disrupt the wider peace.

Therefore, although the Charter and Security Council enforcement powers may exert restraining influences on the use of force in inter-state relations, ongoing geo-political tensions continue to ensure a role for the legal institution of neutrality. Further, the Charter does not regulate hostilities directly. The manner in which Charter obligations entailing force are to be performed is instead regulated by International Humanitarian Law (IHL),[46] which area of international law includes rules of neutrality.[47] However, IHL regulates international armed conflicts far more extensively than it does non-international armed conflicts, as the implementation of IHL during an international conflict carries far broader consequences for neutral states. While states must comply with the Charter's rules on force whenever they adopt coercive measures,

---

41 As argued by Castrén (n 10) 56.
42 For example, civil wars have caused more than 80 per cent of the victims in armed conflict since 1945. ICRC, 'Introduction to Protocol 2 of 1977', www.icrc.org/ihl.nsf/INTRO/475?OpenDocument.
43 See also UN Charter art 12 (Security Council priority in decision-making), art 25 (member state obligations to carry out Security Council decisions) and art 49 (member state positive obligation to afford mutual assistance to accomplish Security Council measures).
44 Cf Luis Miguel Hinojosa Martínez, 'The Legislative Role of the Security Council in its Fight Against Terrorism: Legal, Political and Practical Limits' (2008) 57 *ICLQ* 333.
45 *Military and Paramilitary Activities in and against Nicaragua (Nicaragua v US)* [1986] ICJ Rep 14, ¶ 190.
46 Wolff Heintschel von Heinegg, 'The Current State of International Prize Law' in Post (n 4) 5, 17–25. See also *Legality of the Threat or Use of Nuclear Weapons (Advisory Opinion)* [1996] *ICJ Rep* 226, ¶¶ 88–90.
47 See eg UNSC Res 1973 (17 March 2011), regarding which see Constantine Antonopoulos, '"The Legitimacy to Legitimize": The Security Council Action in Libya under Resolution 1973' (2012) 14 *International Community Law Review* 359.

whether force, sanctions regimes, peacekeeping operations[48] and/or judicial solutions,[49] to name but a few, they must also respect the lawful limits on force as per IHL. As a final point at this stage, neutrality remains an available option during international situations involving force unless the Security Council instructs states expressly to act otherwise. For example, the recent Security Council activism regarding international terrorism may appear to afford neutrality little relevance in the 'war on terror', but relevance is also conditioned by context, as is highlighted below. Alternatively, states may 'participate in an armed conflict, but only on the side of the victim [state] of an armed attack, not on that of the aggressor'.[50]

In contrast, during most non-international conflicts, the situation is rather different, as third states should not intervene, unless perhaps in response to governmental invitation, as occurred in 2011 when Saudi Arabia responded to a request for assistance from Bahrain,[51] or unless the Security Council authorises intervention as per Charter Article 2(7), as occurred in 2011 during the Libyan civil conflict.[52] Moreover, the Charter's silence in general regarding neutrality may not encourage states expressly to declare or apply neutral rights and duties during 'civil war' or other domestic unrest, but the controversies surrounding 'humanitarian intervention', as occurred in 1999 when NATO bombed Serbia,[53] or even during certain large-scale post-9/11 'terror' events in which transnational military force is utilised by states in highly intensive and sustained operations, including to enforce sanctions regimes,[54] may benefit from due consideration of modern rules of neutrality (whether in letter or spirit), as is discussed below, after neutrality in international armed conflicts is first briefly outlined.

3 Neutrality and international armed conflicts

As noted above, IHL constitutes the area of international law which regulates the way in which force is utilised.[55] IHL treaty obligations today enjoy broad acceptance, and most IHL rules are considered to constitute customary international law.[56] The double scrutiny of 'lawfulness'

---

48 See eg UN, 'Peacekeeping Fact Sheet as of 31 August 2015', www.un.org/en/peacekeeping/resources/statistics/factsheet.shtml; UN, Peacekeeping Reports 1995–2015, www.un.org/en/peacekeeping/resources/reports.shtml; UN Secretary-General, 'Report on the Work of the Organization', UN Doc A/64/1 (6 October 2009) pt 2, ¶ 47, www.un.org/en/peacekeeping/documents/pko_2009.pdf (17 peacekeeping operations currently deployed across five continents); UN, 'Peacekeeping Operations: Principles and Guidelines' (2008) 17. Cf UNSC Res 1244 (10 June 1999), regarding which see generally James Summers (ed), *The Kosovo Precedent: Implications for Statehood, Self-Determination and Minority Rights* (Brill 2011).

49 See eg UN Secretary-General, 'The Legal Basis for the Establishment of the International Tribunal: Report pursuant to para 2 of Security Council Resolution 808 (1993)' (3 May 1993), www.icty.org/x/file/Legal%20Library/Statute/statute_re808_1993_en.pdf.

50 Bothe, 'Law of Neutrality' (n 1) ¶ 1104. See also the possibilities offered by UN Charter art 12, and UNGA Res 377(V) (3 November 1950).

51 See eg Martin Chulov, 'Saudi Arabian Troops enter Bahrain as Regime Asks for Help to Quell Uprising' *Guardian* (14 March 2011), www.guardian.co.uk/world/2011/mar/14/saudi-arabian-troops-enter-bahrain.

52 Pursuant to UNSC Res 1973 (17 March 2011).

53 See eg Greenwood 'The Applicability of International Humanitarian Law' (n 14).

54 For example, EU export controls on arms and equipment bound for Syria, starting in May 2011.

55 Gioia (n 4) 55, fn 12, argues that it is implicit in the 1899 and 1907 Hague Conventions, in GCI–IV common art 2 and in the Convention for the Protection of Cultural Property in the Event of Armed Conflict (14 May 1954) 249 UNTS 240 art 18 that laws of war apply whenever war in the material sense exists. See also Castrén (n 10) 36 ('even a prohibited war is a war').

56 See generally Jean-Marie Henckaerts and Louise Doswald-Beck, *Customary International Humanitarian Law* (CUP 2005). See also *Nicaragua* (n 45) ¶ 119.

entailed by IHL regulation of force on the one hand, and Charter Articles 2(4) and 51 state resorts to force on the other, means that an 'unlawful' resort to force pursuant to Charter rules can be executed quite lawfully under IHL rules,[57] and vice versa. This dual approach to 'lawful' force reflects not only the fact that force continues to be utilised by states, for example to solve international disputes,[58] but, further, that legal limits on how force when wielded is utilised are central, including for post-conflict situations and unresisted territorial occupations. IHL parameters in customary international law, military usages, surviving aspects of the 1907 Hague Conventions and the 1949 Geneva Conventions – all of which are applicable in full – in addition to Protocol I of 1977 (where ratified or customary), clearly acknowledge the seriousness of international conflicts.[59] In contrast, non-international conflicts incorporate a far lesser standard of obligation, being regulated by domestic criminal law, minimal aspects of customary law and military usages, Common Article 3 of the four 1949 Geneva Conventions[60] and Additional Protocol II of 1977 (where ratified or customary).[61]

As discussed earlier, rules of neutrality were formulated when war was waged as a central sovereign right, largely in order to coordinate the competing interests of neutral and belligerent states.[62] Naturally, the UN Charter contains different considerations, but as states continue to utilise force in their diplomatic relations, the legal institution of neutrality survives both in customary and in conventional rules, for example in the 1907 Hague Conventions,[63] the four 1949 Geneva Conventions[64] and in Additional Protocol I,[65] with Articles 9 and 19 of the latter broadening the traditional perspectives by reference to 'neutral *or other State which is not a Party to [the] conflict*'. Most fundamentally, the common commercial core of war and neutrality remains, such that neutral rules continue to comprise an important topic in the military manuals of most states, in academic commentary and in judicial decisions.[66] Even so, the political and terminological uncertainties surrounding inter-state uses of force generally permit 'more fundamental' Charter

---

57 See eg Sheikh Wahbe al-Zuhili, 'Islam and International Law' (2005) 87(858) *IRRC* 269, 278–279 (issues of equivalency between IHL rules and specific rules in Islamic Shari'a). See also Katja L H Samuel, *The OIC, the UN, and Counter-Terrorism Law-Making: Conflicting or Cooperative Legal Orders?* (Hart 2013).

58 Cf 'The Chatham House Principles of International Law on the Use of Force in Self-Defence' (2006) 55 *ICLQ* 963.

59 See eg Claus Kreß, 'Some Reflections on the International Legal Framework Governing Transnational Armed Conflicts' (2010) 15(2) *JCSL* 245, 266–267.

60 See eg *Prosecutor v Tadić (Decision on the Defence Motion for Interlocutory Appeal on Jurisdiction)* (Case No IT-91-1-AR72, ICTY Appeals Chamber, 2 October 1995) ¶¶ 113–118 ('[IHL] includes principles or general rules protecting civilians from hostilities in the course of internal armed conflicts'), and ¶ 134 ('customary international law imposes criminal liability for serious violations of Common Article 3').

61 See eg Konstantin Obradović, 'International Humanitarian Law and the Kosovo Crisis' (2000) (82)839 *IRRC* 699 (armed conflict between the KLA and Serbia an APII situation, not terrorism).

62 Wolff Heintschel von Heinegg, '"Benevolent" Third States in International Armed Conflicts: The Myth of the Irrelevance of the Law of Neutrality' in Michael N Schmitt and Jelena Pejic (eds), *International Law and Armed Conflict: Exploring the Fault Lines – Essays in Honour of Yoram Dinstein* (Martinus Nijhoff 2007) 543, 567. See also Declaration Renouncing the Use, in Time of War, of Explosive Projectiles under 400 Grammes Weight ('St Petersburg Declaration') (11 December 1868) 138 CTS 297.

63 See discussion above at nn 24–28.

64 In GCI–IV many aspects of neutrality expressly survive, eg common art 8/8/8/9 (neutrals as Protecting Powers); GCIII art 122 ('neutrals or non-belligerent powers').

65 API arts 2(c), 5, 9(2)(a), 19, 22(2)(a), 31, 37(1), 39(1), 64 and 78(1).

66 As noted by Maria Gavouneli, 'Neutrality: A Survivor?' (2012) 23 *EJIL* 267, 270.

prohibitions to detract from the *equal* legal weight which should be attributable to IHL rules.[67] Nonetheless, whenever states disregard the spirit or letter of Charter provisions, for example by directing overly forceful self-help measures against each other, neutral or other states not party to the conflict retain the option and right to adopt and apply neutral and neutrality-inspired policies in highly flexible ways.[68]

Unfortunately, Charter prohibitions do influence whether or not an 'armed conflict', per se, is even recognised, which often allows states sufficient scope to delay IHL implementation. Uncertainty in this regard during the recent 'war on terror' led the International Law Association's (ILA) Use of Force Committee to study the issue. It concluded categorically that 'States may not, consistently with international law, simply declare that a situation is or is not an armed conflict based on policy preferences.'[69] This conclusion was based on objective grounds, as follows:

> [T]he existence of armed conflict has many significant impacts on the operation of international law beyond the well-known fact that during armed conflict IHL will apply and states party to an armed conflict (or other emergencies) may have the right to derogate from some human rights obligations. In addition, ... the *law of neutrality may be triggered*; arms control agreements are affected, and UN forces engaged in armed conflict will have rights and duties not applicable in operations outside of armed conflict.... [T]he international community embraces a common understanding of armed conflict.[70]

The Committee found naturally that international armed conflict is more easily recognised, but evidence of an armed conflict is equally present whenever intense, organised force is utilised by any two opposing sides. In turn, once the Security Council, regional associations and/or individual states adopt political and/or economic sanctions regimes, neutrality becomes relevant because uninvolved states will encounter consequential impediments to their trade and finance flows.[71] For this reason, as soon as states utilise their military instruments, the relevance of IHL (and, thus, of rules of neutrality) becomes of high concern,[72] not least because 'grave breaches'

---

67 Christopher Greenwood, 'The Relationship between *ius ad bellum* and *ius in bello*' (1983) 9(4) *Review of International Studies* 221. See also Jasmine Moussa, 'Can *jus ad bellum* override *jus in bello*? Reaffirming the Separation of the Two Bodies of Law' (2007) 90(872) *IRRC* 963, 974–981.

68 See eg Bothe, 'Law of Neutrality' (n 1) ¶ 1103.

69 International Law Association, Committee on the Use of Force, 'Final Report on the Meaning of Armed Conflict in International Law', submitted at the International Law Association Annual Conference, The Hague, 15–20 August 2010, 27–28, www.ila-hq.org/en/committees/index.cfm/cid/1022 ('[a]n armed confrontation must reach a minimum level of intensity and the parties involved in the conflict must show a minimum of organisation').

70 Ibid 1 (emphasis added).

71 Such as via sanctions regimes, export controls and measures. For example, pursuant to the 2003 Proliferation Security Initiative the US and its allies have sought to interdict shipments of WMD in international waters. See US Department of State, 'Proliferation Security Initiative', www.state.gov/t/isn/c10390.htm; Matthew Allen Fitzgerald, 'Seizing Weapons of Mass Destruction from Foreign-Flagged Ships on the High Seas under Article 51 of the UN Charter' (2009) 49 *Virginia JIL* 473. Cf the Persian Gulf 'Tanker War' of the 1980s, in which Iran allegedly attacked commercial vessels, warships and neutral vessels which refused to obey stop-and-search requests, regarding which see *Oil Platforms (Iran v US)* [2003] ICJ Rep 161. See also Stacey Henderson, 'Emerging Voices: Protecting the World's Children: R2P and Measures-Less-than-Force' *Opinio Juris* (13 August 2014), www.opiniojuris.org/2014/08/13/emerging-voices-protecting-worlds-children-r2p-measures-less-force (increasing use of intercession in modern armed conflicts may represent an emerging norm in international law).

72 Cf GCI–IV common art 1 with Alberto R Gonzales, 'Decision Re Application of the Geneva Convention on Prisoners of War to the Conflict with Al Qaeda and the Taliban', Memorandum for the President (25 January 2002), www.hereinreality.com/alberto_gonzales_torture_memo.html.

and war crimes must be avoided at all costs. Further, any hostile party's 'struggle for survival', when weighed against the global and human *costs* of excessive uses of state force and/or other serious threat to or breach of international peace and security, should shrink in importance,[73] yet as states seek to form defensive and strategic coalitions, and to divide each other into 'friends' and 'enemies',[74] only stronger states are likely to remain capable of neutrality.

Technical legal questions, for example of the relevance of rules for war or neutrality, are also liable to be politicised – a result inimical to IHL and neutrality alike.[75] It should not be forgotten that neutral rights and duties become relevant 'automatically' whenever IHL is implemented in full, and still, more or less, in accordance with neutrality's most recent codification in the 1907 Hague Conventions:[76] neutral territory remains inviolable from belligerent use subject to certain exceptions, while many maritime provisions today are applied by analogy in aerial warfare, for example medical aircraft belonging to the parties in conflict may overfly or touch down if necessary. Neutral states may be appointed as Protecting Powers and offer their good offices to the belligerents, safeguarding belligerent interests in the treatment of captured service personnel and other detainees. Most fundamentally, neutral states retain rights to defend their neutrality, unless the Security Council has authorised collective action to the contrary, in the absence of which neutrals may or may not choose to cooperate voluntarily with enforcement measures, for example by permitting their merchant ships to be stopped and searched, particularly during the enforcement of an unofficial maritime embargo.

Nonetheless, as certain states become notable for proceeding as if international rules, including those of neutrality, either do not exist or do not apply to them, it may well be that the formal proscription of inter-state force in the UN era is undergoing a substantive sea change. The repeating use of force by coalitions of states, and the increasing number of justifications for utilising that force, sustain a growing tolerance of force in general, which potentially undermines further the guidance that neutral traditions might otherwise provide.[77] The question thus arises as to whether the traditional rationale(s) for implementing neutrality really should – or, indeed 'must' – stop at the threshold between international and non-international armed

---

73 Moussa (n 67) n 43, citing Dapo Akande, 'Nuclear Weapons, Unclear Law? Deciphering the *Nuclear Weapons Advisory Opinion* of the International Court' (1997) 68 *BYBIL* 209.

74 See eg George W Bush, 'Address to a Joint Session of Congress and the Nation' (20 September 2001), www.washingtonpost.com/wp-srv/nation/specials/attacked/transcripts/bushaddress_092001.html: '[e]very nation in every region now has a decision to make: either you are with us, or you are with the terrorists', and '[p]erhaps the NATO charter reflects best the attitude of the world: an attack on one is an attack on all. The *civilized* world is rallying to America's side' (emphasis added). Cf R B J Walker, 'Lines of Insecurity: International, Imperial, Exception' (2006) 37(1) *Security Dialogue* 65, 76–77: '[c]onstruct the other ... as that which must be civilised or destroyed ... and the way is open to affirm ... a singular way of being human'.

75 *Legality of Nuclear Weapons* (n 46) ¶¶ 74 and 88–90, acknowledging the applicability of the principle of neutrality during all international armed conflicts at least.

76 See also *San Remo Manual on International Law Applicable to Armed Conflicts at Sea* (International Institute of Humanitarian Law 1994).

77 See eg Wolff Heintschel von Heinegg, 'The Legality of Maritime Interception/Interdiction Operations within the Framework of Operation' in Richard B Jaques (ed), *Issues in International Law and Military Operations* (US Naval War College 2003) 255, who argues for limitations imposed by laws of naval warfare and maritime neutrality to be respected, even though no international armed conflict exists, during 'Operation Enduring Freedom', which authorises naval and aerial stop-and-search of cargo vessels suspected of transporting or providing supplies or support to al-Qaeda. See also Pierre-Marie Dupuy, 'Back to the Future of a Multilateral Dimension of the Law of State Responsibility for Breaches of "Obligations Owed to the International Community as a Whole"' (2012) 23 *EJIL* 1059.

conflicts. For example, might neutrality be equally useful during *any* high-intensity armed conflict in which a material state of war disrupts diplomatic relations and trade sufficiently to pose very real spillover risks to the wider peace?

4 Neutrality and non-international armed conflicts

Equal state sovereignty is assured by Charter Article 2(1), and bolstered by Article 2(4), protecting states externally against 'aggression', and Article 2(7), protecting states internally against external interference in their domestic affairs. Meanwhile, the legality of states autonomously utilising force is expressly acknowledged in Charter Article 51 rights of external self-defence, and implicitly in Article 2(7) rights to use force domestically. However, the Charter is silent regarding the limits on domestic force, for example to maintain public order, subject to the Article 2(7) proviso that the non-interference principle 'shall not prejudice the application of enforcement measures under Chapter VII'. As noted earlier, this sovereignty-based structure is mirrored in IHL rules which apply far less comprehensively to non-international armed conflicts.[78] In the event of civil war therefore the Security Council may intervene and authorise force, at which point rules of neutrality may also become relevant. Lesser situations of domestic force are far less likely to raise issues implicating neutrality,[79] as observing neutrality could constitute prohibited interference and thus breach Charter Article 2(7). A middle ground occupied by 'humanitarian intervention' in domestic forceful situations is theoretically possible,[80] but given the controversy surrounding the practice, and the sovereignty issues associated with non-international armed conflicts since 1945, it would seem more logical for neutrality to be relevant generally in relation to the *materiality* of any state of war, not least due to neutrality's roles of confining the hostilities, restraining the means and methods of war, protecting continued trade and preserving humanity.

Moreover, while states remain free to participate in an armed conflict on the side of the victim of an armed attack,[81] it is generally assumed that appropriate international 'victims' for

---

78 Malcolm N Shaw, *International Law* (6th edn, CUP 2008) 1148 ('international law treats civil wars as purely internal matters, with the possible exception of self-determination conflicts'). Cf Bothe, 'Law of Neutrality' (n 1) ¶ 1106 (this position is no longer uncontroversial). Cf *Prosecutor v Tadić* (Case No IT-94, ICTY Trial Chamber, 7 May 1997) ¶ 562 (criteria of intensity and organisation distinguish 'an armed conflict from banditry, unorganised and short-lived insurrections, or terrorist activities'); APII art 1(1) and the requirement of rebel control over territory.
79 Cf Kevin Jon Heller, 'The Law of Neutrality Does Not Apply to the Conflict with Al-Qaeda, and It's a Good Thing, Too: A Response to Chang' (2011) 47 *Texas ILJ* 115, and Karl S Chang, 'Rejoinder: Enemy Status and Military Detention: Neutrality Law and Non-International Armed Conflict, Municipal Neutrality Statutes, the UN Charter, and Hostile Intent' (2011) 47 *Texas ILJ* 381.
80 See eg Ramesh Thakur, 'Book Review (Anne Orford, *International Authority and the Responsibility to Protect)*' (2012) 23 *EJIL* 284; Antony Lewis, 'The Responsibility to Protect: A New Response to Humanitarian Suffering?' *e-IR* (6 July 2010), www.e-ir.info/2010/07/06/the-responsibility-to-protect-a-new-response-to-humanitarian-suffering; Jeremy Sarkin, 'The Role of the UN, the AU and Africa's Sub-Regional Organizations in Dealing with Africa's Human Rights Problems: Connecting Humanitarian Intervention and the Responsibility to Protect' (2009) 53 *Journal of African Law* 1; Carlo Focarelli, 'The Responsibility to Protect Doctrine and Humanitarian Intervention: Too Many Ambiguities for a Working Doctrine' (2008) 13 *JCSL* 191; Ramesh Thakur, 'Humanitarian Intervention' in Thomas G Weiss and Sam Daws (eds), *The Oxford Handbook on the United Nations* (OUP 2008) 387. See also UNSC Res 1674 (28 April 2006) ¶ 4 (RTP) and UNSC Res 1973 (17 March 2011) ¶ 4 (RTP and Libya).
81 Bothe, 'Law of Neutrality' (n 1) ¶ 1104.

such purposes are 'states' – a category further limited by issues of recognition and personality.[82] States which intervene to assist 'rebels' militarily elsewhere or otherwise without Security Council authorisation do so at their own risk in terms of Charter legality.[83] A modern reluctance to breach the *jus ad bellum* is accompanied by hesitation to implement neutral rights and duties, but as Charter rules have no direct effect on Common Article 1 of the 1949 Geneva Conventions, the Charter provides only *half* the answer regarding the 'legality' of force. Common Article 1 expressly requires the High Contracting Parties to the 1949 Geneva Conventions to respect IHL *in all circumstances*, including 'case[s] of armed conflict not of an international character occurring in the territory of one of the High Contracting Parties'.[84] Most fundamentally, civil armed conflicts and revolutions are not prohibited by general international law, many non-international armed conflicts may be 'internationalised' by proxy, and armed struggles by 'peoples' for their 'self-determination' may actually constitute *international* armed conflicts,[85] per se. Similarly, the higher the intensity of a non-international armed conflict, the higher the level of IHL obligation implicated,[86] not least because the presence of such factors makes external intervention (and neutrality) more likely.[87]

Customary and case law also indicate that rebels who are able to comply with humanitarian provisions should benefit from IHL;[88] were it otherwise, states could exhibit less restraint domestically with impunity,[89] and characterise the force they used as they wished without

---

82   For example, the unsuccessful Palestinian draft Security Council Resolution, UN Doc S2014/916 (17 December 2014), reproduced at, www.nytimes.com/interactive/2014/12/30/world/middleeast/ United-Nations-Resolution-for-Palestinian-State-Fails.html, tabled by the Council's representative from the Arab League (Jordan), to order Israel to terminate its occupation within two years. Cf UNGA Res 67/19 (29 November 2012) upgrading the status of Palestine to non-member observer state, adopted on the 65th anniversary of UNGA Res 181(11) (29 November 1947) on the Future Government of Palestine. See also the Declaration lodged by the Government of Palestine under Rome Statute art 12(3) on 31 December 2014 and UN Secretary-General, Depositary Notification of Palestine's Accession to Rome Statute, C.N.13.2015.TREATIES-XVIII10 (6 January 2015), https://treaties. un.org/doc/Publication/CN/2015/CN.13.2015-Eng.pdf, cited in ICC Office of the Prosecutor, 'Report on Preliminary Examination Activities (2015)' (12 November 2015) 11, fns 14–15.
83   Greenwood, 'The Applicability of International Humanitarian Law' (n 14) 44–45.
84   GCI–IV common art 3.
85   As per API art 1(4).
86   GCI–IV common art 3(2); APII art 1(2). See also Rome Statute art 8(2)(d) and (f).
87   Cf Heintschel von Heinegg, '"Benevolent" Third States' (n 62) 543; Heintschel von Heinegg, 'Legality of Maritime Interception' (n 77). See also Tess Bridgeman, 'The Law of Neutrality and the Conflict with Al Qaeda' (2010) 85 *NYU Law Review* 1186.
88   For example, *Prosecutor v Boškoski and Tarčulovski* (Case No IT-04-82-T, ICTY Trial Chamber, 10 July 2008) ¶ 196.
89   See eg Luis Lema, 'Torture in Algeria: The Report that was to Change Everything' *Le Temps* (Geneva, 19 August 2005), www.icrc.org/eng/resources/documents/misc/algeria-history-190805.htm; A P V Rogers and Dominic McGoldrick, 'Assassination and Targeted Killing: The Killing of Osama Bin Laden' (2011) 60 *ICLQ* 778; Philip Alston, 'Report of the Special Rapporteur on Extrajudicial, Summary or Arbitrary Executions', UN Doc A/HRC/14/24/Add.6 (28 May 2010). See generally Marc Weller (ed), *The Oxford Handbook of the Use of Force in International Law* (OUP 2015).

external comment.[90] Further, the application alone of domestic criminal laws to 'rebels' and 'terrorists'[91] who utilise organised force and who attempt to operate with restraint, risks the uncoupling via law of domestic force from international rules on state responsibility.[92] The fact that Security Council enforcement powers are under-utilised similarly tempts third states to adopt in-/direct forms of intervention into target state domestic affairs, ranging from premature recognition and the provision of military hardware through to 'humanitarian intervention' and/ or direct assistance. For example, external intervention helped end the Yugoslav dissolution wars of the 1990s. In September 1995, NATO conducted a bombing campaign to prevent Bosnian Serbs from 'ethnically cleansing' Bosnia-Herzegovina of its Muslim population; from 24 March to 8 June 1999, NATO did the same again to prevent ethnic-cleansing by Serbia of Muslims in Kosovo.[93] Therefore, it is precisely during the more complex situations of 'revolution' that third states should base their policies on a strict interpretation of the *jus ad bellum*, particularly those states that wish to remain 'impartial'.

Further, the increased international cooperation in pursuing humanitarian interests witnessed after the Cold War ended did not last, due not least to controversies surrounding the proper scope of the *jus ad bellum* and *jus in bello*, respectively. The successful uses of force by NATO in Bosnia-Herzegovina and Kosovo during the 1990s influenced subsequent international decision-making both positively and negatively regarding external interventions in high-intensity, non-international armed conflicts. With the 9/11 terror attacks on the US in 2001, the issue of applying IHL (and neutrality) to high intensity phases of the 'war on terror' became particularly complex.[94] The revolutions which have since unfolded, in the Middle East, and elsewhere, also have provided textbook lessons of the risks and advantages to states of utilising force whilst giving only minimal if any thought to the limits of IHL, particularly should the mass murder of civilians be contemplated. For example, during the recent revolution in Libya, the Security

90 See eg ICRC, 'International Humanitarian Law and Other Legal Regimes: Interplay in Situations of Violence', Summary Report, XXVIIth Round Table on Current Problems of International Humanitarian Law (November 2003). Consider Lucia Aleni, 'Distinguishing Terrorism from Wars of National Liberation in the Light of International Law: A View from Italian Courts' (2008) 6 *JICJ* 525, discussing *Bouyahia Maher Ben Abdelaziz et al* (Supreme Court of Cassation of Italy, 20 September 2007), www.geneva-academy.ch/RULAC/pdf_state/Abdelaziz.pdf; Elizabeth Chadwick, 'It's War, Jim, But Not as We Know It: A "Reality-Check" for International Laws of War?' (2003) 39 *Crime, Law and Social Change* 233.

91 See eg James Ross, 'Black Letter Abuse: The US Legal Response to Torture since 9/11' (2007) 89(867) *IRRC* 561; Claudia Aradau and Rens van Munster, 'Exceptionalism and the "War on Terror": Criminology Meets International Relations' (2009) 49 *British Journal of Criminology* 686, 698. Cf *Hamdan v Rumsfeld*, 126 SCt 2749, 2795-2796 (2006); Fleur Johns, 'Guantanamo Bay and the Annihilation of the Exception' (2005) 16 *EJIL* 613, 618–619, citing *Rasul v Bush*, 542 US 466 (2004). See also 'Chatham House Principles' (n 58) s F.

92 See eg Anna Leander and Rens van Munster, 'Private Security Contractors in the Debate about Darfur: Reflecting and Reinforcing Neo-Liberal Governmentality' (2007) 21 *International Relations* 201. Cf Colin J Bennett and Kevin D Haggerty (eds), *Security Games: Surveillance and Control at Mega-Events* (Routledge 2012) (corporate, governmental and military cooperation).

93 See General Framework Agreement for Peace in Bosnia and Herzegovina (21 November 1995) 35 ILM 75; Marc Weller, 'The International Response to the Dissolution of the SFRY' (1992) 86 *AJIL* 569; 'Documents Regarding the Conflict in Yugoslavia' (1992) 31 ILM 1421; UNSC Res 757 (31 May 1992), UNSC Res 777 (19 September 1992), UNSC Res 819 (16 April 1993) and UNSC Res 1244 (10 June 1999). See generally Summers (n 48). See also *Accordance with International Law of the Unilateral Declaration of Independence in Respect of Kosovo (Advisory Opinion)* [2010] ICJ Rep 403.

94 See eg Proliferation Security Initiative (n 71), which is designed to prevent the trafficking and supply of WMD and related materials to non-state actors.

Council, in Resolutions 1970 and 1973,[95] felt forced to act and impose a range of enforcement measures, largely on the basis of responsibility to protect (R2P). The Security Council authorised the use of 'all necessary measures' to protect Libyan civilians from government attack, and imposed a no-fly zone, a flight ban, an arms embargo on the high seas, an asset freeze and non-forceful measures as well. On 19 March 2011, France, Italy, the UK and the US launched authorised air and sea strikes, after which NATO assumed overall command of the military operations. This external intervention was accomplished purportedly without interposing third state military forces on Libyan territory,[96] while, due to Security Council authorisation, neutrality was hardly an available option. The Libyan campaign further illustrates well the complexities entailed when an international and non-international armed conflict are waged concurrently. The joint international operation was subsequently terminated by Security Council Resolution 2016 (27 October 2011), while the non-international conflict continues.

5 Security Council deadlock and the future of neutrality

Unfortunately, criticisms of the Libyan operation were voiced subsequently in various quarters, accusing the NATO-led coalition in Libya of exceeding its authority by assisting the rebels to achieve regime change and overthrow the governing Gaddafi regime, yet Security Council authorisations rarely if ever specify how, precisely, they are to be accomplished, and IHL regulates the utilisation of military force in any event.[97] Furthermore, regime change in Libya may indeed have been deemed necessary to protect civilians. The Security Council has been mired in deadlock ever since regarding sanctions or forceful measures in a variety of full-scale civil wars, for example in Syria[98] and in the Ukraine,[99] yet Security Council deadlock simultaneously leaves intact the sovereign state right and discretion to maintain neutrality.[100]

In the alternative to Security Council action, regional and/or unilateral measures are frequently adopted, for example by the US and the EU in recent years, which are often aimed against domestic state situations such as those caused by or occurring in Syria and Russia.[101] These measures are designed to discourage excessive, unlawful uses of force,[102] and, whether in

---

95   UNSC Res 1970 (26 February 2011) and UNSC Res 1973 (17 March 2011).
96   UNSC Res 1973 (17 March 2011) ¶ 4.
97   See Antonopoulos (n 47) 369–370.
98   See eg the unsuccessful draft resolutions and other initiatives listed in Security Council Report, 'UN Documents for Syria', www.securitycouncilreport.org/un-documents/syria. But see UNSC Res 2249 (20 November 2015), UNSC Res 2254 (18 December 2015) and UNSC Res 2258 (22 December 2015).
99   See respectively 'Ukraine Profile: Overview' *BBC News* (13 January 2016), www.bbc.co.uk/news/world-europe-18006246; Robert McCorquodale, 'Explainer: How can Crimea Legally Secede from Ukraine?' *The Conversation* (11 March 2014), www.theconversation.com/explainer-how-can-crimea-legally-secede-from-ukraine-24164. See also UNSC Res 2202 (17 February 2015).
100 Particularly UNSC Res 2249 (20 November 2015). See Wolff Heintschel von Heinegg, 'The Current State of the Law of Naval Warfare: A Fresh Look at the San Remo Manual' in Anthony M Helm, *The Law of War in the 21st Century: Weaponry and the Use of Force* (US Naval War College 2006) 269, 283.
101 See respectively 'Syria Profile: Timeline' *BBC News* (9 December 2015), www.bbc.co.uk/news/world-middle-east-14703995 (disposal of chemical weapon stockpile); 'Ukraine Crisis: EU Extends Russia Sanctions to 2016' *BBC News* (22 June 2015), www.bbc.co.uk/news/world-europe-33221888.
102 In the case of Syria, see also UNHRC, '2015 UNHCR Country Operations Profile: Syrian Arab Republic: Overview', www.unhcr.org/pages/49e486a76.html; Report of the Independent International Commission of Inquiry on the Syrian Arab Republic, UN Doc A/HRC/25/65 (12 February 2014).

situations of embargo, sanctions regimes and/or stop-and-search operations at sea and in airports, normally operate along lines of neutrality developed traditionally, the difference being that today, the operation of such measures helps to reinforce the *jus ad bellum* as much as the *jus in bello*.[103] For example, 'innocent passage' through EU territorial waters can be made conditional on cooperation with regional sanctions regimes, the breach of which risks marine insurance cover.[104] Related developments concern energy production, cyber markets, satellites, etc, which offer 'belligerent' possibilities such as 'information warfare' in highly sophisticated technological environments, but which have yet to alter the fundamentals of neutrality.[105] These fundamentals remain: neutral territory remains inviolate, although in the case of information warfare and cyber attack, small incursions may be unavoidable due to the globalised nature of electronic networks. However, if not authorised expressly by the Security Council, neutral states may restrict or withhold their cooperation to the extent possible.

Therefore, the issue of whether or not war persists as an incurable disease, or, indeed, whether humankind 'seems to need war',[106] must be left for future debate, but there can be little doubt that intense 'armed conflicts' of any type could benefit from the application of essential neutral rules, particularly as civil conflicts in sensitive geo-strategic areas such as Syria are prone to spread.[107] More importantly, perhaps, states which choose voluntarily to intervene in wars occurring elsewhere, whether unilaterally or through regional cooperation, still hesitate to breach neutral rights, which, *inter alia*, discouraged NATO in 1999 from imposing an oil embargo against Serbia.[108] Nonetheless, to the extent that any particular sanctions regime could in fact impact on a neutral state's ability to defend its neutrality, flexibility in approach must remain the key.[109]

---

103 See eg Heintschel von Heinegg, 'Legality of Maritime Interception' (n 77). Cf M D Fink, 'Maritime Embargo Operations: Naval Implementation of UN Sanctions at Sea under Articles 41 and 42 of the UN Charter' (2013) 60 *Netherlands ILR* 73.

104 The unavailability of which can cause havoc to neutral trade. See eg Ian Black and Severin Carrell, 'Russian Arms Shipment Bound for Syria Foiled by Britain's Insurers' *Guardian* (London, 20 June 2012), www.theguardian.com/world/2012/jun/19/syria-arms-shipment-foiled.

105 See eg George K Walker, 'Neutrality and Information Warfare' in Michael N Schmitt and Brian T O'Donnell (eds), *Computer Network Attack and International Law* (US Naval War College 2001) 233; Schmitt *et al* (n 26) which considers the likely impact of data routed through neutral state territory; Michael N Schmitt (ed), *Tallinn Manual on the International Law Applicable to Cyber Warfare* (CUP 2013) (Chapter 7 of which outlines neutral and belligerent rights and duties as regards cyber infrastructures located outside or within belligerent territory, or under neutral control or nationality).

106 Jonathan Turley, 'Big Money behind War: The Military-Industrial Complex' *Al Jazeera* (11 January 2014), www.aljazeera.com/indepth/opinion/2014/01/big-money-behind-war-military-industrial-complex-20141473026736533.html ('new coalition of companies, agencies, and lobbyists').

107 See eg 'Battle for Iraq and Syria in Maps' *BBC News* (10 February 2016), www.bbc.co.uk/news/world-middle-east-27838034.

108 See the discussion on this point in Greenwood, 'The Applicability of International Humanitarian Law' (n 14) and accompanying Commentaries. For the customary position on the legalities of stop and search, see the *San Remo Manual* (n 76) ss 67–71, 93–104, 112–134 and 146–158. Cf Proliferation Security Initiative (n 71). Consider Vaughan Lowe, 'Book Review (L A Ivanashchenko, *Blockade at Sea and Contemporary International Law*)' (1991) 40 *ICLQ* 503 (dubious legality of blockades).

109 See eg 'NATO's relations with Ireland' (26 October 2015), www.nato.int/cps/it/natohq/topics_51979.htm (based on 'practical cooperation'); Margaret Havemann, 'Neutrality in Ireland: The War on Terror, the Use of Shannon Airport, and the Irish Anti-War Movement', Independent Study Project (ISP) Collection Paper 359 (2006), http://digitalcollections.sit.edu/cgi/viewcontent.cgi?article=1361&context=isp_collection. Cf Jonathan Horowitz, 'Reaffirming the Role of Human Rights in a Time of "Global" Armed Conflict' (2015) 30 *Emory International Law Review* 2041 (disregarding neutrality in the context of 'global', albeit non-international, armed conflict).

6 Conclusion

The profitability of war, whether international or non-international, and of neutrality is as crucial in modern times as it ever was.[110] Armed interventions, military occupations, sanctions regimes, counter-terrorist and peacekeeping operations, etc, require adequate resources, meaning the demands of logistics, the financing and equipping of trained military personnel, contracts for rebuilding war-torn territories at war's end and so on, can and do generate lucrative opportunities for trade. In turn, the flexibilities inherent in and tolerated by the institution of neutrality are necessitated by the competitive nature of trade and finance globalisation. The need to source and retain groups of specialists who can provide adequate production, manufacturing, distribution and personnel capabilities for all supply and distribution tasks create both public and private financial incentives and rewards, whether by means of the contracting out of public services, or in terms of the greater likelihood of military success. Such schemes also generate unique organisational structures in which human conflict can be made to appear less socially costly than it actually is.[111] Unfortunately, in combining heightened perceptions of danger, such as those associated with information warfare and cyber hacking,[112] with profit, the risks of ignoring the limits both of IHL and of neutrality multiply.[113]

It has been assumed throughout this discussion that the 1945 UN Charter changed neutrality far less than is sometimes thought, particularly as the central contradiction at the heart of the international legal order is that neither the prohibition of inter-state force nor the regulation of force can prevent force from being utilised. Neutral rights and duties, including the prevention of foreign enlistment,[114] obligations of due diligence and continued rights of peaceful trade, continue to operate in-/directly; to the extent they are useful in wider circumstances, neutral rights and duties operate beyond their notional confinement to international war. To recognise and acknowledge this global usefulness seems only logical, particularly given the alternatives. Neutral states do not deny the fact of conflict, nor do they need necessarily to attempt to prevent conflict. Neutral non-engagement during hostilities simply helps to confine the hostilities in time and space, permitting a wider, notional 'peace', thereby reinforcing the limits of lawful force, without which international peace and security simply would not exist.

---

110 See eg Smedley D Butler, *War Is a Racket* (Round Table 1935).

111 For extreme examples, see Annika van Baar and Wim Huisman, 'The Oven Builders of the Holocaust: A Case Study of Corporate Complicity in International Crimes' (2012) 52 *British Journal of Criminology* 1033; Adam Lebor, 'Never Mind the Czech Gold the Nazis Stole ...' *Telegraph* (London, 31 July 2013), http://uk.finance.yahoo.com/news/never-mind-czech-gold-nazis-202141500.html.

112 See eg Michael N Schmitt, 'International Law in Cyberspace: The Koh Speech and Tallinn Manual Juxtaposed' (2012) 54 *Harvard ILJ Online* 13, www.harvardilj.org/2012/12/online-articles-online_54_schmitt; Wolff Heintschel von Heinegg, 'Territorial Sovereignty and Neutrality in Cyberspace' (2013) 89 *ILS* 123; Walker (n 104).

113 Consider Bridgeman (n 87).

114 See eg UNSC Res 2178 (21 September 2014) (condemning foreign terrorist recruitment by entities such as the Islamic State in Iraq). Cf UNSC Res 2249 (20 November 2015), which stops short of authorising the use of force whilst approving the use of 'all necessary measures' against Islamic State in Iraq and the Levant/Sham (ISIL/ISIS) to prevent and suppress terrorist acts on territory under its control in Syria and Iraq. See eg Dapo Akande and Marko Milanovic, 'The Constructive Ambiguity of the Security Council's ISIS Resolution' *EJIL: Talk!* (21 November 2015), www.ejiltalk.org/the-constructive-ambiguity-of-the-security-councils-isis-resolution.

It should thus be of little concern that the UN Charter is silent as to whether the institution of neutrality survives in the post-1945 era, or, assuming such survival, the precise circumstances in which it does so. Moreover, although IHL codifications make no express provision for laws of neutrality outside international armed conflicts, customary international law most certainly does.[115] What is crucial therefore is that international law continues to develop progressively, that all High Contracting Parties to the 1949 Geneva Conventions respect IHL 'in all circumstances', as per Common Article 1, and that laws of neutrality remain 'automatically applicable' to provide guidance during any situation in which the military instrument is utilised. International peace and security depend on it.

115 See eg above at nn 39, 56 and 77.

Part V

Compliance and enforcement

LOAC's humanitarian objectives make it ill-suited for enforcement through traditional means of reciprocal state action (Chapter 28). As a consequence, a number of actors and mechanisms have been developed with a view to ensuring that parties to a conflict comply with their obligations under LOAC.

For one, the ICRC has played a special role in promoting and monitoring compliance with LOAC for more than 150 years (Chapter 27). But, importantly, the primary responsibility to respect and ensure respect for LOAC rests with states and other parties to conflicts.

Since LOAC is a branch of international law, the breaches of its rules are subject to the doctrine of state responsibility found in general international law. However, achieving the accountability of states through inter-state judicial proceedings has often not been possible, which has increasingly led individuals adversely affected by armed conflict to turn to human rights bodies (Chapter 29). At the same time, there is a developing practice of states making reparations to victims of their own accord and even where there has not necessarily been a breach of the law (Chapter 30).

LOAC is one of the few branches of international law that contemplates the individual criminal responsibility of persons for serious breaches of the law (Chapter 31). To that end, credible allegations of war crimes must be investigated (Chapter 32). War crimes are subject to prosecution before international criminal tribunals (Chapter 33) or domestic courts, and the latter may operate under special jurisdictional principles (Chapter 34).

27

The role of the International Committee of the Red Cross

Kelisiana Thynne

The ICRC has been at the forefront of the development and promotion of international humanitarian law (IHL) since its inception over 150 years ago. The original neutral, independent and
impartial humanitarian organisation, ICRC approaches IHL from a very practical perspective
influenced by instances of violations and vulnerability that its delegates witness directly in armed
conflict. It operates generally on the basis of confidential bilateral dialogue with all parties to the
armed conflicts in which it works to assist and protect the victims of armed conflict – both
combatants *hors de combat* and civilians. Much of that dialogue involves promoting greater
enforcement of IHL in ongoing conflicts. Indeed, the ICRC has often been called – and, in the
past, has occasionally named itself – the 'guardian of IHL'. Nowadays, the ICRC is keen to
separate itself from this nomination and role. It is states and other parties to armed conflicts
which have the obligation to uphold and enforce IHL;[1] Switzerland, not the ICRC, is the
depository of the Geneva Conventions and Additional Protocols. The ICRC wishes to be seen
as a protector and persuasive enforcer of IHL, but not the crutch on which states lean to circumvent their own obligations in the conduct of their armed conflicts. Nonetheless, the ICRC
remains very much at the forefront of promoting and interpreting existing IHL and developing
new or extended principles of IHL, whether confidentially bilaterally in the battlefield, in multilateral treaty negotiations or unilaterally.

The ICRC's position as the original organisation responsible for developing and codifying
IHL (from the very first Geneva Convention in 1864 to the Additional Protocol III of 2005),
its mandate under the Geneva Conventions, as well as its continuing operations in the battlefield, give the ICRC an important and persuasive role in the interpretation and further development of IHL. However, there have been instances over the last ten years where the ICRC has
been seen as too conservative and restrictive in a changing environment; in other circumstances
it has been perceived as being too liberal in its approach to the interpretation of IHL and sometimes seen as going beyond its purely IHL mandate to stray into human rights and law enforcement environments.

In many respects the ICRC's role in promoting and developing IHL has changed over time
depending on the circumstances, the reactions it has garnered from interested parties and its own

---

1 GCI–IV common arts 1, 3; APII art 1.

operational realities. In this regard, the approach of the ICRC remains focused on the practical operations of protecting and assisting victims of both international and non-international armed conflicts and occasionally situations of violence below the threshold of an armed conflict. Therefore, this chapter opens with a brief overview of the ICRC's humanitarian operations before turning to its direct IHL work. The remainder of the chapter frames the work of the ICRC on IHL by reference to its two major spheres of activity: (1) operational pragmatics including monitoring and persuasion in the field in relation to interpretation, implementation and enforcement of IHL; and (2) theoretical and thematic promotion of IHL including training in and implementation of existing IHL as well as progressive development and codification of the law.

1 The ICRC as a humanitarian organisation

The mission of the ICRC is: 'to protect the lives and dignity of victims of armed conflict and other situations of violence and to provide them with assistance. The ICRC also endeavours to prevent suffering by promoting and strengthening humanitarian law and universal humanitarian principles.'[2]

Grounded in the promotion and strengthening of IHL, the ICRC's main reason for being initially was to provide protection and assistance to victims of armed conflict. This section briefly considers the history of the ICRC, its activities and its mandate under IHL.

1.1 History

Founded in 1863, a year before the adoption of the first Geneva Convention, the ICRC was originally termed the Committee for the Relief of War Wounded. It was established by Henry Dunant, whose *A Memory of Solferino*[3] had outlined some years before, his vision for wars where injured and dying soldiers would be tended to by civilians who had been specially trained in peacetime to provide first aid and assistance in wartime. The ICRC was the first iteration of a society determined to provide assistance to those affected by war. Its role was supposed to be one of coordination and support as each country developed its own national aid society. However, it was often difficult for national societies to maintain neutrality from their state authorities; the ICRC was better able to send delegates to a state in which there was a conflict, at a minimum to provide neutral support to the national society on the ground and in many cases to undertake relief work independently with both sides of the conflict.[4] While there are 190 national Red Cross, Red Crescent and (nominally) Red Crystal societies nowadays, supported by the International Federation of Red Cross and Red Crescent Societies,[5] the ICRC exists as the main operator to provide assistance and protection to victims and main coordinator of the Red Cross and Red Crescent Movement in times of armed conflict and other situations of violence, now working in 80 countries.[6]

2 ICRC, 'The ICRC's Mandate and Mission' (29 October 2010), www.icrc.org/eng/who-we-are/mandate/overview-icrc-mandate-mission.htm.
3 Henry Dunant, *A Memory of Soferino* (ICRC 1986) [1862], www.icrc.org/eng/assets/files/publications/icrc-002-0361.pdf .
4 The International Committee of the Red Cross (ICRC): Its Mission and Work, adopted by the Assembly of the ICRC on 19 June 2008 (2008) 91(874) *IRRC* 399, 399.
5 International Federation of Red Cross and Red Crescent Societies, 'Who We Are', www.ifrc.org/en/who-we-are/.
6 ICRC, 'The ICRC Worldwide', www.icrc.org/eng/where-we-work/index.jsp.

The ICRC does not consider itself a non-governmental organisation (NGO); nor is it an inter-governmental organisation. The ICRC is *sui generis*, being both a private Swiss organisation and an international organisation.[7] Primarily, it is composed of a Committee of 25 Swiss citizens which, in accordance with the executive management team, determine the priorities for the organisation and delegate the work to the delegations around the world. The inherent Swiss neutrality is said to give the ICRC added independence. However, the ICRC also has an international mandate. Every four years, all the states parties to the Geneva Conventions join the ICRC, the International Federation of Red Cross and Red Crescent Societies and all 190 national Red Cross and Red Crescent Societies at the International Conference of the Red Cross and Red Crescent. The resolutions and statements arising from that Conference and the Statutes of the International Red Cross and Red Crescent Movement[8] adopted at those Conferences give the ICRC its mandate to proceed for the following four years on particular aspects of IHL and programmes of work identified. The International Red Cross Red Crescent Movement has also given the ICRC its enduring mandate to act as key lead in the Red Cross and Red Crescent Movement in armed conflicts and other situations of violence under the Seville Agreement.[9]

1.2 Mandate

The ICRC is in the privileged position of having a solid mandate to act in international armed conflicts under IHL, specifically the Geneva Conventions; indeed, Geneva Convention IV Article 10 provides

> The provisions of the present Convention constitute no obstacle to the humanitarian activities which the International Committee of the Red Cross or any other impartial humanitarian organization may, subject to the consent of the Parties to the conflict concerned, undertake for the protection of civilian persons and for their relief.

As all states are parties to the Geneva Conventions, all states have a duty in international armed conflict to facilitate, as far as possible, humanitarian access of the ICRC.[10] The ICRC has a broad right of initiative in international armed conflict.[11] It can take on the role of Protecting Power to provide the humanitarian tasks under Geneva Convention IV.[12] It can assist in establishing and marking hospitals and safe zones,[13] and protected persons can apply directly to the ICRC for assistance.[14] In occupied territory, the ICRC might be tasked with providing food, clothing and medical supplies.[15]

---

7 Agreement between the International Committee of the Red Cross and the Swiss Federal Council to Determine the Legal Status of the Committee in Switzerland (19 March 1993) reprinted in (1993) 293 *IRRC* 152, www.icrc.org/eng/resources/documents/misc/57jnx7.htm.

8 Statutes of the International Red Cross and Red Crescent Movement, adopted by the twenty-fifth International Conference of the Red Cross at Geneva in 1986, amended in 1995 and 2006, www.icrc.org/eng/assets/files/other/statutes-en-a5.pdf; see also ICRC, 'The 31st International Conference of the Red Cross and Red Crescent', www.icrc.org/eng/who-we-are/movement/international-conference/index.jsp.

9 Agreement on the Organization of the International Activities of the Components of the International Red Cross and Red Crescent Movement: The Seville Agreement (26 November 1997) reprinted in (1998) 322 *IRRC* 159.

10 GCI–IV art 9.

11 GCI–III art 10; GCIV art 11.

12 GCIV art 11.

13 GCI art 12; GCIV art 14.

14 GCIV art 30.

15 GCIV art 59.

In non-international armed conflicts, the situation is more limited, in that Common Article 3 to the Geneva Conventions gives the ICRC the possibility to 'offer its services' to the parties to the conflict to provide assistance and protection to the victims of armed conflict. The ICRC therefore has to demonstrate its added value to the victims of the conflict and indeed to the parties to the conflict. When at least one party to the conflict is a non-state actor, this becomes difficult. It has increasingly been a challenge for the ICRC to demonstrate its neutrality, impartiality and independence and the true humanitarian nature of its work in many contemporary conflict environments. The militarisation of aid and the blurring of lines between humanitarian and military work have contributed to an upsurge in attacks on humanitarian workers.[16] The ICRC has needed constantly to re-evaluate how it can demonstrate and act out its neutrality, thus protecting its delegates and providing protection and assistance to victims of armed conflict. For example, in Afghanistan in 2003, the ICRC had to reassess its relationship with the armed opposition, when a staff member was brutally killed. The ICRC had been in Afghanistan for almost 20 years, but it had to re-establish its neutrality, when it was perceived by the armed opposition of being too close to the US/Afghan Government coalition.[17] Similarly, the ICRC must establish its neutrality in new conflicts, where religion or race might play a part, by demonstrating its neutrality through gestures rather than words and ensuring that the beneficiaries of aid understand the delicate balance of neutrality and impartiality. For example, the ICRC Head of Delegation in Israel and the Occupied Territories, Jacques de Maio, responded forcefully to allegations that the ICRC was favouring one side over another, and was not doing enough, in the 2014 Gaza conflict.[18]

In its dialogue with all parties to the conflict, the ICRC's confidential approach is most adhered to and most valuable to the organisation. The ICRC presents the allegations confidentially to the authority responsible – whether at the ground level or higher up the chain of command. It does not share the report or allegations with any other party to the conflict – certainly not the opposing party to the conflict, but also not the coalition partners. It does not go to the media on such issues, except where the humanitarian imperative is great, highlighting in broad terms a range of general issues where the ICRC is concerned.[19] Where the ICRC's reports have been made public, as was the cases with its Guantánamo Bay or Abu Ghraib reports, this has been done through a national of the receiving party having leaked the document, and the ICRC has condemned such releases.[20]

This confidentiality sometimes poses difficulties for conflicts where there are multiple parties to the conflict all working together. In some cases, Afghanistan being the most obvious current example, the parties to the conflict are operating so closely together that it is difficult to distinguish between the forces for the purposes of determining accountability. Normally, any allegations as to the violations of the law would be presented to the responsible force, but increasingly the ICRC finds it needs to present allegations to both parties to ensure that there is learning and

---

16 Pierre Krahenbuhl, 'The Militarization of Aid and its Perils' ICRC (22 February 2011), www.icrc.org/eng/resources/documents/article/editorial/humanitarians-danger-article-2011-02-01.htm.

17 See Fiona Terry, 'The International Committee of the Red Cross in Afghanistan: Reasserting the Value of Humanitarian Action' (2011) 98(881) *IRRC* 173.

18 Jacques de Maio, 'No Wonder Gazans are Angry: The Red Cross can't Protect Them' (25 July 2014), www.icrc.org/eng/resources/documents/article/editorial/07-24-gaza-israel-palestine-maio.htm.

19 See eg Jacques de Maio, 'Gaza: ICRC Invokes the Humanitarian Imperative: Stop the Killing!' (29 July 2014), www.icrc.org/eng/resources/documents/statement/2014/07-29-gaza-stop-the-killing.htm.

20 ICRC, 'Persons Detained by the US in Relation to Armed Conflict and the Fight against Terrorism: The Role of the ICRC' (9 January 2012), www.icrc.org/eng/resources/documents/misc/united-states-detention.htm.

understanding about IHL, about the ICRC's role and about the fundamental importance to respect for the law and accountability at lower levels of the forces. Occasionally, coalition partners will set up joint programmes, such as policing programmes or justice programmes as part of their reconstruction plans. Where there may be violations occurring within those programmes, the ICRC may issue a joint report highlighting where there are overlapping areas of concern and responsibility.

Sometimes, the ICRC's confidential, bilateral approach can work in individual cases where IHL does not apply, but humanitarian action is needed. Such situations are often below the threshold of an armed conflict, but there is still a considerable level of violence and, consequently, significant humanitarian concerns. The ICRC maintains a privileged relationship with many states which allows it access to victims of state, criminal or tribal-based violence and attended to their needs, which might not be granted to an organisation which would be more vocal. For example, it has operated several pilot programmes, the most famous being in Rio de Janeiro in the *farvelas*,[21] where the ICRC offers traditional humanitarian assistance to the people in these dangerous quarters. In such cases, human rights and law enforcement principles, rather than IHL, would be discussed. While there may be enthusiasm in some parts of the organisation to expand the protection dialogue, it does mean that the ICRC sometimes delves into areas of political difficulty and could be seen as giving legitimacy to non-state actors in the field of human rights.[22] In such cases, the ICRC is coming to understand that not all activities need to be promoted as in accordance with strict legal principles, particularly the assistance work, but rather acceptance of the need for humanitarian action must be developed first and then legal dialogue engaged in at a much later stage.[23]

When it comes to IHL Article 5 of the Statutes of the International Red Cross and Red Crescent Movement provides for the specific tasks of the ICRC, as determined by all the states parties to the Geneva Conventions, the national societies, the Federation and ICRC itself. Notable roles are

> to undertake the tasks incumbent upon it under the Geneva Conventions, to work for the faithful application of international humanitarian law applicable in armed conflicts and to take cognizance of any complaints based on alleged breaches of that law; ... to work for the understanding and dissemination of knowledge of international humanitarian law applicable in armed conflicts and to prepare any development thereof.[24]

The ICRC can also undertake any role assigned to it by the International Conference.[25] The ICRC has read these provisions to give it the mandate to interpret and codify IHL in areas such as conduct of hostilities, the use of force under IHL, protection of civilians and detainees among other issues. The ICRC has a mandate to work on the development of IHL treaties, whether it instigates such developments or participates in existing processes.

---

21 *Farvelas* are urban shanty towns in Brazil, most often dominated by criminal groups and outside government control and government services. The *farvelas* in which the ICRC works are seven neighbourhoods in Rio de Janeiro: Cantagalo/Pavão-Pavãozinho, Cidade de Deus, Complexo da Maré, Complexo do Alemão, Parada de Lucas, Vigário Geral and Vila Vintém: ICRC, 'Brazil: Mitigating the Effects of Armed Violence' (16 September 2011), www.icrc.org/eng/resources/documents/interview/2011/brazil-interview-2011-09-01.htm.

22 Marion Harroff-Tavel, 'Violence and Humanitarian Action in Urban Areas: New Challenges, New Approaches' (2010) 92(878) *IRRC* 329, 346–348.

23 Ibid.

24 Statutes of the Movement (n 8) art 5(2)(c), (g).

25 Ibid art 5(2)(h).

1.3 Activities

Although the dialogue of the ICRC in many of its 'normal' humanitarian activities is grounded in pure humanitarian response rather than technical IHL terminology, all the activities of the ICRC function under the auspices of IHL. Indeed, the ICRC's activities reflect its mandate and mission statement. A large part of its activities are assistance programmes. These range from economic security programmes, such as micro-credit programmes or agricultural assistance, to health programmes including first aid training, ambulance services, war surgery and support to general hospitals in conflict affected areas. These are 'relief activities' as provided for under the Geneva Conventions. Water and habitation programmes also assist villages to build pumps, or allow detention facilities to access water or implement hygiene programmes for the benefit of the detainees.

Detainees – or, more broadly, persons deprived of their liberty – are one of the three strands of ICRC's protection programme. The other two strands are protection of the civilian population and reuniting families torn apart through war. In protection, perhaps more than any other aspect of its work, the activities of the ICRC are grounded directly in IHL. The ICRC is mandated to establish (and has established) a Central Tracing Agency which can lodge lost family members and try to locate those persons through the network of national societies and its own delegations.[26] The ICRC is also mandated to visit prisoners of war and civilian internees in international armed conflicts.[27] It has carved out a role for itself in commenting on conduct of hostilities through its interpretations of IHL, specifically the Geneva Conventions and Additional Protocols.[28] These last two aspects of its work will be dealt with in more detail in this chapter under Section 2.1 'Persuasion in the field'. More obviously related to IHL is the considerable work done in promoting and strengthening IHL, which is the second part of the mission statement and encompasses the work of the ICRC as set out in the rest of this chapter.

2 Practical engagement

As mentioned above, one of the pillars of the ICRC's mandate is to promote IHL. To the ICRC, promoting IHL means not only talking about it and presenting it to relevant audiences, but also persuading states and other parties to conflicts that IHL is relevant to them and must be upheld. In this section, the practical means that the ICRC uses to uphold and persuade others to uphold IHL are discussed.

2.1 Persuasion in the field

Some would argue that the ICRC's core work is in the field promoting IHL through its protection work.[29] This is where the ICRC's mandate, founded as it is in IHL, surpasses that of other humanitarian organisations. Moreover, its access means that it can comment on IHL violations and promote adherence to IHL in conflict situations. The ICRC works to protect civilians and persons deprived of liberty by directly intervening in particular cases. In both circumstances, the methodology is the same. The ICRC delegates go into the field, hospitals or detention facilities, talk to witnesses or those directly affected, in a confidential manner ('entretien sans témoin' or

---

26 GCIV art 140.
27 GCIII arts 125, 126; GCIV arts 76, 142, 143.
28 GCI–III art 11; GCIV art 12.
29 See eg Alain Aeschlimann, 'Protection of Detainees: ICRC Action Behind Bars' (2005) 87(857) *IRRC* 83.

'interview without witness' in ICRC terminology) and document allegations of violations of IHL. If those violations are 'nominally transmissible', that is the person's name can be mentioned, the case will be brought directly to the authorities. If the person refuses to allow his or her name to be mentioned, usually for fear of recriminations, the ICRC will present the case as part of a group of cases or a pattern of events. The authorities include those potentially directly responsible for violations, such as prison directors or military field commanders. But when allegations are particularly serious or inadequately addressed at the lower level, the delegates may need to bring them to the attention of higher officials – the Minister for Justice, for example, or the commander of an armed force.

The ICRC action on behalf of persons deprived of their liberty focuses for the most part on those detained as part of a conflict – either as criminal detainees charged with offences, prisoners of war (although nowadays there are few who meet such a description) and those interned for security reasons. Jointly with states, the ICRC is working on a project called 'Strengthening International Humanitarian Law', which covers, among other things, detention in non-international armed conflict and the need to define better the status of detainees and the conditions of detention.[30] While the legal basis for detention underpins the ICRC's dialogue with parties to a conflict who are detaining people, the ICRC does not question the basis for detention. Instead, it asks the authorities to ensure that the legal basis is correct for each individual. Therefore, the ICRC treads a fine line between determining what the legal framework is, and questioning whether certain people should be held under that framework.

Then the ICRC turns to conditions of detention and judicial guarantees. Conditions of detention encompass a wide range of issues depending on the state of the prison or detention centre. Sometimes the ICRC will visit all detainees in a particular prison, whether or not they have been put there for security or conflict reasons. This enables the ICRC to see how all detainees are treated and what the conditions of detention are like in the entire facility so as to address any shortcomings. Ill treatment – ranging from degrading treatment to torture – is a constant area of concern. There are also issues of access to outdoor air and exercise, access to education, bedding, clothing, food and water. Each of these has a legal basis in IHL and human rights law, underpinning the practical solutions that the ICRC offers in many cases. Judicial guarantees are the rights to a fair trial outlined in Common Article 3 and in more detail in human rights law. These include access to a lawyer, trial within a reasonable amount of time and exclusion of evidence obtained by torture. When dealing with internment, rather than criminal detention, the ICRC enquires into the procedural safeguards in place to ensure no abuse of process. Such safeguards include regular review of the reasons for detention.[31]

The ICRC's work on the protection of civilians arises from the general protection accorded to civilians who are not directly participating in hostilities and who should not be the subject of attack. The ICRC learns of allegations of attacks on the civilian population in conflicts through victims or witnesses who come to their offices, from persons being treated in hospitals the ICRC supports, and through direct engagement with victims and witnesses when assistance activities are undertaken in the field. The ICRC collects the allegations, tries to interview persons who can corroborate the story and, where possible, visits the site of the alleged attack. Having collected the evidence, the ICRC analyses which rules of IHL related to the conduct of

30 ICRC, 'Strengthening International Humanitarian Law: 31st International Conference of the Red Cross and Red Crescent, Geneva, 28 November to 1 December 2011' (15 December 2011), www.icrc.org/eng/resources/documents/red-cross-crescent-movement/31st-international-conference/31-international-conference-strengthening-ihl-2011-12-29.htm.

31 Jelena Pejic, 'Procedural Principles and Safeguards for Internment/Administrative Detention in Armed Conflict and Other Situations of Violence' (2005) 87(858) *IRRC* 375.

hostilities and the protection of civilians may have been breached. For example, if an attack appears to have taken place against a civilian village, but there is also evidence of combatants in the area, or civilians directly participating in hostilities, the relevant rules might relate to proportionality and precaution in attack or attack on a civilian population.[32] The question of status of civilians and whether they were directly participating in hostilities will also arise.[33] After concluding the legal assessment, the ICRC presents the allegations to the party to the conflict who was allegedly responsible for the attack or violation, and asks that party to investigate. The rank of the official approached will depend upon the severity of the alleged violation or the level of command of the official authorised to order an investigation or hold those responsible accountable.

The ICRC will generally only present allegations of violations of IHL where delegates have collected the evidence themselves and have attempted to verify the facts as far as possible so as to maintain credibility. While this dialogue is fundamentally grounded in IHL, the party's own interpretations of IHL and of conduct of hostilities will always influence the way the party responds. Further, it is difficult from the civilian perspective always to appreciate the difficulties and the split-second decisions that fighters make while under pressure on the battlefield. Therefore, a lot of the dialogue the ICRC engages in is not necessarily to make people accountable for what they have done in the past, but to remind commanders of their IHL obligations and constantly try and persuade them to assess each potential violation to learn lessons so as not to commit such a violation in the future. This involves an acceptance by the party to the conflict of the obligation and the need to train forces in IHL principles, which the ICRC also engages in, as discussed below.

2.2 Domestic implementation and promotion of IHL

The ICRC not only persuades parties to a conflict to uphold IHL, but it also persuades states to have a solid grounding in IHL – as part of their obligation to 'respect and ensure respect' of IHL under Common Article 1 of the Geneva Conventions. The ICRC recognises that in many respects international law does not provide the necessary sticks for enforcement and also that IHL needs some national grounding for it to have any impact in the field. Therefore, the ICRC expends a considerable amount of energy on promoting domestic implementation of IHL, educating and encouraging education of future leaders, and instructing military officers and soldiers on the practical application of IHL in the field. The purpose behind this reflects Henry Dunant's core desire to have people prepared in times of peace to act in times of war to ensure humanitarian principles are upheld.

While the Geneva Conventions are universally ratified, there are many other IHL treaties, including the Additional Protocols which are well behind on universal ratification. Moreover, the ratification of IHL treaties in and of itself does not mean they can be fully implemented and applied in armed conflicts and domestic contexts. Even for monist states, some form of criminal law is required to give effect to the grave breaches provisions of the Geneva Conventions for example. There is a desire for universality of IHL treaties which drives the ratification work of the ICRC – the Geneva Conventions being some of the few universally ratified treaties. Additionally, the principle of universal jurisdiction may apply in some cases to allow prosecution of persons having committed war crimes well beyond the territory of the state in which they com-

---

32 API arts 52, 57.
33 API art 51(3); see also ICRC, *Interpretive Guidance on the Notion of Direct Participation in Hostilities under International Humanitarian Law* (ICRC 2009).

mitted such crimes. If there are no safe havens in the world, many ICRC delegates and some state representatives reason that there will not be a culture of impunity for violations of IHL.[34] In its day to day work, increasingly the ICRC relies on national laws to underpin its interventions on IHL matters with states so as to augment the effect of such dialogue. Through such dialogue, the ICRC has come to realise that some states have problems in terms of the technical expertise and the capacity to undertake domestic implementation of IHL treaties.

In 1996, the ICRC set up an Advisory Service on IHL.[35] While other organisations also work on IHL implementation, the ICRC has a wide coverage of the world outside the usual conflict environment. While the Advisory Services themselves are primarily located in Geneva, there are regional legal advisers in most of the ICRC's regional delegations, who cover up to 25 countries each. The Advisory Service develops draft legislation, collects national legislation and assists states requiring technical expertise to implement their own national legislation on IHL. The ICRC has developed model legislation which covers a wide range of IHL treaties – Geneva Conventions, Anti-Personnel Land Mines Convention, Cluster Munitions Convention and the Hague Convention on the Protection of Cultural Property in Times of Armed Conflict amongst others. The ICRC also assists states implement the Rome Statute, using the Commonwealth Secretariat's model law.[36] It promotes ratification of IHL treaties through dialogue with the relevant law and decision-makers in governments around the world. In many states, the Advisory Service assists in establishing and running national IHL Committees which provide a platform for coordination of various government departments responsible for different aspects of IHL and implementation.

The Advisory Service's regional legal advisers often take the role of the promoters of IHL to academics and students and there are also some dedicated staff members who promote IHL through education. The ICRC recognises that the future leaders will need to know about IHL in case there is any armed conflict in their state when they are the decision-makers; even basic knowledge about the ICRC and the basics of IHL will have benefits. The ICRC assists with moot court competitions promoting enforcement of IHL, gives lectures and provides model curriculums for teaching IHL in universities.[37] Moreover, academics often have important links to government and policy-makers in addition to their role in exploring principles of law more deeply. They are important partners for the ICRC when organising events or seeking greater understanding of IHL principles in the wider community.

Aside from government law-makers and future leaders, a large part of dialogue on and implementation of IHL happens in the armed forces, whether of a state or a non-state actor. In non-international armed conflicts in particular, the ICRC must engage clearly with fighters so that they allow the ICRC access to the victims of armed conflict. The ICRC discusses strategic issues with higher levels of command, including providing confidential assessments of the situation on the ground related to detention and protection of civilians, and, on a day to day basis,

---

34 Kelisiana Thynne, 'The Universality of IHL: Surmounting the Last Bastion of the Pacific' (2010) 41 *Victoria University of Wellington Law Review* 135, 145.

35 See Paul Berman, 'The ICRC's Advisory Service on International Humanitarian Law: The Challenge of National Implementation' (1996) 36(312) *IRRC* 338.

36 Model Law to Implement the Rome Statute of the International Criminal Court, Annex B to the Cover Note: International Criminal Court (ICC) Statute and Implementation of the Geneva Conventions, Provisional Agenda Item 9, Meeting of Commonwealth Law Ministers and Senior Officials, Sydney, Australia, 11–14 July 2011 (May 2011), www.thecommonwealth.org/files/238381/FileName/LMM(11)17PICCStatuteandImplementationoftheGenevaConventions.pdf.

37 ICRC, 'The ICRC Reach out to Universities' (29 October 2010), www.icrc.org/eng/what-we-do/building-respect-ihl/education-outreach/universities/overview-the-icrc-universities.htm.

the ICRC also engages with militaries at checkpoints, at airports or ports, in hospitals and in the field to allow the physical access to victims. The ICRC's dialogue with non-state armed forces is often at a more basic level than with established state militaries, and is included as part of first aid training sessions or food assistance programmes.

The ICRC and militaries are necessarily always working in the same environment, but do not necessarily speak the same language in terms of protection, assistance and conduct of hostilities. Therefore, the ICRC engages former military and police officers to act as Security and Armed Forces delegates.[38] These delegates provide training to militaries and police in conflict environments and also before such forces are deployed. ICRC Security and Armed Forces delegates work with national military trainers on curriculum development and assist in practical exercises to ensure national forces understand the ICRC and its mandate, recognise the independent and neutral role it plays in the battlefield, as well as understand important principles of IHL. Of course, in many instances, the militaries themselves are well able to train their legal advisers and commanders on in-depth principles of IHL, but it is also important for junior officers and soldiers to have some grounding in the basic principles of IHL. After all, it is the front-line forces themselves who will confront split-second operational decisions including, for example, whether or not to shoot a person who may be a civilian or whether or not to allow an ambulance through a checkpoint.

3 Theoretical and thematic engagement

As part of the ICRC's mandate to promote and ensure the faithful application of IHL, it works on the theoretical side of IHL – enhancing existing interpretations of IHL and developing new IHL treaties or principles. This section explores these areas further.

3.1 Interpretations and codification of existing IHL

The ICRC has engaged in many projects of codification and interpretation of IHL starting from the commissioning in the 1950s of the *Commentaries* to the Geneva Conventions and later of the Additional Protocols. The ICRC has approached such tasks in different ways with varying effect – unilaterally, in consultation with a small group of states or under direction from the International Conference.

In 2009, the ICRC released its *Interpretive Guidance on the Notion of Direct Participation in Hostilities*. The study arose out of concerns about the status of civilians and combatants in Afghanistan and Iraq who were often indistinguishable from each other. This confusion as to legal status led to higher civilian casualties and difficulties in determining who and who was not a legitimate target. Under IHL, civilians are protected 'unless and for such time as they directly participate in hostilities'. When a lot of civilians appear to be involved in a conflict the question becomes, who is 'directly participating in hostilities'? in order to determine who is a legitimate target. The ICRC commenced the study with a series of expert roundtables in conjunction with the TMC Asser Institute in The Hague. However, after six roundtables, it was clear there would be no consensus, and the ICRC decided unilaterally to launch its own interpretation of the concept of 'direct participation in hostilities'.

The reaction from most states involved in coalitions in Afghanistan and Iraq was intense and commentators closely associated with such governments objected to the *Interpretative Guidance* on

38 ICRC, 'The ICRC and Weapons Bearers' (29 October 2010), www.icrc.org/eng/what-we-do/ building-respect-ihl/dialogue-weapon-bearers/overview-icrc-weapon-bearers.htm.

a number of grounds. Some challenged the mandate of the ICRC to enter into the domain of conduct of hostilities, the use of force and defining legitimate targets.[39] Others criticised the ICRC's use of the 'threshold of harm'[40] as 'harm which may reasonably be expected to result from an act in the prevailing circumstances'.[41] For example, Schmitt has said that the element of harm 'would exaggerate humanitarian considerations at the expense of military necessity'[42] because it does not include activities which would normally amount to direct participation in hostilities, but do not in fact cause harm.[43] Commentators also suggested that the ICRC had not taken due account of the concept of 'membership of an armed group',[44] which is widely accepted in Western militaries. The suggestion that a civilian regains protection after committing an act of direct participation in hostilities because the civilian loses the protection 'unless, and for such time as' he or she directly participates in hostilities – the so-called 'revolving door' – as unrealistic and giving too great an advantage to the civilian.[45] Interestingly enough, however, the UN Special Rapporteur on Extrajudicial Killing criticised the ICRC for inserting the notion of continuous combat function into the *Interpretative Guidance*, which would override some of the 'revolving door' concerns and, in effect, suggesting an even narrower approach was required for the concept of 'civilians directly participating in hostilities' including a greater focus on human rights.[46]

The ICRC expected the *Interpretative Guidance* be a useful and practical tool in assessing the responses to attacks on civilians – thereby strengthening the principle of distinction.[47] However, while adhering to the principle of distinction, few states have openly shared their targeting procedures and have openly rejected the idea that they will include the ICRC study in their targeting training. Commentators have expressed the opinion that the study will not be used to provide practical guidance.[48] On the other hand, others have suggested that the Guidance is useful in its original purpose, namely to provide guidance, in a field that is still unsettled in law. In any event, given the general reception of the *Interpretative Guidance*, it is certain that the ICRC will not release a similar unilateral report on the basis of solely its own views in the near future.

In the meantime, the ICRC joined with the Government of Switzerland to gather 16 other countries and stakeholders to address concerns around the use of private military and security companies in armed conflicts.[49] While some states criticised this process for including only 17 states, the resulting Montreux Document[50] has been widely accepted by the industry and by

---

39 W Hays Parks, 'Part IX of the ICRC "Direct Participation in Hostilities" Study: No Mandate, No Expertise, and Legally Incorrect' (2010) 42 *NYU JILP* 769, 794–796.

40 Michael N Schmitt, 'Deconstructing Direct Participation in Hostilities: The Constitutive Elements' (2010) 42 *NYU JILP* 697, 719–720, 727.

41 ICRC, *Interpretive Guidance* (n 33) 47.

42 Schmitt (n 40) 714.

43 Ibid 714–719.

44 Kenneth Watkin, 'Opportunity Lost: Organized Armed Groups and the ICRC "Direct Participation in Hostilities" Interpretive Guidance' (2010) 42 *NYU JILP* 641, 643, 649–652.

45 Ibid 686–687; Bill Boothby, '"And For Such Time As": The Time Dimension to Direct Participation in Hostilities' (2010) 42 *NYU JILP* 741, 754, 757–758.

46 Philip Alston, 'Report of the Special Rapporteur on Extrajudicial, Summary or Arbitrary Executions: Addendum: Study on Targeted Killings' UN Doc A/HRC/14/24/Add.6 (28 May 2010) ¶ 20.

47 ICRC, *Interpretive Guidance* (n 33) 5–6.

48 See eg Schmitt (n 40) 699.

49 This topic is discussed in detail in Nelleke van Amstel and Rain Liivoja, 'Private military and security companies' ch 36 in this volume.

50 Montreux Document on Pertinent International Legal Obligations and Good Practices for States related to Operations of Private Military and Security Companies during Armed Conflict (17 September 2008), www.icrc.org/eng/resources/documents/misc/montreux-document-170908.htm.

states that use private military and security companies for a wide variety of functions. Importantly, the Montreux Document does not seek to interpret IHL expansively or create new principles. Rather, it gathers existing principles of IHL, human rights law and other relevant laws to guide 'territorial', 'home' and 'contracting' states, as well as contractors and companies as to how those principles and laws can be applied to the existing issue. Therefore, stakeholders have not expressed the view that the ICRC is dictating the law to them or creating new law.

In 1995, the Intergovernmental Group of Experts for the Protection of War Victims met in Geneva and recommended that the ICRC, in consultation with governments and IHL experts, be tasked with preparing a report on customary rules of IHL applicable in international and non-international armed conflicts. The twenty-sixth International Conference of the Red Cross and Red Crescent endorsed this recommendation and mandated the ICRC to produce such a report. The ICRC started work on collecting examples of state practice and *opinio juris* in the form of legislation, official statements, case law and military manuals from 90 states and also searched ICRC archives and gathered practice from international tribunals and organisations.[51] The ten-year project culminated in the *Customary International Humanitarian Law* study (CIHL). The purpose of the CIHL was to determine which principles of IHL were reflective of customary international law, whether a state had become a party to a relevant treaty or not. The CIHL produced 160 rules, which the authors, and the ICRC, determined on the basis of the collection of state practice and *opinio juris*, to be customary international law. The Study is particularly useful in the determination of which laws apply to non-international armed conflicts where there are relatively few treaty provisions.

Some governments took issue with the CIHL, and particularly some of the rules, arguing primarily that the methodology and collection of materials was weak, that the study conflated state practice and *opinio juris*, and that the CIHL relied on certain state practice which was done as a matter of policy not as a matter of law.[52] Nonetheless, unlike the *Interpretative Guidance* on the direct participation in hostilities, the CIHL was welcomed[53] and, because of its nature, it has proven to be a useful tool for discussion as to whether certain rules of IHL apply in non-international armed conflicts. As Jean-Marie Henckaerts, one of the CIHL's authors said: 'In this process, the study can form the basis of a rich discussion and dialogue on the implementation, clarification and possible development of the law.'[54]

In 2012, the ICRC commenced work on new commentaries to the Geneva Conventions and Additional Protocols to reflect new interpretations and scenarios of IHL as applied in modern conflicts. The publication of the Commentaries to the First Geneva Convention is expected in 2015, after a lengthy peer-review process whereby experts from all over the world (in academic, governmental and military positions) will be asked to comment on the second draft; the first draft is to be intensively reviewed internally to ICRC. This approach is consistent with the need to ensure wider review and support before ICRC issues its own interpretation of existing laws and it will be interesting to see how states will react to these updated interpretations of the fundamental IHL treaties.

---

51 Jean-Marie Henckaerts, 'Study on Customary International Humanitarian Law: A Contribution to the Understanding and Respect for the Rule of Law in Armed Conflict' (2005) 87(857) *IRRC* 175, 185.

52 John B Bellinger III and William J Haynes II, 'A US Government Response to the International Committee of the Red Cross Study *Customary International Humanitarian Law*' (2007) 89(866) *IRRC* 443, 445–446.

53 Ibid 443.

54 Henckaerts (n 51) 197.

3.2 Treaty development

One of the first roles of the ICRC was to organise the diplomatic conference at which 12 states adopted the first Geneva Convention.[55] In a similar vein, the ICRC and the Swiss Government organised and facilitated the diplomatic conferences that negotiated the Geneva Conventions and their Additional Protocols. In addition, the ICRC has attended almost all of the negotiations for other key IHL treaties and has attempted to influence the way those treaties are written. For example, the ICRC was fully engaged in the negotiations for the Rome Statute and the Cluster Munitions Convention, but its relationship with those treaties and the negotiations highlights some tensions in its approaches to IHL issues.

The ICRC has a desire to see IHL violations punished and enforced, as required by each state under the Geneva Conventions. It is this stipulation – that states are responsible for investigation and prosecution of IHL violations that guides the ICRC's work in relation to the ICC. The ICRC welcomed the entry into force of the Rome Statute in 2002.[56] The ICRC has also published a book explaining further the elements of war crimes under the Rome Statute so as to lead to more consistent interpretation.[57] The ICRC promotes the ratification and implementation of the Rome Statute into domestic law, in the understanding that if states have domestic law, they can prosecute possible offenders themselves or cooperate with the ICC, if unable to prosecute those persons themselves. However, as an organisation, it is not generally allowed (and nor are its staff past and present) to give evidence before the ICC, as this could undermine the ICRC's strictly held neutrality. Similarly, in some conflicts, the ICRC does not reference the Rome Statute or the ICC for fear that the ICRC would seem to be promoting the sending of one or both parties to the court and hinder access to victims. Thus the ICRC must tread a fine line between general enthusiasm for the laws which the Rome Statute sets out, and the institution of the ICC.

The ICRC also sought to assist negotiations for the Cluster Munitions Convention through interpretations of existing rules and principles of IHL; for example, the principle of distinction and the prohibition of weapons which cause superfluous and unnecessary suffering. The Cluster Munitions Convention is much less controversial for the ICRC than the Rome Statute. The Convention adheres to the existing principles of IHL and seeks to apply them to a particular type of weapon, while incorporating practical criminal sanctions and victims assistance provisions, which the ICRC promotes.[58] In contrast to its cautious approach to the Rome Statute, the ICRC has strenuously promoted the Cluster Munitions Convention and its IHL principles. Indeed, it was vocal against the previously proposed Protocol on Cluster Munitions to the Convention on Certain Conventional Weapons (CCW), which many of the states that are large weapons producers support. The ICRC stated that the Protocol is not 'an adequate response to the humanitarian problems caused by cluster munitions. Rather, it risks perpetuating many

---

55 Convention for the Amelioration of the Condition of the Wounded in Armies in the Field (22 August 1864) 129 CTS 361.

56 See UNGA Sixth Committee, 57th Session, Summary Record of the 14th Meeting, 14 October 2002, UN Doc A/C.6/57/SR.14 (30 October 2002) ¶¶ 19–25 (statement by Ms Gillard, Observer for the ICRC).

57 Knut Dörmann, *Elements of War Crimes under the Rome Statute of the International Criminal Court: Sources and Commentary* (ICRC/CUP 2003).

58 See eg Statement by Mrs Christine Beerli, Vice-President of the ICRC, 'Convention on Cluster Munitions: Encouraging Results but Challenges Remain' Third Meeting of States Parties to the Convention on Cluster Munitions, Oslo, Norway, 11 September 2012, www.icrc.org/eng/resources/documents/statement/2012/cluster-munitions-statement-2012-09-11.htm.

aspects of these problems.'[59] The reaction by states opposed to the Cluster Munitions Convention, and favouring the Protocol to the CCW, as well as the content of that Protocol, had led the ICRC to suggest that IHL might be in decline.[60] At the time, this decline was also said to be reflected in the failure of states to adopt the Arms Trade Treaty, in which the ICRC was also most active in promoting victim assistance and IHL principles.[61]

However, today, the Arms Trade Treaty has now become a reality, and entered into force in 2014; now the ICRC's task is to support implementation of the IHL criteria. With the continued engagement in and support of states of the Strengthening IHL Project there is little fear at the moment that states will not comply with or continue to develop IHL. The challenge now is to ensure that non-state actors abide by IHL and are engaged in the process of development of IHL, and the ICRC, having worked with these non-state actors is cognisant of the need to engage more closely with them.[62]

4 Conclusion

The ICRC is first and foremost a humanitarian organisation. Distancing itself from its once self-proclaimed title of 'guardian of IHL', the ICRC still works tirelessly to promote IHL, whether through practical means in the field or by supporting the development, codification and interpretation of IHL. It is also in the privileged position of having a close dialogue with all parties to a conflict, and can therefore persuade them to abide by IHL and point out instances when they can learn from violations in the future. The ICRC uses its experience in the field to highlight gaps in IHL and assist in filling them. It also engages in training of militaries, law-makers and potential leaders. However, some states or their legal advisers have rejected ICRC interpretations and suggested that the ICRC does not have a mandate to act. Indeed, as the 'guardians of IHL', the ICRC has often in the past put legal interpretations before practical realities.

The ICRC is recognising increasingly that a balance should be struck between humanitarian persuasion and diplomacy to uphold IHL on the one hand and creating new rules on the other hand. The ICRC is also gradually becoming aware that there is little taste currently for new developments in IHL that are created purely as unilateral interpretations, and that an attempt to force these developments could damage existing principles of IHL. While the ICRC has a clear mandate to work on IHL both in the practical and theoretical sense, it is only states that have the authority to create IHL and it is parties to the conflicts going on around the world that have the responsibility to uphold IHL. One of the challenges for an organisation as old and as

59 Statement by Jakob Kellenberger, President of the International Committee of the Red Cross, 'ICRC Comments on the Draft Protocol on Cluster Munitions and Other issues for the CCW Review Conference' Fourth Review Conference of the States Parties to the Convention on Certain Conventional Weapons (CCW), Geneva, Switzerland, 14-25 November 2011, www.icrc.org/eng/resources/documents/ statement/ccw-statement-2011-11-15.htm.

60 ICRC, 'States Must Insist on Urgent, Effective Action against Cluster Munitions: Interview with Peter Herby, Head of the ICRC's Arms Unit' (10 November 2011), www.icrc.org/eng/resources/documents/interview/2011/cluster-munitions-interview-2011-11-10.htm.

61 ICRC, 'Arms Trade Treaty: Agreement as Urgent as Ever Despite Failure' News Footage ref AV02N (30 July 2012), www.icrc.org/eng/resources/documents/news-footage/2012/arms-trade-treaty-footage.htm.

62 See eg 'ICRC's Conference on Humanitarian Dialogue with Non-State Armed Groups: The Impact of Geopolitical Challenges' (25 February 2014), www.icrc.org/eng/resources/documents/feature/2014/02-25-humanitarium-conference-dialogue-non-state-armed-groups.htm; see also Yves Daccord, 'Is There Still a Place for Impartial Humanitarianism?' Chatham House (4 September 2014), www.chathamhouse.org/node/15213.

well established as the ICRC is to recognise that often a lot more can be done by persuasion over time than by pushing hard for the establishment of specific rules which are subsequently difficult to amend. On the other hand, interpreting the law in an authoritative way, although it may raise the ire of some, leads to openness in discussion and continued development of the law. The ICRC is constantly finding ways to balance and combine the two approaches of persuasiveness in the field and using that practical experience rather than its IHL expertise in house necessarily to work towards codification and treaty development, and to engage more frequently and constructively with different partners nowadays, in order to strengthen IHL and its application.

28
Reciprocity and reprisals

Shane Darcy

Reciprocity plays a significant part in influencing the behaviour of parties to an armed conflict and has had a prominent role in the creation, enforcement and indeed breach of the law of armed conflict. There is little doubt that parties to a conflict are motivated to respect the law by the belief that, for example, treating captured enemy combatants and civilians humanely will lead to similar treatment by one's opponents. Conversely, a failure by one side to respect the law of armed conflict is likely to be met in practice by a similar disregard for the rules. It is not uncommon for parties to an armed conflict to claim that their opponents do not respect the laws of armed conflict and that accordingly they should not be bound by those same laws. It has been said that the parties to the conflict in the Former Yugoslavia 'plead reciprocity with almost pathological insistence in seeking to justify the gravest breaches of international humanitarian law'.[1] Conflicts involving non-state actors, particularly those under the rubric of the 'war on terror', have been especially prone to claims that states involved in such conflicts should not be bound to apply the law of armed conflict given the disregard for groups such as al-Qaeda for the law.[2]

Without question, international law regulating armed conflict has been moving steadily away from the idea of reciprocal obligations to more universal or absolute obligations. That is to say, a party to an armed conflict should generally be considered to be bound by the law of armed conflict irrespective of the conduct of its opponent. Section 1 considers reciprocity in the law of armed conflict, with regard in particular to the application of the law to a situation of armed conflict and the observance of those laws in the event of a breach by an opponent. The great exception to the decline of reciprocity has been provided by the doctrine of belligerent reprisals, whereby a party to an armed conflict might as a last resort deliberately breach the applicable law in response to breaches by the enemy and for the purpose of forcing a return to respect for the law. Recourse to reprisals has been increasingly restricted by the law of armed conflict, but not completely outlawed, and reprisals are one of the remaining vestiges of the legal concept of

---

1 Marco Sassòli, 'Book Review: Dieter Fleck (ed), *The Handbook of Humanitarian Law in Armed Conflict*' (1995) 35(309) *IRRC* 679.

2 See eg John Yoo, 'Terrorists have no Geneva Rights' *Wall Street Journal* (New York, 26 May 2004) A16.

reciprocity within the law of armed conflict. The customary law requirements governing resort to reprisals and the scope of the existing legal prohibitions are set out in Section 2. Reprisals and the broader concept of reciprocity in the law of armed conflict are controversial subjects, generating frequent challenges to the existing law. Section 3 explores the more prominent of these, in particular the role of reciprocity and reprisals in non-international armed conflicts, the scope of permissible reprisals and the challenges presented by the 'war on terror' and asymmetric warfare.

1 Reciprocity in the law of armed conflict

The concept of reciprocity is no stranger to public international law,[3] and although the law of armed conflict is a branch of public international law, it is subject to exceptional rules on reciprocity, largely in light of its humanitarian character. Reciprocity has historically had a significant role in the law of armed conflict, a legal regime 'created by mutual agreement and enforced through the promise and threat of reciprocity'.[4] This section is concerned primarily with the law relating to reciprocity in the context of armed conflict. Consideration will first be given to its role in the initial application of treaty rules to situations of armed conflict. The section will then address the nature of the legal obligations existing under the law of armed conflict and whether these amount to reciprocal undertakings from which parties to an armed conflict are freed in the event of breaches by an opponent. By and large this is not the case, as will be seen, although reprisals can in some sense be considered to be based on such an idea. Finally, reciprocity, as René Provost observes, is 'at once a social, political, and legal phenomenon',[5] and accordingly attention will also be paid to its role in a non-legal sense in influencing compliance with the law of armed conflict.

States have agreed to be bound by treaties of international humanitarian law because 'such texts correspond with their reciprocal and well understood interests'.[6] When Russia proposed a Project for an International Convention on the Laws and Customs of War in 1874, it made clear that the purpose of the endeavour was 'to establish by common accord, upon a basis of complete reciprocity, rules which may be binding on all governments and their armies'.[7] The early laws of war were not intended to apply to 'savages', meaning the inhabitants of colonised territories who resorted to force against the colonial powers.[8] The reciprocity between states is evidenced in rules which limited the application of treaties to those states which are parties to the treaty in question. Article 2 of the 1907 Hague Convention (IV), for example, sets out that its provisions, and those of the attached Hague Regulations (HR), 'do not apply except between Contracting powers, and then only if all the belligerents are parties to the Convention'. The 1949 Geneva Conventions also limit their application 'to all cases of declared war or of any other armed

---

3 Bruno Simma, 'Reciprocity' *MPEPIL* (April 2008); Ernst Schneeberger, 'Reciprocity as a Maxim of International Law' (1948) 37 *Georgetown LJ* 29; Francesco Parisi and Nita Ghei, 'The Role of Reciprocity in International Law' (2003) 36 *Cornell ILJ* 93; D W Greig, 'Proportionality, Reciprocity, and the Law of Treaties' (1994) 34 *Virginia JIL* 295.

4 Eyal Benvenisti, 'The Legal Battle to Define the Law on Transnational Asymmetric Warfare' (2010) 20 *Duke JCIL* 339, 340.

5 René Provost, 'Reciprocity in Human Rights and Humanitarian Law' (1995) 65 *BYBIL* 383, 388.

6 Jean Pictet, 'The Formation of International Humanitarian Law' (1985) (25)244 *IRRC* 3, 21.

7 'Correspondence Respecting the Proposed Conference at Brussels on the Rules of Military Warfare' *United Kingdom Parliamentary Papers,* Miscellaneous No 1 (1874) [c 1010] 5–6.

8 See Frédéric Mégret, 'From "Savages" to "Unlawful Combatants": A Postcolonial Look at International Humanitarian Law's "Other"' in Ann Orford (ed), *International Law and its Others* (CUP 2006) 265.

conflict which may arise between two or more of the High Contracting Parties',[9] although for international armed conflicts involving a non-state party, the states parties remain bound 'in their mutual relations' and 'shall furthermore be bound by the Convention in relation to the said Power, if the latter accepts and applies the provisions thereof'.[10] The practical relevance of this latter provision has been reduced almost to nil, given the near universal ratification of the Geneva Conventions.[11] The right of the High Contracting Parties to the Geneva Conventions to denounce the treaties is circumscribed, in that any denunciation cannot take effect until after the conclusion of a conflict they are engaged in at the time of denunciation.[12]

The crystallisation of rules of international humanitarian law into customary international law limits the use of reciprocity arguments for denying the application of the law of armed conflict, even in the face of denunciation or the involvement of non-state parties. It was argued at Nuremberg that Germany was not bound by the HR because of the so-called general participation clause in Article 2.[13] The International Military Tribunal turned to customary international law, finding that the customary status of the regulations meant they were binding on Germany irrespective of the participation in the war of non-state parties.[14] It is clear that armed conflicts are 'automatically subject to customary humanitarian law, without any condition relating to reciprocity'.[15] According to the ICTY, 'most norms of international humanitarian law, in particular those prohibiting war crimes, crimes against humanity and genocide, are also peremptory norms of international law or *jus cogens*, ie of a non-derogable and overriding character'.[16] The rationale behind obligations *erga omnes* is that such are owed to the international community as a whole, rather than to individual states.

The 1949 Geneva Conventions are also addressed to non-international armed conflicts, and Common Article 3 applies automatically when such a conflict arises on the territory of a High Contracting Party. Reciprocity has no role in the application of Common Article 3, although for Additional Protocol II, the instrument applies only to non-international armed conflict where armed groups control such territory that enables them 'to carry out sustained and concerted military operations and *to implement this Protocol*'.[17] This might suggest a reciprocity requirement for the application of the Protocol,[18] although it is argued that the provision 'corresponds to a capacity requirement on the part of the insurgent rather than the application of immediate reciprocity in non-international armed conflicts'.[19] The ICRC *Commentary* considers there to be 'a degree of realism' involved here, that the armed group 'may reasonably be expected to apply the rules developed in the Protocol'.[20] For non-state actors who may be party to a

---

9 GCI–IV art 2(1).
10 GCI–IV art 2(3).
11 See however Second Protocol to the Hague Convention of 1954 for the Protection of Cultural Property in the Event of Armed Conflict (26 March 1999) 2253 UNTS 212, art 3(2).
12 GCI art 63; GCII art 62; GCIII art 142; GCIV art 158.
13 *US et al v Göring et al*, 1 TMWC 171, 253 (1946).
14 Ibid 253–254. For a critical view, see Sean Watts, 'Reciprocity and the Laws of War' (2009) 50 *Harvard ILJ* 365, 402.
15 Provost, 'Reciprocity' (n 5) 388.
16 *Prosecutor v Kupreškić et al* (Case no IT-95-16-T, ICTY Trial Chamber, 14 January 2000) ¶¶ 519–520.
17 APII art 1(1) (emphasis added).
18 See eg Benvenisti, 'The Legal Battle' (n 4) 341; Leslie C Green, *The Contemporary Law of Armed Conflict* (2nd edn, Manchester University Press 2000) 321.
19 René Provost, 'Asymmetrical Reciprocity and Compliance with the Laws of War' in Benjamin Perrin (ed), *Modern Warfare: Armed Groups, Private Militaries, Humanitarian Organizations, and the Law* (UBC Press 2012) 17, 23.
20 *AP Commentary* ¶ 1352.

conflict under Additional Protocol I, Article 96 requires that they make a unilateral declaration to apply the Conventions and Protocol in order for them to come into force between them and a state party. Those aspects of Additional Protocol I that amount to customary international law would obviously apply to the conflict in question irrespective of ratification by the state or the making of the declaration by the non-state entity.

According to the ICTY, '[t]he defining characteristic of modern international humanitarian law is ... the obligation to uphold key tenets of this body of law regardless of the conduct of enemy combatants'.[21] The concept of negative reciprocity which would allow for a treaty or specific rules to be suspended in the event of a breach by another state is present in international law but no longer holds sway in the law of armed conflict. It is distinguishable from reprisals,[22] discussed below, and was clearly espoused in early documents on the laws of war. The Lieber Code, for example, instructed troops to deny quarter to enemy troops which had done so themselves.[23] A reciprocal element was introduced for the 1925 Gas Protocol through the use of reservations, with many states denying the Protocol's obligations in the event of its breach by another state party.[24] Nevertheless, the aspiration of the 1880 Oxford Manual, 'that each belligerent should conform to the rules of war, without reciprocity on the part of the enemy', has since become a fundamental underpinning of the law of armed conflict.[25] The authoritative ICRC Customary International Humanitarian Law Study states squarely that '[t]he obligation to respect and ensure respect for international humanitarian law does not depend on reciprocity'.[26]

In treaty law, the most significant rejection of reciprocity for the law of armed conflict is evidenced by Common Article 1 of the Geneva Conventions, present also in Additional Protocol I, and the Vienna Convention on the Law of Treaties. Common Article 1 imposes on state parties an obligation 'to respect and to ensure respect for the present Convention in all circumstances'.[27] Geoffrey Best considers that the phrase 'in all circumstances' marked 'the legal death of reciprocity'.[28] The ICRC *Commentary* asserts the 'special character' of each of the Geneva Conventions:

> [I]t is not merely an engagement concluded on a basis of reciprocity, binding each party to the contract only in so far as the other party observes its obligations. It is rather a series of unilateral engagements solemnly contracted before the world as represented by the other Contracting Parties. Each State contracts obligations vis-à-vis itself and at the same time vis-à-vis the others.[29]

---

21 *Kupreškić* (n 16) ¶ 511.

22 Frits Kalshoven, *Belligerent Reprisals* (Martinus Nijhoff 2005 [1971]) 25; Watts (n 14) 385.

23 Instructions for the Government of Armies of the United States in the Field, prepared by Francis Lieber, promulgated as General Orders no 100 by President Lincoln (24 April 1863) art 62 ('Lieber Code').

24 Protocol for the Prohibition of the Use of Asphyxiating, Poisonous or Other Gases, and of Bacteriological Methods of Warfare (7 June 1925) 94 LNTS 6.

25 Oxford Manual on the Laws of War on Land (9 September 1880) art 84.

26 CIHL r 140. See further David Turns, 'Implementation and Compliance' in Elizabeth Wilmshurst and Susan Breau (eds), *Perspectives on the ICRC Study on Customary International Humanitarian Law* (CUP 2007) 354, 360.

27 See further Frits Kalshoven, 'The Undertaking to Respect and Ensure Respect in All Circumstances: From Tiny Seed to Ripening Fruit' (1999) 2 *YBIHL* 3.

28 Geoffrey Best, *War and Law since 1945* (Clarendon Press 1994) 146. See however Ingrid Detter, *The Law of War* (2nd edn, CUP 2000) 404.

29 *GCIII Commentary* 17–18. See also Jean de Preux, 'The Geneva Conventions and Reciprocity' (1985) 25(244) *IRRC* 25.

The law of treaties reinforces the exceptional nature of much of the law of armed conflict. The rules relating to termination or suspension of treaties in the Vienna Convention explicitly 'do not apply to provisions relating to the protection of the human person contained in treaties of a humanitarian character, in particular to provisions prohibiting any form of reprisals against persons protected by such treaties'.[30] Other evidence of the decline of negative reciprocity can be found in the denial of the *tu quoque* defence by international criminal tribunals.[31]

The rationale behind the creation of non-reciprocal obligations under the Geneva Conventions and the Additional Protocols has a strong humanitarian element. As explained by the ICTY:

> norms of international humanitarian law were not intended to protect State interests; they were primarily designed to benefit individuals *qua* human beings. Unlike other international norms, such as those of commercial treaties which can legitimately be based on the protection of reciprocal interests of States, compliance with humanitarian rules could not be made dependent on a reciprocal or corresponding performance of these obligations by other States.[32]

This begs the question as to whether reciprocity here can apply to the law of armed conflict that might not be considered humanitarian in nature. An excerpt from the 2007 US *Naval Handbook* is instructive:

> Some obligations under the law of armed conflict are reciprocal in that they are binding on the parties only so long as both sides continue to comply with them. A major violation by one side will release the other side from all further duty to abide by that obligation. The concept of reciprocity is not applicable to humanitarian rules of law that protect the victims of armed conflict, that is, those persons protected by the 1949 Geneva Conventions.[33]

Sean Watts points to certain Hague-law weapons treaties which he argues might not be covered by the Vienna Convention exception,[34] although arguably restrictions on the use of poisonous gas against enemy personnel can be seen to have a humanitarian element. According to Hersch Lauterpacht, '[i]t is probably true to say that that humanitarian sphere constitutes the bulk of the law of war'.[35]

While respect for the law of armed conflict is generally not contingent on reciprocity in a legal sense, and breaches by an opponent do not justify similar breaches, except perhaps in the limited case of reprisals, it is clear that reciprocity has an important role to play in motivating parties to an armed conflict to observe the relevant rules and principles.[36] This is most apparent

---

30 Vienna Convention on the Law of Treaties (23 May 1969) 1155 UNTS 331, art 60(5).

31 See *Kupreškić* (n 16) ¶¶ 511, 515–517; *Prosecutor v Kunarac et al* (Case no IT-96-23 and IT-96-23/1-A, ICTY Appeals Chamber, 12 June 2002) ¶ 87; *Prosecutor v Martić* (Case no IT-95-11-A, ICTY Appeals Chamber, 8 October 2008) ¶ 111.

32 *Kupreškić* (n 16) ¶ 518.

33 US Navy, US Marine Corps and US Coast Guard, *The Commander's Handbook on the Law of Naval Operations*, NWP 1-14M/MCWP 5-12.1/COMDTPUB P5800.7A (July 2007) s 6.2.5 ('US *Naval Handbook*').

34 Watts (n 14) 423.

35 Hersch Lauterpacht, 'The Limits of the Operations of the Law of War' (1953) 30 *BYBIL* 206, 212–213.

36 Best (n 28) 420; A P V Rogers, *Law on the Battlefield* (3rd edn, Manchester University Press 2012) 349–350; Peter Margulies, 'The Fog of War Reform: Change and Structure in the Law of Armed Conflict after September 11' (2012) 95 *Marquette LR* 1417, 1430.

with regard to the treatment of prisoners of war, with detaining powers likely to treat captured soldiers humanely with the belief that their own soldiers will be similarly treated if captured. The ICRC notes how reciprocity can play a role in encouraging parties to actually go beyond what is provided for under the law of armed conflict.[37] Fear of a reciprocal response might also deter parties to an armed conflict from breaching the law because, as Best observes, a belligerent will 'only forbear from using unlawful means to gain advantage and inflict damages if it knows the other side can and will do the same, or worse, back to them'.[38] It is claimed that the laws of occupation are ineffective because a conquered sovereign is by definition almost unable to retaliate against an occupying power.[39] The negative side of reciprocity is that breaches by one side are likely to lead to breaches by the other, and, according to Canada's *Joint Doctrine Manual*, to 'strengthen your enemy's will to fight to the bitter end'.[40]

Empirical evidence seems to support the utility of reciprocity in enforcing the law of armed conflict.[41] James D Morrow has shown that this is especially the case where states engaged in a conflict are both parties to the relevant treaties.[42] He finds that this joint ratification 'reinforces reciprocity because both sides understand that they are both committed to the treaty standard'.[43] Breaches by either party in such a situation, he concludes, are 'more likely to provoke a response in kind',[44] and democratic countries 'take their legal obligations more seriously than other states, yet are still willing to respond to violations in kind'.[45] Individual soldiers are also likely to retaliate for violations against fellow soldiers, although certain means for responding, such as using chemical weapons would tend to be out of reach of soldiers on the ground.[46] Morrow finds the role of reciprocity in enforcement is complex,[47] and while law is not seen as 'a substitute for reciprocal enforcement; it can aid such enforcement'.[48] Law can act as a means to delay the perhaps inevitable resort to reciprocal behaviour in the face of breaches, in particular those 'indignant retaliatory tit-for-tats which almost always spiral beyond proportionality'.[49] The next section demonstrates, in this regard, how the doctrine of belligerent reprisals has been significantly circumscribed by the law of armed conflict.

2 Belligerent reprisals

Belligerent reprisals are prima facie unlawful actions taken by a party to an armed conflict in response to breaches by an opponent and for the purpose of forcing the enemy to cease its

37 *AP Commentary* 37; *GCIV Commentary* 513.
38 Best (n 28) 420.
39 Eric A Posner, 'Terrorism and the Laws of War' (2004) 5 *Chicago JIL* 423, 430 (footnote omitted).
40 Canada National Defence, *Joint Doctrine Manual: Law of Armed Conflict at the Operational and Tactical Levels* (Office of the Judge Advocate General 2001) s 204(7). See also Rogers (n 36) 349–350; Rüdiger Wolfrum and Dieter Fleck, 'The Enforcement of International Humanitarian Law' in Terry Gill and Dieter Fleck (eds), *The Handbook of International Humanitarian Law* (OUP 2008) 675, 687; Michael D Gottesman, 'Reciprocity and War: A New Understanding of Reciprocity's Role in Geneva Convention Obligations' (2008) 14 *UC Davis Journal of Law and Policy* 147, 148, 171–176.
41 James D Morrow, 'When do States Follow the Laws of War?' (2007) 101 *American Political Science Review* 559, 568.
42 Ibid 561.
43 Ibid.
44 Ibid.
45 Ibid 567.
46 Ibid 561.
47 Ibid 568.
48 Ibid 570.
49 Best (n 28) 146.

unlawful action.[50] They are viewed as a means of enforcing the law of armed conflict and consequently are lawful provided certain conditions are met. These requirements are well established in customary international law and are set out below, as are the ever-expanding categories of persons and objects that are prohibited from being targeted in reprisal action. Reprisals are 'drastic and exceptional measures',[51] which are increasingly restricted but not yet completely outlawed under the law of armed conflict. There is obviously an element of reciprocity in the doctrine of belligerent reprisals, in that it allows for a breach of the law of armed conflict in response to violation of those laws. However, the unlawful action comprising a reprisal might not be of the same type as the original breach and, moreover, it is a temporary violation which must cease once the enemy's violation has ended.[52] Traditional reciprocity, on the other hand, used to allow for the complete suspension or termination of a treaty or particular rules.[53] Belligerent reprisals are frequently addressed in scholarship, military manuals and judicial decisions, but have become far less common in actual practice.

2.1 Customary requirements

The customary international law conditions for belligerent reprisals can be found in the military manuals of some of the largest military powers, each of which emphasises the same key requirements with only minor variations. The 'stringent conditions'[54] are that belligerent reprisals must be for the purpose of law enforcement, in response to a prior violation of the law of armed conflict, as a last resort, authorised from a high level, publicised, conducted in accordance with the principle of proportionality and ceasing upon the enemy's return to observance.

The purpose of reprisals is to enforce the law of armed conflict in the event of a breach of those laws. The UK *Manual of Law of Armed Conflict* allows a reprisal only 'in response to serious and manifestly unlawful acts, committed by an adverse government, its military commanders, or combatants for whom the adversary is responsible'.[55] A reprisal is permitted only in response to a violation of 'the law of war',[56] and breaches of the *jus ad bellum* do not justify belligerent reprisals.[57] Reprisals are responsive measures and accordingly '[a]nticipatory reprisal is not authorized'.[58] If the enemy has already stopped is violation then the justification for reprisal is gone. Australia's *Law of Armed Conflict Manual* (in language borrowed from the UK *Manual*) elaborates:

> if one party to an armed conflict breaches the law but then expresses regret, declares that it will not be repeated and takes measures to punish those immediately responsible, then any action taken by another party in response to the original unlawful act cannot be justified as a reprisal.[59]

---

50 See generally Kalshoven, *Belligerent Reprisals* (n 22); Shane Darcy, 'The Evolution of the Law of Belligerent Reprisals' (2003) 175 *Military LR* 184.
51 *Prosecutor v Martić* (Case no IT-95-11-T, ICTY Trial Chamber, 12 June 2007) ¶ 465.
52 Kalshoven, *Belligerent Reprisals* (n 22) 25.
53 Watts (n 14) 385.
54 CIHL r 145.
55 UK Ministry of Defence, *The Manual of Law of Armed Conflict* (OUP 2004) 419.
56 US Army, *Law of War Handbook* (Judge Advocate General's School 2005) 194.
57 Christopher Greenwood, 'The Twilight of the Law of Belligerent Reprisals' (1989) 20 *Netherlands YBIL* 35, 40–41.
58 US *Naval Handbook* (n 33) s 6.2.4.1.2.
59 Australian Defence Forces, *Law of Armed Conflict* (Department of Defence 2006) ¶ 13.18.

This underscores the temporary nature of reprisals; such measures must end once the original breach has.[60] Reprisals cannot be taken for purposes of revenge or punishment, but rather they serve solely as a means of compelling a law-breaking enemy to cease its unlawful action.[61]

Belligerent reprisals must only be taken as a last resort. The Lieber Code first required 'careful inquiry into the real occurrence, and the character of the misdeeds that may demand retribution',[62] with a modern incarnation adding that reprisals can only follow 'an unsatisfied demand to cease and desist'.[63] According to Canada's *Joint Doctrine Manual*, a party 'must first exhaust other reasonable means of securing compliance in order to justify taking a reprisal'.[64] The US *Naval Handbook* allows reprisals as a last resort only 'when other enforcement mechanisms have failed or would be of no avail'.[65] If reprisals are to be taken they must be publicised and notice given. The ICTY considered that 'reprisals may be exercised only after a prior and formal warning has been given, which has failed to put an end to the violations committed by the adversary'.[66] Publicising a reprisal action is necessary in order to inform the enemy of the purpose of the inherently unlawful action being taken and to offer an opportunity for compliance.[67] The decision to authorise belligerent reprisals is usually reserved for those in the highest political office or military rank. The 1880 Oxford Manual recommended that reprisals 'only be resorted to with the authorization of the commander in chief',[68] and this is explicitly the case in the US.[69] The UK military requires the approval of the Cabinet to engage in a reprisal.[70]

Any reprisal undertaken must be in accordance with the principle of proportionality.[71] The reprisal must be 'proportional to the original violation',[72] but need not match exactly the breach which triggered it:

> Whilst a reprisal need not conform in kind to the act complained of, it may not significantly exceed the adverse party's violation either in degree or effect. Effective but disproportionate acts cannot be justified as reprisals on the basis that only an excessive response will forestall further violations.[73]

German reprisal measures during the Second World War were condemned in the *Einsatzgruppen* case for their 'obvious disproportionality'.[74] Although not mentioned in today's military manuals or the ICRC Study, the 1880 Oxford Manual advocated that belligerent reprisals 'conform in all cases to the laws of humanity and morality'.[75] This is well meaning but hardly realistic given that 'inhumanity ... is more or less by definition a characteristic of belligerent reprisals'.[76] The ICTY

---

60 CIHL commentary to r 145.
61 Ibid.
62 Lieber Code (n 23) art 28.
63 US *Law of War Handbook* (n 56) 194.
64 Canada *Joint Doctrine Manual* (n 40) s 1507(6)(d). See also UK *Manual* (n 55) 419.
65 US *Naval Handbook* (n 33) s 6.2.4.1.5.
66 *Martić* (n 51) ¶ 466.
67 UK *Manual* (n 55) 421.
68 Oxford Manual (n 25) art 86.
69 US *Naval Handbook* (n 33) s 6.2.4.3.
70 UK *Manual* (n 55) 419.
71 *Legality of the Threat or Use of Nuclear Weapons (Advisory Opinion)* [1996] ICJ Rep 226, ¶ 46.
72 US *Naval Handbook* (n 33) s 6.2.4.3.
73 UK *Manual* (n 55) 419.
74 *US v Ohlendorf et al (Einsatzgruppen)* IV TWC 411, 493–494 (1948).
75 Oxford Manual (n 25) art 86.
76 Frits Kalshoven, 'Human Rights, the Law of Armed Conflict, and Reprisals' (1971) 11(121) *IRRC* 183, 189.

found that reprisals should accord with 'the laws of humanity and the dictates of the public conscience', which meant that 'reprisals must be exercised, to the extent possible, in keeping with the principle of the protection of the civilian population in armed conflict and the general prohibition of targeting civilians'.[77] Humanitarian concerns have undoubtedly motivated the near total ban on reprisals against civilians, as described in the next section, as have serious misgivings regarding the effectiveness of reprisals as a sanction of the law of armed conflict.

2.2 Prohibited reprisals

Treaties on the law of armed conflict address belligerent reprisals solely by way of prohibition. The only rule in positive law prior to the Second World War was in the 1929 Prisoners of War Convention, which expressly forbade measures of reprisal against POWs.[78] Reprisal was frequently raised as a defence in the trials conducted after the Second World War, but with little success often owing to the usually disproportionate nature of German reprisals.[79] The 1949 Geneva Conventions introduced reprisal prohibitions for each of the categories of persons and objects protected by those treaties, including wounded, sick and shipwrecked members of armed forces, prisoners of wars, civilians and civilian property in occupied territory.[80] There was no opposition to the introduction of these prohibitions at the 1949 Diplomatic Conference, nor has any High Contracting Party made a reservation to these rules. The same cannot be said for the reprisal prohibitions introduced in Additional Protocol I.

Belligerent reprisals were a source of much debate and disagreement in the 1974–1977 Diplomatic Conference on the Reaffirmation and Development of International Humanitarian Law Applicable in Armed Conflicts.[81] Additional Protocol I as finally agreed expands the list of persons and objects that are protected from reprisals, while an attempt to prohibit reprisals in Additional Protocol II applicable to non-international armed conflicts proved unsuccessful, as discussed below. Additional Protocol I prohibits reprisals against the wounded, sick, shipwrecked and the objects protected by Part II of the instrument, the civilian population or civilians, civilian objects, historic and cultural objects and places of worship, objects indispensable to the survival of the civilian population, the natural environment, works and installations containing dangerous forces and any military objectives at or in the vicinity of these works or installations upon which an attack 'may cause the release of dangerous forces from the works or installations and consequent severe losses among the civilian population'.[82] The 1980 Mines Protocol specifically prohibits their use in reprisal against civilians.[83]

---

77 *Martić* (n 51) ¶ 467.

78 Convention Relative to the Treatment of Prisoners of War (27 July 1929) 118 LNTS 343, art 2(3).

79 See eg *US v List et al* XI TWC 757, 1252–1253 (1948); *US v von Leeb et al* XI TWC 462, 528 (1948); *Einsatzgruppen* (n 74) 493–494; *In re Rauter,* Holland, Special Criminal Court, 4 May 1948, Special Court of Cassation, 12 January 1949, Case no 193 (1949) 16 ADIL 526, 539.

80 GCI art 46; GCII art 47; GCIII art 13(3); GCIV art 33(3). See also Convention for the Protection of Cultural Property in the Event of Armed Conflict (14 May 1954) 249 UNTS 240, art 4(4).

81 See Stanislav E Nahlik, 'Belligerent Reprisals as Seen in the Light of the Diplomatic Conference on Humanitarian Law, Geneva, 1974–1977' (1978) 42 *Law and Contemporary Problems* 36, 43–66.

82 API arts 20, 51(6), 52(1), 53(c), 54(4), 55(2) and 56(4).

83 Protocol (II) on Prohibitions or Restrictions on the Use of Mines, Booby Traps and Other Devices, annexed to the Convention on Prohibitions or Restrictions on the Use of Certain Conventional Weapons which may be Deemed to be Excessively Injurious or to have Indiscriminate Effects (10 October 1980) 1342 UNTS 137, art 2(3).

The list of reprisal prohibitions under treaty law is extensive and when considered in tandem with the requirements of customary international law, severely limits the scope of parties to an international armed conflict to resort to belligerent reprisals. The reprisal prohibitions in the Geneva Conventions are without question part of customary international law.[84] The reprisals rules of Additional Protocol I, however, have not been agreed to by several states and the customary law status of certain provisions is uncertain. The reservation entered by the UK upon ratification of Additional Protocol I is significant:

> If any adverse party makes serious and deliberate attacks, in violation of Article 51 or Article 52 against the civilian population or civilians or against civilian objects, or, in violation of Articles 53, 54 and 55, on objects or items protected by those Articles, the United Kingdom will regard itself as entitled to take measures otherwise prohibited by the Articles in question to the extent that it considers it necessary for the sole purpose of compelling the adverse party to cease committing violations.[85]

The US is not presently a party to Additional Protocol I, partly because of the reprisal rules, and the 2007 *Naval Handbook* states that '[r]eprisals may be taken against enemy armed forces, *enemy civilians other than those in occupied territory*, and enemy property'.[86]

In the *Kupreškić* judgment, an ICTY Trial Chamber referred to 'the absolute character of the prohibition of reprisals against civilian populations' and found that the prohibition of reprisals against civilians in Additional Protocol I was part of customary international law.[87] It had been held in an earlier decision that

> the rule which states that reprisals against the civilian population as such, or individual civilians, are prohibited in all circumstances, even when confronted by wrongful behaviour of the other party, is an integral part of customary international law and must be respected in all armed conflicts.[88]

The ICRC has taken a more circumspect approach:

> Because of existing contrary practice, albeit very limited, it is difficult to conclude that there has yet crystallized a customary rule specifically prohibiting reprisals against civilians during the conduct of hostilities. Nevertheless, it is also difficult to assert that a right to resort to such reprisals continues to exist on the strength of the practice of only a limited number of States, some of which is also ambiguous. Hence, there appears, at a minimum, to exist a trend in favour of prohibiting such reprisals.[89]

Given the progressive restriction of the scope for permissible reprisals over the course of the twentieth century, it would seem inevitable that all civilians will eventually be protected from such actions by the law of armed conflict.

---

84 CIHL rr 146 and 147.
85 UK *Manual* (n 55) 421.
86 US *Naval Handbook* (n 33) s 6.2.4 (emphasis added).
87 *Kupreškić* (n 16) ¶¶ 513, 531.
88 *Prosecutor v Martić (Rule 61 Decision)* (Case no IT-95-11-R.61, ICTY Trial Chamber I, 8 March 1996) ¶¶ 16–17. No mention was made in the Trial or Appeal judgments of the reprisal prohibitions, although there was discussion of the customary requirements: *Martić* (n 51) ¶ 465; *Martić* (n 31) ¶¶ 264–267.
89 CIHL commentary to r 146.

3 Contemporary challenges

The law of armed conflict has progressively moved away from being a legal regime based on reciprocity where law-breaking by an opponent might free a party to an armed conflict from its obligations, by suspending or terminating the applicable rules or allowing for unlawful action under the doctrine of belligerent reprisals. While these legal concepts might be in terminal decline, they have not yet been completely excised from the law of armed conflict.[90] Questions remain regarding the scope of permissible reprisals and whether the doctrine has any place in non-international armed conflicts. Reciprocity has also featured in debates over the application of the Geneva Conventions to persons detained in the 'war on terror', while asymmetrical warfare also presents particular challenges for compliance. This final section seeks to highlight these areas of contention.

That we have not yet arrived at a complete prohibition of belligerent reprisals is evidenced by Rule 145 of the ICRC's *Customary International Humanitarian Law* study: 'Where not prohibited by international law, belligerent reprisals are subject to stringent conditions.' Leaving aside civilians in enemy territory as discussed above, the overwhelming view is that belligerent reprisals are permitted only against military objectives and combatants,[91] a seemingly incongruous position given that these can already be the lawful target of military action.[92] It is conceivable that a reprisal might consist of the use of unlawful weapons or prohibited means or methods of warfare against enemy objects and personnel.[93] George Aldrich considers that a reprisal use of a banned weapon 'is unlikely to be useful or desirable', unless it is a response in kind.[94] In fact, the effectiveness of any reprisal measure is highly debatable, with Frits Kalshoven, the leading scholar on the subject, concluding that they can no longer be seen 'as even moderately effective sanctions of the laws of war'.[95] The US *Naval Handbook* expressly acknowledges that the US has been reluctant to resort to belligerent reprisals because of the risk that they 'will trigger counter-reprisals by the enemy'.[96] Despite claims to the contrary,[97] the wealth of official, judicial and scholarly comment on reprisals is met with a dearth of contemporary practice, with hardly any examples forthcoming in recent decades of unlawful action specifically undertaken as a belligerent reprisal, against any category of persons or objects, and meeting the requirements established in customary international law, including being publicly declared as such.

---

90 Theodor Meron, 'The Humanization of Humanitarian Law' (2000) 94 *AJIL* 239, 251; Adam Roberts, 'The Equal Application of the Laws of War: A Principle under Pressure' (2008) 90(872) *IRRC* 931, 944; Eyal Benvenisti, 'Rethinking the Divide Between *Jus ad Bellum* and *Jus in Bello* in Warfare Against Non-State Actors' (2009) 34 *Yale JIL* 541, 542; Provost, 'Asymmetrical Reciprocity' (n 19); Toni Pfanner, 'Asymmetrical Warfare from the Perspective of Humanitarian Law and Humanitarian Action' (2005) 87(857) *IRRC* 149, 163; Watts (n 14).

91 UK *Manual* (n 55) 419; US *Naval Handbook* (n 33) s 6.2.4; Canada *Joint Doctrine Manual* (n 40) s 1507(5); Turns (n 26) 367.

92 Meron (n 90) 249; Rogers (n 36) 349–350.

93 Greenwood, 'Twilight' (n 57) 65; Françoise Hampson, 'Belligerent Reprisals and the 1977 Protocols to the Geneva Conventions of 1949' (1988) 37 *ICLQ* 818, 829; Frits Kalshoven, 'Belligerent Reprisals Revisited' (1990) 21 *Netherlands YBIL* 43, 70.

94 George H Aldrich, 'Compliance with International Humanitarian Law' (1991) 31(282) *IRRC* 294 302.

95 Kalshoven, *Belligerent Reprisals* (n 22) 25. See further Shane Darcy, 'What Future for the Doctrine of Belligerent Reprisals?' (2002) 5 *YBIHL* 107.

96 US *Naval Handbook* (n 33) s 6.2.4.3.

97 Mark Osiel, *The End of Reciprocity* (CUP 2009) 56; Michael A Newton, 'Reconsidering Reprisals' (2010) 20 *Duke JCIL* 361, 362.

In the context of non-international armed conflicts, the law of armed conflict does not operate on the basis of reciprocity, while the applicability of the doctrine of belligerent reprisals is most uncertain. Although the ICRC had proposed during the drafting of the Geneva Conventions that parties to a non-international armed conflict might observe the full treaties on the basis of reciprocity,[98] Common Article 3 and Additional Protocol II make no mention of reciprocity and apply automatically.[99] The Appeals Chamber of the ICTY has stated that 'internal armed conflict is now the concern of international law without any question of reciprocity'.[100] While the absence of a reciprocity requirement in a legal sense is established,[101] it has been argued that this might deter states from accepting the existence of an internal armed conflict.[102] Views differ as to whether reciprocity acts as an incentive for compliance here, given the imbalance between the parties and the likelihood of the criminalisation of the non-state fighters for taking up arms.[103]

On the matter of belligerent reprisals in non-international armed conflict, the treaty law is silent and it is questioned whether this traditionally inter-state doctrine is even applicable.[104] The ICRC has contended that '[p]arties to non-international armed conflicts do not have the right to resort to belligerent reprisals'.[105] An attempt to introduce a prohibition of reprisals into Additional Protocol II was unsuccessful, and comments by several states' representatives indicated a general view that the doctrine was not relevant in internal conflicts.[106] While belligerent reprisals are not explicitly prohibited in non-international armed conflicts, it cannot be said that they are accordingly permitted. Moreover, measures of reprisal directed by a state against its citizens would undoubtedly run afoul of its obligations under international human rights law. The dubious effectiveness of reprisals as a mean of law enforcement is an additional reason not to import the concept into non-international armed conflicts.[107]

Official rhetoric and scholarly discourse in the aftermath of 11 September 2001 have suggested a renewed role for reciprocity and reprisals in the law of armed conflict. The 'war against terrorism' was said to require 'new thinking in the law of war',[108] which ironically has included attempts to reintroduce the outdated concepts of reciprocity and reprisal. The US Office of

---

98 See Draft Convention for the Protection of Civilian Persons in Time of War, as approved by the XVIIth International Red Cross Conference, *Final Record of the Diplomatic Conference of Geneva of 1949*, vol I, 113, art 2(4).

99 *GCIII Commentary* 35; *AP Commentary* ¶ 1452; CIHL commentary to r 140.

100 *Prosecutor v Hadžihasanović (Interlocutory Appeal on Decision on Joint Challenge to Jurisdiction)* (Case no IT-01-47-PT, ICTY Appeals Chamber, 27 November 2002) ¶ 39.

101 Derek Jinks, 'The Applicability of the Geneva Conventions to the "Global War on Terrorism"' (2005) 46 *Virginia JIL* 165, 191, 193.

102 Provost, 'Reciprocity' (n 5) 393.

103 Compare Report of the Secretary-General to the Security Council on the Protection of Civilians in Armed Conflict, UN Doc S/2009/277 (29 May 2009) ¶ 41; Meron (n 90) 251 with Daphné Richemond-Barak, 'Nonstate Actors in Armed Conflicts: Issues of Distinction and Reciprocity' in William Banks (ed), *New Battlefields/Old Laws: From the Hague Convention to Asymmetric Warfare* (Columbia University Press 2010) 106, 107; Margulies (n 36) 1420.

104 Rogers (n 36) 316; Christopher J Greenwood, 'Reprisals and Reciprocity in the New Law of Armed Conflict' in Michael A Meyer (ed), *Armed Conflict and the New Law* (British Institute of International and Comparative Law 1989) 227, 234; Lindsay Moir, *The Law of Internal Armed Conflict* (CUP 2002) 241.

105 CIHL r 148. See however Turns (n 26) 370.

106 See Shane Darcy, *Collective Responsibility and Accountability under International Law* (Transnational 2007) 166–175.

107 Nicolas Lamp, 'Conceptions of War and Paradigms of Compliance: The "New War" Challenge of International Humanitarian Law' (2011) 16 *JCSL* 225, 249.

108 George W Bush, 'Humane Treatment of Taliban and al Qaeda Detainees' Memorandum from the President (Washington, 7 February 2002) ¶ 1.

Legal Counsel suggested that the Geneva Conventions could be suspended during the Afghanistan conflict if the Taliban were found to be in material breach.[109] John Yoo has emphasised reciprocity, stating that the US observes the Geneva Conventions 'because our opponent does the same with American POWs. That is impossible with al Qaeda.'[110] Colin Powell, however, warned of the danger that denying the application of the Geneva Conventions in Afghanistan would 'reverse over a century of U.S. policy and practice in supporting the Geneva conventions and undermine the protections of the law of war for our troops, both in this specific conflict and in general'.[111] In scholarly writings, reciprocity-based arguments have been used to suggest, for example, that during 'an armed conflict against a terrorist organization that neither accepts nor applies the laws of war, Common Article 2 implies that the State is not bound to accept such laws'.[112] Reprisals have also featured; it has been argued that it would be 'entirely lawful' to execute 'detained unlawful combatants' by way of a reprisal,[113] that reprisals should be permitted against 'semi-civilian' government institutions[114] and that reprisals 'may well be the most moral and humanitarian response to the growing threat of transnational terrorism'.[115]

Reciprocity has been raised as a reason to deny prisoner of war status to certain persons detained in the 'war on terror'. Article 4 of Geneva Convention III requires as a condition for granting such status to members of militias, volunteer corps and organised resistance movements 'belonging to a Party to the conflict' that they conduct operations 'in accordance with the laws and customs of war'.[116] 'To claim the protection of the law', Ruth Wedgwood asserts, 'a side must generally conduct its own military operations in accordance with the laws of war'.[117] The US Office of Legal Counsel considered that al-Qaeda members could not benefit from Article 4 because they 'have clearly demonstrated that they will not follow these basic requirements of lawful warfare'.[118] It was also declared by George W Bush that 'none of the provisions of Geneva apply to our conflict with al-Qaeda in Afghanistan or elsewhere throughout the world', in particular because al-Qaeda was not a High Contracting Party.[119] The US Supreme Court pushed back to some extent by holding that al-Qaeda detainees were to be treated in accordance with Common Article 3.[120]

Scholarly debate has focused on the question of whether the law of armed conflict applies to the 'war on terror', particularly when considered in light of reciprocity.[121] Steven Ratner wrote

---

109 Jay S Bybee, 'Application of Treaties and Laws to al Qaeda and Taliban Detainees' Memorandum for Alberto R Gonzales, Counsel to the President, and William J Haynes II, General Counsel of the Department of Defence (Office of the Assistant Attorney General, Office of Legal Counsel, Department of Justice, 22 January 2002) 10–13.

110 Yoo (n 2). See also Alan Dershowitz, 'The Laws of War weren't Written for this War' *Wall Street Journal* (New York, 12 February 2004).

111 US Department of State, 'Memorandum regarding Draft Decision Memorandum for the President on the Applicability of the Geneva Conventions to the Conflict in Afghanistan' (26 January 2002) 2.

112 Richemond-Barak (n 103) 124.

113 Philip Sutter, 'The Continuing Role for Belligerent Reprisals' (2008) 13 *JCSL* 93, 117; Kalshoven, 'Belligerent Reprisals Revisited' (n 93) 78, 117.

114 Robbie Sabel, 'The Legality of Reciprocity in the War on Terrorism' (2010) 43 *Case Western ILJ* 473, 480–481.

115 Newton (n 97) 369.

116 GCIII art 4(A)(2)(d). See however API art 44.

117 Ruth Wedgwood, 'The Rules of War can't Protect Al-Qaeda' New York Times (New York, 31 December 2001) A11. See also Provost, 'Reciprocity' (n 5) 395.

118 Bybee (n 109) 10.

119 Bush (n 108) ¶ 2(a).

120 *Hamdan v Rumsfeld*, 548 US 557 (2006) 628–631.

121 Jinks (n 101); Posner (n 39) 424. See generally Noam Lubell, 'The War(?) against Al-Qaeda' in Elizabeth Wilmshurst (ed), *International Law and the Classification of Conflicts* (OUP 2012) 421.

that '[w]e cannot have a legal regime where only one side of combatants benefits from the protections of international humanitarian law', although this was not a 'prescription for a free-for-all in the war on terrorism'.[122] In asymmetrical conflicts, reciprocity is seen as particularly problematic. It may not act as an incentive for compliance, given the lack of symmetry between parties in terms of their ability to take prisoners or inflict damage on each other.[123] The premise in much of the literature, that the state is the observant party and the non-state actor the violator,[124] would seem to be an oversimplification given the experience of recent conflicts. As Eyal Benvenisti notes:

> The asymmetric relationship in fact incentivizes both sides to eschew reciprocal considerations: the nonstate actor resorts to terrorism, whereas the stronger regular army is tempted to inflict excessive harm upon noncombatants, to conflate military objectives with killing combatants, and to treat captured combatants as outlaws.[125]

While the law of armed conflict arguably tends to favour the stronger side,[126] and abiding by it might create some disadvantage vis-à-vis a law-breaking opponent, the law is nevertheless 'binding on all parties'.[127] Continued observance by states is recommended, even in the face of breaches, for fear of an even greater fall in observance.[128] Belligerent reprisals would obviously be a perilous option in terms of seeking improved compliance, even aside from the difficult legal questions of whether the doctrine applies in non-international armed conflicts in the first place, and whether the unlawful actions of a state might give a right to reprisal for non-state actors.[129] More desirable suggestions for enhancing respect for the law of armed conflict in such contexts include adopting prisoner-of-war status for members of organised armed groups.[130]

4 Conclusion

The retreat from reciprocity and reprisals in the law of armed conflict has been deliberate and cumulative, steadily restricting the scope for parties to an armed conflict to raise reciprocity in order to avoid legal obligations or for resorting to belligerent reprisals as a means of law enforcement. While reciprocity remains valuable as a practical tool for improving compliance, it is a double-edged sword which can encourage retaliatory action and similar law-breaking and hence is legally limited. The near total outlawing of belligerent reprisals and elimination of reciprocity reinforce the absolute nature of obligations under the law of armed conflict. These developments serve to protect victims of armed conflict and to mitigate conflict by avoiding counter-productive actions of a notoriously degenerative nature.

122 Steven R Ratner, 'The War on Terrorism and International Humanitarian Law' (2006) 14 *Michigan State JIL* 19, 22.
123 Lamp (n 107) 248; Pfanner (n 90) 169; Marco Sassòli, 'The Implementation of International Humanitarian Law: Current and Inherent Challenges' (2007) 10 *YBIHL* 45, 58; Benvenisti, 'The Legal Battle' (n 4) 342.
124 See eg Richemond-Barak (n 103) 122; Osiel (n 97) 1; Sabel (n 114) 473; Dan Belz, 'Is International Humanitarian Law Lapsing into Irrelevance in the War on International Terror?' (2006) 77 *Theoretical Inquiries in Law* 97, 98; Ganesh Sitaraman, 'Counterinsurgency, the War on Terror, and the Laws of War' (2009) 95 *Virginia JIL* 1745, 1748. See however Posner (n 39) 431.
125 Benvenisti, 'Rethinking' (n 90) 545–546. See also Benvenisti, 'The Legal Battle' (n 4) 344.
126 Benvenisti, 'Rethinking' (n 90) 547.
127 Pfanner (n 90) 163.
128 Sitaraman (n 124) 1748, 1827; Belz (n 124) 98.
129 Darcy, *Collective Responsibility* (n 106) 172–175.
130 Provost, 'Asymmetrical Reciprocity' (n 19) 28.

29
State responsibility

Charles Garraway

The issue of state responsibility is one of great importance and diversity. This was one of the first topics adopted by the International Law Commission (ILC) at its first session in 1949. The complexity of the matter however is illustrated by the fact that it was not until 2001 that the Commission was able to adopt the Draft Articles on Responsibility of States for Internationally Wrongful Acts.[1] Even today, those articles have not been adopted in treaty form though it is generally accepted that they represent customary international law.

Articles 1, 2 and 3 of the Draft Articles lay down the general principles of state responsibility. First, there must be a breach of an international obligation. That will be decided by reference to the primary sources such as treaties, customary international law and other sources of international law. Second, that breach must be attributable to a particular state. In principle, this means that the conduct impugned is that of a state's organs of government or its agents. However, there are occasions when the conduct of bodies other than state organs can still be attributable to a state and these are outlined in Articles 8 to 11 of the Draft Articles.

This chapter does not seek to reflect the whole essence of state responsibility across the board. It will concern itself solely with the narrower issue of state responsibility in relation to the law of armed conflict. The armed forces of a state clearly are organs of the state but the law of armed conflict introduced its own rules, long before the ILC took responsibility. However, these rules too are not without their complexity and the subject matter will inevitably cross into other areas of state responsibility. These will be introduced where appropriate but limited in scope to those areas where they impinge on the law of armed conflict and on the conduct of hostilities in general.

1 Early state responsibility

In order to examine this subject, it is necessary to look at the development of the law. Until the attempts to codify the law of armed conflict by way of treaty in the nineteenth century, the law

---

1 Draft Articles on Responsibility of States for Internationally Wrongful Acts, in 'Report of the International Law Commission on the Work of its Fifty-Third Session' UN Doc A/56/10 (November 2001).

was in customary form, unwritten for the most part. War was very much part of international relations but the issue of state responsibility rested primarily on the result of the war. The winner would impose terms on the loser by way of peace treaty or other means. Whole territories changed hands and maps were redrawn. However, responsibility for the conduct of the war was left to the states themselves. International criminal law as we know it today did not exist. War was seen as an offshoot of state sovereignty. As such, the act of going to war was a right of a sovereign state. Aggression, though rife, was not considered as a 'wrong' until the twentieth century.

The codification of the law of armed conflict proceeded down two different but complementary strands. The first, 'Hague Law', dealing principally with the conduct of hostilities, was state-centric and took fully into account the interests of states. It sought to strike a balance between the necessities of war and the laws of humanity.[2] The second strand, 'Geneva law', which grew out of the vision of Henri Dunant after his experiences at the battle of Solferino in 1859, was more victim orientated. This strand could be described as seeking to maximise the protection given to those not, or no longer, taking part in hostilities. The tension between these two approaches, one involving a balancing act between military necessity and humanity and the other seeming to recognise that there is a 'line in the sand'[3] when military necessity can never outweigh humanity, has been apparent in the law ever since.

The early treaties under 'Hague law' were primarily limited to single issues illustrated perhaps by the St Petersburg Declaration itself. No enforcement mechanisms or issues of state responsibility appear in the treaties themselves. However, the Hague Peace Conferences of 1899 and 1907 were wider in scope and hence did look at issues of state responsibility. The earlier Oxford Manual on the Laws of War on Land had made it plain that, for example, in relation to prisoners of war, 'the government into whose hands prisoners have fallen is charged with their maintenance'.[4] However, enforcement was still seen as a matter for domestic law.[5] Whilst the 1899 Hague Convention (II) with Respect to the Laws and Customs of War on Land did not advance on that, the 1907 Convention IV on the same subject did contain a ground-breaking provision in Article 3. This provided that '[a] belligerent party which violates the provisions of the said Regulations shall, if the case demands, be liable to pay compensation. It shall be responsible for all acts committed by persons forming part of its armed forces.'[6] This introduced a form of state civil responsibility for the actions of its armed forces, state agents.

'Geneva law', on the other hand, remained more focused on the individual and did not contain any such provision. For example, the 1929 Geneva Convention for the Amelioration of the Condition of the Wounded and Sick in Armies in the Field placed a number of obligations on governments, including putting an end to violations. However, this was still seen as a matter of penal law. State responsibility was still governed by the embryonic general principles under customary law. These had begun to take shape after the First World War.

---

2 Declaration Renouncing the Use, in Time of War, of Explosive Projectiles under 400 Grammes Weight ('St Petersburg Declaration') (11 December 1868) 138 CTS 297.

3 See speech by Jacob Kellenberger on the 140th Anniversary of the 1868 St Petersburg Declaration (28 November 2008), www.icrc.org/eng/resources/documents/misc/st-petersburg-declaration-281108.htm.

4 Oxford Manual on the Laws of War on Land (9 September 1880) art 69, www.icrc.org/ihl.nsf/FULL/140?OpenDocument.

5 'If any of the foregoing rules be violated, the offending parties should be punished, after a judicial hearing, by the belligerent in whose hands they are' ibid pt III preamble.

6 Hague Convention (IV) regarding the Laws and Customs of Land Warfare (18 October 1907) 205 CTS 277, art 3.

2 The two World Wars

The Treaty of Versailles, at the end of the First World War, was controversial in that, apart from the usual terms which included the dismemberment of the German Empire and its redistribution amongst the victorious Allies, there was a section of the treaty dealing specifically with reparations. This began with a general article (Article 231) stating that:

> The Allied and Associated Governments affirm and Germany accepts the responsibility of Germany and her allies for causing all the loss and damage to which the Allied and Associated Governments and their nationals have been subjected as a consequence of the war imposed upon them by the aggression of Germany and her allies.[7]

It will be noted that Germany was to be held responsible for *all* the loss and damage, regardless of the legality of acts under the law of armed conflict. A Reparation Commission was established[8] and the harshness of Article 231 was partly alleviated by Annex I to Section I which outlined the various heads of damages under which compensation could be claimed.

Whereas clause (1) of the Annex made Germany responsible for *all* damage to civilians arising from belligerent operations by either side, clause (4) was more precise in covering 'maltreatment of prisoners of war'. It would appear therefore that losses incurred through the simple fact of becoming a prisoner of war would not lead to compensation in that there had to be some form of mistreatment.

The reparation terms imposed upon Germany amounted to over $200 billion at 2014 prices. Whilst therefore the severity of the terms to some extent reflected the traditional relationship of victor and vanquished, there was at least lip service, in the reference to 'maltreatment of prisoners of war', to recognition that correct application of the law of armed conflict should not be penalised.

The Second World War was different in that it resulted in the complete disintegration of the Third Reich. At the end of the war, there was no German state. The outcome of the Potsdam Conference was not a treaty in the sense of Versailles but a series of terms imposed upon Germany by the victorious Allies.[9] Germany itself was not represented. Reparations mainly centred on the transfer of manufacturing capability, principally to the Soviet Union. The Paris Peace Treaties of 1947 laid down sums to be paid in reparations by other Axis powers, but these were fixed sums and not premised on particular categories of loss. Germany subsequently paid a substantial sum to Israel as Holocaust reparations, but again this was not linked to specific instances.

There was considerable fear amongst the Allies that imposing too severe an economic burden on Germany could result in a further rise in extremism as had resulted after the First World War. As a result, in the London Debt Agreement of 1953, there was a general deferment of debt payments until the conclusion of a Peace Treaty.[10] Such a treaty was not concluded until 1990[11] and it is interesting to note that the final payment in relation to the First World War debts was not

---

7 Treaty of Peace between the Allied and Associated Powers and Germany (Treaty of Versailles) (28 June 1919) 225 CTS 188, art 231.
8 Ibid art 233.
9 See the Berlin (Potsdam) Conference, Protocol of the Proceedings (1 August 1945), avalon.law.yale.edu/20th_century/decade17.asp.
10 Agreement on German External Debts (27 February 1953) 333 UNTS 3.
11 Treaty on the Final Settlement with Respect to Germany (12 September 1990) 1696 UNTS 115.

made until 2010.[12] In fact the 1990 Treaty on the Final Settlement with Respect to Germany contained no reference to reparations and this has opened the door to subsequent claims by affected groups.

In the case of Japan, the San Francisco Treaty dealt with reparations but recognised that 'the resources of Japan are not presently sufficient, if it is to maintain a viable economy, to make complete reparation for all such damage and suffering and at the same time meet its other obligations'.[13] Interestingly, there was a waiver clause in that

[e]xcept as otherwise provided in the present Treaty, the Allied Powers waive all reparations claims of the Allied Powers, other claims of the Allied Powers and their nationals arising out of any actions taken by Japan and its nationals in the course of the prosecution of the war, and claims of the Allied Powers for direct military costs of occupation.[14]

A specific clause was inserted dealing with prisoners of war whereby funds were to be transferred to the ICRC for distribution to 'appropriate national agencies'.[15] This also was not to prove the end of the matter.

3 Post-war developments

The Cold War inevitably stalled any further developments in this area. Treaty law was scarce and limited primarily to 'Geneva law' and to arms control measures. Insofar as 'Geneva law' was concerned, the core development was the adoption of the four Geneva Conventions of 1949. However, again, they contained little on state responsibility as such. States, in Common Article 1, undertook to 'respect and to ensure respect' for the Conventions 'in all circumstances'.[16] However, the Conventions did not in any way affect the influence of Article 3 of the 1907 Hague Convention. Their concentration was more on penal sanctions with the introduction of the 'grave breach' regime. An important article was, however, also included in all four Conventions providing that: 'No High Contracting Party shall be allowed to absolve itself or any other High Contracting Party of any liability incurred by itself or by another High Contracting Party in respect of breaches referred to in the preceding Article.'[17] The 'preceding Article' deals not only with grave breaches but with 'all acts contrary to the provisions' of the relevant Convention.

The ICRC *Commentary* explains that the purpose of this article, as put forward by the proposers – the Italian delegation – was that '[t]he State ... was responsible for breaches of the Convention, and could not refuse to admit liability on the grounds that the authors of the breaches had been punished. It was, for example, still bound to pay compensation.'[18] The article was only narrowly approved and, despite the Italian explanation, the meaning is not altogether clear.

---

12 See Allan Hall, 'Germany ends World War One Reparations after 92 Years with £59m Final Payment' *Daily Mail* (29 September 2010).
13 Treaty of Peace with Japan (8 September 1951) 136 UNTS 45, art 14.
14 Ibid art 14(b).
15 Ibid art 16.
16 GCI–IV common art 1.
17 GCI art 51; GCII art 52; GCIII art 131; GCIV art 148.
18 *GCI Commentary* 373.

The ICRC view is stated in the *Commentary*:

> In our opinion, the purpose of Article 51 is to prevent the defeated party from being compelled in an armistice agreement or peace treaty to abandon all claims due for infractions committed by persons in the service of the victor. In this matter of material reparation for infractions of the Convention it is not possible, at any rate as the law at present stands, to imagine an injured party being able to bring an action individually against the State in whose service the author of the infraction was. Only a State can put forward such claims against another State. These claims fall in the ordinary way into the category of what are called 'war reparations'. It would seem unfair that individuals should be punished, if the State in whose behalf – and often on the instructions of which – they have acted were absolved of all responsibility.[19]

The view of the law outlined above has been challenged in more modern times.

The 1954 Hague Convention on the Protection of Cultural Property also concentrated primarily on penal sanctions.[20] However, this does not present the full story as the First Protocol to the 1954 Convention[21] dealt with the export and sale of cultural property from occupied territory. The Protocol imposed an obligation (Article 1) on states 'to prevent the exportation, from a territory occupied by it during an armed conflict' of cultural property. There follows a series of other state responsibilities including an obligation to return property exported in breach of Article 1 and to 'pay an indemnity to the holders in good faith of any cultural property' returned under the terms of the Protocol.

The issue of return and indemnity has dogged the art world since the Second World War, particularly in relation to art looted or even 'purchased' from Jewish victims of the Holocaust.[22] The majority of these cases involve private participants, including museums, though in the case of national museums there is a major state interest.

The 1977 Additional Protocols to the 1949 Geneva Conventions sought to bring together 'Hague law' and 'Geneva law'. The grave breach regime in respect of international armed conflict was expanded and the provision contained in the 1907 Hague Convention rephrased in Article 91.[23]

The Commentary seeks to explain how this in fact expands the 1907 Hague Convention because of the changes in the law since that time. It pointed out the difference that the UN Charter had made to responsibility under the *jus ad bellum* but claimed:

> However, this aspect of the problem should remain separate from that of violations committed during the course of the conflict itself, which may have been committed by any one of the Parties involved. The main merit of the present Article 91 is to affirm this, as the above-mentioned article common to the four Conventions had also done.[24]

---

19 Ibid.
20 Convention for the Protection of Cultural Property in the Event of Armed Conflict (14 May 1954) 249 UNTS 240.
21 Protocol for the Protection of Cultural Property in the Event of Armed Conflict (14 May 1954) 249 UNTS 358.
22 See *US v Portrait of Wally*, 105 F Supp 2d 288 (SDNY 2000). For a fuller account of this and other cases, see Thérèse O'Donnell, 'The Restitution of Holocaust Looted Art and Transitional Justice: The Perfect Storm or the Raft of the Medusa?' (2011) 22 *EJIL* 1, 49–80.
23 API art 91.
24 *AP Commentary* ¶ 3650.

The Commentary reflects the law at the time in stating that:

> Apart from exceptional cases, persons with a foreign nationality who have been wronged by the unlawful conduct of a Party to the conflict should address themselves to their own government, which will submit their complaints to the Party or Parties which committed the violation. However, since 1945 a tendency has emerged to recognize the exercise of rights by individuals.[25]

We will see later how that tendency has now developed further. The Commentary also looked at wider compensation and stated that:

> It therefore seems possible that a Party to the conflict could be liable to pay compensation even in a case where no particular violation of the rules of the Conventions and the Protocol, or of another rule of the law of armed conflict, can be imputed to it. However, such liability could not be based on the present article.[26]

Whilst we are still some way from such a strict liability rule, there are growing demands for it.[27]

4 Growth of human rights law

Whilst the law of armed conflict remained focused primarily on a criminal response to violations, a new branch of public international law was developing which was directly concerned with the relationship between states and those within their jurisdiction – human rights law. Energised by the UN, human rights law was seen in its early days as part of the law of peace with no application in time of war where the law of armed conflict remained supreme. However, even a cursory inspection of the actual wording of the various human rights treaties showed that this was not a view that would stand the test of time or critical analysis. Whilst in the Universal Declaration of Human Rights and the International Covenants, there is a noticeable absence of the word 'war', apart from a reference to 'propaganda',[28] the European Convention on Human Rights was different. Article 15, the derogation clause, specifically provided that '[i]n time of war or other public emergency threatening the life of the nation', certain derogations could be made.[29] The implication was that, without derogation, the Convention continued to operate, even in time of war. Of course, in 1950, when the Convention was adopted, 'war' would still be looked upon as inter-state war, international armed conflict. Non-international conflict would be 'other public emergency'. However, it was clear for Europeans from an early stage that human rights law continued to have some applicability in times of armed conflict, both international and non-international.

As has been seen from the ICRC *Commentary* to Additional Protocol I, compensation for violations of the laws of armed conflict was principally seen as a state-on-state matter. Those with claims were usually required to submit them through their government. However, human rights law offered a new channel where, in some circumstances, individual claims could be made

---

25 Ibid ¶ 3657.
26 Ibid ¶ 3661.
27 See the campaign by Center for Civilians in Conflict, civiliansinconflict.org.
28 ICCPR art 20(1).
29 ECHR art 15.

directly against offending states. This new channel was to take some time to develop but the end of the Cold War reopened the debate, not only in relation to existing conflicts but also in relation to the supposed settlement at the end of the Second World War. No longer was there a view that war was a matter for states and that it was therefore for states to decide on any final settlement. Individual rights were also now coming to the fore.

5 Iraq War 1990–1991

However, two conflicts at the end of the twentieth century still reflected the old system. First was the Iraq war of 1990–1991, when, following the invasion and annexation of Kuwait by Iraq under the rule of Saddam Hussein, a multi-national force, led by the US and under the authority of Security Council resolutions, liberated Kuwait and restored the previous government. In April 1991, the Security Council passed a resolution which, *inter alia*, reaffirmed Iraq's liability for the consequences of the invasion and occupation of Kuwait.[30]

The Security Council established a fund for these reparations and appointed a Commission to administer the fund.[31] The Commission operated on the basis of a Report by the Secretary-General[32] which provided that the primary method of submitting claims would be through a state.[33] However, it was realised early on that a large number of people, particularly Palestinians, would be disenfranchised by a strict interpretation of these rules and so a decision was taken to allow an 'appropriate person, authority or body' to act, in lieu of a state, for such claimants.[34]

Whilst the general criteria for claims delineated by the Commission seemed to follow the traditional form that Iraq was liable for all the consequences of the invasion and occupation, whether legal or illegal under the law of armed conflict, the specific listings, though not exclusive, were not so clear.[35] For example, 'illegal detention' was covered but what of 'legal detention'?[36] What was the position of members of the Allied Coalition armed forces who had been killed, wounded or captured? The Governing Council considered this and ruled that there was no general eligibility for compensation but that prisoners of war who had suffered 'mistreatment in violation of international humanitarian law' could lodge claims.[37] This allowance for victims of illegality recognised a distinction between legal and illegal acts under the law of armed conflict.

The UN Compensation Commission received approximately 2.7 million claims seeking approximately US$352.5 billion in compensation for death, injury, loss of or damage to property, commercial claims and claims for environmental damage resulting from Iraq's unlawful invasion and occupation of Kuwait in 1991. As at 24 July 2014, almost $50 billion had been paid out to claimants.[38]

---

30 UNSC Res 687 (3 April 1991) ¶ 16.
31 UNSC Res 692 (20 May 1991).
32 Report of the Secretary General Pursuant to Paragraph 19 of Security Council Resolution 687 (1991), UN Doc S/22559 (2 May 1991).
33 Ibid ¶ 21.
34 Guidelines Relating to Paragraph 19 of the Criteria for Expedited Processing of Urgent Claims, Governing Council of the UN Compensation Commission, UN Doc S/AC.26/1991/5 (23 October 1991).
35 Criteria for Expedited Processing of Urgent Claims, Governing Council of the UN Compensation Commission, UN Doc S/AC.26/1991/1 (2 August 1991) ¶ 18.
36 Ibid.
37 Eligibility for Compensation of Members of the Allied Coalition Armed Forces, Governing Council of the UN Compensation Commission, UN Doc S/AC.26/1992/11 (26 June 1992).
38 For the current position, see UN Compensation Commission, 'Summary of Awards and Current Status of Payments' (21 January 2016), www.uncc.ch/summary-awards-and-current-status-payments.

6 The Ethiopia/Eritrea War 1998–2000

The second conflict that resulted in a claims commission being established was that between Ethiopia and Eritrea from 1998 to 2000. An agreement was signed in Algiers in December 2000 that 'The parties shall permanently terminate military hostilities between themselves.'[39] The Agreement also provided for a Border Commission and a Claims Commission.[40] The mandate of the Commission was unusual in that it was tasked to look into 'violations of international humanitarian law including the 1949 Geneva Conventions, or other violations of international law'.[41] Notably, 'claims arising from the cost of military operations, preparing for military operations, or the use of force' were explicitly excluded unless they involved violations of international humanitarian law.[42] This approach seemed to recognise that only violations of international law could be considered and there was no 'winner takes all' principle at work.

There followed a series of state to state claims and a number of hearings on different issues until the Commission concluded its work in 2009 with its final awards of damages. The Final Awards granted compensation in respect of claims by both Eritrea and Ethiopia for violations of international law previously found by the Commission in its 15 earlier Awards on liability, rendered between 1 July 2003 and 19 December 2005. Eritrea had claimed damages under a number of headings including loss of personal and business property, damage to or destruction of buildings, consequential damages, damage to cultural property, prisoners of war, rape and specifically the displacement of the population of Awgaro.[43] There were also a number of individual claims, as well as more remote headings of damage.

Ethiopia also made claims against Eritrea. However, whereas Eritrea had effectively limited itself to claims under *jus in bello*, Ethiopia also brought claims under *jus ad bellum*. The Commission limited itself to a finding on a single breach of the *jus ad bellum* limited as to place and time.[44] This narrow ruling meant that the Commission had to seek to identify the damages which were proximate to that particular act. This decision of the Commission to tackle the *jus ad bellum* issue at all has been criticised as outside its mandate.[45] It was argued that the 'Claims Commission's powers were designed to cover claims for violations of international humanitarian law or other violations of international law committed during the conflict'.[46]

In its various findings, the Commission made a number of rulings in relation to applicable law, particularly on the extension of customary law. Certainly, the jurisprudence of the Commission will be important in future examinations of how customary law in this field is developing.

In total, the Commission awarded $174,036,520 to Ethiopia and $161,455,000 to Eritrea plus an additional $2,065,865 for individual Eritrean claimants.

---

39 Agreement for the Resettlement of Displaced Persons, as well as Rehabilitation and Peacebuilding (Ethiopia–Eritrea) (12 December 2000) 2138 UNTS 93, art 1.

40 Ibid arts 4 and 5. See the Permanent Court of Arbitration, 'Eritrea-Ethiopia Claims Commission' (17 August 2009), www.pca-cpa.org/showpage.asp?pag_id=1151.

41 Ethiopia–Eritrea Agreement (n 39) art 5(1).

42 Ibid.

43 *Eritrea v Ethiopia (Final Award, Eritrea's Damages Claim)* (2009) 26 RIAA 505.

44 *Eritrea v Ethiopia (Final Award, Ethiopia's Damages Claim)* (2009) 26 RIAA 631, ¶ 282.

45 Christine Gray, 'The Eritrea/Ethiopia Claims Commission Oversteps its Boundaries: A Partial Award?' (2006) 17 *EJIL* 4, 699–721.

46 Ibid 704.

7 Domestic litigation

The end of the Cold War also led to a new trend. The settlements reached at the end of the Second World War were reopened in private litigation. For many years, those who had been prisoners of war of the Japanese had sought further compensation over and above that agreed between states. However, litigation in Japanese courts was continually blocked by government citation of Article 14(b) of the Multilateral Treaty of Peace with Japan.[47]

Japan pointed out that it had transferred some $27 billion in state to state settlements and therefore it was for the recipient states to decide how the money should be dispersed internally. Both Canada and the UK subsequently made payments to surviving prisoners.[48] Similar pressure on Germany led to the German Parliament, in 2000, passing a law setting up a $5 billion claim fund to pay Nazi-era slave and forced labourers, those experimented on and some other Holocaust-related claims.[49] This law did not pay money direct to individuals but to 'partner organisations'.[50] However, this law was deemed not to apply to prisoners of war, who were entitled to be put to work by the detaining power. A number of Italian prisoners, who had been transferred to Germany, denied prisoner of war status and forced to work as slave labour found themselves disqualified on the basis that, whatever had been the Nazi view of their status, they remained prisoners of war in law and therefore were excluded from lodging claims to the fund.

A number of these prisoners began proceedings in the Italian courts against Germany but were faced with claims of sovereign immunity by Germany. The applicants' answer was that such immunity did not apply in cases where the act complained of constituted an international crime. There followed a series of cases which made their way eventually to the Italian Court of Cassation which ruled that the Italian courts did have jurisdiction over the claims against Germany. The decision was based on the argument that, in cases of crimes under international law, the jurisdictional immunity of states should be set aside.[51]

This led to Germany instigating proceedings before the ICJ arguing that

> by allowing civil claims based on violations of international humanitarian law by the German Reich during World War II from September 1943 to May 1945, to be brought against the Federal Republic of Germany, [Italy] committed violations of obligations under international law in that it has failed to respect the jurisdictional immunity which the Federal Republic of Germany enjoys under international law.[52]

Greece applied to intervene following a similar claim in the Greek courts which, though successful, had been unenforceable under Greek law. The Greek claimants had then sought to enforce the judgment before the Italian courts and obtained a legal charge over a villa, property of the German state, near Lake Como.

Italy based its defence in the ICJ on two main arguments. First, Germany was not entitled to sovereign immunity before the Italian courts on the basis of *acta jure imperii* where the torts or

---

47 Treaty of Peace with Japan (n 13).
48 In relation to the UK, see Statement to the House of Commons by Dr Lewis Moonie, Parliamentary Under-Secretary of State for Defence, HC Deb 7 November 2000, vol 356, col 159.
49 Gesetz zur Errichtung Einer Stiftung 'Erinnerung, Verantwortung und Zukunft' (2 August 2000) *BGBl* 2000 I 1263.
50 See *Jurisdictional Immunities of the State (Germany v Italy; Greece Intervening)* [2012] ICJ Rep 143, ¶ 26.
51 Ibid ¶ 29.
52 Ibid ¶ 15.

delicts occasioning death, personal injury or damage to property were committed on the territory of the forum state; second, that, irrespective of where the relevant acts took place, Germany was not entitled to immunity because those acts involved the most serious violations of rules of international law of a peremptory character for which no alternative means of redress was available.[53]

The case gave the opportunity to the Court to review the history of sovereign immunity and in particular how it had developed since the end of the Cold War. It was accepted that the Court must look for a customary law norm to provide an exception to state immunity for *acta jure imperii*.[54]

The Court, after an extensive examination of treaty law, was not satisfied that such a norm existed. The Court also examined domestic law statutes dealing with sovereign immunity and, again, although there were differences between the way in which these statutes dealt with the subject, the Court, even in those cases where there was no general exclusion for acts of armed forces, could find no situation where the legislation had been applied in a case involving the armed forces of a foreign state, acting in the context of an armed conflict.[55]

The judgments of national courts also seemed to confirm the existence of state sovereignty in such cases. The Court examined a large number of cases from a broad spread of countries, not just involving acts arising from the Second World War. In particular, in relation to Italy's second ground, the Court found numerous cases where '[a]rguments to the effect that international law no longer required State immunity in cases of allegations of serious violations of international human rights law, war crimes or crimes against humanity have been rejected by the courts'.[56] These included cases in Canada, France, Slovenia, New Zealand, Poland and the UK. The Court pointed out that:

> against the background of a century of practice in which almost every peace treaty or post-war settlement has involved either a decision not to require the payment of reparations or the use of lump sum settlements and set-offs, it is difficult to see that international law contains a rule requiring the payment of full compensation to each and every individual victim as a rule accepted by the international community of States as a whole as one from which no derogation is permitted.[57]

In conclusion, the Court upheld the claim of Germany that 'the action of the Italian courts in denying Germany the immunity to which the Court has held it was entitled under customary international law constitutes a breach of the obligations owed by the Italian State to Germany'.[58] Although this case seemed to confirm state sovereignty, it was not without dissent. The decision on the immunity of Germany before the Italian courts was reached by twelve votes to three and, as Judge Koroma pointed out whilst voting with the majority:

> Given that the Court's task is to apply the existing law, nothing in the Court's Judgment today prevents the continued evolution of the law on State immunity. In the past century, the law on State immunity has evolved considerably in a manner that has significantly

---

53 Ibid ¶ 61.
54 Ibid ¶ 64.
55 Ibid ¶ 71.
56 Ibid ¶ 85.
57 Ibid ¶ 94.
58 Ibid ¶ 107.

circumscribed the circumstances in which a State is entitled to immunity. It is possible that further exceptions to State immunity will continue to develop in the future. The Court's Judgment applies the law as it exists today.[59]

Judge Keith also, whilst agreeing with the majority, warned that the doctrine of sovereign immunity was 'narrowing'.[60] However, he also laid down the practical reasoning behind the current system of dealing with reparations on a state to state basis.[61]

Those judges who dissented did so for the most part on the grounds that the narrowing of sovereign immunity had already passed the point where states could claim immunity in such cases of admitted international crimes.[62] The decision of the ICJ was acknowledged and followed in subsequent domestic proceedings in Italy.[63]

8 International litigation

But whilst the ICJ seems to have closed the door on individual claims against foreign states proceeding through the domestic courts of the state whose nationals wish to make the claims, the Court has not entirely ruled out holding states responsible for breaches of the law of armed conflict. Indeed, in a series of cases, it has taken an increasingly strong line in relation to violations of the laws of war and human rights law. The trend started with the seminal *Nicaragua* case where the Court held that the US was 'in breach of its obligations under customary international law not to use force against another State'.[64] However, the Court also held that, whilst the US had encouraged the commission by the Contra forces of acts contrary to general principles of humanitarian law,

> [f]or this conduct to give rise to legal responsibility of the United States, it would in principle have to be proved that that State had effective control of the military or paramilitary operations in the course of which the alleged violations were committed.[65]

In this case, the issue was the liability of a state for the actions of non-state actors. The 'effective control' test laid down in the *Nicaragua* case later seemed to be amended by the ICTY in the *Tadić* case.[66] The ICTY Appeals Chamber found the 'effective control' test 'unconvincing'.[67] The Chamber sought to apply a more flexible test.

A distinction was drawn between acts performed by private individuals engaged by a state to perform specific illegal acts where the 'effective control' test would be appropriate, and actions of an organised and hierarchically structured group where a lesser standard, that of 'overall control', would suffice. The Chamber said:

---

59 Ibid Separate Opinion of Judge Koroma, ¶ 7.
60 Ibid Separate Opinion of Judge Keith, ¶ 3.
61 Ibid ¶ 18.
62 Ibid Dissenting Opinion of Judge Cançado Trindade, ¶ 2.
63 Criminal Proceedings against Albers, Court of Cassation (2012) 95 *Rivista di Diritto Internazionale* 1196.
64 *Military and Paramilitary Activities in and against Nicaragua (Nicaragua v US)* [1986] ICJ Rep 14, ¶ 292(4).
65 Ibid ¶ 115.
66 *Prosecutor v Tadić* (Case no IT-94-1-A, ICTY Appeals Chamber, 15 July 1999).
67 Ibid ¶ 116

In order to attribute the acts of a military or paramilitary group to a State, it must be proved that the State wields overall control over the group, not only by equipping and financing the group, but also by coordinating or helping in the general planning of its military activity. Only then can the State be held internationally accountable for any misconduct of the group. However, it is not necessary that, in addition, the State should also issue, either to the head or to members of the group, instructions for the commission of specific acts contrary to international law.[68]

The ICJ, however, did not accept this criticism of its jurisprudence. Whilst in the case of *Democratic Republic of the Congo (DRC) v Uganda*,[69] the issue did not strictly arise as the Court was primarily dealing with the actions of Ugandan forces operating in the DRC, the issue arose again, in more direct form, in the case of *Bosnia v Serbia*.[70] This related to the application of the Genocide Convention of 9 December 1948. Here the Court had to consider the responsibility of Serbia for the massacre at Srebrenica. There was no evidence to show direct involvement by the army of the then Federal Republic of Yugoslavia and it was accepted that neither the Republika Srpska nor the VRS (the army of the Republika Srpska) were *de jure* organs of the FRY or could be equated as such.[71] However, the Court went on to consider as a separate question 'whether, in the specific circumstances surrounding the events at Srebrenica the perpetrators of genocide were acting on the Respondent's instructions or under its direction or control'.[72] This brought in the test of 'effective control' previously laid down in the *Nicaragua* case. The Court here examined the *Tadić* judgment but felt unable to accept it. Whilst it did not reject the *Tadić* test of 'overall control' for the purposes of deciding whether or not a conflict was international, the Court considered that the test

has the major drawback of broadening the scope of State responsibility well beyond the fundamental principle governing the law of international responsibility: a State is responsible only for its own conduct, that is to say the conduct of persons acting, on whatever basis, on its behalf.[73]

It therefore reaffirmed the test of 'effective control' as laid down in the *Nicaragua* case and was not satisfied that the test was met in this case.

It should be noted that this judgment by the Court rested on the specific wording of the Genocide Convention but the ruling on control will apply in wider circumstances. These cases show that the ICJ is prepared to hold states responsible for breaches of the law of armed conflict and human rights law committed by their own state agents and, where the test of 'effective control' is met, by others.

---

68 Ibid ¶ 131.
69 *Armed Activities on the Territory of the Congo (Democratic Republic of the Congo v Uganda)* [2005] ICJ Rep 116.
70 *Application of the Convention on the Prevention and Punishment of the Crime of Genocide (Bosnia and Herzegovina v Serbia and Montenegro)* [2007] ICJ Rep 43.
71 Ibid ¶ 386.
72 Ibid ¶ 397.
73 Ibid ¶ 406.

9 Human rights litigation

Whilst the ICJ has been dealing with inter-state claims, individuals have been finding new ways around the limits imposed by sovereign immunity. The vehicle used has been human rights law. The general applicability of human rights law and its relationship with the law of armed conflict is dealt with elsewhere[74] and so it is not necessary to go into detail here. Suffice it to say for these purposes that there is now little doubt that human rights law and the law of armed conflict both operate during times of armed conflict, though the exact nature of the relationship between the two is not yet entirely clear.

Many violations of the law of armed conflict are also human rights violations and so, by taking advantage of the overlap between the two bodies of law, applicants have managed to find a means of holding states responsible for violations of the law of armed conflict by use of human rights mechanisms. The difficulty is that not all violations of human rights are necessarily violations of the law of armed conflict and thus there is a developing risk that the ECtHR may find a violation of human rights law where the conduct impugned would be legitimate under the law of armed conflict.

The Court has already faced these difficulties in relation to non-international armed conflict. In a number of cases involving Chechnya, the Court was faced with a dilemma. The Russian Federation refused to acknowledge the existence of an armed conflict or to derogate from the Convention itself. The Court stated that

> no martial law and no state of emergency has been declared in Chechnya and no derogation has been made under Article 15 of the Convention. . . . The operation in question therefore has to be judged against a normal legal background. . . . The massive use of indiscriminate weapons . . . cannot be considered compatible with the standard of care prerequisite to an operation of this kind involving the use of force by State agents.[75]

The problem here is that the situation in Chechnya involved high intensity conflict including aerial bombardment. It might be thought somewhat unrealistic to judge this 'against a normal legal background'. Nevertheless, on the facts of the cases, it is unlikely that the conclusions would have been any different whether the reasoning was based on human rights law, as it was, or the law of armed conflict.

For non-international armed conflicts, the issue of 'jurisdiction' is normally moot but it arises directly in international armed conflict and in those non-international armed conflicts where the armed forces of a state are operating outside their own territory. As has been outlined already, the extension of 'jurisdiction' has led to a succession of cases arising from operations by the British armed forces in Iraq from 2003 onwards. A number of the cases arise from allegations that inquiries into deaths occasioned by the armed forces have not been adequately investigated.[76] This avoids any need for the Court to examine the death itself. However, some cases[77] have involved detention and it is here that there might be a clash between human rights law and the law of armed conflict. Article 5 of the European Convention, on the right to liberty, states that '[n]o one shall be deprived of his liberty' save in certain specified circumstances.[78] There is no mention in Article 5 of detention under the Geneva Conventions, either of prisoners of war

---

74 See Noam Lubell and Nancie Prud'homme, 'Impact of human rights law' ch 6 in this volume.
75 *Isayeva v Russia* (App no 57950/00, ECtHR, 24 February 2005) ¶ 191.
76 *Al-Skeini et al v UK* (App no 55721/07, ECtHR Grand Chamber, 7 July 2011).
77 *Al-Jedda v UK* (App no 27021/08, ECtHR Grand Chamber, 7 July 2011).
78 ECHR art 5.

or internees. In Iraq, there had been no attempt by the UK to derogate from the Convention and so the Court had to consider again to what extent they could take into account the law of armed conflict. The Court appeared to look to see if the law of armed conflict imposed an 'obligation' to detain and in holding that detention, certainly under Convention IV, was a 'measure of last resort' and not an obligation, the Court held that the human rights standards continued to apply. The UK does not appear to have placed any heavy reliance on the law of armed conflict in the pleadings, preferring to base the case on Security Council Resolutions, but the possibility of a conflict of laws is raised here as both in cases of detention and, more importantly, in relation to the use of force, the law of armed conflict does not impose 'obligations' either to detain or to use force – the law merely permits such actions. Whether that is sufficient to dislodge human rights obligations remains to be seen.

In the case of *Hassan v United Kingdom*, the Court dealt directly with the interplay between the law of armed conflict and human rights law in relation to detention in international armed conflict indicating that they would be prepared to 'read in' to the Convention authority to detain under the Third or Fourth Geneva Conventions of 1949, whether or not there was a formal derogation in place, provided that the state specifically pleaded such a case. The court would not accept this *proprio motu*.[79]

There are a number of cases due to be heard by the Court arising from the Russia–Georgia conflict and the relationship between human rights law and the law of armed conflict will be tested to the full there.

10 Conclusions

It will be seen that state responsibility for violations of the law of armed conflict is at present in a state of flux. Whilst such responsibility is acknowledged and has been for a long time, it is the means of enforcing that responsibility that is at issue. The traditional view that this is a matter of inter-state relations and that individuals have no rights of their own to pursue claims is under challenge. Whilst the ICJ appears, for the moment, to have upheld that particular view of state sovereignty in *Germany v Italy*, that is being increasingly bypassed in recent times by the use of human rights mechanisms to obtain individual redress. However, human rights law and the law of armed conflict are not the same and the use of such fora is placing strains on the relationship between the two branches of public international law. But until such time as there is a mechanism whereby individual claims arising from allegations of violations of the law of armed conflict can be litigated as such, human rights courts will continue to fill this function.

79 *Hassan v UK* (App no 27950/09, ECtHR Grand Chamber, 16 September 2014).

30

Reparations for violations in armed conflict and the emerging practice of making amends

*Bruce Oswald and Bethany Wellington**

A fundamental principle of humanity is recognising that victims have rights. These rights are especially important in situations of armed conflict because victims are vulnerable to death, physical or psychological harm, loss of income and damage to their property or the environment they live in. Such harm might arise from violations of international humanitarian law (IHL) or international human rights law (IHRL) or from the acts considered necessary and proportional to achieving the military aim. Providing victims with measures to deal with the harm committed is important from a number of perspectives, including the need to deter future violations, protect the interests of victims, realise the rights victims are entitled to, and work towards transitional justice and post-conflict development.[1]

The term 'reparations', in the context of IHL, is 'meant to cover measures that seek to eliminate all the harmful consequences of a violation of rules of international law applicable in armed conflict and to re-establish the situation that would have existed if the violation had not occurred'.[2] It is now settled as a matter of law that a state that has committed a serious violation of IHL is responsible to make reparations for the injury caused by that violation. There are numerous mechanisms through which reparations can be made. As a minimum these include restitution, compensation and satisfaction. However, there are a number of issues concerning reparations that remain unsettled, including whether individuals may claim for violations of IHL or whether claims must be made through states; whether claims are only limited to serious

---

* The authors are very grateful to Ms Carla Ferstman, Ms Sarah Holewinski and Ms Clara Jordan-Baird for their comments concerning this chapter. Bruce Oswald remains grateful to Ms Liz Saltnes for her support.

1 See eg Report of the Secretary-General on the Rule of Law and Transitional Justice in Conflict and Post-Conflict Societies, UN Doc S/2004/616 (23 August 2004) ¶ 54; Report of the Secretary-General on the Rule of Law and Transitional Justice in Conflict and Post-Conflict Societies, UN Doc S/2011/634 (12 October 2011), pt IV, ¶¶ 53 and 68; *Prosecutor v Lubanga (Decision Establishing the Principles and Procedures to be Applied to Reparations)* (Case no ICC-01/04-01/06, Trial Chamber I, 7 August 2012); Campaign for Innocent Victims in Conflict ('CIVIC') (currently the Center for Civilians in Conflict), *Addressing Civilian Harm in Afghanistan: Policies and Practices of International Forces* (15 June 2010), http://civiliansinconflict.org/resources/publications.

2 International Law Association, Declaration of International Law Principles on Reparation for Victims of Armed Conflict (Substantive Issues), Res no 2/2010, art 1.

violations such as war crimes or crimes against humanity; who is entitled to reparations; the forms reparations might take; and whether damages might be punitive in nature.[3] These matters have been dealt with in a variety of fora including treaties and instruments, judgments of international courts, resolutions by international organisations (IGOs) such the UN, and the policies of states, IGOs and civil society.

Alongside reparations, there is an emerging practice for states to make amends to collateral damage victims of military operations, including armed conflict, despite the fact that there is no legal obligation under IHL or IHRL to do so.[4] The term 'amends' as used in this chapter refers to a dignifying gesture such as recognition, apology, monetary payment or in-kind gifts, for incidental harm caused by military operations. In some contexts, ex-gratia cash payments are used as a mechanism for making amends. The practice of making amends is crucial, as it is an important mechanism that offers collateral damage victims a degree of respect, dignity and practical assistance following a death, injury or damage to their property arising from military operations.[5] States and IGOs have developed policies which address how to make amends when the need arises. However, such policies are non-binding, are often developed and applied on an ad hoc basis and are sometimes, it has been argued, insensitive to the plight of those harmed.[6] As the practice of amends develops further, the questions of whether there should be an obligation on states to compensate collateral damage victims of armed conflict, and the importance of making amends in conflict situations, will need to be considered.[7]

Against the background of recognising the growing importance of making reparations and amends for harm in armed conflicts, this chapter is divided into four sections. Section 1 explores the international law framework that governs reparations for violations in armed conflict. Section 2 considers the challenges confronting the development of this area of law. Section 3 discusses the practice of making amends for harm caused during lawful military actions. Section 4 concludes the chapter and reflects on issues regarding reparations and making amends that require further reflection and research. This chapter does not address the issue of *jus ad bellum* reparations.

3 The term 'incidentally injured civilians' is taken from Yael Ronen, 'Avoid or Compensate? Liability for Incidental Injury to Civilians Inflicted during Armed Conflict' (2009) 42 *Vanderbilt JTL* 181.

4 For an excellent article concerning making amends to victims of armed conflict, see Scott T Paul, 'The Duty to make Amends to Victims of Armed Conflict' (2013) 22 *Tulane JICL* 87–117.

5 See eg Sarah Holewinski, 'Making Amends: A New Expectation for Civilian Losses in Armed Conflict' in Daniel Rothbar, Karina Korostelina and Mohammed Cherkaoui (eds), *Civilians and Modern War: Armed Conflict* (1st edn, Routledge 2012), 317–333, 329.

6 See CIVIC (n 1) for a detailed study of the various policies of assistance that were applied in Afghanistan by the International Security Assistance Force (ISAF); and Philip Alston, Report of the Special Rapporteur on Extrajudicial, Summary or Arbitrary Executions, UN Doc A/HRC/14/24 (20 May 2010) ¶¶ 84–88.

7 While the chapter addresses the matter of the practice of states making amends to victims who are characterised as collateral damage victims, the question of whether there should be an obligation on states to compensate collateral damage victims of military conflict is not explored. For further discussion on the obligation of states to pay compensation to victims of collateral damage, see eg Ronen (n 3) 181; Gabriella Blum and Natalie J Lockwood, 'Earthquakes and Wars: The Logic of international Reparations' (2012) *Harvard Public Law and Legal Theory Working Paper Series*, Paper No 12-30; Minako Ichikawa Smart, 'Compensation for Civilian Casualties in Armed Conflicts and Theories of Liability' in Benjamin E Goldsmith and Jurgen Brauer (eds), *Economics of War and Peace: Economic, Legal and Political Perspectives (Contributions to Conflict Management, Peace Economics and Development, Volume 14)* (Emerald Group Publishing Limited 2010) 243.

1 The legal framework for reparations

The legal framework concerning the right to reparation during armed conflict is fragmented in the sense that there are a number of legal regimes that apply. In addition to the general rules of state and IGO responsibility, and IHL, it is now generally accepted that IHRL, international criminal law (ICL), ad hoc agreements, such as peace agreements, resolutions by the UN Security Council and judicial findings also apply to varying degrees.[8]

The right to reparation during armed conflict is founded on the essential principle of international law that a state or an IGO is responsible to make reparations for the injury caused by a violation of an obligation under international law.[9] Injury 'includes any damage, whether material or moral, caused by an internationally wrongful act'[10] of either a state or an IGO. The harm or injury may be direct or indirect. The forms of reparations under the general rules of state and IGO responsibility include restitution,[11] compensation[12] and satisfaction,[13] either singly or in combination.[14]

Restitution, compensation and satisfaction, at least pursuant to the ILC's Draft Articles on State Responsibility and also the ILC's Draft Articles on the Responsibility of International Organisations, are defined as follows.[15]

Restitution requires a state or international organisation to

> re-establish the situation which existed before the wrongful act was committed, provided and to the extent that restitution:
>
> (a) is not materially impossible; [and]
> (b) does not involve a burden out of proportion to the benefit deriving from restitution instead of compensation.[16]

Compensation requires a state or an IGO to 'compensate for the damage ... insofar as such damage is not made good by restitution' and stipulates that '[t]he compensation shall cover any financially assessable damage including loss of profits insofar as it is established'.[17] Satisfaction

---

8 For a more detailed account about reparations in international law, and the practice of states and tribunals, see eg Naomi Roht-Arriaza, 'Reparations in International Law and Practice' in M Cherif Bassiouni (ed), *The Pursuit of International Criminal Justice: A World Study on Conflicts, Victimization, and Post Conflict Justice* (1st edn, Intersentia 2010) 655–698.

9 See Draft Articles on Responsibility of States for Internationally Wrongful Acts, in Report of the International Law Commission on the Work of its Fifty-Third Session, UN Doc A/56/10 (November 2001) ('ARSIWA') art 31; and Draft Articles on the Responsibility of International Organizations, in the Report of the International Law Commission on the Work of its Sixty-Third Session, UN Doc A/66/10 ¶ 87 (2011) ('ARIO') art 31.

10 ARSIWA (n 9) art 31(2); ARIO (n 9) art 31(2). For a more detailed discussion of injury, see James Crawford, *The International Law Commission's Articles on State Responsibility: Introduction, Texts and Commentaries* (CUP 2002) 202–206.

11 See ARSIWA (n 9) art 35; ARIO (n 9) art 35.

12 See ARSIWA (n 9) art 36; ARIO (n 9) art 36

13 See ARSIWA (n 9) art 37; ARIO (n 9) art 37.

14 See ARSIWA (n 9) art 34; ARIO (n 9) art 34.

15 These definitions act as a starting point for understanding the obligation to make full reparations, cf Basic Principles and Guidelines on the Right to a Remedy and Reparation for Victims of Gross Violations on International Human Rights and Serious Violations of International Humanitarian Law, UNGA Res 60/147 (16 December 2005) ('Basic Principles'), which lists the forms of reparation as restitution (¶ 19), compensation (¶ 20), rehabilitation (¶ 21), satisfaction (¶ 22) and guarantees of non-repetition (¶ 23).

16 See ARSIWA (n 9) art 35; ARIO (n 9) art 35.

17 See ARSIWA (n 9) art 36; ARIO (n 9) art 36.

requires a state or an IGO 'to give satisfaction for the injury caused by that act insofar as it cannot be made good by restitution or compensation' and stipulates that satisfaction

> may consist in acknowledgement of the breach, an expression of regret, a formal apology or another appropriate modality ... [and it] shall not be out of proportion to the injury and may not take a form of humiliating the responsible State.[18]

More narrowly, there are two provisions in IHL that deal with compensation during armed conflicts. The oldest provision is in the 1907 Hague Convention (IV). Article 3 of that Convention recognises that a violation of the annexed Hague Regulations by a belligerent party will, if the case demands, give rise to liability to pay compensation.[19] Article 3 was not replicated in the Geneva Conventions and, consequently, unless a state was bound by that article there was no explicit treaty obligation for a state to pay compensation for violations of the Geneva Conventions. It was not until Additional Protocol I that the obligation to pay compensation for violations of the Geneva Conventions and Additional Protocol I was reintroduced explicitly. Article 91 of Additional Protocol I provides: 'A Party to the conflict which violates the provisions of the Conventions or of this Protocol [that is, Protocol I] shall, if the case demands, be liable to pay compensation.'[20] It is now accepted by the ICRC that the rule articulated in Article 3 of Hague Convention (IV) and Article 91 of Additional Protocol I is a customary international law rule applicable in all international armed conflicts.[21] While it is true that there is no corresponding provision for compensation to be found concerning non-international conflicts, the ICRC also argues that the rule applies as an international customary law rule to non-international armed conflicts.[22] No state has publicly denounced the ICRC's statements concerning the customary law status of the rule.

In circumstances where IHRL applies during armed conflict, reparation provisions from that body of law will also apply.[23] The Universal Declaration of Human Rights (UDHR) and the International Covenant on Civil and Political Rights (ICCPR), both general human rights instruments, speak of remedies. The UDHR deals with effective remedies for acts violating fundamental rights;[24] and Articles 2(3)(a) and 9(5) of the ICCPR deal with remedies as well as 'an enforceable right to compensation' for unlawful arrest or detention.[25] The subject matter treaties, such as the Convention Against Torture and Other Cruel, Inhuman or Degrading Treatment or Punishment (CAT) and the International Convention for the Protection of All Persons from Enforced Disappearances (CED) also have provisions concerning reparations. State parties to the CAT now have considerable guidance by way of a General Comment from the Committee Against Torture as to how that Committee envisages the scope and content of Article 14 of that Convention.[26] Thus, where an individual is tortured during an armed conflict the Committee Against Torture would expect states to provide both substantive and procedural redress to the victim. The redress a victim would be entitled to includes restitution, compensation,

---

18 See ARSIWA (n 9) art 37; ARIO (n 9) art 37.
19 HR art 3; see also *Lubanga* (n 1) ¶¶ 184–186.
20 API art 91.
21 See CIHL r 150.
22 Ibid.
23 The ICC in the *Lubanga* decision (n 1) stated more generally that 'the right to reparations is a well-established and basic human right, that is enshrined in universal and regional human rights treaties, and in other international instruments' (185). Noam Lubell and Nancie Prud'homme, 'Impact of human rights law' ch 6 in this volume.
24 UDHR art 8.
25 ICCPR arts 2(3)(a) and 9(5) respectively.
26 Committee against Torture, General comment no 3, CAT/C/GC/3 (13 December 2012).

rehabilitation, satisfaction and the right to truth, and guarantees of non-repetition.[27] The CED is drafted in similar terms to the CAT provision, except that the CED provisions require reparation for victims of enforced disappearances.[28] Further, under the CED reparation includes material and moral damages and other forms of reparations such as restitution, rehabilitation, satisfaction and guarantees of non-repetition.[29]

Amongst the regional human rights treaties the Protocol on the Statute of the African Court of Justice and Human Rights provides that the African Court 'may, if it considers that there was a violation of a human or peoples' right, order any appropriate measures in order to remedy the situation, including granting fair compensation'.[30] The Court is also able to determine 'the nature or extent of the reparation to be made for the breach of an international obligation'.[31] The American Convention on Human Rights requires that a violation of a right or freedom that is protected by the Convention be remedied, and that fair compensation is paid to the injured party.[32] The European Convention for the Protection of Human Rights and Fundamental Freedoms (ECHR) stipulates that, where rights and freedoms protected by that Convention are violated, the victim shall have an effective remedy before a national authority.[33] That Convention also provides for the European Court 'if necessary, [to] afford just satisfaction to the injured party' in circumstances where the internal law of a state party to the ECHR allows only partial reparation.[34]

International criminal law also deals with rights to reparation for victims of armed conflict. For example, the Rome Statute provides that the Court may make orders 'against a convicted person specifying appropriate reparations to, or in respect of, victims, including restitution, compensation and rehabilitation'.[35] We will discuss the application of this provision in the *Lubanga* case in due course.

There are a number of soft law instruments that reinforce these treaty norms, and are relevant to the way in which states, IGOs and civil society view reparations. These include the Basic Principles and Guidelines on the Right to a Remedy and Reparation for Victims of Gross Violations on International Human Rights and Serious Violations of International Humanitarian Law[36] (Basic Principles), the Declaration of International Law Principles on Reparation for

---

27 Ibid 2–5.
28 International Convention for the Protection of All Persons from Enforced Disappearances (CED), UNGA Res 61/177 (20 December 2006) art 24(4). Pursuant to art 24(1) '"victims" includes disappeared persons and any individual who has suffered harm as the direct result of an enforced disappearance'.
29 Ibid art 24(5)(a)–(d).
30 Decision on the Single Legal Instrument on the Merger of the African Court on Human and Peoples' Rights and the African Court of Justice, African Union, Assembly/AU/Dec 196 (XI) (1 July 2008) art 45.
31 Ibid art 28(h).
32 ACHR art 63(1). See also art 25 which concerns judicial protection.
33 Art 13.
34 Ibid art 41.
35 Art 75. Other international criminal tribunals also deal with reparations. The ICTY Rules of Procedure and Evidence, r 106 provides for a victim to bring an action in a national court or other competent body to obtain compensation for crimes within the ICTY's mandate. See also, ICTY Rules of Procedure and Evidence r 105; ICTR Rules of Procedure and Evidence rr 105 and 106; Statute of the SCSL art 14, which applies the ICTR Rules of Procedure and Evidence to the SCSL.
36 Basic Principles (n 15). See also the Paris Principles: Principles and Guidelines on Children Associated With Armed Forces or Armed Groups (February 2007); Guidelines on Justice in Matters involving Child Victims and Witnesses of Crime, ECOSOC Res 2005/20 (22 July 2005); human rights reports such as the Final Report of the Special Rapporteur, Mr Cherif Bassiouni, 'Civil and Political Rights, Including the Questions of: Independence of the Judiciary, Administration of Justice, Impunity' UN Doc E/CN.4/2000/62 (18 January 2000); Commissions of Inquiry established by the UN.

Victims of Armed Conflict (Substantive Issues)[37] (the Substantive Declaration) and the Declaration of International Law Principles on Reparation for Victims of Armed Conflict (Procedural Principles for Reparation Mechanisms)[38] (the Procedural Principles). The Basic Principles provide for remedies for serious violations of IHL and, in that context, they state that victims have a right under international law to – among other things – '[a]dequate, effective and prompt reparation for harm suffered'.[39] Reparations under the Basic Principles take the form of restitution,[40] compensation,[41] rehabilitation,[42] satisfaction[43] and guarantees of non-repetition.[44] The Substantive Declaration considers reparations for victims of armed conflict on the same basis as the general principle of international law, that is: 'measures that seek to eliminate all the harmful consequences of a violation of rules of international law applicable in armed conflict and to re-establish the situation that would have existed if the violation had not occurred'.[45] Reparations under the Substantive Declaration include the forms dealt with by the Basic Principles. The Procedural Principles emphasise the 'right to access an effective mechanism to claim reparation'[46] and the types of mechanisms that should be in place in order to ensure that reparation mechanisms are effective and efficient.

The UN Security Council has considered the issue of reparations for victims in armed conflict. For example, the United Nations Compensation Commission (UNCC), which was established pursuant to Resolution 687 (1991), created a fund to pay claims for 'death or personal injury, or losses of income, support, housing or personal property, or medical expenses or costs of departure as a result of Iraq's unlawful invasion and occupation of Kuwait'.[47] The claims could be based on, among other things, military operations conducted between 2 August 1990 to 2 March 1991, and hostage taking or other illegal detention.[48] The Commission accepted claims from individuals, corporations and governments. In relation to individual claims, for example, where an individual suffered a personal injury, or their spouse, child or parent died as a result of Iraq's invasion and occupation of Kuwait, the Commission awarded compensation ranging from 'US$2,500 for individuals and up to US$10,000 for families'.[49]

The UN Secretary-General has also issued guidance for UN engagement in the 'area of reparations for victims of conflict-related sexual violence'.[50] That guidance aims to provide both

---

37 Declaration of International Law Principles (Substantive Issues) (n 2).
38 International Law Association, Declaration of International Law Principles on Reparation for Victims of Armed Conflict (Procedural Principles for Reparation Mechanisms), Res no 1/2014.
39 Basic Principles (n 15) ¶ 11(b).
40 Ibid ¶ 19.
41 Ibid ¶ 20.
42 Ibid ¶ 21.
43 Ibid ¶ 22.
44 Ibid ¶ 23.
45 *Declaration of International Law Principles (Substantive Issues)* (n 2) art 1.
46 *Declaration of International Law Principles (Procedural Principles for Reparation Mechanisms)* (n 38) Principle 1.
47 See First Session of the Governing Council of the UN Compensation Commission, 'Arrangements for Ensuring Payments to the Compensation Fund' UN Doc S/AC.26/1991/1 (2 August 1991) ¶ 14.
48 Ibid ¶ 18(a) and (e). For more details concerning the Commission and its work, see eg Dinah Shelton, *Remedies in International Human Rights Law* (2nd edn, OUP 2005) 404–412; Linda A Taylor, 'The United Nations Compensation Commission' in Carla Ferstman, Mariana Goetz and Alan Stephens (eds), *Reparations for Victims of Genocide, War Crimes and Crimes against Humanity* (Martinus Nijhoff 2009) 197.
49 United Nations Compensation Commission, 'Category B Claims', www.uncc.ch/claims/b_claims.htm.
50 Guidance Note of the Secretary-General, 'Reparations for Conflict-Related Sexual Violence' (June 2014), www.ohchr.org/Documents/Press/GuidanceNoteReparationsJune-2014.pdf, 2.

policy and operational direction when the UN engages in activities such as implementing, monitoring and evaluating reparation programmes and initiatives that are directed at victims of conflict-related sexual violence. It reinforces the Security Council's resolutions concerning women, peace and security such as Resolutions 1325 (2000) and 2122 (2013), which in part address redress for victims of sexual violence.[51]

Peace agreements have led to systems of reparations being established for victims of armed conflicts. For example, the Eritrea–Ethiopia Claims Commission (EECC), which was established and operated pursuant to Article 5 of an agreement between both states, was authorised to deal with claims resulting from IHL violations that related to the conflict.[52] The EECC awarded Eritrea, for example, compensation of US$4,000,000 for the mistreatment of prisoners of war (POWs) by Ethiopia.[53]

There have been a number of international tribunals that have considered the application of reparations to victims in armed conflict. For example, in the *Wall* opinion, the ICJ concluded that Israel is under an obligation to make reparations, for example by returning land, orchards and other immovable property taken from persons for the purposes of the construction of the wall.[54] Where it is not possible to provide restitution the Court stated that Israel has an obligation to compensate for any material damage.[55] More recently the ICJ concluded in the *Jurisdictional Immunities of the State* case that Germany is immune, as a matter of customary international law, from the jurisdiction of Italian domestic courts for serious IHL violations that were committed by Nazi Germany in Italy between 1943 and 1945.[56] One effect of such jurisdictional immunity is that victims of serious violations of IHL are not able to make individual claims for reparations against Germany.[57]

International criminal courts and tribunals have also considered reparations for serious violations of IHL. For example, in the *Lubanga* case the ICC dealt with the principles and procedures to be applied to reparations.[58] The Court stated that reparations fulfil two main purposes under the Rome Statute: they oblige 'those responsible for serious crimes to repair the harm they caused to the victims and they enable the [Trial] Chamber to ensure that offenders account for their acts'.[59] Some of the other issues that the Court decided upon included the beneficiaries of

---

51 See eg UNSC Res 1325 (31 October 2010) ¶ 10 and UNSC Res 2122 (18 October 2013) ¶ 13. For a more detailed discussion of the UN's role in promoting reparation for victims, see Christine Evans, *The Right to Reparation in International Law for Victims of Armed Conflict* (2nd edn, CUP 2014) pt II.

52 Agreement between the Federal Democratic Republic of Ethiopia and the Government of the State of Eritrea (12 December 2000) 2138 UNTS 94, art 5.

53 Eritrea–Ethiopia Claims Commission, *Final Award* (2009) 26 RIAA 505, pt IX. For a more detailed discussion of the role of peace agreements in promoting reparation for victims of conflicts in Guatemala, Sierra Leone, East Timor and Columbia, see Evans (n 51) pt II.

54 *Legal Consequences of the Construction of a Wall in the Occupied Palestinian Territory (Advisory Opinion)* [2004] ¶¶ 152 and 153. This case concerned the legality of a security wall constructed by Israel along the border (and in some instances, into the territory) of the Occupied Palestinian Territory.

55 Ibid ¶ 153. See also *Armed Activities on the Territory of the Congo (Democratic Republic of the Congo v Uganda)* [2005] ICJ Rep 168, ¶ 258. This case concerned the legality of the violence perpetrated by Uganda against the Democratic Republic of Congo between August 1998 and June 2003.

56 *Jurisdictional Immunities of the State (Germany v Italy: Greece Intervening)* [2002] ICJ Rep 99 ¶ 52. The serious violations of IHL included large-scale killing of civilians in occupied territory, deportations to work as slave labour and denial of prisoner of war status.

57 Ibid. See the dissenting judgments of Judges Trindade and Yusuf.

58 *Lubanga* (n 1).

59 Ibid ¶ 179. For a more detailed discussion concerning reparations pursuant to the Rome Statute, see Conor McCarthy, *Reparations and Victim Support in the International Criminal Court* (2nd edn, CUP 2014) ch 4.

reparations,[60] accessibility and consultation with victims,[61] and the modalities of reparations.[62] In relation to beneficiaries of reparations the Court concluded that reparations may be granted to

> direct and indirect victims ... anyone who attempted to prevent the commission of one or more of the serious crimes under consideration; and those who suffered personal harm as a result of these offences, regardless of whether they participated in the trial proceedings.[63]

A further important conclusion concerning beneficiaries involved the Court's recognition that priority may be given to certain victims based on their vulnerability.[64] The Court decided that a gender-based approach should guide accessibility and consultation with victims;[65] and that the Court should 'consult with victims on issues relating, inter alia, to the identity of beneficiaries, their priorities and the obstacles they have encountered in their attempts to secure reparations'.[66] The Court determined that the modalities of reparation include not only restitution, compensation and rehabilitation but also 'those with a symbolic, preventative or transformative value'.[67]

The European Court of Human Rights has also decided on reparations for violations occurring in armed conflict. For example, in *Al-Skeini*, the Grand Chamber concluded that in deciding reparations its

> guiding principle is equity, which above all involves flexibility and an objective consideration of what is just, fair and reasonable in all the circumstances of the case, including not only the position of the applicant but the overall context in which the breach occurred.[68]

Consequently, the Grand Chamber decided to compensate some of the applicants 'for the distress caused by the lack of a fully independent investigation into the deaths of their relatives ... €17,000 each'.[69]

In light of the above overview of the legal framework concerning reparations, the question arises whether there is a customary international law right for an individual who is a victim of armed conflict to claim reparations. The ICRC has stated that there is a customary international law rule that 'a State responsible for violations of international humanitarian law is required to make full reparation for loss or injury caused'.[70] What is less certain is whether there is an international customary law right for an individual victim of armed conflict to claim reparations. Some academics have argued that there is such a right[71] but there is insufficient opinio juris and state practice outside the realm of treaty obligations to establish that such a right exists.

---

60 Ibid ¶¶ 194–201.
61 Ibid ¶¶ 202–206.
62 Ibid ¶¶ 222–241.
63 Ibid ¶ 194.
64 Ibid ¶ 200.
65 Ibid ¶¶ 202 and 222.
66 Ibid ¶ 206.
67 Ibid ¶ 222 and see also ¶¶ 237–241 for a description of other forms of reparations.
68 *Al-Skeini and Others v The United Kingdom* (App no 55721/07, ECtHR Grand Chamber, 7 July 2011) ¶ 182.
69 Ibid.
70 CIHL r 150.
71 See Christine Evans, *The Right to Reparation in International Law for Victims of Armed Conflict* (1st edn, CUP 2005) 39–42 and 126–127.

2 Challenges in the development of reparations

The above description of the international legal framework surrounding reparations during armed conflict gives rise to a number of controversial matters. First, the traditional approach of both general international law and IHL seems to focus on inter-state claims for reparations. This interpretation is supported by the fact that the commentary to the Draft Articles on State Responsibility makes no reference to individuals having legal standing to make claims for reparation from the offending state. Traditionally, academic writers also fail to mention individual standing when speaking about reparations.[72] While Article 91 of Additional Protocol I does not expressly state that individuals have standing, the commentary does say that 'since 1945 a tendency has emerged to recognise the exercise of rights by individuals',[73] however, those rights only exist through the victims' own government 'which will submit [its] complaints to the Party or Parties which have committed the violation'.[74] In the *Jurisdictional Immunities of the State* case before the ICJ, Judge Yusuf, in his dissenting opinion, asserts that individuals have standing to bring claims for violations of IHL. He argues that neither the law of state responsibility nor IHL 'exclude the right of individuals to make claims for compensation for damages arising from breaches of IHL'.[75] Judge Yusuf makes the point that it is unjust to deny individuals standing to seek remedies from the state responsible for breaches of IHL in instances where victims of violations do not have recourse to compensation from inter-state reparations schemes.[76] Injustice also arises where individuals are stateless and cannot rely on a state to represent their interests in seeking remedies.

In the context of human rights treaties or the Rome Statute, the concerns about individuals having standing to bring claims for IHL violations does not arise.[77] Thus, for breaches such as torture pursuant to the CAT, or war crimes pursuant to the Rome Statue, individuals will have standing to make claims seeking remedies for breaches of IHL. Furthermore, both the Basic Principles and the Substantive Declaration recognise that individuals have standing to claim reparations for breaches of IHL. The concern about stateless individuals having standing to make claims was incorporated in the UNCC Provisional Rules for Claims Procedures.[78] In the context of specialist legal regimes that provide individuals with standing to seek remedies, one complex issue that must be considered is the potential for such regimes to effect the broader right for individuals to claim remedies. This issue arises in instances where a specialist legal regime does not apply. In other words, if an individual cannot make a claim pursuant to a specialist regime, does that mean that the individual should have no standing under general principles of international law? This approach would result in a situation where a victim of torture cannot seek

---

72 See eg Robert Jennings and Arthur Watts, *Oppenheim's International Law* (9th edn, OUP 1992); Ian Brownlie, *Principles of Public International Law* (7th edn, OUP 2008); Gillian Triggs, *International Law: Contemporary Principles and Practices* (2nd edn, LexisNexis Butterworth 2010); Malcolm Shaw, *International Law* (6th edn, CUP 2008); Shelton (n 48).

73 Jean de Preux, 'API Article 91' *API Commentary* ¶ 3657.

74 Ibid.

75 *Germany v Italy: Greece Intervening* (n 56), dissenting Opinion of Judge Yusuf, ¶¶ 18–19. It may also be implied from the majority judgment in the Israeli *Wall* case (n 54) ¶ 153 that individuals have standing to claim for reparations by virtue of the emphasis placed on restitution for individuals where there is no right for individuals to claim compensation.

76 Ibid ¶ 20.

77 See discussion in s 1, above.

78 Sixth Session of the Governing Council of the UN Compensation Commission, 'Provisional Rules for Claims Procedures' UN Doc S/AC.26/1992/10 (26 June 1992) art 5(3).

remedies for torture where the specialist regime does not apply to the situation they are in, because the specialist regime is considered to 'cover the field'.

This issue is closely related to the question of whether groups of individuals have a right to claim collective reparations. There is no singularly accepted definition of what constitutes 'collective reparations' in international law.[79] However, there are a number of international treaty and soft law agreements, and judgments, that indicate that reparations can be collectively awarded to groups of victims.[80] For example, the Basic Principles define victims as 'persons who individually or collectively suffer harm',[81] and Rule 97 of the ICC Rules of Procedure and Evidence enables the Court to award reparations on a collective basis.[82] In the *Lubanga* decision, the ICC emphasised that '[t]here is a growing recognition in international human rights law that victims and groups of victims may apply for and receive reparations',[83] and found that 'a community-based approach ... would be more beneficial and have greater utility than individual awards'.[84] In light of these developments, it will be necessary to consider further the nature of a potential collective right to reparations, the mechanisms through which collective reparations can be enforced and implemented, and the way in which collective rights should interact with individual rights to reparations.[85]

A second issue of concern is the overall content of reparations. For example, do the references to 'compensation' in Article 3 of the Hague Regulations and Article 91 of Additional Protocol I limit reparations to a narrow interpretation which only incorporates 'compensation', or can 'compensation' be interpreted more broadly to encompass other forms of reparation? The commentary to Article 91 suggests that compensation 'refers to the award made to make reparation for a wrong'.[86] The commentary also states that compensation is a remedy that only arises when restitution is not possible.[87] In relation to compensation, the commentary indicates that compensation is generally provided as a 'sum of money which must correspond either to the value of the object for which restitution is not possible, or to an indemnification which is proportional to the loss suffered'.[88] Further, although compensation can be achieved through the provision of services, the commentary emphasises that POWs cannot be used to provide services to the Detaining Power at the cessation of the conflict, as this would be a violation of Article 118 of Geneva Convention III.[89]

---

79 See eg Sylvain Aubry and Maria Isabel Henao-Trip, 'Collective Reparations and the International Criminal Court' Briefing Paper no 2 (Transitional Justice Network, University of Essex August 2011) 2–4, www.essex.ac.uk/tjn/.../Paper_2_Collective_Reparations.pdf; Diana Contreras-Garduño, 'Defining Beneficiaries of Collective Reparations: The Experience of the IACtHR' (2012) 4(3) *Amsterdam Law Forum* 40, 46–48.

80 For a comprehensive discussion of existing soft law, treaties and judgments pertaining to collective reparations, see Friedrich Rosenfeld, 'Collective Reparation for Victims of Armed Conflict' (2010) 92(879) *IRRC* 731.

81 Basic Principles (n 15) ¶ 8.

82 Rules of Procedure and Evidence of the ICC, ICC-ASP/1/3 and Corr 1, pt II.A (9 September 2002) r 97. Rule 97(1) states that 'the Court may award reparations on an individualized basis or, where it deems it appropriate, on a collective basis or both'.

83 *Lubanga* (n 1) ¶ 217.

84 Ibid (n 1) ¶ 274.

85 For a discussion on the challenges of conceptualising a collective right to reparations, see Rosenfeld (n 80).

86 de Preux (n 73) ¶ 3653.

87 Ibid ¶ 3655.

88 Ibid.

89 Ibid.

The list of reparations for violations of IHL therefore includes, at a minimum, restitution and compensation. However, as stated in the *Lubanga* case, the mechanisms of reparations can also include other types of reparations.[90] With the approach taken by the ICC, the Basic Principles, the Substantive Declaration and the Procedural Principles it is arguable that reparations for IHL violations now include other modalities of reparations including rehabilitation, satisfaction and guarantees for non-repetition,[91] and other forms of reparations such as campaigns to assist victims by, for example, 'issuing certificates to acknowledge the harm a particular individual has suffered, ... [and] setting up outreach and promotional programmes that inform victims of the outcome of the trial'.[92]

Although the commentary to Article 91 Additional Protocol I explains that compensation must correspond either to the value of the object or an indemnification, there is no guide as to how value and indemnification are actually decided upon. One reason why it is difficult to establish the exact extent and content of reparations is that the numbers of victims might be too great, and resources available too limited to apply a single standard in all cases.[93]

Another contentious issue is the question of whether reparations for violations of IHL have a punitive component. The ICRC commentary to Article 91 states that 'it is not sufficient for a violation simply to have been committed. For the obligation to make reparation to exist there must also be loss or damage which in most cases will be of material or a personal nature.'[94] This statement implies that punitive damages are a component of reparations. It is argued in *Oppenheim's International Law* that state and tribunal practices demonstrate that penal damages are often a component of reparations.[95] Furthermore, Dinah Shelton asserts that satisfaction can have a punitive role, and also 'functions to redress moral, immaterial, or non-pecuniary damage caused by a state'.[96] On the other hand, Shelton asserts the Draft Articles on State Responsibility approach reparations as having a 'purpose and scope ... [which] is limited to remedial measures, excluding sanctions or punishments such as punitive measures'.[97] Bin Cheng argues that 'the notion of responsibility for an unlawful act implies the principle of ... reparations, but ... it does not cover the infliction of any sanction in the form of a pecuniary penalty'.[98] The Eritrea–Ethiopia Claims Commission has concluded 'that compensation has a limited function. Its role is to restore an injured party, in so far as possible, to the position it would have occupied but for the injury. This function is remedial, not punitive.'[99]

A fourth matter concerning reparations relates to whether claims for reparations are limited to claims for violations of IHL or whether claims may be made for any harm arising out of armed conflict. A plain reading of Article 91 limits compensation to violations of IHL. Similarly, human rights treaties such as the ICCPR and the CAT envisage reparations only arising in the context of violations of rights. Neither IHL nor IHRL has provisions obligating states to assist victims who suffer because of conflict occurring around them, however, there is an increasing

---

90 *Lubanga* (n 1) ¶ 222.
91 See Basic Principles (n 15) ¶¶ 21–23.
92 See *Lubanga* (n 1) ¶ 239.
93 See eg the decision by the Eritrea–Ethiopia Claims Commission (n 53) ¶¶ 22–270, to understand better the types of factors that need to be considered in deciding compensation. See also, the categories of claims established by the UNCC, www.uncc.ch/theclaims.htm.
94 de Preux (n 73) ¶ 3655.
95 Jennings and Watts (n 72) 533.
96 Shelton (n 48) 54.
97 Ibid 86.
98 Bin Cheng, *General Principles of Law as Applied by International Courts and Tribunals* (Stevens & Sons 1953) 236.
99 *Final Award* (n 53) ¶ 26.

recognition that states should make amends to individuals harmed by armed conflict, regardless of whether the harm arose from a violation of IHL or IHRL.[100]

In light of this, a further issue that warrants consideration is the obligation for states to provide assistance for victims who suffer harm, even where that harm is not caused by a violation of IHL. This is not a form of making reparations, as the obligation is not predicated on a state's wrongful act, but is instead contingent on the victim having suffered injury, or damage to property during armed conflict. One example is Article 68 of Geneva Convention III which contains a specific provision that concerns claims for compensation by POWs where they suffer an 'injury or other disability arising out of work' undertaken as a prisoner.[101] POWs may also claim compensation for loss of personal effects, including valuables, which were confiscated by the Detaining Power and subsequently lost by the Detaining Power or not returned to the prisoner at the time of repatriation.[102] Geneva Convention IV articulates the arrangements that must be made by an Occupying Power to ensure that fair value is paid for any requisitioned goods.[103] These requirements place an obligation on states to pay compensation for harm, even where there is no violation of IHL.

More recently, this approach has been broadened to establish an obligation for states to provide assistance to civilians who are harmed by the use of particular weapons. A number of weapons treaties focus on the need to provide redress to all civilian victims, rather than the specific provision of reparations for violations of IHL. For example, the 1997 Ottawa Treaty[104] requires that state parties, who are in a position to do so, provide assistance to care for and rehabilitate civilian victims of anti-personnel mines.[105] Further, the 2003 Protocol on Explosive Remnants of War requires that state parties take steps to remove remnants of explosives at the cessation of a conflict, and provide for the care and rehabilitation of civilian victims of these explosives.[106] The 2008 Convention on Cluster Munitions has also facilitated the provision of medical care and rehabilitation support for civilian victims of cluster munitions.[107] This treaty requires that state parties, who have the capacity, offer support to other states to adhere to their obligations under the treaty.[108] Each of these treaties focuses on (1) the provision of assistance to civilians by the state or party that causes harm as well as other states, including the state in which the injured civilian was harmed, and (2) facilitating assistance for *all* civilian victims of these weapons, rather than predicating assistance on the commission of a violation of IHL.

3 The emerging practice of making amends

These treaty obligations foreshadow the potential for the development of a more complete approach to redressing victims' losses – an approach that facilitates recompense for *all* victims of

100 See discussion in s 3, below.
101 Art 68(1).
102 GCIII art 68(2).
103 GCIV art 55(2).
104 Convention on the Prohibition of the Use, Stockpiling, Production and Transfer of Anti-Personnel Mines and on the Destruction (18 September 1997) 2056 UNTS 211.
105 Ibid art 6(3). See also ICRC, 'Anti-Personnel Mines' (29 October 2010), www.icrc.org/eng/war-and-law/weapons/anti-personnel-landmines/overview-anti-personnel-landmines.htm.
106 Convention on Certain Conventional Weapons, Protocol on Explosive Remnants of War (Protocol V) (28 November 2003). See also ICRC, 'Explosive Remnants of War' (29 October 2010), www.icrc.org/eng/war-and-law/weapons/explosive-remnants-war/overview-explosive-remnants-of-war.htm.
107 Convention on Cluster Munitions (30 May 2008) CCM/ 77, art 5.
108 Ibid art 6.

conflict. There are many collateral damage victims of armed conflicts who have limited, if any, recourse to compensation for the damage they have suffered. These victims are civilians who are killed, or suffer injury or damage to themselves or their property in the course of proportionate and discriminate attacks on legitimate military objects. Historically, these 'collateral damage' victims are cared for by their state, with each state party to the conflict bearing the costs of supporting their civilian casualties.[109] However, with an increasing number of non-international and asymmetrical conflicts,[110] this traditional approach leaves many civilians without the requisite support to recover from their losses.

In this context, many states have sought to refine their military tactics to minimise civilian casualties,[111] and some states have adopted a policy of making amends to collateral damage victims. There is an increasing trend towards recognising that in counter-insurgency warfare, states need to win the 'hearts and minds' of the local population, or at the very least, deter the local population from working actively against the government or coalition forces.[112] These policies are an operational and tactical effort that seeks to garner support for the mission by adopting a more complete approach to redressing victims' losses. States' policies often facilitate the making of amends to collateral damage victims injured in conflict situations, as well as civilians who are injured by armed forces in non-combat situations. They are generally administered on an ad-hoc basis, and there can be significant variation in the approaches taken by different states, even within the same conflict.[113]

As well as states' policies of making amends, IGOs also provide an avenue for victims to receive recompense for loss that results from legitimate military action. The UN pays compensation to victims who suffer injury or damage during UN peacekeeping operations.[114] Compensation was first paid to victims in 1956 during the First United Nations Emergency Force in the Middle-East operation, and also during subsequent UN peacekeeping operations.[115] In 1998, following recommendations from the Secretary-General,[116] the General Assembly established specific guidelines for payment of compensation for damage caused to third parties by the UN.[117] This resolution stipulates that third parties who suffer injury, death

---

109 See eg Smart (n 7) 246–247.
110 See eg ICRC, Report of the 30th International Conference of the Red Cross and Red Crescent (October 2007) 1, 12–13 and Annex 3; Robin Geiß, 'Asymmetric Conflict Structures' (2006) 88(864) *IRRC* 757; Michael John-Hopkins, 'Regulating the Conduct of Urban Warfare: Lessons from Contemporary Asymmetric Armed Conflicts' (2010) 92(878) *IRRC* 469, 469–472.
111 Larry Lewis and Sarah Holewinski, Center for Civilians in Conflict, 'As Pentagon reshapes Fighting Force, Civilian Casualties need to be Considered' *The Hill* (Washington DC, 7 September 2012), http://thehill.com/blogs/congress-blog/foreign-policy/248197-as-pentagon-reshapes-fighting-force-civilian-casualties-need-to-be-considered; US Department of Army, 'Civilian Casualty Mitigation' ATTP 3-37.31 (July 2012).
112 See eg Captain Karin Tackaberry, 'Judge Advocates Play a Major Role in Rebuilding Iraq: The Foreign Claims Act and Implementation of the Commander's Emergency Response Program' (February 2004) *Army Lawyer* 39, 43; Jeremy Joseph, 'Mediation in War: Winning Hearts and Minds using Mediated Condolence Payments' (2007) 23(3) *Negotiation Journal*, 219, 223–224.
113 See eg CIVIC (n 1).
114 For a general discussion on responsibility in peacekeeping operations, see Marten Zwanenburg, *Accountability of Peace Support Operations* (Martinus Nijhoff 2005).
115 Bruce Oswald, Helen Durham and Adrian Bates, *Documents on the Law of UN Peace Operations* (OUP 2010) 323–324.
116 See Report of the Secretary-General, 'Administrative and Budgetary Aspect of the Financing of the United Nations Peacekeeping Operations' UN Doc A/51/389 (20 September 1996); Report of the Secretary-General, 'Administrative and Budgetary Aspects of the Financing of United Nations Peacekeeping Operations' UN Doc A/51/903 (21 May 1997).
117 UNGA Res 52/247 (26 June 1998).

or property damage during UN peacekeeping operations can claim compensation from the UN of up to US$50,000.[118]

However, there are a number of limitations on victims' access to recompense from the UN for damage caused during peacekeeping operations. Claims must be made within six months of the damage or loss being sustained,[119] and non-economic damage, 'such as pain and suffering or moral anguish, as well as punitive or moral damages', is not compensable.[120] Most significantly, compensation is not available for damage caused out of 'operational necessity'.[121] The Secretary-General's Report explains that damage from 'operational necessity' occurs 'where damage results from necessary actions taken by a peacekeeping force in the course of carrying out its operations'.[122] Therefore, although the UN facilitates recompense to victims of its peacekeeping operations, it places considerable limitations on claimants' ability to access compensation.

In relation to the International Security Assistance Force (ISAF) campaign in Afghanistan, NATO developed a policy to guide ISAF troop-contributing states' approach to compensating civilians who suffered injury or property loss during the conflict. Established in 2010, the 'Non-Binding Guidelines for Payments in Combat-Related Cases of Civilian Casualties or Damage to Civilian Property' stipulated that troop-contributing states should seek to 'proactively offer assistance for civilian casualty cases or damages to civilian property, in order to mitigate human suffering'.[123] NATO established the NATO Claims Office to facilitate payment of compensation to civilians injured by NATO forces in non-combat situations in Afghanistan.[124] The International Commission of Inquiry on Libya also recommended that NATO apply the Non-Binding Guidelines to civilian losses in Libya resulting from its operations in that country during the 2011 Libyan armed conflict.[125]

Amends can take the form of financial compensation, however other provisions for the support of collateral damage victims, such as the rebuilding of property, educational opportunities and apologies from the injuring state, may also play a role in making amends.[126] Due to the non-binding nature of these NATO guidelines, the decision to provide recompense to incidentally injured Afghan civilians during the ISAF mission was at the discretion of each state. In all

---

118 UNGA Res 52/247 (26 June 1998) ¶¶ 3, 5 and 9(d). Note that claims over US$50,000 can be paid in 'exceptional circumstances' on the recommendation of the Secretary-General. Ibid ¶ 9(e).

119 Alternatively, claims must be brought within six months of the damage of loss being discovered by the claimant. Ibid ¶ 8.

120 Ibid ¶ 9(b).

121 Ibid ¶ 6.

122 Report of the Secretary-General (1996) (n 116) 13, 14. The Secretary-General articulated four conditions for the existence of 'operational necessity'. These include the requirement that the commander has 'good-faith conviction' of the existence of operational necessity, that the action was 'strictly necessary and not a matter of mere convenience or expediency', that the act was 'executed in pursuance of an operational plan and not the result of a rash individual action' and that the damage was 'proportional to what is strictly necessary in order to achieve the operational goal'. See also, Daphna Shraga, 'UN Peacekeeping Operations: Applicability of International Humanitarian Law and Responsibility for Operations-Related Damage' (2000) 94 AJIL 450, 453.

123 NATO Final Council Approval of Non-Binding Guidelines for Payments in Combat-Related Cases of Civilian Casualties, SG(2010)0377 (9 June 2010) ¶ 2, and Annex ¶ 9. See also NATO, 'NATO Nations Approve Civilian Casualty Guidelines' (NATO Official Texts, 6 August 2010), www.nato.int/cps/en/natolive/official_texts_65114.htm. In March 2012, the UN Human Rights Council recommended that these guidelines be applied by NATO in the Libyan conflict: Report of the 15th Special Session of the Council, UN Doc A/HRC/19/68 (25 February 2011) ¶ 130(b).

124 NATO Claims Policy for Designated Crisis Response Operations, AC/119-N(2004)0058 (5 May 2004).

125 See eg Report of the International Commission of Inquiry on Libya, 2 March 2012 (131(b)).

126 See eg 'Civilian Casualty Mitigation' (n 111) ¶¶ 2-115–2-120. See also Holewinski (n 5) 320.

cases, the states providing these remedies stipulated that by making amends, the state was not admitting legal liability and amends offered were not predicated on any violation of IHL.[127]

The US, the largest troop-contributing state to ISAF,[128] employed a number of mechanisms to facilitate payment of compensation as a form of making amends to incidentally injured Afghan civilians. During the ISAF campaign, three forms of ex gratia payments were made by the US to compensate incidentally injured civilians; *solatia* payments,[129] condolence payments and battle damage payments.[130] US commanders had discretion to make *solatia* payments 'in accordance with local custom … to convey personal feelings of sympathy or condolence' to incidentally injured civilians.[131] In Afghanistan, a maximum of US$2,000 could be paid to victims, funded from commanders' Unit Operations and Maintenance Funds.[132] Condolence payments served the same purpose as *solatia* payments, however commanders had discretion to award up to US$2,500 for death and $2,200 for property damage.[133] Battle damage payments compensated civilians for damage to property caused during combat.[134] In contrast to *solatia* payments, condolence and battle damage payments were made from the Commander's Emergency Response Program.[135] There were limited guidelines for payment of compensation, and commanders had broad discretion on whether to offer compensation to incidentally injured civilians.[136] Alongside ex gratia payments, the US Foreign Claims Act[137] facilitates payment of compensation to civilians who are injured or have suffered damage to their property caused by US forces in non-combat activities.[138]

The UK, another significant ISAF troop contributing nation,[139] also made ex gratia compensation payments to civilians in Afghanistan who were injured or suffered property damage

---

127 See eg NATO Final Council Approval (n 123) ¶ 2, and Annex ¶ 9; US Department of the Army, 'Legal Services Claims Procedures' Pamphlet 27-162 (21 March 2008) ¶ 10-10; Hon Greg Combet, Minister for Defence Materiel and Science, 'Tactical Payments Scheme' (media release), 008/200925 (June 2009), www.defence.gov.au/minister/94tpl.cfm?CurrentId=9198; Defence Act 1903, s 123H.

128 See eg ISAF, 'International Security Assistance Force (ISAF): Key Facts and Figures', www.nato.int/nato_static_fl2014/assets/pdf/pdf_2014_09/20140901_140903-ISAF-Placemat-final.pdf.

129 *Solatia* payments were approved for use by the US military in Afghanistan from October 2005, see US Government Accountability Office, *Military Operations: The Department of Defence's Use of Solatia and Condolence Payments in Iraq and Afghanistan* (May 2007) ('US GAO') 2. *Solatia* payments were also made by the US in Iraq between June 2003 and January 2005 (ibid). See also 'Legal Services Claims Procedures' (n 127) ¶ 10-10; US Department of the Army, 'Money as a Weapons System Afghanistan' USFOR-A Pub 1-06 (March 2012) 86.

130 Condolence and battle damage payments were approved for use in Afghanistan in 2005: US GAO (n 129) 2. This report states that 'units generally follow a similar process for making solatia and condolence payments in Iraq and Afghanistan': ibid 3. See also Amsterdam International Law Clinic, *Monetary Payments for Civilian Harm in International and National Practice* (2 October 2013), commissioned by the Center for Civilians in Conflict, http://civiliansinconflict.org/resources/pub/valuation-of-life, 13–15.

131 'Legal Services Claims Procedures' (n 127) ¶ 10-10.

132 CIVIC (n 1) 5. See also, US GAO (n 129) 13; Amsterdam International Law Clinic (n 130) 15.

133 CIVIC (n 1) 5–6; Amsterdam International Law Clinic (n 130) 15. Note that payments up to US$5,000 may be approved by colonels and US$10,000 by the Deputy Commanding General: CIVIC (n 1) 6; US GAO (n 129) 34.

134 'Money as a Weapons System Afghanistan' (n 129) 85–86.

135 Ibid 85–86; US GAO (n 129) 13; CIVIC (n 1) 5.

136 'Civilian Casualty Mitigation' (n 111) ¶¶ 2-115–2-120; US GAO (n 129) 31–32.

137 Foreign Claims Act, 10 USC § 2734 (2006).

138 For further discussion on the Foreign Claims Act and the distinction between combat and non-combat activities, see Jordan Walerstein, 'Coping with Combat Claims: An Analysis of the Foreign Claims Act's Combat Exclusion' (2009–2010) 11 *Cardozo Journal of Conflict Resolution* 319.

139 ISAF, 'United Kingdom', www.isaf.nato.int/troop-numbers-and-contributions/united-kingdom/index.php.

during the ISAF campaign.[140] Payments were made where the loss had been caused by the negligence of the UK military, and also, in some instances, 'to promote "civil effect"'.[141] Payments could be made by the Common Law Claims and Policy Division of the UK, with the amount paid for deaths ranging from US$201 to US$7,000.[142] Ex gratia claims were paid by Area Claims Officers, who could pay compensation of up to US$115,000 per claim.[143]

Alongside the US and the UK, a number of other NATO member states made ex gratia payments to incidentally injured civilians in Afghanistan during the ISAF campaign. Canadian legal advisers could approve ex gratia payments[144] and compensation was generally made in response to civilian claims lodged at an Operational Coordination Center District.[145] The Netherlands had a formal policy that facilitated ex gratia payments to compensate Afghan civilians for property damage caused by the Dutch forces.[146] Claims under US$500 could be handled directly by commanders, and claims between US$500 and US$1,500 were handled by the Dutch Task Force Uruzgan Legal Advisers.[147] For compensation payments over $1,500 authorisation was required from the Task Force Unit Commander.[148] There were no formal guidelines that indicate the amount of individual payments for injury or death.[149] Poland paid ex gratia compensation during the ISAF campaign in Afghanistan of up to US$2,500.[150] Norway also made compensation payments to civilians, assessed on an individual basis.[151] In contrast, neither Germany nor Italy had any policy to facilitate compensation for civilians in Afghanistan,[152] but, despite this, there were instances of both states awarding ex gratia compensation to incidentally injured civilians.[153]

Australia similarly awarded ex gratia 'act of grace payments' to civilians who were injured or suffered property damage in Afghanistan.[154] These payments required approval from the Australian Finance Minister and therefore commanders had limited capacity to respond immediately to civilian claims.[155] In light of this, the Tactical Payments Scheme was created in 2009 to give commanders discretion to compensate civilians for death, injury or property damage.[156]

At the time of writing, the ISAF campaign is ending and NATO will shortly be transitioning to the 'Resolute Support' campaign in Afghanistan. It remains to be seen how contributing

---

140 CIVIC (n 1) 8.
141 Ibid.
142 Amsterdam International Law Clinic (n 130) 15.
143 Ibid.
144 See Ronen (n 3) 214; Michael Friscolanti, 'What's a Life Worth?' (Macleans 10 January 2011), www2.macleans.ca/2011/01/10/whats-a-life-worth/.
145 CIVIC (n 1) 11.
146 'Standard Operating Procedures' Task Force Uruzgan (April 2009), as cited in CIVIC (n 1) 10.
147 CIVIC (n 1) 10.
148 Amsterdam International Law Clinic (n 130) 12; see also CIVIC (n 1) 10.
149 CIVIC (n 1) 10.
150 Ibid 12; Amsterdam International Law Clinic (n 130) 12.
151 Ibid 13.
152 Ibid 9.
153 Ibid 9.
154 Financial Management and Accountability Act 1997, s 33. See also Ronen (n 3) 215; Holewinski (n 5) 324.
155 Financial Management and Accountability Act 1997, s 33; Emily Bourke, 'Troops Speed Up "Act of Grace Payments" to Afghan Civilians' *The World Today* (ABC News, 2 July 2009), www.abc.net.au/worldtoday/content/2009/s2614822.htm. See also CIVIC (n 1) 12.
156 Defence Legislation Amendment Bill (No 1), 2009. Commanders must be ranked lieutenant colonel or above in order to award payments under the Tactical Payments Scheme. See also Nesam McMillan, 'The Tactical Payment Scheme: Configurations of Life and Death in the Context of War' (2011–2012) 23 *Current Issues in Criminal Justice* 313, 321.

states will approach the challenge of making amends throughout this transition. However, in addition to the practices adopted by ISAF troop contributing nations, there have also been instances of states making ex gratia payments to incidentally injured civilians in other contemporary conflicts. Sarah Holewinski, previously Director of the Center for Civilians in Conflict (previously CIVIC), provides examples of amends made to Yemeni civilians by the Yemeni government, and to Pakistani civilians by the Pakistani government.[157] The Republic of Georgia has made amends to collateral damage victims in South Ossetia.[158] Ex gratia compensation has also been paid by the African Union Mission in Somalia (AMISOM), in at least one instance.[159] In relation to amends made by AMISOM, the UNHCR supported a report released by the Center for Civilians in Conflict in 2011, which called for the creation of a database for civilian injuries in Somalia to facilitate making amends to collateral damage victims.[160] In response to this report, the UNHCR called for 'donors to provide the necessary financial support ... so that an effective policy on making amends can be established by AMISOM'.[161]

These examples of state and IGO practice demonstrate that there is significant variation in the approach taken to compensate incidentally injured civilians.[162] In light of this, at least three non-governmental organisations (NGOs) have engaged with the issue, emphasising the difficulties and inconsistencies that divergent approaches create for victims.[163] Although the practice of making amends to collateral damage victims recognises their suffering and goes some way to redressing their immediate needs, there remains significant scope for further consideration of how this practice can be developed for future conflicts.[164]

---

157 Holewinski (n 5) 325.

158 Ibid.

159 Ibid. For a discussion of the potential for AMISOM to pay compensation to incidentally injured Somalian civilians, see Walter Lotze and Yvonne Kasumba, 'AMISOM and the Protection of Civilians in Somalia' (2012) 2 *Conflict Trends* 17–24, 23.

160 UNHCR and Center for Civilians in Conflict, 'Somali Civilians say they want Recognition for Conflict Losses' (Joint Press Release, 10 November 2011), www.unhcr.org/4ebbcc1efc1.html. See also UNSC Res 2036 (22 February 2012).

161 B Banon, 'Poor Weather and Conflict are Further Exacerbating the Situation for Civilians in Somalia' UNHCR *November 2011 Update*, www.unhcr.org.uk/resources/monthly-updates/november-2011-update/poor-weather-and-conflict-are-further-exacerbating-the-situation-for-civilians-in-somalia.html.

162 For a detailed evaluation of the consistency of current practice in providing monetary payments, both the amounts and methodologies used by the entity offering the payment, see the report by the Center for Civilians in Conflict (n 130).

163 See eg Human Rights Watch, 'Letter to NATO to Investigate Compensation for Civilian Casualties in Afghanistan' (1 April 2009), www.hrw.org/news/2009/04/02/letter-nato-investigate-compensation-civilian-casualties-afghanistan; Amnesty International, 'Human Rights in Afghanistan: Amnesty Briefing for the 2012 NATO Summit' (20 May 2012), www.amnesty.org.uk/press-releases/human-rights-afghanistan-amnesty-briefing-2012-nato-summit; Joint Briefing Paper, 'Nowhere to Turn, the Failure to Protect Civilians in Afghanistan' (18 November 2010), www.oxfam.org/en/policy/nowhere-turn 12; Campaign for Innocent Victims in Conflict, 'Civilian Harm in Somalia: Creating an Appropriate Response' (2011), www.unhcr.org/refworld/pdfid/4ec4bec02.pdf.

164 US Congress, Evidence to US Senate Committee on Appropriations Subcommittee on State and Foreign Relations (Erica Gaston) (Washington DC, 1 April 2009), www.appropriations.senate.gov/ht-state.cfm?method=hearings.view&id=5050563e-c9c1-46b2-9af5-13302e637e6f. For a discussion on the relevance of examples of making amends to establishing a pattern of state practice, see Paul (n 4).

4 Conclusion: future challenges

In some contexts, policies and practice demonstrate the increasing recognition that amends should be made to collateral damage victims for injuries caused to themselves and their families, and damage to their property. However, states and IGOs are not under any legal obligation to make amends to these victims and, although there may be an emerging trend of making amends, it is unclear how this practice will develop in the future. Currently, there appears to be significant scope for states to establish best practices,[165] and a continuing role for IGOs and NGOs in facilitating the development and implementation of these practices.

In contrast, there is a clear obligation on states to make reparations for violations of IHL and IHRL. Recent moves to facilitate reparations directly to individual victims – particularly by the ILC, ICC, ad hoc tribunals and IGOs – reflect a shifting conceptualisation of the obligation to make reparations. By providing reparations directly to individuals and collective groups, rather than states, there is potential for the development of individual and collective rights to reparations in international law.

However, in order to be effective these rights will require procedural mechanisms through which they can be enforced. Given the limited resources available for reparations, the international community faces a number of challenges to the creation of a uniform legal framework through which these rights can be exercised. It will be necessary to determine who is eligible to receive reparations, which violations will be redressed through reparations and what type of reparations can be provided.[166] Further, it will become increasingly important to consider what mechanisms can be established to ensure that victims of violence perpetrated by non-state actors, including collateral damage victims and victims of IHL violations, can be compensated.[167]

In considering these issues, some of the key questions that the international community will grapple with will be those identified by Philip Alston in his report on Extrajudicial, Summary and Arbitrary Executions, notably his emphasis on facilitating the protection of civilians and administration of justice following breaches of IHL and IHRL obligations.[168] Alston's questions serve to emphasise the importance of recognising individual and collective suffering, and enabling the victims to move forward with an acknowledgement that they have been wronged. Although reparations for victims of violations of IHL play an important role in achieving this, for many victims the limitation on accessing compensation for incidental injury appears arbitrary. In light of the growing numbers of 'collateral damage' victims of armed conflict, it may be necessary to consider a more complete approach to reparations, one that maintains the importance of reparations for violations of IHL and IHRL, but also focuses on facilitating redress to *all* victims of armed conflict. Civilians need to know that militaries value the lives of all civilian victims of conflict.[169]

165 For a discussion on the challenges of establishing best practices, see Holewinski (n 5) 327–330.
166 See eg Basic Principles (n 15).
167 Ron Dudai, 'Closing the Gap: Symbolic Reparations and Armed Groups' (September 2011) 93(883) *IRRC* 783.
168 Alston's discussion focuses on international law generally, and is not specific to reparations. Alston (n 6) ¶ 79(d).
169 See Sarah Holewinski, 'Do Less Harm: Protecting and Compensating Civilians in War' (January/ February 2013) *Foreign Affairs* 20.

31
Individual liability in international law

Robert Cryer

International law, on the whole, deals with states.[1] International humanitarian law (IHL), on the other hand, not only imposes duties on states, but also grants certain people (in particular, but not only, 'protected persons' in the Geneva Conventions sense) rights.[2] IHL is not unique in this regard, the law of human rights, for example does the same.[3] IHL, though, also imposes obligations on individuals, and, in certain cases, directly criminalises their violation. This is something international law rarely does.[4] This chapter will investigate the development of this phenomenon, the conditions under which violations of IHL become criminalised and a principle of responsibility that is directly linked to IHL – command responsibility.

1 The development of individual liability for violations of IHL

Although there are many interesting examples of early war crimes trials,[5] the development of direct liability under international law is largely a twentieth century phenomenon. The closest analogy to the modern law of war crimes was the enforcement of the law of war through the law of arms and the law of chivalry from the fourteenth to the sixteenth century.[6] This area of law drew on Roman concepts of the *jus gentium*, and was considered to bind knights irrespective of specific allegiances, and was considered applicable throughout medieval Europe.[7] However,

---

1 Robert Jennings and Arthur Watts (eds), *Oppenheim's International Law* (9th edn, Pearson 1992) 4.
2 See eg *GCI Commentary* 71–75, 82–84; Kate Partlett, *The Individual in the International Legal System: Continuity and Change in International Law* (CUP 2011) ch 3.
3 Partlett (n 2) ch 5. On the overlaps between the two areas, see amongst a vast literature, Symposium, 'The Influence of the European Court of Human Rights on International Criminal Law' (2011) 9 *JICJ* 571.
4 Other examples are aggression, crimes against humanity and genocide. The status of individual acts of torture and terrorism are more controversial. See Robert Cryer, Håkan Friman, Darryl Robinson and Elizabeth Wilmshurst, *An Introduction to International Criminal Law and Procedure* (3rd edn, CUP 2014) ch 14.
5 Timothy L H McCormack, 'From Sun Tzu to the Sixth Committee: The Evolution of an International Criminal Law Regime' in Timothy L H McCormack and Gerry J Simpson (eds), *The Law of War Crimes: National and International Approaches* (Nijhoff 1997) 31.
6 Maurice H Keen, *The Laws of War in the Late Middle Ages* (Keegan Paul 1965) ch 1.
7 Ibid.

direct parallels between the law of arms and modern international criminal law risks anachronism to say the least, and the understanding of what international law is differed greatly from then to now.[8] In addition, much of the criminalisation of the law of war was through domestic decrees such as the code promulgated by Charles VII of Orleans in 1439.[9]

By the time the Vattelian concept of the international legal order became accepted, the general approach to war crimes was largely (although not universally) that they were domestic crimes authorised by international law.[10] It is interesting that the First Geneva Convention of 1864 did not contain a provision on punishment of breaches,[11] even though Gustave Moynier, one of the instigators of the Convention, suggested an international criminal court in 1872.[12] Hague Convention (IV) of 1907 was similarly silent on criminal liability.[13]

Probably the first clear assertion by states that international law directly criminalised violations of IHL came in the 1919 Inter-Allied Commission on the Responsibility of the Authors of the War. Here the majority expressly opined that international law directly imposed liability for war crimes, recommending reliance in courts on '[t]he principles of the law of nations as they result from the usages established among civilised peoples, from the laws of humanity and from the dictates of public conscience'.[14] The Report was not unanimous, though, with both the Japanese and American members dissenting on precisely the question of whether or not there was individual liability in international law.[15] In the end, the Report went unimplemented, and the very few trials that occurred after the First World War in Leipzig were not only unsatisfactory, but based on violations of the German Criminal Code.[16]

During the Second World War, views as to the domestic or international nature of liability were split, although some of the most influential writers (who advised the Allies), tended to take the view that international law did directly criminalise war crimes.[17] Given who had advised the Prosecution at the Nuremberg International Military Tribunal – and the fact that Article 6 of its Statute provided that, *inter alia*, war crimes 'are crimes coming within the jurisdiction of the Tribunal for which there shall be individual responsibility'[18] – it was perhaps unsurprising that the tribunal held that liability was firmly based on international, not domestic law:

---

8 David Kennedy, 'Primitive International Law' (1986) 27 *Harvard ILJ* 1, 1–7.

9 Cited in Theodor Meron, *Henry's Wars and Shakespeare's Laws* (OUP 1993) 149.

10 Robert Cryer, *Prosecuting International Crimes: Selectivity and the International Criminal Law Regime* (CUP 2005) 21–31.

11 Geneva Convention for the Amelioration of the Condition of the Wounded in Armies in the Field (22 August 1864) 1 *AJIL Supp* 90.

12 Christopher K Hall, 'The First Proposal for a Permanent International Criminal Court' (1998) 38 *IRRC* 57.

13 Hague Convention (IV) regarding the Laws and Customs of Land Warfare (18 October 1907) 2 *AJIL Supp* 90.

14 'Report of the Commission on the Responsibility of the Authors of the War and Enforcement' (1920) 14 *AJIL* 95, 122.

15 Ibid 146, 152.

16 See generally Gary J Bass, *Stay the Hand of Vengeance: The Politics of War Crimes Tribunals* (Princeton University Press 2000) ch 3.

17 Hersch Lauterpacht, 'The Law of Nations and the Punishment of War Crimes' (1944) 21 *BYIL* 58; Quincy Wright, 'War Criminals' (1947) 39 *AJIL* 257. A firm view to the contrary was George Manner, 'The Legal Nature and Punishment of Criminal Acts of Violence Contrary to the Laws of War' (1943) 37 *AJIL* 407.

18 Although the provision is not entirely clear, see Kirsten Sellars, *Crimes against Peace and International Law* (CUP 2013) 85–87.

crimes against international law are committed by men, not abstract entities, and only by punishing individuals who commit such crimes can the provisions of international law be enforced ... individuals have international duties which transcend the national obligations of obedience imposed by the individual state.[19]

To a defence argument that the law of war, in particular the 1907 Hague Convention (IV) and the 1929 Geneva Convention, did not provide for individual liability for violations, the tribunal simply responded that 'violation of these provisions constituted crimes for which the guilty individuals were punishable is too well settled to admit argument'.[20] At least with hindsight, this was the point at which direct liability under international law became solidly (and practically) established.[21] After the war, only those who denied the existence of international criminal law in the sense of direct liability for international crimes denied that such liability existed for war crimes.[22]

2 The relationship between IHL and war crimes

Although they are often run together, the law of war crimes and IHL are not coterminous. War crimes are, in essence, a criminalised subset of violations of IHL.[23] The relationship can be described, with all due caveats about domestic analogies, as being similar to the relationship between the civil law of property and the law of theft, the latter being the criminal sphere of the former. Perhaps owing to the domestic nature of early liability for war crimes discussed above, the relationship between war crimes and IHL was not something greatly discussed until the post-war era. As the Statute of the Nuremberg International Military Tribunal (IMT) defined war crimes by reference to a non-exhaustive list of 'violations of the laws and customs of war', the tribunal had little time for the distinction between them and the claim that there was no criminal phase of IHL.

Interestingly, the Statute of the Tokyo IMT was even terser, its Article 5(b) simply describing war crimes as 'violations of the laws and customs of war'. The defence specifically argued that the tribunal was incompetent to try war crimes as the appropriate venue would be a national tribunal of a specially affected state, but the tribunal, to all intents and purposes, ignored the argument.[24] The Majority Opinion in the Tokyo IMT simply followed Nuremberg on all relevant aspects of the law, therefore not really adding to our understanding of the relationship between war crimes and IHL. One of the dissenters, though, Judge Pal, at least implicitly raised the distinction. Although he would have acquitted the defendants of all of the war crimes charges, mostly on the basis that there was no evidence that the specific defendants had ordered or condoned them, the prosecution evidence relating of aspects of the treatment of prisoners of war included orders signed by one of the defendants (Tōjō). In response to this, Pal argued that this was merely an act of state for which there was no individual liability.[25] The dividing line

---

19 *US et al v Göring et al* 1 TMWC 171, 223 (1946).
20 Ibid.
21 *Interlocutory Decision on the Applicable Law: Terrorism, Conspiracy, Homicide, Perpetration, Cumulative Charging* (Case no STL-11-01-17 *bis*, STL Appeals Chamber, 16 February 2011) ¶ 104.
22 One example is Georg Schwarzenberger, 'The Problem of an International Criminal Law' (1950) 3 *Current Legal Problems* 263.
23 See Sandesh Sivakumaran, *The Law of Non-International Armed Conflict* (OUP 2012) 77–83.
24 See Neil Boister and Robert Cryer, *The Tokyo International Military Tribunal: A Reappraisal* (OUP 2008) 178–179.
25 See ibid 188.

between such acts and those which gave rise to individual responsibility was not identified by Pal. Admittedly, the line is not, even now, always clear.

The current, most influential, statement of the conditions for a violation of IHL to be considered a war crime was given by the ICTY in its seminal *Tadić* decision. Here the Appeals Chamber argued that there were four cumulative conditions that had to be fulfilled for a violation to be criminal:

i   the violation must constitute an infringement of a rule of international humanitarian law;
ii the rule must be customary in nature or, if it belongs to treaty law, the required conditions must be met;
iii the violation must be 'serious,' that is to say, it must constitute a breach of a rule protecting important values, and the breach must involve grave consequences for the victim; and
iv the violation must entail, under customary or conventional law, the individual criminal responsibility of the person breaching the rule.[26]

Each of them raises important issues, and they will be discussed in turn.

2.1 The violation must constitute an infringement of a rule of IHL

This condition may sound like a statement of the obvious. However, it is important for two linked reasons. First, it shows that the law of war crimes is parasitic on IHL. For there to be a war crime, a violation of IHL must be shown. The law of war crimes is not hermetically sealed, but reliant on the underlying norms of IHL. As Michael Bothe has said:

> Rules concerning the punishment of 'war crimes' are secondary rules in relation to the primary rules concerning behaviour which is prohibited in case of an armed conflict. Thus, the concept of war crimes is a dynamic concept, as it is bound to change with the development of the primary or substantive rules relating to that behaviour.[27]

The Trial Chamber in the *Tadić* case had argued that owing to the fact that Article 2 of the ICTY's Statute granted them jurisdiction over grave breaches of the Geneva Conventions, they did not need to look at the applicability of those Conventions from the point of view of IHL (that is, that there was an international armed conflict). This was on the basis that the Statute

> has been so drafted as to be self-contained rather than referential, save for the identification of the victims of enumerated acts; that identification and that alone involves going to the Conventions themselves for the definition of 'persons or property protected'.[28]

The Appeals Chamber unambiguously rejected the argument, stating that the Trial Chamber had misinterpreted the extent to which war crimes law relies on IHL, and that war crimes law required all of IHL's conditions to be fulfilled.[29] In this regard it is notable that the Rome Statute of the ICC, when dealing with certain war crimes, expressly requires that the violations are of

---

26 *Prosecutor v Tadić (Decision on Interlocutory Appeal on Jurisdiction)* (Case no IT-94-1-AR72, ICTY Appeals Chamber, 2 October 1995) ¶ 94.
27 Michael Bothe 'War Crimes' in Antonio Cassese, John R W D Jones and Paula Gaeta (eds), *The Rome Statute of the International Criminal Court: A Commentary* (OUP 2000) 379, 381.
28 As cited in *Tadić* (n 26) ¶ 80.
29 Ibid ¶¶ 80–81.

'the laws and customs applicable in … armed conflict, within the established framework of international law'.[30]

The discussion of the Appeals Chamber leads to the second (as mentioned above, strongly linked) aspect of the condition: the relevant part of IHL has to be applicable. In other words that there must be an armed conflict. IHL does not (aside from small aspects relating to dissemination and protection of the protective emblems) apply in peacetime. Hence the ICTY, beginning with *Tadić*, has engaged in considerable and highly influential discussion of what amounts to an armed conflict.[31] In addition, where there is a disjunct in the IHL applicable in international and non-international armed conflict (which will be discussed below), and in different types of non-international armed conflicts,[32] it is necessary to distinguish the substantive law applicable to each type of conflict, and determine whether a specific conflict falls within one or the other category.[33]

2.2 The rule must be customary in nature or, if it belongs to treaty law, the required conditions must be met

This criterion also relates to the applicability of the relevant rule. In international armed conflicts, it is clear that customary IHL law binds all states (aside from persistent objectors)[34] and is therefore applicable to all international armed conflicts. What amounts to customary IHL, though, is the subject of some controversy.[35] In international armed conflicts, however, not all states party to the conflict may be parties to all the relevant treaties, and not all IHL treaties reflect customary law in their entirety. This is the case, most notably, but by no means only, for Additional Protocol I.[36] Where this is the case, the applicable IHL, and thus the applicable law of war crimes, may be different for different participants. In non-international armed conflicts, though, the situation tends to be somewhat less complex, as non-state participants in non-international armed conflicts are considered bound by both customary law and the treaties entered into by the state fighting them.[37]

---

30 Rome Statute art 8(2)(b)(e).

31 See eg Sivakumaran, *The Law of Non-International Armed Conflict* (n 23) chs 5–6.

32 The applicability criteria for common art 3 of the Geneva Conventions, and customary law, on one hand, and APII on the other, are different. See eg Sivakumaran, *The Law of Non-International Armed Conflict* (n 23) ch 5.

33 Although the ICTY has frequently determined that the substantive law is the same, therefore it is unnecessary to make this determination. See Sonja Boelaert-Suominen, 'The Yugoslavia Tribunal and the Common Core of Humanitarian Law Applicable to all Armed Conflicts' (2000) 13 *Leiden JIL* 619.

34 The notion of persistent objector does not play a large role in IHL, but its application cannot be entirely dismissed. See Iain Scobbie, 'The Approach to Customary Law in the Study' in Elizabeth Wilmshurst and Susan Breau (eds), *Perspectives on the ICRC Study on Customary International Law* (CUP 2007) 15, 34–36.

35 Jean-Marie Henckaerts and Louise Doswald-Beck, *Customary International Humanitarian Law* (CUP 2005). For critique, see Yoram Dinstein, *The Conduct of Hostilities under the Law of International Armed Conflict* (2nd edn, CUP 2010) 16; George Aldrich, 'Customary International Humanitarian Law: An Interpretation on Behalf of the International Committee of the Red Cross' (2005) 76 *BYIL* 503.

36 Christopher Greenwood, 'Customary Status of the 1977 Geneva Protocols' in Astrid J M Delissen and Gerard J Tanja (eds), *Humanitarian Law of Armed Conflict: Challenges Ahead* (Nijhoff 1991) 93.

37 There are various asserted bases for this, the most convincing being that the treaties do not require the consent of the relevant rebels or groups: Sandesh Sivakumaran, 'Binding Armed Opposition Groups' (2006) 55 *ICLQ* 369.

There are those who say that treaties, in and of themselves, cannot create criminal liability.[38] If this is the case, violations of, for example, the Geneva Conventions cannot, in and of themselves, create liability for individuals; only customary law could.[39] It is true that when the ICTY was created, the Secretary-General said that the jurisdiction of the ICTY ought to be limited to customary law, owing to the *nullum crimen sine lege* principle.[40] However, the ICTY has not quite kept to that, and the vast majority of state practice accepts that treaty-based violations of IHL can give rise to individual liability.[41] There is nothing conceptually impossible about treaties creating individual liability,[42] the main question is whether or not the particular treaty does, in fact, do so.

2.3 The violation must be 'serious', that is to say, it must constitute a breach of a rule protecting important values, or the breach must involve grave consequences for the victim

There is some state practice to support the proposition that all violations of IHL, no matter how trivial, amount to war crimes.[43] However, the more general view is that there are some IHL norms (such as the requirement that POWs may purchase tobacco at local market prices) that do not readily or appropriately lend themselves to criminalisation.[44] Hence most commentators (and the ICTY) require that the violation be 'serious'. It is worth noting that in the Rome Statute, all of the war crimes included in Article 8(2)(b), (c) and (e) are described as 'serious' (the grave breaches included in Article 8(2)(a) must be serious by definition). The Rome Conference that drafted that provision saw seriousness as an important criterion for the inclusion of a violation of IHL as a war crime.[45]

While the foundations of the requirement are fairly clear, the interpretation of it is more controversial. It has been described as a 'question-begging approach' and not 'operational as a distinguishing criterion'.[46] It is true that 'seriousness' can mean different things, for example, some values may be considered so important that any violation of them is serious; others may depend on the result.[47] In the end 'serious' is an evaluative term, rather than a self-applying one. That said, given in part that prosecutions before international tribunals have not really dealt with minor or technical breaches of IHL, the ICTY has not had practical difficulty with this criterion. Furthermore, interpreting it in a very strict manner (as was arguably done at Rome) could prevent conduct appropriately criminalised as a war crime from being prosecuted.[48]

38 Guénaël Mettraux, *International Crimes and the Ad Hoc Tribunals* (OUP 2005) 7–9.
39 Although some, conversely, doubt whether customary law is specific enough to ground criminal liability: Vladimir Djuro-Degan, 'On the Sources of International Criminal Law' (2005) 4 *Chinese JIL* 45, 67.
40 Report of the Secretary-General Pursuant to Paragraph 2 of Security Council Resolution 808, UN Doc S/25704 (3 May 1993) ¶ 34.
41 Henckaerts and Doswald-Beck (n 35) 572.
42 Marko Milanovic, 'Does the Rome Statute Bind Individuals? (And Why we Should Care)' (2011) 9 *JICJ* 25, 38ff.
43 See that canvassed in Robert Cryer, '*Galić* and the War Crime of Terror Bombing' (2005–2006) 2 *IDF Law Review* 73, 95–96.
44 Cryer, Friman, Robinson and Wilmshurst (n 4) 272.
45 Herman von Hebel and Darryl Robinson, 'Crimes within the Jurisdiction of the Court' in Roy S Lee (ed), *The International Criminal Court: The Making of the Rome Statute* (Kluwer 1999) 79, 104.
46 Georges Abi-Saab, 'The Concept of War Crimes' in Sineho Yee and Tieya Wang (eds), *International Law and the Post-Cold World: Essays in Honour of Li Haopei* (Routledge 2001) 99, 112.
47 Charles Garraway, 'War Crimes' in Wilmshurst and Breau (eds) (n 34) 377, 385.
48 Ibid 386.

2.4 The violation must entail, under customary or conventional law, the individual criminal responsibility of the person breaching the rule

This criterion requires, in addition to the rule being one of applicable IHL and the violation being serious, that there is a separate rule criminalising its violation. It must be said that the ICTY did not provide strong support in state practice for this purported requirement,[49] and it played little (although not an entirely negligible) role in the Rome negotiations.[50] However, it has played a considerable part in the reasoning of the ICTY and, at times, the Special Court for Sierra Leone, though their decisions on this point have not always been the most comprehensively reasoned.[51]

The most detailed analysis of this criterion has been provided by Antonio Cassese.[52] This is not surprising, as he was the President of the Chamber in *Tadić*, which promulgated the test. Cassese thought that there were various ways in which this criterion could be fulfilled. One way for Cassese, was if a treaty expressly criminalised the violation. Others were that case law had previously treated the violation as a war crime, or that the relevant norm had been included in the jurisdiction of an international criminal tribunal. Failing that, Cassese asserted that it was necessary to look at materials such as military manuals and national legislation. If that did not yield a result, he took the view that general principles of criminal justice and the legislation and jurisprudence of the state of nationality of the accused or the territorial state ought to be considered.[53] To a greater extent, what Cassese was suggesting was looking to the sources of international law, namely treaties, customary international law and general principles of law.

2.4.1 Treaties

It is certainly good evidence that a violation of IHL is criminalised when a treaty says so. However, the question is not quite as simple as this might imply.

First, there is the question of what language has to be used for the treaty to have this effect, and the status of the treaty. The paradigmatic examples of treaty rules criminalising violations of IHL are the grave breaches provisions of the Geneva Conventions (as is noted by Cassese).[54] The language of those provisions requires states to criminalise and punish such breaches.[55] Interestingly, although it is now accepted that grave breaches are war crimes, the Conventions themselves do not use the terminology (although Article 85(5) of Additional Protocol I does). In addition, the Geneva Conventions require certain grave breaches to be criminalised in the domestic legal order, which is language more like that of a transnational crime convention than, say, Article 1 of the Genocide Convention, that declares that 'genocide is a crime under international law'.[56]

---

49 Cryer 'Galić' (n 43) 95–96.
50 Von Hebel and Robinson (n 45) 104–105.
51 *Prosecutor v Norman (Decision on Preliminary Motion Based on Lack of Jurisdiction) (Child Recruitment)* (Case no SCSL-2004-14-AR72, SCSL Appeals Chamber, 31 May 2004), including dissenting opinion of Judge Robertson; *Prosecutor v Galić* (Case no IT-98-29-A, ICTY Appeals Chamber, 30 November 2006) ¶¶ 91–98 and dissenting opinion of Judge Schomburg.
52 Antonio Cassese, Paola Gaeta, Laurel Baig, Mary Fan, Christopher Gosnell and Alex Whiting, *Cassese's International Criminal Law* (3rd edn, OUP 2013) 67–70.
53 Ibid 68.
54 Ibid.
55 GCI art 50; GCII art 51; GCIII art 130; GCIV art 147; to which he adds API art 85.
56 On transnational crimes, see Neil Boister, *An Introduction to Transnational Criminal Law* (OUP 2012) ch 2.

Nonetheless, it is practically universally accepted that grave breaches are criminalised by international law.[57]

The second difficulty is with treaties that do not reflect customary international law. It is not, for example, entirely clear that all of Additional Protocol I's grave breaches are necessarily customarily criminal. So difficult issues could arise here, with different war crimes applying to parties to the treaty from non-parties. A further level of complexity may be added if the underlying IHL norm, but not the criminalising norm, is customary where it would only give rise to state responsibility of non-parties.[58]

There is also the question of conduct which falls within the purview of a treaty which expressly criminalises some, but not all, conduct falling under its terms. This is the case with non-grave breaches of the Geneva Conventions. In relation to those conventions, it is accepted that states may criminalise, in addition to grave breaches, other serious violations of the Conventions.[59] Precisely which ones it is not always clear. However, it would be wrong to read the Geneva Conventions *a contrario* as preventing states from criminalising 'non-grave' breaches of the Conventions. To do so would be to confuse what the grave breaches provisions do, which is to require states to assert mandatory universal jurisdiction over those breaches. They are not intended to prevent states from criminalising others.[60] Whether they can assert universal jurisdiction over such offences though, depends on customary law or the universal acceptance of the treaty.[61]

The inclusion of a violation of IHL in the statute of an international criminal tribunal is, for the most part, a sub-category of the situation where a treaty criminalises the conduct (the Statutes of the ICTY and the ICTR being based, in the end, on the UN Charter, and the SCSL Statute and the Rome Statute, being treaties themselves). As mentioned above, this is close to proof that something is criminalised in customary law too, but it is not conclusive, so the relationship to non-parties to those treaties is relevant.[62] Furthermore, particular conduct might not be defined as a war crime in the statute of an international criminal court to the full extent to which (customary) international law provides, as Article 10 of the Rome Statute makes clear.[63] There are customary war crimes that do not find their basis in the Rome Statute, although, again, there is disagreement about what they are.[64]

2.4.2 Customary international law

The other ways (outside general principles) that Cassese suggests for determining this criminalising rule, as a matter of international law, are perhaps best seen as methods of determining customary international law. So, for example, Cassese suggests looking at previous prosecution before national and international criminal tribunals. It is true that previous prosecution is a good *indicium* of criminality, but it must be remembered that international case law, pursuant to Article 38(1)(d) of the ICJ Statute, is strictly speaking only a subsidiary means of determining international law, not a source of it (although its practical influence is, admittedly, stronger than

---

57 James G Stewart, 'Introduction' (2009) 9 *JICJ* 653, 653.
58 Yves Sandoz, 'Penal Aspects of International Humanitarian Law' in M Cherif Bassiouni (ed), *International Criminal Law Volume 1: Sources, Subjects and Concepts* (3rd edn, Brill 2008) 293, 310.
59 As states are required to repress breaches of the Conventions. Ibid 304.
60 Theodor Meron, 'International Criminalization of Internal Atrocities' (1995) 89 *AJIL* 554, 561–565.
61 See generally Luis Benavides, 'Universal jurisdiction over war crimes' ch 35 in this volume.
62 Milanovic (n 42).
63 See also Garraway (n 47).
64 Ibid 387–388.

this would suggest).[65] National case law, it must be said, can be a source of state practice,[66] although case law is perhaps most useful when it seeks to prove customary law, as its argumentation can be adopted later.[67] As Cassese accepts, though, a small number of isolated precedents may not be enough.[68]

When the above (other than national courts) are silent, Cassese suggests that military manuals and national legislation be consulted. These are better seen simply as examples of state practice, of which there are others, and, indeed, this seems to be the way in which they were used in *Tadić*. What is complex here, is upon what basis states may domestically criminalise as war crimes prior to such a criminalising rule being established in customary international law or treaty for the individual rule of IHL? The better view, as implied above, is that a war crime is any 'serious' violation of IHL.

2.4.3 General principles

Failing any of these evidences of customary international law, Cassese suggests general principles of criminal law and the legislation and jurisprudence of the nationality or territoriality state. The reference to general principles of criminal law finds its basis in the *List* case,[69] but how this could form the basis of a rule criminalising a violation of IHL is not entirely clear, unless the idea is that conduct that is domestically criminal ought to be when it is also prohibited by IHL, but that begs the question of what is so criminalised. It is true that the European Convention on Human Rights, for example, in Article 7(2), provides that the prohibition of retroactive criminal law in Article 7(1) 'shall not prejudice the trial and punishment of any person for any act or omission which, at the time when it was committed, was criminal according the general principles of law recognized by civilized nations', although this is generally thought of as a savings clause intended not to cast doubt on the legality of the post-war trials than anything else.

The final idea, of looking at the legislation of the nationality and territoriality state really is a default idea, relating to whether or not the domestic courts and legislation of the nationality and territoriality state criminalise such conduct does not really affect international legal criminalisation, but may go to the fairness or predictability of prosecution from the point of view of the defendant.

2.5 Non-international armed conflicts

Christopher Greenwood has said that since serious violations of IHL applicable in international armed conflicts are criminalised, it is logical that, when IHL expanded to cover non-international armed conflicts, criminalisation occurred along similar lines.[70] But international law is not always made on the basis of logic. As Peter Rowe has said: 'It is difficult to justify, on grounds of logic,

---

65 For details, see Robert Cryer, 'Neither Here nor There? The Status of International Criminal Jurisprudence in the International and UK Legal Orders' in Michael Bohlander and Kaiyan Kaikobad (eds), *International Law and Power: Perspectives on Legal Order and Justice: Essays in Honour of Colin Warbrick* (Brill 2008) 183.

66 James Crawford, *Brownlie's Principles of Public International Law* (8th edn, OUP 2012) 24.

67 Ibid 39–40. For examples, see Robert Cryer, 'Of Custom, Treaties, Scholars and the Gavel: The Impact of the International Criminal Tribunals on the ICRC Customary Study' (2006) 11 *JCSL* 239.

68 Cassese *et al* (n 52) 68. Although framed without an abundance of clarity, it seems that this is an allusion to the sufficiency of such evidence to prove customary law.

69 Ibid 69.

70 Christopher Greenwood, 'International Humanitarian Law and the *Tadić* Case' (1996) 7 *EJIL* 265, 280–281.

a different regime of criminal responsibility for an act depending solely on whether it was committed during an international or a non-international armed conflict. But that is what States did.'[71] Indeed, in the Geneva Conventions, Common Article 3 was not considered to fall within the purview of the grave breaches provisions,[72] and Additional Protocol II (unlike Additional Protocol I) contained nothing on criminal repression at all.[73] There was some state practice to support the extension of the law of war crimes to non-international armed conflicts prior to the 1990s,[74] but there was very significant support for the contrary view amongst commentators,[75] the ICRC[76] and, indeed, the Commission of Inquiry for former Yugoslavia (the '780' Commission) that presaged the ICTY.[77]

The first clear criminalisation of violations of Common Article 3 and Additional Protocol II at the international level came in Article 4 of the Statute of the ICTR, a provision that was considered by the Secretary-General to have criminalised such violations for the first time.[78] The watershed on point though, must be considered to be the ICTY's decision in *Tadić*.[79] Here, having found that the grave breaches provisions do not apply to non-international armed conflicts,[80] the Appeals Chamber determined that, as Article 3 of its Statute granted it jurisdiction over an open-ended list of 'violations of the laws and customs of war', it could prosecute violations of the law of non-international armed conflicts so long as they were criminalised in international law.[81] On the basis of their reading of sources mentioned above, the Appeals Chamber determined that customary international law criminalised certain serious violations of IHL applicable in non-international armed conflicts.[82] This was controversial both on the bench[83] and amongst academics.[84] However, it achieved a remarkable degree of acceptance by states in a short time. The findings in *Tadić* were hugely influential in the negotiations for the

---

71 Colin Warbrick and Peter Rowe, 'The International Criminal Tribunal for Yugoslavia: The Decision of the Appeals Chamber on the Interlocutory Appeal on Jurisdiction in the *Tadic* Case' (1996) 45 *ICLQ* 691, 698.

72 Lindsay Moir, 'Grave Breaches and Internal Armed Conflicts' (2009) 8 *JICJ* 763; Jean-Marie Henckaerts, 'The Grave Breaches Regime as Customary International Law' (2009) 7 *JICJ* 683; although, see Sonja Boelaert-Suominen, 'Grave Breaches, Universal Jurisdiction and Internal Armed Conflicts: Is Customary Law Moving towards a Uniform Enforcement Mechanism for all Armed Conflicts?' (2000) 5 *JCSL* 63.

73 That said, as the ICTY Appeals Chamber pointed out, the absence of express criminalising provisions in IHL treaties did not stop the Nuremberg IMT for declaring individual criminal liability for violations to exist, *Tadić* (n 26) ¶ 128.

74 Very influentially discussed in Meron (n 60), although, see Eve la Haye, *War Crimes in Internal Armed Conflicts* (CUP 2007) ch 4.

75 Peter Rowe, 'War Crimes and the former Yugoslavia: The Legal Difficulties' (1993) 32 *RDMDG* 317, 328–333.

76 Denise Plattner, 'The Penal Repression of Violations of International Humanitarian Law Applicable in Non-International Armed Conflicts' (1990) 278 *IRRC* 409, 414.

77 Final report of the Commission Established Pursuant to Security Council Resolution 780, Annex to Letter dated 24 May 1994 from the Secretary-General to the President of the Security Council, UN Doc S/1994/674, ¶ 42.

78 Report of the Secretary General Pursuant to Paragraph 5 of Security Council Resolution 955, UN Doc S/1995/134 (13 February 1995) ¶ 12.

79 *Tadić* (n 26).

80 Ibid ¶¶ 80–84.

81 Ibid ¶¶ 83–93.

82 Ibid ¶¶ 128–136.

83 Separate Opinion of Judge Li, ¶¶ 10–13.

84 See Greenwood, 'International Humanitarian Law' (n 70), against, Geoffrey R Watson, 'The Humanitarian Law of the Yugoslavia War Crimes Tribunal: Jurisdiction in Prosecutor v Tadić' (1996) 36 *Virginia JIL* 687, 709–728.

Rome Statute,[85] and, since 1998, the position is settled: there is criminal liability for violations of IHL in non-international armed conflicts on the same conditions that apply to the criminalisation of violations in their international counterparts. But, as we have seen above, the interpretation of those conditions can give rise to controversy.

3 Command/superior responsibility[86]

Command responsibility is the responsibility of superiors for crimes committed by their subordinates that they have wrongfully failed to prevent and/or punish. Although its history is lengthy,[87] command responsibility's modern incarnation is often traced to its birth ('in sin') to *US v Yamashita*.[88] Irrespective of the merit and ambit of command responsibility, it is unfortunate that the case is uncertain on many of the most controversial issues relating to the principle. In *Yamashita*, command responsibility was framed as a violation of the laws and customs of war, possibly in itself, rather than as it is seen now, which is as a principle of liability.[89] The principle played practically no role in Nuremberg, but a significant one in the Tokyo IMT.[90]

The principle first received a partial, treaty-based codification in Article 86(2) of Additional Protocol I. This reads:

> The fact that a breach of the Conventions or of this Protocol was committed by a subordinate does not absolve his superiors from penal or disciplinary responsibility, as the case may be, if they knew, or had information which should have enabled them to conclude in the circumstances at the time, that he was committing or was going to commit such a breach and if they did not take all feasible measures within their power to prevent or repress the breach.

This is linked to a more general duty of superiors to exercise command, which is provided for in Article 87(1) of the Protocol:

> The High Contracting Parties and the Parties to the conflict shall require military commanders, with respect to members of the armed forces under their command and other persons under their control, to prevent and, where necessary, to suppress and to report to competent authorities breaches of the Conventions and of this Protocol.

As we will see, the precise relationship between the two is not simple, not least as Article 86 speaks of criminal liability, but Article 87 does not.

---

85 See, *inter alia*, La Haye (n 74) 136; Tamàs Hoffman, 'The Gentle Civilizer of Humanitarian Law: Antonio Cassese and the Creation of the Customary Law of Non-International Armed Conflict' in Carsten Stahn and Larissa van den Herik (eds), *Future Perspectives in International Criminal Justice* (Asser 2009) 58.

86 See generally Guénaël Mettraux, *The Law of Command Responsibility* (OUP 2009); Chantal Meloni, *Command Responsibility in International Criminal Law* (Asser 2010); Elies van Sliedregt, *Individual Criminal Responsibility in International Law* (OUP 2012) ch 8.

87 See W Hays Parks, 'Command Responsibility for War Crimes' (1973) 62 *Military LR* 1, 1–20.

88 *US v Yamashita* 4 TWC 1 (US Military Commission at Manila 1945), 327 US 1 (1946); on it being 'born in sin', see Mettraux (n 86) 5.

89 Although that is not uncontroversial, see Darryl Robinson, 'How Command Responsibility got so Complicated: A Culpability Contradiction, its Obfuscation and a Simple Solution' (2012) 13 *Melbourne JIL* 1.

90 Neil Boister and Robert Cryer, *The Tokyo International Military Tribunal: A Reappraisal* (OUP 2008) 227–236.

After Tokyo, the next international criminal tribunal with jurisdiction over such a form of liability was the ICTY, Article 7(3) of whose Statute (drawing upon, although not quite repeating, the language of Additional Protocol I) provides:

> The fact that [crimes were] committed by a subordinate does not relieve his superior of criminal responsibility if he knew or had reason to know that the subordinate was about to commit such acts or had done so and the superior failed to take the necessary and reasonable measures to prevent such acts or to punish the perpetrators thereof.

The ICTR and SCSL Statutes (Articles 6(3) and 6(3) respectively) are, to all intents and purposes the same. The relevant parts of Article 28 of the ICC Statute, which deals with superior responsibility, are more detailed and deserves quotation in full:

(a) A military commander or person effectively acting as a military commander shall be criminally responsible for crimes within the jurisdiction of the Court committed by forces under his or her effective command and control, or effective authority and control as the case may be, as a result of his or her failure to exercise control properly over such forces, where:

    (i) That military commander or person either knew or, owing to the circumstances at the time, should have known that the forces were committing or about to commit such crimes; and

    (ii) That military commander or person failed to take all necessary and reasonable measures within his or her power to prevent or repress their commission or to submit the matter to the competent authorities for investigation and prosecution.

(b) With respect to superior and subordinate relationships not described in paragraph (a), a superior shall be criminally responsible for crimes within the jurisdiction of the Court committed by subordinates under his or her effective authority and control, as a result of his or her failure to exercise control properly over such subordinates, where:

    (i) The superior either knew, or consciously disregarded information which clearly indicated, that the subordinates were committing or about to commit such crimes;

    (ii) The crimes concerned activities that were within the effective responsibility and control of the superior; and

    (iii) The superior failed to take all necessary and reasonable measures within his or her power to prevent or repress their commission or to submit the matter to the competent authorities for investigation and prosecution.

Although many aspects of command responsibility are complex, the basic elements can be set out fairly briefly. They are (1) a superior and subordinate relationship, (2) the mental element, (3) a failure to take reasonable measures to prevent and/or punish[91] and (4) causation. The customary status of the fourth condition is questionable, but it is clear that it is present in the Rome Statute, which requires that the crimes occur 'as a result' of the failure to control subordinates.

---

91 *Prosecutor v Delalić, Mučić, Delić and Landžo* (Case no IT-96-21-T, ICTY Trial Chamber, 16 November 1998) ¶ 344

3.1 Effective control

Command responsibility arises only in the circumstances where there is effective control of the subordinates, or at least the ability to exercise effective control, given that part of the principle is a failure to supervise subordinates properly. Official position is not, in and of itself, proof of effective control, although it may be good evidence of it.[92] This is for two reasons: the first is that there are circumstances in which a *de jure* superior may, particularly in fast moving conflicts, lose control of his/her subordinates. Indeed breaking lines of command is likely to be one of the aims of the opposing forces.[93] In addition, especially in non-international armed conflicts, given that states are very unlikely to concede any legitimacy to rebel legal order, if it was required that there be a legal, rather than factual, relation on control the principle would only apply to governmental forces. The approach of the ICTY has been to require quite a high level of control in practice,[94] which, according to some, has led to the principle being rarely useful in practice, and not reflecting the fluid nature of modern warfare.[95]

One issue which has proved controversial before the ICTY is whether a person can be held responsible for failing to punish crimes committed prior to them taking up command. The Appeals Chamber rejected that responsibility by a bare majority in the *Hadžihasanović* appeal.[96] This proved controversial inside and outside the Chamber,[97] however, although it has been said that a majority of Appellate thought disagrees with this conclusion, the Appeals Chamber has not formally overruled the decision.[98] Owing to the causation requirement in the Rome Statute, it would not be possible to argue that liability could arise under that treaty for failing to punish offences committed prior to a person taking up command.

Although the principle of command responsibility was developed in the military context, from at least the time of the Tokyo Trial (1948) it has been accepted that the principle applies to civilians although the precise conditions are controversial.[99] The ICTY has traditionally accepted that the test is *mutatis mutandis* the same, that is, effective control, and that the level of control has to be similar to that in military contexts, albeit exercised differently.[100] The Rome Statute emphasises the control aspect, including, in addition to the express requirement of

---

92 *Prosecutor v Delalić, Mučić, Delić and Landžo* (Case no IT-96-21-A, ICTY Appeals Chamber, 20 February 2001) ('*Čelebići Appeal*') ¶ 256, 186–198; *Prosecutor v Bemba Gombo (Decision Pursuant to Article 61(7)(a) and (b) of the Rome Statute on the Charges)* (Case no ICC01/05-01/08, ICC Pre-Trial Chamber III, 15 July 2009) ¶¶ 414–416. See generally Mettraux (n 86) ch 9.

93 Those who argue that Yamashita was not guilty often do so on the basis that he was not in fact in command of his troops at the relevant time, as American forces had cut his lines of communication with them.

94 It is notable that 'substantial influence' is not enough, *Čelebići Appeal* (n 92) ¶ 266.

95 Mark Osiel, 'The Banality of Good: Aligning Incentives Against Mass Atrocity' (2005) 105 *Columbia LR* 1751, 1779ff.

96 *Prosecutor v Hadžihasanović, Alagić and Kubura (Judgment on Interlocutory Appeal Challenging Jurisdiction in Relation to Command Responsibility)* (Case no IT-01-47-AR72, ICTY Appeals Chamber, 16 July 2003) ¶¶ 37–56.

97 See generally Robert Cryer, 'The ad hoc Tribunals and Command Responsibility: A Quiet Earthquake' in Shane Darcy and Joseph Powderly (eds), *Judicial Creativity in International Criminal Tribunals* (OUP 2010) 159; Alphons Orie, 'Stare Decisis in the ICTY Appeal: Successor Responsibility in the Hadžihasanović Case' (2012) 10 *JICJ* 635.

98 *Prosecutor v Orić* (Case no IT-03-68-A, ICTY Appeals Chamber, 3 July 2008) ¶¶ 166–188, Declaration of Judge Shahabuddeen, ¶¶ 2–15.

99 Some also remain slightly uncomfortable about civilian command responsibility, van Sliedregt (n 86) 209.

100 *Prosecutor v Bagilishema* (Case no IT-95-1A-A, ICTY Appeals Chamber, 3 July 2002) ¶ 52.

effective authority and control, that 'the crimes concerned activities that were within the effective responsibility and control of the superior'.[101]

3.2 Mental element

The mental element of command responsibility is an area of considerable controversy, and divergence arguably between customary law, the jurisprudence of the ad hoc tribunals and the Rome Statute.[102] The Rome Statute, controversially, and probably wrongly, also introduced a distinction in the mental element between military and non-military superiors.[103]

The *Yamashia* case, although hardly crystalline in its entirety, set a standard that the commander knew or was at fault in not having known, about the offences.[104] The first time the principle was brought into treaty law, though, in Additional Protocol I, the terminology, which, according to the ICRC's commentary on point, was intended to reflect the post-Second World War case law (admittedly not all of which agreed entirely with *Yamashita*)[105] was not quite the same. As noted above, Article 86 of Additional Protocol I provides that there is to be criminal liability where a superior 'knew, or had information which should have enabled them to conclude' that grave breaches were committed or about to be, and Article 87 of the Protocol provides for positive duties to control and monitor compliance with humanitarian law by superiors. Some argue, with considerable force, that the criminal prohibition in Article 86 receives a clarification in its ambit from the (not expressly criminal) Article 87.[106] This shows the difficulty of interpreting treaties' often ambiguous language when it comes to the interplay of, as well as the extent of, individual criminal liability and state responsibility.

As mentioned above, the language of the ICTY/ICTR/SCSL Statutes draws upon (although is not the same as) that of the Additional Protocol. This language was interpreted by the leading authority in the tribunals (the *Čelebići* case) as meaning:

> [A superior] ... may possess the *mens rea* for command responsibility where: (1) he had actual knowledge, established through direct or circumstantial evidence, that his subordinates were committing or about to commit crimes ... or (2) where he had in his possession information of a nature, which at the least, would put him on notice of the risk of such offences by indicating the need for additional investigation in order to ascertain whether such crimes were committed or were about to be committed by his subordinates.[107]

This was based primarily on the idea that Article 86 on its own, reflected the pre-existing customary standard (which they interpreted quite narrowly).[108] This did not go uncontroverted

---

101 Rome Statute art 28(b)(ii). For discussion of the early ICC case law on point, see William Schabas, *The International Criminal Court: A Commentary on the Rome Statute* (OUP 2010) 460–461.

102 See generally Kai Ambos, *Treatise on International Criminal Law: Volume I: Foundations and General Part* (OUP 2013) 220–228.

103 For critique, see van Sliedregt (n 86) 200–202, 209.

104 Parks (n 87) 14; see Dinstein (n 35) 273–274.

105 See *AP Commentary* 1013–1014. Others are narrower on point, see Michael Bothe, Karl Joseph Partsch and Waldemar Solf, *New Rules for Victims of Armed Conflicts* (Nijhoff 1982) 523–526. For the post-war cases, see 15 TWC 66ff.

106 *API Commentary* 1011; Robert Kolb, 'The Jurisprudence of the Yugoslav and Rwandan Criminal Tribunals on their Jurisdiction and on International Crimes' (2000) 69 *BYBIL* 259, 301.

107 *Čelebići Appeal* (n 92) ¶¶ 223, 241.

108 Ibid ¶ 237 the Appeals Chamber said that 'Article 87 therefore interprets Article 86(2) as far as the duties of the commander or superior are concerned, but the criminal offence based on command responsibility is defined in Article 86(2) only.'

in the ICTY. The Trial Chamber in the *Blaškić* case (which predated the *Čelebići* appeal) which on the basis of its own (broader) reading of custom and the interplay of Articles 86 and 87,[109] took the view that:

> if a commander has exercised due diligence in the fulfilment of his duties yet lacks know-ledge that crimes are about to be or have been committed, such lack of knowledge cannot be held against him. However, taking into account his particular position of command and the circumstances prevailing at the time, such ignorance cannot be a defence where the absence of knowledge is the result of negligence in the discharge of his duties: this com-mander had reason to know within the meaning of the Statute.[110]

Whatever its merits, this is, however, a minority view in the jurisprudence of the ad hoc tribunals. The *Blaškić* finding was notably not upheld by the Appeals Chamber (although the prosecution did not seek to have it affirmed). In the latter appeal the Appeals Chamber also specifically rejected the terminology of negligence for both military and civilian command responsibility.[111]

The Rome Statute, on the other hand, separates off military and civilian command respons-ibility, and applies different mental elements to them. This was introduced late on in the nego-tiations in Rome,[112] and is a departure from customary international law, which does not distinguish military and non-military superiors.[113] For military superiors the Rome Statute estab-lishes a 'should have known' standard. This has been interpreted by a Pre-Trial Chamber of the ICC as creating a negligence standard for liability.[114] Although that chamber accepted that the standard differed from that adopted in *Čelebići*, it also accepted that the relevant criteria were the same.[115]

When it comes to civilian superiors, the Rome Statute requires that the superior knew or 'consciously disregarded information which clearly indicated' that crimes were about to be committed, or had been committed by subordinates. Although this has yet to be the subject of detailed analysis by the ICC itself, it has been suggested that the standard is not far from that adopted for military and non-military superiors by the ICTY.[116] There are reasons to doubt this. Not least, to 'consciously disregard' information which clearly indicated that criminality was afoot is very close to constructive knowledge of that (potential or extant) criminality. In addi-tion, the standard applied by the ad hoc tribunals, which is that possession (not conscious dis-regard) of information (which does not require that it has been read) suffices.

3.3 Failure to take measures

In addition to the requirements above, it is also necessary that the superior fails to take necessary and reasonable measures to prevent the conduct occurring. This is generally a factual enquiry,

---

109 *Prosecutor v Blaškić* (Case no IT-96-14/1-T, ICTY Trial Chamber, 3 March 2000) ¶¶ 319–331.
110 Ibid ¶ 332.
111 *Prosecutor v Blaškić* (Case no IT-96-14/1-A, ICTY Appeals Chamber, 29 July 2004) ¶¶ 58–64; *Bagil-ishema Appeal* (n 100) ¶¶ 34–35
112 Van Sliedregt (n 86) 200–201.
113 Ibid 201–202. Greg Vetter, 'Command Responsibility of Non-Military Superiors in the International Criminal Court (ICC)' (2000) 25 *Yale JIL* 89.
114 *Bemba Gombo* (n 92) ¶ 429.
115 Ibid ¶¶ 432–433.
116 Mettraux (n 86) 195.

which is not easily reduced to abstract analysis, as it relates to the precise powers that a superior has.[117] As was said in the *Blaškić* case, the measures that 'can be taken ... [are those] ... within the competence of a commander as evidenced by the degree of effective control he wielded over his subordinates.... What constitutes such measures is not a matter of substantive law but of evidence'.[118] That said, the ICTY has determined that although disciplinary sanctions against subordinates as opposed to criminal punishment 'cannot be excluded', as fulfilling the duty to punish,[119] for international crimes this is unlikely to be enough.[120] The ICC Statute makes sometimes (but by no means always) submitting the matter to the appropriate prosecutorial organs sufficient.[121] Similarly, a superior is not 'obliged to do the impossible'.[122] The ICC has taken the view that the relevant measures include:

(i) to ensure that the superior's forces are adequately trained in international humanitarian law; (ii) to secure reports that military actions were carried out in accordance with international law; (iii) to issue orders aiming at bringing the relevant practices into accord with the rules of war; (iv) to take disciplinary measures to prevent the commission of atrocities by the troops under the superior's command.[123]

There is no question that some of these could be quite onerous, but, that is the nature of command: with the power and privileges of command come responsibilities. In particular when sending (often young, stressed, nervous and highly armed) subordinates into conflict situations, superiors need to be cautious, and exercise leadership. The *raison d'être* of military discipline is to maintain control, and a failure to do so that leads to international crimes is, in and of itself, culpable.[124]

3.4 Causation

The final, controversial condition of superior responsibility is causation. The ICTY has consistently, albeit not always on consistent grounds, denied that causation is an element of command responsibility.[125] This has primarily been on the basis that failure to punish liability, arising, as it does, after the relevant crimes have occurred, hence cannot strictly be considered to have caused those crimes. The ICC Statute, however, expressly includes a requirement of causation, in that the *chapeau* requires that the crimes occur 'as a result of his or her failure to exercise control

---

117 Although, see Ambos (n 102) 217–220.
118 *Blaškić* Appeal (n 111) ¶ 72.
119 *Prosecutor v Hadžihasanović*, Judgment (Case no IT-01-47-A, ICTY Appeals Chamber, 22 April, 2008) ¶ 33.
120 Ibid ¶¶ 149–155.
121 The ICTY has agreed, *Prosecutor v Halilović* (Case no IT-01-48-A, ICTY Appeals Chamber, 16 October 2007) ¶ 182, although as the Appeals Chamber noted in *Hadžihasanović* (n 119) ¶¶ 149–155, if those authorities are known not to take action, then referral to such authorities may not be sufficient in and of itself. Formal legal competence to take the necessary measures to prevent or repress the crime is not required: see *Prosecutor v Delalić, Mučić, Delić and Landžo* (Case no IT-96-21-T, ICTY Trial Chamber, 16 November 1998) ¶ 395.
122 *Prosecutor v Orić* (Case no IT-03-68-T, ICTY Trial Chamber, 30 June 2006) ¶ 329.
123 *Bemba Gombo* (n 92) ¶ 438.
124 For further discussion on point, see Robert Cryer, 'General Principles of Liability in International Criminal Law' in Dominic McGoldrick, Peter Rowe and Eric Donelly (eds), *The International Criminal Court: Issues of Law, Policy and Practice* (Hart 2004) 233, 260–261.
125 See generally Robinson, 'Command Responsibility' (n 89).

properly over such forces'. This requires that the offences occur as a result of a general failure to exercise control over subordinates. That said, the ICC, in the *Bemba* decision (the first case to express a view on point), did not set a high threshold for causation, saying that it only applied to 'failure to prevent', and 'it is only necessary to prove that the commander's omission increased the risk of the commission of the crimes charged in order to hold him criminally responsible under article 28(a) of the Statute'.[126]

The question of causation is linked to one of the most controversial aspects of superior responsibility: its nature. It is not always made clear in the case law whether or not superior responsibility is a mode of liability in the underlying offences, or a separate form of, in essence more severe form of, dereliction of duty offence, or indeed a form of *sui generis* liability.[127] As has been made clear by, *inter alia*, Judge Shahabuddeen, the appropriate ambit of liability is heavily linked to its conceptualisation.[128] It ought to be said that the vast majority of post-war cases treated the principle as a mode of liability, and the statutes of the various international tribunals treat it as such.[129] One solution, which is to treat superior responsibility as a form of complicity liability, with failure to punish liability being considered a form of complicity in future offences that are encouraged by the impunity granted to the earlier offences, has been suggested by Darryl Robinson.[130] This is an elegant solution, but one which cannot be squared with the practice of the ad hoc tribunals, in that the superiors in cases in which they have been convicted of offences on this basis have been found responsible for all of the offences, not only those later offences that have been (probably) encouraged by the failure to punish earlier offences.

Equally, it could just be the case that the tribunals have misunderstood the nature of the offence, but their practice is more than partially constitutive of our understanding of the principle, and ought not to be dismissed out of hand (not, to be fair, that Robinson does so). This shows the difficulty of developing a coherent principle in the absence of agreement, or reflection on the underlying approaches to criminal liability and principles of culpability.[131]

It is probably the case that the problem with superior responsibility is that the various different forms of it have been lumped together by international criminal law. The knowing failure to prevent offences by a superior is very close to the classic complicity paradigm, whereas the negligent failure to prevent to do so fits less comfortably within that paradigm. Still less so does either knowing (and furthermore) negligent failure to punish. The German legislation on point, which separates out knowing and negligent failures to prevent offences, and failure to punish liability into three different offences,[132] goes a considerable way to dealing with the difficulty of reconciling the various levels of culpability involved in command responsibility with liberal principles of culpability and individual responsibility.[133] But international law is not, as yet, as nuanced.

---

126 *Bemba Gombo* (n 92) ¶¶ 424–425.
127 See generally Cryer *et al* (n 4) 397–400; Mirjan Damaška, 'The Shadow Side of Command Responsibility' (2001) 49 *AJCL* 455, 460–471 and the symposium at (2007) 5 *JICJ* 599–682.
128 *Hadžihasanović* Appeal (n 96) Judge Shahabuddeen, ¶ 33. This also has relevance to liability for failure to punish offences that occurred prior to a superior taking up command, see eg Christopher Greenwood, 'Command Responsibility and the *Hadžihasanović* Decision' (2004) 2 *JICJ* 598.
129 Robinson, 'Command Responsibility' (n 89) 30–35.
130 Ibid *passim*.
131 For critique on this basis, see George Fletcher 'The Theory of Criminal Liability and International Criminal Law' (2012) 10 *JICJ* 1029; Darryl Robinson, 'A Cosmopolitan Liberal Account of International Criminal Law' (2013) 26 *Leiden JIL* 127.
132 German Code of Crimes against International Law, ss 4, 13, 14.
133 Ambos (n 102) 230–231.

4 Conclusion

IHL has various mechanisms of ensuring respect and enforcement.[134] Some, and some of the most important, are non-criminal in nature. Criminal law is, by definition a response to violations, and prevention is better than cure.[135] That said criminal enforcement, through the law of war crimes plays a significant role in IHL, including in its development.[136] The conflation of IHL and the law of war crimes, though, would be a mistake, as it could lead to a diminution in attention given both to the non-criminal means of enforcement, and the important rules of IHL that do not come under the purview of war crimes. This includes broader interpretations and applications of IHL and what amounts to its breach appropriate to state, rather than individual responsibility.[137] War crimes law is but a part of the overall tapestry that makes up IHL. Unfortunately, as we have seen, the relationship is not always a clear one, and the list of war crimes is not one that has come from a systematic thinking through of what ought to be criminal in times of armed conflict, but a hotchpotch of treaty provisions, assertions about customary law, national legislation and judicial decisions. That said, the substantive law of war crimes is tolerably broad, a greater difficulty is persuading states to prosecute such offences equally and fairly, against friend, foe and any other person seriously suspected of having committed such activity.[138] In spite of the creation of the ICC, and the upswing in interest in international criminal law more generally, such a time remains, sadly, some way off.

134 Rüdiger Wolfrum, 'Enforcement of International Humanitarian Law' in Dieter Fleck (ed), *The Handbook of Humanitarian Law in Armed Conflicts* (2nd edn, OUP 2008) ch 14.

135 Hilaire McCoubrey, 'The Concept and Treatment of War Crimes' (1996) 1 *Journal of Armed Conflict Law* 121, 121.

136 Christopher Greenwood, 'The Development of International Humanitarian Law by the International Criminal Tribunal for the Former Yugoslavia' (1998) 2 *Max Planck Yearbook of United Nations Law* 97.

137 Darryl Robinson, 'The Identity Crisis of International Criminal Law' (2008) 21 *Leiden JIL* 925.

138 See eg Timothly L H McCormack, '*Their* Atrocities and *Our* Misdemeanours: The Reticence of States to Try Their "Own Nationals" for International Crimes' in Mark Lattimer and Phillipe Sands (eds), *Justice For Crimes Against Humanity* (Hart 2003) 107.

32

Investigations under international humanitarian law

Sasha Radin and Michael N Schmitt*

Release of the Goldstone Report on Israel's 2008 Operation Cast Lead in Gaza focused the international community's attention on the nature and scope of the duty to investigate alleged breaches of international humanitarian law (IHL).[1] The report controversially condemned the manner in which Israel conducted investigations into IHL violations allegedly committed during the conflict.[2] Several additional reports followed. Chief among these were a Human Rights Watch examination of the conflict generally[3] and a UN Human Rights Council assessment of Israeli and Palestinian investigations.[4] Such reports highlight a growing tendency on the part of governments, international bodies and non-governmental organisations (NGOs) to pronounce on the success or failure of parties to armed conflicts in investigating and prosecuting alleged war crimes.[5] Sensitive to this reality, the Israeli government tasked an independent commission to

---

* This chapter does not reflect the developments since 30 April 2013.

1 Human Rights in Palestine and other Occupied Arab Territories: Report of the United Nations Fact Finding Mission on the Gaza Conflict, UN Doc A/HRC/12/48 (15 September 2009) ('Goldstone Report'). The Goldstone Report was endorsed in HRC Res S-12/1 (21 October 2009) and UNGA Res 64/10 (1 December 2009).

2 Goldstone Report (n 1) ¶ 1823.

3 Human Rights Watch, 'Turning a Blind Eye: Impunity for Laws-of-War Violations during the Gaza War' (April 2010).

4 Report of the Committee of Independent Experts in International Humanitarian and Human Rights Laws to Monitor and Assess any Domestic, Legal or other Proceedings undertaken by both the Government of Israel and the Palestinian side, in the light of General Assembly Resolution 64/254, including the Independence, Effectiveness, Genuineness of these Investigations and their Conformity with International Standards, UN Doc A/HRC/15/50 (23 September 2010) ('Tomuschat Report').

5 See eg Rt Hon Sir William Gage, The Report of the Baha Mousa Inquiry (2011); The Turkel Commission, Report (Part 1) of the Public Commission to Examine the Maritime Incident of 31 May 2010 investigation into the Mavi Mara incident of 2010 (January 2010); Human Rights Watch, 'Unacknowledged Deaths: Civilian Casualties in NATO's Air Campaign in Libya' (May 2012). In addition, a plethora of international fact-finding commissions have been established to look into potential violations in a number of conflicts. See eg Report of the Independent International Commission of Inquiry on the Syrian Arab Republic, UN Doc A/HRC/21/50 (16 August 2012) ¶¶ 5, 6, 141, 142, 146 ('HRC Inquiry on Syria').

examine Israeli compliance with the international law governing investigations.[6] Such scrutiny of the relevant legal norms has led to a more refined understanding of what the duty to investigate under IHL entails. The chapter examines the law governing the duty to investigate and how it operates in cases of possible IHL violations.

1 Applicable law

The rules setting forth the obligation to investigate during an armed conflict derive from both treaty and customary international humanitarian and international human rights law (IHRL). Permeating any analysis of the relevant rules is the crucial question of how these bodies of law interact in the context of investigations. International criminal law and practice has to an extent clarified the applicable law.[7]

1.1 International humanitarian law

1.1.1 International armed conflicts

During international armed conflicts, states have an obligation to ensure compliance with the rules found in the 1949 Geneva Conventions,[8] certain express provisions of which create an implied duty to investigate war crimes. For instance, each of the conventions provides that parties

> shall be under the obligation to search for persons alleged to have committed, or to have ordered to be committed, such grave breaches, and shall bring such persons, regardless of their nationality, before its own courts. It may also, if it prefers, and in accordance with the provisions of its own legislation, hand such persons over for trial to another High Contracting Party concerned, provided such High Contracting Party has made out a *prima facie* case.
>
> Each High Contracting Party shall take measures necessary for the suppression of all acts contrary to the provisions of the present Convention other than the grave breaches.[9]

---

6 The Turkel Commission, Second Report: Israel's Mechanisms for Examining and Investigating Complaints and Claims of Violations of the Laws of Armed Conflict According to International Law (February 2013) ('Turkel Commission II'); For a detailed analysis of the Report, see Michelle Lesh, 'A Critical Discussion of the Second Turkel Report and How It Engages with the Duty to Investigate Under International Law' (2013) 16 YBIHL 119–145.

7 See Amichai Cohen and Yuval Shany, 'Beyond the Grave Breaches Regime: The Duty to Investigate Alleged Violations of International Law Governing Armed Conflicts' (2011) 14 *YBIHL* 43. See also Turkel Commission II (n 6) pt A, ¶¶ 14–17.

8 GCI–IV common art 1.

9 GCIV art 146. Similar wording can be found in GCI art 49; GCII art 50; GCIII art 129. The following acts constitute grave breaches according to art 147 GCIV (see also GCI art 50; GCII art 52; GCIII art 130):

> wilful killing, torture or inhuman treatment, including biological experiments, wilfully causing great suffering or serious injury to body or health, unlawful deportation or transfer or unlawful confinement of a protected person, compelling a protected person to serve in the forces of a hostile Power, or wilfully depriving a protected person of the rights of fair and regular trial prescribed in the present Convention, taking of hostages and extensive destruction and appropriation of property, not justified by military necessity and carried out unlawfully and wantonly.

The obligation to search for and bring to justice those persons believed to have committed grave breaches of the 1949 Geneva Conventions often cannot be fulfilled absent an investigation into the attendant circumstances. In such cases, the duty to investigate arises. The related responsibility to suppress other violations encompasses 'everything which can be done by a state to avoid acts contrary to the Convention being committed or repeated'.[10]

Careful textual analysis of the cited provisions is merited. They create no obligation to take steps to unearth any violation of IHL; rather, the duty to search applies only once an allegation of a grave breach has been levelled or indications otherwise surface that one may have been committed. Moreover, the reference to a prima facie case, albeit not set forth in the context of investigations, suggests that only those allegations or indications of violations that appear sufficiently credible merit investigation.[11] Importantly, the requirement to investigate does not depend on knowing the violator's identity, there is no limitation on the source of the allegation and it applies equally to nationals and enemies.[12]

Additional Protocol I develops the duty to investigate by setting forth the doctrine of command responsibility. Article 86 of the Protocol requires that:

1   The High Contracting Parties and the Parties to the conflict shall repress grave breaches, and take measures necessary to suppress all other breaches, of the Conventions or of this Protocol which result from a failure to act when under a duty to do so.

2   The fact that a breach of the Conventions or of this Protocol was committed by a subordinate does not absolve his superiors from penal or disciplinary responsibility, as the case may be, if they knew, or had information which should have enabled them to conclude in the circumstances at the time, that he was committing or was going to commit such a breach and if they did not take all feasible measures within their power to prevent or repress the breach.

Article 87 further provides that:

1   The High Contracting Parties and the Parties to the conflict shall require military commanders, with respect to members of the armed forces under their command and other persons under their control, to prevent and, where necessary, to suppress and to report to competent authorities breaches of the Conventions and of this Protocol. [...]

3   The High Contracting Parties and Parties to the conflict shall require any commander who is aware that subordinates or other persons under his control are going to commit or have committed a breach of the Conventions or of this Protocol, to initiate such steps as are necessary to prevent such violations of the Conventions or this Protocol, and, where appropriate, to initiate disciplinary or penal action against violators thereof.

As with the analogous provisions of the 1949 Geneva Conventions, the duty to investigate is inherent in Additional Protocol I's obligation that commanders prevent and suppress. It is likewise implied in the obligation to report breaches, take measures necessary to prevent

10   *GCIV Commentary* 594.

11   Michael N Schmitt 'Investigating Violations of International Law in Armed Conflict' (2011) 2 *Harvard NSJ* 39.

12   *GCIII Commentary* 623; *GCIV Commentary* 592–593.

violations and impose disciplinary or penal sanctions on violators.[13] Of course, the precise parameters of the duty to investigate are always contextual.[14]

The contribution of the Additional Protocol I provisions is that they clarify and expand on the general duty to investigate, particularly with respect to the obligations and responsibilities of commanders. For instance, the ICRC Commentary to Article 87 specifies that authority and responsibility of those in command at any level includes:

> informing superior officers of what is taking place in the sector, drawing up a report in the case of a breach, or intervening with a view to preventing a breach from being committed, proposing a sanction to a superior who has disciplinary power, or – in the case of someone who holds such power himself – exercising it, within the limits of his competence, and finally, remitting the case to the judicial authority where necessary with such factual evidence as it was possible to find. In this way ... a commander of a unit would act like an investigating magistrate.[15]

These duties apply to commanders who 'are in a position to establish or ensure the establishment of the facts, which would be the starting point for any action to suppress or punish a breach'.[16] As noted,

> [w]hether they are concerned with the theatre of military operations, occupied territories or places of internment, the necessary measures for the proper application of the Conventions and the Protocol must be taken at the level of the troops, so that a fatal gap between the undertakings entered into by Parties to the conflict and the conduct of individuals is avoided.[17]

In other words, the Additional Protocol I duties fall on the shoulders of those best able to meet them.

The obligation to investigate permeates the chain of command; superior commanders are not relieved of their responsibilities by the existence of corollary duties lower down the chain of command or excused from compliance due to the availability of legal advice.[18] Nor is the obligation limited to those formally in command, to high-ranking commanders or to military personnel.[19] Rather it extends to anyone in de facto command, including civilians and 'the common soldier who takes over as head of the platoon to which he belongs at the moment his

---

13 See eg *Prosecutor v Limaj* (Case no IT-03-66-T, ICTY Trial Chamber, 30 November 2005) ¶ 529; *Prosecutor v Mrkšić* (Case no IT-95-13/1-T, ICTY Trial Chamber, 27 September 2007) ¶ 568; *Prosecutor v Strugar* (Case no IT-01-42-T, ICTY Trial Chamber, 31 January 2005) ¶ 376; *Prosecutor v Boškoski* (Case no IT-04-82-T, 10 July 2008, Trial Chamber II) ¶¶ 418, 420; *Prosecutor v Bemba (Decision on the Confirmation of Charges)* (Case no ICC-01/05-01/08, ICC Pre-Trial Chamber 3, 15 June 2009) ¶¶ 416, 440.

14 *Prosecutor v Blaškić* (Case no IT-95-14-A, ICTY Appeals Chamber, 29 July 2004) ¶¶ 417 420; *Prosecutor v Delalić et al* (Case no IT-96-21-T, ICTY Trial Chamber, 16 November 1998) ¶¶ 394, 395.

15 *AP Commentary* ¶ 3562.

16 Ibid ¶ 3560.

17 Ibid ¶ 3550.

18 Ibid ¶ 3550. API art 82 requires that legal advisers be available to commanders.

19 See eg *Prosecutor v Halilović (Judgment)* (Case no IT-01-48-T, ICTY Trial Chamber, 16 November 2005). See generally Maria Nybondas, *Command Responsibility and its Application to Civilian Superiors* (Asser Press 2010).

commanding officer has fallen and is no longer capable of fulfilling his task'.[20] This obligation is non-delegable.[21]

This system of command responsibility is not intended to supplant the obligations of states. Rather, state responsibility for the structural implementation and enforcement of the duty to investigate and prosecute co-exists with the obligation of commanders to conduct investigations when appropriate.

In contrast to the 1949 Geneva Conventions, certain key states that engage in armed conflict with frequency and intensity, most notably the United States and Israel, are not party to Additional Protocol I.[22] However, the duty to investigate alleged war crimes during situations of international armed conflicts is widely considered to be reflective of customary international law. In particular, the ICRC's Customary International Humanitarian Law Study provides that

> [s]tates must investigate war crimes allegedly committed by their nationals or armed forces, or on their territory, and, if appropriate, prosecute the suspects. They must also investigate other war crimes over which they have jurisdiction and, if appropriate, prosecute the suspects.[23]

No state or international law expert has expressed serious misgiving with this purported restatement of customary law. Moreover, a number of international agreements relevant to conflict situations include, like the 1949 Geneva Conventions, a duty to prosecute or extradite.[24] This requirement, as discussed, incorporates an implied duty to investigate. On the national level, a duty to investigate and prosecute alleged war crimes frequently exists in military manuals.[25]

1.1.2 Non-international armed conflicts

Neither Additional Protocol II nor Common Article 3, the two key sources of law for non-international armed conflicts, contain obligations equivalent to those explicitly and implicitly set forth in the Geneva Conventions and Additional Protocol I. At most, the duty to suppress *all* violations of the conventions would include violations of Common Article 3.[26] However, a

---

20 *AP Commentary* ¶ 3553.
21 Ibid ¶ 3557.
22 To date 168 states have ratified API.
23 CIHL r 158.
24 See eg Convention on the Prevention and Punishment of the Crime of Genocide (9 December 1948) 78 UNTS 277, art 4; Convention against Torture and Other Cruel, Inhumane or Degrading Treatment (10 December 1984) 1465 UNTS 85, art 7; Convention for the Protection of Cultural Property in the Event of Armed Conflict (14 May 1954) 249 UNTS 240, art 28; Convention on the Prohibition of the Development, Production, Stockpiling and Use of Chemical Weapons and on their Destruction (13 January 1993) 1974 UNTS 45, art 7(1); Convention on the Prohibition of the Use, Stockpiling, Production and Transfer of Anti-Personnel Mines and on their Destruction (3 May 1996) 35 ILM 1206, art 14; Convention on the Prohibition of the Use, Stockpiling, Production and Transfer of Anti-Personnel Mines and on their Destruction (18 September 1997) 36 ILM 1507, art 9; Second Protocol to the Hague Convention for the Protection of Cultural Property in the Event of Armed Conflicts (26 March 1999) 38 ILM 769, arts 15–17.
25 See eg the US War Crimes Act, 18 USC § 2441 (2006); UK Ministry of Defence, *The Manual of the Law of Armed Conflict* (OUP 2004) ch 16, S G ('UK *Manual*'); Canadian Office of the Judge Advocate General, Joint Doctrine Manual B-GJ-005-104/FP-201: Law of Armed Conflict at the Operation and Tactical Levels (2003) s 8 ¶ 1621.1.
26 GCI art 49; GCII art 50; GCIII art 129; GCIV art 146.

number of developments in recent years has led to the conclusion that the duty to investigate extends to non-international armed conflicts as a matter of customary international law.

First, treaties such as the 1954 Convention for the Protection of Cultural Property in the Event of Armed Conflict (and its Second Protocol) and the 1993 Chemical Weapons Convention provide that the duty to suppress and prosecute violations applies to both international and non-international armed conflicts.[27] Also significant is the fact that the doctrine of command responsibility has increasingly been treated as applicable in non-international armed conflicts.[28] The Statute of the International Tribunal for Rwanda, created to hold those responsible for war crimes accountable in a non-international armed conflict, includes the doctrine of command responsibility.[29] The Rome Statute of the ICC confirms this trend by not differentiating between international and non-international armed conflicts in laying out the criminal responsibility of superiors who fail to 'prevent or repress [the] commission [of crimes] or to submit the matter to the competent authorities for investigation and prosecution'.[30] Similarly, the Statute's preambular reference to the duty to ensure effective prosecution makes no distinction between international and non-international armed conflicts, despite the fact that the substantive war crimes provisions do.[31] To the extent these responsibilities apply during non-international armed conflicts, the duty to investigate must correspondingly apply. This is the position correctly taken in the ICRC customary law study.[32]

An interesting question is whether the duty to investigate applies to non-state organised armed groups that are party to a non-international armed conflict. Both the ICRC and Turkel Commission II, for example, frame the obligation in terms of a *state's* duty to investigate.[33] And from a practical standpoint, one commentator has accurately noted that non-state organised armed groups might not have the structure or tools required for implementing this duty (although this begs the question of whether the group qualifies as organised).[34] Yet, in a number of cases, the duty has been held to apply to non-state parties. This was the position adopted in the Goldstone Report.[35] UN General Assembly resolutions have also urged the Palestinians to conduct investigations 'in conformity with international standards'.[36] Furthermore, the UN Human Rights Council report on Syria held that the duty to investigate serious violations of IHL applies 'beyond doubt' to 'individuals on either side of the conflict in the Syrian Arab Republic'.[37] In light of such practice and commentary, the most defensible position is that while the duty to investigate is shouldered by all parties to a non-international armed conflict, the manner of compliance will necessarily depend on the resources available. In other words, the legal duty is relative.

---

27 For other conventions that apply all cases of non-international armed conflict, see Cultural Property Convention (n 24) art 28, and Chemical Weapons Convention (n 24) art 7.
28 See eg *Prosecutor v Hadžihasanović* (Case no IT-01-47-T, ICTY Trial Chamber, 15 March 2006) ¶¶ 93, 179.
29 ICTR Statute art 6(1).
30 Rome Statute art 28(b)3.
31 Rome Statute art 8.
32 CIHL r 158.
33 CIHL r 158; Turkel Commission II (n 6) pt A, ¶ 27.
34 See Sandesh Sivakumaren, *The Law of Non-International Armed Conflict* (OUP 2012) 373.
35 Goldstone Report (n 1) ¶ 1804.
36 See eg UNGA Res 64/10 (1 December 2009) ¶ 4; UNGA Res 64/254 (25 March 2010) ¶ 3.
37 HRC Inquiry on Syria (n 5) Annex II, ¶¶ 23, 24.

1.1.3 Triggers for investigation

There are three types of IHL violations: grave breaches,[38] additional war crimes[39] and other violations of international humanitarian law.[40] The Geneva Conventions clearly require investigation into allegations of grave breaches.[41] This obligation is widely understood to extend to the broader category of war crimes[42] and includes both acts and omissions.[43]

Not all violations of IHL are war crimes.[44] A classic example is failure to take feasible measures to reunite family members.[45] As noted, Article 146 of Geneva Convention IV calls for the suppression of violations 'other than the grave breaches' and Article 86 of Additional Protocol I requires parties to the conflict to 'suppress all other breaches'. The Turkel Commission interprets these provisions as including a duty to prevent breaches, regardless of whether they qualify as grave breaches, war crimes or other IHL violations.[46] This is not an unreasonable conclusion to draw in light of states' obligation to 'respect and ensure respect' for the Conventions[47] and to 'suppress all other breaches'.[48] Building upon this view, the Turkel Commission distinguishes between the obligation to *investigate* alleged war crimes and a more general duty to *examine* other violations, entailing less stringent measures.[49]

Some differentiation between responsibilities pertaining to war crimes and those related to other violations finds support in a number of sources.[50] However, the duty to 'examine' violations that do not qualify as war crimes, while constituting good policy, does not have a firm textual basis in international humanitarian law. Indeed, expressions of customary law generally are limited to an obligation to investigate war crimes, and are silent on the question of responsibilities that breaches of other rules may generate.[51] The most defensible view of the *lex lata* is, accordingly, that only war crimes unambiguously give rise to the obligation to investigate under IHL.

In any case, there is no IHL obligation to investigate incidents in the absence of a purported violation. Therefore, for example, there is no requirement to investigate all cases that result in civilian casualties.[52] Unlike human rights law treaties and practice, which view any death as a

38 GCI art 50; GCII art 51; GCIII art 130; GCIV art 147; API art 85.
39 CIHL r 156.
40 See eg API art 86 and GCIV art 146.
41 GCI art 49; GCII art 50; GCIII art 129; GCIV art 146; API arts 86 and 87.
42 Rome Statute art 8(a) and 8(b); CIHL r 158; Turkel Commission II (n 6) pt A, ¶ 25; Tomuschat Report (n 4) ¶ 19; Goldstone Report (n 1) ¶ 1804; Human Rights Watch, *Unacknowledged Deaths* (n 5) 6. UK *Manual* (n 25) ss 16.23, 16.26.
43 API art 86(1). See eg Rome Statute art 28. *AP Commentary* ¶¶ 3529–3536.
44 See also Robert Cryer, 'Individual liability in international law' ch 31 in this volume.
45 API art 74.
46 Turkel Commission II (n 6) pt A, ¶ 23.
47 GCI–GCIV art 1; API art 1(1). See eg Australian Defence Headquarters, Law of Armed Conflict, Australian Defence Doctrine Publication (ADDP) 06.4, ss 13.2, 13.6 (2006).
48 *AP Commentary* ¶ 3530.
49 Turkel Commission II (n 6) pt A, ¶¶ 23, 24, 60.
50 Rome Statute art 8; *AP Commentary* ¶ 3538. See also discussion in Schmitt (n 11) 60.
51 See eg CIHL r 158. *AP Commentary* ¶ 3539, eg equates the obligation to 'suppress' with that to 'repress'.
52 For support, see Turkel Commission II (n 6) pt A, ¶ 51. But note the trend among NGOs to call for investigations into every civilian death in an armed conflict. See eg Human Rights Watch, *Unacknowledged Deaths* (n 5); Amnesty International, *The Battle for Libya: Killings, Disappearances and Torture* (September 2011).

possible breach of the right to life that must be investigated,[53] IHL bestows immunity on combatants for deaths that are in accordance with its strictures. Consequently, the death of an individual, even a civilian, does not per se point to a breach of IHL. Commanders, of course, may nevertheless choose to initiate investigations into any incident out of policy or operational concerns.

As noted, only credible allegations of suspected breaches must be investigated. State practice and the bulk of IHL and IHRL jurisprudence on the matter confirm this duty.[54] The credibility of an allegation will vary depending on the circumstances. For example, previously demonstrated IHL violations by a single unit would enhance the credibility of later allegations of violations by that unit, as might the inexperience of a unit or of soldiers involved in an incident. In this respect, indications of an allegation's credibility must be distinguished from evidence of a breach, as the obligation to search for alleged violations differs from the duty to prosecute.[55] The former depends on the credibility of the allegation, whereas that latter is driven by the legal sufficiency of the evidence. At the point that the allegation is no longer credible the obligation ceases.

It has been suggested that credibility should be assessed on a sliding scale in accordance with the gravity of the crime, with a lesser degree of credibility sufficing for cases involving serious crimes.[56] The justification used to support this suggestion is that IHRL differentiates between two standards of indications – prima facie and credible.[57] However, while the distinction does exist in IHRL, there is no basis for translating it into an IHL norm of 'less than credible' allegations with respect to serious crimes. Indeed, taken to its extreme, such a standard could lead to the view that all deaths must be investigated, a requirement that is at best *lex ferenda*.

It is clear that the source of the allegation is not determinative of the obligation to investigate,[58] although it may bear on the credibility of a claim. Moreover, if a credible reason exists to suspect that a war crime has been committed, an investigation is required even in the absence of an allegation, formal or otherwise.[59] Finally, when neither a credible level of suspicion nor an allegation exist, it is at least arguable that a duty to investigate logically arises if commission of a war crime surfaces as a rational explanation for the occurrence of an out of the ordinary event, such as a large number of unanticipated civilian deaths.[60]

1.2 The relationship between IHRL and IHL

Although IHRL is not the focus of this chapter, the relationship between that body of law and IHL bears directly on the nature and extent of the duty to investigate violations of the latter. A rich source of rules and jurisprudence pertaining to how investigations should be carried out can

---

53 ICCPR art 6(1); ECHR art 2. ECtHR case law, such as *Ergi v Turkey* (App no 23818/94, ECtHR, 28 July 1998) ¶ 82.

54 See eg Australian Department of Defence, Defence Instructions (General) Admin 45-2, Amdt No 1: The Reporting and Management of Notifiable Incidents (26 March 2010) ss 6(a), (b), (e); UK Armed Forces Act 2006 (UK), ss 113(2) and 115(2); US Department of Defense, Directive 2311.01E: DoD Law of War Program (9 May 2006) s 3.2. See also *Assenov v Bulgaria* (App no 90/1997/874/1086, ECtHR, 28 October 1998) ¶¶ 101–102.

55 *GCIV Commentary* 590.

56 Cohen and Shany (n 7) 51–52.

57 Ibid 51–52.

58 Turkel Commission II (n 6) pt A, ¶ 46.

59 Ibid.

60 The Turkel Commission suggests that in such circumstances there is a duty to 'examine' rather than 'investigate'. Ibid ¶¶ 49, 59.

be found in IHRL. The key human rights law instruments in this regard are the International Covenant on Civil and Political Rights (ICCPR)[61] and, for parties thereto, the European Convention on the Protection of Human Rights and Fundamental Freedoms (ECHR).[62] It is well accepted that alleged violations of these treaty norms have to be investigated,[63] and that the investigations must be carried out in an impartial, independent, prompt, effective and transparent way.[64] The question is how these standards, which the Goldstone Report labelled 'universal principles',[65] apply during situations of armed conflict.

As to the interrelationship between IHL and IHRL, the prevailing view is that the latter continues to apply in situations of armed conflict.[66] However, because IHRL and IHL are based on different objects and purposes, they cannot always function congruently. Human rights law is designed to protect individuals from the state's power, and, as such, regulates the relationship between individuals and the state by instituting rules and procedures that safeguard the individual. International humanitarian law, by contrast, is founded on a delicate balance between military necessity and humanity aimed at providing protection to individuals and their property to the extent reasonable in light of the state's goal of achieving its objectives militarily. It regulates relations between states.

The precise way in which these two bodies of law interact during armed conflict is a hotly debated issue.[67] The ICJ held in the *Nuclear Weapons Advisory Opinion* that specialised bodies of law (*lex specialis*) take precedence over more general legal regimes (*lex generalis*).[68] Since IHL specifically addresses situations of armed conflict, its rules are *lex specialis*. Application of this principle can take two forms. First, when a human rights rule contradicts that of IHL, the latter

---

61 ICCPR art 2(2).

62 ECHR art 1 requires that 'the High Contracting Parties shall secure to everyone within their jurisdiction the rights and freedoms defined in Section I of this Convention'.

63 See eg HRC, 'General Comment No 31: Nature of the General Obligation Imposed on States Parties to the Covenant' UN Doc CCPR/C/21/Re.1/Add.13 (26 May 2004) ¶ 15; *McKerr v UK* (App no 28883/95, ECtHR, 4 May 2001) ¶ 111; *Isayeva v Russia* (App no 57950/00, ECtHR, 24 February 2005) ¶¶ 208, 209; *McCann and Others v UK* (App no 18984/91, ECtHR Grand Chamber, 27 September 1995) ¶ 161.

64 See eg UN Basic Principles on the Use of Force and Firearms by Law Enforcement Officials ¶ 22, UN Doc A/CONF.144/28/Rev.1 (27 August to 7 September 1990); UN Principles on the Effective Prevention and Investigation of Extra-Legal, Arbitrary and Summary Executions (Economic and Social Council Resolution 1989/65) ¶ 9, UN Doc E/1989/89 (24 May 1989); UN Basic Principles and Guidelines on the Right to Remedy and Reparations for Victims of Violations of International Human Rights and Serious Violations of International Humanitarian Law, UN Doc A/RES/60/147 (16 December 2005) ('UN Guidelines on the Right to Remedy'); Principles on the Effective Investigation and Documentation of Torture and Other Cruel, Inhuman or Degrading Treatment or Punishment, UNGA Res 55/89 (22 February 2001). Tomuschat Report (n 4) ¶ 30; Human Rights Watch, *Turning a Blind Eye* (n 3) 7. See also *Kaya v Turkey* (App no 158/1996/777/978, ECtHR, 19 February 1998) ¶ 86.

65 Goldstone Report (n 1) ¶ 1814. See also Tomuschat Report (n 4) ¶ 90.

66 See eg *Legality of the Threat or Use of Nuclear Weapons (Advisory Opinion)* [1996] ICJ Rep 226; *Legal Consequences of the Construction of a Wall in the Occupied Palestinian Territories (Advisory Opinion)* [2004] ICJ Rep 136; *Armed Activity on the Territory of the Congo (Democratic Republic of the Congo v Uganda)* [2005] ICJ Rep 168.

67 Contrast eg the Fourth Periodic Report of the United States of America to the United Nations Committee on Human Rights Concerning the International Covenant on Civil and Political Rights, ¶¶ 504–505 (30 December 2011) and HRC, 'General Comment No 31' (n 63). See also Noam Lubell and Nancie Prud'homme, 'Impact of human rights law' ch 6 in this volume.

68 *Nuclear Weapons* (n 66) ¶ 25. See also *Wall* (n 66) ¶ 106; *Armed Activity* (n 66) ¶¶ 216–220.

takes precedence. Second, if the rules are compatible, or there is a lacuna in IHL, human rights law applies but is interpreted in light of IHL.

The latter generally applies to investigations because the human rights standards of effectiveness, promptness, impartiality and independence are fully consistent with the goals underlying the IHL investigation requirements. Moreover, human rights law jurisprudence explicitly recognises the contextual nature of investigations.[69] It is reasonable to conclude, therefore, that general IHRL standards apply to investigations in both law enforcement situations and those of armed conflict, albeit with sensitivity to the unique circumstances of conflict.[70] Of course, a situation qualifying as one of purely law enforcement concern, even if it occurs during an armed conflict, would be governed by IHRL as the *lex specialis*.[71]

State practice on the implementation of these norms varies widely.[72] Ascertaining whether states have adopted particular practices as a matter of policy, domestic law or international law can prove extremely challenging.[73] Accordingly, caution must be exercised when examining state practice as relevant to international legal norms.[74]

2 How should an investigation be carried out?

As indicated, express IHL on the nature of investigations is sparse, while human rights law is generally more granular. However, gaps in IHL cannot be filled by indiscriminately transferring IHRL rules to situations of armed conflict without sensitivity to the differences in the underlying object and purpose of the two bodies of law. In addition, practicalities in situations of armed conflict may make it difficult, and at times impossible, to apply the investigative standards in the same manner as could occur in the peacetime situations generally envisaged for the human rights legal regime. For example, it may not be feasible to gather evidence or locate witnesses amidst hostilities because the necessary equipment is unavailable or opposing forces may control the territory on which the violation is alleged to have taken place. Witness and investigator safety is also a concern, while the personnel and resources necessary to conduct a robust investigation may be required elsewhere for the military mission. The seriousness of the crime can be an additional factor that affects how the standards are implemented because the more severe the crime the greater the legal safeguards to which defendants in disciplinary or criminal proceedings are entitled.[75] The duty to investigate in time of armed conflict must accordingly be interpreted with an elasticity reflecting such realities. Of course, during armed conflict, these factors also influence contextual application of the human rights investigative standards of effectiveness, promptness, impartiality and independence.

---

69 See eg *Isayeva* (n 63) ¶ 210; *Al Skeini v UK* (App no 55721/07, ECtHR Grand Chamber, 7 July 2011) ¶ 168.

70 See eg *Ergi* (n 53) ¶ 85; *Kaya* (n 64) ¶ 91; *Al Skeini* (n 69) ¶ 164; *Isayeva* (n 63) ¶ 209; *Halilovic* (n 19) ¶¶ 97, 98. See also UN Guidelines on the Right to Remedy (n 64) ¶ 3; UNGA Res 64/10 (1 December 2009) and HRC Inquiry on Syria, Annex II (n 5) ¶ 24; Turkel Commission II (n 6) pt A, ¶ 63.

71 See Turkel Commission II (n 6) pt A, ¶¶ 53, 58.

72 See Schmitt (n 11) 56–77 for an extensive survey on the practice of Canada, Australia, the UK and the US with regard to investigations, and Turkel Commission II (n 6) pt B for an in-depth examination of certain state practice. On US practice, see Dick Jackson, 'Reporting and Investigation of Possible, Suspected, or Alleged Violations of the Law of War' (June 2010) *Army Lawyer* 95.

73 See eg US Department of Defense, Directive 2311.01E (n 54) ss 4.4–4.5.

74 Schmitt (n 11) 56, 77, 83. But, see Cohen and Shany (n 7) 65, 66, 74 for a different view.

75 In this regard, see Cohen and Shany (n 7) 48. Note that this point differs from the earlier suggestion that the seriousness of the alleged crime could affect the level of credibility required, see Cohen and Shany (n 7).

2.1 Effectiveness

The requirement that an investigation be 'effective' concerns the manner in which the procedural aspects of the investigation are carried out.[76] There is a duty to be thorough, for example, in the collection of evidence.[77] This has been interpreted under human rights law as an obligation to 'take the reasonable steps available' to secure evidence.[78] As noted, measures that might be reasonably available during peacetime may prove impossible to accomplish on the battlefield.[79]

The duty self-evidently assumes sensitivity to the attendant military realities. To illustrate, an investigator examining an air strike who does not understand weapons options, fuzing, guidance systems, angle of attack, optimal release altitudes, command and control relationships, communications capabilities, tactical options, available intelligence sources, enemy practices, pattern of life analysis, collateral damage estimate methodology, human factors in a combat environment and so forth, will generally be unable to conduct a thorough investigation. Many times, it will also be necessary to have immediate access to a hot battlefield to gather evidence effectively. For these and related reasons, it is often essential that operational personnel participate in the initial investigative process. Correspondingly, the investigator need not be formally trained as such. The same military realities may pose insurmountable obstacles to timely investigations by outside bodies, a fact acknowledged by the UN Human Rights Council when outlining the difficulty its investigators faced in accessing witnesses and victims in Syria.[80]

It is especially crucial to bear in mind the differing purposes of the requirement to investigate in the two bodies of law. In IHL, the investigations are conducted to ensure accountability and to help preclude other violations. By contrast, this duty in IHRL investigations serves in great part to ensure that a person is not tried based on faulty or incomplete evidence. These differing purposes impugn divergent meaning into the notion of effectiveness. In particular, effectiveness in the IHL context involves identifying inculpatory evidence, whereas in the IHRL context the discovery of exculpatory evidence is often the central concern.

2.2 Promptness

Investigations must be prompt in both purely law enforcement situations and those involving potential violations of the law of armed conflict.[81] In IHRL, promptness facilitates the discovery of exculpatory evidence, thereby minimising the need to rely on 'stale' evidence that could disadvantage the accused (as in the case of witnesses who have subsequently become unavailable). By contrast, the underlying purpose of promptness in IHL investigations is to prevent future breaches by removing the violator from the battlefield and holding him or her accountable.

---

76 See eg *Al Skeini* (n 69) ¶ 167; *Assenov* (n 54) ¶ 103; Turkel Commission II (n 6) Part A, ¶¶ 81, 84; Tomuschat Report (n 4) ¶ 24.

77 *Avsar v Turkey* (App no 25657/94, ECtHR, 10 July 2001) ¶ 394; *Al Skeini* (n 69) ¶ 166; *McKerr* (n 63) ¶ 159; *Ristic v Yugoslavia* (Comm no 113/1998, HRC, 11 May 2011) ¶ 8.6.

78 See eg *Kerimova and Others v Russia* (App nos 17170/04, 20792/04, 22448/04, 23360/04, 5681/05 and 5684/05, ECtHR, 3 May 2011) ¶¶ 264, 265; *Isayeva* (n 63) ¶ 212.

79 See eg *Al Skeini* (n 69) ¶¶ 164, 168. See also, Philip Alston, 'Report of the Special Rapporteur on Extrajudicial, Summary or Arbitrary Executions' UN Doc E/CN.4/2006/53 (8 March 2006) ¶ 36.

80 HRC Inquiry on Syria (n 5) ¶¶ 5, 6.

81 See eg Rome Statute art 17(2)(b); GCI Commentary 365, 366; GCIV Commentary 593; *Kerimova* (n 78) ¶ 265; *Al Skeini* (n 69) ¶ 164; *Bazorkina v Russia* (App no 69481/01, ECtHR, 27 July 2006) ¶ 121; *Isayeva* (n 63) ¶ 213.

During an armed conflict the promptness standard must be applied with sensitivity to the context in which the investigation is to take place.[82] In particular, conditions on the battlefield and competing military demands for scarce resources may influence how quickly the investigation can take place.[83] The requirement for promptness tends, therefore, to support the use of immediate onsite fact-finding inquiries carried out by unit personnel despite the fact that they may lack the expertise of professional investigators. Within the constraints of the circumstances, unreasonable delays in the investigation must be avoided.[84]

2.3 Independence

The purpose of the independence requirement is to allow investigators to examine an incident free from undue influence that might affect the results thereof.[85] It is an obligation that applies equally to law enforcement situations and armed conflict. However, its precise scope in times of armed conflict has generated debate, particularly with respect to whether independence from the chain of command or civilian oversight are required. As with the other standards, the specific circumstances of armed conflict affect its application.

European Court of Human Rights (ECtHR) case law has repeatedly interpreted independence to include 'a lack of hierarchical or institutional connection',[86] necessitating 'that the investigating authority [i]s, and [i]s seen to be, operationally independent of the military chain of command'.[87] Moreover, a number of states have reformed their military justice systems to, *inter alia*, create more independence from the chain of command in the course of investigations.[88] Notwithstanding this trend, no requirement exists under IHL that investigators necessarily remain outside the chain of command.

On the contrary, IHL treaties envision the involvement of military commanders in the investigative process, at least during its early stages.[89] Article 87 Additional Protocol I, for example, requires commanders to prevent, suppress and report breaches of Additional Protocol I 'with respect to members of the armed forces under their command and other persons under their control'. This means that the duty of commanders to repress and suppress breaches stems, in part, from their position in the military hierarchy,[90] and that 'the role of commanders is decisive' vis-à-vis the obligation to repress and suppress violations.[91] In fact, as can be seen in the requirement that organised armed groups have a responsible command that enables them to implement IHL,[92] this body of law presumes the existence of a command structure that enables its application.

---

82 See eg *Al Skeini* (n 69) ¶¶ 164, 167.
83 See eg ibid ¶ 167.
84 *Bazorkina* (n 81) ¶ 121. The Goldstone Report found that Israel's operational debriefings do not comply with this requirement. Goldstone Report (n 1) ¶¶ 121, 1820.
85 Philip Alston, 'Report of the Special Rapporteur on Extrajudicial, Summary or Arbitrary Executions' UN Doc A/HRC/14/24/Add.6 (28 May 2010) 25, 33–38.
86 *Al Skeini* (n 69) ¶ 167. See also *Isayeva* (n 63) ¶ 211; *Dadydov and Others v Ukraine* (App nos 17674/02 and 39081/02, ECtHR, 1 July 2010) ¶ 277; *McKerr* (n 63) ¶ 112.
87 *Al Skeini* (n 69) ¶ 169. See also Turkel Commission II (n 6) pt A, ¶¶ 98, 99.
88 See eg UK Armed Forces Act 2006, s 113 requiring the Commanding Officer to notify the Service Police of a suspicion that a serious crime has occurred. See also the Canadian Report of the Somalia Commission of Inquiry (1997).
89 *AP Commentary* ¶ 3562 confirms this interpretation.
90 Ibid ¶ 3562.
91 Ibid ¶ 3550.
92 See APII art 1.

Although some sources have taken a contrary position,[93] these factors augur against any contention that the requirement of independence precludes involvement by members of the command in the investigative process. The election of a number of states to refer allegations of serious violations to criminal justice agencies falling outside the chain of command does not necessarily represent state practice based on *opinio juris*.[94] Such practices are more appropriately characterised as matters of policy or domestic law.

That said, recall that the duty to investigate, as well as its implementation, are always contextual. For instance, the standards may apply differently depending on the position of the person in question.[95] To illustrate, defence lawyers and judges in military trials generally must be more independent of the chain of command than those individuals conducting an investigation of a recent incident on a hot battlefield. Even so, in certain circumstances, investigations within a unit would unambiguously violate the requirement of independence. It would, for example, be unacceptable for a subordinate to investigate the activities of an immediate superior, as doing so could clearly affect the subordinate's investigative conduct. Moreover, such a situation would run counter to IHL's dependence on the command structure to ensure IHL compliance.

Interestingly, in distinguishing between the duty to *investigate* allegations of war crimes and the purported duty to *examine* other violations of IHL, the Turkel Commission concluded that the standard of independence only applies with respect to the former.[96] As noted, the concept of 'examining', and the duties associated therewith, are not clearly resident within IHL.

Several states, in restructuring their military justice systems to comport with a human rights independence standard, have introduced civilian oversight to their military justice systems.[97] In part, this is in response to assertions in the human rights context that a lack of civilian oversight over the military justice system reduces the incentive to implement the standards adequately, and exposes those involved to undue pressure.

While civilian oversight might serve to enhance the independence of the investigative process in certain circumstances, IHL does not prohibit investigations undertaken completely within the province of the military.[98] Therefore, caution should be exercised in drawing conclusions as to the relevance for IHL of the restructured military justice systems.[99] Complicating any assessment as to IHL implications of such IHRL practices is the additional fact that the countries in question have a stronger rule of law tradition than is the global norm, as well as the capacity to dedicate significant resources to the investigative infrastructure.[100] Finally, countries sometimes expressly restructure their military legal systems based on human rights obligations; in such cases it would be incorrect on its face to cite them as evidence of an IHL obligation.[101] Of course, systems that

---

93 See ECtHR case law listed in n 86 and Turkel Commission II (n 6) pt A, ¶ 98.

94 See eg Canadian Forces National Investigation Service, '2007 Annual Report' (2007) 5. Chairman of the Joint Chiefs of Staff, Instruction CJCSI 5810.01C: Implementation of the DoD Law of War Program (30 April 2010) s 6(f)(4)(e)(2)). Armed Forces Act 2006 (UK) s 116.

95 Turkel Commission II (n 6) pt A, ¶¶ 66, 67.

96 Ibid ¶¶ 98–100 and 109–112.

97 Canada in 1997 (National Defence Act, RSC 1985, c N-5); UK in 2006 (Armed Forces Act 2006); Australia in 2010 established a military court outside the chain of command (see Defence Legislation Amendment Act 2006), although this court was ruled as unconstitutional in *Lane v Morrison* [2009] HCA 29.

98 Turkel Commission II (n 6) pt A, ¶ 73; pt D, Recommendation 7, ¶ 47; Tomuschat Report (n 4) ¶ 34.

99 Cohen and Shany (n 7) 69, 70.

100 See n 76 and accompanying text.

101 European states, for example, that are bound by the ECHR by law must comply with its case law.

have implemented civilian oversight will often, although not the direct product of IHL obligations, nevertheless comport with the requirement for independence.

2.4 Impartiality

The obligations of impartiality and independence are distinct, albeit related. Impartiality requires that those investigating an alleged IHL violation have no personal interest in the matter or its resolution.[102] For the most part, this duty is manifested similarly both in law enforcement situations and in those of armed conflict. Thus, for instance, the requirement logically prohibits the involvement of a commander in the investigative process when he or she is personally implicated in a possible violation.[103]

The unique circumstances of the battlefield can give rise to differences in application. For instance, in light of the doctrine of command responsibility, the possibility exists that a commander ordering, conducting or deciding upon an investigation into the conduct of a subordinate will personally benefit, or suffer, from its outcome. Yet, in certain situations the commander might be the *only* individual available initially to investigate the incident. In such a case, the sole alternatives to commander involvement may be the absence of an investigation or unacceptable delay of the investigation.[104] Moreover, recall that under IHL a commander has a duty to investigate.

2.5 Transparency

The IHRL requirement of transparency has two components: that the victims and their families be informed of and involved in investigations and that the public be informed about them.[105] Transparency does not transfer readily as a legal obligation during armed conflict.[106] Not only is the obligation absent from the treaty and customary international law under IHL, it also could place witnesses and investigators at risk, compromise intelligence sources and undermine the military mission by exposing operational tactics, strategy, etc. At times, however, transparency makes good policy and operational sense, particularly during counter-insurgencies or controversial operations.[107]

2.6 Forum for investigation

A criminal investigation need not be launched for every alleged breach; indeed, not all breaches lead to criminal liability. Nor does IHL include an obligation for a specific type of investigation, criminal or administrative.[108] Rather, the requirements depend on the circumstances.[109]

---

102 See eg Rome Statute art 17(2)(c); *Kolevi v Bulgaria* (App no 1108/02, ECtHR, 5 November 2009) ¶¶ 210, 211; *Girgvliani v Georgia* (App no 25091/07, ECtHR, 26 April 2011) ¶ 249. See also Turkel Commission II (n 6) pt A, ¶¶ 75, 98; Tomuschat Report (n 4) ¶¶ 23, 91.
103 See eg Cohen and Shany (n 7) 72, 73.
104 The Turkel Commission concludes that the Military Advocate General's dual role in Israel as both the head of military prosecution and of legal advice generates a perception of partiality and thus recommends restructuring. Turkel Commission II (n 6) pt D, Recommendation 8, ¶¶ 53, 57; pt A, ¶ 75. See also Tomuschat Report (n 4) ¶¶ 53–54. Although such action is likely good policy, there is no basis in IHL for a duty to prevent a perception of impartiality.
105 See eg *McKerr* (n 63) ¶ 148; Turkel Commission II (n 6) pt A, ¶ 106.
106 Turkel Commission II (n 6) Part A, ¶ 106; Tomuschat Report (n 4) ¶ 33.
107 See eg Cohen and Shany (n 7) 64.
108 IHRL case law has also recognised this. See eg Al Skeini (n 69) ¶ 165.
109 See eg *Isayeva* (n 63) ¶ 209; *Al Skeini* (n 69) ¶ 165.

Administrative fact-finding inquiries may be more suitable for situations where, for example, a policy or procedure is being examined, such as targeting guidelines or operational procedures. Fact-finding inquiries immediately after an event may be sufficient, and even necessary, for example, to gather relevant information from witnesses before they disperse. Should a fact-finding inquiry lead to clear evidence of criminal misconduct, then a criminal investigation would usually need to be initiated. IHL does not require routine after-action reports designed to garner information, but if they produce credible indications that a breach may have occurred, further investigation would be necessary. It is very common for different reporting and investigative requirements to co-exist with respect to military operations, even for the same incident.

An unresolved question is whether a non-state body (for example, a contractor or NGO) may satisfy the investigative obligations borne by the parties to the conflict. A reasonable interpretation of the requirement would hold that it may only do so if the investigation is adequately objective and meets all other necessary criteria. Of course, prosecution or disciplinary measures would continue to be the responsibility of the relevant party to the conflict.

3 Conclusions

Summarised, IHL imposes the following requirements for investigations in times of armed conflict:[110]

1   The Geneva Conventions, Additional Protocols and relevant customary international law give rise to a duty to investigate credible allegations of war crimes in both international and non-international armed conflicts. The obligation extends throughout the chain of command and includes those who are de facto in command. Superior commanders are not relieved of their duty by virtue of this fact, nor does the existence of legal advice replace the commander's responsibilities. The law is unclear as to the precise obligations that result from the duty to 'suppress' breaches of IHL other than war crimes.

2   States differ in how they carry out investigations. Domestic norms, policy concerns, human rights law obligations and practical capacity, *inter alia*, influence their investigative process. Therefore, care is merited when attempting to draw normative conclusions based on state practice.

3   Allegations must be credible to trigger the responsibility to conduct an investigation. The credibility of an allegation depends on the attendant circumstances and is to be distinguished from actual evidence of a breach. No restriction exists as to the source of the allegation, as long as it is credible. Investigations may be required absent an allegation if the circumstances reasonably indicate that a war crime might have occurred. There is no obligation under IHL to investigate all incidences of civilian causalities.

4   Human rights law standards of effectiveness, promptness, impartiality and independence apply to investigations in times of armed conflict. The manner in which they apply depends on the specific circumstances. Factors that can influence the requisite depth and scope of the investigation required include the seriousness of the alleged violation, the complexity of a specific case and the degree to which the hostilities interfere with the practical ability to investigate.

5   The requirements of independence and impartiality are questions of fact and scale. There must be no undue interference with, or influence on, the investigation. No prescription for a particular organisational structure exists with respect to the conduct of an investigation.

110 See Schmitt (n 11) 39–40, 43 and 79–82.

Consequently, there is no IHL requirement that those conducting an investigation be outside the chain of command. Although civilian oversight sometimes enhances the independence of the investigative system, IHL does not prohibit investigations (and punishment) undertaken completely within the military system. Those involved in the investigation may have no personal interest in the matter. Thus, while members of a unit that is implicated in an incident may sometimes conduct the investigation, the requirement of impartiality means that subordinate commanders may not investigate their immediate superiors, nor can any individual investigate a situation in which s/he was personally involved.

6   Immediate on-site investigations are appropriate and, at times, necessary, in order to ensure that an investigation is prompt and effective. The results may trigger further investigation or lead to the conclusion that no additional investigation is merited. In cases where the circumstances delay investigation, a standard of reasonableness applies. Investigators need not have formal training in investigative practices; an individual with an operational background may be better suited to carry out an effective investigation under battlefield conditions.

7   No obligation exists to make the investigative process or results public, nor is there a requirement to keep victims involved. Operational or policy considerations may, however, make transparency sensible in the circumstances.

8   There is no duty to use a specific forum or conduct a certain type of investigation. The key is to ensure that the maximum safeguards are applied in a fashion that is reasonable in a given circumstance. Different investigations are commonly carried out successively or simultaneously. However, while the duty to investigate credible allegations of war crimes does not necessarily require a criminal investigation, should a *prima facie* case develop, appropriate disciplinary action or criminal prosecution must be undertaken.

The conclusions set forth above are characterised by a marked degree of abstraction. In contrast, a highly developed set of laws and jurisprudence pertaining to investigations can be found in IHRL. It is well accepted that the IHRL standards of effectiveness, promptness, independence and impartiality also apply in times of armed conflict. Indeed, they are consistent with the duty to investigate found in IHL. However, IHRL standards cannot simply be superimposed on to the IHL framework since the two bodies of law are based upon different foundational premises. Moreover, the realities of armed conflict make it difficult, and at times impossible, to carry out the procedures in the same way as may transpire in situations of relative calm. The standard that ultimately applies to investigations of possible war crimes is one of reasonableness in the surrounding circumstances.

33

Role of international courts and tribunals

*Jackson Nyamuya Maogoto**

States have generally been inclined to regulate the conduct of international armed conflict but disinclined with regard to non-international armed conflict based on the imperatives of safe-guarding tenets of sovereignty – domestic supremacy and freedom from external interference. This has played an important role in limiting law of armed conflict (LOAC)[1] compliance and enforcement. Internally, states have domestic supremacy which encompasses a traditional mono-poly on use of force. On this aspect, prevention of usurpation of governmental authority by non-state actors who may take up arms against the government has always been paramount. States while keen on regulatory frameworks that humanise war have been wary of compliance mechanisms that may adversely interfere with the choice of means and methods in war and thus undermine their expansive domestic prosecutorial prerogative. The net result is that over cen-turies the regulatory framework relating to inter-state LOAC has advanced more than its intra-state counterpart.[2] In effect, thus, the extent to 'which the customary rules are applicable to armed conflict not of an international nature' is often diluted by states with many LOAC viola-tions not seen as readily extending to non-international armed conflicts which affects legal ques-tions as breaches are often domestically prosecuted as ordinary crimes.

Supranational enforcement of LOAC dates back to the middle ages, when the first known war crimes trials were held. In 1474, an ad hoc transnational tribunal of 28 judges (made up of

---

* The author wishes to register his appreciation for the invitation by his former doctoral supervisor and mentor – Professor Tim McCormack – to contribute to this volume. Equally the author wishes to register the privilege of a Visiting Fellowship at the British Institute of International and Comparative Law and access to its facilities at the penultimate phase of this chapter. Any slippages or errors rest solely with the author.

1 The terms law of armed conflict (LOAC) and international humanitarian law (IHL) will be used here interchangeably but to a minimum with LOAC the general term. This is more based on the generality that sometimes LOAC has sought to be distinguished from IHL in some quarters on account of the influence that human rights brought to bear to the regime. This chapter seeks to side-step doctrinal and theoretical argumentations by settling for the use of these terms in general parameters but will note the specifics where relevant.

2 See eg Suzannah Linton, 'Completing the Circle: Accountability for the Crimes of the 1971 Bangladesh War of Liberation' (2010) 21 *Criminal Law Forum* 191, 257; Dieter Fleck, 'Shortcomings of the Grave Breaches Regime' (2009) 7 *JICJ* 833, 835.

representatives of the Hanseatic cities), tried and convicted Peter von Hagenbach for murder, rape, perjury and other crimes in violation of 'the laws of God and man' during his occupation of the town of Breisach on behalf of Charles, the Duke of Burgundy.[3] He was found guilty and executed despite his plea of obedience to the orders of his lord and superior.[4] In that era (and largely to date) the waging of war was a prerogative of states making this historical event even more poignant. For the next five centuries, states resolutely retreated from supranational avenues of LOAC enforcement in favour of domestic mechanisms until the twentieth century when visible precedents of supranational enforcement were manifested in the abortive but ground-breaking attempts at the end of the First World War and the successful efforts post-Second World War.

The Cold War that set in at the end of the Second World War was to oust expected consolidations in enforcement. However by a twist of irony, it was in the early stages of the superpower stand-off that renewed efforts to strengthen compliance and enforcement was entrenched marked with the adoption of the 1949 Geneva Conventions which reaffirmed the obligation to prosecute LOAC breaches. This was echoed some three decades later by Additional Protocol I.[5] The 1949 Geneva Conventions enshrined and stressed the basic obligation that states have obligations to investigate and repress LOAC violations by ensuring existence of specific penalties.[6] As straightforward as this may appear, the prosecutorial terrain is much more convoluted resulting in LOAC breaches being prosecuted in international and national courts in very different ways. Black letter LOAC provisions are often denatured by national prosecutorial endeavours which charge violations differently. Sometimes they are charged as what they should be – war crimes – but often as ordinary crimes like murder or manslaughter with LOAC not mentioned at all.[7] Even '[m]ore controversially, international human rights law has been used directly to regulate internal armed conflict rather than to inform regulation through international humanitarian law'.[8] The end run is that LOAC (particularly as relates to internal conflict) remains peripheral in compliance and enforcement terms as violations while largely clear under LOAC remain contested in enforcement.

In the 1990s as the Cold War waned, the maturation of international criminal law and establishment of supranational penal mechanisms re-energised the judicial enforcement of LOAC breaches. The statutes of the ad hoc international criminal tribunals for the former Yugoslavia and Rwanda (ICTY and ICTR respectively) played a major role in streamlining legal and doctrinal schisms with their mandate to prosecute international crimes directly (including those covered by LOAC) without the interposition of anaemic national law and processes. This radical development was further solidified by the adoption of the Rome Statute of the ICC and several internationalised domestic judicial processes.

The remit of this chapter to enunciate the role of international courts and tribunals in compliance and enforcement is challenging. The focus will be on modern times – loosely defined as practical efforts in the twentieth and twenty-first centuries. The turn of the twentieth century is

3 Leslie C Green, 'Enforcement of the Law in International and Non-International Conflicts: The Way Ahead' (1996) 24 *Denver JILP* 285, 291; Timothy L H McCormack, 'Selective Reaction to Atrocity: War Crimes and the Development of International Criminal Law' (1997) 60 *Albany LR* 681, 702.
4 Ibid.
5 APII was silent on the question of enforcement and imposed no explicit obligations on states parties to prosecute serious breaches.
6 GCI art 49(1); GCII art 50(1); GCIII art 129(1); GCIV art 146(1).
7 Ward Ferdinandusse, 'The Prosecution of Grave Breaches In National Courts' (2009) 7 *JICJ* 723, 741.
8 Francisco Martin, 'Using International Human Rights Law for Establishing a Unified Use of Force Rule in the Law of Armed Conflict' (2001) 64 *Saskatchewan LR* 347.

taken as a baseline for three reasons. First, by then there was a discernible body of LOAC law underpinned by the Hague Conventions[9] which presented a definite codification of various strands of LOAC. Second, it was in this century that the first practical efforts towards supra-national enforcement were taken in the aftermath of two epochal events – the First and Second World Wars. Third, it was in the Cold War period that the next major effort to address new developments in warfare through expansion and clarification of LOAC enforcement was made. This occurred with the adoption of the Geneva Conventions and Additional Protocols supple-mented by a resurgence of human rights and a maturing international criminal law regime. Many cases have found their way into international courts and tribunals, in particular the Inter-national Military Tribunals (IMTs) at the end of the Second World War, the ICJ, with the ad hoc international criminal tribunals established in the 1990s, and the ICC. This chapter eschews a mechanical evaluation of individual cases in favour of an endeavour that focuses on the general tenets distilled from landmark rulings relating to LOAC.

1 The World Wars – the fall and rise of enforcement

1.1 The First World War – international and national inertia

The First World War which commenced in 1914 witnessed one of the largest military mobilisa-tions in history. Four years later, the war came to a halt with the incredible devastation of coun-tries and the extent of the loss of life (soldiers and civilians) revealed. The facts of death and destruction staggered the citizenry of the world including the protagonists.[10] Civil and political outrage in Europe and America prompted calls for trials of political leaders and military person-nel with the ire of the victorious Allied states directed at Germany and Turkey – two pivotal powers that comprised the defeated Central Powers alliance. The call for prosecutions covered widespread and systematic breaches of LOAC. This led to the establishment of the Commission on the Responsibilities of the Authors of War and on Enforcement of Penalties (hereinafter 1919 Allied Commission)[11] intended to be the body that would be the main driver of supra-national prosecutions – a landmark moment in the modern enforcement of LOAC.

By 1920, the Allies had compiled a list of approximately 20,000 Germans who were to be investigated for war crimes.[12] These crimes included torture, use of human shields, rape and indiscriminate sinking of ships by the German navy. The Treaty of Peace Between the Allied and Associated Powers and Germany (Treaty of Versailles)[13] concluded at Versailles on 28 June 1919 provided in Article 227 for the creation of a supranational criminal tribunal to prosecute Kaiser Wilhelm II – the German emperor – for initiating the war.[14] Further and importantly for LOAC enforcement, Articles 228 and 229 provided for the prosecution of German military

---

9 The texts are reproduced in J B Scott (ed), *Texts of the Peace Conferences at The Hague, 1899 and 1907* (Ginn 1908).
10 The total cost in human life was estimated at 22 million dead and eight million casualties. See generally Jackson N Maogoto, *International Criminal Law and State Sovereignty: Versailles to Rome* (Transnational 2003) 35–42.
11 *The Treaties of Peace 1919-1923* (Carnegie Endowment for International Peace 1924) 3; Commission on the Responsibility of the Authors of the War and on Enforcement of Penalties, 'Report Presented to the Preliminary Peace Conference, 29 March 1919' (1920) 14 *AJIL* 95, 96.
12 M Cherif Bassiouni, 'Former Yugoslavia: Investigating Violations of International Humanitarian Law and Establishing an International Criminal Tribunal' (1995) *Fordham ILJ* 1191, 1194.
13 Treaty of Peace between the Allied and Associated Powers and Germany (Treaty of Versailles) (28 June 1919) 225 CTS 188.
14 Ibid art 227.

personnel accused of violating the laws and customs of war before Allied military tribunals or before the military courts of any of the Allies.[15] There is no question that the terrible crimes were covered by LOAC as it then existed, but legal and practical angst revolved around prosecuting the German emperor (a head of state) and, even more, the mooted supranational tribunal to prosecute German soldiers in an age when the act of state and obedience to superior orders doctrines reigned supreme.

The Allies, faced with several legal dilemmas and, exhausted by the war, were apprehensive of trying so many German officials and personnel. On one hand this posed a political risk of antagonising a defeated but major European power, on the other hand it would trample relevant key tenets of international law as it then stood. Subsequently, instead of setting up a supranational tribunal as provided for in Article 228, an agreement was reached allowing the German government to prosecute a limited number of war criminals before the Supreme Court of Germany (*Reichsgericht*) in Leipzig. The original list of 20,000 names was whittled down by the Allies to 896 names. The Germans eventually only initiated trial proceedings against 24 accused and, of these, half were acquitted and just 12 accused were convicted. The outcome of the Leipzig proceedings, while metrically dismal, was nonetheless an important future marker – enforcement of LOAC was not simply a matter of opaque domestic military disciplinary procedures. Ordinary courts were part of the enforcement mechanism. Significantly, supranational penal tribunals would form part of the enforcement regime in disciplining actions that crossed the line between breaches of military discipline and outright criminality under LOAC.

With regard to Turkey, during the First World War, the Turkish Empire[16] carried out the twentieth century's first genocide, slaughtering huge portions of its minority Christian Armenian population.[17] While these actions may seem not to fall strictly within the remit of this chapter, they are worth mentioning particularly as these atrocities were linked to war crimes and breaches of LOAC as they then existed.[18] While the massacres against the Armenians did not technically fall within the category of 'war crimes' to be prosecuted and punished by the Allies,

15 Ibid art 228 states:

> The German Government recognizes the right of the Allied and Associated Powers to bring before military tribunals persons accused of having committed acts in violation of the laws and customs of war. Such persons shall, if found guilty, be sentenced to punishments laid down by law. This provision will apply notwithstanding any proceedings or prosecution before a tribunal in Germany or in the territory of her allies.

> The German Government shall hand over to the Allied and Associated Powers, or to such one of them as shall so request, all persons accused of having committed an act in violation of the laws and customs of war, who are specified either by name or by the rank, office, or employment which they held under the German authorities.

Article 229 states:

> Persons guilty of criminal acts against the nationals of one of the Allied and Associated Powers will be brought before the military tribunals of that Power. Persons guilty of criminal acts against the nationals of more than one of the Allied and Associated Powers will be brought before military tribunals composed of members of the military tribunals of the Powers concerned. In every case the accused will be entitled to name his own counsel.

16 This chapter will not to delve into *realpolitik* nuances of terminology. Often the parlance is the Ottoman Empire but historically this had Turkey as its pivot hence as well referred to as the Turkish Empire.

17 It is to be noted that though Armenians were the main victims (in size and numbers), the Greek and Assyrians – much smaller Christian groups – also suffered.

18 This was an era when concepts and conceptualisations of LOAC breaches and enforcement avenues were evolving.

the scale of the massacres was such that the majority of the members of the 1919 Allied Commission were of the opinion that the Hague Convention (IV) principle, which allowed for reliance upon 'the laws of humanity' and 'dictates of public conscience' whenever clearly defined standards and regulations to deal with grave offences were lacking, applied.[19]

Based on the recommendations of the 1919 Allied Commission, several articles stipulating trial and punishment of those responsible for the Armenian genocide and LOAC violations were incorporated into the Treaty of Peace between the Allied Powers and Turkey (Treaty of Sèvres).[20] Under Article 226, the Turkish government recognised the right of trial and punishment by the Allied Powers, 'notwithstanding any proceedings or prosecution before a tribunal in Turkey' with an obligation that it surrender 'all persons accused of having committed an act in violation of the laws and customs of war.' Under Article 230 of the Treaty, Turkey was also obligated to hand over to the Allied Powers the persons responsible for the massacres committed during the continuance of the state of war on territory that formed part of the Turkish Empire on 1 August 1914 with the Allied Powers reserving the right to designate the tribunal which would try the persons accused of LOAC breaches and crimes against humanity.

The envisaged supranational tribunal initiative was to be derailed in the face of pressure by an ascendant ultra-nationalist Turkish government as a republic emerged from the ruins of the Ottoman Empire that had overplayed its hand. The Allied Powers capitulated and effectively discarded the Treaty of Sèvres when they concluded the Treaty of Lausanne in 1923.[21] This treaty, signed by representatives of Turkey (successor to the Ottoman Empire) on one side and by Britain, France, Italy, Japan, Greece, Romania and the Kingdom of Serbs, Croats and Slovenes (Yugoslavia) on the other, avoided the subject of accountability for war crimes and massacres. What is not often heralded is the fact that, though the supranational penal mechanism initiative collapsed, domestic pressure and political expedience in Turkey played a key role in delivering a measure of justice with a series of domestic trials.[22] Prosecutions by Turkish courts relied on the Ottoman Penal Code and Military Code while drawing strongly on international norms of LOAC for finesse. They resulted in a series of indictments, verdicts and sentences – an extraordinary milestone.[23]

1.2 The Second World War: rise and soar of enforcement – the International Military Tribunals

The establishment of the UN War Crimes Commission (UNWCC)[24] in 1943 constituted the main operative action taken by the Allies to deal with alleged major Axis Powers' war criminals once the Second World War concluded. The UNWCC was tasked with collecting evidence pursuant to the four major Allied Powers' resolute decision on the prosecution and punishment

19 See generally Jackson N Maogoto, *War Crimes and Realpolitik: From World War I into the 21st Century* (Lynne Rienner 2004) ch 2.
20 Treaty of Peace between the Allied Powers and Turkey (Treaty of Sèvres) (10 August 1920) 15 *AJIL Supp* 179.
21 Treaty of Lausanne (24 July 1923) 28 LNTS 12.
22 These targeted: (1) the members of Ittihad's Central Committee; (2) war-time cabinet ministers; (3) a host of provincial governors; (4) high ranking military officers.
23 For an explication, see generally Jackson N Maogoto, 'Reading the Shadows of History: The Bridges between Turkish and Ethiopian "Internationalised" Domestic Crime Trials' in Kevin Jon Heller and Gerry Simpson (eds), *The Hidden Histories of War Crimes Trials* (OUP 2013) 289.
24 This body had no relation to the UN that was to be established in 1945. It was labelled the 'United Nations' as an umbrella term for the leading Allied Powers acting in concert.

of war criminals.[25] The envisaged trials of alleged war criminals were meant to be a comprehensive attempt to unravel and deliver justice regarding the widespread breaches of LOAC and other international crimes specifically committed by the losing Axis Powers targeting Germany and Japan – two pivotal Axis powers.[26] In the course of its existence, the UNWCC amassed thousands of dossiers on alleged war criminals and served as a clearinghouse for information among governments.[27] The information that the UNWCC collected was to form a major basis for the subsequent IMTs convened at Nuremberg and Tokyo and accompanying frameworks for national prosecutions premised on LOAC tenets.

From the perspective of the principle of legality, the easiest of the crimes to define was 'war crimes'. War crimes in Article 6(b) of the Nuremberg Charter[28] included breaches of the laws and customs of war as identified explicitly and implicitly by 1907 Hague Convention (IV)[29] and the 1929 Prisoners of War Convention.[30] Important too was Article 8 of the Nuremberg Charter which removed the accepted defence of 'obedience to superior orders' in favour of individual criminal responsibility to preclude exoneration of defendants from responsibility.[31] Of the 22 high profile defendants who appeared before the Nuremberg IMT, 11 were given the death penalty, three were acquitted, three were sentenced to life imprisonment and four were given sentences of imprisonment ranging from ten to 20 years.

Subsequent to the Nuremberg Charter, the Allies passed Control Council Law No 10 (CCL No 10).[32] This was patterned after the Nuremberg Charter and provided the legal basis for the Allies to prosecute alleged German war criminals in their respective zones of occupation. CCL No 10 authorised the four key zone commanders – one each from France, UK, USSR and US – to set up tribunals for the punishment of war crimes, crimes against peace and crimes against humanity. Prosecutions in the Allied zones of occupation under the auspices of CCL No 10 were more in the nature of domestic as opposed to international prosecutions premised on Allies exercising sovereign power over Germany as a result of the country's unconditional surrender. In the British Zone, military tribunals tried 937 persons, acquitted 260 and sentenced 230 to death. In the US Zone, 177 persons were tried by military tribunals, 24 were sentenced to

---

25 This was as called for by the Moscow Declaration signed in 1943 by the United States, British and Russian leaders. See also UN War Crimes Commission, *The Punishment of War Criminals: Recommendations of the London International Assembly* (HMSO 1944) vol I.

26 The issue of victor's justice has been comprehensively dealt with intensively and extensively in various strands of mainstream scholarly works, hence this chapter will seek to take a narrower line focusing on its remit.

27 The 'dossiers' dealt with 24,453 accused, 9,520 suspects and 2,556 material witnesses: see eg War Office – Judge Advocate General's Office – Military Deputy's Department, *War Crimes, Europe, Card Indexes of Perpetrators, Witnesses and Accused, Second World War* (HMSO 1935–1948).

28 Agreement for the Prosecution and Punishment of the Major War Criminals of the European Axis (London Agreement) (8 August 1945) 82 UNTS 280 annex ('Nuremberg Charter').

29 Hague Convention (IV) regarding the Laws and Customs of Land Warfare (18 October 1907) 205 CTS 277.

30 Convention Relative to the Treatment of Prisoners of War (27 July 1929) 118 LNTS 343. The revised and updated version was one of the four Geneva Conventions of 1949 – GCIII.

31 This was a milestone in accountability as it was contrary to what most military laws provided for at the time the Second World War started.

32 Allied Control Council Law No 10, Punishment of Persons Guilty of War Crimes, Crimes Against Peace and Against Humanity, 20 December 1945, Official Gazette of the Control Council for Germany, No 3, Berlin, 31 January 1946 ('CCL No 10'), reprinted in Benjamin B Ferencz, *An International Criminal Court, a Step toward World Peace: A Documentary History and Analysis* (Oceana 1980) 488.

death, 35 acquitted.[33] In the French Zone, military courts tried 2,107 people, condemned 104 to death, acquitted 404 and gave 1,235 shorter prison terms. The Soviets did not hold such trials in its zone of occupation, but instead tried Nazi military personnel in the USSR for atrocities committed against civilians during Germany's occupation of their territory (the figures remain contested as many were summarily executed).

In the Far East, the history of the Tokyo IMT began with the establishment of the Far Eastern Commission.[34] The Commission provided the political and legal umbrella for prosecution and other policies related to suspected war criminals. The Tokyo Charter[35] followed the broad outline of the Big Four agreement in London that had established the Nuremberg IMT. It provided for the prosecution and punishment of those accused of committing 'crimes against peace', 'war crimes' and 'crimes against humanity'. Twenty-eight Japanese military and political leaders were charged with Class A crimes, and more than 5,700 Japanese nationals were charged with Class B and C crimes. Class A defendants (major political and civilian leaders) faced the Tokyo IMT.[36] Class B and C defendants faced national prosecutions in domestic courts/tribunals that spanned countries and continents: UK, France, the Netherlands and US to Australia, China and Philippines.[37]

The Nuremberg and Tokyo IMTs and their concomitant national trials established plainly and forcefully that the enforcement of LOAC was too important a matter to be left entirely to states. These trials created legal precedents on the supranational enforcement of LOAC breaches. However, the enforcement of LOAC violations was to be stifled by the onset of the Cold War which heralded a system transforming hegemonic struggle that cast a dark shadow over compliance and enforcement of LOAC.

2 The Cold War: a mixed report card – strengthening rules amidst weak enforcement

2.1 Expansion and codification of law of armed conflict

The wartime excess of the Second World War had created fertile ground for the landmark 1949 Geneva Conventions reinforced some three decades later by two Additional Protocols. This addressed the rights of individuals and populations in times of armed conflict, representing a major shift in focus from the methods of warfare to the protection of the victims of war and a preference for standards rather than rules. They marked a redefining moment in international humanitarian law, which was still dominated by the state-centric Hague Laws of the late nineteenth and early twentieth centuries whose deficiencies had been exposed by the two World

---

33 See further, Kevin Jon Heller, *The Nuremberg Military Tribunals and the Origins of International Criminal Law* (OUP 2011).

34 See generally 'Activities of the Far Eastern Commission, Report by the Secretary General 26 February to 10 July 1947' (1947) 16 *US Department of State Bulletin* 804–806.

35 US Department of State, *Trial of the Japanese War Criminals* (Publication 2613, Far Eastern Series 1946) 39–44.

36 See further, Yuki Tanaka, Tim McCormack and Gerry Simpson (eds), *Beyond Victor's Justice? The Tokyo War Crimes Trial Revisited* (Martinus Nijhoff 2011).

37 Over 2,200 trials were held outside Japan against 5,600 Japanese nationals and Japanese collaborators accused of various crimes. More than 4,400 were convicted, and about 1,000 were sentenced to death.

Wars – the shift from state-to-state aspects of international humanitarian law to individual criminal responsibility, and an emphasis on the rights of individuals and populations.[38]

The 1949 Geneva Conventions enshrined an obligation on states to enact legislation necessary to provide effective penal sanctions for persons committing, or ordering to be committed, LOAC breaches and integrating 'universal' jurisdiction into the law.[39] The concept of grave breaches was included in the 1949 Geneva Conventions as part of the effort to strengthen the obligation of states to provide effective penal sanctions against war crimes.[40] The Geneva Conventions were geared to provide an effective punishment regime for war crimes by 'establishing universal jurisdiction in the form of a duty to prosecute or extradite for these crimes'[41] when committed in international armed conflicts.[42] As the Commentary to the Geneva Conventions stated, '[t]he universality of jurisdiction for grave breaches is some basis for the hope that they will not remain unpunished and the obligation to extradite ensures the universality of punishment'.[43] Subsequently to improve effectiveness, this jurisdictional basis was expanded to cover conflicts of a non-international law character with the adoption of Additional Protocol I in 1977.[44] This was intended to counter state reluctance to prosecute violations of LOAC domestically as international crimes in light of emerging practice that favoured penal codes which often (and still) do not mirror violations as crimes under international humanitarian law.[45]

Despite these advances in the LOAC regime, the period was characterised by an absence of prosecutions despite intra-state conflict emerging as a major source of LOAC breaches. The volatile power politics of the Cold War laid down the basis of a turbulent global political order that spawned, perpetuated and propagated inter-state and intra-state wars fomenting regional instability. *Realpolitik* curtailed the expected benefits in compliance and enforcement of LOAC even as conflicts (internal and external) proliferated.

2.2 The International Court of Justice: bark and bite

The primary difference between international and non-international armed conflict is the actors taking part in them. International armed conflicts are traditionally fought between states; non-international armed conflicts are fought between a state and a non-state armed group or between opposing armed groups.[46] The differing actors involved in the two types of armed conflict suggest that certain legal norms cannot be transposed directly from the international armed conflict to the non-international armed conflict without some modification. Thus the extent to which customary rules of LOAC are applicable to armed conflict not of an international nature

---

38 See generally Frits Kalshoven, 'The history of international humanitarian law treaty-making', and Noam Lubell and Nancie Prud'homme, 'Impact of human rights law', respectively chs 2 and 6 in this volume.

39 See generally Robert Cryer, 'Individual liability in international law' and Luis Benavides, 'Universal jurisdiction over war crimes', respectively chs 31 and 34 in this volume; see further Sonja Boelaert-Suominen, 'Grave Breaches, Universal Jurisdiction and Internal Armed Conflict: Is Customary Law Moving towards a Uniform Enforcement Mechanism for All Armed Conflicts?' (2000) 5 *JCSL* 63.

40 For a more detailed evaluation of these efforts, see Rüdiger Wolfrum and Dieter Fleck, 'Enforcement of International Humanitarian Law' in Dieter Fleck (ed), *The Handbook of International Humanitarian Law* (2nd edn, OUP 2008) 675, 678–685.

41 Ferdinandusse (n 7) 723.

42 Arts 49 and 50 GCI; arts 50 and 51 GCII; arts 129 and 130 GCIII; arts 146 and 147 GCIV.

43 *GCIV Commentary* 587.

44 See APII art 85.

45 Ferdinandusse (n 7) 730.

46 See Caitlin Dwyer and Tim McCormack, 'Conflict characterisation' ch 3 in this volume.

is contested.[47] By the 1980s, there was in existence a recognisable body of LOAC relating to non-international armed conflict. However, identification of specific norms and rules was contested at best and disputed at worst[48] despite Common Article 3 of the 1949 Geneva Conventions setting down minimum standards.

The ICJ was the first international court to weigh into the debate on the disjunction between international and non-international conflict norms and the doctrinal schisms. In its 1986 judgment in the *Nicaragua* case,[49] the Court addressed in part the contentious issue of the applicability of Common Article 3 in armed conflict. The Court took the view that the rules contained in Common Article 3 of the Geneva Conventions reflected 'elementary considerations of humanity applicable in international and non-international armed conflicts alike affording protection in both non-international armed conflict and international armed conflict'.[50] A decade later and against the background of the work of the ad hoc international criminal tribunals, the ICJ was confronted with another thorny issue regarding the interplay of international human rights law and humanitarian law. While international human rights law post-Second World War influenced the growth and expansion of LOAC – which had approached stagnation – it also generated some confusion. In its 1996 advisory opinion on *Nuclear Weapons*[51] the ICJ addressed the matter through the prism of *lex specialis* in situations of armed conflict. It noted that 'the right to life must be construed by making a *renvoi* to humanitarian law'[52] in light of its role as a general principle of international law.[53]

3 The 1990s and into the twenty-first century – enforcement takes centre stage with shades and contestations

Despite the progress in LOAC codification, compliance and enforcement remained feeble. Schisms related to the nature of conflict, such as the distinction between grave breaches and war crimes, impacted on enforcement mechanisms despite the customary law position on individual criminal responsibility for serious violations of LOAC. The creation of the two ad hoc international criminal tribunals – ICTY and ICTR – in the early 1990s and the adoption of the Rome Statute in 1998 signalled important changes in enforcement of LOAC. International penal institutions were once again a central plank in the enforcement of LOAC.

3.1 The ad hoc international criminal tribunals

The ad hoc international tribunals addressed and clarified several significant albeit contested paradigms.[54] There had been a tendency, at least among certain states, to deal with the relative lack of treaty obligations for the enforcement of violations of LOAC in non-international armed conflicts, to extend the enforcement regime applicable to international armed conflicts by

---

47 Linton (n 2) 257.
48 See generally Sandesh Sivakumaran, 'Re-Envisaging the International Law of Internal Armed Conflict' (2011) 22 *EJIL* 219, 223.
49 *Military and Paramilitary Activities in and against Nicaragua (Nicaragua v US)* [1986] ICJ Rep 14, ¶ 218.
50 Ibid.
51 Legality of the Threat or Use of Nuclear Weapons (Advisory Opinion) [1996] ICJ Rep 226.
52 See eg William Abresch, 'A Human Rights Law of Internal Armed Conflict: The European Court of Human Rights in Chechnya' (2005) 16 *EJIL* 741, 744.
53 Ibid.
54 The author will dispense with the events leading to the establishment of these two ad hoc international criminal tribunals as they are well covered in general literature. See also generally Cryer (n 39).

analogy. The ICTY dramatically advanced this tendency and greatly contributed to the clarification of laws and customs of war in relation to enforcement of serious violations of the LOAC applicable in non-international armed conflicts. The ICTY Statute encompassed grave breaches in Article 2 while separating them from other serious violations of the laws and customs of war covered in Article 3. The interpretation and application of Article 3 was the basis for judicial pronouncements that advanced the enforcement of violations of LOAC in non-international armed conflict.

In *Tadić*,[55] the first case before the ICTY, the Trial Chamber sought to close the compliance and enforcement gap between international and non-international conflicts. The ICTY discussed whether the grave breaches provisions of the 1949 Geneva Conventions also applied to armed conflicts not of an international character. It noted that: '[w]hat is inhumane, and consequently proscribed, in international wars, cannot but be inhumane and inadmissible in civil strife'.[56] The ICTY Appeals Chamber affirmed this position with its assertion that 'with respect to the minimum rules in Article 3 common to all four Geneva Conventions, the character of the conflict is irrelevant'.[57] The essence of this is captured by Sonja Boelaert-Suominen's assertion that:

> the 'laws or customs of war', referred to in article 3 of the statute were held to constitute a general and residual clause covering all violations of humanitarian law not falling under article 2 or covered by articles 4 and 5, more specifically: (1) violations of the Hague law on international conflicts; (2) infringements of provisions of the Geneva Conventions other than those classified as 'grave breaches' by those Conventions; (3) violations of common article 3 and other customary rules on internal conflicts.[58]

The ICTY gravitated to the position that the grave breaches system encapsulated in the 1949 Geneva Conventions applied to non-international armed conflicts and that personal criminal responsibility for war crimes committed in non-international conflict was just as important as in international armed conflicts. However the ICTY stopped short of endorsing a role for the grave breaches regime in such conflicts and never accepted the application of Article 2 of the ICTY Statute in non-international armed conflicts. The 'expansive interpretation of article 3 of the statute' was construed as a residual basis of jurisdiction that would be invoked 'when more specialised provisions of the statute do not apply'[59] breaking 'new ground in its unequivocal assertion that individual criminal responsibility exists for violations of the laws applicable to internal armed conflicts'.[60]

The influence of international human rights in giving international humanitarian law content and contour was recognised by the ICTY which noted that: 'notions developed in the field of human rights can be transposed in international humanitarian law only if they take into consideration the specificities of the latter body of law'.[61] This was a reflection that in general terms

55 *Prosecutor v Tadić (Decision on the Defence Motion for Interlocutory Appeal on Jurisdiction)* (Case no IT-94-1-AR72, ICTY Appeals Chamber, 2 October 1995) ¶¶ 110–112.

56 Ibid.

57 Declaration on the Granting of Independence to Colonial Countries and Peoples, UNGA Res 1514 (14 December 1960) ¶ 4.

58 Boelaert-Suominen (n 39).

59 Ibid.

60 Ibid.

61 *Prosecutor v Kunarac, Kovač and Vuković* (Case nos IT-96-23-T and IT-96-23/1-T, ICTY Trial Chamber, 22 February 2001) ¶ 471.

both seek to achieve the protection of individuals but 'diverge in terms of the identity and role of the actors as well as sanctions for their violation'.[62] In effect, international human rights law had often been the basis of analysing internal strife that was on the borderline of serious civil upheaval and internal armed conflict.[63]

In *Halilović*,[64] the Trial Chamber stated that Article 3 of the Statute had been defined in the jurisprudence of the tribunal as a general clause covering all violations of international humanitarian law not covered by Articles 2, 4 or 5 of the ICTY Statute, including violations of Article 3 common to the Geneva Conventions and other customary rules on non-international armed conflict.[65] This position was to be echoed the following year in *Hadžihasanović*,[66] albeit with a reservation and a pointer on progression. It was observed that no rules, either in customary or in conventional international law, obligated states to prosecute acts which can be characterised as war crimes solely on the basis of international humanitarian law and thus granting a greater role for national criminal law.[67] The import was that states generally do not initiate proceedings solely on the basis of customary international law meaning it grants them leeway in restricting the prosecution of offences as war crimes.[68] In canvassing the Geneva Conventions and their Additional Protocols the Court seemed to intimate that implicit silence in legal provisions was not fatal but the absence of sufficiently consistent state practice was inclined towards states considering themselves not bound under international law to prosecute domestically and try grave breaches of LOAC.[69] In the author's opinion this was an important pointer to the role that the ICTY attached to clarifying legal provisions vis-à-vis inconsistencies in state practice.

Turning to the ICTR, its mandate fell firmly on the non-international conflict terrain rather than the variegated conflict spectrum the ICTY had to deal with. Article 4 of the ICTR Statute granted the tribunal jurisdiction over serious violations of Common Article 3 and Additional Protocol II. The tribunal was in time to enunciate that a serious violation of the LOAC applicable in non-international armed conflict was, indeed, a war crime.[70] On this basis, the tribunal determined that the acts enumerated in Article 4 of the ICTR Statute constitute serious violations of Common Article 3 and Additional Protocol II, entailing individual criminal responsibility.[71] The ICTR clarified the applicability of Common Article 3 and Additional Protocol II in armed conflicts. Previously 'common article 3 was seen as so vague that its prescriptions could be hardly ascertained and thus could easily be evaded'.[72] The ICTR also contributed to clarifications in assessment of factual situations falling on the periphery of LOAC. The Trial Chamber in the *Akayesu* case reasoned that since the Geneva Conventions and their Additional Protocols primarily aim at protection of victims of armed conflicts, they are 'addressed to persons who by virtue of their authority, are responsible for the outbreak of, or are otherwise engaged in the

62 Sivakumaran (n 48) 240–241.
63 Ibid 235.
64 *Prosecutor v Halilović* (Case no IT-01-48-T, ICTY Trial Chamber, 16 November 2005) ¶ 23.
65 Ibid.
66 *Prosecutor v Hadžihasanović* (Case no IT-01-47-T, ICTY Trial Chamber, 15 March 2006) ¶ 260.
67 Ibid.
68 Ibid ¶¶ 258–259.
69 Ibid 259.
70 See eg *Prosecutor v Rutaganda* (Case no ICTR-96-3, Trial Chamber, 6 December 1999) ¶ 106; *Prosecutor v Kayishema & Ruzindana* (Case no ICTR-95-1, Trial Chamber, 21 May 1999) ¶ 184; *Prosecutor v Bagilishema* (Case no ICTR-95-1A-A, Appeal Chamber, 2 July 2003) ¶ 102.
71 Ibid.
72 Roman Boed, 'Individual Criminal Responsibility for Violations of Article 3 Common to the Geneva Conventions of 1949 and of Additional Protocol II Thereto in the Case Law of the International Criminal Tribunal For Rwanda' (2002) 13 *Criminal Law Forum* 293, 322.

conduct of hostilities'.[73] According to this position, the responsibilities prescribed in these instruments normally fall to members of the armed forces, or to 'individuals who were legitimately mandated and expected, as public officials or agents or persons otherwise holding public authority or de facto representing the Government, to support or fulfil the war efforts'.[74]

The Trial Chamber in *Kayishema and Ruzindana* highlighted that the aim of Common Article 3 and Additional Protocol II is to protect victims of non-international armed conflicts[75] stressing the necessity of establishing a nexus between the alleged crimes and the conflict. This was encapsulated tangentially by the Trial Chamber in its enunciation that international armed conflicts are conflicts conducted by two or more states, whereas non-international armed conflicts are those between a state and a non-state entity. It, however, muddled this with its backhand observation that Common Article 3 and Additional Protocol II have differing thresholds of application.[76]

In sum, the ICTY and the ICTR commencing with their constituting statutes and reinforced by their judicial pronouncements have contributed greatly to the enforcement of LOAC and particularly that applicable to non-international armed conflicts. The tribunals clarified important practical enforcement realities, erased certain perceived black-letter artificialities and emphasised that the law governing internal armed conflict was both ascertainable and enforceable.[77] This is evident in the elucidation of material elements of Common Article 3 and Additional Protocol II as containing penal provisions that fundamentally contribute to promoting enforcement and thus repression of LOAC breaches.[78]

3.2 The International Criminal Court

The Rome Statute advanced the 'criminalisation' of offences committed in non-international armed conflicts by defining 'war crimes' as encompassing violations committed in international as well as in non-international armed conflicts. Boelaert-Suominen reminds us though that:

> [T]his progress needs to be set against the fact that the Statute confirms the existence of the 'two-box approach' in international humanitarian law, that its jurisdictional clauses do not fully reflect the principle of universality, and that the treaty contains plenty of reminders to the principle of legality.[79]

Article 8(1) provides that the ICC will have jurisdiction over war crimes when committed as part of a plan or policy or as part of a large-scale commission of such crimes. Article 8(2) defines acts the Statute considers to be war crimes, Article 8(2)(a) covering war crimes that result from a grave breach of the 1949 Geneva Conventions (this mirrors Article 2 of the ICTY Statute). The list of acts specified in Article 8(2)(b) is applicable in an international armed conflict while Article 8(2)(c) and 8(2)(e) extends the ICC jurisdiction to cover war crimes committed in non-international armed conflicts. This confirms the existence of individual criminal

---

73 *Prosecutor v Akayesu* (Case no ICTR-96-4-T, Trial Chamber, 2 September 1998) ¶ 630.

74 Ibid ¶ 631.

75 *Rutaganda* (n 70) 1999, ¶ 90; *Kayishema and Ruzindana* (n 70) ¶ 189. See also *Prosecutor v Musema* (Case no ICTR-96-13-T, Trial Chamber, 27 January 2000) ¶ 242; *Prosecutor v Bagilishema* (Case no ICTR-95-1A-T, Trial Chamber, 7 June 2001) ¶ 617.

76 *Kayishema and Ruzindana* (n 70) ¶ 170.

77 Boed (n 72) 322.

78 Ibid 305.

79 Boelaert-Suominen (n 39).

responsibility for violations of the corresponding humanitarian standards, regardless of the characterisation of the conflict – a significant development.

However, the structure and content of Article 8 confirm that there is still a recognisable regulatory gap between international and non-international conflicts to 'a certain degree in the distinction between Geneva-type provisions and Hague law type provisions'.[80] It is of note that the first ever Review Conference of the Rome Statute, held in Kampala in 2010, adopted an amendment that expanded the ICC's jurisdiction over war crimes in international armed conflicts to armed conflicts of a non-international character.[81] At Rome, states had granted the Court jurisdiction only over crimes relating to use of prohibited means of warfare if committed in the context of an international armed conflict.[82] At the Review Conference, states parties closed the gap in the Court's jurisdiction by extending customary law provisions relating to LOAC by amending Article 8 of the Rome Statute. This endorsed the applicability of customary LOAC prohibitions within the framework of non-international armed conflicts.[83]

4 Internationalised domestic war crime tribunals

Logically, prosecution of LOAC breaches domestically should be effective as states have control of territory and people. However, national penal provisions and enforcement processes too often fall short in disciplining LOAC breaches. The schism of monism and dualism has always seen a classic structural divide in the reception of international law as a source of law among states. For monist legal orders international law fits relatively easily within formally recognised domestic legal sources; for dualist legal orders, the enabling domestic legislation serves as a conduit and can often restrict the ambit of international law.[84] It is beyond the scope of this chapter to carry out a survey identifying various national legislation and case law. In light of this, it will reflect generally on the Cambodia, Sierra Leone and East Timor trials where the mechanisms, though tied to domestic legal regimes, were in the nature of internationalised LOAC enforcement. They were a hybridisation experiment (a half-way process in enforcing LOAC breaches combining international and national tenets) primarily to compensate for shortcomings in national systems.[85]

The Extraordinary Chambers in the Courts of Cambodia (ECCC) were established to prosecute those most responsible for the atrocities during the Khmer Rouge years (1975–1999).[86] The ECCC law declares that anyone who planned, instigated, ordered, aided and abetted, or committed crimes is individually criminally responsible and expressly limited the ambit of the

---

80 Ibid.

81 See Review Conference of the Rome Statute of the International Criminal Court, Kampala, 31 May to 11 June 2011, Resolution RC/Res 5 (10 June 2010) Annex I.

82 Daniel D N Nsereko, 'The Kampala Review Conference: The Capstone of the Rome System' (2011) 22(3) *Criminal Law Forum* 511, 515–518.

83 See Resolution RC/Res 5 (n 81) preambular ¶¶ 8–9.

84 See generally Timothy L H McCormack, 'Their Atrocities and our Misdemeanours: The Reticence of States to Try their "Own Nationals" for International Crimes' in Mark Lattimer and Philippe Sands (eds), *Justice for Crimes against Humanity* (Hart 2003).

85 See generally Parinaz Kermani Mendez, 'The New Wave of Hybrid Tribunals: A Sophisticated Approach to Enforcing International Humanitarian Law or an Idealistic Solution with Empty Promises?' (2009) *Criminal Law Foum* 53, 54.

86 Law on the Establishment of Extraordinary Chambers in the Courts of Cambodia for the Prosecution of Crimes Committed during the Period of Democratic Kampuchea, UNGA Res 57/228 B (22 May 2003).

Cambodian government to grant amnesties or pardons.[87] The Group of Experts on the ECCC opined that Common Article 3 of the 1949 Geneva Conventions applied to the exclusion of Hague Law on the means and methods of war.[88] However the Special Law does not give the Extraordinary Chambers jurisdiction regarding violations of Common Article 3 of the Geneva Conventions and the laws and customs of war in internal conflicts. Thus an important core of LOAC was not part of the accountability regime despite strong evidence of systematic crimes that are encompassed within LOAC through customary law. The rationale was that the bulk of Khmer Rouge atrocities were committed against Khmer civilians by the government of the day prior to the grave breaches regime encompassed in the Geneva Conventions being extended to non-international conflict through the adoption in 1977 of Additional Protocol I.[89]

In the Asia-Pacific region, the East Timor Serious Crimes legislation created a regime based on the Rome Statute. 'The threshold requirements for the law of war crimes contained in section 6 of UNTAET Regulation 2000/15 were based on article 8 of the Rome Statute of the International Criminal Court'[90] which attempted to balance considerations of war crimes to the situation that had been the basis of its emanation.[91] Claus Kress synthesises the net legal effect astutely.

> Under section 6, the existence of an armed conflict, be it international or non-international, is the fundamental threshold requirement to trigger the applicability of the law of war crimes. This follows from the references to the 'grave breaches of the Geneva Conventions of 12 August 1949' in section 6.1(a), to 'international armed conflict' in section 6.1(b), to 'an armed conflict not of an international character' in section 6.1(c), and to 'armed conflicts not of an international character' in section 6.1(e).[92]

In Africa, after the vicious civil war that raged between the government and the rebel Revolutionary United Front (RUF), the Statute of the SCSL focused on the well-established principle of distinction between civilian and combatant but lacked provision for prosecutions of the laws and customs of war which cover violations of a 'means and methods' variety. The SCSL had jurisdiction over crimes against humanity, serious violations of Common Article 3 and Additional Protocol II, serious violations of international humanitarian law and selected provisions of Sierra Leonean law. This was geared to centre the crimes as encompassed in black-letter provisions relating to serious violations of international humanitarian law rather than laws and customs of war whose deficiencies were exposed by Regulation 2000/15 in East Timor which by importing 'virtually the whole of the ICC Statute's substantive legal provisions' posed problems regarding retroactivity.

---

87 Ibid arts 29, 40.
88 Report of the Group of Experts for Cambodia established pursuant to General Assembly Resolution 52/135, transmitted by the Secretary-General along with his own report, UN Doc A/53/850, S/199/231 (16 March 1999) ¶ 151.
89 API art 85(1).
90 Claus Kress, 'The 1999 Crisis in East Timor and the Threshold of the Law on War Crimes' (2002) *Criminal Law Forum* 409.
91 Linton (n 2) 230.
92 Kress (n 90).

5 Conclusion

Non-international armed conflicts account for greater sources of LOAC breaches but the enforcement remains relatively weak. The normative gap with respect to enforcement, was bridged in the early 1990s when the Commission of Experts appointed to investigate violations of international humanitarian law committed in the former Yugoslavia opined that '[i]t is unlikely that there is any body of customary international law applicable to internal armed conflict which does not find its root in' Common Article 3, Additional Protocol II and Article 19 of the 1954 Hague Convention.[93] Subsequently the ICTY affirmed that under laws and customs of war, penal sanctions for violations of grave breaches provisions under the Geneva Conventions were not restricted to international armed conflict but extended to non-international armed conflict. This tenor is reflected as well by the ICTR in its clarification and enunciation of thresholds regarding the distinction between international and non-international armed conflicts.[94]

International and internationalised courts have played an important role in explication and enforcement of LOAC despite their limited remit in numbers and perpetrators tried. Often, it may not be easy, for example, to find adequate provisions in national criminal codes for some offences. The disjunction of international and non-international conflicts remains a thorny issue. They have exposed and often closed existing gaps by the inactivity of states. States are under clear obligations 'to search for, investigate and repress these violations, either by bringing the perpetrators to their own courts or extraditing them to another state that has made out a prima facie case'.[95] The work of international courts and tribunals is a harbinger of manifest efforts in harmonising prosecutorial approaches and bridging the divide in reception of customary law norms through the work of international courts and tribunals in enunciating the *lex specialis* application of LOAC to the rules provided by humanitarian law. Emblematic of this has been the clarification of the applicability of customary law to international and non-international conflicts trumping state practice that penal sanctions for violations of grave breaches provisions only arose in international armed conflicts.[96]

International courts and tribunals have played a major role in actualising universality as a tenet of prosecuting grave breaches of LOAC. However the reality remains that they seek to target individuals (usually senior) most responsible for violations and are limited in their temporal jurisdiction. This means that many considered low-level offenders are excluded from prosecution. As well, within domestic settings, provisions of law are inconsistent with international norms and the defences available are more extensive than those available under international law. This raises the existence of different prosecutorial approaches and ultimately differential treatment of LOAC violations. However they remain vital to closing the existing gaps caused by the inactivity of national courts as well as the primer for the ascendance in more robust national legal and prosecutorial activity.

---

93 Final Report of the Commission of Experts established pursuant to Security Council Resolution 780 (1992), UN Doc S/1994/674 (24 May 1994) ¶ 52.
94 See eg *Kayishema and Ruzindana* (n 70) ¶ 170.
95 Fleck, 'Shortcomings' (n 2) 849.
96 Linton (n 2) 258. See also Boed (n 72).

34

Universal jurisdiction over war crimes

Luis Benavides

Universal jurisdiction is a fairly old concept in international law.[1] However, during the 1990s some European states revived the principle in their legislations along with a judicial practice in a way that has, at times, been very controversial.[2]

Thus, universal jurisdiction became part of a heated debate between those who love it and those who hate it.[3] Time had to pass to cool things off along with some setbacks in legislation[4] and states' jurisdictional exercise of that principle.[5]

One of the reasons of the controversy surrounding the principle of universality is, in my opinion, that the principle had a qualitative leap of rationale when applied in the late twentieth century.

---

1 Henri Donnedieu de Vabres, *Les Principes Modernes du Droit Pénal International* (Recueil Sirey 1928) 135.

2 Belgium noted that the application of the Act of 16 June 1993 … in practice gave rise to a number of problems. These derived from the combined application of several provisions, namely the possibility of initiating proceedings in absentia, initiating a case by instituting civil indemnification proceedings before an examining magistrate, and the exclusion of immunities as an obstacle to prosecution. This broad field of application entailed a politicization of the law, which was considered improper.

> Report of the Secretary-General prepared on the Basis of Comments and Observations of Governments, the Scope and Application of the Principle of Universal Jurisdiction, UN Doc A/65/181 (17 September 2010) ('SG Report Universal Jurisdiction 2010') ¶ 94

For example, 'Principle of "Universal Jurisdiction" Again divides Assembly's Legal Committee. Delegates; Further Guidance sought from International Law Commission. Aim to Avoid Impunity for Gross Crimes Is Recalled; Concern Expressed that Broadened Scope may bring other Problems, Threaten State Sovereignty' UN Press release, General Assembly, UN Doc GA/L/3415 (12 October 2011).

3 Compare eg Kenneth Roth, 'The Case for Universal Jurisdiction' *Foreign Affairs* (September/October 2001) and Henry Kissinger, 'The Pitfalls of Universal Jurisdiction: Risking Judicial Tyranny' *Foreign Affairs* (July/August 2001).

4 See eg Human Rights Watch, 'Belgium: Universal Jurisdiction Law Repealed', www.hrw.org/news/2003/08/01/belgium-universal-jurisdiction-law-repealed. Center for Justice and Accountability, 'Spanish Congress Enacts Bill Restricting Spain's Universal Jurisdiction Law', www.cja.org/article.php?id=740.

5 For recent setbacks in practice, see for instance, Amnesty International, 'Universal Jurisdiction: Strengthening this Essential Tool of International Justice' (2012) 45–54, www.amnesty.org/en/library/info/IOR53/020/2012/en.

Thus, the first section of this chapter will deal with the analysis of the concept of universal jurisdiction in criminal law;[6] with particular emphasis on the evolution of its rationale.

The second section will deal with a modern conception of war crimes, regardless of the type of conflict in which they might occur.

1 Universal jurisdiction

Universal jurisdiction allows every state to try and punish a person who has committed a particular international crime (*delicta juris gentium*), when the crime was committed outside its territory by a foreigner, against any person or group of persons without any link with the prosecuting state, provided that the criminal is in the state's custody (*judex deprehensionis*) when brought to trial.[7]

I will now deconstruct the above definition.

1.1 'Universal jurisdiction allows every state ...'

Universal jurisdiction has the function of a right; this means that the state may or may not exercise it. It may be argued, however, that since there is a commitment of the international community to prosecute international criminals and to end impunity as is reflected, for example, in the preamble of the ICC Statute, the use of universal jurisdiction becomes, apparently, compulsory in the pursuit of that goal. In our opinion, this is not an *ipso facto* obligation since the state that has custody of the alleged perpetrator may choose between prosecuting the culprit or extraditing him to another state or transferring him to an appropriate international tribunal. This is a sort of *aut dedere aut judicare* rule, which will be discussed later in the analysis. The reason for that is that the state in possession of the alleged culprit may not be well fitted to carry out a universal jurisdiction trial. Universal jurisdiction cases usually demand more economic[8] and human resources than common or normal cases.[9] It also requires an adequate national legal framework; therefore, the importance for the state to harmonise its national legislation to international standards.[10] Moreover, universal jurisdiction cases need to be carried out according to international human rights law (IHRL) standards,[11] which not all states are capable to meet even under normal circumstances. Thus, it seems very difficult to oblige a state to exercise universal jurisdiction when it lacks the necessary capacity to prosecute an international criminal; the same

---

6 Even though some states have established civil or tort universal jurisdiction, it goes outside the scope of the present work. See eg Donald Francis Donovan and Anthea Roberts, 'The Emerging Recognition of Universal Civil Jurisdiction' (2006) 100 *AJIL* 142.

7 See Luis Benavides, 'The Universal Jurisdiction Principle: Nature and Scope' (2001) I *Anuario Mexicano de Derecho Internacional* 19, 28.

8 The budget for the trial of Mr Hissène Habré, former President of the Republic of Chad, in Senegal as adopted by the Donors Round Table in 2010 was set at €8.6 million, in *Questions relating to the Obligation to Prosecute or Extradite (Belgium v Senegal)* [2012] ICJ Rep 33. Senegal held in a Verbal Note of 2007 in the case of Habré that: '[it] require[d] substantial funds which Senegal cannot mobilize without the assistance of the [i]nternational community'. Ibid 29.

9 See, among others, Eugene Kontorovich and Steven Art, 'An Empirical Examination of Universal Jurisdiction for Piracy' (2010) 104 *AJIL* 436.

10 One of the most important harmonisation processes that has taken place is among the state parties to the Rome Statute since basically all of them have enacted legislation to implement the ICC Statute, see www.icc-cpi.int/Menus/ASP/states+parties/. For a compilation of national implementing legislation, see the Coalition for the ICC, www.iccnow.org/?mod=home.

11 SG Report Universal Jurisdiction 2010 (n 2) ¶ 9.

appears to apply in cases when the state is unwilling to prosecute the alleged culprit. Consequently, the alternative obligation of *aut dedere aut judicare* seems to be a better option when a state is unable or unwilling to exercise universal jurisdiction. One thing is clear: there should be no safe haven for international criminals.

At this point, it is important to clarify, due to the persistent confusion that exists, the principles of universal jurisdiction and *aut dedere aut judicare*. Both principles are closely related and sometimes intertwined as bases for the exercise of a state criminal jurisdiction; nevertheless, they are not the same and although they may pursue the same goal, that is, to fight impunity, they have different natures and play different roles in the international criminal system.[12]

The exercise of universal jurisdiction is a right, based on customary international law, which is applied to a special category of international crimes, *delicta juris gentium*, such as piracy, slavery, war crimes, crimes against humanity and genocide. Universal jurisdiction is an exceptional jurisdiction which can be exercised, under certain circumstances, by all the states. On the other hand, *aut dedere aut judicare* is an alternative obligation: prosecute or extradite, usually inserted as a clause in multilateral conventions providing for judicial cooperation and, therefore, only binding among the parties to such treaties.[13] These treaties codify several crimes of international concern such as drug trafficking or terrorism. The customary status of *aut dedere aut judicare* outside the convention obligations is, nevertheless, doubtful.[14]

Although *aut dedere aut judicare* may create the illusion of a conventional universal jurisdiction the truth is that both concepts are different in nature and should not be used synonymously.

Universal jurisdiction does not mean that every state should be looking for all alleged perpetrators of international crimes at all times – that does not happen in reality – but rather that every state could eventually exercise its criminal jurisdiction when in possession of a suspect of international crimes or, as already explained, to use the *aut dedere aut judicare* rule.

Universal jurisdiction is not a primary jurisdiction, it is a jurisdiction that needs to be used as a backup mechanism when the state concerned, usually the territorial state, is unwilling or unable to exercise its criminal jurisdiction or when an international judicial body is not the appropriate forum to try the alleged culprit. International judicial bodies are subsidiary mechanisms of the state's primary criminal jurisdiction; they are able to prosecute only a small number of perpetrators. Although they represent a very powerful deterrent mechanism for international crimes, it is essential for the international rule of law to strengthen national judicial systems to investigate and prosecute international crimes.

The function of universal jurisdiction within the international criminal system is that of a last resort jurisdiction, our last tool to fight impunity. Since universal jurisdiction is of an exceptional nature it should therefore be used exceptionally.

1.2 '... to try and punish a person ...'

Any person, regardless of his position in a state, who commits or participates in the commission of a *delicta jure gentium* is internationally criminally responsible for that crime. Since the *obiter dictum* of the International Military Tribunal (IMT) at Nuremberg, it is nowadays well established as a principle of international law that 'crimes against international law are committed by

12 Originally the distinction between these two principles could be found at Benavides (n 7) 36.
13 For an analysis of treaties with the *aut dedere aut judicare* clause, see among others, M Cherif Bassiouni and Edward Wise, *Aut Dedere aut Judicare, the Duty to Extradite or to Prosecute in International Law* (Martinus Nijhoff 1995) 340.
14 Cf Report of the International Law Commission on its Sixty-Third Session, UN Doc A/66/10 (2010) ¶ 320.

men, not by abstract entities, and only by punishing individuals who committed such crimes can the provisions of international law be enforced'.[15]

This will take us to another issue, the question of immunity regarding *delicta juris gentium*. It is not the intention of this chapter to elaborate fully on all aspects of immunity of high ranking officials, mainly heads of state and government, and ministers of foreign affairs, but simply to point out that from the perspective of a coherent international criminal system, immunities, as well as amnesties, pardons and other similar acts, are incompatible with the main purpose of the system: that is, to prosecute and punish international criminals whatever their position within a state[16] and, with that, to end impunity and to bring justice to the victims of such heinous crimes.

Recent practice shows that while in office high ranking officials may not be subject to universal jurisdiction; however, this is not an impediment for international judicial bodies to exercise their jurisdiction.[17] A call for prudence seems to be the way in which states, willing to exercise universal jurisdiction, should behave regarding incumbent high ranking officials. This does not mean impunity but rather is a matter of timing, as to the best moment to prosecute a criminal and a question as to the suitable mechanism.

Ideally, high ranking officials that commit international crimes should be prosecuted before international tribunals, because part of the rationale for the establishment of international tribunals is to prosecute those who play the most important role in the commission of international crimes. Nevertheless, in cases where that is not possible the states need to step up and prosecute the criminals.

Although not explicitly included in the definition, it is clear that the prosecution and eventual punishment of an international criminal should be subject to IHRL rights standards.

1.3 '… who has committed a particular international crime (delicta juris gentium) …'

Universal jurisdiction applies only to a particular category of crimes called *delicta juris gentium* which are established by general international law. But what is the rationale for this type of crime? In our opinion, these crimes are characterised by the nature of the conduct which affects the international community as a whole.[18]

In its origins, the rationale for the principle of universality was based on value – and space – oriented considerations, and the 'gravity' of the crimes.[19] The crime par excellence subject to the universality principle is piracy.[20] Thus, for instance, in the crime of piracy the value-oriented

---

15 *US et al v Göring et al* 1 TMWC 171, 223 (1946).

16 Ibid

> The principle of international law, which under certain circumstances protects the representatives of a State, cannot be applied to acts which are condemned as criminal by international law. The authors of these rights cannot shelter themselves behind their official position in order to be freed from punishment in appropriate proceedings.

17 See for instance the international arrest warrants issued by the ICC against Mr Omar Hassan Ahmad Al Bashir, currently President of Sudan. *Prosecutor v Al Bashir (First warrant of arrest)* (Case no ICC-02/05-01/09-1, Pre-Trial Chamber I, 4 March 2009); *(Second warrant of arrest)* (Case no ICC-02/05-01/09-95, Pre-Trial Chamber I, 12 July 2010).

18 See eg *Attorney-General of the Government of Israel v Adolf Eichmann* (1968) 36 ILR 290–291.

19 See eg SG Report Universal Jurisdiction 2010 (n 2) ¶ 10.

20 For example, Tullio Treves, 'Piracy, Law of the Sea, and Use of Force: Developments off the Coast of Somalia' (2009) 20 *EJIL* 400. See also UNSC Res 1816 (2 June 2008).

consideration was to protect mainly commercial maritime routes and navigation, which are essential for the international community. The pirate was considered *hostis humani generis*, an enemy of mankind,[21] hence the interest of the international community to suppress that crime and to punish the culprit.

The space-oriented consideration is simply that piracy was committed on the high seas, that is, outside the jurisdiction of any state. At the time, there were few states and an incipient international legal system, with minimum rules and practically no institutions/organisations. Therefore, the exercise of universal jurisdiction does not seem to have created a particular conflict in the international community.

The revival of universal jurisdiction in the twentieth century kept its value-oriented consideration, but it shifted from maritime and commercial issues to human rights, humanitarian law and international criminal law values. The scope of application of the universality principle also expanded to new crimes: crimes against humanity, genocide, war crimes and aggression and, probably, nowadays, to torture.[22] The space-oriented aspect of the principle remained only in relation to the fact that the crime is committed outside the territory of the state willing to exercise universal jurisdiction. International crimes subject to universal jurisdiction are usually committed within the jurisdiction of a state and not on the high seas.

Some questions arise from that evolution including, for instance: At what moment did the rationale for universal jurisdiction change? When did states agree on that change? What are the consequences of that change?

It is not possible to identify a single date, but rather a series of events that contributed to the change of rationale. One of the key moments that reshaped the rationale for universal jurisdiction was delivery of the judgments of the IMT at Nuremberg and the International Military Tribunal for the Far East (IMFTE) at Tokyo. Although, obviously neither the IMT nor the IMFTE were an exercise of universal jurisdiction,[23] both tribunals set the basis for the exercise of the said principle. The legacy of the IMT and IMFTE's judgments is reflected in the 'Principles of International Law Recognized in the Charter of the Nuremberg Tribunal and in the Judgment of the Tribunal', as elaborated by the ILC at the request of the UN General Assembly.[24] These principles could be considered the cornerstone of international criminal law (ICL), and the basis for universal jurisdiction, since they established, among other issues, individual criminal responsibility for the commission of international crimes even in the case of heads of state and high ranking officials and a definition for crimes against peace, humanity and war crimes. The principles also had an impact on the international community as they showed that when international crimes are committed by governments against their own population, international society has a legal interest in their prosecution. Thus, for example, the General Assembly affirmed that '[t]he punishment of the crime of genocide is a matter of international concern'[25] and that the alleged culprits should be punished.

---

21 Hugo Grotius, *De Jure Belli ac Pacis, Libri Tres* (Francis W Kelsey transl, vol 2, Clarendon 1925/1995) 373.

22 The ICJ stated in *Questions relating to the Obligation to Prosecute or Extradite* (n 8) ¶ 93 that 'the prohibition of torture is part of customary international law and it has become a peremptory norm *(jus cogens)*'. This may imply that any state may exercise universal jurisdiction in cases of torture. The Court, however, did not explore this possibility as it only confined its argument to the Convention against Torture's obligations.

23 International law only permits states to exercise universal jurisdiction. International tribunals do not exercise universal jurisdiction *stricto senso* although they might be considered of universal value.

24 Cf UNGA Res 177(II) (21 November 1947) ¶ (a); UN Doc A/CN.4/85 (1947) and YILC Pt II (1950) 374–378.

25 UNGA Res 96(I) (1946).

The second important event was the adoption of the four Geneva Conventions of 1949. Article 1 common to the conventions establishes a system of collective responsibility: 'The High Contracting Parties undertake to respect and to ensure respect for the present Convention in all circumstances.'[26] The ICRC commentary to this article points out that: 'The Contracting Parties are no longer merely required to take the necessary legislative action to prevent or repress violations. They are under obligation to search for, and prosecute, guilty parties, and cannot evade their responsibility.'[27] Article 1 must be read along with Articles 49, 50, 129 and 146 of Geneva Conventions I–IV respectively, each of which establishes a tripartite obligation (1) to enact special legislation on this issue, (2) to search for any person accused of grave breaches of the Convention and (3) to try the alleged culprit or to hand him over for trial to another state concerned.[28]

It is obvious that these are conventional obligations only binding upon state parties; however, due to the universal acceptance of the Geneva Conventions,[29] it is possible to argue that a customary international norm has emerged for the application of universal jurisdiction over war crimes including grave breaches. In fact, in the ICRC's opinion, based on customary international humanitarian law: 'States have the right to vest universal jurisdiction in their national courts over war crimes.'[30] It is worth noting that the ICRC indicates that universal jurisdiction is a 'right' and not an obligation to be exercised:

> The right of States to vest universal jurisdiction in their national courts over war crimes in no way diminishes the obligation of States party to the Geneva Conventions and States party to Additional Protocol I to provide for universal jurisdiction in their national legislation over those war crimes known as 'grave breaches'.[31]

The third event was the creation of the legal and institutional framework for the protection of human rights. It is clear that after the Second World War violations of human rights were not the exclusive interest of the state where they happened. Thus, in the last 50 years we have witnessed the diminishing scope of the state's *domaine reservé* regarding human rights issues and an evolution of the normative and institutional framework for their protection.

It is true that this evolution has not been without setbacks,[32] but there has definitely been progress in the protection of human rights that did not exist before 1945. The first wave in the normative protection of human rights came with adoption of the so-called International Bill of Human Rights.[33] Not much more was done during the first three decades after 1945, due particularly to the inertia into which the UN fell during the Cold War. The second wave of development came precisely once the Cold War was over, as a vast number of international instruments of human rights were enacted after 1989.[34] Yet the institutions that were created (that is, treaty bodies and special procedures) to monitor the fulfilment of states' international obligations

---

26 See Laurence Boisson de Chazournes and Luigi Condorelli, 'Common Article 1 of the Geneva Conventions Revisited: Protecting Collective Interests' (2000) 82 *IRRC* 67.
27 *GCI Commentary* 27.
28 *GCI Commentary* 362.
29 As of December 2015 there were 196 state parties to the GCI–IV. Please see www.icrc.org/IHL.nsf/ (SPF)/party_main_treaties/$File/IHL_and_other_related_Treaties.pdf.
30 CIHL r 157.
31 CIHL r 157.
32 The setbacks are because despite the creation of the said normative and institutional framework they have been unable to stop human rights violations.
33 For a list of international human rights instruments, see eg www2.ohchr.org/english/law.
34 Ibid.

lacked the necessary tools effectively to stop human rights atrocities and, therefore, much of their protection was purely rhetoric.[35] On the other hand, there has been a certain degree of efficiency regarding human rights institutions that deal with *ex post facto* violations of human rights. Those institutions include the European and Inter American Courts of Human Rights[36] decisions of which are compulsory upon the states that have accepted the Courts' contentious jurisdiction. In sum, those instruments and institutions have helped to reshape the *opinio juris* of the international community as to what a state can or cannot do regarding human rights issues.

Nowadays, it is clear that human rights are not left alone to the states.[37] Their violation is a question of concern for the international community and, under certain circumstances, their lack of compliance might be considered a threat to or a breach of international peace and security. For example, the Security Council has applied sanctions in order to eliminate apartheid,[38] return to democracy and respect for human rights (Haiti),[39] respect international human rights and humanitarian law (Yugoslavia)[40] and bring to justice government and militia leaders for human rights violations and international crimes (Sudan),[41] among many other issues. The idea is that massive or gross violations of human rights might amount to international crimes such as crimes against humanity and genocide.[42]

The fourth event came with the armed conflicts of the former Yugoslavia (1990s) and Rwanda (1994). In both cases international tribunals were set up via the UN Security Council.[43] These are particularly important events since they constitute a landmark moment for the institutionalisation of ICL, which lacked an important impetus since the Nuremberg and Tokyo trials. Both UN tribunals also constituted a very important precedent and thrust for the creation of the ICC.

It is interesting to note that since the establishment of the two ad hoc international criminal tribunals, the international community has opted for a two-way approach to the prosecution of international crimes. On one hand, it has developed the institutionalisation of the prosecution of international crimes as evidenced by the ICTY (1993), ICTR (1994), Hybrid Courts of Kosovo (1999), Special Panels of the Dili District Court in East Timor (2000), Special Court for Sierra Leone (2002), ICC (2002), War Crimes Section of the State Court of Bosnia and Herzegovina (2005), Extraordinary Chambers in the Courts of Cambodia (2006) and the Special Tribunal for Lebanon (2007).

On the other hand, there has been an 'explosion' in the exercise of universal jurisdiction at the national level. According to a recent study on this subject there have been more than 1,000 complaints but only 32 have ended up in trials.[44] Only 14 states have exercised universal jurisdictions,

---

35 See eg Emilie M Hafner-Burton and James Ron, 'Human Rights Institutions: Rhetoric and Efficacy' (2007) 44 *Journal of Peace Research* 379.

36 The African Court on Human and Peoples' Rights is so incipient, officially entered into functions in 2006 that still is difficult to measure its impact.

37 See Hersh Lauterpacht, *International Law and Human Rights* (Stevens & Sons 1950) 68.

38 See eg UNSC Res 418, 473, 569, 591, 765, etc.

39 See eg UNSC Res 841, 861, 862, 867, 873, 875, 905, 917, etc.

40 For example, UNSC Res 757, 764, 808, 820, 917, among many more.

41 UNSC Res 1556 (30 July 2004).

42 See eg Stanislav Chernichenko, 'Definition of Gross and Large-Scale Violations of Human Rights as an International Crime' UN Doc E/CN.4/Sub.2/1993/10 (25 October 1993).

43 ICTR: UNSC Res 827 (1993); ICTR: UNSC Res 955 (1994).

44 Maximo Langer, 'The Diplomacy of Universal Jurisdiction: The Political Branches and the Transnational Prosecution of International Crimes' (2011) 105 *AJIL* 1.

all of them western states.[45] In comparison there are so far 123 state parties to the Rome Statute.[46] It is clear, therefore, that the international community has favoured an institutionalised process for the prosecution of international criminals.

Thus, it is the accumulative effect of all the above-mentioned events that have transformed the rationale of universal jurisdiction and the *opinio juris* of states in regard to the nature and scope of the said principle.

This change of rationale was rapidly endorsed by many states;[47] particularly in the 1990s, creating an evolving *opinio juris*[48] to deal with international crimes, not only through international criminal judicial mechanisms,[49] but also through the exercise of the state's jurisdiction, including universal jurisdiction.[50] In this sense, the UN Secretary-General stated in his report on universal jurisdiction:

> [O]ne of the major achievements in international law in recent decades had been the shared understanding that there should be no impunity for serious crimes. International cooperation was constantly being strengthened and new measures taken to ensure that perpetrators of such crimes were brought to justice. These efforts had led to concrete outcomes, giving practical recognition to international criminal jurisdiction, as well as to prosecutions based on universal jurisdiction.[51]

The first test of this new rationale for universal jurisdiction arose in the case of Pinochet and the extradition request to the UK for his trial in Spain, coupled with multiple attempts by Belgium to implement its universal jurisdiction legislation. These cases disrupted the international

---

45 The states that have held trials under the basis of universal jurisdiction in the last two decades are: Australia, Austria, Belgium, Canada, Denmark, Finland, France, Germany, Israel, Netherlands, Norway, Spain, Switzerland, United Kingdom. See Langer (n 44) 42. A recent case was also prosecuted in Sweden, although the defendant was acquitted, www.windsorstar.com/news/Swedish+court+overturns +life+sentence+Serb+acquits+crimes/7720421/story.html. Around 50 per cent of all the culprits have been convicted, Langer (n 44) 43.

46 See www.icc-cpi.int/Menus/ASP/states+parties.

47 This rapid endorsement is what professor Condorelli has called '*coutume grande vitesse*'. Luigi Condorelli, 'La Cour Pénale Internationale : Un Pas de Géant (Pourvu qu'il soit Accompli)' (1999) 103 *RGDIP* 7. It can also be called 'instant custom', Bin Cheng, 'United Nations Resolutions on Outer Space: "Instant" International Customary Law?' (1965) 5 *Indian Journal of International Law* 23 *passim*.

48   Recent developments show, however, that customary rules may come into existence rapidly … it may be due to the urgency of coping with widespread sentiments of moral outrage regarding crimes committed in conflicts, such as those in Rwanda and Yugoslavia … that brought about the rapid formation of a set of customary rules concerning crimes committed in internal conflicts.
        Tullio Treves, 'Customary International Law' (November 2006) *MPEPIL* ¶ 24

49 For instance, the ICTR: UNSC Res 855 (1994); ICTY: UNSC Res 827 (1993); SCSL: UNSC Res 1315 (2000); Extraordinary Chambers in the Courts of Cambodia: UNGA Res 57/228 B (22 May 2003); Crimes Panels of the District Court of Dili: UNSC Res 1272 (25 October 1999); Panels in the courts of Kosovo: UNMIK Reg 2000/64 (15 December 2000); Rome Statute.

50 See the compilation of state practice regarding universal jurisdiction at the Reports of the Secretary-General Prepared on the Basis of Comments and Observations of Governments, the Scope and Application of the Principle of Universal Jurisdiction, UN Docs A/65/181 (17 September 2010), A/66/93 (20 June 2011), A/RES/67/116 (18 December 2012). See also Amnesty International, 'Universal Jurisdiction: A Preliminary Survey of Legislation around the World: 2012 update,' www.amnesty.org/es/ library/info/IOR53/019/2012/en; Amnesty International, 'Universal Jurisdiction' (n 5).

51 SG Report Universal Jurisdiction 2010 (n 2) ¶ 7.

system since they tried to apply the principle of universality without any limits or coherence. Eventually both states had to step back in their exercise of universality.[52]

Unfortunately, the change in rationale of the principle of universality did not come with a change in the functioning of the rest of the international criminal system. The principle of universal jurisdiction had to adapt to the existing system.

1.4 '… when the crime was committed outside its territory by a foreigner, against any person or group of persons without any link with the prosecuting state …'

The main characteristic of universal jurisdiction is the lack of a direct link to the state willing to prosecute the alleged culprit. The usual requirement of such a link comes directly from international law. Practice shows, however, that universal jurisdiction does not exist in a vacuum, that even when international law recognises that states are entitled to exercise this type of jurisdiction, states do need to implement it through national legislation. So far, I am not aware of a single national decision on which a municipal court had applied universal jurisdiction alone, directly from customary international law without reference to municipal law or to a conventional obligation.[53] On the contrary, it seems that the principle of universality works more as an argument to legitimise the decision of national courts rather than the exclusive legal basis for adjudication.

Therefore, the principle of universality should be used with caution. In this sense, it is surprising to note that, according to Amnesty International, many states have provided 'universal jurisdiction' for crimes under national law of international concern such as hostage taking, sale of psychotropic substances, counterfeiting, etc. This, in my opinion, delegitimises and denatures the principle of universal jurisdiction, only creating confusion about it.[54]

The scope and nature of universal jurisdiction is established by general international law, not by the individual acts of states. States may individually try to expand their criminal jurisdiction extraterritorially, however, those extraterritorial actions are not the same as universal jurisdiction.

1.5 '… providing that the criminal is in the state's custody (judex deprehensionis) when brought to trial'

Physical custody of the accused is an operative requirement for the exercise of universal jurisdiction.[55] The reason is that this permits the principle of universality to function better vis-à-vis other rules, for example, immunity for certain state officials (for example, heads of state, ministers of foreign affairs). It represents one of the recent evolutionary aspects of the said principle.

---

52 After Belgium repealed its law on universal jurisdiction on 23 July 2013, the Belgian Cour de Cassation (Belgium's highest court) dismissed the war crimes complaints against former US President Bush, Secretary of State Colin Powell and Israeli Prime Minister Ariel Sharon, ruling that the country no longer had a legal basis to charge them. See eg www.trial-ch.org/fr/ressources/trial-watch/trial-watch/profils/profile/261/action/show/controller/Profile/tab/legal-procedure.html.

53 See SG Report Universal Jurisdiction 2010 (n 2) ¶ 11.

54 Amnesty International, 'Universal Jurisdiction' (n 5).

55 The *judex deprehensionis* principle, could, however, play a procedural role in the context of the *aut dedere aut judicare* rule within some treaties. Convention against Torture and Other Cruel, Inhuman or Degrading Treatment or Punishment (10 December 1984) 1465 UNTS 85, art 4.

Since the principle of universality gives a state the possibility to prosecute and punish a criminal, it seems, therefore, that implicitly the state can also take all necessary steps, for example, the issuance of arrest warrants or requests for inter-state cooperation in providing information or witnesses, in order to accomplish that end. These (the investigation and pre-trial actions) have indeed been very controversial issues regarding the exercise of the principle of universality.[56] It is within this context that the *judex deprehensionis* principle plays a role of self-constraint as a mechanism to avoid some of those controversial issues, particularly when a state purports to apply the principle of universality to high-ranking officials.[57]

2 War crimes

War crimes are a legal category that has evolved over time. In principle, not all violations of the laws and customs of war are war crimes. War crimes are only the most serious violations of what is known nowadays as international humanitarian law (IHL), which is composed of both customary[58] and conventional law.[59] These crimes give rise to individual criminal responsibility, which means that the culprits must face the consequences of their acts either in a national or an international jurisdiction.[60] Moreover, war crimes are not subject to statutory limitations, and no amnesty or pardon may be granted.[61]

Traditionally, IHL has had two sub-legal regimes: one related to international armed conflict and the other to non-international armed conflicts. For international armed conflicts the body of law that regulates them is well developed. It includes, among other rules and instruments, the four Geneva Conventions and their Additional Protocol I. On the other hand, non-international armed conflicts have a very limited number of regulations applicable to them. These are basically Article 3, common to all four Geneva Conventions, and Additional Protocol II. These provisions establish minimum standards of protection for this type of conflict.

Moreover, the Geneva Conventions, along with Additional Protocol I, establish a system of accountability in which state parties are obliged to search for persons alleged to have committed, or to have ordered to be committed, a particular category of violations of the above-mentioned instruments, called grave breaches.[62] The states can prosecute those persons, regardless of their nationality, or, if they prefer, to extradite them to another High Contracting Party concerned,

---

56 Interesting to note, the AU Model National Law on Universal Jurisdiction over International Crimes would theoretically permit initiation of proceedings without the presence of the alleged criminal in the territory of the state willing to exercise universal jurisdiction, although it will not allow trials *in absentia*, www.ejiltalk.org/wp-content/uploads/2012/08/AU-draft-model-law-UJ-May-2012.pdf. See also Dapo Akande, 'The African Union, the ICC and Universal Jurisdiction: Some Recent Developments' *EJIL:Talk!* (29 August 2012), www.ejiltalk.org/the-african-union-the-icc-and-universal-jurisdiction-some-recent-developments.

57 In contrast, as practice shows, when criminals are common citizens or mid-ranking officials the state seeking jurisdiction is more likely to count on the cooperation of the states concerned. See eg Langer (n 44).

58 See CIHL.

59 For a general view of treaty law related to IHL, see www.icrc.org/ihl.

60 See Georges and Rosemary Abi-Saab, 'Les Crimes de Guerre' in Ascensio Hervé, Decaux Emmanuel and Pellet Alain (eds) *Droit International Pénal* (Pedone 2000) 265.

61 See eg Non-Applicability of Statute of Limitations for the Crimes Subject to the Competence of the ICC, and the Convention on the Non-Applicability of Statutory Limitations to War Crimes and Crimes Against Humanity (26 November 1968) 754 UNTS 73, art 29.

62 For a list of the conducts considered grave breaches, see arts 50, 51, 130 and 147 GCI–IV, respectively, and arts 11 and 85 API.

provided such High Contracting Party has made out a prima facie case.[63] This alternative obligation is the so-called *aut dedere aut judicare* principle, which some consider a sort of compulsory universal jurisdiction.[64]

The grave breaches system is applicable only to international armed conflicts and not to non-international ones.[65] This distinction, however, seems to be blurred due to recent developments in ICL and IHL.[66] It is important to note that for violations other than grave breaches the state parties should take all necessary measures for their suppression, but should those measures include the application of universal jurisdiction? The Geneva Conventions remain silent in that respect. Thus, it is left to state practice to give a clear answer in that regard. Hence, violations, other than the serious ones of IHL, might still be punishable at municipal level for the purpose of military discipline or the enforcement of domestic criminal law.

Accordingly, the question is whether war crimes and grave breaches are the same. The answer is both negative and affirmative. Negative, because in principle the term 'breach' gives the impression that the gravity of the act is of less importance than that of a crime. It is clear that although all crimes can be considered breaches of the law, not all breaches amount to crimes. War crimes are serious 'acts and omissions that violate international humanitarian law and are criminalized in international criminal law'.[67] That is the reason why war crimes are considered a distinct category of international crime in their own right. Article 8 of the ICC is an example of that approach. On the other hand, it is true that not all breaches of IHL are war crimes and not all war crimes are grave breaches (although they are all serious breaches), but we return to our first question: are war crimes and grave breaches the same? According to Article 85 of Additional Protocol I, grave breaches 'shall be regarded as war crimes' such that grave breaches can be considered a distinct category of war crimes.[68] In a way, grave breaches have been absorbed by war crimes.[69]

It seems, therefore, that there is a sort of schizophrenic logic behind war crimes *in genere*, meaning war crimes that come from customary and treaty law, and war crimes *in specie* known as grave breaches. Depending on whether the crime is committed within an international or a non-international armed conflict, whether a crime is characterised as a grave breach or not and whether the basis for prosecution is the Geneva Conventions or customary international law, their identification and the precise elements of each could be different.

The ICTY in the *Tadić* case articulated a more elaborate test to identify serious violations of IHL:

(i) the violation must constitute an infringement of a rule of international humanitarian law;

(ii) the rule must be customary in nature or, if it belongs to treaty law, the required conditions must be met ...;

---

63 Cf arts 49, 50, 129 and 146 GCI–IV, respectively.

64 For example, Knut Dörmann, *Elements of War Crimes under the Rome Statute of the International Criminal Court: Sources and Commentary* (CUP 2003) 128–129.

65 Cf *Prosecutor v Tadić (Decision on the Defence Motion for Interlocutory Appeal on Jurisdiction)* (Case no IT-94-1, ICTY Appeals Chamber, 2 October 1995) ¶ 80.

66 See eg Sonja Boelaert-Suominen, 'Grave Breaches, Universal Jurisdiction and Internal Armed Conflicts: Is Customary Law Moving Towards a Uniform Enforcement Mechanism for all Armed Conflicts?' (2000) 5 *JCSL* 63.

67 Georges Abi-Saab, 'The Concept of War Crimes' in Sienho Yee and Wang Tieya (eds), *International Law in the Post-Cold War World* (Routledge 2001) 112.

68 CIHL r 156.

69 Marko Divac Öberg, 'The Absorption of Grave Breaches into War Crimes Law' (2009) 91 *IRRC* 163.

(iii) the violation must be 'serious', that is to say, it must constitute a breach of a rule protecting important values, and the breach must involve grave consequences for the victim. Thus, for instance, the fact of a combatant simply appropriating a loaf of bread in an occupied village would not amount to a 'serious violation of international humanitarian law' although it may be regarded as falling foul of the basic principle laid down in Article 46, paragraph 1, of the Hague Regulations (and the corresponding rule of customary international law) whereby 'private property must be respected' by any army occupying an enemy territory;

(iv) the violation of the rule must entail, under customary or conventional law, the individual criminal responsibility of the person breaching the rule.[70]

In the ICTY's opinion, this analysis is valid regardless of the specific characterisation of the armed conflict as either international or non-international, consequently rendering superfluous the distinction between both types of conflict for the purposes of Article 3 of the ICTY Statute.[71] Unfortunately, the ICTY's *obiter dictum* in this aspect is still *lege ferenda*.

In recent times, however, it has been questioned whether IHL, as it stands today, could still represent an efficient tool against what is now considered 'new types' of conflicts[72] in which the main players are non-state actors.[73]

In our opinion, IHL is an evolving discipline that has to be understood, interpreted and applied in a teleological manner, taking into consideration its main purpose: to protect persons who are not or are no longer participating in the hostilities and to restrict the means and methods of warfare.

Moreover, it is also important to take into consideration that IHL, IHRL and ICL are intertwined disciplines that regulate and protect the individual at the international level. Thus, what is not covered by one discipline in terms of protection or punishment, is covered by another discipline, making international law in that respect a more coherent system.

---

70 *Tadić* (n 65) ¶ 94. Obviously, the ICTY's analysis is regarding its own Statute.
71 Cf *Tadić* (n 65) ¶ 97. See also ¶ 83 of the same case as the ICTY elaborates on the 'possible change in *opinio juris* of States' regarding the grave breaches provisions of art 2 of the ICTY Statute as applicable to both international and non-international armed conflicts. Nevertheless, the ICTY Chamber concluded that 'in the present state of development of the law, art 2 of the Statute only applies to offences committed within the context of international armed conflicts', ¶ 84. Bassiouni holds:

> It is anachronistic that these different legal regimes and sub-regimes apply to the same socially protected interests and reflect the same human and social values, but differ in their applications depending on the legal characterization of the type of conflict. Governments maintain these distinctions for purely political reasons, namely, to avoid giving insurgents any claim or appearance of legal legitimacy. This political rationale is the source for the legal disparities in IHL.
> Cherif Bassiouni, 'The New Wars and the Crisis of Compliance with the Law of Armed Conflict by Non-State Actors' (2008) 98 *Journal of Criminal Law and Criminology* 732

72 See eg Andreas Paulus and Mindia Vashakmadze, 'Asymmetrical War and the Notion of Armed Conflict: A Tentative Conceptualization' (2009) 91 *IRRC* 95; Robin Geiss, 'Asymmetric Conflict Structures' (2006) 88 *IRRC* 757–777.
73 See, among others, Bassiouni (n 71) 711. See also the analysis of the ICRC in this regard. ICRC, 'International Humanitarian Law and the Challenges of Contemporary Armed Conflicts' Official Working Document of the 31st International Conference of the Red Cross and Red Crescent, Geneva (28 November to 1 December 2011), www.icrc.org/eng/resources/documents/report/31-international-conference-ihl-challenges-report-2011-10-31.htm.

3 Conclusions

The principle of universal jurisdiction is a well-established principle in international law. What has been questioned about the principle is not really its existence, but its operation within the international legal system, particularly in relation to other principles and norms of international law. It has also been under scrutiny for its potentially political impact on international relations particularly when the alleged perpetrators are high ranking officials of a state.

The principle of universal jurisdiction has been the object of opposite views. For some, it was a tool to end impunity across the world while, to others, it was like a disease with the potential to disrupt the entire international system.[74] The truth is that neither extreme reflects the reality of the application of the principle.

In the late twentieth century the rationale for the principle of universality evolved in its nature and in the scope of its application. It passed from a principle aimed at the protection of commercial and maritime interests to extend to human rights and IHL considerations.

The revival of the principle of universal jurisdiction was akin to bringing a mammoth to life. The principle of universality was originally created and applied to a world less complex than the one we have today. Once the international community started using the principle of universality in the current international system it had to be adjusted in order to function properly within the system.

In the early 1990s the exercise of universal jurisdiction was quite chaotic, but little by little the application of the principle has settled down and it will be confined to its place within the international criminal system which is that of a criminal jurisdiction to be used exceptionally.

The application of universal jurisdiction in the last 20 years shows a trend in which states, most of them western states, tend to exercise universal jurisdiction against low profile criminals that will not jeopardise international relations. If this tendency continues, most future cases involving the exercise of universal jurisdiction will probably be prosecuted in western societies, simply because they have the resources (material and human) to carry out such an important task.[75]

There has not been a widespread use of the principle of universal jurisdiction, and that situation is unlikely to change despite the existence of many international criminals still at large.[76] States seem to be more particular as to when, against whom and why to exercise universal jurisdiction and to weigh the political consequences of their acts.

War crimes have also experienced a transformation in recent times. It is clear that the traditional demarcation between the rules applicable to international and non-international armed conflicts is eroding. The protection given by IHL should be extended regardless of the particular legal characterisation of the armed conflict.

Universal jurisdiction against war crimes is still a valid basis for the prosecution of these crimes. As already described, alleged war criminals will continue to be prosecuted at the municipal level, but most likely only low profile culprits.

Universal jurisdiction is not a panacea to end impunity in the world, but, if used wisely, it may well contribute to that end.

---

74 Luc Reydams, 'The Rise and Fall of Universal Jurisdiction' in William A Schabas and Nadia Bernaz (eds), *Routledge Handbook of International Criminal Law* (Routledge 2010) 337.

75 At the moment of writing this chapter, the news was that Senegal will set up a special African Union Tribunal to prosecute the former President of Chad, Hissène Habré. If that becomes a reality then we have lost the opportunity to witness the first case of universal jurisdiction from a non-western state. See www.bbc.co.uk/news/world-africa-20791090.

76 Langer (n 44) 45, holds that in the last 20 years around 26 people have been convicted on the basis of universal jurisdiction.

Part VI
Some contemporary issues

As the previous chapters of this book have highlighted, certain aspects of contemporary armed conflicts present challenges for LOAC both in terms of the appropriateness of particular substantive rules and the adequacy of enforcement measures. Some recent developments have raised issues across a number of different areas of LOAC. These developments include the rapid adoption of new technologies for hostile purposes (Chapter 35) and increased reliance of states on private military and security companies (Chapter 36).

Finally, it remains to examine critically Liberalism's insistence on governing war by law (Chapter 37). Does it make any sense? Is it worthwhile?

35

Emerging technologies of warfare

Rain Liivoja, Kobi Leins and Tim McCormack*

Advances in science and technology have had a major impact on the conduct of war throughout history.[1] On a popular view, the development of warfare has been punctuated by so-called 'revolutions in military affairs', periods of rapid change in military thinking and practice; scientific and technological transformations have played a significant role in such change.[2] At the time of writing, we appear to be in the midst of one such revolution in military affairs, namely an information revolution.[3] This revolution has been facilitated by the development of digital computers and their wide adoption in society at large and in military systems in particular.

Assuming that there is an ongoing revolution in military affairs, the question arises as to whether it ought to be accompanied by a 'revolution in military legal affairs',[4] or whether the existing law of armed conflict (LOAC) is capable of accommodating recent technological developments. This chapter does not purport to provide a comprehensive answer to this question, nor does it seek to evaluate the lawfulness or otherwise of specific means or methods of warfare. Rather, it addresses some of the key legal implications and regulatory challenges arising from the military applications of certain types of technology.[5] We begin with information technology and the notion of 'cyber warfare' (Section 1). We then turn to robotics, specifically remotely controlled, automated and autonomous military systems (Section 2). Finally we consider nanotechnology (Section 3). We conclude the chapter with a brief reflection on the formal legal review of new means and methods of warfare in the context of emerging technologies of warfare (Section 4).

* The research for this chapter was supported under Australian Research Council's *Discovery Projects* funding scheme (project number DP130100432) and by a Society in Science – Branco Weiss Fellowship (administered by ETH Zurich). We are grateful to Chris Jenks, Natalia Jevglevskaja, Robert J Mathews, Tim McFarland and Angus Willoughby for comments on an earlier draft. The responsibility for the present text, however, remains ours.
1 See generally Martin van Creveld, *Technology and War: From 2000 BC to the Present* (rev edn, Free Press 1991); Max Boot, *War Made New: Technology, Warfare, and the Course of History, 1500 to Today* (Gotham Books 2006).
2 See the seminal work by Michael G Vickers and Robert C Martinage, 'The Revolution in War' (Center for Strategic and Budgetary Assessments, December 2004).
3 Boot (n 1) 305 et seq.
4 This term has been used, although not specifically in relation to technology, by Charles J Dunlap Jr, 'The Revolution in Military Legal Affairs: Air Force Legal Professionals in 21st Century Conflicts' (2001) 51 *Air Force Law Review* 293.
5 For other broad discussions, see eg Special Issue: New Technologies and Warfare (2012) 94(886) *IRRC* 457; Dan Saxon (ed), *International Humanitarian Law and the Changing Technology of War* (Martinus Nijhoff 2013); Hitoshi Nasu and Robert McLaughlin (eds), *New Technologies and the Law of Armed Conflict* (Asser 2014).

1 Information technology

1.1 Technology

The start of the ongoing information revolution in military affairs can be reasonably precisely dated to the late 1930s and early 1940s. This was the time when the first digital computers were built, many of which were preoccupied by military tasks such as ballistics calculations and code breaking.[6] Of course, computers have developed quite spectacularly from what in hindsight appears to be a rather humble beginning as advanced calculators, into systems that process and store exponentially increasing amounts of data, which is often strategically significant and/or economically valuable.

Also, computers are widely used to exert control over the physical world. Computerised industrial control systems (ICS) are common in many different sectors of industry and infrastructure.[7] A comparatively simple programmable logic controller (PLC) can run a specific device – such as an elevator, a set of traffic lights or an industrial appliance – by 'monitor[ing] the state of input devices and make[ing] decisions based upon a custom program to control the state of output devices'.[8] A distributed control system (DCS) is more complex, coordinating between multiple sub-systems involved in carrying out an entire industrial process, for example, at an oil refinery, water and wastewater treatment plant, power plant or chemical manufacturing plant.[9] Another type of ICS, a supervisory control and data acquisition (SCADA) system, is

> designed to collect field information, transfer it to a central computer facility, and display the information to the operator graphically or textually, thereby allowing the operator to monitor or control an entire system from a central location in near real time.[10]

SCADA systems are widely used in distribution systems, such as water distribution and wastewater collection systems, oil and natural gas pipelines, electrical grids, as well as rail, air traffic control and other public transportation systems.[11]

Computers are routinely connected to each other to form networks. These networks can, in turn, be connected to other networks, ultimately making up the Internet. This allows for the remote access and manipulation of data, such as accessing a website stored on a server or saving documents in the 'cloud'. ICS are also often networked. Indeed, the architecture of DCS and SCADA presumes a degree of interconnection between computers. Also, many ICS are connected to the Internet to facilitate remote access. The same is true for various computerised

---

6 See Martin Campbell-Kelly, Willian Aspray, Nathan Ensmenger and Jeffrey R Yost, *Computer: A History of the Information Machine* (3rd edn, Westview 2013).

7 Keith Stouffer, Suzanne Lightman, Victoria Pilletteri, Marshall Abrams and Adam Hahn, 'NIST Special Publication 800-82: Guide to Industrial Control Systems (ICS) Security' Revision 2 – Final Public Draft (National Institute of Standards and Technology, US Department of Commerce, February 2015).

8 Advance Micro Controllers Inc, 'What is a Programmable Logic Controller (PLC)?' (undated), www.amci.com/tutorials/tutorials-what-is-programmable-logic-controller.asp.

9 Stouffer *et al* (n 7) 2–10.

10 Ibid 2–5.

11 Ibid.

devices, ranging from mobile phones to refrigerators – giving rise to the phenomenon referred to as the 'Internet of Things'.[12]

Computers and networks have vulnerabilities, that is to say flaws or weaknesses in their design or operation, which can be exploited to violate information systems' key security attributes – confidentiality, integrity or availability.[13] A breach of confidentiality entails access to data by an unauthorised person, for instance for the purposes of cyber espionage. This was the case with the alleged copying by Chinese hackers of sensitive design data of the US's F-35 Joint Strike Fighter[14] and the blueprints of the new headquarters of the Australian Secret Intelligence Organisation.[15] A breach of integrity involves the modification of data on the system or the system's configuration. This would include the defacement of websites, as well as the loading by hackers of pro-Daesh videos and messages to the US military's YouTube and Twitter accounts.[16] A violation of availability denies access to data and of services of the system, to those authorised to use them. An example would be the launch of such a number of queries to a system as to overwhelm it and to shut it down or to render it inaccessible, referred to as a denial-of-service attack. Prominent examples include the disabling of governmental websites of Estonia (in April 2007), Georgia (in July/August 2008) and Germany (in January 2015) by cyber activities ostensibly emanating from Russia.[17]

Perhaps more seriously, given the wide use of computerised ICS, cyber operations altering data can provoke real-world physical events. The most prominent example was the use of the Stuxnet virus to infect the ICS of an Iranian uranium enrichment facility; the virus manipulated the rotational speeds of centrifuges, causing them significant damage.[18] It does not require much imagination to envision the potentially catastrophic destruction that could be caused by cyber operations against air traffic control systems, emergency services, dams or nuclear power plants.

1.2 Legal challenges

Since the late 1990s, significant effort has gone into clarifying the international legal framework applicable to hostile cyber operations. Numerous papers and books have appeared on the law of

---

12 See eg Dave Evans, 'The Internet of Things: How the Next Evolution of the Internet is Changing Everything' White Paper (Cisco Internet Business Solutions Group, April 2011); Jacob Morgan, 'A Simple Explanation of "The Internet Of Things"' *Forbes* (13 May 2014), www.forbes.com/sites/jacobmorgan/2014/05/13/simple-explanation-internet-things-that-anyone-can-understand.

13 See eg George Loukas, *Cyber-Physical Attacks: A Growing Invisible Threat* (Butterworth-Heinemann 2015) 2–3.

14 See Siobhan Gorman, August Cole and Yochi Dreazen, 'Computer Spies Breach Fighter-Jet Project' *Wall Street Journal* (21 April 2009).

15 See Ben Grubb, 'Blueprints for New ASIO Headquarters "Stolen"' *The Age* (Melbourne, 27 May 2013).

16 See Mana Raibee, 'US Central Command's YouTube, Twitter Accounts Suspended after Hacking by IS Supporters' *New York Times* (12 January 2015), www.nytimes.com/video/multimedia/1000 00003445205.

17 See Michelle Martin and Erik Kirschbaum, 'Pro-Russian Group Claims Cyber Attack on German Government Websites' *Reuters* (7 January 2015), www.reuters.com/article/2015/01/07/us-germany-cyberattack-idUSKBN0KG15320150107.

18 See eg Holger Stark, 'Mossad's Miracle Weapon: Stuxnet Virus Opens New Era of Cyber War' *Der Spiegel International* (8 August 2011), www.spiegel.de/international/world/mossad-s-miracle-weapon-stuxnet-virus-opens-new-era-of-cyber-war-a-778912.html.

cyber warfare,[19] with the most prominent scholarly publication being the 2013 *Tallinn Manual on the International Law Applicable to Cyber Warfare*,[20] a statement of 95 rules considered to be *lex lata* by an international group of experts meeting at the invitation of the NATO Cooperative Cyber Defence Centre of Excellence.[21]

There appears to be broad agreement on a few important issues. Most fundamentally, hostile cyber operations undertaken by belligerents in the context of an ongoing armed conflict are, like other military operations, governed by LOAC.[22] In particular, where such cyber operations amount to 'attacks' within the meaning of LOAC, they are subject to the key principles of distinction and proportionality, and necessitate the taking of certain precautionary measures.[23]

These general propositions, however well accepted, inexorably lead to further questions. First, which cyber operations amount to 'attacks'? Second, are cyber operations that do not amount to attacks subject to restrictions of LOAC? Third, are cyber operations capable of triggering the application of LOAC in the absence of 'ordinary' hostilities? While we readily acknowledge that a number of further LOAC issues arise from cyber operations, we limit our attention here to these three key questions as they are in some ways foundational to any discussion about the law of cyber hostilities.

1.2.1 Cyber operations as 'attacks'

Additional Protocol I defines 'attacks' as 'acts of violence against the adversary, whether in offence or defence'.[24] According to the prevailing view, it is the anticipated violent effect or consequence of an act that allow it to be characterised as an attack.[25] Commentators point out that the wilful releases of pathogens or toxic chemicals, entailing no overtly violent action, undoubtedly constitute attacks for the purpose of LOAC because of their harmful or even lethal consequences.[26] Thus, the lack of violent action cannot exclude cyber operations from constituting attacks as long as the consequences are violent.

19 See eg Symposia in (2012) 17 *JCSL* 183, (2013) 84 *International Law Studies* 1; Heather Harrison Dinniss, *Cyber Warfare and the Laws of War* (CUP 2012); Marco Roscini, *Cyber Operations and the Use of Force in International Law* (OUP 2014); Jens David Ohlin, Claire Finkelstein and Kevin Govern (eds), *Cyber War: Law and Ethics for Virtual Conflicts* (OUP 2015).

20 *Tallinn Manual on the International Law Applicable to Cyber Warfare* (CUP 2013), https://ccdcoe.org/tallinn-manual.html.

21 For critical comments, see eg Rain Liivoja and Tim McCormack, 'Law in the Virtual Battlespace: The Tallinn Manual and the *Jus in Bello*' (2012) 15 *YBIHL* 45; Dieter Fleck, 'Searching for International Rules Applicable to Cyber Warfare: A Critical First Assessment of the New Tallinn Manual' (2013) 18 *JCSL* 331; Oliver Kessler and Wouter Werner, 'Expertise, Uncertainty, and International Law: A Study of the Tallinn Manual on Cyberwarfare' (2013) 26 *Leiden JIL* 793.

22 See ICRC, 'International Humanitarian Law and the Challenges of Contemporary Armed Conflict' 31st International Conference of the Red Cross and Red Crescent, 28 November to 1 December 2011, Doc 31IC/11/5.1.2 (October 2011) 38; *Tallinn Manual* (n 20) r 20. For further references, see David Turns, 'Cyber War and the Concept of "Attack" in International Humanitarian Law' in Saxon (ed) (n 5) 209, 221 (citing academic works); Cordula Droege, 'Get Off my Cloud: Cyber Warfare, International Humanitarian Law, and the Protection of Civilians' (2012) 94(886) *IRRC* 533, 567 (citing views of states); Roscini, *Cyber Operations* (n 19) 21–22 (citing views of states).

23 See ICRC (n 22) 37; *Tallinn Manual* (n 20) rr 31, 51, 53–59.

24 API art 49(1).

25 Michael N Schmitt, 'Cyber Operations and the *Jus in Bello*: Key Issues' in Raul A Pedrozo and Daria P Wollschlaeger (eds), *International Law and the Changing Character of War* (US Naval War College 2011) 89, 93–94; Roscini, *Cyber Operations* (n 19) 179; for a detailed discussion, see Turns (n 22) 221–224.

26 See eg Schmitt, 'Key Issues' (n 25) 94; Bill Boothby, 'Where do Cyber Hostilities Fit in the International Law Maze?' in Nasu and McLaughlin (eds) (n 5) 59, 60.

There is broad support for the proposition that injury or death to persons, or damage or destruction to objects, amounts to violence, and that cyber operations that are reasonably expected to, or which do, have such consequences amount to attacks.[27] On one view, physical damage of this nature is not merely a sufficient but a necessary condition for a cyber operation to constitute an attack.[28] This reading relies on the literal meaning of the word 'violence' and draws support from the formulation of the principle of proportionality in Additional Protocol I, which speaks of 'loss of civilian life, injury to civilians, damage to civilian objects, or a combination thereof'.[29] According to an alternative view, the disabling of an object, even without causing any physical damage or destruction, also constitutes an attack.[30] The proponents of this approach rely in particular on the definition of military objects in Additional Protocol I, which implies that the capture or neutralisation of an object is a possible aim of an attack.[31]

One construction attempts to reconcile these two approaches. This moves the focus from physical destruction to 'the fact that it [the object] is no longer completely suitable for its intended purpose'.[32] It does so by interpreting the notion of 'damage' to mean 'the loss of functionality that permanently renders the object inoperable or that necessitates some form of repair'.[33] However, even amongst those who adopt this approach to 'damage', there is no unanimity as to the nature or extent of the repair necessary. Circumstances where 'restoration of functionality requires replacement of physical components' seems to be more readily accepted as damage.[34] Going further, some would argue, for example, is that the reloading of 'the operating system or any software essential to operation' would qualify as damage; however, replacing data 'merely stored on the system' would not.[35]

This discussion is closely associated with the problem as to whether data could qualify as an 'object'. If that were the case, the destruction of data could be considered an attack in itself – that is to say, even in the absence of physical damage or loss of functionality of a device. There does not appear to be much support for the data-as-object position.[36] This is unsurprising given that the ICRC *Commentary* to the 1977 Additional Protocols indicates that the word 'object', as used in Additional Protocol I, means 'something that is visible and tangible'.[37] But, as we have argued elsewhere, this corporeal conception of objects under LOAC may be outdated.[38] The economic value of data can be enormous and its permanent destruction may have far more serious consequences than the destruction of some tangible objects. As a result, it may prove

---

27 See *Tallinn Manual* (n 20) r 30.
28 Schmitt, 'Key Issues' (n 25) 94–95; Yoram Dinstein, 'The Principle of Distinction and Cyber War in International Armed Conflicts' (2012) 17 *JCSL* 261, 264.
29 Michael N Schmitt, 'Wired Warfare: Computer Network Attack and *Jus in Bello*' (2002) 84(846) *IRRC* 365, 376–377.
30 Knut Dörmann, 'The Applicability of the Additional Protocols to Computer Network Attacks: An ICRC Approach' in Karin Byström (ed), *International Expert Conference on Computer Network Attacks and the Applicability of International Humanitarian Law, 17–19 November 2004, Stockholm, Sweden: Proceedings of the Conference* (Swedish National Defence College 2005) 139, 142–143; ICRC (n 22) 37.
31 API art 52(2).
32 Michael N Schmitt, 'Rewired Warfare: Rethinking the Law of Cyber Attack' (2014) 96(893) *IRRC* 189, 203.
33 Ibid.
34 *Tallinn Manual* (n 20) commentary to r 30, ¶ 10.
35 Schmitt, 'Rewired Warfare' (n 32) 15.
36 *Tallinn Manual* (n 20) commentary to r 30, ¶ 6. But, see Nils Melzer, 'Cyberwarfare and International Law' UNIDIR Resources (2011) 31.
37 *AP Commentary* ¶ 2008.
38 See Liivoja and McCormack (n 21) 53–54.

difficult in the long run to 'maintain a normative distinction between harm caused to physical objects and that caused to data'.[39]

1.2.2 Cyber operations not amounting to 'attacks'

The vast majority of cyber operations would not meet the fairly restrictive definition of attacks outlined previously. This raises the question whether such operations are subject to any restrictions under LOAC. Notably, Article 48 of Additional Protocol I requires parties to a conflict to 'direct their operations only against military objectives' and Article 57(1) stipulates that, '[i]n the conduct of military operations, constant care shall be taken to spare the civilian population, civilians and civilian objects'. There are, however, differences in opinion as to the significance of the use of the ostensibly broader term 'operations' instead of 'attack' in these provisions.

Some commentators do not hold the choice of terminology to be determinative: they argue that the prohibition contained in Article 48 'is not so much on targeting non-military objectives as it is on *attacking* them, specifically through the use of violence'.[40] This view draws contextual support from the position of Article 48 within the Protocol: the provision introduces a series of more specific articles, all dealing with attacks.[41] Also, according to the ICRC *Commentary* on Article 48, 'the word "operations" should be understood in the context of the whole of the Section [on methods and means of warfare]; it refers to military operations during which violence is used, and not to ideological, political or religious campaigns'.[42] If this line of reasoning is accepted, cyber operations not amounting to attacks are not restricted by the principle of distinction and thus 'are permissible against non-military objectives, such as the population'.[43]

Alternative views note that the drafters' choice to use the term operations instead of attack must have some significance. Those views rely on the ICRC *Commentary* on Article 48 which accepts a dictionary definition whereby '"military operations" refers to all movements and acts related to hostilities that are undertaken by armed forces'.[44] This has led to the argument that the applicability of LOAC restraints on cyber operations depends on whether they constitute part of 'hostilities'.[45] Accordingly, given that 'hostilities' is a broader concept than 'attacks', cyber operations 'directly adversely affecting military operations or military capacity' of the adversary must also be subject to restrictions imposed by LOAC:[46]

> [C]yber operations aiming to disrupt or incapacitate an adversary's computer-controlled radar or weapon systems, logistic supply or communication networks may not directly cause any physical damage, but would certainly qualify as part of the hostilities and, therefore, would have to comply with the rules and principles of [international humanitarian law] governing the conduct of hostilities. The same would apply to cyber operations intruding into the adversary's computer network to delete targeting data, manipulate military orders or change, encrypt, exploit or render useless any other sensitive data with a direct (adverse) impact on the belligerent party's capacity to conduct hostilities.[47]

39 Schmitt, 'Rewired Warfare' (n 32) 16.
40 Schmitt, 'Wired Warfare' (n 29) 376 (original emphasis); see also Turns (n 22) 217; Roscini, *Cyber Operations* (n 19) 178.
41 Schmitt, 'Wired Warfare' (n 29) 376.
42 *AP Commentary* ¶ 1875.
43 Schmitt, 'Wired Warfare' (n 29) 376.
44 *AP Commentary* ¶ 1875.
45 Melzer (n 36) 27.
46 Ibid 28.
47 Ibid 28 (footnotes omitted).

A variation of this approach relies on the commentary to Article 57, which explains that the term '"military operations" should be understood to mean any movements, manœuvres and other activities whatsoever carried out by the armed forces with a view to combat'.[48] Consequently, in order to be subject to the principles of distinction, proportionality and precaution, a cyber operation must be combat related, in other words it 'must be associated with the use of physical force, but it does not have to result in violent consequences itself'.[49]

On either of the broader conceptions of 'operations', however, propaganda, espionage and psychological operations – sometimes compared with sub-attack cyber operations – would not be governed by the principles of distinction, proportionality and precaution because they are neither part of hostilities nor undertaken with a view to combat.[50]

To conclude the discussion about the difference between attacks and operations, it is worthwhile to note that certain persons and objects enjoy special protection under LOAC. In particular, medical personnel, units and transports must be 'respected and protected'.[51] This prohibition 'includes, but is not limited to the prohibition of attacks'.[52] Accordingly, irrespective of what the correct interpretation of the notions of attack and operation may be, any cyber operation that impedes, prevents or otherwise adversely affects the carrying out of humanitarian functions of medical services – for example, altering the GPS data of a medical aircraft or the digital personal records of patients – is prohibited.[53]

1.2.3 Cyber operations as a trigger for armed conflict

The preceding discussion presupposed that an armed conflict was already in existence. The question remains, however, whether cyber operations, in the absence of hostilities involving conventional military means, could constitute an armed conflict and thus trigger the application of LOAC.

Even though the Geneva Conventions and the Additional Protocols apply, according to their own terms, in 'armed conflict', these treaties do not establish what constitutes such a conflict.[54] The now-standard threshold test, reflecting the relevant treaty provisions and customary law, was formulated by the ICTY Appeals Chamber in *Tadić* as follows: 'An armed conflict exists whenever there is a resort to armed force between States or protracted violence between governmental authorities and organized armed groups or between such groups within a State.'[55]

The application of this test to establish the existence of an armed conflict involves a significant preliminary question of attribution. The usual rules of state responsibility apply when determining whether a cyber operation is attributable to a state but demonstrating the requisite link between the operation and a state or a non-state armed group can be difficult.[56] It may well be that cyber operations are undertaken by independent 'hacktivists' whose conduct cannot be

---

48 *AP Commentary* ¶ 2191.
49 Harrison Dinniss (n 19) 201.
50 See Droege (n 22) 556.
51 See in particular API arts 12(1), 15(1), 21, 23(1), 24; cf *Tallinn Manual* (n 20) rr 70–71.
52 See *Tallinn Manual* (n 20) commentary to r 70, ¶ 4.
53 See ibid commentary to r 70, ¶ 4; commentary to r 71, ¶ 3.
54 See GCI–IV common arts 2 and 3; API art 1; APII art 1.
55 *Prosecutor v Tadić (Decision on the Defence Motion for Interlocutory Appeal on Jurisdiction)* (Case no IT-94-1, ICTY Appeals Chamber, 2 October 1995) ¶ 70.
56 See eg Marco Roscini, 'Evidentiary Issues in International Disputes Related to State Responsibility for Cyber Operations' (2015) 50 *Texas International Law Journal* 233.

attributed to any state or a non-state armed group, in which case a situation of armed conflict would not arise, irrespective of the extent of damage caused.

If the attribution problem can be overcome, the question is whether the requirements of the *Tadić* test can be met.

According to the prevailing view, no particular degree of violence or intention is required for the existence of an international armed conflict – all that is necessary is 'a resort to armed force between States'.[57] On this view, where a single cyber operation, launched by one state against another, amounts to an 'attack' as discussed previously, an international armed conflict would be triggered.[58] Admittedly, the uncertainty as to what constitutes an attack in the cyber context would obviously create some difficulties in this context. But were one to accept the competing view that the applicability of LOAC requires a greater extent, duration or intensity of hostilities, even the 2010 Stuxnet operation, which succeeded in causing physical damage to centrifuges in a nuclear fuel processing plant, might not be sufficient to trigger an international armed conflict.[59]

The threshold for a non-international armed conflict is higher: the armed force used must have a certain degree of intensity – in the words of the ICTY, 'protracted violence' – and each non-state armed group involved must have a certain level of organisation.[60] To amount to protracted violence, 'cyber attacks have to be frequent enough to be considered related, [but] they clearly do not have to be continuous'.[61] The requirement of organisation means, for example, that a number of individuals sharing a common purpose, but engaging in cyber operations against a state or a non-state armed group independently of each other, would not constitute an organised armed group.[62] However, a group that operates as a unit in a coordinated fashion – for example, where members of the group have assigned roles and they act upon orders issued virtually from a recognised leader – could be seen as organised, even though the members never meet face to face and may never even discover each other's true identity.[63] An additional difficulty is created, however, by Additional Protocol II: Article 1(1) of the Protocol presumes that an organised armed group is 'under responsible command'. This requirement has been interpreted to mean that the organised armed group 'must be in a position to implement the Protocol'[64] and that this entails 'the possibility to impose discipline'.[65] There is obvious doubt whether a group organised virtually would have the tools to impose the kind of discipline that is typical of military organisations. However, there is room for the argument that the 'responsible command' requirement does not limit the applicability of Common Article 3,[66] and that, at any rate, 'being in a position to implement' the law merely requires 'the organisational *ability* to comply with the obligations of international humanitarian law'.[67]

---

57 See further Caitlin Dwyer and Tim McCormack, 'Conflict characterisation' ch 3 in this volume, s 2.2.

58 See eg Michael Schmitt, 'Classification of Cyber Conflict' (2012) 17 *JCSL* 245, 251–252; see also Roscini, *Cyber Operations* (n 19) 134–135.

59 See *Tallinn Manual* (n 20) commentary to r 22, ¶¶ 12, 14.

60 See further Dwyer and McCormack (n 57) s 2.3.

61 Schmitt, 'Classification' (n 58) 258; see also Roscini, *Cyber Operations* (n 19) 152–153.

62 Schmitt, 'Classification' (n 58) 256; *Tallinn Manual* (n 20) commentary to r 23, ¶ 15.

63 See Schmitt, 'Classification' (n 58) 256; *Tallinn Manual* (n 20) commentary to r 23, ¶¶ 13, 15; for an analysis of different scenarios pertaining to the level of organisation, see Roscini, *Cyber Operations* (n 19) 155–157.

64 *AP Commentary* ¶ 4470.

65 *Prosecutor v Bemba (Decision on the Confirmation of Charges)* (Case no ICC-01/05-01/08, ICC Pre-Trial Chamber III, 15 June 2009) ¶ 234.

66 *Tallinn Manual* (n 20) commentary to r 23, ¶ 14, n 202.

67 See *Prosecutor v Boškoski and Tarćulovski*.
(ICTY-04-82-T, ICTY Judgment, 10 July 2008) ¶ 205.

Whatever the correct interpretation, the intensity and organisation requirements imposed by the LOAC of non-international armed conflicts are significant. Thus the plausible view has been expressed that 'cyber operations alone can trigger a non-international armed conflict in only rare cases'.[68]

2 Robotics

2.1 Technology

The term 'robotics' refers to 'the science and technology of robots'.[69] There is a modicum of agreement that a robot is 'an artificial device that can *sense* its environment and *purposefully act* on or in that environment'.[70] In other words, a robot has *sensors* to monitor the environment, *processors* to make decisions as to how to react to the environment (thus incorporating some degree of programmability or artificial intelligence) and *actuators* to effect change in the environment.[71] What remains controversial, however, is whether a device must have some meaningful degree of autonomy in order to be deemed a robot.[72] Autonomy, in this context, refers to the capacity of the device to undertake some action without intervention from a human operator.[73]

While it is important to appreciate that different devices have different levels of autonomy with respect to each of their functions – being autonomous is a matter of degree[74] – it does not appear to be easy, or particularly helpful in this context, to try to establish a requisite minimal degree of autonomy for something to be called a 'robot'. The field of 'robotics' and the notion of 'robotic technology' are broad enough to cover sophisticated electromechanical systems that rely heavily on a sensing–processing–acting loop but have very limited autonomy. For example, the area of telerobotics deals with devices where high-level cognitive decisions are made by a human operator while the device is responsible for the mechanical implementation of these decisions some distance away.[75] There is, however, very little autonomy involved. For the purposes of this discussion, we take the widest possible view of robotics: we believe that utilising narrow definitions has the potential of ignoring how devices with a greater degree of autonomy are essentially incremental developments of less-sophisticated devices.

Especially in view of a broad definition of the term, military applications of robotics are numerous. One commonplace example is the use of fly-by-wire (FBW) technology on military aircraft. With a FBW system, the connection between the cockpit controls (such as the yoke or joystick, and rudder pedals) on the one hand, and the flight control surfaces and engines on the

---

68 See *Tallinn Manual* (n 20) commentary to r 23, ¶ 7.

69 Bruno Siciliano and Oussama Khatib, 'Introduction' in Bruno Siciliano and Oussama Khatib (eds), *Springer Handbook of Robotics* (Springer 2008) 1, 1.

70 Alan Winfield, *Robotics: A Very Short Introduction* (OUP 2012) 8–9.

71 Cf P W Singer, *Wired for War: The Robotics Revolution and Conflict in the Twenty-First Century* (Penguin 2009) 67; Armin Krishnan, *Killer Robots: Legality and Ethicality of Autonomous Weapons* (Ashgate 2009) 9.

72 Cf US Department of Defense, *Joint Robotics Program Master Plan FY2005* (2005) 1–2 (suggesting that a robot 'works automatically or operates by remote control'); Krishnan (n 71) 9 ('A robot must exhibit some degree of autonomy, even if it is only very limited autonomy.').

73 See Winfield (n 70) 10.

74 See, notably, Thomas B Sheridan and William L Verplank, 'Human and Computer Control of Undersea Teleoperators' Technical Report (Massachusetts Institute of Technology, 14 July 1978).

75 See eg Günter Niemeyer, Carsten Preusche and Gerd Hirzinger, 'Telerobotics' in Bruno Siciliano and Oussama Khatib (eds), *Springer Handbook of Robotics* (Springer 2008) 741, 741.

other hand, is electronic rather than mechanical.[76] Essentially, the same concept is used in many remotely controlled weapon stations (RCWS) – systems controlled by operators who are not in direct (physical) contact with the weapons. For example, a gun turret may be mounted on a vehicle and be controlled by an operator inside. Such systems are widely used both on land, for example on armoured fighting vehicles,[77] as well as on naval vessels.[78]

The rapidly increasing ability to combine robotics with sophisticated sensing systems (radars, electro-optical and infrared sensors) and a communication link has paved the way for advanced remotely controlled military systems. Remotely piloted vehicles (RPVs) are now available in all traditional domains of warfare – land, sea and air.[79] Remotely piloted aircraft (RPA) – also called unmanned aerial vehicles (UAVs) or, popularly, 'drones' – are used widely for intelligence, surveillance and reconnaissance purposes. According to a 2013 report, '[b]oth military and civilian UAVs are in use by almost every country, including nearly 60 with their own manufacturing capability'.[80] RPA carrying weapons, on the other hand, have remained the purview of a considerably smaller number of states: a 2014 report identified 23 states as potentially developing some type of armed RPA.[81] Thus, much of the prominence of RPVs has to do with their extensive use by the US: between 2002 and early 2015, it had carried out more than 500 strikes using RPA, with the greatest number in Pakistan.[82]

Military systems are obtaining an increasing degree of autonomy in relation to some of their functions.[83] For example, some RPA currently in operation, such as the RQ-4 Global Hawk, have a considerable ability to navigate on a pre-defined flight plan without any human intervention. The Northrop Grumman X-47B, a strike fighter-sized RPV prototype, has demonstrated the feasibility of unsupervised aerial refuelling.[84] Certain weapon systems are also capable of operation without continuous control by an operator. Notable examples include 'close-in weapon systems' (CIWS) on naval vessels, and their land-based counterparts, C-RAMs (short for 'counter rocket, artillery and mortar'). In a nutshell, CIWS and C-RAM are rapid-fire, computer-controlled, radar-guided guns designed to engage automatically and defeat incoming missiles and other close-in threats.[85]

---

76 See eg Nick Lee-Frampton, 'Anything but Simple: The F-16's FBW Flight Control System' (January/February 2000) 54(9) *New Zealand Engineering* 13.

77 See eg Ezio Bonsignore and David Eshel, 'Remotely Controlled Weapon Stations: Technologies and Markets' (2009) 33(7) *Military Technology* 52.

78 See eg Luca Peruzzi, 'Remote Control Cannon Proliferation at Sea' (2013) 37(4) *Armada International* 26.

79 For an overview of the technology, see eg US Department of Defense, 'Unmanned Systems Integrated Roadmap FY2013–2038' Ref No 14-S-0553 (2013).

80 'UAV Roundup 2013' (July–August 2013) *Aerospace America* 26, 26; see also Lynn E Davis, Michael J McNerney, James S Chow, Thomas Hamilton, Sarah Harting and Daniel Byma, *Armed and Dangerous? UAVs and U.S. Security* (RAND 2014).

81 Davis *et al* (n 80) 7.

82 The Bureau of Investigative Journalism, 'Get the Data: Drone Wars', www.thebureauinvestigates.com/category/projects/drones/drones-graphs.

83 As the US Defense Science Board has noted,

> [a]utonomy is better understood as a capability (or a set of capabilities) that enables the larger human-machine system to accomplish a given mission, rather than as a 'black box' that can be discussed separately from the vehicle and the mission.
>
> US Defense Science Board, 'Task Force Report: The Role of Autonomy in DoD Systems' (July 2012) 21, http://fas.org/irp/agency/dod/dsb/autonomy.pdf

84 See 'Fueled in Flight: X-47B First to Complete Autonomous Aerial Refueling' *NAVAIR News* (22 April 2015), www.navair.navy.mil/index.cfm?fuseaction=home.NAVAIRNewsStory&id=5880.

85 See eg Raytheon, 'Phalanx Close-In Weapon System: Last Line of Defense for Air, Land and Sea', www.raytheon.com/capabilities/products/phalanx.

2.2 Legal challenges

Philip Alston, the UN Special Rapporteur on Extrajudicial, Summary or Arbitrary Executions, noted in a 2010 report that

> [a]lthough robotic or unmanned weapons technology has developed at astonishing rates, the public debate over the legal, ethical and moral issues arising from its use is at a very early stage, and very little consideration has been given to the international legal framework necessary for dealing with the resulting issues.[86]

The widely reported and often contentious use of RPA for 'targeted killings' has, however, fuelled an intense debate about the legality and morality of remotely controlled weapons.[87]

The single most controversial international law issue in this regard has been the determination of the appropriate regulatory framework. The use of violence in the course of an armed conflict is subject to the restrictions of LOAC. This framework is relatively permissive: in particular, it accepts the lethal targeting of persons on the basis of their status (combatants) or their conduct (direct participation in hostilities), and tolerates civilian deaths insofar as they are incidental to an attack against a legitimate military objective and proportionate to the military advantage expected from the attack.[88] Use of armed force outside an armed conflict, on the other hand, is governed by the fairly restrictive human rights law. Under human rights standards, a state may use lethal force only where 'it is required to protect life ... and there is no other means, such as capture or non-lethal incapacitation, of preventing that threat to life'.[89]

Given the disparity of these standards, the lawfulness of a particular RPV attack would heavily depend on whether LOAC is applicable. The initial issue in this respect is the existence of an armed conflict that would trigger the application of LOAC.[90] But even when there is an armed conflict, LOAC would apply to hostilities only in the context of that armed conflict. Hence, to apply LOAC to a specific attack, there must be a connection between that attack and the armed conflict. This issue has become particularly problematic in relation to US RPA strikes against al-Qaeda in Pakistan: it is unclear whether these can be seen as occurring in the context of an armed conflict, such as the non-international armed conflict against al-Qaeda in Afghanistan.[91]

---

86 Philip Alston (Special Rapporteur on Extrajudicial, Summary or Arbitrary Executions), Interim Report to the General Assembly, UN Doc A/65/32 (23 August 2010) ¶ 29.

87 See eg P W Singer, *Wired For War: The Robotics Revolution and Conflict in the 21st Century* (Penguin 2009); Claire Finkelstein, Jens David Ohlin and Andrew Altman (eds), *Targeted Killings: Law and Morality in an Asymmetrical World* (OUP 2012); Bradley Jay Strawser (ed), *Killing by Remote Control: The Ethics of an Unmanned Military* (OUP 2013); Christian Enemark, *Armed Drones and the Ethics of War: Military Virtue in a Post-Heroic Age* (Routledge 2014); John Kaag and Sarah Kreps, *Drone Warfare* (Polity 2014); Special Issue: Unmanned Vehicles, Legal, Social and Ethical Issues (2012) 21(2) *JLIS*; Special Issue: Legal and Ethical Implications of Drone Warfare (2015) 19(2) *International Journal of Human Rights* 105.

88 See generally Part II of this volume.

89 Philip Alston (Special Rapporteur on Extrajudicial, Summary or Arbitrary Executions), Report to the Human Rights Council, Addendum: Study on Targeted Killings, UN Doc A/HRC/14/24/Add.6 (28 May 2010) ¶ 32.

90 See generally Dwyer and McCormack (n 57).

91 See eg Chris Jenks, 'Law from Above: Unmanned Aerial Systems, Use of Force, and the Law of Armed Conflict' (2010) 85 *North Dakota LR* 649; Ian Henderson and Bryan Cavanagh, 'Unmanned Aerial Vehicles: Do They Pose Legal Challenges?' in Nasu and McLaughlin (eds) (n 5) 193, 200–201.

Where LOAC is applicable, it is doubtful whether remotely controlled weapon systems pose, in and of themselves, any novel issues in terms of rules governing the conduct of hostilities. Weapon-specific rules place no restriction on the development, acquisition or use of weapons that are controlled remotely.[92] Of course, no weapon can be placed lawfully on an RPV that could not be placed lawfully on a manned vehicle. Thus, for example, a state party to the 2008 Convention on Cluster Munitions[93] would be precluded from arming its RPVs with cluster munitions.

Complying with the principles of discrimination and proportionality, and taking precautionary measures, does not appear to be more difficult when launching an attack by means of a weapon carried by an RPV as compared to a comparable manned vehicle. To the contrary, in some circumstances RPVs may enhance compliance with LOAC. Removing the operator from immediate danger and making use of the advanced sensing capabilities of RPVs may allow for more thoroughly considered and accurate targeting decisions.[94] Paradoxically, LOAC may thus encourage the use of RPVs.[95]

An oft-expressed concern in relation to RPVs has to do with the status of their operators under LOAC. While difficulties in classifying persons for the purposes of LOAC are hardly a problem specific to this operational context,[96] it is certainly true that civilian operators of remotely controlled systems can easily become direct participants in hostilities, with all the attendant consequences.[97] This would be the case not only where a remote operator, say, launches an attack from an RPV, but also where the operator of an unarmed RPV passes information about the location of adversary military forces to ground troops for the purposes of launching a land-based attack.

Additional legal and ethical issues arise from the increased autonomy of military systems, which has already generated quite a voluminous body of literature.[98] Broad questions as to the safety of a system will arise from any kind of operation where a human is not in control, such as the unsupervised flight of an RPA along a predetermined flight path – notwithstanding that human-controlled operation might not, on the evidence, be any safer.[99] But a weapon system that can identify targets and launch attacks upon them without attack-specific human oversight generates significant issues under LOAC.

International law does not specifically restrict the degree of autonomy that can be implemented in weapon systems. Thus the key problem is whether the weapon system is capable of

---

92 See eg Meredith Hagger and Tim McCormack, 'Regulating the Use of Unmanned Combat Vehicles: Are General Principles of International Humanitarian Law Sufficient?' (2011) 21 *JLIS* 74, 84–85.

93 (3 December 2008) 2688 UNTS 39.

94 Cf Jenks (n 91) 668–669; Henderson and Cavanagh (n 91) 205–206.

95 See Michael W Lewis and Emily Crawford, 'Drones and Distinction: How IHL Encouraged the Rise of Drones' (2013) 44 *Georgetown JIL* 1127.

96 See eg Nelleke van Amstel and Rain Liivoja, 'Private military and security companies' ch 36 of this volume, s 2 (in relation to employees of private companies).

97 See API arts 51(3); APII art 13(3); Michelle Lesh, 'Direct participation in hostilities' ch 10 in this volume.

98 See eg Patrick Lin, George Bekey and Keith Abney, 'Autonomous Military Robotics: Risk, Ethics, and Design' (Ethics + Emerging Sciences Group, California Polytechnic State University, 20 December 2008); Ronald C Arkin, *Governing Lethal Behaviour in Autonomous Robots* (CRC Press 2009); Krishnan (n 71); Jai Galliott, *Military Robots: Mapping the Moral Landscape* (Ashgate 2015); 'Autonomous Weapon Systems: Technical, Military, Legal and Humanitarian Aspects' Report of the ICRC Expert Meeting, Geneva, 26–28 March 2014 (9 May 2014), www.icrc.org/eng/assets/files/2014/expert-meeting-autonomous-weapons-icrc-report-2014-05-09.pdf.

99 See Chris Jenks, 'False Rubicons, Human Placebos and Increasingly Autonomous Weapon Systems' (forthcoming).

operating in compliance with LOAC. In particular: Can the system adequately distinguish between combatants and civilians, and military objectives and civilian objects? Can the system assess collateral damage? Can the system recognise surrender?

Arguably these are primarily technical challenges, potentially capable of a technical solution, rather than legal problems requiring a regulatory remedy.[100] In any event, one should not assume that any autonomous systems would have to be given the same amount of discretion as a soldier, only to find that the system is incapable of exercising that discretion in conformity with LOAC (especially, assessing the maximum permissible collateral damage). The LOAC compliance of a particular system may be ensured by programming it to identify a very narrow range of objects that by their clearly identifiable nature or behaviour are military objectives (say, submarines or incoming missiles) and to deploy them only where no civilians or civilian objects can be identified in the vicinity. This may well be easier to achieve in some operational settings, such as remote deserts, open oceans and depopulated areas.[101]

Significant legal issues do arise in terms of accountability. In autonomous systems, certain decisions normally made by humans are 'delegated' to the system such that the need for input from a human operator is reduced and the operation of the system is determined by computer software.[102] Yet it would be fanciful to think that the system thereby becomes an accountable agent and human beings are removed from the decision-making process; rather, the nature of the decisions made by humans changes: such decisions will be more general, made ahead of deployment and involve greater degree of forecasting.[103] To put it differently, an autonomous system will have been designed, built, programmed, approved and deployed by people, who will ultimately remain responsible for the 'conduct' of the system. Admittedly, allocating that responsibility between those human actors may be a difficult enterprise. Part of this difficulty results from the assumption underlying LOAC and international criminal law that the operator of a weapon system has ultimate control over it. With autonomous – or, for that matter, other highly advanced – systems that would not necessarily be the case: the designer and programmer could have more control over a system than the person switching it on. Current modes of individual criminal responsibility might not be adequate to reflect this new reality.[104]

Finally, RPVs or autonomous systems can potentially affect other areas of LOAC, for example, the law of occupation. Under LOAC, a territory is considered occupied when it falls under the actual control of the adversary.[105] Traditionally, this has meant 'boots on the ground' – the presence of military personnel exercising authority in the territory. Technology can undoubtedly allow certain kinds of military operations to be carried out without such presence of personnel. This raises the question whether the control potentially exercisable through a combination of RPVs and autonomous systems can be such as to warrant a reinterpretation of certain basic tenets of the law of occupation.

---

100 On the distinction, see Tim McFarland, 'How Should Lawyers Think about Weapon Autonomy?' (2016) *IRRC* (forthcoming).

101 See William H Boothby, *Conflict Law: The Influence of New Weapons Technology, Human Rights and Emerging Actors* (Asser 2014) 111.

102 Cf ibid 105 ('The significant element of autonomy is the ability of the system to decide a course of action from a number of alternatives without depending on human oversight and control.').

103 See McFarland (n 100).

104 See Tim McCormack and Tim McFarland, 'Mind the Gap: Can Developers of Autonomous Weapons Systems be Liable for War Crimes?' (2014) 90 *International Law Studies* 361.

105 HR art 42.

3 Nanotechnology

3.1 Technology

Nanotechnology – conceptualised in the late 1950s, and introduced to a wider audience in the 1970s and 1980s[106] – refers to 'technology at the nanoscale'.[107] The broad term 'technology' includes applications from just about every field of science. Nanoscale, for its part, refers to the size of these applications, and covers a range of one to 100 nanometres.[108] (A nanometre is one-billionth of a metre – a factor of 10^{-9}. To put this in perspective, a nanometre is to a metre what a marble is to the size of the Earth.)[109] Thus, nanotechnology involves the deliberate manipulation of material on the atomic or molecular level to produce novel materials, devices and systems.[110]

Much of nanotechnology is concerned with nanomaterials, that is to say materials that have one or more dimensions on the nanoscale.[111] The most common type of these materials, a nanoparticle, has all three dimensions on the nanoscale.[112] Nanoparticles occur naturally in the environment, such as in volcanic ash, sea spray, clay and milk, and in some man-made substances, such as depleted uranium. In the field of nanotechnology, however, scientists and engineers have an increasingly sophisticated ability to manipulate, design and develop novel nanoparticles.

Chemicals at the nanoparticle size behave differently from chemicals at 'normal size'. They may be more conductive, have stronger bonds or be more chemically reactive than larger particles of the same substance. For example, gold, chemically inert at normal size, can serve as a chemical catalyst at the nanoscale.[113] Furthermore, surface charge – the potential electrical energy between the particle surface and the medium in which it moves[114] – appears to play a greater role at the nanoscale.

As a consequence, substances made of or incorporating nanoparticles may have markedly different, and often enhanced, mechanical, catalytic and thermal properties. Nanoparticles can be utilised, for example, to create more resistant surfaces and to produce active filters to protect against toxic chemical and biological threats. Also, nanotechnology 'helps to enhance specific biological reactions as drug delivery systems help to pass through biological barriers',[115] leading to, *inter alia*, more efficient (targeted) drug delivery, and creating new opportunities for cell imaging.

---

106 See especially Richard Feynman, 'Plenty of Room at the Bottom' (Talk given to the American Physical Society, Pasadena, December 1959), www.pa.msu.edu/~yang/RFeynman_plentySpace.pdf; K Eric Drexler, *Engines of Creation: The Coming Era of Nanotechnology* (Anchor 1986).
107 Jeremy Ramsden, *Nanotechnology: An Introduction* (Elsevier 2011) 2.
108 Ibid.
109 Jennifer Kahn, 'Nanotechnology' *National Geographic* (June 2006) 98.
110 For definitions along these lines, see eg Interagency Working Group on Nanoscience, Engineering and Technology, 'National Nanotechnology Initiative: Leading to the Next Industrial Revolution' (Committee on Technology, National Science and Technology Council, February 2000) 15; The Foresight Institute, 'About Nanotechnology', www.foresight.org/nano.
111 Ramsden (n 107) 101–103.
112 Ibid.
113 See eg Naomi Lubick and Kellyn Betts, 'Silver Socks have Cloudy Lining: Court Bans Widely Used Flame Retardant' (2008) 42 *Environmental Science and Technology* 3910.
114 See International Union of Pure and Applied Chemistry, *Compendium of Chemical Terminology* (2nd edn, Blackwell Scientific Publications 1997).
115 Johann Ach and Beate Luttenberg (eds), *Nanobiotechnology, Nanomedicine and Human Enhancement* (Lit 2008).

What are often referred to as 'nanorobots' are effectively assemblies of atoms that have the ability to trap, transport and alter other atoms. They are 'programmable, potentially self-replicating, molecular machines made of specifically arranged atoms'.[116] Scientists working on this cutting-edge research describe their beneficent vision of a future in which 'nanorobots' would 'cruise around inside the body, communicating with each other and performing various kinds of diagnoses and therapy'.[117] The possibility of using 'nanorobots' to seek out specific organs, and even specific cells, opens up new approaches to much less invasive, highly targeted and hence more effective administration of drugs or of micro-surgical techniques.

As this brief discussion indicates, the applications for nanotechnology are many and they span, *inter alia*, biotechnology, medicine, microelectronics, energy conversion and storage, coatings, textiles, pharmaceuticals, cosmetics, food, manufacturing and security. Many of these applications are already exploited in a wide range of commercial products.[118] For example, gold nanoparticles, mentioned earlier, are used in biosensors, cancer cell imaging and drug delivery to cell membranes.[119]

In the same way that other areas of science and technology can be dual-purpose, there is little doubt that nanotechnology may also be repurposed in a military context: the distinct properties of materials at the nanoscale offer new potential applications for armed conflict. The potential military uses of nanotechnology – both offensive and defensive – have been explored in the literature, although not exhaustively.[120] A notable difficulty in this respect is the futuristic, and sometimes classified, nature of research in this area, which means that potential military nanotechnology applications and estimates of development time frames have to be extrapolated from present science and technology.[121]

While many potential military applications of nanotechnology remain speculative, it is possible to give a few illustrations. The unique properties of matter observed at the nanoscale have been utilised to improve sensors,[122] to enhance protective vests worn by military and paramilitary personnel[123] as well as to develop new types of armour and communication equipment.[124] Nano-enhanced energy storage is being developed with implications for fuel cells, soldier systems, small robots, RPVs and outer space technology.[125] Nanotechnology may

116 Jun Wang and Peter J Dortmans, 'A Review of Selected Nanotechnology Topics and their Potential Military Applications' Report no DSTO-TN-0537 (DSTO Systems Sciences Laboratory 2004) 4.

117 Kristna Weidner,'Nanomotors are Controlled for the First Time, within Living Cells' *Penn State News* (11 February 2014), http://news.psu.edu/story/303296/2014/02/10/research/nanomotors-are-controlled-first-time-inside-living-cells.

118 Maxine McCall, 'Nanoparticles and Nanosafety: The Big Picture' *Conversation* (6 February 2014), http://theconversation.com/nanoparticles-and-nanosafety-the-big-picture-22061.

119 Madhusudhan R Papasani, Guankui Wang and Rodney A Hill, 'Gold Nanoparticles: The Importance of Physiological Principles to Devise Strategies for Targeted Drug Delivery' (2012) 8(6) *Nanomedicine: Nanotechnology, Biology and Medicine* 804.

120 See in particular Wang and Dortmans (n 116); Jürgen Altmann, *Military Nanotechnology* (Routledge 2006); Margaret Kosal, *Nanotechnology for Chemical and Biological Defense* (Springer 2009); Wilson Wong, *Emerging Military Technologies: A Guide to the Issues* (Praeger 2013) ch 5.

121 Altmann (n 120) 71.

122 Margaret Kosal, 'The Security Implications of Nanotechnology' (2013) 66 *Bulletin of the Atomic Scientists* 58.

123 See eg Kanesalingam Sinnppoo, Lyndon Arnold and Rajiv Padhye, 'Application of Wool in High-Velocity Ballistic Protective Fabrics' (2010) 80 *Textile Research Journal* 1083.

124 Wang and Dortmans (n 116).

125 Altmann (n 120) 78–79.

improve the penetration capability and accuracy of projectiles, and enhance camouflaging.[126] Furthermore, given its therapeutic potential, nanotechnology could also 'facilitate weapons based on enhanced delivery mechanisms for toxic substances, on tailored compounds capable of targeting specific physiological functions, and on complex multilayered stealth designs'.[127]

3.2 Legal challenges

Since nanotechnology includes manipulation of chemical and biological functions, specific rules which govern chemical and biological weapons may have relevance where nanotechnology is used in the military context, even though no nanotechnology-derived weapons appear to be in production as yet. In the chemical and biological warfare context, there are at least four broad areas where nanotechnology has regulatory implications: (1) nano-enabled delivery methods, (2) novel nanotechnology-based biochemical weapons, (3) nanoparticles and nanomaterials with toxicological or deleterious health properties and (4) nanotechnology-enabled evasion of medical countermeasures.[128]

The 1925 Geneva Protocol prohibits the use of 'asphyxiating, poisonous or other gases, and of all analogous liquids, materials or devices' and 'bacteriological methods of warfare'.[129] This prohibition is extended by the 1972 Biological Weapons Convention (BWC) and the 1993 Chemical Weapons Convention (CWC) to cover the development, production, acquisition, stockpiling and transfer of biological and chemical weapons respectively.[130] The creation of synthetic DNA has effectively increased the 'continuous biochemical threat spectrum' with the BWC and CWC prohibitions 'overlapping in their coverage of mid-spectrum agents such as toxins and bioregulators'.[131]

To determine their scope of application, the BWC and CWC use broad terms such as 'microbial or other biological agents', 'toxins' and 'toxic chemicals',[132] making the conventions applicable to any new technologies that involve chemical or biological agents used for hostile purposes. The conventions, and the corresponding rules of customary international law, remain applicable regardless of the size of the matter in question.

That said, the BWC is concerned with living organisms and substances produced by such organisms. It has been suggested that artificially created nanoparticles or 'nanorobots' fall within the scope of the BWC prohibition if they replicate the behaviour of known biological agents.[133] On the other hand, nanoparticles that interact with their host through their chemical action on

---

126 Thomas Faunce and Hitoshi Nasu, 'Nanotechnology and the International Law of Weaponry: Towards International Regulation of Nano-Weapons' (2010) 20 *JLIS* 21; Hitoshi Nasu, 'Nano-technology and Challenges to International Humanitarian Law: A Preliminary Legal Assessment' (2012) 94(886) *IRRC* 653.

127 Juan Pardo-Guerra and Francisco Aguayo Ayala, 'Nanotechnology and the International Regime on Chemical and Biological Weapons' (2005) 2 *Law and Business* 1.

128 Kosal, *Chemical and Biological Defense* (n 120) ch 4.

129 Protocol for the Prohibition of the Use of Asphyxiating, Poisonous or Other Gases, and of Bacteriological Methods of Warfare (17 June 1925) 94 LNTS 65.

130 Convention on the Prohibition of the Development, Production, and Stockpiling of Bacteriological (Biological) and Toxin Weapons and on their Destruction (10 April 1972) 1015 UNTS 163, arts 1 and 3; Convention on the Prohibition of the Development, Production, Stockpiling and Use of Chemical Weapons and on their Destruction (13 January 1993) 1974 UNTS 45, art 1.

131 Mark Wheelis and Malcolm Dando, 'Neurobiology: A Case Study for the Imminent Militarization of Biology' (2005) 87(859) *IRRC* 560.

132 BWC art 1(1); CWC art 2(2).

133 Robert Pinson, 'Is Nanotechnology Prohibited by the Biological and Chemical Weapons Conventions?' (2004) 22 *Berkeley Journal of International Law* 279, 298–300.

life processes fall squarely under the prohibition contained in the CWC, regardless of their size.[134]

Significantly, however, the prohibition of biological weapons extends to 'equipment or means of delivery designed to use such [biological] agents or toxins for hostile purposes or in armed conflict' and the definition of chemical weapons expressly includes 'munitions and devices' for the release of toxic chemicals.[135] This would also capture any nanotechnological means of delivering biological agents or toxic chemicals into the human body.

Nanoscale objects can, however, affect human physiology by way of their physical properties rather than by their chemical composition. For example, the inhalation of silver nanofibres has been shown to cause an acute inflammatory reaction in the lungs, with the severity of reaction dependent on the length of the fibre.[136] Also, an accumulation of nanoparticles in the human body – for example the build-up of nanogold, used as an anti-inflammatory agent for conditions such as arthritis[137] – could be manipulated externally (that is, heated) to cause damage to the human body. Finally, 'nanorobots' could potentially be programmed to cause mechanical injury at the cellular level without any biochemical action. The absence of a toxic chemical or disease-causing organism in these instances suggests that the prohibitions contained in the BWC and CWC could be inapplicable. Arguably, however, the broad customary law prohibition of poisoning, codified in the Hague Regulations,[138] would prohibit such uses of nanotechnology.[139] Also, causing tissue damage by means of nanoparticles or 'nanorobots' that due to their size or other properties cannot be detected by industry-standard medical imaging devices may run afoul of the ban on 'any weapon the primary effect of which is to injure by fragments which in the human body escape detection by X-rays'.[140]

Rules and principles on the protection of the environment may also play a role in the use and application of nanotechnology for military purposes. The ENMOD Convention prohibits the 'military or any other hostile use of environmental modification techniques having widespread, long-lasting or severe effects as the means of destruction, damage or injury to any other State Party'[141] and Additional Protocol I bans methods or means of warfare 'which are intended, or may be expected, to cause widespread, long-term and severe damage to the natural environment'.[142] While the precise environmental impact of engineered nanomaterials and nanoparticles remains unclear, there is evidence that at least some of them pose significant risks to the natural environment.[143] This raises the question whether the precautionary principle recognised in environmental law applies equally during times of armed conflict.[144]

---

134 Ibid 300–304.
135 BWC art 1(2); CWC art 2(1)(b)–(c).
136 Anja Schinwald, Fiona A Murphy, Adriele Prina-Mello, Craig A Poland, Fiona Byrne, Dania Movia, James R Glass, Janet C Dickerson, David A Schultz, Chris E Jeffree, William MacNee and Ken Donaldson, 'The Threshold Length for Fibre-Induced Acute Pleural Inflammation: Shedding Light on the Early Events in Asbestos-Induced Mesothelioma' (2012) 128(2) *Toxicological Sciences* 461.
137 Christine T N Pham, 'Nanotherapeutic Approaches for the Treatment of Rheumatoid Arthritis' (2011) 3 *Wiley Interdisciplinary Reviews: Nanomedicine and Nanobiotechnology* 607.
138 HR art 23(a).
139 On the scope of the prohibition on the use of poison and poisoned weapons, see Robert J Mathews, 'Chemical and biological weapons' ch 12 in this volume, in particular s 4.3.
140 Protocol (I) on Non-Detectable Fragments (10 October 1980) 1342 UNTS 168.
141 Convention on the Prohibition of Military or any Other Hostile Use of Environmental Modification Techniques (10 December 1976) 1108 UNTS 151 art I.
142 API art 35(3).
143 See Nasu (n 126) and the sources cited therein.
144 See Laurent Hourcle, 'Environmental Law of War' (2001) 25 *Vermont LR* 653.

4 Weapons review

Article 36 of Additional Protocol I provides an obligation to conduct due diligence in relation to some military applications of technology:

> In the study, development, acquisition or adoption of a new weapon, means or method of warfare, a High Contracting Party is under an obligation to determine whether its employment would, in some or all circumstances, be prohibited by this Protocol or by any other rule of international law applicable to the High Contracting Party.

Even though this provision is contained in Additional Protocol I that is applicable in armed conflict, the effect of Article 36 is such that legal review needs to be undertaken irrespective of whether the state in question is involved in an armed conflict.

Article 36 is broad in scope. In terms of the object of review, it refers to any 'new weapon, means and method of warfare'. This clearly covers, for example, novel projectiles as well as innovative devices for propelling them. The reference to methods of warfare also subjects to legal review military technology that, despite not being directly used to harm the adversary, nonetheless changes the way in which hostilities are undertaken. Thus, for instance, armed RPVs, even if they carry previously known and reviewed weapons, may become new means or methods of warfare and thus subject to a legal review.

Article 36 is also extensive in terms of the relevant legal framework. The review obligation extends well beyond the rules contained in Additional Protocol I itself. The phrase 'any other rule of international law applicable to the High Contracting Party' clearly refers to other LOAC treaties as well as customary international law.[145] Moreover, the ICRC *Commentary* makes it plain that the phrase also 'refers to any agreement on disarmament concluded by the Party concerned, or any other agreement related to the prohibition, limitation or restriction on the use of a weapon or a particular type of weapon, concluded by this Party'.[146] The broad language of Article 36 suggests that the compatibility of weapons, means and methods of warfare with applicable human rights law or environmental law obligations must also be assessed, to the extent that those branches of international law apply in armed conflict.

The broad scope of Article 36 and the complexity of new military platforms can make the legal review of new weapons, means and methods a difficult task. The reviewers of weapons must not only have a thorough knowledge of the applicable law, they must also have an understanding of the 'engineering design, production and testing (or validation) methods, and the way in which the weapon might be employed on the battlefield'.[147] Thus, the obligation under Article 36 necessitates close collaboration between scientists, engineers and lawyers so as to ensure compliance with the requirement to review weapons. Also, given the immediate military applications of some advances in technology, Article 36 reviews may need to be conducted earlier in the development process than previously.

Unfortunately, Article 36 suffers from a striking lack of national implementation. Only a handful of states parties to Additional Protocol I, and two non-parties (the US and Israel), have in place procedures for systematically conducting reviews of new weapons, means and methods of warfare. Even when such reviews are conducted, they do not necessarily reveal all of the

---

145 *AP Commentary* ¶ 1472.
146 Ibid.
147 Alan Backstrom and Ian Henderson, 'New Capabilities in Warfare: An Overview of Contemporary Technological Developments and the Associated Legal and Engineering Issues in Article 36 Weapons Reviews' (2012) 94(886) *IRRC* 483, 484.

relevant legal issues: as pointed out earlier, some emerging technologies raise legal difficulties not in relation to specific prohibitions or restrictions arising under LOAC, arms control law or even human rights law, but because they challenge some of the assumptions that underlie these legal regimes (for example, what constitutes 'attack' or how accountability with respect to systems with a degree of autonomy is implemented). Thus, while a more diligent national application of Article 36 should certainly be welcomed, even broader legal reviews may be necessary for some types of emerging technology.

5 Concluding remarks

Rapid technological developments in the defence sector have justifiably caused concern, especially within civil society and among scholars. This has led to calls for additional regulation. It has been suggested that '[t]he world needs a Geneva Convention for cybercombat'.[148] It has been argued that states should 'control and regulate the proliferation of drones through the judicious use of international law'[149] and that they 'should prohibit the creation of weapons that have full autonomy to decide when to apply lethal force'.[150] It has been claimed that 'there is an urgent need for regulating nano-weapons under the international law of weaponry'[151] and that '[p]ast methods for other technologies are not adequate to deal with nanotechnology'[152] such that reducing the risk of misuse requires both '[t]raditional and innovative new approaches to non-proliferation and counterproliferation'.[153] In short, there appears to be a growing sentiment in some quarters that the existing law is inadequate. Many LOAC specialists, on the other hand, tend to be more optimistic. One commentator concludes that, at least with respect to targeting rules, 'the existing body of law is capable of being applied to novel weapons technologies'.[154]

We take an intermediate position. We believe that much of LOAC is flexible enough to be applied to any weapon technology that might be fielded. That said, some of the current scientific and technological developments do point to weaknesses or uncertainties in the law. Some of these problems could, however, be overcome by more up-to-date interpretations of the current law, rather than the adoption of new, ever-more intricate rules. For instance, in the context of cyber operations, revisiting the meaning of the term 'damage' would help clarify some of the uncertainties. A major difficulty, however, is that the use of emerging technologies – including specifically cyber capabilities and RPVs – constitutes an area where states have been exceedingly reluctant to express their legal views clearly.[155] We share the concern that this

---

148 Karl Rauscher, 'It's Time to Write the Rules of Cyberwar' *IEEE Spectrum* (27 November 2013), http://spectrum.ieee.org/telecom/security/its-time-to-write-the-rules-of-cyberwar.

149 Kaag and Kreps (n 87) 151; Sarah Kreps and Micah Zenko, 'The Next Drone Wars: Preparing for Proliferation' (2014) 93(2) *Foreign Affairs* 68.

150 Human Rights Watch, *Losing Humanity: The Case against Killer Robots* (2012) 46.

151 Faunce and Nasu (n 126) 59; see also Altmann (n 120).

152 Kosal, 'Security Implications' (n 122) 59.

153 Kosal, *Chemical and Biological Defense* (n 120) 8.

154 William H Boothby, 'Legal Challenges of New Technologies: An Overview' in Nasu and McLaughlin (eds) (n 5) 21, 25. Boothby concedes, though that

> if novel technology should emerge which raises humanitarian concerns that cannot easily be addressed by the application of existing law, it would be for the international community of states to decide whether new, specific treaty regulation is required to address such concerns.

155 See Michael N Schmitt and Sean Watts, 'The Decline of International Humanitarian Law: *Opinio Juris* and the Law of Cyber Warfare' (2015) 50 *Texas International Law Journal* 189.

unwillingness to express *opinio juris* will have detrimental effects on the development of LOAC.[156]

Finally, it is worth keeping in mind that efforts to ban outright military applications of particular kinds of technology may have unintended consequences: unqualified restrictions, however well intentioned, can prove to be counter-humanitarian. As regards autonomous systems, for example, it is worth recalling the 1988 incident where the US missile cruiser USS *Vincennes* shot down an Iranian civilian airliner, mistaking it for an attacking military fighter. The disaster could have been avoided, however, had the commander of the *Vincennes* relied on the data supplied by the Aegis Combat System, which was consistent with a civilian aircraft. This suggests that, at least in some situations, an autonomous system would react more appropriately to potential threats than a combatant. RPVs and nanotechnology serve as illustrations of dual-use technology, the regulation of which has its inherent challenges. Any restriction of the use of such technology would need to accommodate the research and development of beneficial (civilian) applications.

156 Ibid.

36

Private military and security companies

Nelleke van Amstel and Rain Liivoja

The past two decades have seen a significant reliance by states on the services of private contractors in sustaining the war-fighting capabilities of national armed forces. While the phenomenon of outsourcing in the military context is by no means new,[1] the expansion of this market in the post-Cold War period has been extraordinary.[2] In particular, the US use of contractors in recent conflicts has risen to such a degree that in Iraq and Afghanistan the number of contracted personnel deployed has been almost constantly higher than the number of troops deployed.[3]

The industry is extremely diverse. Companies providing actual combat services are now few and far between, but it is certainly possible to hire firms to provide all manner of advice and training, and to procure services ranging from logistics and base support to intelligence operations and physical security. Also, different states have different motives and needs for outsourcing: while some have used contractors as a source of expertise and manpower that would otherwise simply not be available, others have seen outsourcing as a way to obtain greater flexibility when planning operations and, most significantly, to cut costs.

Many firms in the marketplace shun the label 'military contractors' and rather describe themselves as providers of 'national security solutions'[4] or 'security services',[5] or explain that they deliver services to 'support the missions of defense and governmental agencies'.[6] Since the way a company chooses to designate itself, or even what services it primarily seeks to provide, is of little significance for LOAC purposes, we refer to all such companies in this chapter as private military and security companies or, for short, PMSCs.

---

1 See eg Erkki Holmila, 'The History of Private Violence' in Rain Liivoja and Andres Saumets (eds), *The Law of Armed Conflict: Historical and Contemporary Perspectives* (Tartu University Press 2012) 45.
2 See generally P W Singer, *Corporate Warriors: The Rise of the Privatized Military Industry* (Cornell University Press 2003; updated edn 2008).
3 See Moshe Schwartz and Jennifer Church, 'Department of Defense's Use of Contractors to Support Military Operations: Background, Analysis, and Issues for Congress' Report no R43074 (Congressional Research Service, 17 May 2013) appendices A and B.
4 L-3 Communications, 'Company Profile', www.l-3com.com/about-l-3/company-profile.html.
5 Academi, 'About Us', www.academi.com/pages/about-us.
6 KBR, 'Business Groups', www.kbr.com/About/Organization.

The increased use of PMSCs has drawn multiple objections and raised numerous concerns – legal and otherwise. On the most general level, the outsourcing of certain heretofore governmental functions has been seen as undermining the role of the state, especially the idea of the state's monopoly on violence.[7] On a more procedural level, the lack of transparency in the outsourcing process and the potential waste of public resources have been a source of concern.[8] Finally, and perhaps most vocally, many have criticised PMSC personnel as being engaged in questionable conduct and lacking in accountability.[9]

We cannot address all these issues in this chapter.[10] We focus on the continued relevance of LOAC in situations of armed conflict where PMSCs are used and the regulatory means by which the existing law is being adapted to accommodate the emergence of a new actor. We begin in section 1 with a brief overview of the recent regulatory initiatives that have been designed to address some of the legal problems associated with PMSCs. In section 2, we consider the application of existing LOAC to PMSCs, in particular the status, obligations and accountability of PMSC personnel under LOAC. Section 3 focuses on the obligations and accountability of states, as the primary actors of international law, with respect to the conduct of PMSCs. Finally, section 4 considers the obligations and accountability of the companies themselves.

1 Regulatory initiatives

1.1 Montreux Document

The first major multilateral attempt to address the perceived lack of regulation of PMSCs was the Montreux Document,[11] finalised in 2008, which aims to define and reaffirm the obligations of states to ensure that PMSCs operating in armed conflicts comply with LOAC and human rights law. Initiated by the ICRC and the Swiss Government, the document outlines and reaffirms existing legal obligations of contracting states, territorial states and home states, and identifies good practices to support states in their national efforts to implement PMSC regulations. Although the document is intended to apply in times of armed conflict, its good practices may inform behaviour in other situations.

The Montreux Document has been well received and, as of December 2015, 53 states and three international organisations (EU, OSCE and NATO) have expressed their support for it.[12] In December 2013, the 'Montreux + 5 conference' took place, which aimed to promote the Montreux Document among interested stakeholders and to help ensure its effective implemen-

---

7 See eg Council of Europe, Parliamentary Assembly, Recommendation 1858 (2009) ¶ 5.

8 See eg Council of Europe (n 7) ¶ 9; Allison Stanger, 'Transparency as a Core Public Value and Mechanism of Compliance' (2012) 31 *Criminal Justice Ethics* 287.

9 See eg Council of Europe (n 7) ¶ 7.

10 For a broader discussion of international law issues involving PMSCs, see eg Simon Chesterman and Chia Lehnardt (eds), *From Mercenaries to Market: The Rise and Regulation of Private Military Companies* (OUP 2007); Francesco Francioni and Natalino Ronzitti (eds), *War by Contract: Human Rights, Humanitarian Law, and Private Contractors* (OUP 2011); Lindsay Cameron and Vincent Chetail, *Privatizing War: Private Military and Security Companies under Public International Law* (CUP 2013).

11 Montreux Document on Pertinent International Legal Obligations and Good Practices for States related to Operations of Private Military and Security Companies during Armed Conflict (17 September 2008), www.icrc.org/eng/assets/files/other/icrc_002_0996.pdf.

12 Swiss Federal Department of Foreign Affairs, 'Participating States of the Montreux Document' (last updated 9 December 2015), www.eda.admin.ch/eda/en/fdfa/foreign-policy/international-law/international-humanitarian-law/private-military-security-companies/participating-states.html.

tation by participating states. A study issued at the occasion, identified a number of challenges relating to the effective implementation of the legal obligations and good practices of the Document.[13] In December 2014, the Montreux Document Forum was established as an intergovernmental forum aiming to strengthen the dialogue among states and international organisations that are participating in the Document. The Forum is a platform for states to exchange on good practices on implementing the Montreux Document in national regulation, and to support outreach and increase awareness for the Document in different regions.[14]

1.2 International code of conduct and its association

Regulation by states only may, however, leave a regulatory and accountability gap; effective government authority and control is not available in all environments in which PMSCs operate, particularly in complex security situations, which may lead to insufficient protection for potential victims of their conduct. In order to ensure commitment to effective rules in such situations, it is important to include companies in standard setting processes. The International Code of Conduct for Private Security Services Providers[15] (ICoC, the Code) was initiated by the Swiss Government in a multi-stakeholder initiative, to complement state regulation in complex environments.[16] Governments, industry and human rights organisations have jointly crafted these commonly agreed standards for the industry.[17] The ICoC includes management policies and human rights-based normative rules and prohibitions. Signed in 2010 by 58 companies, the number of signatory companies rose to 708 by September 2013, when the possibility to become a signatory company was closed and replaced by membership of the ICoC Association (ICoCA):[18] this Association under Swiss law will form an oversight mechanism for compliance with the ICoC,[19] as has been foreseen by the Code and thus committed to by all its signatories.[20] The three core functions of the ICoCA will be (i) the certification of companies, (ii) performance assessment, including reporting and in-field monitoring to ensure that companies continue to apply the Code and (iii) administering a complaints process which can assess whether companies

---

13 Benjamin S Buckland and Anna Marie Burdzy, *Progress and Opportunities, Five Years on: Challenges and Recommendations for Montreux Document Endorsing States* (Geneva Centre for the Democratic Control of Armed Forces 2013).

14 See Montreux Document Forum, www.mdforum.ch.

15 International Code of Conduct for Private Security Service Providers ('ICoC') (9 November 2010), http://icoca.ch/en/the_icoc.

16 'Complex environments' is defined in the ICoC as

> any area experiencing or recovering from unrest or instability, whether due to natural disaster or armed conflict, where the rule of law has been substantially undermined, and in which the capacity of the state authority to handle the situation is diminished, limited, or non-existent.
>
> ICoC (n 15) pt B

17 The ICoC applies to 'Private Security Companies', defined as companies providing 'Security Services', ie

> guarding and protection of persons and objects, such as convoys, facilities, designated sites, property or other places (whether armed or unarmed), or any other activity for which the Personnel of Companies are required to carry or operate a weapon in the performance of their duties.
>
> ICoC (n 15) pt B

This therefore also includes PMSCs.

18 The International Code of Conduct Association, www.icoca.ch.

19 International Code of Conduct Articles of Association (22 February 2013), http://icoca.ch/en/articles_of_association.

20 ICoC (n 15) ¶¶ 7, 8.

deal appropriately, by fair and accessible grievance mechanisms, with any claims of breaches of the Code. This oversight mechanism will play a crucial role in enforcing the incentives for compliance. Consistent with the drafting process for the ICoC, the establishment of the ICoCA was a multi-stakeholder process.

The ICoC and Montreux Document together form the 'Swiss initiatives' expressing the consensus that PMSCs do not operate in a legal vacuum and outlining their obligations to comply with applicable national law and standards of international law.[21] The two instruments are set out for different stakeholders and for different fields of application, and aim to complement effective national regulation. In this way, concerns over a perceived legal void have been replaced by a layered approach to regulation at international and national levels that clearly sets out the responsibilities both of states and of companies.

1.3 UN initiatives

A draft Convention on the Use of Private Security Companies has been considered in different UN forums since first proposed to the Human Rights Council by the Working Group on Mercenaries in 2010.[22] As differences in positions between states on the need for international regulation are considerable, an open-ended intergovernmental working group[23] (OEWG) was created in 2010 in order to discuss this draft further among states. Most recently, in 2015, the mandate of the OEWG was extended for a further two-and-a-half years, but with a clear divergence of views on the topic within the HRC.[24] After one session a year for several years, the achievements of this forum seem to be limited.[25]

In addition to its mandate to elaborate guidelines and study activities of mercenaries and private military and security companies, the Working Group on Mercenaries also has the ability to receive communications from individuals concerning actions of PMSC personnel.[26] Complains against corporations are then, however, referred to the attention of the home state and not dealt with directly.[27]

---

21 See Swiss Federal Department of Foreign Affairs, 'Private Military and Security Companies' (last updated 27 June 2014), www.eda.admin.ch/eda/en/home/topics/intla/humlaw/pse.html.

22 Draft of a Possible Convention on Private Military and Security Companies (PMSCs) for Consideration and Action by the Human Rights Council, HRC 15th session, UN Doc A/HRC/15/25 (2 July 2010) Annex.

23 Full title of the working group is 'Open-ended intergovernmental working group intergovernmental working group to consider the possibility of elaborating an international regulatory framework on the regulation, monitoring and oversight of the activities of private military and security companies'.

24 Renewal of the Mandate of the Open-Ended Intergovernmental Working Group to consider the Possibility of Elaborating an International Regulatory Framework on the Regulation, Monitoring and Oversight of the Activities of Private Military and Security Companies, UN Doc A/HRC/28/L.11 (20 March 2015) (32 in favour, 13 against, two abstaining).

25 See eg Summary of the Third Session of the Open-Ended Intergovernmental Working Group to consider the Possibility of Elaborating an International Regulatory Framework on the Regulation, Monitoring and Oversight of the Activities of Private Military and Security Companies, UN Doc A/HRC/WG.10/3/2 (2 September 2014).

26 For the mandate of this working group, see HRC Res 7/21 (28 March 2008) ¶ 2, which focuses on 'mercenaries, mercenary-related activities and activities of private military and private security companies which have an impact on human rights in general'.

27 See Report of the Working Group on the Use of Mercenaries as a Means of Violating Human Rights and Impeding the Exercise of the Right of Peoples to Self-Determination, UN Doc A/61/341 (13 September 2006) ¶ 20.

A UN initiative with considerable influence on the regulation of PMSCs has been the development of the UN Guiding Principles on Business and Human Rights. It outlines a 'protect, respect, remedy' framework describing how business and states are to address human rights challenges.[28] This framework is increasingly important for any corporation, wherever they may operate.[29]

1.4 EU initiatives

In the EU, policies regarding PMSCs fall under the Common Foreign and Security Policy, which entered into force after the 2007 Treaty of Lisbon. Although there are no regulations specifically aimed at the PMSC industry, EU policies do address the procurement of PMSC services to support EU-led military and humanitarian missions and the export of PMSC services to non-EU member states.

With respect to procurement, the EU produced a concept note in 2014 for contractor support to EU-led military operations which defines and clarifies principles, policies, procedures and responsibilities.[30] For humanitarian missions, the European Commission's Humanitarian and Civil Protection Department (ECHO) has reviewed the management of security for its personnel and produced a Generic Security Guide which gathers common security standards and good practices.[31] The document also analyses the costs and benefits of hiring local PMSCs and concludes that engaging a local private company can have several advantages including reduced administration, more flexibility and immediate guard replacements, as well as some drawbacks, including higher costs and insufficiently trained personnel. ECHO has also produced Humanitarian Aid Guidelines for Procurement, which refer to ethical procurement but lack a specific reference to PMSCs.[32]

In addition to the regulation of procurement, the scope of the EU export control regime may also extend to PMSCs' services leaving the EU. A European Commission regulation stipulates that no dual-use goods may be exported from the EU without export authorisation.[33] If PMSC activities or services fall under the export, transfer or brokering of dual use goods, the regulation may be applicable.[34]

Although the EU examined the harmonisation of laws related to PMSCs operating at the member-state level, PMSCs were excluded from the 2006 Directive on the internal market that harmonised service sectors.[35] The European Commission was to assess, by 28 December 2010,

---

28 Guiding Principles of Business and Human Rights: Implementing the United Nations 'Protect, Respect and Remedy' Framework, UN Doc A/HRC/17/31 (21 March 2011); see further s 4.1, below.

29 Currently, it is being discussed whether an international treaty on business and human rights would be appropriate, for the latest information, www.ohchr.org/EN/HRBodies/HRC/WGTransCorp/Pages/IGWGOnTNC.aspx.

30 European Union Military Committee, 'EU Concept for Contractor Support to EU-led Military Operations' Doc EEAS 00754/14 (4 April 2014).

31 ECHO, 'Generic Security Guide for Humanitarian Organisations' (European Commission 2004).

32 ECHO, 'Guidelines for the Award of Procurement Contracts within the Framework of Humanitarian Aid Actions Financed by the European Union' (European Commission 31 May 2011).

33 Council Regulation (EC) No 428/2009 of 5 May 2009 setting up a Community Regime for the Control of Exports, Transfer, Brokering and Transit of Dual-Use Items [2009] OJ L 134/1.

34 Ibid annex I, quoted in Elke Krahmann and Aida Abzhaparova, 'The Regulation of Private Military and Security Services in the European Union: Current Policies and Future Options' EUI Working Paper AEL (August 2008).

35 Directive 2006/123/EC of the European Parliament and of the Council of 12 December 2006 on Services in the Internal Market [2006] OJ L 376/36; Directorate-General for Internal Market and Services, *Handbook on the Implementation of the Services Directive* (European Communities 2007) 13.

the possibility of presenting proposals for harmonisation in this field; however, the extent of progress in this regard remains unclear. In any event, this would only be relevant to PMSCs that operate within the EU in armed conflict.

2 Status, obligations and accountability of PMSC personnel

The principal LOAC treaties, having been drafted and adopted before the emergence of the PMSC phenomenon in its current form, obviously do not mention PMSCs by name and do not expressly assign rights and obligations to their personnel. The status of such personnel therefore remains to be determined with reference to the general rules of LOAC.

The question as to the status of PMSC personnel defies an easy answer. It is impossible to assess their position as a group because of the diverse nature of their activities and the divergent relationships to their paymasters. The status of PMSC personnel for LOAC purposes thus has to be assessed on a case-by-case basis.[36]

2.1 Status in international armed conflicts

In an international armed conflict, the key question is whether PMSC personnel are combatants or civilians. This distinction is fundamental in that it impacts both on the legitimacy of the individuals as targets of attack as well as the regime of their protection upon capture.[37] Since LOAC defines civilians negatively as persons who are not combatants,[38] it is appropriate to consider eligibility for combatant status first.

Applying the general rules contained in Geneva Convention III, PMSC personnel are combatants if they are either '[m]embers of the armed forces of a Party to the conflict' or, subject to meeting certain further conditions, '[m]embers of other militias and … volunteer corps … belonging to a Party to the conflict'.[39]

As for the first of these two options, membership in the armed forces of a state, or any unit thereof, is a matter for domestic law, leaving states with a considerable degree of flexibility.[40] States have sometimes formally incorporated PMSC into their armed forces in non-international armed conflicts,[41] which implies that such incorporation may also occur in an international armed conflict and would result in combatant status for the relevant personnel. That said, the most significant contracting states are unlikely to resort to formal incorporation as it would defeat the very purpose of outsourcing certain military or security services.[42]

---

36 See Montreux Document (n 11) statement 24.
37 This is explored in more detail elsewhere in this volume: see in particular, introductory notes to Part II; Emily Crawford, 'Combatants' ch 7; Emanuela Chiara-Gillard, 'Protection of civilians in the conduct of hostilities' ch 9; Chris Jenks, 'Detention under the law of armed conflict' ch 17.
38 API art 50(1).
39 GCIII art 4A(1) and (2); the possibility of PMSC personnel being participants in a *levée en masse*, as recognised in GCIII art 4A(6), appears negligible. The definition of API art 43 generally mirrors the one of GCIII art 4 – the biggest difference consists of the exception from the individual obligation to distinguish, under API art 44(3).
40 See Cameron and Chetail (n 10) 390.
41 See s 2.2 below.
42 Michael N Schmitt, 'Humanitarian Law and Direct Participation in Hostilities by Private Contractors or Civilian Employees' (2005) 5 *Chicago JIL* 511, 526–527; Emanuela-Chiara Gillard, 'Business Goes to War: Private Military/Security Companies and International Humanitarian Law' (2006) 88(863) *IRRC* 525, 533; Louise Doswald-Beck, 'Private Military Companies under International Humanitarian Law' in Chesterman and Lehnardt (n 10) 115, 118; Cameron and Chetail (n 10) 391.

Whether PMSC personnel could be equated to members of militias or volunteer groups belonging to a state is a more practical but also more complex issue. Combatant status by virtue of membership in such groups is contingent on the four traditional criteria of irregular armed forces: (i) being commanded by a person responsible for his or her subordinates, (ii) having a fixed sign recognisable at a distance, (iii) carrying arms openly and (iv) conducting operations in accordance with the laws and customs of war.[43] A number of commentators have examined whether PMSCs meet these criteria.[44] While the shared sentiment is that they do not – especially in relation to a 'fixed distinctive sign' – this derives largely from the experience with PMSCs in Iraq or Afghanistan rather than from any insurmountable quality of the criteria. In other words, PMSCs could comply with these criteria if they chose to do so.[45]

The requirements regarding the link between the group and the state potentially create more fundamental problems. The ICRC *Commentary* to Geneva Convention III regards it 'essential that there should be a de facto relationship' between the group and the state.[46] There is no apparent reason for rejecting a contractual arrangement between a PMSC and a state as the basis of such a relationship, though subcontracting could admittedly complicate matters considerably.[47] The ICRC *Commentary* goes on to say that the group must be 'fighting on behalf of a "Party to the conflict"'.[48] What this implies remains unclear. At the very least, the group must actually fight. As Schmitt notes, '[i]f a contractor is not directly participating [in hostilities], and most do not, it is by definition not the sort of group envisaged by Article 4A(2)'.[49] Gillard raises the further question as to whether only PMSCs 'actually hired to fight' could meet the 'belonging to' requirement and takes the view that Article 4A(2) 'would presumably only cover persons hired to carry out activities close to the heart of military operations'.[50] Cameron and Chetail place the bar slightly lower, arguing that the state must at least 'accept' that the group fights on its behalf.[51] On this view, US contractor personnel would find it exceedingly difficult to qualify as combatants under Article 4A(2), as the US generally regards them as civilians accompanying the armed forces (see below) and thus does not accept that they are fighting on behalf of the US.

The ICRC *Commentary* observes that addressing regular and irregular forces separately in paragraphs (1) and (2) of Article 4A reflects 'the principle stated in Article 1 of the 1907 Hague Regulations, which made a distinction between militias and volunteer corps forming part of the army and those which are independent'.[52] From this observation, Schmitt derives the requirement that groups falling under Article 4A(2) must be independent from the armed forces.[53] Arguably, this condition would often not be met by PMSCs, which tend to be highly dependent, at least financially, on their contracting state.[54] But denying combatant status to groups on the basis of their lack of independence finds no support in the actual text of Geneva

43 GCIII art 4A(2).
44 Schmitt (n 42) 529–531; Gillard (n 42) 534–535; Mirko Sossai, 'Status of Private Military Companies' Personnel in the Laws of War: The Question of Direct Participation in Hostilities' (2008) 18 *Italian YBIL* 89, 93; Doswald-Beck (n 42) 119–120; Cameron and Chetail (n 10) 401–406.
45 Doswald-Beck (n 42) 119.
46 *GCIII Commentary* 57.
47 Schmitt (n 42) 528; Gillard (n 42) 534; Doswald-Beck (n 42) 119.
48 Ibid.
49 Schmitt (n 42) 529, fn 71.
50 Gillard (n 42) 534–535
51 Cameron and Chetail (n 10) 395–396.
52 *GCIII Commentary* 57.
53 Schmitt (n 42) 528–529.
54 Ibid.

Convention III.[55] Moreover, if this line of reasoning is accepted, it would lead to the peculiar situation where a PMSC that is sufficiently independent from the armed forces would no longer belong to the state whereas a PMSC so belonging would not be sufficiently independent.

If, as in most cases, contractor personnel do not qualify for combatant status, they are civilians, with all the attendant legal consequences. However, there are a number of sub-categories of civilians, which are subject to a modified legal regime.

Certain civilians are entitled to be treated as POWs upon capture. They are, under Article 4A(4) of Geneva Convention III,

> [p]ersons who accompany the armed forces without actually being members thereof, such as civilian members of military aircraft crews, war correspondents, supply contractors, members of labour units or of services responsible for the welfare of the armed forces, provided that they have received authorization from the armed forces which they accompany, who shall provide them for that purpose with an identity card.[56]

Some PMSC personnel may fall within the confines of this provision.[57] Indeed, the US Department of Defense has instructions in place for authorising contractor personnel to accompany the armed forces and for issuing the relevant identity cards.[58] Commentators agree, however, that only personnel who are not expected to participate directly in hostilities are covered by Article 4A(4).[59]

Two additional observations regarding combatant status are apposite here. First, state practice indicates that a state has no obligation to grant POW status to its own nationals who have been detained while fighting for the adversary.[60] Given the diverse background of PMSC personnel, this may deprive some of them of POW status. Second, if there is doubt as to the entitlement by any captured individual, including PMSC personnel, to POW status – either as a combatant or a civilian accompanying the armed forces – the presumption of entitlement to such status applies until a competent tribunal determines otherwise.[61]

Civilians lose their protection from attack when they take direct part in hostilities.[62] The precise parameters of the notion of direct participation remain subject to debate and, in any event, necessitate a context-specific analysis.[63] That said, some functions that PMSCs might engage in would amount to direct participation: defending lawful military objectives from attack and undertaking military planning on a tactical level (for example, mission planning for aerial operations) would be cases in point.[64]

---

55 Sossai (n 44) 93 is also sceptical about Schmitt's reading of the notion of independence.
56 Cf HR art 13, which refers to 'individuals who follow an army without directly belonging to it', including 'sutlers and contractors'.
57 See Montreux Document (n 11) statement 26(c); see also Giulio Bartolini, 'Private Military and Security Contractors as "Persons who Accompany the Armed Forces"' in Francioni and Ronzitti (n 10) 218.
58 See US DoD Instruction no 3020.41: Contractor Personnel Authorized to Accompany the U.S. Forces (20 December 2011); US DoD Instruction no 1000.01: Identification (ID) Cards Required by the Geneva Conventions (16 April 2012).
59 Gillard (n 42) 537; Doswald-Beck (n 42) 124; Carsten Hoppe, 'Passing the Buck: State Responsibility for Private Military Companies' (2008) 19 *EJIL* 989, 1007.
60 See eg *Public Prosecutor v Koi* [1968] AC 829 (Privy Council, Malaysia).
61 GCIII art 5(2).
62 API art 51(3).
63 See Michelle Lesh, 'Direct participation in hostilities' ch 10 in this volume.
64 For a discussion, see Schmitt (n 42) 536–546.

It has to be stressed that all civilians, including PMSC personnel, retain the right to self-defence, a right recognised in virtually all national legal systems[65] as well as under international law.[66] Under international law, self-defence must serve a lawful aim (the protection of persons and property that is essential for their survival) and be necessary and proportional.[67] The use of force in self-defence should, however, not amount to direct participation in hostilities, which means that the right is likely to be interpreted restrictively.[68]

With regard to civilians accompanying the armed forces, the further question arises as to whether they also lose their entitlement to POW status when directly participating in hostilities. The UK *LOAC Manual* and a number of commentators answer this question in the affirmative.[69] US doctrine, however, takes the opposite view.[70]

Finally, could PMSC personnel be mercenaries?[71] Given that only persons who are 'specifically recruited ... in order to fight in an armed conflict' are mercenaries,[72] few PMSC personnel would qualify. At any rate, the effects of meeting the definition under LOAC are negligible, as the consequences are the same as being a civilian taking a direct part in hostilities:[73] in particular, such persons would be targetable while directly participating in hostilities and could be subject to prosecution for specific warlike acts; but they would be entitled to other guarantees under LOAC protecting civilians. There would, however, be some significance in contexts where one of the two anti-mercenary conventions were applicable,[74] in which case the individual not only would face prosecution for acts committed in the course of directly participating in hostilities but such participation itself would become punishable.

2.2 Status in non-international armed conflicts

Even though combatant status and the attendant entitlement to protection as a POW are alien to the law of non-international armed conflict, the principle of distinction still applies. The distinction is largely 'conduct-based'[75] in the sense that LOAC specifically protects '[p]ersons taking no active part in the hostilities, including members of armed forces who have laid down their arms and those placed *hors de combat* by sickness, wounds, detention, or any other cause'.[76]

---

65 See Petere Haggenmacher, 'Self-Defence as General Principle of Law and its Relation to War' in Arthur Eyffinger, Alan Stephens and Sam Muller (eds), *Self-Defence as Fundamental Principle* (Asser 2009) 14.

66 See eg Rome Statute art 31(1)(c); *Prosecutor v Kordić and Čerkez* (IT-95-14/2-T, ICTY Trial Chamber, 26 February 2001) ¶ 451.

67 Guido den Dekker and Eric P J Myjer, 'The Right to Life and Self-Defence of Private Military and Security Contractors in Armed Conflict' in Francioni and Ronzitti (eds) (n 10) 171, 180.

68 Ibid 181–182.

69 UK Ministry of Defence, *The Manual of the Law of Armed Conflict* (OUP 2004) ¶ 4.3.7; Sossai (n 44) 112; Gillard (n 42) 538; see also Bartolini (n 57) 230–232.

70 US DoD Instruction No 1100.22: Policy and Procedures for Determining Workforce Mix (12 April 2010) 51.

71 See Marina Mancini, Faustin Z Ntoubandi and Thilo Marauhn, 'Old Concepts and New Challenges: Are Private Contractors the Mercenaries of the Twenty-first Century?' in Francioni and Ronzitti (eds) (n 10) 321.

72 API art 47(a). See Gillard (n 42) 569; Doswald-Beck (n 42) 122–123.

73 See Gillard (n 42) 562.

74 International Convention Against the Recruitment, Use, Financing and Training of Mercenaries (4 December 1989) 2163 UNTS 75; OAU Convention for the Elimination of Mercenarism in Africa (3 July 1977) OAU Doc CM/433/Rev.L.Annex I.

75 Cameron and Chetail (n 10) 388.

76 GCI–IV common art 3.

Though Additional Protocol II expressly mentions the category of 'civilians',[77] this notion is identical with that of persons not taking a direct part in hostilities. Thus, when not directly participating in hostilities, PMSC personnel would be protected by Common Article 3, Additional Protocol II (where it applies) and any relevant rules of customary international law.[78] If, however, PMSC personnel fulfil a 'continuous combat function', the direct participation in hostilities would become a permanent state, making them a legitimate military target at all times.[79]

When PMSCs are contracted by a government, their personnel may be incorporated into the armed forces – or, for that matter, some other governmental agencies – as was the case with Executive Outcomes personnel in Sierra Leone during the civil war in 1995–1996.[80] This would grant the PMSC personnel whatever legal privileges and immunities attach to the armed forces or government agencies under domestic law.

2.3 Obligations and accountability of PMSC personnel

The significance of a person's status under LOAC should not be overstated. In particular, such status is wholly irrelevant for the obligation to comply with LOAC and responsibility for violations. In the context of an armed conflict, every person, including PMSC personnel, must comply with LOAC and, having committed a serious violation of LOAC that entails individual criminal responsibility, may be prosecuted for war crimes.[81]

The rules of superior responsibility[82] also apply in the context of PMSCs. Thus, within a particular PMSC, managers incur responsibility for the conduct of their subordinates in the same way as a civilian superior has responsibility for his or her subordinates. That said, whether superior responsibility extends all the way to senior corporate management remains in doubt,[83] as senior management might not have the requisite effective authority and control over those actually undertaking the operations. Furthermore, superior responsibility potentially extends beyond the company and covers persons (whether military commanders or civilian officials) under whose control the PMSC personnel actually work. At the same time, the kind of de facto control required to establish a superior–subordinate relationship under LOAC is unlikely to exist in case of PMSC contract managers.[84]

One obstacle to individual criminal responsibility of PMSC personnel may arise from the lack of jurisdiction over them as a matter of domestic law. While under international law, states can arguably extend their criminal law to cover their contracted personnel even overseas,[85] not

---

77 APII art 13(3).
78 Doswald-Beck (n 42) 126–127.
79 ICRC, *Interpretive Guidance on the Notion of Direct Participation in Hostilities under International Humanitarian Law* (ICRC 2009) 33–36.
80 See Juan Carlos Zarate, 'The Emergence of a New Dog of War: Private International Security Companies, International Law, and the New World Disorder' (1998) 34 *Stanford JIL* 75. See also Agreement for the Provision of Military Assistance between the Independent State of Papua New Guinea and Sandline International (31 January 1997) (envisaging the enrolment of Sandline personnel as 'Special Constables').
81 See Montreux Document (n 11) statement 26(a) and (e).
82 See Rob Cryer, 'Individual liability in international law' ch 31 in this volume; see also Rome Statute art 28.
83 Gillard (n 42) 545.
84 Doswald-Beck (n 42) 136.
85 See Rain Liivoja, 'Service Jurisdiction under International Law' (2010) 11 *Melbourne JIL* 309.

all states take full advantage of this possibility.[86] Where a lack of the contracting state's jurisdiction coincides with immunity from host state jurisdiction, a serious accountability gap emerges.

3 Obligations and accountability of states

The responsibility of a state under international law arises where an act or omission that is attributable to that state amounts to a breach of an obligation of that state under international law.[87] The conduct of private actors that contravenes international law does not generally implicate the state. A mere contractual relationship between a state and a PMSC would not, by itself, suffice as link of attribution.[88]

That said, a state could accrue responsibility for the conduct of PMSCs in two ways.[89] First, where PMSCs – or their employees – become instrumentalities of a state, their conduct can be directly attributed to the state. Second, where direct attribution is lacking, states have certain positive obligations to exercise control and influence over private actors, including PMSCs, and can be responsible for a failure to conduct 'due diligence'.

3.1 Attribution of PMSC conduct

The conduct of a state organ is considered an act of the state.[90] A PMSC would constitute a state organ where it has this status under national law, for example where it is formally incorporated into the armed forces of the state.[91] However, as noted earlier, such incorporation remains relatively uncommon. Alternatively, a PMSC could be regarded a de facto state organ if it was in 'complete dependence' on the state.[92] While an entire PMSC would be unlikely to satisfy this test, a group of PMSC employees in the context of a specific contract and in a particular conflict zone might.[93]

The conduct of a person or entity empowered by the law of a state to exercise elements of the governmental authority is also considered an act of that state.[94] Even though the notion of 'governmental authority' cannot be defined very precisely or exhaustively, it would appear to cover at least some activities that PMSCs may be engaged in, such as provision of security

---

86 Incidentally, such lack of jurisdiction has been cited by some commentators as a reason for denying combatant status to PMSC personnel – they are not under a command responsible if criminal jurisdiction is lacking. Doswald-Beck (n 42) 120–121.

87 Articles on Responsibility of States for Internationally Wrongful Acts, in UN Doc A/55/10, ch IV (2001) ('ARSIWA') arts 1–3; with regard to LOAC, see Charles Garraway, 'State responsibility' ch 29 in this volume.

88 See Montreux Document (n 11) statement 7.

89 Hannah Tonkin, *State Control over Private Military and Security Companies in Armed Conflict* (CUP 2011) 56–57.

90 ARSIWA (n 87) art 4(1).

91 See ARSIWA (n 87) art 4(2); Montreux Document (n 11) statement 7(a).

92 See *Application of the Convention on the Prevention and Punishment of the Crime of Genocide (Bosnia and Herzegovina v Serbia and Montenegro)* [2007] ICJ Reports 43, ¶ 392; *Military and Paramilitary Activities in and against Nicaragua (Nicaragua v US)* [1986] ICJ Reports 14, ¶ 110.

93 For a discussion, see Carsten Hoppe, 'Private Conduct, Public Service? State Responsibility for Violations of International Humanitarian Law Committed by Individuals Providing Coercive Services under a Contract with a State' in Michael J Matheson and Djamchid Momtaz (eds), *Rules and Institutions of International Humanitarian Law Put to the Test of Recent Armed Conflicts* (Martinus Nijhoff 2011) 411, 427–431; Cameron and Chetail (n 10) 142–157.

94 ARSIWA (n 87) art 5; cf Montreux Document (n 11) statement 7(c).

amounting to direct participation in hostilities, detention operations and interrogation.[95] Some form of domestic legislation – such as a legal authorisation to delegate tasks by means of contract – appears to be necessary to meet the 'empowered by law' requirement.[96]

Finally, the conduct carried out by a person or a group of persons in fact acting on the instructions of, or under the direction or control of, a state constitutes an act of that state.[97] The ICJ has distinguished this basis of attribution from the de facto organ approach contemplated above: unlike the de facto organ that requires 'complete dependence' on the state, it suffices that the state has given specific instructions, or has 'effective control', with respect to a particular operation.[98]

A point of further difficulty is that with regard both to state organs and to persons or entities exercising elements of governmental authority, the relevant conduct will be attributable to the state only where the contractor personnel acted in their 'official' capacity in the particular circumstances.[99] The final scenario of instructions or effective control is situation-specific anyway. Thus, this creates a 'responsibility gap' as a state is responsible, at least in an international armed conflict, for all of the acts of the members of its armed forces, however unrelated to their official capacity.[100] Unless PMSC personnel qualify as members of the armed forces, the degree of responsibility of states is reduced through outsourcing.

3.2 Positive obligations with respect to PMSCs

The question of attributing the conduct of PMSCs to a state really only arises with respect to the contracting state. All states, however, potentially have positive obligations in relation to the conduct of PMSCs.

Under LOAC, positive obligations in the broadest sense of the term are anchored in the principle that states must not only respect, but ensure respect for, the law in all circumstances.[101] The steps that states must take in order to ensure respect for LOAC depend on the degree of influence they can exert under the circumstances: while states without any involvement in a particular conflict can resort to diplomatic measures, those more closely involved may need to take more concrete steps to ensure that PMSCs abide by the law.[102]

More specifically, states parties to a conflict have the obligation to 'protect' particular categories of persons and facilities – the wounded, sick and shipwrecked,[103] medical services,[104] prisoners of war[105] and civilians.[106] The ICRC *Commentaries* on the Geneva Conventions suggest

---

95   For a discussion, see Hoppe, 'Private Conduct, Public Service?' (n 93) 433–437; Cameron and Chetail (n 10) 172–204.

96   Hoppe, 'Private Conduct, Public Service?' (n 93) 432.

97   ARSIWA (n 87) art 8; cf Montreux Document (n 11) statement 7(d).

98   See *Bosnian Genocide* (n 92) ¶¶ 399–400; *Nicaragua* (n 92) ¶ 115; Hoppe, 'Private Conduct, Public Service?' (n 93) 439–443.

99   ARSIWA (n 87) arts 5 and 7.

100 See Hague Convention (IV) art 3; API art 91; see also *Armed Activities on the Territory of the Congo (Democratic Republic of the Congo v Uganda)* [2005] ICJ Rep 168, ¶ 213; for a discussion, see Hoppe, 'Private Conduct, Public Service?' (n 93) 445–458; see also Carsten Hoppe, 'Passing the Buck: State Responsibility for Private Military Companies' (2008) 19 *EJIL* 989, 991.

101 GCI–IV art 1; API art 1; for a discussion, see Tonkin (n 89) 124–137; Cameron and Chetail (n 10) 244–251.

102 Cameron and Chetail (n 10) 250.

103 GCI art 12; GCII art 18.

104 GCI arts 19, 24, 25, 35; GCII art 21; GC III arts 36, 37; GCIV arts 18, 21; API arts 8c, 21, 24.

105 GCIII art 13.

106 See GCIV art 27.

that protection in this context includes the duty to take feasible steps to prevent acts of violence against the persons or facilities in question.[107] This duty would undoubtedly extend to providing protection *from* PMSCs where necessary.

Furthermore, according to a rule codified in the Hague Regulations, an occupying power has the obligation to 'take all the measures in his power to restore, and ensure, as far as possible, public order and [civil life]'.[108] In this regard, the US Military Tribunal at Nuremberg found that 'international law places the responsibility upon the commanding general of preserving order, punishing crime, and protecting lives and property within the occupied territory'.[109] The ICJ has more recently held that the occupying power has

> the duty to secure respect for the applicable rules of international human rights law and international humanitarian law, to protect the inhabitants of the occupied territory against acts of violence, and not to tolerate such violence by any third party.[110]

In casu, this entailed for Uganda the 'obligation to take appropriate measures to prevent the looting, plundering and exploitation of natural resources in the occupied territory to cover private persons in this district and not only members of Ugandan military forces'.[111] In the context of PMSCs, it is important to note that this obligation applies not only in relation to PMSCs contracted by the occupying power itself, but with respect to all PMSCs that operate in the territory.[112]

Additionally, states have the obligation to criminalise 'grave breaches' of the Geneva Conventions and to prosecute or extradite persons alleged to have committed such breaches.[113] They also have the obligation take measures necessary for the suppression of all other acts contrary to the provisions of the Conventions.[114] The result is a broad obligation, clearly recognised by the Montreux Document with respect to contracting, territorial and home states alike, to

> take measures to suppress violations of international humanitarian law committed by the personnel of PMSCs through appropriate means such as military regulations, administrative orders and other regulatory measures as well as administrative, disciplinary or judicial sanctions, as appropriate.[115]

4 Obligations and accountability of companies

Companies are traditionally considered to be only bound indirectly by international law, through the national laws of states.[116] Similarly, corporations are not considered to be bound directly by LOAC, which is applicable to states, armed groups and individuals. In the absence of international minimum standards, obligations of PMSCs under national laws differ widely, with only

---

107 See eg *GCI Commentary* 134–135, 152; *GCIII Commentary* 141; *GCIV Commentary* 204.
108 HR art 43.
109 *US v List et al (Hostages Trial)* 11 TWC 1230, 1244 (1948).
110 *Armed Activities on the Territory of the Congo (Democratic Republic of the Congo v Uganda)* [2005] ICJ Rep 168, ¶ 178.
111 Ibid ¶ 248.
112 Cameron and Chetail (n 10) 240.
113 GCI art 41(1)–(2); GCII art 50(1)–(2); GCIII art 129(1)–(2); GCIV art 146(1)–(2).
114 GCI art 41(3); GCII art 50(3); GCIII art 129(3); GCIV art 146(3).
115 Montreux Document (n 11) statements 3(c), 9(c) and 14(c).
116 For a different view, particularly with regard to PMSCs, see Andrew Clapham, 'Human Rights Obligations of Non-State Actors in Conflict Situations' (2006) 88(863) *IRRC* 491.

few countries regulating PMSC operations at home or abroad at all.[117] Rules containing direct obligations on how to operate in accordance with human rights, the incorporation of rules of LOAC and the level of accountability for compliance with those rules, depend largely on the state's national legal system and its willingness to enforce domestic law. In the past decades this lack of possible accountability of corporations at the international level, and minimal accountability provided by traditional state regulatory regimes, has led to a perception that PMSCs operate in a legal void.

4.1 International obligations for companies

When considering obligations on the international level, there exists a growing consensus that rules stemming from human rights law and LOAC are certainly and increasingly relevant for these actors. In the absence of hard law covering international obligations of companies, a number of innovative 'soft-law' initiatives have emerged. Within the development of corporate social responsibility an expectation has emerged that (transnational) corporations should strive to refrain from negatively impacting the rights of individuals with their operations – the responsibility to respect human rights.[118]

Building upon this development, international obligations to be respected by PMSCs have been clarified and consolidated in the above-mentioned ICoC. It outlines human rights and LOAC standards that apply to companies when operating in complex environments.[119] This term refers to areas experiencing or recovering from unrest or instability, whether due to natural disasters or armed conflicts, where the rule of law has been substantially undermined, and in which the capacity of the state authority to handle the situation is diminished, limited or nonexistent.[120] Thus, the ICoC does not strive to apply in situations where the territorial state is willing and able to regulate PMSC conduct effectively, including by enforcing LOAC rules through the national legal system. Instead, it works in a complementary manner to national law. The ICoC, like the Montreux Document, does not create new rules but merely restates existing standards.

Though not strictly legal, there are a number of ways in which the ICoC is intended to become increasingly compelling.

First, the most powerful incentive to compliance stems from procurement policies of clients, meaning that clients require compliance with all provisions of the ICoC in service contracts. This will grant a competitive advantage to those companies willing to commit to the rules. The UN has already made membership of the ICoC a prerequisite to hire private security[121] but also private entities can do this and certain extractive companies have included similar demands in their procurement policy.

Including the obligation to comply with the ICoC in contracts with service providers has as a consequence – besides the loss of or exclusion from obtaining contracts – that a violation of

117 For an overview of national laws regarding PMSC regulation, see 'National Regulations' *Private Security Monitor* (undated), http://psm.du.edu/national_regulation.
118 See Guiding Principles (n 28); Report of the Special Representative of the Secretary-General (SRSG) on the Issue of Human Rights and Transnational Corporations and Other Business Enterprises, UN Doc A/HRC/4/035 (9 February 2007) ¶ 44.
119 ICoC (n 15) ¶ 13.
120 Ibid definitions.
121 UN Department of Safety and Security, Guidelines on the Use of Armed Security Services from Private Security Companies (8 November 2012), www.ohchr.org/Documents/Issues/Mercenaries/WG/StudyPMSC/GuidelinesOnUseOfArmedSecurityServices.pdf.

human rights becomes a reason for contract litigation. Companies do have subjective legal personality under private law, and such litigation could have grave consequences for them.

Additionally, governments can require that the PMSCs they hire obtain ICoCA membership – as Switzerland has done[122] – making compliance with the ICoC provisions effectively an obligation under national law.

Last, there is the important reputational and marketing argument to become a member of the ICoC, as well as an ethical commitment increasingly recognised by companies. In a broader perspective, the development of such Codes of Conducts can, as all soft law, shape future legislation, by setting standards which are increasingly accepted as the norm, which can then be more easily incorporated in law. It raises standards as different corporations within the sector start complying with the Code and it becomes the norm for operations across the board.

As explained above, companies will be held to their commitment to implementation of the human rights and LOAC principles contained in the ICoC through the oversight of the ICoCA. If violations of standards of the ICoC are detected or when the company does not help find accessible and fair grievance mechanisms for victims of alleged violations, the ultimate sanction may be suspension or termination of membership by the ICoCA Board. If indeed clients require membership of the Association, this may have serious commercial loss as a consequence. A public statement of the outcome of ICoCA activities and in particular of suspension or termination of specific companies may influence how and which companies are awarded contracts, which will enforce the reputational incentive.[123]

4.2 Tort/civil liability

Under the current state of the law, corporations are not directly bound by international law, with the exception that companies can be held responsible for violations of *jus cogens* norms, since these impose direct obligations even on corporations.[124]

The lack of corporate accountability under international law has highlighted the possibilities of litigation in national legal systems. As corporations are not criminally liable in many states, focus has turned to civil liability. In order to bring a civil suit, however, a violation of human rights law or LOAC[125] must be framed as a tort or wrongful act under national law, or the capacity to apply rules of international law must have been granted to the national courts, such as under the US Alien Tort Statute (ATS) (discussed below).

---

122 Loi Fédérale sur les Prestations de Sécurité Privées Fournies à l'Étranger [Federal Law on Private Security Services provided Abroad] (27 September 2013), www.admin.ch/opc/fr/federal-gazette/2013/6577.pdf.

123 ICoC Articles of Association (n 19) art 12.2.9.

124 Report of the Independent International Commission of Inquiry on the Syrian Arab Republic, UN Doc A/HRC/19/69 (22 February 2012) ¶ 106; International Law Association, 'Non-State Actors in International Law: Aims, Approach and Scope of Project and Legal Issues' (2010) 17, ¶ 3.2; John Ruggie, 'Promotion and Protection of All Human Rights, Civil, Political, Economic, Social and Cultural Rights, Including the Right to Development: Protect, Respect and Remedy: A Framework for Business and Human Rights' Report of the Special Representative of the Secretary-General on the Issue of Human Rights and Transnational Corporations and Other Business Enterprises, UN Doc A/HRC/8/5 (7 April 2008) (2008 Ruggie Report). See for discussions, Cedric Ryngaert, 'Litigating Abuses Committed by Private Military Companies' (2008) 19 *EJIL* 1038; Clapham (n 116).

125 For an analysis of liability in tort based on LOAC, see Eric Mongelard, 'Corporate Civil Liability for Violations of International Humanitarian Law' (2006) 88(863) *IRRC* 665.

Litigation in the territorial state of the violation – normally a state facing serious security challenges – has obvious difficulties.[126] While filing a civil claim in the home or hiring state of the company may seem more feasible, problems may still arise from the often limited extra-territorial jurisdiction of courts in torts cases. The dearth of successful civil litigation against PMSCs on the national level can be explained in large part by these limitations of national litigation.[127]

One example of tort liability at the national level has been the recent attempts to use the US ATS[128] to hold transnational corporations accountable for violations of international law that have occurred outside the US.[129] ATS creates universal civil jurisdiction for violations of 'the law of nations'. In this way, foreign torts in violation of international law, international human rights in particular, can be prosecuted, irrespective of where the violation took place. However, in a 2013 decision the US Supreme Court ruled that the ATS could not be used on companies merely having a presence in the US, and that there was a presumption against extraterritoriality.[130] The precedent value of this ruling remains to be seen but already seems to have some resonance in the case of a PMSC allegedly involved in the Abu-Ghraib abuses.[131] Recent lawsuits in Canada brought by foreign plaintiffs against Canadian mining companies for the omission to prevent alleged human rights abuses committed by their private security contractors abroad, have created new possibilities to hold corporate entities responsible. The Ontario Superior Court of Justice held in *Choc v Hudbay Minerals Inc* that public statements and commitments to corporate social responsibility (CSR) and international norms like the Voluntary Principles on Security and Human Rights can be used to establish a novel duty of care and thus trigger corporate liability for negligence.[132] In the same decision the court has also signalled a potential shift with regards to the issue of jurisdiction over torts committed by a company's foreign subsidiary, in this case by a PMSC working for a Guatemalan subsidiary of a Canadian company. Previously, jurisdiction was often rejected in these situations on the basis of the *forum non conveniens* doctrine.[133] The court's admission of the *Choc v Hudbay Minerals Inc* case has opened the door for similar cases to be brought before courts in Canada, reinforcing the pressure on

---

126 Courts may not be functioning, and immunities may be agreed for foreign companies, such as was the case in Iraq until 2009.

127 Complications regarding state sovereignty of place of occurrence, on gathering evidence in such environment and costs of finding it, cooperation between forum and territorial state, having violations reported/ detected at all.

128 28 USC § 1350, stating: 'The district courts shall have original jurisdiction of any civil action by an alien for a tort only, committed in violation of the law of nations or a treaty of the United States.'

129 A leading corporate ATS case is the case brought against the US corporation Unocal in relation to its activities in Burma/Myanmar. See *Doe I v Unocal Corp*, 963 F Supp 880 (CD Cal 1997); *National Coalition Government of the Union of Burma v Unocal*, 176 FRD 329 (CD Cal 1997); *Doe v Unocal Corp*, 27 F Supp 2d 1174 (CD Cal 1998), affirmed 248 F 3d 915 (2001); *Doe I v Unocal Corp*, 110 F Supp 2d 1294 (CD Cal 2000); *Doe I v Unocal Corp*, 395 F 3d 3932 (9th Cir 2002). Other cases brought under the ATCA include *Wiwa v Royal Dutch Shell Petroleum*, 626 F Supp 2d 377 (SDNY 2009); *Presbyterian Church of Sudan et al v Talisman Energy* Inc, 582 F 3d 244 (2nd Cir 2009); *Doe I v Nestle USA, Inc*, 766 F 3d 1013 (9th cir 2014).

130 *Kiobel v Royal Dutch Petroleum Co*, 569 US __, 133 S Ct 1659 (2013).

131 See *Al Shimari et al v CACI International Inc et al*, 758 F 3d 516 (4th Cir 2014).

132 *Choc v Hudbay Minerals Inc* [2013] ONSC 1414 ¶ 69. A non-governmental website has been created on the basis of this case to encourage Guatemalan victims to bring their cases before Canadian courts, www.chocversushudbay.com.

133 Susana Mijares Pena, 'Human Rights Violations by Canadian Companies Abroad: *Choc v Hudbay Minerals Inc.*' (2014) 5 *Western Journal of Legal Studies* fn 6.

Canadian companies to adopt appropriate risk management measures to ensure adherence to their CSR principles and international norms.[134]

5 Concluding remarks

The increasing use of private security services has not diminished the importance and applicability of LOAC rules in situations of armed conflict where these actors operate. However, the application of the law on PMSCs and their personnel is often not straightforward. This chapter looked both at the applicability of the traditional framework of LOAC, as well as at different new approaches and initiatives built on LOAC and human rights law which have been developed to clarify the applicable rules, or to find alternative ways to reach commitment of private actors to universally accepted standards of LOAC and human rights.

Going forward, the growing PMSC sector and the diversification of their services and activities will not make their regulation any easier. Application of LOAC rules and protections will depend, as always, on the status and the actions of the actor and the existence of an international or non-international armed conflict. For PMSC personnel this depends on a number of criteria which are not easily determined. New initiatives coming from an influx of the focus on business and human rights, such as the ICoCA, depend to a large extent on the willingness of the actors to accept the applicability of international rules, and the involvement of states to ensure compliance. For now, the engagement of the industry seems promising but much more global support of states and the clients of PMSCs is needed to ensure compliance by and oversight of the private security industry.

From an accountability perspective, developments within national legal systems may be most interesting, but development is slow.

This chapter makes clear that any lack in the governance and accountability of PMSCs is not so much caused by an absence of law, but rather by lack of a clarity surrounding the applicable rules or weaknesses in their implementation. Nevertheless, the assortment of laws, rules and initiatives should be seen together to form a patchwork of norms and standards applicable to PMSCs, no matter in what situation or jurisdiction they may find themselves.

---

134 Two similar lawsuits were filed in British Columbia. Like the first case, *Adolfo Agustín García et al v Tahoe Resources Inc* (2014) is a lawsuit brought by Guatemalan plaintiffs against human rights violations by private security personnel of a Canadian mining company operating in Guatemala. The third lawsuit, however, does not involve private security contractors as alleged perpetrators. Young Park and Rick Moscone, 'Commentary: The Shifting Liability Landscape for Canadian Miners Abroad' *Northern Miner* (29 April 2015), www.northernminer.com/news/commentary-the-shifting-liability-landscape-for-canadian-miners-abroad/1003596651/?&er=NA.

37

The rule of law in war

A liberal project

Louise Arimatsu

In October 2012, following an investigation by the Royal Military Police (RMP), the UK Service Prosecuting Authority (SPA) charged five Royal Marines on suspicion of murder in relation to an incident alleged to have taken place in Helmand, Afghanistan in 2011. The arrests came after a video was discovered on a laptop which appeared to show members of a patrol discussing whether to administer first aid to an injured Taliban fighter. The footage is said to cut out before anything happens; the RMP subsequently confirmed the man had died. Within two weeks of the arrests, a Facebook page, 'Free the 5 Royal Marines Charged with Murdering a Taliban Terrorist' had amassed over 25,000 supporters. Events in support of the defendants were arranged to take place in late October in Edinburgh, Swansea, Norwich and London. Commentaries posted on the Facebook site were incredulous as to why the Marines had been charged with murder: the dead man was an enemy insurgent and the soldiers were engaged in an armed conflict.

Albeit understandable, such sentiments are also troubling. For what they reveal is a lack of understanding as to the law that binds the parties to a conflict and, perhaps more significantly, the reasons upon which the rules are founded. The obligation to disseminate the law of armed conflict (LOAC) falls squarely on states although insofar as educating the general public is concerned, the duty on the part of the state is merely to 'encourage' its study.[1] In contrast, the state

---

1 Geneva Convention for the Amelioration of the Condition of the Wounded and Sick in Armies in the Field (6 July 1906) 202 CTS 144 art 26, and Convention for the Amelioration of the Condition of the Wounded and Sick in Armies in the Field (27 July 1929) 118 LNTS 303 art 27 required states to take the steps necessary to make the Conventions known to the population at large. GCI art 47, GCII art 48, GCIII art 127 and GCIV art 144, and the Hague Convention for the Protection of Cultural Property in the Event of Armed Conflict (14 May 1954) 249 UNTS 240 art 25 require states to include the study of international humanitarian law in their programmes of civilian training 'if possible'. API art 83 requires states to disseminate international humanitarian law as widely as possible and, in particular, to 'encourage the study thereof by the civilian population'. See CIHL commentary to r 143. Despite the rise in the number of universities offering courses on international humanitarian law at graduate level, the discipline continues to be dominated by the military lawyer, acting and retired.

must provide all members of its armed forces with instruction in the law.[2] Thus, for those familiar with the law of armed conflict, not least the soldier, it is common knowledge that a fighter who has been wounded or who is sick – and for *that* reason is *hors de combat*[3] – may *not* be the object of attack. The rule is binding by virtue of customary international law, applicable in international and non-international armed conflict alike, codified in numerous treaty provisions and found in the vast majority, if not all, military manuals.[4] This norm, which dates back to the nineteenth century, prohibits attacks on soldiers *hors de combat* for two distinct reasons. The first is inextricably linked to the logic of warfare itself, founded on the reasoning that since 'the only legitimate object which states should endeavour to accomplish during war is to weaken the military forces of the enemy',[5] there is simply no reason to kill an enemy soldier who is no longer able to participate in the hostilities. This reasoning cuts both ways since all armed forces will have a vested interest in upholding the rule if only to protect its own forces through reciprocal arrangements. Ethical considerations also shape the rule to the extent that it is not because the enemy is wounded but because he is incapable of defending himself that the obligation not to attack arises.[6] Thus the law insists that the soldier re-evaluates the wounded adversary not as part of the *collective* enemy but as an *individual* fellow human being and, in the event that he is no longer capable of defending himself, to treat him with humanity.

Most law of war experts would no doubt opine that this rule exemplifies the 'carefully thought out balance between the principles of military necessity and humanity' and that every

2 The duty of states to teach international humanitarian law to their armed forces was first codified in 1906 Geneva Convention (n 1) art 26 and 1929 Geneva Convention (n 1) art 27. It was subsequently restated in GCI art 47, GCII art 48, GCIII art 127, GCIV art 144, API art 83 and APII art 19, in the Convention for the Protection of Cultural Property (n 1) art 25 and its Second Protocol (26 March 1999) 2253 UNTS 212 art 30, and in CCW art 6, all of which specify that the obligation to teach international humanitarian law to armed forces applies in time of peace as in time of armed conflict. See CIHL commentary to r 142.
3 The literal translation is 'out of combat'. This would include those who do not take, or who no longer take, an active part in the hostilities.
4 The rule was recognised in the 1863 Lieber Code, the 1874 Brussels Declaration and the 1880 Oxford Manual. HR art 23(c) provides that it is especially forbidden 'to kill or wound an enemy who, having laid down his arms, or having no means of defence, has surrendered at discretion'. The prohibition extends to non-international armed conflict by virtue of GCI–IV common art 3 which states

> persons taking no active part in the hostilities, including members of armed forces who have laid down their arms and those placed 'hors de combat' by sickness, wounds, detention, or any other cause, shall in all circumstances be treated humanely, without any adverse distinction founded on race, colour, religion or faith, sex, birth or wealth, or any other similar criteria.

API art 41(1) prohibits attacks against persons recognised as *hors de combat* and art 85(3)(e) provides that such attacks constitute grave breaches of the Protocol. See also Rome Statute art 8(2)(b)(vi) and 8(2)(c). See also James P Benoit, 'Wounded and sick, and medical services' ch 18 in this volume.
5 Declaration Renouncing the Use, in Time of War, of Explosive Projectiles under 400 Grammes Weight ('St Petersburg Declaration') (11 December 1868) 138 CTS 297. See also *AP Commentary* ¶ 1605.
6 See also HR art 23(c) which prohibits especially the killing or wounding of an enemy who no longer has the means of defence. On the other hand, as the commentary to API art 41 makes clear, there is no obligation to abstain from attacking a wounded or sick person who is preparing to fire, or who is actually firing, regardless of the severity of his wounds or sickness: *AP Commentary* ¶ 1620.

rule 'constitutes a dialectical compromise between these two opposing forces'.[7] But even if a legally binding rule was not in place, should we (especially as external observers) not instinctively realise that there is a difference between killing an enemy in the heat of a battle and killing that same enemy if the control we exert over them is such that they are no longer even capable of defending themselves? Or does war and law reframe our perceptions to such a degree that it negates our ability to see the enemy as a fellow human being making judgments of this kind impossible, necessitating a rule?[8] Even the ICRC *Commentary* to the rule acknowledges that 'it would be useless to deny that in the heat of action and under the pressure of events, this rule is not always easy to follow'.[9] The law's unequivocal stance – that to kill or wound persons recognised as *hors de combat* is to commit a war crime – is reassuring and perplexing in equal measure.

It is not uncommon for the parties to a conflict to cross the line between permissible and impermissible behaviour prompting many a cynic to cite the adage attributed to Cicero, *inter arma silent leges*.[10] Blanket criticisms of this sort, whether as a commentary on the lack of man's moral fortitude in situations of extreme adversity or on the law's lack of purchase, nevertheless do not entirely correspond with all contemporary conflicts. Complete disregard for the rules of war may still afflict some wars but this is far from the case in many other conflict situations. In these juridified spaces, belligerents are as keen to claim full compliance with the law of armed conflict as they are to winning the war.[11] As with peace, war too – we are repeatedly reminded – is governed by law and violations will not be tolerated.[12]

In this chapter I suggest that the densely legislated landscape within which contemporary wars are fought is both a symptom and expression of liberalism's insistence on governance by law.[13] To bridge the gap between the fact of war and liberal philosophy – which is inimical to war[14] – liberal states have turned to law weaving their political priorities, in form and content, through the *jus in bello*. In the first section I reflect on the way in which some of liberalism's core principles, including the very notion of the rule of law, have been integrated into LOAC.[15] This process has been disjointed and marked by doubt, partiality and uncertainty each of which finds expression in the law itself. Liberalism's predilection for law often places it in difficulty when

---

7 Michael Schmitt, 'Military Necessity and Humanity in International Humanitarian Law: Preserving the Delicate Balance' (2010) 50 *Virginia JIL* 798. Schmitt notes that 'at times the express or inherent balance between military necessity and humanity may appear illogical, such that one or other ought to be invoked to rebalance an existing rule'. Nevertheless, he continues, 'irrational as it may seem, the rule reflects a *de jure* balance between military necessity and humanity. No adjustment is permissible.' Cf Nobuo Hayashi, 'Basic principles' ch 5 in this volume.

8 As Walzer candidly notes, 'soldiers cannot endure modern warfare for long without blaming someone for their pain and suffering'. Michael Walzer, *Just and Unjust Wars: A Moral Argument with Historical Illustrations* (4th edn, Basic Books 2006) 36.

9 *AP Commentary* ¶ 1601.

10 Translated as 'in times of war, law is silent'.

11 See generally Dale Stephens, 'The Age of Lawfare' in Raul Pedrozo and Daria P Wollschlaeger (eds), *International Law and the Changing Character of War* (US Naval War College 2011) 327.

12 For example, it is now part of the UN Security Council's language when adopting resolutions in respect of conflict situations to remind the parties as to their international humanitarian law obligations.

13 This trend applies to all fields of international law and is not confined to LOAC.

14 Liberal states 'are not at ease with military adventures [since] war of its very nature involves attacks on life ... and it encourages a warrior ethos that draws upon non-liberal motivations'. However, it does not follow that liberals are pacifists. Leverhulme War Programme – Reading University, 'Liberal Wars: Strategy, History, Ideology', www.reading.ac.uk/spirs/Leverhulme/Liberalwars.aspx.

15 Geoffrey Best, *War & Law since 1945* (Clarendon 2002) 9.

confronted by the law's normative contradictions. This theme is taken up in the second section which examines how LOAC is constructed on a series of artificial separations that are perpetually on the brink of collapse. Mediation between conflicting norms often takes the form of strategies that insist on deferring to the technical experts who represent the promise of objectivity and certainty that the law fails to deliver. This always means that the law is never random or contingent. In the final section I suggest that the anxiety generated by LOAC is as much about compliance as non-compliance and explore how this fact is mediated within liberal societies.

1 Liberal ideology and the law of armed conflict: from form to substance

The interaction between law and war has long captivated thinkers from a broad spectrum of disciplines principally because the law's *raison d'être* is to facilitate social peace.[16] Not only is law a means by which to secure peace, it is also regarded as an alternative to war.[17] As Judith Shklar notes, the ultimate spiritual and political struggle is always based on the simple dichotomy between war and law.[18] In view of the fact that law is typically juxtaposed to war, the regulation of war by law – which unavoidably functions to constitute the very violence that in all other respects the law seeks to prohibit – is often regarded as a misnomer. The observation that the law is normalising the very barbarity that it is meant to shun is a critique that is difficult to contest.[19] For the liberal, the disquiet that is aroused by the *jus in bello* is precisely because its aim is to 'channel' rather than to displace violence. Unable to rebuff the criticism but equally unable to transcend violence, liberal states embrace the juridification[20] of war, despite the paradox, insisting on rule-abidance as the *only* way to engage in warfare.

To dismiss the idea of the 'rule of law' in war as an oxymoron is both hasty and counterproductive since whether it is possible to speak of the rule of law in the context of war is contingent on what the term entails. The widespread usage of the phrase would indicate that there is a common understanding as to its content. Yet even a cursory examination of the literature soon

16 See eg Immanuel Kant who maintained that 'the establishment of peace constitutes, not a part of, but the whole purpose of the doctrine of law'. Cited by Francisoco Contreras and Ignacio de la Rasilla, 'On War as Law and Law as War' (2008) 21 *Leiden JIL* 765.

17 The notion of 'lawfare' has prompted a series of polemical exchanges on this topic. See generally the special issue on 'Lawfare!' (2010) 43 (1&2) *Case Western Reserve JIL* 1.

18 Judith N Shklar, 'Political Theory and the Rule of Law' in Judith N Shklar, *Political Thought and Political Thinkers* (Stanley Hoffmann ed, University of Chicago Press 1998) 25.

19 Nathaniel Berman argues that 'rather than opposing violence, the legal construction of war serves to channel violence into certain forms of activity engaged in by certain kinds of people, while excluding other forms engaged in by other people'. Nathaniel Berman, 'Privileging Combat? Contemporary Conflict the Legal Construction of War' (2004) 43 *Columbia JTL* 5.

20 The expression 'juridification' [*Verrechtlichung*] refers quite generally to the tendency towards an increase in formal (or positive, written) law that can be observed in modern society. We can distinguish here between the *expansion* of law, that is, the legal regulation of new, hitherto informally regulated social matters, from the *increasing density* of law, that is, the specialized breakdown of global statements of the legally relevant facts [*Rechtstatbestände*] into more detailed statements.
Jürgen Habermas, *The Theory of Communicative Action* (Beacon 1987) ii, 359

dispels this myth.[21] As scholars writing on the rule of law have acknowledged, one intrinsic problem with the idea is that it has many varied definitions. Although its origin can be traced back to the days of Aristotle,[22] extant understandings of the concept are founded on the principles embedded in liberal orthodoxy which surfaced during the Enlightenment period.[23] The recognition that man was born free and equal – a realisation derived from a rejection of the principles of natural justice – engendered the belief that to prevent arbitrary decisions founded on naked power, individual rights could best be protected by the equal application of the law to citizens and sovereign alike. Liberalism's faith in the rule of law is therefore rooted in its aversion to the tyrannical ruler who would otherwise 'take pleasure from the degradation of those unfortunate enough to be subject to their will'.[24] This reading of the rule of law 'implies no commitment regarding the content of the norms thereby established or the character of the society advanced'[25] since the law's exclusive concern is with constraining power. However, what is required by this 'thin' version of the rule of law is for the laws to be made public, properly enacted, non-retrospective and government – and, in the case of war, governance – by law.[26]

If tyranny presents liberalism with its paramount concern in peace, in conflict the anxiety induced is that much more acute since war always gives rise to a power *over* others. The recognition that it is particularly when individuals fall under the control of the adversary in times of war that a tyrannical relationship is likely to materialise, manifests itself in the plethora of rules that form the bedrock of 'Geneva law'.[27] Described as comprising those rules which provide

---

21 There is a considerable body of literature addressing the rule of law at the national level but comparatively little that engages with the concept as it applies to the international level. This is all the more surprising given the considerable resources that have been allocated to the pursuit of the rule of law by the UN system. There has been some scholarly debate as to whether the rule of law has any place at the international level given its origins within the domestic realm; see eg James Crawford, 'International Law and the Rule of Law' (2003) 24 *Adelaide LR* 5 and Jeremy Waldron, 'Are Sovereigns Entitled to the Benefit of the International Rule of Law?' (2011) 22 *EJIL* 323. Nevertheless, objections to the transplanting of the doctrine are in some respects overstated and might be set aside if the rule of law is understood as a means by which to constrain arbitrary power between states as much as by states. At the international level the rule of law is seen as offering the prospect of enhanced predictability in the relations between states and to that extent, distinguished from, and for that reason preferred to, politics. See J Blum, 'Critical Legal Studies and the Rule of Law' (1990) 38 *Buffalo* 59, 94.

22 See eg Judith Shklar on Aristotle's conception of the rule of law which is nothing more than the rule of reason. Shklar, 'Political Theory and the Rule of Law' (n 18). See also Blandine Kriegel, *The State and the Rule of Law* (Marc A LePain and Jeffrey C Cohen trs, Princeton University Press 1995).

23 Although liberalism was influenced by many of the ideas that emerged during the Enlightenment, the two should not be confused since the latter also produced ideas that were conservative and illiberal. For some leading commentaries on the rule of law, see A V Dicey, *Introduction to the Study of the Law of the Constitution* (Macmillan 1885); Ronald Dworkin, 'Political Judges and the Rule of Law' in Ronald Dworkin, *A Matter of Principle* (Harvard University Press 1985); John Finnis, *Natural Law and Natural Rights* (OUP 1980); Lon L Fuller, *The Morality of Law* (Yale University Press 1964); John Rawls, *A Theory of Justice* (Harvard University Press 1971); Brian Tamanaha, *On the Rule of Law: History, Politics, Theory* (CUP 2004).

24 David Luban, 'Liberalism, Torture, and the Ticking Bomb' (2005) 91 *Virginia LR* 1433.

25 Martti Koskenniemi, 'The Politics of International Law' (1990) 1 *EJIL* 27.

26 Joseph Raz, 'The Rule of Law and its Virtue' in Joseph Raz (ed), *The Authority of Law: Essays on Law and Morality* (OUP 1977).

27 The international law of armed conflict originally developed along two theoretical lines comprising 'Hague law' and 'Geneva law'. The former regulates the use of force in armed conflict while the latter is concerned with protecting the sick, wounded and shipwrecked, civilians and prisoners of war. With the adoption of the API and APII, the two bodies of law were merged. As a consequence, most of the literature since then has not distinguished between the two.

'legal protection of human beings against violence and abuse of power'[28] this extensively codified branch of law is concerned primarily with the treatment of *enemy* civilians and soldiers *hors de combat*. The Geneva Conventions are a concession to liberalism's fear of unadulterated power that war portends. The insistence by liberal states on the governance of war by law is thus predicated on the need to distinguish between legitimate and illegitimate exercise of power, if only to curb arbitrary and despotic rule whether by the enemy or by its own hands. It is precisely because those deemed *hors de combat* are at the complete mercy of the enemy that liberal ideology insists on governance by law. A second conception of the rule of law is one that emphasises the existence of institutions that are legally mandated to uphold and enforce the substantive rules. Under this rubric, a body with the power to enforce coupled with an independent judiciary to apply the law uniformly, fairly and without discrimination, serve as the cornerstone of the concept.[29]

Measured against both the 'thin' and the 'institutional' version of the rule of law, it would appear that the contemporary law of armed conflict is moving in the direction of being reconstituted as an international legal regime founded on the rule of law, albeit in its nascent stage. It is certainly one of the most – if not *the* most – codified branches of international law and treaty rules are increasingly supplemented by ever-bourgeoning customary international law, soft law instruments, codes of conduct and domestic law. Not only have the vast majority of states ratified and incorporated into national law the core instruments that comprise the law of armed conflict,[30] the rules themselves are for the most part publicly promulgated, properly enacted, non-retrospective and accepted as binding on all parties irrespective as to the reasons for war. Insofar as enforcement is concerned, significant challenges still remain. That said, the last two decades have witnessed a proliferation of international, regional and domestic courts and tribunals with jurisdiction to scrutinise the conduct of states and of individuals and to penalise for non-compliance. These developments have propelled an unprecedented turn to law in war and, with it, the revival of one of liberalism's most ambitious projects, international criminal justice. In today's wars the conduct of the belligerents, be they members of the armed forces or organised armed groups, are increasingly judged by reference to legal rules. Conformity with the law is concurrently assessed by UN bodies, the human rights machinery, fact-finding commissions, expert groups, NGOs, the global media, academic and social commentators, and the public. Against this backdrop, it is the liberal state that eagerly claims legitimacy as to their cause through a rhetoric that champions strict adherence to the rules.[31] The inescapable consequence of this liberal agenda is that if the rule of law is to have any traction, liberal societies have no option but to investigate alleged transgressions by its own agents when confronted by evidence that suggests a breach of a rule.

Notwithstanding these developments, for liberal societies, the rule of law has always been more than the operation of certain mechanisms and practices and more than a normative influence on its self-characterisation that rule abidance is a moral way of being in the world.[32]

---

28 Hans-Peter Gasser, 'Protection of the Civilian Population' in Dieter Fleck (ed), *The Handbook of International Humanitarian Law* (2nd edn, OUP 2008) 237.

29 As with the thin version of the rule of law, the institutional version does not require any allegiance to a particular substantive content. These theories have been criticised for having stripped the concept of its original political objectives enabling those holding quite disparate and antithetical views to justify their respective positions by invoking the rule of law without any risk of incoherence.

30 For a useful database, see RULAC, 'Rule of Law in Armed Conflicts Project', www.geneva-academy. ch/RULAC/index.php.

31 See generally Stephens (n 11).

32 Christopher May, 'The Rule of Law and International Political Economy: Starting a Conversation' (2007) 28 *Zeitschrift für Rechtssoziologie* 179.

The most widely held idea of the rule of law in contemporary literature embodies a 'thicker' content in that it encompasses substantive rights, more commonly expressed in the language of human rights law. The content of the rules matters in that the rules are expected to correspond with notions of justice and to further liberalism's core political values, freedom and liberty.[33] Although this version of the rule of law does not fully correspond with the more limited aims of the law of armed conflict, what *is* indisputable is that liberalism's values have nonetheless shaped both the direction and content of the law of armed conflict principally by way of the concepts of 'humanity' and 'dignity' and through liberalism's aversion to cruelty.

The law of war, it is often maintained, is ancient in origin. While that may indeed be the case, the law that we recognise today finds its roots in the mid-nineteenth century with the emergence of international law more broadly as a liberal-internationalist project.[34] Both the Lieber Code, which ultimately led to the evolution of Hague law, and Henry Dunant's *A Memory of Solferino*, which inspired the development of Geneva law, are expressions of an evolutionary liberalism in which humanity as 'a positive normative principle'[35] was first invoked to constrain the conduct of belligerents and to offer some protection to the 'victims' of armed conflict.[36] Over the years, the principle of humanity has prompted the adoption of what is now a significant body of codified law while even a cursory review of contemporary customary international law reveals the extent to which humanitarian considerations are deeply entrenched within the substantive rules.[37] Although states may dispute the customary status of a rule or voice deep ambivalence as to whether a treaty provision exhibits an acceptable balance between

---

33 More recent adaptations by the UN reveal aspirations that attempt to go beyond formalising the relations between states through legal rules although a commitment to a substantive agenda at the international level remains sketchy at best. In practice, what this translates into is a programme directed at strengthening existing international institutions complemented by an agenda that is geared towards encouraging states to sign up to, ratify and implement their treaty obligations. In contrast, the UN's agenda at the national level incorporates a 'thicker' version of the rule of law in which human rights and justice takes centre stage and where assistance is extended – perhaps controversially but unavoidably – on the potential of recipient communities to assimilate liberal values. As defined by the UN, the international rule of law is

> a principle of governance in which all persons, institutions and entities, public and private, including the State itself, are accountable to laws that are publicly promulgated, equally enforced and independently adjudicated, and which are consistent with international human rights norms and standards. It requires, as well, measures to ensure adherence to the principles of supremacy of law, equality before the law, accountability to the law, fairness in the application of the law, separation of powers, participation in decisionmaking, legal certainty, avoidance of arbitrariness and procedural and legal transparency.
>
> The Rule of Law and Transitional Justice in Conflict and Post-Conflict Societies:
> Report of the Secretary-General, UN Doc S/2004/616 (23 August 2004)

34 Martti Koskenniemi, *The Gentle Civilizer of Nations: The Rise and Fall of International Law 1870–1960* (CUP 2008) 11–97.

35 Matthew Zagor, 'Elementary Considerations of Humanity' *Australian National University College of Law Research Paper* No 12-19 (2011) 13, http://papers.ssrn.com/sol3/papers.cfm?abstract_id=2089115.

36 Theodore Meron, 'The Humanisation of Humanitarian Law' (2000) 94 *AJIL* 245. The trend to 'humanise' the law during the first 100 years was not an all-inclusive movement since there were vast numbers of peoples – namely those populations subject to colonial rule – who simply did not fall within the purview of even the most reputable humanitarians of the day. For a critical view, see Burrus Carnhan, 'Lincoln, Lieber and the Laws of War: the Origins and Limits of the Principle of Military Necessity' (1998) 92 *AJIL* 213–231.

37 Commenting on the balance between humanity and military necessity, Schmitt argues: 'since the nineteenth century, [international humanitarian law] has moved steadily in the direction of humanity and away from that of military necessity.' Michael Schmitt, 'Military Necessity and Humanity' (n 7) 805.

military necessity and humanity, what is not questioned is that the rules must be penned to take account of the principle of humanity.[38]

In spite of the fact that liberalism takes many different political forms and has given rise to numerous theoretical positions that diverge significantly,[39] central to its political philosophy is the concept of human dignity. Although the notion of human dignity is more typically associated with human rights law, its presence in the law of armed conflict is irrefutable principally at the moment when an individual falls into the hands of the enemy. As already noted, in such situations the law of armed conflict demands that the state – and more specifically the soldier who acts on its behalf – regard the enemy as an individual and, in so doing, treat them humanely[40] and without discrimination.[41] The concept of human dignity is the implicit bedrock upon which many of the rules on the conditions of internment are founded in respect of both combatants and civilians.

The vice that liberalism ranks the most vicious among all, is cruelty.[42] This is not, as David Luban explains, because liberals are more compassionate but because of the close connection between cruelty and tyranny.[43] The abhorrence of cruelty is 'a powerful part of the liberal consciousness'[44] and manifests itself in the shape of many of the absolute prohibitions contained in the law of armed conflict[45] including the prohibition on torture, cruel or inhuman treatment[46] and starving the civilian population as a method of warfare.[47] It also appears in the guise of two 'cardinal' principles identified by the ICJ that govern the conduct of hostilities: the prohibition on the use of means and methods of warfare which are of a nature to cause superfluous injury or unnecessary suffering and the prohibition on the use of weapons that are by nature

---

38 In contrast, consider the doctrine of *Kriegsraison geht vor Kriegsmanier* (necessity in war overrules the manner of warfare). On the doctrine of *Kriegsraison*, see Geoffrey Best, *Humanity in Warfare: The Modern History of the International Law of Armed Conflicts* (Routledge 1983) 172–179.

39 See Ronald Dworkin, 'Liberalism' in Ronald Dworkin, *A Matter of Principle* (Harvard University Press 2000) 181.

40 The obligation to treat prisoners of war humanely was recognised in the 1863 Lieber Code, the 1874 Brussels Declaration and the 1880 Oxford Manual and codified in HR art 4. The requirement of humane treatment for civilians and person *hors de combat* is also provided in GCI–IV common art 3, GCI art 12, GCII art 12, GCIII art 13, GCIV arts 5 and 27. It is recognised as a fundamental guarantee in API art 75(1) and APII art 4(1). It is regarded as binding under customary international law and reproduced in CIHL r 87.

41 The prohibition is codified in GCI–IV common art 3, GCI art 12, GCII art 12, GCIII art 16, GCIV art 13.

42 Judith Shklar, *Ordinary Vices* (Harvard University Press 1984) 8.

43 David Luban, 'Liberalism, Torture, and the Ticking Bomb' (2005) 91 *Virginia LR* 1438.

44 Shklar, *Ordinary Vices* (n 42) 43.

45 Lieber Code art 16 specifically states,

> Military necessity does not admit of cruelty – that is, the infliction of suffering for the sake of suffering or for revenge, nor of maiming or wounding except in fight, nor of torture to extort confessions. It does not admit of the use of poison in any way, nor of the wanton devastation of a district.

46 GCI–IV common art 3 prohibits 'cruel treatment and torture' and 'outrages upon personal dignity, in particular humiliating and degrading treatment' of civilians and persons *hors de combat*. Torture and cruel treatment are also prohibited by specific provisions of the four Geneva Conventions while 'torture or inhuman treatment' and 'wilfully causing great suffering or serious injury to body or health' constitute grave breaches of GCI–IV and are war crimes under the Rome Statute. The prohibition of torture and outrages upon personal dignity, in particular humiliating and degrading treatment, is recognised as a fundamental guarantee for civilians and persons *hors de combat* by API and APII.

47 API art 54(1).

indiscriminate.[48] Both prohibitions, which are binding on all states by virtue of their customary international law status, serve as the basis upon which a series of concrete rules are founded[49] and have been instrumental in inspiring and shaping treaties to prohibit and limit the use of certain weapons.[50] The prohibition on unnecessary suffering can be traced to the sentiment first expressed in the preamble to the 1868 St Petersburg Declaration that it would be 'contrary to the laws of humanity' to employ arms which 'uselessly aggravate the sufferings of disabled men, or render their death inevitable' since the purpose of military operations is to weaken the military forces of the enemy. If a weapon or the particular use of a weapon causes aggravated suffering with no identifiable military advantage, the suffering inflicted cannot be anything other than unadulterated cruelty.[51] Likewise, the prohibition on indiscriminate weapons functions to prevent, as far as possible, the civilian population from being exposed to unnecessary suffering.[52]

Liberalism's insistence on war by law assumes a foundation of determinate rules framed within a coherent legal system.[53] In the following section I examine the ways in which the law is plagued by and manages uncertainty and indeterminacy and reflect on how the law of armed conflict insists on maintaining its artificial separations to preserve its coherence.[54] The level of ambiguity and incoherence that permeates this body of law is, I suggest, symptomatic of liberalism's disjointed engagement with the law of armed conflict that derives principally from a resignation that to humanise violence is to admit to a failed ambition to transcend violence.

2 Disjunctions

Liberalism's fidelity to the law as a preferable institutional practice over the arbitrariness of politics often serves to minimalise the problems associated with the law's indeterminacy.[55] This feature of the law is particularly alarming for the armed forces which depend upon clarity and certainty as to the law's substance since only then can internal coherence and principled external engagement be maintained. It is therefore not surprising that the law of war is dominated by

48 *Legality of the Threat or Use of Nuclear Weapons (Advisory Opinion)* [1996] ICJ Reports 226, ¶ 78.

49 See eg HR art 23(e) and API art 35(2). It should be emphasised that although LOAC is often expressed in the form of principles, the principles translate into a collection of concrete rules.

50 For example, the prohibition on the use of chemical and biological weapons in the Protocol for the Prohibition of the Use of Asphyxiating, Poisonous or Other Gases, and of Bacteriological Methods of Warfare (17 June 1925) 94 LNTS 65 was originally motivated by this rule.

51 Since attacking civilians is unlawful per se, this prohibition applies to combatants and those taking a direct part in the hostilities.

52 API art 51(4).

53 Coherence is valued because of its connection with predictability and 'only a coherent legal system treats legal subjects equally'; Fragmentation of International Law: Difficulties arising from the Divergence and Expansion of International Law – Report of the Study Group of the International Law Commission: Finalized by Martti Koskenniemi (13 April 2006) UN Doc A/CN.4/L.682, ¶ 491 ('Fragmentation report').

54 Normative conflict is 'endemic' to international law and not an exclusive problem associated with LOAC. 'Lawyers have always had to deal with heterogeneous materials at different levels of generality and with different normative force' as a consequence of the 'spontaneous, decentralized and hierarchical nature of international law-making'. Fragmentation report (n 53) ¶ 486.

55 It is often assumed that law is objective in the sense that it is independent from politics. The law's independence and validity rests on its concreteness and its normativity, but as Koskenniemi has repeatedly shown, on close scrutiny it is impossible to prove that a rule, principle or doctrine is simultaneously both concrete and normative. Koskenniemi, 'The Politics of International Law' (n 25). For a useful critique on the untenable claims to objectivity and formalism by the law, see Roberto Unger, 'The Critical Legal Studies Movement' (1982) 96 *Harvard LR* 561.

specialists who have a tendency to recite the rules with an unmatched certitude founded on dichotomies that give the law a coherent structure. Emphasis is placed on the need to distinguish between war and peace, between international and non-international armed conflict, between combatant and civilian, between military objective and civilian object, between an enemy fighter and person *hors de combat*, since the relevant rules are contingent on such judgments. Repetition of the law's bifurcated edifice dominates the discipline as does the rigorous formulaic mode of analysis shrouding a reality that is ambiguous, uncertain and unstable. On occasion, war does present easy situations within which judgment can be made. Often, however, conflict gives rise to difficult situations – factual and legal – exemplified by the disagreements over how to distinguish between civilians and those who take a direct part in the hostilities; between non-international armed conflict and 'internationalised' non-international armed conflict; between civilian objects and military objectives.

These separations – the very credentials upon which the law is founded – are perpetually on the brink of collapse since even the distinction between war and peace that determines whether LOAC applies is clouded by uncertainty.[56] Take for example, Common Article 2 of the 1949 Geneva Conventions which sets forth the conditions for the applicability of the Conventions and provides:

> The present Convention shall apply to all cases of declared war or of any other armed conflict which may arise between two or more of the High Contracting Parties even if the state of war is not recognized by one of them. The Convention shall also apply to all cases of partial or total occupation of the territory of a High Contracting Party, even if the said occupation meets with no armed resistance.[57]

Prior to the adoption of the Conventions, the applicability of the law was, for the most part, contingent on the arbitrary decisions of states based on political interests. Since the purpose of the treaties was to ensure maximum protection for the victims of war, the ambition of the drafters was to integrate into the text an objective test – the existence of an armed conflict – that would operationalise the law regardless of what states claimed. Over the years, the ICRC has consistently maintained that '[a]ny difference arising between two States and leading to the intervention of armed forces is an armed conflict ... [irrespective of] how long the conflict lasts, or how much slaughter takes place'.[58] Despite (and because there is) agreement as to the customary international law status of the article, the frequent practice on the part of states to dismiss incidents involving uses of force as 'sporadic border clashes' or 'isolated naval incidents' and therefore not to constitute armed conflict exposes the law to the damning critique that it is nothing but a rhetorical gesture. That the very applicability of the law of armed conflict remains

---

56 If a declaration of war once offered guidance as to the existence of an armed conflict operationalising the law of armed conflict, today, that practice is almost obsolete.

57 GCI–IV common art 2.

58 *GCI Commentary* 32. The ICRC *Commentary* to API art 1 reads,

> humanitarian law also covers any dispute between two States involving the use of their armed forces. Neither the duration of the conflict, nor its intensity, play a role: the law must be applied to the fullest extent required by the situation of the persons and objects protected by it.
>
> *AP Commentary* ¶ 62

See also Christopher Greenwood, 'Scope of Application of Humanitarian Law' in Dieter Fleck (ed), *The Handbook of International Humanitarian Law* (2nd edn, OUP 2008) s 201. In contrast, see International Law Association's, 'Final Report on the Meaning of Armed Conflict in International Law' (2010).

contingent on a political judgment – reframed as a threshold question – is hugely troubling for the armed forces given the differences between the legal regimes governing war and peace.[59] The inability of the law of armed conflict to distinguish between war and peace without dissolving into politics is emblematic of a trait that pervades this body of law.

The normative inconsistencies that have been engendered as a consequence of liberalism's unabashed faith in both the production of law and the rule of law are demonstrated most clearly by the relationship between the law of armed conflict and human rights law which also finds its roots in the liberal tradition of thought. The tension between the need to distinguish the two regimes[60] (since that is the very basis upon which the law is founded) and the recognition that they are concurrently applicable, foreclosing the ability to separate, exposes – once again – the law's failure to differentiate between war and peace.[61] The concerns expressed by law of war experts are by and large founded on an anxiety that inadequate attention has been accorded to the extension of human rights law into war that seems to collapse peacetime law into war. These anxieties are not without merit since the conflation of the two regimes has likewise enabled wartime law to collapse into peace, to the dismay of many.[62]

As a progressive liberal project, the presence of human rights law in armed conflict has brought huge rewards. It has pioneered new opportunities through which accountability, redress and justice can be realised;[63] sovereign power can be contested and decisions made during armed conflict that have hitherto remained beyond scrutiny can now be challenged. Nevertheless, for legal advisers to the armed forces and the executive branch the prospect that both legal regimes can apply concurrently has introduced a troubling element of ambiguity that seems to fly in the face of the rule of law itself. Diverging rules makes reconciliation sometimes impossible while judicial decisions have not always contributed to the clarification of the already nebulous relationship between the two legal regimes.[64] Against this backdrop, further complications arise in respect of multinational operations in that individual troop contributing countries have different treaty obligations and views on the customary international law credentials of some rules. In a bid to contain accusations of non-compliance and to 'resolve' the conflict of norm problem, law of war experts are increasingly invoking the *lex specialis* argument as a strategy to reintroduce a separation between the legal regimes. At the same time specialists in the human rights field are familiarising themselves with the language of their competitors in an attempt to shape the discourse through legal

---

59 Charles Garraway, 'To Kill or Not to Kill? Dilemmas on the Use of Force' (2010) 17 *JCSL* 1.

60 In a seminal article which appeared in *AJIL* over a decade ago, Judge Theodor Meron described how the law of armed conflict, 'driven to a large extent by human rights and the principles of humanity' was undergoing radical change. This was most apparent in the ways in which LOAC was evolving from one conceived as an interstate regime to one that allowed for an individual-rights perspective. Despite his general optimism, Meron cautions against conflating the two regimes noting that given the divergent assumptions upon which each body of law is constituted, to speak of the humanisation of humanitarian law was, in many ways, a contradiction in terms. Meron (n 36) 239.

61 *Legal Consequences of the Construction of a Wall in the Occupied Territory (Advisory Opinion)* [2004] ICJ Reports 136, ¶¶ 105–106.

62 For example, consider the disputes over the lawfulness of targeted killings in geographical locations that are not regarded as conflict zones.

63 For example, see the case of *Al-Skeini and Others v UK* (App no 55721/07, ECtHR, 7 July 2011).

64 Jelena Pejic, 'The ECtHR's *Al-Jedda* Judgment: Implications for IHL' (2011) 14 *YIHL* 1237. In contrast to the critical approach adopted by Pejic, claims by other scholars that commanders who are unable to fulfil their legal obligations will simply disregard the law and therefore put civilians at greater risk are not only overstated but counter-productive.

argument.[65] These experts nevertheless resist adopting the structural reasoning of the competing regime in the knowledge that therein lies the catch: to reason as the other is already to lose the argument although to assimilate *only* the vocabulary is to risk being consigned to the periphery.[66]

Indeterminacy and incoherence present particular problems for the law of armed conflict but this does not necessarily mean that the law is random or, for that matter, contingent, since ambiguity is often resolved by deferring judgment to the technocrat. In other words, the law's outcomes are more predictable than imagined not as a consequence of legal doctrine but because there is a relinquishing of judgment to the technician whose opinions always involve an oscillation between determined possibilities. Take, for example, the judgment of the ICTY in the case of *Prosecutor v Gotovina*[67] which centred on Croatia's military offensive in August 1995 to re-take territory which was then under the control of Serbia. In April 2011, the ICTY Trial Chamber found the defendants guilty of the crimes of persecution, deportation and forcible transfer of the civilian population based predominantly, although not exclusively, on its determination that the artillery attacks by the Croatian armed forces were unlawful and essentially a means by which to ethnically cleanse the region of the Serbian population. Pivotal to the case was the legal question of whether the artillery attacks by the Croatian armed forces violated the prohibition on indiscriminate attacks and were therefore unlawful attacks on civilians and civilian objects.[68]

The prohibition on indiscriminate attacks is derived from and represents an implementation of the principle of distinction.[69] The rule's customary international law status is indisputable as is its applicability both to international and to non-international armed conflict.[70] Article 51(4) of Additional Protocol I sets forth the rule in no uncertain terms with the simple statement that 'indiscriminate attacks are prohibited'. The article does not end there in that it further elaborates on what constitutes indiscriminate attacks which are defined as:

(a) those which are not directed at a specific military objective;

(b) those which employ a method or means of combat which cannot be directed at a specific military objective; or

(c) those which employ a method or means of combat the effects of which cannot be limited as required by this Protocol;

and consequently, in each such case, are of a nature to strike military objectives and civilians or civilian objects without distinction.[71]

---

65 For example, see Human Rights Watch, 'Losing Humanity: The Case against Killer Robots' (November 2012) and the response by Michael Schmitt 'Autonomous Weapon Systems and International Humanitarian Law: A Reply to the Critics' (2012) *Harvard NSJ* 1.

66 As the authors of the Fragmentation report (n 53) ¶ 488 observe,

> the law cannot resolve in an abstract way any possible conflict that may arise between different regimes; each has its experts and its ethos, its priorities and preference, its structural bias. Such regimes are institutionally 'programmed' to prioritize particular concerns over others.

67 *Prosecutor v Gotovina et al* (Case no IT-06-90-T, ICTY Trial Camber, 15 April 2011).

68 Ibid ¶ 1911.

69 The principle of distinction is codified in arts 48, 51(2) and 52(2) of API. This article builds on the basic rule enumerated in art 48 of API which states, 'Parties to the conflict shall at all times distinguish between the civilian population and combatants and between civilian objects and military objectives and accordingly shall direct their operations only against military objectives.'

70 CIHL r 11 *Tallinn Manual on the International Law Applicable to Cyber Warfare* (CUP 2013) r 49.

71 The ICRC's *Commentary* to the Protocol revealingly notes that 'the need to achieve a consensus [on art 51(4) and (5)] has led those drafting these provisions to formulate them in a way that is sometimes ambiguous. Several delegates remarked on this when the article was adopted.' *AP Commentary* ¶ 1948.

What and who is protected by the rule is contingent on a clear understanding as to what comprises a 'military objective'.[72] In addition to the armed forces and their members, objects that are lawful 'military objectives' are defined in Article 52 of the Protocol.[73] Also prohibited are attacks using weapons that by their nature cannot be directed at a specific military objective; such weapons are unlawful per se.[74] This prohibition extends to the use of what are otherwise lawful weapons in an indiscriminate manner. Whether a particular means or method is indiscriminate is often inextricably tied to the specific context. For example, the use of certain weapons in environments with few or no civilians would not violate the rule but the use of the same weapon in cities or other densely populated locations would be unlawful.[75] Article 51(5) of the same Protocol provides two examples of indiscriminate attacks: those that treat clearly separated and distinct military objectives located in a town, for example, or another area with a similar concentration of civilians or civilian objects, as a single military objective; and those that cause civilian deaths and damage to civilian objects which would be excessive in relation to the concrete and direct military advantage anticipated. Under scrutiny, the clarity and simplicity of the prohibition as originally expressed dissolves. In practice, whether or not a particular attack complies with the law is often subject to contestation, argument, claim and counter-claim.

The Trial Chamber's resolution to this problem was to identify an objective standard by which judgment could be made. According to the tribunal, the artillery attacks by the forces under Gotovina's command were indiscriminate because the entire town of Knin was treated as a target without discriminating between military and civilian objects. The failure to discriminate could be objectively verified by adopting a presumption that sites damaged as a consequence of an artillery attack that were located more than 200 metres from a legitimate target constituted evidence of an unlawful artillery attack.[76] The articulation of this standard by the tribunal provoked considerable criticism from those in the armed forces and law of war experts on the grounds that the 200 metre standard of acceptable error 'is fundamentally inconsistent with the realities of operational employment of artillery and other fire assets' and 'impossible to satisfy and operationally untenable'.[77] On appeal, and despite dividing three–two on the acquittal in respect

---

72 API art 51(4)(a).

73 API art 52(2) limits military objects 'to those objects which by their nature, location, purpose or use make an effective contribution to military action and whose total or partial destruction, capture or neutralization, in the circumstances ruling at the time, offers a definite military advantage'. In combat conditions, what would otherwise be a civilian object may become a legitimate military objective. In such circumstances an attack would be subject to the proportionality rule and the requirement to take feasible precautions in attack (API art 57). This included the selection of methods and means of attack, timing of the attack, issuing warnings to the civilian population and cancelling an attack when the anticipated harm to civilians or civilian property is considered excessive in relation to the concrete and direct military advantage anticipated.

74 API art 51(4)(b).

75 API art 51(4)(c). An often cited example is the use by Iraq of SCUD missiles that were repeatedly launched at cities during the 1990–1991 Gulf War. Although there were military objectives located within the cities, the missiles were insufficiently accurate reliably to strike any of them.

76 *Prosecutor v Gotovina et al* (n 67) ¶ 1911. The Trial Chamber did not appear to consider whether the use of artillery fire was appropriate in the circumstances. In other words, given the high number of civilians in the towns under attack, could the effects of the artillery fire be reconciled with the principle of distinction?

77 'Application and Proposed *Amicus Curiae* Brief concerning the 15 April 2011 Trial Chamber Judgment and requesting that the Appeals Chamber Reconsider the Findings of Unlawful Artillery Attacks during Operation Storm' submission in *Prosecutor v Gotovina* (Case no IT-06-90-A, 13 January 2012) ¶ 16 B ('Amicus brief'). See also International Humanitarian Law Clinic – Emory University School of Law, 'Operational Law Experts Roundtable on the *Gotovina* Judgment', www.law.emory.edu/index. php?id=5093.

of all the charges, the Appeals Chamber was unanimous in rejecting the 200 metre standard.[78] Nevertheless, the Chamber's equivocal stance on whether the error by the Trial Chamber was one of fact or law has effectively left the law, at best, fuzzy on what constitutes an indiscriminate attack. Above all what this case demonstrates is that the law of armed conflict is never random in that ambiguity is always resolvable by the military technicians and the law of war experts:[79] the message delivered through the Appeals Chamber is that the 200 metre standard is wrong. It is apparent from the judgments and the dissenting opinions that, without exception, the judges were determined to appreciate the specifications of the different types of artillery projectiles and to absorb the complex calculations that are made by the military to factor in variables including, for example, distance, muzzle velocity, wind speed, temperature.[80] Nevertheless, this absorption with the technical details and whether the margin of risk for artillery fire is 200 or 400 metres diverts attention from the fact that the law categorises projectiles that, by their very nature, will 'inevitably produce effects beyond the intended target'[81] as API art 51(4)(c) a *discriminate* weapon; it is their use within a particular context that is all important.

3 A resolution

The rift between the impression conveyed by a rule – as in the case of the prohibition on indiscriminate attacks – and its implementation in fact is often a space in which contestation abounds. For liberal states the most ideologically problematic aspect of LOAC is mediating the anxiety generated by rule compliance rather than non-compliance precisely because civilians are killed and maimed in the course of military operations that are executed in conformity with the rules using weapons that are classified, at least according to LOAC, as discriminate. That liberals experience unease with LOAC is only to be expected given that compliance with the rules exposes liberalism's complicity in facilitating the violence that it seeks to screen through the law's vernacular. The law's betrayal is even more acutely felt by the fact that this body of law is more commonly referred to as international *humanitarian* law conveying an ambition that goes beyond its limited objectives while eliding those aspects of the law that are simply not concerned with humanitarianism.[82]

---

78 *Prosecutor v Gotovina and Markač* (Case no IT-06-90-A, ICTY Appeals Chamber, 16 November 2012). For a useful critical analysis of the judgment by the Appeals Chamber, see Marko Milanovic, 'The Gotivina Omnishambles' *EJIL: Talk!* (18 November 2012), www.ejiltalk.org/the-gotovina-omnishambles/.
79 It is common practice for law of war experts to emphasise repeatedly the complexity of targeting decisions; while such assessment may indeed be a complex exercise, it is doubted that complexity alone has ever precluded a commander from authorising an attack.
80 *Prosecutor v Gotovina et al* (n 67) ¶ 1897.
81 Amicus brief (n 77) ¶ 5: 'artillery and other indirect fire assets, by their very nature involve a range of variables that will inevitably produce effects beyond the intended target'.
82 Many of the rules also reflect the 'practical concerns of states and their armed forces on grounds other than those which may be considered humanitarian'. Adam Roberts and Richard Guelff, *Documents on the Laws of War* (3rd edn, OUP 2000) 2. Schmitt also observes,

> more recently, this body of law has become known as 'international humanitarian law,' in great part through the efforts of the International Committee of the Red Cross (ICRC). Despite its recognition by the ICJ, the label has the marked disadvantage of masking the role military necessity plays in the law governing armed conflict. Nevertheless, it accurately reflects the trend toward according greater weight to the humanitarian features of the law.
>
> Schmitt, 'Military Necessity and Humanity (n 7) 806

Frits Kalshoven and Liesbeh Zegveld, *Constraints on the Waging of War: An Introduction to International* (4th edn, CUP 2011) 1–2.

Typically liberal societies simply avoid the fact that the law is designed to *allow* for the killing of civilians. The line between intentionally attacking civilians and launching an attack against a military objective in the knowledge that civilians will also be killed is a fine one and a distinction that is far more tenuous than many would care to admit. Confronted by the anxiety that compliance engenders, liberal societies direct their attention to non-compliance embracing the international criminal law project and championing the rule of law, both of which correspond with liberalism's political agenda.[83] Paradoxically, it is when the liberal state elects to charge its own soldiers with murder rather than war crimes that attention is inadvertently drawn back to the unresolvable problem that compliance with the law of armed conflict poses.

The humanitarian who delves too deeply into the world of the law of war expert is likely to be disappointed with what is on offer. That said, liberalism's ambition to inject some humanity into war through law has not been a futile exercise. To castigate the law of armed conflict too readily may be to miss the point that

> the essential precondition for the effectiveness of law, in its function as ideology, is that it shall display an independence from gross manipulation and shall seem to be just. It cannot seem to be so without upholding its own logic and criteria of equity; indeed, on occasion, by actually *being* just.[84]

83 The idea of the rule of law is not without its critics who argue that it is nothing more than a doctrine that impedes the pursuit of substantive justice by creating formal equality. Morton J Horwitz, 'The Rule of Law: An Unqualified Human Good?' (1977) 86 *Yale LJ* 561.
84 E P Thompson, *Whigs and Hunters: The Origin of the Black Act* (Breviary Stuff 1975) 263.

Index